1980

Readings in
Western Civilization

Readings in

Fourth Edition

Western Civilization

SELECTED AND EDITED BY

GEORGE H. KNOLES

Stanford University

RIXFORD K. SNYDER

Stanford University

J. B. LIPPINCOTT COMPANY   *Philadelphia*   *New York*

Preface

In preparing this book we have provided a collection of readings to accompany college courses in the History of Western Civilization and in Humanities. We have sought to furnish what a textbook cannot offer: namely, extensive illustrative source materials to amplify and to enrich the textbook assignments and other readings. We have not hesitated to draw upon the rich heritage in the fields of religion, literature, science, and the arts for these selections in our search to find suitable readings to illuminate the more significant aspects of the development of the Western tradition. In preparing this revised edition we have further enriched the offering by adding new materials from the literature of the late Middle Ages and the contemporary world.

In selecting readings we have constantly looked for significant works which lend themselves to use in class discussion. It is this emphasis upon usability in discussion rather than full coverage of all phases of a culture that has led to this particular collection of readings. We have found in our teaching that some of the finest results flowed from class discussion of the issues raised in these sources.

We have included from all ages selections which raise fundamental questions concerning the nature of man, his life, and his ultimate destiny. We have also included materials which raise basic questions concerning the organization of human society. Our aim has been not to avoid the controversial issues of the past nor of the present, but to encourage an intelligent examination of ideas and issues with an eye to developing a critical understanding of the human venture. To do less, it seems to us, would jeopardize our efforts to evoke the latent qualities of leadership in our student bodies. Today's confused and frustrated world needs trained specialists in all areas of human endeavor—scientific and technological, economic, political, social, and cultural. But one of the perils facing our society is this very specialization upon which we must depend. There is a serious danger that the more we train for specialization the less we train for meeting the insistent problems of human association. Our society desperately needs specialists whose philosophy of life is solidly grounded in human and humane principles. We hope, therefore, that this volume will be useful in stimulating the discussion of human affairs so necessary for providing leadership for the free world.

Wherever possible we have included complete works or fairly long selections to allow a fuller acquaintance with the materials chosen. All of the selections appear in the language of the authors or translators; in many cases we have followed spelling and printing styles of these authors or translators. We have neither condensed nor abstracted materials. We have, however, been rigorous in our selections and have omitted much; we have indicated the omissions in the usual manner.

The materials are arranged generally in chronological order; there are some departures from this plan to permit a logical progression within a given section. There is no special virtue in our organization of the sections, and individual instructors will find that assignments can be made to suit their own courses or textbook arrangements.

We have not thought it necessary to furnish elaborate explanatory and interpretive settings for the documents, believing that this can be done better by the instructor or the textbook. On the other hand, we think it helpful to give students adequate directions to assist them in making full use of the readings. The notes preceding each selection direct the students' attention to the significant points or conclusions in the reading. We have not sought to spoon-feed the students; rather we have told them what to look for with the thought that not only will they gain a better insight into the authors' intentions, but will also be better prepared to carry on an intelligent class discussion.

We are indebted to many persons for their helpfulness in the original preparation of this volume and in the present revision. Particularly we wish to thank our former colleague, Professor Max Savelle, now of the University of Washington, who made valuable suggestions during the early stages of our work. Others, especially at Michigan State University, the University of Washington, and Stanford University, gave us the benefit of their critical judgments based on use of the book in their classes.

GEORGE HARMON KNOLES
RIXFORD KINNEY SNYDER

Stanford University

CONTENTS

The Ancient Near East

Greek Civilization

Roman Civilization

The Decline of Classical Civilization

Civilization in the Middle Ages

Renaissance and Reformation

Civilization in the Seventeenth and Eighteenth Centuries

The Revolutionary Era and the Conservative Reaction

Industrialism, Liberalism, and Democracy in the Nineteenth Century

Social and Cultural Trends in the Nineteenth Century

Nationalism, Imperialism, and the War of 1914–1918

Economic, Social, and Political Changes in the Twentieth Century

The Ancient Near East

Properly speaking, the Near East is not a part of the area in which Western Civilization originated and developed. Nevertheless, the region between the western borders of India and the eastern shores of the Mediterranean Sea, including the valley of the Nile, provided the setting for the earliest civilizations, and these first ventures of mankind into more mature methods of living and thinking furnished the background for subsequent cultural developments in the Mediterranean world. Beginning in the millennium 4000–3000 B.C. and extending down through the centuries when Greece and Rome were first emerging, successive civilizations developed and flourished in Egypt, Mesopotamia, Palestine, and Persia. For the most part they were characterized by political absolutism which in turn gave rise to imperial rule over neighboring peoples. This phase of their culture inevitably required the development of legal principles, many of which were codified from time to time. For a variety of reasons, too, the peoples of the Ancient Near East were deeply concerned with religious ideas and with the ceremonies which developed to give expression to them. From these peoples, then, the western world gained certain legalistic and religious concepts which were to influence its civilization materially. A proper approach to the history of Western Civilization should therefore begin with a study of the Ancient Near East.

Hammurabi

The Amorite, Hammurabi (1728–1686 B.C.), succeeded in constructing an empire in Mesopotamia with Babylon as his capital city. In an effort to unify his conquests the king codified and systematized the various and conflicting laws and customs of his lands. This code, cut in a diorite shaft nearly eight feet high, was discovered early in the twentieth century by French archaeologists at Susa, in Persia, to which place it had been carried from Babylon by unknown persons. Provisions of this code continued in use for centuries and exerted considerable influence on Arabic and Islamic law. Comparisons of this code with selections from the Mosaic code to be found in the early books of the Bible will prove informative. In reading the following selections from Hammurabi's compilation, note regulations concerning (1) trial by ordeal, (2) scheduling of fines and punishments on the basis of social classes, (3) slavery and problems arising therefrom, (4) marriage, divorce, alimony, and the protection of children, and (5) business, agriculture, and the professions.

From: THE CODE OF HAMMURABI

1. If a man has accused another of laying a *nêrtu* (death spell?) upon him, but has not proved it, he shall be put to death.

2. If a man has accused another of laying a *kišpu* (spell) upon him, but has not proved it, the accused shall go to the sacred river, he shall plunge into the sacred river, and if the sacred river shall conquer him, he that accused him shall take possession of his house. If the sacred river shall show his innocence and he is saved, his accuser shall be put to death. He that plunged into the sacred river shall appropriate the house of him that accused him.

3. If a man has borne false witness in a trial, or has not established the statement that he has made, if that case be a capital trial, that man shall be put to death.

6. If a man has stolen goods from a temple, or house, he shall be put to death; and he that has received the stolen property from him shall be put to death.

8. If a patrician has stolen ox, sheep, ass, pig, or ship, whether from a temple, or a house, he shall pay thirtyfold. If he be a plebeian, he shall return tenfold. If the thief cannot pay, he shall be put to death.

14. If a man has stolen a child, he shall be put to death.

15. If a man has induced either a male or female slave from the house of a patrician, or plebeian, to leave the city, he shall be put to death.

21. If a man has broken into a house he shall be killed before the breach and buried there.

22. If a man has committed highway robbery and has been caught, that man shall be put to death.

23. If the highwayman has not been caught, the man that has been robbed shall state on oath what he has lost, and the city or district governor in whose territory or district the robbery took place shall restore to him what he has lost.

25. If a fire has broken out in a man's house and one who has come to put it out has coveted the property of the householder and appropriated any of it, that man shall be cast into the self-same fire.

26. If a levy-master, or warrant-officer, who has been detailed on the king's service, has not gone, or has hired a substitute in his place, that levy-master, or warrant-officer, shall be put to

C. H. W. Johns, *Babylonian and Assyrian Laws, Contracts and Letters*, Charles Scribner's Sons, New York, 1904, 44–66. Courtesy of Charles Scribner's Sons.

death and the hired substitute shall take his office.

27. If a levy-master, or warrant-officer, has been assigned to garrison duty, and in his absence his field and garden have been given to another who has carried on his duty, when the absentee has returned and regained his city, his field and garden shall be given back to him and he shall resume his duty.

28. If a levy-master, or warrant-officer, has been assigned to garrison duty, and has a son able to carry on his official duty, the field and garden shall be given to him and he shall carry on his father's duty.

36. The field, garden, or house, of a levy-master, warrant-officer, or tributary shall not be sold.

37. If a man has bought field, garden, or house, of a levy-master, a warrant-officer, or tributary, his title-deed shall be destroyed and he shall lose his money. He shall return the field, garden, or house to its owner.

42. If a man has hired a field to cultivate and has caused no corn to grow on the field, he shall be held responsible for not doing the work on the field and shall pay an average rent.

48. If a man has incurred a debt and a storm has flooded his field or carried away the crop, or the corn has not grown because of drought, in that year he shall not pay his creditor. Further, he shall post-date his bond and shall not pay interest for that year.

53, 54. If a man has neglected to strengthen his dike and has not kept his dike strong, and a breach has broken out in his dike, and the waters have flooded the meadow, the man in whose dike the breach has broken out shall restore the corn he has caused to be lost. [54.] If he be not able to restore the corn, he and his goods shall be sold, and the owners of the meadow whose corn the water has carried away shall share the money.

55. If a man has opened his runnel for watering and has left it open, and the water has flooded his neighbor's field, he shall pay him an average crop.

100. [If an agent has received money of a merchant, he shall write down the amount] and [what is to be] the interest of the money, and when his time is up, he shall settle with his merchant.

102, 103. If the merchant has given money, as a speculation, to the agent, who during his travels has met with misfortune, he shall return the full sum to the merchant. [103.] If, on his travels, an enemy has forced him to give up some of the goods he was carrying, the agent shall specify the amount on oath and shall be acquitted.

104. If a merchant has given to an agent corn, wool, oil, or any sort of goods, to traffic with, the agent shall write down the money value, and shall return that to the merchant. The agent shall then take a sealed receipt for the money that he has given to the merchant.

107. If the principal has overcharged the agent and the agent has [really] returned to his principal whatever his principal gave him, and if the principal has disputed what the agent has given him, that agent shall put his principal on oath before the elders, and the merchant, because he has defrauded the agent, shall pay to the agent sixfold what he misappropriated.

108. If the mistress of a beer-shop has not received corn as the price of beer or has demanded silver on an excessive scale, and has made the measure of beer less than the measure of corn, that beer-seller shall be prosecuted and drowned.

109. If the mistress of a beer-shop has assembled seditious slanderers in her house and those seditious persons have not been captured and have not been haled to the palace, that beer-seller shall be put to death.

110. If a votary, who is not living in the convent, open a beer-shop, or enter a beer-shop for drink, that woman shall be put to death.

117. If a man owes a debt, and he has given his wife, his son, or his daughter [as hostage] for the money, or has handed someone over to work it off, the hostage shall do the work of the creditor's house, but in the fourth year he shall set them free.

122. If a man has given another gold, silver, or any goods whatever, on deposit, all that he gives shall he show to witnesses, and take a bond and so give on deposit.

123. If he has given on deposit without witnesses and bonds, and has been defrauded where he made his deposit, he has no claim to prosecute.

125. If a man has given anything whatever on deposit, and, where he has made his deposit,

something of his has been lost together with something belonging to the owner of the house, either by house-breaking or a rebellion, the owner of the house who is in default shall make good all that has been given him on deposit, which he has lost, and shall return it to the owner of the goods. The owner of the house shall look after what he has lost and recover it from the thief.

128. If a man has taken a wife and has not executed a marriage-contract, that woman is not a wife.

129. If a man's wife be caught lying with another, they shall be strangled and cast into the water. If the wife's husband would save his wife, the king can save his servant.

132. If a man's wife has the finger pointed at her on account of another, but has not been caught lying with him, for her husband's sake she shall plunge into the sacred river.

138. If a man has divorced his wife, who has not borne him children, he shall pay over to her as much money as was given for her bride-price and the marriage-portion which she brought from her father's house, and so shall divorce her.

139. If there was no bride-price, he shall give her one mina of silver, as a price of divorce.

140. If he be a plebeian, he shall give her one-third of a mina of silver.

141. If a man's wife, living in her husband's house, has persisted in going out, has acted the fool, has wasted her house, has belittled her husband, he shall prosecute her. If her husband has said, "I divorce her," she shall go her way; he shall give her nothing as her price of divorce. If her husband has said, "I will not divorce her," he may take another woman to wife; the wife shall live as a slave in her husband's house.

142. If a woman has hated her husband, and has said, "You shall not possess me," her past shall be inquired into, as to what she lacks. If she has been discreet, and has no vice, and her husband has gone out, and has greatly belittled her, that woman has no blame, she shall take her marriage-portion and go off to her father's house.

143. If she has not been discreet, has gone out, ruined her house, belittled her husband, she shall be drowned.

145. If a man has married a votary, and she has not granted him children, and he is determined to marry a concubine, that man shall marry the concubine, and bring her into his house, but the concubine shall not place herself on an equality with the votary.

148. If a man has married a wife and a disease has seized her, if he is determined to marry a second wife, he shall marry her. He shall not divorce the wife whom the disease has seized. In the home they made together she shall dwell, and he shall maintain her as long as she lives.

151. If a woman, who is living in a man's house, has persuaded her husband to bind himself, and grant her a deed to the effect that she shall not be held for debt by a creditor of her husband's; if that man had a debt upon him before he married that woman, his creditor shall not take his wife for it. Also, if that woman had a debt upon her before she entered that man's house, her creditor shall not take her husband for it.

152. From the time that that woman entered into the man's house they together shall be liable for all debts subsequently incurred.

153. If a man's wife, for the sake of another, has caused her husband to be killed, that woman shall be impaled.

159. If a man, who has presented a gift to the house of his prospective father-in-law and has given the bride-price, has afterward looked upon another woman and has said to his father-in-law, "I will not marry your daughter"; the father of the girl shall keep whatever he has brought as a present.

160. If a man has presented a gift to the house of his prospective father-in-law, and has given the bride-price, but the father of the girl has said, "I will not give you my daughter," the father shall return double all that was presented him.

168. If a man has determined to disinherit his son and has declared before the judge, "I cut off my son," the judge shall inquire into the son's past, and, if the son has not committed a grave misdemeanor such as should cut him off from sonship, the father shall [not] disinherit his son.

170. If a man has had children borne to him by his wife, and also by a maid, if the father in his lifetime has said, "My sons," to the chil-

dren whom his maid bore him, and has reckoned them with the sons of his wife; then after the father has gone to his fate, the children of the wife and of the maid shall share equally. The children of the wife shall apportion the shares and make their own selections.

175. If either a slave of a patrician, or of a plebeian, has married the daughter of a free man, and she has borne children, the owner of the slave shall have no claim for service on the children of a free woman. And if a slave, either of a patrician or of a plebeian, has married a free woman and when he married her she entered the slave's house with a marriage-portion from her father's estate, be he slave of a patrician or of a plebeian, and from the time that they started to keep house, they have acquired property; after the slave, whether of a patrician or of a plebeian, has gone to his fate, the free woman shall take her marriage-portion, and whatever her husband and she acquired, since they started house-keeping. She shall divide it into two portions. The master of the slave shall take one half, the other half the free woman shall take for her children.

177. If a widow, whose children are young, has determined to marry again, she shall not marry without consent of the judge. When she is allowed to remarry, the judge shall inquire as to what remains of the property of her former husband, and shall intrust the property of her former husband to that woman and her second husband. He shall give them an inventory. They shall watch over the property, and bring up the children. Not a utensil shall they sell. A buyer of any utensil belonging to the widow's children shall lose his money and shall return the article to its owners.

186. If a man has taken a young child to be his son, and after he has taken him, the child discover his own parents, he shall return to his father's house.

188, 189. If a craftsman has taken a child to bring up and has taught him his handicraft, he shall not be reclaimed. If he has not taught him his handicraft that foster child shall return to his father's house.

195. If a son has struck his father, his hands shall be cut off.

196. If a man has knocked out the eye of a patrician, his eye shall be knocked out.

197. If he has broken the limb of a patrician, his limb shall be broken.

198. If he has knocked out the eye of a plebeian or has broken the limb of a plebeian, he shall pay one mina of silver.

199. If he has knocked out the eye of a patrician's servant, or broken the limb of a patrician's servant, he shall pay half his value.

200. If a patrician has knocked out the tooth of a man that is his equal, his tooth shall be knocked out.

201. If he has knocked out the tooth of a plebeian, he shall pay one-third of a mina of silver.

206. If a man has struck another in a quarrel, and caused him a permanent injury, that man shall swear, "I struck him without malice," and shall pay the doctor.

215. If a surgeon has operated with the bronze lancet on a patrician for a serious injury, and has cured him, or has removed with a bronze lancet a cataract for a patrician, and has cured his eye, he shall take ten shekels of silver.

216. If it be plebeian, he shall take five shekels of silver.

217. If it be a man's slave, the owner of the slave shall give two shekels of silver to the surgeon.

218. If a surgeon has operated with the bronze lancet on a patrician for a serious injury, and has caused his death, or has removed a cataract for a patrician, with the bronze lancet, and has made him lose his eye, his hands shall be cut off.

221. If a surgeon has cured the limb of a patrician, or has doctored a diseased bowel, the patient shall pay five shekels of silver to the surgeon.

224. If a veterinary surgeon has treated an ox, or an ass, for a severe injury, and cured it, the owner of the ox, or the ass, shall pay the surgeon one-sixth of a shekel of silver, as his fee.

225. If he has treated an ox, or an ass, for a severe injury, and caused it to die, he shall pay one-quarter of its value to the owner of the ox, or the ass.

229. If a builder has built a house for a man, and has not made his work sound, and the house he built has fallen, and caused the

death of its owner, that builder shall be put to death.

237. If a man has hired a boat and boatman, and loaded it with corn, wool, oil, or dates, or whatever it be, and the boatman has been careless, and sunk the boat, or lost what is in it, the boatman shall restore the boat which he sank, and whatever he lost that was in it.

240. If a boat, on its course, has run into a boat at anchor, and sunk it, the owner of the boat that was sunk shall estimate on oath whatever was lost in his boat, and the owner of the moving vessel, which sank the boat at anchor, shall make good his boat and what was lost in it.

245. If a man has hired an ox and has caused its death, by carelessness, or blows, he shall restore ox for ox, to the owner of the ox.

250. If a bull has gone wild and gored a man, and caused his death, there can be no suit against the owner.

251. If a man's ox be a gorer, and has revealed its evil propensity as a gorer, and he has not blunted its horn, or shut up the ox, and then that ox has gored a free man and caused his death, the owner shall pay half a mina of silver.

259. If a man has stolen a watering-machine from the meadow, he shall pay five shekels of silver to the owner of the watering-machine.

261. If a man has hired a herdsman, to pasture oxen, or sheep, he shall pay him eight *gur* of corn yearly.

273. If a man has hired a laborer from the beginning of the year to the fifth month, he shall pay six *še* of silver daily; from the sixth month to the close of the year, he shall pay five *še* of silver daily.

The Bible

The Book of Exodus includes materials drawn from different ages and put together about the middle of the fourth century B.C. The chapters selected give the account of the meeting of Moses and Jahweh and the drawing up of a contract between Jahweh and the people of Israel. The Mosaic code, which in this account was made a part of the contract between Jahweh and Moses, dates from before 1000 B.C. and was largely derived from Egyptian and Babylonian codes. A comparison with the Code of Hammurabi (see above p. 3) will be profitable. Note (1) the kind of deity that is represented here, (2) the economic interests and practices of the Israelites, (3) the ethical principles stressed, (4) the terms of the contract between Jahweh and the Israelites, (5) the religious practices prescribed, (6) the boundaries Jahweh set for the future home of the Israelites, (7) the method used to seal the contract, (8) the provisions made to permit Jahweh to move from Mt. Sinai and accompany the people of Israel in their wanderings, and (9) the character of Jahweh as here described.

From: THE SECOND BOOK OF MOSES, CALLED EXODUS

In the third month, when the children of Israel were gone forth out of the land of Egypt, the same day came they into the wilderness of Sinai. For they were departed from Rephidim,

Adapted from the King James version of the Bible.

and were come to the desert of Sinai, and had pitched in the wilderness; and there Israel camped before the mount.

And Moses went up unto God, and the Lord

called unto him out of the mountain, saying, "Thus shalt thou say to the house of Jacob, and tell the children of Israel: 'Ye have seen what I did unto the Egyptians, and how I bare you on eagles' wings, and brought you unto myself. Now therefore, if ye will obey my voice indeed, and keep my covenant, then ye shall be a peculiar treasure unto me above all people: for all the earth is mine. And ye shall be unto me a kingdom of priests, and a holy nation.' These are the words which thou shalt speak unto the children of Israel."

And Moses came and called for the elders of the people, and laid before their faces all these words which the Lord commanded him. And all the people answered together, and said, "All that the Lord hath spoken we will do." And Moses returned the words of the people unto the Lord.

And the Lord said unto Moses, "Lo, I come unto thee in a thick cloud, that the people may hear when I speak with thee, and believe thee forever." And Moses told the words of the people unto the Lord. And the Lord said unto Moses, "Go unto the people, and sanctify them today and tomorrow, and let them wash their clothes, and be ready against the third day, for the third day the Lord will come down in the sight of all the people upon Mount Sinai. And thou shalt set bounds unto the people round about, saying, 'Take heed to yourselves, that ye go not up into the mount, or touch the border of it: whosoever toucheth the mount shall be surely put to death.' There shall not a hand touch it, but he shall surely be stoned, or shot through; whether it be beast or man, it shall not live: when the trumpet soundeth long, they shall come up to the mount."

And Moses went down from the mount unto the people, and sanctified the people; and they washed their clothes. And he said unto the people, "Be ready against the third day: come not at your wives."

And it came to pass on the third day in the morning, that there were thunders and lightnings, and a thick cloud upon the mount, and the voice of the trumpet exceeding loud; so that all the people that was in the camp trembled. And Moses brought forth the people out of the camp to meet with God; and they stood at the nether part of the mount. And Mount Sinai was altogether on a smoke, because the Lord descended upon it in fire; and the smoke thereof ascended as the smoke of a furnace, and the whole mount quaked greatly. And when the voice of the trumpet sounded long, and waxed louder and louder, Moses spake, and God answered him by a voice. And the Lord came down upon Mount Sinai, on the top of the mount: and the Lord called Moses up to the top of the mount; and Moses went up.

And the Lord said unto Moses, "Go down, charge the people, lest they break through unto the Lord to gaze and many of them perish. And let the priests also, which come near to the Lord, sanctify themselves, lest the Lord break forth upon them."

And Moses said unto the Lord, "The people cannot come up to Mount Sinai: for thou chargedst us, saying, 'Set bounds about the mount, and sanctify it.'"

And the Lord said unto him, "Away, get thee down, and thou shalt come up, thou, and Aaron with thee: but let not the priests and the people break through to come up unto the Lord, lest he break forth upon them."

So Moses went down unto the people, and spake unto them.

And God spake all these words, saying, "I am the Lord thy God, which have brought thee out of the land of Egypt, out of the house of bondage.

"Thou shalt have no other gods before me.

"Thou shalt not make unto thee any graven image, or any likeness of any thing that is in heaven above, or that is in the earth beneath, or that is in the water under the earth; thou shalt not bow down thyself to them, nor serve them: for I the Lord thy God am a jealous God, visiting the iniquity of the fathers upon the children unto the third and fourth generation of them that hate me; and showing mercy unto thousands of them that love me, and keep my commandments.

"Thou shalt not take the name of the Lord thy God in vain; for the Lord will not hold him guiltless that taketh his name in vain.

"Remember the sabbath day, to keep it holy. Six days shalt thou labor, and do all thy work: but the seventh day is the sabbath of the Lord thy God: in it thou shalt not do any work, thou, nor thy son, nor thy daughter, thy manservant, nor thy maidservant, nor thy cattle, nor thy stranger that is within thy gates: for in six days the Lord made heaven and earth, the sea, and all that in them is, and rested the seventh day: wherefore the Lord blessed the sabbath day, and hallowed it.

"Honour thy father and thy mother: that thy days may be long upon the land which the Lord thy God giveth thee.

"Thou shalt not kill.

"Thou shalt not commit adultery.

"Thou shalt not steal.

"Thou shalt not bear false witness against thy neighbor.

"Thou shalt not covet thy neighbour's house, thou shalt not covet thy neighbour's wife, nor his manservant, nor his maidservant, nor his ox, nor his ass, nor any thing that is thy neighbour's."

And all the people saw the thunderings, and the lightnings, and the noise of the trumpet, and the mountain smoking: and when the people saw it, they removed, and stood afar off.

And they said unto Moses, "Speak thou with us, and we will hear: but let not God speak with us, lest we die."

And Moses said unto the people, "Fear not: for God is come to prove you, and that his fear may be before your faces, that ye sin not."

And the people stood afar off, and Moses drew near unto the thick darkness where God was. And the Lord said unto Moses, "Thus thou shalt say unto the children of Israel: 'Ye have seen that I have talked with you from heaven. Ye shall not make with me gods of silver, neither shall ye make unto you gods of gold. An altar of earth thou shalt make unto me, and shalt sacrifice thereon thy burnt offerings, and thy peace offerings, thy sheep, and thine oxen: in all places where I record my name I will come unto thee and I will bless thee. And if thou wilt make me an altar of stone, thou shalt not build it of hewn stone: for if thou lift up thy tool upon it, thou hast polluted it.' . . ."

"Now these are the judgments which thou shalt set before them:

"If thou buy a Hebrew servant, six years he shall serve: and in the seventh he shall go out free for nothing. If he came in by himself, he shall go out by himself: if he were married,

then his wife shall go out with him. If his master have given him a wife, and she have borne him sons or daughters; the wife and her children shall be her master's, and he shall go out by himself. And if the servant shall plainly say, 'I love my master, my wife, and my children; I will not go out free': then his master shall bring him unto the judges; he shall also bring him to the door, or unto the door post; and his master shall bore his ear through with an awl; and he shall serve him for ever.

"And if a man sell his daughter to be a maidservant, she shall not go out as the menservants do. If she please not her master, who hath betrothed her to himself, then shall he let her be redeemed: to sell her unto a strange nation he shall have no power, seeing he hath dealt deceitfully with her. And if he hath betrothed her unto his son, he shall deal with her after the manner of daughters. If he take him another wife, her food, her raiment, and her duty of marriage, shall he not diminish. And if he do not these three unto her, then shall she go out free without money.

"He that smiteth a man, so that he die, shall be surely put to death. And if a man lie not in wait, but God deliver him into his hand; then I will appoint thee a place whither he shall flee. But if a man come presumptuously upon his neighbour, to slay him with guile; thou shalt take him from mine altar, that he may die. And he that smiteth his father, or his mother, shall be surely put to death.

"And he that stealeth a man, and selleth him, or if he be found in his hand, he shall surely be put to death.

"And he that curseth his father, or his mother, shall surely be put to death.

"And if men strive together, and one smite another with a stone, or with his fist, and he die not, but keepeth his bed: if he rise again, and walk abroad upon his staff, then shall he that smote him be quit; only he shall pay for the loss of his time, and shall cause him to be thoroughly healed.

"And if a man smite his servant, or his maid, with a rod, and he die under his hand; he shall be surely punished. Notwithstanding, if he continue a day or two, he shall not be punished: for he is his money.

"If men strive, and hurt a woman with child,

so that her fruit depart from her, and yet no mischief follow: he shall be surely punished, according as the woman's husband will lay upon him; and he shall pay as the judges determine. And if any mischief follow, then thou shalt give life for life, eye for eye, tooth for tooth, hand for hand, foot for foot, burning for burning, wound for wound, stripe for stripe.

"And if a man smite the eye of his servant, or the eye of his maid, that it perish; he shall let him go free for his eye's sake. And if he smite out his manservant's tooth, or his maidservant's tooth; he shall let him go free for his tooth's sake.

"If an ox gore a man or a woman, that they die: then the ox shall be surely stoned, and his flesh shall not be eaten; but the owner of the ox shall be quit. But if the ox were wont to push with his horn in time past, and it hath been testified to his owner, and he hath not kept him in, but that he hath killed a man or a woman; the ox shall be stoned, and his owner also shall be put to death. If there be laid on him a sum of money, then he shall give for the ransom of his life whatsoever is laid upon him. . . .

"And if a man shall open a pit, or if a man shall dig a pit, and not cover it, and an ox or an ass fall therein; the owner of the pit shall make it good, and give money unto the owner of them; and the dead beast shall be his.

"And if one man's ox hurt another's, that he die; then they shall sell the live ox, and divide the money of it; and the dead ox also they shall divide. Or if it be known that the ox hath used to push in time past, and his owner hath not kept him in; he shall surely pay ox for ox; and the dead shall be his own.

"If a man shall steal an ox, or a sheep, and kill it, or sell it; he shall restore five oxen for an ox, and four sheep for a sheep. If a thief be found breaking up, and be smitten that he die, there shall no blood be shed for him. If the sun be risen upon him, there shall be blood shed for him: for he should make full restitution; if he have nothing, then he shall be sold for his theft. If the theft be certainly found in his hand alive, whether it be ox, or ass, or sheep; he shall restore double. . . .

"If a man deliver unto his neighbour an ass, or an ox, or a sheep, or any beast, to keep; and

it die, or be hurt, or driven away, no man seeing it: then shall an oath of the Lord be between them both, that he hath not put his hand unto his neighbour's goods; and the owner of it shall accept thereof, and he shall not make it good. And if it be stolen from him, he shall make restitution unto the owner thereof. If it be torn in pieces, then let him bring it for witness, and he shall not make good that which was torn. And if a man borrow ought of his neighbour, and it be hurt, or die, the owner thereof being not with it, he shall surely make it good. But if the owner thereof be with it, he shall not make it good: if it be a hired thing, it came for his hire.

"And if a man entice a maid that is not betrothed, and lie with her, he shall surely endow her to be his wife. If her father utterly refuse to give her unto him, he shall pay money according to the dowry of virgins.

"Thou shalt not suffer a witch to live.

"Whosoever lieth with a beast shall surely be put to death.

"He that sacrificeth unto any god, save unto the Lord only, he shall be utterly destroyed.

"Thou shalt neither vex a stranger, nor oppress him: for ye were strangers in the land of Egypt.

"Ye shall not afflict any widow, or fatherless child. If thou afflict them in any wise, and they cry at all unto me, I will surely hear their cry; and my wrath shall wax hot, and I will kill you with the sword; and your wives shall be widows, and your children fatherless.

"If thou lend money to any of my people that is poor by thee, thou shalt not be to him as a usurer, neither shalt thou lay upon him usury. If thou at all take thy neighbour's raiment to pledge, thou shalt deliver it unto him by that the sun goeth down: for that is his covering only, it is his raiment for his skin: wherein shall he sleep? and it shall come to pass, when he crieth unto me, that I will hear; for I am gracious.

"Thou shalt not revile the gods, nor curse the ruler of thy people. . . .

"And in all things that I have said unto you be circumspect: and make no mention of the name of other gods, neither let it be heard out of thy mouth. . . .

"The first of the firstfruits of thy land thou

shalt bring into the house of the Lord thy God. Thou shalt not seethe a kid in his mother's milk.

"Behold, I send an Angel before thee, to keep thee in the way, and to bring thee into the place which I have prepared. Beware of him, and obey his voice, provoke him not; for he will not pardon your transgressions: for my name is in him. But if thou shalt indeed obey his voice, and do all that I speak; then I will be an enemy unto thine enemies, and an adversary unto thine adversaries. For mine Angel shall go before thee, and bring thee in unto the Amorites, and the Hittites, and the Perizzites, and the Canaanites, the Hivites, and the Jebusites; and I will cut them off. Thou shalt not bow down to their gods, nor serve them, nor do after their works: but thou shalt utterly overthrow them, and quite break down their images.

"And ye shall serve the Lord your God, and he shall bless thy bread, and thy water; and I will take sickness away from the midst of thee. . . . I will send my fear before thee, and will destroy all the people to whom thou shalt come; and I will make all thine enemies turn their backs unto thee. And I will send hornets before thee, which shall drive out the Hivite, the Canaanite, and the Hittite, from before thee. I will not drive them out from before thee in one year; lest the land become desolate, and the beast of the field multiply against thee. By little and little I will drive them out from before thee, until thou be increased, and inherit the land. And I will set thy bounds from the Red sea even unto the sea of the Philistines, and from the desert unto the river: for I will deliver the inhabitants of the land into your hand; and thou shalt drive them out before thee. Thou shalt make no covenant with them, nor with their gods. They shall not dwell in thy land, lest they make thee sin against me: for if thou serve their gods, it will surely be a snare unto thee. . . ."

And Moses came and told the people all the words of the Lord, and all the judgments: and all the people answered with one voice, and said, "All the words which the Lord has said will we do."

And Moses wrote all the words of the Lord, and rose up early in the morning, and builded an altar under the hill, and twelve pillars, according to the twelve tribes of Israel. And he sent young men of the children of Israel, which offered burnt offerings, and sacrificed peace offerings of oxen unto the Lord. . . .

And the Lord said unto Moses, "Come up to me into the mount, and be there: and I will give thee tables of stone, and a law, and commandments which I have written; that thou mayest teach them. . . ."

And Moses went up into the mount, and a cloud covered the mount. And the glory of the Lord abode upon Mount Sinai, and the cloud covered it six days: and the seventh day he called unto Moses out of the midst of the cloud. And the sight of the glory of the Lord was like devouring fire on the top of the mount in the eyes of the children of Israel. And Moses went into the midst of the cloud, and gat him up into the mount: and Moses was in the mount forty days and forty nights.

And the Lord spake unto Moses, saying, "Speak unto the children of Israel, that they bring me an offering: of every man that giveth it willingly with his heart ye shall take my offering. And this is the offering which ye shall take of them; gold, and silver, and brass, and blue, and purple, and scarlet, and fine linen, and goats' hair, and rams' skins dyed red, and badgers' skins, and shittim wood, oil for the light, spices for anointing oil, and for sweet incense, onyx stones, and stones to be set in the ephod, and in the breastplate.

"And let them make me a sanctuary; that I may dwell among them. According to all that I show thee, after the pattern of the tabernacle, and the pattern of all the instruments thereof, even so shall ye make it.

"And they shall make an ark of shittim wood: two cubits and a half shall be the length thereof, and a cubit and a half the breadth thereof, and a cubit and a half the height thereof. And thou shalt overlay it with pure gold, within and without shalt thou overlay it, and shalt make upon it a crown of gold round about. And thou shalt cast four rings of gold for it, and put them in the four corners thereof; and two rings shall be in the one side of it, and two rings in the other side of it. And thou shalt make staves of shittim wood, and overlay them with gold. And thou shalt put the staves into the rings by the sides of the ark, that the ark may be borne with them. The staves shall be in the rings of the ark: they shall not be taken from it. And thou shalt put into the ark the testimony which I shall give thee.

"And thou shalt make a mercy seat of pure gold: two cubits and a half shall be the length thereof, and a cubit and a half the breadth thereof. And thou shalt make two cherubim of gold, of beaten work shalt thou make them, in the two ends of the mercy seat. And make one cherub on the one end, and the other cherub on the other end: even of the mercy seat shall ye make the cherubim on the two ends thereof.

"And the cherubim shall stretch forth their wings on high, covering the mercy seat with their wings, and their faces shall look one to another; toward the mercy seat shall the faces of the cherubim be.

"And thou shalt put the mercy seat above upon the ark; and in the ark thou shalt put the testimony that I shall give thee. And there I will meet with thee, and I will commune with thee from above the mercy seat, from between the two cherubim which are upon the ark of the testimony, of all things which I will give thee in commandment unto the children of Israel. . . ."

The Books of the Kings were put together shortly before the fall of the Kingdom of Judah (ca. 586 B.C.) from earlier records kept by priests and other interested writers. Following their conquest of Canaan, the Israelites gradually succumbed to the culture of the conquered. In this process Jahweh and his worship was neglected for the worship of the agricultural deities abounding in this area. The law of survival applied to the gods of the ancient orient and many lost out in the struggle. Jahweh entered into this conflict for existence and in the dramatic episodes centering around the careers of Elijah and Elisha, He emerged victorious. Henceforth there was little question in the minds of the Israelites as to who their god was to be, and the way was opened for a further refinement of Jahweh's character. In the selections note (1) the subject of the dispute between Ahab and Elijah, (2) the preparations made for the test between Elijah and the priests of Baal, (3) the extent to which apostasy had spread as indicated by the relative numbers of contenders, (4) the results of the contest, (5) Jahweh's approval of the mass murder of priests, (6) the success of Jehu's rebellion against Ahab, (7) Jehu's slaughter of the worshippers of Baal, (8) the desecration of the temple of Baal, and (9) Jehu's reward from Jahweh for his devotion.

From: THE BOOKS OF THE KINGS

And it came to pass after many days, that the word of the Lord came to Elijah in the third year, saying, "Go, show thyself unto Ahab; and I will send rain upon the earth."

And Elijah went to show himself unto Ahab. And there was a sore famine in Samaria. And Ahab called Obadiah, which was the governor of his house. (Now Obadiah feared the Lord greatly: for it was so, when Jezebel cut off the prophets of the Lord, that Obadiah took a hundred prophets, and hid them by fifty in a cave, and fed them with bread and water.)

And Ahab said unto Obadiah, "Go into the land, unto all fountains of water, and unto all brooks: peradventure we may find grass to save the horses and mules alive, that we lose not all the beasts."

So they divided the land between them to pass throughout it: Ahab went one way by himself, and Obadiah went another way by himself. And as Obadiah was in the way, behold, Elijah met him: and he knew him, and fell on his face, and said, "Art thou that my lord Elijah?"

And he answered him, "I am: go, tell thy lord, 'Behold, Elijah is here.'"

And he said, "What have I sinned, that thou wouldst deliver thy servant into the hand of Ahab, to slay me? As the Lord thy God liveth, there is no nation or kingdom, whither my lord hath not sent to seek thee: and when they said, 'He is not there'; he took an oath of the kingdom and nation, that they found thee not. And now thou sayest, 'Go, tell thy lord, "Behold, Elijah is here."' And it shall come to pass, as soon as I am gone from thee, that the Spirit of the Lord shall carry thee whither I know not; and so when I come and tell Ahab, and he cannot find thee, he shall slay me: but I thy servant fear the Lord from my youth. Was it not told my lord what I did when Jezebel slew the prophets of the Lord, how I hid a hundred men of the Lord's prophets by fifty in a cave, and fed them with bread and water? And now thou sayest, 'Go, tell thy lord, "Behold, Elijah is here"': and he shall slay me."

And Elijah said, "As the Lord of hosts liveth, before whom I stand, I will surely show myself unto him today."

So Obadiah went to meet Ahab, and told him: and Ahab went to meet Elijah.

And it came to pass, when Ahab saw Elijah, that Ahab said unto him, "Art thou he that troubleth Israel?"

And he answered, "I have not troubled Israel; but thou, and thy father's house, in that ye have forsaken the commandments of the Lord, and thou hast followed Baalim. Now therefore send, and gather to me all Israel unto Mount Carmel, and the prophets of Baal four hundred and fifty, and the prophets of the groves four hundred, which eat at Jezebel's table."

So Ahab sent unto all the children of Israel, and gathered the prophets together unto Mount Carmel. And Elijah came unto all the people, and said, "How long halt ye between two opinions? If the Lord be God, follow him: but if Baal, then follow him." And the people answered him not a word.

Then said Elijah unto the people, "I, even I only, remain a prophet of the Lord; but Baal's prophets are four hundred and fifty men. Let them therefore give us two bullocks; and let them choose one bullock for themselves, and cut it in pieces, and lay it on wood, and put no fire under: and I will dress the other bullock, and lay it on wood, and put no fire under: and call ye on the name of your gods, and I will call on the name of the Lord: and the God that answereth by fire, let him be God." And all the people answered and said, "It is well spoken."

And Elijah said unto the prophets of Baal, "Choose you one bullock for yourselves, and dress it first; for ye are many; and call on the name of your gods, but put no fire under."

And they took the bullock which was given them, and they dressed it, and called on the name of Baal from morning even until noon, saying, "O Baal, hear us." But there was no voice, nor any that answered. And they leaped upon the altar which was made.

And it came to pass at noon, that Elijah mocked them, and said, "Cry aloud: for he is a god; either he is talking, or he is pursuing, or he is in a journey, or peradventure he sleepeth, and must be awaked."

And they cried aloud, and cut themselves after their manner with knives and lancets, till the blood gushed out upon them. And it came to pass, when midday was past, and they prophesied until the time of the offering of the evening sacrifice, that there was neither voice, nor any to answer, nor any that regarded.

And Elijah said unto all the people, "Come near unto me." And all the people came near unto him. And he repaired the altar of the Lord that was broken down. And Elijah took twelve stones, according to the number of the tribes of the sons of Jacob, unto whom the word of the Lord came, saying, "Israel shall be thy name": and with the stones he built an altar in the name of the Lord: and he made a trench about the altar, as great as would contain two measures of seed. And he put the wood in order, and cut the bullock in pieces, and laid him on the wood, and said, "Fill four barrels with water, and pour it on the burnt sacrifice, and on the wood." And he said, "Do it the second time." And they did it the second time. And he said, "Do it the third time." And they did it the third time. And the water ran round about the altar; and he filled the trench also with water.

And it came to pass at the time of the offering of the evening sacrifice, that Elijah the prophet came near, and said, "Lord God of Abraham, Isaac, and of Israel, let it be known this day that thou art God in Israel, and that I am thy servant, and that I have done all these things at thy word. Hear me, O Lord, hear me, that this people may know that thou art the Lord God, and that thou hast turned their heart back again."

Then the fire of the Lord fell, and consumed the burnt sacrifice, and the wood, and the stones, and the dust, and licked up the water that was in the trench. And when all the people saw it, they fell on their faces: and they said, "The Lord, he is the God; the Lord, he is the God."

And Elijah said unto them, "Take the prophets of Baal; let not one of them escape." And they took them: and Elijah brought them down to the brook Kishon, and slew them there.

And Elijah said unto Ahab, "Get thee up, eat and drink; for there is a sound of abundance of rain."

So Ahab went up to eat and to drink. And Elijah went up to the top of Carmel; and he cast himself down upon the earth, and put his face between his knees, and said to his servant, "Go up now, look toward the sea." And he went up, and looked, and said, "There is nothing." And he said, "Go again seven times."

And it came to pass at the seventh time, that he said, "Behold, there ariseth a little cloud out of the sea, like a man's hand." And he said, "Go up, say unto Ahab, 'Prepare thy chariot, and get thee down, that the rain stop thee not.'"

And it came to pass in the meanwhile, that the heaven was black with clouds and wind, and there was a great rain. And Ahab rode,

and went to Jezreel. And the hand of the Lord was on Elijah; and he girded up his loins, and ran before Ahab to the entrance of Jezreel. . . .

And Ahab had seventy sons in Samaria. And Jehu wrote letters, and sent to Samaria, unto the rulers of Jezreel, to the elders, and to them that brought up Ahab's children, saying, "Now as soon as this letter cometh to you, seeing your master's sons are with you, and there are with you chariots and horses, a fenced city also, and armor; look even out the best and meetest of your master's sons, and set him on his father's throne, and fight for your master's house."

And it came to pass, when the letter came to them, that they took the king's sons, and slew seventy persons, and put their heads in baskets, and sent him them to Jezreel. So Jehu slew all that remained of the house of Ahab in Jezreel, and all his great men, and his kinsfolk, and his priests, until he left him none remaining.

And he arose and departed, and came to Samaria. And as he was at the shearing house in the way, Jehu met with the brethren of Ahaziah king of Judah, and said, "Who are ye?" And they answered, "We are the brethren of Ahaziah; and we go down to salute the children of the king and the children of the queen." And he said, "Take them alive." And they took them alive, and slew them at the pit of the shearing house, even two and forty men; neither left he any of them.

And when he came to Samaria, he slew all that remained unto Ahab in Samaria, till he had destroyed him, according to the saying of the Lord, which he spake to Elijah.

And Jehu gathered all the people together, and said unto them, "Ahab served Baal a little; but Jehu shall serve him much. Now therefore call unto me all the prophets of Baal, all his servants, and all his priests; let none be wanting: for I have a great sacrifice to do to Baal; whosoever shall be wanting, he shall not live." But Jehu did it in subtilty, to the intent that he might destroy the worshippers of Baal.

And Jehu said, "Proclaim a solemn assembly for Baal." And they proclaimed it. And Jehu sent through all Israel: and all the worshippers of Baal came, so that there was not a man left that came not. And they came into the house of

Baal; and the house of Baal was full from one end to another. And he said unto him that was over the vestry, "Bring forth vestments for all the worshippers of Baal." And he brought them forth vestments. And Jehu went, and Jehonadab the son of Rechab, into the house of Baal, and said unto the worshippers of Baal, "Search, and look that there be here with you none of the servants of the Lord, but the worshippers of Baal only."

And when they went in to offer sacrifices and burnt offerings, Jehu appointed fourscore men without, and said, "If any of the men whom I have brought into your hands escape, he that letteth him go, his life shall be for the life of him."

And it came to pass, as soon as he had made an end of offering the burnt offering, that Jehu said to the guard and to the captains, "Go in, and slay them; let none come forth." And they smote them with the edge of the sword; and the guard and the captains cast them out, and went to the city of the house of Baal. And they brought forth the images out of the house of Baal, and burned them. And they brake down the image of Baal, and brake down the house of Baal, and made it a draught house unto this day. Thus Jehu destroyed Baal out of Israel. And the Lord said unto Jehu, "Because thou hast done well in executing that which is right in mine eyes, and hast done unto the house of Ahab according to all that was in mine heart, thy children of the fourth generation shall sit on the throne of Israel."

Following Jahweh's victory over his rivals, the way was prepared for a transformation in the character of Jahweh. Two significant achievements are to be noted in connection with the Hebrew prophetic movement beginning in the eighth century B.C.: the development of the idea that Jahweh is more interested in social justice than mere sacrifice and ritual, and the development of the idea that there is only one God in the universe. The external history of the ancient orient between 800 B.C. and 500 B.C. helped immeasurably to shape the internal history of Hebrew religious thought. For one thing, Israel achieved great pros·perity during the first half of the eighth century B.C., and a situation developed in which the rich became richer and the poor, poorer. The outward prosperity seemed proof that Jahweh was pleased with his people and the rich remembered Him with ever more lavish sacrifices and ritual. A second factor shaping religious thought was the rise and fall of the later empires of antiquity—Assyria, Chaldean Babylonia, and Persia. In an effort to explain the movements of these peoples involving the loss of liberty and destruction of the Hebrew kingdoms, Hebrew prophets extended the tradition of supernatural intervention in their own history to the control by Jahweh of other gods and other peoples in order to fulfill His purposes with respect to the people of Israel.

Amos, a plain, roughly dressed tender of flocks from the grasslands of the southern kingdom, appeared about 760 B.C. in the northern kingdom with a message of impending doom and disaster. The Assyrian armies, he warned, acting as the scourge of Jahweh were about to overrun the land, destroying homes, fields, and flocks because of the violence, oppression, fraud, and corruption practiced on every hand in Israel. Jahweh's pardon cannot be bought by sacrifice and ritual; but He demands justice and righteousness from His people. In reading the selection note (1) Amos's method of first pronouncing doom upon neighboring peoples before including his hearers in the prophecy, (2) the kinds of misdeeds specified in the judgment, (3) the punishments to be visited upon Israel for social injustice, (4) what Amos has Jahweh say regarding sacrifice and ritual, (5) what Jahweh demands of His people, (6) Amos's prophecy of captivity, and (7) what Jahweh's intentions are for the future of Israel after He punishes them.

From: AMOS

Amos said, "The Lord will roar from Zion, and utter his voice from Jerusalem; and the habitations of the shepherds shall mourn, and the top of Carmel shall wither."

Thus saith the Lord: "For three transgressions of Damascus, and for four, I will not turn away the punishment thereof; because they have threshed Gilead with threshing instruments of iron. But I will send a fire into the house of Hazael, which shall devour the palaces of Ben-hadad. I will break also the bar of Damascus, and cut off the inhabitant from the plain of Aven, and him that holdeth the sceptre from the house of Eden: and the people of Syria shall go into captivity unto Kir," saith the Lord.

Thus saith the Lord: "For three transgressions of Gaza, and for four, I will not turn away the punishment thereof; because they carried away captive the whole captivity, to deliver them up to Edom. But I will send a fire on the wall of Gaza, which shall devour the palaces thereof: and I will cut off the inhabitant from Ashdod, and him that holdeth the sceptre from Ashkelon, and I will turn mine hand against Ekron: and the remnant of the Philistines shall perish," saith the Lord God.

Thus saith the Lord: "For three transgressions of Tyrus, and for four, I will not turn away the punishment thereof; because they delivered up the whole captivity to Edom, and remembered not the brotherly covenant. But I will send a fire on the wall of Tyrus, which shall devour the palaces thereof."

Thus saith the Lord: "For three transgres-

sions of Edom, and for four, I will not turn away the punishment thereof; because he did pursue his brother with the sword, and did cast off all pity, and his anger did tear perpetually, and he kept his wrath for ever. But I will send a fire upon Teman, which shall devour the palaces of Bozrah."

Thus saith the Lord: "For three transgressions of the children of Ammon, and for four, I will not turn away the punishment thereof; because they have ripped up the women with child of Gilead, that they might enlarge their border. But I will kindle a fire in the wall of Rabbah, and it shall devour the palaces thereof, with shouting in the day of battle, with a tempest in the day of the whirlwind: and their king shall go into captivity, he and his princes together," saith the Lord.

Thus saith the Lord: "For three transgressions of Moab, and for four, I will not turn away the punishment thereof; because he burned the bones of the king of Edom into lime. But I will send a fire upon Moab, and it shall devour the palaces of Kirioth: and Moab shall die with tumult, with shouting, and with the sound of the trumpet: and I will cut off the judge from the midst thereof, and will slay all the princes thereof with him," saith the Lord.

Thus saith the Lord: "For three transgressions of Judah, and for four, I will not turn away the punishment thereof; because they have despised the law of the Lord, and have not kept his commandments, and their lies caused them to err, after the which their fathers have walked. But I will send a fire upon Judah, and it shall devour the palaces of Jerusalem."

Thus saith the Lord: "For three transgressions of Israel, and for four, I will not turn away the punishment thereof; because they sold the righteous for silver, and the poor for a pair of shoes; that pant after the dust of the earth on the head of the poor, and turn aside the way of the meek: and a man and his father will go in unto the same maid, to profane my holy name: and they lay themselves down upon clothes laid to pledge by every altar, and they drink the wine of the condemned in the house of their god.

"Yet destroyed I the Amorite before them, whose height was like the height of the cedars, and he was strong as the oaks; yet I destroyed his fruit from above, and his roots from beneath. Also I brought you up from the land of Egypt, and led you forty years through the wilderness, to possess the land of the Amorite. And I raised up of your sons for prophets, and of your young men for Nazarites. Is it not even thus, O ye children of Israel?" saith the Lord. "But ye gave the Nazarites wine to drink; and commanded the prophets, saying, 'Prophesy not.'

"Behold, I am pressed under you, as a cart is pressed that is full of sheaves. Therefore the flight shall perish from the swift, and the strong shall not strengthen his force, neither shall the mighty deliver himself: neither shall he stand that handleth the bow; and he that is swift of foot shall not deliver himself: neither shall he that rideth the horse deliver himself. And he that is courageous among the mighty shall flee away naked in that day," saith the Lord.

Hear ye this word which I take up against you, even a lamentation, O house of Israel: "The virgin of Israel is fallen; she shall no more rise: she is forsaken upon her land; there is none to raise her up." For thus saith the Lord God: "The city that went out by a thousand shall leave a hundred, and that which went forth by a hundred shall leave ten, to the house of Israel."

For thus saith the Lord unto the house of Israel, "Seek ye me, and ye shall live: but seek not Beth-el, nor enter into Gilgal, and pass not to Beer-sheba: for Gilgal shall surely go into captivity, and Beth-el shall come to nought."

Seek the Lord, and ye shall live; lest he break out like fire in the house of Joseph, and devour it, and there be none to quench it in Beth-el. Ye who turn judgment to wormwood, and leave off righteousness in the earth, seek him that maketh the seven stars and Orion, and turneth the shadow of death into the morning, and maketh the day dark with night: that calleth for the waters of the sea, and poureth them out upon the face of the earth: the Lord is his name.

Forasmuch therefore as your treading is upon the poor, and ye take from him burdens of wheat: ye have built houses of hewn stone, but ye shall not dwell in them; ye have planted pleasant vineyards, but ye shall not drink wine of them. For I know your manifold transgressions and your mighty sins: they afflict the just, they take a bribe, and they turn aside the poor in the gate from their right. Therefore the prudent shall keep silence in that time; for it is an evil time.

Seek good, and not evil, that ye may live: and so the Lord, the God of hosts, shall be with you, as ye have spoken. Hate the evil, and love the good, and establish judgment in the gate: it may be that the Lord God of hosts will be gracious unto the remnant of Joseph. Therefore the Lord, the God of hosts, the Lord saith thus: "Wailing shall be in all streets; And they shall say in the highways, 'Alas! alas!' And they shall call the husbandman to mourning, and such as are skilful of lamentation to wailing. And in all vineyards shall be wailing: For I will pass through thee," saith the Lord.

"Woe unto you that desire the day of the Lord! To what end is it for you? The day of the Lord is darkness, and not light. As if a man did flee from a lion, and a bear met him; or went into the house, and leaned his hand on the wall, and a serpent bit him. Shall not the day of the Lord be darkness and not light? Even very dark and no brightness in it? I hate, I despise your feast days, and I will not smell in your solemn assemblies. Though ye offer me burnt offerings and your meat offerings, I will not accept them: neither will I regard the peace offerings of your fat beasts. Take thou away from me the noise of thy songs; for I will not hear the melody of thy viols. But let judgment run down as waters, and righteousness as a mighty stream. Have ye offered unto me sacrifices and offerings in the wilderness forty years, O house of Israel? But ye have borne the tabernacle of your Moloch and Chiun your images, the star of your god, which ye made to yourselves. Therefore will I cause you to go into captivity beyond Damascus," saith the Lord, whose name is the God of hosts.

"Are ye not as children of the Ethiopians unto me, O children of Israel?" saith the Lord. "Have not I brought up Israel out of the land of Egypt? And the Philistines from Caphtor, and the Syrians from Kir? Behold, the eyes of the Lord God are upon the sinful kingdom, and I will destroy it from off the face of the earth; saving that I will not utterly destroy the house of Jacob," saith the Lord. "For, lo, I will command, and I will sift the house of Israel among all nations, like as corn is sifted in a sieve, yet shall not the least grain fall upon the earth. All the sinners of my people shall die by the sword, which

say, 'The evil shall not overtake nor prevent us.'

"In that day will I raise up the tabernacle of David that is fallen, and close up the breaches thereof; and I will raise up his ruins, and I will build it as in the days of old: that they may possess the remnant of Edom, and of all the heathen, which are called by my name," saith the Lord that doeth this.

"Behold, the days come," saith the Lord, "that the plowman shall overtake the reaper, and the treader of grapes him that soweth seed; and the mountains shall drop sweet wine, and all the hills shall melt. And I will bring again the captivity of my people of Israel, and they shall build the waste cities, and inhabit them; and they shall plant vineyards, and drink the wine thereof; they shall also make gardens, and eat the fruit of them. And I will plant them upon their land, and they shall no more be pulled up out of their land which I have given them," saith the Lord thy God.

Amos had warned the northern kingdom that Jahweh would punish it for injustice, using the Assyrian host as a scourge of iron. The conquest of Samaria by the Assyrians in 722 B.C. seemed to fulfill this prophecy. Now was Israel being punished by Jahweh for its failure to achieve social justice. Would the southern kingdom heed this plain warning? Isaiah and Micah the Morasthite appeared in Jerusalem to sound the tocsin of impending destruction which Jahweh planned for the entire nation for its failure to heed the demands of justice. Lacking a precise definition of the corporate nature of sin, Isaiah and Micah, nevertheless, stated their conviction in bold terms that the entire community must suffer for its lapses. Although Israel would be chastised, Micah expressed a dream of universal peace that would eventually prevail. This statement represents one of the earliest professions of faith for a peaceful world and is the more significant because it emerged at a time when its fulfillment seemed utterly hopeless. In reading these selections note (1) what social and political wrongs met Jahweh's disapproval, (2) the punishment awaiting Zion and Jerusalem, (3) Micah's dream of universal peace, (4) Jahweh's contrast of how people were remembering Him and what He really desired of them, and (5) the conviction that after punishing them, Jahweh would eventually restore the people of Israel to their privileged position.

From: ISAIAH and MICAH

Hear, O heavens, and give ear, O earth: for the Lord hath spoken: "I have nourished and brought up children, and they have rebelled against me. The ox knoweth his owner, and the ass his master's crib; but Israel doth not know, my people doth not consider."

Ah sinful nation, a people laden with iniquity, a seed of evildoers, children that are corrupters! They have forsaken the Lord, they have provoked the Holy One of Israel unto anger, they are gone away backward.

Why should ye be stricken any more? ye will revolt more and more; the whole head is sick, and the whole heart faint. From the sole of the foot even unto the head there is no soundness in it; but wounds, and bruises, and putrifying sores: they have not been closed, neither bound up, neither mollified with ointment. Your country is desolate, your cities are burned with fire: your land, strangers devour it in your presence, and it is desolate, as overthrown by strangers. And the daughter of Zion is left as a cottage in a vineyard, as a lodge in a garden of cucumbers, as a besieged city. Except the Lord of hosts had left unto us a very small remnant, we should have been as Sodom, and we should have been like unto Gomorrah.

Hear the word of the Lord, ye rulers of Sodom! Give ear unto the law of our God, ye people of Gomorrah! "To what purpose is the multitude of your sacrifices unto me?" Saith the Lord: "I am full of the burnt offerings of rams, and the fat of fed beasts; and I delight not in the blood of bullocks, or of lambs or of he goats. When ye come to appear before me, who hath required this at your hand, to tread my courts? Bring no more vain oblations; incense is an abomination unto me; the new moons and sabbaths, the calling of assemblies, I cannot away with; it is iniquity, even the solemn meeting. Your new moons and your appointed feasts my soul hateth: they are a trouble unto me; I am weary to bear them. And when ye spread forth your hands, I will hide mine eyes from you: Yea, when ye make many prayers, I will not hear: your hands are full of blood. Wash you, make you clean; put away the evil of your doings from before mine eyes; cease to do evil;

learn to do well; seek judgment, relieve the oppressed, judge the fatherless, plead for the widow. Come now, and let us reason together," saith the Lord, "though your sins be as scarlet, they shall be as white as snow; though they be red like crimson, they shall be as wool. If ye be willing and obedient, ye shall eat the good of the land: but if ye refuse and rebel, ye shall be devoured with the sword," for the mouth of the Lord hath spoken it. . . .

Woe unto them that decree unrighteous decrees, and that write grievousness which they have prescribed; to turn aside the needy from judgment, and to take away the right from the poor of my people, that widows may be their prey, and that they may rob the fatherless! And what will ye do in the day of visitation, and in the desolation which shall come from far? To whom will ye flee for help? And where will you leave your glory? Without me they shall bow down under the prisoners, and they shall fall under the slain. For all this his anger is not turned away, but his hand is stretched out still.

O Assyrian, the rod of mine anger, and the staff in their hand is mine indignation. I will send him against a hypocritical nation, and against the people of my wrath will I give him a charge, to take the spoil, and to take the prey, and to tread them down like the mire of the streets. Howbeit he meaneth not so, neither doth his heart think so; but it is in his heart to destroy and cut off nations not a few. For he saith, "Are not my princes altogether kings? Is not Calno as Carchemish? Is not Hamath as Arpad? Is not Samaria as Damascus? As my hand hath found the kingdoms of the idols, and whose graven images did excel them of Jerusalem and of Samaria; shall I not, as I have done unto Samaria and her idols, so do to Jerusalem and her idols?"

ISAIAH

Hear, I pray you, O heads of Jacob, and ye princes of the house of Israel; is it not for you to know judgment? Who hate the good, and love the evil; who pluck off their skin from off them, and their flesh from off their bones; who also eat the flesh of my people, and flay their skin from off them; and they break their bones, and chop them in pieces, as for the pot, and as flesh within the caldron. Then shall they cry unto the Lord, but he will not hear them: he will even hide his face from them at that time, as they have behaved themselves ill in their doings.

Thus saith the Lord concerning the prophets that make my people err, that bite with their teeth, and cry, "Peace"; and he that putteth not into their mouths, they even prepare war against him: "Therefore night shall be unto you, that ye shall not have a vision; and it shall be dark unto you, that ye shall not divine; and the sun shall go down over the prophets, and the day shall be dark over them. Then shall the seers be ashamed, and the diviners confounded: yea, they shall all cover their lips; for there is no answer of God."

But truly I am full of power by the spirit of the Lord, and of judgment and of might, to declare unto Jacob his transgression, and to Israel his sin. Hear this, I pray you, ye heads of the house of Jacob, and princes of the house of Israel, that abhor judgment, and pervert all equity. They build up Zion with blood, and Jerusalem with iniquity. The heads thereof judge for reward, and the priests thereof teach for hire, and the prophets thereof divine for money: yet will they lean upon the Lord, and say, "Is not the Lord among us? None evil can come upon us." Therefore shall Zion for your sake be plowed as a field, and Jerusalem shall become heaps, and the mountain of the house as the high places of the forest.

But in the last days it shall come to pass, that the mountain of the house of the Lord shall be established in the top of the mountains, and it shall be exalted above the hills; and people shall flow unto it. And many nations shall come, and say, "Come, and let us go up to the mountain of the Lord, and to the house of the God of Jacob; and he will teach us of his ways, and we will walk in his paths": for the law shall go forth of Zion, and the word of the Lord from Jerusalem.

And he shall judge among many people, and rebuke strong nations afar off; and they shall beat their swords into plowshares, and their spears into pruninghooks: nation shall not lift up a sword against nation, neither shall they learn war any more. But they shall sit every man under his vine and under his fig tree; and none shall make them afraid: for the mouth of the Lord of hosts hath spoken it. For all people will walk every one in the name of his god, and we will walk in the name of the Lord our God for ever and ever.

"In that day," saith the Lord, "will I assemble her that halteth, and I will gather her that is driven out, and her that I have afflicted; and I will make her that halted a remnant, and her that was cast far off a strong nation": and the Lord shall reign over them in Mount Zion from henceforth, even for ever. . . .

Hear ye now what the Lord saith: "Arise, contend thou before the mountains, and let the hills hear thy voice."

Hear ye, O mountains, the Lord's controversy, and ye strong foundations of the earth: for the Lord hath a controversy with his people, and he will plead with Israel.

"O my people, what have I done unto thee? And wherein have I wearied thee? Testify against me. For I brought thee up out of the land of Egypt, and redeemed thee out of the house of servants; and I sent before thee Moses, Aaron, and Miriam."

Wherewith shall I come before the Lord, and bow myself before the high God? Shall I come before him with burnt offerings, with calves of a year old? Will the Lord be pleased with thousands of rams, or with ten thousands of rivers of oil? Shall I give my firstborn for my transgression, the fruit of my body for the sin of my soul? He hath showed thee, O man, what is good; and what doth the Lord require of thee, but to do justly, and to love mercy, and to walk humbly with thy God? . . .

Woe is me! for I am as when they have gathered the summer fruits, as the grape gleanings of the vintage: there is no cluster to eat: my soul desired the first ripe fruit. The good man is perished out of the earth; and there is none upright among men: they all lie in wait for blood; they hunt every man his brother with a net.

That they may do evil with both hands earnestly, the prince asketh, and the judge asketh for a reward; and the great man, he uttereth his mischievous desire: so they wrap it up. The best of them is as a brier: the most upright is sharper than a thorn hedge: the day of thy watchmen and thy visitation cometh; now shall be their perplexity.

Trust ye not in a friend, put ye not confidence in a guide: keep the doors of thy mouth from her that lieth in thy bosom. For the son dishonoreth the father, the daughter riseth up against her mother, the daughter-in-law against her mother-in-law; a man's enemies are the men of his own house. Therefore I will look unto the Lord; I will wait for the God of my salvation: my God will hear me.

Rejoice not against me, O mine enemy: when I fall, I shall arise; when I sit in darkness, the Lord shall be a light unto me. I will bear the indignation of the Lord, because I have sinned against him, until he plead my cause, and execute judgment for me: he will bring me forth to the light, and I shall behold his righteousness. Then she that is mine enemy shall see it, and shame shall cover her which said unto me, "Where is the Lord thy God?" Mine eyes shall behold her: now shall she be trodden down as the mire of the streets. In the day that thy walls are to be built, in that day shall the decree be far removed. In that day also he shall come even to thee from Assyria, and from the fortified cities, and from the fortress even to the river, and from sea to sea, and from mountain to mountain. Nothwithstanding, the land shall be desolate because of them that dwell therein, for the fruit of their doings.

Feed thy people with thy rod, the flock of thine heritage, which dwell solitarily in the wood, in the midst of Carmel: let them feed in Bashan and Gilead, as in the days of old. According to the days of thy coming out of the land of Egypt will I show unto him marvelous things.

The nations shall see and be confounded at all their might: they shall lay their hand upon their mouth, their ears shall be deaf. They shall lick the dust like a serpent, they shall move out of their holes like worms of the earth: they shall be afraid of the Lord our God, and shall fear because of thee. Who is a God like unto thee, that pardoneth iniquity, and passeth by the transgression of the remnant of his heritage? He retaineth not his anger for ever, because he delighteth in mercy. He will turn again, he will have compassion upon us; he will subdue our iniquities; and thou wilt cast all their sins into the depths of the sea. Thou wilt perform the truth to Jacob, and the mercy to Abraham, which thou hast sworn unto our fathers from the days of old.

MICAH

The disasters of the eighth century had considerably weakened Israel's faith in Jahweh as its divine protector. With the Assyrian conquerors came foreign ways and foreign gods. Other conquering hordes swept over the land, first the Scythian war bands followed by Chaldean Babylonians. In 586 B.C. Nebuchadnezzar appeared before Jerusalem, breached the fortifications, burned the temples and palaces, and deported thousands to Babylon. The Babylonian captivity had many consequences. Jahweh became more of a spiritual entity, disassociated as He was from the familiar scenes of His earlier triumphs. Moreover, with the community shattered by deportation, the personal and individual aspects of religion tended to supplant religion as a community enterprise. In this selection note (1) Ezekiel's statement of individualism in religion, (2) the listing of misdeeds of a social and of a religious nature, (3) the promise of favor to those who repent and, (4) the call for a new life on the part of each man.

From: EZEKIEL

The word of the Lord came unto me again, saying, "What mean ye, that ye use this proverb concerning the land of Israel, saying,

'The fathers have eaten sour grapes,
And the children's teeth are set on edge'?

"As I live," saith the Lord God, "ye shall not have occasion any more to use this proverb in Israel. Behold, all souls are mine; as the soul of the father, so also the soul of the son is mine: the soul that sinneth, it shall die.

"But if a man be just, and do that which is lawful and right, and hath not eaten upon the mountains, neither hath lifted up his eyes to the idols of the house of Israel, neither hath defiled his neighbor's wife, neither hath come near to a menstruous woman, and hath not oppressed any, but hath restored to the debtor his pledge, hath spoiled none by violence, hath given his bread to the hungry, and hath covered the naked with a garment; he that hath not given forth upon usury, neither hath taken any increase, that hath withdrawn his hand from iniquity, hath executed true judgment between man and man, hath walked in my statutes, and hath kept my judgments, to deal truly; he is just, he shall surely live," saith the Lord God.

"If he beget a son that is a robber, a shedder of blood, and that doeth the like to any one of these things, and that doeth not any of those duties, but even hath eaten upon the mountains, and defiled his neighbor's wife, hath oppressed the poor and needy, hath spoiled by violence, hath not restored the pledge, and hath lifted up his eyes to the idols, hath committed abomination, hath given forth upon usury, and hath taken increase: shall he then live? He shall not live: he hath done all these abominations; he shall surely die; his blood shall be upon him.

"Now, lo, if he beget a son, that seeth all his father's sins which he hath done, and considereth, and doeth not such like, that hath not eaten upon the mountains, neither hath lifted up his eyes to the idols of the house of Israel, hath not defiled his neighbor's wife, neither hath oppressed any, hath not withheld the pledge, neither hath spoiled by violence, but hath given his bread to the hungry, and hath covered the naked with a garment, that hath taken off his hand from the poor, that hath not received usury nor increase, hath executed my judgments, hath walked in my statutes; he shall not die for the iniquity of his father, he shall surely live.

"As for his father, because he cruelly oppressed, spoiled his brother by violence, and did that which is not good among his people, lo, even he shall die in his iniquity.

"Yet say ye, 'Why? doth not the son bear the iniquity of the father?' When the son hath done that which is lawful and right, and hath kept all my statutes, and hath done them, he shall surely live. The soul that sinneth, it shall die. The son shall not bear the iniquity of the father, neither shall the father bear the iniquity of the son: the righteousness of the righteous shall be upon him, and the wickedness of the wicked shall be upon him. But if the wicked will turn from all his sins that he hath committed, and keep all my statutes, and do that which is lawful and right, he shall surely live, he shall not die. All his transgressions that he hath committed, they shall not be mentioned unto him: in his righteousness that he hath done he shall live. Have I any pleasure at all that the wicked should die?" saith the Lord God: "and not that he should return from his ways, and live?

"But when the righteous turneth away from his righteousness, and committeth iniquity, and doeth according to all the abominations that the wicked man doeth, shall he live? All his righteousness that he hath done shall not be mentioned: in his trespass that he hath trespassed, and in his sin that he hath sinned, in them shall he die.

"Yet ye say, 'The way of the Lord is not equal.' Hear now, O house of Israel: is not my way equal? Are not your ways unequal? When a righteous man turneth away from his righteousness, and committeth iniquity, and dieth in them; for his iniquity that he hath done shall he die. Again, when the wicked man turneth away from his wickedness that he hath committed, and doeth that which is lawful and right, he shall save his soul alive. Because he considereth, and turneth away from all his transgressions that he hath committed, he shall surely live, he shall not die. Yet saith the house of Israel, 'The way of the Lord is not equal.' O house of Israel, are not my ways equal? Are not your ways unequal? Therefore I will judge you, O house of Israel, every one according to his ways," saith the Lord God. "Repent, and turn yourselves from all your transgressions; so iniquity shall not be your ruin.

"Cast away from you all your transgressions, whereby ye have transgressed; and make you a new heart and a new spirit: for why will ye die, O house of Israel? For I have no pleasure in the death of him that dieth," saith the Lord God: "wherefore turn yourselves, and live ye."

The earlier prophets, whatever kind or degree of superiority they attributed to Jahweh, seemingly never questioned that the gods of other peoples were real; but the prophets after 600 B.C. went far beyond this position, first by asserting that Jahweh was superior to all other gods, and second by proclaiming that there were no other gods. In the writings of the unknown prophet, sometimes known as the Second Isaiah or Deutero-Isaiah, there is pictured a Jahweh of immeasurable might and lofty majesty, before whom everything on earth that lifts itself on high before Him shall be abased. Moreover, Jahweh is here described as sole God, maker of heaven and earth, and ruler of the destinies of men and nations. Such assertions of omnipotence at the very moment of Judah's destruction, which in the eyes of the world represented Jahweh's total defeat, needed explanation. Jahweh had been responsible for the defeat of Israel and Judah; indeed, He had been responsible for putting into motion the empires of antiquity to serve and fulfill His purpose. All of the forces of history were controlled by one universal will. The Second Isaiah answered another troublesome question: How was it possible for the god of a small and relatively unimportant segment of the human family to be sole God of the universe? How, if there be but one God, was it that the Jews alone knew and worshipped Him? God, who was identical with Jahweh, chose Israel and revealed Himself to it so that Israel could be the prophet of the true God to enlighten the Gentile world. In reading the selections note (1) the author's description of God's majesty, (2) his statement of monotheism, (3) the role of Israel as a messenger to the Gentiles, and (4) the nature and mission of the messiah, or anointed one of God.

From: ISAIAH

"Comfort ye, comfort ye my people," saith your God. "Speak ye comfortably to Jerusalem, and cry unto her, that her warfare is accomplished, that her iniquity is pardoned: for she hath received of the Lord's hand double for all her sins."

The voice of him that crieth in the wilderness, "Prepare ye the way of the Lord, make straight in the desert a highway for our God. Every valley shall be exalted, and every mountain and hill shall be made low: and the crooked shall be made straight, and the rough places plain: and the glory of the Lord shall be revealed, and all flesh shall see it together: for the mouth of the Lord hath spoken it."

The voice said, "Cry." And he said, "What shall I cry?"

"All flesh is grass, and all the goodliness thereof is as the flower of the field: the grass withereth, the flower fadeth: because the spirit of the Lord bloweth upon it: surely the people is grass. The grass withereth, the flower fadeth: but the word of our God shall stand for ever."

O Zion, that bringest good tidings, get thee up into the high mountain; O Jerusalem, that bringest good tidings, lift up thy voice with strength; lift it up, be not afraid; say unto the cities of Judah, "Behold your God!"

Behold, the Lord God will come with strong hand, and his arm shall rule for him: behold, his reward is with him, and his work before him. He shall feed his flock like a shepherd: he shall gather the lambs with his arm, and carry them in his bosom, and shall gently lead those that are with young.

Who hath measured the waters in the hollow of his hand, and meted out heaven with the span, and comprehended the dust of the earth in a measure, and weighed the mountains in scales, and the hills in a balance? Who hath directed the Spirit of the Lord, or being his counsellor hath taught him? With whom took he counsel, and who instructed him, and taught him in the path of judgment, and taught him knowledge, and showed to him the way of understanding? Behold, the nations are as a drop of a bucket, and are counted as the small dust of the balance: behold, he taketh up the isles as a very little thing. And Lebanon is not sufficient to burn, nor the beasts thereof sufficient for a burnt offering. All nations before him are as nothing; and they are counted to him less than nothing, and vanity.

To whom then will ye liken God? Or what likeness will ye compare unto him? . . . Have ye not known? Have ye not heard? Hath it not been told you from the beginning? Have ye not understood from the foundations of the earth? It is he that sitteth upon the circle of the earth, and the inhabitants thereof are as grasshoppers; that stretcheth out the heavens as a curtain, and spreadeth them out as a tent to dwell in; that bringeth the princes to nothing; he maketh the judges of the earth as vanity. Yea, they shall not be planted; yea, they shall not be sown; yea, their stock shall not take root in the earth: and he shall also blow upon them, and they shall wither, and the whirlwind shall take them away as stubble.

"To whom then will ye liken me, or shall I be equal?" saith the Holy One. Lift up your eyes on high, and behold who hath created these things, that bringeth out their host by number: he calleth them all by names by the greatness of his might, for that he is strong in power; not one faileth. Why sayest thou, O Jacob, and speakest, O Israel, "My way is hid from the Lord, and my judgment is passed over from my God"?

Hast thou not known? Hast thou not heard, that the everlasting God, the Lord, the Creator of the ends of the earth, fainteth not, neither is weary? There is no searching of his understanding. He giveth power to the faint; and to them that have no might he increaseth strength. Even the youths shall faint and be weary, and the young men shall utterly fall: but they that wait upon the Lord shall renew their strength; they shall mount up with wings as eagles; they shall run, and not be weary; and they shall walk, and not faint. . . .

Thus saith the Lord to his anointed, to Cyrus, whose right hand I have held, to subdue nations before him; and I will loose the loins of kings, to open before him the two-leaved gates; and the gates shall not be shut: "I will go before thee, and make the crooked places straight: I will break in pieces the gates of brass, and cut in sunder the bars of iron; and I will give thee the treasures of darkness, and hidden riches of secret places, that thou mayest know that I, the Lord, which call thee by thy name, am the God of Israel. For Jacob my servant's sake, and Israel mine elect, I have even called thee by thy name; I have surnamed thee, though thou hast not known me. I am the Lord, and there is none else, there is no God beside me; I girded thee, though thou hast not known me: that they may know from the rising of the sun, and from the west, that there is none beside me. I am the Lord, and there is none else. I form the light, and create darkness: I make peace, and create evil: I the Lord do all these things. Drop down, ye heavens, from above, and let the skies pour down righteousness; let the earth open, and let them bring forth salvation, and let righteousness spring up together; I the Lord have created it. Woe unto him that striveth with his Maker! Let the potsherd strive with the potsherds of the earth. Shall the clay say to him that fashioneth it, 'What makest thou?' Or thy work, 'He hath no hands'? Woe unto him that saith unto his father, 'What begettest thou?' Or to the woman, 'What hast thou brought forth?' "

Thus saith the Lord, the Holy One of Israel, and his Maker, "Ask me of things to come concerning my sons, and concerning the work of my hands command ye me. I have made the earth, and created man upon it; I, even my hands, have stretched out the heavens, and all their host have I commanded. I have raised him up in righteousness, and I will direct all his ways; he shall build my city, and he shall let go my captives, not for price nor reward," saith the Lord of hosts.

Thus saith the Lord, "The labor of Egypt, and merchandise of Ethiopia and of the Sabeans, men of stature, shall come over unto thee, and they shall be thine: they shall come after thee; in chains they shall come over, and they shall fall down unto thee, they shall make supplication unto thee, saying, 'Surely God is in thee; and there is none else, there is no God.' "

Verily, thou art a God that hidest thyself, O God of Israel, the Saviour. They shall be ashamed, and also confounded, all of them: they shall go to confusion together that are makers of idols. But Israel shall be saved in the Lord with an everlasting salvation: ye shall not be ashamed nor confounded world without end. . . .

Who hath believed our report? And to whom is the arm of the Lord revealed? For he shall grow up before him as a tender plant, and as a root out of a dry ground: he hath no form nor comeliness; and when we shall see him, there is no beauty that we should desire him. He is despised and rejected of men; a man of sorrows, and acquainted with grief: and we hid as it were our faces from him; he was despised, and we esteemed him not. Surely he hath borne our griefs, and carried our sorrows: yet we did esteem him stricken, smitten of God, and afflicted. But he was wounded for our transgressions, he was bruised for our iniquities: the chastisement of our peace was upon him; and with his stripes we are healed. All we like sheep have gone astray; we have turned every one to his own way; and the Lord hath laid on him the iniquity of us all. He was oppressed, and he was afflicted, yet he opened not his mouth: he is brought as a lamb to the slaughter, and as a sheep before her shearers is dumb, so he openeth not his mouth. He was taken from prison and from judgment: and who shall declare his generation? For he was cut off out of the land of the living: for the transgression of my people was he stricken. And he made his grave with the wicked, and with the rich in his death; because he had done no violence, neither was any deceit in his mouth.

Yet it pleased the Lord to bruise him; he hath put him to grief: when thou shalt make his soul an offering for sin . . . , the pleasure of the Lord shall prosper in his hand. He shall see of the travail of his soul, and shall be satisfied: by his knowledge shall my righteous servant justify many; for he shall bear their iniquities. Therefore will I divide him a portion with the great, and he shall divide the spoil with the strong; because he hath poured out his soul unto death: and he was numbered with the transgressors; and he bore the sin of many, and made intercession for the transgressors.

The Egyptians

From earliest times the Egyptians believed that moral goodness, right-doing, and righteousness pleased both gods and men, while wrong-doing displeased the gods and angered their fellow men. Moreover, evidence suggests that they believed they would be judged after death by a court presided over by a god-judge. These views underwent slow development from vague and undefined beginnings in early Egyptian history to a more certain and definite set of beliefs used in regulating many of the activities of everyday life. Religious thought developed rapidly after the downfall of the Old Kingdom (about 2500 B.C.), and ethics came to be more thoroughly integrated with religion than formerly. The cult of Osiris increased in popularity, partly because of its promise of eternal life not only to kings, but to all men and women; in time Osiris came to be identified with the supreme judge who sat in the Hall of Maāt. In addition to requiring high moral conduct on earth as a prerequisite for an afterlife, certain magic spells and rubrics were considered useful to the soul in its journey to the judgment hall. The title given to one of these collections by modern scholars is The Book of the Dead. This selection (composed about 1500 B.C.) is a part of the declaration which the soul made before Osiris and the judges. In reading it note (1) the salutation to the gods, (2) the actions which refer to the conduct of religious practices, (3) the standards of personal morality, (4) the emphasis upon social justice, and (5) the evidences of magic.

From: THE BOOK OF THE DEAD

Homage to Thee, O Great God, Lord of the city of MAĀTI, I have come unto Thee, O my Lord, and I have brought myself hither that I may gaze upon Thy beauties (or beneficence).

I know Thee, I know Thy Name, I know the name[s] of the Forty-two gods who are with Thee in this Hall of MAĀTI, who live as the warders of sinners [and] who swallow their blood on that day of reckoning up the characters (or dispositions of men) in the presence of UN-NEFER (i.e. OSIRIS). In truth 'REKHTI-MERTI-NEB-MAĀTI' is Thy Name.

Verily I have come unto Thee, I have brought unto Thee MAĀT (i.e. TRUTH, or the LAW), I have crushed for Thee SIN.

1. I have not acted sinfully towards men.
2. I have not oppressed the members of my family.
3. I have not done wrong instead of what is right.
4. I have known no worthless folk.
5. I have not committed abominable acts.
6. I have not made excessive work to be done for me on any day(?).
7. I have [not made] my name to go forth for positions of dignity.
8. I have not domineered over servants.
9. I have not belittled god [or the God].
10. I have not filched the property of the lowly man.
11. I have not done things which are the abominations of the gods.
12. I have not vilified a servant to his master.
13. I have not inflicted pain (or caused suffering).
14. I have not permitted any man to suffer hunger.
15. I have not made any man to weep.
16. I have not committed murder (or slaughter).
17. I have not given an order to cause murder.

E. A. Wallis Budge, From Fetish to God in Ancient Egypt, Oxford University Press, London, 1934, 296–300. Courtesy of the University College, Oxford and Christ College, Cambridge.

18. I have not made men and women to suffer calamities.
19. I have not purloined the oblations in the temples.
20. I have not defrauded the gods of [their] cakes (or offerings).
21. I have not carried off the cakes of the AAKHU (the dead?).
22. I have not committed sodomy.
23. I have not polluted [the sacred waters of the god of my city].
24. I have not made light the bushel.
25. I have not filched from, nor added to, an estate.
26. I have not encroached upon the fields [of others].
27. I have not added to the weights of the scales [to cheat the seller].
28. I have not diminished the weight of the pointer of the scales.
29. I have not snatched away milk from the mouth[s] of children.
30. I have not driven away the cattle from their pastures.
31. I have not snared the geese in the preserves of the gods.
32. I have not fished with bait made of the bodies of fish.
33. I have not stopped water when it should run.
34. I have not made a cutting in a canal of running water.
35. I have not extinguished a fire when it should burn.
36. I have not neglected the times for the chosen offerings.
37. I have not driven away the cattle from the farms of the gods.
38. I have not obstructed the god in his comings forth (or appearances in processions).
39. Hail, USEKH-NEMMAT, coming out from ANNU (HELIOPOLIS), I have not committed sin.
40. Hail, HEPT-SHET, coming out from KHER-ĀBA, I have not robbed.
41. Hail, FENTI, coming out from KHE-MENU (HERMOPOLIS).
42. Hail, AM-KHAIBIT, coming out from QERRTI (ELEPHANTINE?), I have not committed thefts.
43. Hail, NEHA-ḤER, coming out from RE-STAU, I have not slain men and women.
44. Hail, RUTI (SHU-TEFNUT), coming out from heaven, I have not diminished the bushel.
45. Hail, ARITI-F-SHET, coming out from SEKHEM, I have not defrauded.
46. Hail, NEBA, coming out and retreating, I have not plundered sacred property.
47. Hail, SET-QESU, coming out from ḤENSU (HERAKLEOPOLIS), I have not uttered falsehood.
48. Hail, KHEMI, coming out from the Hidden Sanctuary, I have not robbed with violence.
49. Hail, UADJ-NESERT, coming out from HE-T-KA-PTAḤ (MEMPHIS), I have not blasphemed (or cursed god or man).
50. Hail, ḤER-F-ḤA-F, coming out from TEPHET-DJAT, I have not carried away food (?).
51. Hail, QERTI, coming out from AMENT, I have not uttered slanders (or words of backbiting).
52. Hail, TA-RET, coming out from the night, I have not eaten my heart.
53. Hail, HEDJ-ABEHU, coming out from TA-SHE (the FAYYŪM), I have not invaded [on the property of others].
54. Hail, UNEM-SNEF, coming out from the chamber of the block of slaughter, I have not slain a sacred bull.
55. Hail, UNEM-BESKU, coming out from the MĀBET chamber, I have not laid waste ploughed lands.
56. Hail, NEB-MAĀT, coming out from the city of MAĀTI, I have not played the eavesdropper.
57. Hail, THENEMI, coming out from UBAST (BUBASTIS), I have not set my mouth in motion [for mischief].
58. Hail, ĀNTI, coming out from HELIOPO-LIS, I have not been wroth without a cause (?).
59. Hail, TU-TUT-F, coming out from the nome of ĀNDJ-T, I have not lain with a lier with men.
60. Hail, UAMEMTI, coming out from the chamber of slaughter, I have not masturbated.

61. Hail, MA-ANTEF, coming out from PER-MENU, I have not lain with the woman of a man (i.e. another man's wife).

62. Hail, HERI-SERU (?), coming out from NEHAT, I have terrified no man.

63. Hail, NEB-SEKHEM, coming out from GAUI (?), I have not made hot my mouth [I have avoided irascibility].

64. Hail, SHEṬ-KHERU, coming out from URIT, I have not made myself deaf to the admonitions of MAĀT (i.e. the Law).

65. Hail, NEKHEN, coming out from HEQA-ĀNDJ (HELIOPOLIS), I have made no man to weep.

66. Hail, KENEMTI, coming out from KEN-MET, I have reviled no man.

67. Hail, AN-ḤETEP-F, coming out from SAU-T (SAÏS), I have not acted truculently (or with unnecessary violence).

68. Hail, SER-KHERU, coming out from UNSI (?), I have not hurried my heart (i.e. judged hastily, or acted without due thought and consideration).

69. Hail, NEB-HERU, coming out from NEDJF-T, I have not attacked the . . . I have not . . . of the god.

70. Hail, SREKHI, coming out from UTHEN-T, I have not multiplied speech overmuch (?).

71. Hail, NEB-ĀBUI, coming out from SAU-T (SAÏS), I have not acted deceitfully, countenancing evil (or wickedness).

72. Hail, NEFER-TEM, coming out from HE-T-KA-PTAḤ (MEMPHIS), I have not spoken treasonably about the king.

73. Hail, TEM-SEP, coming out from ṬEṬU, I have not fouled water.

74. Hail, ARI-EM-AB-F, coming out from TEBU, I have not made high my voice.

75. Hail, AHI, coming out from NU, I have not blasphemed the god.

76. Hail, UADJ-REKHIT, [coming out from SAU-T], I have not committed acts of arrogance (or 'stinking deeds').

77. Hail, NEHEB-NEFER-T, coming out from his temple, I have not thrust myself forward pridefully.

78. Hail, NEHEB-KAU, coming out from his sanctuary, I have not increased my possessions except through my own property.

79. Hail, DJESER-TEP, coming out from his shrine, the god of the city hath not been cursed through me.

80. Hail, ĀN-Ā-F, [coming out from AU-GERT], I have not belittled the god of [my] city.

I am washed. I am washed. I am washed. I am washed. My purity (?) is the purity of that great BENU which is in ḤENSU (i.e. HANES, HERAKLEOPOLIS). For I am that Nose of the Lord of the Winds (i.e. THOTH), who maketh all mankind to live, on the day of the filling of the UDJAT (i.e. full moon) in ANNU (HELIOPOLIS) in the second month of the season of PERT, the last day [in the presence of the Lord of this land]. I have seen the fullness of the UDJAT (i.e. full moon) in ANNU. Evil shall not happen to me in this land, in the Hall of MAĀTI, because I know the name[s] of these gods who are therein [who are the followers of the Great God].

Greek Civilization

The first people to develop an outstanding civilization on the continent of Europe were the Greeks. Their ancestors had migrated from central Europe, beginning sometime around 2000 B.C., and had conquered the peoples who were already living on the peninsula that was to become their home. When the Greeks arrived on the shores of the Mediterranean, their culture was a primitive one, but it gradually matured, and by 500 B.C. these people entered what has become known as the Golden Age of Greece. They excelled in nearly every phase of human achievement, and in a period of less than 200 years prominent Greeks produced works that have placed their names for all times among the great men of human history. Politically, they developed democratic institutions which in turn made possible an environment conducive to individual expression and creation. Philosophy, in particular, appealed to them, but the search for truth and perfection was not confined to that activity; they carried it into the fields of literature, art, and, in the case of the Alexandrian Greeks, of science as well. By 300 B.C. the Greek Civilization was eclipsed and other peoples took their places of leadership in the Mediterranean world, but subsequent ages have never ceased to study what the Greeks achieved, and thus their contribution to Western Civilization has been continuous as well as profound.

Thucydides

Thucydides (about 471–400 B.C.), one of the world's greatest historians, concluded that the Peloponnesian War, which in many respects was like a civil war among the city states of the Greek world, represented a major event in world history. The Greeks had succeeded in turning back the Persian hosts, thus saving the West from engulfment in a sweeping tide of oriental influences. Victory in the Persian wars released significant creative energies among the Greeks with startling achievements, particularly in the city-state of Athens, which witnessed a flowering of culture and at the same time sought political supremacy among her neighbors. This latter ambition led to the disastrous Peloponnesian Wars which so weakened the Greek states that they became an easy prey to the armies of Alexander. Thucydides, believing that the war had a far-reaching importance, carefully recorded its history. This selection is from the author's account of a funeral oration delivered by the great Athenian leader, Pericles, in which Pericles attempted to explain some of the underlying characteristics of the Athenian spirit. In reading it note (1) the nature of the funerary ceremonies, (2) Pericles' description of Athenian democracy, and (3) the ideals of the Athenian way of life.

From: THE PELOPONNESIAN WAR

In the same winter the Athenians gave a funeral at the public cost to those who had first fallen in this war. It was a custom of their ancestors, and the manner of it is as follows:

Three days before the ceremony, the bones of the dead are laid out in a tent which has been erected; and their friends bring to their relatives such offerings as they please. In the funeral procession cypress coffins are borne in carts, one for each tribe; the bones of the deceased being placed in the coffin of their tribe. Among these is carried one empty bier decked for the missing, that is, for those whose bodies could not be recovered. Any citizen or stranger who pleases, joins in the procession: and the female relatives are there to wail at the burial. The dead are laid in the public sepulchre in the most beautiful suburb of the city, in which those who fall in war are always buried; with the exception of those slain at Marathon, who for their singular and extraordinary valour

were interred on the spot where they fell. After the bodies have been laid in the earth, a man chosen by the state, of approved wisdom and eminent reputation, pronounces over them an appropriate panegyric; after which all retire. Such is the manner of the burying; and throughout the whole of the war, whenever the occasion arose, the established custom was observed. Meanwhile these were the first that had fallen, and Pericles, son of Xanthippus, was chosen to pronounce their eulogium. When the proper time arrived, he advanced from the sepulchre to an elevated platform in order to be heard by as many of the crowd as possible, and spoke as follows:

"Most of my predecessors in this place have commended him who made this speech part of the law, telling us that it is well that it should be delivered at the burial of those who fall in battle. For myself, I should have thought that the worth which had displayed itself in

As translated by R. Crawley in *The Complete Writings of Thucydides, The Peloponnesian War*, The Modern Library, New York, 1934, 102–109. Courtesy of Random House, Inc.

deeds, would be sufficiently rewarded by honours also shown by deeds; such as you now see in this funeral prepared at the people's cost. And I could have wished that the reputations of many brave men were not to be imperilled in the mouth of a single individual, to stand or fall according as he spoke well or ill. For it is hard to speak properly upon a subject where it is even difficult to convince your hearers that you are speaking the truth. On the one hand, the friend who is familiar with every fact of the story, may think that some point has not been set forth with that fulness which he wishes and knows it to deserve; on the other, he who is a stranger to the matter may be led by envy to suspect exaggeration if he hears anything above his own nature. For men can endure to hear others praised only so long as they can severally persuade themselves of their own ability to equal the actions recounted; when this point is passed, envy comes in and with it incredulity. However, since our ancestors have stamped this custom with their approval, it becomes my duty to obey the law and to try to satisfy your several wishes and opinions as best I may.

"I shall begin with our ancestors: it is both just and proper that they should have the honour of the first mention on an occasion like the present. They dwelt in the country without break in the succession from generation to generation, and handed it down free to the present time by their valour. And if our more remote ancestors deserve praise, much more do our own fathers, who added to their inheritance the empire which we now possess, and spared no pains to be able to leave their acquisitions to us of the present generation. Lastly, there are few parts of our dominions that have not been augmented by those of us here, who are still more or less in the vigour of life; while the mother country has been furnished by us with everything that can enable her to depend on her own resources whether for war or for peace. That part of our history which tells of the military achievements which gave us our several possessions, or of the ready valour with which either we or our fathers stemmed the tide of Hellenic or foreign aggression, is a theme too familiar to my hearers for me to dilate on, and I shall therefore pass it by. But

what was the road by which we reached our position, what the form of government under which our greatness grew, what the national habits out of which it sprang; these are questions which I may try to solve before I proceed to my panegyric upon these men; since I think this to be a subject upon which on the present occasion a speaker may properly dwell, and to which the whole assemblage, whether citizens or foreigners, may listen with advantage.

"Our constitution does not copy the laws of neighbouring states; we are rather a pattern to others than imitators ourselves. Its administration favours the many instead of the few; this is why it is called a democracy. If we look to the laws, they afford equal justice to all in their private differences; if to social standing, advancement in public life falls to reputation for capacity, class considerations not being allowed to interfere with merit; nor again does poverty bar the way, if a man is able to serve the state, he is not hindered by the obscurity of his condition. The freedom which we enjoy in our government extends also to our ordinary life. There, far from exercising a jealous surveillance over each other, we do not feel called upon to be angry with our neighbour for doing what he likes, or even to indulge in those injurious looks which cannot fail to be offensive, although they inflict no positive penalty. But all this ease in our private relations does not make us lawless as citizens. Against this fear is our chief safeguard, teaching us to obey the magistrates and the laws, particularly such as regard the protection of the injured, whether they are actually on the statute book, or belong to that code which, although unwritten, yet cannot be broken without acknowledged disgrace.

"Further, we provide plenty of means for the mind to refresh itself from business. We celebrate games and sacrifices all the year round, and the elegance of our private establishments forms a daily source of pleasure and helps to banish the spleen; while the magnitude of our city draws the produce of the world into our harbour, so that to the Athenian the fruits of other countries are as familiar a luxury as those of his own.

"If we turn to our military policy, there also we differ from our antagonists. We throw open our city to the world, and never by alien acts exclude foreigners from any opportunity of learning or observing, although the eyes of an enemy may occasionally profit by our liberality; trusting less in system and policy than to the native spirit of our citizens; while in education, where our rivals from their very cradles by a painful discipline seek after manliness, at Athens we live exactly as we please, and yet are just as ready to encounter every legitimate danger. In proof of this it may be noticed that the Lacedaemonians do not invade our country alone, but bring with them all their confederates; while we Athenians advance unsupported into the territory of a neighbour, and fighting upon a foreign soil usually vanquish with ease men who are defending their homes. Our united force was never yet encountered by any enemy, because we have at once to attend to our marine and to despatch our citizens by land upon a hundred different services; so that, wherever they engage with some such fraction of our strength, a success against a detachment is magnified into a victory over the nation, and a defeat into a reverse suffered at the hands of our entire people. And yet if with habits not of labour but of ease, and courage not of art but of nature, we are still willing to encounter danger, we have the double advantage of escaping the experience of hardships in anticipation and of facing them in the hour of need as fearlessly as those who are never free from them.

"Nor are these the only points in which our city is worthy of admiration. We cultivate refinement without extravagance and knowledge without effeminacy; wealth we employ more for use than for show, and place the real disgrace of poverty not in owning to the fact but in declining the struggle against it. Our public men have, besides politics, their private affairs to attend to, and our ordinary citizens, though occupied with the pursuits of industry, are still fair judges of public matters; for, unlike any other nation, regarding him who takes no part in these duties not as unambitious but as useless, we Athenians are able to judge at all events if we cannot originate, and instead of looking on discussion as a stumbling-block in the way of action, we think it an indispensable preliminary to any wise action at all. Again, in our enterprises we present the singular spectacle of daring and deliberation, each carried to its highest point, and both united in the same persons; although usually decision is the fruit of ignorance, hesitation of reflexion. But the palm of courage will surely be adjudged most justly to those who best know the difference between hardship and pleasure and yet are never tempted to shrink from danger. In generosity we are equally singular, acquiring our friends by conferring, not by receiving favours. Yet, of course, the doer of the favour is the firmer friend of the two, in order by continued kindness to keep the recipient in his debt; while the debtor feels less keenly from the very consciousness that the return he makes will be a payment, not a free gift. And it is only the Athenians who, fearless of consequences, confer their benefits not from calculations of expediency, but in the confidence of liberality.

"In short, I say that as a city we are the school of Hellas; while I doubt if the world can produce a man, who where he has only himself to depend upon, is equal to so many emergencies, and graced by so happy a versatility as the Athenian. And that this is no mere boast thrown out for the occasion, but plain matter of fact, the power of the state acquired by these habits proves. For Athens alone of her contemporaries is found when tested to be greater than her reputation, and alone gives no occasion to her assailants to blush at the antagonist by whom they have been worsted, or to her subjects to question her title by merit to rule. Rather, the admiration of the present and succeeding ages will be ours, since we have not left our power without witness, but have shown it by mighty proofs; and far from needing a Homer for our panegyrist, or other of his craft whose verses might charm for the moment only for the impression which they gave to melt at the touch of fact, we have forced every sea and land to be the highway of our daring, and everywhere, whether for evil or for good, have left imperishable monuments behind us. Such is the Athens for which these men, in the assertion of their resolve not to lose her, nobly fought and died; and well may every one of their survivors be ready to suffer in her cause.

"Indeed if I have dwelt at some length upon the character of our country, it has been to show that our stake in the struggle is not the same as theirs who have no such blessings to lose, and also that the panegyric of the men over whom I am now speaking might be by definite proofs established. That panegyric is now in a great measure complete; for the Athens that I have celebrated is only what the heroism of these and their like have made her, men whose fame, unlike that of most Hellenes, will be found to be only commensurate with their deserts. And if a test of worth be wanted, it is to be found in their closing scene, and this not only in the cases in which it set the final seal upon their merit, but also in those in which it gave the first intimation of their having any. For there is justice in the claim that steadfastness in his country's battles should be as a cloak to cover a man's other imperfections; since the good action has blotted out the bad, and his merit as a citizen more than outweighed his demerits as an individual. But none of these allowed either wealth with its prospect of future enjoyment to unnerve his spirit, or poverty with its hope of a day of freedom and riches to tempt him to shrink from danger. No, holding that vengeance upon their enemies was more to be desired than any personal blessings, and reckoning this to be the most glorious of hazards, they joyfully determined to accept the risk, to make sure of their vengeance and to let their wishes wait; and while committing to hope the uncertainty of final success, in the business before them they thought fit to act boldly and trust in themselves. Thus choosing to die resisting, rather than to live submitting, they fled only from dishonour, but met danger face to face, and after one brief moment, while at the summit of their fortune, escaped, not from their fear, but from their glory.

"So died these men as became Athenians. You, their survivors, must determine to have as unaltering a resolution in the field, though you may pray that it may have a happier issue. And not contented with ideas derived only from words of the advantages which are bound up with the defence of your country, though these would furnish a valuable text to a speaker even before an audience so alive to them as the present, you must yourselves realise the power of Athens, and feed your eyes upon her from day to day, till love of her fills your hearts; and then, when all her greatness shall break upon you, you must reflect that it was by courage, sense of duty, and a keen feeling of honour in action that men were enabled to win all this, and that no personal failure in an enterprise could make them consent to deprive their country of their valour, but they laid it at her feet as the most glorious contribution that they could offer. For this offering of their lives made in common by them all they each of them individually received that renown which never grows old, and for a sepulchre, not so much that in which their bones have been deposited, but that noblest of shrines wherein their glory is laid up to be eternally remembered upon every occasion on which deed or story shall fall for its commemoration. For heroes have the whole earth for their tomb; and in lands far from their own, where the column with its epitaph declares it, there is enshrined in every breast a record unwritten with no tablet to preserve it, except that of the heart. These take as your model, and judging happiness to be the fruit of freedom and freedom of valour, never decline the dangers of war. For it is not the miserable that would most justly be unsparing of their lives; these have nothing to hope for: it is rather they to whom continued life may bring reverses as yet unknown, and to whom a fall, if it came, would be most tremendous in its consequences. And surely, to a man of spirit, the degradation of cowardice must be immeasurably more grievous than the unfelt death which strikes him in the midst of his strength and patriotism!

"Comfort, therefore, not condolence, is what I have to offer to the parents of the dead who may be here. Numberless are the chances to which, as they know, the life of man is subject; but fortunate indeed are they who draw for their lot a death so glorious as that which has caused your mourning, and to whom life has been so exactly measured as to terminate in the happiness in which it has been passed. Still I know that this is a hard saying, especially when those are in question of whom you will constantly be reminded by seeing in the homes of others blessings of which once you also boasted: for grief is felt not so much for the want of what we have never known, as for the loss of that to which we have been long accustomed. Yet you who are still of an age to beget children must bear up in the hope of having others in their stead; not only will they help you to forget those whom you have lost, but will be to the state at once a reinforcement and a security; for never can a fair or just policy be expected of the citizen who does not, like his fellows, bring to the decision the interests and apprehensions of a father. While those of you who have passed your prime must congratulate yourselves with the thought that the best part of your life was fortunate, and that the brief span that remains will be cheered by the fame of the departed. For it is only the love of honour that never grows old; and honour it is, not gain, as some would have it, that rejoices the heart of age and helplessness.

"Turning to the sons or brothers of the dead, I see an arduous struggle before you. When a man is gone, all are wont to praise him, and should your merit be ever so transcendent, you will still find it difficult not merely to overtake, but even to approach their renown. The living have envy to contend with, while those who are no longer in our path are honoured with a goodwill into which rivalry does not enter. On the other hand, if I must say anything on the subject of female excellence to those of you who will now be in widowhood, it will be all comprised in this brief exhortation. Great will be your glory in not falling short of your natural character; and greatest will be hers who is least talked of among the men whether for good or for bad.

"My task is now finished. I have performed it to the best of my ability, and in words, at least, the requirements of the law are now satisfied. If deeds be in question, those who are here interred have received part of their honours already, and for the rest, their children will be brought up till manhood at the public expense: the state thus offers a valuable prize, as the garland of victory in this race of valour, for the reward both of those who have fallen and their survivors. And where the rewards for merit are greatest, there are found the best citizens.

"And now that you have brought to a close your lamentations for your relatives, you may depart."

Plato

Plato (427?–347? B.C.), one of the greatest thinkers of all time, studied under Socrates, and from him he obtained many of his ideas. He wrote a series of dialogues, with his master as the principal character, and it is from this source that most of our knowledge of Socrates is obtained. The Crito relates some of the events that took place while Socrates was in prison for having antagonized certain elements in the Athenian population in the period following the Peloponnesian Wars. In reading the Crito note (1) Crito's message to Socrates, (2) his plan of action, (3) Socrates' reply, (4) the principal characteristics of the good man, (5) the attitude of Socrates toward democracy, and (6) what he considered his responsibility toward the city state.

As translated by Benjamin Jowett in The Dialogues of Plato, 2nd ed., 5 vols., Clarendon Press, Oxford, 1875, I, 383-396. Courtesy of the Jowett Copyright Fund.

THE CRITO

Persons of the Dialogue: *Socrates, Crito.*
Scene: The Prison of Socrates.

Socrates. Why have you come at this hour, Crito? it must be quite early?

Crito. Yes, certainly.

Soc. What is the exact time?

Cr. The dawn is breaking.

Soc. I wonder that the keeper of the prison would let you in.

Cr. He knows me, because I often come, Socrates; moreover, I have done him a kindness.

Soc. And are you only just arrived?

Cr. No, I came some time ago.

Soc. Then why did you sit and say nothing, instead of at once awakening me?

Cr. I should not have liked myself, Socrates, to be in such great trouble and unrest as you are—indeed I should not: I have been watching with amazement your peaceful slumbers; and for that reason I did not awake you, because I wished to minimize the pain. I have always thought you to be of a happy disposition; but never did I see anything like the easy, tranquil manner in which you bear this calamity.

Soc. Why, Crito, when a man has reached my age he ought not to be repining at the approach of death.

Cr. And yet other old men find themselves in similar misfortunes, and age does not prevent them from repining.

Soc. That is true. But you have not told me why you come at this early hour.

Cr. I come to bring you a message which is sad and painful; not, as I believe, to yourself, but to all of us who are your friends, and saddest of all to me.

Soc. What? Has the ship come from Delos, on the arrival of which I am to die?

Cr. No, the ship has not actually arrived, but she will probably be here today, as persons who have come from Sunium tell me that they left her there; and therefore tomorrow, Socrates, will be the last day of your life.

Soc. Very well, Crito; if such is the will of God, I am willing; but my belief is that there will be a delay of a day.

Cr. Why do you think so?

Soc. I will tell you. I am to die on the day after the arrival of the ship.

Cr. Yes; that is what the authorities say.

Soc. But I do not think that the ship will be here until tomorrow; this I infer from a vision which I had last night, or rather only just now, when you fortunately allowed me to sleep.

Cr. And what was the nature of the vision?

Soc. There appeared to me the likeness of a woman, fair and comely, clothed in bright raiment, who called to me and said: O Socrates,

"The third day hence to fertile Phthia shalt thou go."

Cr. What a singular dream, Socrates!

Soc. There can be no doubt about the meaning, Crito, I think.

Cr. Yes; the meaning is only too clear. But, oh! my beloved Socrates, let me entreat you once more to take my advice and escape. For if you die I shall not only lose a friend who can never be replaced, but there is another evil: people who do not know you and me will believe that I might have saved you if I had been willing to give money, but that I did not care. Now, can there be a worse disgrace than this—that I should be thought to value money more than the life of friend? For the many will not be persuaded that I wanted you to escape, and that you refused.

Soc. But why, my dear Crito, should we care about the opinion of the many? Good men, and they are the only persons who are worth considering, will think of these things truly as they occurred.

Cr. But you see, Socrates, that the opinion of the many must be regarded, for what is now happening shows that they can do the greatest evil to any one who has lost their good opinion.

Soc. I only wish it were so, Crito; and that the many could do the greatest evil; for then they would also be able to do the greatest good—and what a fine thing this would be! But in reality they can do neither; for they cannot make a man either wise or foolish; and whatever they do is the result of chance.

Cr. Well, I will not dispute with you; but please to tell me, Socrates, whether you are not acting out of regard to me and your other friends: are you not afraid that if you escape from prison we may get into trouble with the informers for having stolen you away, and lose either the whole or a great part of our property; or that even a worse evil may happen to us? Now, if you fear on our account, be at ease; for in order to save you, we ought surely to run this, or even a greater risk; be persuaded, then, and do as I say.

Soc. Yes, Crito, that is one fear which you mention, but by no means the only one.

Cr. Fear not—there are persons who are willing to get you out of prison at no great cost; and as for the informers, they are far from being exorbitant in their demands—a little money will satisfy them. My means, which are certainly ample, are at your service, and if you have a scruple about spending all mine, here are strangers who will give you the use of theirs; and one of them, Simmias the Theban, has brought a large sum of money for this very purpose; and Cebes and many others are prepared to spend their money in helping you to escape. I say, therefore, do not hesitate on our account, and do not say, as you did in the court, that you will have a difficulty in knowing what to do with yourself anywhere else. For men will love you in other places to which you may go, and not in Athens only; there are friends of mine in Thessaly, if you like to go to them, who will value and protect you, and no Thessalian will give you any trouble. Nor can I think that you are at all justified, Socrates, in betraying your own life when you might be saved; in acting thus you are playing into the hands of your enemies, who are hurrying on your destruction. And further I should say that you are deserting your own children; for you might bring them up and educate them; instead of which you go away and leave them, and they will have to take their chance; and if they do not meet with the usual fate of orphans, there will be small thanks to you. No man should bring children into the world who is unwilling to persevere to the end in their nurture and education. But you appear to be choosing the easier part, not the better and manlier, which would have been more becoming in one who professes to care for virtue in all his actions, like yourself. And, indeed, I am ashamed not only of you, but of us who are your friends, when I reflect that the whole business will be attributed entirely to our want of courage. The trial need never have come on, or might have been managed differently; and this last act, or crowning folly, will seem to have occurred through our negligence and cowardice, who might have saved you, if we had been good for anything; and you might have saved yourself, for there was no difficulty at all. See now, Socrates, how sad and discreditable are the consequences, both to us and you. Make up your mind, then, or rather have your mind already made up, for the time of deliberation is over, and there is only one thing to be done, which must be done this very night, and if we delay at all will be no longer practicable or possible; I beseech you therefore, Socrates, be persuaded by me, and do as I say.

Soc. Dear Crito, your zeal is invaluable, if a right one; but if wrong, the greater the zeal the greater the danger; and therefore we ought to consider whether I shall or shall not do as you say. For I am and always have been one of those natures who must be guided by reason, whatever the reason may be which upon reflection appears to me to be the best; and now that this chance has befallen me, I cannot repudiate my own words: the principles which I have hitherto honoured and revered I still honour, and unless we can at once find other and better principles, I am certain not to agree with you; no, not even if the power of the multitude could inflict many more imprisonments, confiscations, deaths, frightening us like children with hobgoblin terrors. What will be the fairest way of considering the question? Shall I return to your old argument about the opinions of men?—we were saying that some of them are to be regarded, and others not. Now, were we right in maintaining this before I was condemned? And has the argument which was once good now proved to be talk for the sake of talking—mere childish nonsense? That is what I want to consider with your help, Crito: —whether, under my present circumstances, the argument appears to be in any way different or not; and is to be allowed by me or disallowed. That argument, which, as I believe, is maintained by many persons of authority, was to the effect, as I was saying, that the opinions of some men are to be regarded, and of other men not to be regarded. Now you, Crito, are not going to die tomorrow—at least, there is no human probability of this—and therefore you are disinterested and not liable to be deceived by the circumstances in which you are placed. Tell me, then, whether I am right in saying that some opinions, and the opinions of some men only, are to be valued, and that other opinions, and the opinions of other men, are not to be valued. I ask you whether I was right in maintaining this?

Cr. Certainly.

Soc. The good are to be regarded, and not the bad?

Cr. Yes.

Soc. And the opinions of the wise are good, and the opinions of the unwise are evil?

Cr. Certainly.

Soc. And what was said about another matter? Is the pupil who devotes himself to the practice of gymnastics supposed to attend to the praise and blame and opinion of every man, or of one man only—his physician or trainer, whoever he may be?

Cr. Of one man only.

Soc. And he ought to fear the censure and welcome the praise of that one only, and not of the many?

Cr. Clearly so.

Soc. And he ought to act and train, and eat and drink in the way which seems good to his single master who has understanding, rather than according to the opinion of all other men put together?

Cr. True.

Soc. And if he disobeys and disregards the opinion and approval of the one, and regards the opinion of the many who have no understanding, will he not suffer?

Cr. Certainly he will.

Soc. And what will the evil be, whither tending and what affecting, in the disobedient person?

Cr. Clearly, affecting the body; that is what is destroyed by the evil.

Soc. Very good; and is not this true, Crito, of other things which we need not separately enumerate? In questions of just and unjust, fair and foul, good and evil, which are the subjects of our present consultation, ought we to follow the opinion of the many and to fear them; or the opinion of the one man who has understanding? ought we not to fear and reverence him more than all the rest of the world: and if we desert him shall we not destroy and injure that principle in us which may be assumed to be improved by justice and deteriorated by injustice;—there is such a principle?

Cr. Certainly there is, Socrates.

Soc. Take a parallel instance:—if, acting under the advice of those who have no understanding, we destroy that which is improved by health and is deteriorated by disease, would life be worth having? And that which has been destroyed is—the body?

Cr. Yes.

Soc. Could we live, having an evil and corrupted body?

Cr. Certainly not.

Soc. And will life be worth having, if that higher part of man be destroyed, which is improved by justice and depraved by injustice? Do we suppose that principle, whatever it may be in man, which has to do with justice and injustice, to be inferior to the body?

Cr. Certainly not.

Soc. More honourable than the body?

Cr. Far more.

Soc. Then, my friend, we must not regard what the many say of us: but what he, the one man who has understanding of just and unjust, will say, and what the truth will say. And therefore you begin in error when you advise that we should regard the opinion of the many about just and unjust, good and evil, honourable and dishonourable.—"Well," some one will say, "but the many can kill us."

Cr. Yes, Socrates; that will clearly be the answer.

Soc. And it is true: but still I find with surprise that the old argument is unshaken as ever. And I should like to know whether I may say the same of another proposition—that not life, but a good life, is to be chiefly valued?

Cr. Yes, that also remains unshaken.

Soc. And a good life is equivalent to a just and honourable one—that holds also?

Cr. Yes, it does.

Soc. From these premises I proceed to argue the question whether I ought or ought not to try to escape without the consent of the Athenians: and if I am clearly right in escaping, then I will make the attempt; but if not, I will abstain. The other considerations which you mention, of money and loss of character and the duty of educating one's children, are, I fear, only the doctrines of the multitude, who would be as ready to restore people to life, if they were able, as they are to put them to death—and with as little reason. But now, since the argument has thus far prevailed, the only question which remains to be considered is, whether we shall do rightly either in escaping or in suffering others to aid in our escape and paying them in money and thanks, or whether in reality we shall not do rightly; and if the latter, then death or any other calamity which may ensue on my remaining here must not be allowed to enter into the calculation.

Cr. I think that you are right, Socrates; how then shall we proceed?

Soc. Let us consider the matter together, and do you either refute me if you can, and I will be convinced; or else cease, my dear friend, from repeating to me that I ought to escape against the wishes of the Athenians: for I highly value your attempts to persuade me to do so, but I may not be persuaded against my own better judgment. And now please to consider my first position, and try how you can best answer me.

Cr. I will.

Soc. Are we to say that we are never intentionally to do wrong, or that in one way we ought and in another way we ought not to do wrong, or is doing wrong always evil and dishonourable, as I was just now saying, and as has been already acknowledged by us? Are all our former admissions which were made within a few days to be thrown away? And have we, at our age, been earnestly discoursing with one another all our life long only to discover that we are no better than children? Or, in spite of the opinion of the many, and in spite of consequences whether better or worse, shall we insist on the truth of what was then said, that injustice is always an evil and dishonour to him who acts unjustly? Shall we say so or not?

Cr. Yes.

Soc. Then we must do no wrong?

Cr. Certainly not.

Soc. Nor when injured injure in return, as the many imagine; for we must injure no one at all?

Cr. Clearly not.

Soc. Again, Crito, may we do evil?

Cr. Surely not, Socrates.

Soc. And what of doing evil in return for evil, which is the morality of the many—is that just or not?

Cr. Not just.

Soc. For doing evil to another is the same as injuring him?

Cr. Very true.

Soc. Then we ought not to retaliate or render evil for evil to any one, whatever evil we may have suffered from him. But I would have you consider, Crito, whether you really mean what you are saying. For this opinion has never been held, and never will be held, by any considerable number of persons; and those who are agreed and those who are not agreed upon this point have no common ground, and can only despise one another when they see how widely they differ. Tell me, then, whether you agree with and assent to my first principle, that neither injury nor retaliation nor warding off evil by evil is ever right. And shall that be the premise of our argument? Or do you decline and dissent from this? For so I have ever thought, and continue to think; but, if you are of another opinion, let me hear what you have to say. If, however, you remain of the same mind as formerly, I will proceed to the next step.

Cr. You may proceed, for I have not changed my mind.

Soc. Then I will go on to the next point, which may be put in the form of a question:—Ought a man to do what he admits to be right or ought he to betray the right?

Cr. He ought to do what he thinks right.

Soc. But if this is true, what is the application? In leaving the prison against the will of the Athenians, do I wrong any? or rather do I not wrong those whom I ought least to wrong? Do I not desert the principles which were acknowledged by us to be just—what do you say?

Cr. I cannot tell, Socrates; for I do not know.

Soc. Then consider the matter in this way:—

Imagine that I am about to play truant (you may call the proceeding by any name which you like), and the laws and the government come and interrogate me: "Tell us, Socrates," they say, "what are you about? Are you not going by an act of yours to overturn us—the laws, and the whole State, as far as in you lies? Do you imagine that a State can subsist and not be overthrown, in which the decisions of law have no power, but are set aside and trampled upon by individuals?" What will be our answer, Crito, to these and the like words? Any one, and especially a rhetorician, will have a good deal to say on behalf of the law which requires a sentence to be carried out. He will argue that this law should not be set aside; and shall we reply, "Yes, but the State has injured us and given an unjust sentence." Suppose I say that?

Cr. Very good, Socrates.

Soc. "And was that our agreement with you?" the law would answer, "or were you to abide by the sentence of the State?" And if I were to express my astonishment at their words, the law would probably add: "Answer, Socrates, instead of opening your eyes—you are in the habit of asking and answering questions. Tell us,—What complaint have you to make against us which justifies you in attempting to destroy us and the State? In the first place did we not bring you into existence? Your father married your mother by our aid and begat you. Say whether you have any objection to urge against those of us who regulate marriage?" None, I should reply. "Or against those of us who after birth regulate the nurture and education of children, in which you also were trained? Were not the laws which have the charge of education, right in commanding your father to train you in music and gymnastic?" Right, I should reply. "Well, then, since you were brought into the world and nurtured and educated by us, can you deny in the first place that you are our child and slave, as your fathers were before you? And if this is true, you are not on equal terms with us; nor can you think that you have a right to do to us what we are doing to you. Would you have any right to strike or revile or do any other evil to your father or your master, if you had one, because you have been struck or reviled by him, or received some other evil at his hands? —you would not say this? And because we

think right to destroy you, do you think that you have any right to destroy us in return, and your country as far as in you lies? Will you, O professor of true virtue, pretend that you are justified in this? Has a philosopher like you failed to discover that our country is more to be valued and higher and holier far than mother or father or any ancestor, and more to be regarded in the eyes of the gods and of men of understanding? also to be soothed, and gently and reverently entreated when angry, even more than a father, and either to be persuaded, or if not persuaded, to be obeyed? And when we are punished by her, whether with imprisonment or stripes, the punishment is to be endured in silence; and if she lead us to wounds or death in battle, thither we follow as is right; neither may any one yield or retreat or leave his rank, but whether in battle or in a court of law, or in any other place, he must do what his city and his country order him; or he must change their view of what is just: and if he may do no violence to his father or mother, much less may he do violence to his country." What answer shall we make to this, Crito? Do the laws speak truly, or do they not?

Cr. I think that they do.

Soc. Then the laws will say: "Consider, Socrates, if we are speaking truly that in your present attempt you are going to do us an injury. For, having brought you into the world, and nurtured and educated you, and given you and every other citizen a share in every good which we had to give, we further proclaim to any Athenian by the liberty which we allow him, that if he does not like us when he has become of age and has seen the ways of the city, and made our acquaintance, he may go where he pleases and take his goods with him. None of us laws will forbid him or interfere with him. Anyone who does not like us and the city, and who wants to emigrate to a colony or to any other city, may go where he likes, retaining his property. But he who has experience of the manner in which we order justice and administer the State, and still remains, has entered into an implied contract that he will do as we command him. And he who disobeys us is, as we maintain, thrice wrong; first, because in disobeying us he is disobeying his parents; secondly, because we are the authors of his education; thirdly, because he has made an agreement with us that he will duly obey our commands; and he neither obeys them nor convinces us that our commands are unjust; and we do not rudely impose them, but give him the alternative of obeying or convincing us;—that is what we offer, and he does neither.

"These are the sort of accusations to which, as we were saying, you, Socrates, will be exposed if you accomplish your intentions; you, above all other Athenians." Suppose now I ask, why I rather than anybody else? They will justly retort upon me that I above all other men have acknowledged the agreement. "There is clear proof," they will say, "Socrates, that we and the city were not displeasing to you. Of all Athenians you have been the most constant resident in the city, which, as you never leave, you may be supposed to love. For you never went out of the city either to see the games, except once when you went to the Isthmus, or to any other place unless when you were on military service; nor did you travel as other men do. Nor had you any curiosity to know other States or their laws: your affections did not go beyond us and our State: we were your special favourites, and you acquiesced in our government of you; and here in this city you begat your children, which is a proof of your satisfaction. Moreover, you might in the course of the trial, if you had liked, have fixed the penalty at banishment; the State which refuses to let you go now would have let you go then. But you pretended that you preferred death to exile, and that you were not unwilling to die. And now you have forgotten these fine sentiments, and pay no respect to us, the laws, of whom you are the destroyer; and are doing what only a miserable slave would do, running away and turning your back upon the compacts and agreements which you made as a citizen. And, first of all, answer this very question: Are we right in saying that you agreed to be governed according to us in deed, and not in word only? Is that true or not?" How shall we answer, Crito? Must we not assent?

Cr. We cannot help it, Socrates.

Soc. Then will they not say: "You, Socrates, are breaking the covenants and agreements which you made with us at your leisure, not in any haste or under any compulsion or decep-

tion, but after you have had seventy years to think of them, during which time you were at liberty to leave the city, if we were not to your mind, or if our covenants appeared to you to be unfair. You had your choice, and might have gone either to Lacedaemon or Crete, both which States are often praised by you for their good government, or to some other Hellenic or foreign State. Whereas you, above all other Athenians, seemed to be so fond of the State, or, in other words, of us, her laws (and who would care about a State which has no laws?), that you never stirred out of her; the halt, the blind, the maimed were not more stationary in her than you were. And now you run away and forsake your agreements. Not so, Socrates, if you will take our advice; do not make yourself ridiculous by escaping out of the city.

"For just consider, if you transgress and err in this sort of way, what good will you do either to yourself or to your friends? That your friends will be driven into exile and deprived of citizenship, or will lose their property, is tolerably certain; and you yourself, if you fly to one of the neighbouring cities, as, for example, Thebes or Megara, both of which are well governed, will come to them as an enemy, Socrates, and their government will be against you, and all patriotic citizens will cast an evil eye upon you as a subverter of the laws, and you will confirm in the minds of the judges the justice of their own condemnation of you. For he who is a corrupter of the laws is more than likely to be a corrupter of the young and foolish portion of mankind. Will you then flee from well-ordered cities and virtuous men? and is existence worth having on these terms? Or will you go to them without shame, and talk to them, Socrates? And what will you say to them? What you say here about virtue and justice and institutions and laws being the best things among men? Would that be decent of you? Surely not. But if you go away from well-governed States to Crito's friends in Thessaly, where there is great disorder and licence, they will be charmed to hear the tale of your escape from prison, set off with ludicrous particulars of the manner in which you were wrapped in a goatskin or some other disguise, and metamorphosed as the manner is of runaways; but will there be no one to remind you that in your old age you were not ashamed to violate the most sacred laws from a miserable desire of a little more life? Perhaps not, if you keep them in a good temper; but if they are out of temper you will hear many degrading things; you will live, but how?—as the flatterer of all men, and the servant of all men; and doing what?—eating and drinking in Thessaly, having gone abroad in order that you may get a dinner. And where will be your fine sentiments about justice and virtue? Say that you wish to live for the sake of your children—you want to bring them up and educate them—will you take them into Thessaly and deprive them of Athenian citizenship? Is this the benefit which you will confer upon them? Or are you under the impression that they will be better cared for and educated here if you are still alive, although absent from them; for your friends will take care of them? Do you fancy that if you are an inhabitant of Thessaly they will take care of them, and if you are an inhabitant of the other world that they will not take care of them? Nay; but if they who call themselves friends are good for anything, they will—to be sure they will.

"Listen, then, Socrates, to us who have brought you up. Think not of life and children first, and of justice afterwards, but of justice first, that you may be justified before the princes of the world below. For neither will you nor any that belong to you be happier or holier or juster in this life, or happier in another, if you do as Crito bids. Now you depart in innocence, a sufferer and not a doer of evil; a victim, not of the laws but of men. But if you go forth, returning evil for evil, and injury for injury, breaking the covenants and agreements which you have made with us, and wronging those whom you ought least of all to wrong, that is to say, yourself, your friends, your country, and us, we shall be angry with you while you live, and our brethren, the laws in the world below, will receive you as an enemy; for they will know that you have done your best to destroy us. Listen, then, to us and not to Crito."

This, dear Crito, is the voice which I seem to hear murmuring in my ears, like the sound of the flute in the ears of the mystic; that voice, I say, is humming in my ears, and prevents me from hearing any other. And I know that anything more which you may say will be vain. Yet speak, if you have anything to say.

Cr. I have nothing to say, Socrates.

Soc. Leave me then, Crito, to fulfil the will of God, and to follow whither he leads.

Aristotle

Aristotle (384–322 B.C.) was the student of Plato and the third member of the great intellectual triumvirate of ancient Greece. One of the problems to which Greek thinkers inevitably turned was that of human conduct and what was involved in "the good life." Aristotle gave one of the most typically Greek answers to this question of ethics and in so doing made use of the compromise position which he took in philosophy generally. The golden mean that he discussed was the ideal which Greeks customarily sought as a guide to their daily lives, both public and private. It followed naturally that Aristotle associated ethics with the state and not with religion as Christianity subsequently taught. In reading the selections from the Ethics note (1) Aristotle's method of argument, (2) what he regarded as the greatest good in life, (3) how he arrived at that conclusion, (4) how he defined happiness, (5) the formation of moral virtue, (6) the relationship between virtue and pleasure and pain, and (7) what constituted moral virtue.

Adapted from *The Nicomachean Ethics of Aristotle*, translated by F. H. Peters, London, 1886, 1–5; 12–18; 34–52

From: THE NICOMACHEAN ETHICS

Every art and every kind of inquiry, and similarly every act and purpose, seems to aim at some good; and so it has been well said that the good is that at which everything aims. But a difference is observable among these aims or ends. What is aimed at is sometimes the exercise of a faculty, sometimes a certain result beyond that exercise. And where there is an end beyond the act, there the result is better than the exercise of the faculty. Now since there are many kinds of actions and many arts and sciences, it follows that there are many ends also; the end of medicine is health, of shipbuilding, ships, of war, victory, and of economy, wealth. But when several of these are subordinated to some one art or science—as bridle-making and other arts concerned with horsemanship, and this in turn, along with all else the soldier does, to the art of war, and so on—then the end of the master-art is always more desired than the ends of the subordinate arts, since these are pursued for its sake. And this is equally true whether the end in view be the mere exercise of a faculty or something beyond that, as in the case of the sciences just mentioned.

If then in what we do there be some end which we wish for on its own account, choosing all the other ends as means to this, but not every end without exception as a means to something else (for so we should go on indefinitely, and desire would be left void and without object) this evidently will be the good or the best of all goods. And surely from a practical point of view it concerns us much to know this good; for then, like archers shooting at a target, we shall be more likely to get what we want. If this be so, we must try to indicate roughly what it is, and first of all to which of the arts or sciences it belongs. It would seem to belong to the highest art or science, that one which most of all deserves the name of master-art or master-science. Politics seems to answer this description. [Politics for Aristotle covers the whole field of human life; it must determine (a) what is the good and (b) what law can do to promote this good.] For politics prescribes which of the sciences a state needs, and which each man shall study, and how much; and to politics we see subordinated even the highest arts, such as economy [the management of a household], rhetoric, and war. Since then politics makes use of the other practical sciences, and since further it ordains what men are to do and from what to refrain, its end must include the ends or objectives of the others, and this end is the good of man. For though this good is the same for the individual as well as the state, yet the good of the state seems a larger and more perfect thing both to attain and to secure; and glad as one would be to do this service for a single individual, to do it for a people and for a number of city-states is nobler and more divine. This then is the aim of the present inquiry, which is political science.

We must be content if we can attain to so much precision in our statement as the subject will permit, for the same degree of accuracy is no more to be expected in all kinds of reasoning than in all kinds of manufacture. Now what is noble and just (with which political science deals) is so various and uncertain, that some think that these are merely conventional, and not natural, distinctions. There is a similar uncertainty also about what is good, because good things often do people harm; men have before now been ruined by wealth or have lost their lives through courage. Our subject then and our data being of this nature, we must be content if we can indicate roughly and in outline the truth; and if, in dealing with matters not subject to immutable laws, and reasoning from premises that are but probable, we can arrive at probable conclusions. The reader, on his part, should take each of my statements in the same spirit; for it is the mark of an educated man to require, in each kind of study, just so much exactness as the subject permits; it is equally absurd to accept probable reasoning from a mathematician, and to demand scientific proof from an orator.

Now each man can form a judgment about what he knows, and is called a good judge of that—that is of any special matter in which he has received special training. And the man who has received an all-round education is a good judge in general. And hence a young man is not qualified to be a student of politics; for he lacks experience of the affairs of life which form the data and the subject matter of political science. Further, since he is apt to be swayed by his passions, he will derive no benefit from a study whose aim is practical and not speculative. And it makes no difference whether he is young in years or young in character, for the young man's disqualification is not a matter of time, but is due to the fact that feeling or passion rules his life and directs all his desires. Men of this character turn the knowledge they get to no practical account, as we see with those we call incontinent; but those who direct their desires and ambitions by reason will gain much profit from a knowledge of these matters. So much, then, by way of preface as to the student, and the spirit in which he must accept what we say, and the object which we propose to ourselves. . . .

Let us return once more to the question of what this good can be of which we are in search. It seems to be different in different kinds of action and in different arts; it is different in medicine, in war, and in the other arts. What then is the good in each of these? Surely that for the sake of which all else is done. And that in medicine is health, in war is victory, in building is a house—a different thing in each case, but always the end in whatever we do and in whatever we choose. For it is always for the sake of the end that all else is done. If then there be one end of all that man does, this end will be the good achievable in action, and if there be more than one, these will be the goods achievable by action. Our argument has thus come round by a different path to the same point; this we must try to explain more clearly. We see that there are many ends. But some of these are chosen only as means, as wealth, flutes, and the whole class of instruments. And so it is plain that not all ends are final. But the best of all things must be something final. If then there be only one final end, this will be what we are seeking; or if there be more than one, then the most final of them.

Now that which is pursued as an end in itself is more final than that which is pursued as a means to something else, and that which is never chosen as a means than that which is chosen both as an end in itself and as a means,

and that is strictly final which is always chosen as an end in itself and never as a means. Happiness seems more than anything else to answer this description, for we always choose it for itself, and never for the sake of something else; while honor and pleasure and reason, and all virtue or excellence, we choose partly for themselves (for, apart from any result, we should choose each of them), but partly also for the sake of happiness, supposing that they will help to make us happy. But no one chooses happiness for the sake of those things, or as a means to anything else at all.

We seem to be led to the same conclusion when we start from the idea of self-sufficiency. The final good is thought to be self-sufficing or all-sufficing. In applying this term we do not regard a man as an individual leading a solitary life, but we take account also of parents, children, wife, and in short, friends and fellow-citizens generally, since man is naturally a social being. Some limit must indeed be set for this; for if you go on to parents and descendants and friends of friends, you will never come to a stop. But this we will consider further on; for the present we will take self-sufficing to mean what by itself makes life desirable and in want of nothing. And happiness answers this description. And further, happiness is believed to be the most desirable thing in the world, and that not merely as one among other good things. If it were merely one among other good things [so that other things could be added to it] it is plain that the addition of the least of other goods must make it more desirable; for the addition becomes a surplus of good, and of two goods the greater is always more desirable. Thus it seems that happiness is something final and self-sufficing, and is the end of all that man does.

But perhaps the reader thinks that though no one will dispute the statement that happiness is the best thing in the world, yet a still more precise definition of it is needed. This will best be gained by asking, What is the function of man? For as the goodness and the excellence of the flute-player or the sculptor, or the practitioner of any art, and generally of those who have any business to do, lies in the function, so man's good would seem to lie in his function, if he possesses one. But can we suppose that, while a carpenter or a shoemaker has a function and a business of his own, man has no business and no function assigned to him as man by nature? Nay, surely as his several members, eye, hand, and foot, plainly have each its own function, so we must suppose that man also has some function over and above all of these. What then is it? Life evidently he has in common even with the plants, but we want that which is peculiar to man. We must exclude, therefore, the life of mere nutrition and growth. Next to this comes the life of sense; but this too he plainly shares with horses and cattle and all kinds of animals. There remains then the life whereby he acts—the life of his rational nature with its two aspects or divisions, one rational as obeying reason, the other rational as having and exercising reason. But as this expression is ambiguous, we must be understood to mean thereby the life that consists in the exercise of the faculties; for this seems to be more properly entitled to the name. The function of man, then, is the exercise of his soul on one side in obedience to reason, and on the other side with reason. But what is called the function of a man of any profession and the function of a man who is good in that profession are generically the same, that is to say, of a harper and of a good harper; and this holds in all cases without exception, only that in the case of the latter his superior excellence at his work is added; for we say a harper's function is to play the harp, and a good harper's function is to play the harp well. Man's function then being, as we say, a kind of life—that is, the exercise of his faculties and action of various kinds with reason—the good man's function is to do this well and nobly. But the function of anything is done well when it is done in accordance with the proper excellence of that thing. Putting all this together, then, we find that the good of man is the exercise of his faculties in accordance with excellence or virtue, or, if there be more than one, in accordance with the best and most complete virtue. But there must be a full term of years for this exercise; for one swallow or one fine day does not make a spring, nor does one day or any small space of time make a happy or virtuous man.

This, then, may be taken as a rough outline of the good; for this, I think, is the proper method: first to sketch the outline, and then to fill in the details. But it would seem that, the outline once fairly drawn, any one can carry on the work and fit in the several items which time reveals to us or aids us to discover. And this, indeed, is the way in which the arts and sciences have developed, for it requires no unusual genius to fill in the gaps. We must bear in mind, however, what was said earlier, and not demand the same degree of accuracy in all branches of inquiry, but in each case as much as the subject permits and as is proper to that kind of study. The carpenter and the geometer both look for the right angle, but in different ways; the former only wants such an approximation of it as his work requires, but the latter wants to know what constitutes a right angle, or what is its special quality—his aim is to find the truth. And so in other cases we must follow the same course, lest we spend more time on what is immaterial to our purpose than on the real business at hand. Nor must we in all cases alike demand the reason why. Sometimes it is sufficient if the undemonstrated fact be fairly pointed out, as in the case of the first principles of a science. Undemonstrated facts always form the first step or beginning of a science; and these first principles are arrived at some in one way and some in another way, some by induction, others by perception, others by some kind of training. But in each case we must attempt to apprehend them in the proper way, and do our best to define them clearly, for they have great influence upon the subsequent course of an inquiry. A good start is more than half the race, and our starting-point, once found, clears up a number of difficulties. . . .

Excellence or virtue, then, being of two kinds, intellectual and moral, intellectual excellence owes its birth and growth mainly to teaching, and so requires time and experience, while moral excellence is the result of habit or custom (*ethike*), and has accordingly received in our language [Greek] a name formed by a slight change from the word *ethos* (habit). From this it is plain that none of the moral excellencies or virtues is implanted in us by nature; for that which is by nature implanted within us cannot be altered by training. For example, a stone naturally tends to fall downward, and you could not train it to rise upward, though you tried to do so by throwing it up ten thousand times, nor could you train fire to move downward, nor accustom anything which naturally behaves in one way to behave in any other way. The virtues, then, come neither by nature nor contrary to nature, but nature gives us the capacity for acquiring them, and this is developed by training.

Again, where we do things by nature we get the power first, and put this power forth in act afterwards (as we plainly see in the case of the senses); for it is not by constantly seeing and hearing that we acquire those faculties, but, on the contrary, we had the power first and then used it, instead of acquiring the power by use. But we acquire the virtues by doing the acts, as is the case with the arts. We learn an art by doing those things which we wish to do when we have learned the art; we become builders by building, and harpists by playing the harp. And so by doing just and virtuous acts we become just and virtuous, and by doing acts of temperance and courage we become temperate and courageous. This is confirmed by what happens in states; for the legislators make their citizens good by training, and this is the wish of all legislators. Those who do not succeed in this miss their aim, and it is this that distinguishes a good from a bad constitution.

Again, both virtues and vices result from and are formed by the same acts in which they manifest themselves, as is the case also with the arts. It is by playing the harp that good harpers and bad harpers alike are produced; and so it is with builders and the rest, by building well they will become good builders and bad builders by building badly. Indeed, if it were not so, they would not need anybody to teach them, but would all be born either good or bad at their trades. And it is just the same with the virtues also. It is by our conduct in our dealings with other men that we become just or unjust, and by acting in circumstances of danger, and training ourselves to feel fear or confidence, that we become courageous or cowardly. So too with our animal appetites and the passion of anger; for by behaving in this way or in that on occasions with which these passions are concerned, some become temperate and gentle, others profligate and ill-tempered. In a word, the several habits or characters are formed by the same kind of acts as those which they produce. Hence we ought to make certain that our acts be of a particular kind; for the resulting character varies as the acts vary. Instead of making a very small difference whether a man be trained from his youth up in this way or that, it makes a very great difference; indeed, it makes all the difference.

But our present study has not, like the rest, merely a theoretical aim. We are not inquiring simply to learn what excellence or virtue is, but in order to become good; for otherwise our study would be useless. We must ask therefore about these acts, and see of what kind they are to be; for, as we said, it is the acts that determine our habits or character. First of all, then, that they must be in accordance with right reason is a common characteristic of them, which we shall take for granted here, reserving for future discussion the question what this right reason is, and how it is related to the other excellencies or virtues. But let it be understood before we go on, that all reasoning on matters of practice must be in outline merely, and not scientifically exact; for as we said at the beginning the kind of reasoning demanded varies with the subject in hand, and in practical matters and questions of expediency there are no invariable laws, any more than in questions of health. And if our general conclusions are thus inexact, still more inexact is all reasoning about particular cases; for these fall under no system of scientifically established rules or traditional maxims, but the agent must always consider for himself what the special occasion requires, just as in medicine or navigation. In spite of this, however, we must try to give what help we can.

First of all then, we must observe that, in matters of this sort, to fall short and to go beyond are both fatal. To illustrate what we cannot see by what we can see: This is plain in the case of strength and health. Too much and too little exercise alike destroy strength, and to take too much meat and drink, or to take too little, is equally ruinous to health; but the proper amount produces and increases strength and health. So it is with temperance also and courage and the other virtues. The man who shuns and fears everything and never makes a stand becomes a coward; while the man who fears nothing at all, but will face anything, becomes foolhardy. So, too, the man who takes his fill of any kind of pleasure and abstains from none, is self-indulgent; but the man who avoids all pleasures (like a boor) lacks sensibility. For temperance and courage are destroyed both by excess and defect, but are preserved by moderation.

But habits or types of character are not only produced and preserved and destroyed by the same occasions and the same means, but they will also manifest themselves in the same circumstances. This is the case with obvious things like strength. Strength is produced by taking plenty of nourishment and doing plenty of hard work, and the strong man, in turn, has the greatest capacity for these. And the case is the same with the virtues. By abstaining from pleasure we become temperate, and when we have become temperate we are best able to abstain. And so with courage. By habituating ourselves to despise danger, and to face it, we become courageous; and when we have become courageous, we are best able to face danger.

The pleasure or pain that accompanies the acts must be taken as a test of the formed habit or character. He who abstains from the pleasures of the body and rejoices in the abstinence is temperate, while he who is vexed at having to abstain is self-indulgent. And, again, he who faces danger with pleasure, or at any rate, without pain is courageous, but he to whom this is painful is a coward. For moral virtue or excellence is closely concerned with pleasure and pain. It is pleasure that moves us to do what is base and pain that moves us to refrain from what is noble. And therefore, as Plato says, man needs to be so trained from his youth as to find pleasure and pain in the right objects. This is what sound education means. Another reason why virtue has to do with pleasure and pain is that it has to do with actions and passions or affections; but every affection and every act is accompanied by pleasure or pain. This is indicated also by the use of pleasure and pain in correction; they have a kind of curative property, and a cure is effected by administering the opposite of the disease.

Again, as we said before, every type of character or habit is essentially relative to, and concerned with, those things that form it for good or for ill; but it is through pleasure and pain that bad characters are formed—that is to say, through pursuing and avoiding them at the wrong time, or in the wrong manner, or in any other of the various ways of going wrong that may be distinguished. And hence some people go so far as to define the virtues as a kind of impassive or neutral state of mind. But they make a mistake in saying this absolutely, instead of qualifying it by the addition of the right and wrong manner, time, etc. We may lay down, therefore, that this kind of excellence [moral excellence or virtue] makes us do what is best in matters of pleasure and pain, while vice or badness has the contrary effect. The following considerations will throw additional light on the point. There are three kinds of things that move us to choose and three that move us to avoid them. On the one hand, the beautiful or noble, the advantageous, the pleasant. On the other hand, the ugly or base, the hurtful, the painful. Now the good man is apt to go right, and the bad man to go wrong about them all, but especially about pleasure; for pleasure is not only common to man and animals, but also accompanies all pursuit or objects of choice; for even the noble and advantageous appear pleasant.

Again, the feeling of pleasure has been fostered in us all from our infancy by our training, and has thus become so ingrained in our life that it can scarcely be washed out. And, indeed, we all more or less make pleasure our test in judging actions. For this reason too, then, our whole study must be concerned with these matters; since to be pleased and pained in the right or wrong way has great influence on our actions. And lastly, as Heraclitus says, it is harder to fight with pleasure than with wrath; and virtue, like art, is always more concerned with what is harder; for the harder the task, the better is success. For this reason also, then, both moral virtue or excellence and political science must always be concerned with pleasures and pains; for he that behaves rightly with regard to them will be good, and he that behaves badly will be bad. We will take it as established then, that moral virtue or excellence has to do with pleasures and pains; and that the acts which produce virtue develop it, and also, when done differently, destroy it; and that it manifests itself in the same acts which produced it.

But here we may be asked what we mean by saying that men can become just and temperate only by doing what is just and temperate. Surely, it may be said, if their acts are just and temperate, they themselves are already just and temperate, as they are grammarians and musicians if they do what is grammatical and musical. We may answer, I think firstly, that this is not quite the case even with the arts. A man may do something grammatical or write something correctly by chance, or at the prompting of another person. He will not be grammatical till he not only does something grammatical, but also does it like a grammatical person—because of his own knowledge of grammar. But secondly, the virtues are not in this point analogous to the arts. The products of art have their excellence in themselves, and so it is enough if when produced they are of a certain quality; but in the case of the virtues, a man is not said to act justly or temperately or like a just or temperate man if what he does merely be of a certain sort—he must also be in a certain state of mind when he does it. That is to say, first of all he must know what he is doing; secondly he must choose it, and choose it for himself; and thirdly his act must be the expression of a formed and stable character. Now, of these conditions, only one, the knowledge, is necessary for the possession of any art; but for the possession of the virtues, knowledge is of little or no value, while the other conditions that result from repeatedly doing what is just and temperate are not just slightly important, but all-important.

The thing that is done, therefore, is called just or temperate when it is such as the just or temperate man would do; but the man who does it is not just or temperate unless he also does it in the spirit of the just or temperate man. It is right then to say that by doing what is just a man becomes just, and temperate by doing what is temperate, while without doing thus he has no chance of ever becoming good. But most men, instead of doing thus, fly to

theories and fancy that they are philosophizing and that this will make them good, like a sick man who listens attentively to what the doctor says and then disobeys all his orders. This sort of theorizing will no more produce a healthy habit of mind than this sort of treatment will produce a healthy habit of body.

Next we must consider what virtue is. Everything psychical is either (1) a passion or emotion, or (2) a power or faculty, or (3) a habit or a trained faculty; and so virtue must be one of these three. By (1) passion or emotion we mean appetite, anger, fear, confidence, envy, joy, love, hate, longing, emulation, pity, or generally that which is accompanied by pleasure or pain; (2) a power or faculty is that in respect of which we are said to be capable of being affected in any of these ways, as for instance, that in respect of which we are able to be angered or pained or to pity; and (3) a habit or trained faculty is that in respect of which we are well or ill regulated or disposed in the matter of our affections; as, for instance, in the matter of being angered, we are ill regulated if we are too violent or too slack, but if we are moderate in our anger we are well regulated. And so with the rest.

Now neither the virtues nor the vices are passions (1) because we are not called good or bad in respect of our emotions, but are called good or bad in respect of our virtues or vices; (2) because we are neither praised nor blamed in respect of our emotions (a man is not praised for being afraid or angry, nor blamed for being angry simply, but for being angry in a particular way), but we are praised or blamed in respect of our virtues or vices; (3) because we may be angered or frightened without deliberate choice, but the virtues are a kind of deliberate choice, or at least are impossible without it; and (4) because in respect of our emotions we are said to be moved, but in respect of our virtues and vices we are not said to be moved, but to be regulated or disposed in this way or in that way. For these same reasons also they are not powers or faculties; for we are not called either good or bad for being merely capable of emotion, nor are we either praised or blamed for this. And further, while nature gives us our powers or faculties, she does not make us either good or bad. This point, however, we have already treated.

If, then, the virtues be neither emotions nor faculties, it remains for them to be habits or trained faculties.

We have thus found the genus to which virtue belongs; but we want to know, not only that it is a trained faculty, but also what species of trained faculty it is. We may safely assert that the virtue or excellence of a thing causes that thing both to be itself in good condition and to perform its function well. The excellence of the eye, for example, makes both the eye and its work good; for it is by the excellence of the eye that we see well. Similarly the excellence of the horse makes a horse both good in itself and good at running and at carrying its rider and at awaiting the attack of the enemy. If this is true in every case, therefore, the virtue of man also will be the state of character which makes a man good and which makes him do his own work well.

How this is to be done we have already said, but we may exhibit the same conclusion in another way, by inquiring what the nature of this virtue is. Now, if we have any quantity, whether continuous or divisible, it is possible to take either a larger, or a smaller, or an equal amount, and that either absolutely or relatively to our own needs. By an equal or fair amount I understand a mean amount, or one that lies between excess and deficiency. By the absolute mean, or mean relatively to the thing itself, I understand that which is equidistant from both extremes, and this is one and the same for all. By the mean relatively to us I understand that which is neither too much nor too little for us; and this is not one and the same for all. For instance, if ten be larger and two be smaller, if we take six we take the mean relatively to the thing itself [or the arithmetical mean]; for it exceeds one extreme by the same amount by which it is exceeded by the other extreme. This is the mean in arithmetical proportion. But the mean relatively to us cannot be found in this way. If ten pounds of food is too much for a given man to eat, and two pounds too little, it does not follow that the trainer will order six pounds. For that also may perhaps be too much for the man in question or too little; too little for Milo [a famous Greek wrestler], too much for the beginner. The same holds true in running and wrestling. And so we say that generally a master in any art avoids what is too much and what is too little and seeks for the mean and chooses it—not the absolute but the relative mean.

Every art or science, then, perfects its work in this way, looking to the mean and bringing its work up to this standard; so that people are wont to say of a good work that nothing could be taken from it or added to it, implying that excellence is destroyed by excess or deficiency, but secured by observing the mean. And good artists do in fact keep their eyes fixed on this in all that they do. Virtue therefore, since like nature it is more exact and better than any art, must also aim at the mean—virtue of course meaning moral virtue or moral excellence; for it has to do with passions and actions, and it is these that admit of excess and deficiency and the mean. For example, it is possible to feel fear, confidence, desire, anger, pity, and generally to be affected pleasantly and painfully, either too much or too little, in either case wrongly; but to be thus affected at the right times, and on the right occasions, and toward the right persons, and with the right object, and in the right fashion, is the mean course and the best course, and these are characteristics of virtue. And in the same way our outward acts also admit of excess and deficiency, and the mean or intermediate. Virtue then is concerned with feelings or passions and with outward acts, in which excess is wrong and deficiency is also blamed, but the mean is praised and is right; and being praised and being successful are both characteristics of virtue. Virtue, therefore, is a kind of moderation or mean as it aims at the mean or moderate amount.

Again, there are many ways of going wrong (for evil is infinite in nature, to use a figure of the Pythagoreans, while good is finite or limited), but only one way of going right; so that the one is easy and the other hard—easy to miss the mark and hard to hit the mark. On this account also excess and deficiency are characteristic of vice; hitting the mean is characteristic of virtue:

"Goodness is simple, evil takes any shape."

Virtue, then, is a habit or trained faculty of choice, the characteristic of which lies in observing the mean relatively to the persons concerned, and which is guided by reason, that is, by the judgment of the prudent man. And it is a moderation, firstly, inasmuch as it comes in the middle or the mean between two vices, one on the side of excess, the other on the side of deficiency; and secondly, inasmuch as, while these vices fall short of or exceed the mean or intermediate measure in feeling and in action, it finds and chooses the mean, middling, or moderate amount. Regarded in essence, therefore, or according to the definition of its nature, virtue is a moderation or middle state, but viewed in its relation to what is best and right it is the extreme of perfection.

But it is not all actions nor all passions that admit of moderation; there are some whose very names imply badness, as malevolence, shamelessness, envy, and among acts, adultery, theft, murder. These and all other like things are blamed as being bad in themselves, and not merely in their excess or deficiency. It is impossible, therefore, to go right in them; they are always wrong. Rightness and wrongness in such things, adultery for example, does not depend upon whether it is the right woman, at the right time, and in the right way, but the mere doing of any one of them is wrong. It would be equally absurd to look for moderation or excess or deficiency in unjust, cowardly, or self-indulgent conduct; for then there would be moderation in excess or deficiency, and excess in excess, and deficiency in deficiency. The fact is that just as there can be no excess or deficiency in temperance or courage because the mean or moderate amount is, in a sense, an extreme, so in these kinds of conduct also there can be no moderation or excess or deficiency, but the acts are wrong however they be done.

It is not enough, however, to make these general statements about virtue and vice; we must go on and apply them to particulars—that is to the several virtues and vices. For in reasoning about matters of conduct general statements are too vague and do not convey as much truth as particular propositions. It is with particulars that conduct is concerned. Our statements, therefore, when applied to these particulars, should be found to hold good. These particulars then—the several virtues and vices and the several acts and affections with which they deal—we will take from the following [list].

Moderation in the feelings of fear and con-

fidence is courage. Of those that exceed, he that exceeds in fearlessness has no name (as often happens), but he that exceeds in confidence is foolhardy, while he that exceeds in fear, but is deficient in confidence, is cowardly.

Moderation in respect of certain pleasures and also (though to a less extent) certain pains is temperance, while excess is self-indulgence or profligacy. But defectiveness in the matter of these pleasures is hardly ever found, and so this sort of people also have as yet received no name. Let us put them down as devoid of sensibility, or call them insensible.

In the matter of giving and taking money, moderation is liberality, excess and deficiency are prodigality and illiberality. But these two vices exceed and fall short in contrary ways. The prodigal exceeds in spending, but falls short in taking; while the illiberal man exceeds in taking, but falls short in spending. . . . But, besides these, there are other dispositions in the matter of money. There is a moderation which is called magnificence (for the magnificent is not the same as the liberal man; the former deals with large sums, the latter with small), and an excess which is called bad taste or vulgarity, and a deficiency which is called meanness; and these vices differ from those that are opposed to liberality. How they differ will be explained later.

With respect to honor and disgrace, there is a mean or moderation which is high-mindedness, and an excess which may be called vanity, and a deficiency which is little-mindedness. But just as we said that liberality is related to magnificence, differing only in that it deals with small sums, so here there is a virtue related to high-mindedness, and differing only in that it is concerned with small instead of great honors. A man may have a due desire for honor and also more or less than a moderate desire. He that carries this desire to excess is called ambitious, he that has a deficiency is called unambitious, while he that has the proper amount has no special name. There are also no abstract names for the characters, except "ambition" corresponding to ambitious. And on this account those who occupy the extremes lay claim to the middle place. And in common parlance too, the moderate man is sometimes called ambitious and sometimes unambitious, and sometimes the ambitious man is praised and sometimes the unambitious. Why this is so we will explain later. For the present we will continue the plan and enumerate the other types of character.

In the matter of anger also we find excess and deficiency and the mean or moderation. The characters themselves scarcely have recognized names, but as the moderate man is here called gentle, we will call his character gentleness; of those who go into extremes, we may use the term wrathful or irascible for him who exceeds, with wrathfulness or irascibility for the vice, and wrathless for him who is deficient, with wrathlessness for his character.

Besides these, there are three kinds of moderation, bearing some resemblance to one another, and yet different. They all have to do with intercourse in speech and action, but they differ in that one has to do with the truthfulness of this intercourse, while the other two have to do with its pleasantness—one of the two with pleasantness in matters of amusement, the other with pleasantness in all the relations of life. We must therefore speak of these qualities also in order that we may the more plainly see how, in all cases, moderation is praiseworthy, while the extreme courses are neither right nor praiseworthy, but blamable. In these cases also names are for the most part wanting, but we must try here as elsewhere to coin names in order to make our argument clear and easy to follow. In the matter of truth, then, let us call him who observes the mean a true or truthful person, and observance of the mean truth or truthfulness; pretence, when it exaggerates, may be called boasting, and the person a boaster; when it understates, let the names be irony and ironical. With regard to pleasantness in amusement, he who observes the mean we may call witty, and his character wittiness; excess may be called buffoonery, and the man a buffoon; while we may call the deficient person boorish, and boorishness for his character. With regard to pleasantness in the other affairs of life, he who makes himself properly pleasant may be called friendly, and his moderation friendliness; he that exceeds may be called an obsequious person if he have no ulterior motive, but a flatterer if he is looking out for his own advantage; he that is deficient in this respect, and always makes himself disagreeable, may be called a quarrelsome and surly sort of person.

Moreover, in the emotions and passions and in our conduct with regard to them there are ways of observing the mean. For example, shame is not a virtue, but yet the modest man is praised. For in these matters also we speak of this man as observing the mean, of that man as going beyond it (as the shame-faced man whom the least thing makes shy), while he who is deficient in the feeling, or lacks it altogether, is called shameless; but the term modest is applied to him who observes the mean.

Righteous indignation, again, hits the mean between envy and spite or malevolence. These have to do with feelings of pleasure and pain at what happens to our neighbors. A man is called righteously indignant when he feels pain at the sight of undeserved prosperity, but the envious man goes beyond and is pained by the sight of any one in prosperity, while the spiteful or malevolent man is so far from being pained that he actually exults in the sight of prosperous iniquity. . . .

The universal character of Aristotle's interests and the fact that he was a Greek naturally led him to a study of government, and in his Politics we have the results of his thinking in this field. In reading the selections from them note (1) his view concerning the origin of the state, (2) his classification of the forms of government and their perversions, (3) the best form of government ideally and practically, (4) the justification of his choice, and (5) his view as to how the good life could best be realized.

As translated by Benjamin Jowett in *The Politics of Aristotle*, 2 vols., Clarendon Press, Oxford, 1885, I, 1–5; 77–84, 126–131. Courtesy of the Jowett Copyright Fund.

From: THE POLITICS

Every state is a community of some kind, and every community is established with a view to some good; for mankind always act in order to obtain that which they think good. But, if all communities aim at some good, the state or political community, which is the highest of all, and which embraces all the rest, aims at good in a greater degree than any other, and at the highest good.

Some people think that the qualifications of a statesman, king, householder, and master are the same, and that they differ, not in kind, but only in the number of their subjects. For example, the ruler over a few is called a master; over more, the manager of a household; over a still larger number, a statesman or king, as if there were no difference between a great household and a small state. The distinction which is made between the king and the statesman is as follows: When the government is personal, the ruler is a king; when, according to the rules of the political science, the citizens rule and are ruled in turn, then he is called a statesman.

But all this is a mistake; for governments differ in kind, as will be evident to any one who considers the matter according to the method which has hitherto guided us. As in other departments of science, so in politics, the compound should always be resolved into the simple elements or least parts of the whole. We must therefore look at the elements of which the state is composed, in order that we may see in what the different kinds of rule differ from one another, and whether any scientific result can be attained about each one of them.

He who thus considers things in their first growth and origin, whether a state or anything else, will obtain the clearest view of them. In the first place there must be a union of those who cannot exist without each other; namely, of male and female, that the race may continue (and this is a union which is formed, not of deliberate purpose, but because, in common with other animals and with plants, mankind have a natural desire to leave behind them an image of themselves), and of natural ruler and subject, that both may be preserved. For that which can foresee by the exercise of mind is by nature intended to be lord and master, and that which can with its body give effect to such foresight is a subject, and by nature a slave; hence master and slave have the same interest. Now nature has distinguished between the female and the slave. For she is not niggardly, like the smith who fashions the Delphian knife for many uses; she makes each thing for a single use, and every instrument is best made when intended for one and not for many uses. But among barbarians no distinction is made between women and slaves, because there is no natural ruler among them: they are a community of slaves, male and female. Wherefore the poets say—

"It is meet that Hellenes should rule over barbarians";

as if they thought that the barbarian and the slave were by nature one.

Out of these two relationships between man and woman, master and slave, the first thing to arise is the family, and Hesiod is right when he says—

"First house and wife and an ox for the plough,"

for the ox is the poor man's slave. The family is the association established by nature for the supply of men's everyday wants, and the members of it are called by Charondas "companions of the cupboard," and by Epimenides the Cretan, "companions of the manger." But when several families are united, and the association aims at something more than the supply of daily needs, the first society to be formed is the village. And the most natural form of the village appears to be that of a colony from the family, composed of the children and grandchildren, who are said to be suckled with the same milk. And this is the reason why Hellenic states were originally governed by kings; because the Hellenes were under royal rule before they came together, as the barbarians still are. Every family is ruled by the eldest, and therefore in the colonies of the family the kingly form of government prevailed because they were of the same blood. As Homer says:

"Each one gives law to his children and to his wives."

For they lived dispersedly, as was the manner in ancient times. Wherefore men say that the Gods have a king, because they themselves either are or were in ancient times under the rule of a king. For they imagine, not only the forms of the Gods, but their ways of life to be like their own.

When several villages are united in a single complete community, large enough to be nearly or quite self-sufficing, the state comes into existence, originating in the bare needs of life, and continuing in existence for the sake of a good life. And therefore, if the earlier forms of society are natural, so is the state, for it is the end of them, and the nature of a thing is its end. For what each thing is when fully developed, we call its nature, whether we are speaking of a man, a horse, or a family. Besides, the final cause and end of a thing is the best, and to be self-sufficing is the end and the best.

Hence it is evident that the state is a creation of nature, and that man is by nature a political animal. And he who by nature and not by mere accident is without a state, is either a bad man or above humanity; he is like the

"Tribeless, lawless, heartless one,"

whom Homer denounces—the natural outcast is forthwith a lover of war; he may be compared to an isolated piece at draughts.

Now, that man is more of a political animal than bees or any other gregarious animals is evident. Nature, as we often say, makes nothing in vain, and man is the only animal whom she has endowed with the gift of speech. And whereas mere voice is but an indication of pleasure or pain, and is therefore found in other animals (for their nature attains to the perception of pleasure and pain and the intimation of them to one another, and no further), the power of speech is intended to set forth the expedient and inexpedient, and therefore likewise the just and the unjust. And it is a characteristic of man that he alone has any sense of good and evil, of just and unjust, and the like, and the association of living beings who have this sense makes a family and a state.

Further, the state is by nature clearly prior to the family and to the individual, since the whole is of necessity prior to the part; for example, if the whole body be destroyed, there will be no foot or hand, except in an equivocal sense, as we might speak of a stone hand; for when destroyed the hand will be no better than that. But things are defined by their working and power; and we ought not to say that they are the same when they no longer have their proper quality, but only that they have the same name. The proof that the state is a creation of nature and prior to the individual is that the individual, when isolated, is not self-sufficing; and therefore he is like a part in relation to the whole. But he who is unable to live in society, or who has no need because he is sufficient for himself, must be either a beast or a god: he is no part of a state. A social instinct is implanted in all men by nature, and yet he who first founded the state was the greatest of benefactors. For man, when perfected, is the best of animals, but, when separated from law and justice, he is the worst of all; since armed injustice is the more dangerous, and he is equipped at birth with arms, meant to be used by intelligence and virtue, which he may use for the worst ends. Wherefore, if he have not virtue, he is the most unholy and the most savage of animals, and the most full of lust and gluttony. But justice is the bond of men in states, for the administration of justice, which is the determination of what is just, is the principle of order in political society. . . .

We have next to consider whether there is only one form of government or many, and if many, what they are, and how many, and what are the differences between them.

A constitution is the arrangement of magistracies in a state, especially of the highest of all. The government is everywhere sovereign in the state, and the constitution is in fact the government. For example, in democracies the people are supreme, but in oligarchies, the few; and, therefore, we say that these two forms of government also are different: and so in other cases.

First, let us consider what is the purpose of a state, and how many forms of government there are by which human society is regulated. We have already said, in the first part of this treatise, when discussing household management and the rule of a master, that man is by nature a political animal. And therefore, men, even when they do not require one another's help, desire to live together; not but that they are also brought together by their common interests in proportion as they severally attain to any measure of well-being. This is certainly the chief end, both of individuals and of states. And also for the sake of mere life (in which there is possibly some noble element so long as the evils of existence do not greatly overbalance the good) mankind meet together and maintain the political community. And we all see that men cling to life even at the cost of enduring great misfortune, seeming to find in life a natural sweetness and happiness.

There is no difficulty in distinguishing the various kinds of authority; they have been often defined already in discussions outside the school. The rule of a master, although the slave by nature and the master by nature have in reality the same interests, is nevertheless exercised primarily with a view to the interest of the master, but accidentally considers the slave, since, if the slave perish, the rule of the master perishes with him. On the other hand, the government of a wife and children and of a household, which we have called household management, is exercised in the first instance for the good of the governed or for the common good of both parties, but essentially for the good of the governed, as we see to be the case in medicine, gymnastic, and the arts in general, which are only accidentally concerned with the good of the artists themselves. For there is no reason why the trainer may not sometimes practise gymnastics, and the helmsman is always one of the crew. The trainer or the helmsman considers the good of those committed to his care. But, when he is one of the persons taken care of, he accidentally participates in the advantage, for the helmsman is also a sailor, and the trainer becomes one of those in training. And so in politics: when the state is framed upon the principle of equality and likeness, the citizens think that they ought to hold office by turns. Formerly, as is natural, every one would take his turn of service; and then again, somebody else would look after his interest, just as he, while in office, had looked after theirs. But nowadays, for the sake of the advantage which is to be gained from the public revenues and from office, men want to be always in office. One might imagine that the rulers, being sickly, were only kept in health while they continued in office; in that case we may be sure that they would be hunting after places. The conclusion is evident: that governments which have a regard to the common interest are constituted in accordance with strict principles of justice, and are therefore true forms; but those which regard only the interest of the rulers are all defective and perverted forms, for they are despotic, whereas a state is a community of freemen.

Having determined these points, we have next to consider how many forms of government there are, and what they are; and in the first place what are the true forms, for when they are determined the perversions of them will at once be apparent. The words constitution and government have the same meaning, and the government, which is the supreme authority in states, must be in the hands of one, or of a few, or of the many. The true forms of government, therefore, are those in which the one, or the few, or the many, govern with a view to the common interest; but governments which rule with a view to the private interest, whether of the one, or of the few, or of the many, are perversions. For the members of a state, if they are truly citizens, ought to participate in its advantages. Of forms of government in which one rules, we call that which regards the common interests, kingship or royalty; that in which more than one, but not many, rule, aristocracy; and it is so called, either because the rulers are the best men, or because they have at heart the best interests of the state and of the citizens. But when the citizens at large administer the state for the common interest, the government is called by the generic name—a constitution. And there is a reason for this use of language. One man or a few may excel in virtue; but as the number increases it becomes more difficult for them to attain perfection in every kind of virtue, though they may in military virtue, for this is found in the masses. Hence in a constitutional government the fighting-men have the supreme power, and those who possess arms are the citizens.

Of the above-mentioned forms, the perversions are as follows:—of royalty, tyranny; of aristocracy, oligarchy; of constitutional government, democracy. For tyranny is a kind of monarchy which has in view the interest of the monarch only; oligarchy has in view the interest of the wealthy; democracy, of the needy: none of them the common good of all.

But there are difficulties about these forms of government, and it will therefore be necessary to state a little more at length the nature of each of them. For he who would make a philosophical study of the various sciences, and does not regard practice only, ought not to overlook or omit anything, but to set forth the truth in every particular. Tyranny, as I was saying, is monarchy exercising the rule of a master over the political society; oligarchy is when men of property have the government in their hands; democracy, the opposite, when the indigent, and not the men of property, are the rulers. And here arises the first of our difficulties, and it relates to the distinction just drawn. For democracy is said to be the government of the many. But what if the many are men of property and have the power in their hands? In like manner oligarchy is said to be the government of the few; but what if the poor are fewer than the rich, and have the power in their hands because they are stronger? In these cases the distinction which we have drawn between these different forms of government would no longer hold good.

Suppose, once more, that we add wealth to the few and poverty to the many, and name the governments accordingly—an oligarchy is said to be that in which the few and the wealthy, and a democracy that in which the many and the poor are the rulers—there will still be a difficulty. For, if the only forms of government are the ones already mentioned, how shall we describe those other governments also just mentioned by us, in which the rich are the more numerous and the poor are the fewer, and both govern in their respective states?

The argument seems to show that, whether in oligarchies or in democracies, the number of the governing body, whether the greater number, as in a democracy, or the smaller number, as in an oligarchy, is an accident due to the fact that the rich everywhere are few, and the poor numerous. But if so, there is a misapprehension of the causes of the difference between them. For the real difference between democracy and oligarchy is poverty and wealth. Wherever men rule by reason of their wealth, whether they be few or many, that is an oligarchy, and where the poor rule, that is a democracy. But, as a fact, the rich are few and the poor many; for few are well-to-do, whereas freedom is enjoyed by all, and wealth and freedom are the grounds on which the oligarchical and democratical parties respectively claim power in the state.

Let us begin by considering the common definitions of oligarchy and democracy, and what is justice oligarchical and democratical. For all men cling to justice of some kind, but their conceptions are imperfect and they do not express the whole idea. For example, justice is thought by them to be, and is, equality; not, however, for all, but only for equals. And inequality is thought to be, and is, justice; neither is this for all, but only for unequals. When the persons are omitted, then men judge erroneously. The reason is that they are passing judgment on themselves, and most people are bad judges in their own case. And whereas justice implies a relation to persons as well as to things, and a just distribution, as I have already said in the *Ethics,* implies the same ratio between the persons and between the things, they agree about the equality of the things, but dispute about the equality of the persons, chiefly for the reason which I have just given —because they are bad judges in their own affairs; and secondly, because both the parties to the argument are speaking of a limited and partial justice, but imagine themselves to be speaking of absolute justice. For the one party, if they are unequal in one respect, for example wealth, consider themselves to be unequal in all; and the other party, if they are equal in one respect, for example free birth, consider themselves to be equal in all. But they leave out the capital point. For if men met and associated out of regard to wealth only, their share in the state would be proportioned to their property, and the oligarchical doctrine would then seem to carry the day. It would not be just that he who paid one mina should have the same share of a hundred minae, whether of the principal or of the profits, as he who paid the remaining ninety-nine. But a state exists for the sake of a good life, and not for the sake of life only; if life only were the object, slaves and brute animals might form a state, but they cannot, for they have no share in happiness or in a life of free choice. Nor does a state exist for the sake of alliance and security from injustice, nor yet for the sake of exchange and mutual intercourse; for then the Tyrrhenians and the Carthaginians, and all who have commercial treaties with one another, would be the citizens of one state. True, they have agreements about imports, and engagements that they will do no wrong to one another, and written articles of alliance. But there are no magistracies common to the contracting parties who will enforce their engagements; different states have each their own magistracies. Nor does one state take care that the citizens of the other are such as they ought to be, nor see that those who come under the terms of the treaty do no wrong or wickedness at all, but only that they do no injustice to one another. Whereas, those who care for good government take into consideration virtue and vice in states. Whence it may be further inferred that virtue must be the care of a state which is truly so called, and not merely enjoys the name: for without this end the community becomes a mere alliance which differs only in place from alliances of which the members live apart; and law is only a convention, 'a surety to one another of justice,' as the sophist Lycophron says, and has no real power to make the citizens good and just.

This is obvious; for suppose distinct places, such as Corinth and Megara, to be brought together so that their walls touched, still they would not be one city, not even if the citizens had the right to intermarry, which is one of the rights peculiarly characteristic of states. Again, if men dwelt at a distance from one another, but not so far off as to have no intercourse, and

there were laws among them that they should not wrong each other in their exchanges, neither would this be a state. Let us suppose that one man is a carpenter, another a husbandman, another a shoemaker, and so on, and that their number is ten thousand: nevertheless, if they have nothing in common but exchange, alliance, and the like, that would not constitute a state. Why is this? Surely not because they are at a distance from one another: for even supposing that such a community were to meet in one place, but that each man had a house of his own, which was in a manner his state, and that they made alliance with one another, but only against evil-doers; still an accurate thinker would not deem this to be a state, if their intercourse with one another was of the same character after as before their union. It is clear then that a state is not a mere society, having a common place, established for the prevention of mutual crime and for the sake of exchange. These are conditions without which a state cannot exist; but all of them together do not constitute a state, which is a community of families and aggregations of families in well-being, for the sake of a perfect and self-sufficing life. Such a community can only be established among those who live in the same place and intermarry. Hence arise in cities family connections, brotherhoods, common sacrifices, amusements which draw men together. But these are created by friendship, for the will to live together is friendship. The end of the state is the good life, and these are the means towards it. And the state is the union of families and villages in a perfect and self-sufficing life, by which we mean a happy and honourable life.

Our conclusion, then, is that political society exists for the sake of noble actions, and not of mere companionship. Hence they who contribute most to such a society have a greater share in it than those who have the same or a greater freedom or nobility of birth but are inferior to them in political virtue; or than those who exceed them in wealth but are surpassed by them in virtue.

From what has been said it will be clearly seen that all the partisans of different forms of government speak of a part of justice only. . . .

We have now to inquire what is the best

constitution for most states, and the best life for most men, neither assuming a standard of virtue which is above ordinary persons, nor an education which is exceptionally favoured by nature and circumstances, nor yet an ideal state which is an aspiration only, but having regard to the life in which the majority are able to share, and to the form of government which states in general can attain. As to those aristocracies, as they are called, of which we were just now speaking, they either lie beyond the possibilities of the greater number of states, or they approximate to the so-called constitutional government, and therefore need no separate discussion. And in fact the conclusion at which we arrive respecting all these forms rests upon the same grounds. For if what was said in the *Ethics* is true, that the happy life is the life according to virtue lived without impediment, and that virtue is a mean, then the life which is in a mean, and in a mean attainable by every one, must be the best. And the same principles of virtue and vice are characteristic of cities and of constitutions; for the constitution is in a figure the life of the city.

Now in all states there are three elements: one class is very rich, another very poor, and a third in a mean. It is admitted that moderation and the mean are best, and therefore it will clearly be best to possess the gifts of fortune in moderation; for in that condition of life men are most ready to follow rational principle. But he who greatly excels in beauty, strength, birth, or wealth, or on the other hand who is very poor, or very weak, or very much disgraced, finds it difficult to follow rational principle. Of these two the one sort grow into violent and great criminals, the others into rogues and petty rascals. And two sorts of offences correspond to them, the one committed from violence, the other from roguery. Again, the middle class is least likely to shrink from rule, or to be over-ambitious for it; both of which are injuries to the state. Again, those who have too much of the goods of fortune, strength, wealth, friends, and the like, are neither willing nor able to submit to authority. The evil begins at home; for when they are boys, by reason of the luxury in which they are brought up, they never learn, even at school, the habit of obedience. On the other hand, the very poor, who are in the opposite

extreme, are too degraded. So that the one class cannot obey, and can only rule despotically; the other knows not how to command and must be ruled like slaves. Thus arises a city, not of freemen, but of masters and slaves, the one despising, the other envying; and nothing can be more fatal to friendship and good fellowship in states than this: for good fellowship springs from friendship; when men are at enmity with one another, they would rather not even share the same path. But a city ought to be composed, as far as possible, of equals and similars; and these are generally the middle classes. Wherefore the city which is composed of middle-class citizens is necessarily best constituted in respect of the elements of which we say the fabric of the state naturally consists. And this is the class of citizens which is most secure in a state, for they do not, like the poor, covet their neighbours' goods; nor do others covet theirs, as the poor covet the goods of the rich; and as they neither plot against others, nor are themselves plotted against, they pass through life safely. Wisely then did Phocylides pray—"Many things are best in the mean; I desire to be a middle condition in my city."

Thus it is manifest that the best political community is formed by citizens of the middle class, and that those states are likely to be well-administered, in which the middle class is large, and stronger if possible than both the other classes, or at any rate than either singly: for the addition of the middle class turns the scale, and prevents either of the extremes from being dominant. Great then is the good fortune of a state in which the citizens have a moderate and sufficient property; for where some possess much, and the others nothing, there may arise an extreme democracy, or a pure oligarchy; or a tyranny may grow out of either extreme—either out of the most rampant democracy, or out of an oligarchy; but it is not so likely to arise out of the middle constitutions and those akin to them. I will explain the reason of this hereafter, when I speak of the revolutions of states. The mean condition of states is clearly best, for no other is free from faction; and where the middle class is large, there are least likely to be factions and dissensions. For a similar reason large states are less liable to faction than small ones, because in them the middle class is large; whereas in small states it is easy to divide all the citizens into two classes who are either rich or poor, and to leave nothing in the middle. And democracies are safer and more permanent than oligarchies, because they have a middle class which is more numerous and has a greater share in the government; for when there is no middle class, and the poor greatly exceed in number, troubles arise, and the state soon comes to an end. A proof of the superiority of the middle class is that the best legislators have been of a middle condition; for example, Solon, as his own verses testify; and Lycurgus, for he was not a king; and Charondas, and almost all legislators.

These considerations will help us to understand why most governments are either democratical or oligarchical. The reason is that the middle class is seldom numerous in them, and whichever party, whether the rich or the common people, transgresses the mean and predominates, draws the constitution its own way, and thus arises either oligarchy or democracy. There is another reason—the poor and the rich quarrel with one another, and whichever side gets the better, instead of establishing a just or popular government, regards political supremacy as the prize of victory, and the one party sets up a democracy and the other an oligarchy. Further, both the parties which had the supremacy in Hellas looked only to the interest of their own form of government, and established in states, the one, democracies, and the other, oligarchies; they thought of their own advantage, of the public not at all. For these reasons the middle form of government has rarely, if ever, existed, and among a very few only. One man alone of all who ever ruled in Hellas was induced to give this middle constitution to states. But it has now become a habit among the citizens of states, not even to care about equality; all men are seeking for dominion, or, if conquered, are willing to submit.

What then is the best form of government, and what makes it the best, is evident; and of other constitutions, since we say that there are many kinds of democracy and many of oligarchy, it is not difficult to see which has the first and which the second or any other place in the order of excellence, now that we have determined which is the best. For that which is nearest to the best must of necessity be better, and that which is furthest from it worse, if we are judging absolutely and not relatively to given conditions: I say "relatively to given conditions," since a particular government may be preferable, but another form may be better for some people.

Sophocles

S ophocles (496?–406 B.C.) *lived in the period that witnessed the victory of the Greeks over the Persians and the flowering of culture in Athens. One of the great triumvirate of dramatists which included Aeschylus and Euripides, Sophocles interested himself in the perennial human question of how men react to the problems presented by life. In this great tragedy prepared for presentation at one of the annual Dionysian festivals at Athens, Sophocles portrayed the reactions of King Œdipus to the fate outlined for him by the inexorable decree of the gods. In reading this play note (1) that the chorus is used by the author as an additional character to aid in telling the story, (2) the style of writing and the form of the play, (3) evidence of religious thought, (4) the relationship between moral conduct and equivalent rewards and punishments, (5) man's role when confronted by adversity, and (6) evidence of the Greek view of life.*

As translated by Thomas Francklin in *Sophocles*, New York, 1834, 238–288.

ŒDIPUS THE KING

DRAMATIS PERSONÆ

Œdipus, king of Thebes
Jocasta, wife of Œdipus
Creon, brother of Jocasta
Tiresias, a blind prophet of Thebes
A Shepherd from Corinth
A Messenger
An Old Shepherd, formerly belonging to Laius
High Priest of Jupiter
Chorus, composed of the priests and ancient men of Thebes, Theban youths, children of Œdipus, attendants, &c.

ARGUMENT

Laius, king of Thebes, having learned from the oracle of Apollo that he was destined to perish by the hand of his son, commanded his wife Jocasta to destroy her infant as soon as it came into the world. The mother accordingly gave the child to a domestic, with orders to expose him on Mount Cithæron, where he was found by one of the shepherds of Polybus, king of Corinth; who having no children, determined, by the advice of his queen, to keep the boy in ignorance of the circumstances of his birth, and educate him as his own son. When Œdipus had arrived at years of maturity, he went to consult the oracle, which terrified him with the intelligence that he would commit parricide and incest. He now therefore resolved to return to Corinth no more; and travelling towards Phocis, met Laius, and, in a dispute which ensued, slew him. As Œdipus was ignorant of the rank and quality of the man whom he had killed, he was attracted to Thebes by the report of the sphinx; the overthrow of which monster raised him to the throne, while the prophecy was completed by his nuptials with the widow of Laius, by whom he had four children. The Theban territories were at length desolated by a plague, which the oracle declared should cease when the murderer of Laius was banished from Bœotia. After a minute investigation, the dreadful secret was at length divulged; and Jocasta put a period to her existence, while Œdipus deprived himself of sight, and was, at his own request, banished from Thebes by the order of Creon, the brother of Jocasta, who then assumed the reins of government.

ACT I

Scene, Thebes before the palace of Œdipus.
   Œdipus, High Priest of Jupiter
   Œdi. O my loved sons! the youthful progeny
Of ancient Cadmus! wherefore sit you here,
And   suppliant   thus,   with   sacred   boughs
      adorn'd,
Crowd to our altars? Frequent sacrifice,
And prayers, and sighs, and sorrows fill the
      land.
I could have sent to learn the fatal cause:
But see, your anxious sovereign comes himself
To know it all from you: behold your king,
Renowned Œdipus. Do thou, old man
(For best that office suits thy years), inform me
Why you are come. Is it the present ill
That calls you here, or dread of future woe?
Hard were indeed the heart that did not feel
For grief like yours, and pity such distress.
If there be aught that Œdipus can do
To serve his people, know me for your friend.
   Priest. O king! thou seest what numbers
      throng thy altars.
Here, bending sad beneath the weight of years,
The hoary priests, here crowd the chosen
      youth
Of Thebes, with these a weak and suppliant
      train
Of helpless infants: last, in me behold
The minister of Jove: far off thou seest
Assembled multitudes, with laurel crown'd,
To where Minerva's hallow'd temples rise
Frequent repair, or where Ismenus laves
Apollo's sacred shrine. Too well thou know'st,
Thy wretched Thebes, with dreadful storms
      oppress'd,
Scarce lifts her head above the whelming flood:
The teeming earth her blasted harvest mourns,
And on the barren plain the flocks and herds
Unnumber'd perish; dire abortion thwarts
The mother's hopes, and painful she brings
      forth
The half-formed infant; baleful pestilence

Hath laid our city waste; the fiery god
Stalks o'er deserted Thebes; while, with our
    groans
Enrich'd, the gloomy god of Erebus
Triumphant smiles. O Œdipus! to thee
We bend: behold these youths; with me they
    kneel,
And suppliant at thy altars sue for aid,
To thee, the first of men, and only less
Than they, whose favour thou alone canst gain,
The gods above: thy wisdom yet may heal
The deep-felt wounds, and make the powers
    divine
Propitious to us. Thebes long since to thee
Her safety owed, when, from the sphinx de-
    liver'd,
Thy grateful people saw thee, not by man
But by the gods instructed, save the land.
Now, then, thou best of kings! assist us now:
O! by some mortal or immortal aid
Now succour the distress'd! On wisdom oft
And prudent counsels, in the hour of ill,
Success awaits. O dearest prince! support,
Relieve thy Thebes; on thee, its saviour once,
Again it calls: now, if thou wouldst not see
The memory perish of thy former deeds,
Let it not call in vain; but rise, and save.
With happiest omens once, and fair success,
We saw thee crown'd: O! be thyself again,
And may thy will and fortune be the same!
If thou art yet to reign, O king! remember,
A sovereign's riches is a peopled realm;
For what will ships or lofty towers avail,
Unarm'd with men to guard and to defend
    them?
    Œdi. O my unhappy sons! too well I know
Your sad estate; I know the woes of Thebes:
And yet among you lives not such a wretch
As Œdipus; for O! on me, my children!
Your sorrows press. Alas! I feel for you,
My people, for myself, for Thebes, for all.
Think not I slept regardless of your ills;
O no; with many a tear I wept your fate,
And oft in meditation deep revolved
How best your peace and safety to restore.
The only medicine that my thoughts could find
I have administered: Menœceus' son,
The noble Creon, went by my command
To Delphi, from Apollo's shrine to know
What must be done to save this wretched land.
'Tis time he were returned; I wonder much

At his delay: if, when he comes, your king
Perform not all the god enjoins, then say
He is the worst of men.
    Priest.   O king! thy words
Are gracious; and, if right these youths in-
    form me,
Creon is here.
    Œdi.   O Phœbus! grant he come
With tidings cheerful as the smile he wears?
    Priest. He is the messenger of good; for see,
His brows are crown'd with laurel.
    Œdi.   We shall soon
Be satisfied: he comes.

            Enter Creon, Chorus.

                 My dearest Creon!
O! say, what answer bear'st thou from the god?
Or good or ill?
    Cre.   Good, very good; for know,
The worst of ills, if rightly used, may prove
The means of happiness.
    Œdi.   What says my friend?
This answer gives me naught to hope or fear.
    Cre. Shall we retire, or would you that I
    speak
In public here?
    Œdi.   Before them all declare it:
Their woes sit heavier on me than my own.
    Cre. Then mark what I have heard: the god
    commands
That instant we drive forth the fatal cause
Of this dire pestilence, nor nourish here
The accursed monster.
    Œdi.   Who? what monster? how
Remove it?
    Cre.   Or by banishment, or death:
Life must be given for life; for yet his blood
Rests on the city.
    Œdi.   Whose? what means the god?
    Cre. O king! before thee Laius ruled o'er
    Thebes.
    Œdi. I know he did, though I did ne'er be-
    hold him.
    Cre. Laius was slain, and on his murderers
(So Phœbus says) we must have vengeance.
    Œdi.   Where,
Where are the murderers? who shall trace the
    guilt
Buried so long in silence?
    Cre.   Here, he said,

Ev'n in this land: what's sought for may be
found;
But truth, unsearch'd for, seldom comes to
light.
   Œdi. How did he fall, and where? at home,
abroad?
Died he at Thebes, or in a foreign land?
   Cre. He left his palace, fame reports, to seek
Some oracle; since that we ne'er beheld him.
   Œdi. But did no messenger return? Not one
Of all his train, of whom we might inquire
Touching this murder?
   Cre.   One, and one alone,
Came back, who, flying, 'scaped the general
slaughter;
But nothing, save one little circumstance,
Or knew, or e'er related.
   Œdi.   What was that?
Much may be learn'd from that; a little dawn
Of light appearing, may discover all.
   Cre. Laius, attack'd by robbers, and op-
press'd
By number, fell; such is his tale.
   Œdi.   Would they,—
Would robbers do so desperate a deed,
Unbribed and unassisted?
   Cre.   So indeed
Suspicion whisper'd then; but, Laius dead,
No friend was found to vindicate the wrong.
   Œdi. But what strange cause could stop in-
quiry thus
Into the murder of a king?
   Cre.   The sphinx:
Her dire enigma kept our thought intent
On present ills, nor gave us time to search
The past mysterious deed.
   Œdi.   Myself will try
Soon to unveil it: thou, Apollo! well,
And well hast thou, my Creon! lent thy aid;
Your Œdipus shall now perform his part:
Yes, I will fight for Phœbus and my country,
And so I ought; for not to friends alone
Or kindred owe I this, but to myself.
Who murder'd him perchance would murder
me;
His cause is mine; wherefore, my children! rise,
Take hence your suppliant boughs, and sum-
mon here
The race of Cadmus, my assembled people.
Naught shall be left untried: Apollo leads,
And we will rise to joy, or sink for ever.

   Priest. Haste then, my sons! for this we
hither came;
About it quick; and may the god, who sent
This oracle, protect, defend, and save us!
                          [*Exeunt.*

Chorus

Strophe I

O, thou great oracle divine!
Who didst to happy Thebes remove,
   From Delphi's golden shrine,
And in sweet sounds declare the will of Jove;
Daughter of hope! O! soothe my soul to rest,
And calm the rising tumult in my breast.
   Look down, O Phœbus! on thy loved abode;
Speak, for thou know'st the dark decrees of
fate,
Our present and our future state.
   O Delian! be thou still our healing god!

Antistrophe I

Minerva! first on thee I call,
Daughter of Jove, immortal maid;
   Low beneath thy feet we fall:
O! bring thy sister Dian to our aid.
Goddess of Thebes! from thy imperial throne
Look with an eye of gentle pity down;
   And thou, far-shooting Phœbus! once the
friend
   Of this unhappy, this devoted land;
   O! now, if ever, let thy hand
Once more be stretched to save and to defend.

Strophe II

Great Thebes, my sons! is now no more;
   She falls, and ne'er again shall rise;
Naught can her health or strength restore;
   The mighty nation sinks, she droops, she
dies.
Stripp'd of her fruits behold the barren earth:
The half-form'd infant struggles for a birth;
   The mother sinks, unequal to her pain:
      While, quick as birds in airy circles fly,
      Or lightnings from an angry sky,
   Crowds press on crowds to Pluto's dark do-
main.

Antistrophe II

Behold, what heaps of wretches slain,
   Unburied, unlamented lie:

Nor parents now nor friends remain
  To grace their deaths with pious obsequy;
The aged matron and the blooming wife,
Clung to the altars, sue for added life.
  With sighs and groans united, Pæans rise;
    Re-echoed still doth great Apollo's name
    Their sorrows and their wants proclaim
  Frequent to him ascends the sacrifice.

STROPHE III

Haste, then, Minerva! beauteous maid!
  Descend in this afflictive hour;
Haste to thy dying people's aid;
  Drive hence this baneful, this destructive
    power,
Who comes not arm'd with hostile sword or
    shield,
Yet strews with many a corse the ensanguined
  field.
  To Amphitrite's wide-extending bed,
    O! drive me, goddess, from thy favourite
      land;
    Or let him, by thy dread command,
  Bury in Thracian waves his ignominious
  head.

ANTISTROPHE III

  Father of all, immortal Jove!
  O! now thy fiery terrors send;
    From thy dreadful stores above
  Let lightnings blast him, and let thunders
    rend.
And thou, O Lydian king! thy aid impart;
Send from thy golden bow the unerring dart;
  Smile, chaste Diana! on this loved abode,
While Theban Bacchus joins the maddening
    throng.
O god of wine, and mirth, and song!
  Now with thy torch destroy the base, in-
  glorious god.   [*Exeunt.*

ACT II

Œdipus, Chorus, *the People assembled.*

Œdi. Your prayers are heard; and, if you
    will obey
Your king, and hearken to his words, you soon
Shall find relief: myself will heal your woes.
I was a stranger to the dreadful deed,
A stranger ev'n to the report till now;

And yet, without some traces of the crime,
I should not urge this matter; therefore hear
    me.
I speak to all the citizens of Thebes,
Myself a citizen; observe me well:
If any know the murderer of Laius,
Let him reveal it; I command you all;
But if, restrain'd by dread of punishment,
He hide the secret, let him fear no more;
For naught but exile shall attend the crime,
Whene'er confess'd: if by a foreign hand
The horrid deed was done, who points him out
Commands our thanks, and meets a sure re-
    ward;
But if there be who knows the murderer,
And yet conceals him from us, mark his fate,
Which here I do pronounce; let none receive,
Throughout my kingdom, none hold converse
    with him,
Nor offer prayer, nor sprinkle o'er his head
The sacred cup; let him be driven from all,
By all abandon'd, and by all accursed;
For so the Delphic oracle declared:
And therefore to the gods I pay this duty,
And to the dead. O! may the guilty wretch,
Whether alone, or by his impious friends
Assisted, he perform'd the horrid deed,
Denied the common benefits of nature,
Wear out a painful life and, O! if here,
Within my palace I conceal the traitor,
On me and mine alight the vengeful curse!
To you, my people! I commit the care
Of this important business; 'tis my cause,
The cause of Heaven, and your expiring coun-
    try.
Ev'n if the god had naught declared, to leave
This crime unexpiated were most ungrateful:
He was the best of kings, the best of men;
That sceptre now is mine which Laius bore:
His wife is mine; so would his children be,
Did any live; and therefore am I bound,
Ev'n as he were my father, to revenge him.
Yes, I will try to find this murderer:
I owe it to the son of Labdacus,
To Polydorus, Cadmus, and the race
Of great Agenor. O! if yet there are
Who will not join me in the pious deed;
From such may Earth withhold her annual
    store,
And barren be their bed, their life most
    wretched,

And their death cruel as the pestilence
That wastes our city; but on you, my Thebans!
Who wish us fair success, may Justice smile
Propitious, and the gods for ever bless!

Cho. O king! thy imprecation unappall'd
I hear, and join thee, guiltless of the crime,
Nor knowing who committed it. The god
Alone, who gave the oracle, must clear
Its doubtful sense, and point out the offender.

Œdi. 'Tis true; but who shall force the powers divine
To speak their hidden purpose?

Cho.   One thing more,
If I might speak.

Œdi.   Say on, whate'er thy mind
Shall dictate to thee.

Cho.   As among the gods
All-knowing Phœbus, so to mortal men
Doth sage Tiresias in foreknowledge sure
Shine forth pre-eminent: perchance his aid
Might much avail us.

Œdi.   Creon did suggest
The same expedient, and by his advice
Twice have I sent for this Tiresias; much
I wonder that he comes not.

Cho.   'Tis most fitting
We do consult him; for the idle tales
Which rumour spreads are not to be regarded.

Œdi. What are those tales? for naught
 should we despise.

Cho. 'Tis said, some travellers did attack the
 king.

Œdi. It is: but still no proof appears.

Cho.   And yet,
If it be so, thy dreadful execration
Will force the guilty to confess

Œdi.   O no!
Who fears not to commit the crime will ne'er
Be frighted at the curse that follows it.

Cho. Behold, he comes, who will discover
 all!
The holy prophet, see! They lead him hither:
He knows the truth, and will reveal it to us.

Enter Tiresias

Œdi. O sage Tiresias! thou, who knowest all
That can be known, the things of heaven above
And earth below; whose mental eye beholds,
Blind as thou art, the state of dying Thebes,
And weeps her fate; to thee we look for aid;
On thee alone for safety we depend.

This answer, which perchance thou hast not
 heard,
Apollo gave: The plague, he said, should cease,
When those who murder'd Laius were dis-
 cover'd,
And paid the forfeit of their crime by death
Or banishment. O! do not then conceal
Aught that thy art prophetic, from the flight
Of birds or other omens, may disclose.
O! save thyself, save this afflicted city,
Save Œdipus, avenge the guiltless dead
From this pollution! Thou art all our hope;
Remember, 'tis the privilege of man,
His noblest function, to assist the wretched.

Tir. Alas! what misery it is to know,
When knowledge is thus fatal! O Tiresias!
Thou art undone. Would I had never come!

Œdi. What sayest thou? Whence this
 strange dejection? Speak.

Tir. Let me be gone; 'twere better for us
 both
That I retire in silence: be advised.

Œdi. It is ingratitude to Thebes, who bore
And cherish'd thee; it is unjust to all,
To hide the will of Heaven.

Tir.   'Tis rash in thee
To ask, and rash I fear will prove my answer.

Cho. O! do not, by the gods, conceal it from
 us:
Suppliant we all request, we all conjure thee.

Tir. You know not what you ask: I'll not
 unveil
Your miseries to you.

Œdi.   Know'st thou then our fate,
And will not tell it? Mean'st thou to betray
Thy country and thy king?

Tir.   I would not make
Myself and thee unhappy: why thus blame
My tender care, nor listen to my caution!

Œdi. Wretch as thou art, thou wouldst pro-
 voke a stone,
Inflexible and cruel, still implored,
And still refusing.

Tir.   Thou condemn'st my warmth,
Forgetful of thy own.

Œdi.   Who would not rage,
To see an injured people treated thus
With vile contempt?

Tir.   What is decreed by Heaven
Must come to pass, though I reveal it not.

Œdi. Still 'tis thy duty to inform us of it.

Tir. I'll speak no more, not though thine anger swell
Ev'n to its utmost.

Œdi. Nor will I be silent.
I tell thee, once for all, thou wert thyself
Accomplice in this deed; nay more, I think,
But for thy blindness, wouldst with thine own hand
Have done it too.

Tir. 'Tis well; now hear Tiresias:
The sentence, which thou didst thyself proclaim,
Falls on thyself: henceforth shall never man
Hold converse with thee, for thou art accursed;
The guilty cause of this our city's woes.

Œdi. Audacious traitor! think'st thou to escape
The hand of vengeance?

Tir. Yes, I fear thee not;
For truth is stronger than a tyrant's arm.

Œdi. Whence didst thou learn this? Was it from thy art?

Tir. I learn'd it from thyself: thou didst compel me
To speak, unwilling as I was.

Œdi. Once more
Repeat it then, that I may know my fate
More plainly still.

Tir. Is it not plain already,
Or mean'st thou but to tempt me?

Œdi. No; but say,
Speak it again.

Tir. Again then I declare
Thou art thyself the murderer whom thou seek'st.

Œdi. A second time thou shalt not pass unpunish'd.

Tir. What wouldst thou say, if I should tell thee all?

Œdi. Say what thou wilt; for all is false.

Tir. Know then,
That Œdipus, in shameful bonds united
With those he loves, unconscious of his guilt,
Is yet most guilty.

Œdi. Darest thou utter more,
And hope for pardon?

Tir. Yes, if there be strength
In sacred truth.

Œdi. But truth dwells not in thee:
Thy body and thy mind are dark alike,

For both are blind; thy every sense is lost.

Tir. Thou dost upbraid me with the loss of that
For which thyself ere long shall meet reproach
From every tongue.

Œdi. Thou blind and impious traitor!
Thy darkness is thy safeguard, or this hour
Had been thy last.

Tir. It is not in my fate
To fall by thee; Apollo guards his priest.

Œdi. Was this the tale of Creon, or thy own?

Tir. Creon is guiltless, and the crime is thine.

Œdi. O riches, power, dominion, and thou far
Above them all, the best of human blessings,
Excelling wisdom, how doth envy love
To follow and oppress you! This fair kingdom,
Which, by the nation's choice and not my own,
I here possess, Creon, my faithful friend
(For such I thought him once), would now wrest from me,
And hath suborn'd this vile impostor here,
This wand'ring hypocrite, of sharpest sight
When interest prompts, but ignorant and blind
When fools consult him. Tell me, prophet! where
Was all thy art, when the abhorred sphinx
Alarm'd our city? Wherefore did not then
Thy wisdom save us? Then the man divine
Was wanting; but thy birds refused their omens;
Thy god was silent: then came Œdipus,
This poor, unlearned, uninstructed sage,
Who not from birds uncertain omens drew,
But by his own sagacious mind explored
The hidden mystery; and now thou comest
To cast me from the throne my wisdom gain'd,
And share with Creon my divided empire.
But you should both lament your ill-got power,
You and your bold compeer; for thee, this moment,
But that I bear respect unto thy age,
I'd make thee rue thy execrable purpose.

Cho. You both are angry, therefore both to blame:
Much rather should you join, with friendly zeal
And mutual ardour, to explore the will
Of all-deciding Heaven.

Tir. What though thou rulest
O'er Thebes despotic, we are equal here;

I am Apollo's subject, and not thine;
Nor want I Creon to protect me. No;
I tell thee, king! this blind Tiresias tells thee,
Seeing thou seest not, know'st not where thou
    art,
What, or with whom. Canst thou inform me
    who
Thy parents are, and what thy horrid crimes
'Gainst thy own race, the living and the dead?
A father's and a mother's curse attend thee.
Soon shall their furies drive thee from the land,
And leave thee dark like me: what mountain
    then,
Or conscious shore, shall not return the groans
Of Œdipus, and echo to his woes?
When thou shalt look on the detested bed,
And in that haven where thou hopest to rest,
Shalt meet with storm and tempest; then what
    ills
Shall fall on thee and thine! Now vent thy rage
On old Tiresias and the guiltless Creon:
We shall be soon avenged, for ne'er did
    Heaven
Cut off a wretch so base, so vile as thou art.
 Œdi. Must I bear this from thee? Away, be-
  gone!
Home, villain, home!
 Tir.   I did not come to thee
Unsent for.
 Œdi. Had I thought thou wouldst have thus
Insulted me, I had not call'd thee hither.
 Tir. Perhaps thou hold'st Tiresias as a fool
And madman; but thy parents thought me
    wise.
 Œdi. My parents, saidst thou? Speak! who
  were my parents?
 Tir. This day, that gives thee life, shall give
  thee death.
 Œdi. Still dark, and still perplexing are the
  words
Thou utter'st.
 Tir.   'Tis thy business to unriddle,
And therefore thou canst best interpret them.
 Œdi. Thou dost reproach me for my virtues.
 Tir.   They,
And thy good fortune, have undone thee.
 Œdi.   Since
I sav'd the city, I'm content.
 Tir.   Farewell.
Boy, lead me hence.
 Œdi.   Away with him, for here

His presence but disturbs us; being gone,
We shall be happier.
 Tir.   Œdipus! I go;
But first inform thee (for I fear thee not)
Wherefore I came: know, then, I came to tell
    thee,
The man thou seek'st, the man on whom thou
    pour'dst
Thy execrations, ev'n the murderer
Of Laius, now is here; a seeming stranger,
And yet a Theban. He shall suffer soon
For all his crimes: from light and affluence
    driven
To penury and darkness, poor and blind,
Propp'd on his staff, and from his native land
Expell'd, I see him in a foreign clime
A helpless wanderer; to his sons at once
A father and a brother; child and husband
Of her from whom he sprang. Adulterous,
Incestuous parricide! now fare thee well;
Go, learn the truth; and, if it be not so,
Say I have ne'er deserved the name of prophet.

Chorus

STROPHE I

When will the guilty wretch appear,
Whom Delphi's sacred oracle demands;
 Author of crimes too black for mortal ear,
Dipping in royal blood his sacrilegious hands?
Swift as the storm by rapid whirlwinds driven,
Quick let him fly the impending wrath of
    Heaven;
  For lo, the angry son of Jove,
  Arm'd with red lightnings from above,
Pursues the murderer with immortal hate,
And round him spreads the snares of unre-
    lenting fate.

ANTISTROPHE I

From steep Parnassus' rocky cave,
Cover'd with snow, came forth the dread com-
    mand;
 Apollo thence his sacred mandate gave,
To search the man of blood through every
    land.
Silent and sad the weary wanderer roves
O'er pathless rocks and solitary groves,
  Hoping to 'scape the wrath divine
  Denounced from great Apollo's shrine:

Vain hopes to 'scape the fate by Heaven decreed
For vengeance hovers still o'er his devoted
head.

STROPHE II

Tiresias, famed for wisdom's lore,
Hath dreadful ills to Œdipus divined;
　And as his words mysterious I explore,
Unnumber'd doubts perplex my anxious mind:
Now raised by hope, and now with fears op-
press'd,
Sorrow and joy alternate fill my breast.
　　　How should these hapless kings be foes,
　　　When never strife between them rose?
Or why should Laius, slain by hands unknown,
Bring foul disgrace on Polybus' unhappy son?

ANTISTROPHE II

From Phœbus and all-seeing Jove
Naught can be hid of actions here below;
　But earthly prophets may deceitful prove,
And little more than other mortals know.
Though much in wisdom man doth man excel,
In all that's human error still must dwell.
　　　Could he commit the bloody deed,
　　　Who from the sphinx our city freed?
O no! he never shed the guiltless blood;
The sphinx declares him wise, and innocent,
　　　and good.　　　　　　　[Exeunt.

ACT III

Creon, Chorus

Cre. O citizens! with grief I hear your king
Hath blasted the fair fame of guiltless Creon,
And most unjustly brands me with a crime
My soul abhors. While desolation spreads
On every side, and universal ruin
Hangs o'er the land, if I in word or deed
Could join to swell the woes of hapless Thebes,
I were unworthy, nay, I would not wish
To live another day. Alas, my friends!
Thus to be deem'd a traitor to my country,
To you, my fellow-citizens, to all
That hear me; O, 'tis infamy and shame!
I cannot, will not bear it.
　Cho.　　　　　　'Twas the effect
Of sudden anger only; what he said,
But could not think.

Cre.　　　　　Who told him I suborn'd
The prophet to speak falsely? What could raise
This vile suspicion?
　Cho.　　　　　Such he had, but whence
I know not.
　Cre.　　　Talk'd he thus with firm com-
posure
And confidence of mind?
　Cho.　　　　　　I cannot say:
'Tis not for me to know the thoughts of kings,
Or judge their actions: but, behold, he comes.

Enter Œdipus

Œdi. Ha! Creon here? And darest thou thus
approach
My palace? thou, who wouldst have murder'd
me,
And taken my kingdom? By the gods, I ask
thee
(Answer me! traitor), didst thou think me fool
Or coward, that I could not see thy arts,
Or had not strength to vanquish them? What
madness,
What strange infatuation, led thee on,
Without or force or friends, to grasp at empire,
Which only their united force can give?
What wert thou doing?
　Cre.　　　　Hear what I shall answer,
Then judge impartial.
　Œdi.　　　　Thou canst talk it well,
But I shall ne'er attend to thee; thy guilt
Is plain; thou art my deadliest foe.
　Cre.　　　　　　　But hear
What I shall urge.
　Œdi.　　　Say not thou art innocent.
　Cre. If self-opinion, void of reason, seem
Conviction to thee, know, thou err'st most
grossly.
　Œdi. And thou more grossly, if thou
think'st to pass
Unpunish'd for this injury to thy friend.
　Cre. I should not, were I guilty; but what
crime
Have I committed? Tell me.
　Œdi.　　　　　Wert not thou
The man who urged me to require the aid
Of your all-knowing prophet?
　Cre.　　　　　True, I was;
I did persuade you: so I would again.
　Œdi. How long is it since Laius—
　Cre.　　　　　　　Laius? what?

Œdi. Since Laius fell by hands unknown?
Cre.   A long,
Long tract of years.
Œdi.   Was this Tiresias then
A prophet?
Cre.   Ay, in wisdom and in fame,
As now, excelling.
Œdi.   Did he then say aught
Concerning me?
Cre.   I never heard he did.
Œdi. Touching this murder, did you ne'er
    inquire
Who were the authors?
Cre.   Doubtless; but in vain.
Œdi. Why did not the same prophet then
    inform you?
Cre. I know not that, and when I'm igno-
    rant
I'm always silent.
Œdi.   What concerns thyself
At least thou know'st, and therefore shouldst
    declare it.
Cre. What is it? speak; and if 'tis in my
    power,
I'll answer thee.
Œdi.   Thou know'st, if this Tiresias
Had not combined with thee, he would not
    thus
Accuse me as the murderer of Laius.
Cre. What he declares thou best canst tell;
    of me,
What thou requirest, myself am yet to learn.
Œdi. Go, learn it, then; but ne'er shalt
    thou discover
That Œdipus is guilty.
Cre.   Art not thou
My sister's husband?
Œdi.   Granted.
Cre.   Join'd with her,
Thou rulest o'er Thebes.
Œdi.   'Tis true, and all she asks
Most freely do I give her.
Cre.   Is not Creon
In honour next to you?
Œdi.   Thou art, and therefore
The more ungrateful.
Cre.   Hear what I shall plead,
And thou wilt never think so: tell me, prince,
Is there a man who would prefer a throne,
With all its dangers, to an equal rank
In peace and safety? I am not of those

Who choose the name of king before the
    power;
Fools only make such wishes; I have all
From thee, and fearless I enjoy it all.
Had I the sceptre, often must I act
Against my will. Know, then, I am not yet
So void of sense and reason as to quit
A real 'vantage for a seeming good.
Am I not happy? am I not revered,
Embraced, and loved by all? To me they come
Who want thy favour, and by me acquire it:
What then should Creon wish for? Shall he
    leave
All this for empire? Bad desires corrupt
The fairest mind: I never entertain'd
A thought so vile, nor would I lend my aid
To forward such base purposes. But go
To Delphi; ask the sacred oracle
If I have spoke the truth: if there you find
That with the prophet I conspired, destroy
The guilty Creon: not thy voice alone
Shall then condemn me, for myself will join
In the just sentence; but accuse me not
On weak suspicion's most uncertain test.
Justice would never call the wicked good,
Or brand fair virtue with the name of vice,
Unmerited: to cast away a friend
Faithful and just, is to deprive ourselves
Of life and being, which we hold most dear:
But time, and time alone, revealeth all;
That only shows the good man's excellence:
A day sufficeth to unmask the wicked.
    Cho. O king! his caution merits your regard;
Who judge in haste do seldom judge aright.
    Œdi. When they are quick who plot against
    my life,
'Tis fit I should be quick in my defence:
If I am tame and silent, all they wish
Will soon be done, and Œdipus must fall.
    Cre. What wouldst thou have? My banish-
    ment?
Œdi.   Thy death.
Cre. But first inform me wherefore I should
    die.
Œdi. Dost thou rebel then? Wilt thou not
    submit?
Cre. Not when I see thee thus deceived.
Œdi.   'Tis fit
I should defend my own.
Cre.   And so should I.
Œdi. Thou art a traitor.

Cre.   What, if I should prove
I am not so?
    Œdi.   A king must be obey'd.
    Cre. Not if his orders are unjust.
    Œdi.   O Thebes!
O citizens!
    Cre.   I too can call on Thebes:
She is my country.
    Cho.   O! no more, my lords!
For, see, Jocasta comes in happiest hour
To end your contest.

Enter Jocasta

Joc.   Whence this sudden tumult?
O princes! is this well, at such a time
With idle broils to multiply the woes
Of wretched Thebes? Home, home, for shame;
        nor thus
With private quarrel swell the public ruin.
    Cre. Sister! thy husband hath most basely
        used me;
He threatens me with banishment or death.
    Œdi. I do confess it; for he did conspire,
With vile and wicked arts, against my life.
    Cre. O! may I never prosper, but, accursed,
Unpitied, perish if I ever did!
    Joc. Believe him, Œdipus! revere the gods
Whom he contests, if thou dost love Jocasta:
Thy subjects beg it of thee.
    Cho.   Hear, O king!
Consider, we entreat thee.
    Œdi.   What wouldst have?
Think you I'll e'er submit to him?
    Cho.   Revere
His character, his oath, both pleading for him.
    Œdi. But know you what you ask?
    Cho.   We do.
    Œdi.   What is it?
    Cho. We ask thee to believe a guiltless
        friend,
Nor cast him forth dishonour'd thus, on slight
Suspicion's weak surmise.
    Œdi.   Requesting this,
You do request my banishment or death.
    Cho. No, by yon leader of the heavenly host,
The immortal sun, I had not such a thought:
I only felt for Thebes' distressful state,
And would not have it by domestic strife
Imbitter'd thus.
    Œdi.   Why, let him then depart:
If Œdipus must die, or leave his country

For shameful exile, be it so: I yield
To thy request, not his; for hateful still
Shall Creon ever be.
    Cre.   Thy stubborn soul
Bends with reluctance, and when anger fires it,
Is terrible; but natures form'd like thine
Are their own punishment.
    Œdi.   Wilt thou not hence?
Wilt not be gone?
    Cre.   I go: thou know'st me not;
But these will do me justice.   [*Exit* Creon.
    Cho.   Princess! now
Persuade him to retire.
    Joc.   First let me know
The cause of this dissension.
    Cho.   From reports
Uncertain, and suspicions most injurious,
The quarrel rose.
    Joc.   Was the accusation mutual?
    Cho. It was.
    Joc.   What follow'd then?
    Cho.   Ask me no more;
Enough's already known: we'll not repeat
The woes of hapless Thebes.
    Œdi.   You are all blind,
Insensible, unjust; you love me not,
Yet boast your piety.
    Cho.   I said before,
Again I say, that not to love my king
Ev'n as myself would mark me for the worst
Of men; for thou didst save expiring Thebes.
O! rise once more, protect, preserve thy coun-
        try!
    Joc. O king! inform me, whence this strange
        dissension?
    Œdi. I'll tell thee, my Jocasta! (for thou
        know'st
The love I bear thee), what this wicked Creon
Did artfully devise against me.
    Joc.   Speak it,
If he indeed be guilty.
    Œdi.   Creon says
That I did murder Laius.
    Joc.   Spake he this
As knowing it himself, or from another?
    Œdi. He had suborn'd that evil-working
        priest,
And sharpens every tongue against his king.
    Joc. Let not a fear perplex thee, Œdipus!
Mortals know nothing of futurity,
And these prophetic seers are all impostors;

I'll prove it to thee. Know, then, Laius once,
Not from Apollo, but his priests, received
An oracle, which said it was decreed
He should be slain by his own son, the off-
    spring
Of Laius and Jocasta; yet he fell
By strangers, murder'd (for so fame reports)
By robbers in the place where three ways meet.
A son was born; but ere three days had pass'd,
The infant's feet were bored; a servant took,
And left him on the pathless mountain's top,
To perish there: thus Phœbus ne'er decreed
That he should kill his father, or that Laius
(Which much he fear'd) should by his son be
    slain.
Such is the truth of oracles: henceforth
Regard them not. What Heaven would have us
    know
It can with ease unfold, and will reveal it.
    Œdi. What thou hast said, Jocasta! much
      disturbs me:
I tremble at it.
    Joc.   Wherefore shouldst thou fear?
    Œdi. Methought I heard thee say, Laius was
      slain
Where three ways meet.
    Joc.   'Twas so reported then,
And is so still.
    Œdi.   Where happened the misfortune?
    Joc. In Phocis, where the roads unite that
      lead
To Delphi and to Daulia.
    Œdi.   How long since?
    Joc. A little time ere you began to reign
O'er Thebes, we heard it.
    Œdi.   O almighty Jove!
What wilt thou do with me?
    Joc.   Why talk'st thou thus?
    Œdi. Ask me no more; but tell me of this
      Laius,
What was his age and stature?
    Joc.   He was tall;
His hairs just turning to the silver hue;
His form not much unlike thy own.
    Œdi.   O me!
Sure I have call'd down curses on myself
Unknowing.
    Joc.   Ha! what say'st thou, Œdipus?
I tremble while I look on thee.
    Œdi.   O! much
I fear, the prophet saw too well: but say,

One thing will make it clear.
    Joc.   I dread to hear it;
Yet speak, and I will tell thee.
    Œdi.   Went he forth
With few attendants, or a numerous train,
In kingly pomp?
    Joc.   They were but five in all,
The herald with them; but one chariot there,
Which carried Laius.
    Œdi.   O! 'tis but too plain.
Who brought the news?
    Joc.   A servant, who alone
Escaped with life.
    Œdi.   That servant, is he here?
    Joc. O no: his master slain, when he return'd,
And saw thee on the throne of Thebes, with
      prayer
Most earnest he besought me to dismiss him
That he might leave this city, where he wish'd
No longer to be seen, but to retire,
And feed my flocks: I granted his request:
For that and more his honest services
Had merited.
    Œdi.   I beg he may be sent for
Immediately.
    Joc.   He shall; but wherefore is it?
    Œdi. I fear thou hast said too much, and
      therefore wish
To see him.
    Joc.   He shall come: but, O my lord!
Am I not worthy to be told the cause
Of this distress?
    Œdi.   Thou art, and I will tell thee.
Thou art my hope; to whom should I impart
My sorrows but to thee? Know then, Jocasta!
I am the son of Polybus, who reigns
At Corinth, and the Dorian Merope
His queen; there long I held the foremost rank,
Honour'd and happy, when a strange event
(For strange it was, though little meriting
The deep concern I felt) alarm'd me much.
A drunken reveller at a feast proclaim'd
That I was only the supposed son
Of Corinth's king. Scarce could I bear that day
The vile reproach; the next, I sought my
    parents,
And ask'd of them the truth; they too, enraged,
Resented much the base indignity.
I liked their tender warmth, but still I felt
A secret anguish; and, unknown to them,
Sought out the Pythian oracle, in vain.

Touching my parents, nothing could I learn;
But dreadful were the miseries it denounced
Against me: 'twas my fate, Apollo said,
To wed my mother, to produce a race
Accursed and abhorr'd, and last to slay
My father who begat me:—sad decree!
Lest I should e'er fulfil the dire prediction,
Instant I fled from Corinth, by the stars
Guiding my hapless journey, to the place
Where thou report'st this wretched king was
     slain.
But I will tell thee the whole truth: at length,
I came to where the three ways meet; when lo!
A herald, with another man, like him
Whom thou describest, and in a chariot, met
     me.
Both strove with violence to drive me back.
Enraged, I struck the charioteer, when straight,
As I advanced, the old man saw, and twice
Smote me on the head; but dearly soon repaid
The insult on me: from his chariot roll'd,
Prone on the earth, beneath my staff he fell,
And instantly expired; the attendant train
All shared his fate. If this unhappy stranger
And Laius be the same, lives there a wretch
So cursed, so hateful to the gods as I am?
Nor citizen nor alien must receive,
Or converse or communion hold with me,
But drive me forth with infamy and shame:
The dreadful curse pronounced with my own
     lips
Shall soon o'ertake me: I have stain'd the bed
Of him whom I had murder'd; am I then
Aught but pollution? If I fly from hence,
The bed of incest meets me, and I go
To slay my father Polybus, the best,
The tenderest parent; this must be the work
Of some malignant power. Ye righteous gods!
Let me not see that day, but rest in death,
Rather than suffer such calamity.

   Cho. O king! we pity thy distress: but wait
With patience his arrival, and despair not.
   Œdi. That shepherd is my only hope:
     Jocasta!
Would he were here!
   Joc.   Suppose he were; what then?
What wouldst thou do?
   Œdi.   I'll tell thee; if he says
The same as thou dost, I am safe, and guiltless.
   Joc. What said I then?
   Œdi.   Thou saidst, he did report

Laius was slain by robbers: if 'tis true
He fell by numbers, I am innocent,
For I was unattended; if but one
Attack'd and slew him, doubtless I am he.
   Joc. Be satisfied, it must be as he first
Reported it: he cannot change the tale.
Not I alone, but the whole city heard it:
Or grant he should, the oracle was ne'er
Fulfill'd; for Phœbus said, Jocasta's son
Should slay his father; that could never be,
For, O! Jocasta's son long since is dead.
He could not murder Laius; therefore, never
Will I attend to prophecies again.
   Œdi. Right, my Jocasta! but, I beg thee,
     send
And fetch this shepherd; do not fail.
   Joc.   I will,
This moment; come, my lord! let us go in;
I will do nothing but what pleases thee.
                         [*Exeunt.*

Chorus

STROPHE I

Grant me, henceforth, ye powers divine!
   In virtue's purest paths to tread;
   In every word, in every deed,
May sanctity of manners ever shine;
   Obedient to the laws of Jove,
   The laws descended from above;
Which, not like those by feeble mortals given,
   Buried in dark oblivion lie,
   Or, worn by time, decay and die:
But bloom eternal like their native heaven!

ANTISTROPHE I

Pride first gave birth to tyranny:
   That hateful vice, insulting Pride,
   When, every human power defied,
She lifts to glory's height her votary;
   Soon stumbling, from her tottering throne
   She throws the wretched victim down.
But may the god, indulgent, hear my prayer,
   That god whom humbly I adore
   O! may he smile on Thebes once more,
And take its wretched monarch to his care!

STROPHE II

Perish the impious and profane,
   Who, void of reverential fear,
   Nor justice nor the laws revere;

Who leave their god for pleasure or for gain;
   Who swell by fraud their ill-got store;
   Who rob the wretched and the poor.
If vice, unpunish'd, virtue's meed obtain,
   Who shall refrain the impetuous soul,
   The rebel passions who control,
Or wherefore do I lead this choral train?

ANTISTROPHE II

No more to Delphi's sacred shrine
   Need we with incense now repair;
   No more shall Phocis hear our prayer,
Nor fair Olympia see her rites divine;
   If oracles no longer prove
   The power of Phœbus and of Jove.
Great lord of all! from thy eternal throne
   Behold how impious men defame
   Thy loved Apollo's honour'd name:
O! guard his rights, and vindicate thy own.
                        [*Exeunt.*

ACT IV

Jocasta, Chorus

Joc. Sages and rulers of the land! I come
To seek the altars of the gods, and there
With incense and oblations to appease
Offended Heaven. My Œdipus, alas!
No longer wise and prudent, as you all
Remember once he was, with present things
Compares the past, nor judges like himself:
Unnumber'd cares perplex his anxious mind,
And every tale awakes new terrors in him.
Vain is my counsel, for he hears me not.
First then to thee, O Phœbus! (for thou still
Art near to help the wretched), we appeal,
And suppliant beg thee now to grant thy aid
Propitious: deep is our distress; for, O!
We see our pilot sinking at the helm,
And much already fear the vessel lost.

Enter Shepherd *from Corinth*

Shep. Can you instruct me, strangers! which
   way lies
The palace of king Œdipus? himself
I would most gladly see. Can you inform me?
   Cho. This is the palace; he is now within;
Thou seest his queen before thee.
   Shep.   Ever bless'd,
And happy with the happy mayst thou live!
   Joc. Stranger! the same good wish to thee,
   for well

Thy words deserve it: but say, wherefore
   comest thou,
And what's thy news?
   Shep.   To thee, and to thy husband.
Pleasure and joy!
   Joc. What pleasure? and whence art thou?
   Shep. From Corinth: to be brief, I bring thee
   tidings
Of good and evil.
   Joc.   Ha! what mean thy words
Ambiguous?
   Shep.   Know, then, if report say true,
The Isthmian people will choose Œdipus
Their sovereign.
   Joc.   Is not Polybus their king?
   Shep. No; Polybus is dead.
   Joc.   What say'st thou? dead?
   Shep. If I speak falsely, may death seize on
   me!
   Joc. [*to one of her Attendants.*] Why fliest
   thou not to tell thy master? Hence!
What are you now, you oracles divine?
Where is your truth? The fearful Œdipus
From Corinth fled, lest he should slay the king.
This Polybus, who perish'd, not by him,
But by the hand of Heaven.

Enter Œdipus

   Œdi.   My dear Jocasta!
Why hast thou call'd me hither?
   Joc.   Hear this man;
And when thou hear'st him, mark what faith is
   due
To your revered oracles.
   Œdi.   What is he,
And what doth he report?
   Joc.   He comes from Corinth,
And says, thy father, Polybus, is dead.
   Œdi. What say'st thou, stranger? Speak to
   me,
O! speak.
   Shep. If touching this thou first desirest my
   answer,
Know, he is dead.
   Œdi.   How died he? say, by treason,
Or some disease?
   Shep.   Alas! a little force
Will lay to rest the weary limbs of age.
   Œdi. Distemper then did kill him?
   Shep.   That in part,
And part a length of years that wore him down.

Œdi. Now, my Jocasta, who shall henceforth
    trust
To prophecies, and seers, and clamourous birds
With their vain omens? they who had decreed
That I should kill my father? He, thou seest,
Beneath the earth lies buried, while I live
In safety here, and guiltless of his blood:
Unless, perhaps, sorrow for the loss of me
Shorten'd his days, thus only could I kill
My father; but he's gone, and to the shades
Hath carried with him those vain oracles
Of fancied ill, no longer worth my care.

Joc. Did I not say it would be thus?

Œdi.   Thou didst;
But I was full of fears.

Joc.   Henceforth, no more
Indulge them.

Œdi.   But my mother's bed—that still
Must be avoided: I must fly from that.

Joc. Why should man fear, whom chance,
    and chance alone,
Doth ever rule? Foreknowledge all is vain,
And can determine nothing: therefore best
It is to live as fancy leads, at large,
Uncurb'd and only subject to our will.
Fear not thy mother's bed: oft-times in dreams
Have men committed incest; but his life
Will ever be most happy who contemns
Such idle phantoms.

Œdi.   Thou wert right, Jocasta!
Did not my mother live; but as it is,
Spite of thy words, I must be anxious still.

Joc. Think on thy father's death; it is a light
To guide thee here.

Œdi.   It is so; yet I fear,
While she survives him.

Shep.   Who is it you mean?
What woman fear you?

Œdi.   Merope, the wife
Of Polybus.

Shep.   And wherefore fear you her?

Œdi. Know, stranger, a most dreadful oracle
Concerning her affrights me.

Shep.   May I know it,
Or must it be reveal'd to none but thee?

Œdi. O, no, I'll tell thee: Phœbus hath de-
    clared
That Œdipus should stain his mother's bed,
And dip his hands in his own father's blood;
Wherefore I fled from Corinth, and lived here,

In happiness indeed; but still thou know'st
It is a blessing to behold our parents,
And that I had not.

Shep.   Was it for this cause
Thou wert an exile then?

Œdi.   It was; I fear'd
That I might one day prove my father's mur-
    derer.

Shep. What if I come, O king! to banish
    hence
Thy terrors, and restore thy peace?

Œdi.   O stranger!
Couldst thou do this, I would reward thee
    nobly.

Shep. Know, then, for this I came; I came to
    serve,
And make thee happy.

Œdi.   But I will not go
Back to my parents.

Shep.   Son, I see thou know'st not
What thou art doing.

Œdi.   Wherefore think'st thou so?
By Heaven, I beg thee then do thou instruct
    me.

Shep. If thou didst fly from Corinth for this
    cause—

Œdi. Apollo's dire predictions still affright
    me.

Shep. Fear'st thou pollution from thy par-
    ents?

Œdi. That,
And that alone, I dread.

Shep.   Thy fears are vain.

Œdi. Not if they are my parents.

Shep.   Polybus
Was not akin to thee.

Œdi.   What say'st thou? Speak;
Say, was not Polybus my father?

Shep.   No;
No more than he is mine.

Œdi.   Why call me then
His son?

Shep. Because long since I gave thee to him:
He did receive thee from these hands.

Œdi.   Indeed!
And could he love another's child so well?

Shep. He had no children; that persuaded
    him
To take and keep thee.

Œdi.   Didst thou buy me then,

Or am I thine, and must I call thee father?

Shep. I found thee in Cithæron's woody vale.

Œdi. What brought thee there?

Shep. I came to feed my flocks
On the green mountain's side.

Œdi. It seems thou wert
A wandering shepherd.

Shep. Thy deliverer,
I saved thee from destruction.

Œdi. How! what then
Had happen'd to me?

Shep. Thy own feet will best
Inform thee of that circumstance.

Œdi. Alas!
Why call'st thou to remembrance a misfortune
Of so long date?

Shep. 'Twas I who loosed the tendons
Of thy bored feet.

Œdi. It seems, in infancy,
I suffer'd much then.

Shep. To this incident
Thou owest thy name.

Œdi. My father or my mother,
Who did it? Know'st thou?

Shep. He who gave thee to me
Must tell thee that.

Œdi. Then from another's hand
Thou didst receive me?

Shep. Ay, another shepherd.

Œdi. Who was he? Canst thou recollect?

Shep. 'Twas one,
At least so called, of Laius' family.

Œdi. Laius, who ruled at Thebes?

Shep. The same: this man
Was shepherd to King Laius.

Œdi. Lives he still?
And could I see him?

Shep. [*pointing to the Chorus.*] Some of these, perhaps,
His countrymen, may give you information.

Œdi. [*to the Chorus.*] O! speak, my friends! if any of you know
This shepherd; whether still he lives at Thebes,
Or in some neighbouring country; tell me quick,
For it concerns us near.

Cho. It must be he
Whom thou didst lately send for; but the queen

Can best inform thee.

Œdi. Know'st thou, my Jocasta!
Whether the man whom thou didst order hither,
And whom the shepherd speaks of, be the same?

Joc. Whom meant he? for I know not. Œdipus!
Think not so deeply of this thing.

Œdi. Good Heaven
Forbid, Jocasta! I should now neglect
To clear my birth, when thus the path is mark'd
And open to me.

Joc. Do not, by the gods
I beg thee, do not, if thy life be dear,
Make farther search, for I have felt enough
Already from it.

Œdi. Rest thou satisfied:
Were I descended from a race of slaves,
'Twould not dishonour thee.

Joc. Yet hear me; do not,
Once more, I beg thee, do not search this matter.

Œdi. I will not be persuaded: I must search,
And find it too.

Joc. I know it best, and best
Advise thee.

Œdi. That advice perplexes more.

Joc. O! would to Heaven that thou mayst never know
Or who or whence thou art!

Œdi. [*to the Attendant.*] Let some one fetch
That shepherd quick, and leave this woman here
To glory in her high descent.

Joc. Alas!
Unhappy Œdipus! that word alone
I now can speak: remember, 'tis my last.

[*Exit* Jocasta.

Cho. Why fled the queen in such disorder hence?
Sorely distress'd she seemed, and much I fear
Her silence bodes some sad event.

Œdi. Whate'er
May come of that, I am resolved to know
The secret of my birth, how mean soever
It chance to prove: perhaps her sex's pride
May make her blush to find I was not born
Of noble parents; but I call myself

The son of Fortune, my indulgent mother,
Whom I shall never be ashamed to own.
The kindred months, that are, like me, her
    children;
The years, that roll obedient to her will,—
Have raised me from the lowest state to power
And splendour; wherefore, being what I am,
I need not fear the knowledge of my birth.

Chorus

STROPHE

If my prophetic soul doth well divine,
Ere on thy brow tomorrow's sun shall shine,
    Cithæron! thou the mystery shalt unfold:
The doubtful Œdipus, no longer blind,
Shall soon his country and his father find,
        And all the story of his birth be told:
            Then shall we in grateful lays,
            Celebrate our monarch's praise,
And in the sprightly dance our songs tri-
    umphant raise.

ANTISTROPHE

What heavenly power gave birth to thee, O
    king?
From Pan, the god of mountains, didst thou
    spring,
        With some fair daughter of Apollo join'd?
Art thou from him who o'er Cyllene reigns,
Swift Hermes, sporting in Arcadia's plains?
        Some nymph of Helicon did Bacchus find;—
            Bacchus, who delights to rove
            Through the forest, hill, and grove,
And art thou, prince, the offspring of their love?

Enter Œdipus, Shepherd *from Corinth*

Œdi. If I may judge of one whom yet I ne'er
Had converse with, yon old man whom I see
This way advancing, must be that same shep-
    herd
We lately sent for, by his age and mien,
Ev'n as this stranger did describe him to us.
My servants too are with him; but you best
Can say, for you must know him well.
    Cho.   'Tis he,
My lord! the faithful shepherd of King Laius.
    Œdi. [*to the Shepherd from Corinth.*] What
        say'st thou, stranger? is it he?
    Shep.   It is.

Enter Old Shepherd

Œdi. Now answer me, old man! look this
    way; speak;
Didst thou belong to Laius?
    O. Shep.   Sir, I did:
No hireling slave, but in his palace bred,
I serv'd him long.
    Œdi.   What was thy business there?
    O. Shep. For my life's better part I tended
        sheep.
    Œdi. And whither didst thou lead them?
    O. Shep.   To Cithæron,
And to the neighbouring plains.
    Œdi.   Behold this man;
        [*pointing to the Shepherd of Corinth*]
Dost thou remember to have seen him?
    O. Shep.   Whom?
What hath he done?
    Œdi.   Him who now stands before thee;
Call'st thou to mind or converse or connexion
Between you in time past?
    O. Shep.   I cannot say
I recollect it now.
    Shep.   I do not wonder
He should forget me; but I will recall
Some facts of ancient date: he must remember,
When on Cithæron we together fed
Our several flocks, in daily converse join'd,
From spring to autumn, and when winter bleak
Approach'd, retired: I to my little cot
Convey'd my sheep, he to the palace led
His fleecy care. Canst thou remember this?
    O. Shep. I do, but that is long since.
    Shep.   It is so;
But say, good shepherd, canst thou call to mind
An infant, whom thou didst deliver to me,
Requesting me to breed him as my own?
    O. Shep. Ha! wherefore ask'st thou this?
    Shep. [*pointing to* Œdipus] Behold him
        here,
That very child.
    O. Shep.   O! say it not; away!
Perdition on thee!
    Œdi.   Why reprove him thus?
Thou art thyself to blame, old man!
    O. Shep.   In what
Am I to blame, my lord?
    Œdi.   Thou wilt not speak
Touching this boy.

O. Shep.   Alas, poor man! he knows not
What he hath said.

Œdi.   If not by softer means
To be persuaded, force shall wring it from thee.

O. Shep. Treat not an old man harshly.

Œdi. [to the Attendants.]   Bind his hands.

O. Shep. Wherefore, my lord? What wouldst
thou have me do?

Œdi. That child he talks of, didst thou give
it to him?

O. Shep. I did, and would to Heaven I then
had died!

Œdi. Die soon thou shalt, unless thou tell'st
it all.

O. Shep. Say, rather, if I do.

Œdi.   This fellow means
To trifle with us, by his dull delay.

O. Shep. I do not; said I not, I gave the
child?

Œdi. Whence came the boy? Was he thy
own, or who
Did give him to thee?

O. Shep.   From another hand
I had received him.

Œdi.   Say, what hand? from whom?
Whence came he?

O. Shep.   Do not, by the gods! I beg thee,
Do not inquire.

Œdi.   Force me to ask again,
And thou shalt die.

O. Shep.   In Laius' palace born.

Œdi. Son of a slave, or of the king?

O. Shep.   Alas!
'Tis death for me to speak.

Œdi.   And me to hear;
Yet say it.

O. Shep. He was call'd the son of Laius;
But ask the queen, for she can best inform thee.

Œdi. Did she then give the child to thee?

O. Shep.   She did.

Œdi. For what?

O. Shep.   To kill him.

Œdi.   Kill her child! Inhuman
And barbarous mother!

O. Shep.   A dire oracle
Affrighted and constrained her to it.

Œdi.   Ha!
What oracle?

O. Shep.   Which said, her son should slay
His parents.

Œdi. Wherefore gavest thou then the infant
To this old shepherd?

O. Shep.   Pity moved me to it:
I hoped he would have soon convey'd his
charge
To some far distant country: he, alas!
Preserved him but for misery and woe;
For, O my lord! if thou indeed art he,
Thou art of all mankind the most unhappy.

Œdi. O me! at length the mystery's un-
ravell'd:
'Tis plain; 'tis clear; my fate is all determined.
Those are my parents who should not have
been
Allied to me: she is my wife, ev'n she,
Whom nature had forbidden me to wed;
I have slain him who gave me life, and now
Of thee, O light! I take my last farewell,
For Œdipus shall ne'er behold thee more.

[Exeunt.

Chorus

Strophe I

O, hapless state of human race!
How quick the fleeting shadows pass
Of transitory bliss below,
Where all is vanity and woe!
By thy example taught, O prince! we see
Man was not made for true felicity.

Antistrophe I

Thou, Œdipus! beyond the rest
Of mortals wert supremely bless'd;
Whom every hand conspired to raise,
Whom every hand rejoiced to praise;
When from the sphinx thy all-preserving
hand
Stretch'd forth its aid to save a sinking land.

Strophe II

Thy virtues raised thee to a throne,
And grateful Thebes was all thy own:
Alas! how changed that glorious name!
Lost are thy virtues and thy fame.
How couldst thou thus pollute thy father's
bed?
How couldst thou thus thy hapless mother
wed?

ANTISTROPHE II

How could that bed unconscious bear
So long the vile, incestuous pair?
But Time, of quick and piercing sight,
Hath brought the horrid deed to light:
At length Jocasta owns her guilty flame,
And finds a husband and a child the same.

EPODE

Wretched son of Laius! thee
Henceforth may I never see;
But absent shed the pious tear,
And weep thy fate with grief sincere!
For thou didst raise our eyes to life and light,
To close them now in everlasting night.

[*Exeunt.*

ACT V

Messenger, Chorus

Mes. Sages of Thebes, most honour'd and
revered!
If e'er the house of Labdacus was dear
And precious to you, what will be your grief,
When I shall tell the most disastrous tale
You ever heard, and to your eyes present
A spectacle more dreadful than they yet
Did e'er behold? Not the wide Danube's waves,
Nor Phasis' stream, can wash away the stains
Of this polluted palace. The dire crimes,
Long time conceal'd, at length are brought to
light;
But those which spring from voluntary guilt
Are still more dreadful.
Cho. Nothing can be worse
Than what we know already; bring'st thou
more
Misfortunes to us?
Mes. To be brief, the queen,
Jocasta's dead.
Cho. Say, by what hand?
Her own;
And, what's more dreadful, no one saw the
deed:
What I myself beheld, you all shall hear.
Inflamed with rage, soon as she reach'd the
palace,
Instant retiring to the nuptial bed,
She shut the door, then raved and tore her hair,
Called out on Laius dead, and bade him think

On that unhappy son who murder'd him,
And stain'd his bed: then, turning her sad eyes
Upon the guilty couch, she cursed the place
Where she had borne a husband from her hus-
band,
And children from her child: what follow'd
then
I know not, by the cries of Œdipus
Prevented, for on him our eyes were fix'd
Attentive: forth he came, beseeching us
To lend him some sharp weapon, and inform
him
Where he might find his mother and his wife;
His children's wretched mother and his own.
Some ill-designing power did then direct him
(For we were silent) to the queen's apartment:
Forcing the bolt, he rush'd unto the bed,
And found Jocasta, where we all beheld her,
Entangled in the fatal noose; which, soon
As he perceived, loosing the pendent rope,
Deeply he groan'd; and, casting on the ground
His wretched body, show'd a piteous sight
To the beholders. On a sudden thence
Starting, he pluck'd from off the robe she wore
A golden buckle, that adorn'd her side,
And buried in his eyes the sharpen'd point,
Crying, he ne'er again would look on her,
Never would see his crimes or miseries more,
Or those whom, guiltless, he could ne'er be-
hold,
Or those to whom he now must sue for aid.
His lifted eyelids then, repeating still
These dreadful plaints, he tore; while down
his cheeks
Fell showers of blood: such fate the wretched
pair
Sustain'd, partakers in calamity;
Fall'n from a state of happiness (for none
Were happier once than they) to groans and
death,
Reproach, and shame, and every human woe.
Cho. And where is now the poor unhappy
man?
Mes. "Open the doors," he cries, "and let all
Thebes
Behold his parents' murderer!" adding words
Not to be uttered: banish'd now he says
He must be, nor, devoted as he is
By his own curse, remain in this sad place.
He wants a kind conductor, and a friend
To help him now, for 'tis too much to bear.

But you will see him soon; for lo! the doors
Are open'd, and you will behold a sight
That would to pity move his deadliest foe.

Enter Œdipus

Cho. O horrid sight! more dreadful spectacle
Than e'er these eyes beheld! What madness
 urged thee
To this sad deed? What power malignant
 heap'd
On thy poor head such complicated woe?
Unhappy man! Alas! I would have held
Some converse with thee, but thy looks affright
 me:
I cannot bear to speak to thee.
Œdi.   O me!
Where am I, and whence comes the voice I
 hear?
Where art thou, fortune?
Cho.   Changed to misery,
Dreadful to hear, and dreadful to behold.
Œdi. O cruel darkness! endless, hopeless
 night!
Shame, terrors, and unutterable woe!
More painful is the memory of my crimes
Than all the wounds my wild distraction made.
Cho. Thus doubly cursed, O prince! I won-
 der not
At thy affliction.
Œdi.   Art thou here, my friend?
I know thy voice: thou wouldst not leave the
 wretched;
Thou art my faithful, kind assistant still.
Cho. How couldst thou thus deprive thy-
 self of sight?
What madness drove thee to the desperate
 deed?
What god inspired?
Œdi.   Apollo was the cause;
He was, my friends, the cause of all my woes;
But for these eyes myself did quench their
 light;
I want not them. What use were they to me,
But to discover scenes of endless woe?
Cho. 'Tis but too true.
Œdi.   What pleasure now remains
For Œdipus? He cannot joy in aught
To sight or ear delightful. Curse on him,
Whoe'er he was, that loosen'd my bound feet,
And saved me, in Cithæron's vale, from death!
I owe him nothing; had I perish'd then,

Much happier had it been for you, my friends,
And for myself.
Cho.   I too could wish thou hadst.
Œdi. I should not then have murdered
 Laius; then
I had not ta'en Jocasta to my bed:
But now I am a guilty wretch, the son
Of a polluted mother, father now
To my own brother: all that's horrible
To nature is the lot of Œdipus.
Cho. Yet must I blame this cruel act; for,
 sure,
The loss of sight is worse than death itself.
Œdi. I care not for thy counsel or thy praise;
For with what eyes could I have e'er beheld
My honour'd father in the shades below,
Or my unhappy mother, both destroy'd
By me? This punishment is worse than death;
And so it should be. Sweet had been the sight
Of my dear children; them I could have wish'd
To gaze on; but I must never see
Or them, or this fair city, or the palace
Where I was born: deprived of every bliss
By my own lips, which doom'd to banishment
The murderer of Laius, and expelled
The impious wretch, by gods and men ac-
 cursed;—
Could I behold them after this? O, no!
Would I could now with equal ease remove
My hearing too, be deaf as well as blind,
And from another entrance shut out woe!
To want our senses, in the hour of ill,
Is comfort to the wretched. O Cithæron!
Why didst thou e'er receive me, or, received,
Why not destroy, that men might never know
Who gave me birth? O Polybus! O Corinth!
And thou, long time believed my father's pal-
 ace!
O, what a foul disgrace to human nature
Didst thou receive beneath a prince's form!
Impious myself, and from an impious race.
Where is my splendour now? O Daulian path!
The shady forest, and the narrow pass
Where three ways meet, who drank a father's
 blood,
Shed by these hands; do you not still remember
The horrid deed, and what, when here I came,
Follow'd more dreadful? Fatal nuptials! you
Produced me, you returned me to the womb
That bare me: thence relations horrible
Of fathers, sons, and brothers came: of wives,

Sisters, and mothers, sad alliance! all
That man holds impious and detestable.
But what in act is vile, the modest tongue
Should never name. Bury me, hide me, friends,
From every eye! destroy me, cast me forth
To the wide ocean! let me perish there;
Do any thing to shake off hated life.
Seize me! approach, my friends! you need not
    fear,
Polluted though I am, to touch me. None
Shall suffer for my crimes but I alone.
    Cho. In most fit time, my lord, the noble
    Creon
This way advances: he can best determine,
And best advise; sole guardian now of Thebes,
To him thy power devolves.
    Œdi.   What shall I say?
Can I apply to him for aid, whom late
I deeply injured by unjust suspicion?
                    [*Exit Messenger.*

Enter Creon

    Cre. I come not, prince, to triumph o'er thy
    woes
With vile reproach; I pity thy misfortunes:
But, O my Thebans! if you do not fear
The censure of your fellow-citizens,
At least respect the all-creating eye
Of Phœbus, who beholds you thus exposing
To public view a wretch accursed, polluted,
Whom neither earth can bear, nor sun behold,
Nor holy shower besprinkle. Take him hence,
Within the palace: those who are by blood
United should alone be witnesses
Of such calamity.
    Œdi.   O Creon! thou
The best of men, and I the worst! How kind
Thou art to visit me! O! by the gods
Let me entreat thee, since, beyond my hopes,
Thou art so good, now hear me: what I ask
Concerns thee most.
    Cre.   What is it thou desirest
Thus ardently?
    Œdi.   I beg thee banish me
From Thebes this moment, to some land re-
mote,
Where I may ne'er converse with man again.
    Cre. My self had long since done it, but the
    gods
Must be consulted first.
    Œdi.   Their will is known

Already, and their oracle declared
The guilty parricide should die.
    Cre.   It hath;
But, as it is, 'twere better to inquire
What must be done.
    Œdi.   For such a wretch as I,
Wouldst thou again explore the will of Heaven?
    Cre. Thy hapless fate should teach us to
    believe
And reverence the gods.
    Œdi.   Now, Creon, list:
I beg thee, I conjure thee, let a tomb
Be raised, and all due honours paid to her
Who lies within. She was thy sister, Creon.
It is a duty which thou owest: for me,
I cannot hope this city now will deign
To keep me here. O Creon! let me go,
And seek the solitary mountain's top,
My own Cithæron, by my parents doom'd
Long since to be the grave of Œdipus:
There would I die, as they decreed I should.
Alas! I cannot, must not perish yet,
Till I have suffer'd evils worse than death,
For I was only saved to be unhappy;
But I must meet my fate, whate'er it be.
My sons are men, and wheresoever fortune
May place them, cannot want the means of life.
They shall not burden thee; but O, my friend!
What will become of my unhappy daughters,
With tenderest love, beneath a father's hand
Cherish'd so long? O! take them to thy care,
Thou best of men! O! might I but embrace
    them,
But shed a tear o'er their disastrous fate;
Might I be suffer'd but to touch them here;
I should rejoice, and think I saw them still.
But hark! methinks e'en now I hear the voice
Of my dear daughters. Hath the gracious
    Creon,
In pity to my woes, already brought
My children to me? Is it so?
    Cre.   It is:
Thy wishes are prevented; they are here.

Enter Daughters of Œdipus

    Œdi. May Heaven reward thee for this good-
ness to me,
And give thee much more bliss than I have
    known!
Now, my dear children! come towards me,
    come

Towards your father and your—brother: see
These sightless eyes, pierced by my own mad
 hands;
Behold that wretched father who begat you
Unknowingly on her who gave me birth.
I cannot see you now; I can but weep
Your fate, to think what hours of wretchedness
You have to know hereafter. Whither now
Must my poor children fly? From every feast,
Joyless, with grief and shame, shall you return;
And when the time shall come when riper
 years
Should give you to the nuptial bed, who then,
Careless of fame, will let his child partake
The infamy of my abhorred race,
Sprung from a wretch accursed, who kill'd his
 father,
And from the womb that bare him did beget
You, my unhappy daughters? Such reproach
Must still be yours, to virgin solitude
Devoted ever and a barren bed.
Son of Menœceus! thou alone art left
Their father now; for O! Jocasta's dead,
And I am—nothing: do not then forsake
Thy kindred; nor, deserted and forlorn,
Suffer them still, in penury and woe,
To wander helpless, in their tender age.
Remember, they have no support but thee.
O generous prince! have pity on them; give me
Thy friendly hand in promise of thy aid.
To you, my daughters! had your early years
Permitted, I had given my last advice:
Too young for counsel, all I ask of you
Is but to pray the gods that my sad life
May not be long; but yours, my children!
 crown'd

With many days, and happier far than mine.
 Cre. It is enough: go in; thy grief transports
  thee
Beyond all bounds.
 Œdi.   'Tis hard, but I submit.
 Cre. The time demands it; therefore go.
 Œdi.   O Creon!
Know'st thou what now I wish?
 Cre.   What is it? Speak.
 Œdi. That I may quit this fatal place.
 Cre.   Thou ask'st
What Heaven alone can grant.
 Œdi.   Alas! to Heaven
I am most hateful.
 Cre.   Yet shalt thou obtain
What thou desirest.
 Œdi.   Shall I indeed?
 Cre.   Thou shalt;
I never say aught that I do not mean.
 Œdi. Then let me go: may I depart?
 Cre.   Thou mayst;
But leave thy children.
 Œdi.   Do not take them from me.
 Cre. Thou must not always have thy will,
 already
Thou hast suffer'd for it.
 Cho.   Thebans! now behold
The great, the mighty Œdipus, who once
The sphinx's dark enigma could unfold;
Who less to fortune than to wisdom owed;
In virtue, as in rank, to all superior;
Yet fallen at last to deepest misery.
Let mortals hence be taught to look beyond
The present time, nor dare to say a man
Is happy, till the last decisive hour
Shall close his life without the taste of woe.

*P*lato

In the Phaedo Plato takes advantage of the incidents surrounding the death of Socrates to discuss the idea of immortality. In this dialogue he discusses his famous doctrine
of ideas. In reading the selections from the Phaedo
note (1) the moral issue involved in suicide, (2) the goal
of the true philosopher, (3) obstacles to the achievement
of this goal, (4) the discussion of immortality, (5) the
proof of immortality and the doctrine of ideas, and (6) the
similarity of Socrates' death to a Greek tragedy.

As translated by Benjamin Jowett in *The Dialogues of Plato,* 2nd ed., 5 vols., Clarendon Press, Oxford, 1875, I, 429–447; 460–461. Courtesy of the Jowett Copyright Fund.

From: THE PHAEDO

Persons of the Dialogue:

> Phaedo, who is the narrator of the Dialogue to
> Echecrates of Phlius.
> Socrates.
> Attendant of the Prison.
> Apollodorus.
> Simmias.
> Cebes.
> Crito.

Scene: The prison of Socrates.

Place of the Narration:—Phlius.

Echecrates. Were you yourself, Phaedo, in the prison with Socrates on the day when he drank the poison?

Phaedo. Yes, Echecrates, I was.

Ech. I should so like to hear about his death. What did he say in his last hours? We were informed that he died by taking poison, but no one knew anything more; for no Phliusian ever goes to Athens now, and it is a long time since any stranger from Athens has found his way hither; so that we had no clear account.

Phaed. Did you not hear of the proceedings at the trial?

Ech. Yes; some one told us about the trial, and we could not understand why, having been condemned, he should have been put to death, not at the time, but long afterwards. What was the reason of this?

Phaed. An accident, Echecrates: the stern of the ship which the Athenians sent to Delos happened to have been crowned on the day before he was tried.

Ech. What is this ship?

Phaed. It is the ship in which, according to Athenian tradition, Theseus went to Crete when he took with him the fourteen youths, and was the saviour of them and of himself. And they are said to have vowed to Apollo at the time, that if they were saved they would send a yearly mission to Delos. Now this custom still continues, and the whole period of the voyage to and from Delos, beginning when the priest of Apollo crowns the stern of the ship, is a holy season, during which the city is not allowed to be polluted by public executions; and when the vessel is detained by contrary winds, the time spent in going and returning is very considerable. As I was saying, the ship was crowned on the day before the trial, and this was the reason why Socrates lay in prison and was not put to death until long after he was condemned.

Ech. What was the manner of his death, Phaedo? What was said or done? And which of his friends were with him? Or did the authorities forbid them to be present—so that he had no friends near him when he died?

Phaed. No; there were several of them with him.

Ech. If you have nothing to do, I wish that you would tell me what passed, as exactly as you can.

Phaed. I have nothing at all to do, and will try to gratify your wish. To be reminded of Socrates is always the greatest delight to me, whether I speak myself or hear another speak of him.

Ech. You will have listeners who are of the same mind with you, and I hope that you will be as exact as you can.

Phaed. I had a singular feeling at being in his company. For I could hardly believe that I was present at the death of a friend, and therefore I did not pity him, Echecrates; he died so fearlessly, and his words and bearing were so noble and gracious, that to me he appeared blessed. I thought that in going to the other world he could not be without a divine call, and that he would be happy, if any man ever was, when he arrived there; and therefore I did not pity him as might have seemed natural at such an hour. But I had not the pleasure which I usually feel in philosophical discourse (for philosophy was the theme of which we spoke). I was pleased, but in the pleasure there was also a strange admixture of pain; for I reflected that he was soon to die, and this double feeling was shared by us all; we were laughing and weeping by turns, especially the excitable Apollodorus—you know the sort of man?

Ech. Yes.

Phaed. He was quite beside himself; and I and all of us were greatly moved.

Ech. Who were present?

Phaed. Of native Athenians there were, besides Apollodorus, Critobulus and his father Crito, Hermogenes, Epigenes, Aeschines, Antisthenes; likewise Ctesippus of the deme of Paeania, Menexenus, and some others; Plato, if I am not mistaken, was ill.

Ech. Were there any strangers?

Phaed. Yes, there were; Simmias the Theban, and Cebes, and Phaedondes; Euclid and Terpsion, who came from Megara.

Ech. And was Aristippus there, and Cleombrotus?

Phaed. No, they were said to be in Aegina.

Ech. Any one else?

Phaed. I think that these were nearly all.

Ech. Well, and what did you talk about?

Phaed. I will begin at the beginning and endeavour to repeat the entire conversation. On the previous days we had been in the habit of assembling early in the morning at the court in which the trial took place, and which is not far from the prison. There we used to wait talking with one another until the opening of the doors (for they were not opened very early); then we went in and generally passed the day with Socrates. On the last morning we assembled sooner than usual, having heard on the day before when we quitted the prison in the evening that the sacred ship had come from Delos; and so we arranged to meet very early at the accustomed place. On our arrival the jailer who answered the door, instead of admitting us, came out and told us to stay until he called us. "For the Eleven," he said, "are now with Socrates; they are taking off his chains, and giving orders that he is to die today." He soon returned and said that we might come in. On entering we found Socrates just released from chains, and Xanthippe, whom you know, sitting by him, and holding his child in her arms. When she saw us she uttered a cry and said, as women will: "O Socrates, this is the last time that either you will converse with your friends, or they with you." Socrates turned to Crito and said: "Crito, let some one take her home." Some of Crito's people accordingly led her away, crying out and beating herself. And when she was gone,

Socrates, sitting up on the couch, bent and rubbed his leg, saying, as he was rubbing: How singular is the thing called pleasure, and how curiously related to pain, which might be thought to be the opposite of it; for they are never present to a man at the same instant, and yet he who pursues either is generally compelled to take the other; their bodies are two, but they are joined by a single head. And I cannot help thinking that if Aesop had remembered them, he would have made a fable about God trying to reconcile their strife, and how, when he could not, he fastened their heads together; and this is the reason why when one comes the other follows: as I know by my own experience now, when after the pain in my leg which was caused by the chain, pleasure appears to succeed.

Upon this Cebes said: I am glad, Socrates, that you have mentioned the name of Aesop. For it reminds me of a question which has been asked by many, and was asked of me only the day before yesterday by Evenus the poet—he will be sure to ask it again, and therefore if you would like me to have an answer ready for him, you may as well tell me what I should say to him:—he wanted to know why you, who never before wrote a line of poetry, now that you are in prison are turning Aesop's fables into verse, and also composing that hymn in honour of Apollo.

Tell him, Cebes, he replied, what is the truth—that I had no idea of rivalling him or his poems; to do so, as I knew, would be no easy task. But I wanted to see whether I could purge away a scruple which I felt about the meaning of certain dreams. In the course of my life I have often had intimations in dreams "that I should compose music." The same dream came to me sometimes in one form, and sometimes in another, but always saying the same or nearly the same words: "Cultivate and make music," said the dream. And hitherto I had imagined that this was only intended to exhort and encourage me in the study of philosophy, which has been the pursuit of my life, and is the noblest and best of music. The dream was bidding me do what I was already doing, in the same way that the competitor in a race is bidden by the spectators to run when he is already running. But I was not certain of this;

for the dream might have meant music in the popular sense of the word, and being under sentence of death, and the festival giving me a respite, I thought that it would be safer for me to satisfy the scruple, and, in obedience to the dream, to compose a few verses before I departed. And first I made a hymn in honour of the god of the festival, and then considering that a poet, if he is really to be a poet, should not only put together words, but should invent stories, and that I have no invention, I took some fables of Aesop, which I had ready at hand and which I knew—they were the first I came upon—and turned them into verse. Tell this to Evenus, Cebes, and bid him be of good cheer; say that I would have him come after me if he be a wise man, and not tarry; and that today I am likely to be going, for the Athenians say that I must.

Simmias said: What a message for such a man! Having been a frequent companion of his I should say that, as far as I know him, he will never take your advice unless he is obliged.

Why, said Socrates,—is not Evenus a philosopher?

I think that he is, said Simmias.

Then he, or any man who has the spirit of philosophy, will be willing to die; but he will not take his own life, for that is held to be unlawful.

Here he changed his position, and put his legs off the couch on to the ground, and during the rest of the conversation he remained sitting.

Why do you say, enquired Cebes, that a man ought not to take his own life, but that the philosopher will be ready to follow the dying?

Socrates replied: And have you, Cebes and Simmias, who are the disciples of Philolaus, never heard him speak of this?

Yes, but his language was obscure, Socrates.

My words, too, are only an echo; but there is no reason why I should not repeat what I have heard: and, indeed, as I am going to another place, it is very meet for me to be thinking and talking of the nature of the pilgrimage which I am about to make. What can I do better in the interval between this and the setting of the sun?

Then tell me, Socrates, why is suicide held to be unlawful? as I have certainly heard Philolaus, about whom you were just now asking, affirm when he was staying with us at Thebes; and there are others who say the same, although I have never understood what was meant by any of them.

Do not lose heart, replied Socrates, and the day may come when you will understand. I suppose that you wonder why, when other things which are evil may be good at certain times and to certain persons, death is to be the only exception, and why, when a man is better dead, he is not permitted to be his own benefactor, but must wait for the hand of another.

Very true, said Cebes, laughing gently and speaking in his native Boeotian.

I admit the appearance of inconsistency in what I am saying; but there may not be any real inconsistency after all. There is a doctrine whispered in secret that man is a prisoner who has no right to open the door and run away; this is a great mystery which I do not quite understand. Yet I too believe that the gods are our guardians, and that we men are a possession of theirs. Do you not agree?

Yes, I quite agree, said Cebes.

And if one of your own possessions, an ox or an ass, for example, took the liberty of putting himself out of the way when you had given no intimation of your wish that he should die, would you not be angry with him, and would you not punish him if you could?

Certainly, replied Cebes.

Then, if we look at the matter thus, there may be reason in saying that a man should wait, and not take his own life until God summons him, as he is now summoning me.

Yes, Socrates, said Cebes, there seems to be truth in what you say. And yet how can you reconcile this seemingly true belief that God is our guardian and we his possessions, with the willingness to die which you were just now attributing to the philosopher? That the wisest of men should be willing to leave a service in which they are ruled by the gods, who are the best of rulers, is not reasonable; for surely no wise man thinks that when set at liberty he can take better care of himself than the gods take of him. A fool may perhaps think so—he may argue that he had better run away from his master, not considering that his duty is to remain to the end, and not to run away from the good, and that there would be no sense in his running away. The wise man will want to be ever with him who is better than himself. Now this, Socrates, is the reverse of what was just now said; for upon this view the wise man should sorrow and the fool rejoice at passing out of life.

The earnestness of Cebes seemed to please Socrates. Here, said he, turning to us, is a man who is always enquiring, and is not so easily convinced by the first thing which he hears.

And certainly, added Simmias, the objection which he is now making does appear to me to have some force. For what can be the meaning of a truly wise man wanting to fly away and lightly leave a master who is better than himself? And I rather imagine that Cebes is referring to you; he thinks that you are too ready to leave us, and too ready to leave the gods whom you acknowledge to be our good masters.

Yes, replied Socrates; there is reason in what you say. And so you think that I ought to answer your indictment as if I were in a court?

We should like you to do so, said Simmias.

Then I must try to make a more successful defence before you than I did before the judges. For I am quite ready to admit, Simmias and Cebes, that I ought to be grieved at death, if I were not persuaded in the first place that I am going to other gods who are wise and good (of which I am as certain as I can be of any such matters), and secondly (though I am not so sure of this last) to men departed, better than those whom I leave behind; and therefore I do not grieve as I might have done, for I have good hope that there is yet something remaining for the dead, and as has been said of old, some far better thing for the good than for the evil.

But do you mean to take away your thoughts with you, Socrates? said Simmias. Will you not impart them to us?—for they are a benefit in which we too are entitled to share. Moreover, if you succeed in convincing us, that will be an answer to the charge against yourself.

I will do my best, replied Socrates. But you must first let me hear what Crito wants; he has long been wishing to say something to me.

Only this, Socrates, replied Crito:—the attendant who is to give you the poison has been telling me, and he wants me to tell you, that you are not to talk much; talking, he says, increases heat, and this is apt to interfere with the action of the poison; persons who excite themselves are sometimes obliged to take a second or even a third dose.

Then, said Socrates, let him mind his business and be prepared to give the poison twice or even thrice if necessary; that is all.

I knew quite well what you would say, replied Crito; but I was obliged to satisfy him.

Never mind him, he said.

And now, O my judges, I desire to prove to you that the real philosopher has reason to be of good cheer when he is about to die, and that after death he may hope to obtain the greatest good in the other world. And how this may be, Simmias and Cebes, I will endeavour to explain. For I deem that the true votary of philosophy is likely to be misunderstood by other men; they do not perceive that he is always pursuing death and dying; and if this be so, and he has had the desire of death all his life long, why when his time comes should he repine at that which he had been always pursuing and desiring?

Simmias said laughingly: Though not in a laughing humour, you have made me laugh, Socrates; for I cannot help thinking that the many when they hear your words will say how truly you have described philosophers, and our people at home will likewise say that the life which philosophers desire is in reality death, and that they have found them out to be deserving of the death which they desire.

And they are right, Simmias, in thinking so, with the exception of the words "they have found them out"; for they have not found out either what is the nature of that death which the true philosopher deserves, or how he deserves or desires death. But enough of them: —let us discuss the matter among ourselves. Do we believe that there is such a thing as death?

To be sure, replied Simmias.

Is it not the separation of soul and body? And to be dead is the completion of this; when the soul exists in herself, and is released from the body and the body is released from the soul, what is this but death?

Just so, he replied.

There is another question, which will probably throw light on our present enquiry if you and I can agree about it:—Ought the philosopher to care about the pleasures—if they are to be called pleasures—of eating and drinking?

Certainly not, answered Simmias.

And what about the pleasures of love—should he care for them?

By no means.

And will he think much of the other ways of indulging the body, for example, the acquisition of costly raiment, or sandals, or other adornments of the body? Instead of caring about them, does he not rather despise anything more than nature needs? What do you say?

I should say that the true philosopher would despise them.

Would you not say that he is entirely concerned with the soul and not with the body? He would like, as far as he can, to get away from the body and to turn to the soul.

Quite true.

In matters of this sort philosophers, above all other men, may be observed in every sort of way to dissever the soul from the communion of the body.

Very true.

Whereas, Simmias, the rest of the world are of opinion that to him who has no sense of pleasure and no part in bodily pleasure, life is not worth having; and that he who is indifferent about them is as good as dead.

That is also true.

What again shall we say of the actual acquirement of knowledge?—is the body, if invited to share in the enquiry, a hinderer or a helper? I mean to say, have sight and hearing any truth in them? Are they not, as the poets are always telling us, inaccurate witnesses? and yet, if even they are inaccurate and indistinct, what is to be said of the other senses?—for you will allow that they are the best of them?

Certainly, he replied.

Then when does the soul attain truth?—for in attempting to consider anything in company with the body she is obviously deceived.

True.

Then must not true existence be revealed to her in thought, if at all?

Yes.

And thought is best when the mind is gathered into herself and none of these things trouble her—neither sounds nor sights nor pain nor any pleasure,—when she takes leave of the body, and has as little as possible to do with it, when she has no bodily sense or desire, but is aspiring after true being?

Certainly.

And in this the philosopher dishonours the body; his soul runs away from his body and desires to be alone and by herself?

That is true.

Well, but there is another thing, Simmias: Is there or is there not an absolute justice?

Assuredly there is.

And an absolute beauty and absolute good?

Of course.

But did you ever behold any of them with your eyes?

Certainly not.

Or did you ever reach them with any other bodily sense?—and I speak not of these alone, but of absolute greatness, and health, and strength, and of the essence or true nature of everything. Has the reality of them ever been perceived by you through the bodily organs? or rather, is not the nearest approach to the knowledge of their several natures made by him who so orders his intellectual vision as to have the most exact conception of the essence of each thing which he considers?

Certainly.

And he attains to the purest knowledge of them who goes to each with the mind alone, not introducing or intruding in the act of thought sight or any other sense together with reason, but with the very light of the mind in her own clearness searches into the very truth of each; he who has got rid, as far as he can, of eyes and ears and, so to speak, of the whole body, these being in his opinion distracting elements which when they infect the soul hinder her from acquiring truth and knowledge—who, if not he, is likely to attain to the knowledge of true being?

What you say has a wonderful truth in it, Socrates, replied Simmias.

And when real philosophers consider all these things, will they not be led to make a reflection which they will express in words something like the following? "Have we not found," they will say, "a path of thought which seems to bring us and our argument to the conclusion, that while we are in the body, and while the soul is infected with the evils of the body, our desire will not be satisfied, and our desire is of the truth? For the body is a source of endless trouble to us by reason of the mere requirement of food; and is liable also to diseases which overtake and impede us in the search after true being: it fills us full of loves, and lusts, and fears, and fancies of all kinds, and endless foolery, and, in fact, as men say, takes away from us the power of thinking at all. Whence come wars, and fightings, and factions? whence but from the body and the lusts of the body? Wars are occasioned by the love of money, and money has to be acquired for the sake and service of the body; and by reason of all these impediments we have no time to give to philosophy; and, last and worst of all, even if we are at leisure and betake ourselves to some speculation, the body is always breaking in upon us, causing turmoil and confusion in our enquiries, and so amazing us that we are prevented from seeing the truth. It has been proved to us by experience that if we would have pure knowledge of anything we must be quit of the body—the soul in herself must behold things in themselves: and then we shall attain the wisdom which we desire, and of which we say that we are lovers; not while we live, but after death; for if while in company with the body, the soul cannot have pure knowledge, one of two things follows—either knowledge is not to be attained at all, or, if at all, after death. For then, and not till then, the soul will be parted from the body and exist in herself alone. In this present life, I reckon that we make the nearest approach to knowledge when we have the least possible intercourse or communion with the body, and are not surfeited with the bodily nature, but keep ourselves pure until the hour when God himself is pleased to release us. And thus having got rid of the foolishness of the body we shall be pure and hold converse with the pure, and know of ourselves the clear light everywhere, which is no other than the light of truth." For the impure are not permitted to approach the pure. These are the sort of words, Simmias,

which the true lovers of knowledge cannot help saying to one another, and thinking. You would agree; would you not?

Undoubtedly, Socrates.

But, O my friend, if this be true, there is great reason to hope that, going whither I go, when I have come to the end of my journey, I shall attain that which has been the pursuit of my life. And therefore I go on my way rejoicing, and not I only, but every other man who believes that his mind has been made ready and that he is in a manner purified.

Certainly, replied Simmias.

And what is purification but the separation of the soul from the body, as I was saying before; the habit of the soul gathering and collecting herself into herself from all sides out of the body; the dwelling in her own place alone, as in another life, so also in this, as far as she can;—the release of the soul from the chains of the body?

Very true, he said.

And this separation and release of the soul from the body is termed death?

To be sure, he said.

And the true philosophers, and they only, are ever seeking to release the soul. Is not the separation and release of the soul from the body their especial study?

That is true.

And, as I was saying at first, there would be a ridiculous contradiction in men studying to live as nearly as they can in a state of death, and yet repining when it comes upon them.

Clearly.

And the true philosophers, Simmias, are always occupied in the practice of dying, wherefore also to them least of all men is death terrible. Look at the matter thus:—if they have been in every way the enemies of the body, and are wanting to be alone with the soul, when this desire of theirs is granted, how inconsistent would they be if they trembled and repined, instead of rejoicing at their departure to that place where, when they arrive, they hope to gain that which in life they desired—and this was wisdom—and at the same time to be rid of the company of their enemy. Many a man has been willing to go to the world below animated by the hope of seeing there an earthly love, or wife, or son, and conversing with them. And will he who is a true lover of wisdom, and is strongly persuaded in like manner that only in the world below he can worthily enjoy her, still repine at death? Will he not depart with joy? Surely he will, O my friend, if he be a true philosopher. For he will have a firm conviction that there, and there only, he can find wisdom in her purity. And if this be true, he would be very absurd, as I was saying, if he were afraid of death.

He would indeed, replied Simmias.

And when you see a man who is repining at the approach of death, is not his reluctance a sufficient proof that he is not a lover of wisdom, but a lover of the body, and probably at the same time a lover of either money or power, or both?

Quite so, he replied.

And is not courage, Simmias, a quality which is especially characteristic of the philosopher?

Certainly.

There is temperance again, which even by the vulgar is supposed to consist in the control and regulation of the passions, and in the sense of superiority to them—is not temperance a virtue belonging to those only who despise the body, and who pass their lives in philosophy?

Most assuredly.

For the courage and temperance of other men, if you will consider them, are really a contradiction.

How so?

Well, he said, you are aware that death is regarded by men in general as a great evil.

Very true, he said.

And do not courageous men face death because they are afraid of yet greater evils?

That is quite true.

Then all but the philosophers are courageous only from fear, and because they are afraid; and yet that a man should be courageous from fear, and because he is a coward, is surely a strange thing.

Very true.

And are not the temperate exactly in the same case? They are temperate because they are intemperate—which might seem to be a contradiction, but is nevertheless the sort of thing which happens with this foolish temperance. For there are pleasures which they are afraid of losing; and in their desire to keep them, they abstain from some pleasures, because they are overcome by others; and although to be conquered by pleasure is called by men intemperance, to them the conquest of pleasure consists in being conquered by pleasure. And that is what I mean by saying that, in a sense, they are made temperate through intemperance.

Such appears to be the case.

Yet the exchange of one fear or pleasure or pain for another fear or pleasure or pain, and of the greater for the less, as if they were coins, is not the exchange of virtue. O my blessed Simmias, is there not one true coin for which all things ought to be exchanged?—and that is wisdom; and only in exchange for this, and in company with this, is anything truly bought or sold, whether courage or temperance or justice. And is not all true virtue the companion of wisdom, no matter what fears or pleasures or other similar goods or evils may or may not attend her? But the virtue which is made up of these goods, when they are severed from wisdom and exchanged with one another, is a shadow of virtue only, nor is there any freedom or health or truth in her; but in the true exchange there is a purging away of all these things, and temperance, and justice, and courage, and wisdom herself are the purgation of them. The founders of the mysteries would appear to have had a real meaning, and were not talking nonsense when they intimated in a figure long ago that he who passes unsanctified and uninitiated into the world below will lie in a slough, but that he who arrives there after initiation and purification will dwell with the gods. For "many," as they say in the mysteries, "are the thyrsus-bearers, but few are the mystics,"— meaning, as I interpret the words, "the true philosophers." In the number of whom, during my whole life, I have been seeking, according to my ability, to find a place;—whether I have sought in a right way or not, and whether I have succeeded or not, I shall truly know in a little while, if God will, when I myself arrive in the other world—such is my belief. And therefore I maintain that I am right, Simmias and Cebes, in not grieving or repining at parting from you and my masters in this world, for I believe that I shall equally find good masters and friends in another world. But most men do not believe this saying; if then I succeed in convincing you by my defence better than I did the Athenian judges, it will be well.

Cebes answered: I agree, Socrates, in the greater part of what you say. But in what concerns the soul, men are apt to be incredulous; they fear that when she has left the body her place may be nowhere, and that on the very day of death she may perish and come to an end—immediately on her release from the body, issuing forth dispersed like smoke or air and in her flight vanishing away into nothingness. If she could only be collected into herself after she has obtained release from the evils of which you were speaking, there would be good reason to hope, Socrates, that what you say is true. But surely it requires a great deal of argument and many proofs to show that when the man is dead his soul yet exists, and has any force or intelligence.

True, Cebes, said Socrates; and shall I suggest that we converse a little of the probabilities of these things?

I am sure, said Cebes, that I should greatly like to know your opinion about them.

I reckon, said Socrates, that no one who heard me now, not even if he were one of my old enemies, the comic poets, could accuse me of idle talking about matters in which I have no concern:—If you please, then, we will proceed with the enquiry.

Suppose we consider the question whether the souls of men after death are or are not in the world below. There comes into my mind an ancient doctrine which affirms that they go from hence into the other world, and returning hither, are born again from the dead. Now, if it be true that the living come from the dead, then our souls must exist in the other world, for if not, how could they have been born again? And this would be conclusive, if there were any real evidence that the living are only born from the dead; but if this is not so, then other arguments will have to be adduced.

Very true, replied Cebes.

Then let us consider the whole question, not in relation to man only, but in relation to animals generally, and to plants, and to everything of which there is generation, and the proof will be easier. Are not all things which have opposites generated out of their opposites? I mean such things as good and evil, just and unjust—and there are innumerable other opposites which are generated out of opposites. And I want to show that in all opposites there is of necessity a similar alternation; I mean to say, for example, that anything which becomes greater must become greater after being less.

True.

And that which becomes less must have been once greater and then have become less.

Yes.

And the weaker is generated from the stronger, and the swifter from the slower.

Very true.

And the worse is from the better, and the more just is from the more unjust.

Of course.

And is this true of all opposites? and are we convinced that all of them are generated out of opposites?

Yes.

And in this universal opposition of all things, are there not also two intermediate processes which are ever going on, from one to the other opposite, and back again; where there is a greater and a less there is also an intermediate process of increase and diminution, and that which grows is said to wax, and that which decays to wane?

Yes, he said.

And there are many other processes, such as division and composition, cooling and heating, which equally involve a passage into and out of one another. And this necessarily holds of all opposites, even though not always expressed in words—they are really generated out of one another, and there is a passing or process from one to the other of them?

Very true, he replied.

Well, and is there not an opposite of life, as sleep is the opposite of waking?

True, he said.

And what is it?

Death, he answered.

And these, if they are opposites, are generated the one from the other, and have their two intermediate processes also?

Of course.

Now, said Socrates, I will analyze one of the two pairs of opposites which I have mentioned to you, and also its intermediate processes, and you shall analyze the other to me. One of them I term sleep, the other waking. The state of sleep is opposed to the state of waking, and out of sleeping waking is generated, and out of waking, sleeping; and the process of generation is in the one case falling asleep, and in the other waking up. Do you agree?

I entirely agree.

Then suppose that you analyze life and death to me in the same manner. Is not death opposed to life?

Yes.

And they are generated one from the other?

Yes.

What is generated from the living?

The dead.

And what from the dead?

I can only say in answer—the living.

Then the living, whether things or persons, Cebes, are generated from the dead?

That is clear, he replied.

Then the inference is that our souls exist in the world below?

That is true.

And one of the two processes or generations is visible—for surely the act of dying is visible?

Surely, he said.

What then is to be the result? Shall we exclude the opposite process? and shall we suppose nature to walk on one leg only? Must we not rather assign to death some corresponding process of generation?

Certainly, he replied.

And what is that process?

Return to life.

And return to life, if there be such a thing, is the birth of the dead into the world of the living?

Quite true.

Then here is a new way by which we arrive at the conclusion that the living come from the dead, just as the dead come from the living; and this, if true, affords a most certain proof that the souls of the dead exist in some place out of which they come again.

Yes, Socrates, he said; the conclusion seems to flow necessarily out of our previous admissions.

And that these admissions were not unfair, Cebes, he said, may be shown, I think, as follows: If generation were in a straight line only, and there were no compensation or circle in nature, no turn or return of elements into their opposites, then you know that all things would at last have the same form and pass into the same state, and there would be no more generation of them.

What do you mean? he said.

A simple thing enough, which I will illustrate by the case of sleep, he replied. You know that if there were no alternation of sleeping and waking, the tale of the sleeping Endymion would in the end have no meaning, because all other things would be asleep too, and he would not be distinguishable from the rest. Or if there were composition only, and no division of substances, then the chaos of Anaxagoras would come again. And in like manner, my dear Cebes, if all things which partook of life were to die, and after they were dead remained in the form of death, and did not come to life again, all would at last die, and nothing would be alive—what other result could there be? For if the living spring from any other things, and they too die, must not all things at last be swallowed up in death?

There is no escape, Socrates, said Cebes; and to me your argument seems to be absolutely true.

Yes, he said, Cebes, it is and must be so, in my opinion; and we have not been deluded in making these admissions; but I am confident that there truly is such a thing as living again, and that the living spring from the dead, and that the souls of the dead are in existence and that the good souls have a better portion than the evil.

Cebes added: Your favourite doctrine, Socrates, that knowledge is simply recollection, if true, also necessarily implies a previous time in which we have learned that which we now recollect. But this would be impossible unless our soul had been in some place before existing in the form of man; here then is another proof of the soul's immortality. . . .

The lovers of knowledge are conscious that the soul was simply fastened and glued to the body—until philosophy received her, she could only view real existence through the bars of a prison, not in and through herself; she was wallowing in the mire of every sort of ignorance, and by reason of lust had become the principal accomplice in her own captivity. This was her original state; and then, as I was saying, and as the lovers of knowledge are well aware, philosophy, seeing how terrible was her confinement, of which she was herself the cause, received and gently comforted her and sought to release her, pointing out that the eye and the ear and the other senses are full of deception, and persuading her to retire from them, and abstain from all the necessary use of them, and be gathered up and collected into herself, bidding her trust in herself and her own pure apprehension of pure existence, and to mistrust whatever comes to her through other channels and is subject to variation; for such things are visible and tangible, but what she sees in her own nature is intelligible and invisible. And the soul of the true philosopher thinks that she ought not to resist this deliverance, and therefore abstains from pleasures and desires and pains and fears, as far as she is able; reflecting that when a man has great joys or sorrows or fears or desires, he suffers from them, not merely the sort of evil which might be anticipated—as, for example, the loss of his health or property which he has sacrificed to his lusts—but an evil greater far, which is the greatest and worst of all evils, and one of which he never thinks.

What is it, Socrates? said Cebes.

The evil is that when the feeling of pleasure or pain is most intense, every soul of man imagines the objects of this intense feeling to be then plainest and truest: but this is not so, they are really the things of sight.

Very true.

And is not this the state in which the soul is most enthralled by the body?

How so?

Why, because each pleasure and pain is a sort of nail which nails and rivets the soul to the body, until she becomes like the body, and believes that to be true which the body affirms to be true; and from agreeing with the body and having the same delights she is obliged to have the same habits and haunts, and is not likely ever to be pure at her departure to the world below, but is always infected by the body; and so she sinks into another body and there germinates and grows, and has therefore no part in the communion of the divine and pure and simple.

Most true, Socrates, answered Cebes.

And this, Cebes, is the reason why the true lovers of knowledge are temperate and brave; and not for the reason which the world gives.

Certainly not.

Certainly not! The soul of a philosopher will reason in quite another way; she will not ask philosophy to release her in order that when released she may deliver herself up again to the thraldom of pleasures and pains, doing a work only to be outdone again, weaving instead of unweaving her Penelope's web. But she will calm passion, and follow reason, and dwell in the contemplation of her, beholding the true and divine (which is not matter of opinion), and thence deriving nourishment. Thus she seeks to live while she lives, and after death she hopes to go to her own kindred and to that which is like her, and to be freed from human ills. Never fear, Simmias and Cebes, that a soul which has been thus nurtured and has had these pursuits, will at her departure from the body be scattered and blown away by the winds and be nowhere and nothing. . . .

When he had spoken these words, he arose and went into a chamber to bathe; Crito followed him and told us to wait. So we remained behind, talking and thinking of the subject of discourse, and also of the greatness of our sorrow; he was like a father of whom we were being bereaved, and we were about to pass the rest of our lives as orphans. When he had taken the bath his children were brought to him (he had two young sons and an elder one); and the women of his family also came, and he talked to them and gave them a few directions in the presence of Crito; then he dismissed them and returned to us.

Now the hour of sunset was near, for a good deal of time had passed while he was within. When he came out, he sat down with us again after his bath, but not much was said. Soon the jailer, who was the servant of the Eleven, entered and stood by him, saying:—To you, Socrates, whom I know to be the noblest and gentlest and best of all who ever came to this place, I will not impute the angry feeling of other men, who rage and swear at me, when, in obedience to the authorities, I bid them drink the poison—indeed, I am sure that you will not be angry with me; for others, as you are aware, and not I, are to blame. And so fare you well, and try to bear lightly what must needs be—you know my errand. Then bursting into tears he turned away and went out.

Socrates looked at him and said: I return your good wishes, and will do as you bid. Then turning to us, he said, How charming the man is: since I have been in prison he has always been coming to see me, and at times he would talk to me, and was as good to me as could be, and now see how generously he sorrows on my account. We must do as he says, Crito; and therefore let the cup be brought, if the poison is prepared: if not, let the attendant prepare some.

Yet, said Crito, the sun is still upon the hill-tops, and I know that many a one has taken the draught late, and after the announcement has been made to him, he has eaten and drunk, and enjoyed the society of his beloved: do not hurry—there is time enough.

Socrates said: Yes, Crito, and they of whom you speak are right in so acting, for they think that they will be gainers by the delay; but I am right in not following their example, for I do not think that I should gain anything by drinking the poison a little later; I should only be ridiculous in my own eyes for sparing and saving a life which is already forfeit. Please then to do as I say, and not to refuse me.

Crito made a sign to the servant, who was standing by; and he went out, and having been absent for some time, returned with the jailer carrying the cup of poison. Socrates said: You, my good friend, who are experienced in these matters, shall give me directions how I am to proceed. The man answered: You have only to walk about until your legs are heavy, and then to lie down, and the poison will act. At the same time he handed the cup to Socrates, who in the easiest and gentlest manner, without the least fear or change of colour or feature, look-ing at the man with all his eyes, Echecrates, as his manner was, took the cup and said: What do you say about making a libation out of this cup to any god? May I, or not? The man answered: We only prepare, Socrates, just so much as we deem enough. I understand, he

said: but I may and must ask the gods to pros-per my journey from this to the other world—even so—and so be it according to my prayer. Then raising the cup to his lips, quite readily and cheerfully he drank off the poison. And hitherto most of us had been able to control our sorrow; but now when we saw him drinking, and saw too that he had finished the draught, we could no longer forbear, and in spite of my-self my own tears were flowing fast; so that I covered my face and wept, not for him, but at the thought of my own calamity in having to part from such a friend. Nor was I the first; for Crito, when he found himself unable to re-strain his tears, had got up, and I followed; and at that moment, Apollodorus, who had been weeping all the time, broke out in a loud and passionate cry which made cowards of us all. Socrates alone retained his calmness: What is this strange outcry? he said. I sent away the women mainly in order that they might not misbehave in this way, for I have been told that a man should die in peace. Be quiet then, and have patience. When we heard his words we were ashamed, and refrained our tears; and he walked about until, as he said, his legs began to fail, and then he lay on his back, ac-cording to directions, and the man who gave him the poison now and then looked at his feet and legs; and after a while he pressed his foot hard, and asked him if he could feel; and he said, No; and then his leg, and so upwards and upwards, and showed us that he was cold and stiff. And he felt them himself, and said: When the poison reaches the heart, that will be the end. He was beginning to grow cold about the groin, when he uncovered his face, for he had covered himself up, and said—they were his last words—he said: Crito, I owe a cock to Asclepius; will you remember to pay the debt? The debt shall be paid, said Crito; is there any-thing else? There was no answer to this ques-tion; but in a minute or two a movement was heard, and the attendants uncovered him; his eyes were set, and Crito closed his eyes and mouth.

Such was the end, Echecrates, of our friend; concerning whom I may truly say, that of all men of his time whom I have known, he was the wisest and justest and best.

Plato

Plato (see p. 35) in The Republic (his best-known and probably most characteristic work) deals with the relationships of life and speculation, politics, and philosophy. Believing in the existence of an ideal world above and beyond the world of everyday reality, Plato outlined a perfect state which would in his judgment embody the idea of justice and which would correct the weaknesses and defects of Athenian democracy recently made manifest in Sparta's defeat of Athens. The dialogue takes place at the home of Cephalus at the Piraeus and is narrated by Socrates the day after it took place. The selection opens with Socrates speaking to Glaucon concerning the rulers or guardians of the state. In reading the selection, note (1) the characteristics to be looked for in the guardians, (2) how the guardians are chosen, (3) the fiction to be used in justifying the selection of guardians and the divisions of society, (4) the established way of life of the guardians, (5) Socrates's justification of the guardians' way of life, (6) how the state would defend itself, (7) the treatment of women and children and Socrates's justification thereof, (8) the provisions for insuring the continued high quality of citizens and the long-range results to be expected from such a program, (9) the meaning and import of the allegory of the cave, (10) the implied freedom for the guardians who have achieved understanding, and (11) their obligation to return to society and accept the responsibilities of governing.

From: THE REPUBLIC

There can be no doubt that the elder must rule the younger.

Clearly.

And that the best of these must rule.

That is also clear.

Now, are not the best husbandmen those who are most devoted to husbandry?

Yes.

And as we are to have the best of guardians for our city, must they not be those who have most the character of guardians?

Yes.

And to this end they ought to be wise and efficient, and to have a special care of the State?

True.

And a man will be most likely to care about that which he loves?

To be sure.

And he will be most likely to love that which he regards as having the same interests with himself, and that of which the good or evil fortune is supposed by him at any time most to affect his own?

Very true, he replied.

Then there must be a selection. Let us note among the guardians those who in their whole life show the greatest eagerness to do what is for the good of their country, and the greatest repugnance to do what is against her interests.

As translated by Benjamin Jowett in *The Republic of Plato*, 3rd ed., Clarendon Press, Oxford, 1888, 100–112; 141; 143; 150; 151–160; 170–171; 214–222; 245–247. Courtesy of the Jowett Copyright Fund.

Those are the right men.

And they will have to be watched at every age, in order that we may see whether they preserve their resolution, and never, under the influence either of force or enchantment, forget or cast off their sense of duty to the State.

How cast off? he said.

I will explain to you, I replied. A resolution may go out of a man's mind either with his will or against his will; with his will when he gets rid of a falsehood and learns better, against his will whenever he is deprived of a truth.

I understand, he said, the willing loss of a resolution; the meaning of the unwilling I have yet to learn.

Why, I said, do you not see that men are unwillingly deprived of good, and willingly of evil? Is not to have lost the truth an evil, and to possess the truth a good? and you would agree that to conceive things as they are is to possess the truth?

Yes, he replied; I agree with you in thinking that mankind are deprived of truth against their will.

And is not this involuntary deprivation caused either by theft, or force, or enchantment?

Still, he replied, I do not understand you.

I fear that I must have been talking darkly, like the tragedians. I only mean that some men are changed by persuasion and that others forget; argument steals away the hearts of one class, and time of the other; and this I call theft. Now you understand me?

Yes.

Those again who are forced, are those whom the violence of some pain or grief compels to change their opinion.

I understand, he said, and you are quite right.

And you would also acknowledge that the enchanted are those who change their minds either under the softer influence of pleasure, or the sterner influence of fear?

Yes, he said; everything that deceives may be said to enchant.

Therefore, as I was just now saying, we must enquire who are the best guardians of their own conviction that what they think the interest of the State is to be the rule of their lives. We must watch them from their youth upwards, and make them perform actions in which they are most likely to forget or to be deceived, and he who remembers and is not deceived is to be selected, and he who fails in the trial is to be rejected. That will be the way?

Yes.

And there should also be toils and pains and conflicts prescribed for them, in which they will be made to give further proof of the same qualities.

Very right, he replied.

And then, I said, we must try them with enchantments—that is the third sort of test—and see what will be their behaviour: like those who take colts amid noise and tumult to see if they are of a timid nature, so must we take our youth amid terrors of some kind, and again pass them into pleasures, and prove them more thoroughly than gold is proved in the furnace, that we may discover whether they are armed against all enchantments, and of a noble bearing always, good guardians of themselves and of the music which they have learned, and retaining under all circumstances a rhythmical and harmonious nature, such as will be most serviceable to the individual and to the State. And he who at every age, as boy and youth and in mature life, has come out of the trial victorious and pure, shall be appointed a ruler and guardian of the State; he shall be honoured in life and death, and shall receive sepulture and other memorials of honour, the greatest that we have to give. But him who fails, we must reject. I am inclined to think that this is the sort of way in which our rulers and guardians should be chosen and appointed. I speak generally, and not with any pretension to exactness.

And, speaking generally, I agree with you, he said.

And perhaps the word 'guardian' in the fullest sense ought to be applied to this higher class only who preserve us against foreign enemies and maintain peace among our citizens at home, that the one may not have the will, or the others the power, to harm us. The young men whom we before called guardians may be more properly designated auxiliaries and supporters of the principles of the rulers.

I agree with you, he said.

How then may we devise one of those needful falsehoods of which we lately spoke—just one royal lie which may deceive the rulers, if that be possible, and at any rate the rest of the city?

What sort of lie? he said.

Nothing new, I replied; only an old Phoenician tale of what has often occurred before now in other places, (as the poets say, and have made the world believe,) though not in our time, and I do not know whether such an event could ever happen again, or could now even be made probable, if it did.

How your words seem to hesitate on your lips!

You will not wonder, I replied, at my hesitation when you have heard.

Speak, he said, and fear not.

Well then, I will speak, although I really know not how to look you in the face, or in what words to utter the audacious fiction, which I propose to communicate gradually, first to the rulers, then to the soldiers, and lastly to the people. They are to be told that their youth was a dream, and the education and training which they received from us, an appearance only; in reality during all that time they were being formed and fed in the womb of the earth, where they themselves and their arms and appurtenances were manufactured; when they were completed, the earth, their mother, sent them up; and so, their country being their mother and also their nurse, they are bound to advise for her good, and to defend her against attacks, and her citizens they are to regard as children of the earth and their own brothers.

You had good reason, he said, to be ashamed of the lie which you were going to tell.

True, I replied, but there is more coming; I have only told you half. Citizens, we shall say to them in our tale, you are brothers, yet God has framed you differently. Some of you have the power of command, and in the composition of these he has mingled gold, wherefore also they have the greatest honour; others he has made of silver, to be auxiliaries; others again who are to be husbandmen and craftsmen he has composed of brass and iron; and the species will generally be preserved in the children. But as all are of the same original stock, a golden parent will sometimes have a silver son, or a silver parent a golden son. And God proclaims as a first principle to the rulers, and above all else, that there is nothing which they should so anxiously guard, or of which they are to be such good guardians, as of the purity of the race. They should observe what elements mingle in their offspring; for if the son of a golden or silver parent has an admixture of brass and iron, then nature orders a transposition of ranks, and the eye of the ruler must not be pitiful towards the child because he has to descend in the scale and become a husbandman or artisan, just as there may be sons of artisans who having an admixture of gold or silver in them are raised to honour, and become guardians or auxiliaries. For an oracle says that when a man of brass or iron guards the State, it will be destroyed. Such is the tale; is there any possibility of making our citizens believe in it?

Not in the present generation, he replied; there is no way of accomplishing this; but their sons may be made to believe in the tale, and their sons' sons, and posterity after them.

I see the difficulty, I replied; yet the fostering of such a belief will make them care more for the city and for one another. Enough, however, of the fiction, which may now fly abroad upon the wings of rumour, while we arm our earth-born heroes, and lead them forth under the command of their rulers. Let them look round and select a spot whence they can best suppress insurrection, if any prove refractory within, and also defend themselves against enemies, who like wolves may come down on the fold from without; there let them encamp, and when they have encamped, let them sacrifice to the proper Gods and prepare their dwellings.

Just so, he said.

And their dwellings must be such as will shield them against the cold of winter and the heat of summer.

I suppose that you mean houses, he replied.

Yes, I said; but they must be the houses of soldiers, and not of shop-keepers.

What is the difference? he said.

That I will endeavour to explain, I replied. To keep watch-dogs, who, from want of discipline or hunger, or some evil habit or other, would turn upon the sheep and worry them, and behave not like dogs but wolves, would be a foul and monstrous thing in a shepherd?

Truly monstrous, he said.

And therefore every care must be taken that our auxiliaries, being stronger than our citizens, may not grow to be too much for them and become savage tyrants instead of friends and allies?

Yes, great care should be taken.

And would not a really good education furnish the best safeguard?

But they are well-educated already, he replied.

I cannot be so confident, my dear Glaucon, I said; I am much more certain that they ought to be, and that true education, whatever that may be, will have the greatest tendency to civilize and humanize them in their relations to one another, and to those who are under their protection.

Very true, he replied.

And not only their education, but their habitations, and all that belongs to them, should be such as will neither impair their virtue as guardians, nor tempt them to prey upon the other citizens. Any man of sense must acknowledge that.

He must.

Then now let us consider what will be their way of life, if they are to realize our idea of them. In the first place, none of them should have any property of his own beyond what is absolutely necessary; neither should they have a private house or store closed against any one who has a mind to enter; their provisions should be only such as are required by trained warriors, who are men of temperance and courage; they should agree to receive from the citizens a fixed rate of pay, enough to meet the expenses of the year and no more; and they will go to mess and live together like soldiers in a camp. Gold and silver we will tell them that they have from God; the diviner metal is within them, and they have therefore no need of the dross which is current among men, and ought not to pollute the divine by any such earthly admixture; for that commoner metal has been the source of many unholy deeds, but their own is undefiled. And they alone of all the citizens may not touch or handle silver or gold, or be under the same roof with them, or wear them,

or drink from them. And this will be their salvation, and they will be the saviours of the State. But should they ever acquire homes or lands or moneys of their own, they will become housekeepers and husbandmen instead of guardians, enemies and tyrants instead of allies of the other citizens; hating and being hated, plotting and being plotted against, they will pass their whole life in much greater terror of internal than of external enemies, and the hour of ruin, both to themselves and to the rest of the State, will be at hand. For all which reasons may we not say that thus shall our State be ordered, and that these shall be the regulations appointed by us for our guardians concerning their houses and all other matters?

Yes, said Glaucon.

Here Adeimantus interposed a question: How would you answer, Socrates, said he, if a person were to say that [for their own good] you are making these people miserable, and that they are the cause of their own unhappiness; the city in fact belongs to them, but they are none the better for it; whereas other men acquire lands, and build large and handsome houses, and have everything handsome about them, offering sacrifices to the gods on their own account, and practising hospitality; moreover, as you were saying just now, they have gold and silver, and all that is usual among the favourites of fortune; but our poor citizens are no better than mercenaries who are quartered in the city and are always mounting guard?

Yes, I said; and you may add that they are only fed, and not paid in addition to their food, like other men; and therefore they cannot, if they would, take a journey of pleasure; they have no money to spend on a mistress or any other luxurious fancy, which, as the world goes, is thought to be happiness; and many other accusations of the same nature might be added.

But, said he, let us suppose all this to be included in the charge.

You mean to ask, I said, what will be our answer?

Yes.

If we proceed along the old path, my belief, I said, is that we shall find the answer. And our answer will be that, even as they are, our guardians may very likely be the happiest of men; but that our aim in founding the State was not the disproportionate happiness of any one class, but the greatest happiness of the whole; we thought that in a State which is ordered with a view to the good of the whole we should be most likely to find justice, and in the ill-ordered State injustice: and, having found them, we might then decide which of the two is the happier. At present, I take it, we are fashioning the happy State, not piecemeal, or with a view of making a few happy citizens, but as a whole; and by-and-by we will proceed to view the opposite kind of State. Suppose that we were painting a statue, and some one came up to us and said, Why do you not put the most beautiful colours on the most beautiful parts of the body—the eyes ought to be purple, but you have made them black—to him we might fairly answer, Sir, you would not surely have us beautify the eyes to such a degree that they are no longer eyes; consider rather whether, by giving this and the other features their due proportion, we make the whole beautiful. And so I say to you, do not compel us to assign to the guardians a sort of happiness which will make them anything but guardians; for we too can clothe our husbandmen in royal apparel, and set crowns of gold on their heads, and bid them till the ground as much as they like, and no more. Our potters also might be allowed to repose on couches, and feast by the fireside, passing round the winecup, while their wheel is conveniently at hand, and working at pottery only as much as they like; in this way we might make every class happy—and then, as you imagine, the whole State would be happy. But do not put this idea into our heads; for, if we listen to you, the husbandman will be no longer a husbandman, the potter will cease to be a potter, and no one will have the character of any distinct class in the State. Now this is not of much consequence where the corruption of society, and pretension to be what you are not, is confined to cobblers; but when the guardians of the laws and of the government are only seeming and not real guardians, then see how they turn the State upside down; and on the other hand they alone have the power of giving order and happiness to the State. We mean our guardians to be true saviours and not the destroyers of the State, whereas our opponent is thinking of peasants at

a festival, who are enjoying a life of revelry, not of citizens who are doing their duty to the State. But, if so, we mean different things, and he is speaking of something which is not a State. And therefore we must consider whether in appointing our guardians we would look to their greatest happiness individually, or whether this principle of happiness does not rather reside in the State as a whole. But if the latter be the truth, then the guardians and auxiliaries, and all others equally with them, must be compelled or induced to do their own work in the best way. And thus the whole State will grow up in a noble order, and the several classes will receive the proportion of happiness which nature assigns to them.

I think that you are quite right.

I wonder whether you will agree with another remark which occurs to me.

What may that be?

There seem to be two causes of the deterioration of the arts.

What are they?

Wealth, I said, and poverty.

How do they act?

The process is as follows: When a potter becomes rich, will he, think you, any longer take the same pains with his art?

Certainly not.

He will grow more and more indolent and careless?

Very true.

And the result will be that he becomes a worse potter?

Yes; he greatly deteriorates.

But, on the other hand, if he has no money, and cannot provide himself with tools or instruments, he will not work equally well himself, nor will he teach his sons or apprentices to work equally well.

Certainly not.

Then, under the influence either of poverty or of wealth, workmen and their work are equally liable to degenerate?

That is evident.

Here, then, is a discovery of new evils, I said, against which the guardians will have to watch, or they will creep into the city unobserved.

What evils?

Wealth, I said, and poverty; the one is the

parent of luxury and indolence, and the other of meanness and viciousness, and both of discontent.

That is very true, he replied; but still I should like to know, Socrates, how our city will be able to go to war, especially against an enemy who is rich and powerful, if deprived of the sinews of war.

There would certainly be a difficulty, I replied, in going to war with one such enemy; but there is no difficulty where there are two of them.

How so? he asked.

In the first place, I said, if we have to fight, our side will be trained warriors fighting against an army of rich men.

That is true, he said.

And do you not suppose, Adeimantus, that a single boxer who was perfect in his art would easily be a match for two stout and well-to-do gentlemen who were not boxers?

Hardly, if they came upon him at once.

What, not, I said, if he were able to run away and then turn and strike at the one who first came up? And supposing he were to do this several times under the heat of a scorching sun, might he not, being an expert, overturn more than one stout personage?

Certainly, he said, there would be nothing wonderful in that.

And yet rich men probably have a greater superiority in the science and practise of boxing than they have in military qualities.

Likely enough.

Then we may assume that our athletes will be able to fight with two or three times their own number?

I agree with you, for I think you right.

And suppose that, before engaging, our citizens send an embassy to one of the two cities, telling them what is the truth: Silver and gold we neither have nor are permitted to have, but you may; do you therefore come and help us in war, and take the spoils of the other city: Who, on hearing these words, would choose to fight against lean wiry dogs, rather than, with the dogs on their side, against fat and tender sheep?

That is not likely; and yet there might be a danger to the poor State if the wealth of many States were to be gathered into one.

But how simple of you to use the term State at all of any but our own!

Why so?

You ought to speak of other States in the plural number; not one of them is a city, but many cities, as they say in the game. For indeed any city, however small, is in fact divided into two, one the city of the poor, the other of the rich; these are at war with one another; and in either there are many smaller divisions, and you would be altogether beside the mark if you treated them all as a single State. But if you deal with them as many, and give the wealth or power or persons of the one to the others, you will always have a great many friends and not many enemies. And your State, while the wise order which has now been prescribed continues to prevail in her, will be the greatest of States, I do not mean to say in reputation or appearance, but in deed and truth, though she number not more than a thousand defenders. A single State which is her equal you will hardly find, either among Hellenes or barbarians, though many that appear to be as great and many times greater.

That is most true, he said.

And what, I said, will be the best limit for our rulers to fix when they are considering the size of the State and the amount of territory which they are to include, and beyond which they will not go?

What limit would you propose?

I would allow the State to increase so far as is consistent with unity; that, I think, is the proper limit.

Very good, he said.

Here then, I said, is another order which will have to be conveyed to our guardians: Let our city be accounted neither large nor small, but one and self-sufficing.

And surely, said he, this is not a very severe order which we impose upon them.

And the other, said I, of which we were speaking before is lighter still,—I mean the duty of degrading the offspring of the guardians when inferior, and of elevating into the rank of guardians the offspring of the lower classes, when naturally superior. The intention was, that, in the case of the citizens generally, each individual should be put to the use for which nature intended him, one to one work, and then every man would do his own business, and be one and not many; and so the whole city would be one and not many.

Yes, he said; that is not so difficult.

The regulations which we are prescribing, my good Adeimantus, are not, as might be supposed, a number of great principles, but trifles all, if care be taken, as the saying is, of the one great thing,—a thing, however, which I would rather call, not, great, but sufficient for our purpose.

What may that be? he asked.

Education, I said, and nurture: If our citizens are well educated, and grow into sensible men, they will easily see their way through all these, as well as other matters which I omit; such, for example, as marriage, the possession of women and the procreation of children, which will all follow the general principle that friends have all things in common, as the proverb says.

That will be the best way of settling them.

Also, I said, the State, if once started well, moves with accumulating force like a wheel. For good nurture and education implant good constitutions, and these good constitutions taking root in a good education improve more and more, and this improvement affects the breed in man as in other animals. . . . What sort of community of women and children is this which is to prevail among our guardians? And how shall we manage the period between birth and education, which seems to require the greatest care? Tell us how these things will be. . . .

For men born and educated like our citizens, the only way, in my opinion, of arriving at a right conclusion about the possession and use of women and children is to follow the path on which we originally started, when we said that the men were to be the guardians and watchdogs of the herd.

True.

Let us further suppose the birth and education of our women to be subject to similar or nearly similar regulations; then we shall see whether the result accords with our design.

What do you mean?

What I mean may be put into the form of a question, I said: Are dogs divided into hes and shes, or do they both share equally in hunting and in keeping watch and in the other duties of dogs? Or do we entrust to the males the entire and exclusive care of the flocks, while we leave the females at home, under the idea that the bearing and suckling their puppies is labour enough for them?

No, he said, they share alike; the only difference between them is that the males are stronger and the females weaker.

But can you use different animals for the same purpose, unless they are bred and fed in the same way?

You cannot.

Then, if women are to have the same duties as men, they must have the same nurture and education?

Yes.

The education which was assigned to the men was music and gymnastic.

Yes.

Then women must be taught music and gymnastic and also the art of war, which they must practise like the men?

That is the inference, I suppose. . . .

The law, I said, which is the sequel of this and of all that has preceded, is to the following effect,—'that the wives of our guardians are to be common, and their children are to be common, and no parent is to know his own child, nor any child his parent.' . . .

I do not think, I said, that there can be any dispute about the very great utility of having wives and children in common; the possibility is quite another matter, and will be very much disputed. . . . If you have no objection, I will endeavour with your help to consider the advantages of the measure; and hereafter the question of possibility.

I have no objection; proceed.

First, I think that if our rulers and their auxiliaries are to be worthy of the name which they bear, there must be willingness to obey in the one and the power of command in the other; the guardians must themselves obey the laws, and they must also imitate the spirit of them in any details which are entrusted to their care.

That is right, he said.

You, I said, who are their legislator, having selected the men, will now select the women and give them to them;—they must be as far as possible of like natures with them; and they must live in common houses and meet at common meals. None of them will have anything specially his or her own; they will be together, and will be brought up together, and will associate at gymnastic exercises. And so they will be drawn by a necessity of their natures to have intercourse with each other—necessity is not too strong a word, I think?

Yes, he said;—necessity, not geometrical, but another sort of necessity which lovers know, and which is far more convincing and constraining to the mass of mankind.

True, I said; and this, Glaucon, like all the rest, must proceed after an orderly fashion; in a city of the blessed, licentiousness is an unholy thing which the rulers will forbid.

Yes, he said, and it ought not to be permitted.

Then clearly the next thing will be to make matrimony sacred in the highest degree, and what is most beneficial will be deemed sacred?

Exactly.

And how can marriages be made most beneficial?—that is a question which I put to you, because I see in your house dogs for hunting, and of the nobler sort of birds not a few. Now, I beseech you, do tell me, have you ever attended to their pairing and breeding?

In what particulars?

Why, in the first place, although they are all of a good sort, are not some better than others?

True.

And do you breed from them all indifferently, or do you take care to breed from the best only?

From the best.

And do you take the oldest or the youngest, or only those of ripe age?

I choose only those of ripe age.

And if care was not taken in the breeding, your dogs and birds would greatly deteriorate?

Certainly.

And the same of horses and of animals in general?

Undoubtedly.

Good heavens! my dear friend, I said, what consummate skill will our rulers need if the same principle holds of the human species!

Certainly, the same principle holds; but why does this involve any particular skill?

Because, I said, our rulers will often have to practice upon the body corporate with medicines. Now you know that when patients do not require medicines, but have only to be put under a regimen, the inferior sort of practitioner is deemed to be good enough; but when medicine has to be given, then the doctor should be more of a man.

That is quite true, he said; but to what are you alluding?

I mean, I replied, that our rulers will find a considerable dose of falsehood and deceit necessary for the good of their subjects: we were saying that the use of all these things regarded as medicines might be of advantage.

And we were very right.

And this lawful use of them seems likely to be often needed in the regulations of marriages and births.

How so?

Why, I said, the principle has been already laid down that the best of either sex should be united with the best as often, and the inferior with the inferior, as seldom as possible; and that they should rear the offspring of the one sort of union, but not of the other, if the flock is to be maintained in first-rate condition. Now these goings on must be a secret which the rulers only know, or there will be a further danger of our herd, as the guardians may be termed, breaking out into rebellion.

Very true.

Had we not better appoint certain festivals at which we will bring together the brides and bridegrooms, and sacrifices will be offered and suitable hymeneal songs composed by our poets: the number of weddings is a matter which must be left to the discretion of the rulers, whose aim will be to preserve the average of population? There are many other things which they will have to consider, such as the effects of wars and diseases and any similar agencies, in order as far as this is possible to prevent the State from becoming either too large or too small.

Certainly, he replied.

We shall have to invent some ingenious kind of lots which the less worthy may draw on each occasion of our bringing them together, and then they will accuse their own ill-luck and not the rulers.

To be sure, he said.

And I think that our braver and better youth, besides their other honours and rewards, might have greater facilities of intercourse with women given them; their bravery will be a reason, and such fathers ought to have as many sons as possible.

True.

And the proper officers, whether male or female or both, for offices are to be held by women as well as by men—

Yes—

The proper officers will take the offspring of the good parents to the pen or fold, and there they will deposit them with certain nurses who dwell in a separate quarter; but the offspring of the inferior, or of the better when they chance to be deformed, will be put away in some mysterious, unknown place, as they should be.

Yes, he said, that must be done if the breed of the guardians is to be kept pure.

They will provide for their nurture, and will bring the mothers to the fold when they are full of milk, taking the greatest possible care that no mother recognises her own child; and other wet-nurses may be engaged if more are required. Care will also be taken that the process of suckling shall not be protracted too long; and the mothers will have no getting up at night or other trouble, but will hand over all this sort of thing to the nurses and attendants.

You suppose the wives of our guardians to have a fine easy time of it when they are having children.

Why, said I, and so they ought. Let us, however, proceed with our scheme. We were saying that the parents should be in the prime of life?

Very true.

And what is the prime of life? May it not be defined as a period of about twenty years in a woman's life, and thirty in a man's?

Which years do you mean to include?

A woman, I said, at twenty years of age may begin to bear children to the State, and continue to bear them until forty; a man may begin at five-and-twenty, when he has passed the point at which the pulse of life beats quickest, and continue to beget children until he be fifty-five.

Certainly, he said, both in men and women

those years are the prime of physical as well as of intellectual vigour.

Any one above or below the prescribed ages who takes part in the public hymeneals shall be said to have done an unholy and unrighteous thing; the child of which he is the father, if it steals into life, will have been conceived under auspices very unlike the sacrifices and prayers, which at each hymeneal priestesses and priests and the whole city will offer, that the new generation may be better and more useful than their good and useful parents, whereas his child will be the offspring of darkness and strange lust.

Very true, he replied.

And the same law will apply to any one of those within the prescribed age who forms a connection with any woman in the prime of life without the sanction of the rulers; for we shall say that he is raising up a bastard to the State, uncertified and unconsecrated.

Very true, he replied.

This applies, however, only to those who are within the specified age: after that we allow them to range at will, except that a man may not marry his daughter or his daughter's daughter, or his mother or his mother's mother; and women, on the other hand, are prohibited from marrying their sons or fathers, or son's son or father's father, and so on in either direction. And we grant all this, accompanying the permission with strict orders to prevent any embryo which may come into being from seeing the light; and if any force a way to the birth, the parents must understand that the offspring of such an union cannot be maintained, and arrange accordingly.

That also, he said, is a reasonable proposition. But how will they know who are fathers and daughters, and so on?

They will never know. The way will be this: —dating from the day of the hymeneal, the bridegroom who was then married will call all the male children who are born in the seventh and the tenth month afterwards, his sons, and the female children his daughters, and they will call him father, and he will call their children his grandchildren, and they will call the elder generation grandfathers and grandmothers. All who were begotten at the time when their fathers and mothers came together will be called their brothers and sisters, and these, as I was saying, will be forbidden to intermarry. This, however, is not to be understood as an absolute prohibition of the marriage of brothers and sisters; if the lot favours them, and they receive the sanction of the Pythian oracle, the law will allow them.

Quite right, he replied.

Such is the scheme, Glaucon, according to which the guardians of our State are to have their wives and families in common. And now you would have the argument show that this community is consistent with the rest of our polity, and also that nothing can be better— would you not?

Yes, certainly.

Shall we try to find a common basis by asking of ourselves what ought to be the chief aim of the legislator in making laws and in the organization of a State,—what is the greatest good, and what is the greatest evil, and then consider whether our previous description has the stamp of the good or of the evil?

By all means.

Can there be any greater evil than discord and distraction and plurality where unity ought to reign? or any greater good than the bond of unity?

There cannot.

And there is unity where there is community of pleasures and pains—where all the citizens are glad or grieved on the same occasions of joy and sorrow?

No doubt.

Yes; and where there is no common but only private feeling a State is disorganized—when you have one half of the world triumphing and the other plunged in grief at the same events happening to the city or the citizens?

Certainly.

Such differences commonly originate in a disagreement about the use of the terms 'mine' and 'not mine,' 'his' and 'not his.'

Exactly so.

And is not that the best-ordered State in which the greatest number of persons apply the terms 'mine' and 'not mine' in the same way to the same thing?

Quite true.

Or that again which most nearly approaches to the condition of the individual—as in the body, when but a finger of one of us is hurt, the whole frame, drawn towards the soul as a centre and forming one kingdom under the ruling power therein, feels the hurt and sympathizes all together with the part affected, and we say that the man has a pain in his finger; and the same expression is used about any other part of the body, which has a sensation of pain at suffering or of pleasure at the alleviation of suffering.

Very true, he replied; and I agree with you that in the best-ordered State there is the nearest approach to this common feeling which you describe.

Then when any one of the citizens experiences any good or evil, the whole State will make his case their own, and will either rejoice or sorrow with him?

Yes, he said, that is what will happen in a well-ordered State.

It will now be time, I said, for us to return to our State and see whether this or some other form is most in accordance with these fundamental principles.

Very good.

Our State like every other has rulers and subjects?

True.

All of whom will call one another citizens?

Of course.

But is there not another name which people give to their rulers in other States?

Generally they call them masters, but in democratic States they simply call them rulers.

And in our State what other name besides that of citizens do the people give the rulers?

They are called saviours and helpers, he replied.

And what do the rulers call the people?

Their maintainers and foster-fathers.

And what do they call them in other States?

Slaves.

And what do the rulers call one another in other States?

Fellow-rulers.

And what in ours?

Fellow-guardians.

Did you ever know an example in any other State of a ruler who would speak of one of his colleagues as his friend and of another as not being his friend?

Yes, very often.

And the friend he regards and describes as one in whom he has an interest, and the other as a stranger in whom he has no interest?

Exactly.

But would any of your guardians think or speak of any other guardian as a stranger?

Certainly he would not; for every one whom they meet will be regarded by them either as a brother or sister, or father or mother, or son or daughter, or as the child or parent of those who are thus connected with him.

Capital, I said; but let me ask you once more: Shall they be a family in name only; or shall they in all their actions be true to the name? For example, in the use of the word 'father,' would the care of a father be implied and the filial reverence and duty and obedience to him which the law commands; and is the violator of these duties to be regarded as an impious and unrighteous person who is not likely to receive much good either at the hands of God or of man? Are these to be or not to be the strains which the children will hear repeated in their ears by all the citizens about those who are intimated to them to be their parents and the rest of their kinsfolk?

These, he said, and none other; for what can be more ridiculous than for them to utter the names of family ties with the lips only and not to act in the spirit of them?

Then in our city the language of harmony and concord will be more often heard than in any other. As I was describing before, when any one is well or ill, the universal word will be 'with me it is well' or 'it is ill.'

Most true.

And agreeably to this mode of thinking and speaking, were we not saying that they will have their pleasures and pains in common?

Yes, and so they will.

And they will have a common interest in the same thing which they will alike call 'my own,' and having this common interest they will have a common feeling of pleasure and pain?

Yes, far more so than in other States.

And the reason of this, over and above the general constitution of the State, will be that the guardians will have a community of women and children?

That will be the chief reason.

And this unity of feeling we admitted to be the greatest good, as was implied in our own comparison of a well-ordered State to the relation of the body and the members, when affected by pleasure or pain?

That we acknowledged, and very rightly.

Then the community of wives and children among our citizens is clearly the source of the greatest good to the State?

Certainly.

And this agrees with the other principle which we were affirming,—that the guardians were not to have houses or lands or any other property; their pay was to be their food, which they were to receive from the other citizens, and they were to have no private expenses; for we intended them to preserve their true character of guardians.

Right, he replied.

Both the community of property and the community of families, as I am saying, tend to make them more truly guardians; they will not tear the city in pieces by differing about 'mine' and 'not mine'; each man dragging any acquisition which he has made into a separate house of his own, where he has a separate wife and children and private pleasures and pains; but all will be affected as far as may be by the same pleasures and pains because they are all of one opinion about what is near and dear to them, and therefore they all tend towards a common end.

Certainly, he replied.

And as they have nothing but their persons which they can call their own, suits and complaints will have no existence among them; they will be delivered from all those quarrels of which money or children or relations are the occasion.

Of course they will.

Neither will trials for assault or insult ever be likely to occur among them. For that equals should defend themselves against equals we shall maintain to be honourable and right; we shall make the protection of the person a matter of necessity.

That is good, he said.

Yes; and there is a further good in the law; viz. that if a man has a quarrel with another he will satisfy his resentment then and there, and not proceed to more dangerous lengths.

Certainly.

To the elder shall be assigned the duty of ruling and chastising the younger.

Clearly.

Nor can there be a doubt that the younger will not strike or do any other violence to an elder, unless the magistrates command him; nor will he slight him in any way. For there are two guardians, shame and fear, mighty to prevent him: shame, which makes men refrain from laying hands on those who are to them in the relation of parents; fear, that the injured one will be succoured by the others who are his brothers, sons, fathers.

That is true, he replied.

Then in every way the laws will help the citizens to keep the peace with one another?

Yes, there will be no want of peace.

And as the guardians will never quarrel among themselves there will be no danger of the rest of the city being divided either against them or against one another. . . .

Until philosophers are kings, or the kings and princes of this world have the spirit and power of philosophy, and political greatness and wisdom meet in one, and those commoner natures who pursue either to the exclusion of the other are compelled to stand aside, cities will never have rest from their evils—no, nor the human race, as I believe—and then only will this our State have a possibility of life and behold the light of day. Such was the thought, my dear Glaucon, which I would fain have uttered if it had not seemed too extravagant; for to be convinced that in no other State can there be happiness private or public is indeed a hard thing.

Socrates, what do you mean? I would have you consider that the word which you have uttered is one at which numerous persons, and very respectable persons too, in a figure pulling off their coats all in a moment, and seizing any weapon that comes to hand, will run at you might and main, before you know where you are, intending to do heaven knows what; and if you don't prepare an answer, and put yourself in motion, you will be 'pared by their fine wits', and no mistake.

You got me into the scrape, I said.

And I was quite right; however, I will do all I can to get you out of it; but I can only

give you good-will and good advice, and, perhaps, I may be able to fit answers to your questions better than another—that is all. And now, having such an auxiliary, you must do your best to show the unbelievers that you are right.

I ought to try, I said, since you offer me such invaluable assistance. And I think that, if there is to be a chance of our escaping, we must explain to them whom we mean when we say that philosophers are to rule in the State; then we shall be able to defend ourselves: There will be discovered to be some natures who ought to study philosophy and to be leaders in the State; and others who are not born to be philosophers, and are meant to be followers rather than leaders. . . .

And now, I said, let me show in a figure how far our nature is enlightened or unenlightened: —Behold! human beings living in an underground den, which has a mouth open towards the light and reaching all along the den; here they have been from their childhood, and have their legs and necks chained so that they cannot move, and can only see before them, being prevented by the chains from turning round their heads. Above and behind them a fire is blazing at a distance, and between the fire and the prisoners there is a raised way; and you will see, if you look, a low wall built along the way, like the screen which marionette players have in front of them, over which they show the puppets.

I see.

And do you see, I said, men passing along the wall carrying all sorts of vessels, and statues and figures of animals made of wood and stone and various materials, which appear over the wall? Some of them are talking, others silent.

You have shown me a strange image, and they are strange prisoners.

Like ourselves, I replied; and they see only their own shadows, or the shadows of one another, which the fire throws on the opposite wall of the cave?

True, he said; how could they see anything but the shadows if they were never allowed to move their heads?

And of the objects which are being carried in like manner they would only see the shadows?

Yes, he said.

And if they were able to converse with one another, would they not suppose that they were naming what was actually before them?

Very true.

And suppose further that the prison had an echo which came from the other side, would they not be sure to fancy when one of the passers-by spoke that the voice which they heard came from the passing shadow?

No question, he replied.

To them, I said, the truth would be literally nothing but the shadows of the images.

That is certain.

And now look again, and see what will naturally follow if the prisoners are released and disabused of their error. At first, when any of them is liberated and compelled suddenly to stand up and turn his neck round and walk and look towards the light, he will suffer sharp pains; the glare will distress him, and he will be unable to see the realities of which in his former state he had seen the shadows; and then conceive some one saying to him, that what he saw before was an illusion, but that now, when he is approaching nearer to being and his eye is turned towards more real existence, he has a clearer vision,—what will be his reply? And you may further imagine that his instructor is pointing to the objects as they pass and requiring him to name then,—will he not be perplexed? Will he not fancy that the shadows which he formerly saw are truer than the objects which are now shown to him?

Far truer.

And if he is compelled to look straight at the light, will he not have a pain in his eyes which will make him turn away to take refuge in the objects of vision which he can see, and which he will conceive to be in reality clearer than the things which are now being shown to him?

True, he said.

And suppose once more, that he is reluctantly dragged up a steep and rugged ascent, and held fast until he is forced into the presence of the sun himself, is he not likely to be pained and irritated? When he approaches the light his eyes will be dazzled, and he will not be able to see anything at all of what are now called realities.

Not all in a moment, he said.

He will grow accustomed to the sight of the upper world. And first he will see the shadows best, next the reflections of men and other objects in the water, and then the objects themselves; then he will gaze upon the light of the moon and the stars and the spangled heaven; and he will see the sky and the stars by night better than the sun or the light of the sun by day?

Certainly.

Last of all he will be able to see the sun, and not mere reflections of him in the water, but he will see him in his own proper place, and not in another; and he will contemplate him as he is.

Certainly.

He will then proceed to argue that this is he who gives the season and the years, and is the guardian of all that is in the visible world, and in a certain way the cause of all things which he and his fellows have been accustomed to behold?

Clearly, he said, he would first see the sun and then reason about him.

And when he remembered his old habitation, and the wisdom of the den and his fellow-prisoners, do you not suppose that he would felicitate himself on the change, and pity them?

Certainly, he would.

And if they were in the habit of conferring honours among themselves on those who were quickest to observe the passing shadows and to remark which of them went before, and which followed after, and which were together; and who were therefore best able to draw conclusions as to the future, do you think that he would care for such honours and glories, or envy the possessors of them? Would he not say with Homer,

'Better to be the poor servant of a poor master,' and to endure anything, rather than think as they do and live after their manner?

Yes, he said, I think that he would rather suffer anything than entertain these false notions and live in this miserable manner.

Imagine once more, I said, such an one coming suddenly out of the sun to be replaced in his old situation; would he not be certain to have his eyes full of darkness?

To be sure, he said.

And if there were a contest, and he had to

compete in measuring the shadows with the prisoners who had never moved out of the den, while his sight was still weak, and before his eyes had become steady (and the time which would be needed to acquire this new habit of sight might be very considerable), would he not be ridiculous? Men would say of him that up he went and down he came without his eyes; and that it was better not even to think of ascending; and if any one tried to loose another and lead him up to the light, let them only catch the offender, and they would put him to death.

No question, he said.

This entire allegory, I said, you may now append, dear Glaucon, to the previous argument; the prison-house is the world of sight, the light of the fire is the sun, and you will not misapprehend me if you interpret the journey upwards to be the ascent of the soul into the intellectual world according to my poor belief, which, at your desire, I have expressed—whether rightly or wrongly, God knows. But, whether true or false, my opinion is that in the world of knowledge the idea of good appears last of all, and is seen only with an effort; and, when seen, is also inferred to be the universal author of all things beautiful and right, parent of light and of the lord of light in this visible world, and the immediate source of reason and truth in the intellectual; and that this is the power upon which he who would act rationally either in public or private life must have his eye fixed.

I agree, he said, as far as I am able to understand you.

Moreover, I said, you must not wonder that those who attain to this beatific vision are unwilling to descend to human affairs; for their souls are ever hastening into the upper world where they desire to dwell; which desire of theirs is very natural, if our allegory may be trusted.

Yes, very natural.

And is there anything surprising in one who passes from divine contemplations to the evil state of man, misbehaving himself in a ridiculous manner; if, while his eyes are blinking and before he has become accustomed to the surrounding darkness, he is compelled to fight in courts of law, or in other places, about the images or the shadows of images of justice, and is endeavouring to meet the conceptions of those who have never yet seen absolute justice?

Anything but surprising, he replied.

Any one who has common sense will remember that the bewilderments of the eyes are of two kinds, and arise from two causes, either from coming out of the light or from going into the light, which is true of the mind's eye, quite as much as of the bodily eye; and he who remembers this when he sees any one whose vision is perplexed and weak, will not be too ready to laugh; he will first ask whether that soul of man has come out of the brighter life, and is unable to see because unaccustomed to the dark, or having turned from darkness to the day is dazzled by excess of light. And he will count the one happy in his condition and state of being, and he will pity the other; or, if he have a mind to laugh at the soul which comes from below into the light, there will be more reason in this than in the laugh which greets him who returns from above out of the light into the den.

That, he said, is a very just distinction.

But then, if I am right, certain professors of education must be wrong when they say that they can put a knowledge into the soul which was not there before, like sight into blind eyes.

They undoubtedly say this, he replied.

Whereas, our argument shows that the power and capacity of learning exists in the soul already; and that just as the eye was unable to turn from darkness to light without the whole body, so too the instrument of knowledge can only by the movement of the whole soul be turned from the world of becoming into that of being, and learn by degrees to endure the sight of being, and of the brightness and best of being, or in other words, of the good.

Very true.

And must there not be some art which will effect conversion in the easiest and quickest manner; not implanting the faculty of sight, for that exists already, but has been turned in the wrong direction, and is looking away from the truth?

Yes, he said, such an art may be presumed.

And whereas the other so-called virtues of the soul seem to be akin to bodily qualities, for even when they are not originally innate they can be implanted later by habit and exercise, the virtue of wisdom more than anything else contains a divine element which always remains, and by this conversion is rendered useful and profitable; or, on the other hand, hurtful and useless. Did you never observe the narrow intelligence flashing from the keen eye of a clever rogue—how eager he is, how clearly his paltry soul sees the way to his end; he is the reverse of blind, but his keen eye-sight is forced into the service of evil, and he is mischievous in proportion to his cleverness?

Very true, he said.

But what if there had been a circumcision of such natures in the days of their youth; and they had been severed from those sensual pleasures, such as eating and drinking, which, like leaden weights, were attached to them at their birth, and which drag them down and turn the vision of their souls upon the things that are below—if, I say, they had been released from these impediments and turned in the opposite direction, the very same faculty in them would have seen the truth as keenly as they see what their eyes are turned to now.

Very likely.

Yes, I said; and there is another thing which is likely, or rather a necessary inference from what has preceded, that neither the uneducated and uninformed of the truth, nor yet those who never make an end of their education, will be able ministers of State; not the former, because they have no single aim of duty which is the rule of all their actions, private as well as public; nor the latter, because they will not act at all except upon compulsion, fancying that they are already dwelling apart in the islands of the blest.

Very true, he replied.

Then, I said, the business of us who are the founders of the State will be to compel the best minds to attain that knowledge which we have already shown to be the greatest of all— they must continue to ascend until they arrive at the good; but when they have ascended and seen enough we must not allow them to do as they do now.

What do you mean?

I mean that they remain in the upper world: but this must not be allowed; they must be made to descend again among the prisoners in the den, and partake of their labours and honours, whether they are worth having or not.

But is not this unjust? He said; ought we to give them a worse life, when they might have a better?

You have again forgotten, my friend, I said, the intention of the legislator, who did not aim at making any one class in the State happy above the rest; the happiness was to be in the whole State, and he held the citizens together by persuasion and necessity, making them benefactors of the State, and therefore benefactors of one another; to this end he created them, not to please themselves, but to be his instruments in binding up the State.

True, he said, I had forgotten.

Observe, Glaucon, that there will be no injustice in compelling our philosophers to have a care and providence of others; we shall explain to them that in other States, men of their class are not obliged to share in the toils of politics: and this is reasonable, for they grow up at their own sweet will, and the government would rather not have them. Being self-taught, they cannot be expected to show any gratitude for a culture which they have never received. But we have brought you into the world to be rulers of the hive, kings of yourselves and of the other citizens, and have educated you far better and more perfectly than they have been educated, and you are better able to share in the double duty. Wherefore each of you, when his turn comes, must go down to the general underground abode, and get the habit of seeing in the dark. When you have acquired the habit, you will see ten thousand times better than the inhabitants of the den, and you will know what the several images are, and what they represent, because you have seen the beautiful and just and good in their truth. And thus our State, which is also yours, will be a reality, and not a dream only, and will be administered in a spirit unlike that of other States, in which men fight with one another about shadows only and are distracted in the struggle for power, which in their eyes is a great good. Whereas the truth is that the State in which the rulers are most reluctant to govern is always the best and most quietly governed, and the State in which they are most eager, the worst. . . .

Quite true, he replied.

And will our pupils, when they hear this, refuse to take their turn at the toils of State, when they are allowed to spend the greater part of their time with one another in the heavenly light?

Impossible, he answered; for they are just men, and the commands which we impose upon them are just; there can be no doubt that every one of them will take office as a stern necessity, and not after the fashion of our present rulers of State.

Yes, my friend, I said; and there lies the point. You must contrive for your future rulers another and a better life than that of a ruler, and then you may have a well-ordered State; for only in the State which offers this, will they rule who are truly rich, not in silver and gold, but in virtue and wisdom, which are the true blessings of life. Whereas if they go to the administration of public affairs, poor and hungering after their own private advantage, thinking that hence they are to snatch the chief good, order there can never be; for they will be fighting about office, and the civil and domestic broils which thus arise will be the ruin of the rulers themselves and of the whole State.

Most true, he replied. . . .

And so, Glaucon, we have arrived at the conclusion that in the perfect State wives and children are to be in common; and that all education and the pursuits of war and peace are also to be common, and the best philosophers and the bravest warriors are to be their kings?

That, replied Glaucon, has been acknowledged.

Yes, I said; and we have further acknowledged that the governors, when appointed themselves, will take their soldiers and place them in houses such as we were describing, which are common to all, and contain nothing private, or individual; and about their property, you remember what we agreed?

Yes, I remember that no one was to have any of the ordinary possessions of mankind; they were to be warrior athletes and guardians, receiving from the other citizens, in lieu of annual payment, only their maintenance, and they were to take care of themselves and of the whole State.

Aristarchus

Aristarchus of Samos was a great astronomer of the Hellenistic age. In the third century B.C. he made one of the most accurate computations of the size of the sun and the moon and their distance from the earth. After this work had been published, he became convinced that the sun was the center around which the earth and the planets revolved. The first of the two selections is in Aristarchus' own words, while the second is quoted by Archimedes. In reading them note (1) the advanced knowledge of the nature of the universe possessed by these scientists, and (2) the rationalists' approach to investigating and analyzing the universe of reality.

From: HYPOTHESES

The moon receives its light from the sun.

The earth is in the relation of a point and center of the sphere in which the moon moves.

The distance of the sun from the earth is greater than 18 times, but less than 20 times, the distance of the moon (from the earth).

The diameter of the moon is less than

G. W. Botsford and E. G. Sihler, eds., *Hellenic Civilization*, Columbia University Press, New York, 1915, 639–640. Courtesy of Columbia University Press.

$\frac{2}{45}$ but greater than $\frac{1}{30}$ of the distance of the center of the moon from our eye.

The diameter of the sun has to the diameter of the earth a ratio greater than 19:3 but less than 43:6.

The sun has to the moon a ratio greater than 5832:1 but less than 8000:1.

[The Heliocentric Theory.] The term *world,* as it is defined by most astronomers, is here designed to signify a sphere of the heavens, whose center coincides with the center of the earth, and whose semi-diameter is the distance from the center of the earth to the center of the sun. This definition of the term *world,* as given in the writings of other astronomers, Aristarchus of Samos refutes, and has given it a far more extensive signification; for according to his hypothesis, neither the fixed stars nor the sun are subject to any motion; but the earth annually revolves round the sun in the circumference of a circle, in the center of which the sun remains fixed. The sphere of the fixed stars, too, whose center he supposes to coincide with the sun's, is of such immense magnitude that the circle, in whose periphery the earth is supposed to revolve round the sun, bears no greater proportion to the distance of the fixed stars than the center of a sphere does to its superficies [surface].

Eratosthenes

Eratosthenes (276–196(?) B.C.), one of the great scientists of the Hellenistic age, was librarian at Alexandria, and was particularly interested in astronomy and geography. Although it was a well-known fact in his day that the earth was round, its exact size had not been determined, but Eratosthenes made the closest calculation that had yet been reached. This description of his computation is not in his own words, but was written by Cleomedes in the second century A.D. In reading this selection note (1) the understanding displayed of the universe, (2) the method used to calculate the total circumference, and (3) the results of his computation.

From: CONCERNING THE CIRCULAR MOTION OF THE HEAVENLY BODIES

Under the same meridian, he says, lie Syene and Alexandria. Since then the greatest (lines) in the universe are the meridians, the spherical lines lying under them on the earth must necessarily be the greatest. Consequently whatever extent the theory (of Eratosthenes) will demonstrate for the spherical line running through Syene and Alexandria, so extensive also will be the greatest spherical line of the earth. He then says: And it is so, that Syene lies under the summer solstice. Whenever therefore the sun, having passed into Cancer and, effecting the summer solstice, is precisely at the zenith point of the sky, the gnomon of the sundial necessarily becomes shadowless, in accordance with the exact perpendicular of the sun standing overhead; and it is reasonable that this should happen to the extent of three hundred stadia in diameter. At Alexandria at the same hour the gnomons of the sundials cast a shadow, since this city lies more to the north than Syene. Inasmuch as these cities lie under the same meridian and the greatest spherical line, if we draw the arc from the apex of the shadow of the sundial to the base itself of the sundial which is in Alexandria, this arc will prove a

G. W. Botsford and E. G. Sihler, eds., *Hellenic Civilization,* Columbia University Press, New York, 1915, 636–637. Courtesy of Columbia University Press.

segment of the greatest spherical line in the concave sundial, since the concave surface of the sundial lies under the largest spherical line. If consequently we were to conceive straight lines extended through the earth from each of the sundials, they will meet at the centre of the earth. Since then the sundial at Syene lies perpendicularly under the sun, if we conceive in addition a straight line drawn from the sun to the apex of the style of the sundial, then the line drawn from the sun to the centre of the earth will prove *one* straight line. If then we conceive another straight line from the apex of the shadow of the gnomon drawn up to the sun from the concave dial in Alexandria, this one and the aforesaid straight line will prove to be parallel, passing from different parts of the sun to different parts of the earth. Into these (lines), which are parallel, the line drawn from the centre of the earth to the dial at Alexandria falls as a straight line, so as to render the alternate angles equal. Of these (angles) the one is at the centre of the earth

through the meeting of the straight lines which were drawn from the apex of its shadow. The other angle results through the meeting of (the lines drawn) from the apex of the dial at Alexandria and the line drawn upward from the apex of its shadow to the sun through the contact with it. Upon this is constructed the circular line which has been circumscribed from the apex of the shadow of the gnomon to its base; and upon that at the centre of the earth the (line) which passes from Syene to Alexandria. Similar then are the arcs to each other, namely, those based on equal angles. The relation therefore which the line in the concave has to its own circle is the same as the relation of the line drawn from Syene to Alexandria. The line in the concave is to be $\frac{1}{50}$ of its own circle; therefore necessarily also the distance from Syene to Alexandria must be $\frac{1}{50}$ of the largest circle of earth; and this is (a distance) of 5,000 stadia. The whole circle therefore amounts to 250,000 stadia.

Such is the computation of Eratosthenes.

Roman Civilization

While the Greeks were developing their glorious civilization in the eastern Mediterranean, the Romans were consolidating their position politically on the Italian peninsula and throughout the western Mediterranean generally. War and politics occupied much of their time and energy, and it was only natural that their civilization was dominated by these two activities. Their great men of letters wrote of the excellent qualities of Roman generals and statesmen, and inevitably Roman literature came to be an expression of the national character. When the empire was finally consolidated, and the administration established, Rome's intellectuals turned to other cultural outlets. Here, however, they were unable to create much that was original, but rather they fell back upon the cultural patterns which the Greeks had established. Thus in their epic poetry, their philosophy, their drama, and even in their art they built upon the achievements of the Greeks. Only in government, law, and engineering did the Romans excel, and in these fields the demands of imperial rule over alien peoples made it almost mandatory that they should do so. It was in construction, government, and jurisprudence, then, that the Roman world worked out its greatest contributions to Western Civilization.

Polybius

Polybius (about 205–123 B.C.) was a Greek historian who became interested in the imperial expansion of Rome while a captive in that city. He made an exhaustive study of the written sources and then sought in his Histories to interpret the facts in the light of personal travel to the sites of the events, and through practical experience in politics and warfare. He placed particular importance upon the institutions under which society lived as a determining force in the course of events. In the sixth book he discussed the Roman constitution as one of the factors contributing to Rome's imperial success. In reading the selections from it note (1) the motive of Polybius in writing this book, (2) the appeal for the student of history in the study of events, (3) the influence of Aristotle upon Polybius, (4) the elements of strength in the Roman government, (5) Polybius' feelings toward the Athenian government, (6) the fundamental attributes in every state by which it may be evaluated, (7) Roman practices to preserve the strength of the state, (8) the author's implied forecast of Rome's future, and (9) the extent to which Polybius was an objective historian.

From: THE HISTORIES

I am aware that some will be at a loss to account for my interrupting the course of my narrative for the sake of entering upon the following disquisition on the Roman constitution. But I think that I have already in many passages made it fully evident that this particular branch of my work was one of the necessities imposed on me by the nature of my original design; and I pointed this out with special clearness in the preface which explained the scope of my history. I there stated that the feature of my work which was at once the best in itself, and the most instructive to the students of it, was that it would enable them to know and fully realise in what manner, and under what kind of constitution, it came about that nearly the whole world fell under the power of Rome in somewhat less than fifty-three years, —an event certainly without precedent. This being my settled purpose, I could see no more fitting period than the present for making a pause, and examining the truth of the remarks about to be made on this constitution. In private life if you wish to satisfy yourself as to the badness or goodness of particular persons, you would not, if you wish to get a genuine test, examine their conduct at a time of uneventful repose, but in the hour of brilliant success or conspicuous reverse. For the true test of a perfect man is the power of bearing with spirit and dignity violent changes of fortune. An examination of a constitution should be conducted in the same way: and therefore being unable to find in our day a more rapid or more signal change than that which has happened to Rome, I reserved my disquisition on its constitution for this place. . . .

What is really educational and beneficial to students of history is the clear view of the causes of events, and the consequent power of choosing the better policy in a particular case. Now in every practical undertaking by a state we must regard as the most powerful agent for success or failure the form of its constitution; for from this as from a fountainhead all con-

As translated by Evelyn S. Shuckburgh in *The Histories of Polybius*, 2 vols., Macmillan and Company, London and New York, 1889, I, 458–459; 466–467; 474–475; 494–501; 506–507. Courtesy of The Macmillan Company.

ceptions and plans of action not only proceed, but attain their consummation. . . .

I am fully conscious that to those who actually live under this constitution I shall appear to give an inadequate account of it by the omission of certain details. Knowing accurately every portion of it from personal experience, and from having been bred up in its customs and laws from childhood, they will not be struck so much by the accuracy of the description, as annoyed by its omissions; nor will they believe that the historian has purposely omitted unimportant distinctions, but will attribute his silence upon the origin of existing institutions or other important facts to ignorance. What is told they depreciate as insignificant or beside the purpose; what is omitted they desiderate as vital to the question: their object being to appear to know more than the writers. But a good critic should not judge a writer by what he leaves unsaid, but from what he says: if he detects misstatement in the latter, he may then feel certain that ignorance accounts for the former; but if what he says is accurate, his omissions ought to be attributed to deliberate judgment and not to ignorance. So much for those whose criticisms are prompted by personal ambition rather than by justice. . . .

Another requisite for obtaining a judicious approval for an historical disquisition, is that it should be germane to the matter in hand; if this is not observed, though its style may be excellent and its matter irreproachable, it will seem out of place, and disgust rather than please. . . .

As for the Roman constitution, it had three elements, each of them possessing sovereign powers: and their respective share of power in the whole state had been regulated with such a scrupulous regard to equality and equilibrium, that no one could say for certain, not even a native, whether the constitution as a whole were an aristocracy or democracy or despotism. And no wonder: for if we confine our observation to the power of the Consuls we should be inclined to regard it as despotic; if on that of the Senate, as aristocratic; and if finally one looks at the power possessed by the people it would seem a clear case of a democracy. What the exact powers of these several parts were,

and still, with slight modifications, are, I will now state.

The Consuls, before leading out the legions, remain in Rome and are supreme masters of the administration. All other magistrates, except the Tribunes, are under them and take their orders. They introduce foreign ambassadors to the Senate; bring matters requiring deliberation before it; and see to the execution of its decrees. If, again, there are any matters of state which require the authorisation of the people, it is their business to see to them, to summon the popular meetings, to bring the proposals before them, and to carry out the decrees of the majority. In the preparations for war also, and in a word in the entire administration of a campaign, they have all but absolute power. It is competent to them to impose on the allies such levies as they think good, to appoint the Military Tribunes, to make up the roll for soldiers and select those that are suitable. Besides they have absolute power of inflicting punishment on all who are under their command while on active service: and they have authority to expend as much of the public money as they choose, being accompanied by a Quaestor who is entirely at their orders. A survey of these powers would in fact justify our describing the constitution as despotic,—a clear case of royal government. Nor will it affect the truth of my description, if any of the institutions I have described are changed in our time, or in that of our posterity: and the same remarks apply to what follows.

The Senate has first of all the control of the treasury, and regulates the receipts and disbursements alike. For the Quaestors cannot issue any public money for the various departments of the state without a decree of the Senate, except for the service of the Consuls. The Senate controls also what is by far the largest and most important expenditure, that, namely, which is made by the Censors every *lustrum* for the repair or construction of public buildings; this money cannot be obtained by the Censors except by the grant of the Senate. Similarly all crimes committed in Italy requiring a public investigation, such as treason, conspiracy, poisoning, or wilful murder, are in the hands of the Senate. Besides, if any individual or state among the Italian allies requires a controversy to be settled, a penalty to be assessed, help or protection to be afforded, —all this is the province of the Senate. Or again, outside Italy, if it is necessary to send an embassy to reconcile warring communities, or to remind them of their duty, or sometimes to impose requisitions upon them, or to receive their submission, or finally to proclaim war against them,—this too is the business of the Senate. In like manner the reception to be given to foreign ambassadors in Rome, and the answers to be returned to them, are decided by the Senate. With such business the people have nothing to do. Consequently, if one were staying at Rome when the Consuls were not in town, one would imagine the constitution to be a complete aristocracy: and this has been the idea entertained by many Greeks, and by many kings as well, from the fact that nearly all the business they had with Rome was settled by the Senate.

After this one would naturally be inclined to ask what part is left for the people in the constitution, when the Senate has these various functions, especially the control of the receipts and expenditure of the exchequer; and when the Consuls, again, have absolute power over the details of military preparation, and an absolute authority in the field? There is, however, a part left the people, and it is a most important one. For the people are the sole fountain of honour and of punishment; and it is by these two things and these alone that dynasties and constitutions and, in a word, human society are held together: for where the distinction between them is not sharply drawn both in theory and practice, there no undertaking can be properly administered,—as indeed we might expect when good and bad are held in exactly the same honour. The people then are the only court to decide matters of life and death; and even in cases where the penalty is money, if the sum to be assessed is sufficiently serious, and especially when the accused have held the higher magistracies. And in regard to this arrangement there is one point deserving especial commendation and record. Men who are on trial for their lives at Rome, while sentence is in process of being voted,—if even only one of the tribes whose votes are needed to ratify the sentence has not voted,—have the

privilege at Rome of openly departing and condemning themselves to a voluntary exile. Such men are safe at Naples or Praeneste or at Tibur, and at other towns with which this arrangement has been duly ratified on oath.

Again, it is the people who bestow offices on the deserving, which are the most honourable rewards of virtue. It has also the absolute power of passing or repealing laws; and, most important of all, it is the people who deliberate on the question of peace or war. And when provisional terms are made for alliance, suspension of hostilities, or treaties, it is the people who ratify them, or the reverse.

These considerations again would lead one to say that the chief power in the state was the people's, and that the constitution was a democracy.

Such, then, is the distribution of power between the several parts of the state. I must now show how each of these several parts can, when they choose, oppose or support each other.

The Consul, then, when he has started on an expedition with the powers I have described, is to all appearance absolute in the administration of the business in hand; still he has need of the support both of people and Senate, and, without them, is quite unable to bring the matter to a a successful conclusion. For it is plain that he must have supplies sent to his legions from time to time; but without a decree of the Senate they can be supplied neither with corn, nor clothes, nor pay, so that all the plans of a commander must be futile, if the Senate is resolved either to shrink from danger or hamper his plans. And again, whether a Consul shall bring any undertaking to a conclusion or no depends entirely upon the Senate: for it has absolute authority at the end of a year to send another Consul to supersede him, or to continue the existing one in his command. Again, even to the successes of the generals the Senate has the power to add distinction and glory, and on the other hand to obscure their merits and lower their credit. For these high achievements are brought in tangible form before the eyes of the citizens by what are called "triumphs." But these triumphs the commanders cannot celebrate with proper pomp, or in some cases celebrated at all, unless the Senate concurs and grants the necessary money. As for the people, the Consuls are pre-eminently obliged to court their favour, however distant from home may be the field of their operations; for it is the people, as I have said before, that ratify, or refuse to ratify, terms of peace and treaties; but most of all because when laying down their office they have to give an account of their administration before it. Therefore in no case is it safe for the Consuls to neglect either the Senate or the good-will of the people.

As for the Senate, which possesses the immense power I have described, in the first place it is obliged in public affairs to take the multitude into account, and respect the wishes of the people; and it cannot put into execution the penalty for offences against the republic, which are punishable with death, unless the people first ratify its decrees. Similarly even in matters which directly affect the senators,—for instance, in the case of a law diminishing the Senate's traditional authority, or depriving senators of certain dignities and offices, or even actually cutting down their property,—even in such cases the people have the sole power of passing or rejecting the law. But most important of all is the fact that, if the Tribunes interpose their veto, the Senate not only is unable to pass a decree, but cannot even hold a meeting at all, whether formal or informal. Now, the Tribunes are always bound to carry out the decree of the people, and above all things to have regard to their wishes: therefore, for all these reasons the Senate stands in awe of the multitude, and cannot neglect the feelings of the people.

In like manner the people on their part are far from being independent of the Senate, and are bound to take its wishes into account both collectively and individually. For contracts, too numerous to count, are given out by the Censors in all parts of Italy for the repairs or construction of public buildings; there is also the collection of revenue from many rivers, harbours, gardens, mines, and land—everything, in a word, that comes under the control of the Roman government: and in all these the people at large are engaged; so that there is scarcely a man, so to speak, who is not interested either as a contractor or as being employed in the works. For some purchase the contracts from the Censors for themselves; and others go partners with them; while others again go security for these contractors, or actually pledge their property to the treasury for them. Now over all these transactions the Senate has absolute control. It can grant an extension of time; and in case of unforeseen accident can relieve the contractors from a portion of their obligation, or release them from it altogether, if they are absolutely unable to fulfil it. And there are many details in which the Senate can inflict great hardships, or, on the other hand, grant great indulgences to the contractors: for in every case the appeal is to it. But the most important point of all is that the judges are taken from its members in the majority of trials, whether public or private, in which the charges are heavy. Consequently, all citizens are much at its mercy; and being alarmed at the uncertainty as to when they may need its aid, are cautious about resisting or actively opposing its will. And for a similar reason men do not rashly resist the wishes of the Consuls, because one and all may become subject to their absolute authority on a campaign.

The result of this power of the several estates for mutual help or harm is a union sufficiently firm for all emergencies, and a constitution than which it is impossible to find a better. For whenever any danger from without compels them to unite and work together, the strength which is developed by the State is so extraordinary, that everything required is unfailingly carried out by the eager rivalry shown by all classes to devote their whole minds to the need of the hour, and to secure that any determination come to should not fail for want of promptitude; while each individual works, privately and publicly alike, for the accomplishment of the business in hand. Accordingly, the peculiar constitution of the State makes it irresistible, and certain of obtaining whatever it determines to attempt. Nay, even when these external alarms are past, and the people are enjoying their good fortune and the fruits of their victories, and, as usually happens, growing corrupted by flattery and idleness, show a tendency to violence and arrogance,—it is in these circumstances, more than ever, that the constitution is seen to possess within itself the power of correcting abuses. For when any one of the three classes becomes puffed up, and manifests an inclination to be contentious and unduly encroaching, the mutual interdependency of all the three, and the possibility of the pretensions of any one being checked and thwarted by the others, must plainly check this tendency: and so the proper equilibrium is maintained by the impulsiveness of the one part being checked by its fear of the other. . . .

Nearly all historians have recorded as constitutions of eminent excellence those of Lacedaemonia, Crete, Mantinea, and Carthage. Some have also mentioned those of Athens and Thebes. The former I may allow to pass; but I am convinced that little need be said of the Athenian and Theban constitutions: their growth was abnormal, the period of their zenith brief, and the changes they experienced unusually violent. Their glory was a sudden and fortuitous flash, so to speak; and while they still thought themselves prosperous, and likely to remain so, they found themselves involved in circumstances completely the reverse. The Thebans got their reputation for valour among the Greeks, by taking advantage of the senseless policy of the Lacedaemonians, and the hatred of the allies towards them, owing to the valour of one, or at most two, men who were wise enough to appreciate the situation. Since fortune quickly made it evident that it was not the peculiarity of their constitution, but the valour of their leaders, which gave the Thebans their success. For the great power of Thebes notoriously took its rise, attained its zenith, and fell to the ground with the lives of Epaminondas and Pelopidas. We must therefore conclude that it was not its constitution, but its men, that caused the high fortune which it then enjoyed.

A somewhat similar remark applies to the Athenian constitution also. For though it perhaps had more frequent interludes of excellence, yet its highest perfection was attained during the brilliant career of Themistocles; and having reached that point it quickly declined, owing to its essential instability. For the Athenian demos is always in the position of a ship without a commander. In such a ship, if fear of the enemy, or the occurrence of a storm,

induce the crew to be of one mind and to obey the helmsman, everything goes well; but if they recover from this fear, and begin to treat their officers with contempt, and to quarrel with each other because they are no longer all of one mind,—one party wishing to continue the voyage, and the other urging the steersman to bring the ship to anchor; some letting out the sheets, and others hauling them in, and ordering the sails to be furled,—their discord and quarrels make a sorry show to lookers on; and the position of affairs is full of risk to those on board engaged on the same voyage: and the result has often been that, after escaping the dangers of the widest seas, and the most violent storms, they wreck their ship in harbour and close to shore. And this is what has often happened to the Athenian constitution. For, after repelling, on various occasions, the greatest and most formidable dangers by the valour of its people and their leaders, there have been times when, in periods of secure tranquillity, it has gratuitously and recklessly encountered disaster. Therefore I need say no more about either it, or the Theban constitution: in both of which a mob manages everything on its own unfettered impulse—a mob in the one city distinguished for headlong outbursts of fiery temper, in the other trained in long habits of violence and ferocity. . . .

To my mind, then, there are two things fundamental to every state, in virtue of which its powers and constitution become desirable or objectionable. These are customs and laws. Of these the desirable are those which make men's private lives holy and pure, and the public character of the state civilised and just. The objectionable are those whose effect is the reverse. As, then, when we see good customs and good laws prevailing among certain people, we confidently assume that, in consequence of them, the men and their civil constitution will be good also, so when we see private life full of covetousness, and public policy of injustice, plainly we have reason for asserting their laws, particular customs, and general constitution to be bad. . . .

Now the Carthaginian constitution seems to me originally to have been well contrived in these most distinctively important particulars. For they had kings, and the Gerusia had the powers of an aristocracy, and the multitude were supreme in such things as affected them; and on the whole the adjustment of its several parts was very like that of Rome and Sparta. But about the period of its entering on the Hannibalian war the political state of Carthage was on the decline, that of Rome improving. For whereas there is in every body, or polity, or business a natural stage of growth, zenith, and decay; and whereas everything in them is at its best at the zenith; we may thereby judge of the difference between these two constitutions as they existed at that period. For exactly so far as the strength and prosperity of Carthage preceded that of Rome in point of time, by so much was Carthage then past its prime, while Rome was exactly at its zenith, as far as its political constitution was concerned. In Carthage therefore the influence of the people in the policy of the state had already risen to be supreme, while at Rome the Senate was at the height of its power: and so, as in the one, measures were deliberated upon by the many, in the other, by the best men, the policy of the Romans in all public undertakings proved the stronger; on which account, though they met with capital disasters, by force of prudent counsels they finally conquered the Carthaginians in the war.

If we look however at separate details, for instance at the provisions for carrying on a war, we shall find that whereas for a naval expedition the Carthaginians are the better trained and prepared—as it is only natural with a people with whom it has been hereditary for many generations to practise this craft, and to follow the seaman's trade above all nations in the world—yet, in regard to military service on land, the Romans train themselves to a much higher pitch than the Carthaginians. The former bestow their whole attention upon this department: whereas the Carthaginians wholly neglect their infantry, though they do take some slight interest in the cavalry. The reason for this is that they employ foreign mercenaries, the Romans, native and citizen levies. It is in this point that the latter polity is preferable to the former. They have their hopes of freedom ever resting on the courage of mercenary troops: The Romans on the valour of their own citizens and the aid of their allies. The result is that even if the Romans have suffered a defeat at first, they renew the war with undiminished forces, which the Carthaginians cannot do. For, as the Romans are fighting for country and children, it is impossible for them to relax the fury of their struggle; but they persist with obstinate resolution until they have overcome their enemies. What has happened in regard to their navy is an instance in point. In skill the Romans are much behind the Carthaginians, as I have already said; yet the upshot of the whole naval war has been a decided triumph for the Romans, owing to the valour of their men. For although nautical science contributes largely to success in sea-fights, still it is the courage of the marines that turns the scale most decisively in favour of victory. The fact is that Italians as a nation are by nature superior to Phoenicians and Libyans both in physical strength and courage; but still their habits also do much to inspire the youth with enthusiasm for such exploits. One example will be sufficient of the pains taken by the Roman state to turn out men ready to endure anything to win a reputation in their country for valour.

Whenever one of their illustrious men dies, in the course of his funeral, the body with all its paraphernalia is carried into the forum to the rostra, as a raised platform there is called, and sometimes is propped upright upon it so as to be conspicuous, or, more rarely, is laid upon it. Then with all the people standing round, his son, if he has left one of full age and he is there, or, failing him, one of his relations, mounts the rostra and delivers a speech concerning the virtues of the deceased, and the successful exploits performed by him in his lifetime. By these means the people are reminded of what has been done, and made to see it with their own eyes—not only such as were engaged in the actual transactions but those also who were not—and their sympathies are so deeply moved, that the loss appears not to be confined to the actual mourners, but to be a public one affecting the whole people. After the burial and all the usual ceremonies have been performed, they place the likeness of the deceased in the most conspicuous spot in his house, surmounted by a wooden canopy or shrine. This likeness consists of a mask made to represent the deceased with extraordinary fidelity both in shape and colour. These likenesses they display at public sacrifices adorned with much care. And when any illustrious member of the family dies, they carry these masks to the funeral, putting them on men whom they thought as like the originals as possible in height and other personal peculiarities. And these substitutes assume clothes according to the rank of the person represented: if he was a Consul or Praetor, a toga with purple stripes; if a Censor, whole purple; if he had also celebrated a triumph or performed any exploit of that kind, a toga embroidered with gold. These representatives also ride themselves in chariots, while the fasces and axes, and all the other customary insignia of the particular offices, lead the way, according to the dignity of the rank in the state enjoyed by the deceased in his lifetime; and on arriving at the rostra they all take their seats on ivory chairs in their order. There could not easily be a more inspiring spectacle than this for a young man of noble ambitions and virtuous aspirations. For can we conceive any one to be unmoved at the sight of all the likenesses collected together of the men who have earned glory, all as it were living and breathing? Or what could be a more glorious spectacle?

Besides, the speaker over the body about to be buried, after having finished the panegyric of this particular person, starts upon the others whose representatives are present, beginning with the most ancient, and recounts the successes and achievements of each. By this means the glorious memory of brave men is continually renewed; the fame of those who have performed any noble deed is never allowed to die; and the renown of those who have done good service to their country becomes a matter of common knowledge to the multitude, and part of the heritage of posterity. But the chief benefit of the ceremony is that it inspires young men to shrink from no exertion for the general welfare, in the hope of obtaining the glory which awaits the brave. And what I say is confirmed by this fact. Many Romans have volunteered to decide a whole battle by single combat; not a few have deliberately accepted certain death, some in time of war to secure the safety of the rest, some in time of peace to preserve the safety of the commonwealth. There have also been instances of men in office putting their own sons to death, in defiance of every custom and law, because they rated the interest of their country higher than those of natural ties even with their nearest and dearest. There are many stories of this kind, related of many men in Roman history; but one will be enough for our present purpose; and I will give the name as an instance to prove the truth of my words.

The story goes that Horatius Cocles, while fighting with two enemies at the head of the bridge over the Tiber, which is the entrance to the city on the north, seeing a large body of men advancing to support his enemies, and fearing that they would force their way into the city, turned round, and shouted to those behind him to hasten back to the other side and break down the bridge. They obeyed him: and whilst they were breaking the bridge, he remained at his post receiving numerous wounds, and checked the progress of the enemy: his opponents being panic-stricken, not so much by his strength as by the audacity with which he held his ground. When the bridge had been broken down, the attack of the enemy was stopped; and Cocles then threw himself into the river with his armour on and deliberately sacrificed his life, because he valued the safety of his country and his own future reputation more highly than his present life, and the years of existence that remained to him. Such is the enthusiasm and emulation for noble deeds that are engendered among the Romans by their customs.

Again the Roman customs and principles regarding money transactions are better than those of the Carthaginians. In the view of the latter, nothing is disgraceful that makes for gain; with the former nothing is more disgraceful than to receive bribes and to make profit by improper means. For they regard wealth obtained from unlawful transactions to be as much a subject of reproach, as a fair profit from the most unquestioned source is of commendation. A proof of the fact is this: The Carthaginians obtain office by open bribery, but among the Romans the penalty for it is death. With such a radical difference, therefore, between the rewards offered to virtue among the two peoples, it is natural that the ways adopted for obtaining them should be different also.

But the most important difference for the better which the Roman commonwealth appears to me to display is in their religious beliefs. For I conceive that what in other nations is looked upon as a reproach, I mean a scrupulous fear of the gods, is the very thing which keeps the Roman commonwealth together. To such an extraordinary height is this carried among them, both in private and public business, that nothing could exceed it. Many people might think this unaccountable; but in my opinion their object is to use it as a check upon the common people. If it were possible to form a state wholly of philosophers, such a custom would perhaps be unnecessary. But seeing that every multitude is fickle, and full of lawless desires, unreasoning anger, and violent passion, the only resource is to keep them in check by mysterious terrors and scenic efforts of this sort. Wherefore, to my mind, the ancients were not acting without purpose or at random, when they brought in among the vulgar those opinions about the gods, and the belief in the punishments in Hades: much rather do I think that men nowadays are acting rashly and foolishly in rejecting them. This is the reason why, apart from anything else, Greek statesmen, if entrusted with a single talent, though protected by ten checking-clerks, as many seals, and twice as many witnesses, yet cannot be induced to keep faith: whereas among the Romans, in their magistracies and embassies, men have the handling of a great amount of money, and yet from pure respect to their oath keep their faith intact. And, again, in other nations it is a rare thing to find a man who keeps his hands out of the public purse, and is entirely pure in such matters: but among the Romans it is a rare thing to detect a man in the act of committing such a crime. . . .

That to all things, then, which exist there is ordained decay and change I think requires no further arguments to show: for the inexorable course of nature is sufficient to convince us of it.

But in all polities we observe two sources of decay existing from natural causes, the one external, the other internal and self-produced. The external admits of no certain or fixed definition, but the internal follows a definite order. What kind of polity, then, comes naturally first, and what second, I have already stated in such a way, that those who are capable of taking in the whole drift of my argument can henceforth draw their own conclusions as to the future of the Roman polity. For it is quite clear, in my opinion. When a commonwealth, after warding off many great dangers, has arrived at a high pitch of prosperity and undisputed power, it is evident that, by the lengthened continuance of great wealth within it, the manner of life of its citizens will become more extravagant; and that the rivalry for office, and in other spheres of activity, will become fiercer than it ought to be. And as this state of things goes on more and more, the desire of office and the shame of losing reputation, as well as the ostentation and extravagance of living, will prove the beginning of a deterioration. And of this change the people will be credited with being the authors, when they become convinced that they are being cheated by some from avarice, and are puffed up with flattery by others from love of office. For when that comes about, in their passionate resentment and acting under the dictates of anger, they will refuse to obey any longer, or to be content with having equal powers with their leaders, but will demand to have all or far the greatest themselves. And when that comes to pass the constitution will receive a new name, which sounds better than any other in the world, liberty or democracy; but, in fact, it will become that worst of all governments, mob-rule.

With this description of the formation, growth, zenith, and present state of the Roman polity, and having discussed also its difference, for better and worse, from other polities, I will now at length bring my essay on it to an end.

Plutarch

Plutarch (46?–120?), a Greek moralist and biographer, wrote a series of books each containing lives of one Greek and one Roman, followed by a comparison of the two (many of the comparisons are lacking, either lost or not completed). The author was primarily concerned with depicting character rather than delineating the intricacies of political intrigue and state building. Caius Julius Caesar (100–44 B.C.) lived during a period of civil strife between the Senate and the popular party at Rome. He associated himself with the latter group in its efforts to break down the walls of privilege which the Senate sought to preserve under the cloak of republican institutions. In 50 B.C. the conflict reached a climax when Caesar, fresh from his Gallic triumphs, sought election to the consulship while still in his province. His enemies raised legal difficulties against his ambitions, and Pompey, as sole consul, became his principal antagonist. In 49 B.C. Caesar led his legions across the Rubicon River, the boundary of his province, and the civil war was on. Caesar defeated Pompey and eventually achieved supreme power. In reading Plutarch's biography, note (1) the means Caesar used to gain popularity, (2) his political machinations, (3) evidence of his ambition, (4) his military ability and his methods of cultivating leadership, (5) Plutarch's explanation of why the Romans made Caesar dictator for life, (6) Caesar's treatment of his opponents, (7) Caesar's achievements and plans for Rome, (8) the causes of Caesar's downfall, (9) the incidents leading to and the aftermath of Caesar's murder, (10) evidences of belief in the intervention of the supernatural in everyday occurrences, and (11) the extent to which Plutarch understood the forces producing the concentration and consolidation of power at Rome.

From: THE LIVES

. . . In his pleadings at Rome, his eloquence soon obtained him great credit and favor, and he won no less upon the affections of the people by the affability of his manners and address, in which he showed a tact and consideration beyond what could have been expected at his age; and the open house he kept, the entertainments he gave, and the general splendor of his manner of life contributed little by little to create and increase his political influence. His enemies slighted the growth of it at first, presuming it would soon fail when his money was gone; whilst in the meantime it was growing up and flourishing among the common people. When his power at last was established and not to be overthrown, and now openly

As translated by John Dryden and revised by A. H. Clough in *Plutarch's Lives. The Translation called Dryden's. Corrected from the Greek and Revised,* Boston: Little, Brown, and Company, 1888, IV, 259–262; 267–268; 271–274; 313–319; 321–328.

tended to the altering of the whole constitution, they were aware too late that there is no beginning so mean, which continued application will not make considerable, and that despising a danger at first, will make it at last irresistible. Cicero was the first who had any suspicions of his designs upon the government, and, as a good pilot is apprehensive of a storm when the sea is most smiling, saw the designing temper of the man through this disguise of good-humor and affability, and said, that in general, in all he did and undertook, he detected the ambition for absolute power, "but when I see his hair so carefully arranged, and observe him adjusting it with one finger, I cannot imagine it should enter into such a man's thoughts to subvert the Roman state.". . .

The first proof he had of the people's goodwill to him, was when he received by their suffrages a tribuneship in the army, and came out on the list with a higher place than Caius Popilius. A second and clearer instance of their favor appeared upon his making a magnificent oration in praise of his aunt Julia, wife to Marius, publicly in the forum, at whose funeral he was so bold as to bring forth the images of Marius, which nobody had dared to produce since the government came into Sylla's hands, Marius's party having from that time been declared enemies of the State. When some who were present had begun to raise a cry against Cæsar, the people answered with loud shouts and clapping in his favor, expressing their joyful surprise and satisfaction at his having, as it were, brought up again from the grave those honors of Marius, which for so long a time had been lost to the city.

It had always been the custom at Rome to make funeral orations in praise of elderly matrons, but there was no precedent of any upon young women till Cæsar first made one upon the death of his own wife. This also procured him favor, and by this show of affection he won upon the feelings of the people, who looked upon him as a man of great tenderness and kindness of heart.

After he had buried his wife, he went as quæstor into Spain under one of the prætors, named Vetus, whom he honored ever after, and made his son his own quæstor, when he himself came to be prætor. After this employment was

ended, he married Pompeia, his third wife, having then a daughter by Cornelia, his first wife, whom he afterwards married to Pompey the Great. He was so profuse in his expenses, that before he had any public employment, he was in debt thirteen hundred talents, and many thought that by incurring such expense to be popular, he changed a solid good for what would prove but a short and uncertain return; but in truth he was purchasing what was of the greatest value at an inconsiderable rate. When he was made surveyor of the Appian Way, he disbursed, besides the public money, a great sum out of his private purse; and when he was ædile, he provided such a number of gladiators, that he entertained the people with three hundred and twenty single combats, and by his great liberality and magnificence in theatrical shows, in processions, and public feastings, he threw into the shade all the attempts that had been made before him, and gained so much upon the people, that every one was eager to find out new offices and new honors for him in return for his munificence.

There being two factions in the city, one that of Sylla, which was very powerful, the other that of Marius, which was then broken and in a very low condition, he undertook to revive this and to make it his own. And to this end, whilst he was in the height of his repute with the people for the magnificent shows he gave as ædile, he ordered images of Marius, and figures of Victory, with trophies in their hands, to be carried privately in the night and placed in the capitol. Next morning, when some saw them bright with gold and beautifully made, with inscriptions upon them, referring them to Marius's exploits over the Cimbrians, they were surprised at the boldness of him who had set them up, nor was it difficult to guess who it was. The fame of this soon spread and brought together a great concourse of people. Some cried out that it was an open attempt against the established government thus to revive those honors which had been buried by the laws and decrees of the senate; that Cæsar had done it to sound the temper of the people whom he had prepared before, and to try whether they were tame enough to bear his humor, and would quietly give way to his innovations. On the other hand, Marius's party took courage, and it was incredible how numerous they were suddenly seen to be, and what a multitude of them appeared and came shouting into the capitol.

Many, when they saw Marius's likeness, cried for joy, and Cæsar was highly extolled as the one man, in the place of all others, who was a relation worthy of Marius. Upon this the senate met, and Catulus Lutatius, one of the most eminent Romans of that time, stood up and inveighed against Cæsar, closing his speech with the remarkable saying, that Cæsar was now not working mines, but planting batteries to overthrow the state. But when Cæsar had made an apology for himself, and satisfied the senate, his admirers were very much animated, and advised him not to depart from his own thoughts for any one, since with the people's good favor he would ere long get the better of them all, and be the first man in the commonwealth. . . .

Cæsar, in the meantime, being out of his prætorship, had got the province of Spain, but was in great embarrassment with his creditors, who, as he was going off, came upon him, and were very pressing and importunate. This led him to apply himself to Crassus, who was the richest man in Rome, but wanted Cæsar's youthful vigor and heat to sustain the opposition against Pompey. Crassus took upon him to satisfy those creditors who were most uneasy to him, and would not be put off any longer, and engaged himself to the amount of eight hundred and thirty talents, upon which Cæsar was now at liberty to go to his province. In his journey, as he was crossing the Alps, and passing by a small village of the barbarians with but few inhabitants, and those wretchedly poor, his companions asked the question among themselves by way of mockery, if there were any canvassing for offices there; any contention which should be uppermost, or feuds of great men one against another. To which Cæsar made answer seriously, "For my part, I had rather be the first man among these fellows, than the second man in Rome."

It is said that another time, when free from business in Spain, after reading some part of the history of Alexander, he sat a great while very thoughtful, and at last burst out into tears. His friends were surprised, and asked him the reason of it. "Do you think," said he, "I have not just cause to weep, when I consider that Alexander at may age had conquered so many nations, and I have all this time done nothing that is memorable?"

As soon as he came into Spain he was very active, and in a few days had got together ten new cohorts of foot in addition to the twenty which were there before. With these he marched against the Calaici and Lusitani and conquered them, and advancing as far as the ocean, subdued the tribes which never before had been subject to the Romans.

Having managed his military affairs with good success, he was equally happy in the course of his civil government. He took pains to establish a good understanding amongst the several states, and no less care to heal the differences between debtors and creditors. He ordered that the creditor should receive two parts of the debtor's yearly income, and that the other part should be managed by the debtor himself, till by this method the whole debt was at last discharged. This conduct made him leave his province with a fair reputation; being rich himself, and having enriched his soldiers, and having received from them the honorable name of Imperator. . . .

Thus far have we followed Cæsar's actions before the wars of Gaul. After this, he seems to begin his course afresh, and to enter upon a new life and scene of action. And the period of those wars which he now fought, and those many expeditions in which he subdued Gaul, showed him to be a soldier and general not in the least inferior to any of the greatest and most admired commanders who had ever appeared at the head of armies. For if we compare him with the Fabii, the Metelli, the Scipios, and with those who were his contemporaries, or not long before him, Sylla, Marius, the two Luculli, or even Pompey himself, whose glory, it may be said, went up at that time to heaven for every excellence in war, we shall find Cæsar's actions to have surpassed them all. One he may be held to have outdone in consideration of the difficulty of the country in which he fought, another in the extent of territory which he conquered; some, in the number and strength of the enemies whom he defeated; one man, because of the wildness and perfidiousness of the tribes whose good-will he conciliated, another in his humanity and clemency to those he overpowered; others, again, in his gifts and kindnesses to his soldiers; all alike in the number of the battles which he fought and the enemies whom he killed. For he had not pursued the wars in Gaul full ten years, when he had taken by storm above eight hundred towns, subdued three hundred states, and of the three millions of men, who made up the gross sum of those with whom at several times he engaged, he had killed one million, and taken captive a second.

He was so much master of the good-will and hearty service of his soldiers, that those who in other expeditions were but ordinary men displayed a courage past defeating or withstanding when they went upon any danger where Cæsar's glory was concerned. Such a one was Acilius, who, in the sea-fight before Marseilles, had his right hand struck off with a sword, yet did not quit his buckler out of his left, but struck the enemies in the face with it, till he drove them off, and made himself master of the vessel. Such another was Cassius Scæva, who, in a battle near Dyrrhachium, had one of his eyes shot out with an arrow, his shoulder pierced with one javelin, and his thigh with another; and having received one hundred and thirty darts upon his target, called to the enemy, as though he would surrender himself. But when two of them came up to him, he cut off the shoulder of one with a sword, and by a blow over the face forced the other to retire, and so with the assistance of his friends, who now came up, made his escape.

Again, in Britain, when some of the foremost officers had accidentally got into a morass full of water, and there were assaulted by the enemy, a common soldier, whilst Cæsar stood and looked on, threw himself into the midst of them, and after many signal demonstrations of his valor, rescued the officers, and beat off the barbarians. He himself, in the end, took to the water, and with much difficulty, partly by swimming, partly by wading, passed it, but in the passage lost his shield. Cæsar and his officers saw it and admired, and went to meet him with joy and acclamation. But the soldier, much dejected and in tears, threw himself down at Cæsar's feet, and begged his pardon for having let go his buckler. Another time in Africa, Scipio having taken a ship of Cæsar's in which Granius Petro, lately appointed quæstor, was sailing, gave the other passengers as free prize to his soldiers, but thought fit to offer the quæstor his life. But he said it was not usual for Cæsar's soldiers to take, but give mercy, and having said so, fell upon his sword and killed himself.

This love of honor and passion for distinction were inspired into them and cherished in them by Cæsar himself, who, by his unsparing distribution of money and honors, showed them that he did not heap up wealth from the wars for his own luxury, or the gratifying his private pleasures, but that all he received was but a public fund laid by for the reward and encouragement of valor, and that he looked upon all he gave to deserving soldiers as so much increase to his own riches. Added to this, also, there was no danger to which he did not willingly expose himself, no labor from which he pleaded an exemption. His contempt of danger was not so much wondered at by his soldiers, because they knew how much he coveted honor. But his enduring so much hardship, which he did to all appearance beyond his natural strength, very much astonished them. For he was a spare man, had a soft and white skin, was distempered in the head, and subject to an epilepsy, which, it is said, first seized him at Corduba. But he did not make the weakness of his constitution a pretext for his ease, but rather used war as the best physic against his indispositions; whilst, by indefatigable journeys, coarse diet, frequent lodging in the field, and continual laborious exercise, he struggled with his diseases and fortified his body against all attacks. He slept generally in his chariots or litters, employing even his rest in pursuit of action. In the day he was thus carried to the forts, garrisons, and camps, one servant sitting with him, who used to write down what he dictated as he went, and a soldier attending behind him with his sword drawn. He drove so rapidly, that when he first left Rome, he arrived at the river Rhone within eight days. He had been an expert rider from his childhood; for it was usual with him to sit with his hands joined together behind his back, and so to put his horse to its full speed. And in this way he disciplined himself so far as to be able to dictate letters from on horseback, and to give directions to two who took notes at the same time, or, as Oppius says, to more. And it is thought that he was the first who contrived means for communicating with friends by cipher, when either press of business, or the large extent of the city, left him no time for a personal conference about matters that required dispatch. . . .

His countrymen, conceding all to his fortune, and accepting the bit, in the hope that the government of a single person would give them time to breathe after so many civil wars and calamities, made him dictator for life. This was indeed a tyranny avowed, since his power now was not only absolute, but perpetual too. Cicero made the first proposals to the senate for conferring honors upon him, which might in some sort be said not to exceed the limits of ordinary human moderation. But others, striving which should deserve most, carried them so excessively high, that they made Cæsar odious to the most indifferent and moderate sort of men, by the pretention and extravagance of the titles which they decreed him. His enemies, too, are thought to have had some share in this, as well as his flatterers. It gave them advantage against him, and would be their justification for any attempt they should make upon him; for since the civil wars were ended, he had nothing else that he could be charged with. And they had good reason to decree a temple to Clemency, in token of their thanks for the mild use he made of his victory. For he not only pardoned many of those who fought against him, but, further, to some gave honors and offices; as particularly to Brutus and Cassius, who both of them were prætors. Pompey's images that were thrown down, he set up again, upon which Cicero also said that by raising Pompey's statues he had fixed his own.

When his friends advised him to have a guard, and several offered their service, he would not hear of it; but said it was better to suffer death once, than always to live in fear of it. He looked upon the affections of the people to be the best and surest guard, and entertained them again with public feasting, and general distributions of corn; and to gratify his army, he sent out colonies to several places, of which the most remarkable were Carthage and Corinth; which as before they had been ruined at the same time, so now were restored and re-peopled together.

As for the men of high rank, he promised to some of them future consulships and prætorships, some he consoled with other offices and honors, and to all held out hopes of favor by the solicitude he showed to rule with the general good-will; insomuch that upon the death of Maximus one day before his consulship was ended, he made Caninius Revilius consul for that day. And when many went to pay the usual compliments and attentions to the new consul, "Let us make haste," said Cicero, "lest the man be gone out of his office before we come."

Cæsar was born to do great things, and had a passion after honor, and the many noble exploits he had done did not now serve as an inducement to him to sit still and reap the fruit of his past labors, but were incentives and encouragements to go on, and raised in him ideas of still greater actions, and a desire of new glory, as if the present were all spent. It was in fact a sort of emulous struggle with himself, as it had been with another, how he might outdo his past actions by his future.

In pursuit of these thoughts, he resolved to make war upon the Parthians, and when he had subdued them, to pass through Hyrcania; thence to march along by the Caspian Sea to Mount Caucasus, and so on about Pontus, till he came into Scythia; then to overrun all the countries bordering upon Germany, and Germany itself; and so to return through Gaul into Italy, after completing the whole circle of his intended empire, and bounding it on every side by the ocean. While preparations were making for this expedition, he proposed to dig through the isthmus on which Corinth stands; and appointed Anienus to superintend the work. He had also a design of diverting the Tiber, and carrying it by a deep channel directly from Rome to Circeii, and so into the sea near Tarracina, that there might be a safe and easy passage for all merchants who traded to Rome. Besides this, he intended to drain all the marshes by Pomentium and Setia, and gain ground enough from the water to employ many thousands of men in tillage. He proposed further to make great mounds on the shore nearest Rome, to hinder the sea from breaking in upon the land, to clear the coast at Ostia of all the hidden rocks and shoals that made it unsafe for shipping, and to form ports and harbors, fit to receive the large number of vessels that would frequent them.

These things were designed without being carried into effect; but the reformation of the calendar, in order to rectify the irregularity of time, was not only projected with great scientific ingenuity, but was brought to its completion, and proved of very great use. For it was not only in ancient times that the Romans had wanted a certain rule to make the revolutions of their months fall in with the course of the year, so that their festivals and solemn days for sacrifice were removed by little and little, till at last they came to be kept at seasons quite the contrary to what was at first intended, but even at this time the people had no way of computing the solar year; only the priests could say the time, and they, at their pleasure, without giving any notice, slipped in the intercalary month, which they called Mercedonius. Numa was the first who put in this month, but his expedient was but a poor one and quite inadequate to correct all the errors that arose in the returns of the annual cycles, as we have shown in his life. Cæsar called in the best philosophers and mathematicians of his time to settle the point, and out of the systems he had before him, formed a new and more exact method of correcting the calendar, which the Romans use to this day, and seem to succeed better than any nation in avoiding the errors occasioned by the inequality of the cycles. Yet even this gave offence to those who looked with an evil eye on his position, and felt oppressed by his power. Cicero, the orator, when some one in his company chanced to say, the next morning Lyra would rise, replied, "Yes, in accordance with the edict," as if even this were a matter of compulsion.

But that which brought upon him the most apparent and mortal hatred was his desire of being king; which gave the common people the first occasion to quarrel with him, and proved the most specious pretence to those who had been his secret enemies all along. Those, who would have procured him that title, gave

it out, that it was foretold in the Sibyls' books that the Romans should conquer the Parthians when they fought against them under the conduct of a king, but not before. And one day, as Cæsar was coming down from Alba to Rome, some were so bold as to salute him by the name of king; but he, finding the people disrelish it, seemed to resent it himself, and said his name was Cæsar, not king. Upon this, there was a general silence, and he passed on looking not very well pleased or contented.

Another time, when the senate had conferred on him some extravagant honors, he chanced to receive the message as he was sitting on the rostra, where, though the consuls and prætors themselves waited on him, attended by the whole body of the senate, he did not rise, but behaved himself to them as if they had been private men, and told them his honors wanted rather to be retrenched than increased. This treatment offended not only the senate, but the commonalty too, as if they thought the affront upon the senate equally reflected upon the whole republic; so that all who could decently leave him went off, looking much discomposed. Cæsar, perceiving the false step he had made, immediately retired home; and laying his throat bare, told his friends that he was ready to offer this to any one who would give the stroke. But afterwards he made the malady from which he suffered the excuse for his sitting, saying that those who are attacked by it lose their presence of mind if they talk much standing; that they presently grow giddy, fall into convulsions, and quite lose their reason. But this was not the reality, for he would willingly have stood up to the senate, had not Cornelius Balbus, one of his friends, or rather flatterers, hindered him. "Will you not remember," said he, "you are Cæsar, and claim the honor which is due to your merit?"

He gave a fresh occasion of resentment by his affront to the tribunes. The Lupercalia were then celebrated, a feast at the first institution belonging, as some writers say, to the shepherds, and having some connection with the Arcadian Lycæa. . . . Cæsar, dressed in a triumphal robe, seated himself in a golden chair at the rostra to view this ceremony. Antony, as consul, was one of those who ran this course, and when he came into the forum, and the people made way for him, he went up and reached to Cæsar a diadem wreathed with laurel. Upon this, there was a shout, but only a slight one, made by the few who were planted there for that purpose; but when Cæsar refused it, there was universal applause. Upon the second offer, very few, and upon the second refusal, all again applauded. Cæsar finding it would not take, rose up, and ordered the crown to be carried into the capitol. Cæsar's statues were afterwards found with royal diadems on their heads. Flavius and Marullus, two tribunes of the people, went presently and pulled them off, and having apprehended those who first saluted Cæsar as king, committed them to prison. The people followed them with acclamations, and called them by the name of Brutus, because Brutus was the first who ended the succession of kings, and transferred the power which before was lodged in one man into the hands of the senate and people. Cæsar so far resented this, that he displaced Marullus and Flavius; and in urging his charges against them, at the same time ridiculed the people, by himself giving the men more than once the names of Bruti, and Cumæi [implying stupidity and dullness]. . . .

In this juncture, Decimus Brutus, surnamed Albinus, one whom Cæsar had such confidence in that he made him his second heir, who nevertheless was engaged in the conspiracy with the other Brutus and Cassius, fearing lest if Cæsar should put off the senate to another day, the business might get wind, spoke scoffingly and in mockery of the diviners, and blamed Cæsar for giving the senate so fair an occasion of saying he had put a slight upon them, for that they were met upon his summons, and were ready to vote unanimously, that he should be declared king of all the provinces out of Italy, and might wear a diadem in any other place but Italy, by sea or land. If any one should be sent to tell them they might break up for the present, and meet again when Calpurnia should chance to have better dreams, what would his enemies say? Or who would with any patience hear his friends, if they should presume to defend his government as not arbitrary and tyrannical? But if he was possessed so far as to think this day unfortunate, yet it were more decent to go himself to the senate, and to ad-

journ it in his own person. Brutus, as he spoke these words, took Cæsar by the hand, and conducted him forth. He was not gone far from the door, when a servant of some other person's made towards him, but not being able to come up to him, on account of the crowd of those who pressed about him, he made his way into the house, and committed himself to Calpurnia, begging of her to secure him till Cæsar returned, because he had matters of great importance to communicate to him. . . .

The place which was destined for the scene of this [Cæsar's] murder, in which the senate met that day, was the same in which Pompey's statue stood, and was one of the edifices which Pompey had raised and dedicated with his theatre to the use of the public, plainly showing that there was something of a supernatural influence which guided the action, and ordered it to that particular place. Cassius, just before the act, is said to have looked towards Pompey's statue, and silently implored his assistance, though he had been inclined to the doctrines of Epicurus. But this occasion and the instant danger, carried him away out of all his reasonings, and filled him for the time with a sort of inspiration. As for Antony, who was firm to Cæsar, and a strong man, Brutus Albinus kept him outside the house, and delayed him with a long conversation contrived on purpose.

When Cæsar entered, the senate stood up to show their respect to him, and of Brutus's confederates, some came about his chair and stood behind it, others met him, pretending to add their petitions to those of Tillius Cimber, in behalf of his brother, who was in exile; and they followed him with their joint supplications till he came to his seat. When he was sat down, he refused to comply with their requests, and upon their urging him further, began to reproach them severally for their importunities, when Tillius, laying hold of his robe with both his hands, pulled it down from his neck, which was the signal for the assault. Casca gave him the first cut, in the neck, which was not mortal nor dangerous, as coming from one who at the beginning of such a bold action was probably very much disturbed. Cæsar immediately turned about, and laid his hand upon the dagger and kept hold of it. And both of them at the same time cried out, he that received the blow, in Latin, "Vile Casca, what does this mean?" and he that gave it, in Greek, to his brother, "Brother, help!" Upon this first onset, those who were not privy to the design were astonished, and their horror and amazement at what they saw were so great that they durst not fly nor assist Cæsar, nor so much as speak a word. But those who came prepared for the business enclosed him on every side, with their naked daggers in their hands. Which way soever he turned, he met with blows, and saw their swords levelled at his face and eyes, and was encompassed, like a wild beast in the toils, on every side. For it had been agreed they should each of them make a thrust at him, and flesh themselves with his blood; for which reason Brutus also gave him one stab in the groin.

Some say that he fought and resisted all the rest, shifting his body to avoid the blows, and calling out for help, but that when he saw Brutus's sword drawn, he covered his face with his robe and submitted, letting himself fall, whether it were by chance, or that he was pushed in that direction by his murderers, at the foot of the pedestal on which Pompey's statue stood, and which was thus wetted with his blood. So that Pompey himself seemed to have presided, as it were, over the revenge done upon his adversary, who lay here at his feet, and breathed out his soul through his multitude of wounds, for they say he received three and twenty. And the conspirators themselves were many of them wounded by each other, whilst they all levelled their blows at the same person.

When Cæsar was dispatched, Brutus stood forth to give a reason for what they had done, but the senate would not hear him, but flew out of doors in all haste, and filled the people with so much alarm and distraction, that some shut up their houses, others left their counters and shops. All ran one way or the other, some to the place to see the sad spectacle, others back again after they had seen it. Antony and Lepidus, Cæsar's most faithful friends, got off privately, and hid themselves in some friends' houses. Brutus and his followers, being yet hot from the deed, marched in a body from the senate-house to the capitol with their drawn swords, not like persons who thought of escaping, but with an air of confidence and as-

surance, and as they went along, called to the people to resume their liberty, and invited the company of any more distinguished people whom they met. And some of these joined the procession and went up along with them, as if they also had been of the conspiracy, and could claim a share in the honor of what had been done. As, for example, Caius Octavius and Lentulus Spinther, who suffered afterwards for their vanity, being taken off by Antony and the young Cæsar, and lost the honor they desired, as well as their lives, which it cost them, since no one believed they had any share in the action. For neither did those who punished them profess to revenge the fact, but the ill-will.

The day after, Brutus with the rest came down from the capitol, and made a speech to the people, who listened without expressing either any pleasure or resentment, but showed by their silence that they pitied Cæsar and respected Brutus. The senate passed acts of oblivion for what was past, and took measures to reconcile all parties. They ordered that Cæsar should be worshipped as a divinity, and nothing, even of the slightest consequence, should be revoked, which he had enacted during his government. At the same time they gave Brutus and his followers the command of provinces, and other considerable posts. So that all people now thought things were well settled, and brought to the happiest adjustment.

But when Cæsar's will was opened, and it was found that he had left a considerable legacy to each one of the Roman citizens, and when his body was seen carried through the market-place all mangled with wounds, the multitude could no longer contain themselves within the bounds of tranquillity and order, but heaped together a pile of benches, bars, and tables, which they placed the corpse on, and setting fire to it, burnt it on them. Then they took brands from the pile, and ran some to fire the houses of the conspirators, others up and down the city, to find out the men and tear them to pieces, but met, however, with none of them, they having taken effectual care to secure themselves. . . .

Cæsar died in his fifty-sixth year, not having survived Pompey above four years. That empire and power which he had pursued through the whole course of his life with so much hazard, he did at last with much difficulty compass, but reaped no other fruits from it than the empty name and invidious glory. But the great genius which attended him through his lifetime, even after his death remained as the avenger of his murder, pursuing through every sea and land all those who were concerned in it, and suffering none to escape, but reaching all who in any sort or kind were either actually engaged in the fact, or by their counsels any way promoted it.

The most remarkable of mere human coincidences was that which befell Cassius, who, when he was defeated at Philippi, killed himself with the same dagger which he had made use of against Cæsar. . . . The phantom which appeared to Brutus showed the murder was not pleasing to the gods. . . . (While campaigning against Antony and Cæsar in Asia Minor a specter appeared before Brutus saying they would meet at Philippi. Brutus won the first engagement.) The night before the second battle, the same phantom appeared to him again. . . . He presently understood his destiny was at hand, and expressed himself to all the danger of the battle. Yet he did not die in the fight, but seeing his men defeated, got up to the top of a rock, and there presenting his sword to his naked breast, and assisted, as they say, by a friend, who helped him to give the thrust, met his death.

Vergil

Vergil (70 B.C.–19 A.D.) gained considerable attention as an author during the reign of Augustus. Much of his writing survived the collapse of the Roman Empire and is still read with pleasure throughout the learned world. Partially inspired by the achievements of the Augustan age and partially prompted by the emperor himself, Vergil wrote his greatest work, The Aeneid. The story is that of the founding of Rome by the mythical Aeneas, but the theme is really the epic of Rome—the virtues which had made it great, and the destiny which was naturally hers. The books of the poem describe the adventurous wanderings of Aeneas and his fellow Trojans from the ruins of Troy to the site of the city of Rome. In the fifth book Vergil tells of the commemoration of the first anniversary of the death of Aeneas' father, Anchises, at a Trojan community in Sicily and the near collapse of the entire expedition. In book six, the Cumaean Sibyl (guardian of the secrets of Apollo) conducts the hero into hell. After passing through its various areas, Aeneas finally meets his father who tells him of the future of Rome and the men who will contribute to its greatness. In reading this selection note (1) the character of Aeneas; (2) evidences of Greek influences upon Vergil and the Romans; (3) the nature of the commemoration ceremonies for Anchises; (4) the cause of the crisis in the affairs of the expedition and the resolution of the crisis; (5) the crimes committed by those suffering torture in the underworld; (6) descriptions of the souls of great Romans waiting to be born; (7) the peculiar destiny of Rome in contrast to other states; and (8) efforts to link Rome with a glorious past.

From: THE AENEID

Meanwhile Aeneas and the fleet were holding
The sure course over the sea, cutting the waters
That darkened under the wind. . . .
   They were out of sight of land, with only sea
Around them on all sides, alone with ocean,
Ocean and sky, when a cloud, black-blue,
   loomed over
With night and tempest in it; the water rough-
   ened
In shadow, and the pilot Palinurus . . .
Turned to Aeneas: "With a sky like this,
I'd have no hope of reaching Italy, . . .
Let us change the course, and follow. I remem-
   ber
Fraternal shores near by, the land of Eryx,
Sicilian harbors; we were here before
If I recall my stars. " Aeneas answered:
"I saw it long ago, the will of the winds,
The uselessness of struggle. Change the course,
Steer to the land most welcome to me; there
My friend Acestes dwells, and there my father
Anchises lies at rest. What better land
To rest our weary ships?" They made for the
   harbor,
With favoring wind, a swift run over the water,
A happy turn to a familiar shore. . . .
A good night's rest, and a bright morning fol-
   lowed,
And from the shore Aeneas called his comrades,
Stood on a little rise of ground, and told them:
"Great sons of Dardanus, heaven-born, a year
Draws to an end, a year ago we buried
My father in this land, and consecrated
Sorrowful altars to his shade. The day
Comes round again, which I shall always cher-
   ish,
Always lament, with reverence, in the mourn-
   ing,
For the gods' will. If I were held, an exile,
In the Gaetulian quicksands, or a captive
In some Greek ship or city, I would honor
This day with solemn rites, and pile the altars
With sacrificial offering. But now,—
This must be heaven's purpose—we have en-
   tered
A friendly harbor. Come, then, all of us,

Let us be happy in our celebration,
Let us pray for winds, and that the god here-
   after
Receive his rites in temples for his honor
Built in the city we found. Two heads of oxen
Acestes gives each vessel; bring the gods
Of our own household, and the ones Acestes
Pays worship to. Nine days from now, if dawn
Comes bright and shining over the world of
   men,
There will be games, a contest for the boats,
A foot-race, javelin-throw or archery, a battle
With rawhide gloves; let all attend, competing
For victory's palm and prize. And now, in si-
   lence,
Garland the brow with leaves."
                     He bound his temples
With Venus' myrtle, and the others followed,
Acestes, Helymus, and young Iulus,
And the other lads, and Aeneas, from the meet-
   ing,
Moved to Anchises' tomb, and many thousands
Came thronging there. He poured libation,
   duly,
Bowls of pure wine, and milk, and victim-blood,
And strewed bright flowers, praying: "Holy
   father,
Hail, once again; hail once again, O ashes,
Regained in vain; hail, holy shade and spirit!
Hail, from a son, destined to seek alone
The fated fields, Italian soil, alone
To seek, whatever it is, Ausonian Tiber. . . ."
Two sheep he sacrificed, two swine, two heifers,
Poured wine, invoked the spirit of his father,
And the shade loosed from Acheron. His com-
   rades
Also bring gifts, whatever they can, slay bull-
   ocks,
Load altars high; others prepare the kettles,
Sprawl on the greensward, keep the live coals
   glowing
Under the roasting-spits, and the meat turn-
   ing. . . .
   [After the games] . . . fortune changed, not
   keeping faith; for Juno,
While the ritual of sport went on, sent Iris,

As translated by Rolfe Humphries in *The Aeneid of Virgil, A Verse Translation* (New York: Charles Scribner's Sons, 1951), pp. 113–16; 132–75. Reprinted by permission.

With a fair wind, to the Trojan fleet. She was
  angry,
Still, and the ancient grudge unsatisfied,
And Iris, over her thousand-colored rainbow,
Ran her swift path, unseen, beheld the crowd,
Surveyed the shore, harbor and fleet deserted,
While far off on the lonely coast the women
Mourned for Anchises lost, weeping and watch-
  ing
The unfathomable deep. "For weary people,
Alas! how much remains, of shoal and ocean!"
So ran the common sigh. They crave a city,
They are tired of bearing the vast toil of sailing,
And into their midst came Iris, versed in mis-
  chief,
Laying aside her goddess-guise, becoming
Old Beroe, Doryclus' wife, who sometime
Had children, fame, and lineage. Now Iris,
Resembling her, came down to the Trojan
  mothers.
"Alas for us!" she cried, "on whom the Greeks
Never laid hands, to drag us down to death
Before our native walls! Unfortunate people,
For what is fortune saving us, what doom,
What dying? It is seven weary summers
Since Troy's destruction, and still we wander
  over
All lands, all seas, with rocks and stars forever
Implacable, as we go on pursuing
A land that flees forever over the waters.
Here lived our brother Eryx, here we find
A welcomer, king Acestes; who forbids us
To found the walls, to build our city here? . . .
  Come with me, burn
These vessels of ill-omen. Let me tell you,
I have been given warnings; in a dream
I saw Cassandra, she was giving me firebrands,
Here seek your Troy, here is your home, she
  told me;
It is time for us to act, be quick about it!
Neptune himself, with fire on these four altars,
Provides the method, and the resolution."
  She was the first to seize a brand; she raised it
Above here head, and swung it, streaming and
  glowing,
And flung it forth. The women, for a moment,
Stood in bewilderment . . . [then]
They cried aloud; tore fire from the hearths and
  altars;
Made tinder of the altar-decorations,

The garlandry and wreaths. And the fire, let
  loose,
Rioted over thwarts and oars and rigging.
  To theatre and tomb Eumelus brought
Word of the ships on fire; and the men could
  see
The black ash billowing in the smoky cloud. . . .
  Aeneas hurried
With others to the troubled camp. The women
Scattered and fled along the shore, in terror
And guilt, wherever they could, to hiding-
  places
In woods or caves in the rock; they are ashamed
Of daylight and their deed; Juno is shaken
Out of their hearts, and they recognize their
  own.
That does not stop the fire; it burns in fury
Under wet oak, tow smoulders, and the stub-
  born
Steam eats the keels away, destruction seizing
On deck and hull, and water can not quench it,
Nor any strength of men. Tearing his garment
Loose from his shoulders, Aeneas prays to
  heaven:—
"Almighty Jove, if the Trojans are not hateful
To the last man, if any record of goodness
Alleviates human trouble, let our fleet
Escape this flame, O father; save from doom
This little Trojan remnant; or with lightning,
If I deserve it, strike us down forever!"
He had scarcely spoken, when a cloudburst fell
Full force, with darkness and black tempest
  streaming,
And thunder rumbling over plain and hillock,
The whole sky pouring rain; the ships were
  drowned
With water from above, the half-burnt timbers
Were soaked, and the hiss of steam died out;
  four vessels
Were gone, the others rescued from disaster.
  And now Aeneas, stunned by the bitter evil,
Was troubled at heart, uncertain, anxious, griev-
  ing:
What could be done? forget the call of the fates
And settle here in Sicily, or keep on
To the coast of Italy? An old man, Nautes,
Whom Pallas had instructed in deep wisdom,
Gave him the answer. "Goddess-born, wherever
Fate pulls or hauls us, there we have to follow;
Whatever happens, fortune can be beaten

By nothing but endurance. We have here
A friend, Acestes, Trojan-born, divine
In parentage; make him an ally in counsel,
Partner in enterprise; to him hand over
The ones whose ships are lost, and all the weary,
The sick and tired, the old men, and the mothers
Who have had too much of the sea, and the
faint-hearted,
Whose weariness may find a city for them
Here in this land; Acesta, let them call it."
The old man's words still troubled him; the
mind
Was torn this way and that. Night rode the
heavens
In her dark chariot, and there came from the
darkness
The image of Anchises, speaking to him
In words of comfort:—"Son, more dear to me
Than life, when life was mine; son, sorely
troubled
By Trojan fate, I come at Jove's command,
Who drove the fire away, and from the heaven
Has taken pity. Obey the words of Nautes,
He gives the best of counsel; the flower of the
youth,
The bravest hearts, lead on to Italy.
There will be trouble there, a rugged people
Must be subdued in Latium. Come to meet me,
First, in the lower world; come through Avernus
To find me, son. Tartarus' evil prison
Of gloomy shades I know not, for I dwell
Among the happy spirits in Elysium.
Black sheep are good for sacrifice. The Sibyl,
A holy guide, will lead the way, foretelling
The race to come, the given walls. Farewell,
My son; the dewy night is almost over,
I feel the breath of the morning's cruel horses."
He spoke, and vanished, smoke into airy thin-
ness,
From the cries of his son, who woke, and roused
the embers
Of the drowsing altar-fires, with meal and
censer
Propitiating Vesta, making worship
To Trojan household gods.
                                And called Acestes
And the Trojan counsellors, told them of Jove
And his good father's orders, the decision
He has reached at last. They all agree, Acestes
Accepts the trust. They make a roll for the city,
The women-folk, the people willing to linger,

The unadventurous; and they make ready
The thwarts again, replace the fire-scorched
timbers,
Fit out new oars and rigging. There are not
many,
But a living company, for war brave-hearted.
Aeneas ploughs the limits for the city,
Sets out new homes, Ilium, again, and Troy,
A kingdom welcome to Acestes, senate
And courts, and laws, established; and a shrine
High on the crest of Eryx, is given Venus,
Near the high stars, and a priest assigned as
warden
To the wide boundaries of Anchises' grove. . . .
It is time to loose the cables. At the bow
He stands, his temples garlanded with olive,
Makes to the sea libation of wine and entrails,
And the wind comes up astern, and they sweep
the waters
In happy rivalry.
                        But meanwhile Venus,
Driven by worry, went to Neptune, pouring
Complaints from a full heart. . . .
                        And Neptune answered:—
"None has a better right to trust my kingdom
Than the goddess born of the sea-foam. And I
have earned
This confidence. I have often checked the anger
Of sea and sky. And the rivers of Troy are wit-
ness
I have helped on land as well, and saved
Aeneas . . .
Have done with fear; he will reach in safety
The haven of Avernus; the prayer is granted.
Let one be lost in the flood, one life alone
Be given for the many."
                        This comfort given,
To bring the goddess joy, he yoked his horses,
Gold bridle, foaming bit, and sent them flying
With the lightest touch of the reins, skimming
the surface
In the bright blue car; and the waves went
down, the axle
Subdued the swell of the wave, and storm-
clouds melted
To nothing in the sky . . .
So that Aeneas, in his turn, was happy,
Less anxious at heart. The masts are raised,
and sail
Stretched from the halyards; right and left they
bend

The canvas to fair winds: at the head of the fleet
Rides Palinurus, and the others follow,
As ordered, close behind him; dewy night
Has reached mid-heaven, while the sailors, sleeping,
Relax on the hard benches under the oars,
All calm, all quiet. And the god of Sleep
Parting the shadowy air, comes gently down,
Looking for Palinurus, bringing him,
A guiltless man, ill-omened dreams. He settles
On the high stern, a god disguised as a man,
Speaking in Phorbas' guise, "O Palinurus,
The fleet rides smoothly in the even weather,
The hour is given for rest. Lay down the head,
Rest the tired eyes from toil. I will take over
A little while." But Palinurus, barely
Lifting his eyes, made answer: "Trust the waves,
However quiet? Trust a peaceful ocean?
Put faith in such a monster? Never! I
Have been too often fooled by the clear stars
To trust Aeneas to their faithless keeping."
And so he clung to the tiller, never loosed
His hand from the wood, his eyes from the fair heaven.
But lo, the god over his temples shook
A bough that dripped with dew from Lethe, steeped
With Stygian magic, so the swimming eyes,
Against his effort close, blink open, close
Again, and slumber takes the drowsy limbs.
Bending above him, leaning over, the god
Shoves him, still clinging to the tiller, calling
His comrades vainly, into the clear waves.
And the god is gone like a bird to the clear air,
And the fleet is going safely over its journey
As Neptune promised. But the rocks were near,
The Siren-cliffs, most perilous of old,
White with the bones of many mariners,
Loud with their hoarse eternal warning sound.
Aeneas starts from sleep, aware, somehow
Of a lost pilot, and a vessel drifting,
Himself takes over guidance, with a sigh
And heartache for a friend's mishap, "Alas,
Too trustful in the calm of sea and sky,
O Palinurus, on an unknown shore,
You will be lying, naked."
Mourning for Palinurus, he drives the fleet
To Cumae's coast-line; the prows are turned, the anchors

Let down, the beach is covered by the vessels.
Young in their eagerness for the land in the west,
They flash ashore; some seek the seeds of flame
Hidden in veins of flint, and others spoil
The woods of tinder, and show where water runs.
Aeneas, in devotion, seeks the heights
Where stands Apollo's temple, and the cave
Where the dread Sibyl dwells, Apollo's priestess,
With the great mind and heart, inspired revealer
Of things to come. They enter Diana's grove,
Pass underneath the roof of gold.
                                    The story
Has it that Daedalus fled from Minos' kingdom,
Trusting himself to wings he made, and travelled
A course unknown to man, to the cold north,
Descending on this very summit; here,
Earth-bound again, he built a mighty temple,
Paying Apollo homage, the dedication
Of the oarage of his wings. On the temple doors
He carved, in bronze, Androgeos' death, and the payment
Enforced on Cecrops' children, seven sons
For sacrifice each year: there stands the urn,
The lots are drawn—facing this, over the sea,
Rises the land of Crete: the scene portrays
Pasiphae in cruel love, the bull
She took to her by cunning, and their offspring,
The mongrel Minotaur, half man, half monster,
The proof of lust unspeakable; and the toil
Of the house is shown, the labyrinthine maze
Which no one could have solved, but Daedalus
Pitied a princess' love, loosened the tangle,
Gave her a skein to guide her way. His boy,
Icarus, might have been here, in the picture,
And almost was——his father had made the effort
Once, and once more, and dropped his hands; he could not
Master his grief that much. The story held them;
They would have studied it longer, but Achates
Came from his mission; with him came the priestess,
Deiphobe, daughter of Glaucus, who tends the temple
For Phoebus and Diana; she warned Aeneas:

"It is no such sights the time demands; far better
To offer sacrifice, seven chosen bullocks,
Seven chosen ewes, a herd without corruption."
They were prompt in their obedience, and the priestess
Summoned the Trojans to the lofty temple.

The rock's vast side is hollowed into a cavern,
With a hundred mouths, a hundred open portals,
Whence voices rush, the answers of the Sibyl.
They had reached the threshold, and the virgin cried:
"It is time to seek the fates; the god is here,
The god is here, behold him." And as she spoke
Before the entrance, her countenance and color
Changed, and her hair tossed loose, and her heart was heaving,
Her bosom swollen with frenzy; she seemed taller,
Her voice not human at all, as the god's presence
Drew nearer, and took hold on her. "Aeneas,"
She cried, "Aeneas, are you praying?
Are you being swift in prayer? Until you are,
The house of the gods will not be moved, nor open
Its mighty portals." More than her speech, her silence
Made the Trojans cold with terror, and Aeneas
Prayed from the depth of his heart: "Phoebus Apollo,
Compassionate ever, slayer of Achilles
Through aim of Paris' arrow, helper and guide
Over the seas, over the lands, the deserts,
The shoals and quicksands, now at last we have come
To Italy, we hold the lands which fled us:
Grant that thus far, no farther, a Trojan fortune
Attend our wandering. And spare us now,
All of you, gods and goddesses, who hated
Troy in the past, and Trojan glory. I beg you,
Most holy prophetess, in whose foreknowing
The future stands revealed, grant that the Trojans—
I ask with fate's permission—rest in Latium
Their wandering storm-tossed gods. I will build a temple,
In honor of Apollo and Diana,
Out of eternal Marble, and ordain

Festivals in their honor, and for the Sibyl
A great shrine in our kingdom, and I will place there
The lots and mystic oracles for my people
With chosen priests to tend them. Only, priestess,
This once, I pray you, chant the sacred verses
With your own lips; do not trust them to the leaves,
The mockery of the rushing wind's disorder."

But the priestess, not yet subject to Apollo,
Went reeling through the cavern, wild, and storming
To throw the god, who presses, like a rider,
With bit and bridle and weight, tames her wild spirit,
Shapes her to his control. The doors fly open,
The hundred doors, of their own will, fly open,
And through the air the answer comes:—"O Trojans,
At last the dangers of the sea are over;
That course is run, but graver ones are waiting
On land. The sons of Dardanus will reach
The kingdom of Lavinia—be easy
On that account—the sons of Dardanus, also,
Will wish they had not come there. War, I see,
Terrible war, and the river Tiber foaming
With streams of blood. There will be another Zanthus,
Another Simois, and Greek encampment,
Even another Achilles, born in Latium,
Himself a goddess' son. And Juno further
Will always be there: you will beg for mercy,
Be poor, turn everywhere for help. A woman
Will be the cause once more of so much evil,
A foreign bride, receptive to the Trojans,
A foreign marriage. Do not yield to evil,
Attack, attack, more boldly even than fortune
Seems to permit. An offering of safety,—
Incredible!—will come from a Greek city."

So, through the amplifiers of her cavern,
The hollow vaults, the Sibyl cast her warnings,
Riddles confused with truth; and Apollo rode her,
Reining her rage, and shaking her, and spurring
The fierceness of her heart. The frenzy dwindled,
A little, and her lips were still. Aeneas
Began:—"For me, no form of trouble, maiden,
Is new, or unexpected; all of this

I have known long since, lived in imagination.
One thing I ask: this is the gate of the kingdom,
So it is said, where Pluto reins, the gloomy
Marsh where the water of Acheron runs over.
Teach me the way from here, open the portals
That I may go to my belovèd father,
Stand in his presence, talk with him. I brought him,
Once, on these shoulders, through a thousand weapons
And following fire, and foemen. He shared with me
The road, the sea, the menaces of heaven,
Things that an old man should not bear; he bore them,
Tired as he was. And he it was who told me
To come to you in humbleness. I beg you
Pity the son, the father. You have power,
Great priestess, over all; it is not for nothing
Hecate gave you this dominion over
Avernus' groves. If Orpheus could summon
Eurydice from the shadows with his music,
If Pollux could save his brother, coming, going,
Along this path,—why should I mention Theseus,
Why mention Hercules? I, too, descended
From the line of Jupiter." He clasped the altar,
Making his prayer, and she made answer to him:
"Son of Anchises, born of godly lineage,
By night, by day, the portals of dark Dis
Stand open: it is easy, the descending
Down to Avernus. But to climb again,
To trace the footsteps back to the air above,
There lies the task, the toil. A few, beloved
By Jupiter, descended from the gods,
A few, in whom exalting virtue burned,
Have been permitted. Around the central woods
The black Cocytus glides, a sullen river;
But if such love is in your heart, such longing
For double crossing of the Stygian lake,
For double sight of Tartarus, learn first
What must be done. In a dark tree there hides
A bough, all golden, leaf and pliant stem,
Sacred to Proserpine. This all the grove
Protects, and shadows cover it with darkness.
Until this bough, this bloom of light, is found,
No one receives his passport to the darkness
Whose queen requires this tribute. In succession,

After the bough is plucked, another grows,
Gold-green with the same metal. Raise the eyes,
Look up, reach up the hand, and it will follow
With ease, if fate is calling; otherwise,
No power, no steel, can loose it. Furthermore,
(Alas, you do not know this!), one of your men
Lies on the shore, unburied, a pollution
To all the fleet, while you have come for counsel
Here to our threshold. Bury him with honor;
Black cattle slain in expiation for him
Must fall before you see the Stygian kingdoms,
The groves denied to living men."

Aeneas,
With sadness in his eyes, and downcast heart,
Turned from the cave, and at his side Achates
Accompanied his anxious meditations.
They talked together: who could be the comrade
Named by the priestess, lying there unburied?
And they found him on dry sand; it was Misenus,
Aeolus' son, none better with the trumpet
To make men burn for warfare. He had been
Great Hector's man-at-arms; he was good in battle
With spear as well as horn, and after Hector
Had fallen to Achilles, he had followed
Aeneas, entering no meaner service.
Some foolishness came over him; he made
The ocean echo to the blare of his trumpet
That day, and challenged the sea-gods to a contest
In martial music, and Triton, jealous, caught him,
However unbelievable the story,
And held him down between the rocks, and drowned him
Under the foaming waves. His comrades mourned him,
Aeneas most of all, and in their sorrow
They carry out, in haste, the Sibyl's orders,
Construct the funeral altar, high as heaven,
They go to an old wood, and the pine-trees fall
Where wild beasts have their dens, and holm-oak rings
To the stroke of the axe, and oak and ash are riven
By the splitting wedge, and rowan-trees come rolling

Down the steep mountain-side. Aeneas helps
 them,
And cheers them on; studies the endless forest,
Takes thought, and prays: "If only we might
 see it,
That golden bough, here in the depth of the
 forest,
Bright on some tree. She told the truth, our
 priestess,
Too much, too bitter truth, about Misenus."
No sooner had he spoken than twin doves
Came flying down before him, and alighted
On the green ground. He knew his mother's
 birds,
And made his prayer, rejoicing,—"Oh, be lead-
 ers,
Wherever the way, and guide me to the grove
Where the rich bough makes rich the shaded
 ground.
Help me, O goddess-mother!" And he paused,
Watching what sign they gave, what course
 they set.
The birds flew on a little, just ahead
Of the pursuing vision; when they came
To the jaws of dank Avernus, evil-smelling,
They rose aloft, then swooped down the bright
 air,
Perched on the double tree, where the off-color
Of gold was gleaming golden through the
 branches.
As mistletoe, in the cold winter, blossoms
With its strange foliage on an alien tree,
The yellow berry gilding the smooth branches,
Such was the vision of the gold in leaf
On the dark holm-oak, so the foil was rustling,
Rattling, almost, the bract in the soft wind
Stirring like metal. Aeneas broke it off
With eager grasp, and bore it to the Sibyl.
 Meanwhile, along the shore, the Trojans
 mourned,
Paying Misenus' dust the final honors.
A mighty pyre was raised, of pine and oak,
The sides hung with dark leaves, and somber
 cypress
Along the front, and gleaming arms above.
Some made the water hot, and some made
 ready
Bronze caldrons, shimmering over fire, and
 others
Lave and anoint the body, and with weeping
Lay on the bier his limbs, and place above them
Familiar garments, crimson color; and some

Take up the heavy burden, a sad office,
And, as their fathers did, they kept their eyes
Averted, as they brought the torches nearer.
They burn gifts with him, bowls of oil, and
 viands,
And frankincense; and when the flame is quiet
And the ashes settle to earth, they wash the
 embers
With wine, and slake the thirsty dust. The
 bones
Are placed in a bronze urn by Corynaeus,
Who, with pure water, thrice around his com-
 rades
Made lustral cleansing, shaking gentle dew
From the fruitful branch of olive; and they
 said
Hail and farewell! And over him Aeneas
Erects a mighty tomb, with the hero's arms,
His oar and trumpet, where the mountain rises
Memorial for ever, and named Misenus.
 These rites performed, he hastened to the
 Sibyl.
There was a cavern, yawning wide and deep,
Jagged, below the darkness of the trees,
Beside the darkness of the lake. No bird
Could fly above it safely, with the vapor
Pouring from the black gulf (the Greeks have
 named it
Avernus, or A-Ornos, meaning *birdless*),
And here the priestess for the slaughter set
Four bullocks, black ones, poured the holy
 wine
Between the horns, and plucked the topmost
 bristles
For the first offering to the sacred fire,
Calling on Hecate, a power in heaven,
A power in hell. Knives to the throat were
 driven,
The warm blood caught in bowls. Aeneas of-
 fered
A lamb, black-fleeced, to Night and her great
 sister,
A sterile heifer for the queen; for Dis
An altar in the night, and on the flames
The weight of heavy bulls, the fat oil pouring
Over the burning entrails. And at dawn,
Under their feet, earth seemed to shake and
 rumble,
The ridges move, and bitches bay in darkness,
As the presence neared. The Sibyl cried a
 warning,
"Keep off, keep off, whatever is unholy,

Depart from here! Courage, Aeneas; enter
The path, unsheathe the sword. The time is
  ready
For the brave heart." She strode out boldly,
  leading
Into the open cavern, and he followed.
  Gods of the world of spirit; silent shadows,
Chaos and Phlegethon, areas of silence,
Wide realms of dark, may it be right and proper
To tell what I have heard, this revelation
Of matters buried deep in earth and darkness!
  Vague forms in lonely darkness, they were
    going
Through void and shadow, through the empty
  realm
Like people in a forest, when the moonlight
Shifts with a baleful glimmer, and shadow
  covers
The sky, and all the colors turn to blackness.
At the first threshold, on the jaws of Orcus,
Grief and avenging Cares have set their
  couches,
And pale Diseases dwell, and sad Old Age,
Fear, evil-counselling Hunger, wretched Need,
Forms terrible to see, and Death, and Toil,
And Death's own brother, Sleep, and evil Joys,
Fantasies of the mind, and deadly War,
The Furies' iron chambers, Discord, raving,
Her snaky hair entwined in bloody bands.
An elm-tree loomed there, shadowy and huge,
The aged boughs outspread, beneath whose
  leaves,
Men say, the false dreams cling, thousands on
  thousands.
And there are monsters in the dooryard, Cen-
  taurs,
Scyllas, of double shape, the beast of Lerna,
Hissing most horribly, Briareus,
The hundred-handed giant, a Chimaera
Whose armament is fire, Harpies, and Gorgons,
A triple-bodied giant. In sudden panic
Aeneas drew his sword, the edge held forward,
Ready to rush and flail, however blindly,
Save that his wise companion warned him, say-
  ing
They had no substance, they were only
  phantoms
Flitting about, illusions without body.
  From here, the road turns off to Acheron,
River of Hell; here, thick with muddy whirling,
Cocytus boils with sand. Charon is here,
The guardian of these mingling waters, Charon,

Uncouth and filthy, on whose chin the hair
Is a tangled mat, whose eyes protrude, are
  burning,
Whose dirty cloak is knotted at the shoulder.
He poles a boat, tends to the sail, unaided,
Ferrying bodies in his rust-hued vessel.
Old, but a god's senility is awful
In its raw greenness. To the bank come throng-
  ing
Mothers and men, bodies of great-souled he-
  roes,
Their life-time over, boys, unwedded maidens,
Young men whose fathers saw their pyres burn-
  ing,
Thick as the forest leaves that fall in autumn
With early frost, thick as the birds to landfall
From over the seas, when the chill of the year
  compels them
To sunlight. There they stand, a host, imploring
To be taken over first. Their hands, in longing,
Reach out for the farther shore. But the gloomy
  boatman
Makes choice among them, taking some, and
  keeping
Others far back from the stream's edge. Aeneas,
Wondering, asks the Sibyl, "Why the crowd-
  ing?
What are the spirits seeking? What distinction
Brings some across the livid stream, while oth-
  ers
Stay on the farther bank?" She answers, briefly:
"Son of Anchises, this is the awful river,
The Styx, by which the gods take oath; the
  boatman
Charon; those he takes with him are the buried,
Those he rejects, whose luck is out, the grave-
  less.
It is not permitted him to take them over
The dreadful banks and hoarse-resounding
  waters
Till earth is cast upon their bones. They haunt
These shores a hundred restless years of waiting
Before they end postponement of the crossing."
Aeneas paused, in thoughtful mood, with pity
Over their lot's unevenness; and saw there,
Wanting the honor given the dead, and griev-
  ing,
Leucaspis, and Orontes, the Lycian captain,
Who had sailed from Troy across the stormy
  waters,
And drowned off Africa, with crew and vessel,
And there was Palinurus, once his pilot,

Who, not so long ago, had been swept over,
Watching the stars on the journey north from
    Carthage.
The murk was thick; Aeneas hardly knew him,
Sorrowful in that darkness, but made question:
"What god, O Palinurus, took you from us?
Who drowned you in the deep? Tell me. Apollo
Never before was false, and yet he told me
You would be safe across the seas, and come
Unharmed to Italy; what kind of promise
Was this, to fool me with?" But Palinurus
Gave him assurance:—"It was no god who
    drowned me,
No falsehood on Apollo's part, my captain,
But as I clung to the tiller, holding fast
To keep the course, as I should do, I felt it
Wrenched from the ship, and I fell with it,
    headlong.
By those rough seas I swear, I had less fear
On my account than for the ship, with rudder
And helmsman overboard, to drift at the
    mercy
Of rising seas. Three nights I rode the waters,
Three nights of storm, and from the crest of a
    wave,
On the fourth morning, sighted Italy,
I was swimming to land, I had almost reached
    it, heavy
In soaking garments; my cramped fingers strug-
    gled
To grasp the top of the rock, when barbarous
    people,
Ignorant men, mistaking me for booty,
Struck me with swords; waves hold me now, or
    winds
Roll me along the shore. By the light of heaven,
The lovely air, I beg you, by your father,
Your hope of young Iulus, bring me rescue
Out of these evils, my unconquered leader!
Cast over my body earth—you have the
    power—
Return to Velia's harbor,—or there may be
Some other way—your mother is a goddess,
Else how would you be crossing this great river,
This Stygian swamp?—help a poor fellow, take
    me
Over the water with you, give a dead man
At least a place to rest in." But the Sibyl
Broke in upon him sternly:—"Palinurus,
Whence comes this mad desire? No man, un-
    buried,
May see the Stygian waters, or Cocytus,

The Furies' dreadful river; no man may come
Unbidden to this bank. Give up the hope
That fate is changed by praying, but hear this,
A little comfort in your harsh misfortune:
Those neighboring people will make expiation,
Driven by signs from heaven, through their
    cities
And through their countryside; they will build
    a tomb,
Thereto bring offerings yearly, and the place
Shall take its name from you, Cape Palinurus."
So he was comforted a little, finding
Some happiness in the promise.
                            And they went on,
Nearing the river, and from the stream the boat-
    man
Beheld them cross the silent forest, nearer,
Turning their footsteps toward the bank. He
    challenged:—
"Whoever you are, O man in armor, coming
In this direction, halt where you are, and tell
    me
The reason why you come. This is the region
Of shadows, and of Sleep and drowsy Night;
I am not allowed to carry living bodies
In the Stygian boat; and I must say I was sorry
I ever accepted Hercules and Theseus
And Pirithous, and rowed them over the lake,
Though they were sons of gods and great in
    courage,
One of them dared to drag the guard of Hell,
Enchained, from Pluto's throne, shaking in
    terror,
The others to snatch our queen from Pluto's
    chamber."
The Sibyl answered briefly: "No such cunning
Is plotted here; our weapons bring no danger.
Be undisturbed: the hell-hound in his cavern
May bark forever, to keep the bloodless
    shadows
Frightened away from trespass; Proserpine,
Untouched, in pureness guard her uncle's
    threshold.
Trojan Aeneas, a man renowned for goodness,
Renowned for nerve in battle, is descending
To the lowest shades; he comes to find his fa-
    ther.
If such devotion has no meaning to you,
Look on this branch at least, and recognize it!"
And with the word she drew from under her
    mantle
The golden bough; his swollen wrath subsided.

No more was said; he saw the bough, and
  marvelled
At the holy gift, so long unseen; came sculling
The dark-blue boat to the shore, and drove the
  spirits,
Lining the thwarts, ashore, and cleared the
  gangway,
And took Aeneas aboard; as that big man
Stepped in, the leaky skiff groaned under the
  weight,
And the strained seams let in the muddy water,
But they made the crossing safely, seer and
  soldier,
To the far margin, colorless and shapeless,
Grey sedge and dark-brown ooze. They heard
  the baying
Of Cerberus, that great hound, in his cavern
  crouching,
Making the shore resound, as all three throats
Belled horribly; and serpents rose and bristled
Along the triple neck. The priestess threw him
A sop with honey and drugged meal; he opened
The ravenous throat, gulped, and subsided,
  filling
The den with his huge bulk. Aeneas, crossing,
Passed on beyond the bank of the dread river
Whence none return.

             A wailing of thin voices
Came to their ears, the souls of infants crying,
Those whom the day of darkness took from the
  breast
Before their share of living. And there were
  many
Whom some false sentence brought to death.
  Here Minos
Judges them once again; a silent jury
Reviews the evidence. And there are others,
Guilty of nothing, but who hated living,
The suicides. How gladly, now, they would
  suffer
Poverty, hardship, in the world of light!
But this is not permitted; they are bound
Nine times around by the black unlovely river;
Styx holds them fast.

           They came to the Fields of
  Mourning,
So-called, where those whom cruel love had
  wasted
Hid in secluded pathways, under myrtle,
And even in death were anxious. Procris,
  Phaedra,
Eriphyle, displaying wounds her son

Had given her, Caeneus, Laodamia,
Caeneus, a young man once, and now again
A young man, after having been a woman.
And here, new come from her own wound, was
  Dido,
Wandering in the wood. The Trojan hero,
Standing near by, saw her, or thought he saw
  her,
Dim in the shadows, like the slender crescent
Of moon when cloud drifts over. Weeping, he
  greets her:—
"Unhappy Dido, so they told me truly
That your own hand had brought you death.
  Was I—
Alas!—the cause? I swear by all the stars,
By the world above, by everything held sacred
Here under the earth, unwillingly, O queen,
I left your kingdom. But the gods' commands,
Driving me now through these forsaken places,
This utter night, compelled me on. I could not
Believe my loss would cause so great a sorrow.
Linger a moment, do not leave me; whither,
Whom, are you fleeing? I am permitted only
This last word with you."

            But the queen, unmoving
As flint or marble, turned away, her eyes
Fixed on the ground: the tears were vain, the
  words,
Meant to be soothing, foolish; she turned away,
His enemy forever, to the shadows
Where Sychaeus, her former husband, took her
With love for love, and sorrow for her sorrow.
And still Aeneas wept for her, being troubled
By the injustice of her doom; his pity
Followed her going.

           They went on. They came
To the farthest fields, whose tenants are the
  warriors,
Illustrious throng. Here Tydeus came to meet
  him,
Parthenopaeus came, and pale Adrastus,
A fighter's ghost, and many, many others,
Mourned in the world above, and doomed in
  battle,
Leaders of Troy, in long array; Aeneas
Sighed as he saw them: Medon; Polyboetes,
The priest of Ceres; Glaucus; and Idaeus
Still keeping arms and chariot; three
  brothers,
Antenor's sons; Thersilochus; a host
To right and left of him, and when they see
  him,

One sight is not enough; they crowd around
him,
Linger, and ask the reasons for his coming.
But Agamemnon's men, the Greek battalions,
Seeing him there, and his arms in shadow
gleaming,
Tremble in panic, turn to flee for refuge,
As once they used to, toward their ships, but
where
Are the ships now? They try to shout, in terror;
But only a thin and piping treble issues
To mock their mouths, wide-open.
                                    One he knew
Was here, Deiphobus, a son of Priam,
With his whole body mangled, and his features
Cruelly slashed, and both hands cut, and ears
Torn from his temples, and his nostrils slit
By shameful wounds. Aeneas hardly knew him,
Shivering there, and doing his best to hide
His marks of punishment; unhailed, he hailed
him:—
"Deiphobus, great warrior, son of Teucer,
Whose cruel punishment was this? Whose li-
cense
Abused you so? I heard, it seems, a story
Of that last night, how you had fallen, weary
With killing Greeks at last; I built a tomb,
Although no body lay there, in your honor,
Three times I cried, aloud, over your spirit,
Where now your name and arms keep guard. I
could not,
Leaving my country, find my friend, to give him
Proper interment in the earth he came from."
And Priam's son replied:—"Nothing, dear com-
rade,
Was left undone; the dead man's shade was
given
All ceremony due. It was my own fortune
And a Spartan woman's deadliness that sunk
me
Under these evils; she it was who left me
These souvenirs. You know how falsely happy
We were on that last night; I need not tell you.
When that dread horse came leaping over
our walls,
Pregnant with soldiery, she led the dancing,
A solemn rite, she called it, with Trojan
women
Screaming their bacchanals; she raised the
torches
High on the citadel; she called the Greeks.

Then—I was worn with trouble, drugged in
slumber,
Resting in our ill-omened bridal chamber,
With sleep as deep and sweet as death upon
me—
Then she, that paragon of helpmates, deftly
Moved all the weapons from the house; my
sword,
Even, she stole from underneath my pillow,
Opened the door, and called in Menelaus,
Hoping, no doubt, to please her loving hus-
band,
To win forgetfulness of her old sinning.
It is quickly told: they broke into the chamber,
The two of them, and with them, as accom-
plice,
Ulysses came, the crime-contriving bastard.
O gods, pay back the Greeks; grant the peti-
tion
If goodness asks for vengeance! But you,
Aeneas,
A living man—what chance has brought you
here?
Vagrant of ocean, god-inspired,—which are
you?
What chance has worn you down, to come, in
sadness,
To these confusing sunless dwelling-places?"
  While they were talking, Aurora's rosy car
Had halfway crossed the heaven; all their time
Might have been spent in converse, but the
Sibyl
Hurried them forward:—"Night comes on,
Aeneas;
We waste the hours with tears. We are at the
crossroad,
Now; here we turn to the right, where the path-
way leads
On to Elysium, under Pluto's ramparts.
Leftward is Tartarus, and retribution,
The terminal of the wicked, and their dungeon."
Deiphobus left them, saying, "O great priestess,
Do not be angry with me; I am going;
I shall not fail the roll-call of the shadows.
Pride of our race, go on; may better fortune
Attend you!" and, upon the word, he vanished.
  As he looked back, Aeneas saw, to his left,
Wide walls beneath a cliff, a triple rampart,
A river running fire, Phlegethon's torrent,
Rocks roaring in its course, a gate, tremen-
dous,

Pillars of adamant, a tower of iron,
Too strong for men, too strong for even gods
To batter down in warfare, and behind them
A Fury, sentinel in bloody garments,
Always on watch, by day, by night. He heard
Sobbing and groaning there, the crack of the
    lash,
The clank of iron, the sound of dragging shack-
    les.
The noise was terrible; Aeneas halted,
Asking, "What forms of crime are these, O
    maiden?
What harrying punishment, what horrible out-
    cry?"
She answered:—"O great leader of the Tro-
    jans,
I have never crossed that threshold of the
    wicked;
No pure soul is permitted entrance thither,
But Hecate, by whose order I was given
Charge of Avernus' groves, my guide, my
    teacher,
Told me how gods exact the toll of vengeance.
The monarch here, merciless Rhadamanthus,
Punishes guilt, and hears confession; he forces
Acknowledgment of crime; no man in the
    world,
No matter how cleverly he hides his evil,
No matter how much he smiles at his own sly-
    ness,
Can fend atonement off; the hour of death
Begins his sentence. Tisiphone, the Fury,
Leaps at the guilty with her scourge; her ser-
    pents
Are whips of menace as she calls her sisters.
Imagine the gates, on jarring hinge, rasp open,
You would see her in the doorway, a shape, a
    sentry,
Savage, implacable. Beyond, still fiercer,
The monstrous Hydra dwells; her fifty throats
Are black, and open wide, and Tartarus
Is black, and open wide, and it goes down
To darkness, sheer deep down, and twice the
    distance
That earth is from Olympus. At the bottom
The Titans crawl, Earth's oldest breed, hurled
    under
By thunderbolts; here lie the giant twins,
Aloeus' sons, who laid their hands on heaven
And tried to pull down Jove; Salmoneus here
Atones for high presumption,—it was he

Who aped Jove's noise and fire, wheeling his
    horses
Triumphant through his city in Elis, cheering
And shaking the torch, and claiming divine
    homage,
The arrogant fool, to think his brass was
    lightning,
His horny-footed horses beat out thunder!
Jove showed him what real thunder was, what
    lightning
Spoke from immortal cloud, what whirlwind
    fury
Came sweeping from the heaven to overtake
    him.
Here Tityos, Earth's giant son, lies sprawling
Over nine acres, with a monstrous vulture
Gnawing, with crooked beak, vitals and liver
That grow as they are eaten; eternal anguish,
Eternal feast. Over another hangs
A rock, about to fall; and there are tables
Set for a banquet, gold with royal splendor,
But if a hand goes out to touch the viands,
The Fury drives it back with fire and yelling.
Why name them all, Pirithous, the Lapiths,
Ixion? The roll of crime would take forever.
Whoever, in his lifetime, hated his brother,
Or struck his father down; whoever cheated
A client, or was miserly—how many
Of these there seem to be!—whoever went
To treasonable war, or broke a promise
Made to his lord, whoever perished, slain
Over adultery, all these, walled in,
Wait here their punishment. Seek not to know
Too much about their doom. The stone is rolled,
The wheel keeps turning; Theseus forever
Sits in dejection; Phlegyas, accursed,
Cries through the halls forever: *Being warned,
Learn justice; reverence the gods!* The man
Who sold his country is here in hell; the man
Who altered laws for money; and a father
Who knew his daughter's bed. All of them
    dared,
And more than dared, achieved, unspeakable
Ambitions. If I had a hundred tongues,
A hundred iron throats, I could not tell
The fullness of their crime and punishment."
And then she added:—"Come: resume the
    journey,
Fulfill the mission; let us hurry onward.
I see the walls the Cyclops made, the portals
Under the archway, where, the orders tell us,

Our tribute must be set." They went together
Through the way's darkness, came to the doors, and halted,
And at the entrance Aeneas, having sprinkled
His body with fresh water, placed the bough
Golden before the threshold. The will of the goddess
Had been performed, the proper task completed.
   They came to happy places, the joyful dwelling,
The lovely greenery of the groves of the blessèd.
Here ampler air invests the fields with light,
Rose-colored, with familiar stars and sun.
Some grapple on the grassy wrestling-ground
In exercise and sport, and some are dancing,
And others singing; in his trailing robe
Orpheus strums the lyre; the seven clear notes
Accompany the dance, the song. And heroes
Are there, great-souled, born in the happier years,
Ilus, Assaracus; the city's founder,
Prince Dardanus. Far off, Aeneas wonders,
Seeing the phantom arms, the chariots,
The spears fixed in the ground, the chargers browsing,
Unharnessed, over the plain. Whatever, living,
The men delighted in, whatever pleasure
Was theirs in horse and chariot, still holds them
Here under the world. To right and left, they banquet
In the green meadows, and a joyful chorus
Rises through groves of laurel, whence the river
Runs to the upper world. The band of heroes
Dwell here, all those whose mortal wounds were suffered
In fighting for the fatherland; and poets,
The good, the pure, the worthy of Apollo;
Those who discovered truth and made life nobler;
Those who served others—all, with snowy fillets
Binding their temples, throng the lovely valley.
And these the Sibyl questioned, most of all
Musaeus, for he towered above the center
Of that great throng:—"O happy souls, O poet,
Where does Anchises dwell? For him we come here,
For him we have traversed Erebus' great rivers."
And he replied:—"It is all our home, the shady

Groves, and the streaming meadows, and the softness
Along the river-banks. No fixed abode
Is ours at all; but if it is your pleasure,
Cross over the ridge with me; I will guide you there
By easy going." And so Musaeus led them
And from the summit showed them fields, all shining,
And they went on over and down.
   Deep in a valley of green, father Anchises
Was watching, with deep earnestness, the spirits
Whose destiny was light, and counting them over,
All of his race to come, his dear descendants,
Their fates and fortunes and their works and ways,
And as he saw Aeneas coming toward him
Over the meadow, his hands reached out with yearning,
He was moved to tears, and called:—"At last, my son,—
Have you really come, at last? and the long road nothing
To a son who loves his father? Do I, truly,
See you, and hear your voice? I was thinking so,
I was hoping so, I was counting off the days,
And I was right about it. O my son!
What a long journey, over land and water,
Yours must have been! What buffeting of danger!
I feared, so much, the Libyan realm would hurt you."
And his son answered:—"It was your spirit, father,
Your sorrowful shade, so often met, that led me
To find these portals. The ships ride safe at anchor,
Safe in the Tuscan sea. Embrace me, father;
Let hand join hand in love; do not forsake me."
And as he spoke, the tears streamed down. Three times
He reached out toward him, and three times the image
Fled like the breath of the wind or a dream on wings.
   He saw, in a far valley, a separate grove
Where the woods stir and rustle, and a river,

The Lethe, gliding past the peaceful places,
And tribes of people thronging, hovering over,
Innumerable as the bees in summer
 Working the bright-hued flowers, and the
  shining
Of the white lilies, murmuring and humming.
Aeneas, filled with wonder, asks the reason
For what he does not know, who are the peo-
 ple
In such a host, and to what river coming?
Anchises answers:—"These are spirits, ready
Once more for life; they drink of Lethe's water
The soothing potion of forgetfulness.
I have longed, for long, to show them to you,
 name them,
Our children's children; Italy discovered,
So much the greater happiness, my son."
"But, O my father, is it thinkable
That souls would leave this blessedness, be
 willing
A second time to bear the sluggish body,
Trade Paradise for earth? Alas, poor wretches,
Why such a mad desire for light?" Anchises
Gives detailed answer: "First, my son, a spirit
Sustains all matter, heaven and earth and
 ocean,
The moon, the stars; mind quickens mass, and
 moves it.
Hence comes the race of man, of beast, of
 wingèd
Creatures of air, of the strange shapes which
 ocean
Bears down below his mottled marble surface.
All these are blessed with energy from heaven;
The seed of life is a spark of fire, but the
 body
A clod of earth, a clog, a mortal burden.
Hence humans fear, desire, grieve, and are joy-
 ful,
And even when life is over, all the evil
Ingrained so long, the adulterated mixture,
The plagues and pestilences of the body
Remain, persist. So there must be a cleansing,
By penalty, by punishment, by fire,
By sweep of wind, by water's absolution,
Before the guilt is gone. Each of us suffers
His own peculiar ghost. But the day comes
When we are sent through wide Elysium,
The Fields of the Blessed, a few of us, to lin-
 ger
Until the turn of time, the wheel of ages,

Wears off the taint, and leaves the core of
 spirit
Pure sense, pure flame. A thousand years pass
 over
And the god calls the countless host to Lethe
Where memory is annulled, and souls are will-
 ing
Once more to enter into mortal bodies."
 The discourse ended; the father drew his son
And his companion toward the hum, the center
Of the full host; they came to rising ground
Where all the long array was visible,
Anchises watching, noting, every comer.
"Glory to come, my son, illustrious spirits
Of Dardan lineage, Italian offspring,
Heirs of our name, begetters of our future!
These I will name for you and tell our
 fortunes. . . .
". . . there will be a son of Mars; his mother
Is Ilia, and his name is Romulus. . . .
Under his auspices Rome, that glorious city,
Will bound her power by earth, her pride by
 heaven,
Happy in hero sons, one wall surrounding
Her seven hills, even as Cybele, riding
Through Phrygian cities, wears her crown of
 towers. . . .
Turn the eyes now this way; behold the Ro-
 mans,
Your very own. These are Iulus' children,
The race to come. One promise you have heard
Over and over: here is its fulfillment,
The son of a god, Augustus Caesar, founder
Of a new age of gold, in lands where Saturn
Ruled long ago; he will extend his empire
Beyond the Indies, beyond the normal measure
Of years and constellations, where high Atlas
Turns on his shoulders the star-studded world.
Maeotia and the Caspian seas are trembling
As heaven's oracles predict his coming,
And all the seven mouths of Nile are troubled.
Not even Hercules, in all his travels,
Covered so much of the world, from Eryman-
 thus
To Lerna; nor did Bacchus, driving his tigers
From Nysa's summit. How can hesitation
Keep us from deeds to make our prowess
 greater? . . .
[See] the avenger Brutus, proud of spirit,
Restorer of the balance. He shall be
First holder of the consular power; his children

Will stir up wars again, and he, for freedom
And her sweet sake, will call down judgment
    on them,
Unhappy, however future men may praise him,
In love of country and intense ambition.
    "There . . . [is] stern Torquatus,
The man with the axe, and Camillus, the re-
    gainer
Of standards lost. And see those two, resplend-
    ent
In equal arms, harmonious friendly spirits
Now, in the shadow of night, but if they ever
Come to the world of light, alas, what warfare,
What battle-lines, what slaughter they will
    fashion,
Each for the other, one from Alpine ramparts
Descending, and the other ranged against him
With armies from the east, father and son
Through marriage, Pompey and Caesar. O my
    children,
Cast out the thoughts of war, and do not mur-
    der
The flower of our country. O my son,
Whose line descends from heaven, let the
    sword
Fall from the hand, be leader in forbearing!
    Who would pass over,
Without a word, Cossus, or noble Cato,
The Gracchi, or those thunderbolts of warfare,
The Scipios, Libya's ruin, or Fabricius
Mighty with little, or Serranus, ploughing
The humble furrow? My tale must hurry on:
I see the Fabii next, and their great Quintus
Who brought us back an empire by delaying.
Others, no doubt, will better mould the bronze
To the semblance of soft breathing, draw, from
    marble,
The living countenance; and others plead
With greater eloquence, or learn to measure,
Better than we, the pathways of the heaven,
The risings of the stars: remember, Roman,
To rule the people under law, to establish
The way of peace, to battle down the haughty,
To spare the meek. Our fine arts, these, for-
    ever."
    Anchises paused a moment, and they mar-
    velled,
And he went on:—"See, how Marcellus tri-
    umphs,
Glorious over all, with the great trophies
Won when he slew the captain of the Gauls,

Leader victorious over leading foeman.
When Rome is in great trouble and confusion
He will establish order, Gaul and Carthage
Go down before his sword, and triple trophies
Be given Romulus in dedication."
    There was a young man going with Mar-
    cellus,
Brilliant in shining armor, bright in beauty,
But sorrowful, with downcast eyes. Aeneas
Broke in, to ask his father: "Who is this youth
Attendant on the hero? A son of his?
One of his children's children? How the crowd
Murmurs and hums around him! what distinc-
    tion,
What presence, in his person! But dark night
Hovers around his head with mournful shadow.
Who is he father?" And Anchises answered:—
"Great sorrow for our people! O my son,
Ask not to know it. This one fate will only
Show to the world; he will not be permitted
Any long sojourn. Rome would be too mighty,
Too great in the gods' sight, were this gift hers.
What lamentation will the field of Mars
Raise to the city! Tiber, gliding by
The new-built tomb, the funeral state, bear
    witness!
No youth from Trojan stock will ever raise
His ancestors so high in hope, no Roman
Be such a cause for pride. Alas for goodness,
Alas for old-time honor, and the arm
Invincible in war! Against him no one,
Whether on foot or foaming horse, would come
In battle and depart unscathed. Poor boy,
If you should break the cruel fates; if only—
You are to be Marcellus. Let me scatter
Lilies, or dark-red flowers, bringing honor
To my descendant's shade; let the gift be of-
    fered,
However vain the tribute."
    So through the whole wide realm they went
    together,
Anchises and his son; from fields of air
Learning and teaching of the fame and glory,
The wars to come, the toils to face, or flee from,
Latinus' city and the Latin peoples,
The love of what would be.
                There are two portals,
Twin gates of Sleep, one made of horn, where
    easy
Release is given true shades, the other gleam-
    ing

White ivory, whereby the false dreams issue
To the upper air. Aeneas and the Sibyl
Part from Anchises at the second portal.

He goes to the ships, again, rejoins his com-
    rades,
Sails to Caieta's harbor, and the vessels
Rest on their mooring-lines.

Cicero

*Marcus Tullius Cicero (104–43 B.C.) played a promi-
nent part in the political and intellectual life of
Rome during the last days of the Republic. In the period of
civil strife he identified himself with the aristocratic party
supporting the Republic in opposition to Julius Caesar.
Cicero studied and wrote both in the fields of government
and philosophy, and in The Laws he brought the two together to form a well-known and very influential treatise on
the origin and nature of law. Like the culture he represented, Cicero lacked originality, but also like his culture,
he successfully synthesized many of the ideals of Hellenic
and Hellenistic culture with the practical achievements of
Roman political life. Cicero promoted the classic statement
of the idea of natural law which exerted so much influence
on the thought of the middle ages and of the eighteenth
century. In reading the selections note (1) Cicero's basic
assumptions regarding the universe, God, and man, (2)
evidences of Stoicism and Platonism, (3) his description
of nature's endowment to humanity, (4) his arguments in
favor of human equality, (5) his belief concerning the ultimate force behind law, (6) his rule for distinguishing a
good from a bad law, (7) his effort to establish absolutes
of goodness, law, justice, etc., and (8) his attitude toward
man-made enactments contrary to the law of nature.*

From: THE LAWS

Marcus.—But the whole subject of universal
law and jurisprudence must be comprehended
in this discussion, in order that this which we
call civil law, may be confined in some one
small and narrow space of nature. For we shall
have to explain the true nature of moral justice,
which must be traced back from the nature of
man. And laws will have to be considered by
which all political states should be governed.
And last of all, shall we have to speak of those
laws and customs of nations, which are framed
for the use and convenience of particular countries, (in which even our own people will not
be omitted,) which are known by the title of
civil laws.

Quintus.—You take a noble view of the subject, my brother, and go to the fountainhead,
in order to throw light on the subject of our
consideration; and those who treat civil law
in any other manner, are not so much pointing
out the paths of justice as those of litigation.

Marcus.—That is not quite the case, my
Quintus. It is not so much the science of law
that produces litigation, as the ignorance of it.

As translated by C. D. Yonge in *M. Tullius Cicero, On the Nature of the Gods; On Divination; On Fate; On the Republic; On the Laws; and On Standing for the Consulship,* G. Bell and Sons, Ltd., London, 1911, 406–421; 430–435.
Courtesy of G. Bell and Sons, Ltd.

But more of this by-and-by. At present let us examine the first principles of Right.

Now, many learned men have maintained that it springs from law. I hardly know if their opinion be not correct, at least according to their own definition; for "law," say they, "is the highest reason implanted in nature, which prescribes those things which ought to be done, and forbids the contrary." And when this same reason is confirmed and established in men's minds, it is then law.

They therefore conceive that prudence is a law, whose operation is to urge us to good actions, and restrain us from evil ones. And they think, too, that the Greek name for law (νόμος), which is derived from νέμω, to distribute, implies the very nature of the thing, that is, to give every man his due. The Latin name, *lex*, conveys the idea of selection, *a legendo*. According to the Greeks, therefore, the name of law implies an equitable distribution: according to the Romans, an equitable selection. And, indeed, both characteristics belong peculiarly to law.

And if this be a correct statement, which it seems to me for the most part to be, then the origin of right is to be sought in the law. For this is the true energy of nature,—this is the very soul and reason of a wise man, and the test of virtue and vice. But since all this discussion of ours relates to a subject, the terms of which are of frequent occurrence in the popular language of the citizens, we shall be sometimes obliged to use the same terms as the vulgar, and to call that law, which in its written enactments sanctions what it thinks fit by special commands or prohibitions.

Let us begin, then, to establish the principles of justice on that supreme law, which has existed from all ages before any legislative enactments were drawn up in writing, or any political governments constituted. . . . Shall we, then, seek for the origin of justice at its fountainhead? When we have discovered which, we shall be in no doubt to what these questions which we are examining ought to be referred. . . . Since, then, we wish to maintain and preserve the constitution of that republic which Scipio . . . has proved to be the best, and since all our laws are to be accommodated to the kind of political government there described, we must also treat of the general principles of morals and manners, and not limit ourselves on all occasions to written laws; but I purpose to trace back the origin of right from nature itself, who will be our best guide in conducting the whole discussion.

Atticus.—You will do right, and when she is our guide it is absolutely impossible for us to err.

Marcus.—Do you then grant, my Atticus (for I know my brother's opinion already), that the entire universe is regulated by the power of the immortal Gods, that by their nature, reason, energy, mind, divinity, or some other word of clearer signification, if there be such, all things are governed and directed? for if you will not grant me this, that is what I must begin by establishing.

Atticus.—I grant you all you can desire. But owing to this singing of birds and babbling of waters, I fear my fellow-learners can scarcely hear me.

Marcus.—You are quite right to be on your guard; for even the best men occasionally fall into a passion, and they will be very indignant if they hear you denying the first article of that notable book, entitled "The Chief Doctrines of Epicurus," in which he says "that God takes care of nothing, neither of himself nor of any other being!"

Atticus.—Pray proceed, for I am waiting to know what advantage you mean to take of the concession I have made you.

Marcus.—I will not detain you long. This is the bearing which they have on our subject. This animal—prescient, sagacious, complex, acute, full of memory, reason, and counsel, which we call man—has been generated by the supreme God in a most transcendent condition. For he is the only creature among all the races and descriptions of animated beings who is endued with superior reason and thought, in which the rest are deficient. And what is there, I do not say in man alone, but in all heaven and earth, more divine than reason, which, when it becomes right and perfect, is justly termed wisdom?

There exists, therefore, since nothing is better than reason, and since this is the common property of God and man, a certain aboriginal rational intercourse between divine and human natures. But where reason is common, there right reason must also be common to the same parties; and since this right reason is what we call law, God and men must be considered as associated by law. Again, there must also be a communion of right where there is a communion of law. And those who have law and right thus in common, must be considered members of the same commonwealth.

And if they are obedient to the same rule and the same authority, they are even much more so to this one celestial regency, this divine mind and omnipotent deity. So that the entire universe may be looked upon as forming one vast commonwealth of gods and men. And, as in earthly states certain ranks are distinguished with reference to the relationships of families, according to a certain principle which will be discussed in its proper place, that principle, in the nature of things, is far more magnificent and splendid by which men are connected with the Gods, as belonging to their kindred and nation.

For when we are reasoning on universal nature, we are accustomed to argue (and indeed the truth is just as it is stated in that argument) that in the long course of ages, and the uninterrupted succession of celestial revolutions, there arrived a certain ripe time for the sowing of the human race; and when it was sown and scattered over the earth, it was animated by the divine gift of souls. And as men retained from their terrestrial origin those other particulars by which they cohere together, which are frail and perishable, their immortal spirits were ingenerated by the Deity. From which circumstance it may be truly said, that we possess a certain consanguinity, and kindred, and fellowship with the heavenly powers. And among all the varieties of animals, there is not one except man which retains any idea of the Divinity. And among men, themselves, there is no nation so savage and ferocious as not to admit the necessity of believing in a God, however ignorant they may be what sort of God they ought to believe in. From whence we conclude that every man must recognize a Deity, who has any recollection and knowledge of his own origin.

Now, the law of virtue is the same in God and man, and in no other disposition besides them. This virtue is nothing else than a nature perfect in itself, and wrought up to the most consummate excellence. There exists, therefore, a similitude between God and man. And as this is the case, what connexion can there be which concerns us more nearly, and is more certain?

Therefore, nature has supplied such an abundance of supplies suited to the convenience and use of men, that the things which are thus produced appear to be designedly bestowed on us, and not fortuitous productions. Nor does this observation apply only to the fruits and vegetables which gush from the bosom of the earth, but likewise to cattle and the beasts of the field, some of which, it is clear, were intended for the use of mankind, others for propagation, and others for the food of man. Innumerable arts have likewise been discovered by the teaching of nature, whom reason has imitated, and thus skilfully discovered all things necessary to the happiness of life.

With respect to man, this same bountiful nature hath not merely allotted him a subtle and active spirit, but also physical senses, like so many servants and messengers. And she has laid bare before him the obscure but necessary explanation of many things, which are, as it were, the foundation of practical knowledge; and in all respects she has given him a convenient figure of body, suited to the bent of the human character. For while she has kept down the countenances of other animals, and fixed their eyes on their food, she has bestowed on man alone an erect stature, and prompted him to the contemplation of heaven, the ancient home of his kindred immortals. So exquisitely, too, has she fashioned the features of the human face, as to make them indicate the most recondite thoughts and sentiments. For our eloquent eyes speak forth every impulse and passion of our souls; and that which we call *expression*, which cannot exist in any other animal but man, betrays all our feelings, the power of which was well known to the Greeks, though they have no name for it.

I will not enlarge on the wonderful faculties and qualities of the rest of the body, the modulation of the voice, and the power of oratory, which is the greatest instrument of influence upon human society. For these matters do not all belong to the present occasion or the present subject, and I think that Scipio has already sufficiently explained them in those books of mine which you have read.

Since, then, the Deity has been pleased to create and adorn man to be the chief and president of all terrestrial creatures, so it is evident, without further argument, that human nature has also made very great advances by its own intrinsic energy; that nature, which without any other instruction than her own, has developed the first rude principles of the understanding, and strengthened and perfected reason to all the appliances of science and art.

Atticus.—Oh ye immortal Gods! to what a distance back are you tracing the principles of justice! However, you are discoursing in such a style that I will not show any impatience to hear what I expect you to say on the Civil Law. But I will listen patiently, even if you spend the whole day in this kind of discourse; for assuredly these, which perhaps you are embracing in your argument for the sake of others, are grander topics than even the subject itself for which they prepare the way.

Marcus.—You may well describe these topics as grand, which we are now briefly discussing. But of all the questions which are ever the subject of discussion among learned men, there is none which it is more important thoroughly to understand than this, that man is born for justice, and that law and equity have not been established by opinion, but by nature. This truth will become still more apparent if we investigate the nature of human association and society.

For there is no one thing so like or so equal to another, as in every instance man is to man. And if the corruption of customs, and the variation of opinions, did not induce an imbecility of minds, and turn them aside from the course of nature, no one would more nearly resemble himself than all men would resemble all men. Therefore, whatever definition we give of man, will be applicable to the whole human race. And this is a good argument that there is no dissimilarity of kind among men; because if this were the case, one definition could not include all men.

In fact, reason, which alone gives us so many advantages over beasts, by means of which we conjecture, argue, refute, discourse, and accomplish and conclude our designs, is assuredly common to all men; for the faculty of acquiring knowledge is similar in all human minds, though the knowledge itself may be endlessly diversified. By the same senses we all perceive the same objects, and those things which move the senses at all, do move in the same way the senses of all men. And those first rude elements of intelligence which, as I before observed, are the earliest developments of thought, are similarly impressed upon all men; and that faculty of speech which is the interpreter of the mind, agrees in the ideas which it conveys, though it may differ in the words by which it expresses them. And therefore there exists not a man in any nation, who, if he adopts nature for his guide, may not arrive at virtue.

Nor is this resemblance which all men bear to each other remarkable in those things only which are in accordance with right reason, but also in errors. For all men alike are captivated by pleasure, which, although it is a temptation to what is disgraceful, nevertheless bears some resemblance to natural good; for, as by its delicacy and sweetness it is delightful, it is through a mistake of the intellect adopted as something salutary.

And by an error scarcely less universal, we shun death as if it were a dissolution of nature, and cling to life because it keeps us in that existence in which we were born. Thus, likewise, we consider pain as one of the greatest evils, not only on account of its present asperity, but also because it seems the precursor of mortality. Again, on account of the apparent resemblance between renown with honour, those men appear to us happy who are honoured, and miserable who happen to be inglorious. In like manner our minds are all similarly susceptible of inquietudes, joys, desires, and fears; nor if different men have different opinions, does it follow that those who deify dogs and cats, do not labour under superstition equally with other nations, though they may differ from them in the forms of its manifestation.

Again, what nation is there which has not a regard for kindness, benignity, gratitude, and mindfulness of benefits? What nation is there in which arrogance, malice, cruelty, and unthankfulness, are not reprobated and detested? And while this uniformity of opinions proves that the whole race of mankind is united together, the last point is that a system of living properly makes men better. If what I have said meets your approbation, I will proceed; or if any doubts occur to you, we had better clear them up first.

Atticus.—There is nothing which strikes us, if I may reply for both of us.

Marcus.—It follows, then, that nature made us just that we might share our goods with each other, and supply each other's wants. You observe in this discussion, whenever I speak of nature, I mean nature in its genuine purity, but that there is, in fact, such corruption engendered by evil customs, that the sparks, as it were, of virtue which have been given by nature are extinguished, and that antagonist vices arise around it and become strengthened.

But if, as nature prompts them to, men would with deliberate judgment, in the words of the poet, "being men, think nothing that concerns mankind indifferent to them," then would justice be cultivated equally by all. For to those to whom nature has given reason, she has also given right reason, and therefore also law, which is nothing else than right reason enjoining what is good, and forbidding what is evil. And if nature has given us law, she hath also given us right. But she has bestowed reason on all, therefore right has been bestowed on all. And therefore did Socrates deservedly execrate the man who first drew a distinction between utility and nature, for he used to complain that this error was the source of all human vices, to which this sentence of Pythagoras refers—"The things belonging to friends are common"—and that other, "Friendly equality." From whence it appears, that when a wise man has displayed this benevolence which is so extensively and widely diffused towards one who is endowed with equal virtue, then that phenomenon takes place which is altogether incredible to some people, but which is a necessary consequence, that he loves himself not more dearly than he loves his friend. For how can a difference of interests arise where all interests are similar? If there could be ever so minute a difference of interests, then there would be an end of even the nature of friendship, the real meaning of which is such, that there is no friendship at all the moment that a person prefers anything happening to himself rather than to his friend. . . .

But in conformity with the method of philosophers (I do not mean the older sages of philosophy, but those modern ones, who have erected a magazine, as it were, of wisdom), those questions which were formerly discussed loosely and unconstrainedly, are now examined with strictness and distinctness. Nor will these men allow that we have done justice to the subject which we have now before us, unless we demonstrate in a distinct discussion that right is a part of nature. . . .

But were it the fear of punishment, and not the nature of the thing itself, that ought to restrain mankind from wickedness, what, I would ask, could give villains the least uneasiness, abstracting from all fears of this kind? And yet none of them was ever so audaciously impudent, but what he either denied that the action in question had been committed by him, or pretended some cause or other for his just indignation, or sought a defence of his deed in some right of nature. And if the wicked dare to appeal to this principle, with what respect ought not good men to treat them?

But if either direct punishment, or the fear of it, be what deters men from a vicious and criminal course of life, and not the turpitude of the thing itself, then none can be guilty of injustice, and the greatest offenders ought rather to be called imprudent than wicked.

On the other hand, those among us who are determined to the practice of goodness, not by its own intrinsic excellence, but for the sake of some private advantage, are cunning rather than good men. For what will not that man do in the dark who fears nothing but a witness and a judge? Should he meet a solitary individual in a desert place, whom he can rob of a large sum of money, and altogether unable to defend himself from being robbed, how will he behave? In such a case our man, who is just and honourable from principle and the nature of the thing itself, will converse with the stranger, assist him, and show him the way. But he who does nothing for the sake of another, and measures everything by the advantage it brings to itself, it is obvious, I suppose, how such a one will act; and should he deny that he would kill the man, or rob him of his treasure, his reason for this cannot be that he apprehends there is any moral turpitude in such actions, but only because he is afraid of a discovery, that is to say, that bad consequences will thence ensue— a sentiment this at which not only learned men but even clowns must blush.

It is therefore an absurd extravagance in some philosophers to assert, that all things are necessarily just which are established by the civil laws and the institutions of nations. Are then the laws of tyrants just, simply because they are laws? Suppose the thirty tyrants of Athens had imposed certain laws on the Athenians? Or, suppose again that these Athenians were delighted with these tyrannical laws, would these laws on that account have been considered just? For my own part, I do not think such laws deserve any greater estimation than that passed during our own interregnum, which ordained that the dictator should be empowered to put to death with impunity whatever citizens he pleased, without hearing them in their own defence.

For there is but one essential justice which cements society, and one law which establishes this justice. This law is right reason, which is the true rule of all commandments and prohibitions. Whoever neglects this law, whether written or unwritten, is necessarily unjust and wicked.

But if justice consists in submission to written laws and national customs, and if, as the same school affirms, everything must be measured by utility alone, he who thinks that such conduct will be advantageous to him will neglect the laws, and break them if it is in his power. And the consequence is, that real justice has really no existence if it have not one by nature, and if that which is established as such on account of utility is overturned by some other utility.

But if nature does not ratify law, then all the virtues may lose their sway. For what becomes of generosity, patriotism, or friendship? Where will the desire of benefiting our neighbours, or the gratitude that acknowledges kindness, be able to exist at all? For all these virtues proceed from our natural inclination to love mankind. And this is the true basis of justice, and without this not only the mutual charities of men, but the religious services of the Gods, would be at an end; for these are preserved, as I imagine, rather by the natural sympathy which subsists between divine and human beings, than by mere fear and timidity.

But if the will of the people, the decrees of the senate, the adjudications of magistrates, were sufficient to establish rights, then it might become right to rob, right to commit adultery, right to substitute forged wills, if such conduct were sanctioned by the votes or decrees of the multitude. But if the opinions and suffrages of foolish men had sufficient weight to outbalance the nature of things, then why should they not determine among them, that what is essentially bad and pernicious should henceforth pass for good and beneficial? Or why, since law can make right out of injustice, should it not also be able to change evil into good?

But we have no other rule by which we may be capable of distinguishing between a good or a bad law than that of nature. Nor is it only right and wrong which are discriminated by nature, but generally all that is honourable is by this means distinguished from all that is shameful; for common sense has impressed in our minds the first principles of things, and has given us a general acquaintance with them, by which we connect with virtue every honourable quality, and with vice all that is disgraceful.

But to think that these differences exist only in opinion, and not in nature, is the part of an idiot. For even the virtue of a tree or a horse, in which expression there is an abuse of terms, does not exist in our opinion only, but in nature; and if that is the case, then what is honourable and disgraceful, must also be discriminated by nature.

For if opinion could determine respecting the character of universal virtue, it might also decide respecting particular or partial virtues. But who will dare to determine that a man is prudent and cautious, not from his general conduct, but from some external appearances? For virtue evidently consists in perfect reason, and this certainly resides in nature. Therefore so does all honour and honesty in the same way.

For as what is true and false, creditable and discreditable, is judged of rather by their essential qualities than their external relations; so the consistent and perpetual course of life, which is virtue, and the inconsistency of life, which is vice, are judged of according to their own nature,—and that inconstancy must necessarily be vicious.

We form an estimate of the opinions of youths, but not by their opinions. Those virtues and vices which reside in their moral natures must not be measured by opinions. And so of all moral qualities, we must discriminate between honourable and dishonourable by reference to the essential nature of the things themselves.

The good we commend, must needs contain in itself something commendable; for as I before stated, goodness is not a mode of opinion, but of nature. For if it were otherwise, opinion alone might constitute virtue and happiness, which is the most absurd of suppositions. And since we judge of good and evil by their nature, and since good and evil are the first principles of nature, certainly we should judge in the same manner of all honourable and all shameful things, referring them all to the law of nature.

But we are often too much disturbed by the dissensions of men and the variation of opinions. And because the same thing does not happen with reference to our senses, we look upon them as certain by nature. Those objects, indeed, which sometimes present to us one appearance, sometimes another, and which do not always appear to the same people in the same way, we term fictions of the senses; but it is far otherwise. For neither parent, nor nurse, nor master, nor poet, nor drama, deceive our senses; nor do popular prejudices seduce them from the truth. But all kinds of snares are laid for the mind, either by those errors which I have just enumerated, which, taking possession of the young and uneducated, imbue them deeply, and bend them any way they please; or by that pleasure which is the imitator of goodness, being thoroughly and closely implicated with all our senses—the prolific mother of all evils. For she so corrupts us by her blandishments, that we no longer perceive some things which are essentially excellent, because they have none of this deliciousness and pruriency.

It follows that I may now sum up the whole of this argument by asserting, as is plain to every one from these positions which have been already laid down, that all right and all that is honourable is to be sought for its own sake. In truth, all virtuous men love justice and equity for what they are in themselves; nor is it like a good man to make a mistake, and love that which does not deserve their affection. Right, therefore, is desirable and deserving to be cultivated for its own sake; and if this be true of right, it must be true also of justice. What then shall we say of liberality? Is it exercised gratuitously, or does it covet some reward and recompense? If a man does good without expecting any recompense for his kindness, then it is gratuitous: if he does expect compensation, it is a mere matter of traffic. Nor is there any doubt that he who truly deserves the reputation of a generous and kind-hearted man, is thinking of his duty, not of his interest. In the same way the virtue of justice demands neither emolument nor salary, and therefore we desire it for its own sake. And the case of all the moral virtues is the same, and so is the opinion formed of them.

Besides this, if we weigh virtue by the mere utility and profit that attend it, and not by its own merit, the one virtue which results from such an estimate will be in fact a species of vice. For the more a man refers all his actions especially to his own advantage, the further he recedes from probity; so that they who measure virtue by profit, acknowledge no other virtue than this, which is a kind of vice. For who can be called benevolent, if no one ever acts kindly for the sake of another? And where are we to find a grateful person, if those who are disposed to be so can find no benefactor to whom they can show gratitude? What will become of sacred friendship, if we are not to love our friend for his own sake with all our heart and soul, as people say, if we are even to desert and discard him, as soon as we despair of deriving any further assistance or advantage from him? What can be imagined more inhuman than this conduct? But if friendship ought rather to be cultivated on its own account, so also for the same reason are society, equality, and justice desirable for their own sakes. If this be not so, then there can be no such thing as justice at all; for the most unjust thing of all is to seek a reward for one's just conduct.

What then shall we say of temperance, sobriety, continence, modesty, bashfulness, and chastity? Is it the fear of infamy, or the dread of judgments and penalties, which prevent men from being intemperate and dissolute? Do men then live in innocence and moderation, only to be well spoken of, and to acquire a certain fair reputation? Modest men blush even to speak of indelicacy. And I am greatly ashamed of those philosophers, who assert that there are no vices to be avoided but those which the laws have branded with infamy. For what shall I say? Can we call those persons truly chaste, who abstain from adultery merely from the fear of public exposure and that disgrace which is only one of its many evil consequences? For what can be either praised or blamed with reason, if you depart from that great law and rule of nature, which makes the difference between right and wrong? Shall corporal defects, if they are remarkable, shock our sensibilities, and shall those of the soul make no impression on us?—of the soul, I say, whose turpitude is so evidently proved by its vices. For what is there more hideous than avarice, more brutal than lust, more contemptible than cowardice, more base than stupidity and folly? Well, then, are we to call those persons unhappy, who are conspicuous for one or more of these, on account of some injuries, or disgraces, or sufferings to which they are exposed, or on account of the moral baseness of their sins? And we may apply the same test in the opposite way to those who are distinguished for their virtue.

Lastly, if virtue be sought for on account of some other things, it necessarily follows that there is something better than virtue. Is it money, then? is it fame, or beauty, or health? all of which appear of little value to us when we possess them; nor can it be by any possibility certainly known how long they will last. Or is it (what it is shameful even to utter) that basest of all, pleasure? Surely not; for it is in the contempt and disdain of pleasure that virtue is most conspicuous. . . .

Let us, then, once more examine, before we come to the consideration of particular laws, what is the power and nature of law in general; lest, when we come to refer everything to it, we occasionally make mistakes from the employment of incorrect language, and show ourselves ignorant of the force of those terms which we ought to employ in the definition of laws.

Quintus.—This is a very necessary caution, and the proper method of seeking truth.

Marcus.—This, then, as it appears to me, has been the decision of the wisest philosophers,—that law was neither a thing contrived by the genius of man, nor established by any decree of the people, but a certain eternal principle, which governs the entire universe, wisely commanding what is right and prohibiting what is wrong. Therefore they called that aboriginal and supreme law the mind of God, enjoining or forbidding each separate thing in accordance with reason. On which account it is, that this law, which the Gods have bestowed on the human race, is so justly applauded. For it is the reason and mind of a wise Being equally able to urge us to good and to deter us from evil.

Quintus.—You have, on more than one occasion, already touched on this topic. But before you come to treat of the laws of nations, I wish you would endeavour to explain the force and power of this divine and celestial law, lest the torrent of custom should overwhelm our understanding, and betray us into the vulgar method of expression.

Marcus.—From our childhood we have learned, my Quintus, to call such phrases as this, "that a man appeals to justice, and goes to law," and many similar expressions, law, but, nevertheless, we should understand that these, and other similar commandments and prohibitions, have sufficient power to lead us on to virtuous actions and to call us away from vicious ones. Which power is not only far more ancient than any existence of states and peoples, but is coeval with God himself, who beholds and governs both heaven and earth. For it is impossible that the divine mind can exist in a state devoid of reason; and divine reason must necessarily be possessed of a power to determine what is virtuous and what is vicious. Nor, because it was nowhere written, that one man should maintain the pass of a bridge against the enemy's whole army, and that he should order the bridge behind him to be cut down, are we therefore to imagine that the valiant Cocles did not perform this great exploit agreeably to the laws of nature and the dictates of true bravery. Again, though in the reign of Tarquin there was no written law concerning adultery, it does not therefore follow that Sextus Tarquinius did not offend against the eternal law when he committed a rape on Lucretia, daughter of Tricipitinus. For, even then he had the light of reason deduced from the nature of things, that incites to good actions and dissuades from evil ones; and which does not begin for the first time to be a law when it is drawn up in writing, but from the first moment that it exists. And this existence of moral obligation is coeternal with that of the divine mind. Therefore, the true and supreme law, whose commands and prohibitions are equally authoritative, is the right reason of the Sovereign Jupiter.

Quintus.—I grant you, my brother, that whatever is just is also at all times the true law; nor can this true law either be originated or abrogated by the written forms in which decrees are drawn up.

Marcus.—Therefore, as that Divine Mind, or reason, is the supreme law, so it exists in the mind of the sage, so far as it can be perfected in man. But with respect to civil laws, which are drawn up in various forms, and framed to meet the occasional requirements of the people, the name of law belongs to them not so much by right as by the favour of the people. For men prove by some such arguments as the following, that every law which deserves the name of a law, ought to be morally good and laudable. It is clear, say they, that laws were originally made for the security of the people, for the preservation of states, for the peace and happiness of society; and that they who first framed enactments of that kind, persuaded the people that they would write and publish such laws only as should conduce to the general morality and happiness, if they would receive and obey them. And then such regulations, being thus settled and sanctioned, they justly entitled *Laws.* From which we may reasonably conclude, that those who made unjustifiable and pernicious enactments for the

people, acted in a manner contrary to their own promises and professions, and established anything rather than *laws,* properly so called, since it is evident that the very signification of the word *law,* comprehends the whole essence and energy of justice and equity.

I would, therefore, interrogate you on this point, my Quintus, as those philosophers are in the habit of doing. If a state wants something for the want of which it is reckoned no state at all, must not that something be something good?

Quintus.—A very great good.

Marcus.—And if a state has no law, is it not for that reason to be reckoned no state at all?

Quintus.—We must needs say so.

Marcus.—We must therefore reckon law among the very best things.

Quintus.—I entirely agree with you.

Marcus.—If, then, in the majority of nations, many pernicious and mischievous enactments are made, which have no more right to the name of law than the mutual engagements of robbers, are we bound to call them laws? For as we cannot call the recipes of ignorant and unskilful empirics, who give poisons instead of medicines, the prescriptions of a physician, so likewise we cannot call that the true law of a people, of whatever kind it may be, if it enjoins what is injurious, let the people receive it as they will. For law is the just distinction between right and wrong, made conformable to that most ancient nature of all, the original and principal regulator of all things, by which the laws of men should be measured, whether they punish the guilty or protect and preserve the innocent. . . .

Let this, therefore, be a fundamental principle in all societies, that the Gods are the supreme lords and governors of all things,—that all events are directed by their influence, and wisdom, and Divine power; that they deserve very well of the race of mankind; and that they likewise know what sort of person every one really is; that they observe his actions, whether good or bad; that they take notice with what feelings and with what piety he attends to his religious duties, and that they are sure to make a difference between the good and the wicked.

For when once our minds are confirmed in

these views, it will not be difficult to inspire them with true and useful sentiments. For what can be more true than that no man should be so madly presumptuous as to believe that he has either reason or intelligence, while he does not believe that the heaven and the world possess them likewise, or to think that those things which he can scarcely comprehend by the greatest possible exertion of his intellect, are put in motion without the agency of reason?

In truth, we can scarcely reckon him a man, whom neither the regular courses of the stars, nor the alternations of day and night, nor the temperature of the seasons, nor the productions that nature displays for his use and enjoyment, urge to gratitude towards heaven.

And as those beings which are furnished with reason are incomparably superior to those which want it, and as we cannot say, without impiety, that anything is superior to the universal Nature, we must therefore confess that divine reason is contained within her. And who will dispute the utility of these sentiments, when he reflects how many cases of the greatest importance are decided by oaths; how much the sacred rites performed in making treaties tend to assure peace and tranquillity; and what numbers of people the fear of divine punishment has reclaimed from a vicious course of life; and how sacred the social rights must be in a society where a firm persuasion obtains the immediate intervention of the immortal Gods, both as witnesses and judges of our actions? Such is the "preamble of the law," to use the expression of Plato.

Marcus Aurelius

Marcus Aurelius (121–180 A.D.), the last of the good emperors, achieved fame both as a governor and as a student of philosophy. He attempted, with considerable success, to apply the principles of the Hellenistic philosophy of Stoicism to the problems of empire. A man of lofty ideals and fine character, he was naturally attracted by the strict ethics of Stoicism and by its emphasis on universal brotherhood. The Thoughts of Marcus Aurelius revealed these interests. In reading the selections from them note particularly (1) the basis for his belief in universal brotherhood, (2) the rules he established to govern his own daily conduct, (3) his ideas on law and political bodies, (4) his views on death, (5) his thoughts concerning the relationship between nature and man, and (6) his concept of the nature and importance of mind.

From: THE THOUGHTS OF MARCUS AURELIUS

Every morning repeat to thyself: I shall meet with a busybody, an ingrate, and a bully; with treachery, envy, and selfishness. All these vices have fallen to their share because they know not good and evil. But I have contemplated the nature of the good and seen that it is the beautiful; of evil, and seen that it is deformity; of the sinner, and seen that it is kindred to my own—kindred, not because he shares the same flesh and blood and is sprung from the same seed, but because he partakes of the same reason and the same spark of divinity. How then can any of these harm me? For none can involve me in the shameful save my-

As translated by John Jackson in *The Thoughts of Marcus Aurelius Antonius*, in the World's Classics, Oxford University Press, London, 1906, 8–10; 23–24; 75; 113–121. Courtesy of the Oxford University Press.

self. Or how can I be angered with my kith and kin, or cherish hatred towards them?

For we are all created to work together, as the members of one body—feet, hands, and eyelids, or the upper and nether teeth. Whence, to work against each other is contrary to nature;—but this is the very essence of anger and aversion.

This thing that I call "myself" is compact of flesh, breath, and reason. Thou art even now in the throes of death; despise therefore the flesh. It is but a little blood, a few bones, a paltry net woven from nerves and veins and arteries. Consider next thy breath. What a trifle it is! A little air, and this for ever changing: every minute of every hour we are gasping it forth and sucking it in again!

Only reason is left us. Consider thus: Thou art striken in years; then suffer it not to remain a bond-servant; suffer it not to be puppet-like, hurried hither and thither by impulses that take no thought of thy fellow-man; suffer it not to murmur at destiny in the present or look askance at it in the future.

The works of God are full of providence; the works of Fortune are not independent of Nature, but intertwisted and intertwined with those directed by providence. Thence flow all things. Co-factors, too, are necessity and the common welfare of the whole universe whereof thou art part. Now whatever arises from the nature of the whole, and tends to its well-being, is good also for every part of that nature. But the well-being of the universe depends on change, not merely of the elementary, but also of the compound. Let these dogmas suffice thee, if dogmas thou must have; but put off that thirst for books, and see thou die of good cheer, not with murmurs on thy lips, but blessing God truthfully and with all thy heart.

Bethink thee how long thou hast delayed to do these things; how many days of grace heaven hath vouchsafed thee and thou neglected. Now is the time to learn at last what is the nature of the universe whereof thou art part; what of the power that governs the universe, whereof thou art an emanation. Forget not there is a boundary set to thy time, and that if thou use it not to uncloud thy soul it will anon be gone, and thou with it, never to return again.

Let it be thy hourly care to do stoutly what thy hand findeth to do, as becomes a man and a Roman, with carefulness, unaffected dignity, humanity, freedom, and justice. Free thyself from the obsession of all other thoughts; for free thyself thou wilt, if thou but perform every action as though it were the last of thy life, without light-mindedness, without swerving through force of passion from the dictates of reason, without hypocrisy, without self-love, without chafing at destiny.

Thou seest how few things are needful for man to live a happy and godlike life: for, if he observe these, heaven will demand no more.

Abase thee, abase thee, O my soul! The time is past for exalting thyself. Man hath but a single life; and this thou hast well nigh spent, reverencing not thyself, but dreaming thy happiness is situate in the souls of others!

Why suffer the incidence of things external to distract thee? Make for thyself leisure to learn something new of good, and cease this endless round.—And here beware lest the wheel only reverse its motion. For fools, too, are they who have worn out their lives in action, yet never set before themselves a goal to which they could direct every impulse—nay, every thought.

Thou mayest search, but wilt hardly find a man made wretched through failing to read another's soul; whereas he who fails to ponder the motions of his own must needs be wretched.

Let me ever be mindful what is the nature of the universe, and what my own; how the latter is related to the former, and what part it is of what whole.—And forget not that there is none that can forbid thee to be ever, in deed and word, in harmony with the nature whereof thou art part. . . .

If the intellectual part of us is common to all, so is the reason which gives us our status as rational beings. Granted this, the reason which bids us do or not do must needs be common also. Hence it follows that there is one law; and if the law be one, we are all fellow-subjects, and, as such, members of one body-politic: that is, the universe is a species of state.—For what other conceivable political community is there, of which the whole human race can be said to be citizens?—And from this city of the universe must proceed those very faculties of intellect and reason, with our conception of law. There is no other possible source; but precisely as the earthly part of myself has been assigned me from some universal earth, and the fluid from the contrary element, while breath, warmth, and heat must each have had their proper fount, in virtue of the axiom that nothing can come from nothing any more than it can return from nothing,—so too must the intellect have had its definite origin.

Death is akin to birth in that both are mysteries of nature: in the one there is composition; in the other, decomposition: in both the antecedent and resultant elements are the same. —At all events, it is not a thing to be ashamed of, for in it there is nothing save what is consonant with the nature of rational life, and nothing that is repugnant to the laws of our being.

It is a matter of nature and necessity for men of this type to act as they do.—And, in general, remember the truth that, in a little while, both thou and he will be no more; and yet, a little while, and not so much as your names will be left. . . .

As universal Nature has given every rational being practically all her other powers, so too we are indebted to her for this: that just as she herself converts every obstacle in her path, and every attempt at resistance, to her own ends, assigns them to their proper place in destiny, and makes them part of herself, so each rational being has the power to convert any impediment into material for itself, and to use it for whatever purpose it had in view.

Trouble not thyself by pondering life in its entirety. Strive not to comprehend in one view the nature and number of the burdens that, belike, will fall to thy share. Rather, as each occasion arises in the present put this question to thyself: "Where lies the unbearable, unendurable part of this task?" Confession will put thee to the blush! Next recall to mind that neither past nor future can weigh thee down, only the present. And the present will shrink to littleness if thou but set it apart, assign it its boundaries, and then ask thy mind if it avail not to bear even this! . . .

All the objects thou prayest it may be thine to reach after many days are, even now, within thy power, if thou wilt but stretch forth thy hand to take them: in other words, if thou wilt

leave the past to itself, entrust the future to providence, and content thyself with conforming the present to holiness and justice. Holiness, that thou mayest rest content with the lot Nature assigns thee; for she bare it for thee and thee for it. Justice, that thy words may be the words of truth, free and undisguised; that thy every act may conform to law and equity; and that naught may impede thee, whether it be another's wickedness, his thoughts of thee, and his words, or the sensations of this circumscribing flesh, which, being the sufferer, may be left to look to itself. Accordingly, whensoever thou shalt draw nigh to thy journey's end, leave all else behind thee, reserve thy reverence for reason and the celestial part of thyself, and fear not because sooner or later thou must cease to live, but rather lest life by Nature's laws be yet to begin:—this do, and thou wilt be a man worthy of the universe that gave thee birth, no longer a stranger on thy native soil, no longer a dullard to whom the events of every day are marvels of the unexpected, and no longer a mere dependent on this thing or that!

God views the minds of all men in their nakedness, stripped of the casings and husks and impurities of the material. For, solely in virtue of the intellectual part of Himself, He touches directly the human intellect that emanates from Him and has flowed into these bodies of ours. So train thou thyself to do likewise, and thou shalt be quit of this sore distraction of thine. For he who has no eyes for our fleshly covering surely will not trouble himself with the contemplation of a man's house, raiment, fame, or aught else of these outer trappings and stage decorations!

There are three things whereof thou art compound: body, breath, and mind. Of these the first two are thine in so far as it is thy duty to assume their stewardship; but the third alone is thine absolutely. Wherefore, if thou wilt put away from thyself and thy mind all that others do or say, all thou thyself hast said or done, all disturbing thoughts of the future, all the vicissitudes of thy fleshly garment and its conjunct breath, with all that the circumfluent vortex whirls along, so that the intellective power, exempt and purified from the things of destiny, may dwell free and master in its own household, practising justice of action, resigned to all that chances, and speaking the truth,—if, I say, "thou wilt put aside from this reason of thine all accretions born of the fleshly affections, all time to come, and all time past, likening thyself to the Empedoclean globe— that perfect sphere rejoicing with great joy in its stability,"—and striving to live only the life thou livest, in other words the present, then the power will be thine to pass the span that is left between thee and death in calmness and cheerfulness and content with the godhead that resides within thee.

I have often marvelled how it is that every one loves himself more than the rest of human kind, yet values his own opinion of himself less than that of others. At all events, were some god or some sage to stand by a man and bid him entertain no idea, no thought, within himself without simultaneously uttering it aloud, he could not abide the ordeal for a single day. So true it is that we have more respect for our neighbours and their thoughts of us than we have for ourselves! . . .

The universe must be governed either by a foreordained destiny,—an order that none may overstep,—by a merciful providence, or by a chaos of chance devoid of a ruler. If the theory of an insuperable fate be true, why struggle against it? If providence watches over all and may be inclined to mercy, render thyself worthy of celestial aid. But if leaderless chaos be all, rest content that in the midst of this storm-swept sea Reason still dwells and rules within thee. And if the tide swirl thee away, let it take thy flesh and spirit, with all the rest; for Reason it cannot take. Or shall the light in the lanthorn shine and its radiance be dimmed only by extinction, and the truth, the justice, the temperance, that abide within thee, die out in darkness before death shall overtake thee?

If a man seem to thee to have sinned, ask: How do I know whether this deed of his be a sin or no? But granted he has sinned, is it certain that he has not voluntarily condemned himself? For remorse may be genuine without finding vent in tears and tearings of cheeks.

Reflect, moreover, that he who will not have the vicious man indulge his vice is on a level with him who would forbid the fig-tree's juice to be bitter, prohibit the child from crying, or

the horse from neighing, and veto all else that is inevitable. For what can the man do but sin, with a character such as he has? If then thou hast strength and skill, heal this!

If the act become thee not, do it not! If the word be false, say it not! . . .

Reflect that, in a little while, thou shalt be nothingness and no place shall know thee, nor shall anything be of all that now thou seest, nor any man of those who are now in life. For all things are by nature framed to change, transmute, and decay, that others may rise to fill their places. . . .

There are three things ever to be kept in mind. First, whatever thou doest, see it be done not at random, but so that Justice herself could not have acted otherwise; and remember that all external contingencies are dispensations either of chance or providence, and that it is folly to blame the former, and impiety to accuse the latter. Second, ponder the progress of every being from its generation to the hour when it receives a soul, and thence again to the time when it renders back that soul, together with the elements whereof all things are compound, and into which they must be dissolved. Third, reflect that were some sudden power to bear thee aloft to a pinnacle, whence thou couldst survey human life in all its multifariousness, after gaining withal a glimpse at the multitude of creatures that people the surrounding air and ether, the sight would inspire thee with contempt; and, oft as the ascent might be repeated, the same spectacle would always meet thy gaze: monotony of form and brevity of time. These are the objects of our pride! . . .

To show vexation at aught is to forget that all things take place by the fiat of universal Nature; that the sin which troubles thee is another's, not thine; and that all that happens always has happened, always will happen, and everywhere is happening in exactly the same way. It is to forget the ties of kindred that unite the individual to the rest of his kind;— a kindred based not on community of flesh and blood and seed, but of reason;—to forget that the intelligence wherewith every man is endowed is divine, and an emanation from the Deity; that nothing belongs to ourselves alone, but children, body, and even soul are all sprung from the same source; that all is opinion; and, finally, that each of us lives the present moment alone, and that this is all he loses.

Continually revolve the fate of men whom circumstances have driven to bitterness; men who have known the heights of glory, the depths of calamity and enmity, or any extreme of fortune you will. Then ask: "Where is it all now?" Vapour, dust and ashes; a tale that is told or a tale that has ceased to be told!

And let this bring up all the stories of the life Fabius Catullinus led in the country, Lucius Lupus in his parks, Stertinius at Baiae, Tiberius in Capreae, and Rufus at Velia—in a word, all the classic instances of arrogance pursuing its ends. Reflect how vulgar all their efforts were, and how much more philosophic it is for a man to use the materials at his disposal in order to render himself just and temperate, and a follower in the divine footsteps. But let this be done in simplicity; for of all forms of pride the most intolerable is that which smoulders under a self-styled humility.

When men ask: "Where hast thou seen these gods thou art so eager to worship? Or what proof hast thou that they exist?" My answer is: "First of all, they *are* visible even to the bodily eye; and in the second place, I have not seen my soul, yet I have none the less veneration for it. And so it is with the gods. From all the instances, in which I am every moment experiencing their power, I conclude they exist and bow before them."

The salvation of life is to contemplate every object in its entirety, and see what it is in essence, what is the formal element in it, and what the material; and to do the right, and speak the truth, in all sincerity of heart. What then is left, save to enjoy life, adding one good deed to another so that not the briefest interval is left bare of good?

There is one light of the sun, though it be interrupted by walls, mountains, and impediments innumerable. There is one universal substance, though it be broken up into a myriad of bodies, each with its peculiar qualities. There is one soul, though the natures and the limits of the individual among which it is distributed are legion. And there is one intellective soul, though it seems divided.

Now the other parts of the objects enumerated—for instance, spirit and matter—lack sensation and have no natural connexion one with the other. Yet even these are held in unison by the intellectual faculty and that power which compels them to gravitate towards the same point. But it is a peculiar property of the mind that its motion is ever to its kindred mind; with this it combines, and the feeling for community suffers no interruption.

What seekest thou?—Life?—But what wilt thou have? Perception? Impulse? Growth? The ensuing cessation of growth? The power of speech? Or the faculty of thought?—Which of these seems worthy of thy desire? Then, if they are all despicable, turn to the one thing left, and follow Reason and God. But it is directly antagonistic to this resolve for a man to value the things of life, or to shrink from the thought of being deprived thereof by death.

What an infinitely little part of the endless, unbroken tract of time has been allotted to each of us! What a trifling section of the universal substance and the universal soul! And what a tiny clod of the whole earth is the space whereon thou creepest! Think of all this and deem nothing great, save to do whatsoever the nature of thyself prescribes, and to suffer whatsoever the nature of the Whole brings thee.

To what end is thy ruling faculty applying itself? Herein is all. For the rest of things, be they subject to our will or independent thereof, are but death and vapour.

It is a potent stimulus to contempt of death to reflect that even they who class pleasure as a good, and pain as an evil, have dared to despise it.

The man who counts nothing good save that which comes in due season, who recks not whether the sum of his actions according to right reason shall be greater or less, and who cares not a jot whether he has viewed the universe for many years or few, cannot look on death as a thing of terror.

Friend, thou hast been a citizen in this great city; and what matters it whether for five years or three? The law is the same for us all. Where is the hardship, then, if it be no tyrant's stroke, no unjust judge, that sends thee into exile, but the same Nature that brought thee hither, even as the master of the show dismisses the mummer that he put on the stage? . . .

The Decline of Classical Civilization

Although Rome, by eclipsing the Greeks, had become the standard bearer of classical civilization, she proved to be unequal to the task of maintaining it, and gradually corruption, licentiousness, and waste began to characterize the lives of many in high places of authority. Economic maladjustments likewise began to appear in various parts of the Empire, and slowly but surely Rome's greatness began to decline. These conditions, together with the unsatisfying spiritual and moral character of the official Roman religion, furnished an ideal environment for the rapid spread of Christianity, a new religion which had emerged in the eastern Mediterranean from the bosom of the Hebrew faith. As Christianity spread westward, it brought with it certain oriental characteristics which, together with the uncertainties of life in the declining Empire, led to an increasing popularity of monasticism and a generally otherworldly outlook on life. As Rome's position gradually weakened, other powers emerged upon the Mediterranean scene to assume what Rome could no longer maintain. Thus in the East the Byzantine emperors and the followers of Mohammed inherited political and cultural leadership, while in the West the primitive Germanic peoples began their long struggle to build modern Western Civilization on the ruins of the Roman Empire.

Suetonius

Gaius Suetonius Tranquillus (about 75–150 A.D.) lived during a critical period in Roman history. Politically and culturally the empire reached its greatest development and entered into its long decline during his life. As Latin secretary to the Emperor Hadrian he had access to important archives, and as a student of human nature he was in a favorable position to gather material on the great men of the era. In The Lives of the Twelve Caesars he wrote an accurate and impartial account of the early emperors. Primarily biographical in character, they nevertheless inevitably revealed some of the factors that contributed to the decline of Rome. These selections are from the section on Nero, emperor from 54 to 68 A.D. In reading them note (1) Nero's early character and training, (2) his interest in music, (3) evidences of brutality in the life of the times, (4) Nero's depravity and extravagance, (5) the economic effects of his squanderings, (6) the political results of his superstitious fears, (7) the social and economic effects of the burning of Rome, and (8) the circumstances of his death.

From: THE LIVES OF THE TWELVE CAESARS

Nero was born at Antium nine months after the death of Tiberius, on the eighteenth day before the Kalends of January, just as the sun rose, so that he was touched by its rays almost before he could be laid upon the ground. Many people at once made many direful predictions from his horoscope, and a remark of his father, Domitius, was also regarded as an omen. For, while receiving the congratulations of his friends, he said that nothing that was not abominable and a public bane could be born of Agrippina and himself. Another manifest indication of Nero's future unhappiness occurred on his naming day. For, when Gaius Caesar was asked by his sister to give the child whatever name he liked, he looked at his uncle Claudius, who later became Emperor and adopted Nero, and said that he gave him his name. This he did, not seriously, but in jest, and Agrippina scorned the proposal, because at that time Claudius was one of the laughing-stocks of the court.

At the age of three he lost his father, being left heir to a third of his estate. But even this he did not receive in full, since his fellow heir Gaius seized all the property. Then his mother was banished too, and he was brought up at the house of his aunt Lepida almost in actual want, under two tutors, a dancer and a barber. But when Claudius became emperor, Nero not only recovered his father's property, but was also enriched by an inheritance from his step-father, Passienus Crispus. When his mother was recalled from banishment and reinstated, he became so prominent through her influence that it leaked out that Messalina, wife of Claudius, had sent emissaries to strangle him as he was taking his noonday nap, regarding him as a rival of Britannicus. An addition to this bit of gossip is, that the would-be assassins were frightened away by a snake which darted out from under his pillow. The only foundation for this tale was, that there was found in his bed near the pillow the slough of a serpent. All the same, at his mother's desire he had the skin enclosed in a golden bracelet, and wore it for a long time on his right arm. But when at last the memory of his mother grew hateful to him,

As translated by Joseph Gavorse in Suetonius, *The Lives of the Twelve Caesars,* The Modern Library, New York, 1931, 244–245; 252–253; 255–268; 273–274; 276–278. Courtesy of Random House, Inc.

he threw it away, and afterwards in the time of his extremity sought it again in vain.

While he was still a young, half-grown boy he took part in the game of Troy at a performance in the Circus with great self-possession and success. In the eleventh year of his age he was adopted by Claudius and consigned to the training of Annaeus Seneca, who was then already a Senator. They say that on the following night Seneca dreamed that he was teaching Gaius Caligula, and Nero soon proved the dream prophetic by revealing the cruelty of his disposition at the earliest possible opportunity. For merely because his brother Britannicus had, after his adoption, greeted him as usual as Ahenobarbus, he tried to convince his father that Britannicus was a changeling. Also when his aunt Lepida was accused, he publicly gave testimony against her, to gratify his mother, who was using every effort to ruin Lepida. . . .

Having gained some knowledge of music in addition to the rest of his early education, as soon as he became Emperor he sent for Terpnus, the greatest master of the lyre in those days, and after listening to him sing after dinner for many successive days until late at night, he little by little began to practice himself, neglecting none of the exercises which artists of that kind are in the habit of following, to preserve or strengthen their voices. For he used to lie upon his back and hold a leaden plate on his chest, purge himself by the syringe and by vomiting, and deny himself fruits and all foods injurious to the voice. Finally encouraged by his progress, although his voice was weak and husky, he began to long to appear on the stage, and every now and then in the presence of his intimate friends he would quote a Greek proverb meaning "Hidden music counts for nothing." And he made his début at Naples, where he did not cease singing until he had finished the number which he had begun, even though the theater was shaken by a sudden earthquake shock. In the same city he sang frequently and for several successive days. Even when he took a short time to rest his voice, he could not keep out of sight but went to the theater after bathing and dined in the orchestra with the people all about him, promising them in Greek, that when he had wetted his whistle a bit, he would ring out something good and loud. He was greatly taken too with the rhythmic applause of some Alexandrians, who had flocked to Naples from a fleet that had lately arrived, and summoned more men from Alexandria. Not content with that, he selected some young men of the order of Knights and more than five thousand sturdy young commoners, to be divided into groups and learn the Alexandrian styles of applause, which they called "the bees," "the roof-tiles," and "the bricks." These men were noticeable for their thick hair and fine apparel. Their left hands were bare and without rings, and they played thin "claques" vigorously whenever Nero sang. The leaders of these bands were paid four hundred thousand sesterces each [$16,400.00]. . . .

While he was singing no one was allowed to leave the theater even for the most urgent reasons. And so it is said that some women gave birth to children there, while many who were worn out with listening and applauding, secretly leaped from the side of the theater, since the gates at the entrance were closed, or feigned death and were carried out as if for burial. The trepidation and anxiety with which he took part in the contests, his keen rivalry of his opponents and his awe of the judges, can hardly be credited. As if his rivals were of quite the same station as himself, he used to show respect to them and try to gain their favor, while he slandered them behind their backs, sometimes assailed them with abuse when he met them, and even bribed those who were especially proficient. . . .

On his way back from [the singing contests in] Greece, he entered Naples through a breach made in the city wall, as is customary with victors in the sacred games, since it was at that city he had made his début as an artist. In like manner he entered Antium, then Albanum, and finally Rome. But at Rome he rode in the chariot which Augustus had used in his triumphs in days gone by, and wore a purple robe and a Greek cloak adorned with stars of gold, bearing on his head the Olympic crown and holding the Pythian crown in his right hand, while the rest were carried before him with inscriptions telling where he had won them and against what competitors, and giving the titles of the songs or the subject of the plays. His chariot was followed by his claque as by the escort of a triumphal procession, who shouted that they were the attendants of Augustus and the soldiers of his triumph. Having had the arch of the Circus Maximus taken down, he made his way through it across the Velabrum and the Forum to the Palatine and the temple of Apollo. All along the route victims were slain, the streets were sprinkled from time to time with perfume, while birds, ribbons, and sweetmeats were showered upon him. He placed the sacred crowns in his bedchambers around his couches, as well as statues representing him in the guise of a lyreplayer, which was the device he had stamped on a coin. So far from neglecting or relaxing his practice of the art after this, he never addressed the soldiers except by letter or in a speech delivered by another, to save his voice. He never did anything for amusement or in earnest without a teacher of voice at his side to warn him to spare his vocal organs and hold a handkerchief to his mouth. To many men he offered his friendship or announced his hostility, according as they had applauded him lavishly or grudgingly.

Although at first his acts of wantonness, lust, extravagance, avarice, and cruelty were gradual and secret, and might be condoned as follies of youth, yet even then their nature was such that no one doubted that they were defects of his character and not due to his time of life. No sooner was twilight over than he would slip on the disguise of a cap or a wig and go to the taverns or range about the streets playing pranks, which however were very far from harmless. For he used to beat men as they came home from dinner, stabbing any who resisted him and throwing them into the sewers. He would even break into shops and rob them, setting up a market in the Palace, where he divided the booty which he took, sold it at auction, and then squandered the proceeds. In the scuffles which took place on such occasions he often ran the risk of losing his eyes or even his life, for he was beaten almost to death by a man of the senatorial order whose wife he had handled indecently. Warned by this, he never afterwards ventured to appear in public at that hour without having Tribunes follow him at a distance and unobserved. Even in the daytime he would be carried privately

to the theater in a sedan, where he would take a place in the upper part of the proscenium from which he not only witnessed the brawls of the pantomimic actors but also egged them on. When they came to blows and stones and pieces of broken benches began to fly about he himself threw many missiles at the people and even broke a Praetor's head.

Little by little, however, as his vices grew stronger, he dropped jesting and secrecy and with no attempt at disguise openly broke out into worse crime.

He prolonged his revels from midday to midnight, often livening himself by a warm plunge, or, if it were summer, into water cooled with snow. Sometimes too he closed the inlets of the Naumachia and banqueted there in public, or in the Campus Martius, or in the Circus Maximus, waited on by harlots and dancing girls from all over the city. Whenever he drifted down the Tiber to Ostia, or sailed about the Gulf of Baiae, booths were set up at intervals along the banks and shores, fitted out as brothels and eating-houses, before which were matrons who played the part of bawds and hostesses, soliciting him from every side to come ashore. He also coerced his friends to give him banquets, one of whom spent four million sesterces on a dinner at which turbans were the favor, and another a considerably larger sum on one at which roses were distributed. . . .

I have heard from some men that it was his unshaken conviction that no man was chaste or pure in any part of his body, but that most of them concealed their vices and cleverly drew a veil over them; and that therefore he pardoned all other faults in those who confessed to him their lewdness.

He thought that there was no other way of enjoying riches and money than by riotous extravagance, declaring that only stingy and niggardly fellows kept a correct account of what they spent, while fine and genuinely magnificent gentlemen wasted and squandered. Nothing in his uncle Gaius so excited his envy and admiration as the fact that he had in so short a time run through the vast wealth which Tiberius had left him. Accordingly he made presents and wasted money without stint. On Tiridates, though it would seem hardly within belief, he spent eight hundred thousand sesterces a day, and on his departure presented him with more than a hundred millions. He gave the lyre-player Menecrates and the gladiator Spiculus properties and residences equal to those of men who had celebrated triumphs. He enriched the monkey-faced usurer Paneros with estates in the country and in the city and had him buried with almost regal splendor. He never wore the same garment twice. He played at dice for four hundred thousand sesterces a point. He fished with a golden net drawn by cords woven of purple and scarlet threads. It is said that he never made a journey with less than a thousand carriages, his mules shod with silver and their drivers clad in wool of Canusium, attended by a train of Mazaces and couriers with bracelets and trappings.

There was nothing however in which he was more ruinously prodigal than in building. He made a palace extending all the way from the Palatine to the Esquiline, which at first he called the House of Passage, but when it was burned shortly after its completion and rebuilt, the Golden House. Its size and splendor will be sufficiently indicated by the following details. Its vestibule was high enough to contain a colossal statue of the Emperor a hundred and twenty feet high. So large was this house that it had a triple colonnade a mile long. There was a lake in it too, like a sea, surrounded with buildings to represent cities, besides tracts of country, varied by tilled fields, vineyards, pastures and woods, with great numbers of wild and domestic animals. In the rest of the house all parts were overlaid with gold and adorned with jewels and mother-of-pearl. There were dining-rooms with fretted ceilings of ivory, whose panels could turn and shower down flowers and were fitted with pipes for sprinkling the guests with perfumes. The main banquet hall was circular and constantly revolved day and night, like the heavens. He had baths supplied with sea water and sulphur water. When the edifice was finished in this style and he dedicated it, he deigned to say nothing more in the way of approval than that he was at last beginning to be housed like a human being.

He also began a pool, extending from Misenum to the lake of Avernus, roofed over and enclosed in colonnades, into which he planned to turn all the hot springs in every part of Baiae. He likewise projected a canal to extend from Avernus all the way to Ostia, to enable the journey to be made by ship yet not by sea: its length was to be a hundred and sixty miles and its breadth sufficient to allow ships with five banks of oars to pass each other. For the execution of these projects he had given orders that the prisoners all over the empire should be transported to Italy, and that those who were convicted even of capital crimes should be punished in no other way than by sentence to this work.

He was led to such mad extravagance, in addition to his confidence in the resources of the empire, by the hope of a vast hidden treasure, suddenly inspired by the assurance of a Roman Knight, who declared positively that the enormous wealth which Queen Dido had taken with her of old in her flight from Tyre was hidden away in huge caves in Africa and could be recovered with but trifling labor.

When this hope proved false, he resorted to false accusations and robbery, being at the end of his resources and so utterly impoverished that he was obliged to postpone and defer even the pay of the soldiers and the rewards due to the veterans.

First of all he made a law, that instead of one-half, five-sixths of the property of deceased freedmen should be made over to him, if without good and sufficient reason they bore the name of any family with which he himself was connected. Further, that the estates of those who were ungrateful to their Emperor should belong to the privy purse, and that the lawyers who had written or dictated such wills should not go unpunished. Finally, that any word or deed on which an informer could base an action should come under the law against treason. He demanded the return of the rewards which he had given in recognition of the prizes conferred on him by any city in any competition. Having forbidden the use of amethystine or Tyrian purple dyes, he secretly sent a man to sell a few ounces on a market day and then closed the shops of all the dealers. It is even said that when he saw a matron in the audience at one of his recitals clad in the forbidden color he pointed her out to his agents, who dragged her out and stripped her on the spot, not only of her garment, but also of her property. He never appointed any one to an office without adding: "You know what my needs are," and "Let us see to it that no one possesses anything." At last he stripped many temples of their gifts and melted down the images of gold and silver, including those of the guardian Gods of Rome which, however, Galba soon afterwards restored.

He began his career of parricide and murder with Claudius, for even if he was not the instigator of the Emperor's death, he was at least privy to it, as he openly admitted. For he used afterwards to laud mushrooms, the vehicle in which the poison was administered to Claudius, as "the food of the Gods," as the Greek proverb has it. At any rate, after Claudius' death he vented on him every kind of insult, in act and word, charging him now with folly and now with cruelty. . . . And he disregarded many of his decrees and acts as the work of a madman and a dotard. Finally, he neglected to enclose the place where his body was burned except with a low and mean wall.

He attempted the life of Britannicus by poison, not less from jealousy of his voice (for it was more agreeable than his own) than from fear that he might sometime win a higher place than himself in the people's regard because of the memory of his father. He procured the potion from an arch-poisoner, one Locusta, and when the effect was slower than he anticipated, merely physicking Britannicus, he called the woman to him and flogged her with his own hand, charging that she had administered a medicine instead of a poison. When she said in excuse that she had given a smaller dose to shield him from the odium of the crime, he replied: "It's likely that I am afraid of the Julian law." So he forced her to mix as swift and instant a potion as she knew how in his own room before his very eyes. Then he tried it on a kid, and as the animal lingered for five hours, had the mixture steeped again and again and threw some of it before a pig. The beast instantly fell dead, whereupon he ordered that the poison be taken to the dining-room and given to Britannicus. The boy dropped dead at the very first taste, but Nero lied to his guests and declared that he was seized with the falling sickness, to which he was subject,

and the next day had him hastily and unceremoniously buried in a pouring rain. He rewarded Locusta for her eminent services with a full pardon and large estates in the country, and actually sent her pupils.

His mother offended him by too strict surveillance and criticism of his words and acts, but at first he confined his resentment to frequent endeavors to bring upon her a burden of unpopularity by pretending that he would abdicate the throne and go off to Rhodes. Then depriving her of all her honors and of her guard of Roman and German soldiers, he even forbade her to live with him and drove her from the Palace. After that he passed all bounds in harrying her, bribing men to annoy her with lawsuits while she remained in the city, and after she had retired to the country, to pass her house by land and sea and break her rest with abuse and mockery. At last terrified by her violence and threats, he determined to have her life, and after thrice attempting it by poison and finding that she had made herself immune by antidotes, he tampered with the ceiling of her bedroom, contriving a mechanical device for loosening its panels and dropping them upon her while she slept. When this leaked out through some of those connected with the plot, he devised a collapsible boat, to destroy her by shipwreck or by the falling in of its cabin. Then he pretended a reconciliation and invited her in a most cordial letter to come to Baiae and celebrate the feast of Minerva with him. On her arrival, instructing his captains to wreck the galley in which she had come, by running into it as if by accident, he detained her at a banquet, and when she would return to Bauli, offered her his contrivance in place of the craft which had been damaged, escorting her to it in high spirits and even kissing her breasts as they parted. The rest of the night he passed sleepless in intense anxiety, awaiting the outcome of his design. On learning that everything had gone wrong and that she had escaped by swimming, driven to desperation he secretly had a dagger thrown down beside her freedman Lucius Agermus, when he joyfully brought word that she was safe and sound. He then ordered that the freedman be seized and bound, on the charge of having been hired by her to kill the Emperor, and that his mother be put to death, giving out that she had committed suicide to escape the consequences of her detected guilt. Trustworthy authorities add still more gruesome details: that he hurried off to view the corpse, handled her limbs, criticizing some and commending others, and that becoming thirsty meanwhile, he took a drink. . . .

Indeed there is no kind of relationship that he did not violate in his career of crime. He put to death Antonia, daughter of Claudius, for refusing to marry him after Poppaea's death, charging her with an attempt at revolution. And he treated in the same way all others who were in any way connected with him by blood or by marriage. Among these was the young Aulus Plautius, whom he forcibly defiled before his death, saying "Let my mother come now and kiss my successor," openly charging that Agrippina had loved Plautius and that this had roused him to hopes of the throne. Rufrius Crispinus, a mere boy, his stepson and the child of Poppaea, he ordered to be drowned by the child's own slaves while he was fishing, because it was said that he used to play at being a general and an Emperor. He banished his nurse's son Tuscus, because when Procurator in Egypt, he had bathed in some baths which were built for a visit of Nero's. He drove his tutor, Seneca, to suicide, although when the old man often pleaded to be allowed to retire and offered to give up his estates, he had sworn most solemnly that he did wrong to suspect him and that he would rather die than harm him. He sent poison to Burrus, Prefect of the Guard, in place of a throat medicine which he had promised him. The old and wealthy freedmen who had helped him first to his adoption and later to the throne, and aided him by their advice, he killed by poison, administered partly in their food and partly in their drink.

Those outside his family he assailed with no less cruelty. It chanced that a comet had begun to appear on several successive nights, a thing which is commonly believed to portend the death of great rulers. Worried by this, and learning from the astrologer Balbillus that Kings usually averted such omens by the sacrifice of some illustrious person, thus bringing the danger foreboded to their own persons onto the heads of their chief men, he resolved on the death of all the eminent men of the State, indeed, all the more firmly, and with some semblance of justice, after the discovery of two conspiracies. The earlier and more dangerous of these was that of Piso at Rome; the other was set on foot by Vinicius at Beneventum and detected there. The conspirators made their defense in triple sets of fetters, some voluntarily admitting their guilt, some even maintaining they were trying to do him a favor, saying that there was no way except by death that they could help a man disgraced by every kind of wickedness. The children of those who were condemned were banished or put to death by poison or starvation. A number are known to have been slain all together at a single meal along with their preceptors and attendants, while others were prevented from earning their daily bread. . . .

But he showed no greater mercy to the people or the walls of his capital. When some one in a general conversation said: "When I am dead, be earth consumed by fire," he rejoined "Nay, rather while I live," and his action was wholly in accord. For under cover of displeasure at the ugliness of the old buildings and the narrow, crooked streets, he set fire to the city so openly that several ex-consuls did not venture to lay hands on his household servants although they caught them on their estates with tow and firebrands, while some granaries near the Golden House, on a plot of ground he particularly desired, were demolished by engines of war and then set on fire, because their walls were of stone. For six days and seven nights destruction raged, while the people were driven for shelter to monuments and tombs. At that time, besides an immense number of apartment houses, the private houses of leaders of old were burned, still adorned with trophies of victory, and the temples of the Gods vowed and dedicated by the Kings and later in the Punic and Gallic wars, and whatever else interesting and noteworthy had survived from antiquity. Viewing the conflagration from the tower of Maecenas and exulting, as he said, in "the beauty of the flames," he sang the whole of the "Sack of Troy," dressed up in his regular stage costume. Furthermore, to gain from this calamity, too, all the spoil and booty possible, while promising the removal of the debris and dead bodies free of cost, he allowed no one to approach the ruins of his own property. And from the contributions which he not only received, but even demanded, he nearly bankrupted the provinces and exhausted the resources of individuals. . . .

When he had thus aroused the hatred of all, there was no form of insult to which he was not subjected. A lock of hair was placed on the head of his statue with the inscription in Greek: "Now there is a real contest and you must at last surrender." To the neck of another statue a sack was tied and with it the words: "I have done what I could, but you have earned the sack." People wrote on the columns that by his singing he had stirred up even the Gauls. When night came on, many men pretended to be wrangling with their slaves and kept calling out for a vindicator.

In addition he was frightened by manifest portents from dreams, auspices and omens, both old and new. He had never been in the habit of dreaming before he killed his mother. But after that he had such nightmares as: that he was steering a ship and the helm was wrenched from his hands; that he was dragged by his wife Octavia into thickest darkness; that now he was covered with a swarm of winged ants; or again, that the statues of all the heroes dedicated in Pompey's theater had surrounded him and blocked his way; that a Spanish steed of which he was very fond was changed into the form of an ape in the hinder parts of its body, and its head, which alone remained unaltered, gave forth tuneful neighs. The doors of the Mausoleum flew open of their own accord, and a voice was heard from within summoning him by name. After his domestic Gods had been adorned on the Kalends of January, they fell to the ground in the midst of the preparations for the sacrifice. . . .

At last, while his companions one and all urged him to save himself as soon as possible from the indignities that threatened him, he bade them dig a grave in his presence, proportioned to the size of his own person, collect any bits of marble that could be found, and at the same time bring water and wood for presently disposing of his body. As each of these things was done, he wept and said again and again: "What an artist the world is losing!"

While he hesitated, a letter was brought to Phaon by one of his couriers. Nero snatching it from his hand read that he had been pronounced a public enemy by the Senate, and that they were seeking him to punish him in the ancient fashion. And he asked what manner of punishment that was. When he learned that the criminal was stripped naked, fastened by the neck in a forked stake and then beaten to death with rods, in mortal terror he seized two daggers which he had brought with him, and then, after trying the point of each, put them up again, pleading that the fated hour had not yet come. Now he would beg Sporus to begin to lament and wail, and now entreat some one to help him take his life by setting him the example. Anon he reproached himself for his cowardice in such words as these: "To live despoiled, disgraced—this does not become Nero, does not become him—one should be resolute at such times—come, rouse thyself!" And now the horsemen were at hand who had orders to take him off alive. When he heard them, he quavered: "The trampling of swift-footed studs is in my ear," and drove a dagger into his throat, aided by Epaphroditus, his private secretary. He was all but dead when a Centurion rushed in, and as he placed a cloak to the wound, pretending that he had come to aid him, Nero merely gasped: "Too late!" and "This is fidelity!" With these words he was gone, his eyes so set and starting from their sockets that all who saw him shuddered with horror. First and beyond all else he had forced from his companions a promise to let no one have his head, but to contrive in some way that he be buried unmutilated. And this was granted by Icelus, Galba's freedman, who had shortly before been released from the bondage to which he was consigned at the beginning of the revolt.

He was buried at a cost of two hundred thousand sesterces and laid out in white robes embroidered with gold, which he had worn on the Kalends of January. His ashes were deposited by his nurses, Egloge and Alexandria, accompanied by his mistress Acte, in the family tomb of the Domitii on the summit of the Hill of Gardens, which is visible from the Campus Martius. In that monument his sarcophagus of porphyry, with an altar of marble from Luna standing above it, is enclosed by a balustrade of Thasian stone.

He was about the average height, his body marked with spots and malodorous, his hair light blond, his features regular rather than attractive, his eyes blue and somewhat weak, his neck overthick, his belly prominent, and his legs very slender. His health was good, for though indulging in every kind of riotous excess, he was ill but three times in all during the fourteen years of his reign, and even then not enough to give up wine or any of his usual habits. He was utterly shameless in the care of his person and in his dress, always having his hair arranged in tiers of curls, and during the trip to Greece also letting it grow long and hang down behind. And he often appeared in public in a dinner-gown, with a handkerchief bound about his neck, ungirt and unshod.

The Bible

The Gospel of Matthew was composed a few years after the writing attributed to Mark, and the author was therefore able to use the earlier work for much of the account. The outstanding feature of the later work is the emphasis it placed on the teachings of Jesus, notably in the Sermon on the Mount. The distinctive literary style of this famous passage stands out from the remainder of the Gospel and gives credence to the belief that these are the actual utterances of Jesus. In reading the Sermon on the Mount note (1) the beatitudes, (2) the moral code of Jesus, (3) His attitude toward the teaching of the prophets, (4) the similarities and the differences between His teachings and the law of Moses, and (5) any aspects of His teachings that might lead to conflict with the prevailing Jewish religious beliefs.

From: THE GOSPEL ACCORDING TO ST. MATTHEW

And seeing the multitudes, he went up into a mountain: and when he was set, his disciples came unto him: and he opened his mouth, and taught them, saying,

"Blessed are the poor in spirit:
For theirs is the kingdom of heaven.

Blessed are they that mourn:
For they shall be comforted.

Blessed are the meek:
For they shall inherit the earth.

Blessed are they which do hunger and thirst after righteousness:
For they shall be filled.

Blessed are the merciful:
For they shall obtain mercy.

Blessed are the pure in heart:
For they shall see God.

Blessed are the peacemakers:
For they shall be called the children of God.

Blessed are they which are persecuted for righteousness' sake:
For theirs is the kingdom of heaven.

Blessed are ye, when men shall revile you, and persecute you, and shall say all manner of evil against you falsely, for my sake.

Adapted from the King James version of the Bible.

Rejoice, and be exceeding glad: for great is your reward in Heaven: for so persecuted they the prophets which were before you.

"Ye are the salt of the earth: but if the salt have lost his savour, wherewith shall it be salted? It is thenceforth good for nothing, but to be cast out, and to be trodden under foot of men.

"Ye are the light of the world. A city that is set on a hill cannot be hid. Neither do men light a candle, and put it under a bushel, but on a candlestick; and it giveth light unto all that are in the house. Let your light so shine before men, that they may see your good works, and glorify your Father which is in heaven.

"Think not that I am come to destroy the law, or the prophets: I am not come to destroy, but to fulfil. For verily I say unto you, 'Till heaven and earth pass, one jot or one tittle shall in no wise pass from the law, till all be fulfilled.' Whosoever therefore shall break one of these least commandments, and shall teach men so, he shall be called the least in the kingdom of heaven: but whosoever shall do and teach them, the same shall be called great in the kingdom of heaven. For I say unto you, 'Except your righteousness shall exceed the righteousness of the scribes and Pharisees, ye shall in no case enter into the kingdom of heaven.'

"Ye have heard that it was said by them of old time, 'Thou shalt not kill'; and whosoever shall kill shall be in danger of the judgment. But I say unto you, 'Whosoever is angry with his brother without a cause shall be in danger of the judgment: and whosoever shall say to his brother, "Raca" [worthless], shall be in danger of the council: but whosoever shall say, "Thou fool," shall be in danger of hell fire.' Therefore if thou bring thy gift to the altar, and there rememberest that thy brother hath ought against thee; leave there thy gift before the altar, and go thy way; first be reconciled to thy brother, and then come and offer thy gift. Agree with thine adversary quickly, while thou art in the way with him; lest at any time the adversary deliver thee to the judge, and the judge deliver thee to the officer, and thou be cast into prison. Verily I say unto thee, 'Thou shalt by no means come out thence, till thou hast paid the uttermost farthing.'

"Ye have heard that it was said by them of old time, 'Thou shalt not commit adultery.' But I say unto you, 'Whosoever looketh on a woman to lust after her hath committed adultery with her already in his heart. And if thy right eye offend thee, pluck it out, and cast it from thee: for it is profitable for thee that one of thy members should perish, and not that thy whole body should be cast into hell. And if thy right hand offend thee, cut it off, and cast it from thee: for it is profitable for thee that one of thy members should perish, and not that thy whole body should be cast into hell.' It hath been said, 'Whosoever shall put away his wife, let him give her a writing of divorcement.' But I say unto you, 'Whosoever shall put away his wife, saving for the cause of fornication, causeth her to commit adultery: and whosoever shall marry her that is divorced committeth adultery.'

"Again, ye have heard that it hath been said by them of old time, 'Thou shalt not forswear thyself, but shalt perform unto the Lord thine oaths.' But I say unto you, 'Swear not at all; neither by heaven; for it is God's throne: nor by the earth; for it is his footstool: neither by Jerusalem; for it is the city of the great King. Neither shalt thou swear by thy head, because thou canst not make one hair white or black. But let your communication be, "Yea, yea"; "Nay, nay": for whatsoever is more than these cometh of evil.'

"Ye have heard that it hath been said, 'An eye for an eye, and a tooth for a tooth.' But I say unto you, 'Resist not evil: but whosoever shall smite thee on thy right cheek, turn to him the other also. And if any man will sue thee at the law, and take away thy coat, let him have thy cloak also. And whosoever shall compel thee to go a mile, go with him twain. Give to him that asketh thee, and from him that would borrow of thee turn not thou away.'

"Ye have heard that it hath been said, 'Thou shalt love thy neighbour, and hate thine enemy.' But I say unto you, 'Love your enemies, bless them that curse you, do good to them that hate you, and pray for them which despitefully use you, and persecute you; that ye may be the children of your Father which is in heaven: for he maketh his sun to rise on the evil and on the good, and sendeth rain on the just and on the unjust.' For if ye love them which love you, what reward have ye? Do not even the publicans the same? And if ye salute your brethren only, what do ye more than others? Do not even the publicans so? Be ye therefore perfect, even as your Father which is in heaven is perfect.

"Take heed that ye do not your alms before men, to be seen of them: otherwise ye have no reward of your Father which is in heaven. Therefore when thou doest thine alms, do not sound a trumpet before thee, as the hypocrites do in the synagogues and in the streets, that they may have glory of men. Verily I say unto you, 'They have their reward.' But when thou doest alms, let not thy left hand know what thy right hand doeth: that thine alms may be in secret: and thy Father which seeth in secret himself shall reward thee openly.

"And when thou prayest, thou shalt not be as the hypocrites are: for they love to pray standing in the synagogues and in the corners of the streets, that they may be seen of men. Verily I say unto you, 'They have their reward.' But thou, when thou prayest, enter into thy closet, and when thou hast shut thy door, pray to thy Father which is in secret; and thy Father which seeth in secret shall reward thee openly. But when ye pray, use not vain repetitions, as the heathen do: for they think that they shall be heard for their much speaking. Be not ye therefore like unto them: for your Father knoweth what things ye have need of, before ye ask him. After this manner therefore pray ye:

" 'Our Father which art in heaven,
Hallowed be thy name.
Thy kingdom come.
Thy will be done
In earth, as it is in heaven.

Give us this day
Our daily bread.
And forgive us our debts,
As we forgive our debtors.
And lead us not into temptation,
But deliver us from evil:

For thine is the kingdom,
And the power,
And the glory,
Forever. Amen.'

"For if ye forgive men their trespasses, your heavenly Father will also forgive you: but if ye forgive not men their trespasses, neither will your Father forgive your trespasses.

"Moreover, when ye fast, be not, as the hypocrites, of a sad countenance: for they disfigure their faces, that they may appear unto men to fast. Verily I say unto you, 'They have their reward.' But thou, when thou fastest, anoint thine head, and wash thy face; that thou appear not unto men to fast, but unto thy Father which is in secret: and thy Father, which seeth in secret, shall reward thee openly.

"Lay not up for yourselves treasures
upon earth,
Where moth and rust doth corrupt,
And where thieves break through and
steal:

But lay up for yourselves treasures in
heaven,
Where neither moth nor rust doth corrupt,
And where thieves do not break through
nor steal.

For where your treasure is, there will your heart be also.

"The light of the body is the eye: if therefore thine eye be single, thy whole body shall be full of light. But if thine eye be evil, thy whole body shall be full of darkness. If therefore the light that is in thee be darkness, how great is that darkness!

"No man can serve two masters: for either he will hate the one, and love the other; or else he will hold to the one, and despise the other. Ye cannot serve God and mammon.

"Therefore I say unto you, 'Take no thought for your life, what ye shall eat, or what ye shall drink; nor yet for your body, what ye shall put on.' Is not the life more than meat, and the body than raiment? Behold the fowls of the air: for they sow not, neither do they reap, nor gather into barns; yet your heavenly

Father feedeth them. Are ye not much better than they? Which of you by taking thought can add one cubit unto his stature? And why take ye thought for raiment? Consider the lilies of the field, how they grow; they toil not, neither do they spin: and yet I say unto you that even Solomon in all his glory was not arrayed like one of these.

"Wherefore, if God so clothe the grass of the field, which today is, and tomorrow is cast into the oven, shall he not much more clothe you, O ye of little faith? Therefore take no thought, saying, 'What shall we eat?' or, 'What shall we drink?' or, 'Wherewithal shall we be clothed?' (For after all these things do the Gentiles seek:) for your heavenly Father knoweth that ye have need of all these things. But seek ye first the kingdom of God, and his righteousness; and all these things shall be added unto you. Take therefore no thought for the morrow: for the morrow shall take thought for the things of itself. Sufficient unto the day is the evil thereof.

"Judge not, that ye be not judged. For with what judgment ye judge, ye shall be judged: and with what measure ye mete, it shall be measured to you again. And why beholdest thou the mote that is in thy brother's eye, but considerest not the beam that is in thine own eye? Or how wilt thou say to thy brother, 'Let me pull out the mote out of thine eye'; and, behold a beam is in thy own eye? Thou hypocrite, first cast out the beam out of thine own eye; and then shalt thou see clearly to cast out the mote out of thy brother's eye.

"Give not that which is holy unto the dogs,
     Neither cast ye your pearls before swine,
Lest they trample them under their feet,
And turn again and rend you.

Ask, and it shall be given you;
Seek, and ye shall find;
Knock, and it shall be opened unto you:

For every one that asketh receiveth;
And he that seeketh findeth;
And to him that knocketh it shall be opened.

Or what man is there of you, whom if his son ask bread, will he give him a stone? Or if he ask a fish, will he give him a serpent? If ye then, being evil, know how to give good gifts unto your children, how much more shall your Father which is in heaven give good things to them that ask him? Therefore all things whatsoever ye would that men should do to you, do ye even so to them: for this is the law and the prophets.

"Enter ye in at the strait gate: for wide is the gate, and broad is the way, that leadeth to destruction, and many there be which go in thereat: because strait is the gate, and narrow is the way, which leadeth unto life, and few there be that find it.

"Beware of false prophets, which come to you in sheep's clothing, but inwardly they are ravening wolves. Ye shall know them by their fruits. Do men gather grapes of thorns, or figs of thistles? Even so every good tree bringeth forth good fruit; but a corrupt tree bringeth forth evil fruit. A good tree cannot bring forth evil fruit, neither can a corrupt tree bring forth good fruit. Every tree that bringeth not forth good fruit is hewn down, and cast into the fire. Wherefore by their fruits ye shall know them.

"Not every one that saith unto me, 'Lord, Lord,' shall enter into the kingdom of heaven; but he that doeth the will of my Father which is in heaven. Many will say to me in that day, 'Lord, Lord, have we not prophesied in thy name? And in thy name have cast out devils? And in thy name done many wonderful works?' And then will I profess unto them, 'I never knew you: depart from me, ye that work iniquity.'

"Therefore whosoever heareth these sayings of mine, and doeth them, I will liken him unto a wise man, which built his house upon a rock: and the rain descended, and the floods came and the winds blew, and beat upon that house; and it fell not; for it was founded upon a rock. And every one that heareth these sayings of mine, and doeth them not, shall be likened unto a foolish man, which built his house upon the sand: and the rain descended, and the floods came, and the winds blew, and beat upon that house; and it fell: and great was the fall of it."

And it came to pass, when Jesus had ended these sayings, the people were astonished at his doctrine for he taught them as one having authority, and not as the scribes.

John of Patmos (not to be confused with John the Baptist or the Apostle John), probably wrote his account of the life of Jesus early in the second century A.D., thus providing us with the latest of the four Gospels. Internal evidence suggests that the writer had acquaintance with Greek philosophy, particularly the philosophy associated with the teachers at Alexandria who emphasized the great gulf existing between man and God and the necessity of an intermediary to bridge this gulf. This Gospel represented Jesus as the divine Son of God who appeared among men in the flesh, rather than the human Messiah hoped for by the Jews. In reading the selections note (1) the contrast in the style of writing compared with the earlier Gospels, (2) the use of symbolism, (3) the identification of Jesus with the Alexandrian idea of Logos [Word], the Mithraic concept of Light, and the Hebrew notion of the sacrificial Lamb, (4) the origin of Jesus and the treatment of His birth, (5) Jesus' discussion of His future while at the Last Supper, (6) the relationship between Jesus and God, (7) the emphasis given to mystic love between God and man, (8) the nature and purpose of the Holy Ghost, and (9) the contrast between Mark's and John's description of the death of Jesus.

From: THE GOSPEL ACCORDING TO ST. JOHN

In the beginning was the Word, and the Word was with God, and the Word was God. The same was in the beginning with God. All things were made by him; and without him was not any thing made that was made. In him was life; and the life was the light of men. And the light shineth in darkness; and the darkness comprehended it not.

There was a man sent from God, whose name was John. The same came for a witness, to bear witness of the Light, that all men through him might believe. He was not that Light, but was sent to bear witness of that Light. That was the true Light, which lighteth every man that cometh into the world. He was in the world, and the world was made by him, and the world knew him not. He came unto his own, and his own received him not. But as many as received him, to them gave he power to become the sons of God, even to them that believe on his name: which were born, not of blood, nor of the will of the flesh, nor of the will of man, but of God. And the Word was made flesh, and dwelt among us (and we beheld his glory, the glory as of the only begotten of the Father), full of grace and truth.

John bore witness of him, and cried, saying, "This was he of whom I spoke, 'He that cometh after me is preferred before me: for he was before me.' " And of his fulness have all we received, and grace for grace. For the law was given by Moses, but grace and truth came by Jesus Christ. No man hath seen God at any time; the only begotten Son, which is in the bosom of the Father, he hath declared him. And this is the record of John, when the Jews sent priests and Levites from Jerusalem to ask him, "Who art thou?" And he confessed, and denied not; but confessed, "I am not the Christ."

And they asked him, "What then? Art thou Elias?"

And he saith, "I am not."

"Art thou that prophet?"

And he answered, "No."

Then said they unto him, "Who art thou?

that we may give an answer to them that sent us. What sayest thou of thyself?"

He said, "I am the voice of one crying in the wilderness, 'Make straight the way of the Lord,' as said the prophet Esaias."

And they which were sent were of the Pharisees. And they asked him, and said unto him, "Why baptizest thou then, if thou be not that Christ, nor Elias, neither that prophet?"

John answered them, saying, "I baptize with water: but there standeth one among you, whom ye know not; he it is, who coming after me is preferred before me, whose shoe's latchet I am not worthy to unloose."

These things were done in Bethabara beyond Jordan, where John was baptizing.

The next day John seeth Jesus coming unto him, and saith, "Behold the Lamb of God, which taketh away the sin of the world! This is he of whom I said, 'After me cometh a man which is preferred before me: for he was before me.' And I knew him not: but that he should be made manifest to Israel, therefore am I come baptizing with water."

And John bore record, saying, "I saw the Spirit descending from heaven like a dove, and it abode upon him. And I knew him not: but he that sent me to baptize with water, the same said unto me, 'Upon whom thou shalt see the Spirit descending, and remaining on him, the same is he which baptizeth with the Holy Ghost.' And I saw, and bore record that this is the Son of God."

Again the next day after, John stood, and two of his disciples, and looking upon Jesus as he walked, he saith, "Behold the Lamb of God!"

And the two disciples heard him speak, and they followed Jesus. Then Jesus turned, and saw them following, and saith unto them, "What seek ye?"

They said unto him, "Rabbi" (which is to say, being interpreted, "Master"), "where dwellest thou?"

He saith unto them, "Come and see."

They came and saw where he dwelt, and abode with him that day: for it was about the tenth hour.

One of the two which heard John speak, and followed him, was Andrew, Simon Peter's brother. He first findeth his own brother Simon, and saith unto him, "We have found the Messias, which is, being interpreted, the Christ." And he brought him to Jesus. And when Jesus beheld him, he said, "Thou art Simon the son of Jona: thou shalt be called Cephas," which is by interpretation "a stone.". . .

Now before the feast of the passover, when Jesus knew that his hour was come that he should depart out of this world unto the Father, having loved his own which were in the world, he loved them unto the end. And supper being ended, the devil having now put into the heart of Judas Iscariot, Simon's son, to betray him, Jesus, knowing that the Father had given all things into his hands, and that he was come from God, and went to God, riseth from supper, and laid aside his garments; and took a towel, and girded himself. After that, he poureth water into a basin, and began to wash the disciples' feet, and to wipe them with the towel wherewith he was girded. Then cometh he to Simon Peter: and Peter saith unto him, "Lord, dost thou wash my feet?" Jesus answered and said unto him, "What I do thou knowest not now; but thou shalt know hereafter." Peter saith unto him, "Thou shalt never wash my feet." Jesus answered him, "If I wash thee not, thou hast no part with me." Simon Peter saith unto him, "Lord, not my feet only, but also my hands and my head." Jesus saith to him, "He that is washed needeth not save to wash his feet, but is clean every whit: and ye are clean, but not all." For he knew who should betray him; therefore said he, "Ye are not all clean." So after he had washed their feet, and had taken his garments, and was set down again, he said unto them, "Know ye what I have done to you? Ye call me Master and Lord: and ye say well; for so I am. If I then, your Lord and Master, have washed your feet; ye also ought to wash one another's feet. For I have given you an example, that ye should do as I have done to you. Verily, verily, I say unto you, 'The servant is not greater than his lord; neither he that is sent greater than he that sent him. . . .'"

When Jesus had thus said, he was troubled in spirit, and testified, and said, "Verily, verily, I say unto you that one of you shall betray me."

Then the disciples looked one on another, doubting of whom he spoke. Now there was leaning on Jesus' bosom one of his disciples, whom Jesus loved. Simon Peter therefore beckoned to him, that he should ask who it should be of whom he spoke. He then lying on Jesus' breast saith unto him, "Lord, who is it?"

Jesus answered, "He it is, to whom I shall give a sop, when I have dipped it." And when he had dipped the sop, he gave it to Judas Iscariot, the son of Simon. And after the sop Satan entered into him. Then said Jesus unto him, "That thou doest, do quickly." Now no man at the table knew for what intent he spoke this unto him. For some of them thought, because Judas had the bag, that Jesus had said unto him, "Buy those things that we have need of against the feast"; or, that he should give something to the poor. He then, having received the sop, went immediately out: and it was night.

Therefore, when he was gone out, Jesus said, "Now is the Son of Man glorified, and God is glorified in him. If God be glorified in him, God shall also glorify him in himself, and shall straightway glorify him. Little children, yet a little while I am with you. Ye shall seek me: and as I said unto the Jews, 'Whither I go, ye cannot come'; so now I say to you. A new commandment I give unto you: that ye love one another; as I have loved you, that ye also love one another. By this shall all men know that ye are my disciples, if ye have love one to another."

Simon Peter said unto him, "Lord, whither goest thou?"

Jesus answered him, "Whither I go, thou canst not follow me now; but thou shalt follow me afterwards."

Peter said unto him, "Lord, why cannot I follow thee now? I will lay down my life for thy sake."

Jesus answered him, "Wilt thou lay down thy life for my sake? Verily, verily, I say unto thee, 'The cock shall not crow, till thou hast denied me thrice.'

"Let not your heart be troubled: ye believe in God, believe also in me. In my Father's house are many mansions: if it were not so, I would have told you. I go to prepare a place for you. And if I go and prepare a place for you, I will come again, and receive you unto myself; that where I am, there ye may be also.

And whither I go ye know, and the way ye know."

Thomas saith unto him, "Lord, we know not whither thou goest; and how can we know the way?"

Jesus saith unto him, "I am the way, the truth, and the life: no man cometh unto the Father, but by me. If ye had known me, ye should have known my Father also: and from henceforth ye know him, and have seen him."

Philip saith unto him, "Lord, show us the Father, and it sufficeth us."

Jesus saith unto him, "Have I been so long time with you, and yet hast thou not known me, Philip? He that hath seen me hath seen the Father; and how sayest thou then, 'Show us the Father'? Believest thou not that I am in the Father, and the Father in me? The words that I speak unto you I speak not of myself: but the Father that dwelleth in me, he doeth the works. Believe me that I am in the Father, and the Father in me: or else believe me for the very works' sake. Verily, verily, I say unto you, 'He that believeth in me, the works that I do shall he do also; and greater works than these shall he do; because I go unto my Father.' And whatsoever ye shall ask in my name, that will I do, that the Father may be glorified in the Son. If ye shall ask any thing in my name, I will do it.

"If ye love me, keep my commandments. And I will pray the Father, and he shall give you another Comforter, that he may abide with you for ever; even the Spirit of truth; whom the world cannot receive, because it seeth him not, neither knoweth him: but ye know him; for he dwelleth with you, and shall be in you. I will not leave you comfortless: I will come to you. Yet a little while, and the world seeth me no more; but ye see me: because I live, ye shall live also. At that day ye shall know that I am in my Father, and ye in me, and I in you. He that hath my commandments, and keepeth them, he it is that loveth me: and he that loveth me shall be loved of my Father, and I will love him, and will manifest myself to him."

Judas (not Iscariot) saith unto him, "Lord, how is it that thou wilt manifest thyself unto us, and not unto the world?"

Jesus answered and said unto him, "If a man

love me, he will keep my words: and my Father will love him, and we will come unto him, and make our abode with him. He that loveth me not keepeth not my sayings: and the word which ye hear is not mine, but the Father's which sent me.

"These things have I spoken unto you, being yet present with you. But the Comforter, which is the Holy Ghost, whom the Father will send in my name, he shall teach you all things, and bring all things to your remembrance, whatsoever I have said unto you. . . ."

Pilate . . . brought Jesus forth, and sat down in the judgment seat in a place that is called the Pavement, but, in Hebrew, Gabbatha. And it was the preparation of the passover, and about the sixth hour: and he saith unto the Jews, "Behold your King!"

But they cried out, "Away with him, away with him, crucify him!"

Pilate saith unto them, "Shall I crucify your King?"

The chief priests answered, "We have no king but Caesar."

Then delivered he him therefore unto them to be crucified. And they took Jesus, and led him away. And he bearing his cross went forth into a place called the place of a skull, which is called, in the Hebrew, Golgotha, where they crucified him, and two others with him, on either side one, and Jesus in the midst. And Pilate wrote a title, and put it on the cross. And the writing was JESUS OF NAZARETH, THE KING OF THE JEWS. This title then read many of the Jews: for the place where Jesus was crucified was nigh to the city: and it was written in Hebrew, and Greek, and Latin.

Then said the chief priests of the Jews to Pilate, "Write not, 'The King of the Jews'; but that he said, 'I am King of the Jews.'"

Pilate answered, "What I have written I have written."

Then the soldiers, when they had crucified Jesus, took his garments, and made four parts, to every soldier a part; and also his coat: now the coat was without seam, woven from the top throughout. They said therefore among themselves, "Let us not rend it, but cast lots for it, whose it shall be": that the scripture might be fulfilled, which saith,

"They parted my raiment among them,
And for my vesture they did cast lots."

These things therefore the soldiers did.

Now there stood by the cross of Jesus his mother, and his mother's sister, Mary the wife of Cleophas, and Mary Magdalene. When Jesus therefore saw his mother, and the disciple standing by, whom he loved, he saith unto his mother, "Woman, behold thy son!" Then saith he to the disciple, "Behold thy mother!" And from that hour that disciple took her unto his own home.

After this, Jesus knowing that all things were now accomplished, that the scripture might be fulfilled, saith, "I thirst." Now there was set a vessel full of vinegar: and they filled a sponge with vinegar, and put it upon hyssop, and put it to his mouth. When Jesus therefore had received the vinegar, he said, "It is finished": and he bowed his head, and gave up the ghost. . . .

The Acts of the Apostles relates the history of the early church following the death of Jesus. It was written by the author of the Gospel of Luke and carried on the story of the establishment of the Kingdom of God. The group of Apostles felt a spiritual solidarity with the departed Jesus through the Holy Spirit, which was strongly emphasized through the narrative. The author also stressed the missionary spirit implicit in the teachings of Jesus, and the efforts of His followers to spread the new faith throughout the Roman Empire. Thus The Acts of the Apostles served both as a sequel to the Gospels and as a background for the writings of Paul. In the selections note (1) the author's explanation

*for the religious experiences on the day of Pentecost, (2)
Peter's ideas on the relationship between Jesus and God,
(3) the ceremonies observed by the Apostles and early
Christians, (4) the nature of and reasons for early Christian
organization, (5) the people among whom the Apostles
carried on their early missionary work, (6) Saul's experience
on the Damascus road, (7) the work for which Saul was
selected, (8) Peter's dream and his interpretation of it to
Cornelius, (9) the nature of the dispute between the teachers from Judaea and Paul and Barnabas, and (10) the settlement of this dispute at Jerusalem and the ultimate significance of this solution to Christianity.*

From: THE ACTS OF THE APOSTLES

And when the day of Pentecost was fully
come, they were all with one accord in one
place. And suddenly there came a sound from
heaven as of a rushing mighty wind, and it
filled all the house where they were sitting.
And there appeared unto them cloven tongues
like as of fire, and it sat upon each of them.
And they were all filled with the Holy Ghost,
and began to speak with other tongues, as the
Spirit gave them utterance.

And there were dwelling at Jerusalem Jews,
devout men, out of every nation under heaven.
Now when this was noised abroad, the multitude came together, and were confounded, because that every man heard them speak in his
own language. And they were all amazed and
marvelled, saying one to another, "Behold, are
not all these which speak Galilaeans? And how
hear we every man in our own tongue, wherein
we were born? Parthians, and Medes, and
Elamites, and the dwellers in Mesopotamia,
and in Judaea, and Cappadocia, in Pontus,
and Asia, Phrygia, and Pamphylia, in Egypt,
and in the parts of Libya about Cyrene, and
strangers of Rome, Jews and proselytes, Cre-
tans and Arabians, we do hear them speak in
our tongues the wonderful works of God." And
they were all amazed, and were in doubt, saying one to another, "What meaneth this?"
Others mocking said, "These men are full of
new wine."

But Peter, standing up with the eleven, lifted
up his voice, and said unto them, "Ye men of
Judaea, and all ye that dwell at Jerusalem, be

this known unto you, and hearken to my
words: for these are not drunken, as ye suppose, seeing it is but the third hour of the day.
But this is that which was spoken by the
prophet Joel·

' "And it shall come to pass in the last
        days," saith God,
    "I will pour out of my Spirit upon all
        flesh:
    And your sons and your daughters shall
        prophesy,
    And your young men shall see visions,
    And your old men shall dream dreams:
    And on my servants and on my hand-
        maidens
    I will pour out in those days of my
        Spirit;
    And they shall prophesy:
    And I will show wonders in heaven
        above,
    And signs in the earth beneath;
    Blood, and fire, and vapour of smoke:
    The sun shall be turned into darkness,
    And the moon into blood,
    Before that great and notable day of
        the Lord come:
    And it shall come to pass,
    That whosoever shall call on the name
        of the Lord shall be saved." '

"Ye men of Israel, hear these words: Jesus
of Nazareth, a man approved of God among
you by miracles and wonders and signs, which
God did by him in the midst of you, as ye your-

selves also know: him, being delivered by the determinate counsel and foreknowledge of God, ye have taken, and by wicked hands have crucified and slain. . . . This Jesus hath God raised up, whereof we all are witnesses. Therefore being by the right hand of God exalted, and having received of the Father the promise of the Holy Ghost, he hath shed forth this, which ye now see and hear. . . . Therefore let all the house of Israel know assuredly that God hath made that same Jesus, whom ye have crucified, both Lord and Christ."

Now when they heard this, they were pricked in their heart, and said unto Peter and to the rest of the apostles, "Men and brethren, what shall we do?" Then Peter said unto them, "Repent, and be baptized every one of you in the name of Jesus Christ for the remission of sins, and ye shall receive the gift of the Holy Ghost. For the promise is unto you, and to your children, and to all that are afar off, even as many as the Lord our God shall call." And with many other words did he testify and exhort, saying, "Save yourselves from this untoward generation."

Then they that gladly received his word were baptized: and the same day there were added unto them about three thousand souls. And they continued steadfastly in the apostles' doctrine and fellowship, and in breaking of bread, and in prayers. And fear came upon every soul: and many wonders and signs were done by the apostles. And all that believed were together, and had all things common; and sold their possessions and goods, and parted them to all men, as every man had need. And they, continuing daily with one accord in the temple, and breaking bread from house to house, did eat their meat with gladness and singleness of heart, praising God, and having favour with all the people. And the Lord added to the church daily such as should be saved. . . .

And the multitude of them that believed were of one heart and of one soul: neither said any of them that ought of the things which he possessed was his own; but they had all things common. And with great power gave the apostles witness of the resurrection of the Lord Jesus: and great grace was upon them all. Neither was there any among them that lacked: for as many as were possessors of lands or houses sold them, and brought the prices of the things that were sold, and laid them down at the apostles' feet: and distribution was made unto every man according as he had need. And Joses, who by the apostles was surnamed Barnabas (which is, being interpreted, "the son of consolation"), a Levite, and of the country of Cyprus, having land, sold it, and brought the money, and laid it at the apostles' feet.

And by the hands of the apostles were many signs and wonders wrought among the people (and they were all with one accord in Solomon's porch. And of the rest durst no man join himself to them: but the people magnified them. And believers were the more added to the Lord, multitudes both of men and women); insomuch that they brought forth the sick into the streets, and laid them on beds and couches, that at the least the shadow of Peter passing by might overshadow some of them. There came also a multitude out of the cities round about unto Jerusalem, bringing sick folks, and them which were vexed with unclean spirits: and they were healed every one. Then the high priest rose up, and all they that were with him (which is the sect of the Sadducees), and were filled with indignation, and laid their hands on the apostles, and put them in the common prison.

But the angel of the Lord by night opened the prison doors, and brought them forth, and said, "Go, stand and speak in the temple to the people all the words of this life.". . .

And in those days, when the number of the disciples was multiplied, there arose a murmuring of the Grecians against the Hebrews, because their widows were neglected in the daily ministration. Then the twelve called the multitude of the disciples unto them, and said, "It is not reason that we should leave the word of God, and serve tables. Wherefore, brethren, look ye out among you seven men of honest report, full of the Holy Ghost and wisdom, whom we may appoint over this business. But we will give ourselves continually to prayer, and to the ministry of the word."

And the saying pleased the whole multitude: and they chose Stephen, a man full of faith and of the Holy Ghost, and Philip, and Prochurus, and Nicanor, and Timon, and Parmenas, and Nicolas a proselyte of Antioch: whom they set before the apostles: and when they had prayed, they laid their hands on them. And the word of God increased; and the number of the disciples multiplied in Jerusalem greatly; and a great company of the priests were obedient to the faith. And Stephen, full of faith and power, did great wonders and miracles among the people.

Then there arose certain of the synagogue, which is called the synagogue of the Libertines, and Cyrenians, and Alexandrians, and of them of Cilicia and of Asia, disputing with Stephen. And they were not able to resist the wisdom and the spirit by which he spoke. Then they suborned men, which said, "We have heard him speak blasphemous words against Moses, and against God."

And they stirred up the people, and the elders, and the scribes, and came upon him, and caught him, and brought him to the council, and set up false witnesses, which said, "This man ceaseth not to speak blasphemous words against this holy place, and the law: for we have heard him say that this Jesus of Nazareth shall destroy this place, and shall change the customs which Moses delivered us."

And all that sat in the council, looking steadfastly on him, saw his face as it had been the face of an angel.

Then said the high priest, "Are these things so?"

And he said, "Men, brethren, and fathers, hearken. . . . Ye stiffnecked and uncircumcised in heart and ears, ye do always resist the Holy Ghost: as your fathers did, so do ye. Which of the prophets have not your fathers persecuted? And they have slain them which showed before the coming of the Just One; of whom ye have been now the betrayers and murderers: who have received the law by the disposition of angels, and have not kept it."

When they heard these things, they were cut to the heart, and they gnashed on him with their teeth.

But he, being full of the Holy Ghost, looked up steadfastly into heaven, and saw the glory of God, and Jesus standing on the right hand of God, and said, "Behold, I see the heavens opened, and the Son of Man standing on the right hand of God."

Then they cried out with a loud voice, and stopped their ears, and ran upon him with one accord, and cast him out of the city, and stoned him: and the witnesses laid down their clothes at a young man's feet, whose name was Saul.

And they stoned Stephen, calling upon God, and saying, "Lord Jesus, receive my spirit." And he kneeled down and cried with a loud voice, "Lord, lay not this sin to their charge." And when he had said this, he fell asleep. And Saul was consenting unto his death.

And at that time there was a great persecution against the church which was at Jerusalem; and they were all scattered abroad throughout the regions of Judaea and Samaria, except the apostles. And devout men carried Stephen to his burial, and made great lamentations over him. As for Saul, he made havoc of the church, entering into every house, and haling men and women committed them to prison. Therefore they that were scattered abroad went everywhere preaching the word. . . .

And Saul, yet breathing out threatenings and slaughter against the disciples of the Lord, went unto the high priest, and desired of him letters to Damascus to the synagogues, that if he found any of this way, whether they were men or women, he might bring them bound unto Jerusalem.

And as he journeyed, he came near Damascus: and suddenly there shone round about him a light from heaven, and he fell to the earth, and heard a voice saying unto him, "Saul, Saul, why persecutest thou me?"

And he said, "Who art thou, Lord?"

And the Lord said, "I am Jesus whom thou persecutest: it is hard for thee to kick against the pricks."

And he trembling and astonished said, "Lord, what wilt thou have me to do?"

And the Lord said unto him, "Arise, and go into the city, and it shall be told thee what thou must do."

And the men which journeyed with him stood speechless, hearing a voice, but seeing no man. And Saul arose from the earth; and when his eyes were opened, he saw no man: but they led him by the hand, and brought him into Damascus. And he was three days without sight; and neither did eat nor drink.

And there was a certain disciple at Damascus, named Ananias; and to him said the Lord in a vision, "Ananias!" And he said, "Behold, I am here, Lord."

And the Lord said unto him, "Arise, and go into the street which is called Straight, and enquire in the house of Judas for one called Saul, of Tarsus: for, behold, he prayeth, and hath seen in a vision a man named Ananias coming in, and putting his hand on him, that he might receive his sight."

Then Ananias answered, "Lord, I have heard by many of this man, how much evil he hath done to thy saints at Jerusalem: and here he hath authority from the chief priests to bind all that call on thy name."

But the Lord said unto him, "Go thy way: for he is a chosen vessel unto me, to bear my name before the Gentiles, and kings, and the children of Israel: for I will show him how great things he must suffer for my name's sake."

And Ananias went his way, and entered into the house; and putting his hands on him said, "Brother Saul, the Lord, even Jesus, that appeared unto thee in the way as thou camest, hath sent me, that thou mightest receive thy sight, and be filled with the Holy Ghost."

And immediately there fell from his eyes as it had been scales: and he received sight forthwith, and arose, and was baptized. And when he had received meat, he was strengthened.

Then was Saul certain days with the disciples which were at Damascus. And straightway he preached Christ in the synagogues, that he is the Son of God. But all that heard him were amazed, and said, "Is not this he that destroyed them which called on this name in Jerusalem, and came hither for that intent, that he might bring them bound unto the chief priests?"

But Saul increased the more in strength, and confounded the Jews which dwelt at Damascus, proving that this is very Christ. And after that many days were fulfilled, the Jews took counsel to kill him: but their laying await was known of Saul. And they watched the gates day and night to kill him. Then the disciples took him by night, and let him down by the wall in a basket.

And when Saul was come to Jerusalem, he essayed to join himself to the disciples: but they were all afraid of him, and believed not that he was a disciple. But Barnabas took him, and brought him to the apostles, and declared unto them how he had seen the Lord in the way, and that he had spoken to him, and how he had preached boldly at Damascus in the name of Jesus. And he was with them coming in and going out at Jerusalem. And he spoke boldly in the name of the Lord Jesus, and disputed against the Grecians: but they went about to slay him. Which when the brethren knew, they brought him down to Caesarea, and sent him forth to Tarsus. . . .

There was a certain man in Caesarea called Cornelius, a centurion of the band called the Italian band, a devout man, and one that feared God with all his house, which gave much alms to the people, and prayed to God always. He saw in a vision, evidently about the ninth hour of the day, an angel of God coming in to him, and saying unto him, "Cornelius!"

And when he looked on him, he was afraid, and said, "What is it, Lord?"

And he said unto him, "Thy prayers and thine alms are come up for a memorial before God. And now send men to Joppa, and call for one Simon, whose surname is Peter. He lodgeth with one Simon a tanner, whose house is by the sea side: he shall tell thee what thou oughtest to do."

And when the angel which spoke unto Cornelius was departed, he called two of his household servants, and a devout soldier of them that waited on him continually; and when he had declared all these things unto them, he sent them to Joppa.

On the morrow, as they went on their journey, and drew nigh unto the city, Peter went upon the housetop to pray about the sixth hour: and he became very hungry, and would have eaten: but while they made ready, he fell into a trance, and saw heaven opened, and a certain vessel descending unto him, as it had been a great sheet knit at the four corners, and let down to the earth: wherein were all manner of fourfooted beasts of the earth, and wild beasts, and creeping things, and fowls of the air. And there came a voice to him, "Rise, Peter; kill, and eat."

But Peter said, "Not so, Lord; for I have never eaten any thing that is common or unclean."

And the voice spoke unto him again the second time, "What God hath cleansed, that call not thou common."

This was done thrice: and the vessel was received up again into heaven.

Now while Peter doubted in himself what this vision which he had seen should mean, behold, the men which were sent from Cornelius had made enquiry for Simon's house, and stood before the gate, and called, and asked whether Simon, which was surnamed Peter, were lodged there. . . . Then called he them in, and lodged them. And on the morrow Peter went away with them, and certain brethren from Joppa accompanied him. And the morrow after they entered into Caesarea. And Cornelius waited for them, and had called together his kinsmen and near friends. And as Peter was coming in, Cornelius met him, and fell down at his feet, and worshipped him. But Peter took him up, saying, "Stand up; I myself also am a man."

And as he talked with him, he went in, and found many that were come together. And he said unto them, "Ye know how that it is an unlawful thing for a man that is a Jew to keep company, or come unto one of another nation; but God hath showed me that I should not call any man common or unclean. Therefore came I unto you without gainsaying, as soon as I was sent for: I ask therefore for what intent ye have sent for me?"

And Cornelius said, "Four days ago I was fasting until this hour; and at the ninth hour I prayed in my house, and, behold, a man stood before me in bright clothing, and said, 'Cornelius, thy prayer is heard, and thine alms are had in remembrance in the sight of God. Send therefore to Joppa, and call hither Simon, whose surname is Peter; he is lodged in the house of one Simon a tanner by the sea side: who, when he cometh, shall speak unto thee.' Immediately therefore I sent to thee; and thou hast well done that thou art come. Now therefore are we all here present before God, to hear all things that are commanded thee of God."

Then Peter opened his mouth, and said, "Of a truth I perceive that God is no respecter of persons: but in every nation he that feareth him, and worketh righteousness, is accepted with him. The word which God sent unto the children of Israel, preaching Jesus Christ (he is Lord of all), that word, I say, ye know, which was published throughout all Judaea, and began from Galilee, after the baptism which John preached: how God anointed Jesus of Nazareth with the Holy Ghost and with power: who went about doing good, and healing all that were oppressed of the devil; for God was with him. And we are witnesses of all things which he did both in the land of the Jews, and in Jerusalem; whom they slew and hanged on a tree. Him God raised up the third day, and showed him openly: not to all the people, but unto witnesses chosen before of God, even to us, who did eat and drink with him after he rose from the dead. And he commanded us to preach unto the people, and to testify that it is he which was ordained of God to be the Judge of the quick and dead. To him give all the prophets witness, that through his name whosoever believeth in him shall receive remission of sins."

While Peter yet spoke these words, the Holy Ghost fell on all them which heard the word. And they of the circumcision which believed were astonished, as many as came with Peter, because that on the Gentiles also was poured out the gift of the Holy Ghost. For they heard them speak with tongues, and magnify God. Then answered Peter, "Can any man forbid water, that these should not be baptized, which have received the Holy Ghost as well as we?"

And he commanded them to be baptized in the name of the Lord. Then prayed they him to tarry certain days. . . .

Now there were in the church that was at Antioch certain prophets and teachers; as Barnabas, and Simeon that was called Niger, and Lucius of Cyrene, and Manaen, which had been brought up with Herod the tetrarch, and Saul. As they ministered to the Lord, and fasted, the Holy Ghost said, "Separate me Barnabas and Saul for the work whereunto I have called them." And when they had fasted and prayed, and laid their hands on them, they sent them away. . . .

And certain men which came down from Judaea taught the brethren, and said, "Except ye be circumcised after the manner of Moses, ye cannot be saved."

When therefore Paul and Barnabas had no small dissension and disputation with them, they determined that Paul and Barnabas, and certain other of them, should go up to Jerusalem unto the apostles and elders about this question. And being brought on their way by the church, they passed through Phenice and Samaria, declaring the conversion of the Gentiles: and they caused great joy unto all the brethren. And when they were come to Jerusalem, they were received of the church, and of the apostles and elders, and they declared all things that God had done with them. But there rose up certain of the sect of the Pharisees which believed, saying that it was needful to circumcise them, and to command them to keep the law of Moses.

And the apostles and elders came together for to consider of this matter. And when there had been much disputing, Peter rose up, and said unto them, "Men and brethren, ye know how that a good while ago God made choice among us, that the Gentiles by my mouth should hear the word of the gospel, and believe. And God, which knoweth the hearts, bore them witness, giving them the Holy Ghost, even as he did unto us; and put no difference between us and them, purifying their hearts by faith. Now therefore why tempt ye God, to put a yoke upon the neck of the disciples, which neither our fathers nor we were able to bear? But we believe that through the grace of the Lord Jesus Christ we shall be saved, even as they."

Then all the multitude kept silence, and gave audience to Barnabas and Paul, declaring what miracles and wonders God had wrought among the Gentiles by them. And after they had held their peace, James answered, saying, "Men and brethren, hearken unto me: Simeon hath declared how God at the first did visit the Gentiles, to take out of them a people for his name. And to this agree the words of the prophets. Wherefore my sentence is, that we trouble not them, which from among the Gen-

tiles are turned to God: but that we write unto them, that they abstain from pollutions of idols, and from fornication, and from things strangled, and from blood. . . ."

Then pleased it the apostles and elders, with the whole church, to send chosen men of their own company to Antioch with Paul and Barnabas; namely, Judas surnamed Barsabas, and Silas, chief men among the brethren: and they wrote letters by them after this manner:

> The apostles and elders and brethren send greeting unto the brethren which are of the Gentiles in Antioch and Syria and Cilicia:
>
> Forasmuch as we have heard, that certain which went out from us have troubled you with words, subverting your souls, saying, "Ye must be circumcised, and keep the law": to whom we gave no such commandment: it seemed good unto us, being assembled with one accord, to send chosen men unto you with our beloved Barnabas and Paul, men that have hazarded their lives for the name of our Lord Jesus Christ. We have sent therefore Judas and Silas, who shall also tell you the same things by mouth. For it seemed good to the Holy Ghost, and to us, to lay upon you no greater burden than these necessary things; that ye abstain from meats offered to idols, and from blood, and from things strangled, and from fornication: from which if ye keep yourselves, ye shall do well.
>
> Fare ye well.

So when they were dismissed, they came to Antioch: and when they had gathered the multitude together, they delivered the epistle: which when they had read, they rejoiced for the consolation. And Judas and Silas, being prophets also themselves, exhorted the brethren with many words, and confirmed them. And after they had tarried there a space, they were let go in peace from the brethren unto the apostles. Notwithstanding it pleased Silas to abide there still. Paul also and Barnabas continued in Antioch, teaching and preaching the word of the Lord, with many others also. . . .

Paul (10 A.D.?–65 A.D.?), a Jew of the Dispersion, brought up to believe in the necessity of a strict observance of the Law (Jewish ritualism), experienced conversion to Christianity following a period of persistent activity persecuting Christians. He had become acquainted not only with oriental religious beliefs and rites but also had some contact with Greek philosophy, particularly Stoicism. Intense by nature, he became the first great Christian missionary, and established many new congregations, especially in Asia Minor and in Greece. His letters to these congregations, together with The Acts of the Apostles, give us some indication of Paul's Christianity, which appeared quite different from that presented in the Gospel of Mark. Paul elaborated, apparently for the first time, the concept of Jesus as a deity whose death upon the cross paid to God the penalty-price demanded for the wrong-doing of mankind. Man could achieve salvation only by faith and the grace of God, made available through the sacrifice of Jesus. Paul is also noted for his social ethic which is beautifully expressed in chapter 13. In the selections from this Epistle note (1) Paul's asceticism, (2) his conclusions concerning the nature and purpose of the Lord's Supper, (3) his universalism, (4) his views on charity or Christian love, (5) his doctrine of the atonement, and (6) Paul's Platonic idealism.

From: THE FIRST EPISTLE OF PAUL TO THE CORINTHIANS

Unto the Church of God which is at Corinth, to them that are sanctified in Christ Jesus, called to be saints, with all that in every place call upon the name of Jesus Christ our Lord, both theirs and ours. . . .

Now concerning virgins I have no commandment of the Lord: yet I give my judgment, as one that hath obtained mercy of the Lord to be faithful. . . . Art thou bound unto a wife? Seek not to be loosed. Art thou loosed from a wife? Seek not a wife. But and if thou marry, thou hast not sinned; and if a virgin marry, she hath not sinned. Nevertheless such shall have trouble in the flesh: but I spare you. . . .

But I would have you without carefulness. He that is unmarried careth for the things that belong to the Lord, how he may please the Lord: but he that is married careth for the things that are of the world, how he may please his wife. There is a difference also between a wife and a virgin. The unmarried woman careth for the things of the Lord, that she may be holy both in body and in spirit: but she that is married careth for the things of the world, how she may please her husband. And this I speak for your own profit; not that I may cast a snare upon you, but for that which is comely, and that ye may attend upon the Lord without distraction. But if any man think that he behaveth himself uncomely toward his virgin, if she pass the flower of her age, and need so require, let him do what he will, he sinneth not: let them marry. Nevertheless he that standeth steadfast in his heart, having no necessity, but hath power over his own will, and hath so decreed in his heart that he will keep his virgin, doeth well. . . .

Now in this that I declare unto you I praise you not, that ye come together not for the better, but for the worse. For first of all, when ye come together in the church, I hear that there be divisions among you; and I partly believe it.

For there must be also heresies among you, that they which are approved may be made manifest among you.

When ye come together therefore into one place, this is not to eat the Lord's supper. For in eating, every one taketh before other his own supper: and one is hungry and another is drunken. What? Have ye not houses to eat and to drink in? Or despise ye the church of God, and shame them that have not? What shall I say to you? Shall I praise you in this? I praise you not.

For I have received of the Lord that which also I delivered unto you, that the Lord Jesus the same night in which he was betrayed took bread: and when he had given thanks, he broke it and said, "Take, eat: this is my body, which is broken for you: this do in remembrance of me." After the same manner also he took the cup, when he had supped, saying, "This cup is the new testament in my blood: this do ye, as oft as ye drink it, in remembrance of me." For as often as ye eat this bread, and drink this cup, ye do show the Lord's death till he come. Wherefore whosoever shall eat this bread, and drink this cup of the Lord, unworthily, shall be guilty of the body and blood of the Lord. But let a man examine himself, and so let him eat of that bread, and drink of that cup. . . .

Now concerning spiritual gifts, brethren, I would not have you ignorant. Ye know that ye were Gentiles, carried away unto these dumb idols, even as ye were led. Wherefore I give you to understand, that no man speaking by the Spirit of God calleth Jesus accursed: and that no man can say that Jesus is the Lord, but by the Holy Ghost.

Now there are diversities of gifts, but the same Spirit. And there are differences of administrations, but the same Lord. And there are diversities of operations, but it is the same God which worketh all in all. But the manifestation of the Spirit is given to every man to profit withal. For to one is given by the Spirit the word of wisdom; to another the word of knowledge by the same Spirit; to another faith by the same Spirit; to another the gifts of healing by the same Spirit; to another the working of miracles; to another prophecy; to another discerning of spirits; to another divers kinds of tongues; to another the interpretation of tongues; but all these worketh that one and the selfsame Spirit, dividing to every man severally as he will.

For as the body is one, and hath many members, and all the members of that one body, being many, are one body: so also is Christ. For by one Spirit are we all baptized into one body, whether we be Jews or Gentiles, whether we be bond or free; and have been all made to drink into one Spirit. For the body is not one member, but many.

If the foot shall say, "Because I am not the hand, I am not of the body; is it therefore not of the body . . . ?" Now ye are the body of Christ, and members in particular. And God hath set some in the church, first apostles, secondarily prophets, thirdly teachers, after that miracles, then gifts of healings, helps, governments, diversities of tongues. Are all apostles? Are all prophets? Are all teachers? Are all workers of miracles? Have all the gifts of healing? Do all speak with tongues? Do all interpret? But covet earnestly the best gifts: and yet show I unto you a more excellent way.

Though I speak with the tongues of men and of angels, and have not charity, I am become as sounding brass, or a tinkling cymbal. And though I have the gift of prophecy, and understand all mysteries, and all knowledge; and though I have all faith, so that I could remove mountains, and have not charity, I am nothing. And though I bestow all my goods to feed the poor, and though I give my body to be burned, and have not charity, it profiteth me nothing. Charity suffereth long, and is kind; charity envieth not; charity vaunteth not itself, is not puffed up, doth not behave itself unseemly, seeketh not her own, is not easily provoked, thinketh no evil; rejoiceth not in iniquity, but rejoiceth in the truth; beareth all things, believeth all things, hopeth all things, endureth all things. Charity never faileth: but whether there be prophecies, they shall fail; whether there be tongues, they shall cease; whether there be knowledge, it shall vanish away. For we know in part, and we prophesy in part. But when that which is perfect is come, then that which is in part shall be done away. When I was a child, I spoke as a child, I understood as a child, I thought as a child: but when I became a man, I put away childish things. For now we see through a glass, darkly; but then face to face: now I know in part; but then shall I know even as also I am known. And now abideth faith, hope, charity, these three; but the greatest of these is charity. . . .

Moreover, brethren, I declare unto you the gospel which I preached unto you, which also ye have received, and wherein ye stand; by which also ye are saved, if ye keep in memory what I preached unto you, unless ye have believed in vain. For I delivered unto you first of all that which I also received, how that Christ died for our sins according to the scriptures; and that he was buried, and that he rose again the third day according to the scriptures: and that he was seen of Cephas, then of the twelve: after that, he was seen of above five hundred brethren at once; of whom the greater part remain unto this present, but some are fallen asleep. After that, he was seen of James; then of all the apostles. And last of all he was seen of me also, as of one born out of due time. For I am the least of the apostles, that am not meet to be called an apostle, because I persecuted the church of God. But by the grace of God I am what I am: and his grace which was bestowed upon me was not in vain; but I laboured more abundantly than they all: yet not I, but the grace of God which was with me. Therefore whether it were I or they, so we preach and so ye believed.

Now if Christ be preached that he rose from the dead, how say some among you that there is no resurrection of the dead? But if there be no resurrection of the dead, then is Christ not risen: and if Christ be not risen, then is our preaching vain, and your faith is also vain. Yea, and we are found false witnesses of God; because we have testified of God that he raised up Christ: whom he raised not up, if so be that the dead rise not. For if the dead rise not, then is not Christ raised: and if Christ be not raised, your faith is vain; ye are yet in your sins. Then they also which are fallen asleep in Christ are perished. If in this life only we have hope in Christ, we are of all men most miserable.

But now is Christ risen from the dead, and become the firstfruits of them that slept. For since by man came death, by man came also the resurrection of the dead. For as in Adam all die, even so in Christ shall all be made alive. . . .

But some man will say, "How are the dead raised up? And with what body do they come?" Thou fool, that which thou sowest is not quickened, except it die: and that which thou sowest, thou sowest not that body that shall be, but bare grain, it may chance of wheat, or of some other grain: but God giveth it a body as it hath pleased him, and to every seed his own body. All flesh is not the same flesh: but there is one kind of flesh of men, another flesh of beasts, another of fishes, and another of birds. There are also celestial bodies, and bodies terrestrial: but the glory of the celestial is one, and the glory of the terrestrial is another. There is one glory of the sun, and another glory of the moon, and another glory of the stars: for one star differeth from another star in glory. So also is the resurrection of the dead. It is sown in corruption; it is raised in incorruption; it is sown in dishonour; it is raised in glory; it is sown in weakness; it is raised in power: it is sown a natural body: it is raised a spiritual body. There is a natural body, and there is a spiritual body. . . .

Now this I say, brethren, that flesh and blood cannot inherit the kingdom of God; neither doth corruption inherit incorruption. Behold, I show you a mystery; we shall not all sleep, but we shall all be changed, in a moment, in the twinkling of an eye, at the last trump: for the trumpet shall sound, and the dead shall be raised incorruptible, and we shall be changed. For this corruptible must put on incorruption, and this mortal must put on immortality. So when this corruptible shall have put on incorruption, and this mortal shall have put on immortality, then shall be brought to pass the saying that is written, "Death is swallowed up in victory. O death, where is thy sting? O grave, where is thy victory?" The sting of death is sin; and the strength of sin is the law. But thanks be to God, which giveth us the victory through our Lord Jesus Christ. Therefore, my beloved brethren, be ye steadfast, unmovable, always abounding in the work of the Lord, forasmuch as ye know that your labour is not in vain in the Lord. . . . My love be with you all in Christ Jesus.

Augustine

Augustine (354–430 A.D.), Bishop of Hippo in North Africa, came to be the most influential Christian philosopher among the early Church Fathers. By the time Augustine appeared Christianity had undergone a rapid development from an obscure oriental sect to the official religion of the empire. Augustine gave the most satisfactory answer to the problem of the relationship of Christianity to classical culture. The Confessions, written in 397, in addition to giving an insight into the aspects of Christianity that appealed to the fourth and fifth century mind, revealed the principal steps by which Augustine found peace and happiness in Christianity. In reading the selections note (1) aspects of Augustine's youth and the influences which helped shape his character, (2) his life at Carthage and how he regarded it, (3) how he came to love philosophy, (4) his interest in Manicheanism and why he ultimately rejected its teachings, (5) what he found in Platonism and how he adapted it to Christianity, (6) his view of the role of Jesus in Christianity, and (7) his description of his conversion and of its results.

From: THE CONFESSIONS OF ST. AUGUSTINE

HOW HE WAS DRIVEN TO LEARN FROM WRONG MOTIVES, WHICH YET GOD TURNED TO GOOD

Yet in my boyhood (which my parents thought a less dangerous age than that of adolescence) I did not love learning, and I hated being driven towards it; yet I was driven, and it was well for me, though I was not doing well: for I would not learn except perforce. Now no one does well against his will, even if what he does is well. Nor were those who drove me doing well, yet was I well dealt with by Thee, O my God. For they could discern no other use for the learning, which they forced upon me, than the gratification of the insatiable craving for gilded poverty and shameful glory.

But Thou, who numberest every hair of our heads, didst turn to my profit the error of those who forced me to learn; and my own error, my reluctance to learn, Thou turnedst to my chastisement, for well did I deserve to suffer, who was so small a child, and yet so great a sinner. And so by the hands of those who did me ill, Thou wast doing me well, and by my own sin thou wast justly requiting me. For Thou hast commanded that an ill-regulated mind should be its own punishment; and it is so.

IN WHAT STUDIES HE FOUND MOST DELIGHT

But even now I cannot understand why I hated Greek, which I was taught in my earliest school-days. Because I loved Latin—the literature, I mean, not the grammar. For the first lessons of the Latin schools, in which one learns to read, write and multiply, I thought as dull and penal as Greek from first to last. Now why was this, if not from sin and vanity of life, because I was flesh and a spirit that goeth and returneth not? For certainly the first lessons, which formed in me the enduring

As translated by C. Bigg in *The Confessions of Saint Augustine*, 12th ed., Methuen and Company, Ltd., London, 1929, 52–65; 89–103; 149–152; 232–246; 278–291. Courtesy of Methuen and Company, Ltd.

power of reading books and writing what I choose, were better, because more solid, than the later, in which I was obliged to learn by heart the wanderings of Æneas, forgetting my own wanderings, and to weep for the death of Dido, who slew herself for love, while I looked with dry eyes on my own most unhappy death, wandering far from Thee, O God, my Life. For what is so pitiful as an unhappy wretch who pities not himself, who has tears for the death of Dido, because she loved Æneas, but none for his own death, because he loves not Thee!

O God, the light of my heart, Thou hidden bread of my soul, Thou mighty Husband of my mind and of the bosom of my thought, I loved Thee not. I liveth in adultery away from Thee, and all men cried unto me, Well done! well done! For the friendship of this world is adultery against Thee. Well done! well done! men cry, till one is ashamed not to be even as they. For this I had no tears, but I could weep for Dido, "slain with the sword and flying to the depths," while I was myself flying from Thee into the depths of Thy creation, earth returning to earth. And, if I was forbidden to read these tales, I grieved; because I might not read what caused me grief. Such lessons were thought more elevating and profitable than mere reading or writing. What madness is this!

But now let Thy truth, O my God, cry aloud in my soul, and say unto me Not so, not so; the earlier teaching was the better. For, lo, I would far rather forget the wanderings of Æneas, and everything of the kind, than how to read and write. Truly over the door of the grammar-school there hangs a curtain, yet is that curtain the shroud of falsehood, not the veil of mysteries. Let not those, whom no longer I fear, cry out against me, while I confess unto Thee, O my God, the promptings of my soul, and acquiesce in the condemnation of my evil ways, that I may love Thy good ways. Let not the buyers or sellers of grammar cry out against me. Because if I were to ask them whether the poet speaks the truth, when he says that Æneas came to Carthage, the unlearned would answer that they do not know, the learned that he does not.

But, if I were to ask how the name of Æneas is spelled, all who have learned spelling would answer rightly, in accordance with the convention by which men have regulated the use of the alphabet. And again, if I were to ask which it would be most inconvenient to forget, the art of reading and writing or these poetic fictions, who does not see what answer a man would be obliged to give, unless he had wholly forgotten himself? I was sinning then when, as a boy, I preferred those vanities to more useful arts, or rather when I loved the one and hated the other. "One and one two, two and two four" I thought a wearisome drone, but the wooden horse teeming with armed men, the flames of Troy, the ghost of Creusa—these were the vain delights that enchanted me.

HOW HE HATED GREEK

Why then did I hate my Greek literature, which was full of such songs? For Homer also weaves these fables with a skilful hand, nor is any vanity so delightful as his. Yet he was distasteful to me as a boy, and so I think would Virgil be to Greek boys, if they were compelled to learn him in the same way, that is to say, by dint of drudgery. The drudgery of acquiring a foreign tongue turned all the sweetness of the Grecian myths into gall. For I knew none of the words, and I was forced to master them by menaces and punishment. There was a time when I knew no Latin words, when I was an infant; but I learned them by merely attending, without fear or pain, amid caresses, laughter and joy, from nurses, friends, and playmates.

I learned them, I say, without the dread of punishment to spur me on, because my own heart was eager to bring its ideas to light, and could not do so till I had acquired some little store of phrases, not from teachers but from talkers, in whose ears I in turn was travailing to express my thoughts. It is plain, then, that the freedom of curiosity is a far better instructor in language than the compulsion of fear. Yet fear restrains the vagaries of curiosity by Thy laws, O God, Thy laws which begin with the schoolmaster's rod, and end with the martyr's fiery trial, Thy laws which have power to mingle a wholesome bitterness in our cup, calling us back to Thee, away from the fatal delights that tempted us to leave Thee.

A PRAYER FOR THE LOVE OF GOD

Hear, O Lord, my petition and suffer not my soul to faint beneath Thy chastisement. Suffer me not to faint in confessing to Thee the loving-kindness, whereby Thou didst rescue me from all my evil ways. Be Thou sweeter to me than all the allurements which I once pursued: that I may love Thee with all my strength, and clasp Thy hand with all my heart, so that I may be delivered from all temptation even unto the end.

For behold, O Lord, my King and my God, to Thy service I devote whatever useful thing I learned as a boy, my speaking, my writing, my reading, my arithmetic. For, when I learned vain things, Thou wast disciplining me, and the sin of my delight in those vanities. Thou hast forgiven. For even in them I learned many useful words, words that can be used with effect in matters that are not vain; and that is the safe path for boys to walk in.

HE DISAPPROVES OF THE WAY IN WHICH BOYS ARE TAUGHT

But woe to thee thou torrent of Use and Wont! Who can resist thee? How long wilt thou not be dried up, how long wilt thou sweep away the sons of Eve into that vast and stormy sea, which scarcely those who have embarked upon the Tree can cross in safety? Was it not in thy book that I read of Jove, the thunderer and the adulterer? Yet how could he be both? These tales were told only that the forged thunder might help and exculpate real adulterers. Which of our long-robed professors would listen patiently to a man, made out of the same dust as themselves, who should cry "These are fictions; Homer made God like man! Would he had rather made man like God." But to speak the whole truth, these fictions, for such they are, ascribe divinity to debauched men, in order that debauchery might no longer be counted debauchery, and that the libertine might seem to emulate, not the worst of men but the very Gods in heaven.

Yet, thou hellish torrent, the sons of men are tossed about in thee, and pay high fees to learn these lessons. And is it not a great disaster, when such instruction is given publicly in the market-place, in sight of the laws which promise the apt scholar a salary much higher than his fees? Thou roarest against thy rocks crying, "I teach words; I give eloquence, the power of persuasive expression." But is it so? Should we not understand these words, "shower of gold," "lap," "trick," "temples of heaven," unless Terence brought upon the stage a profligate youth, justifying his uncleanness by the example of Jove, as he gloats over a picture painted on the wall, a picture to illustrate the tale how "Jove rained into the lap of Danae a shower of gold, and so the girl was tricked?" See how he emboldens his lust by use of a divine authority!

"Aye, and what a God," he goes on, "he who shakes the temples of heaven with the crashing thunder. Was not I, poor man, to follow suit? That I did, right merrily." Certainly you need not sin in the same way to learn those words more easily, but by the words you learn to sin more boldly. I blame, not the words, which are, indeed, elect and precious vessels of thought, but the wine of error, which in them was held to our lips by drunken teachers. If we did not drink, we were beaten; nor could we appeal to any sober judge. And yet, O my God, in whose sight all my reminiscences are now free from dread, I conned these fables willingly, and, alas, with delight, and for this I was pronounced a hopeful scholar.

FURTHER STRICTURES ON THE WAY IN WHICH BOYS ARE TAUGHT LITERATURE

Suffer me also, O my God, to tell in what absurdities I frittered away my talent, which was Thy gift. One task was set me that sorely troubled my mind, that under promise of praise or of censure, and even of stripes, I should declaim the speech of Juno, wrathful and sad, because she could not drive away from Italy the Teucrian King. I had been told that Juno had never uttered the words, but we were all compelled to trace the wandering footprints of the poet's fancy, and say in bald prose what he had sung in verse. And he spoke his piece with most applause, who best acted the passions of wrath and sorrow, with due respect to the dignity of the character, and clothed the sentiments in appropriate words.

Now why did it befall me, O my true life, my God, that my recitation was applauded above those of my equals and classmates? Are not such triumphs but vapour and wind? Was there no other field in which my talent and my tongue might have found occupation? Thy praises, O Lord, Thy praises, displayed in Thy Holy Scriptures, should have propped the climbing vine of my heart; it should not have blown loose amid idle trifles, a sport for the fowls of the air. For there is more than one way of sacrificing to the fallen angels.

MEN OBEY THE LAWS OF GRAMMAR, AND DISOBEY THE LAWS OF GOD

But what wonder, if I plunged into vanities and abandoned Thy house, O my God, when I was taught to emulate men, who blushed for a barbarism or a solecism in the expression of some harmless fact, but plumed themselves on the purity and perspicacity, the fluency and brilliance of the speech, in which they revealed their own pollution. Thou seest these things, O Lord, long-suffering and plenteous in mercy and in truth, Thou seest and keepest silence. Wilt Thou keep silence for ever? Even now Thou dost pluck out of this bottomless pit the soul that seeketh Thee, and thirsteth for Thy pleasures, and saith unto Thee, "I have sought Thy face; Thy face, Lord, will I seek." For I had gone far from Thy face in the darkness of my heart.

For not by the movement of our feet, and not by spaces that can be measured, do we fly from Thee or return to Thee? Did that younger son of Thine hire horse or chariot or ship, did he fly on real wings, or walk with real legs to that far-off land where he spent in riotous living all that Thou gavest at his setting forth? In love Thou gavest, O Father; in greater love Thou forgavest the returning prodigal. A lustful heart is that far-off land, a land of darkness, far from Thy face. Behold, O Lord, behold

patiently, as is Thy wont, how scrupulously men observe the covenant of letters and syllables received from the speakers of old, how carelessly they disobey the eternal covenant of everlasting life received from Thee. One who believes and teaches the time-honoured laws of pronunciation, if against the rule of grammar he says "'uman" for "human," gives more offence to his fellow-creatures than if, in violation of Thy laws, he hated the human race, to which he himself belongs. As if, forsooth, an enemy were more deadly than the hatred which regards him as an enemy, or as if a man by his malice could destroy another more utterly than he destroys his own soul.

Assuredly the laws of language are not written so deeply on our hearts as the rule of conscience: "Do not to another what thou wouldst not that he should do unto thee." How dost Thou hide Thyself, O God, Thou only great, that dwellest in high places in silence, and by an unfailing ordinance sendest penal blindness on lawless passion. A man seeking the glory of eloquence, in presence of a man who is judge, surrounded by bystanders who are men, while he inveighs against his adversary with the bitterest hatred, will be most carefully on his guard lest by a slip of the tongue he should say "men was," but will take no care at all lest, through the madness of his own soul, a man should perish from among men.

HOW THE VICES OF BOYHOOD PASS OVER INTO LATER LIFE

Such was the threshold of my moral life, such my training for this scene of strife. I was more afraid of uttering a barbarism than of envying those who did not. All these faults I confess unto Thee, O my God, but they were thought merits by those whose approbation was my standard of excellence. For I could not see the gulf of vileness in which I was cast away from Thine eyes. For in those eyes who was viler than I? nay, even the vile condemned me, for I practised innumerable deceits on my pedagogue, my masters, my parents, from love of play, from a passion for idle diversions, from a restless desire to imitate the follies of the theatre.

I even stole more than once from my father's cellar, and from the table, at the bidding of my greediness, or that I might have something to give to other boys, who sold me their play, though they loved it as much as I. And in my play I often sought to get the mastery by cheating, when I was myself mastered by the vain desire to excel. Yet what did I so detest as the very tricks which I played upon others, and what did I so angrily denounce, when I found them out? But, if I was myself found out, I would fly into a passion rather than give way.

Is this the innocence of boyhood? It is not, O Lord, it is not. I cry to Thee for pardon, O my God. As we disobeyed pedagogues and masters for nuts and balls and sparrows, so in riper years we disobey governors and kings for gold, for manors, for slaves; and so heavier penalties take the place of the cane. It was then humility, symbolised by the littleness of childhood, which Thou wast commending, when Thou saidst, "Of such is the Kingdom of Heaven."

HE GIVES THANKS TO GOD
FOR THE BLESSINGS OF BOYHOOD

And yet, O Lord my God, Thou best and most excellent Creator and Ruler of the world, I should owe Thee thanks, even though Thou hadst wished that I should never be more than boy. For I was; I was alive; I could feel; I could guard my personality, the imprint of that mysterious unity from which my being was derived; by my inner sense I could warrant the accuracy of my outer senses; I found delight in truth, even in little things and in reflections upon little things; I could not bear to make mistakes; my memory was retentive, my speech refined; friendship consoled me; pain, dishonour, ignorance I was able to avoid. Surely every part of such a creature calls for wonder and praise.

But all this is the bounty of my God and not my own; and all these capacities are good; and I am the sum of them. Truly, then, He who made me is good, and very good; and to Him will I give loud thanks for all the good that belonged to me, even as a boy. For my sin was just this, that I sought for pleasure, grandeur, reality, not in Him but in His creatures, my-self and others, and thus fell headlong into sorrow, confusion, error. Thanks be unto Thee, O my God, my joy, my glory, and my confidence. Thanks be unto Thee for all Thy gifts; but do Thou keep them safe for me. For then Thou wilt keep me safe, and Thy gifts will increase and be perfected; and I shall be with Thee, for even my being is Thy gift. . . .

HOW HE WAS CAUGHT BY LOVE,
WHICH HE PURSUED

Next I went to Carthage, where debauchery bubbled around me like a frying-pan. I was not yet in love, but I loved the idea of love, and a deep-felt want made me hate myself, because I wanted less than I should. I sought something to love, loving as I say the idea of love, and hated the tranquil path, where there are no mouse-traps. For my inward man was famished for want of the inward food, Thyself, O my God, yet had I no appetite and felt no desire for the meat that perisheth not; and that not because I was full but because I was empty, and therefore disdained it. And thus my soul was sick and smitten with boils, and rushed desperately out of doors, seeking, like Job, to scrape itself with the things of sense. And yet, if these things of sense had had no soul, I could not have loved them. To love and to be loved was sweet to me, but sweeter still if I enjoyed the person that I loved.

And so I polluted the brook of friendship with the sewage of lust, and darkened its clear shining with smoke from hell, and yet, vile and disreputable as I was, my vanity was inordinate, and I aspired to be known for my fashion and my wit. Also I plunged headlong into love, whose fetters I longed to wear. O my God, my Merciful One, how good Thou wast, and with what gall didst Thou embitter that cup of sweetness! For I was beloved; I attained my wish, the bondage of clandestine fruition, and proudly riveted around myself the chain of woe; then was I scourged with the red-hot iron rods of jealousy, suspicion, fears, anger, and quarrels.

HIS LOVE FOR TRAGEDIES

The stage also bewitched me, and its manifold pictures of my misery added fuel to my fire. Why is it that men desire to be saddened by the representation of tragic misfortunes, which they do not in the least desire to suffer? Yet the spectator does desire to be saddened by them, and the sadness is the very pleasure that he seeks. Surely this is wretched folly. For in proportion as a man's emotions are less wholesome, the more deeply is he moved by the passion of tragedy. Yet, when a man actually feels this passion, we call his state misery. When he participates in it by way of sympathy, we call it pity. But now what pity can there be for the puppets of the stage? No one expects the spectator to help them; he is only asked to shed a tear, and the more tears he sheds, the more he encourages the actor of an idle tale. And, if these old-world or imaginary calamities are acted in such a way that he cannot shed a tear at all, he goes home disgusted and critical; otherwise he keeps his seat, listens with all his ears, and enjoys the luxury of weeping. Do men then delight in tears and grief? Surely not, but in joy. Or shall we say that, though misery is painful, pity is pleasant, and that because there is no pity without grief, we seek grief for the sake of pity. So that the love of grief also runs from the brook of friendship.

But whither does that brook flow? Why does it fall into a torrent of boiling pitch, into seething pools of horrid lust, where by its own free will it loses the crystal purity of its heavenly source, and is changed into the nature of that hateful flood? Are we then to banish pity? By no means. There are times, then, when we must delight in grief. But beware of uncleanness, O my soul, for fear of my God and Guardian, the God of our fathers, who is to be praised and exalted above all for evermore. Beware of uncleanness. For even now I am not pitiless. But while in the old days in the theatre I envied the lovers who enjoyed the forbidden fruits of love—though but in the mimicry of the stage—and grieved with a kind of pity when they were forced to part, and found the pity as pleasant as the joy, now I pity him who rejoices in his wicked success, and do not pity him who has lost—what?—a ruinous pleasure, a miserable happiness.

Now certainly this is a juster pity, but there is no pleasure in its grief. For, though it is the approved office of charity to grieve over the wretched, a truly pitiful man would far rather see nothing to grieve over. One who really and sincerely pities, cannot want people to be wretched, in order that he may pity them, unless there is such a thing as malevolent benevolence, which is an impossibility. Grief, then, may sometimes be right, but never desirable. And this Thou teachest us, O Lord God, who lovest the soul with a love far purer than ours, and whose pity is diviner than ours, because it feels no grief. But who is sufficient for these things? However, wretched man that I was, I loved sorrow in those days; I sought an outlet for pity in the fictitious woes of a dancer, and always that part liked me best which wrung tears from my eyes. What wonder, if the lost and wilful sheep was taken by the murrain? Thence came my delight in troubles—not such as pierce the heart, for I would not for the world have suffered what I was so eager to behold—but idle tales which glance upon the surface—yet they tore my flesh like claws, and left behind them an angry swelling and a festering sore. Is such a life worth calling life, O my God?

IN THE RHETORIC SCHOOL HE TOOK NO PART IN THE DOINGS OF THE WRECKERS

And always Thy faithful mercy hovered over me from afar. O in what wickednesses did I consume away! How did I follow my profane Curiosity, till it led me into the very depths of unbelief, into the deceitful worship of devils to whom my misdeeds were a sacrifice! And always Thou wast scourging me. I was not afraid to think of my lust, and plan a scheme for securing the deadly fruit of sin, even within the walls of Thy church during the celebration of Thy mysteries. For this Thou didst chastise me with heavy penalties, yet not as my fault deserved, O my God, my surpassing Mercy, my Refuge from the awful tormentors among whom I wandered with stubborn neck, fleeing farther and farther from Thee, loving my own ways not Thine, loving a runagate freedom.

My studies also, liberal studies they were called, drew me to look towards the Law Courts and to aspire to success at the bar, where the craftiest is the most honourable.

Such is the blindness of men, who ever glory in their blindness. And now I had reached the top of the school of rhetoric. Proud enough I was, and puffed up with conceit, yet far quieter than I had been, O Lord, Thou knowest. I would take no part at all in the wild doings of the Wreckers, a cruel and devilish name, which was looked upon as the stamp of the best set. I lived amongst them, feeling a kind of impudent shame, because I could not keep pace with them. I went about with them, and of some of them I made friends; yet I always disliked their way of going on, their "wreckings," their wanton attacks upon the shyness of freshmen, and the unprovoked affronts with which they carried on their malignant amusement. Nothing could be more like the conduct of devils, and what name could be fitter for them than Wreckers? They themselves were wrecked and broken to begin with, and the lying spirits were cozening and seducing them, while they were finding delight in flouting and deceiving others.

THE HORTENSIUS OF CICERO ROUSED IN HIM A GREAT LOVE OF PHILOSOPHY

Among such comrades in those years of indiscretion, I was studying books of rhetoric, wherein I desired to excel, seeking through the joys of vanity a flashy and reprobate success, and in the usual course I had entered upon a book by one Cicero whose tongue all men admire, though not his heart. It was the *Hortensius,* a treatise in which he extols the study of philosophy. That book changed my mind, changed my very prayers to Thee, O Lord, and altered my wishes and aspirations. From that moment vain hopes ceased to charm, and with a strange and heartfelt passion I began to long for the immortality of wisdom. Thenceforth began my upward way, and my return towards Thee. For I did not apply that book to the sharpening of my tongue, an accomplishment which it seemed hard to purchase at my mother's cost—for I was in my nineteenth year and my father had died two years before—I did not, I say, apply it to the sharpening of my tongue, for what the book itself commended was not the style but the substance of speech.

How did I burn, O my God, how did I burn to soar away from earth to Thee; yet I knew not what Thou wast doing to me. For wisdom is Thine. The love of wisdom with which those pages inspired me is called in Greek "philosophy." There are some who mislead by philosophy, tricking out their own errors with a high, attractive, and honourable title, and in this book Cicero censures and confutes nearly all these erroneous teachers of his own or earlier times. How distinctly does he preach the wholesome admonition, which Thy Spirit gives by the mouth of Thy good and pious servant: "Beware lest any man spoil you through philosophy and vain deceit, after the tradition of men, after the rudiments of the world and not after Christ. For in Him dwelleth all the fullness of the God-head bodily."

At that time, Thou knowest, O Light of my heart, these words of the Apostle were not yet known to me; yet the one point that came home to me in Cicero's book was the advice not to run after this school or that, but to love, and seek, and pursue, and clasp, and never let go Wisdom herself, wherever I found her. I was strongly moved, and kindled, and inflamed by these words; and one thing only damped my zeal, that the Name of Christ was not mentioned there. For this Name, according to Thy lovingkindness, O Lord, this Name of my Saviour, Thy Son, my infant heart had sucked in with my mother's milk, and there it still was, hidden safe away. So that any book which did not use that Name—cultivated, polished, profound as it might be—could not wholly master me.

HE DISDAINED SACRED SCRIPTURE BECAUSE OF ITS STYLE

And so I determined to read the sacred Scriptures, and find out what they were like. And behold I found a thing not known to the proud, nor laid open to children, but lowly in mien, lofty in operation, and veiled in mysteries. I was not such that I could enter into it, or bow my head at its approach. For I did not feel what I have just described, when first I read the Scriptures. They seemed to me to be far inferior to the dignity of Tully. My extravagance disliked their self-restraint, and my eye could not pierce their hidden depths. In truth it is the nature of that Book to grow with the growth of the babe. But I disdained to be a babe, and in my swelling pride fancied that I was grown-up.

HOW HE WAS CAUGHT BY THE MANICHEES

And so I fell among a sort of men vain and brain-sick, carnal and verbose, in whose mouths were snares of the Devil and lime for silly birds, made up of the syllables of Thy Name, and that of our Lord Jesus Christ, and that of the Paraclete our Comforter, the Holy Ghost. These Names were never off their lips; the sound was there, and the movement of the tongue, but the heart within was void of truth. "The Truth, the Truth," they were always saying, and often said to me, but it was not in them; they taught lies, not only of Thee who art the true Truth, but of the elements of this world, Thy creatures. But, indeed, I ought not to have heeded philosophers, even though they spoke truth about Thy works: I ought to have passed them by for love of Thee, my Father, supremely good, Thou Fairness of all that is fair. O Truth, Truth, how did the inmost marrow of my soul sigh for Thee even then, while those word-mongers were ringing the changes on Thy name in all those ponderous tomes! These were the dainty dishes wherein, when I was hungering for Thee, they served up to me the sun and moon, beautiful works indeed, but Thy works, not Thyself nor even Thy first works. For Thy spiritual world came before these material creatures, bright and heavenly though they be.

I hungered and thirsted not even for those, Thy first works, but for Thee, O Truth, in whom is no variableness, neither shadow of turning, yet still they set before me in those dainty dishes a banquet of delusions. Far better were it to love the sun we see (which to our eyes, at any rate, is real) than these fictions of a mind deceived by the eyes. And yet I fed on them because I took them for Thee, but not with appetite, because I could not find in them Thy savour. For Thou wast not those fictions, nor did they nourish, nay, they starved me. How like is food in dreams to real food! yet the dreamer is not fed, for it is a dream.

But these meats were not like Thee in any way, as Thou didst warn me even then; for they were material notions, imaginary things, far less certain than the real things, which we see with our natural eyes, in earth or sky. These the birds and beasts see as well as we; and they are far more real than those creatures of the imagination. And again, those imaginations are far more real than the infinite series of sublime nonentities which we build upon them. However, with these empty husks was I then fed, yet not fed.

But Thou, my Love, for whom I faint that I may be made strong, art neither these bodies which we see, though they be in heaven, nor those which we see not, for Thou art their Creator, nor dost Thou count them among Thy chiefest works. How far art Thou, then, from those notions that I believed in, notions of bodies which do not exist at all. For our abstract conceptions of bodies which do exist are more certain than they, and the bodies themselves are more certain still, yet Thou art none of these. Thou art not even the soul, which is the life of bodies, so that the life of bodies is better and more certain than the bodies themselves. But Thou art the life of souls, the life of lives, having life in Thyself, and never changest, O Life of my soul. Where wast Thou then? How far away from me? while I was banished far away from Thee, deprived even of the husks of the swine which I was feeding with husks. For the fables of the grammarian and the poet were far better than this deceitful stuff. Beyond a doubt verses and songs about Medea's flight through the air are more profitable than the five elements variously transformed because of the five caves of darkness, which have no existence, and slay him that believes in them. From verses and songs I can find real nutriment, and, as for Medea and her flight, even if I sang about it, I did not maintain that it was true. And when others sang about it, I did not believe them. But these absurdities I did believe.

Alas! alas! by what steps was I brought down to the depths of hell! toiling and chafing for lack of truth, and all, O my God (for unto Thee do I confess it, who hadst pity on me, even when I did not confess), all because I was seeking for Thee by the carnal senses, and not by that intelligence in which Thou madest me superior to the beasts. But Thou wast lower than my lowest depth and higher than my highest height. And so I happened upon that brazen and witless woman of whom Solomon speaks in his parable, sitting on a chair at the entrance of the door, and crying: "Eat gladly of hidden bread and drink sweet stolen water." She corrupted me because she found me rambling abroad in the lust of the eye, and ruminating such food as I had procured for myself thereby.

THE ABSURDITY OF THE MANICHEAN DOCTRINE, WHICH HE PROFESSED

For, knowing not the true Being, I was so shaken by quips and quiddities that I had no answer for these silly deceivers when they asked me what is the origin of evil? whether God is limited by a bodily form? whether he has hair and nails? whether polygamists, homicides, offerers of bloody sacrifices, can be regarded as righteous men? These doubts confused my ignorance; I turned my back on truth and thought I was looking for it, because I did not know that evil is the privation of good and next door to non-existence. How could I see this, when my eye could see nothing but bodies, and my mind nothing but materialised ideas?

I did not understand that God is a spirit, who has no parts that can be measured, whose being is not a bulk, because bulk is less in the part than in the whole, and, even if it be infinite, is less in some definite portion than in its infinity, and cannot be wholly everywhere like God, who is spirit. And I had not the least conception in what we are like God, or whether Scripture was right in saying that we are in the image of God. Nor did I know the true inner righteousness, which judges not conventionally but by the upright law of Almighty God, whereby the customs of countries and times are adapted to the countries and the times, though the law is the same everywhere and always. I did not see that by this law Abraham and Isaac and Jacob and Moses and David and all who are praised by the mouth of God were righteous; though they were counted unrighteous

by foolish men, judging by man's day, and measuring the morality of the whole human race by the petty rule of their own morality, just as if one, who knew nothing about armour, should fasten a greave on his head and shoe his foot with a helmet, and then complain because they do not fit; or as if, when a holiday has been proclaimed for the afternoon, he should make a disturbance because he may not open his shop after twelve o'clock, though it was lawful in the morning; or as if in some great household, having discovered that one slave was allowed to handle things which the butler might not touch, or that things might be done in the stable which were forbidden in the dining room, he should make angry complaints, that in one house and in one family all have not the same office at the same time.

Such are they who are indignant, when they hear that some things were lawful for the righteous in old times, which are not permitted now; or that God for temporary reasons gave the ancients one commandment, us another, though we both obey the same righteousness; or when they see that in one man, in one day, in one house, different offices suit different members, that what was right just now is not right when the clock has struck, that what is done, nay, must be done, in one room is properly forbidden and punished in another. Is justice then capricious or changeable? No, but the times, over which justice presides, do not run evenly, because they are times. So men, whose days upon earth are few, quarrel with the past and accept the present, because they cannot actually see the connection between the laws that governed ages and nations of old and those that are now in operation; while they can see individuals, days, houses, in which different things at different moments are suitable to different members, parts, or persons.

All these things I neither knew nor considered; they forced themselves upon my eyes, but I could not see them. I wrote poems, in which I was not allowed to put any foot I pleased wherever I liked; each metre had its own regulations, and, even in the same line, the same foot would not suit all places. Yet the art of poetry did not make its principles to suit the case, but comprised all in one. Still I did not perceive that justice, which those good and holy men obeyed, comprises all in one in a far more excellent and admirable way; that, without changing in any degree, it yet gives out its precepts, not all at once, but with due respect to the changes of the times. And in my blindness I condemned the holy patriarchs; though they not only regulated the present by the command and inspiration of God, but moreover foretold the future as God revealed it unto them. . . .

OF FAUSTUS THE MANICHEAN, AND OF THE BLINDNESS OF PHILOSOPHERS WHO KNOW THE CREATURE YET KNOW NOT THE CREATOR

I will describe in the sight of my God the twenty-ninth year of my age. There was then at Carthage a Manichean bishop Faustus, a great snare of the devil, who entrapped many by the bait of his eloquence. This I admired; but I was beginning to distinguish the charm of words from the truth of things, which I was eager to learn, nor did I consider so much the beauty of the dish, as the kind of meat which their famous Faustus served up to me. For fame had run before him, as of one skilled in all honourable learning, and especially well versed in the liberal sciences.

And, since I was well read in the philosophers and had a good memory for their principles, I began to compare some of their doctrines with the tedious fables of the Manichees, and it struck me that probability was on the side of the philosophers, whose power reached so far that they were able to form a fair judgment of the world, although they did not find the Sovereign Lord of these His works. For Thou art great, O Lord, and hast respect unto the lowly, but the proud Thou beholdest afar off. Thou drawest near to none but the contrite in heart, nor canst Thou be found by the proud, even though by inquisitive skill they number the stars and the sand, and map out the spaces of the constellations, and track the orbits of the heavenly bodies. For it is by mind and intelligence, which Thou bestowest, that they investigate these things. Much they have found out; they have foretold even beforehand the day, the hour, the extent of eclipses of those

bright luminaries, the sun and moon: their calculations did not fail, and it came to pass as they foretold: they wrote down the rules they had discovered, so that to this day they may be read, and from them may be calculated in what year, in what month, on what day of the month, at what hour of the day, in what portion of its light, sun or moon will be eclipsed, and it will come to pass just as is predicted.

And men who know not, wonder and are amazed; and men who know are boastful and lifted up; in their ungodly pride they withdraw from Thy light into the shadow of eclipse; they can foresee the eclipse of the sun, and cannot see their own. For they do not ask, as religious men should, whence comes the intelligence whereby they investigate. And when they discover that Thou didst make them, they do not give themselves up to Thee, that Thou mayest preserve what Thou didst make, nor do they sacrifice unto Thee what they have made of themselves—slaying their high thoughts like fowls of the air, and their subtleties (wherein they dart along the secret paths of the deep) like fishes of the sea, and their lusts like beasts of the field—that Thou, O God, who art a consuming fire, shouldest burn up their dead cares and renew them unto immortality.

But they know not the Way, Thy Word, by whom Thou didst create the things that are numbered, and the men who number them, and the senses by which they perceive what they number, and the intelligence whereby they number; nor do they know that of Thy Wisdom there is no number. But Thy Only Begotten Himself was made unto us wisdom and righteousness and sanctification, and was numbered amongst us, and paid tribute unto Caesar. They know not this Way, and deem that they are shining among the stars on high; and, lo, they have fallen to earth, and their foolish heart is darkened. Much that is true do they teach about creation, but the Truth, the Artificer of creation, they do not piously seek, and therefore they find not. Or if they find, they know God, yet glorify Him not as God, neither are thankful, but become vain in their imaginations: they profess themselves to be wise, claiming Thy attributes for their own, and hence, in the perversity of blindness, they ascribe to Thee those attributes that are their own, heaping lies upon Thee who art the Truth, changing the glory of the incorruptible God into an image made like to corruptible man, and to birds, and four-footed beasts and creeping things, changing Thy truth into a lie, and worshipping and serving the creature more than the Creator.

Yet I remembered many a true saying of the philosophers about creation, and I saw reason in their calculations, in the orderly sequence of times, and in the manifest attestation of the stars. This I compared with the doctrines of Manichaeus, who in his voluminous folly wrote many books on these matters. And here I could see no reason about the solstice, or the equinox, or eclipses, or whatever I had learned in books of secular philosophy. I was ordered to believe, but the ideas did not correspond with, nay, they contradicted, the rational theories established by mathematics, and indeed by the evidence of my own eyes. . . .

HOW IN THE PLATONIC BOOKS HE FOUND THE DIVINITY OF THE ETERNAL WORD, BUT NOT THE HUMILITY OF THE INCARNATE WORD

And first of all, willing to teach me how Thou dost resist the proud and givest grace to the humble, and how mercifully Thou hast made known to men the way of humility, in that Thy Word was made flesh and dwelt among men, Thou didst procure for me, through the agency of one puffed up with enormous vanity, certain books of the Platonists translated from the Greek into Latin. And therein I found, not indeed these precise words, but precisely the same truth fortified with many and divers arguments, that "in the beginning was the Word, and the Word was with God, and the Word was God, and the same was in the beginning with God; all things were made by Him, and without Him was nothing made that was made; in Him is life, and the life was the light of men, and the light shineth in darkness, and the darkness comprehended it not." Further, that the soul of man, though it bears witness to the light, is not itself that light, but God, the Word of God, is the true light that lighteth every man that cometh into the world. And that "He was in the world, and the world was made by Him, and the world knew Him not." But that "He came unto His own, and His own received Him not; but as many as received Him, to them gave He power to become the sons of God, even to them that believe on His name,"—this I could not find there.

Also I found there that God the Word "was born, not of flesh, nor of blood, nor of the will of a man, nor of the will of the flesh, but of God." But that "the Word was made flesh and dwelt among us," this I found not there. I could discover in these books, though it was expressed in other and in varying phrases, that "the Son was in the form of the Father, and thought it not robbery to be equal with God," because by nature He was that same substance. But that "He emptied Himself, taking upon Him the form of a servant, being made in the likeness of men; and, being found in fashion as a man, He humbled Himself, and became obedient unto death, even the death of the Cross; wherefore also God exalted Him from the dead, and gave Him a Name, which is above every name; that at the name of Jesus every knee should bow, of things in heaven, and things in earth, and things under the earth, and that every tongue should confess that the Lord Jesus Christ is in the glory of God the Father"—this those books do not contain.

For that, before all times and above all times, Thy only begotten Son abideth unchangeable and co-eternal with Thee, and that of His fullness all souls receive, in order that they may be blessed, and that by participation of the eternal wisdom they are renewed, in order that they may be wise, this is there. But that in due time He died for the ungodly, that Thou sparedst not Thine Only Son but deliveredst Him up for us all, this is not there. For Thou hast hidden these things from the wise, and revealed them unto babes, that they that labor and are heavy laden might come unto Him, and He might refresh them, because He is meek and lowly in heart, and the meek He guideth in judgment, and the gentle He teacheth His ways, looking upon our lowliness and troubles, and forgiving all our sins. But those who strut in the buskin of what they deem higher knowledge, will not listen to Him who saith, "Learn of me, for I am meek and lowly in heart, and ye shall find rest unto your souls," and though they know God, yet they glorify Him not as God, nor are thankful, but become vain in their imaginations, and their foolish heart is darkened; professing themselves to be wise, they became fools.

And therefore, as I read there also, they had changed the glory of Thy incorruptible nature into idols and many kinds of images, into the likeness of the image of corruptible man, and birds, and four-footed beasts and creeping things, to wit, that flesh of Egypt for which Esau lost his birthright; for Thy first-born people worshipped the head of a beast instead of Thee, turning in heart back towards Egypt, and bowing down their soul, Thy likeness, before the likeness of a calf that eateth hay. These things found I there, but I would not eat of them. For it pleased Thee, O Lord, to take away the reproach of inferiority from Jacob that the elder should serve the younger, and Thou calledst the Gentiles into Thine inheritance.

And I had come to Thee from the Gentiles; and my mind was set upon the gold which Thou willedst Thy people to carry off from Egypt, for it was Thine wherever it was. And Thou didst say unto the Athenians by the mouth of Thy Apostles that in Thee we live and move and have our being, as certain also of their own poets have said. And surely these books came from thence. But my mind was not set on the idols of the Egyptians, which they fashioned of Thy gold, changing the truth of God into a lie, and worshipping and serving the creature more than the Creator.

AUGUSTINE BEGINS MORE CLEARLY TO DISCERN DIVINE TRUTH

And, being by these books admonished to return into myself, I entered into the secret closet of my soul, guided by Thee; and this I could do because Thou wast my helper. I entered, and beheld with the mysterious eye of my soul the light that never changes, above the eye of my soul, above my intelligence. It was not the common light which all flesh can see, nor was it greater yet of the same kind, as if the light of day were to grow brighter and brighter and flood all space. It was not like this, but something altogether different from any earthly illumination. Nor was it above my intelligence in the same way as oil is above water, or heaven above earth, but it was higher because it made me, and I was lower because made by it. He who knows the truth knows that Light, and he who knows that Light knows Eternity. Love knows that Light.

O eternal Truth, and true Love, and lovely Eternity, Thou art my God; unto Thee do I sigh night and day. When first I knew Thee, Thou didst take hold of me, so that I could see there was something to be seen, though I was not yet fit to see it. And Thou didst beat back my weak sight, dazzling me with Thy splendour, and I thrilled with love and dread, and I perceived that I was far away from Thee in the land of unlikeness, as if I heard Thy voice from on high crying unto me, "I am the Food of the full-grown; become a man, and Thou shalt feed on me. Nor shalt Thou change Me into thine own substance, as thou changest the food of thy flesh, but thou shalt be changed into Mine." And I understood that Thou dost chasten man for iniquity, and hast made my soul to consume away like a spider's web. And I said, "Is truth, then, nothing, because it is not diffused through space finite or infinite?" And Thou didst cry from afar, "Nay, not so; I AM THAT I AM." And I heard as the heart heareth, and there was left no room for doubt. Sooner could I doubt my own existence than think that Truth is not, for it is clearly seen and understood by means of the things which are made.

HOW THE CREATURES ARE AND ARE NOT

And I beheld all the things that are beneath Thee, and I saw that they are neither wholly real nor wholly unreal; they are real in so far as they came from Thee, they are unreal because they are not what Thou art. For that alone is truly real which abides unchanged. It is good then for me to hold me fast by God, because if I abide not in Him, I cannot abide in myself. But He, abiding in Himself, maketh all things new. And Thou art the Lord my God, because my goods are nothing unto Thee.

ALL THAT IS, IS GOOD

And it was made clear to me that all things that are corrupted are good. They could not be corrupted, if they were chief goods, nor unless they were goods; because, if they were chief goods, they would be incorruptible, and if they were not goods at all, there would be nothing in them that could be corrupted. For corruption does harm, and it can do harm only by diminishing goodness. Either then corruption does no harm, which is impossible, or all things that are corrupted are deprived of good, and this is most certainly true. But, if they are deprived of all good, they will cease to exist. For, if they exist and can be no further corrupted, they will be better because henceforth they remain incorruptible.

Now what can be more monstrous than to maintain that, by losing all good, they have become better. If then they are deprived of all good, they will cease to exist. Therefore, so long as they exist, they are good. Therefore, all that exists is good. And so that evil, whose origin I was seeking, is not a substance; because if it were a substance, it would be good. For either it would be an incorruptible substance, that is to say, a chief good, or a corruptible substance, which could not be corrupted unless it were good. And so I saw, and saw clearly that all that Thou hast made is good; and there are no substances at all which Thou didst not make. And because Thou didst not make all things equal, each by itself is good, and the sum of all is very good; for our God made all things very good.

ALL CREATION PRAISES GOD

And to Thee there is no such thing as evil, and even to Thy creation as a whole there is not, because there is nothing beyond it that can burst in and destroy the law which Thou hast imposed upon it. In the details there are things which, because they suit not some parts, are counted evil, yet these same things suit other parts, and are good to them, and are good in themselves. And all these things which are not suitable to one another, are yet suitable to that lower half of creation called earth, which has its own windy and cloudy sky of like nature with itself.

What folly, then, would it be to think that nothing exists except this world of sense. For, if I saw this world alone, I should long indeed for a better, yet should I be bound to praise Thee for this world alone. For, that Thou art to be praised on earth, the dragons do show and all deeps, fire, hail, snow, ice, and stormy wind fulfilling Thy word; mountains and all hills, fruitful trees and all cedars; beasts and all cattle, creeping things and feathered fowl; kings of the earth and all people, princes and all judges of the earth; young men and maidens, old men and children praise Thy Name. But seeing that in heaven all Thy angels praise Thee, praise Thee, O God, in the height, and all Thy hosts, sun and moon, all stars and light, the heaven of heavens and the waters that be above the heavens praise Thy Name, seeing this, I say, I no longer desired a better world, because my thought ranged over all, and with a sounder judgment I reckoned that things above were better than things below, yet that all creation together was better than the things above.

THE SANE MIND FINDS NOTHING EVIL IN GOD'S CREATION

There is no health in those who find fault with any part of Thy creation, as there was no health in me, when I found fault with many of Thy works. And, because my soul did not dare to find fault with God, it denied that the faults it found were Thy handiwork. Thus it had wandered into the notion of two substances, and could find no rest, and talked a strange language. And, escaping from that error, it had made for itself a God extended through infinite space, and thought it to be Thee, and set it up in its heart, and became once more the temple of its own idol, abominable in Thy sight. But Thou didst soothe my brain, though I knew it not, and closed my eyes lest they should behold vanity, and thus by slow degrees my folly ceased and fell asleep. And I awoke in Thee and beheld Thee infinite, yet not in such a manner as I had supposed, and this vision was not derived from the flesh.

HOW THERE IS TRUTH AND FALSE-HOOD IN CREATION

And I looked upon other things, and I saw that all that is finite owes to Thee its existence in Thee; yet it is in Thee not as it is in space, but because Thou holdest all things in the hand of Thy truth: and that all things are true in so far as they are; and that falsehood is nothing, except the existence in thought of that which is not. And I saw that everything bears fit relation, not only to its place but to its time; and that Thou, who alone art Eternal, didst not begin to work after the lapse of innumerable ages, because no time, either of past or of future, could come or go, except by Thy working and abiding.

HOW ALL THAT IS CREATED IS GOOD, THOUGH IT MAY NOT SUIT EVERYTHING

And I felt and realized that it is nothing strange, if bread, which is sweet, is a punishment to the diseased palate, and light, which is lovely to healthy eyes, is hateful to the sick. And the wicked find fault with Thy justice, as they do with the viper and the worm, yet these are good, though belonging only to the lower order of Thy creation. And there is the proper place of the wicked also, the more unlike they are to Thee; yet do they belong also to the higher order, the more they become like Thee. And I asked what wickedness was, and I found that it was no substance, but a perversity of will, which turns aside from Thee, O God, the supreme substance, to desire the lowest, flinging away its inner treasure and boasting itself an outcast.

WHAT IT IS THAT HOLDS MAN BACK FROM THE KNOWLEDGE OF THE DIVINE

And I marvelled to find that now I loved Thee, and not a phantasm in Thy stead. And I could not stand still to enjoy my God, but was swept up to Thee by Thy beauty, and again torn away from Thee by my own weight, and fell back with a groan into the world of sense; and the weight was carnal use and wont. But Thy memory dwelt with me, nor did I doubt in the least that there was One for me to cleave to, only I doubted whether I was as yet able to cleave to Him, forasmuch as the corruptible body presseth down the soul, and the earthly tabernacle weigheth down the mind that museth upon many things. Most certain I was that Thy invisible things are clearly seen from the constitution of the world, being understood through the things that are made, even Thy eternal power and Godhead.

For when I asked how I could estimate the beauty of bodies, whether celestial or terrestrial, and what rule was ready to my hand so that I could judge correctly of changeable things and say This ought to be thus, that ought to be otherwise—when I asked, I say, how it was possible for me to judge in this way, it was clear that I had found the unchangeable and true eternity of truth above my own changeable intelligence. Thus step by step was I led upwards, from bodies to the soul which perceives by means of the bodily senses, and thence to the soul's inward faculty, to which bodily sense reports external facts, and this belongs even to beasts, and thence again to the reasoning power, to whose judgment is referred the knowledge received by the bodily senses.

And when this power also within me found itself changeable, it lifted itself up to its own intelligence, and withdrew its thoughts from experience, abstracting itself from the contradictory throng of sensuous images, that it might find out what that light was wherein it was bathed, when it cried out that beyond doubt the unchangeable was better than the changeable, and how it came to know the unchangeable, which it must have known in some way or another, for otherwise it could not have preferred it so confidently to the changeable. And thus, with the flash of one hurried glance, it attained to the vision of THAT WHICH IS. And then at last I saw Thy invisible things understood by means of the things that are made, but I could not sustain my gaze; my weakness was dashed back, and I was relegated to my ordinary experience, bearing with me nothing but a loving remembrance, cherishing, as it were, the fragrance of those viands which I was not yet able to feed upon.

CHRIST THE ONLY WAY
TO SALVATION

So I cast about for some way to attain a strength that should be able to enjoy Thee; nor could I find any, until I embraced the mediator between God and man, the Man Christ Jesus, who is over all, God blessed for ever, who calleth me and saith, "I am the Way, the Truth, and the Life," who mingleth Himself with flesh, and is the food which I was as yet unable to receive, because the Word was made Flesh, that Thy all-creative wisdom might become milk for us babes. For as yet I did not humbly hold the humble Lord Jesus, nor did I know what His weakness was meant to teach us. For Thy Word, the Eternal Truth, far exalted above the higher parts of Thy creation, lifteth up His subjects towards Himself, but in the lower parts hath built for Himself a humble dwelling of our clay, that so He might pull down from themselves and win over to Himself those whom He is to make subject, lowering their pride and heightening their love, that they might not stray farther afield in self-confidence, but rather be made weak, seeing before their feet the Godhead made weak by sharing our coats of skins, and that they might cast themselves wearily upon It, and be uplifted by Its rising. . . .

HE GOES INTO THE GARDEN.
WHAT BEFELL HIM THERE

Disordered in look and mind by this desperate wrestle with my own soul in the secret chambers of my own heart, I fell upon Alypius crying out, "What has come to us? What means this tale that thou hast heard? Simple men arise and take heaven by violence, and we with all our heartless learning—see how we are wallowing in flesh and blood. Shall we stand still because they have taken the lead? Shall we not follow if we could not lead?" I scarcely knew what I said, and flung away, leaving him staring in silent astonishment. For my voice

was changed; my face, eyes, colour, tone expressed my meaning more clearly than my words.

There was a garden to our lodging, of which we were free, as indeed we were of the whole house. For our host, the master of the house, did not live there. Thither the tumult of my breast drove me, where no one could interrupt the duel into which I had entered with myself, until it should reach the issue which Thou alone couldest foresee. I was mad, unto salvation; I was dying, unto life; I knew what evil thing I was; what good thing I was soon to be I knew not. I fled then into the garden, and Alypius followed me step for step. For I had no secret wherein he did not share, and how could he leave me in such distress? We sat down, as far from the house as possible. I was groaning in spirit, shaken with a gust of indignation, because I could not enter into Thy Will and Covenant, O my God; yet all my bones were crying out that this was the way, the best of all ways, and no ship is needed for that way, nor chariot, no, nor feet, for it is not so far as from the house to the spot where we were seated.

For to go along that road, aye, and to reach the goal, is all one with the will to go; but it must be a strong and single will, not a broken-winged wish fluttering hither and thither, rising with one pinion, struggling and falling with the other. In fine, in the midst of that passionate indecision, I was doing many things which men sometimes will, yet cannot perform, because they have lost a limb, because their limbs are bound with fetters, or enfeebled by disease, or incapacitated in some other way. If I tore my hair, or beat my brow, or clasped my hands about my knees, it was because I willed to do so. Yet I might have willed in vain, if the nerves had not obeyed my bidding. Many things then I did, in which will and power to do were not the same, yet did not that one thing which seemed to me infinitely more desirable, which, before long, I should have power to will, because, before long, I should certainly will to will it. For in this the power of willing is the power of doing, and yet I could not do it. And so my body lent a ready obedience to the slightest desire of the soul, moving its limbs in instant compliance, while my soul could not aid itself in carrying out its great resolve, which needed but resolve to accomplish it.

WHY THE MIND IS NOT OBEYED WHEN IT COMMANDS ITSELF

Now whence and why is this strange anomaly? Let Thy mercy shine as the light; and suffer me to ask, if perchance I may find an answer amid the dark places of human chastisement, and the midnight of the contrition of the sons of Adam. Whence is this anomaly and why? Mind commands body, and there is instant obedience; mind commands mind, and there is rebellion. Mind commands the hand to move, and so facile is the process that you can hardly distinguish the order from its fulfilment; now the mind is mind and the hand is body. Mind commands mind to will, and, though it is one, it will not hear. Whence and why is this anomaly? I say it commands to will; and it would not command unless it did will, and yet its command is inoperative.

But it does not will wholly, and therefore it does not command wholly. For it commands, in so far as it wills, and its command is not executed, in so far as it does not will. For the will commands that there should be a will, and not another will but itself. Certainly it is not the full will that commands, hence it is not the very thing that it commands. For if it were the full will, it would not even command itself to be, because it would be already. And so this "will and will not" is no anomaly, but a sickness of the mind, which is weighed down by evil habit, and cannot rise wholly when uplifted by truth. And so there are two wills, because one of them is not whole, and one of them possesses what the other lacks.

AGAINST THE MANICHEANS, WHO, BECAUSE THERE ARE TWO CONTRARY WILLS, AFFIRM THE EXISTENCE OF TWO CONTRARY NATURES

Let them perish from Thy presence, O God, yea, and they do perish, those vain talkers and seducers of the soul, who, because they have observed that in the act of deliberation there are two wills, maintain that there are two minds of differing natures, the one good and the other bad. They themselves are bad, while they hold these bad ideas, yet will they become good, if they see the truth and assent unto the truth, that Thy Apostle may say to them, "Ye were sometimes darkness, but now are ye light in the Lord." For these Manichees, wishing to be light not in the Lord but in themselves, imagining the essence of the soul to be the essence of God, have become thicker darkness than they were, for in their dread arrogance they have gone farther away from Thee, from Thee, the true Light which lighteth every man that cometh into the world. Mark what you say, and blush for shame. Draw near unto Him and be lightened, and your faces shall not be ashamed. Who was it that willed, who was it that could not will, when I was deliberating whether I should not at once serve the Lord my God, as I had long purposed to do? Was it not I, I myself? I could not fully will, I could not fully will not. And so I was at war with myself, and dragged asunder by myself. And the strife was against my will, yet it showed not the presence of a second mind, but the punishment of the one I had. Therefore it was no more I that wrought it, but sin that dwelt in me, the punishment of a sin that was more voluntary, because I was a son of Adam. For, if there are as many opposing natures as opposing wills, there will be not two but many more.

If a man deliberates whether he shall go to their conventicle or to the theatre they cry, "See, he has two natures; the good one draws him to us, the evil drags him back. For how else shall we account for this halting between conflicting wills?" But I say that both wills are bad, that which draws him to them, not less than that which drags him back to the theatre. They naturally think it a good will which pulls in their direction. But suppose one of our people is tossed about between two wills, to go to the theatre or to go to our church—will they not be puzzled what to say? Either they must reluctantly confess that the will which carries a man to our church is as good as that which carries their own professors and adherents to theirs, or they must allow that two evil natures and two evil minds are fighting in one man, and in this case their favourite doctrine that one is good and the other evil falls to the ground, or they must be converted to the truth, and cease to deny that, when a man deliberates, one soul is agitated by opposing wills. Let them then no longer maintain that, when two wills are contending in one man, two antagonistic minds, one good and one evil, are struggling over two antagonistic substances, created by two antagonistic principles.

For Thou, O God of truth, dost reprove and confute and convict them, for both wills may be bad, as when a man deliberates whether he shall murder by poison or by knife; whether he shall seize upon this field or the other, supposing that he cannot get both; whether he shall purchase pleasure by wantonness, or keep his money through covetousness; whether he shall go to the theatre or the circus, if there are shows at both on the same day; and there may be a third course open to him, for there may be a chance of robbing a house, and even a fourth, for there may be an opportunity of committing adultery as well.

Suppose that all these objects present themselves at the same time, and are all equally desired, yet cannot all be secured together, in this case they rend the mind with four conflicting wills, or even more, if there are more objects of desire. Yet they would not say that all these are different substances. The case is the same with good wills. For I ask them whether it is good to find sober delight in reading the Apostle, or in a psalm, or in discoursing upon the Gospel. They will say that each is good. What then if all are equally delightful, and all at the same time? Are not different wills distracting the heart, when we consider which we shall prefer? All are good, but they are in conflict, till one is chosen, and the will is no longer divided between many objects but poured in its full strength upon that one. So also, when eternity attracts us from above and the pleasure of earthly goods pulls us down from below, the soul does not will either the one or the other with all its force, but it is the same soul; and the reason why it is so vexed and torn is that truth forces it to love the better, while custom will not suffer it to cast away the worse.

THE FLESH WRESTLED WITH THE SPIRIT IN AUGUSTINE

Thus was I sick and tormented, reproaching myself more bitterly than ever, rolling and writhing in my chain till it should be wholly broken, for at present, though all but snapped, it still held me fast. And Thou, O Lord, wast urgent in my inmost heart, plying with austere mercy the scourges of fear and shame, lest I should fail once more, and the remnant of my worn and slender fetter, instead of breaking, should grow strong again, and bind me harder than ever. For I kept saying within myself, "O let it be now, let it be now;" and as I spoke the word I was on the verge of resolution. I was on the point of action, yet acted not; still I did not slip back into my former indifference, but stood close and took fresh breath. I tried again, and came a little nearer and a little nearer, I could all but touch and reach the goal, yet I did not quite reach or touch it, because I still shrank from dying unto death and living unto life, and the worse, which was ingrained, was stronger in me than the better, which was untrained. And the moment, which was to make me different, affrighted me more the nearer it drew, but it no longer repelled or daunted, it only chilled me.

Trifles of trifles and vanities of vanities, my old mistresses, held me back; they caught hold of the garment of my flesh and whispered in my ear, "Can you let us go? and from that instant we shall see you no more for ever; and from that instant this and that will be forbidden you for ever." What did they mean, O my God, what did they mean by "this and that"? O let Thy mercy guard the soul of Thy servant from the vileness, the shame that they meant! As I heard them, they seemed to have shrunk to half their former size. No longer did they meet me face to face with open contradiction, but muttered behind my back, and, when I moved away, plucked stealthily at my coat to make me look back. Yet, such was my indecision, that they prevented me from breaking loose, and shaking myself free, and running after the voice that called me away; for strong habit supported them, asking me, "Do you think you can live without them?"

But the voice of Habit had lost its persuasion. For in that quarter to which I had set my face and was fain to fly, there dawned upon me the chaste dignity of Continence, calm and cheerful but not wanton, modestly alluring me to come and doubt not, holding out to welcome and embrace me her pious hands full of good examples. There might I see boys and girls, a goodly array of youth and of every age, grave widows and aged virgins, and in every one of them all was Continence herself, not barren but a fruitful mother of children, of joys born of Thee, her husband, O Lord. And she smiled upon me with a challenging smile, as if she would say, "Canst not thou do what these have done? Was it their power, was it not that of the Lord their God, that gave them strength? The Lord their God gave me unto them. Thou standest on thyself, and therefore standest not. Cast thyself on Him; fear not; He will not flinch, and thou wilt not fall. Cast thyself boldly upon Him; He will sustain thee, and heal thee." And I blushed, for still I heard the whispers of the daughters of vanity, and still I hung in the wind. And again she seemed to say, "Stop thine ears against thy unclean members upon earth, that they may be mortified. They tell thee of delights, but not according to the law of the Lord thy God." Such was the debate that raged in my heart, myself battling against myself. Alypius kept close to my side and waited in silence to see the issue of my strange agitation.

HOW BY A VOICE AND BY THE WORDS OF THE APOSTLE HE WAS WHOLLY CONVERTED

Now, when deep reflection brought forth from its secret stores the whole cloud of my misery, and piled it up in the sight of my heart, there rose a whirlwind, carrying with it a violent burst of tears. And hereupon I rose and left Alypius, till my weeping and crying should be spent. For solitude seemed fitter for tears. So I went farther off, till I could feel that even his presence was no restraint upon me. Thus it was with me, and he guessed my feelings. I suppose I had said something before I started up; and he noticed that my voice was fraught with tears. So he remained upon the bench lost in wonder. I flung myself down under a figtree, and gave my tears free course, and the floods of mine eyes broke forth, an acceptable sacrifice in Thy sight. And I cried unto Thee incessantly, not in these words, but to this purpose, "And Thou, O Lord, how long? How long, O Lord; wilt Thou

be angry for ever? O remember not our iniquities of old times." For I felt that I was held fast by them, and I went on wailing, "How long, how long? tomorrow and tomorrow? Why not now? Why not this hour make an end of my vileness?"

Thus I spoke, weeping in bitter contrition of heart, when, lo, I heard a voice from the neighbouring house. It seemed as if some boy or girl, I knew not which, was repeating in a kind of chant the words, "Take and read, take and read." Immediately, with changed countenance, I began to think intently whether there was any kind of game in which children sang those words; but I could not recollect that I had ever heard them. I stemmed the rush of tears, and rose to my feet; for I could not think but that it was a divine command to open the Bible, and read the first passage I lighted upon. For I had heard that Antony had happened to enter a church at the moment when this verse of the Gospel was being read, "Go, sell all that thou hast and give to the poor, and thou shalt have treasure in heaven; and come and follow Me," that he had taken these words home to himself, and by this oracle been converted to Thee on the spot.

I ran back then to the place where Alypius was sitting; for, when I quitted him I had left the volume of the Apostle lying there. I caught it up, opened it, and read in silence the passage on which my eyes first fell, "Not in rioting and drunkenness, not in chambering and wantonness, not in strife and envying: but put ye on the Lord Jesus Christ, and make not provision for the flesh to fulfil the lusts thereof." No further would I read, nor was it necessary. As I reached the end of the sentence, the light of peace seemed to be shed upon my heart, and every shadow of doubt melted away. I put my finger, or some other mark, between the leaves, closed the volume, and with calm countenance told Alypius. And then he revealed to me his own feelings, which were unknown to me. He asked to see what I had read. I shewed him the text, and he read a little further than I had done, for I knew not what followed. What followed was this: "Him that is weak in the faith receive." This he explained to me as applying to himself. These words of warning gave him strength, and with good purpose and resolve, following the bent of his moral character, which had always been much better than mine, without any painful hesitation, he cast in his lot with me. Immediately we went in to my mother, and to her great joy told her what had happened. But, when we explained to her how it had come to pass, she was filled with exultation and triumph, and blessed Thee, who art able to do above that we ask or think. For she saw that Thou hadst granted her far more than she had ever asked for me in all her tearful lamentations. For so completely didst Thou convert me to Thyself that I desired neither wife nor any hope of this world, but set my feet on the rule of faith, as she had seen me in her vision so many years ago. So Thou didst turn her mourning into joy, joy fuller by far than she had ventured to pray for, dearer and purer by far than that which she had hoped to find in the children of my flesh.

Augustine wrote The City of God between 413 and 426 in order to explain the tragic and incomprehensible capture of Rome by Alaric in 410. Augustine answered those who charged that the gods sent Alaric to punish the Romans for deserting the old religious worship and accepting Christianity. He placed the destruction of Rome into a cosmic plan of history designed by God. Drawing on Paul and Platonic thought, Augustine developed a theory of history in which two societies—good and evil, light and dark, the other world and this world—struggled for supremacy. In reading the selections note (1) the purpose of his work, (2) intimations of the doctrine of predestination, (3) the attitude toward God's providence, (4) the "definition" of Man, (5) the significance of original sin and the need of God's grace, (6) the nature of the two cities, (7) the discussion of the supreme good, (8) the vision of the City of God, and (9) the use of allegory.

From: *THE CITY OF GOD*

PREFACE, EXPLAINING HIS DESIGN IN UNDERTAKING THIS WORK

The glorious city of God is my theme in this work, which you, my dearest son Marcellinus, suggested, and which is due to you by my promise. I have undertaken its defence against those who prefer their own gods to the Founder of this city,—a city surpassingly glorious, whether we view it as it still lives by faith in this fleeting course of time, and sojourns as a stranger in the midst of the ungodly, or as it shall dwell in the fixed stability of its eternal seat, which it now with patience waits for, expecting until "righteousness shall return unto judgment," and it obtain, by virtue of its excellence, final victory and perfect peace. A great work this, and an arduous; but God is my helper. . . .

WHAT SUBJECTS ARE TO BE HANDLED IN THE FOLLOWING DISCOURSE

But I have still some things to say in confutation of those who refer the disasters of the Roman republic to our religion, because it prohibits the offering of sacrifices to the gods.

As translated by Marcus Dods in Philip Schaff, ed., *Select Library of the Nicene and Post-Nicene Fathers,* Charles Scribner's Sons, New York, 1899, II, 1; 21–22; 82; 93; 205; 245; 249; 262; 282–283; 401; 406–407; 412–413; 509–511. Courtesy of Charles Scribner's Sons.

For this end I must recount all, or as many as may seem sufficient, of the disasters which befell that city and its subject provinces, before these sacrifices were prohibited; for all these disasters they would doubtless have attributed to us, if at that time our religion had shed its light upon them, and had prohibited their sacrifices. I must then go on to show what social well-being the true God, in whose hand are all kingdoms, vouchsafed to grant to them that their empire might increase. I must show why He did so, and how their false gods, instead of at all aiding them, greatly injured them by guile and deceit. And, lastly, I must meet those who, when on this point convinced and confuted by irrefragable proofs, endeavor to maintain that they worship the gods, not hoping for the present advantages of this life, but for those which are to be enjoyed after death. And this, if I am not mistaken, will be the most difficult part of my task, and will be worthy of the loftiest argument; for we must then enter the lists with the philosophers, not the mere common herd of philosophers, but the most renowned, who in many points agree with ourselves, as regarding the immortality of the soul, and that the true God created the world, and by His providence rules all He has created. But as they differ from us on other points, we must not shrink from the task of exposing their errors, that, having refuted the gainsaying of the wicked with such ability as God may vouchsafe, we may assert the city of God, and true piety, and the worship of God, to which alone the promise of true and everlasting felicity is attached. Here, then, let us conclude, that we may enter on these subjects in a fresh book. . . .

THAT THE TIMES OF ALL KINGS AND KINGDOMS ARE ORDAINED BY THE JUDGMENT AND POWER OF THE TRUE GOD

Therefore that God, the author and giver of felicity, because He alone is the true God, Himself gives earthly kingdoms both to good and bad. Neither does He do this rashly, and, as it were, fortuitously,—because He is God, not fortune,—but according to the order of things and times, which is hidden from us, but thoroughly known to Himself; which same order of times, however, He does not serve as subject to it, but Himself rules as lord and appoints as governor. Felicity He gives only to the good. Whether a man be a subject or a king makes no difference; he may equally either possess or not possess it. And it shall be full in that life where kings and subjects exist no longer. And therefore earthly kingdoms are given by Him both to the good and the bad; lest His worshippers, still under the conduct of a very weak mind, should covet these gifts from Him as some great things. And this is the mystery of the Old Testament, in which the New was hidden, that there even earthly gifts are promised: those who were spiritual, understanding even then, although not yet openly declaring, both the eternity which was symbolized by these earthly things, and in what gifts of God true felicity could be found. . . .

CONCERNING THE UNIVERSAL PROVIDENCE OF GOD IN THE LAWS OF WHICH ALL THINGS ARE COMPREHENDED

Therefore God supreme and true, with His Word and Holy Spirit (which three are one), one God omnipotent, creator and maker of every soul and of every body; by whose gift all are happy who are happy through verity and not through vanity; who made man a rational animal consisting of soul and body, who, when he sinned, neither permitted him to go unpunished, nor left him without mercy; who has given, to the good and to the evil, being (in common with stones), vegetable life (in common with trees), sensuous life (in common with brutes), intellectual life (in common with angels alone); from whom is every mode, every species, every order; from whom are measure, number, weight; from whom is everything which has an existence in nature, of whatever kind it be, and of whatever value; from whom are the seeds of forms and the forms of seeds, and the motion of seeds and of forms; who gave also to flesh its origin, beauty, health, reproductive fecundity, disposition of members, and the salutary concord of its parts; who also to the irrational soul has given memory, sense, appetite, but to the rational soul, in addition to these, has given intelligence and will; who has not left, not to speak of heaven and earth, angels and men, but not even the entrails of the smallest and most contemptible animal, or the feather of a bird, or the little flower of a plant, or the leaf of a tree, without an harmony, and, as it were, a mutual peace among all its parts;—that God can never be believed to have left the kingdoms of men, their dominations and servitudes, outside of the laws of His providence. . . .

OF THIS PART OF THE WORK, WHEREIN WE BEGIN TO EXPLAIN THE ORIGIN AND END OF THE TWO CITIES

The city of God we speak of is the same to which testimony is borne by that Scripture, which excels all the writings of all nations by its divine authority, and has brought under its influence all kinds of minds, and this not by a casual intellectual movement, but obviously by an express providential arrangement. For there it is written, "Glorious things are spoken of thee, O city of God." And in another psalm we read, "Great is the Lord, and greatly to be praised in the city of our God, in the mountain of His holiness, increasing the joy of the whole earth." And, a little after, in the same psalm, "As we have heard, so have we seen in the city of the Lord of hosts, in the city of our God. God has established it for ever." And in another, "There is a river the streams whereof shall make glad the city of our God, the holy place of the tabernacles of the Most High. God is in the midst of her, she shall not be moved." From these and similar testimonies, all of which it were tedious to cite, we have learned that there is a city of God, and its Founder has inspired us with a love which makes us covet its citizenship. To this Founder of the holy city the citizens of the earthly city prefer their own gods, not knowing that He is the God of gods, not of false, i.e., of impious and proud gods, who, being deprived of His unchangeable and freely communicated light, and so reduced to a kind of poverty-stricken power, eagerly grasp at their own private privileges, and seek divine honors from their deluded subjects; but of the pious and holy gods, who are

better pleased to submit themselves to one, than to subject many to themselves, and who would rather worship God than be worshipped as God. But to the enemies of this city we have replied in the ten preceding books, according to our ability and the help afforded by our Lord and King. Now, recognizing what is expected of me, and not unmindful of my promise, and relying, too, on the same succor, I will endeavor to treat of the origin, and progress, and deserved destinies of the two cities (the earthly and the heavenly, to wit), which, as we said, are in this present world commingled, and as it were entangled together. And, first, I will explain how the foundations of these two cities were originally laid, in the difference that arose among the angels. . . .

OF THE FALL OF THE FIRST MAN, THROUGH WHICH MORTALITY HAS BEEN CONTRACTED

Having disposed of the very difficult questions concerning the origin of our world and the beginning of the human race, the natural order requires that we now discuss the fall of the first man (we may say of the first men), and of the origin and propagation of human death. For God had not made man like the angels, in such a condition that, even though they had sinned, they could none the more die. He had so made them, that if they discharged the obligations of obedience, an angelic immortality and a blessed eternity might ensue, without the intervention of death; but if they disobeyed, death should be visited on them with just sentence—which, too, has been spoken to in the preceding book. . . .

OF THE LIFE OF MORTALS, WHICH IS RATHER TO BE CALLED DEATH THAN LIFE

For no sooner do we begin to live in this dying body, than we begin to move ceaselessly towards death. For in the whole course of this life (if life we must call it) its mutability tends towards death. Certainly there is no one who is not nearer it this year than last year, and tomorrow than today, and today than yesterday, and a short while hence than now, and now than a short while ago. For whatever time we live is deducted from our whole term of life, and that which remains is daily becoming less and less; so that our whole life is nothing but a race towards death, in which no one is allowed to stand still for a little space, or to go somewhat more slowly, but all are driven forwards with an impartial movement, and with equal rapidity. For he whose life is short spends a day no more swiftly than he whose life is longer. But while the equal moments are impartially snatched from both, the one has a nearer and the other a more remote goal to reach with this their equal speed. It is one thing to make a longer journey, and another to walk more slowly. He, therefore, who spends longer time on his way to death does not proceed at a more leisurely pace, but goes over more ground. . . .

THAT THE DISOBEDIENCE OF THE FIRST MAN WOULD HAVE PLUNGED ALL MEN INTO THE ENDLESS MISERY OF THE SECOND DEATH, HAD NOT THE GRACE OF GOD RESCUED MANY

We have already stated in the preceding books that God, desiring not only that the human race might be able by their similarity of nature to associate with one another, but also that they might be bound together in harmony and peace by the ties of relationship, was pleased to derive all men from one individual, and created man with such a nature that the members of the race should not have died, had not the two first (of whom the one was created out of nothing, and the other out of him) merited this by their disobedience; for by them so great a sin was committed, that by it the human nature was altered for the worse, and was transmitted also to their posterity, liable to sin and subject to death. And the kingdom of death so reigned over men, that the deserved penalty of sin would have hurled all headlong even into the second death, of which there is no end, had not the undeserved grace of God saved some therefrom. And thus it has come to pass, that though there are very many and great nations all over the earth, whose rites and customs, speech, arms, and dress, are distin-

guished by marked differences, yet there are no more than two kinds of human society, which we may justly call two cities, according to the language of our Scriptures. The one consists of those who wish to live after the flesh, the other of those who wish to live after the spirit; and when they severally achieve what they wish, they live in peace, each after their kind. . . .

OF THE NATURE OF THE TWO CITIES, THE EARTHLY AND THE HEAVENLY

Accordingly, two cities have been formed by two loves: the earthly by the love of self, even to the contempt of God; the heavenly by the love of God, even to the contempt of self. The former, in a word, glories in itself, the latter in the Lord. For the one seeks glory from men; but the greatest glory of the other is God, the witness of conscience. The one lifts up its head in its own glory; the other says to its God, "Thou art my glory, and the lifter up of mine head." In the one, the princes and the nations it subdues are ruled by the love of ruling; in the other, the princes and the subjects serve one another in love, the latter obeying, while the former take thought for all. The one delights in its own strength, represented in the persons of its rulers; the other says to its God, "I will love Thee, O Lord, my strength." And therefore the wise men of the one city, living according to man, have sought for profit to their own bodies or souls, or both, and those who have known God "glorified Him not as God, neither were thankful, but became vain in their imaginations, and their foolish heart was darkened; professing themselves to be wise,"— that is, glorying in their own wisdom, and being possessed by pride,—"they became fools, and changed the glory of the incorruptible God into an image made like to corruptible man, and to birds, and four-footed beasts, and creeping things." For they were either leaders or followers of the people in adoring images, "and worshipped and served the creature more than the Creator, who is blessed for ever." But in the other city there is no human wisdom, but only godliness, which offers due worship to the true God, and looks for its reward in the society of the saints, of holy angels as well as holy men, "that God may be all in all.". . .

WHAT THE CHRISTIANS BELIEVE REGARDING THE SUPREME GOOD AND EVIL, IN OPPOSITION TO THE PHILOSOPHERS, WHO HAVE MAINTAINED THAT THE SUPREME GOOD IS IN THEMSELVES

If, then, we be asked what the city of God has to say upon these points, and, in the first place, what its opinion regarding the supreme good and evil is, it will reply that life eternal is the supreme good, death eternal the supreme evil, and that to obtain the one and escape the other we must live rightly. And thus it is written, "The just lives by faith," for we do not as yet see our good, and must therefore live by faith; neither have we in ourselves power to live rightly, but can do so only if He who has given us faith to believe in His help do help us when we believe and pray. As for those who have supposed that the sovereign good and evil are to be found in this life, and have placed it either in the soul or the body, or in both, or to speak more explicitly, either in pleasure or in virtue, or in both; in repose or in virtue, or in both; in pleasure and repose, or in virtue, or in all combined; in the primary objects of nature, or in virtue, or in both,— all these have, with a marvelous shallowness, sought to find their blessedness in this life and in themselves. Contempt has been poured upon such ideas by the Truth, saying by the prophet, "The Lord knoweth the thoughts of men" (or, as the Apostle Paul cites the passage, "The Lord knoweth the thoughts of the *wise*") "that they are vain.". . .

THE REWARD PREPARED FOR THE SAINTS AFTER THEY HAVE ENDURED THE TRIAL OF THIS LIFE

But not even the saints and faithful worshippers of the one true and most high God are safe from the manifold temptations and deceits of the demons. For in this abode of weakness, and in these wicked days, this state of anxiety has also its use, stimulating us to seek with keener longing for that security where peace is complete and unassailable. There we shall enjoy the gifts of nature, that is to say, all that God the Creator of all natures has bestowed upon ours,—gifts not only good, but eternal,— not only of the spirit, healed now by wisdom, but also of the body renewed by the resurrection. There the virtues shall no longer be struggling against any vice or evil, but shall enjoy the reward of victory, the eternal peace which no adversary shall disturb. This is the final blessedness, this the ultimate consummation, the unending end. Here, indeed, we are said to be blessed when we have such peace as can be enjoyed in a good life; but such blessedness is mere misery compared to that final felicity. When we mortals possess such peace as this mortal life can afford, virtue, if we are living rightly, makes a right use of the advantages of this peaceful condition; and when we have it not, virtue makes a good use even of the evils a man suffers. But this is true virtue, when it refers all the advantages it makes a good use of, and all that it does in making good use of good and evil things, and itself also, to that end in which we shall enjoy the best and greatest peace possible. . . .

WHAT PRODUCES PEACE, AND WHAT DISCORD, BETWEEN THE HEAVENLY AND EARTHLY CITIES

But the families which do not live by faith seek their peace in the earthly advantages of this life; while the families which live by faith look for those eternal blessings which are promised, and use as pilgrims such advantages of time and of earth as do not fascinate and divert them from God, but rather aid them to endure with greater ease, and to keep down the number of those burdens of the corruptible body which weigh upon the soul. Thus the things necessary for this mortal life are used by both kinds of men and families alike, but each has its own peculiar and widely different aim in using them. The earthly city, which does not live by faith, seeks an earthly peace, and the end it proposes, in the well-ordered concord of civic obedience and rule, is the combination of men's wills to attain the things which are helpful to this life. The heavenly city, or rather the part of it which sojourns on earth and lives by faith, makes use of this peace only because it must, until this mortal condition which necessitates it shall pass away. Consequently, so long as it lives like a captive and a stranger in the earthly city, though it has already received the promise of redemption, and the gift of the Spirit as the earnest of it, it makes no scruple to obey the laws of the earthly city, whereby the things necessary for the maintenance of this mortal life are administered; and thus, as this life is common to both cities, so there is a harmony between them in regard to what belongs to it. But, as the earthly city has had some philosophers whose doctrine is condemned by the divine teaching, and who, being deceived either by their own conjectures or by demons, supposed that many gods must be invited to take an interest in human affairs, and assigned to each a separate function and a separate department,—to one the body, to another the soul; and in the body itself, to one the head, to another the neck, and each of the other members to one of the gods; and in like manner, in the soul, to one god the natural capacity was assigned, to another education, to another anger, to another lust; and so the various affairs of life were assigned,—cattle to one, corn to another, wine to another, oil to another, the woods to another, money to another, navigation to another, wars and victories to another, marriages to another, births and fecundity to another, and other things to other gods: and as the celestial city, on the other hand, knew that one God only was to be worshipped, and that to Him alone was due that service which . . . can be given only to a god, it has come to pass that the two cities could not have common laws of religion, and that the heavenly city has been compelled in this matter to dissent, and to become obnoxious to those who think differently, and to stand the brunt of their anger and hatred and persecutions, except in so far as the minds of their enemies have been alarmed by the multitude of the Christians and quelled by the manifest protection of God accorded to them. This heavenly city, then, while it sojourns on earth, calls citizens out of all nations, and gathers together a society of pilgrims of all languages, not scrupling about diversities in the manners, laws, and institutions whereby earthly peace is secured and maintained, but recognizing that, however various these are, they all tend to one and the same end of earthly peace. It therefore is so far from rescinding and abolishing these diversities, that it even preserves and adopts them, so long only as no hindrance to the worship of the one supreme and true God is thus introduced. Even the heavenly city, therefore, while in its state of pilgrimage, avails itself of the peace of earth, and, so far as it can without injuring faith and godliness, desires and maintains a common agreement among men regarding the acquisition of the necessaries of life, and makes this earthly peace bear upon the peace of heaven; for this alone can be truly called and esteemed the peace of the reasonable creatures, consisting as it does in the perfectly ordered and harmonious enjoyment of God and of one another in God. When we shall have reached that peace, this mortal life shall give place to one that is eternal, and our body shall be no more this animal body which by its corruption weighs down the soul, but a spiritual body feeling no want, and in all its members subjected to the will. In its pilgrim state the heavenly city possesses this peace by faith; and by this faith it lives righteously when it refers to the attainment of that peace every good action towards God and man; for the life of the city is a social life. . . .

OF THE ETERNAL FELICITY OF THE CITY OF GOD, AND OF THE PERPETUAL SABBATH

How great shall be that felicity, which shall be tainted with no evil, which shall lack no good, and which shall afford leisure for the praises of God, who shall be all in all! For I know not what other employment there can be where no lassitude shall slacken activity, nor any want stimulate to labor. I am admonished also by the sacred song, in which I read or hear the words, "Blessed are they that dwell in Thy house, O Lord; they will be still praising Thee." All the members and organs of the incorruptible body, which now we see to be suited to various necessary uses, shall contribute to the praises of God; for in that life necessity shall have no place, but full, certain, secure, everlasting felicity. For all those parts of the bodily harmony, which are distributed through the whole body, within and without, and of which I have just been saying that they at present elude our observation, shall then be discerned; and, along with the other great and marvellous discoveries which shall then kindle rational minds in praise of the great Artificer, there shall be the enjoyment of a beauty which appeals to the reason. What power of movement such bodies shall possess, I have not the audacity rashly to define, as I have not the ability to conceive. Nevertheless, I will say that in any case, both in motion and at rest, they shall be, as in their appearance, seemly; for into that state nothing which is unseemly shall be admitted. One thing is certain, the body shall forthwith be wherever the spirit wills, and the spirit shall will nothing which is unbecoming either to the spirit or to the body. True honor shall be there, for it shall be denied to none who is worthy, nor yielded to any unworthy; neither shall any unworthy person so much as sue for it, for none but the worthy shall be there. True peace shall be there, where no one shall suffer opposition either from himself or any other. God Himself, who is the Author of virtue, shall there be its reward; for, as there is nothing greater or better, He has promised Himself. What else was meant by His word through the prophet, "I will be your God, and ye shall be my people," than, I shall be their satisfaction, I shall be all that men honorably desire,—life, and health, and nourishment, and plenty, and glory, and honor, and peace, and all good things? This, too, is the right interpretation of the saying of the apostle, "That God may be all in all." He shall be the end of our desires who shall be seen without end, loved without cloy, praised without weariness. This outgoing of affection, this employment, shall certainly be, like eternal life itself, common to all.

But who can conceive, not to say describe, what degrees of honor and glory shall be awarded to the various degrees of merit? Yet it cannot be doubted that there shall be degrees. And in that blessed city there shall be this great blessing, that no inferior shall envy any superior, as now the archangels are not envied by the angels, because no one will wish to be what he has not received, though bound in strictest concord with him who has received; as in the body the finger does not seek to be the eye, though both members are harmoniously included in the complete structure of the body. And thus, along with his gift, greater or less, each shall receive this further gift of contentment to desire no more than he has.

Neither are we to suppose that because sin shall have no power to delight them, free will must be withdrawn. It will, on the contrary, be all the more truly free, because set free from delight in sinning to take unfailing delight in not sinning. For the first freedom of will which man received when he was created upright consisted in an ability not to sin, but also in an ability to sin; whereas this last freedom of will shall be superior, inasmuch as it shall not be able to sin. This, indeed, shall not be a natural ability, but the gift of God. For it is one thing to be God, another thing to be a partaker of God. God by nature cannot sin, but the partaker of God receives this inability from God. And in this divine gift there was to be observed this gradation, that man should first receive a free will by which he was able not to sin, and at last a free will by which he was not able to sin,—the former being adapted to the acquiring of merit, the latter to the enjoying of the reward. But the nature thus constituted, having sinned when it had the ability to do so, it is by a more abundant grace that it is delivered so as to reach that freedom in which it cannot sin. For as the first immortality which Adam lost by sinning consisted in his being able not to die, while the last shall consist in his not being able to die; so the first free will consisted in his being able not to sin, the last in his not being able to sin. And thus piety and justice shall be as indefeasible as happiness. For certainly by sinning we lost both piety and happiness; but when we lost happiness, we did not lose the love of it. Are we to say that God Himself is not free because He cannot sin? In that city, then, there shall be free will, one in all the citizens, and indivisible in each, delivered from all ill, filled with all good, enjoying indefeasibly the delights of eternal joys, oblivious of sins, oblivious of sufferings, and yet not so oblivious of its deliverance as to be ungrateful to its Deliverer.

The soul, then, shall have an intellectual remembrance of its past ills; but, so far as regards sensible experience, they shall be quite forgotten. For a skillful physician knows, indeed, professionally almost all diseases; but experimentally he is ignorant of a great number which he himself has never suffered from. As, therefore, there are two ways of knowing evil things,—one by mental insight, the other by sensible experience, for it is one thing to understand all vices by the wisdom of a cultivated mind, another to understand them by the foolishness of an abandoned life,—so also there are two ways of forgetting evils. For a well-instructed and learned man forgets them one way, and he who has experimentally suffered from them forgets them another,—the former by neglecting what he has learned, the latter by escaping what he has suffered. And in this latter way the saints shall forget their past ills, for they shall have so thoroughly escaped them all, that they shall be quite blotted out of their experience. But their intellectual knowledge, which shall be great, shall keep them acquainted not only with their own past woes, but with the eternal sufferings of the lost. For if they were not to know that they had been miserable, how could they, as the Psalmist says, for ever sing the mercies of God? Certainly that city shall have no greater joy than the celebration of the grace of Christ, who redeemed us by His blood. There shall be accomplished the words of the psalm, "Be still, and know that I am God." There shall be the great Sabbath which has no evening, which God celebrated among His first works, as it is written, "And God rested on the seventh day from all His works which He had made. And God blessed the seventh day, and sanctified it; because that in it He had rested from all His work which God began to make." For we shall ourselves be the seventh day, when we shall be filled and replenished with God's blessing and sanctification. There shall we be still, and know that He is God; that He is that which we ourselves aspired to be when we fell away from Him, and listened to the voice of the seducer, "Ye shall be as gods," and so abandoned God, who would have made us as gods, not by deserting Him, but by participating in Him. For without Him what have we accomplished, save to perish in His anger? But when we are restored by Him, and perfected with greater grace, we shall have eternal leisure to see that He is God, for we shall be full of Him when He shall be all in all. For even our good works, when they are understood to be rather His than ours, are imputed to us that we may enjoy this Sabbath rest. For if we attribute them to ourselves, they shall be servile; for it is said of the Sabbath, "Ye shall do no servile work in it." Wherefore also it is said by Ezekiel the prophet, "And I gave them my Sabbaths to be a sign between me and them, that they might know that I am the Lord who sanctify them." This knowledge shall be perfected when we shall be perfectly at rest, and shall perfectly know that He is God.

This Sabbath shall appear still more clearly if we count the ages as days, in accordance with the periods of time defined in Scripture, for that period will be found to be the seventh. The first age, as the first day, extends from Adam to the deluge; the second from the deluge to Abraham, equalling the first, not in length of time, but in the number of generations, there being ten in each. From Abraham to the advent of Christ there are, as the evangelist Matthew calculates, three periods, in each of which are fourteen generations,—one period from Abraham to David, a second from David to the captivity, a third from the captivity to the birth of Christ in the flesh. There are thus five ages in all. The sixth is now passing, and cannot be measured by any number of generations, as it has been said, "It is not for you to know the times, which the Father hath put in His own power." After this period God shall rest as on the seventh day, when He shall give us (who shall be the seventh day) rest in Himself. But there is not now space to treat of these ages; suffice it to say that the seventh shall be our Sabbath, which shall be brought to a close, not by an evening, but by the Lord's day, as an eighth and eternal day, consecrated by the resurrection of Christ, and prefiguring the eternal repose not only of the spirit, but also of the body. There we shall rest and see, see and love, love and praise. This is what shall be in the end without end. For what other end do we propose to ourselves than to attain to the kingdom of which there is no end?

I think I have now, by God's help, discharged my obligation in writing this large work. Let those who think I have said too little, or those who think I have said too much, forgive me; and let those who think I have said just enough join me in giving thanks to God. Amen.

Benedict of Nursia

The author of this code of monastic rules, Benedict of Nursia (480–543), lived at a time when the Roman Empire in the West disappeared and new barbarian kingdoms took its place. Christian monasticism had its origins in the East and migrated to the West. The new institution which flourished in the environment of Egypt and the Near East had difficulty adjusting to the different climate and cultural soil of Italy, Germany, France, and Britain. Leaders interested in practicing a religious life noted that a more careful regulation of living conditions for monks was necessary for survival in the physical and social climate of Western Europe. The Rule of St. Benedict proved to be successful in holding groups of men together in a community and providing them not only with leadership but also assurance of sufficient food, clothing, and shelter to enable them to continue their devotions. The rule was widely copied and used throughout Western Europe. In reading the selections, note (1) the qualities of character and leadership to be sought in an abbot, (2) the use of scripture to support the rule, (3) the suggestions for enlisting the aid of the community in policy making and the justification therefor, (4) the reasons given for the rule of obedience, (5) the justification for and the means of promoting humility in the community, (6) the arrangements for sleeping, feeding, working, and practicing the religious life, (7) the method of receiving new recruits, (8) the means used to acquaint the novice with his new, sacred responsibilities. (9) the provisions of the rule of obedience, and (10) the suggestions for promoting the spirit of the community.

From: THE RULE OF ST. BENEDICT

WHAT THE ABBOT SHOULD BE

An abbot to be fit to rule a monastery should ever remember what he is called, and in his acts illustrate his high calling. For in a monastery he is considered to take the place of Christ, since he is called by His name as the apostle saith, *Ye have received the spirit of the adoption of sons, whereby we cry, Abba, Father.* Therefore the abbot should neither teach, ordain, nor require anything against the command of our Lord (God forbid!), but in the minds of his disciples let his orders and teaching be mingled with the leaven of divine justice.

As translated by Cardinal Gasquet in *The Rule of Saint Benedict*, London: Chatto and Windus, 1936, 9–16; 22–23; 26–27; 30–35; 53–54; 57–58; 64–66; 72–74; 84–87; 94–97; 99–102; 121–123.

The abbot should ever be mindful that at the dread judgment of God there will be inquiry both as to his teaching and as to the obedience of his disciples. Let the abbot know that any lack of goodness, which the master of the family shall find in his flock, will be accounted the shepherd's fault. On the other hand, he shall be acquitted in so far as he shall have shown all the watchfulness of a shepherd over a restless and disobedient flock: and if as their pastor he shall have employed every care to cure their corrupt manners, he shall be declared guiltless in the Lord's judgment, and he may say with the prophet, *I have not hidden Thy justice in my heart; I have told Thy truth and Thy salvation; but they contemned and despised me.* And then in the end shall death be inflicted as a meet punishment upon the sheep which have not responded to his care. When, therefore, any one shall receive the name of abbot, he ought to rule his disciples with a twofold teaching: that is, he should first show them in deeds rather than words all that is good and holy. To such as are understanding, indeed, he may expound the Lord's behests by words; but to the hard-hearted and to the simple-minded he must manifest the divine precepts in his life. Thus, what he has taught his disciples to be contrary to God's law, let him show in his own deeds that such things are not to be done, lest preaching to others *he himself become a castaway,* and God say unto him thus sinning, *Why dost thou declare My justices, and take My testament in thy mouth? Thou hast hated discipline, and cast My speeches behind thee.* And *Thou, who didst see the mote in thy brother's eye, hast thou not seen the beam that is in thine own?*

Let him make no distinction of persons in the monastery. Let not one be loved more than another, save such as be found to excel in obedience or good works. Let not the free-born be put before the serf-born in religion, unless there be other reasonable cause for it. If upon due consideration the abbot shall see such cause he may place him where he pleases; otherwise let all keep their own places, because *whether bond or free we are all one in Christ,* and bear an equal burden of service under one Lord: *for with God there is no accepting of persons.* For one thing only are we preferred by Him, if we are found better than others in good works and more humble. Let the abbot therefore have equal love for all, and let all, according to their deserts, be under the same discipline.

The abbot in his teaching should always observe that apostolic rule which saith, *Reprove, entreat, rebuke.* That is to say, as occasions require he ought to mingle encouragement with reproofs. Let him manifest the sternness of a master and the loving affection of a father. He must reprove the undisciplined and restless severely, but he should exhort such as are obedient, quiet and patient, for their better profit. We charge him, however, to reprove and punish the stubborn and negligent. Let him not shut his eyes to the sins of offenders; but, directly they begin to show themselves and to grow, he must use every means to root them up utterly, remembering the fate of Heli, the priest of Silo. To the more virtuous and apprehensive, indeed, he may for the first or second time use words of warning; but in dealing with the stubborn, the hard-hearted, the proud and the disobedient, even at the very beginning of their sin, let him chastise them with stripes and with bodily punishment, knowing that it is written, *The fool is not corrected with words.* And again, *Strike thy son with a rod and thou shalt deliver his soul from death.*

The abbot ought ever to bear in mind what he is and what he is called; he ought to know that to whom more is entrusted, from him more is exacted. Let him recognize how difficult and how hard a task he has undertaken, to rule souls and to make himself a servant to the humours of many. One, forsooth, must be led by gentle words, another by sharp reprehension, another by persuasion; and thus shall he so shape and adapt himself to the character and intelligence of each, that he not only suffer no loss in the flock entrusted to his care, but may even rejoice in its good growth. Above all things let him not slight nor make little of the souls committed to his care, heeding more fleeting, worldly and frivolous things; but let him remember always that he has undertaken the government of souls, of which he shall also have to give an account. And that he may not complain of the want of temporal means, let him remember that it is written, *Seek first the kingdom of God, and His justice, and all things shall be given to you.* And again, *Nothing is wanting to such as fear Him.*

He should know that whoever undertakes the government of souls must prepare himself to account for them. And however great the number of the brethren under him may be, let him understand for certain that at the Day of Judgment he will have to give to our Lord an account of all their souls as well as of his own. In this way, by fearing the inquiry concerning his flock which the Shepherd will hold, he is solicitous on account of others' souls as well as of his own, and thus whilst reclaiming other men by his corrections, he frees himself also from all vice.

ON TAKING COUNSEL OF THE BRETHREN

Whenever any weighty matters have to be transacted in the monastery let the abbot call together all the community and himself propose the matter for discussion. After hearing the advice of the brethren let him consider it in his own mind, and then do what he shall judge most expedient. We ordain that all must be called to council, because the Lord often reveals to a younger member what is best. And let the brethren give their advice with all humble subjection, and presume not stiffly to defend their own opinion. Let them rather leave the matter to the abbot's discretion, so that all submit to what he shall deem best. As it becometh disciples to obey their master, so doth it behove the master to dispose of all things with forethought and justice.

In all things, therefore, every one shall follow the Rule as their master, and let no one rashly depart from it. In the monastery no one is to be led by the desires of his own heart, neither shall any one within or without the monastery presume to argue wantonly with his abbot. If he presume to do so let him be subjected to punishment according to the Rule. . . .

ON OBEDIENCE

The first degree of humility is prompt obedience. This is required of all who, whether by reason of the holy servitude to which they are pledged, or through fear of hell, or to attain to the glory of eternal life, hold nothing more dear than Christ. Such disciples delay not in doing what is ordered by their superior, just as if the command had come from God. Of such our Lord says, *At the hearing of the ear he hath obeyed me.* And to the teachers He likewise says, *He that heareth you, heareth me.*

For this reason such disciples, surrendering forthwith all they possess, and giving up their own will, leave unfinished what they were working at, and with the ready foot of obedience in their acts follow the word of command. . . . These take the narrow way, of which the Lord saith, *Narrow is the way which leads to life.* . . .

ON HUMILITY

Brethren, Holy Scripture cries out to us, saying, *Every one who exalteth himself shall be humbled, and he who humbleth himself shall be exalted.* In this it tells us that every form of self-exaltation is a kind of pride, which the prophet declares he carefully avoided, where he says, *Lord, my heart is not exalted, neither are my eyes lifted up; neither have I walked in great things, nor in wonders above myself.* And why? *If I did not think humbly, but exalted my soul: as a child weaned from his mother, so wilt Thou reward my soul.*

Wherefore, brethren, if we would scale the summit of humility, and swiftly gain the heavenly height which is reached by our lowliness in this present life, we must set up a ladder of climbing deeds like that which Jacob saw in his dream, whereon angels were descending and ascending. Without doubt that descending and ascending is to be understood by us as signifying that we descend by exalting ourselves and ascend by humbling ourselves. But the ladder itself thus set up is our life in this world, which by humility of heart is lifted by our Lord to heaven. Our body and soul we may indeed call the sides of the ladder in which our divine vocation has set the divers steps of humility and discipline we have to ascend.

The first step of humility, then, is reached when a man, with the fear of God always before his eyes, does not allow himself to forget, but is ever mindful of all God's commandments. . . .

The second step of humility is reached when any one not loving self-will takes no heed to satisfy his own desires, but copies in his life what our Lord said, *I came not to do My own will, but the will of Him Who sent Me.* . . .

The third step of humility is reached when a man, for the love of God, submits himself with all obedience to a superior, imitating our Lord, of whom the apostle saith, *He was made obedient even unto death.*

The fourth step of humility is reached when any one in the exercise of his obedience patiently and with a quiet mind bears all that is inflicted on him, things contrary to nature, and even at times unjust, and in suffering all these he neither wearies nor gives over the work. . . .

The fifth step of humility is reached when a monk manifests to his abbot, by humble confession, all the evil thoughts of his heart and his secret faults. . . .

The sixth step of humility is reached when a monk is content with all that is mean and vile; and in regard to everything enjoined him accounts himself a poor and worthless workman, saying with the prophet, *I have been brought to nothing, and knew it not. I have become as a beast before Thee, and I am always with Thee.*

The seventh step of humility is reached when a man not only confesses with his tongue that he is most lowly and inferior to others, but in his inmost heart believes so. . . .

The eighth step of humility is reached when a monk does nothing but what the common rule of the monastery, or the example of his seniors, enforces.

The ninth step of humility is reached when a monk restrains his tongue from talking, and, practising silence, speaks not till a question be asked him. . . .

The tenth step of humility is attained to when one is not easily and quickly moved to laughter, for it is written, *The fool lifteth his voice in laughter.*

The eleventh step of humility is reached when a monk, in speaking, do so quietly and without laughter, humbly, gravely and in a few words and not with a loud voice, for it is written, *A wise man is known by a few words.*

The twelfth step of humility is reached when a monk not only has humility in his heart, but even shows it also exteriorly to all who behold him. Thus, whether he be in the oratory at the "Work of God," in the monastery, or in the garden, on a journey, or in the fields, or wheresoever he be, sitting, standing or walking, always let him, with head bent and eyes fixed on the ground, bethink himself of his sins and imagine that he is arraigned before the dread judgment of God. . . .

HOW THE MONKS ARE TO SLEEP

All shall sleep in separate beds and each shall receive, according to the appointment of his abbot, bedclothes, fitted to the condition of his life. If it be possible let them all sleep in a common dormitory, but if their great number will not allow this they may sleep in tens or twenties, with seniors to have charge of them. Let a candle be constantly burning in the room until morning, and let the monks sleep clothed and girt with girdles or cords; but they are not to have knives by their sides in their beds, lest perchance they be injured while sleeping. In this way the monks shall always be ready to rise quickly when the signal is given and hasten each one to come before his brother to the Divine Office, and yet with all gravity and modesty.

The younger brethren are not to have their beds next to each other, but amongst those of the elders. When they rise for the Divine Office let them gently encourage one another, because of the excuses made by those that are drowsy. . . .

WHAT CARE THE ABBOT SHOULD HAVE OF THE EXCOMMUNICATED

Let the abbot take every possible care of the offending brethren, for *They that are well need not the physician, but they that are sick.* Like a wise physician, therefore, he ought to make use of every remedy; he should send some of the older and wiser brethren as comforters, to console, as it were, in secret their wayward brother, and win him to make humble satisfaction. And let them comfort him that he be not overwhelmed by too great sorrow, but as the apostle saith, *Let charity be confirmed in him and let all pray for him.* . . .

OUGHT MONKS TO HAVE ANYTHING OF THEIR OWN?

Above all others, let this vice be extirpated in the monastery. No one, without leave of the abbot, shall presume to give, or receive, or keep as his own, anything whatever: neither book, nor tablets, nor pen: nothing at all. For monks are men who can claim no dominion even over their own bodies or wills. All that is necessary, however, they may hope from the Father of the monastery; but they shall keep nothing which the abbot has not given or allowed. All things are to be common to all, as it is written, *Neither did any one say or think that aught was his own.* Hence if any one shall be found given to this most wicked vice let him be admonished once or twice, and if he do not amend let him be subjected to correction.

WHETHER ALL OUGHT TO RECEIVE NECESSARY THINGS UNIFORMLY

It is written, *Distribution was made to every one, according as he had need.* By this we do not mean that there is to be a personal preference (which God forbid), but a consideration for infirmities. In this wise let him who needs less thank God and be not distressed, and let him who requires more be humiliated because of his infirmity, and not puffed up by the mercy that is shown him: so all the members shall be in peace. Above all things let not the pest of murmuring, for whatever cause, by any word or sign, be manifested. If any one shall be found faulty in this, let him be subjected to the most severe punishment. . . .

OF THE AMOUNT OF FOOD

We believe that it is enough to satisfy just requirement if in the daily meals, at both the sixth and ninth hours, there be at all seasons of the year two cooked dishes, so that he who cannot eat of the one may make his meal of the other. Therefore two dishes of cooked food must suffice for all the brethren, and if there be any fruit or young vegetables these may be added to the meal as a third dish. Let a pound weight of bread suffice for each day, whether there be one meal or two, that is, for both dinner and supper. If there is to be supper a third of the pound is to be kept back by the cellarer and given to the brethren at that meal.

If, however, the community has been occupied in any great labour it shall be at the will, and in the power of the abbot, if he think fit, to increase the allowance, so long as every care be taken to guard against excess, and that no monk be incapacitated by surfeiting. For nothing is more contrary to the Christian spirit than gluttony, as our Lord declares, *Take heed to yourselves lest perhaps your hearts be overcharged with surfeiting.* And the same quantity shall not be given to young children, but a lesser amount than to those older; frugality being maintained in everything. All, save the very weak and sick, are to abstain wholly from eating the flesh of quadrupeds.

OF THE MEASURE OF DRINK

Every one hath his proper gift from God, one thus, another thus. For this reason the amount of other people's food cannot be determined without some misgiving. Still, having regard to the weak state of the sick, we think that a pint of wine a day is sufficient for any one. But let those to whom God gives the gift of abstinence know that they shall receive their proper reward. If either local circumstances, the amount of labour, or the heat of summer require more, it can be allowed at the will of the prior, care being taken in all things that gluttony and drunkenness creep not in. . . .

OF DAILY MANUAL LABOUR

Idleness is an enemy of the soul. Because this is so the brethren ought to be occupied at specified times in manual labour, and at other fixed hours in holy reading. We therefore think that both these may be arranged for as follows: from Easter to the first of October, on coming out from Prime, let the brethren labour till about the fourth hour. From the fourth till close upon the sixth hour let them employ themselves in reading. On rising from table after the sixth hour let them rest on their beds in strict silence;

but if any one shall wish to read, let him do so in such a way as not to disturb any one else.

Let *None* be said somewhat before the time, about the middle of the eighth hour, and after this all shall work at what they have to do till evening. If, however, the nature of the place or poverty require them to labour at gathering in the harvest, let them not grieve at that, for then are they truly monks when they live by the labour of their hands, as our Fathers and the Apostles did. Let everything, however, be done with moderation for the sake of the faint-hearted.

From the first of October till the beginning of Lent let the brethren be occupied in reading till the end of the second hour. At that time *Tierce* shall be said, after which they shall labour at the work enjoined them till *None*. At the first signal for the *Hour of None* all shall cease to work, so as to be ready when the second signal is given. After their meal they shall be employed in reading or on the psalms.

On the days of Lent, from the morning till the end of the third hour, the brethren are to have time for reading, after which let them work at what is set them to do till the close of the tenth hour. During these Lenten days let each one have some book from the library which he shall read through carefully. These books are to be given out at the beginning of Lent.

It is of much import that one or two seniors be appointed to go about the monastery at such times as the brethren are free to read, in order to see that no one is slothful, given to idleness or foolish talking instead of reading, and so not only makes no profit himself but also distracts others. If any such be found (which God forbid) let him be corrected once or twice, and if he amend not let him be subjected to regular discipline of such a character that the rest may take warning. Moreover one brother shall not associate with another at unsuitable hours.

On Sunday also, all, save those who are assigned to various offices, shall have time for reading. If, however, any one be so negligent and slothful as to be unwilling or unable to read or meditate, he must have some work given him, so as not to be idle. For weak brethren, or those of delicate constitutions, some work or craft shall be found to keep them from idleness, and yet not such as to crush them by the heavy labour or to drive them away. The weakness of such brethren must be taken into consideration by the abbot. . . .

WHETHER A MONK MAY RECEIVE LETTERS OR PRESENTS

It is by no means lawful, without the abbot's permission, for any monk to receive or give letters, presents, and gifts of any kind to any one, whether parent or other, and not even to one of the brethren. If anything is sent to a monk from his parents he shall not venture to receive it unless the abbot be first told. If he order it to be accepted he may appoint the person to whom it shall be given. And let not the brother, to whom perchance it was sent, be grieved, lest an opening be given to the devil. He who shall dare to do otherwise shall be subjected to regular discipline.

OF THE CLOTHES AND SHOES OF THE BRETHREN

Let clothing suitable to the locality and the temperature be given to the brethren, for in cold regions more is needed, and less in warm. The determination of all these things is in the hands of the abbot. We believe, however, that in ordinary places it will be enough for each monk to have a cowl and tunic; in winter the cowl being of thicker stuff, in summer of finer or old cloth. He should have also a scapular for working purposes, and shoes and stockings for the feet.

Monks must not grumble at the colour or coarseness of these things; they shall be such as can be procured in the district where they live, or such as can be bought at the cheapest price.

Let the abbot see to their dimensions, that they be not too short, but of the proper length for those who use them. When receiving new clothes the monks shall always give back the old ones at the same time, to be put away in the clothes-room for the poor. For it is sufficient that a monk have two tunics and two cowls, as well for night wear as for the convenience of washing. Anything beyond this is superfluous, and must be cut off. Their shoes also, and whatever is worn out, they shall return on getting new things. Those who are sent on a journey shall get hosen from the wardrobe, which, on their return, when washed, they shall restore. Let their cowls and tunics on such occasions be somewhat better than those in ordinary use. These they shall receive from the wardrobe when starting and restore on their return.

A mattress, blanket, coverlet and pillow are to suffice for bedding. The beds shall be frequently searched by the abbot to guard against the vice of hoarding. And if any one be found in possession of something not allowed by the abbot let him be subjected to the severest punishment. And to uproot this vice of appropriation let all that is necessary be furnished by the abbot, that is, cowl, tunic, shoes, stockings, girdle, knife, pen, needle, handkerchief and tablets. By this every pretext of necessity will be taken away. The abbot, however, should always bear in mind that sentence in the Acts of the Apostles, *And distribution was made to every one according as he had need.* He should, therefore, consider the infirmities of such as need something, and not regard the ill-will of the envious. In all his decisions let him ponder upon the retribution of God. . . .

THE MANNER OF RECEIVING THE BRETHREN TO RELIGION

Any one on first coming to the religious life should not find the entrance made easy, but as the apostle saith, *Try the spirits, if they be of God.* If, however, the newcomer continues to knock, and for four or five days shows a patient bearing, both of the harshness shown him and of the difficulty made about admitting him, and persist in his petition he shall then be allowed to enter the guest-place for a few days. After that let him be in the noviciate, where he shall meditate and eat and sleep.

And let a senior, such as has the skill of winning souls, be appointed to watch carefully over him, to discover whether he truly seeks God and is eager for the Divine Office, for obedience and humiliations. Let all the rigour and austerity of our journey to God be put clearly before him. If he promise to continue in a steadfast perseverance, at the end of two months the entire Rule shall be read to him, and let him be told, "See the law under which you wish to fight, if you can observe it enter upon the life; if you cannot you are free to depart."

If he still persevere let him be brought back to the noviciate and again tried in all patience. And after the lapse of six months let the Rule be read to him again, that he may fully know the kind of life he is entering upon. If he yet persevere, after four months the Rule shall be read to him once more. If after due deliberation he shall then promise to keep all the law and to do whatever is commanded of him, let him be received into the community, knowing that he is now under the law of the Rule, so that he can henceforth neither leave the monastery nor withdraw his neck from the yoke of the Rule which after so long a deliberation he was free to have taken or refused.

When he is to be admitted into the community let him in the oratory, and in the presence of all, promise before God and His saints stability, amendment of manners and obedience, in order that if at any time he shall act otherwise he may know that he shall be condemned by Him Whom he mocketh. He shall draw up the form of his promise in the name of the saints, whose relics are reposing there, and of the abbot there present. Let him write out this form himself, or at least, if he is uneducated another at his request must write it for him, and to this the novice himself shall set his mark and with his own hand lay it upon the altar.

After he has placed it there let the novice immediately begin the verse, *Uphold me, O Lord, according to Thy word, and I shall live, and let me not be confounded in my expectation.* This verse the community shall repeat three times, adding at the end, *Glory be to the Father,* etc. Then the brother novice shall cast himself at the feet of all, asking their prayers, and from that time he shall be counted as one of the community. If he has any property he must first either give it to the poor, or by formal gift make it over to the monastery without any reservation for himself, since he must know that he has henceforth no power even over his own body. Let him, therefore, forthwith be divested in the oratory of his own garments and be clothed in those of the monastery. The clothes he has taken off, however, are to be kept in the wardrobe, so that if (which God forbid) he should, by the persuasion of the devil, resolve to leave the monastery he may be stripped of his monastic dress and expelled. . . .

THAT THE BRETHREN BE OBEDIENT TO EACH OTHER

The excellent virtue of obedience is to be shown by all, not to the abbot only, but to the brethren who shall also mutually obey each other, knowing that by this path of obedience they shall go to God. The commands of the abbot, or other superiors constituted by him, having the first place (for to these we do not allow any private orders to be preferred) the juniors shall obey their seniors with all charity and diligence. If any one be found contentious let him be punished.

If a brother be rebuked for even the least thing by the abbot, or by any prior (*i.e.* superior), or if he shall perceive that the mind of any superior is, however slightly, moved against him, or in anger with him, let him with-

out delay prostrate himself at his feet, and remain offering satisfaction until the feeling be removed and he receive a blessing. If any one be found too proud to do this let him be expelled from the monastery.

OF THE GOOD ZEAL MONKS SHOULD HAVE

As there is an evil and bitter emulation which separates from God and leads to hell, so there is a good spirit of emulation which frees from vices and leads to God and life everlasting. Let monks therefore practise this emulation with most fervent love; that is to say, let them *in honour prevent one another*, let them bear most patiently with each other's infirmities, whether of body or of manner. Let them contend with one another in their obedience. Let no one follow what he thinks most profitable to himself, but rather what is best for another. Let them show brotherly charity with a chaste love. Let them fear God and love their abbot with sincere and humble affection, and set nothing whatever before Christ, Who can bring us unto eternal life.

Tacitus

‖n 89 A.D. *the Roman historian Tacitus (55?–117?) spent some time in Germany, probably as an official of the imperial government. While there he observed the customs and manners of the Germanic peoples and wrote down the results in his Germania. Tacitus greatly admired the virile qualities of these primitive people, and as a moralist he inevitably stressed their virtues as an example for the luxury-loving Romans. In reading the selection note (1) German political and social institutions, (2) how they made their living, and (3) any indication that Tacitus might have been biased in his interpretation of these people.*

From: THE EARLY GERMANS

Germany proper is separated from the Gauls, the Rhaetians and the Pannonians by the Rhine and the Danube, from the Sarmatians and Dacians partly by the mountains, partly by their mutual fears. The ocean washes its other boundaries, forming deep bays and embracing large islands where various tribes and their kings have become known to us through

Arthur C. Howland, *Translations and Reprints from the Original Sources of European History*, VI, no. 3. *The Early Germans* (Second Edition), University of Pennsylvania Press, Philadelphia, n.d., 4–16. Courtesy of the University of Pennsylvania Press.

the disclosures of recent war. The Rhine takes its rise in the steep and inaccessible fastnesses of the Rhaetian Alps, and, bending slightly to the west, flows into the northern ocean. The Danube, pouring down from the gently sloping ridge of Mount Abnoba, passes the borders of many nations, and finally forces its way through six outlets into the Black Sea; a seventh channel is swallowed up by the marshes.

I should say that the Germans themselves were an indigenous people, without any subsequent mixture of blood through immigration or friendly intercourse; for in ancient times it was by sea and not by land that those who wished to change their homes wandered, and the ocean, hostile, as it were, and of boundless extent on the further side, is rarely traversed by ships from our part of the world. And not to mention the danger of the terrible and unknown sea, who indeed would leave Asia or Africa or Italy to seek Germany with its wild scenery, its harsh climate, its sullen manners and aspect, unless, indeed, it were his native country? They tell in their ancient songs, the only kind of tradition and history that they have, how Tuisto, a god sprung from the earth and his son Mannus were the originators and founders of their race. Mannus is supposed to have had three sons from whose names those nearest the ocean are called *Ingaevones,* those in the middle country, *Hermiones,* and the others, *Istaevones.* Certain people assert with the freedom permitted in discussing ancient times that there were many descendants of the god, and many tribal names, such as *Marsi, Gambrivii, Suebi, Vandilii,* and that these were their true and ancient names. But the name Germany, they say, is modern and of recent application, since those who first crossed the Rhine and expelled the Gauls, and who are now called *Tungri,* were then named Germans; thus what had been a tribal, not a national name, spread little by little, so that later they all adopted the newly-coined appellation that was first employed by the conquerors to inspire fear and called themselves Germans.

They say that Hercules himself once visited them, and when about to go into battle they sing of him as the first of all heroes. They have also certain songs, by the intonation of which (*barditus,* as it is called) they excite their courage, while they divine the fortune of the coming battle from the sound itself. They inspire or feel terror according to the character of the cheering, though what harmony there is in the shouting is one of valor rather than of voices. The effect they particularly strive for is that of a harsh noise, a wild and confused roar, which they attain by putting their shields to their mouths so that the reverberation swells their deep, full voices. Ulysses, too, is thought by some to have reached this ocean in those long and fabulous wanderings of his, and to have been cast upon the shores of Germany. They say he built and named Asciburgium, a town on the banks of the Rhine still inhabited; nay even that an altar consecrated by him and inscribed with the name of his father, Laertes, has been found at the same place, and that certain monuments and tombs with Greek letters on them still exist within the confines of Germany and Rhaetia. I have no mind to argue either for or against the truth of these statements; let each one believe or reject them as he feels inclined.

I myself subscribe to the opinion of those who hold that the German tribes have never been contaminated by intermarriage with other nations, but have remained peculiar and unmixed and wholly unlike other people. Hence the bodily type is the same among them all, notwithstanding the extent of their population. They all have fierce blue eyes, reddish hair and large bodies fit only for sudden exertion; they do not submit patiently to work and effort and cannot endure thirst and heat at all, though cold and hunger they are accustomed to because of their climate.

In general the country, though varying here and there in appearance, is covered over with wild forests or filthy swamps, being more humid on the side of Gaul but bleaker toward Noricum and Pannonia. It is suitable enough for grain but does not permit the cultivation of fruit trees; and, though rich in flocks and herds, these are for the most part small, the cattle not even possessing their natural beauty nor spreading horns. The people take pride in possessing a large number of animals, these being their sole and most cherished wealth. Whether it was in mercy or wrath that the gods denied them silver and gold, I know not. Yet I would not affirm that no vein of German soil produces silver or gold; for who has examined? They do not care for their possession and use as much as might be expected. There are to be seen among them vessels of silver that have been presented as gifts to their ambassadors and chiefs, but they are held in no more esteem than vessels of earthenware; however, those nearest to us prize gold and silver because of its use in trade, and they recognize certain of our coins as valuable and choose those The people of the interior practice barter and exchange of commodities in accordance with the simple and ancient custom. They like the old and well-known coins, those with milled edges bearing the stamp of a two-horse chariot. They are more anxious also for silver coins than for gold, not because of any special liking, but because a number of silver coins is more convenient in purchasing cheap and common articles.

Not even iron is abundant, as is shown by the character of their weapons. Some few use swords or long spears, but usually they carry javelins, called in their language *framea*, tipped with a short narrow piece of iron but so sharp and so easy to handle that as occasion demands they employ the same weapon for fighting at close range or at a distance. A horseman is content with a shield or a javelin, but the footmen, either nude or lightly clad in a small cloak, rain missiles, each man having many and hurling them to a great distance. There is no particular adornment to their weapons except that their shields are distinguished by the most carefully chosen colors. A few wear cuirasses, but hardly any have helmets of metal or leather. Their horses are noted neither for their beauty nor their speed, nor are they trained to perform evolutions, as with us. They move straight ahead or make a single turn to the right, the wheel being executed with such perfect alignment that no man drops behind the one next to him. One would say that on the whole their chief strength lies in their infantry. A picked body of these are chosen from among all the youth and placed in advance of the line where they fight mixed with the horsemen, since their swiftness makes them fully equal to engaging in a cavalry contest. Their number is fixed; there are a hundred from each canton, and from this circumstance they take their name among their own people, so that what

was at first a number is now become an appellation of honor. The main body of troops is drawn up in wedge-shaped formation. To yield ground, provided you press forward subsequently, is considered a mark of prudence rather than a sign of cowardice. They carry off the bodies of the fallen even where they are not victorious. It is the greatest ignominy to have left one's shield on the field, and it is unlawful for a man so disgraced to be present at the sacred rites or to enter the assembly; so that many after escaping from battle have ended their shame with the halter.

They choose their kings on account of their ancestry, their generals for their valor. The kings do not have free and unlimited power and the generals lead by example rather than command, winning great admiration if they are energetic and fight in plain sight in front of the line. But no one is allowed to put a culprit to death or to imprison him, or even to beat him with stripes except the priests, and then not by way of a punishment or at the command of the general but as though ordered by the god who they believe aids them in their fighting. Certain figures and images taken from their sacred groves they carry into battle, but their greatest incitement to courage is that a division of horse or foot is not made up by chance or by accidental association, but is formed of families and clans; and their dear ones are close at hand so that the wailings of the women and the crying of the children can be heard during the battle. These are for each warrior the most sacred witnesses of his bravery, these his dearest applauders. They carry their wounds to their mothers and their wives, nor do the latter fear to count their number and examine them while they bring them food and urge them to deeds of valor.

It is related how on certain occasions their forces already turned to flight and retreating have been rallied by the women who implored them by their prayers and bared their breasts to their weapons, signifying thus the captivity close awaiting them, which is feared far more intensely on account of their women than for themselves; to such an extent indeed that those states are more firmly bound in treaty among whose hostages maidens of noble family are also required. Further, they believe that the sex has a certain sanctity and prophetic gift, and they neither despise their counsels nor disregard their answers. We ourselves in the reign of the divine Vespasian saw Valaeda, who was considered for a long time by many as a sort of divinity; and formerly also Albruna and many others were venerated, though not out of servility nor as though they were deified mortals.

Among the gods they worship Mercury most of all, to whom it is lawful to offer human sacrifices also on stated days. Hercules and Mars they placate by the sacrifice of worthy animals. Some of the *Suebi* sacrifice to Isis. The reason for this foreign rite and its origin I have not discovered, except that the image fashioned like a galley shows that the cult has been introduced from abroad. On the other hand they hold it to be inconsistent with the sublimity of the celestials to confine the gods in walls made by hands, or to liken them to the form of any human countenance. They consecrate woods and sacred groves to them and give the names of the deities to that hidden mystery which they perceive by faith alone.

They pay as much attention as any people to augury and lots. The method of casting lots is uniform. They cut off a branch from a fruit-bearing tree and divide it into small wands marked with certain characters. These they throw at random on a white cloth. Then the priest of the tribe, if it is a matter concerning the community, or the father of the family in case it is a private affair, calling on the gods and keeping his eyes raised toward the sky, takes up three of the lots, one at a time, and then interprets their meaning according to the markings before mentioned. If they have proven unfavorable there can be no further consultation that day concerning that particular matter; but if they are favorable, the confirmation of auspices is further demanded. Even the practice of divination from the notes and flight of birds is known; but it is peculiar to this people to seek omens and warnings from horses also. These sacred animals are white and never defiled by labor, being kept at public expense in the holy groves and woods. They are yoked to the sacred chariot by the priest and the king or chief of the tribe, who accompany them and take note of their neighing and

snorting. In no other kind of divination is there greater confidence placed either by the common people or by the nobles; for the priests are considered merely the servants of the gods, but the horses are thought to be acquainted with their counsels. They have another sort of divination whereby they seek to know the result of serious wars. They secure in any way possible a captive from the hostile tribe and set him to fight with a warrior chosen from their own people, each using the weapons of his own country. The victory of the one or the other is accepted as an indication of the result of the war.

Concerning minor matters the chiefs deliberate, but in important affairs all the people are consulted, although the subjects referred to the common people for judgment are discussed beforehand by the chiefs. Unless some sudden and unexpected event calls them together, they assemble on fixed days either at the new moon or the full moon, for they think these the most auspicious times to begin their undertakings. They do not reckon time by the number of days, as we do, but by the number of nights. So run their appointments, their contracts; the night introduces the day, so to speak. A disadvantage arises from their regard for liberty in that they do not come together at once as if commanded to attend, but two or three days are wasted by their delay in assembling. When the crowd is sufficient they take their places fully armed. Silence is proclaimed by the priests, who have on these occasions the right to keep order. Then the king or a chief addresses them, each being heard according to his age, noble blood, reputation in warfare and eloquence, though more because he has the power to persuade than the right to command. If an opinion is displeasing they reject it by shouting; if they agree to it they clash with their spears. The most complimentary form of assent is that which is expressed by means of their weapons.

It is also allowable in the assembly to bring up accusations, and to prosecute capital offenses. Penalties are distinguished according to crime. Traitors and deserters are hung to trees. Weaklings and cowards and those guilty of infamous crimes are cast into the mire of swamps with a hurdle placed over their heads.

This difference of penalty looks to the distinction that crime should be punished publicly while infamy should be hidden out of sight. Lighter offences also are punished according to their degree, the guilty parties being fined a certain number of horses or cattle. A part of the fine goes to the king or the tribe, part to the injured party or his relatives. In these same assemblies are chosen the magistrates who decide suits in the cantons and villages. Each one has the assistance of a hundred associates as advisers and with power to decide.

They undertake no business whatever either of a public or a private character save they be armed. But it is not customary for any one to assume arms until the tribe has recognized his competence to use them. Then in a full assembly some one of the chiefs or the father or relatives of the youth invest him with the shield and spear. This is the sign that the lad has reached the age of manhood; this is his first honor. Before this he was only a member of a household, hereafter he is a member of the tribe. Distinguished rank or the great services of their parents secure even for mere striplings the claim to be ranked as chiefs. They attach themselves to certain more experienced chiefs of approved merit; nor are they ashamed to be looked upon as belonging to their followings. There are grades even within the train of followers assigned by the judgment of its leader. There is great rivalry among these companions as to who shall rank first with the chief, and among the chiefs as to who shall have the most and the bravest followers. It is an honor and a source of strength always to be surrounded by a great band of chosen youths, for they are an ornament in peace, a defence in war. It brings reputation and glory to a leader not only in his own tribe but also among the neighboring peoples if his following is superior in numbers and courage; for he is courted by embassies and honored by gifts, and often his very fame decides the issue of wars.

When they go into battle it is a disgrace for the chief to be outdone in deeds of valor and for the following not to match the courage of their chief; furthermore, for any one of the followers to have survived his chief and come unharmed out of a battle is life-long infamy and reproach. It is in accordance with their most sacred oath of allegiance to defend and protect him and to ascribe their bravest deeds to his renown. The chief fights for victory; the men of his following, for their chief. If the tribe to which they belong sinks into the lethargy of long peace and quiet, many of the noble youths voluntarily seek other tribes that are still carrying on war, because a quiet life is irksome to the Germans and they gain renown more readily in the midst of perils, while a large following is not to be provided for except by violence and war. For they look to the liberality of their chief for their war-horse and their deadly and victorious spear; the feasts and entertainments, however, furnished them on a homely but liberal scale, fall to their lot as mere pay. The means for this bounty are acquired through war and plunder. Nor could you persuade them to till the soil and await the yearly produce so easily as you could induce them to stir up an enemy and earn glorious wounds. Nay, even they think it tame and stupid to acquire by their sweat what they can purchase by their blood.

In the intervals of peace they spend little time in hunting, but much in idleness, given over to sleep and eating; all the bravest and most warlike doing nothing, while the hearth and home and the care of the fields is given over to the women, the old men, and the various infirm members of the family. The masters lie buried in sloth by that strange contradiction of nature that causes the same men to love indolence and hate peace. It is customary for the several tribesmen to present voluntary offerings of cattle and grain to the chiefs which, though accepted as gifts of honor, also supply their wants. They are particularly delighted in the gifts of neighboring tribes, not only those sent by individuals, but those presented by states as such,—choice horses, massive arms, embossed plates and armlets. We have now taught them to accept money also.

It is well known that none of the German tribes live in cities, nor even permit their dwellings to be closely joined to each other. They live separated and in various places, as a spring or a meadow or a grove strikes their fancy. They lay out their villages, not as with us in connected or closely-joined houses, but each one surrounds his dwelling with an open space, either as a protection against conflagration or because of their ignorance of the art of building. They do not even make use of rough stones or tiles. They use for all purposes undressed timber, giving no beauty or comfort. Some parts they plaster carefully with earth of such purity and brilliancy as to form a substitute for painting and designs in color. They are accustomed also to dig out subterranean caves which they cover over with great heaps of manure as a refuge against the cold and a place for storing grain, for retreats of this sort render the extreme cold of their winters bearable and, whenever an enemy has come upon them, though he lays waste the open country, he is either ignorant of what is hidden underground or else it escapes him for the very reason that it has to searched for.

Generally their only clothing is a cloak fastened with a clasp, or if they haven't that, with a thorn; this being their only garment, they pass whole days about the hearth or near a fire. The richest of them are distinguished by wearing a tunic, not flowing as is the case among the Sarmatians and Parthians, but close-fitting and showing the shape of their limbs. There are those, also, who wear the skins of wild beasts, those nearest the Roman border in a careless manner, but those further back more elegantly, as those do who have no better clothing obtained by commerce. They select certain animals, and stripping off their hides sew on them patches of spotted skins taken from those strange beasts that the distant ocean and the unknown sea bring forth. The women wear the same sort of dress as the men except that they wrap themselves in linen garments which they adorn with purple stripes and do not lengthen out the upper part of the tunic into sleeves, but leave the arms bare the whole length. The upper part of their breasts is also exposed. However, their marriage code is strict, and in no other part of their manners are they to be praised more than in this. For almost alone among barbarian peoples they are content with one wife each, excepting those few who because of their high position rather than out of lust enter into more than one marriage engagement.

The wife does not bring a dowry to the husband, but the husband to the wife. The parents and relatives are present at the ceremony and examine and accept the presents,—gifts not suited to female luxury nor such as a young bride would deck herself with, but oxen, a horse and bridle and a shield together with a spear and sword. In consideration of these offerings the wife is accepted, and she in her turn brings her husband a gift of weapons. This they consider as the strongest bond, these as their mystic rites, their gods of marriage. Lest the woman should think herself excluded from aspiring to share in heroic deeds and in the dangers of war, she is admonished by the very initiatory ceremonies of matrimony that she is becoming the partner of her husband's labors and dangers, destined to suffer and to dare with him alike in peace and in war. The yoke of oxen, the caparisoned horse, the gift of arms, give this warning. So must she live, so must she die. What things she receives she must hand down to her children worthy and untarnished and such that future daughters-in-law may receive them and pass them on to her grandchildren.

Thus they live in well-protected virtue, uncorrupted by the allurements of shows or the enticement of banquets. Men and women alike know not the secrecy of correspondence. Though the race is so numerous, adultery is very rare, its punishment being immediate and inflicted by the injured husband. He cuts off the woman's hair in the presence of her kinsfolk, drives her naked from his house and flogs her through the whole village. Indeed, the loss of chastity meets with no indulgence; neither beauty, youth, nor wealth can procure the guilty woman a husband, for no one there laughs at vice, nor is corrupting and being corrupted spoken of as the way of the world. Those tribes do better still where only the virgins marry and where the hope and aspiration of married life is done with once for all. They accept one husband, just as they have one body and one life, that they may have no thought beyond this, no further desire; that their love may be as it were not for the married state, but for the husband. To limit the number of children or to put any of the later children to death is considered a crime, and with them good customs are of more avail than good laws elsewhere.

In every household the children grow up naked and unkempt into that lusty frame and those sturdy limbs that we admire. Each mother nurses her own children; they are not handed over to servants and paid nurses. The lord and the slave are in no way to be distinguished by the delicacy of their bringing up. They live among the same flocks, they lie on the same ground, until age separates them and valor distinguishes the free born. The young men marry late and their vigor is thereby unimpaired. Nor is the marriage of girls hastened. They have the same youthful vigor, the same stature as the young men. Thus well-matched and strong when they marry, the children reproduce the robustness of their parents. An uncle shows the same regard for his sister's children as does their own father. Some tribes consider this relationship more sacred and binding than any other, and in taking hostages lay special stress upon it on the ground that they secure thus a stronger hold on the mind and a wider pledge for the family. A man's heirs and successors, however, are his own children, and no wills are made. If there are no children the next heirs are the brothers, then come the paternal and maternal uncles. The more relatives a man has and the greater the number of his connections, the more honored is his old age. Childlessness has no advantages.

A German is required to adopt not only the feuds of his father or of a relative, but also their friendships, though the enmities are not irreconcilable. For even homicide is expiated by the payment of a certain number of cattle, and the whole family accept the satisfaction, a useful practice as regards the state because feuds are more dangerous where there is no strong legal control.

No other race indulges more freely in entertainments and hospitality. It is considered a crime to turn any mortal man away from one's door. According to his means, each one receives those who come with a well-furnished table. When his food has been all eaten up, he who had lately been the host becomes the guide and companion of his guest to the next house, which they enter uninvited. There is no distinction between guests; they are all received with like consideration. No one makes any difference between friend and stranger so far as concerns the rights of hospitality. If the guest on going away asks for any gift, it is customary to grant it to him, and the host on

his side feels the same freedom from constraint in making a request. They take great pleasure in presents, but they do not reckon them as favors nor do they put themselves under obligations in accepting them.

As soon as they awake from sleep, which they prolong till late in the day, they bathe, usually in warm water as their winter lasts a great part of the year. After the bath they take food, each sitting in a separate seat and having a table to himself. Then they proceed to their business, or not less often to feasts, fully armed. It is no disgrace to spend the whole day and night in drinking. Quarreling is frequent enough as is natural among drunken men, though their disputes are rarely settled by mere wrangling but oftener by bloodshed and wounds. Yet it is at their feasts that they consult about reconciling enemies, forming family alliances, electing chiefs, and even regarding war and peace, as they think that at no other time is the mind more open to fair judgment or more inflamed to mighty deeds. A race without natural or acquired cunning still continues to disclose the secret thoughts of the heart in the freedom of festivity. Therefore at such a time the minds of all are free and unconstrained. On the next day the matter is reconsidered and a particular advantage is secured on each occasion. They take counsel when they are unable to practice deception; they decide when they cannot be misled.

A liquor for drinking bearing a certain resemblance to wine is made by the process of fermentation from barley or other grain. Those next the border also buy wine. Their food is of a simple kind, wild fruit, fresh game, or curdled milk. They satisfy their hunger without elaborate preparation and without the use of condiments. In the matter of thirst they do not use the same temperance. If you should indulge their love of drink by furnishing them as much as they wanted, they might be conquered more easily by their vices than by arms.

As to games, but one and the same kind is seen in all their gatherings. Naked youths who make profession of this exhibition leap and dance among swords and spears that threaten their lives. Constant practice has given them skill, skill has given grace. Still they do not indulge in this pastime with a view to profit. The pleasure of the spectators is the reward for their recklessness, however daring. They indulge in games of chance, strange as it may seem, even when sober, as one of their serious occupations, with such great recklessness in their gains and losses that when everything else is gone they stake their liberty and their own persons on the last and decisive throw. The loser goes into voluntary slavery, Though he may be the younger and stronger of the two, he suffers himself to be bound and led away. Such is their stubbornness in a bad practice. They themselves call it honor. They sell slaves of this description to others that they may not feel the shame of such a success.

But they do not employ slaves as we do with distinct functions prescribed throughout the establishment. Each has his own domicile and rules his own house. The Lord exacts a certain amount of grain or cloth or a certain number of cattle as in the case of a tenant and this is the extent of his servitude. Other duties, those of the household, are performed by the lord's wife and children. To beat a slave or to punish him with chains and task work is rare. They occasionally kill one, not in the severity of discipline, but impetuously and in sudden wrath as they would kill an enemy, except that the deed goes without punishment. Freedmen do not rank much above slaves; they are not of much account in the household and never in the state, except only in those tribes that are ruled by kings. For there they are elevated above the free born and the nobles. The inferior position of the freedman elsewhere is the mark of the free state.

To trade with capital and to let it out at interest is unknown, and so it is ignorance rather than legal prohibition that protects them. Land is held by the villages as communities according to the number of the cultivators, and is then divided among the freemen according to their rank. The extent of their territories renders this partition easy. They cultivate fresh fields every year and there is still land to spare. They do not plant orchards nor lay off meadow-lands nor irrigate gardens so as to require of the soil more than it would naturally bring forth of its own richness and extent. Grain is the only tribute exacted from their land, whence they do not divide the year into as many seasons as we do. The terms winter, spring and summer have a meaning with them, but the name and blessings of autumn are unknown.

There is no pomp in the celebration of their funerals. The only custom they observe is that the bodies of illustrious men should be burned with certain kinds of wood. They do not heap garments and perfumes upon the funeral pile. In every case a man's arms are burned with him, and sometimes his horse also. They believe that stately monuments and sculptured columns oppress the dead with their weight; the green sod alone covers their graves. Their tears and lamentations are quickly laid aside; sadness and grief linger long. It is fitting for women to mourn, for men to remember.

Such are the facts I have obtained in general concerning the origin and customs of the Germans as a whole. . . .

Eginhard

Eginhard (about 770–840 A.D.), a monk who lived at the court of Charlemagne, survived the great emperor by a period of thirty years. During that time he wrote a short biography of the man who claimed to be the heir of the Roman emperors in the West. The work contained some errors, but is nevertheless valuable as the best contemporary account of this important monarch. In reading this biography note (1) the emperor's character; (2) education; (3) family relationships; (4) career; (5) political achievements; (6) how he became emperor; (7) cultural elements derived from Greek, Roman, Christian, and Germanic traditions; and (8) the spirit of his age.

As translated by A. J. Grant in *Early Lives of Charlemagne by Eginhard and the Monk of St. Gall,* The King's Classics, Alexander Moring, Ltd., The De La More Press, London, 1905, 4–50. Courtesy of Alexander Moring, Ltd.

THE LIFE OF THE EMPEROR CHARLES

Having made up my mind to write an account of the life and conversation, and to a large extent of the actions of my lord and patron, King Charles, of great and deservedly glorious memory, I have compressed my task within the narrowest possible limits. My aim has been on the one hand to insert everything of which I have been able to find an account; and on the other to avoid offending the fastidious by telling each new incident at wearisome length. Above all, I have tried to avoid offending in this new book those who look down upon even the monuments of antiquity written by learned and eloquent men.

There are, I do not doubt, many men of learning and leisure who feel that the life of the present day must not be utterly neglected, and that the doings of our own time should not be devoted to silence and forgetfulness as wholly unworthy of record; who, therefore, have such love of fame that they would rather chronicle the great deeds of others in writings, however poor, than, by abstaining from writing, allow their name and reputation to perish from the memory of mankind. But, even so, I have felt that I ought not to hold my hand from the composition of this book, for I knew that no one could write of these events more truthfully than I could, since I was myself an actor in them, and, being present, knew them from the testimony of my own eyes; while I could not certainly know whether anyone else would write them or no. I thought it better, therefore, to join with others in committing this story to writing for the benefit of posterity rather than to allow the shades of oblivion to blot out the life of this King, the noblest and greatest of his age, and his famous deeds, which the men of later times will scarcely be able to imitate.

Another reason, and not, I think, a foolish one, occurred to me, which even by itself would have been strong enough to persuade me to write—the care, I mean, that was taken with my upbringing, and the unbroken friendship which I enjoyed with the King himself and his children from the time when first I began to live at his Court. For in this way he has so bound me to himself, and has made me his debtor both in life and death, that I should most justly be considered and condemned as ungrateful if I were to forget all the benefits that he conferred upon me and were to pass over in silence the great and glorious deeds of a man who was so kind to me; if I were to allow his life to remain as unchronicled and unpraised, as if he had never lived, when that life deserves not merely the efforts of my poor talents, which are insignificant, small and almost non-existent, but all the eloquence of a Cicero.

So here you have a book containing the life of that great and glorious man. There is nothing for you to wonder at or admire except his deeds; unless, indeed, it be that I, a barbarian, and little versed in the Roman tongue, have imagined that I could write Latin inoffensively and usefully, and have become so swollen with impudence as to despise Cicero's words when, speaking about Latin writers in the first book of the Tusculans, he says: "If a man commits his thoughts to paper when he can neither arrange them well nor write them agreeably, nor furnish pleasure of any kind to the reader, he is recklessly misusing both his leisure and his paper." The great orator's opinion would, perhaps, have deterred me from writing if I had not fortified myself with the reflection that I ought to risk the condemnation of men, and bring my poor talents into peril by writing, rather than spare my reputation and neglect this great man's memory.

THE PREFACE ENDS: THE BOOK BEGINS

The race of the Merovings from which the Franks were accustomed to choose their kings is reckoned as lasting to King Hilderich, who, by the order of Stephen, the Roman Pontiff, was deposed, tonsured, and sent into a monastery. But this race, though it may be regarded as finishing with him, had long since lost all power, and no longer possessed anything of importance except the empty royal title. For the wealth and power of the kingdom was in the hands of the Praefects of the Court, who were called Mayors of the Palace, and exercised entire sovereignty. The King, contented with the mere royal title, with long hair and flowing beard, used to sit upon the throne and act the part of a ruler, listening to ambassadors, whencesoever they came, and giving them at their departure, as though of his own power, answers which he had been instructed or commanded to give. But this was the only function that he performed, for besides the empty royal title and the precarious life income which the Praefect of the Court allowed him at his pleasure he had nothing of his own except one estate with a very small revenue, on which he had his house, and from which he drew the few servants who performed such services as were necessary and made him a show of deference. Wherever he had to go he travelled in a waggon, drawn in rustic style by a pair of oxen, and driven by a cowherd. In this fashion he used to go to the palace and to the general meetings of the people, which were held yearly for the affairs of the kingdom; in this fashion he returned home. But the Praefect of the Court looked after the administration of the kingdom and all that had to be done or arranged at home or abroad.

When Hilderich was deposed, Pippin, the father of King Charles, was performing the duties of Mayor of the Palace as if by hereditary right. For his father Charles, who put down the tyrants who were claiming dominion for themselves through all Frankland, and so crushed the Saracens, when they were attempting to conquer Gaul, in two great battles (the one in Aquitania, near the city of Poitiers, the other near Narbonne, on the river Birra), that he forced them to return into Spain—his father Charles had nobly administered the same office, and had inherited it from his father, Pippin. For the people did not usually give this honour except to such as were distinguished for the renown of their family and the extent of their wealth.

This office, then, was handed down from his father and his grandfather to Pippin, the father of King Charles, and to his brother, Carloman. He exercised it for some years conjointly with his brother Carloman on terms of the greatest harmony, still in nominal subordina-

tion to the above-mentioned King Hilderich. But then his brother, Carloman, for some unknown cause, but probably fired with love of the contemplative life, abandoned the toilsome administration of a temporal kingdom and retired to Rome in search of peace. There he changed his dress, and, becoming a monk in the monastery upon Mount Soracte, built near the church of the blessed Sylvester, enjoyed for some years the quiet that he desired, with many brethren, who joined themselves to him for the same purpose. But as many of the nobles of Frankland came on pilgrimage to Rome to perform their vows, and, unwilling to pass by one who had once been their lord, interrupted the peace that he most desired by frequent visits, he was compelled to change his abode. For, seeing that the number of his visitors interfered with his purpose, he left Mount Soracte and retired to the monastery of Saint Benedict, situated in the camp of Mount Cassino, in the province of Samnium. There he occupied what remained to him of this temporal life in religious exercises.

But Pippin, after he was made King instead of Mayor of the Palace by the authority of the Roman Pontiff, exercised sole rule over the Franks for fifteen years, or rather more. Then, after finishing the Aquitanian war, which he had undertaken against Waifar, Duke of Aquitania, and had carried on for nine consecutive years, he died at Paris of the dropsy, and left behind him two sons, Charles and Carloman, to whom by divine will the succession of the kingdom came. For the Franks called a solemn public assembly, and elected both of them to be kings, on the understanding that they should equally divide the whole kingdom, but that Charles should receive for his special administration that part which his father Pippin had held, while Carloman received the territories ruled by their uncle Carloman. The conditions were accepted, and each received the share of the kingdom that was allotted to him. Harmony was maintained between the two brothers, though not without difficulty; for many partisans of Carloman tried to break their alliance, and some even hoped to engage them in war. But the course of events proved that the danger to Charles was imaginary rather than real. For, upon the death of Carloman, his wife with her sons and some of the leading nobles fled to Italy, and, for no obvious reason, passed over her husband's brother, and placed herself and her children under the protection of Desiderius, King of the Lombards. Carloman, after ruling the kingdom for two years conjointly with Charles, died of disease, and Charles, upon the death of Carloman, was made sole king with the consent of all the Franks.

It would be foolish of me to say anything about his birth and infancy, or even about his boyhood, for I can find nothing about these matters in writing, nor does anyone survive who claims to have personal knowledge of them. I have decided, therefore to pass on to describe and illustrate his acts and his habits and the other divisions of his life without lingering over the unknown. I shall describe first his exploits both at home and abroad, then his habits and interests, and lastly the administration of the kingdom and the end of his reign, omitting nothing that demands or deserves to be recorded.

HIS EXPLOITS AT HOME AND ABROAD

Of all the wars that he waged that in Aquitania, begun, but not finished, by his father, was the first that he undertook, because it seemed easy of accomplishment. His brother was still alive, and was called upon for assistance, and, though he failed to provide the help that he promised, Charles prosecuted the enterprise that he had undertaken with the utmost energy, and would not desist or slacken in his task before, by perseverance and continuous effort, he had completely reached the end after which he strove. For he forced Hunold, who after the death of Waifar had attempted to occupy Aquitania and renew the almost finished war, to abandon Aquitania and retire into Gascony. Even there he did not allow him to remain, but crossed the Garonne, and sent ambassadors to Lupus, Duke of the Gascons, ordering him to surrender the fugitive, and threatening him with war unless he did so at once. Lupus, more wisely, not only surrendered Hunold but also submitted himself

and the province over which he presided to the power of Charles.

When the Aquitanian trouble was settled and the war finished, when, too, his partner in the kingdom had withdrawn from the world's affairs, he undertook a war against the Lombards, being moved thereto by the entreaties and the prayers of Hadrian, Bishop of the City of Rome. Now, this war, too, had been undertaken by his father at the supplication of Pope Stephen, under circumstances of great difficulty, inasmuch as certain of the chiefs of the Franks, whose advice he was accustomed to ask, so strongly resisted his wishes that they openly declared that they would leave their King to return home. But now Charles undertook the war against King Haistulf, and most swiftly brought it to an end. For, though his reasons for undertaking the war were similar to, and, indeed, the same as those of his father, he plainly fought it out with a very different energy, and brought it to a different end. For Pippin, after a siege of a few days at Pavia, forced King Haistulf to give hostages, and restore to the Romans the towns and fortresses that he had taken from them, and to give a solemn promise that he would not attempt to regain what he had surrendered. But King Charles, when once he had begun the war, did not stop until he had received the surrender of King Desiderius, whom he had worn down after a long siege; until he had forced his son Adalgis, in whom the hopes of his people seemed to be centred, to fly not only from his kingdom but from Italy; until he had restored to the Romans all that had been taken from them; until he had crushed Hruodgausus, Praefect of the Duchy of Friuli, who was attempting a revolution; until, in fine, he had brought all Italy under his rule, and placed his son Pippin as king over the conquered country. I should describe here the difficulties of the passage of the Alps and the vast toil with which the Franks found their way through the pathless mountain ridges, the rocks that soared to heaven, and the sharply-pointed cliffs, if it were not that my purpose in the present work is rather to describe Charles's manner of life than to chronicle the events of the wars that he waged. The sum of this war was the conquest of Italy, the transportation and perpetual exile of King Desiderius, the expulsion of his son Adalgis from Italy, power taken from the kings of the Lombards and restored to Hadrian, the Ruler of the Roman Church.

When this war was ended, the Saxon war, which seemed dropped for a time, was taken up again. Never was there a war more prolonged nor more cruel than this, nor one that required greater efforts on the part of the Frankish peoples. For the Saxons, like most of the races that inhabit Germany, are by nature fierce, devoted to the worship of demons and hostile to our religion, and they think it no dishonour to confound and transgress the laws of God and man. There were reasons, too, which might at any time cause a disturbance of the peace. For our boundaries and theirs touch almost everywhere on the open plain, except where in a few places large forests or ranges of mountains are interposed to separate the territories of the two nations by a definite frontier; so that on both sides murder, robbery, and arson were of constant occurrence. The Franks were so irritated by these things that they thought it was time no longer to be satisfied with retaliation but to declare open war against them.

So war was declared, and was fought for thirty years continuously with the greatest fierceness on both sides, but with heavier loss to the Saxons than the Franks. The end might have been reached sooner had it not been for the perfidy of the Saxons. It is hard to say how often they admitted themselves beaten and surrendered as suppliants to King Charles; how often they promised to obey his orders, gave without delay the required hostages, and received the ambassadors that were sent to them. Sometimes they were so cowed and broken that they promised to abandon the worship of devils and willingly to submit themselves to the Christian religion. But though sometimes ready to bow to his commands they were always eager to break their promise, so it is impossible to say which course seemed to come more natural to them, for from the beginning of the war there was scarcely a year in which they did not both promise and fail to perform.

But the high courage of the King and the constancy of his mind, which remained unshaken by prosperity and adversity, could not be conquered by their changes nor forced by weariness to desist from his undertakings. He never allowed those who offended in this way to go unpunished, but either led an army himself, or sent one under the command of his counts, to chastise their perfidy and inflict a suitable penalty. So that at last, when all who had resisted had been defeated and brought under his power, he took ten thousand of the inhabitants of both banks of the Elbe, with their wives and children, and planted them in many groups in various parts of Germany and Gaul. And at last the war, protracted through so many years, was finished on conditions proposed by the King and accepted by them; they were to abandon the worship of devils, to turn from their national ceremonies, to receive the sacraments of the Christian faith and religion, and then, joined to the Franks, to make one people with them.

In this war, despite its prolongation through so many years, he did not himself meet the enemy in battle more than twice—once near the mountain called Osning, in the district of Detmold, and again at the river Hasa—and both these battles were fought in one month, with an interval of only a few days. In these two battles the enemy were so beaten and cowed that they never again ventured to challenge the King nor to resist his attack unless they were protected by some advantage of ground.

In this war many men of noble birth and high office fell on the side, both of the Franks and Saxons. But at last it come to an end in the thirty-third year, though in the meanwhile so many and such serious wars broke out against the Franks in all parts of the world, and were carried on with such skill by the King, that an observer may reasonably doubt whether his endurance of toil or his good fortune deserves the greater admiration. For the war in Italy began two years before the Saxon war, and though it was prosecuted without intermission, no enterprise in any part of the world was dropped, nor was there anywhere a truce in any struggle, however difficult. For this King, the wisest and most high-minded of all who in that age ruled over the nations of the world, never refused to undertake or prosecute any enterprise because of the labour involved, nor withdrew from it through fear of its danger. He understood the true character of each task that he undertook or carried through, and thus was neither broken by adversity nor misled by the false flatteries of good fortune.

Whilst the war with the Saxons was being prosecuted constantly and almost continuously he placed garrisons at suitable places on the frontier, and attacked Spain with the largest military expedition that he could collect. He crossed the Pyrenees, received the surrender of all the towns and fortresses that he attacked, and returned with his army safe and sound, except for a reverse which he experienced through the treason of the Gascons on his return through the passes of the Pyrenees. For while his army was marching in a long line, suiting their formation to the character of the ground and the defiles, the Gascons placed an ambuscade on the top of the mountain—where the density and extent of the woods in the neighbourhood rendered it highly suitable for such a purpose—and then, rushing down into the valley beneath, threw into disorder the last part of the baggage train and also the rearguard which acted as a protection to those in advance. In the battle which followed the Gascons slew their opponents to the last man. Then they seized upon the baggage, and under cover of the night, which was already falling, they scattered with the utmost rapidity in different directions. The Gascons were assisted in this feat by the lightness of their armour and the character of the ground where the affair took place. In this battle Eggihard, the surveyor of the royal table; Anselm, the Count of the Palace; and Roland, Praefect of the Breton frontier, were killed along with many others. Nor could this assault be punished at once, for when the deed had been done the enemy so completely disappeared that they left behind them not so much as a rumour of their whereabouts.

He conquered the Bretons, too, who dwelt in the extreme west of France by the shores of the ocean. They had been disobedient, and he, therefore, sent against them an expedition, by which they were compelled to give hostages and promise that they would henceforth obey his orders.

Then later he himself entered Italy with an army, and, passing through Rome, came to Capua, a city of Campania. There he pitched his camp, and threatened the men of Beneventum with war unless they surrendered. But Aragis, Duke of that people, prevented this war by sending his sons Rumold and Grimold to meet the King with a large sum of money. He asked the King to receive his children as hostages, and promised that he and his people would obey all the commands of the King, except only that he would not come himself into the King's presence. Charles, considering rather the advantage of the people than their Duke's obstinacy, received the hostages who were offered him, and as a great favour consented to forego a personal interview. He kept the younger of the two children as a hostage and sent back the elder one to his father. Then he sent ambassadors to require and receive oaths of fidelity from the Beneventans and from Aragis, and so came back to Rome. There he spent some days in the veneration of the holy places, and then returned to Gaul.

Then the Bavarian war broke out suddenly, and was swiftly ended. It was caused by the pride and folly of Tassilo, Duke of Bavaria; for upon the instigation of his wife, who thought that she might revenge through her husband the banishment of her father Desiderius, King of the Lombards, he made an alliance with the Huns, the eastern neighbours of the Bavarians, and not only refused obedience to King Charles but even dared to challenge him in war. The high courage of the King could not bear his overweening insolence, and he forthwith called a general levy for an attack on Bavaria, and came in person with a great army to the river Lech, which separates Bavaria from Germany. He pitched his camp upon the banks of the river, and determined to make trial of the mind of the Duke before he entered the province. But Duke Tassilo saw no profit either for himself or his people in stubbornness, and threw himself upon the King's mercy. He gave the hostages who were demanded, his own son Theodo among the number, and further promised upon oath that no one should ever persuade him again to fall away from his allegiance to the King. And thus a war which seemed likely to grow into a very great one came to a most swift ending. But Tassilo was subsequently summoned into the King's presence, and was not allowed to return, and the province that he ruled was for the future committed to the administration not of dukes but of counts.

When these troubles had been settled, he waged war against the Slavs, whom we are accustomed to call Wilzi, but who properly—that is, in their own tongue—are called Welatabi. Here the Saxons fought along with the other allied nations who followed the King's standards, though their loyalty was feigned and far from sincere. The cause of the war was that the Wilzi were constantly invading and attacking the Abodriti, the former allies of the Franks, and refused to obey the King's commands to desist from their attacks. There is a gulf stretching from the western sea towards the East, of undiscovered length, but nowhere more than a hundred miles in breadth, and often much narrower. Many nations occupy the shores of this sea. The Danes and the Swedes, whom we call the Northmen, hold its northern shore and all the islands in it. The Slavs and the Aisti and various other nations inhabit the eastern shore, amongst whom the chief are these Welatabi against whom then the King waged war. He so broke and subdued them in a single campaign, conducted by himself, that they thought it no longer wise to refuse to obey his commands.

The greatest of all his wars, next to the Saxon war, followed this one—that, namely, which he undertook against the Huns and the Avars. He prosecuted this with more vigour than the rest and with a far greater military preparation. However, he conducted in person only one expedition into Pannonia, the province then occupied by the Avars; the management of the rest he left to his son Pippin, and the governors of the provinces, and in some cases to his counts and lieutenants. These carried on the war with the greatest energy, and finished it after eight years of fighting. How many battles were fought there and how much blood was shed is still shown by the deserted and uninhabited condition of Pannonia, and

the district in which stood the palace of the Kagan is so desolate that there is not so much as a trace of human habitation. All the nobles of the Huns were killed in this war, all their glory passed away; their money and all the treasures that they had collected for so long were carried away. Nor can the memory of man recall any war waged against the Franks by which they were so much enriched and their wealth so increased. Up to this time they were regarded almost as a poor people, but now so much gold and silver were found in the palace, such precious spoils were seized by them in their battles, that it might fairly be held that the Franks had righteously taken from the Huns what they unrighteously had taken from other nations. Only two of the nobles of the Franks were killed in this war. Eric, the Duke of Friuli, was caught in an ambuscade laid by the townsmen of Tharsatica, a maritime town of Liburnia. And Gerold, the Governor of Bavaria, when he was marshalling his army to fight with the Huns in Pannonia, was killed by an unknown hand, along with two others, who accompanied him as he rode along the line encouraging the soldiers by name. For the rest, the war was almost bloodless so far as the Franks were concerned, and most fortunate in its result, although so difficult and protracted.

After this, the Saxon war ended in a settlement as lasting as the struggle had been protracted. The wars with Bohemia and Luneburg which followed were soon over; both of them were swiftly settled under the command of the younger Charles.

The last war of all that Charles undertook was against those Northmen, who are called Danes, who first came as pirates, and then ravaged the coasts of Gaul and Germany with a greater naval force. Their King, Godofrid, was puffed up with the vain confidence that he would make himself master of all Germany. He looked upon Frisia and Saxony as his own provinces. He had already reduced his neighbours, the Abodriti, to obedience, and had forced them to pay him tribute. Now he boasted that he would soon come to Aix, the seat of the King's Court, with a mighty force. His boast, however idle, found some to believe it; it was thought that he would certainly have made some such attempt if he had not been prevented by a sudden death. For he was killed by one of his own followers, and so ended both his life and the war that he had begun.

These, then, are the wars this mighty King waged during the course of forty-seven years—for his reign extended over that period—in different parts of the world with the utmost skill and success. By these wars he so nobly increased the kingdom of the Franks, which was great and strong when he inherited it from his father Pippin, that the additions he made almost doubled it. For before his time the power of the Frankish kingdom extended only over that part of Gaul which is bounded by the Rhine, the Loire, and the Balearic Sea; and that part of Germany which is inhabited by the so-called eastern Franks and which is bounded by Saxony, the Danube, the Rhine, and the river Saal, which stream separates the Thuringians and the Sorabs; and, further, over the Alamanni and the Bavarians. But Charles, by the wars that have been mentioned, conquered and made tributary the following countries:—First, Aquitania and Gascony, and the whole Pyrenean range, and the country of Spain as far as the Ebro, which rising in Navarre and passing through the most fertile territory of Spain, falls into the Balearic Sea, beneath the walls of the city of Tortosa; next, all Italy from Augusta Praetoria as far as lower Calabria, where are the frontiers of the Greeks and Beneventans, a thousand miles and more in length; next, Saxony, which is a considerable portion of Germany, and is reckoned to be twice as broad and about as long as that part of Germany which is inhabited by the Franks; then both provinces of Pannonia and Dacia, on one side of the river Danube, and Histria and Liburnia and Dalmatia, with the exception of the maritime cities which he left to the Emperor of Constantinople on account of their friendship and the treaty made between them; lastly, all the barbarous and fierce nations lying between the Rhine, the Vistula, the Ocean, and the Danube, who speak much the same language, but in character and dress are very unlike. The chief of these last are the Welatabi, the Sorabi, the Abodriti, and the Bohemians;

against these he waged war, but the others, and by far the larger number, surrendered without a struggle.

The friendship, too, which he established with certain kings and peoples increased the glory of his reign.

Aldefonsus, King of Gallaecia and Asturica, was joined in so close an alliance with him that whenever he sent letters or ambassadors to Charles he gave instructions that he should be called "the man" of the Frankish King.

Further, his rich gifts had so attached the kings of the Scots to his favour that they always called him their lord and themselves his submissive servants. Letters are still in existence sent by them to Charles in which those feelings towards him are clearly shown.

With Aaron, the King of the Persians, who ruled over all the East, with the exception of India, he entertained so harmonious a friendship that the Persian King valued his favour before the friendship of all the kings and princes in the world, and held that it alone deserved to be cultivated with presents and titles. When, therefore, the ambassadors of Charles, whom he had sent with offerings to the most holy sepulchre of our Lord and Saviour and to the place of His resurrection, came to the Persian King and proclaimed the kindly feelings of their master, he not only granted them all they asked but also allowed that sacred place of our salvation to be reckoned as part of the possessions of the Frankish King. He further sent ambassadors of his own along with those of Charles upon the return journey, and forwarded immense presents to Charles—robes and spices, and the other rich products of the East—and a few years earlier he had sent him at his request an elephant, which was then the only one he had.

The Emperors of Constantinople, Nicephorus, Michael, and Leo, too, made overtures of friendship and alliance with him, and sent many ambassadors. At first Charles was regarded with much suspicion by them, because he had taken the imperial title, and thus seemed to aim at taking from them their empire; but in the end a very definite treaty was made between them, and every occasion of quarrel on either side thereby avoided. For the Romans and the Greeks always suspected the Frankish power; hence, there is a well-known Greek proverb: "The Frank is a good friend but a bad neighbour."

Though he was so successful in widening the boundaries of his kingdom and subduing the foreign nations he, nevertheless, put on foot many works for the decoration and convenience of his kingdom, and carried some to completion. The great church dedicated to Mary, the holy Mother of God, at Aix, and the bridge, five hundred feet in length, over the great river Rhine near Mainz, may fairly be regarded as the chief of his works. But the bridge was burnt down a year before his death, and though he had determined to rebuild it of stone instead of wood it was not restored, because his death so speedily followed. He began also to build palaces of splendid workmanship —one not far from the city of Mainz, near a town called Ingelheim; another at Nimeguen, on the river Waal, which flows along the south of the Batavian island. And he gave special orders to the bishops and priests who had charge of sacred buildings that any throughout his realm, which had fallen into ruin through age should be restored, and he instructed his agents to see that his orders were carried out.

He built a fleet, too, for the war against the Northmen, constructing ships for this purpose near those rivers which flow out of Gaul and Germany into the northern ocean. And because the Northmen laid waste the coasts of Gaul and Germany by their constant attacks he planted forts and garrisons in all harbours and at the mouths of all navigable rivers, and prevented in this way the passage of the enemy. He took the same measures in the South, on the shore of Narbonne and Septimania, and also along all the coasts of Italy as far as Rome, to hold in check the Moors, who had lately begun to make piratical excursions. And by reason of these precautions Italy suffered no serious harm from the Moors, nor Gaul and Germany from the Northmen, in the days of Charles; except that Centumcellae, a city of Etruria, was betrayed into the hands of the Moors and plundered, and in Frisia certain islands lying close to Germany were ravaged by the Northmen.

PRIVATE LIFE AND CHARACTER OF CHARLEMAGNE

I have shown, then, how Charles protected and expanded his kingdom and also what splendour he gave to it. I shall now go on to speak of his mental endowments, of his steadiness of purpose under whatever circumstances of prosperity or adversity, and of all that concerns his private and domestic life.

As long as, after the death of his father, he shared the kingdom with his brother he bore so patiently the quarrelling and restlessness of the latter as never even to be provoked to wrath by him. Then, having married at his mother's bidding the daughter of Desiderius, King of the Lombards, he divorced her, for some unknown reason, a year later. He took in marriage Hildigard, of the Suabian race, a woman of the highest nobility, and by her he had three sons—viz., Charles and Pippin and Ludovicus, and three daughters—Hrotrud and Bertha and Gisla. He had also three other daughters—Theoderada and Hiltrud and Hruodhaid. Two of these were the children of his wife Fastrada, a woman of the eastern Franks or Germans; the third was the daughter of a concubine, whose name has escaped my memory. On the death of Fastrada he married Liutgard, of the Alemannic race, by whom he had no children. After her death he had four concubines—namely, Madelgarda, who bore him a daughter of the name of Ruothild; Gersuinda, of Saxon origin, by whom he had a daughter of the name of Adolthrud; Regina, who bore him Drogot and Hugo; and Adallinda, who was the mother of Theoderic.

His mother, Bertrada, lived with him to old age in great honour. He treated her with the utmost reverence, so that no quarrel of any kind ever arose between them—except in the matter of the divorce of the daughter of King Desiderius, whom he had married at her bidding. Bertrada died after the death of Hildigard, having lived to see three grandsons and as many granddaughters in her son's house. Charles had his mother buried with great honour in the same great church of St. Denys in which his father lay.

He had only one sister, Gisla, who from

childhood was dedicated to the religious life. He treated her with the same affectionate respect as his mother. She died a few years before Charles's own death in the monastery in which she had passed her life.

In educating his children he determined to train them, both sons and daughters, in those liberal studies to which he himself paid great attention. Further, he made his sons, as soon as their age permitted it, learn to ride like true Franks, and practise the use of arms and hunting. He ordered his daughters to learn wool work and devote attention to the spindle and distaff, for the avoidance of idleness and lethargy, and to be trained to the adoption of high principles.

He lost two sons and one daughter before his death—namely, Charles, his eldest; Pippin, whom he made King of Italy; and Hruotrud, his eldest daughter, who had been betrothed to Constantine, the Emperor of the Greeks. Pippin left one son, Bernard, and five daughters—Adalheid, Atula, Gundrada, Berthaid, and Theoderada. In his treatment of them Charles gave the strongest proof of his family affection, for upon the death of his son he appointed his grandson Bernard to succeed him, and had his granddaughters brought up with his own daughters.

He bore the deaths of his two sons and of his daughter with less patience than might have been expected from his usual stoutness of heart, for his domestic affection, a quality for which he was as remarkable as for courage, forced him to shed tears. Moreover, when the death of Hadrian, the Roman Pontiff, whom he reckoned as the chief of his friends, was announced to him, he wept for him as though he had lost a brother or a very dear son. For he showed a very fine disposition in his friendships: he embraced them readily and maintained them faithfully, and he treated with the utmost respect all whom he had admitted into the circle of his friends.

He had such care of the upbringing of his sons and daughters that he never dined without them when he was at home, and never travelled without them. His sons rode along with him, and his daughters followed in the rear. Some of his guards, chosen for this very purpose, watched the end of the line of march

where his daughters travelled. They were very beautiful, and much beloved by their father, and, therefore, it is strange that he would give them in marriage to no one, either among his own people or of a foreign state. But up to his death he kept them all at home, saying that he could not forego their society. And hence the good fortune that followed him in all other respects was here broken by the touch of scandal and failure. He shut his eyes, however, to everything, and acted as though no suspicion of anything amiss had reached him, or as if the rumour of it had been discredited.

He had by a concubine a son called Pippin—whom I purposely did not mention along with the others—handsome, indeed, but deformed. When Charles, after the beginning of the war against the Huns, was wintering in Bavaria, this Pippin pretended illness, and formed a conspiracy against his father with some of the leaders of the Franks, who had seduced him by a vain promise of the kingdom. When the design had been detected and the conspirators punished Pippin was tonsured and sent to the monastery of Prumia, there to practise the religious life, to which in the end he was of his own will inclined.

Another dangerous conspiracy had been formed against him in Germany at an earlier date. The plotters were some of them blinded and some of them maimed, and all subsequently transported into exile. Not more than three lost their lives, and these resisted capture with drawn swords, and in defending themselves killed some of their opponents. Hence, as they could not be restrained in any other way, they were cut down.

The cruelty of Queen Fastrada is believed to be the cause and origin of these conspiracies. Both were caused by the belief that, upon the persuasion of his cruel wife, he had swerved widely from his natural kindness and customary leniency. Otherwise his whole life long he so won the love and favour of all men both at home and abroad that never was the slightest charge of unjust severity brought against him by anyone.

He had a great love for foreigners, and took such pains to entertain them that their numbers were justly reckoned to be a burden not only to the palace but to the kingdom at large.

But, with his usual loftiness of spirit, he took little note of such charges, for he found in the reputation of generosity and in the good fame that followed such actions a compensation even for grave inconveniences.

His body was large and strong; his stature tall but not ungainly, for the measure of his height was seven times the length of his own feet. The top of his head was round; his eyes were very large and piercing. His nose was rather larger than is usual; he had beautiful white hair; and his expression was brisk and cheerful; so that, whether sitting or standing, his appearance was dignified and impressive. Although his neck was rather thick and short and he was somewhat corpulent, this was not noticed owing to the good proportions of the rest of his body. His step was firm and the whole carriage of his body manly; his voice was clear, but hardly so strong as you would have expected. He had good health, but for four years before his death was frequently attacked by fevers, and at last was lame of one foot. Even then he followed his own opinion rather than the advice of his doctors, whom he almost hated, because they advised him to give up the roast meat to which he was accustomed, and eat boiled instead. He constantly took exercise both by riding and hunting. This was a national habit; for there is hardly any race on the earth that can be placed on equality with the Franks in this respect. He took delight in the vapour of naturally hot waters, and constantly practised swimming, in which he was so proficient that no one could be fairly regarded as his superior. Partly for this reason he built his palace at Aix, and lived there continuously during the last years of his life up to the time of his death. He used to invite not only his sons to the bath but also his nobles and friends, and at times even a great number of his followers and bodyguards.

He wore the national—that is to say, the Frankish—dress. His shirts and drawers were of linen, then came a tunic with a silken fringe, and hose. His legs were cross-gartered and his feet enclosed in shoes. In winter-time he defended his shoulders and chest with a jerkin made of the skins of otters and ermine. He was clad in a blue cloak, and always wore a sword, with the hilt and belt of either gold or silver.

Occasionally, too, he used a jewelled sword, but this was only on the great festivals or when he received ambassadors from foreign nations. He disliked foreign garments, however beautiful, and would never consent to wear them, except once at Rome on the request of Pope Hadrian, and once again upon the entreaty of his successor, Pope Leo, when he wore a long tunic and cloak, and put on shoes made after the Roman fashion. On festal days he walked in procession in a garment of gold cloth, with jewelled boots and a golden girdle to his cloak, and distinguished further by a diadem of gold and precious stones. But on other days his dress differed little from that of the common people.

He was temperate in eating and drinking, but especially so in drinking; for he had a fierce hatred of drunkenness in any man, and especially in himself or in his friends. He could not abstain so easily from food, and used often to complain that fasting was injurious to his health. He rarely gave large banquets, and only on the high festivals, but then he invited a large number of guests. His daily meal was served in four courses only, exclusive of the roast, which the hunters used to bring in on spits, and which he ate with more pleasure than any other food. During the meal there was either singing or a reader for him to listen to. Histories and the great deeds of men of old were read to him. He took delight also in the books of Saint Augustine, and especially in those which are entitled the City of God. He was so temperate in the use of wine and drink of any kind that he rarely drank oftener than thrice during dinner.

In summer, after his midday meal, he took some fruit and a single draught, and then, taking off his clothes and boots, just as he was accustomed to do at night, he would rest for two or three hours. At night he slept so lightly that he would wake, and even rise, four or five times during the night.

When he was putting on his boots and clothes he not only admitted his friends, but if the Count of the Palace told him there was any dispute which could not be settled without his decision he would have the litigants at once brought in, and hear the case, and pronounce on it just as if he were sitting on the tribunal.

He would, moreover, at the same time transact any business that had to be done that day or give any orders to his servants.

In speech he was fluent and ready, and could express with the greatest clearness whatever he wished. He was not merely content with his native tongue but took the trouble to learn foreign languages. He learnt Latin so well that he could speak it as well as his native tongue; but he could understand Greek better than he could speak it. His fluency of speech was so great that he even seemed sometimes a little garrulous.

He paid the greatest attention to the liberal arts, and showed the greatest respect and bestowed high honours upon those who taught them. For his lessons in grammar he listened to the instruction of Deacon Peter of Pisa, an old man; but for all other subjects Albinus, called Alcuin, also a deacon, was his teacher—a man from Britain, of the Saxon race, and the most learned man of his time. Charles spent much time and labour in learning rhetoric and dialectic, and especially astronomy, from Alcuin. He learnt, too, the art of reckoning, and with close application scrutinised most carefully the course of the stars. He tried also to learn to write, and for this purpose used to carry with him and keep under the pillow of his couch tablets and writing-sheets that he might in spare moments accustom himself to the formation of letters. But he made little advance in this strange task, which was begun too late in life.

He paid the most devout and pious regard to the Christian religion, in which he had been brought up from infancy. And, therefore, he built the great and most beautiful church at Aix, and decorated it with gold and silver and candelabras and with wicket-gates and doors of solid brass. And, since he could not procure marble columns elsewhere for the building of it, he had them brought from Rome and Ravenna. As long as his health permitted it he used diligently to attend the church both in the morning and evening, and during the night, and at the time of the Sacrifice. He took the greatest care to have all the services of the church performed with the utmost dignity, and constantly warned the keepers of the building not to allow anything improper or dirty either to be brought into or to remain in the building. He provided so great a quantity of gold and silver vessels, and so large a supply of priestly vestments, that at the religious services not even the door-keepers, who form the lowest ecclesiastical order, had to officiate in their ordinary dress. He carefully reformed the manner of reading and singing; for he was thoroughly instructed in both, though he never read publicly himself, nor sang except in a low voice and with the rest of the congregation.

He was most devout in relieving the poor and in those free gifts which the Greeks call alms. For he gave it his attention not only in his own country and in his own kingdom, but he also used to send money across the sea to Syria, to Egypt, to Africa—to Jerusalem, Alexandria, and Carthage—in compassion for the poverty of any Christians whose miserable condition in those countries came to his ears. It was for this reason chiefly that he cultivated the friendship of kings beyond the sea, hoping thereby to win for the Christians living beneath their sway some succour and relief.

Beyond all other sacred and venerable places he loved the church of the holy Apostle Peter at Rome, and he poured into its treasury great wealth in silver and gold and precious stones. He sent innumerable gifts to the Pope; and during the whole course of his reign he strove with all his might (and, indeed, no object was nearer to his heart than this) to restore to the city of Rome her ancient authority, and not merely to defend the church of Saint Peter but to decorate and enrich it out of his resources above all other churches. But although he valued Rome so much, still, during all the forty-seven years that he reigned, he only went there four times to pay his vows and offer up his prayers.

But such were not the only objects of his last visit; for the Romans had grievously outraged Pope Leo, had torn out his eyes and cut off his tongue, and thus forced him to throw himself upon the protection of the King. He, therefore, came to Rome to restore the condition of the church, which was terribly disturbed, and spent the whole of the winter there. It was then that he received the title of Emperor and Augustus, which he so disliked at first that he affirmed that he would not have entered the church on that day—though it was the chief festival of the church—if he could have foreseen the design of the Pope. But when he had taken the title he bore very quietly the hostility that it caused and the indignation of the Roman emperors. He conquered their ill-feeling by his magnanimity, in which, doubtless, he far excelled them, and sent frequent embassies to them, and called them his brothers.

When he had taken the imperial title he noticed many defects in the legal systems of his people; for the Franks have two legal systems differing in many points very widely from one another, and he, therefore, determined to add what was lacking, to reconcile the differences, and to amend anything that was wrong or wrongly expressed. He completed nothing of all his designs beyond adding a few capitularies, and those unfinished. But he gave orders that the laws and rules of all nations comprised within his dominions which were not already written out should be collected and committed to writing.

He also wrote out the barbarous and ancient songs, in which the acts of the kings and their wars were sung, and committed them to memory. He also began a grammar of his native language.

He gave the months names in his own tongue, for before his time they were called by the Franks partly by Latin and partly by barbarous names. He also gave names to the twelve winds, whereas before not more than four, and perhaps not so many, had names of their own. Of the months, he called January Winter-month, February Mud-month, March Spring-month, April Easter-month, May Joy-month, June Plough-month, July Hay-month, August Harvest-month, September Wind-month, October Vintage-month, November Autumn-month, December Holy-month. The following are the names which he gave to the winds:—The Subsolanus (east) he called East Wind; the Eurus (east by south) East-South Wind; the Euroauster (south by east) South-East Wind; the Auster (south) South Wind; the Austro-Afric (south by west) South-West Wind; the Afric (west by south) West-South Wind; the Zephyr (west) West Wind; the

Corus (west by north) West-North Wind; the Circius (north by west) North-West Wind; Septentrion (north) North Wind; the Aquilon (north by east) North-East Wind; the Vulturnus (east by north) East-North Wind.

At the very end of his life, when already he was feeling the pressure of old age and sickness, he summoned his own son Lewis, King of Aquitania, the only surviving son of Hildigard, and then solemnly called together the Frankish nobles of his whole kingdom; and then, with the consent of all, made Lewis partner in the whole kingdom and heir to the imperial title. After that, putting the diadem on his head, he ordered them to salute him "Imperator" and Augustus. This decision of his was received by all present with the greatest favour, for it seemed to them a divine inspiration for the welfare of the realm. It added to his dignity at home and increased the terror of his name abroad.

He then sent his son back to Aquitania, and himself, though broken with old age, proceeded to hunt, as his custom was, not far from the palace of Aix, and after spending the rest of the autumn in this pursuit he came back to Aix about the beginning of November. Whilst he was spending the winter there he was attacked by a sharp fever, and took to his bed. Then, following his usual habit, he determined to abstain from food, thinking that by such self-discipline he would be able either to cure or alleviate the disease. But the fever was complicated by a pain in the side which the Greeks call pleurisy; and, as Charles still persisted in fasting, and only very rarely drank something to sustain his strength, seven days after he had taken to his bed he received holy communion, and died, in the seventy-second year of his life and in the forty-seventh year of his reign, on the fifth day before the Kalends of February, at the third hour of the day.

His body was washed and treated with the usual ceremonies, and then, amidst the greatest grief of the whole people, taken to the church and buried. At first there was some doubt as to where he should rest, since he had given no instructions during his lifetime. But at length all were agreed that he could be buried nowhere more honourably than in the great church which he had built at his own expense in the same town, for the love of our Lord God Jesus Christ and the honour of His holy and ever-virgin Mother. There he was buried on the same day on which he died. A gilded arch was raised above the tomb, with his statue, and an inscription. The inscription ran as follows:—

"Beneath this tomb lies the body of Charles, the great and orthodox Emperor, who nobly expanded the kingdom of the Franks and reigned prosperously for forty-seven years. He departed this life, more than seventy years of age, in the eight hundred and fourteenth year of our lord, in the seventh indiction, on the fifth day before the Kalends of February."

There were many prodigies to show that his end drew near, and he as well as others understood the meanings of their warnings. During all the three last years of his life there were constant eclipses of sun and moon, and a black coloured spot appeared in the sun for the space of seven days. The gallery which he had built, of great size and strength, between the palace and the church, suddenly, on Ascension Day, fell in ruins down to the foundations. Also, the wooden bridge over the Rhine near Mainz, which he had built with wonderful skill, and the labour of ten years, so that it seemed as though it would last for ever, was accidentally set on fire, and in three hours burnt so far that not a plank remained except those that were covered by the water. Further, when he was making his last expedition in Saxony against Godofrid, King of the Danes, as he was moving out of camp and beginning his march before sunrise, he suddenly saw a meteor rush across the heavens with a great blaze and pass from right to left through the clear sky. Whilst all were wondering what this sign meant, suddenly the horse that he was riding fell head foremost, and threw him so violently to the ground that the girdle of his cloak was broken, and his sword belt slipped from it. When his attendants ran up to help him they found him disarmed and disrobed. His javelin, too, which he was holding in his hand at the time of his fall, fell twenty paces and more away from him. Moreover, the palace at Aix was frequently shaken, and in houses where he lived there was a constant creaking in the fretted ceilings. The church in which he was afterwards buried was struck by lightning, and the golden apple that adorned the summit of the roof was thrown down by a thunder-stroke, and fell upon the Bishop's house, which adjoined the church. In the same church an inscription was written on the edge of the circular space which ran round the inside of the church between the upper and lower arches, saying by whom the sacred edifice had been built. And in the last line occurred the words: "Carolus Princeps." Some noticed that in the very year in which Charles died, and a few months before his death, the letters of the word "princeps" were so destroyed as to be quite invisible. But he either refused to notice or despised all these omens as though they had no connection at all with anything that concerned him. . . .

Civilization in the Middle Ages

As classical civilization declined, Europe underwent a gradual change in all aspects of life. By the year 1000 these developments had produced a new era which historians generally have called the later Middle Ages. The social and economic life of the common people centered around the institution of manorialism, while feudalism furnished one of the elements in the political organization. The idea of a universal empire for western Europe survived the collapse of Rome and persisted into modern times. The papacy and the rulers of the Holy Roman Empire vied with one another in an effort to restore such an institution under the respective leadership of each. Christianity permeated every aspect of the culture of the period. Philosophy, literature, art, and even science were brought into a harmonious synthesis with Christian doctrine, further strengthening the unity of Christendom, and offering little opportunity for variation therefrom. Occasionally, however, individuals expressed views in poetry, in government, and even in religion which deviated from the medieval synthesis. While persons within Europe were formulating new ideas and grasping for new intellectual horizons, a few men like Marco Polo were actually going out and discovering what the world beyond Europe was like.

Manorial Documents

Duuring the Middle Ages, the manor was the basic unit of social and economic life in much of Europe. It furnished the nobility with the bulk of their income and gave to the peasants both a place to live and the means of subsistence. As early as the thirteenth century, however, the revival of trade and the reappearance of a money economy began to undermine the long-established relationship between the lord of the manor and his serfs. As a result of these changes money payments began to supplement payments in service and produce; and gradually, too, both lord and bondsman found advantages in terminating the relationship. In the following documents note (1) the methods of paying for manorial holdings, (2) the practice of summarizing the services in terms of money, (3) restrictions placed upon the villeins, (4) the lord's facilities in the manor house, (5) the statement freeing the serf, William of Wythington, (6) his privileges and obligations, and (7) the relationship between the manor and the clergy.

A DESCRIPTION OF THE MANOR OF BERNEHORNE (1307)

Extent of the manor of Bernehorne, made on Wednesday following the feast of St. Gregory the pope, in the thirty-fifth year of the reign of King Edward, in the presence of Brother Thomas, keeper of Marley, John de la More, and Adam de Thruhlegh, clerks, on the oath of William de Gocecoumbe, Walter le Parker, Richard le Knyst, Richard the son of the latter, Andrew of Estone, Stephen Morsprich, Thomas Brembel, William of Swynham, John Pollard, Roger le Glide, John Syward, and John de Lillingewist, who say that there are all the following holdings: . . .

John Pollard holds a half acre in Aldithewisse and owes 18d. at the four terms, and owes for it relief and heriot.

John Suthinton holds a house and 40 acres of land and owes 3s. 6d. at Easter and Michaelmas.

William of Swynham holds 1 acre of meadow in the thicket of Swynham and owes 1d. at the feast of Michaelmas.

Ralph of Leybourne holds a cottage and 1 acre of land in Pinden and owes 3s. at Easter and Michaelmas, and attendance at the court in the manor every three weeks, also relief and heriot.

Richard Knyst of Swynham holds 2 acres and a half of land and owes yearly 4s.

William of Knelle holds 2 acres of land in Aldithewisse and owes yearly 4s.

Roger le Glede holds a cottage and 3 roods of land and owes 2s. 6d. Easter and Michaelmas.

Alexander Hamound holds a little piece of land near Aldewisse and owes 1 goose of the value of 2d.

The sum of the whole rent of the free tenants, with the value of the goose, is 18s. 9d.

They say, moreover, that John of Cayworth holds a house and 30 acres of land, and owes yearly 2s. at Easter and Michaelmas; and he owes a cock and two hens at Christmas of the value of 4d.

And he ought to harrow for 2 days at the Lenten sowing with one man and his own horse and his own harrow, the value of the work being 4d.; and he is to receive from the lord on each day 3 meals, of the value of 5d., and then the lord will be at a loss of 1d. Thus his harrowing is of no value to the service of the lord.

And he ought to carry the manure of the

E. P. Cheyney, ed., *Translations and Reprints from the Original Sources of European History,* III, no. 5, *English Manorial Documents,* University of Pennsylvania Press, Philadelphia, n.d., 8–13; 31–32. Courtesy of the University of Pennsylvania Press.

lord for 2 days with one cart, with his own 2 oxen, the value of the work being 8*d.*; and he is to receive from the lord each day 3 meals at the value as above. And thus the service is worth 3*d.* clear.

And he shall find one man for 2 days, for mowing the meadow of the lord, who can mow, by estimation, 1 acre and a half, the value of the mowing of an acre being 6*d.*: the sum is therefore 9*d.* And he is to receive each day 3 meals of the value given above. And thus that mowing is worth 4*d.* clear.

And he ought to gather and carry that same hay which he has cut, the price of the work being 3*d.*

And he shall have from the lord 2 meals for 1 man, of the value of 1½*d.* Thus the work will be worth 1½*d.* clear.

And he ought to carry the hay of the lord for 1 day with a cart and 3 animals of his own, the price of the work being 6*d.* And he shall have from the lord 3 meals of the value of 2¼*d.* And thus the work is worth 3½*d.* clear.

And he ought to carry in autumn beans or oats for 2 days with a cart and 3 animals of his own, the value of the work being 12*d.* And he shall receive from the lord each day 3 meals of the value given above. And thus the work is worth 7*d.* clear.

And he ought to carry wood from the woods of the lord as far as the manor, for two days in summer, with a cart and 3 animals of his own, the value of the work being 9*d.* And he shall receive from the lord each day 3 meals of the price given above. And thus the work is worth 4*d.* clear.

And he ought to find 1 man for 2 days to cut heath, the value of the work being 4*d.*, and he shall have 3 meals each day of the value given above: and thus the lord will lose, if he receives the service, 3*d.* Thus that mowing is worth nothing to the service of the lord.

And he ought to carry the heath which he has cut, the value of the work being 5*d.* And he shall receive from the lord 3 meals at the price of 2¼*d.* And thus the work will be worth 2¼*d.* clear.

And he ought to carry to Battle, twice in the summer season, each time half a load of grain, the value of the service being 4*d.* And he shall receive in the manor each time 1 meal of the value of 2*d.* And thus the work is worth 2*d* clear.

The totals of the rents, with the value of the hens, is 2*s*, 4*d.*

The total of the value of the works is 2*s*. 3½*d.*, owed from the said John yearly.

William of Cayworth holds a house and 30 acres of land and owes at Easter and Michaelmas 2*s.* rent. And he shall do all customs just as the aforesaid John of Cayworth.

William atte Grene holds a house and 30 acres of land and owes in all things the same as the said John.

Alan atte Felde holds a house and 16 acres of land (for which the sergeant pays to the court of Bixley 2*s.*), and he owes at Easter and Michaelmas 4*s.*, attendance at the manor court, relief, and heriot.

John Lyllingwyst holds a house and 4 acres of land and owes at the two terms 2*s.*, attendance at the manor court, relief, and heriot.

The same John holds 1 acre of land in the fields of Hoo and owes at the two periods 2*s.*, attendance, relief, and heriot.

Reginald atte Denne holds a house and 18 acres of land and owes at the said periods 18*d.*, attendance, relief, and heriot.

Robert of Northehou holds 3 acres of land at Saltcote and owes at the said periods attendance, relief, and heriot.

Total of the rents of the villeins, with the value of the hens, 20*s.*

Total of all the works of these three villeins, 6*s.* 10½*d.*

And it is to be noted that none of the above-named villeins can give their daughters in marriage, nor cause their sons to be tonsured, nor can they cut down timber growing on the lands they hold, without license of the bailiff or sergeant of the lord, and then for building purposes and not otherwise. And after the death of any one of the aforesaid villeins, the lord shall have as a heriot his best animal, if he had any; if, however, he have no living beast, the lord shall have no heriot, as they say. The sons or daughters of the aforesaid villeins shall give, for entrance into the holding after the death of their predecessors, as much as they give of rent per year.

Sylvester, the priest, holds 1 acre of meadow adjacent to his house and owes yearly 3*s.*

Total of the rent of tenants for life, 3s.

Petronilla atte Holme holds a cottage and a piece of land and owes at Easter and Michaelmas—; also, attendance, relief, and heriot.

Walter Herying holds a cottage and a piece of land and owes at Easter and Michaelmas 18d., attendance, relief, and heriot.

Isabella Mariner holds a cottage and owes at the feast of St. Michael 12d., attendance, relief, and heriot.

Jordan atte Melle holds a cottage and 1½ acres of land and owes at Easter and Michaelmas 2s., attendance, relief, and heriot.

William of Batelesmere holds 1 acre of land with a cottage and owes at the feast of St. Michael 3d., and 1 cock and 1 hen at Christmas of the value of 3d., attendance, relief, and heriot.

John le Man holds half an acre of land with a cottage and owes at the feast of St. Michael 2s., attendance, relief, and heriot.

John Werthe holds 1 rood of land with a cottage and owes at the said term 18d., attendance, relief, and heriot.

Geoffrey Caumbreis holds half an acre and a cottage and owes at the said term 18d., attendance, relief, and heriot.

William Hassok holds 1 rood of land and a cottage and owes at the said term 18d., attendance, relief, and heriot.

The same man holds 3½ acres of land and owes yearly at the feast of St. Michael 3s. for all.

Roger Doget holds half an acre of land and a cottage, which were those of R. the miller, and owes at the feast of St. Michael 18d., attendance, relief, and heriot.

Thomas le Brod holds 1 acre and a cottage and owes at the said term 3s., attendance, relief, and heriot.

Agnes of Cayworth holds half an acre and a cottage and owes at the said term 18d., attendance, relief, and heriot. . . .

Total of the rents of the said cottagers, with the value of the hens, 34s. 6d.

And it is to be noted that all the said cottagers shall do as regards giving their daughters in marriage, having their sons tonsured, cutting down timber, paying heriot, and giving fines for entrance, just as John of Cayworth and the rest of the villeins above mentioned.

Note: Fines and penalties, with heriots and reliefs, are worth yearly 5s.

AN ENGLISH MANOR HOUSE (1256)

He received also a sufficient and handsome hall well ceiled with oak. On the western side is a worthy bed, on the ground a stone chimney, a wardrobe, and a certain other small chamber; at the eastern end is a pantry and a buttery. Between the hall and the chapel is a side room. There is a decent chapel covered with tiles, a portable altar, and a small cross. In the hall are four tables on trestles. There are likewise a good kitchen well covered with tiles, with a furnace and ovens, one large, the other small, for cakes, two tables, and alongside the kitchen a small house for baking. Also a new granary covered with oak shingles, and a building in which the dairy is contained; though it is divided. Likewise a chamber suited for clergymen and a necessary chamber. Also a henhouse. These are within the inner gate.

Likewise outside of that gate are an old house for the servants, a good stable, long and divided, and to the east of the principal building, beyond the smaller stable, a solar for the use of the servants. Also a building in which is contained a bed; also two barns, one for wheat and one for oats. These buildings are enclosed with a moat, a wall, and a hedge. Also beyond the middle gate is a good barn, and a stable for cows and another for oxen, these old and ruinous. Also beyond the outer gate is a pigsty.

FREEING OF A SERF (1278)

To all the faithful of Christ to whom the present writing shall come, Richard, by the divine permission, abbot of Peterborough and of the Convent of the same place, eternal greeting in the Lord:

Let all know that we have manumitted and liberated from all yoke of servitude William, the son of Richard of Wythington, whom previously we have held as our born bondman, with his whole progeny and all his chattels, so that neither we nor our successors shall be able to require or exact any right or claim in the said William, his progeny, or his chattels. But the same William, with his whole progeny and all his chattels, shall remain free and quit and without disturbance, exaction, or any claim on the part of us or our successors by reason of any servitude forever.

We will, moreover, and concede that he and his heirs shall hold the messuages, land, rents, and meadows in Wythington which his ancestors held from us and our predecessors, by giving and performing the fine which is called *merchet* for giving his daughter in marriage, and tallage from year to year according to our will,—that he shall have and hold these for the future from us and our successors freely, quietly, peacefully, and hereditarily, by paying to us and our successors yearly 40s. sterling, at the four terms of the year, namely: at St. John the Baptist's day 10s., at Michaelmas 10s., at Christmas 10s., and at Easter 10s., for all service, exaction, custom, and secular demand; saving to us, nevertheless, attendance at our court of Castre every three weeks, wardship, and relief, and outside service of our lord the king, when they shall happen.

And if it shall happen that the said William or his heirs shall die at any time without an heir, the said messuage, land, rents, and meadows with their appurtenances shall return fully and completely to us and our successors. Nor will it be allowed to the said William or his heirs to give, sell, alienate, mortgage, or encumber in any way, the said messuage, land, rents, and meadows, or any part of them, by which the said messuage, land, rents, and meadows should not return to us and our successors in the form declared above. And if this should occur later, their deed shall be declared null, and what is thus alienated shall come to us and our successors. . . .

Given at Borough, for the love of Lord Robert of good memory, once abbot, our predecessor and maternal uncle of the said William. and at the instance of the good man, Brother Hugh of Mutton, relative of the said abbot Robert, A.D. 1278, on the eve of Pentecost.

The English Barons

From the time of the Norman conquest of England in 1066, the powerful barons of the island kingdom had been kept under control by their monarchs, who had gradually succeeded in strengthening and centralizing the royal power. Beginning with the reign of the unpopular king John in 1199, however, the English nobility began to resist and to demand a restoration of their feudal privileges. Disputes with church officials, military defeats in France, and discontent among the London merchants over excessive royal expenditures all helped to weaken John's despotic rule. On June 15, 1215, he was forced to meet with his hostile barons and grant them certain feudal privileges which were written into Magna Carta. Originally the charter's provisions applied only to the small minority of freemen in England, but subsequent confirmations enhanced its importance until it came to be considered as an integral part of the English constitution, guaranteeing certain fundamental liberties. In reading Magna Carta note (1) the rights granted the English church, (2) the clauses clarifying the various feudal relationships, (3) the guarantees of legal and judicial privileges, (4) the political and civil liberties mentioned, (5) any clauses affecting Englishmen other than the nobility, and (6) methods provided for enforcing the provisions of the charter.

W. S. McKechnie, *Magna Carta* . . . , J. Maclehose and Sons, Glasgow, 1914, 216 ff. Courtesy of Hector McKechnie and J. Maclehose and Sons.

MAGNA CARTA

PREAMBLE

John, by the grace of God, king of England, lord of Ireland, duke of Normandy and Aquitaine, and count of Anjou, to the archbishops, bishops, abbots, earls, barons, justiciars, foresters, sheriffs, stewards, servants, and to all his bailiffs and liege subjects, greeting. Know that, having regard to God and for the salvation of our souls, and those of all our ancestors and heirs, and unto the honour of God and the advancement of holy Church, and for the reform of our realm, [we have granted as underwritten] by advice of our venerable fathers, Stephen, archbishop of Canterbury, primate of all England and cardinal of the holy Roman Church, Henry archbishop of Dublin, William of London, Peter of Winchester, Jocelyn of Bath and Glastonbury, Hugh of Lincoln, Walter of Worcester, William of Coventry, Benedict of Rochester, bishops; of master Pandulf, subdeacon and member of the household of our lord the Pope, of brother Aymeric, master of the Knights of the Temple in England, and of the illustrious men William Marshal, earl of Pembroke, William, earl of Salisbury, William, earl Warenne, William, earl of Arundel, Alan of Galloway, constable of Scotland, Waren Fitz Gerald, Peter Fitz Herbert, Hubert de Burgh, seneschal of Poitou, Hugh de Neville, Matthew Fitz Herbert, Thomas Basset, Alan Basset, Philip d'Aubigny, Robert of Roppesley, John Marshal, John Fitz Hugh, and others, our liegemen.

1. In the first place we have granted to God, and by this our present charter confirmed for us and our heirs for ever that the English church shall be free, and shall have her rights entire, and her liberties inviolate; and we will that it be thus observed; which is apparent from this that the freedom of elections, which is reckoned most important and very essential to the English church, we, of our pure and unconstrained will, did grant, and did by our charter confirm and did obtain the ratification of the same from our lord, Pope Innocent III, before the quarrel arose between us and our barons: and this we will observe, and our will is that it be observed in good faith by our heirs for ever. We have also granted to all freemen of our kingdom, for us and our heirs forever, all the underwritten liberties, to be had and held by them and their heirs, of us and our heirs forever.

2. If any of our earls or barons, or others holding of us in chief by military service shall have died, and at the time of his death his heir shall be full of age and owe "relief" he shall have his inheritance on payment of the ancient relief, namely the heir or heirs of an earl, £100 for a whole earl's barony; the heir or heirs of a baron, £100 for a whole barony; the heir or heirs of a knight, 100s. at most for a whole knight's fee; and whoever owes less let him give less, according to the ancient custom of fiefs.

3. If, however, the heir of any one of the aforesaid has been under age and in wardship, let him have his inheritance without relief and without fine when he comes of age.

4. The guardian of the land of an heir who is thus under age, shall take from the land of the heir nothing but reasonable produce, reasonable customs, and reasonable services, and that without destruction or waste of men or goods; and if we have committed the wardship of the lands of any such minor to the sheriff, or to any other who is responsible to us for its issues, and he has made destruction or waste of what he holds in wardship, we will take of him amends, and the land shall be committed to two lawful and discreet men of that fee, who shall be responsible for the issues to us or to him to whom we shall assign them; and if we have given or sold the wardship of any such land to anyone and he has therein made destruction or waste, he shall lose that wardship, and it shall be transferred to two lawful and discreet men of that fief, who shall be responsible to us in like manner as aforesaid.

5. The guardian, moreover, so long as he has the wardship of the land, shall keep up the houses, parks, fishponds, stanks, mills, and other things pertaining to the land, out of the issues of the same land; and he shall restore to the heir, when he has come to full age, all

his land, stocked with ploughs and "wainage,'" according as the season of husbandry shall require, and the issues of the land can reasonably bear.

6. Heirs shall be married without disparagement, yet so that before the marriage takes place the nearest in blood to that heir shall have notice.

7. A widow, after the death of her husband, shall forthwith and without difficulty have her marriage portion and inheritance; nor shall she give anything for her dower, or for her marriage portion, or for the inheritance which her husband and she held on the day of the death of that husband; and she may remain in the house of her husband for forty days after his death, within which time her dower shall be assigned to her.

8. No widow shall be compelled to marry, so long as she prefers to live without a husband; provided always that she gives security not to marry without our consent, if she holds of us, or without the consent of the lord of whom she holds, if she holds of another.

9. Neither we nor our bailiffs shall seize any land or rent for any debt, so long as the chattels of the debtor are sufficient to repay the debt; nor shall the sureties of the debtor be distrained so long as the principal debtor is able to satisfy the debt; and if the principal debtor shall fail to pay the debt, having nothing wherewith to pay it, then the sureties shall answer for the debt; and let them have the lands and rents of the debtor, if they desire them, until they are indemnified for the debt which they have paid for him, unless the principal debtor can show proof that he is discharged thereof as against the said sureties.

10. If one who has borrowed from the Jews any sum, great or small, die before that loan be repaid, the debt shall not bear interest while the heir is under age, of whomsoever he may hold; and if the debt fall into our hands, we will not take anything except the principal sum contained in the bond.

11. And if anyone die indebted to the Jews, his wife shall have her dower and pay nothing of that debt; and if any children of the deceased are left under age, necessaries shall be provided for them in keeping with the holding of the deceased; and out of the residue the debt shall be paid, reserving, however, service due to feudal lords; in like manner let it be done touching debts due to others than Jews.

12. No scutage nor aid shall be imposed on our kingdom, unless by common counsel of our kingdom, except for ransoming our person, for making our eldest son a knight, and for once marrying our eldest daughter; and for these there shall not be levied more than a reasonable aid. In like manner it shall be done concerning aids from the city of London.

13. And the city of London shall have all its ancient liberties and free customs, as well by land as by water; furthermore, we decree and grant that all other cities, boroughs, towns, and ports shall have all their liberties and free customs.

14. And for obtaining the common counsel of the kingdom anent the assessing of an aid, except in the three cases aforesaid, or of a scutage, we will cause to be summoned the archbishops, bishops, abbots, earls, and greater barons, severally by our letters; and we will moreover cause to be summoned generally, through our sheriffs and bailiffs, all others who hold of us in chief, for a fixed date, namely, after the expiry of at least forty days, and at a fixed place; and in all letters of such summons we will specify the reason of the summons. And when the summons has thus been made, the business shall proceed on the day appointed, according to the counsel of such as are present, although not all who were summoned have come.

15. We will not for the future grant to any one licence to take an aid from his own free tenants, except to ransom his body, to make his eldest son a knight, and once to marry his eldest daughter; and on each of these occasions there shall be levied only a reasonable aid.

16. No one shall be distrained for performance of greater service for a knight's fee, or for any other free tenement, than is due therefrom.

17. Common pleas shall not follow our court, but shall be held in some fixed place.

18. Inquests of *novel disseisin*, of *mort d'ancestor*, and of *darrein presentment*, shall not be held elsewhere than in their own county-courts, and that in manner following,—We, or, if we should be out of the realm, our chief

justiciar, will send two justiciars through every county four times a year, who shall, along with four knights of the county chosen by the county, hold said assizes in the county court, on the day and in the place of meeting of that court.

19. And if any of the said assizes cannot be taken on the day of the county court, let there remain of the knights and freeholders, who were present at the county court on that day, as many as may be required for the efficient making of judgments, according as the business be more or less.

20. A freeman shall not be amerced for a slight offence, except in accordance with the degree of the offence; and for a grave offence he shall be amerced in accordance with the gravity of the offence, yet saving always his "contenement"; and a merchant in the same way, saving his "merchandise"; and a villein shall be amerced in the same way, saving his "wainage"—if they have fallen into our mercy: and none of the aforesaid amercements shall be imposed except by the oath of honest men of the neighbourhood.

21. Earls and barons shall not be amerced except through their peers, and only in accordance with the degree of the offence.

22. A clerk shall not be amerced in respect of his lay holding except after the manner of the others aforesaid; further, he shall not be amerced in accordance with the extent of his ecclesiastical benefice.

23. No village or individual shall be compelled to make bridges at river banks, except those who from of old were legally bound to do so.

24. No sheriff, constable, coroners, or others of our bailiffs, shall hold pleas of our Crown.

25. All counties, hundreds, wapentakes, and trithings, except our demesne manors, shall remain at the old rents, and without any additional payment.

26. If any one holding of us a lay fief shall die, and our sheriff or bailiff shall exhibit our letters patent of summons for a debt which the deceased owed to us, it shall be lawful for our sheriff or bailiff to attach and catalogue chattels of the deceased, found upon the lay fief, to the value of that debt, at the sight of lawworthy men, provided always that nothing whatever

be thence removed until the debt which is evident shall be fully paid to us; and the residue shall be left to the executors to fulfil the will of the deceased; and if there be nothing due from him to us, all chattels shall go to the deceased, saving to his wife and children their reasonable shares.

27. If any freeman shall die intestate, his chattels shall be distributed by the hands of his nearest kinsfolk and friends, under supervision of the church, saving to every one the debts which the deceased owed to him.

28. No constable or other bailiff of ours shall take corn or other provisions from any one without immediately tendering money therefor, unless he can have postponement thereof by permission of the seller.

29. No constable shall compel any knight to give money in lieu of castle-guard, when he is willing to perform it in his own person, or if he himself cannot do it from any reasonable cause, then by another responsible man. Further, if we have led or sent him upon military service, he shall be relieved from guard in proportion to the time during which he has been on service because of us.

30. No sheriff or bailiff of ours, or other person, shall take the horses or carts of any freeman for transport duty, against the will of the said freeman.

31. Neither we nor our bailiffs shall take, for our castles or for any other work of ours, wood which is not ours, against the will of the owner of that wood.

32. We will not retain beyond one year and one day, the lands of those who have been convicted of felony, and the lands shall thereafter be handed over to the lords of the fiefs.

33. All kydells [fish-weirs] for the future shall be removed altogether from Thames and Medway, and throughout all England, except upon the sea shore.

34. The writ which is called *praecipe* shall not for the future be issued to anyone, regarding any tenement whereby a freeman may lose his court.

35. Let there be one measure of wine throughout our whole realm; and one measure of ale; and one measure of corn, to wit, "the London quarter"; and one width of cloth whether dyed, or russet, or "halberget," to wit,

two ells within the selvedges; of weights also let it be as of measures.

36. Nothing in future shall be given or taken for a writ of inquisition of life or limbs, but freely it shall be granted, and never denied.

37. If anyone holds of us by fee-farm, by socage, or by burgage, and holds also land of another lord by knight's service, we will not by reason of that fee-farm, socage, or burgage, have the wardship of the heir, or of such land of his as is of the fief of that other; nor shall we have wardship of that fee-farm, socage, or burgage, unless such fee-farm owes knight's service. We will not by reason of any small serjeanty which anyone may hold of us by the service of rendering to us knives, arrows, or the like, have wardship of his heir or of the land which he holds of another lord by knight's service.

38. No bailiff for the future shall, upon his own unsupported complaint, put anyone to his "law," without credible witnesses brought for this purpose.

39. No freeman shall be taken or [and] imprisoned or disseised or exiled or in any way destroyed, nor will we go upon him nor send upon him, except by the lawful judgment of his peers or [and] by the law of the land.

40. To no one will we sell, to no one will we refuse or delay, right or justice.

41. All merchants shall have safe and secure exit from England, and entry to England, with the right to tarry there and to move about as well by land as by water, for buying and selling by the ancient and right customs, quit from all evil tolls, except in time of war such merchants as are of the land at war with us. And if such are found in our land at the beginning of the war, they shall be detained, without injury to their bodies or goods, until information be received by us, or by our chief justiciar, how the merchants of our land found in the land at war with us are treated; and if our men are safe there, the others shall be safe in our land.

42. It shall be lawful in future for any one excepting always those imprisoned or outlawed in accordance with the law of the kingdom, and natives of any country at war with us, and merchants, who shall be treated as is above provided to leave our kingdom and to return, safe and secure by land and water, ex-

cept for a short period in time of war, on grounds of public policy—reserving always the allegiance due to us.

43. If anyone holding of some escheat, such as the honour of Wallingford, Nottingham, Boulogne, Lancaster, or of other escheats which are in our hands and are baronies, shall die, his heir shall give no other relief, and perform no other service to us than he would have done to the baron, if that barony had been in the baron's hand; and we shall hold it in the same manner in which the baron held it.

44. Men who dwell without the forest need not henceforth come before our justiciars of the forest upon a general summons, except those who are impleaded, or who have become sureties for any person or persons attached for forest offences.

45. We will appoint as justices, constables, sheriffs, or bailiffs only such as know the law of the realm and mean to observe it well.

46. All barons who have founded abbeys, concerning which they hold charters from the kings of England, or of which they have long-continued possession, shall have the wardship of them, when vacant, as they ought to have.

47. All forests that have been made such in our time shall forthwith be disafforested; and a similar course shall be followed with regard to river-banks that have been placed "in defence" by us in our time.

48. All evil customs connected with forests and warrens, foresters and warreners, sheriffs and their officers, river-banks and their wardens, shall immediately be inquired into in each county by twelve sworn knights of the same county chosen by the honest men of the same county, and shall, within forty days of the said inquest, be utterly abolished, so as never to be restored, provided always that we previously have intimation thereof, or our justiciar, if we should not be in England.

49. We will immediately restore all hostages and charters delivered to us by Englishmen, as sureties of the peace or of faithful service.

50. We will entirely remove from their bailiwicks, the relations of Gerard of Athée so that in future they shall have no bailiwick in England; namely, Engelard of Cigogné, Peter, Guy, and Andrew of Chanceaux, Guy of Cigogné,

Geoffrey of Martigny with his brothers, Philip Mark with his brothers and his nephew Geoffrey, and the whole brood of the same.

51. As soon as peace is restored, we will banish from the kingdom all foreign-born knights, cross-bowmen, serjeants, and mercenary soldiers, who have come with horses and arms to the kingdom's hurt.

52. If any one has been dispossessed or removed by us, without the legal judgment of his peers, from his lands, castles, franchises, or from his right, we will immediately restore them to him; and if a dispute arise over this, then let it be decided by the five-and-twenty barons of whom mention is made below in the clause for securing the peace. Moreover, for all those possessions, from which any one has, without the lawful judgment of his peers, been disseised or removed, by our father, King Henry, or by our brother, King Richard, and which we retain in our hand or which are possessed by others, to whom we are bound to warrant them, we shall have respite until the usual term of crusaders; excepting those things about which a plea has been raised, or an inquest made by our order, before our taking of the cross; but as soon as we return from our expedition or if perchance we desist from the expedition we will immediately grant full justice therein.

53. We shall have, moreover, the same respite and in the same manner in rendering justice concerning the disafforestation or retention of those forests which Henry our father and Richard our brother afforested, and concerning the wardship of lands which are of the fief of another, namely, such wardships as we have hitherto had by reason of a fief which anyone held of us by knight's service, and concerning abbeys founded on other fiefs than our own, in which the lord of the fee claims to have right; and when we have returned, or if we desist from our expedition, we will immediately grant full justice to all who complain of such things.

54. No one shall be arrested or imprisoned upon the appeal of a woman, for the death of any other than her husband.

55. All fines made with us unjustly and against the law of the land, and all amercements imposed unjustly and against the law of the land, shall be entirely remitted, or else it

shall be done concerning them according to the decision of the five-and-twenty barons of whom mention is made below in the clause for securing the peace, or according to the judgment of the majority of the same, along with the aforesaid Stephen, archbishop of Canterbury, if he can be present, and such others as he may wish to bring with him for this purpose, and if he cannot be present the business shall nevertheless proceed without him, provided always that if any one or more of the aforesaid five-and-twenty barons are in a similar suit, they shall be removed as far as concerns this particular judgment, others being substituted in their places after having been selected by the rest of the same five-and-twenty for this purpose only, and after having been sworn.

56. If we have disseised or removed Welshmen from lands or liberties, or other things, without the legal judgment of their peers in England or in Wales, they shall be immediately restored to them; and if a dispute arise over this, then let it be decided in the marches by the judgment of their peers; for tenements in England according to the law of England, for tenements in Wales according to the law of Wales, and for tenements in the marches according to the law of the marches. Welshmen shall do the same to us and ours.

57. Further, for all those possessions from which any Welshman has, without the lawful judgment of his peers, been disseised or removed by King Henry our father, or King Richard our brother, and which we retain in our hand or which are possessed by others, to whom we are bound to warrant them, we shall have respite until the usual term of crusaders; excepting those things about which a plea has been raised or an inquest made by our order before we took the cross; but as soon as we return, or if perchance we desist from our expedition, we will immediately grant full justice in accordance with the laws of the Welsh and in relation to the foresaid regions.

58. We will immediately give up the son of Llywelyn and all the hostages of Wales, and the charters delivered to us as security for the peace.

59. We will do towards Alexander, King of Scots, concerning the return of his sisters and

his hostages, and concerning his franchises, and his right, in the same manner as we shall do toward our other barons of England, unless it ought to be otherwise according to the charters which we hold from William his father, formerly King of Scots; and this shall be according to the judgment of his peers in our court.

60. Moreover, all these aforesaid customs and liberties, the observance of which we have granted in our kingdom as far as pertains to us towards our men, shall be observed by all of our kingdom, as well clergy as laymen, as far as pertains to them towards their men.

61. Since, moreover, for God and the amendment of our kingdom and for the better allaying of the quarrel that has arisen between us and our barons, we have granted all these concessions, desirous that they should enjoy them in complete and firm endurance for ever, we give and grant to them the underwritten security, namely, that the barons choose five-and-twenty barons of the kingdom, whomsoever they will, who shall be bound with all their might, to observe and hold, and cause to be observed, the peace and liberties we have granted and confirmed to them by this our present Charter, so that if we, or our justiciar, or our bailiffs or any one of our officers, shall in anything be at fault toward anyone, or shall have broken any one of the articles of the peace or of this security, and the offence be notified to four barons of the foresaid five-and-twenty, the said four barons shall repair to us or our justiciar, if we are out of the realm, and, laying the transgression before us, petition to have that transgression redressed without delay. And if we shall not have corrected the transgression or, in the event of our being out of the realm, if our justiciar shall not have corrected it within forty days, reckoning from the time it has been intimated to us or to our justiciar, if we should be out of the realm, the four barons aforesaid shall refer that matter to the rest of the five-and-twenty barons, and those five-and-twenty barons shall, together with the community of the whole land, distrain and distress us in all possible ways, namely, by seizing our castles, lands, possessions, and in any other way they can, until redress has been obtained as they deem fit, saving harmless **our**

own person, and the persons of our queen and children; and when redress has been obtained, they shall resume their old relations toward us. And let whoever in the country desires it, swear to obey the orders of the said five-and-twenty barons for the execution of all the aforesaid matters, and along with them, to molest us to the utmost of his power, and we publicly and freely grant leave to every one who wishes to swear, and we shall never forbid anyone to swear. All those, moreover, in the land who of themselves and of their own accord are unwilling to swear to the twenty-five to help them in constraining and molesting us, we shall by our command compel the same to swear to the effect foresaid. And if any one of the five-and-twenty barons shall have died or departed from the land, or be incapacitated in any other manner which would prevent the foresaid provisions being carried out, those of the said twenty-five barons who are left shall choose another in his place according to their own judgment, and he shall be sworn in the same way as the others. Further, in all matters, the execution of which is intrusted to these twenty-five barons, if perchance these twenty-five are present and disagree about anything, or if some of them, after being summoned, are unwilling or unable to be present, that which the majority of those present ordain or command shall be held as fixed and established, exactly as if the whole twenty-five had concurred in this; and the said twenty-five shall swear that they will faithfully observe all that is aforesaid, and cause it to be observed with all their might. And we shall procure nothing from anyone, directly or indirectly, whereby any part of these concessions and liberties might be revoked or diminished; and if any such thing has been procured, let it be void and null, and we shall never use it personally or by another.

62. And all the ill-will, hatreds, and bitterness that have arisen between us and our men, clergy and lay, from the date of the quarrel, we have completely remitted and pardoned to everyone. Moreover, all trespasses occasioned by the said quarrel, from Easter in the sixteenth year of our reign till the restoration of peace, we have fully remitted to all, both clergy and laymen, and completely forgiven. **as**

far as pertains to us. And, on this head, we have caused to be made for them letters testimonial patent to the lord Stephen, archbishop of Canterbury, of the lord Henry, archbishop of Dublin, of the bishops aforesaid, and of Master Pandulf as touching this security and the concessions aforesaid.

63. Wherefore it is our will, and we firmly enjoin, that the English Church be free, and that the men in our kingdom have and hold all the aforesaid liberties, rights, and concessions, well and peaceably, freely and quietly, fully

and wholly, for themselves and their heirs, of us and our heirs, in all respects and in all places for ever, as is aforesaid. An oath, moreover, has been taken, as well on our part as on the part of the barons, that all these conditions aforesaid shall be kept in good faith and without evil intent. Given under our hand—the above-named and many others being witnesses —in the meadow which is called Runnymede, between Windsor and Staines, on the fifteenth day of June, in the seventeenth year of our reign.

Geoffrey Chaucer

Geoffrey Chaucer (about 1340–1400) was an English poet, soldier, and diplomat of the later Middle Ages, who spent much of his life in study, travel, and the observation of society. During his visits to Italy he read extensively both in classical Latin and in contemporary Italian writings, thus coming into contact with the beginnings of the Renaissance. As a consequence, Chaucer's poems are not only excellent descriptions of medieval life, but they also reflect some of the characteristics of the trend toward a new outlook on life. He is best known for the Canterbury Tales in which he assembled an imaginary group of English pilgrims on their way to visit the shrine of the martyred Thomas Becket. The following selections are from the "Prologue" and the "Pardoner's Tale." In reading them note (1) Chaucer's relationship to the group of pilgrims, (2) the classes of medieval society assembled, (3) their array and occupations, (4) the methods Chaucer used to portray individual character and the character of the English nation, (5) evidences of classical influence on Chaucer, (6) devices he used to emphasize the individual quality of the tales, (7) the Host's proposal and offer, (8) the Pardoner's occupation, (9) the sins he condemned in his sermon, (10) evidences of his hypocrisy, (11) the moral of his tale, and (12) his relations with the other pilgrims.

From: THE CANTERBURY TALES

THE PROLOGUE

When the sweet showers of April fall and shoot
Down through the drought of March to pierce
   the root,
Bathing every vein in liquid power

From which there springs the engendering of
   the flower,
When also Zephyrus with his sweet breath
Exhales an air in every grove and heath
Upon the tender shoots, and the young sun
His half-course in the sign of the *Ram* has run,

As translated by Nevill Coghill in Geoffrey Chaucer, *The Canterbury Tales*, Penguin Books, Baltimore, 1952, 25–40; 42–48; 265–282. Permission of Penguin Books, Ltd., Baltimore and London.

And the small fowl are making melody
That sleep away the night with open eye
(So nature pricks them and their heart en-
gages)
Then people long to go on pilgrimages
And palmers long to seek the stranger strands
Of far-off saints, hallowed in sundry lands,
And specially, from every shire's end
In England, down to Canterbury they wend
To seek the holy blissful martyr, quick
In giving help to them when they were sick.
    It happened in that season that one day
In Southwark, at *The Tabard,* as I lay
Ready to go on pilgrimage and start
For Canterbury, most devout at heart,
At night there came into that hostelry
Some nine and twenty in a company
Of sundry folk happening then to fall
In fellowship, and they were pilgrims all
That towards Canterbury meant to ride.
The rooms and stables of the inn were wide;
They made us easy, all was of the best.
And shortly, when the sun had gone to rest,
By speaking to them all upon the trip
I was admitted to their fellowship
And promised to rise early and take the way
To Canterbury, as you heard me say.
    But none the less, while I have time and
    space,
Before my story takes a further pace,
It seems a reasonable thing to say
What their condition was, the full array
Of each of them, as it appeared to me,
According to profession and degree,
And what apparel they were riding in;
And at a Knight I therefore will begin.
    There was a KNIGHT, a most distinguished
    man,
Who from the day on which he first began
To ride abroad had followed chivalry,
Truth, honor, greatness of heart and courtesy.
He had done nobly in his sovereign's war
And ridden into battle, no man more,
As well in Christian as in heathen places,
And ever honored for his noble graces. . . .
He was of sovereign value in all eyes.
And though so much distinguished, he was
    wise
And in his bearing modest as a maid.
He never yet a boorish thing had said
In all his life to any, come what might;

He was a true, a perfect gentle-knight.
    Speaking of his appearance, he possessed
Fine horses, but he was not gaily dressed.
He wore a fustian tunic stained and dark
With smudges where his armor had left mark;
Just home from service, he had joined our
    ranks
To do his pilgrimage and render thanks.
    He had his son with him, a fine young
    SQUIRE,
A lover and cadet, a lad of fire
With curly locks, as if they had been pressed.
He was some twenty years of age, I guessed.
In stature he was of a moderate length,
With wonderful agility and strength.
He'd seen some service with the cavalry
In Flanders and Artois and Picardy
And had done valiantly in little space
Of time, in hope to win his lady's grace.
He was embroidered like a meadow bright
And full of freshest flowers, red and white.
Singing he was, or fluting all the day;
He was as fresh as is the month of May.
Short was his gown, the sleeves were long and
    wide;
He knew the way to sit a horse and ride.
He could make songs and poems and recite,
Knew how to joust and dance, to draw and
    write.
He loved so hotly that till dawn grew pale
He slept as little as a nightingale.
Courteous he was, lowly and serviceable,
And carved to serve his father at the table.
    There was a YEOMAN with him at his side,
No other servant; so he chose to ride.
This Yeoman wore a coat and hood of green,
And peacock-feathered arrows, bright and keen
And neatly sheathed, hung at his belt the
    while
—For he could dress his gear in yeoman
    style,
His arrows never drooped their feathers low—
And in his hand he bore a mighty bow.
His head was like a nut, his face was brown.
He knew the whole of woodcraft up and down.
A saucy brace was on his arm to ward
It from the bow-string, and a shield and sword
Hung at one side, and at the other slipped
A jaunty dirk, spear-sharp and well-equipped.
A metal of St. Christopher he wore
Of shining silver on his breast, and bore

A hunting-horn, well slung and burnished
    clean,
That dangled from a baldrick of bright green.
He was a proper forester I guess.

    There also was a NUN, a Prioress;
Simple her way of smiling was and coy.
Her greatest oath was only 'By St. Loy!'
And she was known as Madam Eglantyne.
And well she sang a service, with a fine
Intoning through her nose, as was most seemly,
And she spoke daintily in French, extremely,
After the school of Stratford-atte-Bowe;
French in the Paris style she did not know.
At meat her manners were well taught withal;
No morsel from her lips did she let fall,
Nor dipped her fingers in the sauce too deep;
But she could carry a morsel up and keep
The smallest drop from falling on her breast.
For courtliness she had a special zest.
And she would wipe her upper lip so clean
That not a trace of grease was to be seen
Upon the cup when she had drunk; to eat,
She reached a hand sedately for the meat.
She certainly was very entertaining,
Pleasant and friendly in her ways, and strain-
    ing
To counterfeit a courtly kind of grace,
A stately bearing fitting to her place. . . .
    Another NUN, the chaplain at her cell,
Was riding with her, and *three Priests* as well.

    There was a MONK, a leader of the fashions;
Inspecting farms and hunting were his pas-
    sions,
A manly man, to be an Abbot able,
Many the dainty horses in his stable;
His bridle, when he rode, a man might hear
Jingling in a whistling wind as clear,
Aye, and as loud as does the chapel bell
Where my lord Monk was Prior of the cell.
The Rule of good St. Benet or St. Maur
As old and strict he tended to ignore;
He let go by the things of yesterday
And followed the new world's more spacious
    way. . . .

    There was a FRIAR, a wanton one and merry,
A Limiter, a very festive fellow.
In all Four Orders there was none so mellow
As he in flattery and dalliant speech.
He'd fixed up many a marriage, giving each
Of his young women what he could afford her.
He was a noble pillar to his Order.

Highly beloved and intimate was he
With County folk wherever he might be,
And worthy city women with possessions;
For he was qualified to hear confessions,
Or so he said, with more than priestly scope;
He had a special license from the Pope.
Sweetly he heard his penitents at shrift
With pleasant absolution, for a gift. . . .

    There was a MERCHANT with a forking
    beard
And motley dress; high on his horse he sat,
Upon his head a Flemish beaver hat
And on his feet daintily buckled boots.
He told of his opinions and pursuits
In solemn tones, and how he never lost.
The sea should be kept free at any cost
(He thought) upon the Harwich-Holland
    ranges.
He was expert at dabbling in exchanges.
This estimable Merchant so had set
His wits to work, none knew he was in debt,
He was so stately in negotiation,
Loan, bargain and commercial obligation.
He was an excellent fellow all the same;
To tell the truth I do not know his name.

    There was an OXFORD CLERIC too, a stu-
    dent,
Long given to Logic, longer than was prudent;
The horse he had was leaner than a rake,
And he was not too fat, I undertake,
But had a hollow look, a sober air;
The thread upon his overcoat was bare.
He had found no preferment in the church
And he was too unworldly to make search.
He thought far more of having by his bed
His twenty books all bound in black and red,
Of Aristotle and philosophy
Than of gay music, fiddles or finery.
Though a philosopher, as I have told,
He had not found the stone for making
    gold. . . .

    A SERGEANT AT THE LAW who paid his calls,
Wary and wise, for clients at St. Paul's
There also was, of noted excellence.
Discreet he was, a man to reverence,
Or so he seemed, his sayings were so wise.
He often had been Justice of Assize
By letters patent, and in full commission.
His fame and learning and his high position
Had won him many a robe and many a fee.
There was no such conveyancer as he. . . .

A land-owner, a FRANKLIN, had appeared;
White as a daisy-petal was his beard.
A sanguine man, high-colored and benign,
He loved a morning sop of cake in wine.
He lived for pleasure and had always done,
For he was Epicurus' very son,
In whose opinion sensual delight
Was the one true felicity in sight.
As noted as St. Julian was for bounty
He made his household free to all the County.
His bread, his ale were finest of the fine
And no one had a better stock of wine.
His house was never short of bake-meat pies,
Of fish and flesh, and these in such supplies
It positively snowed with meat and drink
And all the dainties that a man could think.
According to the seasons of the year
Changes of dish were ordered to appear.
He kept fat partridges in coops, beyond,
Many a bream and pike were in his pond. . . .
    A HABERDASHER, a DYER, a CARPENTER,
A WEAVER and a CARPET-MAKER were
Among our ranks, all in the livery
Of one impressive guild-fraternity.
They were so trim and fresh their gear would
    pass
For new. Their knives were not tricked out
    with brass
But wrought with purest silver, which
    avouches
A like display on girdles and on pouches.
Each seemed a worthy burgess, fit to grace
A guild-hall with a seat upon the dais. . . .
    They had a COOK with them who stood alone
For boiling chicken with a marrow-bone,
Sharp flavoring-powder and a spice for savor.
He could distinguish London ale by flavor,
And he could roast and seethe and broil and
    fry,
Make good thick soup and bake a tasty pie.
But a great pity, as it seemed to me,
Was that he had an ulcer on his knee.
As for blancmange, he made it with the best.
    There was a SKIPPER hailing from far west;
He came from Dartmouth, so I understood.
He rode a farmer's horse as best he could,
In a woolen gown that reached his knee.
A dagger on a lanyard falling free
Hung from his neck under his arm and down.
The summer heat had tanned his color brown,
And certainly he was an excellent fellow.

Many a draught of vintage, red and yellow,
He'd drawn at Bordeaux, while the vintner
    slept.
Few were the rules his tender conscience kept.
If, when he fought, the enemy vessel sank,
He sent his prisoners home; they walked the
    plank.
As for his skill in reckoning his tides,
Currents and many another risk besides,
Moons, harbors, pilots, he had such dispatch
That none from Hull to Carthage was his
    match. . . .
    A DOCTOR too emerged as we proceeded;
No one alive could talk as well as he did
On points of medicine and of surgery,
For, being grounded in astronomy,
He watched his patient's favorable star
And, by his Natural Magic, knew what are
The lucky hours and planetary degrees
For making charms and magic effigies.
The cause of every malady you'd got
He knew, and whether dry, cold, moist or hot;
He knew their seat, their humor and condition.
He was a perfect practicing physician.
These causes being known for what they were,
He gave the man his medicine then and
    there. . . .
    A worthy WOMAN from beside BATH city
Was with us, somewhat deaf, which was a
    pity.
In making cloth she showed so great a bent
She bettered those of Ypres and of Ghent.
In all the parish not a dame dared stir
Towards the altar steps in front of her,
And if indeed they did, so wroth was she
As to be quite put out of charity.
Her kerchiefs were of finely woven ground;
I dared have sworn they weighed a good ten
    pound,
The ones she wore on Sunday, on her head.
Her hose were of the finest scarlet red
And gartered tight; her shoes were soft and
    new.
Bold was her face, handsome, and red in hue.
A worthy woman all her life, what's more
She'd have five husbands, all at the church
    door,
Apart from other company in youth;
No need just now to speak of that, for-
    sooth.
And she had thrice been to Jerusalem,

Seen many strange rivers and passed over
    them;
She'd been to Rome and also to Boulogne,
St. James of Compostella and Cologne,
And she was skilled in wandering by the way.
She had gap-teeth, set widely, truth to say.
Easily on an ambling horse she sat
Well wimpled up, and on her head a hat
As broad as is a buckler or a shield;
She had a flowing mantle that concealed
Large hips, her heels spurred sharply under
    that.
In company she liked to laugh and chat
And knew the remedies for love's mischances,
An art in which she knew the oldest dances.

    A holy-minded man of good renown
There was, and poor, the PARSON to a town,
Yet he was rich in holy thought and work.
He also was a learned man, a clerk,
Who truly knew Christ's gospel and would
    preach it
Devoutly to parishioners, and teach it.
Benign and wonderfully diligent,
And patient when adversity was sent
(For so he proved in great adversity)
He much disliked extorting tithe or fee,
Nay rather he preferred beyond a doubt
Giving to poor parishioners round about
From his own goods and Easter offerings.
He found sufficiency in little things.
Wide was his parish, with houses far asunder,
Yet he neglected not in rain or thunder,
In sickness or in grief, to pay a call
On the remotest whether great or small
Upon his feet, and in his hand a stave.
This noble example to his sheep he gave,
First following the word before he taught it,
And it was from the gospel he had caught it.
This little proverb he would add thereto
That if gold rust, what then will iron do?
For if a priest be foul in whom we trust
No wonder that a common man should rust;
And shame it is to see—let priests take stock—
A shitten shepherd and a snowy flock.
The true example that a priest should give
Is one of cleanness, how the sheep should live.
He did not set his benefice to hire
And leave his sheep encumbered in the mire
Or run to London to earn easy bread
By singing masses for the wealthy dead,
Or find some Brotherhood and get enrolled.

He stayed at home and watched over his fold
So that no wolf should make the sheep mis-
    carry.
He was a shepherd and no mercenary.
Holy and virtuous he was, but then
Never contemptuous of sinful men,
Never disdainful, never too proud or fine,
But was discreet in teaching and benign.
His business was to show a fair behavior
And draw men thus to Heaven and their
    Saviour,
Unless indeed a man were obstinate;
And such, whether of high or low estate,
He put to sharp rebuke to say the least.
    I think there never was a better priest.
He sought no pomp or glory in his dealings,
No scrupulosity had spiced his feelings.
Christ and His Twelve Apostles and their lore
He taught, but followed it himself before.

    There was a PLOWMAN with him there, his
    brother.
Many a load of dung one time or other
He must have carted through the morning
    dew.
He was an honest worker, good and true,
Living in peace and perfect charity,
And, as the gospel bade him, so did he,
Loving God best with all his heart and mind
And then his neighbor as himself, repined
At no misfortune, slacked for no content,
For steadily about his work he went
To thrash his corn, to dig or to manure
Or make a ditch; and he would help the poor
For love of Christ and never take a penny
If he could help it, and, as prompt as any,
He paid his tithes in full when they were due
On what he owned, and on his earnings too.
He wore a tabard smock and rode a mare.

    There was a REEVE, also a MILLER, there,
A College MANCIPLE from the Inns of Court,
A papal PARDONER and, in close consort,
A Church-Court SUMMONER, riding at a trot,
And finally myself—that was the lot.
    The MILLER was a chap of sixteen stone,
A great stout fellow big in brawn and bone.
He did well out of them, for he could go
And win the ram at any wrestling show.
Broad, knotty and short-shouldered, he would
    boast
He could heave any door off hinge and post,
Or take a run and break it with his head.

His beard, like any sow or fox, was red
And broad as well, as though it were a spade;
And, at its very tip, his nose displayed
A wart on which there stood a tuft of hair
Red as the bristles in an old sow's ear.
His nostrils were as black as they were wide,
He had a sword and buckler at his side,
His mighty mouth was like a furnace door.
A wrangler and buffoon, he had a store
Of tavern stories, filthy in the main.
His was a master-hand at stealing grain. . . .
 There was a Summoner with us in the place
Who had a fire-red cherubinny face,
For he had carbuncles. His eyes were narrow,
He was as hot and lecherous as a sparrow.
Black, scabby brows he had, and a thin beard.
Children were afraid when he appeared. . . .
 He and a gentle Pardoner rode together,
A bird from Charing Cross of the same feather,
Just back from visiting the Court of Rome.
He loudly sang 'Come hither, love, come
 home!'
The Summoner sang deep seconds to this song,
No trumpet ever sounded half so strong.
This Pardoner had hair as yellow as wax
Hanging down smoothly like a hank of flax.
In driblets fell his locks behind his head
Down to his shoulders which they overspread;
Thinly they fell, like rat-tails, one by one.
He wore no hood upon his head, for fun;
The hood inside his wallet had been stowed,
He aimed at riding in the latest mode;
But for a little cap his head was bare
And he had bulging eye-balls, like a hare.
He'd sewed a holy relic on his cap;
His wallet lay before him on his lap,
Brimful of pardons come from Rome all hot.
He had the same small voice a goat has got.
His chin no beard had harbored, nor would
 harbor,
Smoother than ever chin was left by barber.
I judge he was a gelding, or a mare.
As to his trade, from Berwick down to Ware
There was no pardoner of equal grace,
For in his trunk he had a pillow-case
Which he asserted was Our Lady's veil.
He said he had a gobbet of the sail
Saint Peter had the time when he made bold
To walk the waves, till Jesu Christ took hold.
He had a cross of metal set with stones
And, in a glass, a rubble of pigs' bones.

And with these relics, any time he found
Some poor up-country parson to astound,
On one short day, in money down, he drew
More than the parson in a month or two,
And by his flatteries and prevarication
Made monkeys of the priest and congregation.
But still to do him justice first and last
In church he was a noble ecclesiast.
How well he read a lesson or told a story!
But best of all he sang an Offertory,
For well he knew that when that song was
 sung
He'd have to preach and tune his honey-
 tongue
And (well he could) win silver from the
 crowd.
That's why he sang so merrily and loud.
 Now I have told you shortly, in a clause,
The rank, the array, the number and the cause
Of our assembly in this company
In Southwark, at that high-class hostelry
Known as *The Tabard*, close beside *The Bell*.
And now the time has come for me to tell
How we behaved that evening; I'll begin
After we had alighted at the Inn,
Then I'll report our journey, stage by stage,
All the remainder of our pilgrimage.
But first I beg of you, in courtesy,
Not to condemn me as unmannerly
If I speak plainly and with no concealings
And give account of all their words and deal-
 ings,
Using their very phrases as they fell.
For certainly, as you all know so well,
He who repeats a tale after a man
Is bound to say, as nearly as he can,
Each single word, if he remembers it,
However rudely spoken or unfit,
Or else the tale he tells will be untrue,
The things invented and the phrases new.
He may not flinch although it were his brother,
If he says one word he must say the other.
And Christ Himself spoke broad in Holy Writ,
And as you know there's nothing there unfit,
And Plato says, for those with power to read,
'The word should be as cousin to the deed.'
Further I beg you to forgive it me
If I neglect the order and degree
And what is due to rank in what I've planned.
I'm short of wit as you will understand.
 Our Host gave us great welcome; everyone

Was given a place and supper was begun.
He served the finest victuals you could think,
The wine was strong and we were glad to
     drink.
A very striking man our Host withal,
And fit to be a marshal in a hall.
His eyes were bright, his girth a little wide;
There is no finer burgess in Cheapside.
Bold in his speech, yet wise and full of tact,
There was no manly attribute he lacked,
What's more he was a merry-hearted man.
After our meal he jokingly began
To talk of sport, and, among other things
After we'd settled up our reckonings,
He said as follows: 'Truly, gentlemen,
You're very welcome and I can't think when
—Upon my word I'm telling you no lie—
I've seen a gathering here that looked so spry,
No, not this year, as in this tavern now.
I'd think you up some fun if I knew how.
And, as it happens, a thought has just occurred
And it will cost you nothing, on my word.
You're off to Canterbury—well, God speed!
Blessed St. Thomas answer to your need!
And I don't doubt, before the journey's done
You mean to while the time in tales and fun.
Indeed, there's little pleasure for your bones
Riding along and all as dumb as stones.
So let me then propose for your enjoyment,
Just as I said, a suitable employment.
And if my notion suits and you agree
And promise to submit yourselves to me
Playing your parts exactly as I say
Tomorrow as you ride along the way,
Then by my father's soul (and he is dead)
If you don't like it you can have my head!
Hold up your hands, and not another word.'
     Well, our consent of course was not de-
          ferred,
It seemed not worth a serious debate;
We all agreed to it at any rate
And bade him issue what commands he would.
'My lords,' he said, 'now listen for your good,
And please don't treat my notion with disdain.
This is the point, to make it short and plain.
Each one of you shall help to make things slip
By telling two stories on the outward trip
To Canterbury, that's what I intend,
And, on the homeward way to journey's end
Another two, tales from the days of old;
And then the man whose story is best told,

That is to say who gives the fullest measure
Of good morality and general pleasure,
He shall be given a supper, paid by all,
Here in this tavern, in this very hall,
When we come back again from Canterbury.
And in the hope to keep you bright and merry
I'll go along with you myself and ride
All at my own expense and serve as guide.
I'll be the judge, and those who won't obey
Shall pay for what we spend upon the way.
Now if you all agree to what you've heard
Tell me at once without another word,
And I will make arrangements early for it.'
     Of course we all agreed, in fact we swore it
Delightedly, and made entreaty too
That he should act as he proposed to do,
Become our Governor in short, and be
Judge of our tales and general referee,
And set the supper at a certain price.
We promised to be ruled by his advice
Come high, come low; unanimously thus
We set him up in judgment over us.
More wine was fetched, the business being
     done;
We drank it off and up went everyone
To bed without a moment of delay.
     Early next morning at the spring of day
Up rose our Host and roused us like a cock,
Gathering us together in a flock,
And off we rode, at slightly faster pace
Than walking, to St. Thomas' watering-place;
And there our Host drew up, began to ease
His horse, and said, 'Now, listen if you please,
My lords! Remember what you promised me.
If evensong and matins will agree
Let's see who shall be first to tell a tale.
And as I hope to drink good wine and ale
I'll be your judge. The rebel who disobeys,
However much the journey costs, he pays.
Now draw for cut and then we can depart;
The man who draws the shortest cut shall start.
My Lord the Knight,' he said, 'step up to me
And draw your cut, for that is my decree.
And come you near, my Lady Prioress,
And you, Sir Cleric, drop your shamefastness,
No studying now! A hand from every man!'
Immediately the draw for lots began
And to tell shortly how the matter went,
Whether by chance or fate or accident,
The truth is this, the cut fell to the Knight,
Which everybody greeted with delight.

And tell his tale he must, as reason was
Because of our agreement and because
He too had sworn. What more is there to say?
For when the good man saw how matters lay,
Being by wisdom and obedience driven
To keep a promise he had freely given,
He said, 'Since it's for me to start the game,
Why, welcome be the cut in God's good name!
Now let us ride, and listen to what I say.'
And at the word we started on our way. . . .
[The tales of the Knight and others preceding
the Pardoner are omitted.]

THE PARDONER'S TALE

The Pardoner's Prologue

'My lords,' he said, 'in churches where I preach
I cultivate a haughty kind of speech
And ring it out as roundly as a bell;
I've got it all by heart, the tale I tell.
I have a text, it always is the same
And always has been, since I learnt the game,
Old as the hills and fresher than the grass,
Radix malorum est cupiditas.
    'But first I make pronouncement whence I
      come,
Show them my bulls in detail and in sum,
And flaunt the papal seal for their inspection
As warrant for my bodily protection,
That none may have the impudence to irk
Or hinder me in Christ's most holy work.
And then I tell them, as occasion calls,
Some anecdotes of popes and cardinals,
Of patriarchs and even bishops too,
And speak some words in Latin—just a few—
To put a saffron tinge upon my preaching
And stir devotion with a spice of teaching.
Then I bring all my long glass bottles out
Cram-full of bones and ragged bits of clout,
Relics they are, at least for such are known.
Then, cased in metal, I've a shoulder-bone,
Belonging to a sheep, a holy Jew's.
"Good men," I say, "take heed, for here is
    news.
Take but this bone and dip it in a well;
If cow or calf, if sheep or ox should swell
From eating adders or from being stung,
Take water from that well and wash its tongue,
And it will then recover. Furthermore,
Where there is pox or scab or other sore,
All animals that water at that well

Are cured at once. Take note of what I tell.
If the good man—the owner of the stock—
Goes once a week, before the crow of cock,
Fasting, and takes a draught of water too,
Why then, according to that holy Jew,
He'll find his cattle multiply and sell.
    ' "And it's a cure for jealousy as well;
For if your husband's prone to jealous wroth,
Use the same water when you make his broth
And he will always trust you. It's a curtain
On your behavior, though he knew for certain
That several clergy had enjoyed your love.
    ' "Now look; I have a mitten here, a glove.
Whoever wears this mitten on his hand
Will multiply his grain. He sows his land
And up will come abundant wheat or oats,
Providing that he gives me a few groats.
    ' "Good men and women, here's a word of
      warning;
If there is anyone in church this morning
Guilty of sin so far beyond expression
Revolting he's ashamed to make confession,
Or if some woman young or old's in touch
With man, and cuckolding her husband, such
Shall neither have the power nor the grace
To offer to my relics in this place.
But those who can acquit themselves of blame
Can all come up and offer in God's name,
And I will shrive them by the authority
Committed in this papal bull to me."
    'That trick's been worth a hundred marks a
     year
Since I became a Pardoner, never fear.
I stand up in my pulpit with a frown
Like any priest, and when they've all sat down
I preach upon the text you heard before
And tell a hundred lying mockeries more.
I take great pains, and stretching out my neck
To east and west I crane about and peck,
Just like a pigeon sitting on a barn.
My hands and tongue together spin the yarn
And all my antics are a joy to see.
The curse of avarice and cupidity
Is all my sermon, for it frees the pelf.
Out come the pence, and specially for myself,
For my exclusive purpose is to win
And not at all to castigate their sin.
Once dead what matter how their souls may
    fare?
They can go blackberrying, for all I care!
    'Believe me, many a sermon or devotive

Exordium issues from an evil motive.
Some titillate their folk by flattery
Gaining promotion by hypocrisy;
Some preach from vanity and some from hate.
For want of other methods of debate
I sometimes choose a victim for my tongue
And as he can't escape he sits there stung
By slanderous defamation. Thus he's paid
For injuring me, or others of my trade.
For though I never mention him by name
The congregation guesses all the same
From certain hints that everybody knows,
And so I take revenge upon our foes
And spit my venom forth, while I profess
Holy and true—or seeming holiness.
  'But let me briefly make my purpose plain;
I preach for nothing but for greed of gain
And use the same old text, as bold as brass,
Radix malorum est cupiditas.
The vice on which I pour my emphasis
Is what I live by, namely avarice.
And yet however guilty of that sin
Myself, with others I have power to win
Then from it, I can bring them to repent;
But that is not my principal intent.
Covetousness is both the root and stuff
Of all I preach. That ought to be enough.
  'Well, then I give examples thick and fast
From bygone times, old stories from the past;
A yokel mind loves stories from of old,
Being the kind it can repeat and hold.
What! Do you think, as long as I can preach
And get their silver for the things I teach,
That I will live in poverty, from choice?
That's not the counsel of my inner voice!
No! Let me preach and beg from kirk to kirk
And never do an honest job of work,
No, nor make baskets like St. Paul to gain
A livelihood. I do not preach in vain.
Why copy the apostles? Why pretend?
I must have wool, cheese, wheat, and cash to
    spend,
Though it were given me by the poorest lad
Or poorest village widow, though she had
A string of starving children, all agape.
No, let me drink the liquor of the grape
And keep a jolly wench in every town!
  'But listen, gentlemen; to bring things down
To a conclusion, would you like a tale?
Now, as I've drunk a draught of corn-ripe ale,
By God it stands to reason I can strike

On some good story that you all will like.
For, though I am a wholly vicious man,
Don't think I can't tell moral tales. I can!
Here's one I often preach when out for win-
    ning;
Now please be quiet. Here is the beginning.'

THE PARDONER'S TALE

In Flanders once there was a company
Of youngsters haunting vice and ribaldry,
Riot and gambling, stews and public-houses
Where each with harp, guitar or lute carouses,
Dancing and dicing day and night, and bold
To eat and drink far more than they can hold,
Doing thereby the devil sacrifice
Within that devil's temple of cursed vice,
Abominable in superfluity,
With oaths so damnable in blasphemy
That it's a grisly thing to hear them swear.
Our dear Lord's body they will rend and tear
As if the Jews had rent Him not enough;
And at the sin of others every tough
Will laugh, and presently the dancing-girls,
Small pretty ones, come in and shake their
    curls,
With youngsters selling fruit, and ancient
    bawds,
And girls with cakes and music, devil's gauds
To kindle and blow the fires of lechery
That are so close annexed to gluttony.
Witness the Bible, which is most express
That lust is bred of wine and drunkenness.
  Look how the drunken and unnatural Lot
Lay with his daughters, though he knew it not;
He was too drunk to know what he was doing.
  Take Herod too, his tale is worth pursuing.
Replete with wine and feasting, he was able
To give the order at his very table
To kill the innocent Baptist, good St. John.
  Seneca has a thought worth pondering on;
No difference, he says, that he can find
Between a madman who has lost his mind
And one who is habitually mellow
Except that madness, when it takes a fellow,
Lasts longer, on the whole, than drunkenness.
O cursed gluttony, our first distress!
Cause of our first confusion, first temptation,
The very origin of our damnation,
Till Christ redeemed us with his blood again!
O infamous indulgence! Cursed stain
So dearly bought! And what has it been worth?

Gluttony has corrupted all the earth.
  Adam, our father, and his wife no less,
From Paradise to labor and distress
Were driven for that vice, they were indeed.
While she and Adam fasted, so I read,
They were in Paradise; when he and she
Ate of the fruit of that forbidden tree
They were at once cast forth in pain and woe.
O gluttony, it is to thee we owe
Our griefs! O if we knew the maladies
That follow on excess and gluttonies,
Sure we would diet, we would temper pleasure
In sitting down at table, show some measure!
Alas the narrow throat, the tender mouth!
Men labor east and west and north and south
In earth, in air, in water—Why, d'you think?
To get a glutton dainty meat and drink!
How well of this St. Paul's Epistle treats!
'Meats for the belly, belly for the meats,
But God shall yet destroy both it and them.'
Alas, the filth of it! If we contemn
The name, how far more filthy is the act!
A man who swills down vintages in fact
Makes a mere privy of his throat, a sink
For cursed superfluities of drink!
  So the Apostle said, whom tears could
    soften:
'Many there are, as I have told you often,
And weep to tell, whose gluttony sufficed
To make them enemies of the cross of Christ,
Whose ending is destruction and whose God
Their belly!' O thou belly! stinking pod
Of dung and foul corruption, that canst send
Thy filthy music forth at either end,
What labor and expense it is to find
Thy sustenance! These cooks that strain and
    grind
And bray in mortars, transubstantiate
God's gifts into a flavor on a plate
To please a lecherous palate. How they batter
Hard bones to put some marrow on your
    platter,
Spicery, root, bark, leaf—they search and
    cull it
In the sweet hope of flattering a gullet!
Nothing is thrown away that could delight
Or whet anew lascivious appetite.
Be sure a man whom such a fare entices
Is dead indeed, though living in his vices.
  Wine is a lecherous thing and drunkenness
A squalor of contention and distress.
O drunkard, how disfigured is thy face,

How foul thy breath, how filthy thy embrace!
And through thy drunken nose a stertorous
    snort
Like 'samson-samson'—something of the sort.
Yet Samson never was a man to swig.
You totter, lurch and fall like a stuck pig,
Your manhood's lost, your tongue is in a burr.
Drunkenness is the very sepulcher
Of human judgment and articulation.
He that is subject to the domination
Of drink can keep no secrets, be it said.
Keep clear of wine, I tell you, white or red,
Especially Spanish wines which they provide
And have on sale in Fish Street and Cheap-
    side.
That wine mysteriously finds its way
To mix itself with others—shall we say
Spontaneously?—that grow in neighboring re-
    gions.
Out of the mixture fumes arise in legions,
So when a man has had a drink or two,
Though he may think he is at home with you
In Cheapside, I assure you he's in Spain
Where it was made, at Lepé I maintain,
Not even at Bordeaux. He's soon elate
And very near the 'samson-samson' state.
  But seriously, my lords, attention, pray!
All the most notable acts, I dare to say,
And victories in the Old Testament,
Won under God who is omnipotent,
Were won in abstinence, were won in prayer.
Look in the Bible, you will find it there.
  Or else take Atilla the Conqueror;
Died in his sleep, a manner to abhor,
In drunken shame and bleeding at the nose.
A general should live sober, I suppose.
Moreover call to mind and ponder well
What was commanded unto Lemuel
—Not Samuel but Lemuel I said—
Read in the Bible, that's the fountain-head,
And see what comes of giving judges drink.
No more of that. I've said enough, I think.
  Having put gluttony in its proper setting
I wish to warn you against dice and betting.
Gambling's the very mother of robbed purses
Lies, double-dealing, perjury, and curses,
Manslaughter, blasphemy of Christ, and waste
Of time and money. Worse, you are debased
In public reputation, put to shame.
'A common gambler' is a nasty name.
  The more exalted such a man may be
So much the more contemptible is he.

A gambling prince would be incompetent
To frame a policy of government,
And he will sink in general opinion
As one unfit to exercise dominion.

    Stilbon, that wise ambassador whose mission
Took him to Corinth, was of high position;
Sparta had sent him with intent to frame
A treaty of alliance. When he came,
Hoping for reinforcement and advice,
It happened that he found them all at dice,
Their very nobles; so he quickly planned
To steal away, home to his native land.
He said, 'I will not lose my reputation
Or compromise the honor of my nation
By asking dicers to negotiate.
Send other wise ambassadors of state,
For on my honor I would rather die
Than be a means for Corinth to ally
With gamblers; Corinth, glorious in honor,
Shall take no such alliances upon her
As dicers make, by any act of mine!'
He showed his sense in taking such a line.

    Again, consider King Demetrius;
The King of Parthia—history has it thus—
Sent him a pair of golden dice in scorn,
To show he reckoned him a gambler born
Whose honor, if unable to surmount
The vice of gambling, was of no account.
Lords can amuse themselves in other ways
Honest enough, to occupy their days.

      Now let me speak a word or two of
      swearing
And perjury; the Bible is unsparing.
It's an abominable thing to curse
And swear, it says; but perjury is worse.
Almighty God has said, 'Swear not at all,'
Witness St. Matthew, and you may recall
The words of Jeremiah, having care
To what he says of lying: 'Thou shalt swear
In truth, in judgment and in righteousness.'
But idle swearing is a sin, no less.
Behold and see the tables of the Law
Of God's Commandments, to be held in
      awe;
Look at the third where it is written plain,
'Thou shalt not take the name of God in vain.'
You see He has forbidden swearing first;
Not murder, no, nor other thing accurst
Comes before that, I say, in God's commands.
That is the order; he who understands
Knows that the third commandment is just
      that.

And in addition, let me tell you flat,
Vengeance on him and all his house shall fall
That swears outrageously, or swears at all.
'God's precious heart and passion, by God's
      nails
And by the blood of Christ that is at Hailes,
Seven's my luck, and yours is five and three;
God's blessed arms! If you play false with me
I'll stab you with my dagger!' Overthrown
By two small dice, two bitching bits of bone,
They reach rage, perjury, cheating, homicide.
O for the love of Jesu Christ who died
For us, abandon curses, small or great!
But, sirs, I have a story to relate.

    It's of three rioters I have to tell
Who, long before the morning service bell,
Were sitting in a tavern for a drink.
And as they sat, they heard the hand-bell
      clink
Before a coffin being borne to church.
One called the tavern-lad and with a lurch
Said to him, 'Run along and ask—look spry—
Whose corpse is in that coffin passing by;
And see you get the name correctly too.'
'Sir,' said the boy, 'no need, I promise you;
Two hours before you came here I was told.
He was a friend of yours in days of old,
But suddenly killed last night in an attack,
There on the bench, dead drunk and on his
      back.
There came a privy thief, they call him Death,
Who kills us all round here, and in a breath
He speared him through the heart; he never
      stirred.
And then Death went his way without a word.
He's killed a thousand in the present plague,
And, sir, it doesn't do to be too vague
If you should meet him; you had best be wary.
Be on your guard with such an adversary,
Be primed to meet him everywhere you go,
That's what my mother said. It's all I know.'

    The publican joined in with, 'By St. Mary.
What the child says is right; you'd best be
      wary,
This very year he killed, in a large village
A mile away, man, woman, serf at tillage,
Page in the household, children—all there
      were.
Yes, I imagine that he lives round there.
It's well to be prepared in these alarms,
He might do dirt on you.' 'What's that? God's
      arms!'

The rioter said, 'Is he so fierce to meet?
I'll search for him, by Jesus, street by street.
God's blessed bones! I'll register a vow!
Here, chaps! The three of us together now,
Hold up your hands, like me, and we'll be
    brothers
In this affair, and each defend the others.
We'll kill this double-crosser Death, I say;
Away with him as he has made away
With all our friends. God's dignity! To-night!'
    They made their bargain, swore with ap-
    petite,
These three, to live and die for one another
As brother-born might swear to his born
    brother.
And up they started in their drunken rage
And made towards this village which the page
And publican had spoken of before.
Many and grisly were the oaths they swore,
Tearing Christ's blessed body to a shred;
'If we can only catch him, Death is dead!'
    When they had gone not fully half a mile,
Just as they were about to cross a stile,
They came upon a very poor old man
Who humbly greeted them and thus began,
'God look to you, my lords, and give you quiet!'
To which the proudest of these men of riot
Gave back the answer, 'What, old fool? Give
    place!
Why are you all wrapped up except your face?
Why live so long? Isn't it time to die?'
    The old, old fellow looked him in the eye
And said, 'Because I never yet have found,
Though I have walked to India, searching
    round
Village and city on my pilgrimage,
One who would change his youth to have my
    age.
And so my age is mine and must be still
Upon me, for such time as God may will.
    'Not even Death, alas, will take my life;
So, like a wretched prisoner at strife
Within himself, I walk alone and wait
About the earth, which is my mother's gate,
Knock-knocking with my staff from night to
    noon
And crying, "Mother, open to me soon!
Look at me, mother, won't you let me in?
See how I wither, flesh and blood and skin!
Alas! When will these bones be laid to rest?
Mother, I would exchange—for that were
    best—
The wardrobe in my chamber, standing there

So long, for yours! Aye, for a shirt of hair
To wrap me in!" She has refused her grace,
Whence comes the pallor of my withered face.
    'But it dishonored you when you began
To speak so roughly, sir, to an old man,
Unless he had injured you in word or deed.
It says in holy writ, as you may read,
"Thou shalt rise up before the hoary head
And honor it." And therefore be it said
"Do no more harm to an old man than you,
Being now young, would have another do
When you are old"—if you should live till
    then.
And so may God be with you, gentlemen,
For I must go whither I have to go.'
    'By God,' the gambler said, 'you shan't do
    so,
You don't get off so easy, by St. John!
I heard you mention, just a moment gone,
A certain traitor Death who singles out
And kills the fine young fellows hereabout.
And you're his spy, by God! You wait a bit.
Say where he is or you shall pay for it,
By God and by the Holy Sacrament!
I say you've joined together by consent
To kill us younger folk, you thieving swine!'
    'Well, sir,' he said, 'if it be your design
To find out Death, turn up this crooked way
Towards that grove. I left him there to-day
Under a tree, and there you'll find him wait-
    ing.
He isn't one to hide for all your prating.
You see that oak? He won't be far to find.
And God protect you that redeemed mankind,
Aye, and amend you!' Thus that ancient man.
    At once the three young rioters began
To run, and reached the tree, and there they
    found
A pile of golden florins on the ground,
New-coined, eight bushels of them as they
    thought.
No longer was it Death those fellows sought,
For they were all so thrilled to see the sight,
The florins were so beautiful and bright,
That down they sat beside the precious pile.
The wickedest spoke first after a while.
'Brothers,' he said, 'you listen to what I say.
I'm pretty sharp, although I joke away.
It's clear that Fortune has bestowed this
    treasure
So as to let us live our lives in pleasure.
Light come, light go! We'll spend it as we
    ought.

God's precious dignity! Who would have
    thought
This morning was to be our lucky day?
  'If one could only get the gold away,
Back to my house, or else to yours, perhaps—
For as you know, the gold is ours, chaps—
We'd all be at the top of fortune, hey?
But certainly it can't be done by day.
People would call us robbers—a strong gang,
So our own property would make us hang.
No; we must bring this treasure back by night
Some prudent way, and keep it out of sight.
And so as a solution I propose
We draw for lots and see the way it goes.
The one who draws the longest, lucky man,
Shall run to town as quickly as he can
To fetch us bread and wine—but keep things
    dark—
While two remain in hiding here to mark
Our heap of treasure. If there's no delay,
When night comes down we'll carry it away,
All three of us, wherever we have planned.'

  He gathered lots and hid them in his hand
Bidding them draw for where the luck should
    fall.
It fell upon the youngest of them all,
And off he ran at once towards the town.

  As soon as he had gone the first sat down
And thus began a parley with the other:
'You know that you can trust me as a brother;
Let me point out the advantage to you there.
Our friend has gone, as you are well aware,
And here's a lot of gold that is to be
Divided equally amongst us three.
Nevertheless, if I could shape things thus
So that we shared it out—the two of us—
Wouldn't you take it as a friendly turn?'

  'How?' said the other. 'Maybe I can learn,
But still he knows the gold's with me and you;
What can we tell him? What are we to do?'

  'Is it a bargain,' said the first, 'or no?
For I can tell you in a word or so
What's to be done to bring the thing about.'
'Trust me,' the other said, 'you needn't doubt
My word. I won't betray you, I'll be true.'

  'Well,' said his friend, 'you see that we are
    two,
And two are twice as powerful as one.
Now look; when he comes back, get up in fun
And have a wrestle with him, just a rag;
Then I'll jump up and slice him through the
    bag
While he is struggling, thinking it a game;

You draw your dagger too and do the same.
Then all this money will be ours to spend,
Divided equally of course, dear friend.
Then we can gratify our lusts and fill
The day with dicing at our own sweet will.'
Thus these two miscreants agreed to slay
The third and youngest, as you heard me say.

  The youngest, as he ran towards the town,
Kept turning over, rolling up and down
Within his heart the beauty of those bright
New florins, saying, 'Lord, to think I might
Have all that treasure to myself alone!
Could there be anyone beneath the throne
Of God so happy as I then should be?'

  And so the Fiend, our common enemy,
Was given power to put it in his thought
That there was always poison to be bought,
And that with poison he could kill his friends.
To men in such a state the Devil sends
Thoughts of this kind, and has a full permis-
    sion
To lure them on to sorrow and perdition;
For this young man was utterly content
To kill them both and never to repent.

  And on he ran, he had no thought to tarry,
Came to the town, found an apothecary
And said, 'Sell me some poison if you will,
I have a lot of rats I want to kill
And there's a polecat too about my yard
That takes my chickens and it hits me hard;
But I'll get even, as is only right,
With vermin that destroy a man by night.'

  The chemist answered, 'I've a preparation
Which you shall have, and by my soul's salva-
    tion
If any living creature eat or drink
A mouthful, ere he has the time to think,
Though he took less than makes a grain of
    wheat,
You'll see him fall down dying at your feet;
Yes, die he must, and in so short a while
You'd hardly have the time to walk a mile,
The poison is so strong, you understand.'

  This cursed fellow grabbed into his hand
The box of poison and away he ran
Into a neighboring street, and found a man
Who lent him three large bottles. He withdrew
And deftly poured the poison into two.
He kept the third one clean, as well he might,
For his own drink, meaning to work all night
Stacking the gold and carrying it away.
And when this rioter, this devil's clay,
Had filled his bottles up with wine, all three,

Then back to join his comrades sauntered he.
Why make a sermon of it? Why waste
breath?
Exactly in the way they'd planned his death
They fell on him and slew him, two to one.
Then said the first of them when this was
done,
'Now for a drink. Sit down and let's be merry,
For later on there'll be the corpse to bury.'
And, as it happened, reaching for a sup,
He took a bottle full of poison up
And drank; and his companion, nothing loth,
Drank from it also, and they perished both.
There is, in Avicenna's long relation
Concerning poison and its operation,
Trust me, no ghastlier section to transcend
What these two wretches suffered at their end.
Thus these two murderers received their due,
So did the treacherous young poisoner too.
O cursed sin! O blackguardly excess!
O treacherous homicide! O wickedness!
O gluttony that lusted on and diced!
O blasphemy that took the name of Christ
With habit-hardened oaths that pride began!
Alas, how comes it that a mortal man,
That thou, to thy Creator, Him that wrought
thee,
That paid His precious blood for thee and
bought thee,
Art so unnatural and false within?
Dearly beloved, God forgive your sin
And keep you from the vice of avarice!
My holy pardon frees you all of this,
Provided that you make the right approaches,
That is with sterling, rings, or silver brooches.
Bow down your heads under this holy bull!
Come on, you women, offer up your wool!
I'll write your name into my ledger; so!
Into the bliss of Heaven you shall go.
For I'll absolve you by my holy power,
You that make offering, clean as at the hour
When you were born. . . . That, sirs, is how
I preach.
And Jesu Christ, soul's healer, aye, the leech
Of every soul, grant pardon and relieve you
Of sin, for that is best, I won't deceive you.
One thing I should have mentioned in my
tale,
Dear people. I've some relics in my bale
And pardons to, as full and fine I hope
As any in England, given me by the Pope.

If there be one among you that is willing
To have my absolution, for a shilling
Devoutly given, come! and do not harden
Your hearts, but kneel in humbleness for
pardon;
Or else, receive my pardon as we go.
You can renew it every town or so,
Always provided that you still renew
Each time, and in good money, what is due.
It is an honor for you to have found
A pardoner with his credentials sound,
Who can absolve you, as you ply the spur,
In any accident that may occur.
For instance—we are all at Fortune's beck—
Your horse may throw you down and break
your neck.
What a security it is to all
To have me here among you and at call
With pardon for the lowly and the great,
When soul leaves body for the future state!
And I advise our Host here to begin,
The most enveloped of you all in sin.
Come forward, Host, you shall be first to pay,
And kiss my holy relics right away.
Only a groat. Come on, unbuckle your purse!'
'No, no,' said he, 'not I, and may the curse
Of Christ descend upon me if I do!
You'll have me kissing your old breeches too
And swear they were the relic of a saint
Although your fundament supplied the paint!
Now by St. Helen and the Holy Land
I wish I had your cullions in my hand
Instead of relics in a reliquarium;
Have them cut off and I will help to carry 'em.
We'll have them shrined for you in a hog's
turd.'
The Pardoner said nothing, not a word;
He was so angry that he couldn't speak.
'Well,' said our Host, 'if you're for showing
pique,
I'll joke no more, not with an angry man.'
The worthy Knight immediately began,
Seeing the fun was getting rather rough,
And said, 'No more, we've all had quite
enough.
Now, Master Pardoner, perk up, look cheerly!
And you, Sir Host, whom I esteem so dearly,
I beg of you to kiss the Pardoner.
'Come, Pardoner, draw nearer, my dear sir.
Let's laugh again and keep the ball in play.'
They kissed, and we continued on our way.

Dante Alighieri

D ante Alighieri (1265–1321) was a Florentine who wrote the Divina Commedia, one of the greatest literary works in the Italian language. He was also very active in the political life of the day, and was one of those who opposed the extension of the pope's secular power. When the papacy in its struggle with the Holy Roman Empire triumphed in Dante's native city, however, the great writer was forced into exile. Convinced that factional political strife should be removed from Italy, he wrote De Monarchia to espouse the cause of unity under the temporal rule of the emperor. In taking this stand, Dante was not opposed to the Church, as such, but only to some of its claims to complete supremacy in Christendom. In the following selections note (1) the question Dante proposed to investigate, (2) the three classes of men who opposed the truth he sought to establish, (3) the arguments advanced to support the supremacy of the papacy, (4) how Dante attempted to refute these claims, (5) the character of the authorities he cited in his arguments, and (6) the source and character of the claims he made for the emperor.

From: DE MONARCHIA

"He has shut the lions' mouths and they have not hurt me; inasmuch as before Him righteousness was found in me." In beginning this work I proposed to investigate three questions as far as the subject-matter would allow. For the first two questions this has been done satisfactorily in the foregoing books, I believe. We must now consider the third, the truth of which may, however, be a cause of indignation against me, since it cannot be brought forth without causing certain men to blush. But since Truth from her immutable throne demands it; and Solomon entering his forest of *Proverbs,* and marking out his own conduct, entreats that we "meditate upon truth and abhor wickedness;" and our teacher of morals, the Philosopher, admonishes us to sacrifice whatever is most precious for truth's sake: therefore, gaining assurance from the words of Daniel, wherein the power of God is shown as a shield for defenders of truth, and "putting on the breastplate of faith" according to the admonition of Paul, in the warmth of that coal taken from the heavenly altar by one of the Seraphim and touched to the lips of Isaiah, I will engage in the present conflict, and by the arm of Him who with His blood liberated us from the power of darkness, I will cast the ungodly and the liar from the arena, while the world looks on. Wherefore should I fear, when the Spirit, coeternal with the Father and the Son, says by the mouth of David, "The righteous shall be in everlasting remembrance, he shall not be afraid of evil tidings"?

The question pending investigation, then, concerns two great luminaries, the Roman Pontiff and the Roman Prince: and the point at issue is whether the authority of the Roman Monarch, who, as proved in the second book, is rightful Monarch of the world, derives from God directly, or from some vicar or minister of God, by whom I mean the successor of Peter, veritable keeper of the keys of the kingdom of heaven. . . .

As translated by Aurelia Henry in *The De Monarchia of Dante Alighieri,* Houghton Mifflin Company, Boston and New York, 1904, 135–137; 140–148; 164–182; and 196–206. Courtesy of Dr. Paul Henry Reinhardt and Houghton Mifflin Company.

In entering on this third question, let us bear in mind that the truth of the first was made manifest in order to abolish ignorance rather than contention. But the investigation of the second had reference alike to ignorance and contention. Indeed, we are ignorant of many things concerning which we do not contend: the geometrician does not know the square of the circle, but he does not contend about it; the theologian does not know the number of the angels, but he renders it no cause for quarrel; the Egyptian knows naught of the civilization of Scythia, but does not therefore make the civilization a source of strife.

Now the truth of the third question has to do with so keen a contention that, whereas ignorance generally causes the discord, here the discord causes ignorance. For it always happens to men who will things before rationally considering them that, their desire being evil, they put behind them the light of reason; as blind men they are led about by their desire, and stubbornly deny their blindness. Whence it often occurs not only that falsehood has her own patrimony, but that many men going out from her boundaries run through strange camps, where, neither understanding nor being understood at all, they provoke some to wrath, some to disdain, and not a few to laughter.

Three classes of men struggle hardest against the truth which we would establish.

First the Chief Pontiff, Vicar of our Lord Jesus Christ and successor to Peter, he to whom we should render not what is due to Christ but what is due to Peter, he, perchance in his zeal for the keys, together with some pastors of Christian flocks, and others moved solely, I believe, by their zeal for Mother Church, contradict the truth I am about to declare. They contradict it, perchance, from zeal, I repeat, not from pride.

But others in their inveterate cupidity have quenched the light of reason, and call themselves sons of the Church, although they are of their father the devil. Not only do they arouse controversy in regard to this question, but, despising the very name of the most sacred Princehood, impudently deny the first principles of this and the previous questions.

The third class, called Decretalists, utterly ignorant and unregardful of Theology and Philosophy, depending entirely on the *Decretals* (which, I grant, are deserving of veneration), and I presume trusting in the ultimate supremacy of these, derogate from the imperial power. Nor is it to be wondered at, for I have heard one of them aver and insolently maintain that ecclesiastical traditions are the foundation of faith. Let those dispel this error of thought from mortal minds whom the world doubts not to have believed in Christ, the Son of God, ere ecclesiastical traditions were, believed in Him either to come, or present, or having already suffered, and believing hoped, and hoping burned with love, and burning with love were made co-heirs with Him.

And that such mistaken thinkers may be wholly shut out from the present discussion, it must be observed that some of the Scriptures take precedence of the Church, some are equivalent to the Church, and some subordinate to it.

Those taking precedence of the Church are the Old and New Testaments, which, as the Prophet says, "were commanded for ever," and to which the Church refers in saying to the Bridegroom, "Draw me after thee."

Equivalent to the Church are those Councils so worthy of reverence, and in the midst of which no believer doubts the presence of Christ; for we have, according to Matthew's testimony, the words spoken to His disciples at His ascension into heaven: "Lo, I am with you alway, even unto the end of the world." In addition, there are the writings of the Doctors, Augustine, and others, and whosoever doubts the aid of the Holy Spirit therein has never seen their fruits, or if he has seen, has never tasted them.

Subordinate to the Church are the traditions called Decretals, which, while they must be revered for their apostolic authority, must nevertheless be held unquestionably inferior to the fundamental Scriptures, seeing that Christ rebuked the priests for not so doing. When they had inquired, "Why do thy disciples transgress the tradition of the elders?" (for they had omitted the washing of hands) Christ answered, as Matthew testifies, "Why do ye also transgress the commandment of God by your tradition?" Here the inferiority of tradition is clearly implied.

If, as we believe, traditions of the Church are subordinate to the Church, authority necessarily accrues not to the Church through traditions, but to traditions through the Church. And I repeat, those who have faith in traditions alone are excluded from this discussion. For they who would hunt down this truth must start in their search from those writings whence the authority of the Church emanates.

Others must likewise be excluded who, decked in the plumage of ravens, boast themselves white sheep of the Master's flock. In order to carry out their crimes, these sons of impiety defile their mother, banish their brethren, and scorn judgments brought against them. Why should reason be sought in behalf of these whose passions prevent them from understanding our basic principle?

There remains, then, the controversy with those only who, led by a certain zeal for their Mother the Church, are blind to the truth we are seeking. And with them, confident in that reverence which a loyal and loving son owes to father and mother, to Christ and the Church, to the Shepherd and all who profess the Christian religion, I enter in this book into combat for the preservation of truth. . . .

From the same gospel they quote the saying of Christ to Peter, "Whatsoever thou shalt loose on earth shall be loosed in heaven," and understand this saying to refer alike to all the Apostles, according to the text of Matthew and John. They reason from this that the successor of Peter has been granted of God power to bind and loose all things, and then infer that he has power to loose the laws and decrees of the Empire, and to bind the laws and decrees of the temporal kingdom. Were this true, their inference would be correct.

But we must reply to it by making a distinction against the major premise of the syllogism which they employ. Their syllogism is this: Peter had power to bind and loose all things; the successor of Peter has like power with him; therefore the successor of Peter has power to loose and bind all things. From this they infer that he has power to loose and bind the laws and decrees of the Empire.

I concede the minor premise, but the major

only with distinction. Wherefore I say that "all," the symbol of the universal, which is implied in "whatsoever," is never distributed beyond the scope of the distributed term. When I say, "All animals run," the distribution of "all" comprehends whatever comes under the genus "animal." But when I say, "All men run," the symbol of the universal only refers to whatever comes under the term "man." And when I say, "All grammarians run," the distribution is narrowed still further.

Therefore we must always determine what it is over which the symbol of the universal is distributed; then, from the recognized nature and scope of the distributed term, will be easily apparent the extent of the distribution. Now, were "whatsoever" to be understood absolutely when it is said, "Whatsoever thou shalt bind," he would certainly have the power they claim; nay, he would have even greater power, he would be able to loose a wife from her husband, and, while the man still lived, bind her to another—a thing he can in no wise do. He would be able to absolve me, while impenitent—a thing which God himself cannot do.

So it is evident that the distribution of the term under discussion is to be taken, not absolutely, but relatively to something else. A consideration of the concession to which the distribution is subjoined will make manifest this related something. Christ said to Peter, "I will give unto thee the keys of the kingdom of heaven"; that is, "I will make thee doorkeeper of the kingdom of heaven." Then He adds, "and whatsoever," that is, "everything which," and He means thereby, "Everything which pertains to that office thou shalt have power to bind and loose." And thus the symbol of the universal which is implied in "whatsoever" is limited in its distribution to the prerogative of the keys of the kingdom of heaven. Understood thus, the proposition is true, but understood absolutely, it is obviously not. Therefore I conclude that although the successor of Peter has authority to bind and loose in accordance with the requirements of the prerogative granted to Peter, it does not follow, as they claim, that he has authority to bind and loose the decrees or statutes of Empire, unless they prove that this also belongs to the office of the keys. But we shall demonstrate farther on that the contrary is true.

They quote also the words in Luke which Peter addressed to Christ, saying, "Behold, here are two swords," and they assert that the two ruling powers were predicted by those two swords, and because Peter declared they were "where he was," that is, "with him," they conclude that according to authority these two ruling powers abide with Peter's successor.

To refute this we must show the falsity of the interpretation on which the argument is based. Their assertion that the two swords which Peter designated signify the two ruling powers before spoken of, we deny outright, because such an answer would have been at variance with Christ's meaning, and because Peter replied in haste, as usual, with regard to the mere external significance of things.

A consideration of the words preceding it and of the cause of the words will show that such an answer would have been inconsistent with Christ's meaning. Let it be called to mind that this response was made on the day of the feast, which Luke mentions earlier, saying, "Then came the day of unleavened bread, when the passover must be killed." At this feast Christ had already foretold His impending passion, in which He must be parted from His disciples. Let it be remembered also that when these words were uttered, all the twelve disciples were together; wherefore a little after the words just quoted Luke says, "And when the hour was come, He sat down, and the twelve Apostles with Him." Continuing the discourse from this place he reaches the words, "When I sent you without purse, and scrip, and shoes, lacked ye anything?" And they answered, "Nothing." Then said He unto them, "But now, he that hath a purse, let him take it, and likewise his scrip: and he that hath no sword, let him sell his garment, and buy one." The meaning of Christ is clear enough here. He did not say, "Buy or procure two swords," but "twelve;" for it was in order that each of the twelve disciples might have one that He said to them, "He that hath no sword, let him buy one." And He spake thus to forewarn them of the persecution and contempt the future **should** bring, as though He would say, "While I **was with** you ye were welcomed, now shall ye

be turned away. It behooves you, therefore, to prepare for yourselves those things which before I denied to you, but for which there is present need." If Peter's reply to these words had carried the meaning ascribed to it, the meaning would have been at variance with that of Christ, and Christ would have censured him, as He did oftentimes, for his witless answers. However, He did not do so, but assented, saying to him, "It is enough," meaning, "I speak because of necessity; but if each cannot have a sword, two will suffice."

And that Peter usually spoke of the external significance of things is shown in his quick and unthinking presumption, impelled, I believe, not only by the sincerity of his faith, but by the purity and simplicity of his nature. To this characteristic presumption all those who write of Christ bear witness.

First, Matthew records that when Jesus had inquired of the disciples: "Whom say ye that I am?" before all the others Peter replied, "Thou art Christ, the Son of the living God." He also records that when Christ was telling His disciples how He must go to Jerusalem and suffer many things, Peter took Him and began to rebuke Him, saying, "Be it far from thee, Lord: this shall not be unto thee." Then Christ, turning to him, said in reproof, "Get thee behind me, Satan." Matthew also writes that on the Mount of Transfiguration, in the presence of Christ, Moses, and Elias, and the two sons of Zebedee, Peter said, "Lord, it is good for us to be here. If thou wilt, let us make here three tabernacles, one for thee, one for Moses, and one for Elias." Matthew further writes that when the disciples were on the ship in the night, and Christ walked on the water, Peter said, "Lord, if it be thou, bid me come unto thee on the water." And that when Christ predicted how all His disciples should be offended because of Him, Peter answered, "Though all men shall be offended because of thee, yet will I never be offended." And afterwards, "Though I should die with thee, yet will I not deny thee." And this statement Mark confirms, while Luke writes that, just before the words we have quoted concerning the swords, Peter had said to Christ, "Lord, I am ready to go with thee, both into prison and to death."

John tells of him, that when Christ desired

to wash his feet, Peter asked, "Lord, dost thou wash my feet?" and then said, "Thou shalt never wash my feet." He further relates how Peter smote with his sword the servant of the High Priest, an account in which the four Evangelists agree. And John tells how when Peter came to the sepulchre and saw the other disciples lingering at the door, he entered in straightway; and again when after the resurrection Jesus stood on the shore and Peter "heard that it was the Lord, he girt his fisher's coat unto him (for he was naked), and did cast himself into the sea." Lastly, he recounts that when Peter saw John, he said to Jesus, "Lord, and what shall this man do?"

It is a source of joy to have summed up this evidence of our Head Shepherd, in praise of his singleness of purpose. From all this it is obvious that when he spoke of the two swords, his answer to Christ was unambiguous in meaning.

Even if the words of Christ and Peter are to be accepted typically, they cannot be interpreted in the sense these men claim, but rather as referring to the sword concerning which Matthew writes: "Think not that I am come to send peace on earth: I came not to send peace, but a sword. For I am come to set a man at variance against his father," and what follows. This He accomplished in word and deed, wherefore Luke tells Theophilus of all "that Jesus began to do and teach." Such was the sword Christ enjoined them to buy, and Peter made answer that already they had two with them. As we have shown, they were ready for words and for works to bring to pass those things which Christ proclaimed He had come to do by the sword.

In addition, some persons affirm that the Emperor Constantine, healed of leprosy by the intercession of Sylvester, then the Supreme Pontiff, gave to the Church the very seat of Empire, Rome, together with many imperial dignities. Wherefore they argue that no one has power to assume these dignities except he receives them from the Church, to whom it is asserted they belong. And from this it would fairly follow, as they desire, that one authority is dependent on the other.

So having stated and refuted the arguments which seemed to be rooted in divine commu-

nications, it now remains to set forth and disprove those rooted in Roman deeds and human reason. We have just spoken of the first of these, whose syllogism runs thus: Those things which belong to the Church no one can rightly possess, unless granted them by the Church; and this we concede. The ruling power of Rome belongs to the Church; therefore no one can rightly possess it unless granted it by the Church. And the minor premise they prove by the facts mentioned above concerning Constantine.

This minor premise, then, I deny. Their proof is no proof, for Constantine had not the power to alienate the imperial dignity, nor had the Church power to receive it. Their insistent objection to what I say can be met thus. No one is free to do through an office assigned him anything contrary to the office, for thereby the same thing, in virtue of being the same, would be contrary to itself, which is impossible. But to divide the Empire would be contrary to the office assigned the Emperor, for as is easily seen from the first book of the treatise, his office is to hold the human race subject to one will in all things. Therefore, division of his Empire is not allowed an Emperor. If, as they claim, certain dignities were alienated by Constantine from the Empire and ceded to the power of the Church, the "seamless coat" would have been rent, which even they had not dared to mutilate who with their spears pierced Christ, the very God. Moreover, as the Church has its own foundation, so has the Empire its own. The foundation of the Church is Christ, as the Apostle writes to the Corinthians: "Other foundation can no man lay than that is laid, which is Jesus Christ." He is the rock on which the Church is founded, but the foundation of the Empire is human Right. Now I say that as the Church cannot act contrary to its foundation, but must be supported thereby, according to that verse of the *Canticles*: "Who is she that cometh up from the desert, abounding in delights, leaning on her beloved?" so the Empire cannot act in conflict with human Right. Therefore the Empire may not destroy itself, for, should it do so, it would act in conflict with human Right. Inasmuch as the Empire consists in the indivisibility of universal Monarchy, and inasmuch as an apportionment of the Empire would destroy it, it is evident that division is not allowed to him who discharges imperial duty. And it is proved, from what has been previously said, that to destroy the Empire would be contrary to human Right.

Besides, every jurisdiction exists prior to its judge, since the judge is ordained for the jurisdiction, and not conversely. As the Empire is a jurisdiction embracing in its circuit the administration of justice in all temporal things, so it is prior to its judge, who is Emperor; and the Emperor is ordained for it, not conversely. Clearly the Emperor, as Emperor, cannot alter the Empire, for from it he receives his being and state. So I say, either he was Emperor when he made the concession they speak of to the Church, or he was not. If he was not, it is plain that he had no power to grant anything with regard to the Empire. And if he was, then as Emperor he could not have done this, for the concession would have narrowed his jurisdiction.

Further, if one Emperor has power to cut away one bit from the jurisdiction of the Empire, another may do the same for like reason. And since temporal jurisdiction is finite, and every finite thing may be consumed by finite losses, the possibility of annihilating primal jurisdiction would follow. But this is inconceivable.

And since he who confers a thing has the relation of agent, and he on whom it is conferred the relation of patient, according to the Philosopher in the fourth book to *Nicomachus*, then in order for a grant to be legal, proper qualification is essential not only in the giver, but in the recipient. Indeed, it seems that the acts of agents exist potentially in a properly qualified patient. But the Church was utterly disqualified for receiving temporal power by the express prohibitive command in Matthew: "Provide neither gold, nor silver, nor brass in your purses, nor scrip for your journey," etc. For although we learn from Luke of the mitigation of this order regarding certain things, yet I am unable to find that sanction was given the Church to possess gold and silver, subsequent to the prohibition. Wherefore if the Church had not power to receive, even had Constantine power to bestow, temporal authority, the action

would nevertheless be impossible, because of the disqualification of the patient. It is demonstrated, then, that neither could the Church accept by way of possession, nor could Constantine confer by way of alienation. However, the Emperor did have power to depute to the protectorship of the Church a patrimony and other things, as long as his supreme command, the unity of which suffers no impairment, remained unchanged. And the Vicar of God had power to receive such things, not for possession, but for distribution on behalf of the Church of its fruits to the poor of Christ. We are not ignorant that thus the Apostles did.

Still further, our opponents say that Pope Hadrian called Charles the Great to the aid of himself and the Church, because of oppression by the Lombards in the reign of Desiderius their king, and that from the Pope Charles received the dignity of Empire, notwithstanding the fact that Michael held imperial sway at Constantinople. Wherefore they declare that after Charles all Roman Emperors were advocates of the Church, and must be called to office by the Church. From this would follow the relationship between the Church and Empire which they desire to prove.

To refute this argument, I answer that their premise in it is a mere nullity, for usurpation of right does not create a right. If it did, the same method would show the dependency of ecclesiastical authority on the Empire, after the Emperor Otto restored Pope Leo, and deposed Benedict, sending him in exile to Saxony. . . .

Although by the method of reduction to absurdity it has been shown . . . that the authority of Empire has not its source in the Chief Pontiff, yet it has not been fully proved, save by an inference, that its immediate source is God, seeing that if the authority does not depend on the Vicar of God, we conclude that it depends on God Himself. For a perfect demonstration of the proposition we must prove directly that the Emperor, or Monarch, of the world has immediate relationship to the Prince of the universe, who is God.

In order to realize this, it must be understood that man alone of all beings holds the middle place between corruptibility and incorruptibility, and is therefore rightly compared by philosophers to the horizon which lies between the two hemispheres. Man may be considered with regard to either of his essential parts, body or soul. If considered in regard to the body alone, he is perishable; if in regard to the soul alone, he is imperishable. So the Philosopher spoke well of its incorruptibility when he said in the second book *on the Soul*, "And this only can be separated as a thing eternal from that which perishes."

If man holds a middle place between the perishable and imperishable, then, inasmuch as every mean shares the nature of the extremes, man must share both natures. And inasmuch as every nature is ordained for a certain ultimate end, it follows that there exists for man a two-fold end, in order that as he alone of all beings partakes of the perishable and the imperishable, so he alone of all beings should be ordained for two ultimate ends. One end is for that in him which is perishable, the other for that which is imperishable.

Ineffable Providence has thus designed two ends to be contemplated of man: first, the happiness of this life, which consists in the activity of his natural powers, and is prefigured by the terrestrial Paradise; and then the blessedness of life everlasting, which consists in the enjoyment of the countenance of God, to which man's natural powers may not attain unless aided by divine light, and which may be symbolized by the celestial Paradise.

To these states of blessedness, just as to diverse conclusions, man must come by diverse means. To the former we come by the teachings of philosophy, obeying them by acting in conformity with the moral and intellectual virtues; to the latter through spiritual teachings which transcend human reason, and which we obey by acting in conformity with the theological virtues, Faith, Hope, and Charity. Now the former end and means are made known to us by human reason, which the philosophers have wholly explained to us; and the latter by the Holy Spirit, which has revealed to us supernatural but essential truth through the Prophets and Sacred Writers, through Jesus Christ, the coeternal Son of God, and through His disciples. Nevertheless, human passion would cast all these behind, were not men, like horses, astray in their brutishness, held to the road by bit and rein.

Wherefore a twofold directive agent was necessary to man, in accordance with the twofold end; the Supreme Pontiff to lead the human race to life eternal by means of revelation, and the Emperor to guide it to temporal felicity by means of philosophic instruction. And since none or few—and these with exceeding difficulty—could attain this port, were not the waves of seductive desire calmed, and mankind made free to rest in the tranquillity of peace, therefore this is the goal which he whom we call the guardian of the earth and Roman Prince should most urgently seek; then would it be possible for life on this mortal threshing-floor to pass in freedom and peace. The order of the world follows the order inherent in the revolution of the heavens. To attain this order it is necessary that instruction productive of liberality and peace should be applied by the guardian of the realm, in due place and time, as dispensed by Him who is the ever present Watcher of the whole order of the heavens. And He alone foreordained this order, that by it in His providence He might link together all things, each in its own place.

If this is so, and there is none higher than He, only God elects and only God confirms. Whence we may further conclude that neither those who are now, nor those who in any way whatsoever have been, called Electors have the right to be so called; rather should they be entitled heralds of divine providence. Whence it is that those in whom is vested the dignity of proclamation suffer dissension among themselves at times, when, all or part of them being shadowed by the clouds of passion, they discern not the face of God's dispensation.

It is established, then, that the authority of temporal Monarchy descends without mediation from the fountain of universal authority. And this fountain, one in its purity of source, flows into multifarious channels out of the abundance of its excellence.

Methinks I have now approached close enough to the goal I had set myself, for I have taken the kernels of truth from the husks of falsehood, in that question which asked whether the office of Monarchy was essential to the welfare of the world, and in the next which made inquiry whether the Roman people rightfully appropriated the Empire, and in the last which sought whether the authority of the Monarch derived from God immediately, or from some other. But the truth of this final question must not be restricted to mean that the Roman Prince shall not be subject in some degree to the Roman Pontiff, for felicity that is mortal is ordered in a measure after felicity that is immortal.

Wherefore let Caesar honor Peter as a first-born son should honor his father, so that, refulgent with the light of paternal grace, he may illumine with greater radiance the earthly sphere over which he has been set by Him who alone is Ruler of all things spiritual and temporal.

Peter Abelard

Peter Abelard (1074–1142) was a French monk, scholar, and philosopher who sought to apply logic to the teachings of the medieval church. Of a naturally skeptical frame of mind, he objected strenuously to the practice of citing numerous authorities in order to prove a religious truth. He was particularly struck by the obvious contradictions on matters of doctrine to be found in the writings of the early church fathers. In his famous work, Sic et Non, he presented one hundred and fifty-eight points of dogma, and then showed how the authorities contradicted themselves on each point. He maintained that logic could satisfactorily explain these discrepancies, thus attempting to bring reason to the support of faith. As a result of Abelard's work, theologians since his day have had to do more than merely quote authority to achieve a rational justification of faith. In reading the following summary of Sic et Non note (1) the explanations suggested for the many seeming contradictions in the writings of the church fathers, (2) the possibility of the fathers erring, (3) the position Abelard took in regard to the scriptures, (4) his statement of what he had done, (5) his opinion regarding Aristotle, and (6) the types of questions on which he found conflicting opinions.

From: SIC ET NON

There are many seeming contradictions and even obscurities in the innumerable writings of the church fathers. Our respect for their authority should not stand in the way of an effort on our part to come at the truth. The obscurity and contradictions in ancient writings may be explained upon many grounds, and may be discussed without impugning the good faith and insight of the fathers. A writer may use different terms to mean the same thing, in order to avoid a monotonous repetition of the same word. Common, vague words may be employed in order that the common people may under-

James Harvey Robinson, *Readings in European History.* . . . 2 vols., Ginn and Company, Boston, 1904, I, 450–452. Courtesy of Ginn and Company.

stand; and sometimes a writer sacrifices perfect accuracy in the interest of a clear general statement. Poetical, figurative language is often obscure and vague.

Not infrequently, apocryphal works are attributed to the saints. Then, even the best authors often introduce the erroneous views of others and leave the reader to distinguish between the true and the false. Sometimes, as Augustine confesses in his own case, the fathers ventured to rely upon the opinions of others.

Doubtless, the fathers might err; even Peter, the prince of the apostles, fell into error; what wonder that the saints do not always show themselves inspired? The fathers did not themselves believe that they, or their companions, were always right. Augustine found himself mistaken in some cases and did not hesitate to retract his errors. He warns his admirers not to look upon his letters as they would upon the Scriptures, but to accept only those things which, upon examination, they find to be true.

All writings belonging to this class are to be read with full freedom to criticise, and with no obligation to accept unquestioningly; otherwise the way would be blocked to all discussion, and posterity be deprived of the excellent intellectual exercise of debating difficult questions of language and presentation. But an explicit exception must be made in the case of the Old and New Testaments. In the Scriptures, when anything strikes us as absurd, we may not say that the writer erred, but that the scribe made a blunder in copying the manuscripts, or that there is an error in interpretation, or that the passage is not understood. The fathers make a very careful distinction between the Scriptures and later works. They advocate a discriminating, not to say suspicious, use of the writings of their own contemporaries.

In view of these considerations, I have ventured to bring together various dicta of the holy fathers, as they came to mind, and to formulate certain questions which were suggested by the seeming contradictions in the statements. These questions ought to serve to excite tender readers to a zealous inquiry into truth and so sharpen their wits. The master key of knowledge is, indeed, a persistent and frequent questioning. Aristotle, the most clear-sighted of all the philosophers, was desirous above all things else to arouse this questioning spirit, for in his *Categories* he exhorts a student as follows: "It may well be difficult to reach a positive conclusion in these matters unless they be frequently discussed. It is by no means fruitless to be doubtful on particular points." By doubting we come to examine, and by examining we reach the truth.

[The following will serve as examples of the questions Abelard raised in the *Yea and Nay:*]

Should human faith be based upon reason, or no?

Is God one, or no?

Is God a substance, or no?

Does the first Psalm refer to Christ, or no?

Is sin pleasing to God, or no?

Is God the author of evil, or no?

Is God all-powerful, or no?

Can God be resisted, or no?

Has God free will, or no?

Was the first man persuaded to sin by the devil, or no?

Was Adam saved, or no?

Did all the apostles have wives except John, or no?

Are the flesh and blood of Christ in very truth and essence present in the sacrament of the altar, or no?

Do we sometimes sin unwillingly, or no?

Does God punish the same sin both here and in the future, or no?

Is it worse to sin openly than secretly, or no?

Council of Florence

The sacraments, representing outward signs of inward grace, were, according to Christian tradition, instituted by Christ. In the first centuries of the church's development little attention was given to a scholarly interpretation of them, and neither their number nor their character was accurately expressed. With the revival of learning in the eleventh and twelfth centuries, however, and the development of skepticism in regard to contradictory Christian teaching, a renewed interest in the sacraments developed. In the twelfth century Peter Lombard in his Book of Sentences defined apparently for the first time the number of the sacraments as seven. In 1439, at the Council of Florence the sacraments were both enumerated and defined in the Decree for the Armenians. In reading this decree note (1) the number and character of the sacraments, (2) the three things necessary to make them effective, (3) the persons qualified to administer the various sacraments and the benefits derived from each, and (4) the sources from which the nature of the sacraments was derived.

From: THE DECREE FOR THE ARMENIANS

We have drawn up in the briefest form a statement of the truth concerning the seven sacraments, so that the Armenians, now and in future generations, may more easily be instructed therein.

There are seven sacraments under the new law: that is to say, baptism, confirmation, the mass, penance, extreme unction, ordination, and matrimony. These differ essentially from the sacraments of the old law; for the latter do not confer grace, but only typify that grace which can be given by the passion of Christ alone. But these our sacraments both contain grace and confer it upon all who receive them worthily.

The first five sacraments are intended to secure the spiritual perfection of every man individually; the two last are ordained for the governance and increase of the Church. For through baptism we are born again of the spirit; through confirmation we grow in grace and are strengthened in the faith; and when we have been born again and strengthened we are fed by the divine food of the mass; but if, through sin, we bring sickness upon our souls, we are made spiritually whole by penance; and by extreme unction we are healed, both spiritually and corporeally, according as our souls have need; by ordination the Church is governed and multiplied spiritually; by matrimony it is materially increased.

To effect these sacraments three things are necessary: the things [or symbols], that is, the "material"; the words, that is, the "form"; and the person of the "ministrant," who administers the sacrament with the intention of carrying out what the Church effects through him. If any of these things be lacking, the sacrament is not accomplished.

Three of these sacraments—baptism, confirmation, and ordination—impress indelibly upon the soul a character, a certain spiritual sign, distinct from all others; so they are not

James Harvey Robinson, *Readings in European History.* . . . 2 vols., Ginn and Company, Boston, 1904, I, 348–354. Courtesy of Ginn and Company.

repeated for the same person. The other four do not imprint a character upon the soul, and admit of repetition.

Holy baptism holds the first place among all the sacraments because it is the gate of spiritual life; for by it we are made members of Christ and of the body of the Church. Since through the first man death entered into the world, unless we are born again of water, and of the spirit, we cannot, so saith Truth, enter into the kingdom of heaven. The material of this sacrament is water, real and natural—it matters nothing whether it be cold or warm. Now the form is: "I baptize thee in the name of the Father, and of the Son, and of the Holy Ghost.". . .

The ministrant of this sacrament is the priest, for baptism belongs to his office. But in case of necessity not only a priest or deacon may baptize, but a layman or a woman —nay, even a pagan or a heretic, provided he use the form of the Church and intend to do what the Church effects. The efficacy of this sacrament is the remission of all sin, original sin and actual, and of all penalties incurred through this guilt. Therefore no satisfaction for past sin should be imposed on those who are baptized; but if they die before they commit any sin, they shall straightway attain the kingdom of heaven and the sight of God.

The second sacrament is confirmation. The material is the chrism made from oil, which signifies purity of conscience, and from balsam, which signifies the odor of fair fame; and it must be blessed by the bishop. The form is: "I sign thee with the sign of the cross and confirm thee with the chrism of salvation, in the name of the Father, and of the Son, and of the Holy Ghost." The proper ministrant of this sacrament is the bishop. While a simple priest avails to perform the other anointings, this one none can confer save the bishop only; for it is written of the apostles alone that by the laying on of hands they gave the Holy Ghost, and the bishops hold the office of the apostles. We read in the Acts of the Apostles, when the apostles who were at Jerusalem heard how Samaria had received the word of God, they sent to them Peter and John; who, when they were

come, prayed that they might receive the Holy Ghost; for as yet it was fallen upon none of them,—they were only baptized in the name of the Lord Jesus. Then they laid hands upon them and they received the Holy Ghost. Now, in place of this laying on of hands, confirmation is given in the Church. Yet we read that sometimes, for reasonable and urgent cause, by dispensation from the Holy See, a simple priest has been permitted to administer confirmation with a chrism prepared by a bishop.

In this sacrament the Holy Ghost is given to strengthen us, as it was given to the apostles on the day of Pentecost, that the Christian may confess boldly the name of Christ. And therefore he is confirmed upon the brow, the seat of shame, that he may never blush to confess the name of Christ and especially his cross, which is a stumbling-block to the Jews and foolishness to the Gentiles, according to the apostle. Therefore he is signed with the sign of the cross.

The third sacrament is the eucharist. The material is wheaten bread and wine of the grape, which before consecration should be mixed very sparingly with water; because, according to the testimony of the holy fathers and doctors of the Church set forth in former times in disputation, it is believed that the Lord himself instituted this sacrament with wine mixed with water, and also because this corresponds with the accounts of our Lord's passion. For the holy Pope Alexander, fifth from the blessed Peter, says, "In the offerings of sacred things made to God during the solemnization of the mass, only bread and wine mixed with water are offered up. Neither wine alone nor water alone may be offered up in the cup of the Lord, but both mixed, since it is written that both blood and water flowed from Christ's side."

Moreover the mixing of water with the wine fitly signifies the efficacy of this sacrament, namely, the union of Christian people with Christ, for water signifies "people," according to the passage in the Apocalypse which says, "many waters, many people." And Julius, second pope after the blessed Sylvester, says: "According to the provisions of the canons the cup of the Lord should be offered filled with wine mixed with water, because a people is signified by the water, and in the wine is manifested the blood of Christ. Therefore when the wine and water are mixed in the cup the people are joined to Christ, and the host of the faithful is united with him in whom they believe."

Since, therefore, the holy Roman Church, instructed by the most blessed apostles Peter and Paul, together with all the other churches of the Greeks and Latins in which glowed the light of sanctity and of doctrine, has from the beginning of the nascent Church observed this custom and still observes it, it is quite unseemly that any region whatever should depart from this universal and rational observance. We decree, therefore, that the Armenians likewise shall conform themselves with the whole Christian world, and that their priests shall mix a little water with the wine in the cup of oblation.

The form of this sacrament is furnished by the words of the Saviour when he instituted it, and the priest, speaking in the person of Christ, consummates this sacrament. By virtue of these words, the substance of the bread is turned into the body of Christ and the substance of the wine into his blood. This is accomplished in such wise that the whole Christ is altogether present under the semblance of the bread and altogether under the semblance of the wine. Moreover, after the consecrated host and the consecrated wine have been divided, the whole Christ is present in any part of them. The benefit effected by this sacrament in the souls of those who receive it worthily is the union of man with Christ. And since, through grace, man is made one body with Christ and united in his members, it follows that through this sacrament grace is increased in those who partake of it worthily. Every effect of material food and drink upon the physical life, in nourishment, growth, and pleasure, is wrought by this sacrament for the spiritual life. By it we recall the beloved memory of our Saviour; by it we are withheld from evil, and strengthened in good, and go forward to renewed growth in virtues and graces.

The fourth sacrament is penance. The material, as we may say, consists in the acts of penitence, which are divided into three parts.

The first of these is contrition of the heart, wherein the sinner must grieve for the sins he has committed, with the resolve to commit no further sins. Second comes confession with the mouth, to which it pertains that the sinner should make confession to his priest of all the sins he holds in his memory. The third is satisfaction for sins according to the judgment of the priest, and this is made chiefly by prayer, fasting, and almsgiving. The form of this sacrament consists in the words of absolution which the priest speaks when he says, "I absolve thee," etc.; and the minister of this sacrament is the priest, who has authority to absolve either regularly or by the commission of a superior The benefit of this sacrament is absolution from sins.

The fifth sacrament is extreme unction, and the material is oil of the olive, blessed by a bishop. This sacrament shall not be given to any except the sick who are in fear of death. They shall be anointed in the following places: the eyes on account of the sight, the ears on account of the hearing, the nostrils on account of smell, the mouth on account of taste and speech, the hands on account of touch, the feet on account of walking, and the loins as the seat of pleasure. The form of this sacrament is as follows: "Through this holy unction and his most tender compassion, the Lord grants thee forgiveness for whatever sins thou hast committed by the sight,"—and in the same way for the other members. The minister of this sacrament is a priest. The benefit is even the healing of the mind and, so far as is expedient, of the body also. Of this sacrament the blessed apostle James says: "Is any sick among you? Let him call for the elders of the church and let them pray over him, anointing him with oil in the name of the Lord: and the prayer of faith shall save the sick, and the Lord shall raise him up; and if he have committed sins, they shall be forgiven him."

The sixth sacrament is ordination. The material for the priesthood is the cup with the wine and the paten with the bread; for the deaconate, the books of the Gospel; for the subdeaconate, an empty cup placed upon an empty paten; and in like manner, other offices are conferred by giving to the candidates those things which pertain to their secular ministrations. The form for priests is this: "Receive the power to offer sacrifice in the Church for the living and the dead, in the name of the Father, and of the Son, and of the Holy Ghost." And so for each order the proper form shall be used, as fully stated in the Roman pontifical. The regular minister of this sacrament is a bishop; the benefit, growth in grace, to the end that whosoever is ordained may be a worthy minister.

The seventh sacrament is matrimony, the type of the union of Christ and the Church, according to the apostle, who saith, "This is a great mystery; but I speak concerning Christ and the church." The efficient cause of marriage is regularly the mutual consent uttered aloud on the spot. These advantages are to be ascribed to marriage: first, the begetting of children and their bringing up in the worship of the Lord; secondly, the fidelity that husband and wife should each maintain toward the other; thirdly, the indissoluble character of marriage, for this typifies the indissoluble union of Christ and the Church. Although for the cause of adultery separation is permissible, for no other cause may marriage be infringed, since the bond of marriage once legitimately contracted is perpetual.

Thomas Aquinas

Thomas Aquinas (1225–1274) accepted, as did other scholastic philosophers of his day, the challenge to Christian learning resulting from the large-scale introduction of Greek and Arabic science to the West at the moment when Peter Lombard, Gratian, and others had produced a definitive formulation of truth revealed by God in the Scriptures. By the thirteenth century, Latin learning had been absorbed without detriment to the church; could the same task be accomplished for Greek and Arabic learning? Many churchmen recoiled from the problem of attempting a reconciliation of these apparent irreconcilables; but to their eternal credit such scholars as Albert Magnus and his pupil, Thomas Aquinas, convinced that there could be no real conflict between revealed truth and rational truth, took the whole of knowledge as their province and systematically brought it into subjection to Christian theology. The great achievement of Thomas was in demonstrating that the truths of Christianity were not inconsistent with the secular learning of the Greeks and Arabs. In his greatest work, the Summa Theologica, from which the following selection is taken, Thomas raised 631 questions and answered each by quoting from authorities and by the use of logic. Contrary opinions were elaborated, followed by a harmonizing conclusion. In the Summa, Thomas answered 10,000 objections to his conclusions. In the selection, note (1) Thomas's scholastic method, (2) his answers to whether the existence of God is self-evident and whether it can be demonstrated that God exists, (3) the objections to the existence of God, and (4) the proof from authority and logic.

As translated by the Fathers of the English Dominican Province in *The "Summa Theologica" of St. Thomas Aquinas,* Benziger Brothers, New York, 1911, Part I, First Number, Q. II, 19–27. Courtesy of Benziger Brothers.

WHETHER GOD EXISTS

FIRST ARTICLE.

WHETHER THE EXISTENCE OF GOD IS SELF-EVIDENT?

We proceed thus to the First Article:—

Objection 1. It seems that the Existence of God is self-evident. Those things are said to be self-evident to us the knowledge of which is naturally implanted in us, as we can see in regard to first principles. But the Damascene says that, *the knowledge of God is naturally implanted in all.* Therefore the Existence of God is self-evident.

Obj. 2. Further, those things are said to be self-evident which are known as soon as the terms are known, which the Philosopher says is true of the first principles of demonstration. Thus, when the nature of a whole and of a part is known, it is at once recognized that every whole is greater than its part. But as soon as the signification of the word 'God' is understood, it is at once seen that God exists. For by this word is signified that thing than which nothing greater can exist. But that which exists actually and mentally is greater than that which exists only mentally. Therefore, because as soon as the word 'God' is understood it exists mentally, it also follows that it exists actually. Therefore the proposition that God exists is self-evident.

Obj. 3. Further, the existence of Truth is self-evident; for whoever denies the existence of Truth concedes that Truth does not exist. Now, if Truth does not exist, then the proposition 'Truth does not exist' is true. But if there is anything true, there must be Truth. God is Truth itself: *I am the way, the truth, and the life.* Therefore the proposition that God exists is self-evident.

On the contrary, No one can mentally admit the opposite of what is self-evident; as is clear from the Philosopher, concerning the first principles of demonstration. The opposite of the proposition 'God is' can be mentally admitted: *The fool hath said in his heart, There is no God.* Therefore, that God exists is not self-evident.

I answer that, A thing can be self-evident in either of two ways; on the one hand, self-evident in itself, though not to us; on the other, self-evident in itself, and to us. A proposition is self-evident because the predicate is included in the notion of the subject, as 'Man is an animal,' for animal is contained in the formal idea of man. If, therefore, the essence of the predicate and subject be known to all, the proposition will be self-evident to all; as is clear with regard to the first principles of demonstration, the terms of which are common things that no one is ignorant of, such as being and non-being, whole and part, and such like. If there are some to whom the essence of the predicate and subject are unknown, the proposition will be self-evident in itself, but not to those who do not know the meaning of the predicate and subject of the proposition. Therefore, it happens, as Boethius says, that there are some mental concepts self-evident only to the learned, as that incorporeal substances are not in space. Therefore I say that this proposition, 'God exists,' of itself is self-evident, for the predicate is the same as the subject; because God is His Own Existence. For as much as we do not know the Essence of God, the proposition is not self-evident to us; but needs to be proved by such things as are more evident to us, though less evident in their nature—namely, by effects.

Reply Obj. 1. To know that God exists in a general and indefinite way is implanted in us by nature, inasmuch as God is man's beatitude. For man naturally desires happiness, and what is naturally desired by a man must be naturally known to him. This, however, is not to know absolutely that God exists; as to know that someone is approaching is not the same as to know that Peter is approaching, even though it is Peter who is approaching; for many there are who imagine that man's perfect good (which is happiness) consists in riches, and others in pleasures, and others in something else.

Reply Obj. 2. Perhaps not everyone who hears this word 'God' may understand it to signify something than which nothing better can be imagined, seeing that some have believed God to be a body. Yet, granted that everyone understands that by this word 'God' is signified something than which nothing greater can be imagined, nevertheless, it does not therefore follow that he understands that what the word signifies exists actually, but only that it exists mentally. Nor can it be argued logically that it actually exists, unless it be admitted that there exists something than which nothing greater can be imagined; and this precisely is not admitted by those who hold that God does not exist.

Reply Obj. 3. The existence of truth in a general way is self-evident, but the existence of a Primal Truth is not self-evident to us.

SECOND ARTICLE.

WHETHER IT CAN BE DEMONSTRATED THAT GOD EXISTS?

We proceed thus to the Second Article:—

Objection 1. It seems that the existence of God cannot be demonstrated; for it is an article of Faith that God exists. But what is of Faith cannot be demonstrated, because a demonstration produces knowledge; whereas Faith is of the unseen. (Heb. xi, 1). Therefore it cannot be demonstrated that God exists.

Obj. 2. Further, the essence is the middle term of demonstration. But we cannot know in what God's essence consists, but solely in what it does not consist, as the Damascene says. Therefore we cannot demonstrate that God exists.

Obj. 3. Further, if the existence of God were demonstrated, this could only be from His effects. But the effects are not proportionate to Him, since He is infinite and His effects are finite; and between the finite and infinite there is no proportion. Therefore, since a cause cannot be demonstrated by an effect not proportionate to it, it seems that the existence of God cannot be demonstrated.

On the contrary, The Apostle says: *The invisible things of God are clearly seen, being understood by the things that are made.* But this would not be unless the existence of God could be demonstrated through the things that are made; for the first thing we must know of anything is, whether it exists.

I answer that, Demonstration can be made in two ways: One is through the cause, and is called *a priori,* and this is to argue from what is prior absolutely. The other is through the effect, and is called a demonstration *a posteriori;* this is to argue from what is prior relatively only to us. When an effect is better known to us than its cause, from the effect we proceed to the knowledge of the cause. From every effect the existence of a proportionate cause can be demonstrated, so long as its effects are better known to us. Since every effect depends upon its cause, if the effect exists, the cause must have pre-existed. Hence the existence of God, in so far as it is not self-evident to us, can be demonstrated from those of His effects which are known to us.

Reply Obj. 1. The existence of God and other like truths about God, which can be known by natural reason, are not articles of Faith, but are preambles to the articles; for Faith presupposes natural knowledge, even as grace presupposes nature, and perfection something that can be perfected. Nevertheless, there is nothing to prevent a man, who cannot grasp its proof, accepting, as a matter of Faith, something in itself capable of being known and demonstrated.

Reply Obj. 2. When the existence of a cause is demonstrated from an effect, this effect takes the place of the definition of the cause in proof of the cause's existence. This is especially the case in regard to God, because, in order to prove the existence of anything, it is necessary to accept as a middle term the meaning of the word, and not its essence, for the question of its essence follows on the question of its existence. The names given to God are derived from His effects; consequently, in demonstrating the existence of God from His effects, we may take for the middle term the meaning of the word 'God.'

Reply Obj. 3. From effects not proportionate to the cause no perfect knowledge of that cause can be obtained. Yet from every effect the existence of the cause can be clearly demonstrated, and so we can demonstrate the existence of God from His effects; though from them we cannot perfectly know God as He is in His Own Essence.

THIRD ARTICLE.

WHETHER GOD EXISTS?

We proceed thus to the Third Article:—

Objection 1. It seems that God does not exist; because if one of two contraries be infinite, the other would be altogether destroyed. But the word 'God' means that He is infinite goodness. If, therefore, God existed, there would be no evil discoverable; but there is evil in the world. Therefore God does not exist.

Obj. 2. Further, it is superfluous to suppose that what can be accounted for by a few principles has been produced by many. But it seems that everything that appears in the world can be accounted for by other principles, supposing God did not exist. For all natural things can be reduced to one principle, which is nature; and all things that happen intentionally can be reduced to one principle, which is human reason, or will. Therefore there is no need to suppose God's existence.

On the contrary, It is said in the person of God: *I am Who am* (Exod. iii. 14).

I answer that, The existence of God can be proved in five ways.

The first and more manifest way is the argument from motion. It is certain and evident to our senses that some things are in motion. Whatever is in motion is moved by another, for nothing can be in motion except it have a potentiality for that towards which it is being moved; whereas a thing moves inasmuch as it is in act. By 'motion' we mean nothing else than the reduction of something from a state of potentiality into a state of actuality. Nothing, however, can be reduced from a state of potentiality into a state of actuality, unless by something already in a state of actuality. Thus that which is actually hot as fire, makes wood, which is potentially hot, to be actually hot, and thereby moves and changes it. It is not possible that the same thing should be at once in a state of actuality and potentiality from the same point of view, but only from different points of view. What is actually hot cannot simultane-

ously be only potentially hot; still, it is simultaneously potentially cold. It is therefore impossible that from the same point of view and in the same way anything should be both moved and mover, or that it should move itself. Therefore, whatever is in motion must be put in motion by another. If that by which it is put in motion be itself put in motion, then this also must needs be put in motion by another, and that by another again. But this cannot go on to infinity, because then there would be no first mover, and, consequently, no other mover—seeing that subsequent movers only move inasmuch as they are put in motion by the first mover; as the staff only moves because it is put in motion by the hand. Therefore it is necessary to arrive at a First Mover, put in motion by no other; and this everyone understands to be God.

The second way is from the formality of efficient causation. In the world of sense we find there is an order of efficient causation. There is no case known (neither is it, indeed, possible) in which a thing is found to be the efficient cause of itself; for so it would be prior to itself, which is impossible. In efficient causes it is not possible to go on to infinity, because in all efficient causes following in order, the first is the cause of the intermediate cause, and the intermediate is the cause of the ultimate cause, whether the intermediate cause be several, or one only. To take away the cause is to take away the effect. Therefore, if there be no first cause among efficient causes, there will be no ultimate cause, nor any intermediate. If in efficient causes it is possible to go on to infinity, there will be no first efficient cause, neither will there be an ultimate effect, nor any intermediate efficient causes; all of which is plainly false. Therefore it is necessary to put forward a First Efficient Cause, to which everyone gives the name of God.

The third way is taken from possibility and necessity, and runs thus. We find in nature things that could either exist or not exist, since they are found to be generated, and to corrupt; and, consequently, they can exist, and then not exist. It is impossible for these always to exist, for that which can one day cease to exist must at some time have not existed. Therefore, if everything could cease to exist, then at one time there could have been nothing in existence. If this were true, even now there would be nothing in existence, because that which does not exist only begins to exist by something already existing. Therefore, if at one time nothing was in existence, it would have been impossible for anything to have begun to exist; and thus even now nothing would be in existence—which is absurd. Therefore, not all beings are merely possible, but there must exist something the existence of which is necessary. Every necessary thing either has its necessity caused by another, or not. It is impossible to go on to infinity in necessary things which have their necessity caused by another, as has been already proved in regard to efficient causes. Therefore we cannot but postulate the existence of some being having of itself its own necessity, and not receiving it from another, but rather causing in others their necessity. This all men speak of as God.

The fourth way is taken from the gradation to be found in things. Among beings there are some more and some less good, true, noble, and the like. But 'more' and 'less' are predicated of different things, according as they resemble in their different ways something which is in the degree of 'most,' as a thing is said to be hotter according as it more nearly resembles that which is hottest; so that there is something which is truest, something best, something noblest, and, consequently, something which is uttermost being; for the truer things are, the more truly they exist. What is most complete in any genus is the cause of all in that genus; as fire, which is the most complete form of heat, is the cause whereby all things are made hot.

Therefore there must also be something which is to all beings the cause of their being, goodness, and every other perfection; and this we call God.

The fifth way is taken from the governance of the world; for we see that things which lack intelligence, such as natural bodies, act for some purpose, which fact is evident from their acting always, or nearly always, in the same way, so as to obtain the best result. Hence it is plain that not fortuitously, but designedly, do they achieve their purpose. Whatever lacks intelligence cannot fulfil some purpose, unless it be directed by some being endowed with intelligence and knowledge; as the arrow is shot to its mark by the archer. Therefore some intelligent being exists by whom all natural things are ordained towards a definite purpose; and this being we call God.

Reply Obj. 1. As Augustine says: *Since God is wholly good, He would not allow any evil to exist in His works, unless His omnipotence and goodness were such as to bring good even out of evil.* This is part of the infinite goodness of God, that He should allow evil to exist, and out of it produce good.

Reply Obj. 2. Since nature works for a determinate end under the direction of a higher agent, whatever is done by nature must needs be traced back to God, as to its first cause. So also whatever is done designedly must also be traced back to some higher cause other than human reason or will, for these can suffer change and are defective; whereas things capable of motion and of defect must be traced back to an immovable and self-necessary first principle.

French Epic

The Song of Roland *is a French legendary epic dating from the time of Charlemagne. It is based on historical fact, however, for in 778 the emperor invaded Spain but was forced to withdraw when word reached him of a Saxon revolt in the north. During the retreat through the Pyrenees, a part of his force was ambushed in a narrow defile and annihilated. These events have been idealized in the poem into a heroic description of feudal loyalty and of the virtues of the feudal warrior. Twelve vassals, of whom*

Roland was one, are depicted as the leaders of the finest section of the Frankish army. In the face of overwhelming odds and only to assure vengeance and not for personal security, Roland finally sounded his horn and gave the alarm to the main body of the Franks. The poem lifts medieval feudalism out of its legalistic, contractual pattern, and makes of it a living, personal relationship which involved much more than the mechanical fulfillment of obligations. The lines present in a vivid and moving manner the loyalty and devotion implicit in vassalage and homage—a loyalty suggestive of modern patriotism to one's country. In reading the passage note (1) the description of the highly personalized relationship between Roland and his sword, Durendal, (2) evidences of the close comradeship between Roland and Oliver, (3) indications of the devoted vassalage to Charlemagne, (4) the activities of the archbishop, (5) the number of pagans slain by the Franks, (6) the description of the forces of the Saracen king, Marsilies, (7) the tragic deaths of the companions of Roland and Oliver, (8) evidences of the crusading zeal aroused against the pagans, (9) the discussion between Roland and Oliver about sounding the olifant and the meaning of vassalage, (10) the treachery of Guenes and his disgrace, (11) the death of Oliver, and (12) the final deeds of the archbishop and Roland on the field of battle.

From: THE SONG OF ROLAND

Great is the battle and crowded the mellay,
Nor does Count Roland stint of his strokes
    this day;
While the shaft holds he wields his spear
    amain—
Fifteen great blows ere it splinters and breaks.
Then his bare brand, his Durendal, he takes;
Against Chernubles he spurs his steed in haste,
Splits through the helm with carbuncles ablaze,
Through the steel coif, and through scalp and
    through brain
'Twixt the two eyes he cleaves him through
    the face;
Through the bright byrny close-set with rings
    of mail,
Right through the body, through the fork and
    the reins,
Down through the saddle with its beaten gold
    plates,

Through to the horse he drives the cleaving
    blade,
Seeking no joint through the chine carves his
    way,
Flings horse and man dead on the grassy plain.
"Foul befal, felon, that e'er you sought this
    fray!
Mahound," quoth he, "shall never bring you
    aid.
Villains like you seek victory in vain."

The County Roland throughout the field goes
    riding;
With Durendal, good sword, he stabs and
    slices,
The toll he takes of Saracens is frightful.
Would you had seen him, dead man on dead
    man piling.

As translated by Dorothy L. Sayers in *The Song of Roland, A New Translation*, Baltimore: Penguin Books, 1957, 103–144.

Seen the bright blood about his pathway lying!
Bloody his hauberk and both his arms with
  fighting,
His good horse bloody from crest to withers
  likewise;
Oliver too doth never cease from striking,
And the Twelve Peers are not a whit behind-
  hand,
And all the French are hammering and smiting;
The Paynims fall, some dead and others dying.
Quoth the Archbishop: "Right blessed be our
  knighthood";
He shouts "Mountjoy!" war-cry of Charles the
  mighty.

And Oliver goes riding through the press;
His spear is broken, only the shaft is left.
Against a Paynim, Malun, he rides addrest,
Smashes the shield with flowers and gold be-
  decked,
Both of his eyes he smites out of his head,
So that his brains around his feet are spread,
And flings the corpse amid sev'n hundred dead.
Turgis he's slain, and slain Esturgot next,
Till to the grips the spear-shaft splits in shreds.
Roland cries out: "What are you doing, friend?
I'd give no groat for sticks in such a stead!
Here iron avails, and steel and nothing else.
Where is your sword that Hauteclaire is y-
  clept,
With its gold hilts and pummel crystal-
  gemmed?"
"I've had no time to draw," Oliver said,
"I've been so busy with striking right and left."

Dan Oliver has drawn his goodly brand,
As his friend Roland so urgently demands;
Now will he prove him a stout knight of his
  hands!
He smites a Paynim, Justin of Val Ferrat;
Clean through the middle the skull of him he
  cracks,
The saffron byrny splits, and his breast and
  back,
And saddle, brave with gems and golden
  bands,
And through the spine the horse in sunder
  hacks,
And dead on field flings all before him flat.

"I'll call you brother," quoth Roland, "after
  that!
'Tis for such strokes our Emperor loves a man."
The shout "Mountjoy!" goes up on every hand.

Fiercer and still more fierce the battle grows;
Both French and Paynims deal wondrous
  heavy strokes,
Some in attacking, and some in parrying blows.
How many spears are bloodied there and
  broke!
What gonfalons, what banners rent and strown!
How many French in flower of youth laid low,
Whom wives and mothers shall never more be-
  hold,
Nor those of France who wait them on the
  road!
King Charlemayn must weep and wail for
  woe;
What help in that? he cannot save his folk.
Ill did Count Guènes serve Carlon, when he
  rode
To Saragossa and all his people sold;
Thereby he lost life and limbs of his own
When at Aix after they judged him to the rope,
And of his kin thirty were hanged also,
Who ne'er had thought such death should be
  their dole.

Fierce is the battle and wondrous grim the
  fight.
Both Oliver and Roland boldly smite,
Thousands of strokes the stout Archbishop
  strikes,
The whole Twelve Peers are not a whit behind,
And the French ranks lay on with all their
  might.
Heaped by the hundred thousands of Paynims
  lie,
None can escape unless he turns and flies,
Will he or nill he, there must he leave his
  life.
There France must lose the noblest of her
  knights,
They'll see no more their kindred and their
  sires,
Nor Charles, who scans the pass with anxious
  eyes.
Throughout all France terrific tempests rise,

Thunder is heard, the stormy winds blow high,
Unmeasured rain and hail fall from the sky,
While thick and fast flashes the levin bright,
And true it is the earth quakes far and wide.
Far as from Saintes to Michael-of-the-Tide,
From Besançon to Wissant Port, you'd find
There's not a house but the walls crack and
rive.
Right at high noon a darkness falls like night,
Save for the lightning there's not a gleam of
light;
None that beholds it but is dismayed for fright,
And many say: "This is the latter time,
The world is ending, and the Great Doom is
nigh."
They speak not true, they cannot read the
signs:
'Tis Roland's death calls forth this mighty cry.

The French have fought with valour and suc-
cess;
By scores and thousands lie Paynim corpses
spread,
Of hundred thousand scarce two will fight
again.
Quoth the Archbishop: "Right valiant are our
men,
The like of these hath no lord under heav'n.
Thus it is written in the Gestes of the French:
Our Emperor's power was never rivalled yet."
They search the field for their maimed and
their dead,
With grief and sorrow the eyes of them are wet,
With love and pity for their kindred and
friends.
Now falls upon them Marsile with all his
strength.

The King Marsile comes riding up a gorge
With all his army about him in great force;
He has assembled twenty huge battle-hordes.
Such flash of helms with gems and gold
adorned!
Such shields, such byrnies with burnished saf-
fron wrought!
Sev'n hundred trumpets are sounding the as-
sault;
Through all the country the noise of them goes
forth.

"Brother," quoth Roland, "friend Oliver, sweet
lord,
It is our death false Ganelon has sworn;
The treason's plain, it can be hid no more;
A right great vengeance the Emperor will let
fall.
But we must bide a fearful pass of war.
No man has ever beheld the like before.
I shall lay on with Durendal my sword,
You, comrade, wield that great Hauteclaire of
yours.
In lands how many have we those weapons
borne!
Battles how many victoriously fought!
Ne'er shall base ballad be sung of them in hall!"

Marsile beholds his slaughtered chivalry.
He bids his trumpets and horns sound instantly
And then sets forward with his great company.
Then first rides out a Saracen, Abisme,
In all that host was none more vile than he,
With evil vice and crimes he's dyed full deep,
In Mary's Child, God's Son, he's no belief,
And black he is as melted pitch to see.
Better he loves murder and treachery
Then all the gold that is in Galicie
None ever saw him in mirth or jollity;
But bold he is and rash to a degree,
And for that reason he's loved by King Marsile.
He bears a dragon to rally his meinie.
The good Archbishop observes him, much dis-
pleased,
He'd like to hit him on sight, that's how he
feels,
And to himself he says quite quietly:
"This Sarsen looks right heretic to me.
'Twere best by far to go and kill the beast;
I never loved cowards nor coward deeds."

Th' Archbishop opens the battle up anew;
He rides a charger that from Grossayle he took
(That was a king in Denmark, whom he slew).
A steed he is swiftly-running and smooth,
Flat in the knee and hollow in the hoof,
Short in the thigh and ample in the croup,
Long in the flank and the back well set up,
White of his tail and yellow of his plume,
Small of his ears and his head tawny-hued;
Here is a horse no courser could outdo.

Him the Archbishop, of his valour right good,
Spurs on Abisme, and none shall stay his mood.
He rides to strike him on his target of proof
Wondrous with topaz and amethyst to boot,
With carbuncle ablaze, and beryl blue
(Emir Galafe gave it him for a boon
Whom in Val Metas a devil gave it to.)
Turpin lays on, nor spares; I tell you true,
After he hit it it was not worth a sou!
From flank to flank he spits his body through,
And flings him dead wherever he finds room.
The French all cry: "A valiant blow and
    shrewd!
Right strong to save is our Archbishop's crook!"

Now can the French count up the Paynim
    might;
They see it filling the plains from side to side.
They urge on Roland and Oliver likewise
And the Twelve Peers to flee for all their lives;
To whom straightway the Prelate speaks his
    mind:
"Barons, my lords, these shameful thoughts
    put by;
By God I charge you, hold fast and do not fly,
Lest brave men sing ill songs in your despite.
Better it were to perish in the fight.
Soon, very soon we all are marked to die,
None of us here will see to-morrow's light;
One thing there is I promise you outright:
To you stand open the gates of Paradise,
There with the holy sweet Innocents to bide."
His words so fill them with courage and delight
There's none among them but shouts "Mount-
    joy" on high.

A Saracen, of Saragossa Town
Was there, the lord of half that city round—
Climborin namely, that traitor false and foul
Which took the oath of Ganelon the Count
And then for friendship kissed him upon the
    mouth
And with his helm and carbuncle endowed;
Our Fatherland he swore he'd disrenown,
And from the Emperor would snatch away the
    crown.
Now he comes riding on Barbëmouche his
    mount—
Fleeter was never swallow nor falcon found—

Slacks rein, spurs hard its mettle to arouse,
On Engelier the Gascon forward bounds.
Buckler nor byrny avails against him now,
Into the midriff lance-point and pennon plough,
From breast to back the shaft runs through
    and out,
A whole spear's length he hurls him dead on
    ground.
"Fit for destruction is all this gear!" he shouts;
"Paynims, strike hard! carve your way through
    the rout!"
"God!" say the French, "one of our best is
    down!"

Count Roland calls to Oliver his friend:
"Fair sir, companion, see, Engelier is dead;
No better man had we for knightliness."
The Count replies: "God give me fair revenge!"
In his steed's flanks the golden spurs he sets,
He grasps Hauteclaire, whose steel is all dyed
    red,
He deals the Paynim a mighty stroke and
    dread,
Twists out the blade, down falls the Saracen;
The Adversary bears off his soul to Hell.
Then he goes on, slays Duke Alfayen next,
From Escababa he hews away the head,
And seven Arabs unhorses then pell-mell:
That lot at least will never fight again.
"My friend is angry," the County Roland
    said:
"Fighter for fighter he matches me right well;
'Tis for such strokes King Carlon loves us best!"
Aloud he cries: "Strike on, my valiant men!"

Elsewhere, behold a Paynim, Valdabron,
Was godfather to King Marsilion;
He owns a navy four hundred dromonds
    strong,
And to his service no seaman but is bond.
He captured Salem by fraud in times bygone,
And sacked the Temple of good King Solomon,
Murdering there the Patriarch by the font.
He took the oath of County Ganelon,
And sword and mangons gave him as pledge
    thereon.
He rides a horse that he calls Gramimond,
Never of speed was peregrine more prompt.
With the sharp spur he urges it headlong;

The great Duke Samson straightway he falls
    upon.
He splits the shield, he bursts the habergeon,
Drives through his body spear-head and gon-
    falon,
Flings him from saddle a full spear's length
    alone:
"Paynims!" he cries, "we'll beat them yet! Lay
    on!"
"God!" say the French, "there's a brave baron
    gone!"

When the Count Roland sees Samson thus laid
    low
Well may you guess how he is grieved of soul.
He spurs his horse and speeds to smite the foe
With Durendal, more worth than finest gold.
By might and main the Baron deals the stroke
Full on the helm that is all gemmed with gold;
The skull he splits, byrny and breast are broke,
Cloven the saddle, that is all gemmed with
    gold;
Through the beast's back deep down the
    weapon goes;
Like it or leave it, he has destroyed them both.
The Paynims say: "This is a bitter blow!"
"I love you not," quoth Roland, "by my troth;
Yours is the outrage, yours is the lying boast!"

An African there was of Afric, too,
Was called Malquiant, the son of King Mal-
    cude;
Harnessed he is in gold from head to foot,
None in the sun so glitters to the view,
He rides a horse that he calls Saut-Perdu;
No steed could rival the swiftness of its hoofs.
He strikes Anseïs in mid-shield square and true,
He shears away the scarlet and the blue,
Rips the mailed skirt of the hauberk of proof,
Into the body drives the steel and the wood.
The Count falls dead, his days have met their
    doom.
The French all say: "Brave lord, alack for
    you!"

Archbishop Turpin goes riding through the
    field;
Ne'er was mass sung by any tonsured priest
That of his body could do such valiant deeds!

He hails the Paynim: "God send the worst to
    thee!
Thou hast slain one for whom my whole heart
    grieves."
Into a gallop he urges his good steed,
He strikes him hard on his Toledo shield,
And lays him dead upon the grassy green.

There was a Paynim, and Grandoyne was he
    called,
King Capuel's son, from Cappadocia's shores,
Mounted on Marmor, for so he names his horse,
Swifter of speed than any bird that soars.
He slacks the rein and he goes spurring forth,
And runs to strike Gerin with all his force.
From off his neck he splits the red shield shorn,
From off his body he rips the byrny torn,
Into his heart the pennon blue he's borne,
And down he flings him dead on a rocky tor.
Gerin his comrade he smites down afterward,
Berenger next, Guy of St Antoine fall;
And then he strikes the mighty duke Astorge,
(Envers-on-Rhône and Valence called him
    lord),
And lays him dead; for joy the Paynims roar;
The French all say: "What loss we have to
    mourn!"

The County Roland grips fast his blood-red
    blade;
Well has he heard how the French are dis-
    mayed;
His heart grieves so, 'tis like to split in twain.
He hails the Paynim: "God send thee all His
    plagues!
Thou hast slain one for whom I'll make thee
    pay!"
He spurs his horse that gladly runs apace;
Let win who may, they're at it, face to face.

The Prince Grandoyne was a good knight and
    gallant,
Strong of his hands and valorous in battle;
Athwart him now comes Roland the great
    captain;
He'd never met him, but he knew him in-
    stanter.
By his proud aspect, and by his noble stature,
His haughty looks, and his bearing and manner.

He cannot help it, a mortal fear unmans him;
Fain would he fly, but what's the good? he cannot.
The Count assails him with such ferocious valour
That to the nasal the whole helmet is shattered,
Cloven the nose and the teeth and the palate,
The jaz'rain hauberk and the breastbone and backbone,
Both silver bows from off the golden saddle;
Horseman and horse clean asunder he slashes,
Lifeless he leaves them and the pieces past patching.
The men of Spain fall a-wailing for sadness:
The French all cry: "What strokes! and what a champion!"

Fierce is the battle and marvellous and great.
The Frenchmen ply their burnished spears amain.
There had you seen how many men in pain,
How many wounded and bleeding there and slain!
Heaped up pell-mell they lie, on back or face.
The Saracens cannot endure the strain;
Will they or nill they they flee across the plain,
And the French forces with all their might give chase.

Wondrous the battle, and it grows faster yet;
The French fight on with rage and fury fell,
They lop off wrists, hew ribs and spines to shreds,
They cleave the harness through to the living flesh;
On the green ground the blood runs clear and red.
[The Paynims say: "We cannot stand the stress,]
French Fatherland, be curst of Máhomet!
Your sons are bravest of all the sons of men."
There's none of them but cries: "Marsile to help!
Ride, ride, O King, for we are hard bested."

Roland the Count calls out to Olivere:
"Fair sir, companion, confess that for this gear
Our lord Archbishop quits him like any peer;

Earth cannot match him beneath the heavens' sphere,
Well does he know to handle lance and spear."
The Count replies: "Let's aid him now and here!"
At this the French lay on the lustier,
Hard are their strokes, the fight is very fierce,
And for the Christians the losses are severe.
Who then had seen Roland and Olivere
Smite with their swords and through all the press pierce!
And the Archbishop goes thrusting with his spear.
Of those they slew the numbers are writ clear
In many charters and tales of chroniclers:
More than four thousand as in the Geste appears.
Four great assaults they've borne with right good cheer;
Then comes a fifth, doleful and dread and drear.
All the French knighthood has fallen in career;
Sixty alone by God's grace persevere;
These ere they die will sell their bodies dear.

When County Roland sees all his brave men down,
To Oliver his friend he cries aloud:
"For God's sake, comrade, fair sir, what think you now?
See what good knights lie here upon the ground!
Well may we pity this fair sweet France of ours,
Thus left so barren of all her knighthood's flower.
Why aren't you here, O friend and Emperour?
Oliver, brother, what way is to be found?
How send him news of what is come about?"
Oliver said: "And how should I know how?
I'd rather die than we should lose renown."

"I'll sound," quoth Roland, "my Olifant straightway;
When Carlon hears, passing through Gate of Spain,
I pledge my word, the French will turn again."
Quoth Oliver: "It would be foul disdain,
And to your kindred the reproach would be great:
All their lives long they'd not live down the shame.

When I desired you, why then you said me
 nay;
If now you do it, of me you'll get no praise.
Blow if you will—such conduct is not brave.
Nay, but how deep in blood your arms are
 bathed!
The Count replies: "I've struck good blows this
 day."

Said Roland then: "Full grievous is this fight.
I'll sound my horn, and Charles will hear the
 cry."
Quoth Oliver: " 'Twould ill beseem a knight.
I asked you, comrade, and you refused, for
 pride.
Had Charles been here, then all would have
 gone right;
He's not to blame, nor the men at his side.
Now by my beard (quoth he) if e'er mine eyes
Again behold my sister Aude the bright,
Between her arms never you think to lie."

Quoth Roland: "Why so angry with me,
 friend?"
And he: "Companion, you got us in this mess.
There is wise valour, and there is recklessness:
Prudence is worth more than foolhardiness.
Through your o'erweening you have destroyed
 the French;
Ne'er shall we do service to Charles again.
Had you but given some heed to what I said,
My lord had come, the battle had gone well,
And King Marsile had been captured or dead.
Your prowess, Roland, is a curse on our heads.
No more from us will Charlemayn have help,
Whose like till Doomsday shall not be seen of
 men.
Now you will die, and fair France will be
 shent;
Our loyal friendship is here brought to an end;
A bitter parting we'll have ere this sun set."

When the Archbishop thus hears them in dis-
 pute,
With his gold spurs he pricks his steed anew,
Draws near to them and utters this rebuke:
"Lord Oliver, and you, Lord Roland, too,
Let's have no quarrel, o'God's name, 'twixt
 you two.

It will not save us to sound the horn, that's
 true;
Nevertheless, 'twere better so to do.
Let the King come; his vengeance will be rude;
None shall to Spain ride home with merry
 news.
After, our French will light them down on foot,
Seek out our bodies and limbs in sunder hewn,
Lay us on biers borne upon sumpter-mules,
And weep for us with grief right pitiful;
In the church-close we shall have burial due,
And not be food for dogs and swine and
 wolves."
Quoth Roland, "Sir, your words are right and
 good."

Roland has set Olifant to his lips,
Firmly he holds it and blows it with a will.
High are the mountains, the blast is long and
 shrill,
Thirty great leagues the sound went echoing.
King Carlon heard it and all who rode with
 him.
"Lo, now, our men are fighting," quoth the
 King.
Guènes retorts: "If any man said this
Except yourself, it were a lie, methinks."

The County Roland with pain and anguish
 winds
His Olifant, and blows with all his might.
Blood from his mouth comes spurting scarlet-
 bright
He's burst the veins of his temples outright.
From hand and horn the call goes shrilling
 high:
King Carlon hears it who through the passes
 rides,
Duke Naimon hears, and all the French beside.
Quoth Charles: "I hear the horn of Roland cry!
He'd never sound it but in the thick of fight."
"There is no battle," Count Ganelon replies;
"You're growing old, your hair is sere and
 white,
When you speak thus, you're talking like a
 child.
Full well you know Roland's o'erweening pride;
'Tis strange that God endures him so long time!
Took he not Noples against your orders quite?
The Paynims made a sally from inside,

And there gave battle to Roland the great
    knight;
So he swilled down the field—a brave device
To keep the bloodstains from coming to your
    eyes!
For one small hare he'll blow from morn till
    night;
Now to the Peers he's showing-off in style.
Who dare attack him? No man beneath the sky!
Ride on, ride on! Why loiter here the while?
Our Fathers' land lies distant many a mile."

Count Roland's mouth with running blood is
    red;
He's burst asunder the temples of his head;
He sounds his horn in anguish and distress.
King Carlon hears, and so do all the French.
Then said the King: "This horn is long of
    breath.
" 'Tis blown," quoth Naimon, "with all a brave
    man's strength;
Battle there is, and that I know full well.
He that would stay you is but a traitor fell.
To arms! let sound your battle-cry to heav'n!
Make haste to bring your gallant household
    help!
You hear how Roland makes desperate lament!"

The Emperor Charles lets sound his horns aloft.
The French light down and arm themselves
    anon
With helm and hauberk and gilded swords
    girt on;
Goodly their shields, their lances stiff and
    strong,
Scarlet and white and blue the gonfalons.
Straightway to horse the warrior lords have
    got;
Swift through the passes they spur and never
    stop.
Each unto other they speak and make response:
"Might we reach Roland ere he were dead and
    gone,
We'ld strike good strokes beside him in the
    throng."
What use is that? They have delayed too long.

Vespers draws on and shining is the day;
Against the sun glitters their armed array,
Hauberk and helm flash back a mighty blaze,
So many shields their painted flowers display,
Such store of spears with gilded pennons gay!
The Emperor rides right wrathful on his way.
And all the French in anger and dismay;
There is not one but weeps for very rage;
For Roland's sake they're grievously afraid.
The King arrests Count Ganelon straightway;
He's turned him over to the cooks in his train;
The master-cook he calls, Besgun by name:
"Guard me him well, as fits a man so base,
For all my house this villain has betrayed!"
Besgun takes charge, with five-score kitchen
    knaves,
The best and worst that serve in that estate.
They pluck the beard from off his chin and
    face,
With four sound thumps each gives him a good
    baste,
With sticks and faggots they pound him and
    they paste,
And round his neck they fasten a strong chain,
Right well they chain him like a bear in a cage;
Now on a pack-horse they've hoisted him in
    shame;
Till Carlon want him 'tis they will keep him
    safe.

Huge are the hills and shadowy and high,
Deep in the vales the living streams run by.
The trumpets sound before them and behind,
All with one voice to Olifant reply.
In wrath of heart the Emperor Carlon rides,
And all the French in sorrow and in ire;
There's none but grieves and weeps from out
    his eyes;
They all pray God to safeguard Roland's life
Till they may come to battle by his side;
Once they are with him they'll make it a great
    fight.
What use is that? their prayers are empty quite,
Too long they've lingered, they cannot come in
    time.

King Charlemayn rides on in anger grim,
Over his byrny flows the white beard of him;
All the French barons beside him spur full
    swift;
There's none of them but is with fury filled
Not to be aiding Roland the Paladin

Now that he's fighting the Spanish Sarrasins.
He's hurt so sore, I fear he cannot live.
God! and what men, those sixty with him still!
Better had never nor captain nor yet king.

Roland surveys the mountains and the fells;
How many French he sees there lying dead!
Like a good knight he makes them this lament:
"Barons, my lords, may God of His largesse
Bring all your souls to Paradise the blest,
Amid bright flowers to make their hallowed
    beds!
I never saw braver or truer men.
So long you served me unceasingly and well,
So many lands conquered for Carlon's realm!
The Emperor bred you alas! to what sad end!
O dearest land, fair nursery of the French,
By what hard hap art thou this day bereft!
Barons of France, for me you go to death,
Nought can I give you of safeguard or defence;
Now aid you God, who ne'er failed any yet!
Oliver, brother, you shall not lack my help.
Though none should slay me I'll die of grief no
    less;
Sweet sir, companion, let's go and fight afresh!"

The County Roland returns into the field
And like a warrior his Durendal he wields;
Faldron de Puy through the midriff he cleaves
With four-and-twenty besides, of great esteem.
Never on vengeance was any man so keen.
E'en as the deer before the deerhound flees
So before Roland the Paynims show their heels.
Quoth the Archbishop: "Well done, well done
    indeed!
Valour like this becomes a knight of breed
That bears his arms and sits a goodly steed;
Forward and fierce in battle should he be,
Else he's not worth a single penny-piece,
Best he turn monk in monastery meek
And for our sins pray daily on his knees."
Quoth Roland: "Strike, spare none of them,"
    saith he.
At this the French renew the fight with speed;
Therein the Christians endure great loss and
    grief.

When it is known no prisoners will be made

Men fight back fiercely, and stubborn is the
    fray;
Therefore the French grow very lions for rage.
Here comes Marsile, e'en as a baron brave,
Riding a horse, and Gaignun is its name.
Full upon Bevon he rides and spurs amain,
That held all Beaune and Dijon for domain.
The shield he shatters, and the hauberk he
    breaks,
And lays him dead, he need not strike again.
And Ivon next and Ivor too, his mate,
And Gerard too of Roussillon he slays.
Roland the Count, who is not far away,
Cries to the Paynim: "God damn your soul, I
    say!
These my companions by treason you have
    slain!
Ere we go hence a bitter price you'll pay,
And you shall learn the name of my good
    blade!"
He rides to strike him, e'en as a baron brave;
From his sword-arm he shears the hand away.
And Jurfaret the Fair he next waylays,
Marsilion's son, and slices off his pate.
The Paynims cry: "Mahound! Mahound to aid!
Venge us on Carlon, all you gods of our faith!
Into our land he's sent this evil race!
Come life come death they'll never quit the
    place."
Then one to other cries: "Fly then! fly in haste!"
An hundred thousand have fled the field
    straightway;
They'll not return, call after them who may.

What help is that? Marsile has taken flight,
Yet there remains his uncle Marganice,
That governs Carthage, Alfrere and Garamile,
And Ethiope, a land accursed and vile.
In his command are all the Negro tribes;
Thick are their noses, their ears are very wide;
Full fifty thousand are gathered in their lines,
Boldly and fast and furiously they ride,
Yelling aloud the Paynim battle-cry.
Then Roland said: "Here are we doomed to
    die;
Full well I know we cannot long survive.
Fail not, for shame, right dear to sell your
    lives.
Lift up, my lords, your burnished blades and
    fight!

Come life, come death, the foe shall pay the
    price,
Lest we should bring fair France into despite!
When on this field Carlon my lord sets eyes
He'll see what toll we've taken of their might:
Fifteen dead Paynims for each of us he'll find;
Nor fail to bless us for this our great emprise."

When Roland looks on these accursed tribes-
    men—
As black as ink from head to foot their hides
    are,
With nothing white about them but their grind-
    ers—
Then said the Count: " 'Tis true beyond denial,
Right well I know it, this day shall death be-
    tide us.
I'll to the throng; Frenchmen, fight on beside
    me!"
Quoth Oliver: "The devil take the hindmost!"
The French hear this and once more fall
    a-fighting.

When Paynims see how few the French are
    grown
They plume themselves, puffed up with pride
    and hope:
"Now to the Emperor," they say, "his crimes
    come home!"
Marganice comes, riding a sorrel colt;
He spurs him hard with rowels all of gold,
And from behind deals Oliver a blow;
Deep in his back the burnished mail is broke,
That the spear's point stands forth at his breast-
    bone.
He saith to him: "You've suffered a sore stroke;
Charlemayn sent you to the pass for your woe.
Foul wrong he did us, 'tis good he lose his
    boast:
I've well requited our loss on you alone."

Oliver feels that he is hurt to death;
He grasps his sword Hauteclaire the keen of
    edge,
Smites Marganice on his high golden helm,
Shearing away the flowers and crystal gems,
Down to the teeth clean splits him through the
    head,

Shakes loose the blade and flings him down
    and dead;
Then saith: "Foul fall you, accursèd Paynim
    wretch!
Charles has had losses, so much I will confess:
But ne'er shall you, back to the land you left,
To dame or damsel return to boast yourself
That e'er you spoiled me to the tune of two
    pence,
Or made your profit of me or other men."
This done, to Roland he cries aloud for help.

Oliver feels he's wounded mortally;
His thirst for vengeance can never glutted
    be.
Amid the press he strikes right valiantly;
He breaks asunder the spear-shaft and the
    shield,
Splits chines and saddles and lops off hands
    and feet.
Whoso had seen him hew Paynims piece from
    piece,
Throw one on other their bodies down in heaps,
Might well remember that flower of knightly
    deeds!
And Carlon's war-cry he fails not to repeat,
But still "Mountjoy!" goes shouting loud and
    clear.
He calls to Roland his comrade and his peer:
"Sir, my companion, draw nigh and stand with
    me;
We must this day be parted to our grief."

Oliver's face, when Roland on him looks,
Is grey and ghastly, discoloured, wan with
    wounds,
His bright blood sprays his body head to foot;
Down to the ground it runs from him in pools.
"God!" says the Count, "I know not what to
    do!
Fair sir, companion, woe worth your mighty
    mood!—
Ne'er shall be seen a man to equal you.
Alas, fair France! what valiant men and
    true
Must thou bewail this day, cast down and
    doomed!
Bitter the loss the Emperor has to rue!"
So much he says, and in the saddle swoons.

See Roland now swooning in saddle laid,
And Oliver that unto death is maimed;
He's bled so much that his eyes are all glazed,
Or far or near he can see nothing straight,
Nor recognise a single living shape;
So when he comes to where his comrade waits,
On the gold helm he smites at him amain,
Down to the nasal he splits the jewelled plates,
Only his head is not touched by the blade.
Then Roland, stricken, lifts his eyes to his face,
Asking him low and mildly as he may:
"Sir, my companion, did you mean it that way?
Look, I am Roland, that loved you all my days;
You never sent me challenge or battle-gage."
Quoth Oliver: "I cannot see you plain;
I know your voice; may God see you and save.
And I have struck you; pardon it me, I pray."
Roland replies: "I have taken no scathe;
I pardon you, myself and in God's name."
Then each to other bows courteous in his place.
With such great love thus is their parting made.

Oliver feels the coming pangs of death;
Both of his eyes are turning in his head,
Now he is blind wholly, and wholly deaf.
He lights from horse and to his knees he gets
And makes confession aloud, and beats his
    breast,
Then clasps his hands and lifts them up to
    Heav'n;
In Paradise he prays God give him rest,
And France the Fair and Carlon prays Him
    bless,
And his companion Roland above all men.
His heart-strings crack, he stoops his knightly
    helm,
And sinks to earth, and lies there all his length.
Dead is the Count, his days have reached their
    end.
The valiant Roland weeps for him and laments,
No man on earth felt ever such distress.

When Roland sees his friend and comrade die,
And on the ground face down beholds him lie,
With tender words he bids him thus goodbye:
"Sir, my companion, woe worth your valiant
    might!
Long years and days have we lived side by side,

Ne'er didst thou wrong me nor suffer wrong of
    mine.
Now thou art dead I grieve to be alive."
Having thus said, the Marquis swoons out-
    right
On his steed's back, that Veillantif is hight;
He's kept from falling by the gold stirrups
    bright;
Go as he may, they hold him still upright.

Or ever Roland comes to himself again
And has recovered and rallied from his faint,
Fearful disaster his fortunes have sustained;
All of the French are lost to him and slain;
Sole, the Archbishop and Walter Hum remain.
Walter has come down from the heights
    again;
Well has he striven against the men of Spain,
His men are dead, mown down by Paynim
    blades;
Will he or nill he, he flees towards the vale,
And upon Roland he cries aloud for aid:
"Where art thou, where, great county, warrior
    brave?
While thou wast there I never was dismayed.
Walter am I, who Maëlgut o'ercame,
Nephew am I to Droön white with age;
Thou for my valour wast wont to love me aye!
My lance is shattered, my shield is split in
    twain,
Battered and broken is my hauberk of mail,
A spear has pierced me [through the midst of
    my reins;]
Death is upon me, yet dear I made them
    pay."
Lo! at that word Roland hears him and wakes;
He spurs his horse and comes to him in haste.

Roland is filled with grief and anger sore;
In the thick press he now renews his war.
Of those of Spain he's overthrown a score,
And Walter six, the Archbishop five more.
The Paynims say: "These men are worst of all!
Let none escape alive; look to it, lords!
Who fears the onset, let shame be his reward!
Who lets these go, may he be put to scorn!"
Then once again the hue and cry breaks forth;
From every side pour in the Paynim hordes.

The County Roland is mighty of his mood,
Walter de Hum well-famed for knightlihood,
And the Archbishop a warrior tried and
proved;
Betwixt their valours there's not a pin to choose.
In the thick press they smite the Moorish crew.
A thousand Paynims dismount to fight on
foot,
And forty thousand horsemen they have, to
boot,
Yet 'gainst these three, my troth! they fear to
move.
They hurl against them their lances from aloof,
Javelins, jereeds, darts, shafts and spears they
loose.
In the first shock brave Walter meets his doom.
Turpin of Rheims has his shield split in two,
His helm is broken, his head has ta'en a wound,
His hauberk's pierced, the mail-rings burst and
strewn,
By four sharp spears his breast is stricken
through,
Killed under him his horse rolls neck and croup;
Th' Archbishop's down, woe worth the bitter
dule.

Turpin of Rheims, finding himself o'erset,
With four sharp lance-heads stuck fast within
his breast,
Quickly leaps up, brave lord, and stands erect.
He looks on Roland and runs to him and
says
Only one word: "I am not beaten yet!
True man failed never while life in him was
left."
He draws Almace, his steel-bright brand keen-
edged;
A thousand strokes he strikes amid the press.
Soon Charles shall see he spared no foe he met,
For all about him he'll find four hundred men,
Some wounded, some clean through the body
cleft,
And some of them made shorter by the head.
So tells the Geste; so he that fought there tells:
The worthy Giles, whom God with marvels
blessed,
In Laön minster thus-wise the charter penned;
Who knows not this knows nought of what be-
fel.

The County Roland fights bravely as he may,
But his whole body in heat and sweat is bathed,
And all his head is racked with grievous pain
From that great blast which brake his temples'
veins.
Fain would he know if Charles is bringing
aid;
His Olifant he grasps, and blows full faint.
The Emperor halts, hearing the feeble strain:
"My lords," quoth he, "this tells a woeful tale;
Roland my nephew is lost to us this day,
That call proclaims his breath is nigh to fail.
Whoso would reach him must ride with des-
perate haste.
Sound through the host! bid every trumpet
play!"
Full sixty thousand so loud their clarions bray
The hills resound, the valleys ring again.
The Paynims hear, no lust to laugh have they:
"We'll soon have Charles to reckon with," they
say.

The Paynims say: "The Emperor's turned
about;
Of those of France hark how the trumpets
sound!
If Carlon comes, we shall have rack and rout,
If Roland lives, once more he'll war us down,
We shall not keep one foot of Spanish ground."
Straightway four hundred helmed warriors
rally round,
The finest fighters that in the field are found;
A fearful onslaught they'll make upon the
Count;
Truly Lord Roland has got his work cut out.

Whenas Count Roland sees their assault begin,
Right fierce he makes him, and strong and
meancing;
While life is in him he'll never quail or quit.
He sits his horse that is named Veillantif,
Into his flanks the golden spurs he pricks
And sets upon them where most the press is
thick.
The Lord Archbishop, brave Turpin, rides with
him.
Paynim to Paynim cries: "Comrade, go to it!
Have we not heard the Frankish trumpets ring?

Charles is returning, the great, the mighty
    king!"

The County Roland ne'er loved a recreant,
Nor a false heart, nor yet a braggart jack,
Nor knight that was not a good man of his
    hands.
He cried to Turpin, the Churchman militant,
"Sir, you're on foot, I'm on my horse's back;
For love of you here will I make my stand,
And side by side we'll take both good and bad.
I'll not desert you for any mortal man.
Go we together these Paynims to attack;
The mightiest blows are those of Durendal."
Quoth the Archbishop: " 'Twere shame our
    strokes to slack;
Carlon is coming, our vengeance shall not lack."

The Paynims say: "Why were we ever born?
Woe worth the while! our day of doom has
    dawned.
Now have we lost our peerage and our lords,
The mighty Carlon comes on with all his force,
Of those of France we hear the shrilling horns,
The cry 'Mountjoy!' sounds fearfully abroad.
So grim of mood is Roland in his wrath
No man alive can put him to the sword.
Let fly at him, and then give up the war."
So they let fly; spears, lances they outpour,
Darts and jereeds and feathered shafts galore.
The shield of Roland is pierced and split and
    scored,
The mail-rings riven, and all his hauberk torn,
Yet in his body he is not touched at all,
Though under him, with thirty wounds and
    more,
His Veillantif is stricken dead and falls.
The Paynims flee, abandoning the war;
Count Roland's left amid the field, unhorsed.
In wrath and grief away the Paynims fly;

Backward to Spain with headlong haste they
    hie.
The County Roland cannot pursue their flight,
Veillantif's lost, he has no steed to ride;
Will he or nill he, he must on foot abide,
He's turned to aid Archbishop Turpin's plight,
And from his head the gilded helm untied,

Stripped off the hauberk of subtle rings and
    bright,
And all to pieces has cut the bliaut fine
Wherewith to bandage his wounds that gape
    so wide.
Then to his breast he clasps and lifts him light
And gently lays him upon the green hill-side,
With fair soft speech entreating on this wise:
"Ah, noble sir, pray give me leave awhile;
These friends of ours, we loved so well in life,
We must not leave them thus lying where they
    died.
I will go seek them, find, and identify,
And lay them here together in your sight."
"Go and return," the Bishop makes reply;
"Thanks be to God, this field is yours and
    mine."

Roland departs and through the field is gone;
Alone he searches the valleys and high rocks.
[And there he finds Ivor, and there Ivon],
Gerier and Gerin, the good companions,
[And Engelier whom Gascony begot];
And he has found Berenger and Oton,
And after finds Anseïs and Samson,
And finds Gerard the Old, of Roussillon.
He lifts them up, brave baron, one by one,
To the Archbishop he carries them anon,
And by his knees ranges them all along.
The Bishop weeps, he cannot stint thereof;
He lifts his hand and gives them benison,
And after saith: "Alack, brave champions!
May your souls rest with the all-glorious God
In Paradise, amid the rose-blossoms.
I too am dying and sorrow for my lot,
Who the great Emperor no more may look
    upon."

Roland once more unto the field repairs,
And has sought out his comrade Oliver.
Close to his breast he lifts him, and with care
As best he may to the Archbishop bears
And on his shield lays with the others there;
The Bishop signs and shrives them all with
    prayer.
With tears renewed their sorrow is declared,
And Roland saith: "Fair fellow Oliver,
You were own son unto Duke Renier
That held the marches of the Vale of Runers.

To shatter shield or break lance anywhere,
And from their seat proud men to overbear,
And cheer the brave with words of counsel fair,
And bring the cruel to ruin and despair,
No knight on earth was valiant as you were."

The County Roland, seeing his peers lie dead,
And Oliver, who was his dearest friend,
Begins to weep for ruth and tenderness;
Out of his cheeks the colour all has fled,
He cannot stand, he is so deep distressed,
He swoons to earth, he cannot help himself.
"Alas, for pity, sweet lord!" the Bishop saith.

When the Archbishop saw Roland faint and
    fallen,
So sad was he, he never had been more so;
He reaches out; he's taken Roland's horn up.
In Ronceval there runs a stream of water;
Fain would he go there and fetch a little for
    him.
With feeble steps he turns him thither, falt'ring;
He is so weak, that he cannot go forward,
For loss of blood he has no strength to call on.
Ere one might cover but a rood's length in
    walking
His heart has failed him, he has fallen face-
    foremost;
The pangs of death have seized him with great
    torment.

The County Roland has rallied from his faint,
Gets to his feet, though he's in grievous pain,
And looks about him over hill, over vale.
Beyond his comrades, upon the grass-green
    plain,
There he beholds the noble baron laid,
The great Archbishop, vice-gerent of God's
    name.
He beats his breast with eyes devoutly raised,
With folded hands lifted to Heaven he prays
That God will give him in Paradise a place.
Turpin is dead that fought for Charlemayn;
In mighty battles, and in preaching right brave,
Still against Paynims a champion of the
    Faith;
Blest mote he be, the Lord God give him
    grace!

The County Roland sees the Archbishop lie;
He sees his bowels gush forth out of his side
And on his brow the brain laid bare to sight.
Midst of his breast where the key-bones di-
    vide,
Crosswise he lays his comely hands and white,
And thus laments him as native use requires:
"Ah, debonair, thou good and noble knight!
Now I commend thee to the great Lord of
    might,
Servant more willing than thee He shall not
    find.
Since the Apostles no prophet was thy like,
For to maintain the Faith, and win mankind.
May thy soul meet no hindrance in her flight!
May Heaven's gate to her stand open wide!"

Now Roland feels that he is at death's door;
Out of his ears the brain is running forth.
Now for his peers he prays God call them
    all,
And for himself St Gabriel's aid implores;
Then in each hand he takes, lest shame befal,
His Olifant and Durendal his sword.
Far as a quarrel flies from a cross-bow drawn,
Toward land of Spain he goes, to a wide lawn,
And climbs a mound where grows a fair tree
    tall,
And marble stones beneath it stand by four.
Face downward there on the green grass he
    falls,
And swoons away, for he is at death's door.

High are the hills and very high the trees
    are;
Four stones there are set there, of marble
    gleaming.
The County Roland lies senseless on the green-
    sward.
A Saracen is there, watching him keenly;
He has feigned death, and lies among his peo-
    ple,
And has smeared blood upon his breast and
    features.
Now he gets up and runs towards him fleetly;
Strong was he, comely and of valour exceed-
    ing.
Now in his rage and in his overweening
He falls on Roland, his arms and body seizing;

He saith one word: "Now Carlon's nephew's
beaten.
I'll take his sword, to Araby I'll reive it."
But as he draws it Roland comes to, and feels
him.

Roland has felt his good sword being stol'n;
Opens his eyes and speaks this word alone:
"Thou'rt none of ours, in so far as I know."
He takes his horn, of which he kept fast hold,
And smites the helm, which was all gemmed
with gold;
He breaks the steel and the scalp and the bone,
And from his head batters his eyes out both,
And dead on ground he lays the villain low;
Then saith: "False Paynim, and how wast thou
so bold,
Foully or fairly, to seize upon me so?
A fool he'll think thee who hears this story
told.
Lo, now! the mouth of my Olifant's broke;
Fallen is all the crystal and the gold."

Now Roland feels his sight grow dim and
weak;
With his last strength he struggles to his feet;
All the red blood has faded from his cheeks.
A grey stone stands before him at his knee:
Ten strokes thereon he strikes, with rage and
grief;
It grides, but yet nor breaks nor chips the steel.
"Ah!" cries the Count, "St Mary succour me!
Alack the day, Durendal, good and keen!
Now I am dying, I cannot fend for thee.
How many battles I've won with you in field!
With you I've conquered so many goodly fiefs
That Carlon holds, the lord with the white
beard!
Let none e'er wield you that from the foe would
flee—
You that were wielded so long by a good liege!
The like of you blest France shall never see."

Count Roland smites the sardin stone amain.
The steel grides loud, but neither breaks nor
bates.
Now when he sees that it will nowise break
Thus to himself he maketh his complaint:

"Ah, Durendal! so bright, so brave, so gay!
How dost thou glitter and shine in the sun's
rays!
When Charles was keeping the vales of Mo-
riane,
God by an angel sent to him and ordained
He should bestow thee on some count-capi-
tayne.
On me he girt thee, the noble Charlemayn.
With this I won him Anjou and all Bretayn,
With this I won him Poitou, and conquered
Maine;
With this I won him Normandy's fair terrain,
And with it won Provence and Acquitaine,
And Lombardy and all the land Romayne,
Bavaria too, and the whole Flemish state,
And Burgundy and all Apulia gained;
Constantinople in the King's hand I laid;
In Saxony he speaks and is obeyed;
With this I won Scotland, [Ireland and
Wales,]
And England, where he set up his domain;
What lands and countries I've conquered by its
aid,
For Charles to keep whose beard is white as
may!
Now am I grieved and troubled for my
blade;
Should Paynims get it, 'twere worse than all
death's pains.
Dear God forbid it should put France to
shame!"

Count Roland smites upon the marble stone;
I cannot tell you how he hewed it and smote;
Yet the blade breaks not nor splinters, though
it groans;
Upward to heaven it rebounds from the blow.
When the Count sees it never will be broke,
Then to himself right softly he makes moan:
"Ah, Durendal, fair, hallowed, and devote,
What store of relics lie in thy hilt of gold!
St Peter's tooth, St Basil's blood, it holds,
Hair of my lord St Denis, there enclosed,
Likewise a piece of Blessed Mary's robe;
To Paynim hands 'twere sin to let you go;
You should be served by Christian men
alone,
Ne'er may you fall to any coward soul!
Many wide lands I conquered by your strokes

For Charles to keep whose beard is white as
    snow,
Whereby right rich and mighty is his throne."

Now Roland feels death press upon him hard;
It's creeping down from his head to his heart.
Under a pine-tree he hastens him apart,
There stretches him face down on the green
    grass,
And lays beneath him his sword and Olifant.
He's turned his head to where the Paynims
    are,
And this he doth for the French and for
    Charles,
Since fain is he that they should say, brave
    heart,
That he has died a conquerer at last. . . .

Now Roland feels his time is at an end;
On the steep hill-side, toward Spain he's turned
    his head,
And with one hand he beats upon his breast;
Saith: "*Mea culpa;* Thy mercy, Lord, I beg
For all the sins, both the great and the less,
That e'er I did since first I drew my breath
Unto this day when I'm struck down by death."
His right-hand glove he unto God extends;
Angels from Heaven now to his side descend.

The County Roland lay down beneath a pine;
To land of Spain he's turned him as he lies,
And many things begins to call to mind:
All the broad lands he conquered in his time,
And fairest France, and the men of his line,
And Charles his lord, who bred him from a
    child;
He cannot help but weep for them and sigh.
Yet of himself he is mindful betimes;

He beats his breast and on God's mercy cries:
"Father most true, in whom there is no lie,
Who didst from death St Lazarus make to rise,
And bring out Daniel safe from the lions' might,
Save Thou my soul from danger and despite
Of all the sins I did in all my life.". . .
His right-hand glove he's tendered unto Christ,
And from his hand Gabriel accepts the sign.
Straightway his head upon his arm declines;
With folded hands he makes an end and dies.
God sent to him His Angel Cherubine,
And great St Michael of Peril-by-the-Tide;
St Gabriel too was with them at his side;
The County's soul they bear to Paradise.

Roland is dead, in Heaven God hath his soul.
The Emperor Charles rides in to Roncevaux.
No way there is therein, nor any road,
No path, no yard, no foot of naked mould
But there some French or Paynim corpse lies
    strown.
Charles cries: "Where are you, fair nephew?
    Out, harò!
Where's the Archbishop? is Oliver laid low?
Where are Gerin, Gerier his playfellow,
And Berenger, and the good Count Othone?
Ivor and Ives, so well I loved them both?
Where's Engelier, the Gascon great of note?
Samson the Duke, and Anseïs the Bold?
And where is Gerard of Roussillon the
    Old? . . .
"God!" says the King, "how bitter my reproach,
That I was absent when they struck the first
    blow!"
He plucks his beard right angerly and wroth;
Barons and knights all weep and make their
    moan,
Full twenty thousand swoon to the ground for
    woe;
Naimon the Duke is grieved with all his soul.

Thomas Aquinas

Thomas Aquinas (*see note on page 275*) *in Of Cheating and Of the Sin of Usury was concerned with ethical problems raised within Christendom resulting from the
revival of trade, industry, and town life culminating in the
urban civilization of the thirteenth century. The new capitalism, fostered by the revival of trade, came under the*

close scrutiny of the church and many practices of the burghers were condemned outright. Many prime capitalistic virtues ran counter to the spiritual principles of Christianity and its founder. In Of Cheating Thomas raised and answered such questions as "Is it lawful to sell a thing for more than its worth?" and "Is it lawful in trading to sell a thing at a higher price than was paid for it?" In reading this selection, note (1) the basis for Thomas's conclusion that it is unlawful to sell a thing for more than its worth, (2) obligations of sellers and buyers relating to things exchanged, (3) the various categories of trade and what kinds of trade are just and what kinds are unjust, and (4) Thomas's method of argument compared with the method of present-day economists.

In Of Sin and Usury, Thomas drew some fine distinctions between just and unjust practices, yet it can be observed that in treating economic practices he made a serious effort to harmonize the traditional anti-capitalistic views of Christianity with the newer demands of the expanding middle classes coming into prominence for the first time in 800 years. In reading this selection note (1) Thomas's answer and explanation to the question of whether usury (lending money for profit) is sinful, (2) how he dealt with the problem of practices designed to circumvent the churchs' prohibitions against usury, (3) under what circumstances proceeds from usury are lawfully acquired, (4) what a man should do with profits made by usury, and (5) the relative degree of guilt in lending and borrowing at usurious rates.

From: *OF CHEATING and OF THE SIN OF USURY*

OF CHEATING, WHICH IS COMMITTED IN BUYING AND SELLING

We must now consider those sins which relate to voluntary commutations. First, we shall consider cheating, which is committed in buying and selling: secondly, we shall consider usury, which occurs in loans. In connection with the other voluntary commutations no special kind of sin is to be found distinct from rapine and theft.

Under the first head there are four points of inquiry: (1) Of unjust sales as regards the price; namely, whether it is lawful to sell a thing for more than its worth? (2) Of unjust

sales on the part of the thing sold. (3) Whether the seller is bound to reveal a fault in the thing sold? (4) Whether it is lawful in trading to sell a thing at a higher price than was paid for it?

First Article.

Whether it is Lawful to Sell a Thing for More Than its Worth?

We proceed thus to the First Article:—

Objection 1. It seems that it is lawful to sell a thing for more than its worth. For in the commutations of human life, civil laws determine that which is just. Now according to

As translated by the Fathers of the English Dominican Province in *The "Summa Theologica" of St. Thomas Aquinas*, R. and T. Washbourne, Ltd., London, 1918, Part II, Second Number, QQ. LXXVII–LXXVIII, 317–341. Courtesy of Benziger Brothers.

these laws it is just for buyer and seller to deceive one another: and this occurs by the seller selling a thing for more than its worth, and the buyer buying a thing for less than its worth. Therefore it is lawful to sell a thing for more than its worth.

Obj. 2. Further, That which is common to all would seem to be natural and not sinful. Now Augustine relates that the saying of a certain jester was accepted by all: *You wish to buy for a song and to sell at a premium,* which agrees with the saying of Prov. XX. 14: *It is naught, it is naught, saith every buyer: and when he is gone away, then he will boast.* Therefore it is lawful to sell a thing for more than its worth.

Obj. 3. Further, It does not seem unlawful if that which honesty demands be done by mutual agreement. Now, according to the Philosopher, in the friendship which is based on utility, the amount of the recompense for a favour received should depend on the utility accruing to the receiver: and this utility sometimes is worth more than the thing given, for instance if the receiver be in great need of that thing, whether for the purpose of avoiding a danger, or of deriving some particular benefit. Therefore, in contracts of buying and selling, it is lawful to give a thing in return for more than its worth.

On the contrary, It is written: *All things . . . whatsoever you would that men should do to you, do you also to them.* But no man wishes to buy a thing for more than its worth. Therefore no man should sell a thing to another man for more than its worth.

I answer that, It is altogether sinful to have recourse to deceit in order to sell a thing for more than its just price, because this is to deceive one's neighbor so as to injure him. Hence Tully says: *Contracts should be entirely free from double-dealing; the seller must not impose upon the bidder, nor the buyer upon one that bids against him.*

But, apart from fraud, we may speak of buying and selling in two ways. First, as considered in themselves, and from this point of view, buying and selling seem to be established for the common advantage of both parties, one of whom requires that which belongs to the other, and vice versa, as the Philosopher states. Now whatever is established for the common advantage, should not be more of a burden to any one party than to another, and consequently all contracts between them should observe equality of thing and thing. Again, the quality of a thing that comes into human use is measured by the price given for it, for which purpose money was invented, as stated in *Ethic. V.* Therefore, if either the price exceed the quantity of the thing's worth, or, conversely, the thing exceed the price, there is no longer the equality of justice: and consequently, to sell a thing for more than its worth, or to buy it for less than its worth, is in itself unjust and unlawful.

Secondly we may speak of buying and selling, considered as accidentally tending to the advantage of one party, and to the disadvantage of the other: for instance, when a man has great need of a certain thing, while another man will suffer if he be without it. In such a case the just price will depend not only on the thing sold, but on the loss which the sale brings on the seller. And thus it will be lawful to sell a thing for more than it is worth in itself, though the price paid be not more than it is worth to the owner. Yet if the one man derive a great advantage by becoming possessed of the other man's property, and the seller be not at a loss through being without that thing, the latter ought not to raise the price, because the advantage accruing to the buyer, is not due to the seller, but to a circumstance affecting the buyer. Now no man should sell what is not his, though he may charge for the loss he suffers.

On the other hand if a man find that he derives great advantage from something he has bought, he may, of his own accord, pay the seller something over and above: and this pertains to his honesty.

Reply Obj. 1. As stated above, human law is given to the people among whom there are many lacking virtue, and it is not given to the virtuous alone. Hence human law was unable to forbid all that is contrary to virtue; and it suffices for it to prohibit whatever is destructive of human intercourse, while it treats other matters as though they were lawful, not by approving of them, but by not punishing them. Accordingly, if without employing deceit the seller disposes of his goods for more than their worth, or the buyer obtains them for less than their worth, the law looks upon this as licit, and provides no punishment for so doing, unless the excess be too great, because then even human law demands restitution to be made, for instance if a man be deceived in regard of more than half the amount of the just price of a thing.

On the other hand the Divine law leaves nothing unpunished that is contrary to virtue. Hence, according to the Divine law, it is reckoned unlawful if the equality of justice be not observed in buying and selling: and he who has received more than he ought must make compensation to him that has suffered loss, if the loss be considerable. I add this condition, because the just price of things is not fixed with mathematical precision, but depends on a kind of estimate, so that a slight addition or subtraction would not seem to destroy the equality of justice.

Reply Obj. 2. As Augustine says: *This jester, either by looking into himself or by his experience of others, thought that all men are inclined to wish to buy for a song and sell at a premium. But since in reality this is wicked, it is in every man's power to acquire that justice whereby he may resist and overcome this inclination.* And then he gives the example of a man who gave the just price for a book to a man who through ignorance asked a low price for it. Hence it is evident that this common desire is not from nature but from vice, wherefore it is common to many who walk along the broad road of sin.

Reply Obj. 3. In commutative justice we consider chiefly real equality. On the other hand, in friendship based on utility we consider equality of usefulness, so that the recompense should depend on the usefulness accruing, whereas in buying it should be equal to the thing bought.

SECOND ARTICLE.

WHETHER A SALE IS RENDERED UNLAWFUL THROUGH A FAULT IN THE THING SOLD?

We proceed thus to the Second Article:—

Objection 1. It seems that a sale is not rendered unjust and unlawful through a fault in the thing sold. For less account should be taken of the other parts of a thing than of what belongs to its substance. Yet the sale of a thing does not seem to be rendered unlawful through a fault in its substance: for instance, if a man sell instead of the real metal, silver or gold produced by some chemical process, which is adapted to all the human uses for which silver and gold are necessary, for instance in the making of vessels and the like. Much less therefore will it be an unlawful sale if the thing be defective in other ways.

Obj. 2. Further, Any fault in the thing, affecting the quantity, would seem chiefly to be opposed to justice which consists in equality. Now quantity is known by being measured: and the measures of things that come into human use are not fixed, but in some places are greater, in others less, as the Philosopher states. Therefore, just as it is impossible to avoid defects on the part of the thing sold, it seems that a sale is not rendered unlawful through the thing sold being defective.

Obj. 3. Further, the thing sold is rendered defective by lacking a fitting quality. But in order to know the quality of a thing, much science is required that is lacking in most buyers. Therefore a sale is not rendered unlawful by a fault (in the thing sold).

On the contrary, Ambrose says: *It is manifestly a rule of justice that a good man should not depart from the truth, nor inflict on anyone an unjust injury, nor have any connection with fraud.*

I answer that, A threefold fault may be found pertaining to the thing which is sold. One, in respect of the thing's substance: and if the seller be aware of a fault in the thing he is selling, he is guilty of a fraudulent sale, so that the sale is rendered unlawful. Hence we find it written against certain people: *Thy silver is turned into dross, thy wine is mingled with water:* because that which is mixed is defective in its substance.

Another defect is in respect of quantity which is known by being measured: wherefore if anyone knowingly make use of a faulty measure in selling, he is guilty of fraud, and the sale is illicit. Hence it is written: *Thou shalt not have divers weights in thy bag, a greater and a less: neither shall there be in thy house a greater bushel and a less,* and further on: *For the Lord . . . abhorreth him that doth these things, and He hateth all injustice.*

A third defect is on the part of the quality, for instance, if a man sell an unhealthy animal as being a healthy one: and if anyone do this knowingly he is guilty of a fraudulent sale, and the sale, in consequence, is illicit.

In all these cases not only is the man guilty of a fraudulent sale, but he is also bound to restitution. But if any of the foregoing defects be in the thing sold, and he knows nothing about this, the seller does not sin, because he does that which is unjust materially, nor is his deed unjust, as shown above. Nevertheless he is bound to compensate the buyer, when the defect comes to his knowledge. Moreover what has been said of the seller applies equally to the buyer. For sometimes it happens that the seller thinks his goods to be specifically of lower value, as when a man sells gold instead of copper, and then if the buyer be aware of this, he buys it unjustly and is bound to restitution: and the same applies to a defect in quantity as to a defect in quality.

Reply Obj. 1. Gold and silver are costly not only on account of the usefulness of the vessels and other like things made from them, but also on account of the excellence and purity of their substance. Hence if the gold and silver produced by alchemists has not the true specific nature of gold and silver, the sale thereof is fraudulent and unjust, especially as real gold and silver can produce certain results by their natural action, which the counterfeit gold and silver of alchemists cannot produce. Thus the true metal has the property of making people joyful, and is helpful medicinally against certain maladies. Moreover real gold can be employed more frequently, and lasts longer in its condition of purity than counterfeit gold. If, however, real gold were to be produced by alchemy, it would not be unlawful to sell it for the genuine article, for nothing prevents art from employing certain natural causes for the production of natural and true effects, as Augustine says of things produced by the art of the demons.

Reply Obj. 2. The measures of saleable commodities must needs be different in different places, on account of the difference of supply: because where there is greater abundance, the measures are wont to be larger. However in each place those who govern the state must determine the just measures of things saleable,

with due consideration for the conditions of place and time. Hence it is not lawful to disregard such measures as are established by public authority or custom.

Reply Obj. 3. As Augustine says the price of things saleable does not depend on their degree of nature, since at times a horse fetches a higher price than a slave; but it depends on their usefulness to man. Hence it is not necessary for the seller or buyer to be cognisant of the hidden qualities of the thing sold, but only of such as render the thing adapted to man's use, for instance, that the horse be strong, runs well and so forth. Such qualities the seller and buyer can easily discover.

THIRD ARTICLE.

WHETHER THE SELLER IS BOUND TO STATE THE DEFECTS OF THE THING SOLD?

We proceed thus to the Third Article:

Objection 1. It seems that the seller is not bound to state the defects of the thing sold. For since the seller does not bind the buyer to buy, he would seem to leave it to him to judge of the goods offered for sale. Now judgment about a thing and knowledge of that thing belong to the same person. Therefore it does not seem imputable to the seller if the buyer be deceived in his judgment, and be hurried into buying a thing without carefully inquiring into its condition.

Obj. 2. Further, it seems foolish for anyone to do what prevents him carrying out his work. But if a man states the defects of the goods he has for sale, he prevents their sale: wherefore Tully pictures a man as saying: *Could anything be more absurd than for a public crier, instructed by the owner, to cry: "I offer this unhealthy house for sale"?* Therefore the seller is not bound to state the defects of the thing sold.

Obj. 3. Further, Man needs more to know the road of virtue than to know the faults of things offered for sale. Now one is not bound to offer advice to all or to tell them the truth about matters pertaining to virtue, though one should not tell anyone what is false. Much less therefore is a seller bound to tell the faults of what he offers for sale, as though he were counselling the buyer.

Obj. 4. Further, If one were bound to tell the faults of what one offers for sale, this would only be in order to lower the price. Now sometimes the price would be lowered for some other reason, without any defect in the thing sold: for instance, if the seller carry wheat to a place where wheat fetches a high price, knowing that many will come after him carrying wheat; because if the buyers knew this they would give a lower price. But apparently the seller need not give the buyer this information. Therefore, in like manner, neither need he tell him the faults of the goods he is selling.

On the contrary, Ambrose says: *In all contracts the defects of the saleable commodity must be stated; and unless the seller make them known, although the buyer may have acquired a right to them, the contract is voided on account of the fraudulent action.*

I answer that, It is always unlawful to give anyone an occasion of danger or loss, although a man need not always give another the help or counsel which would be for his advantage in any way; but only in certain fixed cases, for instance when someone is subject to him, or when he is the only one who can assist him. Now the seller who offers goods for sale, gives the buyer an occasion of loss or danger, by the very fact that he offers him defective goods, if such defect may occasion loss or danger to the buyer:—loss, if, by reason of this defect, the goods are of less value, and he takes nothing off the price on that account:—danger, if this defect either hinder the use of the goods or render it hurtful, for instance, if a man sells a lame for a fleet horse, a tottering house for a safe one, rotten or poisonous food for wholesome. Wherefore if suchlike defects be hidden, and the seller does not make them known, the sale will be illicit and fraudulent, and the seller will be bound to compensation for the loss incurred.

On the other hand, if the defect be manifest, for instance if a horse have but one eye, or if the goods, though useless to the buyer, be useful to someone else, provided the seller take as much as he ought from the price, he is not bound to state the defect of the goods, since perhaps, on account of that defect the buyer might want him to allow a greater rebate than he need. Wherefore the seller may look to his own indemnity, by withholding the defect of the goods.

Reply Obj. 1. Judgment cannot be pronounced save on what is manifest: for a man judges according to his knowledge. Hence if the defects of the goods offered for sale be hidden, judgment of them is not sufficiently left with the buyer unless such defects be made known to him. The case would be different if the defects were manifest.

Reply Obj. 2. There is no need to publish beforehand by the public crier the defects of the goods one is offering for sale, because if he were to begin by announcing its defects, the bidders would be frightened to buy, through ignorance of other qualities that might render the thing good and serviceable. Such defect ought to be stated to each individual that offers to buy: and then he will be able to compare the various points one with the other, the good with the bad: for nothing prevents that which is defective in one respect being useful in many others.

Reply Obj. 3. Although a man is not bound, strictly speaking, to tell everyone the truth about matters pertaining to virtue, yet he is so bound in a case when, unless he tells the truth, his conduct would endanger another man in detriment to virtue: and so it is in this case.

Reply Obj. 4. The defect in a thing makes it of less value now than it seems to be: but in the case cited, the goods are expected to be of less value at a future time, on account of the arrival of other merchants, which was not foreseen by the buyers. Wherefore the seller, since he sells his goods at the price actually offered him, does not seem to act contrary to justice through not stating what is going to happen. If, however, he were to do so, or if he lowered his price, it would be exceedingly virtuous on his part: although he does not seem to be bound to do this as a debt of justice.

FOURTH ARTICLE.

WHETHER, IN TRADING, IT IS LAWFUL TO SELL A THING AT A HIGHER PRICE THAN WHAT WAS PAID FOR IT?

We proceed thus to the Fourth Article:—

Objection 1. It seems that it is not lawful, in trading, to sell a thing for a higher price than we paid for it. For Chrysostom says on

Matth. XXI. 12: *He that buys a thing in order that he may sell it, entire and unchanged, at a profit, is the trader who is cast out of God's temple.* Cassiodorus speaks in the same sense in his commentary on Ps. LXX. 15, *Because I have not known learning,* or *trading* according to another version: *What is trade,* says he, *but buying at a cheap price with the purpose of retailing at a higher price?* and he adds: *Such were the tradesmen whom Our Lord cast out of the temple.* Now no man is cast out of the temple except for a sin. Therefore suchlike trading is sinful.

Obj. 2. Further, It is contrary to justice to sell goods at a higher price than their worth, or to buy them for less than their value, as shown above. Now if you sell a thing for a higher price than you paid for it, you must either have bought it for less than its value, or sell it for more than its value. Therefore this cannot be done without sin.

Obj. 3. Further, Jerome says: *Shun, as you would the plague, a cleric who from being poor has become wealthy, or who, from being a nobody has become a celebrity.* Now trading would not seem to be forbidden to clerics except on account of its sinfulness. Therefore it is a sin in trading, to buy at a low price and to sell at a higher price.

On the contrary, Augustine commenting on Ps. LXX. 15, *Because I have not known learning,* says: *The greedy tradesman blasphemes over his losses; he lies and perjures himself over the price of his wares. But these are vices of the man, not of the craft, which can be exercised without these vices.* Therefore trading is not in itself unlawful.

I answer that, A tradesman is one whose business consists in the exchange of things. According to the Philosopher, exchange of things is twofold; one, natural as it were, and necessary, whereby one commodity is exchanged for another, or money taken in exchange for a commodity, in order to satisfy the needs of life. Suchlike trading, properly speaking, does not belong to tradesmen, but rather to housekeepers or civil servants who have to provide the household or the state with the necessaries of life. The other kind of exchange is either that of money for money, or of any commodity for money, not on account of the necessities of life, but for profit, and this kind of exchange, properly speaking, regards tradesmen, according to the Philosopher. The former kind of exchange is commendable because it supplies a natural need: but the latter is justly deserving of blame, because, considered in itself, it satisfies the greed for gain, which knows no limit and tends to infinity. Hence trading, considered in itself, has a certain debasement attaching thereto, in so far as, by its very nature, it does not imply a virtuous or necessary end. Nevertheless gain which is the end of trading, though not implying, by its nature, anything virtuous or necessary, does not, in itself, connote anything sinful or contrary to virtue: wherefore nothing prevents gain from being directed to some necessary or even virtuous end, and thus trading becomes lawful. Thus, for instance, a man may intend the moderate gain which he seeks to acquire by trading for the upkeep of his household, or for the assistance of the needy: or again, a man may take to trade for some public advantage, for instance, lest his country lack the necessaries of life, and seek gain, not as an end, but as payment for his labour.

Reply Obj. 1. The saying of Chrysostom refers to the trading which seeks gain as a last end. This is especially the case where a man sells something at a higher price without its undergoing any change. For if he sells at a higher price something that has changed for the better, he would seem to receive the reward of his labour. Nevertheless the gain itself may be lawfully intended, not as a last end, but for the sake of some other end which is necessary or virtuous, as stated above.

Reply Obj. 2. Not everyone that sells at a higher price than he bought is a tradesman, but only he who buys that he may sell at a profit. If, on the contrary, he buys not for sale but for possession, and afterwards, for some reason wishes to sell, it is not a trade transaction even if he sell at a profit. For he may lawfully do this, either because he has bettered the thing, or because the value of the thing has changed with the change of place or time, or on account of the danger he incurs in transferring the thing from one place to another, or again in having it carried by another. In this sense neither buying nor selling is unjust.

Reply Obj. 3. Clerics should abstain not only from things that are evil in themselves, but even from those that have an appearance of evil. This happens in trading, both because it is directed to worldly gain, which clerics should despise, and because trading is open to so many vices, since *a merchant is hardly free from sins of the lips.* There is also another reason, because trading engages the mind too much with worldly cares, and consequently withdraws it from spiritual cares; wherefore the Apostle says: *No man being a soldier to God entangleth himself with secular businesses.* Nevertheless it is lawful for clerics to engage in the first mentioned kind of exchange, which is directed to supply the necessaries of life, either by buying or by selling.

OF THE SIN OF USURY, WHICH IS COMMITTED IN LOANS.

We must now consider the sin of usury, which is committed in loans: and under this head there are four points of inquiry: (1) Whether it is a sin to take money as a price for money lent, which is to receive usury? (2) Whether it is lawful to lend money for any other kind of consideration, by way of payment for the loan? (3) Whether a man is bound to restore just gains derived from money taken in usury? (4) Whether it is lawful to borrow money under a condition of usury?

First Article.

Whether it is a Sin to Take Usury for Money Lent?

We proceed thus to the First Article:—

Objection 1. It seems that it is not a sin to take usury for money lent. For no man sins through following the example of Christ. But Our Lord said of Himself: *At My coming I might have exacted it,* i.e. the money lent, *with usury.* Therefore it is not a sin to take usury for lending money.

Obj. 2. Further, According to Ps. XVIII. 8, *The law of the Lord is unspotted,* because, to wit, it forbids sin. Now usury of a kind is allowed in the Divine law, according to Deut. XXIII. 19, 20: *Thou shalt not fenerate to thy brother money, nor corn, nor any other thing, but to the stranger:* nay more, it is even prom-

ised as a reward for the observance of the Law, according to Deut. XXVIII. 12: *Thou shalt fenerate to many nations, and shalt not borrow of any one.* Therefore it is not a sin to take usury.

Obj. 3. Further, In human affairs justice is determined by civil laws. Now civil law allows usury to be taken. Therefore it seems to be lawful.

Obj. 4. Further, The counsels are not binding under sin. But, among other counsels we find: *Lend, hoping for nothing thereby.* Therefore it is not a sin to take usury.

Obj. 5. Further, It does not seem to be in itself sinful to accept a price for doing what one is not bound to do. But one who has money is not bound in every case to lend it to his neighbour. Therefore it is lawful for him sometimes to accept a price for lending it.

Obj. 6. Further, Silver made into coins does not differ specifically from silver made into a vessel. But it is lawful to accept a price for the loan of a silver vessel. Therefore it is also lawful to accept a price for the loan of a silver coin. Therefore usury is not in itself a sin.

Obj. 7. Further, Anyone may lawfully accept a thing which its owner freely gives him. Now he who accepts the loan, freely gives the usury. Therefore he who lends may lawfully take the usury.

On the contrary, It is written: *If thou lend money to any of thy people that is poor, that dwelleth with thee, thou shalt not be hard upon them as an extortioner, nor oppress them with usuries.*

I answer that, To take usury for money lent is unjust in itself, because this is to sell what does not exist, and this evidently leads to inequality which is contrary to justice.

In order to make this evident, we must observe that there are certain things the use of which consists in their consumption: thus we consume wine when we use it for drink, and we consume wheat when we use it for food. Wherefore in suchlike things the use of the thing must not be reckoned apart from the thing itself, and whoever is granted the use of the thing, is granted the thing itself; and for this reason, to lend things of this kind is to transfer the ownership. Accordingly if a man wanted to sell wine separately from the use of the wine, he would be selling the same thing twice, or he would be selling what does not exist, wherefore he would evidently commit a sin of injustice. In like manner he commits an injustice who lends wine or wheat, and asks for double payment, viz. one, the return of the thing in equal measure, the other, the price of the use, which is called usury.

On the other hand there are things the use of which does not consist in their consumption: thus to use a house is to dwell in it, not to destroy it. Wherefore in such things both may be granted: for instance, one man may hand over to another the ownership of his house while reserving to himself the use of it for a time, or vice versa, he may grant the use of the house, while retaining the ownership. For this reason a man may lawfully make a charge for the use of his house, and, besides this, revendicate the house from the person to whom he has granted its use, as happens in renting and letting a house.

Now money, according to the Philosopher was invented chiefly for the purpose of exchange: and consequently the proper and principal use of money is its consumption or alienation whereby it is sunk in exchange. Hence it is by its very nature unlawful to take payment for the use of money lent, which payment is known as usury: and just as a man is bound to restore other ill-gotten goods, so is he bound to restore the money which he has taken in usury.

Reply Obj. 1. In this passage usury must be taken figuratively for the increase of spiritual goods which God exacts from us, for He wishes us ever to advance in the goods which we receive from Him: and this is for our own profit not for His.

Reply Obj. 2. The Jews were forbidden to take usury from their brethren, i.e. from other Jews. By this we are given to understand that to take usury from any man is evil simply, because we ought to treat every man as our neighbour and brother, especially in the state of the Gospel, whereto all are called. Hence it is said without any distinction in Ps. XIV. 5: *He that hath not put out his money to usury,* and: *Who hath not taken usury.* They were permitted, however, to take usury from foreigners, not as though it were lawful, but in

order to avoid a greater evil, lest, to wit, through avarice to which they were prone according to Is. LVI. II, they should take usury from the Jews who were worshippers of God.

Where we find it promised to them as a reward, *Thou shalt fenerate to many nations,* etc., fenerating is to be taken in a broad sense for lending, as in Eccles. XXIX. 10, where we read: *Many have refused to fenerate, not out of wickedness,* i.e. they would not lend. Accordingly the Jews are promised in reward an abundance of wealth, so that they would be able to lend to others.

Reply Obj. 3. Human laws leave certain things unpunished, on account of the condition of those who are imperfect, and who would be deprived of many advantages, if all sins were strictly forbidden and punishments appointed for them. Wherefore human law has permitted usury, not that it looks upon usury as harmonizing with justice, but lest the advantage of many should be hindered. Hence it is that in civil law it is stated that *those things according to natural reason and civil law which are consumed by being used, do not admit of usufruct,* and that *the senate did not (nor could it) appoint a usufruct to such things, but established a quasi-usufruct,* namely by permitting usury. Moreover the Philosopher, led by natural reason, says that *to make money by usury is exceedingly unnatural.*

Reply Obj. 4. A man is not always bound to lend, and for this reason it is placed among the counsels. Yet it is a matter of precept not to seek profit by lending: although it may be called a matter of counsel in comparison with the maxims of the Pharisees, who deemed some kinds of usury to be lawful, just as love of one's enemies is a matter of counsel. Or again, He speaks here not of the hope of usurious gain, but of the hope which is put in man. For we ought not to lend or do any good deed through hope in man, but only through hope in God.

Reply Obj. 5. He that is not bound to lend, may accept repayment for what he has done, but he must not exact more. Now he is repaid according to equality of justice if he is repaid as much as he lent. Wherefore if he exacts more for the usufruct of a thing which has no other use but the consumption of its substance, he exacts a price of something non-existent: and so his exaction is unjust.

Reply Obj. 6. The principal use of a silver vessel is not its consumption, and so one may lawfully sell its use while retaining one's ownership of it. On the other hand the principal use of silver money is sinking it in exchange, so that it is not lawful to sell its use and at the same time expect the restitution of the amount lent. It must be observed, however, that the secondary use of silver vessels may be an exchange, and such use may not be lawfully sold. In like manner there may be some secondary use of silver money; for instance, a man might lend coins for show, or to be used as security.

Reply Obj. 7. He who gives usury does not give it voluntarily simply, but under a certain necessity, in so far as he needs to borrow money which the owner is unwilling to lend without usury.

Second Article.

Whether it is Lawful to ask for any Other Kind of Consideration for Money Lent?

We proceed thus to the Second Article:—

Objection 1. It seems that one may ask for some other kind of consideration for money lent. For everyone may lawfully seek to indemnify himself. Now sometimes a man suffers loss through lending money. Therefore he may lawfully ask for or even exact something else besides the money lent.

Obj. 2. Further, As stated in *Ethic.* V. one is in duty bound by a point of honour, to repay anyone who has done us a favour. Now to lend money to one who is in straits is to do him a favour for which he should be grateful. Therefore the recipient of a loan, is bound by a natural debt to repay something. Now it does not seem unlawful to bind oneself to an obligation of the natural law. Therefore it is not unlawful, in lending money to anyone, to demand some sort of compensation as a condition of the loan.

Obj. 3. Further, Just as there is real remuneration, so is there verbal remuneration, and remuneration by service, as a gloss says on Isa. XXXIII. 15: *Blessed is he that shaketh his hands*

from all bribes. Now it is lawful to accept service or praise from one to whom one has lent money. Therefore in like manner it is lawful to accept any other kind of remuneration.

Obj. 4. Further, Seemingly the relation of gift to gift is the same as of loan to loan. But it is lawful to accept money for money given. Therefore it is lawful to accept repayment by loan in return for a loan granted.

Obj. 5. Further, The lender, by transferring his ownership of a sum of money removes the money further from himself than he who entrusts it to a merchant or craftsman. Now it is lawful to receive interest for money entrusted to a merchant or craftsman. Therefore it is also lawful to receive interest for money lent.

Obj. 6. Further, A man may accept a pledge for money lent, the use of which pledge he might sell for a price: as when a man mortgages his land or the house wherein he dwells. Therefore it is lawful to receive interest for money lent.

Obj. 7. Further, It sometimes happens that a man raises the price of his goods under guise of loan, or buys another's goods at a low figure; or raises his price through delay in being paid, and lowers his price that he may be paid the sooner. Now in all these cases there seems to be payment for a loan of money: nor does it appear to be manifestly illicit. Therefore it seems to be lawful to expect or exact some consideration for money lent.

On the contrary, Among other conditions requisite in a just man it is stated that he *hath not taken usury and increase.*

I answer that, According to the Philosopher, *a thing is reckoned as money if its price can be measured by money.* Consequently, just as it is a sin against justice, to take money, by tacit or express agreement, in return for lending money or anything else that is consumed by being used, so also is it a like sin, by tacit or express agreement to receive anything whose price can be measured by money. Yet there would be no sin in receiving something of the kind, not as exacting it, nor yet as though it were due on account of some agreement tacit or expressed, but as a gratuity: since, even before lending the money, one could accept a gratuity, nor is one in a worse condition through lending.

On the other hand it is lawful to exact compensation for a loan, in respect of such things as are not appreciated by a measure of money, for instance, benevolence, and love for the lender, and so forth.

Reply Obj. 1. A lender may without sin enter an agreement with the borrower for compensation for the loss he incurs of something he ought to have, for this is not to sell the use of money but to avoid a loss. It may also happen that the borrower avoids a greater loss than the lender incurs, wherefore the borrower may repay the lender with what he has gained. But the lender cannot enter an agreement for compensation, through the fact that he makes no profit out of his money: because he must not sell that which he has not yet and may be prevented in many ways from having.

Reply Obj. 2. Repayment for a favour may be done in two ways. In one way, as a debt of justice; and to such a debt a man may be bound by a fixed contract: and its amount is measured according to the favour received. Wherefore the borrower of money or any such thing the use of which is its consumption is not bound to repay more than he received in loan: and consequently it is against justice if he be obliged to pay back more. In another way a man's obligation to repayment for favour received is based on a debt of friendship, and the nature of this debt depends more on the feeling with which the favour was conferred than on the greatness of the favour itself. This debt does not carry with it a civil obligation, involving a kind of necessity that would exclude the spontaneous nature of such a repayment.

Reply Obj. 3. If a man were, in return for money lent, as though there had been an agreement tacit or expressed, to expect or exact repayment in the shape of some remuneration of service or words, it would be the same as if he expected or exacted some real remuneration, because both can be priced at a money value, as may be seen in the case of those who offer for hire the labour which they exercise by work or by tongue. If on the other hand the remuneration by service or words be given not as an obligation, but as a favour, which is not to be appreciated at a money value, it is lawful to take, exact, and expect it.

Reply Obj. 4. Money cannot be sold for a greater sum than the amount lent, which has to be paid back: nor should the loan be made with a demand or expectation of aught else but of a feeling of benevolence which cannot be priced at a pecuniary value, and which can be the basis of a spontaneous loan. Now the obligation to lend in return at some future time is repugnant to such a feeling, because again an obligation of this kind has its pecuniary value. Consequently it is lawful for the lender to borrow something else at the same time, but it is unlawful for him to bind the borrower to grant him a loan at some future time.

Reply Obj. 5. He who lends money transfers the ownership of the money to the borrower. Hence the borrower holds the money at his own risk and is bound to pay it all back: wherefore the lender must not exact more. On the other hand he that entrusts his money to a merchant or craftsman so as to form a kind of society, does not transfer the ownership of his money to them, for it remains his, so that at his risk the merchant speculates with it, or the craftsman uses it for his craft, and consequently he may lawfully demand as something belonging to him, part of the profits derived from his money.

Reply Obj. 6. If a man in return for money lent to him pledges something that can be valued at a price, the lender must allow for the use of that thing towards the repayment of the loan. Else if he wishes the gratuitous use of that thing in addition to repayment, it is the same as if he took money for lending, and that is usury; unless perhaps it were such a thing as friends are wont to lend to one another gratis, as in the case of the loan of a book.

Reply Obj. 7. If a man wish to sell his goods at a higher price than that which is just, so that he may wait for the buyer to pay, it is manifestly a case of usury: because this waiting for the payment of the price has the character of a loan, so that whatever he demands beyond the just price in consideration of this delay, is like a price for a loan, which pertains to usury. In like manner if a buyer wishes to buy goods at a lower price than what is just, for the reason that he pays for the goods before they can be delivered, it is a sin of usury;

because again this anticipated payment of money has the character of a loan, the price of which is the rebate on the just price of the goods sold. On the other hand if a man wishes to allow a rebate on the just price in order that he may have his money sooner, he is not guilty of the sin of usury.

THIRD ARTICLE.

WHETHER A MAN IS BOUND TO RESTORE WHATEVER PROFITS HE HAS MADE OUT OF MONEY GOTTEN BY USURY?

We proceed thus to the Third Article:—

Objection 1. It seems that a man is bound to restore whatever profits he has made out of money gotten by usury. For the Apostle says: *If the root be holy, so are the branches.* Therefore likewise if the root be rotten so are the branches. But the root was infected with usury. Therefore whatever profit is made therefrom is infected with usury. Therefore he is bound to restore it.

Obj. 2. Further, It is laid down: *Property accruing from usury must be sold, and the price repaid to the persons from whom the usury was extorted.* Therefore, likewise, whatever else is acquired from usurious money must be restored.

Obj. 3. Further, That which a man buys with the proceeds of usury is due to him by reason of the money he paid for it. Therefore he has no more right to the thing purchased than to the money he paid. But he was bound to restore the money gained through usury. Therefore he is also bound to restore what he acquired with it.

On the contrary, A man may lawfully hold what he has lawfully acquired. Now that which is acquired by the proceeds of usury is sometimes lawfully acquired. Therefore it may be lawfully retained.

I answer that, As stated above, there are certain things whose use is their consumption, and which do not admit of usufruct, according to law. Wherefore if suchlike things be extorted by means of usury, for instance money, wheat, wine and so forth, the lender is not bound to restore more than he received (since what is acquired by such things is the fruit not of the thing but of human industry), unless indeed the other party by losing some of his own goods be injured through the lender retaining them: for then he is bound to make good the loss.

On the other hand there are certain things whose use is not their consumption: such things admit of usufruct, for instance house or land property and so forth. Wherefore if a man has by usury extorted from another his house or land, he is bound to restore not only the house or land but also the fruits accruing to him therefrom, since they are the fruits of things owned by another man and consequently are due to him.

Reply Obj. 1. The root has not only the character of matter, as money made by usury has; but has also somewhat the character of an active cause, in so far as it administers nourishment. Hence the comparison fails.

Reply Obj. 2. Further, Property acquired from usury does not belong to the person who paid usury, but to the person who bought it. Yet he that paid usury has a certain claim on that property just as he has on the other goods of the usurer. Hence it is not prescribed that such property should be assigned to the persons who paid usury, since the property is perhaps worth more than what they paid in usury, but it is commanded that the property be sold, and the price be restored, of course according to the amount taken in usury.

Reply Obj. 3. The proceeds of money taken in usury are due to the person who acquired them not by reason of the usurious money as instrumental cause, but on account of his own industry as principal cause. Wherefore he has more right to the goods acquired with usurious money than to the usurious money itself.

FOURTH ARTICLE.

WHETHER IT IS LAWFUL TO BORROW MONEY UNDER A CONDITION OF USURY?

We proceed thus to the Fourth Article:—

Objection 1. It seems that it is not lawful to borrow money under a condition of usury. For the Apostle says that they *are worthy of death . . . not only they that do these sins, but they also that consent to them that do them.* Now he that borrows money under a condition of usury consents in the sin of the usurer, and gives him an occasion of sin. Therefore he sins also.

Obj. 2. Further, For no temporal advantage ought one to give another an occasion of committing a sin: for this pertains to active scandal, which is always sinful, as stated above. Now he that seeks to borrow from a usurer gives him an occasion of sin. Therefore he is not to be excused on account of any temporal advantage.

Obj. 3. Further, It seems no less necessary sometimes to deposit one's money with a usurer than to borrow from him. Now it seems altogether unlawful to deposit one's money with a usurer, even as it would be unlawful to deposit one's sword with a madman, a maiden with a libertine, or food with a glutton. Neither therefore is it lawful to borrow from a usurer.

On the contrary, He that suffers injury does not sin, according to the Philosopher, wherefore justice is not a mean between two vices, as stated in the same book. Now a usurer sins by doing an injury to the person who borrows from him under a condition of usury. Therefore he that accepts a loan under a condition of usury does not sin.

I answer that, It is by no means lawful to induce a man to sin, yet it is lawful to make use of another's sin for a good end, since even God uses all sin for some good, since He draws some good from every evil, as stated in the *Enchiridion.* Hence when Publicola asked whether it were lawful to make use of an oath taken by a man swearing by false gods (which is a manifest sin, for he gives Divine honour to them) Augustine answered that he who uses, not for a bad but for a good purpose, the oath of a man that swears by false gods, is a party, not to his sin of swearing by demons, but to his good compact whereby he kept his word. If, however, he were to induce him to swear by false gods, he would sin.

Accordingly we must also answer to the question in point that it is by no means lawful to induce a man to lend under a condition of usury: yet it is lawful to borrow for usury from a man who is ready to do so and is a usurer by profession; provided the borrower have a good end in view, such as the relief of his own or another's need. Thus too it is lawful for a man who has fallen among thieves to point out his property to them (which they sin in taking) in order to save his life, after the example of the ten men who said to Ismahel: *Kill us not: for we have stores in the field.*

Reply Obj. 1. He who borrows for usury does not consent to the usurer's sin but makes use of it. Nor is it the usurer's acceptance of usury that pleases him, but his lending, which is good.

Reply Obj. 2. He who borrows for usury gives the usurer an occasion, not for taking usury, but for lending; it is the usurer who finds an occasion of sin in the malice of his heart. Hence there is passive scandal on his part, while there is no active scandal on the part of the person who seeks to borrow. Nor is this passive scandal a reason why the other person should desist from borrowing if he is in need, since this passive scandal arises not from weakness or ignorance, but from malice.

Reply Obj. 3. If one were to entrust one's money to a usurer lacking other means of practising usury; or with the intention of making a greater profit from his money by reason of the usury, one would be giving a sinner matter for sin, so that one would be a participator in his guilt. If, on the other hand, the usurer to whom one entrusts one's money has other means of practising usury, there is no sin in entrusting it to him that it may be in safer keeping, since this is to use a sinner for a good purpose.

St. Bonaventure

Bonaventure (1221–1274) epitomizes the intense interest in Christian mysticism that persisted during the later Middle Ages along with the equally strong concern with rationalism as a support to faith (exemplified by his colleague at the University of Paris, Thomas Aquinas). Bonaventure was born in Italy, entered the Franciscan Order, studied and taught at Paris, and in 1257 became General of the Franciscan Order. Two years later he wrote The Journey of the Mind to God based upon the Platonic belief that the things of this world are useful in revealing to man the ultimate source of being. The Journey of the Mind to God is a road map, as it were, elaborating the three stages of the soul's flight to the great unknown: first, finding the signs of God's presence in the material world; second, seeing God's image in the soul; and third, the direct contemplation of God. At journey's end the soul achieves "peace in eternal life, or eternal life in peace." In reading the following selection, note (1) the elaborate and specific analysis of the means by which the soul moves from the world of sense to the supreme good, (2) the arguments used to demonstrate the contention that God's footprints are to be found in creation and that it is possible to see God in these footprints, (3) the means suggested whereby God's image might be reconstructed in the soul and the best aid or guide for this purpose, (4) the steps necessary to achieve a vision of the timeless things of God, and (5) the suggestions given for the final steps into "the shaft of light that flashes out from the divine."

From: THE JOURNEY OF THE MIND TO GOD

PROLOGUE

At the outset I invoke the Source whence all enlightenment descends to man, the Father of light from whom is "every best gift and every perfect gift." Through the Son of God, our Lord Jesus Christ, I appeal to the Eternal Father that by the intercession of the most holy Virgin Mary, Mother of the same God and Lord, Christ Jesus, and by that of Blessed Francis, our guide and father, He might impart to us the "spirit of wisdom and revelation" so as to direct our feet in the ways of that peace which surpasseth all understanding. It was the gospel of this peace our Lord Jesus Christ preached; it was peace such as this He gave to men. Following in the footsteps of the Master, our father St Francis, went through life preaching peace at the beginning and end of every discourse, wishing peace to all whom he met on the way, and sighing after ecstatic peace in every elevation of his mind like a citizen of that Jerusalem, whereof it is said by that Man of Peace who was peaceful with them that hated peace: "Seek ye those things which are for the peace of Jerusalem." For he knew that only in peace

As translated by Father James in *The Franciscan Vision; Translation of St Bonaventure's Itinerarium Mentis in Deum.* London: Burns Oates and Washbourne Ltd., 1937, 9–10; 13–20; 23–25; 32–40; 45–54; 56–73.

stands the throne of Solomon, as it is written: "In peace is his dwelling-place, and his habitation is in Sion."

Inspired by the example of the Blessed Francis, I sought after this peace with ardent longing—I, a sinner, who, though in all respects unworthy, have succeeded, the seventh in the order of time, to the general ministry of the brethren. It happened that as this desire came vehemently to me, and I longed for peace, God led me, in the thirty-third year after the death of Francis, to Mount Alvernia as to a place of quiet. While I abode there and was pondering over certain elevations of the human mind to God, the associations of the place brought before me that miracle which on this very spot had happened to the Blessed Francis when he saw a winged seraph in the image of the Crucified. It occurred to me that the vision vouchsafed to St Francis typified the uplifting of our father in contemplation and the manner of his rapture suggested itself to my mind. . . .

DEGREES OF THE SOUL'S ASCENT: GOD'S FOOTPRINTS IN CREATION

"Happy the man whose help is from Thee, when he hath set pilgrimages in his heart through the Valley of Tears, to the goal he hath fixed." Since happiness is nothing else but the enjoyment of the Supreme Good, and the Supreme Good is above us, no one can be happy who does not rise beyond himself. This raising up of man is to be understood, of course, of mind and heart and not of body, and since there is question of reaching above himself on the part of man, he must be helped by supernatural strength and be lifted up by a higher power that stoops to raise him. However much then a man's inward steps are ordered and progress made, it is of no avail unless accompanied by help from on high. But divine aid is at hand for those who seek it with a devout and humble heart, and sigh for it in this Valley of Tears; this is done by fervent prayer. Prayer is, therefore, the source and origin of every upward progress that has God for goal. Wherefore, Dionysius in his "Mystical Theology," wishing to instruct us in these transcendent workings of the soul sets down prayer as the first condition. Let us each, therefore, have recourse to prayer and say to our Lord God: "Lead me, O Lord, on Thy path, that I may walk in Thy truth. Let my heart rejoice that it feareth Thy name."

By so praying we are led to discern the degrees of the soul's ascent to God. For, inasmuch as, in our present condition, this universe of things is a ladder whereby we may ascend to God, since among these things some are God's footprints, some God's image, some corporeal, some spiritual, some temporal, some eternal, and, hence, some outside of us, and some inside, it follows that if we are to attain to the contemplation of the First Principle and Source of all things, in Himself altogether spiritual, eternal, and above us, we must begin with God's footprints which are corporeal, temporal and outside us and so enter on the Way that leads to God. We enter in within our own souls, which are images of the eternal God, spiritual and interior to us, and this is to enter into the Truth of God. Finally, we must reach out beyond and above ourselves to the region of the eternal and supereminently spiritual and look to the First Principle of all, and that is to enjoy the knowledge of God in reverential contemplation of His Majesty. . . .

In direct relation with this threefold progress of the soul to God, the human mind has three fundamental attitudes or outlooks. The first is towards corporeal things without, and in this respect it is designated as animal or simply sensual; the next is where it enters in within itself to contemplate itself, and here it ranks as spirit; the third is where its upward glance is beyond itself, and then it is designated "mens" or mind. In all three ways the human soul must prepare to raise itself to God so that it may love Him with the whole mind, with all its heart, and with its whole soul, for in this consists the fullness of the Law and the highest Christian Wisdom.

But since every one of the aforesaid modes is doubled, according as we come to consider God as Alpha, and as Omega, or according as we come to contemplate God in each as in and through a mirror, or because each of these modes of contemplation may be joined with another, or operative simply and purely in itself, so it is necessary that these three primary grades should be raised to the number six;

whence, as God completed the universal world in six days, and rested on the seventh, so the smaller world of man is led in the most orderly way, by six successive grades of illumination, to the quiet of contemplation. A symbol of this may be seen in the six steps that led to the throne of Solomon; in the six-winged Seraphim which Isaiah beheld in vision; in the six days after which God called Moses from the midst of darkness; and in the six days after which, as we read in Matthew, Christ led His disciples up into a mountain, and was transfigured before them.

Corresponding to the six degrees of the soul's ascent to God there are within the soul six kinds of faculties or powers by which we rise from depths to the heights, from external to things internal, from things of time to those of eternity, to wit, sense, imagination, reason, intellect, intelligence, and the fine point or apex of the soul. These powers we have implanted in us by nature; by sin deformed, they are reformed through grace; and they must be purified by justice, exercised by knowledge, and made perfect by wisdom.

In his primitive constitution man was created by God capable of untroubled contemplation, and for that reason was placed by God in a "garden of delights." But, turning his back on the true light in order to pursue the mutable good, he found himself, through his own fault, diminished and removed from his pristine stature. With him the whole human race, through original sin, was afflicted in a twofold manner: the human mind by ignorance and the human body by concupiscence. As a result man, blinded and bent down, sits in darkness and sees not the light of heaven, unless he be strengthened against concupiscence by grace with justice, and against ignorance by knowledge with wisdom. All this is done by Jesus Christ, "who of God is made unto us wisdom and justice and sanctification and redemption." He, being the Power and Wisdom of God, the Incarnate Word full of grace and truth, is the Author of both grace and truth. He it is who infuses the grace of charity which, when it comes "from a pure heart, and a good conscience, and an unfeigned faith," is capable of ordering the whole soul according to the threefold aspect above mentioned. He also taught the knowledge of truth according to the triple mode of

theology: by symbolic theology in which He teaches us how we might rightly use sensible things, by theology properly so called wherein we learn the use of things intelligible, and by mystical theology through contact with which we may be raised aloft to things unspeakable.

Whoso, therefore, would set out in quest of God must first leave aside such sins as deform nature, and engage in the exercise of the aforesaid powers of his soul. By prayer he may hope for grace which will readjust his powers in harmony; in a holy life he must seek for purifying justice; in meditation he will seek that knowledge which enlighteneth; in contemplation he will acquire perfecting wisdom. Therefore, just as no one comes to wisdom save through grace, justice, and knowledge, so no one comes to contemplation save by clear-sighted meditation, by a holy life and devout prayer. As grace is the foundation of an upright will, and of a clear-sighted enlightened reason, so we must first pray, then live holily, and, thirdly, we must look long and attentively at the manifestations of truth; and so attending, we must rise, step by step, until we reach the high mountain where God of gods is seen in Sion.

Since it is imperative first to make the ascent of Jacob's Ladder before we can hope to descend, let us place the first step of the ascent at the bottom holding up this whole sensible world before us as a mirror, through which we may rise to God, the supreme Craftsman. In that way we shall be true Israelites passing forth from the land of Egypt to the land of promise, and also true Christians going forth from this world to the Father, and lovers of Wisdom who answer the Call which says: "Come unto me all ye that desire me, and be ye filled with mine offspring." "For from the greatness and beauty of created things, their Creator may be seen and known."

The supreme wisdom, power, and benevolence of the Creator are reflected in all created things. This is intimated in a threefold manner by the adjustment of external and internal senses in man. The bodily senses minister to the mind, whether it be engaged in rational investigation, in docile faith, or in intellectual contemplation. In contemplation it considers the actual existence of things; in faith it examines the unfolding of events; and in reasoning it surmises their potential pre-excellence.

The first point of view, which is that of contemplation, considering things in themselves, discerns in them weight, number, and measure: weight which marks the point to which they tend, number whereby they are distinguished, and measure whereby they are limited. Hereby it sees in things mode, species, order, as well as substance, virtue and action, from which the mind may arise, as from footprints, to the knowledge of the power, wisdom and boundless goodness of the Creator.

The second point of view, which is that of faith, when it considers the universe goes on to reflect upon its origin, its course, and its end. For "by faith we understand that the world was framed by the word of God." By faith we know that the three epochs—of nature, of the law, and of grace—have succeeded one another in order. By faith we know that the world will terminate with a final judgment. In the first, we observe God's power; in the second, His providence; and in the third, His justice.

The third point of view, that of reason, when it investigates the universe recognises that some things have only being, others being and life, and others possess not only being and life, but knowledge and discernment. This gives us three levels of reality, ranging from lowest to highest. From this viewpoint, also, it is clear that some things are merely corporeal, and some partly corporeal and partly spiritual, while others, ranking highest in perfection and dignity, are purely spiritual. Likewise some things, it is seen, are mutable and corruptible, such as terrestrial things; others are mutable and incorruptible, such as celestial bodies; whence it may be concluded that some things are both immutable and incorruptible, such as supercelestial things. From these visible things, therefore, the human mind rises up to consider the power and goodness and wisdom of God in whom reside Being and Life and Intelligence, in a purely spiritual, incorruptible, and immutable state. . . .

THE MIRROR OF THE MATERIAL WORLD

Speaking of the material world, of sensible things as a mirror wherein God is reflected, we must now proceed to make a distinction. It is possible for the soul to rise to the contemplation of God from a consideration of His footprints in the universe, but it is also possible to see God *in* these footprints, as it were, for God is there by virtue of His essence, His power, and His presence. This new approach leads to a deeper contemplation than that hitherto entertained; it marks a step forward, a second step, in the soul's pursuit of God which brings the soul to contemplate God in all those creatures that appear to it through its outward bodily senses.

We must observe, therefore, that the microcosm of the sensible world enters the microcosm of the soul through the portals of the senses; the soul reacts by apprehension, by fruition, and by judgment. The matter may be looked at in this way. There are in the sensible world some things that are sources in regard to others, there are others which are mere products, and others still which regulate both sources and products. Simple bodies, such as the heavenly bodies and the four elements, must be ranked amongst the first classes since from these elements, by the power of light which neutralises any contrariety in such mixed elements, are generated and produced whatever things are the result of natural operations. Minerals, vegetables, sensible things, and human bodies, being composed of the elements, belong to the class of things generated or produced. Exercising a kind of governance over such sensible realities, there are spiritual substances ranging from the souls of brutes which are altogether immersed in bodies to rational souls which are separable from the body up to spirits that are entirely separate, which are called Intelligences by philosophers but are known as Angels amongst us. The duty of moving the heavenly bodies devolves upon these Intelligences according to the philosophers, and for that reason the administration of the universe is ascribed to them. From the First Cause, God, they receive an influx of His power which they pour out again in their task of administration which regards the natural constitution and consistency of the universe. Theologians also ascribe to them the guiding of the universe according to the command of God, having in view especially the universe of redemption and its works, and in this context the Angels are called "ministering spirits, sent to minister for them who shall receive the inheritance of salvation."

Man, therefore, who is called the microcosm, is endowed with five senses through the gates of which knowledge of all things in the material world enters his soul. Through the sense of sight enter the sublime and luminous bodies together with all other coloured things; through the sense of touch come solid and earthly bodies; through the three intermediate senses, corresponding bodies: through taste, the aqueous, through hearing, the aerial, through smell, the vapourable, which are a mixture of humid and aerial and fiery as is clear from the fumes liberated by the spices. The portals of sense give entrance not only to simple bodies but also to things mixed and compounded of those. Seeing then that by means of the senses we perceive not only their proper sensible objects which are light, sound, smell, taste and the four primary qualities which are known by touch, but also the common sensibles such as number, magnitude, figure, rest and motion; seeing also that everything which is moved, is moved by something else, while certain things move and rest from themselves as do the animals, the senses which reveal to us the motions of the bodies in the universe around us lead us on to a knowledge of spiritual motions as from effects to a knowledge of their causes. . . .

We have now treated of the two first degrees of the soul's ascent to God. In these two steps by which we are led to contemplate God in His footprints, in the manner of two descending wings about His feet, we are taught that all the created things of this material world around us lead the soul of the contemplative and the wise man to the eternal God. The reason to be assigned for this is that sensible things in their totality are simply shadows, echoes, symbols, footprints, images and mirrors, signs divinely given and set before us for the beholding of God, their most powerful, wise and excellent First Principle, the eternal Source and Light and Fountain of all plenitude, of all art Efficient, Exemplary and Intelligent Cause. These things, I say, are so many "exemplata" or samples set before minds uncultured and immersed in the life of sense, so that from things seen they may pass to things invisible . . .

The visible creatures of the material world point to, and signify, the invisible things of God, partly because God is the Origin, Exemplar and End of all created things (and every effect is a sign of its cause, an example of its exemplar, and an indication of the end to which it leads), partly by its own representative power, partly also from prophetic prefiguring, partly from angelic action, and partly also by virtue of divine institution. By nature every creature is a figure and a symbol of divine Wisdom of which it is a likeness. But this is especially true of such things as are taken up by Holy Scripture or such as are employed by the Holy Spirit for the purpose of constituting them pre-figurations of spiritual things to come; particularly does it apply to those creatures in whose likeness God, through the ministry of His angels, appeared; but most especially is this verified of those things employed by God not only as signs merely but as sacraments as well.

From all this we gather that "the invisible things of God, since the creation of the world, are clearly seen, being perceived through the things that are made," so that those people who will not consider these things and come to behold and bless and love God in all things are inexcusable since they do not wish to pass from darkness to the wondrous light of God. But thanks be to God, through Jesus Christ, who has brought us from the region of darkness into His wondrous light, so that by those lights given to us in the external world we may be prompted and disposed to re-enter the sanctuary of our souls to behold in the mirror of our minds the reflection of God's own Light.

THE IMAGE OF GOD IN THE SOUL'S NATURAL POWERS

The two stages of the soul's ascent to God just described, wherein we beheld God mirrored in the external world, have guided us to the point where we experience the impulse to enter in within the sanctuary of our souls, there to see God reflected in His image. This third step must now be taken, so that entering in within ourselves we shall leave behind us the outer courts, as it were, to stand in the holy place which surrounds the Holy of Holies itself. There we shall behold the reflection of God as in the light of some candelabrum which reveals the radiance of the Holy Trinity emanating from the surface of our souls. Enter, therefore, into thyself and realise that thy soul loves itself most fervently. This it could not do did it not first know itself, and to know itself it must be present to itself by memory since nothing is assimilated by intellect unless it is remembered. Conclude from this that a trinity of powers adorns thy soul and for this inference depend not on the corporeal eyes of thy body but upon the spiritual eye of thy mind. When you go on to examine the workings and the inclinations of these powers of thy soul, you will be led to see God reflected in yourself, and by means of His image impressed upon the powers of your soul you will come to behold God as "through a glass in a dark manner.". . .

Passing on to the intellectual power of the human soul it is to be remarked that the function of this faculty is to perceive the meaning of terms, proportions and inferences. The meaning of terms it grasps when it knows by means of definition what any particular thing is. Definition, however, is not possible except by reference to some higher and wider notions, and these in turn lead us to some still higher genus, until ultimately we arrive at the very highest and most general ideas without a knowledge of which the more restricted notions contained under them cannot be definitely understood. Unless we know, therefore, what Being as Being is, we are not in a position fully to understand the definition of any particular substance. Nor can Being as Being be known unless it is envisaged in its most general conditions which are unity, truth, and goodness. Being may be considered in many ways: as complete and incomplete, perfect and imperfect, actual and potential, simple and conditioned, as a whole or in part, as static and dynamic, as from itself and as caused, as pure Being and as composite, as absolute and conditioned, as prior and posterior, as immutable and mutable, as simple and composite. But it is a general principle that the imperfect and that which is privative or negative may be understood only in terms of something positive. So the human reason cannot reach a full and final explanation of created things unless it is aided by an understanding of

the most pure, actual, complete and absolute Being, in other words, unless it reaches out to the utterly simple and eternal Being of God in whose mind are to be found the ultimate ground and reason of all things. How indeed could the human mind surmise that the particular things with which it comes in contact are defective and incomplete did it not possess some knowledge of a Being who is utterly devoid of imperfection? And the same argument applies to the other conditions of created things above specified. The human intellect may be truly said to know the meaning of propositions when it knows with certainty that they are true. It may then be said really to know since in such an assent it cannot be deceived, and since the object of its affirmation cannot be conceived to be otherwise the truth of its judgment must be something immutable. The human mind, however, being itself mutable, it follows that this apprehension of something entirely unalterable is possible only when it sees things in some other light that shines upon it unchangeably. Now such a light cannot possibly emanate from things created. Hence it is that the human mind knows things in the illumination of that light that "enlighteneth every man coming into this world"; and "this is the true light, the Word, which in the beginning was with God." In the matter of inference and reasoning, the human mind is aware of the validity of its processes when it sees that its conclusions follow necessarily from the premises given. This necessity will be found not only in the case of terms that are themselves necessary, but also in contingent matters as well as in things that are actually non-existent. Thus in the proposition, "If a man runs, he moves," the truth of the proposition is independent of the fact that man exists at all or not: if he runs, he moves. It follows that the necessity of inference is not to be derived from the actual existence of things outside us since such existence is contingent, nor yet from the existence of things in the human mind since in the event of their non-reality such an existence would be merely fictitious. It follows that to explain this necessity found in human reasoning we must have recourse to the prototypes of things in the art of God. There we shall find in the divine representation of things according to their aptitudes and mutual relations the ultimate ground of all necessity. For as Augustine says in his treatise, *De Vera Religione,* the mind of every man who rightly reasons is lit by that truth and endeavours to attain to it. From which it will be evident that the human mind is intimately associated with eternal truth itself, for without its teaching it would be impossible for the mind of man to know anything with certitude. Thou mayst, therefore, by means of thyself come to see the Truth which teaches thee, if thou art not impeded by passions and phantasms which come like clouds between thee and the radiance of Truth's light. . . .

GOD'S IMAGE RECONSTITUTED BY GRACE IN THE SOUL

The human soul may be not only a means whereby we come to behold God, the First Principle of all things, but it may lodge within itself this Principle so that we may come to the contemplation of God within ourselves. This is a form of vision, besides, which surpasses the previous one and constitutes the fourth degree of contemplation. When it is said that God is so near and intimate to us it will seem strange that so few people find Him. But the explanation is not far to seek. The soul does not succeed in entering in within itself when its memory is full of cares that distract its attention from itself. It is prevented also by the fact that its intelligence is crowded with phantasms which cloud its insight. Further, the attraction exercised upon it by things of sense draws it away and does not allow it to return to itself in a desire for inward delectation and spiritual joy. In a word, man is so deeply plunged in the life of sense that he cannot possibly discover within himself the Image of God.

Where a man falls, there must he lie, unless someone intervenes to raise him up. In the same way man must have lain, chained by the life of the senses and unable to come to the contemplation of his soul and of eternal truth within it, were it not for the intervention of Truth Itself. Taking unto Itself a human form in Jesus Christ, becoming, as it were, a ladder between earth and heaven, Truth repaired God's original ladder smashed in Adam. No matter how enlightened a man may be either by nature or by acquired knowledge, he cannot come to the contemplation of his inmost self or experience delight in the Lord except it be through the mediation of Jesus Christ, who says: "I am the door; by me if any man enter in he shall be saved and shall go in and out and shall find pastures." But the approach to this door is conditioned by our faith in Him, our hope in Him, and our love: by faith, hope, and charity. If, therefore, we are to re-enter in within ourselves, as into a long-lost paradise, and come to a fruition of the truth, we must enter by the door of faith, hope, and charity, virtues that are based on the mediation between God and man of His Son, Christ Jesus, who is, as it were, the Tree of Life in the garden of Paradise.

God's Image in the soul of man, then, must be re-constituted by means of the three theological virtues, faith, hope, and charity. These virtues purify, enlighten and perfect the soul, thus repairing God's broken Image, fitting out the soul for the heavenly Jerusalem and constituting it a unit of the Church militant which is the offspring of the heavenly Jerusalem as is suggested by the Apostle: "That Jerusalem which is above is free, which is our mother." The soul, therefore, that has faith and hope in Christ, and is adorned with Charity in Him, the Word of the Father, incarnate, uncreated and inspired, "the way, the truth and the life," has advanced in its quest in a threefold manner. By faith in Christ, the uncreated Word and Splendour of the Father, the soul recaptures two mystical senses of hearing and vision: hearing, to accept the sayings of Christ, and vision, with which to contemplate the splendours of His light. By the virtue of hope, the soul sighs for the coming of the Word proceeding from the Father, and in this longing and attachment begins anew to experience the sweet odour of Christ as by a veritable sense of smell. Finally, by love for Christ, hastening to embrace the Word Incarnate who comes, the soul receives in return from Him such heavenly delight that in a very ecstasy of love it finds itself anew experiencing such a relish and feeling of intimacy as can be only compared with the physical senses of taste and touch. The soul adorned with these new mystical senses is like the Spouse in the Canticle of Canticles, delighting with all its senses in the presence of its Bridegroom, celebrating in song its union with God, and for its purpose employing the medium of this Canticle of Canticles composed for those who reach the fourth degree of contemplation. The understanding of all this is beyond the grasp of people who have not actually experienced it; the experience itself is something ineffable and cannot be expressed in rational terms or exhausted by reflective considerations. In this degree of contemplation the soul is equipped with mystical senses for no other purpose than this experimental knowledge of God whereby it may behold that which is supremely beautiful, hear that which is deepest harmony, sense the most transcendent odour, taste a sweetness source of all other sweetness, and experience the intimacies of contact with the Source of all delights. Possessed of these mystic senses, the soul is disposed for ecstatic raptures of devotion, exultation and delight, as is suggested by three sets of phrases from the Canticle of Canticles. Of these, the first is uttered in a fullness of devotion and the soul is likened to a rod of smoke from the perfumes of myrrh and frankincense. The second, in an excess of exultation, sees the soul as like the dawn, like the moon, like the sun itself, raised up mystically to receive its Bridegroom. The third suggests the rapture when the soul in an ecstasy of joy leans upon its Beloved, gently breathing in the delight of Him.

At this stage the soul in its hierarchical character is prepared for the goal of its efforts which is that heavenly Jerusalem, with its divinely ordered hierarchy, into which it must enter. The very prime condition of this ultimate issue is that this supernal Jerusalem first descend into the heart of man, as John in his Apocalypse saw, and bestow upon the soul its own ordered and hierarchical character. This is brought about by the reconstitution of God's Image in the soul by grace and the theological virtues, by the addition of those mystic senses to which we have referred and by the rapturous elevations of the soul which follow, so that the human spirit now reflects the hierarchic order of the heavenly Jerusalem, being purified, enlightened and perfected. But if this hierarchy of heaven is to be reflected in the soul, it must, in addition, show forth the presence of heaven's nine choirs in an ordered

series which will consist of vocation, communication, persuasion, ordination, invigoration, command, acceptance, revelation and unction. The three first-named of these have regard to the nature of the human soul; the three following grades to the soul's industry and activity; the last three bear a direct relation to grace. Possessing these, the soul when it enters in within itself finds itself in presence of the heavenly Jerusalem, where it beholds the orders of the angels and reflected in these orders God who, dwelling in them, is the Source of all their actions. Little wonder that St Bernard should write to Eugenius:

God in the Seraphim loves as charity; God in the Cherubim knows as truth; in the Thrones He sits in equity; in the Dominations He prevails as majesty; He rules in Principalities as power; in the Virtues He reflects His virtue; in the Archangels He spreads His light; in the Angels His piety shines.

Thus entering within ourselves to find God as He is present to us in all those gifts which are the outcome of His most generous bounty we begin to learn how truly God is "all in all."

To attain to this degree of contemplation the indispensable and principal aid is the divinely inspired Sacred Scripture, just as for the preceding degree philosophy was the chief prerequisite. For the Scriptures inculcate chiefly the necessity of repairing what was lost by sin and of re-constructing the broken order of things. The virtues of faith, hope, and charity occupy accordingly a prominent place therein. This is especially true of charity. Of this St Paul says: "The end of the law is charity from a pure heart, and a good conscience, and an unfeigned faith." He also declares that charity is "the fulfilment of the law." Our Saviour inculcates the same truth when He says that "the whole law and the prophets" depend upon the two precepts, the love of God and the love of one's neighbour. These two forms of love are found united in the one true Bridegroom of the Church, Christ Jesus, who is at once our Neighbour and our God, who is our Brother and Lord, at once our Friend and our King, the uncreated Word Incarnate, our Creator and Re-Creator, Alpha and Omega. Christ is also the supreme High Priest who purifies, enlightens and perfects His Spouse, the Church, in its entirety and in every individual holy soul.

It is with Christ in this sense, and with His Church in its saintly hierarchy, that Scripture is chiefly concerned, urging men to be purified, enlightened and perfected according to the threefold law, the natural law, the written law, and the law of grace. Thus by the Mosaic law men may be said to be purified, by the prophetic revelations they are enlightened, and by the evangelical message they are brought to perfection. We may put it in another way. There is in Scripture a threefold meaning or significance: the metaphorical, by which men are purified and led to a more upright life; the allegorical, which illuminates the understanding; the anagogical, which intoxicates the soul with deep draughts of wisdom. All this is brought about by the different preparations we have just been describing. We began with the three theological virtues, then came the mystical senses, followed in turn by three forms of rapture, and finally came the many acts of the mind which fall into a hierarchical design. By these, indeed, as by so many steps, we enter in within our souls to behold God in the glories of the saints, and to rest therein, as in a bridal chamber, docile to the bidding of the divine Bridegroom not to stir until the impulse to awaken arises.

We have ascended two of the intermediary steps in the soul's progress towards the contemplation of God within it. In this there is the suggestion of the two wings, extending from the body, and poised as if for flight. In the first place, recall how we can pass to the contemplation of God when we regard our souls in their natural powers, with their activities, their inclinations, and acquired habits, as mirrors wherein God's perfection is reflected: this constituted the third degree or gradient in the soul's ascent to God. Secondly, we reached the fourth degree when we came to consider the soul, no longer in its mere natural state but as perfected by the life of grace, when we saw in turn the infused virtues, the mystical senses and supernatural raptures. The path stretches out before us, definitely marked and ordered, passing from purification to enlightenment and finally to perfection. The Scriptures light the way in partial revelations that pass from angel

to man according to the dictum of St Paul, "the law was ordained by angels in the hand of a mediator." In fine, the order and hierarchy that had to be introduced into the disposition of the soul for its ascent reflected the hierarchic choirs which are found in the heavenly Jerusalem.

The effect of all this progressive enlightenment on the soul is that it becomes the dwelling-place of divine Wisdom. The daughter and spouse and friend of God, a member of Christ the Head, and sister and co-heir with Him, the soul is made the sanctuary of the Holy Spirit, a temple grounded in faith, raised on hope, and dedicated to God in its own sanctity as well as in that of its conjoint body. All this is accomplished by the perfectly sincere love of Christ which is "poured forth in our hearts by the Holy Ghost who is given to us" and without which we cannot know the secret things of God. For as "no one can know the things of a man save the spirit of man, which is in him, even so the things of God none knoweth save the Spirit of God." Let us, therefore, be rooted and grounded in love, so that we may be able to comprehend, with all the saints, what is the length of eternity, the breadth of liberality, the height of majesty, and the depth of discerning Wisdom.

THE NAME OF GOD AND MIRROR OF THE DIVINE UNITY: BEING

God may be sought in the universe around us or in the inner world of our own soul. In the visible world we behold His footprints; in our souls we discern His image. It is also possible to seek Him in contemplation by raising the eyes of our mind to the light that descends upon us from on high, the light of eternal truth which illumines the minds of men. Seeking God in the visible world in the first degree of contemplation it is as if we stood in the outer court that leads to the tabernacle. Practising the second degree of contemplation, we have advanced a step nearer to the sanctuary; we stand, as it were, in the holy place itself. But it is to those only who reach the third degree of contemplation that it is given to enter, in company with the High Priest, into the Holy of Holies. There they will behold overshadowing the

Seat of Mercy two cherubim with outstretched wings from which they may learn that to the invisible and timeless things of God there are two approaches: the one absolute, wherein God is considered in His nature and essence; the other relative, which takes account of God's Personal properties.

In the first approach our minds are turned towards God as He exists in His proper essence and we feel that our first designation of Him must be: "He who is." But in the second approach we are led to view Him under the guise of goodness and then it seems that God's first name is simply "The Good." In these approaches our attitude is borne out by the two Testaments. In the Old, stress was laid upon the unity of the Godhead, as may be seen from God's reply to Moses, "I am who am," whereas in the New, the emphasis falls upon the presence of a plurality of Persons in God, as may be deduced from the manner of conferring Baptism "in the name of the Father, and of the Son, and of the Holy Ghost." And the Master, Christ, holding out to the young man, who had observed the Law, the offer of a more perfect life, spoke as if God's principal and exclusive attribute was that of goodness. "No one is good but God alone." Damascene, therefore, following Moses, declared that "He who is" must be looked upon as God's chief designation, whereas Dionysius, following Christ, says that God's proper name and designation is "The Good."

Beginning, therefore, with the contemplation of God's essential unity, it is necessary to direct our attention to the concept of Being. Being so certainly exists that it cannot be conceived as not existing. Only in a perfect flight from nothingness is Being to be found in all its purity, for Being and nothingness are absolutely opposed. . . .

Open the eyes of your mind then to Being in all its purity and be persuaded that it represents something absolutely underived. We must necessarily consider as first what cannot be said to originate in nothingness or in another. For if Being is not, absolutely speaking, first in all things, originating from itself and due to no other thing, then what is? Being presents itself to your mind as altogether free from non-being and therefore is it without beginning, without end, eternal. Nor does it allow of the

presence in itself of that which is not itself and is, therefore, without composition and perfectly simple. And since possibility presupposes non-being of some sort, Being excludes it and appears as supremely and completely actual. So you may justly account Being as devoid of imperfection and therefore absolutely perfect, and as indivisible and therefore supremely one. Summing up, it may be said that Being in its entire purity, simple and absolute, is primary, eternal, superlatively simple, actual, perfect, and unity itself.

All these things concerning Being are so certain that the opposite of them cannot be thought by anyone who understands what is implied by Being. Besides, these attributes of Being may be shown to flow from one of them as from their source. For if we take Being as Being absolutely, then it is primordial, that is, it imposes itself as something which is not to be derived from anything else and yet is not to be thought of as the cause of itself, from which it follows that it must be conceived as eternal. Since it is thus primordial and eternal, no composition can mar its perfection and therefore it must be utterly simple. But granted these characters of primacy, eternity and simplicity, Being must also exclude possibility and therefore must be equated with Pure Act. But if Being as Being is primordial, eternal, simple and entirely in act, is it not absolutely perfect? To Being so endowed nothing is lacking and nothing can be superadded. To repeat, Being is primordial, eternal, actual, and perfect. Therefore we reason that it is supereminently one, unique. Of any particular thing we may predicate many things, but of Being only can we say simply "it abounds" or designate it "superabundance" with reference to all other things. Accordingly, if we predicate all we have discerned to characterise Being of God we find He is primordial, eternal, simple, actual, perfect. So perfect indeed is He that we cannot consider Him as not existing or to be anything but God, one unique God. "Hear, therefore, O Israel, the Lord our God is one God." Should you see this in pure simplicity of heart you will be enlightened to some extent with the illumination of eternal light.

Nor yet have we thoroughly exhausted the content of Being; there is still scope for wonder and admiration. Being is at once first and last, eternal yet of the living present, simple yet greatest, at once utterly actual and immutable, altogether perfect and infinite, endowed with the highest unity yet all-pervading. Examining all this in simplicity of heart, still further light is in store for you when you reflect further that Being is an end precisely because it is a beginning. Seeing that it is ultimate in the order of origins and that it acts by reason of itself, Being must likewise necessarily enjoy the position of Ultimate End in regard to everything that exists. Being thus ranks as the beginning and end of all things, the Alpha and Omega. Being is also of the living present just because it is eternal, for the idea of eternity connotes that there is nothing to limit Being, that no deficiency or mutability disturbs its full possession of itself, and therefore that past and future are not predicable of it but that it is entirely in the enduring present. Likewise the magnitude of Being, its possession of the greatest possible perfection, is implied in Being's simplicity. Perfection of operation goes hand in hand with the simple nature of the principle whence it proceeds, the reason being, that the more unified and compact the principle of activity is, the more nearly does its efficacy approach infinitude. The immutability of Being follows from its utter actuality. This entire actuality of Being raises it to the perfection of Pure Act and it is inconceivable that that which is entirely in act should either lose or acquire anything, hence Being is immutable. The immensity of Being follows from its perfection. Nothing can be conceived greater than that which is perfect, nothing nobler, nothing of greater dignity, or we may say simply that than the perfect nothing greater can be conceived, hence Being enjoys the attribute of immensity. But endowed with such characters, Being must necessarily be infinite, extending to every mode of reality in virtue of its very unity. The unity of Being, whereby it is the One which explains the multiple in all its forms, goes to show that as the Principle upon which all things depend Being must be regarded as the universal Cause of all things. Hence it is that Being is at once the efficient, the exemplary and the final cause of things inasmuch as it is "the cause of existence, the ground of understanding, the norm of life." Being therefore pervades the universe of reality not as the essence of things but as the altogether transcendent, universal, and sufficient Cause whose efficacy is in the highest degree infinite and manifold in its effects because of its own utter unity of essence.

To repeat, in virtue of its absolute actuality and entire simplicity, Being is the origin and consummate end of all. Because it is at once eternal and of the living present, Being pervades and circumscribes all forms of duration as if it were both centre and circumference at once. Altogether simple and the most perfect, Being is at once entirely immanent in things and entirely transcendent; it is "the intelligible sphere whose centre is every where and whose circumference is nowhere." As pure actuality and entirely immutable, it moves all things else, remaining itself unmoved. Because of its perfection and immensity Being is immanent to all things without being included in them and outside all things without being excluded from them; it transcends all things and is not for that reason merely raised above them, and it is below the depths of things without being degraded. But because it is in the highest degree One and yet present to the many things of creation, Being may be said to be "All in All" even though the universe is plural and Being is one. This is so because of the utterly simple unity, the perfectly serene truth, and the entirely sincere goodness that are to be found in Being, which go to show that in Being reside all power, the ultimate prototypes of created things and the utmost communicability, so that Being is at once the efficient, the exemplary and the final cause of all: from Being proceed all things, through Being are made things that are made, and everything is ordained to Being as to the Final End. And because Being is omnipotent and omniscient, in every conceivable way good, to behold it perfectly is to be in possession of perfect bliss, as was declared to Moses: "I will make all my goodness pass before thee."

THE TRIUNE GOD MIRRORED IN THE GOOD

Having contemplated God in His essential nature, let us now proceed to consider God as a Trinity of divine Persons. Then the second

Cherub shall take his place beside the first. For as the concept of being is that which underlies all other notions and leads us to the vision of God in His essential attributes, so the concept of goodness will be the chief instrument by which we come to an appreciation of the divine nature in that diffusiveness which characterises its emanations.

Take the concept of goodness and see what is implied in it. Pushed to its supreme degree, as that which simply speaking is the best, then it is to be identified with something which cannot possibly be improved upon. Obviously it would be wrong to think of such as non-existent. If that were the case, it would no longer be supremely good, seeing that it is better to exist than not to exist. Moreover, conceived in this way the good must also appear to us as a trinity and a unity. For the diffusiveness which characterises all goodness must also be found in the Supreme Good. But in its highest form this diffusiveness must be at once actual and intrinsic, substantial and hypostatic, natural and voluntary, free and necessary, indeficient and perfect. In the Supreme Good there are two real processions, consubstantial and hypostatic, the one by generation, the other by inspiration. In each case the resultant principles are co-equal with their Sources and like in nature: in the one an eternal principle is begotten, in the other, this principle acting with its Source as co-principle, simultaneously loving and beloved, there is a further procession as the breath of their common love. Thus we have the Father and the Son and the Holy Ghost. Were these processions not found in God we should not be in the presence of diffusiveness in its highest form and could not therefore speak of God as the highest and most Supreme Good. In appreciating this divine profusion we must not be misled by the notion of diffusiveness in time which is merely a pin-point, or the centre as compared with the circumference of a circle, in relation to diffusion of eternal goodness. There is little difficulty in conceiving something greater than the diffusion of created things in time. But no diffusion of goodness can be conceived greater than this, that there is a communication of the whole substance in the one act of self-diffusion. God would not be the supreme form of goodness, therefore, if in reality, or to our way of looking at things, He did not possess this diffusion of Himself in the communication of His entire nature. Visualise for yourself, if you can at all, the Good in its absolute purity and you will find that it is the pure act of a principle reaching out in charity where there is something absolutely gratuitous, yet constrained, in its love, where its diffusiveness is the most complete both from the viewpoint of its nature and its will, where it utters a Word that pre-eminently contains everything, and breathes forth a Gift which contains all other gifts. Once you have realised the supreme communicability of the Good in its highest form you will see why a Trinity of Persons, Father, Son, and Holy Ghost, is so necessary to the unity of God. And in that same Trinity, according as you obtain partial views of It, it will be seen that the knowledge of one attribute leads to that of another. Starting with the idea of the Good in its supreme form, you see that the idea of communicability enters into it so that it must be supremely diffusive. That being so, its diffusiveness must be also substantial. This in turn leads the mind to a realisation of the similitude in nature between the principle and that produced, so that we are led from this likeness in nature to the further ideas of co-equality, co-eternity and co-intimacy of the Three Divine Persons. All this carries the mind on to the idea of circumincession, by which is meant that each Person of the Holy Trinity so penetrates the other that the Three Divine Persons are indissolubly united in substance, in power and in action.

Be not deceived, however, by the apparent clarity and simplicity of this vision into believing that you have fathomed the very depths of the Incomprehensible God. Reflected well upon, the six characteristics just referred to may well raise the soul into an ecstasy of wonder. Only think of this, that in the Supreme Good there is not only complete communication of Self but that this communication is accompanied with a distinction of Persons; that while there is consubstantiality there is likewise a plurality of subsistent Beings; that the similitude of Their nature does not exclude diversity of Persons; that Their co-equality is not inconsistent with a certain hierarchy of order; that though co-eternal the Persons are due to emanation; that there is stupendous co-intimacy of Persons together with the diffusiveness of the Good. What greater object of wonder could there be found than this? Nevertheless, what has been said may be predicated, with certainty, of the Holy Trinity, no matter how astounding it may appear. Consider the Transcendent Good now from the viewpoint of origins and distinctions. For this idea of origin and distinction is no less really found in the Trinity than the idea of self-communication and diffusiveness. Self-diffusion, remember, does not mean that a part only is communicated; all that is possessed, in fact, is transferred. So that there is a real distinction between that which proceeds and that whence it proceeds, though this distinction is not one in essence but is based on a difference of properties. Maintaining the unity of the divine essence, it is only in virtue of Their properties that the Persons in God are distinct. But because these properties are really personal there is an actual plurality of Persons. Taking up the question of origin, it must be said that the processions in God are processions of origin, and the order amongst the divine Persons is one of origin, not of time. In no way is there any implication of local change in the idea of emanation but simply of gratuitous inspiration by reason of the authority of the producer, a mission of authority the same as that held by anyone who sends. Yet this diversity does not destroy unity. Unity is saved by the substance which is one, and beneath diversity of Persons there is unity of essence, of form of divinity, of existence and infinitude. Pondered over one by one, these aspects of the Supreme Good supply the mind with something to enable it to reach a vision of the truth; by comparisons and contrasts its wonder will be greatly stimulated; but if the soul is to pass on from wonder to the intimacies of contemplation, let it consider further.

In Scripture we read that the Cherubim looked one towards the other: "Let one cherub be on the one side, and the other on the other. Let them cover both sides of the propitiatory, spreading their wings and covering the oracle, and let them look one towards the other, their faces being turned towards the propitiatory wherewith the ark is to be covered." This mutual regarding of each other is not without its mystical significance. For in this mutual beholding they simultaneously turn their faces towards the Seat of Mercy, thus fulfilling the Lord's own words in St John: "This is eternal life, that they should know thee the only true God, and Jesus Christ whom thou hast sent." Not only must God's essential attributes and personal properties be considered in themselves but also in relation to that closest union of God and man, the Hypostatic Union of the Man-God, Jesus Christ.

Place yourself in spirit in the exact position of the Cherub who enjoys a vision of God in His essential attributes and marvel at the many antinomies that come before his mind: the divine Being is at once first and last, eternal yet of the living present, entirely simple in His nature yet boundless and without limit, entirely everywhere yet nowhere localised, absolute in His perfection and unchanging, absolutely perfect without excess or defect yet immense and boundlessly infinite, supereminently one yet many in His way, containing in Himself all things that are, all power, all truth, all goodness. Then gaze with amazement at the Seat of Mercy. He who is the First Principle of all things is seen united to the last among things created; made on the sixth day of divine creating, man is joined to God, man born in the fullness of time, of a virgin, is linked with the Eternal. The supremely Simple is associated with that which is composite; Pure Act, completely actualised in Himself, becomes one with a being capable of both suffering and death; Infinity Itself is wedded to that which is finite. Thus it is that side by side we see absolute Unity and all-inclusive Perfection cohabiting with man, a composite and distinct from other things, in Jesus Christ.

Put yourself now in the place of the other Cherub who contemplates God in His personal properties, in His Trinity of Persons, and marvel at the harmony that underlies the co-existence of communicability and personal properties, of consubstantial unity and number, of sameness of nature and distinction of Persons, of co-equality and hierarchy, of co-eternity and production, of co-intimacy and emanation. By the Father is the Son begotten; by Both is the Holy Spirit breathed forth. Yet the Holy Ghost is ever with the Father and the Son and never abandons either. So while you gaze in wonderment at the Seat of Mercy realise what takes place in Christ, that in Him the unity of His Person co-exists with a trinity of substances and a duality of natures, and in Him there is no disharmony despite a plurality of wills. Of Christ, though He possess many properties, the divine and human may be predicated, and with the Father and the Holy Ghost, though possessed of varying degrees of nobility, Christ is still worthy of equal adoration. Ranking with Them in co-equal exaltation above all things, despite the diversity of dignity, Christ also enjoys with Them complete dominion over things, notwithstanding a diversity of powers.

Here in deliberations such as these does the human soul come to the perfection of its illumination. It arrives, so to speak, at the sixth day of creation when it begins to behold man made in the image and likeness of God. For if an image be but the expression of a likeness, then beholding Christ the Son of God, the Image of the invisible God, we begin to see our humanity so highly exalted by its intimacy with God, that seeing at once in Him the first and the last, the highest and the lowest, the circumference and the centre, the Alpha and the Omega, the Uncaused and the caused, the Creator and the creature, in a word, the hidden and the revealed, we may be said to have reached the summit of our illumination in its sixth degree and on the sixth day, as it were, of the soul's journey to God. Nothing then remains but the quiet and rest of the seventh day when the soul will cease from "all work which it hath done" to enjoy the ecstasy of contemplation.

THE QUIET OF CONTEMPLATION

In its progress towards the possession of God the soul has now passed through six stages. The number of these gradients in the journey of the soul is not without its own significance. Six steps led up to the throne of Solomon and to peace where, as in some inner Jerusalem, the true man of peace reposed in peace of soul. Six wings, too, enveloped the Seraph thereby suggesting to us a picture of the true contemplative raised up from things of earth and enlightened by supernal wisdom. And in six days was the labour of creation completed before the rest of the Sabbath supervened. Recall these six stages of human progress towards the quiet of contemplation. In the first, the soul was led to God by going out to external things to admire in them the work of God's creative power. Then, looking at creation, the soul beheld God's footprints upon the world's surface: the material world became a mirror in which it beheld its God. Next, turning its attention inwards to itself, the soul began to reach God from a consideration of itself as God's created image, and then a further step was made when it began to behold God in the mirror of its renovated being. Whereupon, the soul was led to raise its gaze above and beyond itself, seeking, as it were, the light of God's countenance and rejoicing in its own progress. But no rest was possible until it found God in His own reflected light, for all this progress was achieved in a degree suitable for those who are still pilgrims on the way to God and who must depend upon their own efforts to scale the heights of contemplation. But when the soul shall have reached the sixth step and begun to contemplate the First and Highest Principle of all and Jesus Christ, the Mediator of God and man, then it shall have contact with spiritual things, so sublime that any comparison with created things becomes impossible, and so deeply mysterious that all intellectual keenness is unavailing. Then it will be swept up not only beyond the wonders of all creation but out of its very self and above it. By means of Jesus Christ, the Way, the Door, the Ladder, shall this transition be affected, for He is, as it were, the Seat of Mercy, placed over the ark of God, and the Sacrament hidden from the ages.

With face fully turned towards this Seat of Mercy, seeing Him hanging on the Cross, in faith, hope, charity, devotion, delight, exaltation, appreciation, praise and jubilation, the soul is ready to celebrate its Passover, that is, its transition from things of time to the eternal, passing over, by the power of the Cross, the Red Sea into the desert where it will begin to taste the hidden manna, there to rest in the tomb of Christ to all appearance dead yet experiencing, in so far as a pilgrim may, what was promised on the hill of Calvary to the good thief: "This day thou shalt be with Me in paradise."

This was the vision of Blessed Francis on the lofty mountain where he was raised into an ecstasy of contemplation and upon which I thought out the things here written. To him appeared a six-winged Seraph fastened to a Cross. From the companion who was with him when these things happened and when he was taken up by God in ecstasy, I and many others have gathered this account. In this, Blessed Francis, another Jacob become Israel, is for us a perfect model of the contemplative life, just as hitherto he had proved himself outstanding in the life of action, so that more by the force of his example than by word, God invited the truly spiritual to seek after such quiet of contemplation and ecstasy of soul as was experienced by him on Mount Alvernia.

If this transition, however, is to be genuine and perfect, then must all labour on the part of the soul's reasoning faculty cease and the soul's deep affection be centred in God and transformed, as it were, into Him. So mysterious and sublime is this experience that none save he to whom it has been given knows anything of it, that nobody receives except he who desires it, and this desire comes to him only whose whole being is inflamed by the fire of the Holy Spirit sent by Christ upon the earth. Hence it is that the "hidden things" of God were revealed, as the Apostle says, by the Holy Ghost.

Since, therefore, to arrive at this rapturous state of soul nature is of no avail and human industry of comparatively little value, little heed must be paid to inquiry but much to unction, little account must be taken of human language but much of internal experience of joy, attention must be weaned away from words and writing so as to concentrate on God's Gift to man, His Holy Spirit. In a word, the human soul must turn away its eyes from all created essences to fix them on the uncreated Essence of the Father, the Son and the Holy Ghost; the words of Dionysius must well up within it and address themselves to the Triune God: "O supereminent and transcendent Holy Trinity, Inspiration of all Christian philosophy, direct our steps to the unknown, sublime, and resplendent heights of mystic utterances. On these heights are to be found the new, the absolutely unquestionable and unchanging mysteries of theology hidden away, as it were, in the obscurity of excessively lightsome darkness and illuminating silence. Here on these heights, so resplendent in their excessive light, men are enlightened and spiritual souls are filled with the splendours of the true good." These things we address to God. But to the friend to whom this writing is directed we also speak and say: Do thou, O friend, push on boldly to the mystic vision, abandon the work of the senses and the operations of the reasoning faculty, leave aside all things visible and invisible, being and non-being, and cleave as far as possible, and imperceptibly, to the Unity of Him who transcends all essences and all knowledge. In this immeasurable and absolute elevation of soul, forgetting all created things and liberated from them, thou shalt rise above thyself and beyond all creation to find thyself within the shaft of light that flashes out from the divine, mysterious darkness.

But if thou wouldst know how such things are accomplished, then ask grace, not learning; desire, not understanding; the groanings of prayer, not industry in study; the Spouse, not the master; God, not man; obscurity, not clarity. Seek not so much light as fire which inflames one totally, filling the soul with unction and ardent desires, and raising it out of its very self aloft to God. This fire is indeed God whose "furnace is in Jerusalem." It was kindled on earth by the Man, Jesus, in the fervour of His most ardent passion. In this fervour he participates who can say: "My soul hath chosen strangling and my bones death." He shall see God who chooses such a death, for it is undoubtedly true that "Man shall not see me and live." Let us die, therefore, and by the door of death enter into this darkness. Let us impose silence on our anxieties, our concupiscences, and upon the working of our imagination. Let us, with Christ crucified, pass from this world to the Father, that when He shall be revealed to us we may say with Philip: "It is enough for us." Let us listen with St Paul to the words: "My grace is sufficient for thee." Let us cry out exultingly with David: "My flesh and my heart faileth, but God is the strength of my heart and my portion for ever." "Blessed be the Lord forevermore; and let all the people say: Amen and Amen."

Renaissance and Reformation

By the fifteenth century the civilization of the Middle Ages was undergoing a profound change. One of the important influences bringing this about was the age of exploration which opened up new intellectual and geographical horizons to the people of Europe. Scholars began to study with renewed interest the writings of classical authors, and new humanistic and secular influences affected Europeans. Gradually men strove for greater individual expression, independent of the patterns which had formerly been so well established. Men began to think more intently in terms of pleasant living in the world about them, rather than the means of achieving the hereafter. One of the fields of cultural expression where this was most apparent was in art. Renaissance sculptors, painters, and architects created a new age of beauty that has not been surpassed by any subsequent period. In literature, too, a new interest in secular themes developed, and occasionally this trend went so far as to ridicule organized Christianity. This development, together with the growing individualism and the study of the early Christian dogma by some of the humanists, finally resulted in a revolt against the Catholic Church, itself, the institution which had been so influential in achieving the cultural unity of the Middle Ages. Before the challenge was over, new churches had been established, which protested against both the teachings and the practices of the Catholic Church, and the Age of the Reformation had forever broken the unity of Christendom.

Christopher Columbus

Christopher Columbus (1451–1506) was a native of Genoa who at an early age took up the life of a sailor. In 1492 he made his famous voyage under the sponsorship of Ferdinand and Isabella of Spain. This expedition was the climax of years of ambition on Columbus' part to reach the Orient via the route to the west. This letter was written on the return voyage to Gabriel Sanchez, an officer of the Spanish royal treasury. In reading it note (1) references which indicate Columbus' belief that he had arrived in the east, (2) his description of the islands he visited and other evidences of a scientific interest, (3) the articles he mentioned suited to trade, (4) his observation concerning facilities for commerce in the islands, (5) the customs and beliefs of the natives, (6) the opportunities he saw for missionary activity, and (7) any indication of imperial motives.

From: A LETTER TO GABRIEL SANCHEZ

As I know that it will afford you pleasure that I have brought my undertaking to a successful result, I have determined to write you this letter to inform you of everything that has been done and discovered in this voyage of mine.

On the thirty-third day after leaving Cadiz I came into the Indian Sea, where I discovered many islands inhabited by numerous people. I took possession of all of them for our most fortunate King by making public proclamation and unfurling his standard, no one making any resistance. To the first of them I have given the name of our blessed Saviour, trusting in whose aid I had reached this and all the rest; but the Indians call it Guanahani. To each of the others also I gave a new name, ordering one to be called Sancta Maria de Concepcion, another Fernandina, another Hysabella, another Johana; and so with all the rest. As soon as we reached the island which I have just said was called Johana, I sailed along its coast some considerable distance toward the west, and found it to be so large, without any apparent end, that I believed it was not an island, but a continent, a province of Cathay. But I saw neither towns nor cities lying on the seaboard, only some villages and country farms, with whose inhabitants I could not get speech, because they fled as soon as they beheld us. I continued on, supposing I should come upon some city or country houses. At last, finding that no discoveries rewarded our further progress, and that this course was leading us toward the north, which I was desirous of avoiding, as it was now winter in these regions, and it had always been my intention to proceed southwards, and the winds also were favorable to such desires, I concluded not to attempt any other adventures; so, turning back, I came again to a certain harbor, which I had remarked. From there I sent two of our men into the country to learn whether there was any king or cities in that land. They journeyed for three days, and found innumerable people and habitations, but small and having no fixed government, on which account they returned. Meanwhile I had learned from some Indians whom I had seized at this place, that this country was really an island. Consequently, I continued along toward the east, as much as 322 miles, always hugging the shore, where was the very extremity of the island. From there I saw another island to the eastwards, distant 54 miles from this Johana, which I named Hispana, and proceeded to it, and directed my course for 564 miles east by north as it were, just as I had done at Johana.

The island called Johana, as well as the others in its neighborhood, is exceedingly fertile. It has numerous harbors on all sides, very safe and wide, above comparison with any I have ever seen. Through it flow many very broad and health-giving rivers; and there are in it numerous very lofty mountains. All these islands are very beautiful, and of quite different shapes, easy to be traversed, and full of the greatest variety of trees reaching to the stars. I think these never lose their leaves, as I saw them looking as green and lovely as they are wont to be in the month of May in Spain. Some of them were in leaf, and some in fruit; each flourishing in the condition its nature required. The nightingale was singing and various other little birds, when I was rambling among them in the month of November. There are also in the island called Johana seven or eight kinds of palms, which as readily surpass ours in height and beauty as do all the other trees, herbs, and fruits. There are also wonderful pine-woods, fields, and extensive meadows, birds of various kinds, and honey, and all the different metals except iron.

In the island, which I have said before was called Hispana, there are very lofty and beautiful mountains, great farms, groves and fields, most fertile both for cultivation and for pasturage, and well adapted for constructing buildings. The convenience of the harbors in this island, and the excellence of the rivers, in volume and salubrity, surpass human belief, unless one should see them. In it the trees, pasture-lands, and fruits differ much from those of Johana. Besides, this Hispana abounds in various kinds of spices, gold, and metals. The inhabitants of both sexes of this and of all the other islands I have seen, or of which I have any knowledge, always go as naked as they came into the world, except that some of the women cover parts of their bodies with leaves or branches, or a veil of cotton, which they prepare themselves for this purpose. They are all, as I said before, unprovided with any sort of iron, and they are destitute of arms, which are entirely unknown to them, and for which they are not adapted; not on account of

any bodily deformity, for they are well made, but because they are timid and full of terror. They carry, however, canes dried in the sun in place of weapons, upon whose roots they fix a wooden shaft, dried and sharpened to a point. But they never dare to make use of these, for it has often happened, when I have sent two or three of my men to some of their villages to speak with the inhabitants, that a crowd of Indians has sallied forth; but, when they saw our men approaching, they speedily took to flight, parents abandoning their children, and children their parents. This happened not because any loss or injury had been inflicted upon any of them. On the contrary, I gave whatever I had, cloth and many other things, to whomsoever I approached, or with whom I could get speech, without any return being made to me; but they are by nature fearful and timid. But, when they see that they are safe, and all fear is banished, they are very guileless and honest, and very liberal of all they have. No one refuses the asker anything that he possesses; on the contrary, they themselves invite us to ask for it. They manifest the greatest affection toward all of us, exchanging valuable things for trifles, content with the very least thing or nothing at all. But I forbade giving them a very trifling thing and of no value, such as bits of plates, dishes, or glass, also nails and straps; although it seemed to them, if they could get such, that they had acquired the most beautiful jewels in the world. For it chanced that a sailor received for a single strap as much weight of gold as three gold solidi; and so others for other things of less price, especially for new blancas, and for some gold coins, for which they gave whatever the seller asked; for instance, an ounce and a half or two ounces of gold, or thirty or forty pounds of cotton, with which they were already familiar. So, too, for pieces of hoops, jugs, jars, and pots they bartered cotton and gold like beasts. This I forbade, because it was plainly unjust; and I gave them many beautiful and pleasing things, which I had brought with me, for no return whatever, in order to win their affection, and that they might become Christians and inclined to love our King and Queen and Princes and all the people of Spain, and that they might be eager to search for and gather and give to us what they abound in and we greatly need.

They do not practise idolatry; on the contrary, they believe that all strength, all power, in short, all blessings, are from Heaven, and that I have come down from there with these ships and sailors; and in this spirit was I received everywhere, after they had got over their fear. They are neither lazy nor awkward, but, on the contrary, are of an excellent and acute understanding. Those who have sailed these seas give excellent accounts of everything; but they have never seen men wearing clothes, or ships like ours.

As soon as I had come into this sea, I took by force some Indians from the first island, in order that they might learn from us, and at the same time tell us what they knew about affairs in these regions. This succeeded admirably; for in a short time we understood them and they us both by gesture and signs and words, and they were of great service to us. They are coming now with me, and have always believed that I have come from heaven, notwithstanding the long time they have been, and still remain, with us. They were the first who told this wherever we went, one calling to another, with a loud voice, "Come, come, you will see men from heaven." Whereupon both women and men, children and adults, young and old, laying aside the fear they had felt a little before, flocked eagerly to see us, a great crowd thronging about our steps, some bringing food, and others drink, with greatest love and incredible good will.

In each island are many boats made of solid wood; though narrow, yet in length and shape similar to our two-bankers, but swifter in motion, and managed by oars only. Some of them are large, some small, and some of medium size; but most are larger than a two-banker rowed by eighteen oars. With these they sail to all the islands, which are innumerable, engaging in traffic and commerce with each other. I saw some of these biremes, or boats, which carried seventy or eighty rowers. In all these islands there is no difference in the appearance of the inhabitants, and none in their customs and language, so that all understand one another. This is a circumstance most favorable for what I believe our most serene King especially desires, that is, their conversion to the holy faith of Christ; for which, indeed, so far as I could understand they are very ready and prone.

I have told already how I sailed in a straight course along the island of Johana from west to east 322 miles. From this voyage and the extent of my journeyings I can say that this Johana is larger than England and Scotland together. For beyond the aforesaid 322 miles, in that portion which looks toward the west, there are two more provinces, which I did not visit. One of them the Indians called Anan, and its inhabitants are born with tails. These provinces extend 180 miles, as I learned from the Indians, whom I am bringing with me, and who are well acquainted with all these islands.

The distance around Hispana is greater than all Spain from Colonia to Fontarabia; as is readily proved, because its fourth side, which I myself traversed in a straight course from west to east, stretches 540 miles. This island is to be coveted, and not to be despised when acquired. As I have already taken possession of all the others, as I have said, for our most invincible King, and the rule over them is entirely committed to the said King, so in this one I have taken special possession of a certain large town, in a most convenient spot, well suited for all profit and commerce, to which I have given the name of the Nativity of our Lord; and there I ordered a fort to be built forthwith, which ought to be finished now. In it I left as many men as seemed necessary, with all kinds of arms, and provisions sufficient for more than a year; also a caravel and men to build others, skilled not only in this trade, but in others. I secured for them good will and remarkable friendship of the king of the island; for these people are very affectionate and kind, so much so that the aforesaid king took a pride in my being called his brother. Although they should change their minds, and wish to harm those who have remained in the fort, they cannot, because they are without arms, go naked, and are too timid; so that, in truth, those who hold the aforesaid fort can lay waste the whole of that island, without any danger to themselves, provided they do not violate the rules and instructions I have given them.

In all these islands, as I understand, every man is satisfied with only one wife, except the princes or kings, who are permitted to have 20. The women appear to work more than the men, but I could not well understand whether they have private property or not; for I saw that what every one had was shared with the others, especially meals, provisions, and such things. I found among them no monsters, as very many expected, but men of great deference and kind; nor are they black like the Ethiopians, but they have long, straight hair. They do not dwell where the rays of the sun have most power, although the sun's heat is very great there, as this region is twenty-six degrees distant from the equinoctial line. From the summits of the mountains there comes great cold, but the Indians mitigate it by being inured to the weather, and by the help of very hot food, which they consume frequently and in immoderate quantities.

I saw no monsters, neither did I hear accounts of any such except in an island called Charis, the second as one crosses over from Spain to India, which is inhabited by a certain race regarded by their neighbors as very ferocious. They eat human flesh, and make use of several kinds of boats by which they cross over to all the Indian islands, and plunder and carry off whatever they can. But they differ in no respect from the others except in wearing their hair long after the fashion of women. They make use of bows and arrows made of reeds, having pointed shafts fastened to the thicker portion, as we have before described. For this reason they are considered to be ferocious, and the other Indians consequently are terribly afraid of them; but I consider them of no more account than the others. They have intercourse with certain women who dwell alone upon the island of Mateurin, the first as one crosses from Spain to India. These women follow none of the usual occupations of their sex; but they use bows and arrows like those of their husbands, which I have described, and protect themselves with plates of copper, which is found in the greatest abundance among them.

I was informed that there is another island larger than the aforesaid Hispana, whose in-habitants have no hair; and that there is a greater abundance of gold in it than in any of the others. Some of the inhabitants of these islands and of the others I have seen I am bringing over with me to bear testimony to what I have reported. Finally, to sum up in a few words the chief results and advantages of our departure and speedy return, I make this promise to our most invincible Sovereigns, that, if I am supported by some little assistance from them, I will give them as much gold as they have need of, and in addition spices, cotton, and mastic, which is found only in Chios, and as much aloes-wood, and as many heathen slaves as their Majesties may choose to demand; besides these, rhubarb and other kinds of drugs, which I think the men I left in the fort before alluded to have already discovered, or will do so; as I have myself delayed nowhere longer than the winds compelled me, except while I was providing for the construction of a fort in the city of Nativity, and for making all things safe.

Although these matters are very wonderful and unheard of, they would have been much more so if ships to a reasonable amount had been furnished me. But what has been accomplished is great and wonderful, and not at all proportionate to my deserts, but to the sacred Christian faith, and to the piety and religion of our Sovereigns. For what the mind of man could not compass, the spirit of God has granted to mortals. For God is wont to listen to his servants who love his precepts, even in impossibilities, as has happened to me in the present instance, who have accomplished what human strength has hitherto never attained. For, if any one has written or told anything about these islands, all have done so either obscurely or by guesswork, so that it has almost seemed to be fabulous.

Therefore let King and Queen and Princes, and their most fortunate realms, and all other Christian provinces, let us all return thanks to our Lord and Saviour Jesus Christ, who has bestowed so great a victory and reward upon us; let there be processions and solemn sacrifices prepared; let the churches be decked with festal boughs; let Christ rejoice upon earth as he rejoices in heaven, as he foresees that so many souls of so many people heretofore lost are to be saved; and let us be glad not only for the exaltation of our faith, but also for the increase of temporal prosperity, in which not only Spain, but all Christendom is about to share.

As these things have been accomplished, so have they been briefly narrated. Farewell.

CHRISTOPHER COLOM,
Admiral of the Ocean Fleet.

Lisbon, March 14th [1493].

Niccolò Machiavelli

Niccolò Machiavelli (1469–1527) was a Florentine statesman and one of the outstanding writers on the theory of the state in early modern times. Keenly anxious to see Italy united, he opposed the papal claims to temporal power and advocated the doctrine of secular absolutism, of which his Prince was the personification. He differed with those who asserted that the state's principal objective was a moral one, and insisted that ethics must be divorced from politics. He advocated rather the doctrine that the ruler is justified in following any course which will serve the state. Machiavelli has been widely criticized for his views, and his name has become synonymous with political duplicity. In fairness to the man, however, his writings should be analyzed in terms of the political and social conditions of his age, and not by those of the present day. In reading the selections from The Prince note (1) the sources of Machiavelli's knowledge, (2) his proposal for ruling a conquered people accustomed to governing themselves, (3) how to measure a state's power, (4) a ruler's duty concerning the study of war, (5) his cynical views of human nature, (6) his discussion of the utility of cruelty, (7) his views concerning a prince keeping good faith, (8) the problem of free will versus chance, (9) his views of the barbarians and their influence on his thinking, (10) evidences of an immoral or amoral view toward politics, and (11) the relevance of the last chapter to his motivation in writing.

From: THE PRINCE

Niccolò Machiavelli
to
Lorenzo the Magnificent
Son of Piero Di Medici

It is customary for those who wish to gain the favour of a prince to endeavour to do so by offering him gifts of those things which they hold most precious, or in which they know him to take especial delight. In this way princes are often presented with horses, arms, cloth of gold, gems, and such-like ornaments worthy of their grandeur. In my desire, however, to offer to Your Highness some humble testimony of my devotion, I have been unable to find among my possessions anything which I hold so dear or esteem so highly as that knowledge of the deeds of great men which I have acquired

As translated by Luigi Ricci, revised by E. R. P. Vincent in Niccolò Machiavelli, *The Prince*, The World's Classics, Oxford University Press, London, 1935, 20–21; 47–49; 65–67; 73–80; 111–119. Courtesy of the Oxford University Press.

through a long experience of modern events and a constant study of the past.

With the utmost diligence I have long pondered and scrutinised the actions of the great, and now I offer the results to Your Highness within the compass of a small volume: and although I deem this work unworthy of Your Highness's acceptance, yet my confidence in your humanity assures me that you will receive it with favour, knowing that it is not in my power to offer you a greater gift than that of enabling you to understand in a very short time all those things which I have learnt at the cost of privation and danger in the course of many years. I have not sought to adorn my work with long phrases or high-sounding words or any of those superficial attractions and ornaments with which many writers seek to embellish their material, as I desire no honour for my work but such as the novelty and gravity of its subject may justly deserve. Nor will it, I trust, be deemed presumptuous on the part of a man of humble and obscure condition to attempt to discuss and direct the government of princes; for in the same way that landscape painters station themselves in the valleys in order to draw mountains or high ground, and ascend an eminence in order to get a good view of the plains, so it is necessary to be a prince to know thoroughly the nature of the people, and one of the populace to know the nature of princes.

May I trust, therefore, that Your Highness will accept this little gift in the spirit in which it is offered; and if Your Highness will deign to peruse it, you will recognise in it my ardent desire that you may attain to that grandeur which fortune and your own merits presage for you.

And should Your Highness gaze down from the summit of your lofty position towards this humble spot, you will recognise the great and unmerited sufferings inflicted on me by a cruel fate. . . .

THE WAY TO GOVERN CITIES OR DOMINIONS THAT, PREVIOUS TO BEING OCCUPIED, LIVED UNDER THEIR OWN LAWS

When those states which have been acquired are accustomed to live at liberty under their own laws, there are three ways of holding them.

The first is to despoil them; the second is to go and live there in person; the third is to allow them to live under their own laws, taking tribute of them, and creating within the country a government composed of a few who will keep it friendly to you. Because this government, being created by the prince, knows that it cannot exist without his friendship and protection, and will do all it can to keep them. What is more, a city used to liberty can be more easily held by means of its citizens than in any other way, if you wish to preserve it.

There is the example of the Spartans and the Romans. The Spartans held Athens and Thebes by creating within them a government of a few; nevertheless they lost them. The Romans, in order to hold Capua, Carthage, and Numantia, ravaged them, but did not lose them. They wanted to hold Greece in almost the same way as the Spartans held it, leaving it free and under its own laws, but they did not succeed; so that they were compelled to lay waste many cities in that province in order to keep it, because in truth there is no sure method of holding them except by despoiling them. And whoever becomes the ruler of a free city and does not destroy it, can expect to be destroyed by it, for it can always find a motive for rebellion in the name of liberty and of its ancient usages, which are forgotten neither by lapse of time nor by benefits received; and whatever one does or provides, so long as the inhabitants are not separated or dispersed, they do not forget that name and those usages, but appeal to them at once in every emergency, as did Pisa after being so many years held in servitude by the Florentines. But when cities or provinces have been accustomed to live under a prince, and the family of that prince is extinguished, being on the one hand used to obey, and on the other not having their old prince, they cannot unite in choosing one from among themselves, and they do not know how to live in freedom, so that they are slower to take arms, and a prince can win them over with greater facility and establish himself securely. But in republics there is greater life, greater hatred, and more desire for vengeance; they do not and cannot cast aside the memory of their ancient liberty, so that the surest way is either to lay them waste or reside in them. . . .

HOW THE STRENGTH OF ALL STATES SHOULD BE MEASURED

In examining the character of these principalities it is necessary to consider another point, namely, whether the prince has such a position as to be able in case of need to maintain himself alone, or whether he has always need of the protection of others. The better to explain this I would say, that I consider those capable of maintaining themselves alone who can, through abundance of men or money, put together a sufficient army, and hold the field against any one who assails them; and I consider to have need of others, those who cannot take the field against their enemies, but are obliged to take refuge within their walls and stand on the defensive. We have already discussed the former case and will speak of it in future as occasion arises. In the second case there is nothing to be said except to encourage such a prince to provision and fortify his own town, and not to trouble about the surrounding country. And whoever has strongly fortified his town and, as regards the government of his subjects, has proceeded as we have already described and will further relate, will be attacked with great reluctance, for men are always averse to enterprises in which they foresee difficulties, and it can never appear easy to attack one who has his town stoutly defended and is not hated by the people.

The cities of Germany are absolutely free, have little surrounding country, and obey the emperor when they choose, and they do not fear him or any other potentate that they have about them. They are fortified in such a manner that every one thinks that to reduce them would be tedious and difficult, for they all have the necessary moats and bastions, sufficient artillery, and always keep food, drink, and fuel for one year in the public storehouses. Beyond which, to keep the lower classes satisfied, and without loss to the commonwealth, they have always enough means to give them work for one year in these employments which form the nerve and life of the town, and in the industries by which the lower classes live. Military exercises are still held in high reputation, and many regulations are in force for maintaining them.

A prince, therefore, who possesses a strong city and does not make himself hated, cannot be assaulted; and if he were to be so, the assailant would be obliged to retire shamefully; for so many things change, that it is almost impossible for any one to maintain a siege for a year with his armies idle. And to those who urge that the people, having their possessions outside and seeing them burnt, will not have patience, and the long siege and self-interest will make them forget their prince, I reply that a powerful and courageous prince will always overcome those difficulties by now raising the hopes of his subjects that the evils will not last long, now impressing them with fear of the enemy's cruelty, now by dextrously assuring himself of those who appear too bold. Besides which, the enemy would naturally burn and ravage the country on first arriving and at the time when men's minds are still hot and eager to defend themselves, and therefore the prince has still less to fear, for after some time, when people have cooled down, the damage is done, the evil has been suffered, and there is no remedy, so that they are the more ready to unite with their prince, as it appears that he is under an obligation to them, their houses having been burnt and their possessions ruined in his defence.

It is the nature of men to be as much bound by the benefits that they confer as by those they receive. From which it follows that, everything considered, a prudent prince will not find it difficult to uphold the courage of his subjects both at the commencement and during a state of siege, if he possesses provisions and means to defend himself. . . .

THE DUTIES OF A PRINCE WITH REGARD TO THE MILITIA

A prince should therefore have no other aim or thought, nor take up any other thing for his study, but war and its organisation and discipline, for that is the only art that is necessary to one who commands, and it is of such virtue that it not only maintains those who are born princes, but often enables men of private fortune to attain to that rank. And one sees, on the other hand, that when princes think more of luxury than of arms, they lose their state. The chief cause of the loss of states is the contempt of this art, and the way to acquire them is to be well versed in the same.

Francesco Sforza, through being well armed, became, from private status, Duke of Milan; his sons, through wishing to avoid the fatigue and hardship of war, from dukes became private persons. For among other evils caused by being disarmed, it renders you contemptible; which is one of those disgraceful things which a prince must guard against, as will be explained later. Because there is no comparison whatever between an armed and a disarmed man; it is not reasonable to suppose that one who is armed will obey willingly one who is unarmed; or that any unarmed man will remain safe among armed servants. For one being disdainful and the other suspicious, it is not possible for them to act well together. And therefore a prince who is ignorant of military matters, besides the other misfortunes already mentioned, cannot be esteemed by his soldiers, nor have confidence in them.

He ought, therefore, never to let his thoughts stray from the exercise of war; and in peace he ought to practise it more than in war, which he can do in two ways: by action and by study. As to action, he must, besides keeping his men well disciplined and exercised, engage continually in hunting, and thus accustom his body to hardships; and meanwhile learn the nature of the land, how steep the mountains are, how the valleys debouch, where the plains lie, and understand the nature of rivers and swamps. To all this he should devote great attention. This knowledge is useful in two ways. In the first place, one learns to know one's country, and can the better see how to defend it. Then by means of the knowledge and experience gained in one locality, one can easily understand any other that it may be necessary to observe; for the hills and valleys, plains and rivers of Tuscany, for instance, have a certain resemblance to those of other provinces, so that from a knowledge of the country in one province one can easily arrive at a knowledge of others. And that prince who is lacking in this skill is wanting in the first essentials of a leader; for it is this which teaches how to find the enemy, take up quarters, lead armies, plan battles and lay siege to towns with advantage.

Philopoemen, prince of the Achaei, among other praises bestowed on him by writers, is lauded because in times of peace he thought of nothing but the methods of warfare, and when he was in the country with his friends, he often stopped and asked them: If the enemy were on that hill and we found ourselves here with our army, which of us would have the advantage? How could we safely approach him maintaining our order? If we wished to retire, what ought we to do? If they retired, how should we follow them? And he put before them as they went along all the contingencies that might happen to an army, heard their opinion, gave his own, fortifying it by argument; so that thanks to these constant reflections there could never happen any incident when actually leading his armies for which he was not prepared.

But as to exercise for the mind, the prince ought to read history and study the actions of eminent men, see how they acted in warfare, examine the causes of their victories and defeats in order to imitate the former and to avoid the latter, and above all, do as some men have done in the past, who have imitated some one, who has been much praised and glorified, and have always kept his deeds and actions before them, as they say Alexander the Great imitated Achilles, Caesar Alexander, and Scipio Cyrus. And whoever reads the life of Cyrus written by Xenophon, will perceive in the life of Scipio how gloriously he imitated the former, and how, in chastity, affability, humanity, and liberality Scipio conformed to those qualities of Cyrus as described by Xenophon.

A wise prince should follow similar methods and never remain idle in peaceful times, but industriously make good use of them, so that when fortune changes she may find him prepared to resist her blows, and to prevail in adversity. . . .

OF CRUELTY AND CLEMENCY, AND WHETHER IT IS BETTER TO BE LOVED OR FEARED

Proceeding to the other qualities before named, I say that every prince must desire to be considered merciful and not cruel. He must, however, take care not to misuse this mercifulness. Cesare Borgia was considered cruel, but his cruelty had brought order to the Romagna, united it, and reduced it to peace and fealty. If this is considered well, it will be seen that he was really much more merciful than the Florentine people, who, to avoid the name of cruelty, allowed Pistoia to be destroyed. A prince, therefore, must not mind incurring the charge of cruelty for the purpose of keeping his subjects united and faithful; for, with a very few examples, he will be more merciful than those who, from excess of tenderness, allow disorders to arise, from whence spring bloodshed and rapine; for these as a rule injure the whole community, while the executions carried out by the prince injure only individuals. And of all princes, it is impossible for a new prince to escape the reputation of cruelty, new states being always full of dangers. Wherefore Virgil through the mouth of Dido says:

Res dura, et regni novitas me talia cogunt
Moliri, et late fines custode tueri.

Nevertheless, he must be cautious in believing and acting, and must not be afraid of his own shadow, and must proceed in a temperate manner with prudence and humanity, so that too much confidence does not render him incautious, and too much diffidence does not render him intolerant.

From this arises the question whether it is better to be loved more than feared, or feared more than loved. The reply is, that one ought to be both feared and loved, but as it is difficult for the two to go together, it is much safer to be feared than loved, if one of the two has to be wanting. For it may be said of men in general that they are ungrateful, voluble, dissemblers, anxious to avoid danger, and covetous of gain; as long as you benefit them, they are entirely yours; they offer you their blood, their goods, their life, and their children, as I have before said, when the necessity is remote; but when it approaches, they revolt. And the prince who has relied solely on their words, without making other preparations, is ruined; for the friendship which is gained by purchase and not through grandeur and nobility of spirit is bought but not secured, and at a pinch is not to be expended in your service. And men have less scruple in offending one who makes himself loved than one who makes himself feared;

for love is held by a chain of obligation which, men being selfish, is broken whenever it serves their purpose; but fear is maintained by a dread of punishment which never fails.

Still, a prince should make himself feared in such a way that if he does not gain love, he at any rate avoids hatred; for fear and the absence of hatred may well go together, and will be always attained by one who abstains from interfering with the property of his citizens and subjects or with their women. And when he is obliged to take the life of any one, let him do so when there is a proper justification and manifest reason for it; but above all he must abstain from taking the property of others, for men forget more easily the death of their father than the loss of their patrimony. Then also pretexts for seizing property are never wanting, and one who begins to live by rapine will always find some reason for taking the goods of others, whereas causes for taking life are rarer and more fleeting.

But when the prince is with his army and has a large number of soldiers under his control, then it is extremely necessary that he should not mind being thought cruel; for without this reputation he could not keep an army united or disposed to any duty. Among the noteworthy actions of Hannibal is numbered this, that although he had an enormous army, composed of men of all nations and fighting in foreign countries, there never arose any dissension either among them or against the prince, either in good fortune or in bad. This could not be due to anything but his inhuman cruelty, which together with his infinite other virtues, made him always venerated and terrible in the sight of his soldiers, and without it his other virtues would not have sufficed to produce that effect. Thoughtless writers admire on the one hand his actions, and on the other blame the principal cause of them.

And that it is true that his other virtues would not have sufficed may be seen from the case of Scipio (famous not only in regard to his own times, but all times of which memory remains), whose armies rebelled against him in Spain, which arose from nothing but his excessive kindness, which allowed more licence to the soldiers than was consonant with military discipline. He was reproached with this in the senate by Fabius Maximus, who called him a corrupter of the Roman militia. Locri having been destroyed by one of Scipio's officers was not revenged by him, nor was the insolence of that officer punished, simply by reason of his easy nature; so much so, that some one wishing to excuse him in the senate, said that there were many men who knew rather how not to err, than how to correct the errors of others. This disposition would in time have tarnished the fame and glory of Scipio had he persevered in it under the empire, but living under the rule of the senate this harmful quality was not only concealed but became a glory to him.

I conclude, therefore, with regard to being feared and loved, that men love at their own free will, but fear at the will of the prince, and that a wise prince must rely on what is in his power and not on what is in the power of others, and he must only contrive to avoid incurring hatred, as has been explained.

IN WHAT WAY PRINCES MUST KEEP FAITH

How laudable it is for a prince to keep good faith and live with integrity, and not with astuteness, every one knows. Still the experience of our times shows those princes to have done great things who have had little regard for good faith, and have been able by astuteness to confuse men's brains, and who have ultimately overcome those who have made loyalty their foundation.

You must know, then, that there are two methods of fighting, the one by law, the other by force: the first method is that of men, the second of beasts; but as the first method is often insufficient, one must have recourse to the second. It is therefore necessary for a prince to know well how to use both the beast and the man. This was covertly taught to rulers by ancient writers, who relate how Achilles and many others of those ancient princes were given to Chiron the centaur to be brought up and educated under his discipline. The parable of this semi-animal, semi-human teacher is meant to indicate that a prince must know how to use both natures, and that the one without the other is not durable.

A prince being thus obliged to know well how to act as a beast must imitate the fox and the lion, for the lion cannot protect himself from traps, and the fox cannot defend himself from wolves. One must therefore be a fox to recognise traps, and a lion to frighten wolves. Those that wish to be only lions do not understand this. Therefore, a prudent ruler ought not to keep faith when by so doing it would be against his interest, and when the reasons which made him bind himself no longer exist. If men were all good, this precept would not be a good one; but as they are bad, and would not observe their faith with you, so you are not bound to keep faith with them. Nor have legitimate grounds ever failed a prince who wished to show colourable excuse for the non-fulfilment of his promise. Of this one could furnish an infinite number of modern examples, and show how many times peace has been broken, and how many promises rendered worthless, by the faithlessness of princes, and those that have been best able to imitate the fox have succeeded best. But it is necessary to be able to disguise this character well, and to be a great feigner and dissembler; and men are so simple and so ready to obey present necessities, that one who deceives will always find those who allow themselves to be deceived.

I will only mention one modern instance. Alexander VI did nothing else but deceive men, he thought of nothing else, and found the occasion for it; no man was ever more able to give assurances, or affirmed things with stronger oaths, and no man observed them less; however, he always succeeded in his deceptions, as he well knew this aspect of things.

It is not, therefore, necessary for a prince to have all the above-named qualities, but it is very necessary to seem to have them. I would even be bold to say that to possess them and always to observe them is dangerous, but to appear to possess them is useful. Thus it is well to seem merciful, faithful, humane, sincere, religious, and also to be so; but you must have the mind so disposed that when it is needful to be otherwise you may be able to change to the opposite qualities. And it must be understood that a prince, and especially a new prince, cannot observe all those things which are considered good in men, being often obliged, in order to maintain the state, to act against faith, against charity, against humanity, and against religion. And, therefore, he must have a mind disposed to adapt itself according to the wind, and as the variations of fortune dictate, and, as I said before, not deviate from what is good, if possible, but be able to do evil if constrained.

A prince must take great care that nothing goes out of his mouth which is not full of the above-named five qualities, and, to see and hear him, he should seem to be all mercy, faith, integrity, humanity, and religion. And nothing is more necessary than to seem to have this last quality, for men in general judge more by the eyes than by the hands, for every one can see, but very few have to feel. Everybody sees what you appear to be, few feel what you are, and those few will not dare to oppose themselves to the many, who have the majesty of the state to defend them; and in the actions of men, and especially of princes, from which there is no appeal, the end justifies the means. Let a prince therefore aim at conquering and maintaining the state, and the means will always be judged honourable and praised by every one, for the vulgar is always taken by appearances and the issue of the event; and the world consists only of the vulgar, and the few who are not vulgar are isolated when the many have a rallying point in the prince. A certain prince of the present time, whom it is well not to name, never does anything but preach peace and good faith, but he is really a great enemy to both, and either of them, had he observed them, would have lost him state or reputation on many occasions. . . .

HOW MUCH FORTUNE CAN DO IN HUMAN AFFAIRS AND HOW IT MAY BE OPPOSED

It is not unknown to me how many have been and are of opinion that worldly events are so governed by fortune and by God, that men cannot by their prudence change them, and that on the contrary there is no remedy whatever, and for this they may judge it to be useless to toil much about them, but let things be ruled by chance. This opinion has been more held in our day, from the great changes that have been seen, and are daily seen, be-

yond every human conjecture. When I think about them, at times I am partly inclined to share this opinion. Nevertheless, that our free-will may not be altogether extinguished, I think it may be true that fortune is the ruler of half our actions, but that she allows the other half or thereabouts to be governed by us. I would compare her to an impetuous river that, when turbulent, inundates the plains, casts down trees and buildings, removes earth from this side and places it on the other; every one flees before it, and everything yields to its fury without being able to oppose it; and yet though it is of such a kind, still when it is quiet, men can make provision against it by dykes and banks, so that when it rises it will either go into a canal or its rush will not be so wild and dangerous. So it is with fortune, which shows her power where no measures have been taken to resist her, and directs her fury where she knows that no dykes or barriers have been made to hold her. And if you regard Italy, which has been the seat of these changes, and who has given the impulse to them, you will see her to be a country without dykes or banks of any kind. If she had been protected by proper measures, like Germany, Spain, and France, this inundation would not have caused the great changes that it has, or would not have happened at all.

This must suffice as regards opposition to fortune in general. But limiting myself more to particular cases, I would point out how one sees a certain prince to-day fortunate and to-morrow ruined, without seeing that he has changed in character or otherwise. I believe this arises in the first place from the causes that we have already discussed at length; that is to say, because the prince who bases himself entirely on fortune is ruined when fortune changes. I also believe that he is happy whose mode of procedure accords with the needs of the times, and similarly he is unfortunate whose mode of procedure is opposed to the times. For one sees that men in those things which lead them to the aim that each one has in view, namely, glory and riches, proceed in various ways; one with circumspection, another with impetuosity, one by violence, another by cunning, one with patience, another with the reverse; and each by these diverse ways may arrive at his aim. One sees also two cautious men, one of whom succeeds in his designs, and the other not, and in the same way two men succeed equally by different methods, one being cautious, the other impetuous, which arises only from the nature of the times, which does or does not conform to their method of procedure. From this it results, as I have said, that two men, acting differently, attain the same effect, and of two others acting in the same way, one attains his goal and not the other. On this depend also the changes in prosperity, for if it happens that time and circumstances are favourable to one who acts with caution and prudence he will be successful, but if time and circumstances change he will be ruined, because he does not change his mode of procedure. No man is found so prudent as to be able to adapt himself to this, either because he cannot deviate from that to which his nature disposes him, or else because having always prospered by walking in one path, he cannot persuade himself that it is well to leave it; and therefore the cautious man, when it is time to act suddenly, does not know how to do so and is consequently ruined; for if one could change one's nature with time and circumstances, fortune would never change.

Pope Julius II acted impetuously in everything he did and found the times and conditions so in conformity with that mode of procedure, that he always obtained a good result. Consider the first war that he made against Bologna while Messer Giovanni Bentivogli was still living. The Venetians were not pleased with it, neither was the King of Spain, France was conferring with him over the enterprise, notwithstanding which, owing to his fierce and impetuous disposition, he engaged personally in the expedition. This move caused both Spain and the Venetians to halt and hesitate, the latter through fear, the former through the desire to recover the entire kingdom of Naples. On the other hand, he engaged with him the King of France, because seeing him make this move and desiring his friendship in order to put down the Venetians, that king judged that he could not refuse him his troops without manifest injury. Thus Julius by his impetuous move achieved what no other pontiff with the utmost human prudence would

have succeeded in doing, because, if he had waited till all arrangements had been made and everything settled before leaving Rome, as any other pontiff would have done, it would never have succeeded. For the King of France would have found a thousand excuses, and the others would have inspired him with a thousand fears. I will omit his other actions, which were all of this kind and which all succeeded well, and the shortness of his life did not suffer him to experience the contrary, for had times followed in which it was necessary to act with caution, his ruin would have resulted, for he would never have deviated from these methods to which his nature disposed him.

I conclude then that fortune varying and men remaining fixed in their ways, they are successful so long as these ways conform to circumstances, but when they are opposed then they are unsuccessful. I certainly think that it is better to be impetuous than cautious, for fortune is a woman, and it is necessary, if you wish to master her, to conquer her by force; and it can be seen that she lets herself be overcome by the bold rather than by those who proceed coldly. And therefore, like a woman, she is always a friend to the young, because they are less cautious, fiercer, and master her with greater audacity.

EXHORTATION TO LIBERATE ITALY FROM THE BARBARIANS

Having now considered all the things we have spoken of, and thought within myself whether at present the time was not propitious in Italy for a new prince, and if there was not a state of things which offered an opportunity to a prudent and capable man to introduce a new system that would do honour to himself and good to the mass of the people, it seems to me that so many things concur to favour a new ruler that I do not know of any time more fitting for such an enterprise. And if, as I said, it was necessary in order that the power of Moses should be displayed that the people of Israel should be slaves in Egypt, and to give scope for the greatness and courage of Cyrus that the Persians should be oppressed by the Medes, and to illustrate the pre-eminence of Theseus that the Athenians should be dispersed, so at the present time, in order that the might of an Italian genius might be recognised, it was necessary that Italy should be reduced to her present condition, and that she should be more enslaved than the Hebrews, more oppressed than the Persians, and more scattered than the Athenians; without a head, without order, beaten, despoiled, lacerated, and overrun, and that she should have suffered ruin of every kind.

And although before now a gleam of hope has appeared which gave hope that some individual might be appointed by God for her redemption, yet at the highest summit of his career he was thrown aside by fortune, so that now, almost lifeless, she awaits one who may heal her wounds and put a stop to the pillaging of Lombardy, to the rapacity and extortion in the Kingdom of Naples and in Tuscany, and cure her of those sores which have long been festering. Behold how she prays God to send some one to redeem her from this barbarous cruelty and insolence. Behold her ready and willing to follow any standard if only there be some one to raise it. There is nothing now she can hope for but that your illustrious house may place itself at the head of this redemption, being by its power and fortune so exalted, and being favoured by God and the Church, of which it is now the ruler. Nor will this be very difficult, if you call to mind the actions and lives of the men I have named. And although those men were rare and marvellous, they were none the less men, and each of them had less opportunity than the present, for their enterprise was not juster than this, nor easier, nor was God more their friend than He is yours. Here is a just cause; "iustum enim est bellum quibus necessarium, et pia arma ubi nulla nisi in armis spes est." Here is the greatest willingness, nor can there be great difficulty where there is great willingness, provided that the measures are adopted of those whom I have set before you as examples. Besides this, unexampled wonders have been seen here performed by God, the sea has been opened, a cloud has shown you the road, the rock has given forth water, manna has rained, and everything has contributed to your greatness, the remainder must be done by you. God will not do everything, in order not to deprive us of free-will and the portion of the glory that falls to our lot.

It is no marvel that none of the before-mentioned Italians have done that which it is to be hoped your illustrious house may do; and if in so many revolutions in Italy and so many warlike operations, it always seems as if military capacity were extinct, this is because the ancient methods were not good, and no one has arisen who knew how to discover new ones. Nothing does so much honour to a newly-risen man than the new laws and measures which he introduces. These things, when they are well based and have greatness in them, render him revered and admired, and there is not lacking scope in Italy for the introduction of every kind of new organisation. Here there is great virtue in the members, if it were not wanting in the heads. Look how in duels and in contests of a few the Italians are superior in strength, dexterity, and intelligence. But when it comes to armies they make a poor show; which proceeds entirely from the weakness of the leaders, for those that know are not obeyed, and every one thinks that he knows, there being hitherto nobody who has raised himself so high both by valour and fortune as to make the others yield. Hence it comes about that for so long a time, in all the wars waged during the last twenty years, whenever there has been an entirely Italian army it has always been a failure, as witness first Taro, then Alexandria, Capua, Genoa, Vailà, Bologna, and Mestri.

If your illustrious house, therefore, wishes to follow those great men who redeemed their countries, it is before all things necessary, as the true foundation of every undertaking, to provide yourself with your own forces, for you cannot have more faithful, or truer and better soldiers. And although each one of them may be good, they will united become even better when they see themselves commanded by their prince, and honoured and favoured by him. It is therefore necessary to prepare such forces in order to be able with Italian prowess to defend the country from foreigners. And although both the Swiss and Spanish infantry are deemed terrible, none the less they each have their defects, so that a third method of array might not only oppose them, but be confident of overcoming them. For the Spaniards cannot sustain the attack of cavalry, and the Swiss have to fear infantry which meets them with resolution equal to their own. From which it has resulted, as will be seen by experience, that the Spaniards cannot sustain the attack of French cavalry, and the Swiss are overthrown by Spanish infantry. And although a complete example of the latter has not been seen, yet an instance was furnished in the battle of Ravenna, where the Spanish infantry attacked the German battalions, which are organised in the same way as the Swiss. The Spaniards, through their bodily agility and aided by their bucklers, had entered between and under their pikes and were in a position to attack them safely without the Germans being able to defend themselves; and if the cavalry had not charged them they would have utterly destroyed them. Knowing therefore the defects of both these kinds of infantry, a third kind can be created which can resist cavalry and need not fear infantry, and this will be done by the choice of arms and a new organisation. And these are the things which, when newly introduced, give reputation and grandeur to a new prince.

This opportunity must not, therefore, be allowed to pass, so that Italy may at length find her liberator. I cannot express the love with which he would be received in all those provinces which have suffered under these foreign invasions, with what thirst for vengeance, with what steadfast faith, with what love, with what grateful tears. What doors would be closed against him? What people would refuse him obedience? What envy could oppose him? What Italian would withhold allegiance? This barbarous domination stinks in the nostrils of every one. May your illustrious house therefore assume this task with that courage and those hopes which are inspired by a just cause, so that under its banner our fatherland may be raised up, and under its auspices be verified that saying of Petrarch:

> Valour against fell wrath
> Will take up arms; and be the com-
> bat quickly sped!
> For, sure, the ancient worth,
> That in Italians stirs the heart, is not
> yet dead.

Benvenuto Cellini

Benvenuto Cellini (1500–1571), the Florentine goldsmith, was in many ways typical of the Renaissance. He lived life to the fullest extent, and was above all else a child of will rather than a man of reason. Crimes, pranks, love, and art all blended together in his life to form a rich pattern of emotional existence. Thus his Autobiography serves as an invaluable document of the characteristics of his age. In reading the selections from it note (1) his motives in writing this work, (2) the discussion of his ancestry, (3) the nature of his craftsmanship in Rome, (4) the classes of people who patronized him, (5) his estimate of himself, (6) his relations with the papacy, (7) the commissions he performed for the French king, and (8) the description of the casting of the statue of Perseus.

From: THE AUTOBIOGRAPHY OF BENVENUTO CELLINI

All men of whatsoever quality they be, who have done anything of excellence, or which may properly resemble excellence, ought, if they are persons of truth and honesty, to describe their life with their own hand; but they ought not to attempt so fine an enterprise till

As translated by John Addington Symonds in *Autobiography of Benvenuto Cellini*, 2nd ed., London, 1888, 1–4; 34–51; 114–116; 310–320; 416–427.

they have passed the age of forty. This duty occurs to my own mind, now that I am travelling beyond the term of fifty-eight years, and am in Florence, the city of my birth. Many untoward things can I remember, such as happen to all who live upon our earth; and from those adversities I am now more free than at any previous period of my career—nay, it seems to me that I enjoy greater content of soul and health of body than ever I did in bygone years. I can also bring to mind some pleasant goods and some inestimable evils, which, when I turn my thoughts backward, strike terror in me, and astonishment that I should have reached this age of fifty-eight, wherein, thanks be to God, I am still travelling prosperously forward.

It is true that men who have laboured with some show of excellence, have already given knowledge of themselves to the world; and this alone ought to suffice them; I mean the fact that they have proved their manhood and achieved renown. Yet one must needs live like others; and so in a work like this there will always be found occasion for natural bragging, which is of divers kinds, and the first is that a man should let others know he draws his lineage from persons of worth and most ancient origin.

I am called Benvenuto Cellini, son of Maestro Giovanni, son of Andrea, son of Cristofano Cellini; my mother was Madonna Elisabetta, daughter to Stefano Granacci; both parents citizens of Florence. It is found written in chronicles made by our ancestors of Florence, men of old time and of credibility, even as Giovanni Villani writes, that the city of Florence was evidently built in imitation of the fair city of Rome; and certain remnants of the Colosseum and the Baths can yet be traced. These things are near Santa Croce. The Capitol was where is now the Old Market. The Rotunda is entire, which was made for the temple of Mars, and is now dedicated to our Saint John. That thus it was, can very well be seen, and cannot be denied; but the said buildings are much smaller than those of Rome. He who caused them to be built, they say, was Julius Caesar, in concert with some noble Romans, who, when Fiesole had been stormed and taken, raised a city in

this place, and each of them took in hand to erect one of these notable edifices.

Julius Caesar had among his captains a man of highest rank and valour, who was called Fiorino of Cellino, which is a village about two miles distant from Monte Fiascone. Now this Fiorino took up his quarters under the hill of Fiesole, on the ground where Florence now stands, in order to be near the river Arno, and for the convenience of the troops. All those soldiers and others who had to do with the said captain used then to say: "Let us go to Fiorenze"; as well because the said captain was called Fiorino, as also because the place he had chosen for his quarters was by nature very rich in flowers. Upon the foundation of the city, therefore, since this name struck Julius Caesar as being fair and apt, and given by circumstance, and seeing furthermore that flowers themselves bring good augury, he appointed the name of Florence for the town. He wished besides to pay his valiant captain this compliment; and he loved him all the more for having drawn him from a very humble place, and for the reason that so excellent a man was a creature of his own. The name that learned inventors and investigators of such etymologies adduce, as that Florence is flowing at the Arno, cannot hold; seeing that Rome is flowing at the Tiber, Ferrara is flowing at the Po, Lyons is flowing at the Saone, Paris is flowing at the Seine, and yet the names of all these towns are different, and have come to them by other ways.

Thus then we find; and thus we believe that we are descended from a man of worth. Furthermore, we find that there are Cellinis of our stock in Ravenna, that most ancient town of Italy, where too are plenty of gentle folk. In Pisa also there are some, and I have discovered them in many parts of Christendom; and in this state also the breed exists, men devoted to the profession of arms; for not many years ago a young man, called Luca Cellini, a beardless youth, fought with a soldier of experience and a most valorous man, named Francesco da Vicorati, who had frequently fought before in single combat. This Luca, by his own valour, with sword in hand, overcame and slew him, with such bravery and stoutness that he moved the folk to wonder, who were expecting quite the contrary issue; so that I glory in tracing my descent from men of valour.

As for the trifling honours which I have gained for my house, under the well-known conditions of our present ways of living, and by means of my art, albeit the same are matters of no great moment, I will relate these in their proper time and place, taking much more pride in having been born humble and having laid some honourable foundation for my family, than if I had been born of great lineage and had stained or overclouded that by my base qualities. So then I will make a beginning by saying how it pleased God I should be born. . . .

At Siena I waited for the mail to Rome which I afterwards joined; and when we passed the Paglia, we met a courier carrying news of the new Pope, Clement VII. Upon my arrival in Rome, I went to work in the shop of the master-goldsmith Santi. He was dead; but a son of his carried on the business. He did not work himself, but entrusted all his commissions to a young man named Lucagnolo from Iesi, a country fellow, who while yet a child had come into Santi's service. This man was short but well proportioned, and was a more skilful craftsman than any one whom I had met with up to that time; remarkable for facility and excellent in design. He executed large plate only; that is to say, vases of the utmost beauty, basins, and such pieces. Having put myself to work there, I began to make some candelabra for the Bishop of Salamanca, a Spaniard. They were richly chased so far as that sort of work admits. A pupil of Raffaello da Urbino called Gian Francesco, and commonly known as Il Fattore, was a painter of great ability; and being on terms of friendship with the Bishop, he introduced me to his favour, so that I obtained many commissions from that prelate, and earned considerable sums of money.

During that time I went to draw, sometimes in Michel Agnolo's chapel, and sometimes in the house of Agostino Chigi of Siena, which contained many incomparable paintings by the hand of that great master Raffaello. This I did on feast-days, because the house was then inhabited by Messer Gismondo, Agostino's

brother. They plumed themselves exceedingly when they saw young men of my sort coming to study in their palaces. Gismondo's wife, noticing my frequent presence in that house— she was a lady as courteous as could be, and of surpassing beauty—came up to me one day, looked at my drawings, and asked me if I was a sculptor or a painter; to whom I said I was a goldsmith. She remarked that I drew too well for a goldsmith; and having made one of her waiting-maids bring a lily of the finest diamonds set in gold, she showed it to me, and bade me value it. I valued it at 800 crowns. Then she said I had very nearly hit the mark, and asked me whether I felt capable of setting the stones really well. I said that I should much like to do so, and began before her eyes to make a little sketch for it, working all the better because of the pleasure I took in conversing with so lovely and agreeable a gentlewoman. When the sketch was finished, another Roman lady of great beauty joined us; she had been above, and now descending to the ground-floor, asked Madonna Porzia what she was doing there. She answered with a smile: "I was amusing myself by watching this worthy young man at his drawing; he is as good as he is handsome." I had by this time acquired a trifle of assurance, mixed, however, with some honest bashfulness; so I blushed and said: "Such as I am, lady, I shall ever be most ready to serve you." The gentlewoman, also slightly blushing, said: "You know well that I want you to serve me"; and reaching me the lily, told me to take it away; and gave me besides twenty golden crowns which she had in her bag, and added: "Set me the jewel after the fashion you have sketched, and keep for me the old gold in which it is now set." On this the Roman lady observed: "If I were in that young man's body, I should go off without asking leave." Madonna Porzia replied that virtues rarely are at home with vices, and that if I did such a thing, I should strongly belie my good looks of an honest man. Then turning round, she took the Roman lady's hand, and with a pleasant smile said: "Farewell, Benvenuto." I stayed on a short while at the drawing I was making, which was a copy of a Jove by Raffaello. When I had finished it and left the house, I set myself to making a little model of wax, in order to show how the jewel would look when it was completed. This I took to Madonna Porzia, whom I found with the same Roman lady. Both of them were highly satisfied with my work, and treated me so kindly that, being somewhat emboldened, I promised the jewel should be twice as good as the model. Accordingly I set hand to it, and in twelve days I finished it in the form of a fleur-de-lys, as I have said above, ornamenting it with little masks, children, and animals, exquisitely enamelled, whereby the diamonds which formed the lily were more than doubled in effect.

While I was working at this piece, Lucagnolo, of whose ability I have before spoken, showed considerable discontent, telling me over and over again that I might acquire far more profit and honour by helping him to execute large plate, as I had done at first. I made him answer that, whenever I chose, I should always be capable of working at great silver pieces; but that things like that on which I was now engaged were not commissioned every day; and beside their bringing no less honour than large silver plate, there was also more profit to be made by them. He laughed me in the face, and said: "Wait and see, Benvenuto; for by the time that you have finished that work of yours, I will make haste to have finished this vase, which I took in hand when you did the jewel; and then experience shall teach you what profit I shall get from my vase, and what you will get from your ornament." I answered that I was very glad indeed to enter into such a competition with so good a craftsman as he was, because the end would show which of us was mistaken. Accordingly both the one and the other of us, with a scornful smile upon our lips, bent our heads in grim earnest to the work, which both were now desirous of accomplishing; so that after about ten days, each had finished his undertaking with great delicacy and artistic skill.

Lucagnolo's was a huge silver piece, used at the table of Pope Clement, into which he flung away bits of bone and the rind of divers fruits, while eating; an object of ostentation rather than necessity. The vase was adorned with two fine handles, together with many masks, both small and great, and masses of lovely foliage, in as exquisite a style of elegance as could be imagined; on seeing which I said it was the most beautiful vase that ever I set eyes on. Thinking he had convinced me, Lucagnolo replied: "Your work seems to me no less beautiful, but we shall soon perceive the difference between the two." So he took his vase and carried it to the Pope, who was very well pleased with it, and ordered at once that he should be paid at the ordinary rate of such large plate. Meanwhile I carried mine to Madonna Porzia, who looked at it with astonishment, and told me I had far surpassed my promise. Then she bade me ask for my reward whatever I liked; for it seemed to her my desert was so great that if I craved a castle she could hardly recompense me; but since that was not in her hands to bestow, she added laughing that I must beg what lay within her power. I answered that the greatest reward I could desire for my labour was to have satisfied her ladyship. Then smiling in my turn, and bowing to her, I took my leave, saying I wanted no reward but that. She turned to the Roman lady and said: "You see that the qualities we discerned in him are companied by virtues, and not vices." They both expressed their admiration, and then Madonna Porzia continued: "Friend Benvenuto, have you never heard it said that when the poor give to the rich, the devil laughs?" I replied: "Quite true! and yet, in the midst of all his troubles, I should like this time to see him laugh"; and as I took my leave, she said that this time she had no will to bestow on him that favour.

When I came back to the shop, Lucagnolo had the money for his vase in a paper packet; and on my arrival he cried out: "Come and compare the price of your jewel with the price of my plate." I said that he must leave things as they were till the next day, because I hoped that even as my work in its kind was not less excellent than his, so I should be able to show him quite an equal price for it.

On the day following, Madonna Porzia sent a major-domo of hers to my shop, who called me out, and putting into my hands a paper packet full of money from his lady, told me that she did not choose the devil should have his whole laugh out: by which she hinted that the money sent me was not the entire payment merited by my industry, and other messages were added worthy of so courteous a lady. Lucagnolo, who was burning to compare his packet with mine, burst into the shop; then in the presence of twelve journeymen and some neighbours, eager to behold the result of this competition, he seized his packet, scornfully exclaiming "Ou! ou!" three or four times, while he poured his money on the counter with a great noise. They were twenty-five crowns in giulios; and he fancied that mine would be four or five crowns *di moneta*. I for my part, stunned and stifled by his cries, and by the looks and smiles of the bystanders, first peeped into my packet; then, after seeing that it contained nothing but gold, I retired to one end of the counter, and, keeping my eyes lowered and making no noise at all, I lifted it with both hands suddenly above my head, and emptied it like a mill hopper. My coin was twice as much as his; which caused the onlookers, who had fixed their eyes on me with some derision, to turn round suddenly to him and say: "Lucagnolo, Benvenuto's pieces, being all of gold and twice as many as yours, make a far finer effect." I thought for certain that, what with jealousy and what with shame, Lucagnolo would have fallen dead upon the spot; and though he took the third part of my gain, since I was a journeyman (for such is the custom of the trade, two-thirds fall to the workman and one-third to the masters of the shop), yet inconsiderate envy had more power in him than avarice: it ought indeed to have worked quite the other way, he being a peasant's son from Iesi. He cursed his art and those who taught it him, vowing that thenceforth he would never work at large plate, but give his whole attention to those whoreson gewgaws, since they were so well paid. Equally enraged on my side, I answered that every bird sang its own note; that he talked after the fashion of the hovels he came from; but that I dared to swear that I should succeed with ease in making his lubberly lumber, while he would never be successful in my whoreson gewgaws. Thus I flung off in a passion, telling him that I would soon show him that I spoke truth. The bystanders openly declared against him, holding him for a lout, as indeed he was, and me for a man, as I had proved myself.

Next day, I went to thank Madonna Porzia, and told her that her ladyship had done the opposite of what she said she would; for that while I wanted to make the devil laugh, she had made him once more deny God. We both laughed pleasantly at this, and she gave me other commissions for fine and substantial work.

Meanwhile, I contrived, by means of a pupil of Raffaello de Urbino, to get an order from the Bishop of Salamanca for one of those great water-vessels called *acquereccia*, which are used for ornaments to place on sideboards. He wanted a pair made of equal size; and one of them he intrusted to Lucagnolo, the other to me. Giovan Francesco, the painter I have mentioned, gave us the design. Accordingly I set hand with marvellous good-will to this piece of plate, and was accommodated with a part of his workshop by a Milanese named Maestro Giovan Piero della Tacca. Having made my preparations, I calculated how much money I should need for certain affairs of my own, and sent all the rest to assist my poor father.

It so happened that just when this was being paid to him in Florence, he stumbled upon one of those Radicals who were in the Eight at the time when I got into that little trouble there. It was the very man who had abused him so rudely, and who swore that I should certainly be sent into the country with the lances. Now this fellow had some sons of very bad morals and repute; wherefore my father said to him: "Misfortunes can happen to anybody, especially to men of choleric humour when they are in the right, even as it happened to my son; but let the rest of his life bear witness how virtuously I have brought him up. Would God, for your well-being, that your sons may act neither worse nor better toward you than mine do to me. God rendered me able to bring them up as I have done; and where my own power could not reach, 'twas He who rescued them, against your expectation, out of your violent hands." On leaving the man, he wrote me all this story, begging me for God's sake to practise music at times, in order that I might not lose the fine accomplishment which he had taught me with such trouble. The letter so overflowed with expressions of the tenderest fatherly affection, that I was moved to tears of filial piety, resolving, before he died, to gratify him amply with regard to music. Thus God grants us those lawful blessings which we ask in prayer, nothing doubting.

While I was pushing forward Salamanca's vase, I had one little boy as help, whom I had taken at the entreaty of friends, and half against my own will, to be my workman. He was about fourteen years of age, bore the name of Paulino, and was son to a Roman burgess, who lived upon the income of his property. Paulino was the best-mannered, the most honest, and the most beautiful boy I ever saw in my whole life. His modest ways and actions, together with his superlative beauty and his devotion to myself, bred in me as great an affection for him as a man's breast can hold. This passionate love led me oftentimes to delight the lad with music; for I observed that his marvellous features, which by complexion wore a tone of modest melancholy, brightened up, and when I took my cornet, broke into a smile so lovely and so sweet, that I do not marvel at the silly stories which the Greeks have written about the deities of heaven. Indeed, if my boy had lived in those times, he would probably have turned their heads still more. He had a sister named Faustina, more beautiful, I verily believe, than that Faustina about whom the old books gossip so. Sometimes he took me to their vineyard, and, so far as I could judge, it struck me that Paulino's good father would have welcomed me as a son-in-law. This affair led me to play more than I was used to do.

It happened at that time that one Giangiacomo of Cesena, musician in the Pope's band, and a very excellent performer, sent word through Lorenzo, the trumpeter of Lucca, who is now in our Duke's service, to inquire whether I was inclined to help them at the Pope's Ferragosto, playing soprano with my cornet in some motets of great beauty selected by them for that occasion. Although I had the greatest desire to finish the vase I had begun, yet since music has a wondrous charm of its own, and also because I wished to please my old father, I consented to join them. During eight days be-

fore the festival we practised two hours a day together; then on the first of August we went to the Belvedere, and while Pope Clement was at table, we played those carefully studied motets so well that his Holiness protested he had never heard music more sweetly executed or with better harmony of parts. He sent for Giangiacomo, and asked him where and how he had procured so excellent a cornet for soprano, and inquired particularly who I was. Giangiacomo told him my name in full. Whereupon the Pope said: "So, then, he is the son of Maestro Giovanni?" On being assured I was, the Pope expressed his wish to have me in his service with the other bandsmen. Giangiacomo replied: "Most blessed Father, I cannot pretend for certain that you will get him, for his profession, to which he devotes himself assiduously, is that of a goldsmith, and he works in it miraculously well, and earns by it far more than he could by playing." To this the Pope added: "I am the better inclined to him now that I find him possessor of a talent more than I expected. See that he obtains the same salary as the rest of you; and tell him from me to join my service, and that I will find work enough by the day for him to do in his other trade." Then stretching out his hand, he gave him a hundred golden crowns of the Camera in a handkerchief, and said: "Divide these so that he may take his share."

When Giangiacomo left the Pope, he came to us, and related in detail all that the Pope had said; and after dividing the money between the eight of us, and giving me my share, he said to me: "Now I am going to have you inscribed among our company." I replied: "Let the day pass; tomorrow I will give my answer." When I left them, I went meditating whether I ought to accept the invitation, inasmuch as I could not but suffer if I abandoned the noble studies of my art. The following night my father appeared to me in a dream, and begged me with tears of tenderest affection, for God's love and his, to enter upon this engagement. Methought I answered that nothing would induce me to do so. In an instant he assumed so horrible an aspect as to frighten me out of my wits, and cried: "If you do not, you will have a father's curse; but if you do, may you be ever blessed by me!" When I woke, I ran, for very fright, to have myself inscribed. Then I wrote to my old father, telling him the news, which so affected him with extreme joy that a sudden fit of illness took him, and well-nigh brought him to death's door. In his answer to my letter, he told me that he too had dreamed nearly the same as I had.

Knowing now that I had gratified my father's honest wish, I began to think that everything would prosper with me to a glorious and honourable end. Accordingly, I set myself with indefatigable industry to the completion of the vase I had begun for Salamanca. That prelate was a very extraordinary man, extremely rich, but difficult to please. He sent daily to learn what I was doing; and when his messenger did not find me at home, he broke into fury, saying that he would take the work out of my hands and give it to others to finish. This came of my slavery to that accursed music. Still I laboured diligently night and day, until, when I had brought my work to a point when it could be exhibited, I submitted it to the inspection of the Bishop. This so increased his desire to see it finished, that I was sorry I had shown it. At the end of three months I had it ready, with little animals and foliage and masks, as beautiful as one could hope to see. No sooner was it done than I sent it by the hand of my workman, Paulino, to show that able artist Lucagnolo, of whom I have spoken above. Paulino, with the grace and beauty which belonged to him, spoke as follows: "Messer Lucagnolo, Benvenuto bids me say that he has sent to show you his promises and your lumber, expecting in return to see from you his gewgaws." This message given, Lucagnolo took up the vase, and carefully examined it; then he said to Paulino: "Fair boy, tell your master that he is a great and able artist, and that I beg him to be willing to have me for a friend, and not to engage in aught else." The mission of that virtuous and marvellous lad caused me the greatest joy; and then the vase was carried to Salamanca, who ordered it to be valued. Lucagnolo took part in the valuation, estimating and praising it far above my own opinion. Salamanca, lifting up the vase, cried like a true Spaniard: "I swear by God that I will take as long in paying him as he has lagged in making it." When I heard

this, I was exceedingly put out, and fell to cursing all Spain and every one who wished well to it.

Amongst other beautiful ornaments, this vase had a handle, made all of one piece, with most delicate mechanism, which, when a spring was touched, stood upright above the mouth of it. While the prelate was one day ostentatiously exhibiting my vase to certain Spanish gentlemen of his suite, it chanced that one of them, upon Monsignor's quitting the room, began roughly to work the handle, and as the gentle spring which moved it could not bear his loutish violence it broke in his hand. Aware what mischief he had done, he begged the butler who had charge of the Bishop's plate to take it to the master who had made it, for him to mend it, and promised to pay what price he asked, provided it was set to rights at once. So the vase came once more into my hands, and I promised to put it forthwith in order, which indeed I did. It was brought to me before dinner; and at twenty-two o'clock the man who brought it returned, all in a sweat, for he had run the whole way, Monsignor having again asked for it to show to certain other gentlemen. The butler, then, without giving me time to utter a word, cried: "Quick, quick, bring the vase." I, who wanted to act at leisure and not to give it up to him, said that I did not mean to be so quick. The serving-man got into such a rage that he made as though he would put one hand to his sword, while with the other he threatened to break the shop open. To this I put a stop at once with my own weapon, using therewith spirited language, and saying: "I am not going to give it to you! Go and tell Monsignor, your master, that I want the money for my work before I let it leave this shop." When the fellow saw he could not obtain it by swaggering, he fell to praying me, as one prays to the Cross, declaring that if I would only give it up, he would take care I should be paid. These words did not make me swerve from my purpose; but I kept on saying the same thing. At last, despairing of success, he swore to come with Spaniards enough to cut me in pieces. Then he took to his heels; while I, who inclined to believe partly in their murderous attack, resolved that I would defend myself with courage. So I got an admirable little gun ready, which I used for shooting game, and muttered to myself: "He who robs me of my property and labour may take my life too, and welcome." While I was carrying on this debate in my own mind, a crowd of Spaniards arrived, led by their major-domo, who, with the headstrong rashness of his race, bade them go in and take the vase and give me a good beating. Hearing these words, I showed them the muzzle of my gun, and prepared to fire, and cried in a loud voice: "Renegade Jews, traitors, is it thus that one breaks into houses and shops in our city of Rome? Come as many of you thieves as like, an inch nearer to this wicket, and I'll blow all their brains out with my gun." Then I turned the muzzle toward their major-domo, and making as though I would discharge it, called out: "And you big thief, who are egging them on, I mean to kill you first." He clapped spurs to the jennet he was riding, and took flight headlong. The commotion we were making stirred up all the neighbours, who came crowding round, together with some Roman gentlemen who chanced to pass, and cried: "Do but kill the renegades, and we will stand by you." These words had the effect of frightening the Spaniards in good earnest. They withdrew, and were compelled by the circumstances to relate the whole affair to Monsignor. Being a man of inordinate haughtiness, he rated the members of his household, both because they had engaged in such an act of violence, and also because, having begun, they had not gone through with it. At this juncture the painter, who had been concerned in the whole matter, came in, and the Bishop bade him go and tell me that if I did not bring the vase at once, he would make mince-meat of me; but if I brought it, he would pay its price down. These threats were so far from terrifying me, that I sent him word I was going immediately to lay my case before the Pope.

In the meantime, his anger and my fear subsided; whereupon, being guaranteed by some Roman noblemen of high degree that the prelate would not harm me, and having assurance that I should be paid, I armed myself with a large poniard and my good coat of mail, and betook myself to his palace, where he had drawn up all his household. I entered, and

Paulino followed with the silver vase. It was just like passing through the Zodiac, neither more nor less; for one of them had the face of the lion, another of the scorpion, a third of the crab. However, we passed onward to the presence of the rascally priest, who spouted out a torrent of such language as only priests and Spaniards have at their command. In return I never raised my eyes to look at him, nor answered word for word. That seemed to augment the fury of his anger; and causing paper to be put before me, he commanded me to write an acknowledgment to the effect that I had been amply satisfied and paid in full. Then I raised my head, and said I should be very glad to do so when I had received the money. The Bishop's rage continued to rise; threats and recriminations were flung about; but at last the money was paid, and I wrote the receipt. Then I departed, glad at heart and in high spirits.

When Pope Clement heard the story—he had seen the vase before, but it was not shown him as my work—he expressed much pleasure and spoke warmly in my praise, publicly saying that he felt very favourably toward me. This caused Monsignor Salamanca to repent that he had hectored over me; and in order to make up our quarrel, he sent the same painter to inform me that he meant to give me large commissions. I replied that I was willing to undertake them, but that I should require to be paid in advance. This speech too came to Pope Clement's ears, and made him laugh heartily. Cardinal Cibo was in the presence, and the Pope narrated to him the whole history of my dispute with the Bishop. Then he turned to one of his people, and ordered him to go on supplying me with work for the palace. Cardinal Cibo sent for me, and after some time spent in agreeable conversation, gave me the order for a large vase, bigger than Salamanca's. I likewise obtained commissions from Cardinal Cornaro, and many others of the Holy College, especially Ridolfi and Salviati; they all kept me well employed, so that I earned plenty of money.

Madonna Porzia now advised me to open a shop of my own. This I did; and I never stopped working for that excellent and gentle lady, who paid me exceedingly well, and by whose means perhaps it was that I came to make a figure in the world.

I contracted close friendship with Signor Gabriello Ceserino, at that time Gonfalonier of Rome, and executed many pieces for him. One, among the rest, is worthy of mention. It was a large golden medal to wear in the hat. I engraved upon it Leda with her swan; and being very well pleased with the workmanship, he said he should like to have it valued, in order that I might be properly paid. Now, since the medal was executed with consummate skill, the valuers of the trade set a far higher price on it than he had thought of. I therefore kept the medal, and got nothing for my pains. The same sort of adventures happened in this case as in that of Salamanca's vase. But I shall pass such matters briefly by, lest they hinder me from telling things of greater importance.

Since I am writing my life, I must from time to time diverge from my profession in order to describe with brevity, if not in detail, some incidents which have no bearing on my career as artist. On the morning of St. John's Day I happened to be dining with several men of our nation, painters, sculptors, goldsmiths, amongst the most notable of whom was Rosso and Gianfrancesco, the pupil of Raffaello. I had invited them without restraint or ceremony to the place of our meeting; and they were all laughing and joking, as is natural when a crowd of men come together to make merry on so great a festival. It chanced that a light-brained swaggering young fellow passed by; he was a soldier of Rienzo da Ceri, who, when he heard the noise that we were making, gave vent to a string of opprobrious sarcasms upon the folk of Florence. I, who was the host of those great artists and men of worth, taking the insult to myself, slipped out quietly without being observed, and went up to him. I ought to say that he had a punk of his there, and was going on with his stupid ribaldries to amuse her. When I met him, I asked if he was the rash fellow who was speaking evil of the Florentines. He answered at once: "I am that man." On this I raised my hand, struck him in the face, and said: "And I am *this* man." Then we each of us drew our sword with spirit; but the fray had

hardly begun when a crowd of persons intervened, who rather took my part than not, hearing and seeing that I was in the right.

On the following day a challenge to fight with him was brought me, which I accepted very gladly, saying that I expected to complete this job far quicker than those of the other art I practised. So I went at once to confer with a fine old man called Bevilacqua, who was reputed to have been the first sword of Italy, because he had fought more than twenty serious duels and had always come off with honour. This excellent man was a great friend of mine; he knew me as an artist, and had also been concerned as intermediary in certain ugly quarrels between me and others. Accordingly, when he had learned my business, he answered with a smile: "My Benvenuto, if you had an affair with Mars, I am sure you would come out with honour, because through all the years that I have known you, I have never seen you wrongfully take up a quarrel." So he consented to be my second, and we repaired with sword in hand to the appointed place; but no blood was shed, for my opponent made the matter up, and I came with much credit out of the affair. I will not add further particulars; for though they would be very interesting in their own way, I wish to keep both space and words for my art, which has been my chief inducement to write as I am doing, and about which I shall have only too much to say.

The spirit of honourable rivalry impelled me to attempt some other masterpiece, which should equal, or even surpass, the productions of that able craftsman, Lucagnolo, whom I have mentioned. Still I did not on this account neglect my own fine art of jewellery; and so both the one and the other wrought me much profit and more credit and in both of them I continued to produce things of marked originality. There was at that time in Rome a very able artist of Perugia named Lautizio, who worked only in one department, where he was sole and unrivalled throughout the world. You must know that at Rome every cardinal has a seal, upon which his title is engraved, and these seals are made just as large as a child's hand of about twelve years of age; and, as I have already said, the cardinal's title is engraved upon the seal together with a great many ornamental figures. A well-made article of the kind fetches a hundred, or more than a hundred crowns. This excellent workman, like Lucagnolo, roused in me some honest rivalry, although the art he practised is far remote from the other branches of goldsmithery, and consequently Lautizio was not skilled in making anything but seals. I gave my mind to acquiring his craft also, although I found it very difficult; and, unrepelled by the trouble which it gave me, I went on zealously upon the path of profit and improvement.

There was in Rome another most excellent craftsman of ability, who was a Milanese named Messer Caradosso. He dealt in nothing but chiselled medals, made of plates of metal, and such-like things. I have seen of his some paxes in half relief, and some Christs a palm in length wrought of the thinnest golden plates, so exquisitely done that I esteemed him the greatest master in that kind I had ever seen, and envied him more than all the rest together. There were also other masters who worked at medals carved in steel, which may be called the models and true guides for those who aim at striking coins in the most perfect style. All these divers arts I set myself with unflagging industry to learn.

I must not omit the exquisite art of enamelling, in which I have never known any one excel save a Florentine, our countryman, called Amerigo. I did not know him, but was well acquainted with his incomparable masterpieces. Nothing in any part of the world or by any craftsman that I have seen, approached the divine beauty of their workmanship. To this branch too I devoted myself with all my strength, although it is extremely difficult, chiefly because of the fire, which, after long time and trouble spent in other processes, has to be applied at last, and not infrequently brings the whole to ruin. In spite of its great difficulties, it gave me so much pleasure that I looked upon them as recreation; and this came from the special gift which the God of nature bestowed on me, that is to say, a temperament so happy and of such excellent parts that I was freely able to accomplish whatever it pleased me to take in hand. The various departments of art which I have described are very different one from the other, so that a man who excels in one of them, if he undertakes the others, hardly ever achieves the same success; whereas I strove with all my power to become equally versed in all of them: and in the proper place I shall demonstrate that I attained my object. . . .

I went on applying myself with the utmost diligence upon the gold-work for Pope Clement's button. He was very eager to have it, and used to send for me two or three times a week, in order to inspect it; and his delight in the work was always increased. Often would he rebuke and scold me, as it were, for the great grief in which my brother's loss had plunged me; and one day, observing me more downcast and out of trim than was proper, he cried aloud: "Benvenuto, oh! I did not know that you were mad. Have you only just learned that there is no remedy against death? One would think that you were trying to run after him." When I left the presence, I continued working at the jewel and the dies for the Mint; but I also took to watching the arquebusier who shot my brother, as though he had been a girl I was in love with. The man had formerly been in the light cavalry, but afterwards had joined the arquebusiers as one of the Bargello's corporals; and what increased my rage was that he had used these boastful words: "If it had not been for me, who killed that brave young man, the least trifle of delay would have resulted in his putting us all to flight with great disaster." When I saw that the fever caused by always seeing him about was depriving me of sleep and appetite, and was bringing me by degrees to sorry plight, I overcame my repugnance to so low and not quite praiseworthy an enterprise, and made my mind up one evening to rid myself of the torment. The fellow lived in a house near a place called Torre Sanguigua, next door to the lodging of one of the most fashionable courtesans in Rome, named Signora Antea. It had just struck twenty-four, and he was standing at the house-door, with his sword in hand, having risen from supper. With great address I stole up to him, holding a large Pistojan dagger, and dealt him a back-handed stroke, with which I meant to cut his head clean off; but as he turned round very suddenly, the blow fell upon the point of his left shoulder and broke the the bone. He sprang up, dropped his sword, half-stunned with the great pain, and took to flight. I followed after, and in four steps caught him up, when I lifted my dagger above his head, which he was holding very low, and hit him in the back exactly at the juncture of the nape-bone and the neck. The poniard entered this point so deep into the bone, that, though I used all my strength to pull it out, I was not able. For just at that moment four soldiers with drawn swords sprang out from Antea's lodging, and obliged me to set hand to my own sword to defend my life. Leaving the poniard then, I made off, and fearing I might be recognised took refuge in the palace of Duke Alessandro, which was between Piazza Navona and the Rotunda. On my arrival, I asked to see the Duke; who told me that, if I was alone, I need only keep quiet and have no further anxiety, but go on working at the jewel which the Pope had set his heart on, and stay eight days indoors. He gave this advice the more securely, because the soldiers had now arrived who interrupted the completion of my deed; they held the dagger in their hand, and were relating how the matter happened, and the great trouble they had to pull the weapon from the neck and head-bone of the man, whose name they did not know. Just then Giovan Bandini came up, and said to them: "That poniard is mine, and I lent it to Benvenuto, who was bent on revenging his brother." The soldiers were profuse in their expressions of regret at having interrupted me, although my vengeance had been amply satisfied.

More than eight days elapsed, and the Pope did not send for me according to his custom. Afterwards he summoned me through his chamberlain, the Bolognese nobleman I have already mentioned, who let me, in his own modest manner, understand that his Holiness knew all, but was very well inclined toward me, and that I had only to mind my work and keep quiet. When we reached the presence, the Pope cast so menacing a glance towards me, that the mere look of his eyes made me tremble. Afterwards, upon examining my work, his countenance cleared, and he began to praise me beyond measure, saying that I had done a vast amount in a short time. Then,

looking me straight in the face, he added: "Now that you are cured, Benvenuto, take heed how you live." I, who understood his meaning, promised that I would. Immediately upon this, I opened a very fine shop in the Banchi, opposite Raffaello, and there I finished the jewel after the lapse of a few months. . . .

On our way to the lodgings of the King [Francis I of France] we passed before those of the Cardinal of Ferrara. Standing at his door, he called to me and said: "Our most Christian monarch has of his own accord assigned you the same appointments which his Majesty allowed the painter Lionardo da Vinci, that is, a salary of seven hundred crowns; in addition, he will pay you for all the works you do for him; also for your journey hither he gives you five hundred golden crowns, which will be paid you before you quit this place." At the end of this announcement, I replied that those were offers worthy of the great King he was. The messenger, not knowing anything about me, and hearing what splendid offers had been made me by the King, begged my pardon over and over again. Pagolo and Ascanio exclaimed: "It is God who has helped us to get back into so honoured a go-cart!"

On the day following I went to thank the King, who ordered me to make the models of twelve silver statues, which were to stand as candelabra round his table. He wanted them to represent six gods and six goddesses, and to have exactly the same height as his Majesty, which was a trifle under four cubits. Having dictated this commission, he turned to his treasurer, and asked whether he had paid me the five hundred crowns. The official said that he had received no orders to that effect. The King took this very ill, for he had requested the Cardinal to speak to him about it. Furthermore, he told me to go to Paris and seek out a place to live in, fitted for the execution of such works; he would see that I obtained it.

I got the five hundred crowns of gold, and took up my quarters at Paris in a house of the Cardinal of Ferrara. There I began, in God's name, to work, and fashioned four little waxen models, about two-thirds of a cubit each in height. They were Jupiter, Juno, Apollo, and Vulcan. In this while the King returned to

Paris; whereupon I went to him at once, taking my models with me, and my two prentices, Ascanio and Pagolo. On perceiving that the King was pleased with my work, and being commissioned to execute the Jupiter in silver of the height above described, I introduced the two young men, and said that I had brought them with me out of Italy to serve his Majesty; for inasmuch as they had been brought up by me, I could at the beginning get more help from them than from the Paris workmen. To this the King replied that I might name a salary which I thought sufficient for their maintenance. I said that a hundred crowns of gold apiece would be quite proper, and that I would make them earn their wages well. This agreement was concluded. Then I said that I had found a place which seemed to me exactly suited to my industry; it was his Majesty's own property, and called the Little Nello. The Provost of Paris was then in possession of it from his Majesty; but since the Provost made no use of the castle, his Majesty perhaps might grant it me to employ in his service. He replied upon the instant: "That place is my own house, and I know well that the man I gave it to does not inhabit it or use it. So you shall have it for the work you have to do." He then told his lieutenants to install me in the Nello. This officer made some resistance, pleading that he could not carry out the order. The King answered in anger that he meant to bestow his property on whom he pleased, and on a man who would serve him, seeing that he got nothing from the other; therefore he would hear no more about it. The lieutenant then submitted that some small force would have to be employed in order to effect an entrance. To which the King answered: "Go, then, and if a small force is not enough, use a great one."

The officer took me immediately to the castle, and there put me in possession, not, however, without violence; after that he warned me to take very good care that I was not murdered. I installed myself, enrolled serving-men, and bought a quantity of pikes and partisans; but I remained for several days exposed to grievous annoyances, for the Provost was a great nobleman of Paris, and all the other gentlefolk took part against me; they attacked me with such insults that I could hardly hold my own against them. I must not omit to mention that I entered the service of his Majesty in the year 1540, which was exactly the year in which I reached the age of forty.

The affronts and insults I received made me have recourse to the King, begging his Majesty to establish me in some other place. He answered: "Who are you, and what is your name?" I remained in great confusion, and could not comprehend what he meant. Holding my tongue thus, the King repeated the same words a second time angrily. Then I said my name was Benvenuto. "If, then, you are the Benvenuto of whom I have heard," replied the King, "act according to your wont, for you have my full leave to do so." I told his Majesty that all I wanted was to keep his favour; for the rest, I knew of nothing that could harm me. He gave a little laugh, and said: "Go your ways, then; you shall never want my favour." Upon this he told his first secretary, Monsignor di Villerois, to see me provided and accommodated with all I needed.

This Villerois was an intimate friend of the Provost, to whom the castle had been given. It was built in a triangle, right up against the city walls, and was of some antiquity, but had no garrison. The building was of considerable size. Monsignor di Villerois counselled me to look about for something else, and by all means to leave this place alone, seeing that its owner was a man of vast power, who would most assuredly have me killed. I answered that I had come from Italy to France only in order to serve that illustrious King; and as for dying, I knew for certain that die I must; a little earlier or a little later was a matter of supreme indifference to me.

Now Villerois was a man of the highest talent, exceptionally distinguished in all points, and possessed of vast wealth. There was nothing he would not gladly have done to harm me, but he made no open demonstration of his mind. He was grave, and of a noble presence, and spoke slowly, at his ease. To another gentleman, Monsignor di Marmagna, the treasurer of Languedoc, he left the duty of molesting me. The first thing which this man did was to look out the best apartments in the castle, and have them fitted up for himself. I told him that the King had given me the place to serve him in, and that I did not choose it should be occupied by any but myself and my attendants. The fellow, who was haughty, bold, and spirited, replied that he meant to do just what he liked; that I should run my head against a wall if I presumed to oppose him, and that Villerois had given him authority to do what he was doing. I told him that, by the King's authority given to me, neither he nor Villerois could do it. When I said that he gave vent to offensive language in French, whereat I retorted in my own tongue that he lied. Stung with rage, he clapped his hand upon a little dagger which he had; then I set my hand also to a large dirk which I always wore for my defence, and cried out: "If you dare to draw, I'll kill you on the spot." He had two servants to back him, and I had my two lads. For a moment or two Marmagna stood in doubt, not knowing exactly what to do, but rather inclined to mischief, and muttering: "I will never put up with such insults." Seeing then that the affair was taking a bad turn, I took a sudden resolution, and cried to Pagolo and Ascanio: "When you see me draw my dirk, throw yourselves upon those servingmen, and kill them if you can; I mean to kill this fellow at the first stroke, and then we will decamp together, with God's grace." Marmagna, when he understood my purpose, was glad enough to get alive out of the castle.

All these things, toning them down a trifle, I wrote to the Cardinal of Ferrara, who related them at once to the King. The King, deeply irritated, committed me to the care of another officer of his bodyguard who was named Monsignor lo Iscontro d'Orbech. By him I was accommodated with all that I required in the most gracious way imaginable.

After fitting up my own lodgings in the castle and the workshop with all conveniences for carrying on my business, and putting my household upon a most respectable footing, I began at once to construct three models exactly of the size which the silver statues were to be. These were Jupiter, Vulcan, and Mars. I moulded them in clay, and set them well up on irons; then I went to the King, who disbursed three hundred pounds weight of silver, if I remember rightly, for the commencement of the undertaking. While I was getting these things ready, we brought the little vase and oval basin to completion, which had been several months in hand. Then I had them richly gilt, and they showed like the finest piece of plate which had been seen in France.

Afterwards I took them to the Cardinal, who thanked me greatly; and, without requesting my attendance, carried and presented them to the King. He was delighted with the gift, and praised me as no artist was ever praised before. In return, he bestowed upon the Cardinal an abbey worth seven thousand crowns a year, and expressed his intention of rewarding me too. The Cardinal, however, prevented him, telling his Majesty that he was going ahead too fast, since I had as yet produced nothing for him. The King, who was exceedingly generous, replied: "For that very reason will I put heart and hope into him." The Cardinal, ashamed at his own meanness, said: "Sire, I beg you to leave that to me; I will allow him a pension of at least three hundred crowns when I have taken possession of the abbey." He never gave me anything; and it would be tedious to relate all the knavish tricks of this prelate. I prefer to dwell on matters of greater moment.

When I returned to Paris, the great favour shown me by the King made me a mark for all men's admiration. I received the silver and began my statue of Jupiter. Many journeymen were now in my employ; and the work went onward briskly day and night; so that, by the time I had finished the clay models of Jupiter, Vulcan, and Mars, and had begun to get the silver statue forward, my workshop made already a grand show.

The King now came to Paris, and I went to pay him my respects. No sooner had his Majesty set eyes upon me than he called me cheerfully, and asked if I had something fine to exhibit at my lodging, for he would come to inspect it. I related all I had been doing; upon which he was seized with a strong desire to come. Accordingly, after his dinner, he set off with Madame de Tampes, the Cardinal of Lorraine, and some other of his greatest nobles, among whom were the King of Navarre, his cousin, and the Queen, his sister; the Dauphin and Dauphiness also attended him; so that upon that day the very flower of the French court came to visit me. I had been some time at home, and was hard at work. When the King arrived at the door of the castle, and heard our hammers going, he bade his company keep silence. Everybody in my house was busily employed, so that the unexpected entrance of his Majesty took me by surprise. The first thing he saw on coming into the great hall was myself with a huge plate of silver in my hand, which I was beating for the body of my Jupiter; one of my men was finishing the head, another the legs; and it is easy to imagine what a din we made between us. It happened that a little French lad was working at my side, who had just been guilty of some trifling blunder. I gave the lad a kick, and, as my good luck would have it, caught him with my foot exactly in the fork between his legs, and sent him spinning several yards, so that he came stumbling up against the King precisely at the moment when his Majesty arrived. The King was vastly amused, but I felt covered with confusion. He began to ask me what I was engaged upon, and told me to go on working; then he said that he would much rather have me not employ my strength on manual labour, but take as many men as I wanted, and make them do the rough work; he should like me to keep myself in health, in order that he might enjoy my services through many years to come. I replied to his Majesty that the moment I left off working I should fall ill; also that my art itself would suffer, and not attain the mark I aimed at for his Majesty. Thinking that I spoke thus only to brag, and not because it was the truth, he made the Cardinal of Lorraine repeat what he had said; but I explained my reasons so fully and clearly, that the Cardinal perceived my drift; he then advised the King to let me labour as much or little as I liked.

Being very well satisfied with what he had seen, the King returned to his palace, after bestowing on me too many marks of favour to be here recorded. On the following day he sent for me at his dinner-hour. The Cardinal of Ferrara was there at meat with him. When I arrived, the King had reached his second course; he began at once to speak to me, saying, with a pleasant cheer, that having now so

fine a basin and jug of my workmanship, he wanted an equally handsome salt-cellar to match them; and begged me to make a design, and to lose no time about it. I replied: "Your Majesty shall see a model of the sort even sooner than you have commanded; for while I was making the basin, I thought there ought to be a salt-cellar to match it; therefore I have already designed one, and if it is your pleasure, I will at once exhibit my conception." The King turned with a lively movement of surprise and pleasure to the lords in his company —they were the King of Navarre, the Cardinal of Lorraine, and the Cardinal of Ferrara—exclaiming as he did so: "Upon my word, this is a man to be loved and cherished by every one who knows him." Then he told me that he would very gladly see my model.

I set off, and returned in a few minutes; for I had only to cross the river, that is, the Seine. I carried with me the wax model which I had made in Rome at the Cardinal of Ferrara's request. When I appeared again before the King and uncovered my piece, he cried out in astonishment: "This is a hundred times more divine a thing than I had ever dreamed of. What a miracle of a man! He ought never to stop working." Then he turned to me with a beaming countenance, and told me that he greatly liked the piece, and wished me to execute it in gold. The Cardinal of Ferrara looked me in the face, and let me understand that he recognised the model as the same which I had made for him in Rome. I replied that I had already told him I should carry it out for one who was worthy of it. The Cardinal, remembering my words, and nettled by the revenge he thought that I was taking on him, remarked to the King: "Sire, this is an enormous undertaking; I am only afraid that we shall never see it finished. These able artists who have great conceptions in their brain are ready enough to put the same in execution without duly considering when they are to be accomplished. I therefore, if I gave commission for things of such magnitude, should like to know when I was likely to get them." The King replied that if a man was so scrupulous about the termination of a work, he would never begin anything at all; these words he uttered with a certain look, which implied that such enterprises were not for folk of little spirit. I then began to say my say: "Princes who put heart and courage in their servants, as your Majesty does by deed and word, render undertakings of the greatest magnitude quite easy. Now that God has sent me so magnificent a patron, I hope to perform for him a multitude of great and splendid masterpieces." "I believe it," said the King, and rose from table. Then he called me into his chamber, and asked how much gold was wanted for the salt-cellar. "A thousand crowns," I answered. He called his treasurer at once, who was the Viscount of Orbec, and ordered him that very day to disburse to me a thousand crowns of good weight and old gold.

When I left his Majesty, I went for the two notaries who had helped me in procuring silver for the Jupiter and many other things. Crossing the Seine, I then took a small hand-basket, which one of my cousins, a nun, had given me on my journey through Florence. It made for my good fortune that I took this basket and not a bag. So then, thinking I could do the business by daylight, for it was still early, and not caring to interrupt my workmen, and being indisposed to take a servant with me, I set off alone. When I reached the house of the treasurer, I found that he had the money laid out before him, and was selecting the best pieces as the King had ordered. It seemed to me, however, that that thief of a treasurer was doing all he could to postpone the payment of the money; nor were the pieces counted out until three hours after nightfall.

I meanwhile was not wanting in despatch, for I sent word to several of my journeymen that they should come and attend me, since the matter was one of serious importance. When I found that they did not arrive, I asked the messenger if he had done my errand. The rascal of a groom whom I had sent replied that he had done so, but that they had answered that they could not come; he, however, would gladly carry the money for me. I answered that I meant to carry the money myself. By this time the contract was drawn up and signed. On the money being counted, I put it all into my little basket, and then thrust my arm through the two handles. Since I did this with some difficulty, the gold was well shut in, and

I carried it more conveniently than if the vehicle had been a bag. I was well armed with shirt and sleeves of mail, and having my sword and dagger at my side, made off along the street as quick as my two legs would carry me.

Just as I left the house, I observed some servants whispering among themselves, who also went off at a round pace in another direction from the one I took. Walking with all haste, I passed the bridge of the Exchange, and went up along a wall beside the river which led to my lodging in the castle. I had just come to the Augustines—now this was a very perilous passage, and though it was only five hundred paces distant from my dwelling, yet the lodging in the castle being quite as far removed inside, no one could have heard my voice if I had shouted—when I saw four men with four swords in their hands advancing to attack me. My resolution was taken in an instant. I covered the basket with my cape, drew my sword, and seeing that they were pushing hotly forward, cried aloud: "With soldiers there is only the cape and sword to gain; and these, before I give them up, I hope you'll get not much to your advantage." Then crossing my sword boldly with them, I more than once spread out my arms, in order that, if the ruffians were put on by the servants who had seen me take my money, they might be led to judge I was not carrying it. The encounter was soon over; for they retired step by step, saying among themselves in their own language: "This is a brave Italian, and certainly not the man we are after; or if he be the man, he cannot be carrying anything." I spoke Italian, and kept harrying them with thrust and slash so hotly that I narrowly missed killing one or the other. My skill in using the sword made them think I was a soldier rather than a fellow of some other calling. They drew together and began to fall back, muttering all the while beneath their breath in their own tongue. I meanwhile continued always calling out, but not too loudly, that those who wanted my cape and blade would have to get them with some trouble. Then I quickened pace, while they still followed slowly at my heels; this augmented my fear, for I thought I might be falling into an ambuscade, which would have cut me off in front as well as rear. Accordingly, when I was at the distance of a hundred paces from my home, I ran with all my might, and shouted at the top of my voice: "To arms, to arms! out with you, out with you! I am being murdered." In a moment four of my young men came running, with four pikes in their hands. They wanted to pursue the ruffians, who could still be seen; but I stopped them, calling back so as to let the villains hear: "Those cowards yonder, four against one man alone, had not pluck enough to capture a thousand golden crowns in metal, which have almost broken this arm of mine. Let us haste inside and put the money away; then I will take my big two-handed sword, and go with you whithersoever you like." We went inside to secure the gold; and my lads, while expressing deep concern for the peril I had run, gently chided me, and said: "You risk yourself too much alone; the time will come when you will make us all bemoan your loss." A thousand words and exclamations were exchanged between us; my adversaries took to flight; and we all sat down and supped together with mirth and gladness, laughing over those great blows which fortune strikes, for good as well as evil, and which, what time they do not hit the mark, are just the same as though they had not happened. It is very true that one says to oneself: "You will have had a lesson for next time." But that is not the case; for fortune always comes upon us in new ways, quite unforeseen by our imagination. . . .

Having succeeded so well with the cast of the Medusa, I had great hope of bringing my Perseus through; for I had laid the wax on, and felt confident that it would come out in bronze as perfectly as the Medusa. The waxen model produced so fine an effect, that when the Duke saw it and was struck with its beauty— whether somebody had persuaded him it could not be carried out with the same finish in metal, or whether he thought so for himself— he came to visit me more frequently than usual, and on one occasion said: "Benvenuto, this figure cannot succeed in bronze; the laws of art do not admit of it." These words of

his Excellency stung me so sharply that I answered: "My lord, I know how very little confidence you have in me; and I believe the reason of this is that your most illustrious Excellency lends too ready an ear to my calumniators, or else indeed that you do not understand my art." He hardly let me close the sentence when he broke in: "I profess myself a connoisseur, and understand it very well indeed." I replied: "Yes, like a prince, not like an artist; for if your Excellency understood my trade as well as you imagine, you would trust me on the proofs I have already given. These are, first, the colossal bronze bust of your Excellency, which is now in Elba; secondly, the restoration of the Ganymede in marble, which offered so many difficulties and cost me so much trouble, that I would rather have made the whole statue new from the beginning; thirdly, the Medusa, cast by me in bronze, here now before your Excellency's eyes, the execution of which was a greater triumph of strength and skill than any of my predecessors in this fiendish art have yet achieved. Look you, my lord! I constructed that furnace anew on principles quite different from those of other founders; in addition to many technical improvements and ingenious devices, I supplied it with two issues for the metal, because this difficult and twisted figure could not otherwise have come out perfect. It is only owing to my intelligent insight into means and appliances that the statue turned out as it did; a triumph judged impossible by all the practitioners of this art. I should like you furthermore to be aware, my lord, for certain, that the sole reason why I succeeded with all those great and arduous works in France under his most admirable Majesty King Francis, was the high courage which that good monarch put into my heart by the liberal allowances he made me, and the multitude of work-people he left at my disposal. I could have as many as I asked for, and employed at times above forty, all chosen by myself. These were the causes of my having there produced so many masterpieces in so short a space of time. Now then, my lord, put trust in me; supply me with the aid I need. I am confident of being able to complete a work which will delight your soul. But if your Excellency goes on disheartening me, and does not advance me the assistance which is absolutely required, neither I nor any man alive upon this earth can hope to achieve the slightest thing of value."

It was as much as the Duke could do to stand by and listen to my pleadings. He kept turning first this way and then that; while I, in despair, poor wretched I, was calling up remembrance of the noble state I held in France, to the great sorrow of my soul. All at once he cried: "Come, tell me, Benvenuto, how is it possible that yonder splendid head of Medusa, so high up there in the grasp of Perseus, should ever come out perfect?" I replied upon the instant: "Look you now, my lord! If your Excellency possessed that knowledge of the craft which you affirm you have, you would not fear one moment for the splendid head you speak of. There is good reason, on the other hand, to feel uneasy about this right foot, so far below and at a distance from the rest." When he heard these words, the Duke turned, half in anger, to some gentlemen in waiting, and exclaimed: "I verily believe that this Benvenuto prides himself on contradicting everything one says." Then he faced round to me with a touch of mockery, upon which his attendants did the like, and began to speak as follows: "I will listen patiently to any argument you can possibly produce in explanation of your statement, which may convince me of its probability." I said in answer: "I will adduce so sound an argument that your Excellency shall perceive the full force of it." So I began: "You must know, my lord, that the nature of fire is to ascend, and therefore I promise you that Medusa's head will come out famously; but since it is not in nature of fire to descend, and I must force it downwards six cubits by artificial means, I assure your Excellency upon this most convincing ground of proof that the foot cannot possibly come out. It will, however, be quite easy for me to restore it." "Why, then," said the Duke, "did you not devise it so that the foot should come out as well as you affirm the head will?" I answered: "I must have made a much larger furnace, with a conduit as thick as my leg; and so I might have forced the molten metal by its own

weight to descend so far. Now, my pipe, which runs six cubits to the statue's foot, as I have said, is not thicker than two fingers. However, it was not worth the trouble and expense to make a larger; for I shall easily be able to mend what is lacking. But when my mould is more than half full, as I expect, from this middle point upwards, the fire ascending by its natural property, then the heads of Perseus and Medusa will come out admirably; you may be quite sure of it." After I had thus expounded these convincing arguments, together with many more of the same kind, which it would be tedious to set down here, the Duke shook his head and departed without further ceremony.

Abandoned thus to my own resources, I took new courage, and banished the sad thoughts which kept recurring to my mind, making me often weep bitter tears of repentance for having left France; for though I did so only to revisit Florence, my sweet birthplace, in order that I might charitably succour my six nieces, this good action, as I well perceived, had been the beginning of my great misfortune. Nevertheless, I felt convinced that when my Perseus was accomplished, all these trials would be turned to high felicity and glorious well-being.

Accordingly I strengthened my heart, and with all the forces of my body and my purse, employing what little money still remained to me, I set to work. First I provided myself with several loads of pinewood from the forests of Serristori, in the neighbourhood of Montelupo. While these were on their way, I clothed my Perseus with the clay which I had prepared many months beforehand, in order that it might be duly seasoned. After making its clay tunic (for that is the term used in this art) and properly arming it and fencing it with iron girders, I began to draw the wax out by means of a slow fire. This melted and issued through numerous air-vents I had made; for the more there are of these, the better will the mould fill. When I had finished drawing off the wax, I constructed a funnel-shaped furnace all round the model of my Perseus. It was built of bricks, so interlaced, the one above the other, that numerous apertures were left for the fire to exhale at. Then I began to lay on wood by degrees, and kept it burning two whole days and nights. At length, when all the wax was gone, and the mould was well baked, I set to work at digging the pit in which to sink it. This I performed with scrupulous regard to all the rules of art. When I had finished that part of my work, I raised the mould by windlasses and stout ropes to a perpendicular position, and suspending it with the greatest care one cubit above the level of the furnace, so that it hung exactly above the middle of the pit, I next lowered it gently down into the very bottom of the furnace, and had it firmly placed with every possible precaution for its safety. When this delicate operation was accomplished, I began to bank it up with the earth I had excavated; and, ever as the earth grew higher, I introduced its proper air-vents, which were little tubes of earthenware, such as folk use for drains and such-like purposes. At length, I felt sure that it was admirably fixed, and that the filling-in of the pit and the placing of the air-vents had been properly performed. I also could see that my work-people understood my method, which differed very considerably from that of all the other masters in the trade. Feeling confident, then, that I could rely upon them, I next turned to my furnace, which I had filled with numerous pigs of copper and other bronze stuff. The pieces were piled according to the laws of art, that is to say, so resting one upon the other that the flames could play freely through them, in order that the metal might heat and liquefy the sooner. At last I called out heartily to set the furnace going. The logs of pine were heaped in, and, what with the unctuous resin of the wood and the good draught I had given, my furnace worked so well that I was obliged to rush from side to side to keep it going. The labour was more than I could stand; yet I forced myself to strain every nerve and muscle. To increase my anxieties, the workshop took fire, and we were afraid lest the roof should fall upon our heads; while, from the garden, such a storm of wind and rain kept blowing in, that it perceptibly cooled the furnace.

Battling thus with all these untoward circumstances for several hours, and exerting myself beyond even the measure of my powerful constitution, I could at last bear up no longer, and a sudden fever, of the utmost possible intensity, attacked me. I felt absolutely obliged to go and fling myself upon my bed. Sorely against my will having to drag myself away from the spot, I turned to my assistants, about ten or more in all, what with master-founders, hand-workers, country-fellows, and my own special journeymen, among whom was Bernardino Mannellini of Mugello, my apprentice through several years. To him in particular I spoke: "Look, my dear Bernardino, that you observe the rules which I have taught you; do your best with all despatch, for the metal will soon be fused. You cannot go wrong; these honest men will get the channels ready; you will easily be able to drive back the two plugs with this pair of iron crooks; and I am sure that my mould will fill miraculously. I feel more ill than I ever did in all my life, and verily believe that it will kill me before a few hours are over." Thus, with despair at heart, I left them, and betook myself to bed.

No sooner had I got to bed, than I ordered my serving-maids to carry food and wine for all the men into the workshop; at the same time I cried: "I shall not be alive to-morrow." They tried to encourage me, arguing that my illness would pass over, since it came from excessive fatigue. In this way I spent two hours battling with the fever, which steadily increased, and calling out continually, "I feel that I am dying." My housekeeper, who was named Mona Fiore de Castel del Rio, a very notable manager and no less warm-hearted, kept chiding me for my discouragement; but, on the other hand, she paid me every kind attention which was possible. However, the sight of my physical pain and moral dejection so affected her, that, in spite of that brave heart of hers, she could not refrain from shedding tears; and yet, so far as she was able, she took good care I should not see them. While I was thus terribly afflicted, I beheld the figure of a man enter my chamber, twisted in his body into the form of a capital S. He raised a lamentable, doleful voice, like one who announces their last hour to men condemned to die upon the scaffold, and spoke these words: "O Benvenuto! your statue is spoiled, and there is no hope whatever of saving it." No sooner had I heard the shriek of that wretch than I gave a howl which might have been heard from the sphere of flame. Jumping from my bed, I seized my clothes and began to dress. The maids, and my lad, and every one who came around to help me, got kicks or blows of the fist, while I kept crying out in lamentation "Ah, traitors! enviers! This is an act of treason, done by malice prepense! But I swear by God that I will sift it to the bottom, and before I die will leave such witness to the world of what I can do as shall make a score of mortals marvel."

When I had got my clothes on, I strode with soul bent on mischief toward the workshop; there I beheld the men, whom I had left erewhile in such high spirits, standing stupefied and downcast. I began at once and spoke: "Up with you! Attend to me! Since you have not been able or willing to obey the directions I gave you, obey me now that I am with you to conduct my work in person. Let no one contradict me, for in cases like this we need the aid of hand and hearing, not of advice." When I had uttered these words, a certain Maestro Alessandro Lastricati broke silence and said: "Look you, Benvenuto, you are going to attempt an enterprise which the laws of art do not sanction, and which cannot succeed." I turned upon him with such fury and so full of mischief, that he and all the rest of them exclaimed with one voice: "On then! Give orders! We will obey your least commands, so long as life is left in us." I believe they spoke thus feelingly because they thought I must fall shortly dead upon the ground. I went immediately to inspect the furnace, and found that the metal was all curdled; an accident which we express by "being caked." I told two of the hands to cross the road, and fetch from the house of the butcher Capretta, a load of young oak-wood, which had lain dry for above a year; this wood had been previously offered me by Madame Ginevra, wife of the said Capretta. So soon as the first armfuls arrived, I began to fill the grate beneath the furnace. Now oak-wood of that kind heats more powerfully than any other sort of tree; and for this reason, where a slow fire is wanted, as in the case of gun-foundry, alder or pine is preferred. Accordingly, when the logs took fire, oh! how the cake began to stir beneath that awful heat, to glow and sparkle in a blaze! At the same time I kept stirring up the channels, and sent men upon the roof to stop the conflagration, which had gathered force from the increased combustion in the furnace; also I caused boards, carpets, and other hangings to be set up against the garden, in order to protect us from the violence of the rain.

When I had thus provided against these several disasters, I roared out first to one man and then to another; "Bring this thing here! Take that thing there!" At this crisis, when the whole gang saw the cake was on the point of melting, they did my bidding, each fellow working with the strength of three. I then ordered half a pig of pewter to be brought, which weighed about sixty pounds, and flung it into the middle of the cake inside the furnace. By this means, and by piling on wood and stirring now with pokers and now with iron rods, the curdled mass rapidly began to liquefy. Then, knowing I had brought the dead to life again, against the firm opinion of those ignoramuses, I felt such vigour fill my veins, that all those pains of fever, all those fears of death, were quite forgotten.

All of a sudden an explosion took place, attended by a tremendous flash of flame, as though a thunderbolt had formed and been discharged amongst us. Unwonted and appalling terror astonied every one, and me more even than the rest. When the din was over and the dazzling light extinguished, we began to look each other in the face. Then I discovered that the cap of the furnace had blown up, and the bronze was bubbling over from its source beneath. So I had the mouths of my mould immediately opened, and at the same time drove in the two plugs which kept back the molten metal. But I noticed that it did not flow as rapidly as usual, the reason being probably that the fierce heat of the fire we kindled had consumed its base alloy. Accordingly I sent for all my pewter platters, porringers, and dishes, to the number of some two hundred pieces, and had a portion of them cast, one by one, into the channels, the rest into the furnace. This expedient succeeded, and every one could now perceive that my bronze was in most perfect liquefaction, and my mould was filling;

whereupon they all with heartiness and happy cheer assisted and obeyed by bidding, while I, now here, now there, gave orders, helped with my own hands, and cried aloud: "O God! Thou that by Thy immeasurable power didst rise from the dead, and in Thy glory didst ascent to heaven!". . . even thus in a moment my mould was filled; and seeing my work finished, I fell upon my knees, and with all my heart gave thanks to God.

After all was over, I turned to a plate of salad on a bench there, and ate with hearty appetite, and drank together with the whole crew. Afterwards I retired to bed, healthy and happy, for it was now two hours before morning, and slept as sweetly as though I had never felt a touch of illness. My good housekeeper, without my giving any orders, had prepared a fat capon for my repast. So that, when I rose, about the hour for breaking fast, she presented herself with a smiling countenance, and said: "Oh! is that the man who felt that he was dying? Upon my word, I think the blows and kicks you dealt us last night, when you were so enraged, and had that demon in your body as it seemed, must have frightened away your mortal fever! The fever feared that it might catch it too, as we did!" All my poor household, relieved in like measure from anxiety and overwhelming labour, went at once to buy earthen vessels in order to replace the pewter I had cast away. Then we dined together joyfully; nay, I cannot remember a day in my whole life when I dined with greater gladness or a better appetite.

After our meal I received visits from the several men who had assisted me. They exchanged congratulations, and thanked God for our success, saying they had learned and seen things done which other masters judged impossible. I too grew somewhat glorious; and deeming I had shown myself a man of talent, indulged a boastful humour. So I thrust my hand into my purse, and paid them all to their full satisfaction.

That evil fellow, my mortal foe, Messer Pier Francesco Ricci, major-domo of the Duke, took great pains to find out how the affair had gone. In answer to his questions, the two men whom I suspected of having caked my metal for me, said I was no man, but of a certainty some

powerful devil, since I had accomplished what no craft of the art could do; indeed they did not believe a mere ordinary fiend could work such miracles as I in other ways had shown. They exaggerated the whole affair so much, possibly in order to excuse their own part in it, that the major-domo wrote an account to the Duke, who was then in Pisa, far more marvellous and full of thrilling incidents than what they had narrated.

After I had let my statue cool for two whole days, I began to uncover it by slow degrees. The first thing I found was that the head of Medusa had come out most admirably, thanks to the air-vents; for, as I had told the Duke, it is the nature of fire to ascend. Upon advancing farther, I discovered that the other head, that, namely, of Perseus, had succeeded no less admirably; and this astonished me far more, because it is at a considerably lower level than that of the Medusa. Now the mouths of the mould were placed above the head of Perseus and behind his shoulders; and I found that all the bronze my furnace contained had been exhausted in the head of this figure. It was a miracle to observe that not one fragment remained in the orifice of the channel, and that nothing was wanting to the statue. In my great astonishment I seemed to see in this the hand of God arranging and controlling all.

I went on uncovering the statue with success, and ascertained that everything had come out in perfect order, until I reached the foot of the right leg on which the statue rests. There the heel itself was formed, and going farther, I found the foot apparently complete. This gave me great joy on the one side, but was half unwelcome to me on the other, merely because I had told the Duke that it could not come out. However, when I reached the end, it appeared that the toes and a little piece above them were unfinished, so that about half the foot was wanting. Although I knew that this would add a trifle to my labour, I was very well pleased, because I could now prove to the Duke how well I understood my business. It is true that far more of the foot than I expected had been perfectly formed; the reason of this was that, from causes I have recently described, the bronze was hotter than our rules of art prescribe; also that I had been obliged to supplement the alloy with my pewter cups and platters, which no one else, I think, had ever done before.

Having now ascertained how successfully my work had been accomplished, I lost no time in hurrying to Pisa, where I found the Duke. He gave me a most gracious reception, as did also the Duchess; and although the major-domo had informed them of the whole proceedings, their Excellencies deemed my performance far more stupendous and astonishing when they heard the tale from my own mouth.

When I arrived at the foot of Perseus, and said it had not come out perfect, just as I previously warned his Excellency, I saw an expression of wonder pass over his face, while he related to the Duchess how I had predicted this beforehand. Observing the princes to be so well disposed towards me, I begged leave from the Duke to go to Rome. He granted it in most obliging terms, and bade me return as soon as possible to complete his Perseus; giving me letters of recommendation meanwhile to his ambassador, Averardo Serristori. We were then in the first years of Pope Giulio de Monti. . . .

Dante Alighieri

Dante (see p. 263) in The Divine Comedy describes his imaginary journey through Hell, Purgatory, and Paradise. The appeal of this lengthy poem during the past six hundred years has been extraordinary, and interest in it in our own day has increased rather than diminished. It represents a unique summary and synthesis of medieval culture; it is full of the learning of Dante's day and suggests the remarkable breadth and depth of the scholarship that prevailed during the transition from the Middle Ages to the Renaissance. The poem was originally written in Italian rather than Latin as was usually customary and represented one of the earlier uses of a vernacular tongue for a major cultural work. The selection is from what has come to be called Dante's beatific vision. In reading it, note (1) Dante's allegorical usage, (2) Beatrice's discourse on creation and the fall of the angels, (3) her censure of preachers and the sale of indulgences, (4) Dante's ascent to the tenth heaven and his portrayal of the empyrean, (5) his description of the angels and his invocation to God, (6) the change of guides and the implied reason therefor, (7) the ranking of saints and the occupants of heaven, (8) Bernard's prayer to the virgin, and (9) the picturing of the beatific vision.

From: THE DIVINE COMEDY

CANTO 29

When the twinborn children of Latona,
Surmounted by the Ram and by the Scales,
Share the horizon as a common belt,
As long as from the time the zenith holds
The two in perfect balance, till they break
The equipoise by changing hemispheres:

As translated by Lawrence Grant White in Dante Alighieri, *The Divine Comedy: The Inferno, Purgatorio, and Paradiso, A New Translation into English Blank Verse,* New York: Pantheon Books, 1948, 179–188.

So long stood Beatrice without a word,
A smile illumining her countenance,
Her gaze upon that point which mastered me.
She said: "I'll tell what thou dost wish to hear;
I ask it not, for I already see it
Where every *when* and every *where* are cen-
    tred.
   " 'Twas not that we might gain still greater
    good—
Which is not possible—but so that He
Might in His radiance declare, 'I am,'
That in eternity, outside of time,
Outside of every other comprehension,
Eternal Love unfolded in new loves.
Nor e'er this was He in idleness:
Neither *before* nor *after* yet existed
When God Himself upon the waters moved.
Now form and matter, simple and combined,
Took on existence that had no defect,
Like triple arrows from a three-stringed
    bow. . . .
   "But we digress enough. Now turn thine
    eyes
Once more to that straight path which we have
    left:
Thus may our way be shortened with the time.
The angels grow to such a mighty throng
That never yet had mortal thought or speech
Sufficient compass for describing it.
If thou but think on that which is revealed
By Daniel, thou wilt see that in his 'thousands'
A multiple determinate lies hid.
The Primal Light irradiating all
Is thus received in just as many ways
As there are splendors which to it are joined.
Affection follows action that conceives,
Hence it is, the sweetness of their love
Will glow with heat of varying amount.
   "Behold the vastness of the eternal good,
Since it has made itself so many mirrors
By which its virtue is distributed—
One in itself, remaining as before!"

CANTO 30

Perchance six thousand miles away from us
The sixth bright hour is glowing, while our
    world
Inclines its shadow almost to the level;
And now midheaven changes, far above,
So that a star fades out of earthly sight.
And as the brightest handmaid of the sun

Advances nearer us, in like proportion
The whitening sky shuts out each star in turn,
Until the fairest one has disappeared.
   Not otherwise did that triumphant choir,
Which e'er disports itself around the point
That overcame me, and appears enclosed
By that which it encloses, melt away.
Therefore, to turn my eyes on Beatrice,
Love and the empty sky alike constrained me.
If all that hitherto was said of her
Were concentrated in one eulogy,
'Twould not suffice to tell about that instant.
The beauty I beheld was far beyond
All human measure; thus I am convinced
That God alone can know its full degree.
I know that I am vanquished on this score:
No comic poet, or a tragic one,
Was e'er so fully mastered by his theme.
For as the sun will most affect the eye
That trembles most before it, even so
Remembrance of that smile affects my spirit.
   From that day I saw her first on earth
Until the moment when I saw her now,
The sequence of my song has run its course:
Now must my effort cease from all attempt
Of following her beauty in my verse—
Like any artist pushed beyond his powers!
   Now she who merits worthier heralding
Than that of my poor trumpet, which must
    now
Bring to a close its arduous theme, spoke forth
With voice and gesture like a ready leader's:
"We now have issued from the largest sphere
Into that heaven of purest light composed—
Light intellectual, with love transfused;
Love of true good, transfused throughout with
    joy;
Joy that surpasses every sweet delight.
Here wilt thou behold two mighty armies
Of paradise; and one in that same form
Which it will have upon the Judgment Day."
Much as a sudden lightning flash darts forth
Which overcomes our sight, so that the eye
Loses its power to see the clearest objects:
Just so a vivid light shone round about,
And left me veiled in such a dazzling glare
That nothing else was visible to me.
   "The love that gives its quiet to this heaven
E'er flashes forth a welcome such as this,
To make the candle worthy of the flame."
No sooner had these brief words come to me,

Than I perceived that I was raised above
The limits of my own intelligence.
So great was my new vision's added strength
That any light which ever was conceived
Were not too bright for me to bear its fire.
The light I saw was like a blazing river—
A streaming radiance set between two banks
Enamelled with the wonders of the spring.
And from that stream proceeded living sparks
Which set themselves in flowers on every side,
And glowed like rubies in a golden setting—
Until, as if o'ercome by that sweet scent,
They plunged again into the gleaming flood,
Whence others issued forth to take their place.
"That high desire that now enkindles thee
So that thou seekest knowledge of this sight,
Pleases the more, the more it is intense.
But ere so great a thirst in thee be slaked,
Thou first must drink the water of this stream."
Thus spoke to me that sun which gives me light.
And then: "The river, and the topazes
That enter in and issue forth from it—
The smiling flowers—are shadows of the truth.
They are not difficult to comprehend:
Defect of this inheres in thee alone,—
For thou hast not as yet sufficient vision."

No babe, awakening later than its wont,
E'er turned its face to take its mother's milk
With greater eagerness than now I strove
To make even better mirrors of my eyes,
Stooping toward that flood which flows its
     course
In order that therein we may be bettered.
And even as my eyelids drank of it,
It seemed at once to change its very form,
Becoming circular instead of oblong.
Much as a crowd of people who are masked,
And then appear again in aspect new
When they have doffed their borrowed sem-
     blances:
Just so the flowers and those sparkling jewels
Were changed into a greater jubilee,
So that both courts of heaven were manifest.
Splendor of God, by whose immortal light
I saw that triumph of the realm of truth,
Vouchsafe to me the power to tell of it!
On high there shines a brilliance that dis-
     plays
The sight of God to whatsoever creature
Finds its peace in sight of Him alone.

It spreads into a circle of such width,
That its circumference would be too large
To form a girdle round the sun itself.
Its whole appearance issues from a beam
Reflected from the primum mobile,
From which it takes its life and potency.
And as a hillside decked with leaves and
     flowers
Is mirrored in the water at its base,
As though to see itself thus glorified:
Just so, above that light on every hand,
Were mirrored, in a multitude of thrones,
All those of us who have returned on high.
And if the lowest grade reflects such light,
How vast indeed must be the amplitude
Of this great rose, in its remotest petals!
My sight embraced its fullest height and
     breadth,
So that the quality and quantity
Of all that joy to me was manifest.
For *near* or *far* means nothing in that region;
And where God's power is thus immediate,
The laws of nature are of no avail.

Into the yellow of th' eternal rose—
Which opens outward, rising tier on tier,
And breathes a breath of everlasting spring—
Did Beatrice—like one who holds his peace
And yet would speak—conduct me, as she
     said:
"Behold, the countless hosts arrayed in white,
Behold how great the circuit of our city!
Behold our seats, so peopled with the blest
That few henceforward are awaited here!
"On that great seat whereon thine eyes are
     fixed,
By reason of the crown placed over it,
Ere thou thyself wilt join this marriage feast,
Will sit the soul, erstwhile imperial,
Of Henry, who to straighten Italy
Will come ere she be reconciled to good.
For blind cupidity, bewitching you,
Has made you even as a little child
Who drives away his nurse, and dies of hunger.
Then one will rule as Prefect in the church
Who openly and secretly refuses
To take the road beside him and advance.
But God will not endure him there for long:
For he will be thrust downward to that place
Where Simon Magus writhes for his deserts;
He of Anaga will be lower yet."

CANTO 31

Thus, in the semblance of a snow-white rose,
There was displayed to me the saintly throng
That Christ, with His own blood, had made
  his bride.
That other host—who, as they fly, behold
And sing His glory, which enamors them,
His goodness, which has given them such glory
Just like a swarm of bees, which at one time
Alight upon the flowers, and then again
Return to where their savory toil is stored,
Descended to the heart of that vast flower,
So bright with leaves, thence rising up again
To where their love eternally abides.

  Their countenances were of living flame,
Their wings of finest gold; the rest of them
Was whiter than the whiteness of the snow.
When they went to the flower, from rank to
  rank,
They left there something of the peace and
  love
Which they had gathered while they fanned
  their sides.
Nor did the presence of this flying host
Between the flower and all the thrones above,
Obstruct the vision, or impair its splendor—
Because the Light Divine strikes through all
  things
According to their merit, so that naught
Can ever be impediment to it,
This kingdom so secure, so filled with joy,
Peopled with ancient and with modern folk,
Centres its love and vision on one mark.

  O Trinal Light, which in a single star
Givest them all such rapture, seeing Thee,
Look down in pity on our strife below!
If barbarians, coming from a land
That every day is covered by Callisto
As she revolves beside her cherished son,
Looking at Rome and her great monuments,
While Lateran still ruled all mortal things,
Were wonder-struck at such a spectacle,
Imagine with what wonder I was filled,
Who came from earthly things to things divine,
From time unto eternity itself—
From Florence, to a people just and sane!
In truth, between my wonder and my joy,
I felt no wish to listen or to speak.

  Like a pilgrim, who will find refreshment

In gazing round the temple of his vows,
Hoping some day to tell about its wonders:
Just so, as I walked through that living light
I led my eyes to look upon the ranks
That were above, below, and round about.
Faces I saw, conducive unto love,
Lit by Another's radiance and their own,
And actions graced with every dignity.

  Till then, my contemplation had embraced
Only the general form of paradise,
Without regarding any single part.
Now with rekindled zeal I turned around
To ask some information of my lady,
On things regarding which I stood in doubt.
I purposed one thing, and another answered:
I saw not Beatrice, but an aged man,
Clad in the raiment of those glorious saints.
His eyes and cheeks betokened love benign;
His kindly mien was full of tenderness
That would be fitting to a tender father.
"Where, where is she?" I hastily cried out.

  And he: "To put an end to thy desire,
I here am sent by Beatrice to thee.
Look up—there on the third array of seats
Below the highest rank—and thou wilt see her
Upon that throne allotted by her worth."

  Without response I lifted up my eyes,
And saw her as she made herself a crown,
Reflecting on herself the eternal rays.

  From that highest region of the thunder,
An eye upon the bottom of the sea,
Down in the ocean's nethermost recess,
Is not so far as I was then from her.
Howbeit, this was naught to me: her image,
Unblurred by aught between, was shining
  clear.

  "O lady in whose aid my hope is strong,
And who to save my erring soul didst deign
To leave thy footprints in the soil of hell!
I now can recognize the grace and virtue
Of all the many things that I have seen
By reason of thy goodness and thy power.
From servitude to freedom thou has led
  me,
By every path that lay within thy means
For the accomplishment of such a task.
Preserve in me thy own magnificence,
So that my spirit, which thou has made whole,
May, pleasing thee, be loosened from the
  body."

Such was my prayer; and she, though far
    away,
Appeared to smile, and look again on me:
Then she turned back to that Eternal Fount.
    Now spoke the saint: "So that thou mayst
    complete
Thy journey to perfection,—to which end
Prayer and holy love have sent me here,
Fly with thine eyes around this lovely garden:
The sight of it will make thy vision fit
To rise still higher through God's radiant light.
The Queen of Heaven, for whom I burn with
    love,
Will grant us every grace within her power,
Because I am her faithful servant Bernard."
    Even as one who from Croatia comes,
Perchance, to look on our Veronica,
And who is never sated by the sight,
But says in thought, the while it is exposed,
"Lord Jesus, Verigod of Verigod,
Was this the aspect of thy countenance?"
E'en so was I, while I was marvelling
At that great love of him who in the world
By contemplation tasted of that peace.
    "O Son of grace," he said, "this blessedness
Will ne'er be known to thee, if thou retain
Thy gaze below here, on the lower places:
Seek out the most remote of all the rings
Till thou behold, upon her throne, the Queen
To whom this realm is subject and devoted."
    I lifted up my eyes. Even as at dawn,
That portion of the sky toward the east
Surpasses that in which the sun declines,
Just so, as mountain overtops a vale,
I saw a portion of the distant circles
Surpassing in its brilliance all the rest.
And as the region whence there will emerge
That pole which Phaethon once drove so ill,
Flames most, while either side is not so bright:
'Twas even so, that oriflamme of peace
Seemed brighter in the centre; in like manner,
Its flame grew less pronounced to right and
    left.
At its heart, with pinions far outstretched,
Were countless thousands of rejoicing angels;
Differing each in movement and in light.
I saw there, beaming with a happy smile
Upon their sports and songs, a shining beauty
That was a joy to all the other saints.
But even if I had such wealth in speech
As in imagination, I would shrink

From trying to describe its loveliness.
And Bernard, seeing that mine eyes were fixed
Attentive on its glowing warmth, now turned
His own with such affection to it, that I flamed,
With ardor new, to gaze on it once more.

CANTO 32

Intent upon the source of his delight,
The contemplator willingly assumed
The office of a teacher, and began:
"That wound anointed and closed up by Mary,
Was opened when inflicted on mankind
By that fair woman who is at her feet.
Beneath her, in the circle which is formed
By that third row of seats, is Beatrice,
With Rachel by her side, as thou canst see.
Rebecca, Sarah, Judith, also her
Honored as great-grandmother to the singer
Who once cried *Miserere* for his guilt,
Thou canst also see, if thou but look
From rank to rank in gradual descent,
The while I name the petals, one by one.
    "Downward from the seventh tier of seats,
And upward, sits a band of Hebrew women,
Dividing all the tresses of the flower.
Thereby they form a wall that thus divides
The holy stair, according to the view
Of Christ that those of either faith professed.
Upon this side, where all the petals blossom,
Are seated those who held as their belief
That Christ was yet to come to save the world;
Upon the other side, where thou canst see
Those empty spaces in the semicircles,
Sit those whose faith knew Christ already
    come.
Even as on this side, the glorious throne
Of Her who reigns in heaven, and the rest
Seated below Her, form a line of severance:
There, opposite, behold the great John's seat—
That martyr who endured the wilderness
And hell itself for two years afterward—
Augustine, Francis, Benedict, and others,
Below him, are allotted to those seats
From rank to rank as far as where we stand.
    "Behold God's foresight, wondrous and
    supreme!
This garden will be filled in equal measure
By those two aspects of the faith divine.
And further know that downward from that
    tier,

Crossing the middle of the two arrays,
The thrones are filled by those who earn their
    seats
By reason not of merit of their own,
But that of others, in a certain manner:
For these are souls that were released by death
Ere they had power to exercise their wills.
This thou canst see if thou their features scan,
And hear the childish accents of their speech.
    "Thou art in doubt, and yet thou keepest
      silence!
But I will loose from thee those mighty bonds
In which thou art by faulty reason held.
Within the ample confines of this realm,
No particle of chance can find a place:
No more, indeed, can sorrow, hunger, thirst.
Whatever thou beholdest has been set
By the eternal order; so that here
The ring conforms exactly to the finger.
Therefore it is, that all this multitude
Who have been swiftly garnered to true life,
Are not thus graduated *sine causa*.
The King through whom this kingdom is at rest
In such great love, and in such great delight
That man can never dare to hope for more,
Creating all our minds in His glad aspect,
Gives them grace according to His will,
In varying measure: let the fact suffice.
Now this is clearly manifest to you
By those twin brothers in the Holy Writ,
Who in their mother's womb in anger stirred.
Hence the Light on high must crown us fitly,
Awarding grace in different degrees,
Even as the different hair that crowned their
    heads.
Therefore they sit in graduated tiers,
Not in accordance with their earthly ways,
But following the keenness of their vision.
    "Moreover, in the early centuries,
The parents' faith alone in Christ to come,
Combined with innocence, insured salvation.
But after those first ages were complete,
It was required that males be circumcised,
To make more powerful their feeble wings.
But later, when the time of grace had come,
This innocence of children unbaptized,
And therefore lacking Christ, was held below.
    "Upon that face most like to that of Christ,
Do thou now gaze: for its supernal radiance
Alone can make thee fit to look on Christ."
    I saw such gladness raining down on Her,

Carried by those fair Intelligences
Created but to fly across that height,
That whatsoever I had seen e'er this
Held me not suspended in such wonder,
Nor showed to me such likeness unto God.
That love who had come down to Her before,
Spread out his shining wings in front of Her,
And sang: *Ave Maria, gratia plena!*
In answer to this canticle divine
The blessed court responded on all sides,
And every countenance was more serene.
    "O sainted father, who for my sole sake
Deigning to come to me, hast left
The eternal bliss of thy allotted place!
Who is that angel gazing in the eyes
Of Heaven's bright Queen, with look of so
    much love
That he appears as though he were aflame?"
Thus again I sought the blessed words
Of him who drew his beauty forth from Mary,
As from the sun the morning star draws light.
    And he to me: "All confidence and grace
Existing in an angel or a soul,
Exist in him, and we would have it so;
For he it is who bore the palm to Mary,
At that great moment when the Son of God
Vouchsafed to weight Himself with our great
    load.
    "But now do thou come onward with thine
    eye,
Even as I go forward with my speech
To name the great patricians of this court.
Those two who yonder sit in greater bliss,
Through being closest to the Heavenly Em-
    press,
Are, as it were, the two roots of this rose.
In him who sits beside her on the left
Behold that ancient sire from whose rash tast-
    ing
Mankind has tasted so much bitterness.
See on the right the venerable father
Of Holy Church, to whom below on earth
Christ gave in trust the keys of this fair rose.
And he who ere he died beheld the grief
Of that fair bride—the bride who had been
    won
By virtue of the nails and of the spear—
Sits on one side; upon the other rests
That leader in whose time was sent the manna
To feed his thankless, fickle, stubborn folk.
And there, across from Peter, Anna sits—

So well content to look upon her daughter,
Who as she sings hosanna, holds her gaze.
And opposite the father of mankind
Lucia sits, who unto thee sent down
Thy lady, when thy brow was bent to fall.
    "But since thy vision's time is nearly spent,
We now will stop—much as a skillful tailor,
Who cuts the gown according to his cloth;
And we will gaze upon the Primal Love,
That, looking toward Him, thou mayst pene-
    trate
As far as possible through His effulgence.
And yet, lest thou perchance shouldst back-
    ward slip,
When thinking to advance by thine own wings,
'Tis needful that thou gather grace by prayer—
Sweet grace from her who has the power to
    aid.
Do thou here follow me with thy affection
So that thy heart depart not from my speech."
Then he began his holy orison.

CANTO 33

O Virgin Mother, daughter of thy Son,
Humbler and more exalted than all others,
Predestined object of the eternal will!
Thou gavest such nobility to man
That He who made mankind did not disdain
To make Himself a creature of His making.
Within thy womb, that love was re-enkindled
Whose heat has germinated this fair flower,
To blossom thus in everlasting peace.
Thou art our noonday torch of charity;
And down below thou art for mortal men
The living fount of hope. Thou art so great,
O Lady, and thou art of so much worth,
That whoso hopes for grace, not knowing thee,
Asks that his wish should fly without its wings.
And thy benignity not only gives
Its succor to the suppliant, but oftentimes
Will lavishly anticipate his plea.
In thee is mercy, and magnificence,
And pity, for in thee is concentrate
Whatever good there be in any creature.
    "This man, who from the nethermost abyss
Of all the universe, as far as here,
Has seen the spiritual existences,
Now asks thy grace, so thou wilt grant him
    strength
That he may with his eyes uplift himself

Still higher toward the ultimate salvation.
And I, who ne'er for my own vision burned
As I now burn for his, proffer to thee
All my prayers—and pray they may suffice—
That thou wilt scatter from him every cloud
Of his mortality, with thine own prayers,
So that the bliss supreme may be revealed.
And furthermore I beg of thee, O Queen
Thou hast the power to do whate'er thou wilt,
After his vision to keep his love still pure.
May thy protection quell his human passions!
Lo, Beatrice and many a blessed soul
Entreat thee, with clasped hands, to grant my
    wish!"
    Those eyes so loved and reverenced by God,
Were fixed upon the suppliant, and showed
How greatly She is pleased by earnest prayers.
Then they were turned to that eternal light
Whose depth, one must believe, no other eye
Has vision clear enough to penetrate.
    And I—who now was drawing near the end
Of all desires—ended, as was meet,
Within myself the ardor of my longing.
Here Bernard smiled and made a sign to me
That I should look on high; but I indeed
Was doing what he wished, of my own will,
Because my vision, being purified,
Was piercing more and more within the rays
Of light sublime, which in itself is true.
Thenceforward, no mere human speech could
    tell
My vision's added power: for memory
And speech are both o'ercome by such excess.
    Just as a man who sees things in a dream,
Will still retain impression of his feelings
Although the rest return not to his mind,
So now am I: for though my vision fades,
The sweetness growing from it yet distills
Its essence in the wellsprings of my heart.
Thus the snow is melted in the sun;
And thus the Sibyl's oracle was lost,
Written on leaves so light upon the wind.
    O Light Supreme, that art so far exalted
Above our mortal ken! Lend to my mind
A little part of what Thou didst appear,
And grant sufficient power unto my tongue
That it may leave for races yet unborn,
A single spark of Thy almighty flame!
For if Thou wilt come back to my remem-
    brance,
That I may sing Thy glory in these lines,

The more Thy victory will be explained.
  I think the keenness of the living ray
That I withstood would have bewildered me,
If once my eyes had turned aside from it.
And I recall that for that very reason
I was emboldened to endure so much,
Until my gaze was joined unto His good.
  Abundant grace, by which I could presume
To fix my eyes upon the Eternal Light
Sufficiently to see the whole of it!
  I saw that in its depths there are enclosed,
Bound up with love in one eternal book,
The scattered leaves of all the universe—
Substance, and accidents, and their relations,
As though together fused in such a way
That what I speak of is a single light.
The universal form of this commingling
I think I saw, for when I tell of it
I feel that I rejoice so much the more.
One moment brought me more oblivion
Than five-and-twenty centuries could cast
Upon those argonauts whose shadow once
Made Neptune wonder. Even thus my mind,
Enraptured, gazed attentive, motionless,
And grew the more enkindled as it gazed.
  For in the presence of those radiant beams
One is so changed, that 'tis impossible
To turn from it to any other sight—
Because the good, the object of the will,
Is all collected there. Outside of it
That is defective which is perfect there.
Henceforth my speech will fall still further
    short
Of what I recollect, as 'twere a babe's,
Wetting his tongue upon his mother's breast.
  There was no other than a single semblance

Within that Living Light on which I gazed,
For that remains forever what it was;
And yet by reason of my vision's power,
Which waxed the stronger in me as I looked,
That semblance seemed to change, and I as
    well.
  For within the substance, deep and radiant,
Of that Exalted Light, I saw three rings
Of one dimension, yet of triple hue.
One seemed to be reflected by the next,
As Iris is by Iris; and the third
Seemed fire, shed forth equally by both.
How powerless is speech—how weak, com-
    pared
To my conception, which itself is trifling
Beside the mighty vision that I saw!
  O Light Eternal, in Thyself contained!
Thou only know'st Thyself, and in Thyself
Both known and knowing, smilest on Thy-
    self!
  That very circle which appeared in Thee,
Conceived as but reflection of a light,
When I had gazed on it awhile, now seemed
To bear the image of a human face
Within itself, of its own coloring—
Wherefore my sight was wholly fixed on it.
Like a geometer, who will attempt
With all his power and mind to square the
    circle,
Yet cannot find the principle he needs:
Just so was I, at that phenomenon.
I wished to see how image joined to ring,
And how the one found place within the other.
Too feeble for such flights were my own wings;
But by a lightning flash my mind was struck—
And thus came the fulfilment of my wish. . . .

François Rabelais

rançois Rabelais (1490–1553), a contemporary of Cellini, was a Frenchman who gave expression to an aspect
of the Renaissance which was particularly characteristic of
the movement in the north. Although he studied for the
priesthood, he gave up a career in the church in order to
gain the intellectual and personal freedom he so passionately desired. While still a clergyman he had displayed a
deep interest in classical writings, particularly those of the
Greeks, and this humanistic interest may have been the
determining factor in his decision to return to secular life.

He bitterly resented both the asceticism of the Catholic clergy and the puritanism of the Calvinists, for he wanted to live life fully, with the body as well as with the mind. He used his ability as a writer to satirize some of the things he disliked in the world about him. Gargantua and Pantagruel were members of an imaginary dynasty of giant kings, and around these characters Rabelais has woven his story of satire. In reading this selection note (1) the type of personnel admitted to the abbey, (2) the description of the edifice, (3) the inscription on the great gate, (4) the activities pursued by the inmates, (5) the apparel of the nuns, (6) the rule of the order, (7) the discussion of the effects of restraint, and (8) the relationship between the training in the abbey and life in the secular world.

From: GARGANTUA AND PANTAGRUEL

HOW GARGANTUA CAUSED TO BE BUILT FOR THE MONK THE ABBEY OF THELEME

There was left only the monk to provide for, whom Gargantua would have made Abbot of Seville, but he refused it. He would have given him the Abbey of Bourgueil, or of Sanct Florent which was better, or both, if it pleased him; but the monk gave him a very peremptory answer, that he would never take upon him the charge nor government of monks. For how shall I be able, said he, to rule over others, that have not full power and command over myself? If you think I have done you, or may hereafter do any acceptable service, give me leave to found an abbey after my own mind and fancy. The notion pleased Gargantua very well, who thereupon offered him all the country of Theleme by the river of Loire till within two leagues of the great forest of Port-Huaulx. The monk then requested Gargantua to institute his religious order contrary to all others. First, then, said Gargantua, you must not build a wall about your convent, for all other abbeys are strongly walled and mured about. See, said the monk, and not without cause (seeing wall and mur signify but one and the same thing); where there is mur before and mur behind, there is store of murmur, envy, and mutual conspiracy. Moreover, seeing there are certain convents in the world whereof the custom is, if any woman come in, I mean chaste and honest women, they immediately sweep the ground which they have trod upon; therefore was it ordained, that if any man or woman entered into religious orders should by chance come within this new abbey, all the rooms should be thoroughly washed and cleansed through which they had passed. And because in all other monasteries and nunneries all is compassed, limited and regulated by hours, it was decreed that in this new structure there should be neither clock nor dial, but that according to the opportunities and incident occasions, all their hours should be disposed of; for, said Gargantua, the greatest loss of time that I know is to count the hours. What good comes of it? Nor can there be any greater dotage in the world than for one to guide and direct his courses by the sound of a bell, and not by his own judgment and discretion.

Item, Because at that time they put no women into nunneries but such as were either purblind, blinkards, lame, crooked, ill-favoured, misshapen, fools, senseless, spoiled, or corrupt; nor encloistered any men but those that were either sickly, subject to defluxions, ill-bred louts, simple sots, or peevish trouble-houses. But to the purpose, said the monk. A woman that is neither fair nor good, to what use serves she? To make a nun of, said Gar-

François Rabelais, *Gargantua and Pantagruel*, edited by Donald Douglas, The Modern Library, New York, 1928, 131–147. Courtesy of Random House, Inc.

gantua. Yea, said the monk, and to make shirts and smocks. Therefore was it ordained that into this religious order should be admitted no women that were not fair, well-featured, and of a sweet disposition; nor men that were not comely, personable, and well conditioned.

Item, Because in the convents of women, men come not but underhand, privily, and by stealth, it was therefore enacted that in this house there shall be no women in case there be not men, nor men in case there be not women.

Item, Because both men and women that are received into religious orders after the expiring of their noviciate or probation year were constrained and forced perpetually to stay there all the days of their life, it was therefore ordered that all whatever, men or women, admitted within this abbey, should have full leave to depart with peace and contentment whensoever it should seem good to them so to do.

Item, For that the religious men and women did ordinarily make three vows, to wit, those of chastity, poverty and obedience, it was therefore constituted and appointed that in this convent they might be honourably married, that they might be rich, and live at liberty. In regard of the legitimate time of the persons to be initiated, and years under and above which they were not capable of reception, the women were to be admitted from ten till fifteen, and the men from twelve till eighteen.

HOW THE ABBEY OF THE THELEMITES WAS BUILT AND ENDOWED

For the fabric and furniture of the abbey Gargantua caused to be delivered out in ready money seven and twenty hundred thousand, eight hundred and one and thirty of those golden rams of Berry which have a sheep stamped on the one side and a flowered cross on the other; and for every year, until the whole work was completed, he allotted three score nine thousand crowns of the sun, and as many of the seven stars, to be charged all upon the receipt of the custom. For the foundation and maintenance thereof for ever, he settled a perpetual free-farm-rent of three and twenty hundred, three score and nine thousand, five hundred and fourteen rose nobles, exempted from all homage, fealty, service, or burden whatsoever, and payable every year at the gate of the abbey; and of this by letters patent passed a very good grant. The architecture was in a figure hexagonal, and in such a fashion that in every one of the six corners there was built a great round tower of threescore foot in diameter, and were all of a like form and bigness. Upon the north side ran along the river of Loire, on the bank whereof was situated the tower called Arctic. Going towards the east, there was another called Calaer,—the next following Anatole,—the next Mesembrine, —the next Hesperia, and the last Criere. Every tower was distant from other the space of three hundred and twelve paces. The whole edifice was everywhere six storeys high, reckoning the cellars underground for one. The second was arched after the fashion of a basket-handle; the rest were ceiled with pure wainscot, flourished with Flanders fretwork, in the form of the foot of a lamp, and covered above with fine slates, with an endorsement of lead, carrying the antique figures of little puppets and animals of all sorts, notably well suited to one another, and gilt, together with the gutters, which, jutting without the walls from betwixt the crossbars in a diagonal figure, painted with gold and azure, reached to the very ground, where they ended into great conduit-pipes, which carried all away into the river from under the house.

This same building was a hundred times more sumptuous and magnificent than ever was Bonnivet, Chambourg, or Chantilly; for there were in it nine thousand, three hundred and two and thirty chambers, every one whereof had a withdrawing room, a handsome closet, a wardrobe, an oratory, and neat passage, leading into a great and spacious hall. Between every tower in the midst of the said body of building there was a pair of winding, such as we now call lantern, stairs, whereof the steps were part of porphyry, which is a dark red marble spotted with white, part of Numidian stone, which is a kind of yellowishly-streaked marble upon various colours and part of serpentine marble, with light spots on a dark green ground, each of those steps being two and twenty foot in length and three fingers thick, and the just number of twelve betwixt every rest, or, as we now term it, landing-place. In every resting-place were two fair antique arches where the light came in: and by those they went into a cabinet, made even with and of the breadth of the said winding, and the reascending above the roofs of the house ended conically in a pavilion. By that vise or winding they entered on every side into a great hall, and from the halls into the chambers. From the Arctic tower unto the Criere were the fair great libraries in Greek, Latin, Hebrew, French, Italian, and Spanish, respectively distributed in their several cantons, according to the diversity of these languages. In the midst there was a wonderful scalier or winding-stair, the entry whereof was without the house, in a vault or arch six fathom broad. It was made in such symmetry and largeness that six men-at-arms with their lances in their rests might together in a breast ride all up to the very top of all the palace. From the tower Anatole to the Mesembrine were fair spacious galleries, all coloured over and painted with the ancient prowesses, histories, and descriptions of the world. In the midst thereof there was likewise such another ascent and gate as we said there was on the river-side. Upon that gate was written in great antique letters that which followeth.

THE INSCRIPTION SET UPON THE GREAT GATE OF THELEME

Here enter not vile bigots, hypocrites,
Externally devoted apes, base snites,
Puffed-up, wry-necked beasts, worse than the
    Huns,
Or Ostrogoths, forerunners of baboons:
Cursed snakes, dissembled varlets, seeming
    sancts,
Slipshod cafards, beggars pretending wants,
Fat chuffcats, smell-feast knockers, doltish
    gulls,
Out-strouting cluster-fists, contentious bulls,
Fomenters of divisions and debates,
Elsewhere, not here, make sale of your deceits.
    Your filthy trumperies
    Stuffed with pernicious lies
      (Not worth a bubble),
      Would do but trouble

    Our earthly paradise,
    Your filthy trumperies.
Here enter not attorneys, barristers,
Nor bridle-champing law practitioners:
Clerks, commissaries, scribes, nor pharisees,
Wilful disturbers of the people's ease:
Judges, destroyers, with an unjust breath,
Of honest men, like dogs, even unto death.
Your salary is at the gibbet-foot:
Go drink there! for we do not here fly out
On those excessive courses, which may draw
A waiting on your courts by suits in law.
    Lawsuits, debates, and wrangling
    Hence are exiled, and jangling.
      Here we are very
      Frolic and merry,
    And free from all entangling,
    Lawsuits, debates, and wrangling.
Here enter not base pinching usurers,
Pelf-lickers, everlasting gatherers,
Gold-graspers, coin-gripers, gulpers of mists,
Niggish deformed sots, who, though your
    chests
Vast sums of money should to you afford,
Would ne'ertheless add more unto that hoard,
And yet not be content,—you clunchfist das-
    tards,
Insatiable fiends, and Pluto's bastards,
Greedy devourers, chichy sneakbill rogues,
Hell-mastiffs gnaw your bones, you ravenous
    dogs.
    You beastly-looking fellows,
    Reason doth plainly tell us
      That we should not
      To you allot
    Room here, but at the gallows,
    You beastly-looking fellows.
Here enter not fond makers of demurs
In love adventures, peevish, jealous curs,
Sad pensive dotards, raisers of garboils,
Hags, goblins, ghosts, firebrands of household
    broils,
Nor drunkards, liars, cowards, cheaters, clowns,
Thieves, cannibals, faces o'ercast with frowns,
Nor lazy slugs, envious, covetous,
Nor blockish, cruel, nor too credulous,—
Here mangy, pocky folks shall have no place,
No ugly lusks, nor persons of disgrace.
    Grace, honour, praise, delight,
    Here sojourn day and night.
      Sound bodies lined
      With a good mind,

Do here pursue with might
Grace, honour, praise, delight.
Here enter you and welcome from our hearts,
All noble sparks endowed with gallant parts.
This is the glorious place which bravely shall
Afford wherewith to entertain you all.
Were you a thousand, here you shall not
want
For anything; for what you'll ask we'll grant.
Stay here you lively, jovial, handsome, brisk,
Gay, witty, frolic, cheerful, merry, frisk,
Spruce, jocund, courteous, furtherers of trades,
And in a word, all worthy, gentle blades.
  Blades of heroic breasts
  Shall taste here of the feasts,
    Both privily
    And civilly
  Of the celestial guests,
  Blades of heroic breasts.
Here enter you, pure, honest, faithful, true
Expounders of the Scriptures old and new.
Whose glosses do not blind our reason, but
Make it to see the clearer, and who shut
Its passages from hatred, avarice,
Pride, factions, covenants, and all sort of vice.
Come, settle here a charitable faith,
Which neighbourly affection nourisheth.
And whose light chaseth all corrupters hence,
Of the blest word, from the aforesaid sense.
  The holy sacred Word,
  May it always afford
    T' us all in common,
    Both man and woman,
  A spiritual shield and sword,
  The holy sacred Word.
Here enter you all ladies of high birth,
Delicious, stately, charming, full of mirth,
Ingenious, lovely, miniard, proper, fair,
Magnetic, graceful, splendid, pleasant, rare,
Obliging, sprightly, virtuous, young, salacious,
Kind, neat, quick, feat, bright, compt, ripe,
    choice, dear, precious,
Alluring, courtly, comely, fine, complete,
Wise, personable, ravishing and sweet,
Come joys enjoy. The Lord celestial
Hath given enough wherewith to please us all.
  Gold give us, God forgive us,
  And from all woes relieve us;
    That we the treasure
    May reap of pleasure,
  And shun whate'er is grievous,
  Gold give us, God forgive us.

WHAT MANNER OF DWELLING THE THELEMITES HAD

In the middle of the lower court there was a stately fountain of fair alabaster. Upon the top thereof stood the three graces, with their cornucopias, or horns of abundance, and did jet out the water at their breasts, mouth, ears, eyes, and other open passages of the body. The inside of the buildings in this lower court stood upon great pillars of chalcedony stone, and porphyry marble, made archways after a goodly antique fashion. Within those were spacious galleries, long and large, adorned with curious pictures, the horns of bucks and unicorns: with rhinoceroses, water horses called hippopotamus, the teeth and tusks of elephants, and other things well worth the beholding. The lodging of the ladies, for so we may call those gallant women, took up all from the tower Arctic unto the gate Mesembrine. The men possessed the rest. Before the said lodging of the ladies, that they might have their recreation, between the first two towers, on the outside, were placed the tilt-yard, the barriers of lists for tournaments, the hippodrome or riding-court, the theatre or public playhouse, and natatory or place to swim in, with most admirable baths in three stages, situated above one another, well furnished with all necessary accommodation, and store of myrtle-water. By the riverside was the fair garden of pleasure, and in the midst of that the glorious labyrinth. Between the two other towers were the courts for the tennis and the balloon. Towards the tower Criere stood the orchard, full of all fruit-trees, set and ranged in a quincuncial order. At the end of that was the great park, abounding with all sorts of venison. Betwixt the third couple of towers were the butts and marks for shooting with a snap-work gun, an ordinary bow for common archery, or with a crossbow. The office-houses were without the tower Hesperia, of one storey high. The stables were beyond the offices, and before them stood the falconry, managed by ostrich-keepers and falconers very expert in the art, and it was yearly supplied and furnished by the Canadians, Venetians, Sarmates, now called Muscoviters, with all sorts of most excellent hawks, eagles, gerfalcons, goshawks, sacres, laniers, falcons, sparrowhawks, marlins, and all other kinds of them, so gentle and perfectly well manned, that, flying of themselves sometimes from the castle for their own disport, they would not fail to catch whatever they encountered. The venery, where the beagles and hounds were kept, was a little farther off, drawing towards the park.

All the halls, chambers and closets or cabinets were richly hung with tapestry and hangings of divers sorts, according to the variety of the seasons of the year. All the pavements and floors were covered with green cloth. The beds were all embroidered. In every back-chamber or withdrawing room there was a looking-glass of pure crystal set in a frame of fine gold, garnished all about with pearls, and was of such greatness that it would represent to the full the whole lineaments and proportion of the person that stood before it. At the going out of the halls which belong to the ladies' lodgings were the perfumers and trimmers through whose hands the gallants passed when they were to visit the ladies. Those sweet artificers did every morning furnish the ladies' chambers with the spirit of roses, orange-flower water, and angelica; and to each of them gave a little precious casket, vapouring forth the most odoriferous exhalations of the choicest aromatical scents.

HOW THE MEN AND WOMEN OF THE RELIGIOUS ORDER OF THELEME WERE APPARELLED

The ladies at the foundation of this order were apparelled after their own pleasure and liking; but, since that of their own accord and freewill they have reformed themselves, their accoutrements were in manner as followeth. They wore stockings of scarlet crimson, or ingrained purple dye, which reached just three inches above the knee, having a list beautified with exquisite embroideries and rare incisions of the cutter's art. The garters were of the colour of their bracelets, and circled the knee a little, both over and under. Their shoes, pumps and slippers, were either of red, violet, or crimson-velvet, pinked and jagged like lobster's wattles.

Next to their smock they put on the pretty kirtle or vasquin of pure silk camblet: above

that went the taffety or tabby farthingale, of white, red, tawny, grey, or of any other colour. Above this taffety petticoat they had another of cloth of tissue or brocade, embroidered with fine gold and interlaced with needlework, or as they thought good, and according to the temperature and disposition of the weather, had their upper coats of satin, damask or velvet, and these either orange, tawny, green, ash-coloured, blue, yellow, bright-red, crimson or white, and so forth; or had them a cloth of gold, cloth of silver, or some other choice stuff, enriched with purple, or embroidered according to the dignity of the festival days and times wherein they wore them.

Their gowns being still correspondent to the season, were either of cloth of gold frizzled with a silver raised work; of red satin covered with gold purple; of tabby, or taffety, white, blue, black, tawny, &c., of silk serge, silk camblet, velvet, cloth of silver, silver tissue, cloth of gold, gold wire, figured velvet, or figured satin, tinselled and overcast with golden threads, in divers variously purfled draughts.

In summer, some days, instead of gowns, they wore light handsome mantles, made either of the stuff of the aforesaid attire, or like Moresco rugs, of violet velvet frizzled, with a raised work of gold upon silver purl, or with a knotted cord-work of gold embroidery, everywhere garnished with little Indian pearls. They always carried a fair pannache, or plume of feathers, of the colour of their muff, bravely adorned and tricked out with glistening spangles of gold. In the winter time they had their taffety gowns of all colours, as above-named, and those lined with rich furrings of hindwolves, or speckled-lynxes, black-spotted weasels, martlet skins of Calabria, sables and other costly furs of an inestimable value. Their beads, rings, bracelets, collars, carcanets, and neck-chains were all of precious stones, such as carbuncles, rubies, baleus, diamonds, sapphires, emeralds, turquoises, garnets, agates, beryls, and excellent margarites. Their head-dressing also varied with the season of the year, according to which they decked themselves. In winter, it was of the French fashion; in the spring, of the Spanish; in summer, of the fashion of Tuscany, except only upon the holy days and Sundays, at which times they were accoutred in the French mode, because they accounted it more honourable and better befitting the garb of a matronal pudicity.

The men were apparelled after their fashion. Their stockings were of tamine or of cloth serge, of white, black, scarlet, or some other ingrained colour. Their breeches were of velvet, of the same colour with their stockings, or very near, embroidered and cut according to their fancy. Their doublet was of cloth of gold, of cloth of silver, of velvet, satin, damask, taffeties, &c., of the same colours, cut, embroidered, and suitably trimmed up in perfection. The points were of silk of the same colours; the tags were of gold well enamelled. Their coats and jerkins were of cloth of gold, cloth of silver, gold tissue or velvet embroidered, as they thought fit. Their gowns were every whit as costly as those of the ladies. Their girdles were of silk, of the colour of their doublets. Every one had a gallant sword by his side, the hilt and the handle whereof were gilt, and the scabbard of velvet, of the colour of his breeches, with a chape of gold, and pure goldsmith's work. The dagger was of the same. Their caps or bonnets were of black velvet, adorned with jewels and buttons of gold. Upon that they wore a white plume, most prettily and minion-like parted by so many rows of gold spangles, at the end whereof hung dangling in a more sparkling resplendency, fair rubies, emeralds, diamonds, &c., but there was such a sympathy betwixt the gallants and the ladies, that every day they were apparelled in the same livery. And that they might not miss, there were certain gentlemen appointed to tell the youths every morning what vestments the ladies would on that day wear: for all was done according to the pleasure of the ladies. In these so handsome clothes, and habiliments so rich, think not that either one or other of either sex did waste any time at all; for the masters of the wardrobes had all their raiments and apparel so ready for every morning, and the chamber-ladies so well skilled, that in a trice they would be dressed, and completely in their clothes from head to foot. And to have those accoutrements with the more conveniency, there was about the wood of Theleme, a row of houses of the extent of half a league, very neat and cleanly, wherein dwelt the gold-

smiths, lapidaries, jewellers, embroiderers, tailors, gold-drawers, velvet-weavers, tapestry-makers and upholsterers, who wrought there every one in his own trade, and all for the aforesaid jolly friars and nuns of the new stamp. They were furnished with matter and stuff from the hands of the Lord Nausiclete, who every year brought them seven ships from the Perlas and Cannibal Islands, laden with ingots of gold, with raw silk, with pearls and precious stones. And if any margarites, called unions, began to grow old and lose somewhat of their natural whiteness and lustre, those with their art they did renew, by tendering them to eat to some pretty cocks, as they use to give casting unto hawks.

HOW THE THELEMITES WERE GOVERNED, AND OF THEIR MANNER OF LIVING

All their life was spent not in laws, statutes, or rules, but according to their own free will and pleasure. They rose out of their beds when they thought good; they did eat, drink, labour, sleep, when they had a mind to it, and were disposed for it. None did awake them, none did offer to constrain them to eat, drink, nor to do any other thing; for so had Gargantua established it. In all their rule and strictest tie of their order there was but this one clause to be observed,

DO WHAT THOU WILT.

Because men that are free, well-born, well-bred, and conversant in honest companies, have naturally an instinct and spur that prompteth them unto virtuous actions, and withdraws them from vice, which is called honour. Those same men, when by base subjection and constraint, they are brought under and kept down, turn aside from that noble disposition by which they formerly were inclined to virtue, to shake off and break that bond of servitude wherein they are so tyrannously enslaved; for it is agreeable with the nature of man to long after things forbidden and to desire what is denied us.

By this liberty they entered into a very laudable emulation to do all of them what they saw did please one. If any of the gallants or ladies should say, Let us drink, they would all drink. If any one of them said, Let us play, they all played. If one said, Let us go a-walking into the fields, they went all. If it were to go a-hawking or a-hunting, the ladies mounted upon dainty well-paced nags, seated in a stately palfrey saddle, carried on their lovely fists, miniardly begloved every one of them, either a sparrowhawk or a laneret or a marlin, and the young gallants carried the other kinds of hawks. So nobly were they taught, that there was neither he nor she amongst them but could read, write, sing, play upon several musical instruments, speak five or six several languages, and compose in them all very quaintly, both in verse and prose. Never were seen so valiant knights, so noble and worthy, so dextrous and skilful both on foot and ahorseback, more brisk and lively, more

nimble and quick, or better handling all manner of weapons than were there. Never were seen ladies so proper and handsome, so miniard and dainty, less forward or more ready with their hand and with their needle in every honest and free action belonging to that sex, than were there. For this reason, when the time came that any man of the said abbey, either at the request of his parents, or for some other cause, had a mind to go out of it, he carried along with him one of the ladies, namely, her whom he had before that chosen for his mistress, and [they] were married together. And if they had formerly in Theleme lived in good devotion and amity, and did continue therein and increase it to a greater height in their state of matrimony, they did entertain that mutual love till the very last day of their life, in no less vigour and fervency than at the very day of their wedding.

Desiderius Erasmus

Desiderius Erasmus (1466–1536), a Dutch scholar with a vital interest in the Greek classics, represented the more intellectual phases of the Renaissance and the break from medieval scholaticism. Being a sincere Catholic priest, deeply interested in theology, he translated and edited, in true humanist tradition, the New Testament from the Greek, thereby developing further his erudite theological background. Using the knowledge acquired from his critical study of the early Christian record, he found much to condemn in the fruitless writings of the theologians and in the artificial ritualism of institutionalized Christianity. He considered that both of these developments had corrupted the simple teachings of Jesus and in his writings sought to expose the errors into which he considered the Church had fallen. In Praise of Folly is a delightfully straightforward satire in which Erasmus used a feminine personality, Folly, to expose many of the weaknesses and contradictions in the lives of the men of his time. In reading the selections note (1) the discussion of the efficacy of saints, (2) the observations on indulgences and the character of those who purchased them, (3) the part played by priests in popularizing saints and indulgences, (4) the value of the disputations carried on by the scholastic theologians, and (5) the activity of monks in relation to the teachings of Christ.

James Harvey Robinson, *Readings in European History*. . . ., 2 vols., Ginn and Company, Boston, 1906, II, **41–46.** Courtesy of Ginn and Company.

From: *IN PRAISE OF FOLLY*

To this same class of fools belong those who beguile themselves with the silly but pleasing notion that if they look upon a picture or image of St. Christopher,—that huge Polyphemus,—they will not die that day; or that he who salutes an image of St. Barbara with the proper form of address will come back from battle safe; or that one who approaches St. Erasmus on certain days with wax candles and prayers will soon be rich. They have found a new Hercules in St. George,—a sort of second Hippolytus. They seem to adore even his horse, which is scrupulously decked out with gorgeous trappings, and additional offerings are constantly being made in the hope of gaining new favors. His bronze helmet one would think half divine, the way people swear by it.

And what shall I say of those who comfortably delude themselves with imaginary pardons for their sins, and who measure the time in purgatory with an hour glass into years, months, days, hours, with all the precision of a mathematical table? There are plenty, too, who, relying upon certain magical little certificates and prayers,—which some pious imposter devised either in fun or for the benefit of his pocket,—believe that they may procure riches, honor, future happiness, health, perpetual prosperity, long life, a lusty old age,—nay, in the end, a seat at the right hand of Christ in heaven; but as for this last, it matters not how long it be deferred: they will content themselves with the joys of heaven only when they must finally surrender the pleasures of this world, to which they lovingly cling.

The trader, the soldier, and the judge think that they can clean up the Augean stable of a lifetime, once for all, by sacrificing a single coin from their ill-gotten gains. They flatter themselves that all sorts of perjury, debauchery, drunkenness, quarrels, bloodshed, imposture, perfidy, and treason can be compounded for by contract and so adjusted that, having paid off their arrears, they can begin a new score.

How foolish, or rather how happy, are those who promise themselves more than supernal happiness if they repeat the verses of the seven holy psalms! Those magical lines are supposed to have been taught to St. Bernard by a demon, who seems to have been a wag; but he was not very clever, and, poor fellow, was frustrated in his attempt to deceive the saint. These silly things which even I, Folly, am almost ashamed of, are approved not only by the common herd but even by the teachers of religion.

How foolish, too, for religious bodies each to give preference to its particular guardian saint! Nay, each saint has his particular office allotted him, and is addressed each in his special way: this one is called upon to alleviate toothache; that, to aid in childbirth; others, to restore a stolen article, bring rescue to the shipwrecked, or protect cattle,—and so on with the rest, who are much too numerous to mention. A few indeed among the saints are good in more than one emergency, especially the Holy Virgin, to whom the common man now attributes almost more than to her Son.

And for what, after all, do men petition the saints except for foolish things? Look at the votive offerings which cover the walls of certain churches and with which you see even the ceiling filled; do you find any one who expresses his gratitude that he has escaped Folly or because he has become a whit wiser? One perhaps was saved from drowning, another recovered when he had been run through by his enemy; another, while his fellows were fighting, ran away with expedition and success; another, on the point of being hanged, escaped, through the aid of some saintly friend of thieves, and lived to relieve a few more of those whom he believed to be overburdened with their wealth. . . .

These various forms of foolishness so pervade the whole life of Christians that even the priests themselves find no objection to admitting, not to say fostering, them, since they do not fail to perceive how many tidy little sums accrue to them from such sources. But what if some odious philosopher should chime in and say, as is quite true: "You will not die badly if you live well. You are redeeming your sins when you add to the sum that you contribute a hearty detestation of evil doers: then you may spare yourself tears, vigils, invocations, fasts, and all that kind of life. You may rely upon any saint to aid you when once you begin to imitate his life."

As for the theologians, perhaps the less said the better on this gloomy and dangerous theme, since they are a style of man who show themselves exceeding supercilious and irritable unless they can heap up six hundred conclusions about you and force you to recant; and if you refuse, they promptly brand you as a heretic,— for it is their custom to terrify by their thunderings those whom they dislike. It must be confessed that no other group of fools are so reluctant to acknowledge Folly's benefits toward them, although I have many titles to their gratitude, for I make them so in love with themselves that they seem to be happily exalted to the third heaven, whence they look down with something like pity upon all other mortals, wandering about on the earth like mere cattle.

Then they hedge themselves about with such an array of magisterial definitions, conclusions, corollaries, propositions explicate and implicate, and do so abound in subterfuges, that chains forged by Vulcan himself could not hold them so firm but that they could escape by one of those distinctions which enable them to cut all knots as easily as with a two-edged ax, so readily do they think up and rattle out new and prodigious terms and expressions.

Finally, the theologians are at their best when they are explaining (in their own opinion) such deep mysteries as: How was the world founded and brought into order? How is original sin transmitted to posterity? . . . How can the accidents subsist in the eucharist without their substance? Nay, these are trite and easy questions. The great and illustrious theologians, as they dub themselves, will only awaken when something like the following is proposed: Does supernatural generation require time for its accomplishment? Has Christ a double relation of sonship? Is the proposition possible, "God the Father hates the Son"? Might God have chosen to assume the form of a woman, a devil, an ass, a gourd, or a stone? . . .

St. Paul, they admit, was distinguished for his faith, but nevertheless when he said, "Faith is the substance of things hoped for, the evidence of things not seen," he defined it but inaccurately. He may have excelled in charity, yet he fails to limit and define it with dialectic precision in his first letter to the Corinthians, Chapter XIII. The disciples administered the eucharist reverently, and yet had they been asked about the *terminus a quo* and the *terminus ad quem* of transubstantiation; as to how a body can be in two places at the same time; of the differences which exist between Christ's body in heaven, on the cross, and in the holy wafer; or at what point does transsubstantiation occur, since the prayer through which it is effected is, as a *quantitas discreta*, in a state of flux,—asked of these matters the apostles would not have replied with the acuteness with which the followers of Scotus distinguish and define these subtleties.

The apostles knew the mother of Jesus, but who of them could philosophically prove how she was preserved from the sin of Eve, as do our divines? Peter received the keys, and from one who would not commit them to unworthy hands, but whether or not he knew how one could have the key of knowledge without knowledge itself, he certainly never discussed the matter. The apostles baptized, but never taught the formal, material, efficient, or final cause of baptism, nor do they mention delible or indelible characters. . . . The apostles inculcated grace, but never distinguished between *gratia gratis data* and *gratia gratificans*. They exhorted to good works, but did not perceive the distinction between *opus operans* and *opus operatum*. They frequently urge charity upon us without dividing "infused" from "acquired," or explaining whether charity be an accident or a substance, a created or an uncreated thing.

Next to the theologians in their self-satisfaction may be ranked those who are commonly called the religious and the monks, both terms quite wide of the truth, since a good part of them are a long ways from religion, and as for the monks (whose name suggests solitude), they are to be met in every byway. I do not see who could be more miserable than they unless Folly came to their aid in many ways. Although every one so execrates that stripe of man that even a casual meeting with them is regarded as ominous, yet they have a magnificent idea of their own virtues. First they deem it the most exalted piety to have let learning so completely alone that they cannot even read. Then when they bray out the psalms —which they cannot understand—in the churches, they flatter themselves that they are delighting the ears of the saints with their sweet harmonies. Some of them laud their beggary and filth as great virtues and loudly clamor for bread from door to door. They beset the inns, coaches, and ships, not a little to the prejudice of other beggars. . . .

The greater part of the monks exhibit such confidence in ceremonies and trivial human traditions that one would think a single heaven would scarce suffice as a worthy reward for their merits. They little think that Christ will put them off with a "Who hath required these things at your hands?" and will call them to account only for the stewardship of his legacy of love. One will confidently call attention to his paunch, filled with all kinds of fish; another will pour out a hundred bushels of psalms; a

third will enumerate his myriad fastings and will tell how a single meal nearly killed him; a fourth will produce as many ceremonies as would fill seven merchant ships; a fifth will plead that for threescore years he never so much as touched money except he fingered it through double thick gloves; a sixth will bring along his hood so old and nasty that no sailor would venture to protect himself with it. . . . But Christ shall interrupt their boastings: "Woe unto you, scribes and Pharisees! I left you one great precept, but of that alone I hear nothing from you. I told you plainly in my gospel, with no disguising parables, that my Father's kingdom was promised, not for cowls, petitions, and fastings, but for deeds of love. I know them not who rely on their own merits."

When the monks and friars shall hear these things and shall see simple sailors and carters preferred to them, how shall their faces fall as they look at one another!

Martin Luther

Martin Luther (1483–1546) was a German religious leader who played an important role in the Protestant revolt which, during the sixteenth century, brought about a permanent division within the Christian community. Luther, on November 1, 1517, posted ninety-five articles on the door of the castle church at Wittenberg, initiating a widespread discussion of theology and ecclesiastical politics. Luther's theological position differed little from that of Calvin; each believed that man was saved by God's grace directly rather than indirectly by the rites, ceremonies, and good works which he performed. Good works did not purchase salvation for a man; a saved man performed good works. Knowledge of that salvation came through faith in God's promise of redemption to those predestined to eternal life. Unlike France, where Calvin had his origins, Germany was ripe for revolt against the ecclesiastical as well as moral authority of the Roman Church. In his "Address to the Christian Nobility of the German Nation," (1520) Luther not only phrased well the mounting dissatisfaction with the politico-religious dictation from Rome, but helped to crystallize opinion against the Church. The selections from Luther emphasize the political and economic aspects of the revolt, while the selections from Calvin emphasize the revolt against the spiritual and moral authority of Rome. The two compliment each other and might well be read together. In reading the selections from Luther note (1) Luther's reliance upon a direct and uncomplicated reading of the Bible, (2) evidence of the simplicity of his Christian faith, (3) the bases of his attack upon the ecclesiastical hierarchy, (4) his argument against dividing humanity into two classes, one subordinate to the other, (5) his attack upon the papal claim of sole right to interpret the Bible, (6) his demolition of the claim that only the Pope can call a council, (7) his efforts to belittle the hierarchy and to expose it as a fraud, and (8) his appeals to national sentiment.

From: ADDRESS TO THE CHRISTIAN NOBILITY OF THE GERMAN NATION

INTRODUCTION

The first thing that we must do is to consider the matter with great earnestness, and, whatever we attempt, not to trust in our own strength and wisdom alone, even if the power of all the world were ours; for God will not endure that a good work should be begun trusting to our own strength and wisdom. He destroys it; it is all useless, as we read in Psalm xxxiii., "There is no king saved by the multitude of a host; a mighty man is not delivered by much strength.". . . We must renounce all confidence in our natural strength, and take the matter in hand with humble trust in God; we must seek God's help with earnest prayer, and have nothing before our eyes but the misery and wretchedness of Christendom, irrespective of what punishment the wicked may deserve. If we do not act thus, we may begin the game with great pomp; but when we are well in it, the spirits of evil will make such confusion that the whole world will be immersed in blood, and yet nothing be done. Therefore let us act in the fear of God and prudently. The greater the might of the foe, the greater is the misfortune, if we do not act in the fear of God and with humility. If popes and Romanists have hitherto, with the devil's

help, thrown kings into confusion, they may still do so, if we attempt things with our own strength and skill, without God's help.

THE THREE WALLS OF THE ROMANISTS

The Romanists have, with great adroitness, drawn three walls round themselves, with which they have hitherto protected themselves, so that no one could reform them, whereby all Christendom has fallen terribly.

Firstly, if pressed by the temporal power, they have affirmed and maintained that the temporal power has no jurisdiction over them, but, on the contrary, that the spiritual power is above the temporal.

Secondly, if it were proposed to admonish them with the Scriptures, they objected that no one may interpret the Scriptures but the Pope.

Thirdly, if they are threatened with a council, they pretend that no one may call a council but the Pope.

Thus they have secretly stolen our three rods, so that they may be unpunished, and intrenched themselves behind these three walls, to act with all the wickedness and malice, which we now witness. And whenever they

As translated by C. A. Buchheim in Martin Luther, "Address to the Christian Nobility of the German Nation Respecting the Reformation of the Christian Estate," in *The Harvard Classics*, New York: P. F. Collier and Son, 1910, XXXVI, 263–268; 270–279; 266–287.

have been compelled to call a council, they have made it of no avail by binding the princes beforehand with an oath to leave them as they were, and to give moreover to the Pope full power over the procedure of the council, so that it is all one whether we have many councils or no councils, in addition to which they deceive us with false pretences and tricks. So grievously do they tremble for their skin before a true, free council; and thus they have overawed kings and princes, that these believe they would be offending God, if they were not to obey them in all such knavish, deceitful artifices.

Now may God help us, and give us one of those trumpets that overthrew the walls of Jericho, so that we may blow down these walls of straw and paper, and that we may set free our Christian rods for the chastisement of sin, and expose the craft and deceit of the devil, so that we may amend ourselves by punishment and again obtain God's favour.

THE FIRST WALL

That the Temporal Power has no Jurisdiction over the Spiritualty

Let us, in the first place, attack the first wall.

It has been devised that the Pope, bishops, priests, and monks are called the *spiritual estate*, princes, lords, artificers, and peasants are the *temporal estate*. This is an artful lie and hypocritical device, but let no one be made afraid by it, and that for this reason: that all Christians are truly of the spiritual estate, and there is no difference among them, save of office alone. As St. Paul says (1 Cor. xii.), we are all one body, though each member does its own work, to serve the others. This is because we have one baptism, one Gospel, one faith, and are all Christians alike; for baptism, Gospel, and faith, these alone make spiritual and Christian people.

As for the unction by a pope or a bishop, tonsure, ordination, consecration, and clothes differing from those of laymen—all this may make a hypocrite or an anointed puppet, but never a Christian or a spiritual man. Thus we are all consecrated as priests by baptism, as St. Peter says: "Ye are a royal priesthood, a holy nation" (1 Peter ii. 9); and in the book of Revelations: "and hast made us unto our God (by Thy blood) kings and priests" (Rev. v. 10). For, if we had not a higher consecration in us than pope or bishop can give, no priest could ever be made by the consecration of pope or bishop, nor could he say the mass, or preach, or absolve. Therefore the bishop's consecration is just as if in the name of the whole congregation he took one person out of the community, each member of which has equal power, and commanded him to exercise this power for the rest; in the same way as if ten brothers, co-heirs as king's sons, were to choose one from among them to rule over their inheritance, they would all of them still remain kings and have equal power, although one is ordered to govern.

And to put the matter even more plainly, if a little company of pious Christian laymen were taken prisoners and carried away to a desert, and had not among them a priest consecrated by a bishop, and were there to agree to elect one of them, born in wedlock or not, and were to order him to baptise, to celebrate the mass, to absolve, and to preach, this man would as truly be a priest, as if all the bishops and all the popes had consecrated him. That is why in cases of necessity every man can baptise and absolve, which would not be possible if we were not all priests. This great grace and virtue of baptism and of the Christian estate they have quite destroyed and made us forget by their ecclesiastical law. In this way the Christians used to choose their bishops and priests out of the community; these being afterwards confirmed by other bishops, without the pomp that now prevails. So was it that St. Augustine, Ambrose, Cyprian, were bishops.

Since, then, the temporal power is baptised as we are, and has the same faith and Gospel, we must allow it to be priest and bishop, and account its office an office that is proper and useful to the Christian community. For whatever issues from baptism may boast that it has been consecrated priest, bishop, and pope, although it does not beseem every one to exercise these offices. For, since we are all priests alike, no man may put himself forward or take upon himself, without our consent and election, to do that which we have all alike power to do. For, if a thing is common to all, no man may take it to himself without the wish and command of the community. And if it should happen that a man were appointed to one of these offices and deposed for abuses, he would be just what he was before. Therefore a priest should be nothing in Christendom but a functionary; as long as he holds his office, he has precedence of others; if he is deprived of it, he is a peasant or a citizen like the rest. Therefore a priest is verily no longer a priest after deposition. But now they have invented *characteres indelebiles,* and pretend that a priest after deprivation still differs from a simple layman. They even imagine that a priest can never be anything but a priest—that is, that he can never become a layman. All this is nothing but mere talk and ordinance of human invention.

It follows, then, that between laymen and priests, princes and bishops, or, as they call it, between spiritual and temporal persons, the only real difference is one of office and function, and not of estate; for they are all of the same spiritual estate, true priests, bishops, and popes, though their functions are not the same —just as among priests and monks every man has not the same functions. And this, as I said above, St. Paul says (Rom. xii.; 1 Cor. xii.), and St. Peter (1 Peter ii.): "We, being many, are one body in Christ, and severally members one of another." Christ's body is not double or twofold, one temporal, the other spiritual. He is one Head, and He has one body.

We see, then, that just as those that we call spiritual, or priests, bishops, or popes, do not differ from other Christians in any other or higher degree but in that they are to be concerned with the word of God and the sacraments—that being their work and office—in the same way the temporal authorities hold the sword and the rod in their hands to punish the wicked and to protect the good. A cobbler, a smith, a peasant, every man, has the office and function of his calling, and yet all alike are consecrated priests and bishops, and every man should by his office or function be useful and beneficial to the rest, so that various kinds of work may all be united for the furtherance of body and soul, just as the members of the body all serve one another. . . .

THE SECOND WALL

That no one may interpret the Scriptures but the Pope

The second wall is even more tottering and weak: that they alone pretend to be considered masters of the Scriptures; although they learn nothing of them all their life. They assume authority, and juggle before us with impudent words, saying that the Pope cannot err in matters of faith, whether he be evil or good, albeit they cannot prove it by a single letter. That is why the canon law contains so many heretical and unchristian, nay unnatural, laws; but of these we need not speak now. For whereas they imagine the Holy Ghost never leaves them, however unlearned and wicked they may be, they grow bold enough to decree whatever they like. But were this true, where were the need and use of the Holy Scriptures? Let us burn them, and content ourselves with the unlearned gentlemen at Rome, in whom the Holy Ghost dwells, who, however, can dwell in pious souls only. If I had not read it, I could never have believed that the devil should have put forth such follies at Rome and find a following.

But not to fight them with our own words, we will quote the Scriptures. St. Paul says, "If anything be revealed to another that sitteth by, let the first hold his peace" (1 Cor. xiv. 30). What would be the use of this commandment, if we were to believe him alone that teaches or has the highest seat? Christ Himself says, "And they shall be all taught of God." (St. John vi 45). Thus it may come to pass that the Pope and his followers are wicked and not true Christians, and not being taught by God, have no true understanding, whereas a common man may have true understanding. Why should we then not follow him? Has not the Pope often erred? Who could help Christianity, in case the Pope errs, if we do not rather believe another who has the Scriptures for him?

Therefore it is a wickedly devised fable— and they cannot quote a single letter to confirm it—that it is for the Pope alone to interpret the Scriptures or to confirm the interpretation of them. They have assumed the authority of their own selves. And though they say that this authority was given to St. Peter when the keys were given to him, it is plain enough that the keys were not given to St. Peter alone, but to the whole community. Besides, the keys were not ordained for doctrine or authority, but for sin, to bind or loose; and what they claim besides this from the keys is mere invention. But what Christ said to St. Peter: "I have prayed for thee that thy faith fail not" (St. Luke xxii. 32), cannot relate to the Pope, inasmuch as the greater part of the Popes have been without faith, as they are themselves forced to acknowledge; nor did Christ pray for Peter alone, but for all the Apostles and all Christians, as He says, "Neither pray I for these alone, but for them also which shall believe on Me through their word" (St. John xvii.). Is not this plain enough? . . .

THE THIRD WALL

That no one may call a council but the Pope

The third wall falls of itself, as soon as the first two have fallen; for if the Pope acts contrary to the Scriptures, we are bound to stand by the Scriptures, to punish and to constrain him, according to Christ's commandment, "Moreover, if thy brother shall trespass against thee, go and tell him his fault between thee and him alone; if he shall hear thee, thou hast gained thy brother. But if he will not hear thee, then take with thee one or two more, that in the mouth of two or three witnesses every word may be established. And if he shall neglect to hear them, tell it unto the Church; but if he neglect to hear the Church, let him be unto thee as a heathen man and a publican" (St. Matt. xviii. 15–17). Here each member is commanded to take care for the other; much more then should we do this, if it is a ruling member of the community that does evil, who by his evil-doing causes great harm and offence to the others. If then I am to accuse him before the Church, I must collect the Church together. Moreover, they can show nothing in the Scriptures giving the Pope sole power to call and confirm councils; they have nothing but their own laws; but these hold good only so long as they are not injurious to Christianity and the laws of God. Therefore, if the Pope deserves punishment, these laws cease to bind us, since

Christendom would suffer, if he were not punished by a council. Thus we read (Acts xv.) that the council of the Apostles was not called by St. Peter, but by all the Apostles and the elders. But if the right to call it had lain with St. Peter alone, it would not have been a Christian council, but a heretical *conciliabulum*. Moreover, the most celebrated council of all— that of Nicaea—was neither called nor confirmed by the Bishop of Rome, but by the Emperor Constantine; and after him many other emperors have done the same, and yet the councils called by them were accounted most Christian. But if the Pope alone had the power, they must all have been heretical. Moreover, if I consider the councils that the Pope has called, I do not find that they produced any notable results.

Therefore when need requires, and the Pope is a cause of offence to Christendom, in these cases whoever can best do so, as a faithful member of the whole body, must do what he can to procure a true free council. This no one can do so well as the temporal authorities, especially since they are fellow-Christians, fellow-priests, sharing one spirit and one power in all things, and since they should exercise the office that they have received from God without hindrance, whenever it is necessary and useful that it should be exercised. Would it not be most unnatural, if a fire were to break out in a city, and every one were to keep still and let it burn on and on, whatever might be burnt, simply because they had not the mayor's authority, or because the fire perchance broke out at the mayor's house? Is not every citizen bound in this case to rouse and call in the rest? How much more should this be done in the spiritual city of Christ, if a fire of offence breaks out, either at the Pope's government or wherever it may! The like happens if an enemy attacks a town. The first to rouse up the rest earns glory and thanks. Why then should not he earn glory that descries the coming of our enemies from hell and rouses and summons all Christians? . . .

And now I hope the false, lying spectre will be laid with which the Romanists have long terrified and stupefied our consciences. And it will be seen that, like all the rest of us, they are subject to the temporal sword; that they have no authority to interpret the Scriptures by force without skill; and that they have no power to prevent a council, or to pledge it in accordance with their pleasure, or to bind it beforehand, and deprive it of its freedom; and that if they do this, they are verily of the fellowship of antichrist and the devil, and have nothing of Christ but the name.

Of the Matters To Be Considered in the Councils

Let us now consider the matters which should be treated in the councils, and with which popes, cardinals, bishops, and all learned men should occupy themselves day and night, if they love Christ and His Church. But if they do not do so, the people at large and the temporal powers must do so, without considering the thunders of their excommunications. For an unjust excommunication is better than ten just absolutions, and an unjust absolution is worse than ten just excommunications. Therefore let us rouse ourselves, fellow-Germans, and fear God more than man, that we be not answerable for all the poor souls that are so miserably lost through the wicked, devilish government of the Romanists, and that the dominion of the devil should not grow day by day, if indeed this hellish government can grow any worse, which, for my part, I can neither conceive nor believe.

1. It is a distressing and terrible thing to see that the head of Christendom, who boasts of being the vicar of Christ and the successor of St. Peter, lives in a worldly pomp that no king or emperor can equal, so that in him that calls himself most holy and most spiritual there is more worldliness than in the world itself. He wears a triple crown, whereas the mightiest kings only wear one crown. If this resembles the poverty of Christ and St. Peter, it is a new sort of resemblance. They prate of its being heretical to object to this; nay, they will not even hear how unchristian and ungodly it is. But I think that if he should have to pray to God with tears, he would have to lay down his crowns; for God will not endure any arrogance. His office should be nothing else than to weep and pray constantly for Christendom and to be an example of all humility.

However this may be, this pomp is a stumbling-block, and the Pope, for the very salvation of his soul, ought to put it off, for St. Paul says, "Abstain from all appearance of evil" (1 Thess. v. 21), and again, "Provide things honest in the sight of all men" (2 Cor. viii. 21). A simple mitre would be enough for the pope: wisdom and sanctity should raise him above the rest; the crown of pride he should leave to antichrist, as his predecessors did some hundreds of years ago. They say, He is the ruler of the world. This is false; for Christ, whose vicegerent and vicar he claims to be, said to Pilate, "My kingdom is not of this world" (John xviii. 36). But no vicegerent can have a wider dominion than his Lord, nor is he a vicegerent of Christ in His glory, but of Christ crucified, as St. Paul says, "For I determined not to know anything among you save Jesus Christ, and Him crucified" (2 Cor. ii. 2), and "Let this mind be in you, which was also in Christ Jesus, who made Himself of no reputation, and took upon Himself the form of a servant" (Phil. ii. 5, 7). Again, "We preach Christ crucified" (1 Cor. i.). Now they make the Pope a vicegerent of Christ exalted in heaven, and some have let the devil rule them so thoroughly that they have maintained that the Pope is above the angels in heaven and has power over them, which is precisely the true work of the true antichrist.

2. What is the use in Christendom of the people called "cardinals"? I will tell you. In Italy and Germany there are many rich convents, endowments, fiefs, and benefices, and as the best way of getting these into the hands of Rome, they created cardinals, and gave them the sees, convents, and prelacies, and thus destroyed the service of God. That is why Italy is almost a desert now: the convents are destroyed, the sees consumed, the revenues of the prelacies and of all the churches drawn to Rome; towns are decayed, the country and the people ruined, because there is no more any worship of God or preaching; why? Because the cardinals must have all the wealth. No Turk could have thus desolated Italy and overthrown the worship of God.

Now that Italy is sucked dry, they come to Germany and begin very quietly; but if we look on quietly Germany will soon be brought into the same state as Italy. We have a few cardinals already. What the Romanists mean thereby the drunken Germans are not to see until they have lost everything—bishoprics, convents, benefices, fiefs, even to their last farthing. Antichrist must take the riches of the earth, as it is written (Dan. xi. 8, 39, 43). They begin by taking off the cream of the bishoprics, convents and fiefs; and as they do not dare to destroy everything as they have done in Italy, they employ such holy cunning to join together ten or twenty prelacies, and take such a portion of each annually that the total amounts to a considerable sum. The priory of Würzburg gives one thousand guilders; those of Bamberg, Mayence, Treves, and others also contribute. In this way they collect one thousand or ten thousand guilders, in order that a cardinal may live at Rome in a state like that of a wealthy monarch.

After we have gained this, we will create thirty or forty cardinals on one day, and give one St. Michael's Mount, near Bamberg, and likewise the see of Würzburg, to which belong some rich benefices, until the churches and the cities are desolated; and then we shall say, We are the vicars of Christ, the shepherds of Christ's flocks; those mad, drunken Germans must submit to it. I advise, however, that there be made fewer cardinals, or that the Pope should have to support them out of his own purse. It would be amply sufficient if there were twelve, and if each of them had an annual income of one thousand guilders.

What has brought us Germans to such a pass that we have to suffer this robbery and this destruction of our property by the Pope? If the kingdom of France has resisted it, why do we Germans suffer ourselves to be fooled and deceived? It would be more endurable if they did nothing but rob us of our property; but they destroy the Church and deprive Christ's flock of their good shepherds, and overthrow the service and word of God. Even if there were no cardinals at all, the Church would not perish, for they do nothing for the good of Christendom; all they do is to traffic in and quarrel about prelacies and bishoprics, which any robber could do as well.

3. If we took away ninety-nine parts of the Pope's Court and only left one hundredth, it would still be large enough to answer questions on matters of belief. Now there is such a swarm of vermin at Rome, all called papal, that Babylon itself never saw the like. There are more than three thousand papal secretaries alone; but who shall count the other office-bearers, since there are so many offices that we can scarcely count them, and all waiting for German benefices, as wolves wait for a flock of sheep? I think Germany now pays more to the Pope than it formerly paid the emperors; nay, some think more than three hundred thousand guilders are sent from Germany to Rome every year, for nothing whatever; and in return we are scoffed at and put to shame. Do we still wonder why princes, noblemen, cities, foundations, convents, and people grow poor? We should rather wonder that we have anything left to eat.

Now that we have got well into our game, let us pause a while and show that the Germans are not such fools as not to perceive or understand this Romish trickery. I do not here complain that God's commandments and Christian justice are despised at Rome; for the state of things in Christendom, especially at Rome, is too bad for us to complain of such high matters. Nor do I even complain that no account is taken of natural or secular justice and reason. The mischief lies still deeper. I complain that they do not observe their own fabricated canon law, though this is in itself rather mere tyranny, avarice, and worldly pomp, than a law. This we shall now show.

Long ago the emperors and princes of Germany allowed the Pope to claim the *annates* from all German benefices; that is, half of the first year's income from every benefice. The object of this concession was that the Pope should collect a fund with all this money to fight against the Turks and infidels, and to protect Christendom, so that the nobility should not have to bear the burden of the struggle alone, and that the priests should also contribute. The popes have made such use of this good simple piety of the Germans that they have taken this money for more than one hundred years, and have now made of it a regular tax and duty; and not only have they accumulated nothing, but they have founded out of it many posts and offices at Rome, which are paid by it yearly, as out of a ground-rent.

Whenever there is any pretence of fighting the Turks, they send out some commission for collecting money, and often send out indulgences under the same pretext of fighting the Turks. They think we Germans will always remain such great and inveterate fools that we will go on giving money to satisfy their unspeakable greed, though we see plainly that neither *annates,* nor absolution money, nor any other—not one farthing—goes against the Turks, but all goes into the bottomless sack. They lie and deceive, form and make covenants with us, of which they do not mean to keep one jot. And all this is done in the holy name of Christ and St. Peter.

This being so, the German nation, the bishops and princes, should remember that they are Christians, and should defend the people, who are committed to their government and protection in temporal and spiritual affairs, from these ravenous wolves in sheep's clothing that profess to be shepherds and rulers; and since the *annates* are so shamefully abused, and the covenants concerning them not carried out, they should not suffer their lands and people to be so piteously and unrighteously flayed and ruined; but by an imperial or a national law they should either retain the *annates* in the country, or abolish them altogether. For since they do not keep to the covenants, they have no right to the *annates;* therefore bishops and princes are bound to punish this thievery and robbery, or prevent it, as justice demands. And herein should they assist and strengthen the Pope, who is perchance too weak to prevent this scandal by himself, or, if he wishes to protect or support it, restrain and oppose him as a wolf and tyrant; for he has no authority to do evil or to protect evil-doers. Even if it were proposed to collect any such treasure for use against the Turks, we should be wise in future, and remember that the German nation is more fitted to take charge of it than the Pope, seeing that the German nation by itself is able to provide men enough, if the money is forthcoming. This matter of the *annates* is like many other Romish pretexts. Oh, what a trafficking and plundering is there! One would think that the canon laws were only so many money-snares, from which he must free himself who would become a Christian man. . . . Oh,

what a poor treasury is the toll on the Rhine compared with this holy house!

Let no one think that I say too much. It is all notorious, so that even at Rome they are forced to own that it is more terrible and worse than one can say. I have said and will say nothing of the infernal dregs of private vices. I only speak of well-known public matters, and yet my words do not suffice. Bishops, priests, and especially the doctors of the universities, who are paid to do it, ought to have unanimously written and exclaimed against it. Yea, if you will turn the leaf you will discover the truth.

I have still to give a farewell greeting. These treasures, that would have satisfied three mighty kings, were not enough for this unspeakable greed, and so they have made over and sold their traffic to Fugger at Augsburg, so that the lending and buying and selling sees and benefices, and all this traffic in ecclesiastical property, has in the end come into the right hands, and spiritual and temporal matters have now become one business. Now I should like to know what the most cunning would devise for Romish greed to do that it has not done, except that Fugger might sell or pledge his two trades, that have now become one. I think they must have come to the end of their devices. For what they have stolen and yet steal in all countries by bulls of indulgences, letters of confession, letters of dispensation, and other *confessionalia,* all this I think mere bungling work, and much like playing toss with a devil in hell. Not that they produce little, for a mighty king could support himself by them; but they are as nothing compared to the other streams of revenue mentioned above. I will not now consider what has become of that indulgence money; I shall inquire into this another time, for *Campofiore* and *Belvedere* and some other places probably know something about it.

Meanwhile, since this devilish state of things is not only an open robbery, deceit, and tyranny of the gates of hell, but also destroys Christianity body and soul, we are bound to use all our diligence to prevent this misery and destruction of Christendom. If we wish to fight the Turk, let us begin here, where they are worst. If we justly hang thieves and be-head robbers, why do we leave the greed of Rome so unpunished, that is the greatest thief and robber that has appeared or can appear on earth, and does all this in the holy name of Christ and St. Peter? Who can suffer this and be silent about it? Almost everything that they possess has been stolen or got by robbery, as we learn from all histories. Why, the Pope never bought those great possessions, so as to be able to raise well-nigh ten hundred thousand ducats from his ecclesiastical offices, without counting his gold mines . . . and his land. He did not inherit it from Christ and St. Peter; no one gave it or lent it him; he has not acquired it by prescription. Tell me, where can he have got it? You can learn from this what their object is when they send out legates to collect money to be used against the Turk.

John Calvin

J ohn Calvin (1509–1564) was a Protestant leader who was born in France but was forced by persecution to flee to Switzerland where he took a prominent position in the reform movement. He had been trained for the law and it was inevitable, perhaps, that he should become concerned with matters of religious doctrines. In his Institutes of the Christian Religion Calvin developed the most logical presentation of Protestant theology ever written, and it became a guide both for study and discussion. The entire work was based upon Calvin's belief and faith in the infallible authority of the Bible literally interpreted. In reading the selections taken from this work note (1) Calvin's discussion of the relative authority of the Scriptures and the Church, (2) the evidences he gave to establish the authorship of the Scriptures, (3) the role of God as creator and governor of the world and of mankind, (4) the answer Calvin gave to those who claimed that man could not be held responsible for his evil actions, (5) his description of Christian liberty, (6) his exposition and justification of the doctrine of predestination, (7) Calvin's concept of the Church, (8) the two types of people who may be found in every congregation, (9) the reasons Calvin advanced for attendance at divine services, (10) the number and true nature of the sacraments according to the Bible, and (11) the limits he placed on a Christian's duty to obey civil rulers.

From: THE INSTITUTES OF THE CHRISTIAN RELIGION

Before I proceed any further, it is proper to introduce some remarks on the authority of the Scripture, not only to prepare the mind to regard it with due reverence, but also to remove every doubt. For, when it is admitted to be a declaration of the word of God, no man

As translated by John Allen in John Calvin, *Institutes of the Christian Religion*, 7th American edition, 2 vols., Presbyterian Board of Christian Education, Philadelphia, 1936, I, 85–86; 88–92; 217–218; 225–226; 236–239; 270–271; 273–274; II, 76–77; 280–281; 295–296; 730–732. Used by permission.

can be so deplorably presumptuous, unless he be also destitute of common sense and of the common feelings of men, as to dare to derogate from the credit due to the speaker. But since we are not favoured with daily oracles from heaven, and since it is only in the Scriptures that the Lord hath been pleased to preserve his truth in perpetual remembrance, it obtains the same complete credit and authority with believers, when they are satisfied of its divine origin, as if they heard the very words pronounced by God himself. The subject, indeed, merits a diffuse discussion, and a most accurate examination. But the reader will pardon me, if I attend rather to what the design of this work admits, than to what the extensive nature of the present subject requires. But there has very generally prevailed a most pernicious error, that the Scriptures have only so much weight as is conceded to them by the suffrages of the Church; as though the eternal and inviolable truth of God depended on the arbitrary will of men. For thus, with great contempt of the Holy Spirit, they inquire, Who can assure us that God is the author of them? Who can with certainty affirm, that they have been preserved safe and uncorrupted to the present age? Who can persuade us that this book ought to be received with reverence, and that expunged from the sacred number, unless all these things were regulated by the decisions of the Church? It depends, therefore, (say they) on the determination of the Church, to decide both what reverence is due to the Scripture, and what books are to be comprised in its canon. Thus sacrilegious men, while they wish to introduce an unlimited tyranny, under the name of the Church, are totally unconcerned with what absurdities they embarrass themselves and others, provided they can extort from the ignorant this one admission, that the Church can do every thing. But, if this be true, what will be the condition of those wretched consciences, which are seeking a solid assurance of eternal life, if all the promises extant concerning it rest only on the judgment of men? Will the reception of such an answer cause their fluctuations to subside, and their terrors to vanish? Again, how will the impious ridicule our faith, and all men call it in question, if it be understood to possess only a precarious authority depending on the favour of men! . . .

It must be maintained, as I have before asserted, that we are not established in the belief of the doctrine till we are indubitably persuaded that God is its Author. The principal proof, therefore, of the Scriptures is every where derived from the character of the Divine Speaker. The prophets and apostles boast not of their own genius, or any of those talents which conciliate the faith of the hearers; nor do they insist on arguments from reason; but bring forward the sacred name of God, to compel the submission of the whole world. We must now see how it appears, not from probable supposition, but from clear demonstration, that this use of the Divine name is neither rash nor fallacious. Now, if we wish to consult the true interest of our consciences; that they may not be unstable and wavering, the subjects of perpetual doubt; that they may not hesitate at the smallest scruples,—this persuasion must be sought from a higher source than human reasons, or judgments, or conjectures—even from the secret testimony of the Spirit. It is true that, if we were inclined to argue the point, many things might be adduced which certainly evince, if there be any God in heaven, that he is the Author of the Law, and the Prophecies, and the Gospel. Even though men of learning and deep judgment rise up in opposition, and exert and display all the powers of their minds in this dispute, yet, unless they are wholly lost to all sense of shame, this confession will be extorted from them, that the Scripture exhibits the plainest evidences that it is God who speaks in it, which manifests its doctrine to be Divine. And we shall soon see, that all the books of the sacred Scripture very far excel all other writings. If we read it with pure eyes and sound minds, we shall immediately perceive the majesty of God, which will subdue our audacious contradictions, and compel us to obey him. Yet it is acting a preposterous part, to endeavour to produce sound faith in the Scripture by disputations. Though, indeed, I am far from excelling in peculiar dexterity or eloquence, yet, if I were to contend with the most subtle despisers of God, who are ambitious to display their wit and their skill in weakening the authority of Scripture, I trust I should be able, without difficulty, to silence their obstreperous clamour. And, if it were of any use to attempt a refutation of their cavils, I would easily demolish the boasts which they mutter in secret corners. But though any one vindicates the sacred word of God from the aspersions of men, yet this will not fix in their hearts that assurance which is essential to true piety. Religion appearing, to profane men, to consist wholly in opinion, in order that they may not believe any thing on foolish or slight grounds, they wish and expect it to be proved by rational arguments, that Moses and the prophets spake by Divine inspiration. But I reply, that the testimony of the Spirit is superior to all reason. For as God alone is a sufficient witness of himself in his own word, so also the word will never gain credit in the hearts of men, till it be confirmed by the internal testimony of the Spirit. It is necessary, therefore, that the same Spirit, who spake by the mouths of the prophets, should penetrate into our hearts, to convince us that they faithfully delivered the oracles which were divinely instrusted to them. And this connection is very suitably expressed in these words: "My Spirit that is upon thee, and my word which I have put in thy mouth, shall not depart out of thy mouth, nor out of the mouth of thy seed, nor out of the mouth of thy seed's seed, for ever." Some good men are troubled that they are not always prepared with clear proof to oppose the impious, when they murmur with impunity against the divine word; as though the Spirit were not therefore denominated a "seal," and "an earnest," for the confirmation of the faith of the pious; because, till he illuminate their minds, they are perpetually fluctuating amidst a multitude of doubts.

Let it be considered, then, as an undeniable truth, that they who have been inwardly taught by the Spirit, feel an entire acquiescence in the Scripture, and that it is self-authenticated, carrying with it its own evidence, and ought not to be made the subject of demonstration and arguments from reason; but it obtains the credit which it deserves with us by the testimony of the Spirit. For though it conciliate our reverence by its internal majesty, it never seriously affects us till it is confirmed by the Spirit in our hearts. Therefore, being illuminated by him, we now believe the Divine original of the Scripture, not from our own judgment or that of others, but we esteem the certainty, that we have received it from God's own mouth by the ministry of men, to be superior to that of any human judgment, and equal to that of an intuitive perception of God himself in it. We seek not arguments or probabilities to support our judgment, but submit our judgments and understandings as to a thing concerning which it is impossible for us to judge; and that not like some persons, who are in the habit of hastily embracing what they do not understand, which displeases them as soon as they examine it, but because we feel the firmest conviction that we hold an invincible truth; nor like those unhappy men who surrender their minds captives to superstitions, but because we perceive in it the undoubted energies of the Divine power, by which we are attracted and inflamed to an understanding and voluntary obedience, but with a vigour and efficacy superior to the power of any human will or knowledge. With the greatest justice, therefore, God exclaims by Isaiah, that the prophets and all the people were his witnesses; because, being taught by prophecies, they were certain that God had spoken without the least fallacy or ambiguity. It is such a persuasion, therefore, as requires no reasons; such a knowledge as is supported by the highest reason, in which, indeed, the mind rests with greater security and constancy than in any reasons; it is, finally, such a sentiment as cannot be produced but by a revelation from heaven. I speak of nothing but what every believer experiences in his heart, except that my language falls far short of a just explication of the subject. I pass over many things at present, because this subject will present itself for discussion again in another place. Only let it be known here, that that alone is true faith which the Spirit of God seals in our hearts. And with this one reason every reader of modesty and docility will be satisfied: Isaiah predicts that "all the children" of the renovated Church "shall be taught of God." Herein God deigns to confer a singular privilege on his elect, whom he distinguishes from the rest of mankind. For what is the beginning of true learning but a prompt alacrity to hear the voice of God? By the mouth of Moses he demands our attention in these terms: "Say not in thine heart, Who shall ascend into heaven? or, Who shall descend into the deep? The word is even in thy mouth." If God hath determined that this treasury of wisdom shall be reserved for his children, it is neither surprising nor absurd, that we see so much ignorance and stupidity among the vulgar herd of mankind. By this appellation I designate even those of the greatest talents and highest rank, till they are incorporated into the Church. Moreover, Isaiah, observing that the prophetical doctrine would be incredible, not only to aliens, but also to the Jews, who wished to be esteemed members of the family, adds, at the same time, the reason —Because the arm of the Lord will not be revealed to all. Whenever, therefore, we are disturbed at the paucity of believers, let us, on the other hand, remember that none, but those to whom it was given, have any apprehension of the mysteries of God. . . .

To represent God as a Creator only for a moment, who entirely finished all his work at once, were frigid and jejune; and in this it behoves us especially to differ from the heathen, that the presence of the Divine power may appear to us no less in the perpetual state of the world than in its first origin. For although the minds even of impious men, by the mere contemplation of earth and heaven, are constrained to rise to the Creator, yet faith has a way peculiar to itself to assign to God the whole praise of creation. To which purpose is that assertion of an Apostle before cited, that it is only "through faith that we understand the worlds were framed by the word of God"; because, unless we proceed to his providence, we have no correct conception of the meaning of this article, "that God is the Creator"; however we may appear to comprehend it in our minds, and to confess it with our tongues. The carnal sense, when it has once viewed the power of God in the creation, stops there; and when it proceeds the furthest, it only examines and considers the wisdom, and power, and goodness, of the Author in producing such a work, which spontaneously present themselves to the view even of those who are unwilling to ob-

serve them. In the next place, it conceives of some general operation of God in preserving and governing it, on which the power of motion depends. Lastly, it supposes that the vigour originally infused by God into all things is sufficient for their sustentation. But faith ought to penetrate further. When it has learned that he is the Creator of all things, it should immediately conclude that he is also their perpetual governor and preserver; and that not by a certain universal motion, actuating the whole machine of the world, and all its respective parts, but by a particular providence sustaining, nourishing, and providing for every thing which he has made. . . .

But as we know that the world was made chiefly for the sake of mankind, we must also observe this end in the government of it. The Prophet Jeremiah exclaims, "I know that the way of man is not in himself: it is not in man that walketh to direct his steps." And Solomon: "Man's goings are of the Lord: how can a man then understand his own way?" Now, let them say that man is actuated by God according to the bias of his nature, but that he directs that influence according to his own pleasure. If this could be asserted with truth, man would have the free choice of his own ways. That, perhaps, they will deny, because he can do nothing independently of the power of God. But since it is evident that both the Prophet and Solomon ascribe to God choice and appointment, as well as power, this by no means extricates them from the difficulty. But Solomon, in another place, beautifully reproves this temerity of men, who predetermine on an end for themselves, without regard to God, as though they were not led by his hand: "The preparation of the heart in man," says he, "and the answer of the tongue, is from the Lord." It is, indeed, a ridiculous madness for miserable men to resolve on undertaking any work independently of God, whilst they cannot even speak a word but what he chooses. Moreover, the Scripture, more fully to express that nothing is transacted in the world but according to his destination, shows that those things are subject to him which appear most fortuitous. For what would you be more ready to attribute to chance, than when a limb broken off from a tree kills a passing traveller? But very different is the decision of the Lord, who acknowledges that he has delivered him into the hand of the slayer. Who, likewise, does not leave lots to the blindness of fortune? Yet the Lord leaves them not, but claims the disposal of them himself. He teaches us that it is not by any power of their own that lots are cast into the lap and drawn out; but the only thing which could be ascribed to chance, he declares to belong to himself. To the same purpose is another passage from Solomon: "The poor and the deceitful man meet together: the Lord enlighteneth the eyes of them both." For although the poor and the rich are blended together in the world, yet, as their respective conditions are assigned to them by Divine appointment, he suggests that God, who enlightens all, is not blind, and thus exhorts the poor to patience; because those who are discontented with their lot, are endeavouring to shake off the burden imposed on them by God. Thus also another Prophet rebukes profane persons, who attribute it to human industry, or to fortune, that some men remain in obscurity, and others rise to honours: "Promotion cometh neither from the east, nor from the west, nor from the south. But God is the Judge; he putteth down one, and setteth up another." Since God cannot divest himself of the office of a judge, hence he reasons, that it is from the secret counsel of God, that some rise to promotion, and others remain in contempt. . . .

Those who have learned this modesty, will neither murmur against God on account of past adversities, nor charge him with the guilt of their crimes, like Agamemnon, in Homer, who says, "The blame belongs not to me, but to Jupiter and Fate." Nor will they, as if hurried away by the Fates, under the influence of despair, put an end to their own lives, like the young man whom Plautus introduces as saying, "The condition of our affairs is inconstant; men are governed by the caprice of the Fates; I will betake myself to a precipice, and there destroy my life and every thing at once." Nor will they excuse their flagitious actions by ascribing them to God, after the example of another young man introduced by the same poet, who says, "God was the cause; I believe it was the Divine will. For had it not been so, I know it would not have happened." But they will rather search the Scripture, to learn what is pleasing to God, that by the guidance of the Spirit they may strive to attain it; and at the same time, being prepared to follow God whithersoever he calls them, they will exhibit proofs in their conduct that nothing is more useful than a knowledge of this doctrine. Some profane men foolishly raise such a tumult with their absurdities, as almost, according to a common expression, to confound heaven and earth together. They argue in this manner: If God has fixed the moment of our death, we cannot avoid it; therefore all caution against it will be but lost labour. One man dares not venture himself in a way which he hears is dangerous, lest he should be assassinated by robbers; another sends for physicians, and wearies himself with medicines, to preserve his life; another abstains from the grosser kinds of food, lest he should injure his valetudinary constitution; another dreads to inhabit a ruinous house; and men in general exert all their faculties in devising and executing methods by which they may attain the object of their desires. Now, either all these things are vain remedies employed to correct the will of God, or life and death, health and disease, peace and war, and other things which, according to their desires or aversions, men industriously study to obtain or to avoid, are not determined by his certain decree. Moreover they conclude, that the prayers of the faithful are not only superfluous, but perverse, which contain petitions that the Lord will provide for those things which he has already decreed from eternity. In short, they supersede all deliberations respecting futurity, as opposed to the providence of God, who, without consulting men, has decreed whatever he pleased. And what has already happened they impute to the Divine providence in such a manner as to overlook the person, who is known to have committed any particular act. Has an assassin murdered a worthy citizen? they say he has executed the counsel of God. Has any one been guilty of theft or fornication? because he has done what was foreseen and ordained by the Lord, he is the minister of his providence. Has a son, neglecting all remedies, carelessly waited the death of his father? it was impossible for him to resist God, who had decreed this event from eternity. Thus by these persons all crimes are denominated virtues, because they are subservient to the ordination of God. . . .

The same persons inconsiderably and erroneously ascribe all past events to the absolute providence of God. For since all things which come to pass are dependent upon it, therefore, say they, neither thefts, nor adulteries, nor homicides, are perpetrated without the intervention of the Divine will. Why, therefore, they ask, shall a thief be punished for having pillaged him whom it has pleased the Lord to chastise with proverty? Why shall a homicide be punished for having slain him whose life the Lord had terminated? If all such characters are subservient to the Divine will, why shall they be punished? But I deny that they serve the will of God. For we cannot say, that he who is influenced by a wicked heart, acts in obedience to the commands of God, while he is only gratifying his own malignant passions. That man obeys God, who, being instructed in his will, hastens whither God calls him. Where can we learn his will, but in his word? Therefore in our actions we ought to regard the will of God, which is declared in his word. God only requires of us conformity to his precepts. If we do any thing contrary to them, it is not obedience, but contumacy and transgression. But it is said, if he would not permit it, we should not do it. This I grant. But do we perform evil actions with the design of pleasing him? He gives us no such command. We precipitate ourselves into them, not considering what is his will, but inflamed with the violence of our passions, so that we deliberately strive to oppose him. In this manner even by criminal actions we subserve his righteous ordination; because, in the infinite greatness of his wisdom, he well knows how to use evil instruments for the accomplishment of good purposes. . . .

Nor, to enable us to understand this subject, have we any need to enter on that tedious dispute, with which the fathers were not a little perplexed, whether the soul of a son proceeds by derivation or transmission from the soul of the father, because the soul is the principal seat of the pollution. We ought to be satisfied with this, that the Lord deposited with Adam the endowments he chose to confer on the human nature; and therefore that when he lost the favours he had received, he lost them not only for himself, but for us all. Who will be solicitous about a transmission of the soul, when he hears that Adam received the ornaments that he lost, no less for us than for himself? that they were given, not to one man only, but to the whole human nature? There is nothing absurd therefore, if, in consequence of his being spoiled of his dignities, that nature be destitute and poor; if, in consequence of his being polluted with sin, the whole nature be infected with the contagion. From a putrefied root, therefore, have sprung putrid branches, which have transmitted their putrescence to remoter ramifications. For the children were so vitiated in their parent, that they became contagious to their descendants: there was in Adam such a spring of corruption, that it transfused from parents to children in a perpetual stream. But the cause of the contagion is not in the substance of the body or of the soul; but because it was ordained by God, that the gifts which he conferred on the first man should by him be preserved or lost both for himself and for all his posterity. . . .

We have now to treat of Christian liberty, an explanation of which ought not to be omitted in a treatise which is designed to comprehend a compendious summary of evangelical doctrine. For it is a subject of the first importance, and unless it be well understood, our consciences scarcely venture to undertake any thing without doubting, experience in many things hesitation and reluctance, and are always subject to fluctuations and fears. But especially it is an appendix to justification, and affords no small assistance towards the knowledge of its influence. Hence they who sincerely fear God will experience the incomparable advantage of that doctrine, which impious scoffers pursue with their railleries; because in the spiritual intoxication with which they are seized, they allow themselves the most unbounded impudence. Wherefore this is the proper time to introduce the subject; and though we have slightly touched upon it on some former occasions, yet it was useful to defer the full discussion of it to this place; because, as soon as any mention is made of Christian liberty, then either inordinate passions rage, or violent emotions arise, unless timely opposition be made to those wanton spirits, who must nefariously corrupt things which are otherwise the best. For some, under the pretext of this liberty, cast off all obedience to God, and precipitate themselves into the most unbridled licentiousness; and some despise it, supposing it to be subversive of all moderation, order, and moral distinctions. What can we do in this case, surrounded by such difficulties? Shall we entirely discard Christian liberty, and so preclude the occasion of such dangers? But, as we have observed, unless this be understood, there can be no right knowledge of Christ, or of evangelical truth, or of internal peace of mind. We should rather exert ourselves to prevent the suppression of such a necessary branch of doctrine, and at the same time to obviate those absurd objections which are frequently deduced from it.

Christian liberty, according to my judgment, consists of three parts. The first part is, that the consciences of believers, when seeking an assurance of their justification before God, should raise themselves above the law, and forget all the righteousness of the law. For since the law, as we have elsewhere demonstrated, leaves no man righteous, either we must be excluded from all hope of justification, or it is necessary for us to be delivered from it, and that so completely as not to have any dependence on works. For he who imagines, that in order to obtain righteousness he must produce any works, however small, can fix no limit or boundary, but renders himself a debtor to the whole law. Avoiding, therefore, all mention of the law, and dismissing all thought of our own works, in reference to justification, we must embrace the Divine mercy alone, and turning our eyes from ourselves, fix them solely on Christ. For the question is, not how we can be righteous, but how, though unrighteous and unworthy, we can be considered as righteous. And the conscience that desires to attain any certainty respecting this, must give no admission to the law. Nor will this authorize any one to conclude, that the law is of no use to be-

lievers, whom it still continues to instruct and exhort, and stimulate to duty, although it has no place in their consciences before the tribunal of God. For these two things, being very different, require to be properly and carefully distinguished by us. The whole life of Christians ought to be an exercise of piety, since they are called to sanctification. . . .

The second part of Christian liberty, which is dependent on the first, is, that their consciences do not observe the law, as being under any legal obligation; but that, being liberated from the yoke of the law, they yield a voluntary obedience to the will of God. For being possessed with perpetual terrors, as long as they remain under the dominion of the law, they will never engage with alacrity and promptitude in the service of God, unless they have previously received this liberty. . . .

The third part of Christian liberty teaches us, that we are bound by no obligation before God respecting external things, which in themselves are indifferent; but that we may indifferently sometimes use, and at other times omit them. And the knowledge of this liberty also is very necessary for us; for without it we shall have no tranquillity of conscience, nor will there be any end of superstitions. Many in the present age think it a folly to raise any dispute concerning the free use of meats, of days, and of habits, and similar subjects, considering these things as frivolous and nugatory; but they are of greater importance than is generally believed. For when the conscience has once fallen into the snare, it enters a long and inextricable labyrinth, from which it is afterwards difficult to escape; if a man begin to doubt the lawfulness of using flax in sheets, shirts, handkerchiefs, napkins, and table cloths, neither will he be certain respecting hemp, and at last he will doubt of the lawfulness of using tow; for he will consider with himself whether he cannot eat without table cloths or napkins, whether he cannot do without handkerchiefs. If any one imagine delicate food to be unlawful, he will ere long have no tranquillity before God in eating brown bread and common viands, while he remembers that he might support his body with meat of a quality still inferior. If he hesitate respecting good wine, he will afterwards be unable with any peace of conscience to drink the most vapid; and at last he will not presume even to touch purer and sweeter water than others. In short, he will come to think it criminal to step over a twig that lies across his path. For this is the commencement of no trivial controversy; but the dispute is whether the use of certain things be agreeable to God, whose will ought to guide all our resolutions and all our actions. The necessary consequence is, that some are hurried by despair into a vortex of confusion, from which they see no way of escape; and some, despising God, and casting off all fear of him, make a way of ruin for themselves. For all, who are involved in such doubts, which way soever they turn their views, behold something offensive to their consciences presenting itself on every side. . . .

The covenant of life not being equally preached to all, and among those to whom it is preached not always finding the same reception, this diversity discovers the wonderful depth of the Divine judgment. Nor is it to be doubted that this variety also follows, subject to the decision of God's eternal election. If it be evidently the result of the Divine will, that salvation is freely offered to some, and others are prevented from attaining it,—this immediately gives rise to important and difficult questions, which are incapable of any other explication, than by the establishment of pious minds in what ought to be received concerning election and predestination—a question, in the opinion of many, full of perplexity; for they consider nothing more unreasonable, than that, of the common mass of mankind, some should be predestined to salvation, and others to destruction. But how unreasonably they perplex themselves will afterwards appear from the sequel of our discourse. Besides, the very obscurity which excites such dread, not only displays the utility of this doctrine, but shows it to be productive of the most delightful benefit. We shall never be clearly convinced as we ought to be, that our salvation flows from the fountain of God's free mercy, till we are acquainted with his eternal election, which illus-

trates the grace of God by this comparison, that he adopts not all promiscuously to the hope of salvation, but gives to some what he refuses to others. Ignorance of this principle evidently detracts from the Divine glory, and diminishes real humility. But according to Paul, what is so necessary to be known, never can be known, unless God, without any regard to works, chooses those whom he has decreed. "At this present time also, there is a remnant according to the election of grace. And if by grace, then it is no more of works; otherwise, grace is no more grace. But if it be of works, then it is no more grace; otherwise, work is no more work." If we need to be recalled to the origin of election, to prove that we obtain salvation from no other source than the mere goodness of God, they who desire to extinguish this principle, do all they can to obscure what ought to be magnificently and loudly celebrated, and to pluck up humility by the roots. In ascribing the salvation of the remnant of the people to the election of grace, Paul clearly testifies, that it is then only known that God saves whom he will of his mere good pleasure, and does not dispense a reward to which there can be no claim. They who shut the gates to prevent any one from presuming to approach and taste this doctrine, do no less injury to man than to God; for nothing else will be sufficient to produce in us suitable humility, or to impress us with a due sense of our great obligations to God. Nor is there any other basis for solid confidence, even according to the authority of Christ, who, to deliver us from all fear, and render us invincible amidst so many dangers, snares, and deadly conflicts, promises to preserve in safety all whom the Father has committed to his care. Whence we infer, that they who know not themselves to be God's peculiar people will be tortured with continual anxiety; and therefore, that the interest of all believers, as well as their own, is very badly consulted by those who, blind to the three advantages we have remarked, would wholly remove the foundation of our salvation. And hence the Church rises to our view, which otherwise, as Bernard justly observes, could neither be discovered nor recognized among creatures, being in two respects wonderfully concealed in the bosom of a blessed predestination, and in the mass of a miserable damnation. But before I enter on the subject itself, I must address some preliminary observations to two sorts of persons. The discussion of predestination—a subject of itself rather intricate—is made very perplexed, and therefore dangerous, by human curiosity, which no barriers can restrain from wandering into forbidden labyrinths, and soaring beyond its sphere, as if determined to leave none of the Divine secrets unscrutinized or unexplored. As we see multitudes every where guilty of this arrogance and presumption, and among them some who are not censurable in other respects, it is proper to admonish them of the bounds of their duty on this subject. First, then, let them remember that when they inquire into predestination, they penetrate the inmost recesses of Divine wisdom, where the careless and confident intruder will obtain not satisfaction to his curiosity, but will enter a labyrinth from which he will find no way to depart. For it is unreasonable that man should scrutinize with impunity those things which the Lord has determined to be hidden in himself; and investigate, even from eternity, that sublimity of wisdom which God would have us to adore and not comprehend, to promote our admiration of his glory. The secrets of his will which he determined to reveal to us, he discovers in his word; and these are all that he foresaw would concern us or conduce to our advantage. . . .

Predestination, by which God adopts some to the hope of life, and adjudges others to eternal death, no one, desirous of the credit of piety, dares absolutely to deny. But it is involved in many cavils, especially by those who make foreknowledge the cause of it. We maintain, that both belong to God; but it is preposterous to represent one as dependent on the other. When we attribute foreknowledge to God, we mean that all things have ever been, and perpetually remain, before his eyes, so that to his knowledge nothing is future or past, but all things are present; and present in such a manner, that he does not merely conceive of them from ideas formed in his mind, as things remembered by us appear present to our minds, but really beholds and sees them as if actually placed before him. And this foreknowledge extends to the whole world, and to all the creatures. Predestination we call the eternal decree of God, by which he has determined in himself, what he would have to become of every individual of mankind. For they are not all created with a similar destiny; but eternal life is foreordained for some, and eternal damnation for others. Every man, therefore, being created for one or the other of these ends, we say, he is predestinated either to life or to death. This God has not only testified in particular persons, but has given a specimen of it in the whole posterity of Abraham, which should evidently show the future condition of every nation to depend upon his decision. . . .

From what has been said, I conceive it must now be evident what judgment we ought to form respecting the Church, which is visible to our eyes, and falls under our knowledge. For we have remarked that the word *Church* is used in the sacred Scriptures in two senses. Sometimes, when they mention the Church, they intend that which is really such in the sight of God, into which none are received but those who by adoption and grace are the children of God, and by the sanctification of the Spirit are the true members of Christ. And then it comprehends not only the saints at any one time resident on earth, but all the elect who have lived from the beginning of the world. But the word *Church* is frequently used in the Scriptures to designate the whole multitude, dispersed all over the world, who profess to worship one God and Jesus Christ, who are initiated into his faith by baptism, who testify their unity in true doctrine and charity by a participation of the sacred supper, who consent to the word of the Lord, and preserve the ministry which Christ has instituted for the purpose of preaching it. In this Church are included many hypocrites, who have nothing of Christ but the name and appearance; many persons ambitious, avaricious, envious, slanderous, and dissolute in their lives, who are tolerated for a time, either because they cannot be convicted by a legitimate process, or because discipline is not always maintained with sufficient vigour. As it is necessary, therefore, to believe that Church, which is invisible to us, and known to God alone, so this Church, which is visible to men, we are commanded to honour, and to maintain communion with it.

As far, therefore, as was important for us to know it, the Lord has described it by certain marks and characters. It is the peculiar prerogative of God himself to "know them that are his," as we have already stated from Paul. And to guard against human presumption ever going to such an extreme, the experience of every day teaches us how very far his secret judgments transcend all our apprehensions. For those who seemed the most abandoned, and were generally considered past all hope, are recalled by his goodness into the right way; while some, who seemed to stand better than others, fall into perdition. "According to the secret predestination of God," therefore as Augustine observes, "there are many sheep without the pale of the Church, and many wolves within." For he knows and seals those who know not either him or themselves. Of those who externally bear his seal, his eyes alone can discern who are unfeignedly holy, and will persevere to the end; which is the completion of salvation. On the other hand, as he saw it to be in some measure requisite that we should know who ought to be considered as his children, he has in this respect accommodated himself to our capacity. And as it was not necessary that on this point we should have an assurance of faith, he has substituted in its place a judgment of charity, according to which we ought to acknowledge as members of the Church all those who by a confession of faith, an exemplary life, and a participation of the sacraments, profess the same God and Christ with ourselves. But the knowledge of the body itself being more necessary to our salvation, he has distinguished it by more clear and certain characters. . . .

Here are three things, therefore, worthy of our observation. First, that whatever holiness may distinguish the children of God, yet such is their condition as long as they inhabit a mortal body, that they cannot stand before

God without remission of sins. Secondly, that this benefit belongs to the Church; so that we cannot enjoy it unless we continue in its communion. Thirdly, that it is dispensed to us by the ministers and pastors of the Church, either in the preaching of the gospel, or in the administration of the sacraments; and that this is the principal exercise of the power of the keys, which the Lord has conferred on the society of believers. Let every one of us, therefore, consider it as his duty, not to seek remission of sins any where but where the Lord has placed it. Of public reconciliation, which is a branch of discipline, we shall speak in its proper place. . . .

The readers may now see, collected into a brief summary, almost every thing that I have thought important to be known respecting these two sacraments; the use of which has been enjoined on the Christian Church from the commencement of the New Testament until the end of time; that is to say, baptism, to be a kind of entrance into the Church, and an initiatory profession of faith; and the Lord's supper, to be a continual nourishment, with which Christ spiritually feeds his family of believers. Wherefore, as there is but "one God, one Christ, one Faith," one Church, the body of Christ, so there is only "one baptism" and that is never repeated; but the supper is frequently distributed, that those who have once been admitted into the Church, may understand that they are continually nourished by Christ. Beside these two, as no other sacrament has been instituted by God, so no other ought to be acknowledged by the Church of believers. For that it is not left to the will of man to institute new sacraments, will be easily understood if we remember what has already been very plainly stated—that sacraments are appointed by God for the purpose of instructing us respecting some promise of his, and assuring us of his good-will towards us; and if we also consider, that no one has been the counsellor of God, capable of affording us any certainty respecting his will, or furnishing us any assurance of his disposition towards us, what he chooses to give or to deny us. Hence it follows, that no one can institute a sign to be a testimony respecting any determination or promise of his; he alone can furnish us a testimony respecting himself by giving a sign. I will express myself in terms more concise, and perhaps more homely, but more explicit—that there can be no sacrament unaccompanied with a promise of salvation. All mankind, collected in one assembly, can promise us nothing respecting our salvation. Therefore they can never institute or establish a sacrament.

Let the Christian Church, therefore, be content with these two, and not only neither admit nor acknowledge any other at present, but neither desire nor expect any other to the end of the world. For as the Jews, beside the ordinary sacraments given to them, had also several others, differing according to the varying circumstances of different periods, such as the manna, the water issuing from the rock, the brazen serpent, and the like, they were admonished by this variation not to rest in such figures, which were of short duration, but to expect from God something better, which should undergo no change and come to no end. But our case is very different: to us Christ has been revealed, "in whom are hid all the treasures of wisdom and knowledge," in such abundance and profusion, that to hope or desire any new accession to these treasures would really be to displease God, and provoke his wrath against us. We must hunger after Christ, we must seek, contemplate, and learn him alone, till the dawning of that great day, when our Lord will fully manifest the glory of his kingdom, and reveal himself to us, so that "we shall see him as he is." And for this reason, the dispensation under which we live is designated in the Scriptures as "the last time," "these last times," "the last days," that no one may deceive himself with a vain expectation of any new doctrine or revelation. For "God, who at sundry times and in divers manners spake in time past unto the fathers by the prophets, hath, in these last days, spoken unto us by his Son," who alone is able to "reveal the Father," and who, indeed, "hath declared him" fully, as far as is necessary for our happiness, while "now we see" him "through a glass darkly." As men are not left at liberty to institute new sacraments in the Church of God, so it were to be wished that as little as possible of human invention should be mixed with those which have been instituted by God. For as wine is diluted and lost by an infusion of water, and as a whole mass of meal contracts acidity from a sprinkling of leaven, so the purity of Divine mysteries is only polluted when man makes any addition of his own. And yet we see, as the sacraments are observed in the present day, how very far they have degenerated from their original purity. There is every where an excess of pageantries, ceremonies, and gesticulations; but no consideration or mention of the word of God, without which even the sacraments themselves cease to be sacraments. And the very ceremonies which have been instituted by God are not to be discerned among such a multitude of others, by which they are overwhelmed. In baptism, how little is seen of that which ought to be the only conspicuous object—I mean baptism itself? And the Lord's supper has been completely buried since it has been transformed into the mass; except that it is exhibited once a year, but in a partial and mutilated form. . . .

But in the obedience which we have shown to be due to the authority of governors, it is always necessary to make one exception, and that is entitled to our first attention,—that it do not seduce us from obedience to him, to whose will the desires of all kings ought to be subject, to whose decrees all their commands ought to yield, to whose majesty all their sceptres ought to submit. And, indeed, how preposterous it would be for us, with a view to satisfy men, to incur the displeasure of him on whose account we yield obedience to men! The Lord, therefore, is the King of kings; who, when he has opened his sacred mouth, is to be heard alone, above all, for all, and before all; in the next place, we are subject to those men who preside over us; but no otherwise than in him. If they command any thing against him, it ought not to have the least attention; nor, in this case, ought we to pay any regard to all that dignity attached to magistrates; to which no injury is done when it is subjected to the unrivalled and supreme power of God.

Convocation of the Clergy

The Thirty-nine Articles of the Church of England were adopted in the early years of Queen Elizabeth's reign (1558–1603). They constitute the essential doctrine of the English Established Church and reflect the compromise reached in the English Reformation between the extremes of the Protestant revolt on the one hand and the traditional Roman Catholic position on the other. In reading them note (1) the relationship between God, the Son, and the Holy Ghost, (2) the authority placed in Holy Scripture, (3) the position taken on the historic Christian creeds, (4) the definition of original sin, (5) the relative importance of good works and faith in the justification of man before God, (6) the consideration of predestination and election, (7) the position taken on Christian universalism, (8) the "Romish" doctrines and practices which are condemned, (9) the number and nature of the sacraments, (10) the relationship between civil authority and the clergy, and (11) the attitude expressed concerning property and charity.

From: THE THIRTY-NINE ARTICLES

ARTICLES OF RELIGION

Article I. *Of Faith in the Holy Trinity.*

There is but one living and true God, everlasting, without body, parts, or passions; of infinite power, wisdom, and goodness; the Maker, and Preserver of all things both visible and invisible. And in unity of this Godhead there be three Persons, of one substance, power, and eternity; the Father, the Son, and the Holy Ghost.

Art. II. *Of the Word or Son of God, which was made very Man.*

The Son, which is the Word of the Father, begotten from everlasting of the Father, the very and eternal God, and of one substance with the Father, took Man's nature in the womb of the blessed Virgin, of her substance: so that two whole and perfect Natures, that is to say, the Godhead and Manhood, were joined together in one Person, never to be divided, whereof is one Christ, very God, and

very Man; who truly suffered, was crucified, dead, and buried, to reconcile his Father to us, and to be a sacrifice, not only for original guilt, but also for all actual sins of men.

Art. III. *Of the going down of Christ into Hell.*

As Christ died for us, and was buried, so also is it to be believed, that he went down into Hell.

Art. IV. *Of the Resurrection of Christ.*

Christ did truly rise again from death, and took again his body, with flesh, bones, and all things appertaining to the perfection of Man's nature; wherewith he ascended into Heaven, and there sitteth, until he return to judge all Men at the last day.

Art. V. *Of the Holy Ghost.*

The Holy Ghost, proceeding from the Father and the Son, is of one substance, majesty, and glory, with the Father and the Son, very and eternal God.

The Book of Common Prayer, London, n.d., 621–633.

Art. VI. *Of the Sufficiency of the Holy Scriptures for Salvation.*

Holy Scripture containeth all things necessary to salvation: so that whatsoever is not read therein, nor may be proved thereby, is not to be required of any man, that it should be believed as an article of the Faith, or be thought requisite or necessary to salvation. In the name of the Holy Scripture we do understand those canonical Books of the Old and New Testament, of whose authority was never any doubt in the Church. . . .

Art. VII. *Of the Old Testament.*

The Old Testament is not contrary to the New: for both in the Old and New Testament everlasting life is offered to Mankind by Christ, who is the only Mediator between God and Man, being both God and Man. Wherefore they are not to be heard, which feign that the old Fathers did look only for transitory promises. Although the Law given from God by Moses, as touching Ceremonies and Rites, do not bind Christian men, nor the Civil precepts thereof ought of necessity to be received in any commonwealth; yet notwithstanding, no Christian man whatsoever is free from the obedience of the Commandments which are called Moral.

Art. VIII. *Of the Three Creeds.*

The Three Creeds, *Nicene* Creed, *Athanasius's* Creed, and that which is commonly called the *Apostles'* Creed, ought thoroughly to be received and believed: for they may be proved by most certain warrants of Holy Scripture.

Art. IX. *Of Original or Birth-Sin.*

Original Sin standeth not in the following of *Adam* (as the *Pelagians* do vainly talk); but it is the fault and corruption of the Nature of every man, that naturally is engendered of the offspring of *Adam;* whereby man is very far gone from original righteousness, and is of his own nature inclined to evil, so that the flesh lusteth always contrary to the spirit; and therefore in every person born into this world, it deserveth God's wrath and damnation. And this infection of nature doth remain, yea in them that are regenerated; whereby the lust of the flesh, called in Greek, *phronema sarkos,* which some do expound the wisdom, some sensuality, some the affection, some the desire, of the flesh, is not subject to the Law of God. And although there is no condemnation for them that believe and are baptized; yet the Apostle doth confess, that concupiscence and lust hath of itself the nature of sin.

Art. X. *Of Free-Will.*

The condition of Man after the fall of *Adam* is such, that he cannot turn and prepare himself, by his own natural strength and good works, to faith, and calling upon God: Wherefore we have no power to do good works pleasant and acceptable to God, without the grace of God by Christ preventing us, that we may have a good will, and working with us, when we have that good will.

Art. XI. *Of the Justification of Man.*

We are accounted righteous before God, only for the merit of our Lord and Saviour Jesus Christ by Faith, and not for our own works or deservings. Wherefore, that we are justified by Faith only, is a most wholesome Doctrine, and very full of comfort, as more largely is expressed in the Homily of Justification.

Art. XII. *Of Good Works.*

Albeit that Good Works, which are the fruits of Faith, and follow after Justification, cannot put away our sins, and endure the severity of God's Judgment; yet are they pleasing and acceptable to God in Christ, and do spring out necessarily of a true and lively Faith; insomuch that by them a lively Faith may be as evidently known as a tree discerned by the fruit.

Art. XIII. *Of Works before Justification.*

Works done before the grace of Christ, and the Inspiration of his Spirit, are not pleasant to God, forasmuch as they spring not of faith in Jesus Christ, neither do they make men meet to receive grace, or (as the School-authors say) deserve grace of congruity: yea rather, for that they are not done as God hath willed and commanded them to be done, we doubt not but they have the nature of sin.

Art. XIV. *Of Works of Supererogation.*

Voluntary Works besides, over and above, God's Commandments, which they call Works of Supererogation, cannot be taught without arrogancy and impiety: for by them men do declare, that they do not only render unto God as much as they are bound to do, but that they do more for his sake, than of bounden duty is required: whereas Christ saith plainly, When ye have done all that are commanded to you, say, We are unprofitable servants.

Art. XV. *Of Christ alone without Sin.*

Christ in the truth of our nature was made like unto us in all things, sin only except, from which he was clearly void, both in his flesh, and in his spirit. He came to be the Lamb without spot, who, by sacrifice of himself once made, should take away the sins of the world, and sin, as Saint *John* saith, was not in him. But all we the rest, although baptized, and born again in Christ, yet offend in many things; and if we say we have no sin, we deceive ourselves, and the truth is not in us.

Art. XVI. *Of Sin after Baptism.*

Not every deadly sin willingly committed after Baptism is sin against the Holy Ghost, and unpardonable. Wherefore the grant of repentance is not to be denied to such as fall into sin after Baptism. After we have received the Holy Ghost, we may depart from grace given, and fall into sin, and by the grace of God we may arise again, and amend our lives. And therefore they are to be condemned, which say, they can no more sin as long as they live here, or deny the place of forgiveness to such as truly repent.

Art. XVII. *Of Predestination and Election.*

Predestination to Life is the everlasting purpose of God, whereby (before the foundations of the world were laid) he hath constantly decreed by his counsel secret to us, to deliver from curse and damnation those whom he hath chosen in Christ out of mankind, and to bring them by Christ to everlasting salvation, as vessels made to honour. Wherefore, they which be endued with so excellent a benefit of God, be called according to God's purpose by his Spirit working in due season: they through Grace obey the calling: they be justified freely: they be made sons of God by adoption: they be made like the image of his only-begotten Son Jesus Christ: they walk religiously in good works, and at length, by God's mercy, they attain to everlasting felicity.

As the godly consideration of Predestination, and our Election in Christ, is full of sweet, pleasant, and unspeakable comfort to godly persons, and such as feel in themselves the working of the Spirit of Christ, mortifying the works of the flesh, and their earthly members, and drawing up their mind to high and heavenly things, as well because it doth greatly establish and confirm their faith of eternal Salvation to be enjoyed through Christ, as because it doth fervently kindle their love towards God: So, for curious and carnal persons, lacking the Spirit of Christ, to have continually before their eyes the sentence of God's Predestination, is a most dangerous downfall, whereby the Devil doth thrust them either into desperation, or into wretchlessness of most unclean living, no less perilous than desperation.

Furthermore, we must receive God's promises in such wise, as they be generally set forth to us in Holy Scripture: and, in our doings, that Will of God is to be followed, which we have expressly declared unto us in the Word of God.

Art. XVIII. *Of Obtaining Eternal Salvation only by the Name of Christ.*

They also are to be had accursed that presume to say, That every man shall be saved by the Law or Sect which he professeth, so that he be diligent to frame his life according to that Law, and the light of Nature. For Holy Scripture doth set out unto us only the Name of Jesus Christ, whereby men must be saved.

Art. XIX. *Of the Church.*

The visible Church of Christ is a congregation of faithful men, in the which the pure Word of God is preached, and the Sacraments be duly ministered according to Christ's ordinance, in all those things that of necessity are requisite to the same.

As the Church of *Jerusalem, Alexandria,* and *Antioch,* have erred; so also the Church of

Rome hath erred, not only in their living and manner of Ceremonies, but also in matters of Faith.

Art. XX. *Of the Authority of the Church.*

The Church hath power to decree Rites or Ceremonies, and authority in Controversies of Faith: and yet it is not lawful for the Church to ordain any thing that is contrary to God's Word written, neither may it so expound one place of Scripture, that it be repugnant to another. Wherefore, although the Church be a witness and a keeper of Holy Writ, yet, as it ought not to decree any thing against the same, so besides the same ought it not to enforce any thing to be believed for necessity of Salvation.

Art. XXI. *Of the Authority of General Councils.*

General Councils may not be gathered together without the commandment and will of Princes. And when they be gathered together (forasmuch as they be an assembly of men, whereof all be not governed with the Spirit and Word of God), they may err, and sometimes have erred, even in things pertaining unto God. Wherefore things ordained by them as necessary to salvation have neither strength nor authority, unless it may be declared that they be taken out of Holy Scripture.

Art. XXII. *Of Purgatory.*

The Romish Doctrine concerning Purgatory, Pardons, Worshipping and Adoration, as well of Images as of Reliques, and also Invocation of Saints, is a fond thing, vainly invented, and grounded upon no warranty of Scripture, but rather repugnant to the Word of God.

Art. XXIII. *Of Ministering in the Congregation.*

It is not lawful for any man to take upon him the office of publick preaching, or ministering the Sacraments in the Congregation, before he be lawfully called, and sent to execute the same. And those we ought to judge lawfully called and sent, which be chosen and called to this work by men who have publick authority given unto them in the Congregation, to call and send Ministers into the Lord's vineyard.

Art. XXIV. *Of Speaking in the Congregation in such a Tongue as the People Understandeth.*

It is a thing plainly repugnant to the Word of God, and the custom of the Primitive Church, to have publick Prayer in the Church, or to minister the Sacraments, in a tongue not understanded of the people.

Art. XXV. *Of the Sacraments.*

Sacraments ordained of Christ be not only badges or tokens of Christian men's profession, but rather they be certain sure witnesses, and effectual signs of grace, and God's good will towards us, by the which he doth work invisibly in us, and doth not only quicken, but also strengthen and confirm our Faith in him.

There are two Sacraments ordained of Christ our Lord in the Gospel, that is to say, Baptism, and the Supper of the Lord.

Those five commonly called Sacraments, that is to say, Confirmation, Penance, Orders, Matrimony, and Extreme Unction, are not to be counted for Sacraments of the Gospel, being such as have grown partly of the corrupt following of the Apostles, partly are states of life allowed in the Scriptures; but yet have not like nature of Sacraments with Baptism, and the Lord's Supper, for that they have not any visible sign or ceremony ordained of God.

The Sacraments were not ordained of Christ to be gazed upon, or to be carried about, but that we should duly use them. And in such only as worthily receive the same they have a wholesome effect or operation: but they that receive them unworthily, purchase to themselves damnation, as Saint *Paul* saith.

Art. XXVI. *Of the Unworthiness of the Ministers, which Hinders not the Effect of the Sacraments.*

Although in the visible Church the evil be ever mingled with the good, and sometimes the evil have chief authority in the Ministration of the Word and Sacraments, yet forasmuch as they do not the same in their own name, but in Christ's, and do minister by his commission and authority, we may use their Ministry, both in hearing the Word of God, and in the receiving of the Sacraments. Neither is the effect of Christ's ordinance taken away by their wickedness, nor the grace of God's gifts diminished from such as by faith and rightly, do receive the Sacraments ministered unto them; which be effectual, because of Christ's institution and promise, although they be ministered by evil men.

Nevertheless, it appertaineth to the discipline of the Church, that enquiry be made of evil Ministers, and that they be accused by those that have knowledge of their offences; and finally, being found guilty, by just judgment be deposed.

Art. XXVII. *Of Baptism.*

Baptism is not only a sign of profession, and mark of difference, whereby Christian men are discerned from others that be not christened, but it is also a sign of Regeneration or new-birth, whereby, as by an instrument, they that receive Baptism rightly are grafted into the Church; the promises of the forgiveness of sin, and of our adoption to be the sons of God by the Holy Ghost, are visibly signed and sealed; Faith is confirmed, and Grace increased by virtue of prayer unto God.

The Baptism of young Children is in any wise to be retained in the Church, as most agreeable with the institution of Christ.

Art. XXVIII. *Of the Lord's Supper.*

The Supper of the Lord is not only a sign of love that Christians ought to have among themselves one to another; but rather it is a Sacrament of our Redemption by Christ's death: insomuch that to such as rightly, worthily, and with faith, receive the same, the Bread which we break is a partaking of the Body of Christ; and likewise the Cup of Blessing is a partaking of the Blood of Christ.

Transubstantiation (or the change of the substance of Bread and Wine) in the Supper of the Lord, cannot be proved by Holy Writ; but is repugnant to the plain words of Scripture, overthroweth the nature of a Sacrament, and hath given occasion to many superstitions.

The Body of Christ is given, taken, and eaten, in the Supper, only after an heavenly and spiritual manner. And the mean whereby the Body of Christ is received and eaten in the Supper, is Faith.

The Sacrament of the Lord's Supper was not by Christ's ordinance reserved, carried about, lifted up, or worshipped.

Art. XXIX. *Of the Wicked which eat not the Body of Christ in the Use of the Lord's Supper.*

The Wicked, and such as be void of a lively faith, although they do carnally and visibly press with their teeth (as Saint *Augustine* saith) the Sacrament of the Body and Blood of Christ; yet in no wise are they partakers of Christ: but rather, to their condemnation, do eat and drink the sign or Sacrament of so great a thing.

Art. XXX. *Of Both Kinds.*

The Cup of the Lord is not to be denied to the Lay-people: for both the parts of the Lord's Sacrament, by Christ's ordinance and commandment, ought to be ministered to all Christian men alike.

Art. XXXI. *Of the One Oblation of Christ Finished upon the Cross.*

The Offering of Christ once made is that perfect redemption, propitiation, and satisfaction, for all the sins of the whole world, both original and actual; and there is none other satisfaction for sin, but that alone. Wherefore the sacrifices of Masses, in the which it was commonly said, that the Priest did offer Christ for the quick and the dead, to have remission of pain or guilt, were blasphemous fables, and dangerous deceits.

Art. XXXII. *Of the Marriage of Priests.*

Bishops, Priests, and Deacons, are not commanded by God's Law, either to vow the estate of single life, or to abstain from marriage: therefore it is lawful also for them, as for all other Christian men, to marry at their own discretion, as they shall judge the same to serve better to godliness.

Art. XXXIII. *Of Excommunicate Persons, how They are to be Avoided.*

That person which by open denunciation of the Church is rightly cut off from the unity of the Church, and excommunicated, ought to be taken of the whole multitude of the faithful, as an Heathen and Publican, until he be openly reconciled by penance, and received into the Church by a Judge that hath authority thereunto.

Art. XXXIV. *Of the Traditions of the Church.*

It is not necessary that traditions and ceremonies be in all places one, or utterly like; for at all times they have been divers, and may be changed according to the diversities of countries, times, and men's manners, so that nothing be ordained against God's Word. Whosoever, through his private judgment, willingly and purposely, doth openly break the Traditions and Ceremonies of the Church, which be not repugnant to the Word of God, and be ordained and approved by common authority, ought to be rebuked openly (that others may fear to do the like), as he that offendeth against the common order of the Church, and hurteth the authority of the Magistrate, and woundeth the consciences of the weak brethren.

Every particular or national Church hath authority to ordain, change, and abolish, ceremonies or rites of the Church ordained only by man's authority, so that all things be done to edifying.

Art. XXXV. *Of Homilies.*

The Second Book of Homilies, the several titles whereof we have joined under this Article, doth contain a godly and wholesome Doctrine, and necessary for these times, as doth the former Book of Homilies, which were set forth in the time of *Edward* the Sixth; and therefore we judge them to be read in Churches by the Ministers, diligently and distinctly, that they may be understanded of the people.

Art. XXXVI. *Of Consecration of Bishops and Ministers.*

The Book of Consecration of Archbishops and Bishops, and Ordering of Priests and Deacons, lately set forth in the time of *Edward* the Sixth, and confirmed at the same time by authority of Parliament, doth contain all things necessary to such Consecration and Ordering: neither hath it anything, that of itself is superstitious and ungodly. And therefore whosoever are consecrated or ordered according to the Rites of that Book, since the second year of the forenamed King *Edward* unto this time, or hereafter shall be consecrated or ordered according to the same Rites; we decree all such to be rightly, orderly, and lawfully consecrated and ordered.

Art. XXXVII. *Of the Civil Magistrates.*

The King's Majesty hath the chief power in this Realm of *England,* and other his Dominions, unto whom the chief Government of all Estates of this Realm, whether they be Ecclesiastical or Civil, in all causes doth appertain, and is not, nor ought to be, subject to any foreign Jurisdiction.

Where we attribute to the King's Majesty the chief government, by which Titles we understand the minds of some slanderous folks to be offended; we give not to our Princes the ministering either of God's Word, or of the Sacraments, the which thing the Injunctions also lately set forth by *Elizabeth* our Queen do most plainly testify; but that only prerogative, which we see to have been given always to all godly Princes in Holy Scriptures by God himself; that is, that they should rule all estates and degrees committed to their charge by God, whether they be Ecclesiastical or Temporal, and restrain with the civil sword the stubborn and evil-doers.

The Bishop of *Rome* hath no jurisdiction in this Realm of *England.*

The Laws of the Realm may punish Christian men with death, for heinous and grievous offences.

It is lawful for Christian men, at the commandment of the Magistrate, to wear weapons, and serve in the wars.

Art. XXXVIII. *Of Christian Men's Goods, which are not Common.*

The Riches and Goods of Christians are not common, as touching the right, title, and possession of the same, as certain Anabaptists do falsely boast. Notwithstanding, every man ought, of such things as he possesseth, liberally to give alms to the poor, according to his ability.

Art. XXXIX. *Of a Christian Man's Oath.*

As we confess that vain and rash Swearing is forbidden Christian men by our Lord Jesus Christ, and *James* his Apostle, so we judge, that Christian Religion doth not prohibit, but that a man may swear when the Magistrate requireth, in a cause of faith and charity, so it be done according to the Prophet's teaching, in justice, judgment, and truth.

Council of Trent

Between 1545 and 1564 the Catholic Church held a general council in the city of Trent. During that time a total of 25 sessions were called and important decisions reached about the vital religious issues of the Reformation period. The procedure followed was to discuss problems at some length, then to set forth the accepted view of the Church in a series of chapters, and finally to draw up a list of canons anathematizing those who held contrary views. In reading the selected chapters and canons note (1) the purposes for which the council was called, (2) the decree concerning the edition of the Bible to be considered authentic and who was to interpret it, (3) the position taken on original sin, (4) the admonition concerning predestination, (5) the canons treating with the number and character of the sacraments, (6) the attitude taken on the doctrine of transubstantiation, (7) the measures adopted affecting the lives and habits of the clergy, (8) the description of the character and ranks of the clergy, (9) the decision concerning the place of relics, saints, and images in religious practices, and (10) the position taken on the controversial issue of indulgences.

From: THE DECREES OF THE COUNCIL OF TRENT

DECREE TOUCHING THE OPENING OF THE COUNCIL

Doth it please you,—unto the praise and glory of the holy and undivided Trinity, Father, and Son, and Holy Ghost; for the increase and exaltation of the Christian faith and religion; for the extirpation of heresies; for the peace and union of the Church; for the reformation of the Clergy and Christian people; for the depression and extinction of the enemies of the Christian name,—to decree and declare that the sacred and general council of Trent do begin, and hath begun?

They answered: It pleaseth us.

DECREE CONCERNING THE EDITION, AND THE USE, OF THE SACRED BOOKS

Moreover, the same sacred and holy Synod, —considering that no small utility may accrue to the Church of God, if it be made known which out of all the Latin editions, now in circulation, of the sacred books, is to be held as authentic,—ordains and declares, that the said old and vulgate edition, which, by the lengthened usage of so many ages, has been approved of in the Church, be, in public lectures, disputations, sermons and expositions, held as authentic; and that no one is to dare, or presume to reject it under any pretext whatever.

Furthermore, in order to restrain petulant spirits, It decrees, that no one, relying on his own skill, shall,—in matters of faith, and of morals pertaining to the edification of Christian doctrine,—wrestling the sacred Scripture to his own senses, presume to interpret the said sacred Scripture contrary to that sense which holy mother Church,—whose it is to judge of the true sense and interpretation of the holy Scriptures,—hath held and doth hold; or even contrary to the unanimous consent of the Fathers; even though such interpretations were

As translated by J. Waterworth in *The Canons and Decrees of the Sacred and Œcumenical Council of Trent. . . .* London, 1848, 12; 19–23; 39–40; 54–55; 78; 82–84; 116–117; 158–159; 162–163; 173–174; 233–235; 270–271; 277–278.

never (intended) to be at any time published. Contraveners shall be made known by their Ordinaries, and be punished with the penalties by law established.

DECREE CONCERNING ORIGINAL SIN

That our Catholic *faith, without which it is impossible to please God,* may, errors being purged away, continue in its own perfect and spotless integrity, and that the Christian people may not *be carried about with every wind of doctrine;* whereas that old serpent, the perpetual enemy of mankind, amongst the very many evils with which the Church of God is in these our times troubled, has also stirred up not only new, but even old, dissensions touching original sin, and the remedy thereof; the sacred and holy, oecumenical and general Synod of Trent,—lawfully assembled in the Holy Ghost, the three same legates of the Apostolic See presiding therein,—wishing now to come to the reclaiming of the erring, and the confirming of the wavering,—following the testimonies of the sacred Scriptures, of the holy Fathers, of the most approved councils, and the judgment and consent of the Church itself, ordains, confesses, and declares these things touching the said original sin:

1. If any one does not confess that the first man, Adam, when he had transgressed the commandment of God in Paradise, immediately lost the holiness and justice wherein he had been constituted; and that he incurred, through the offence of that prevarication, the wrath and indignation of God, and consequently death, with which God had previously threatened him, and, together with death, captivity under his power who thenceforth *had the empire of death, that is to say, the devil,* and that the entire Adam, through that offence of prevarication, was changed, in body and soul, for the worse; let him be anathema.

2. If any one asserts, that the prevarication of Adam injured himself alone, and not his posterity; and that the holiness and justice, received of God, which he lost, he lost for himself alone, and not for us also; or that he, being defiled by the sin of disobedience, has only transfused death, and pains of the body, into the whole human race, but not sin also, which is the death of the soul; let him be anathema: —whereas he contradicts the apostle who says: *By one man sin entered into the world, and by sin death, and so death passed upon all men, in whom all have sinned.*

3. If any one asserts, that this sin of Adam, —which in its origin is one, and being transfused into all by propagation, not by imitation, is in each one as his own,—is taken away either by the powers of human nature, or by any other remedy than the merit of the *one mediator, our Lord Jesus Christ, who hath reconciled us to God in his own blood, made unto us justice, sanctification, and redemption;* or if he denies that the said merit of Jesus Christ is applied, both to adults and to infants, by the sacrament of baptism rightly administered in the form of the Church; let him be anathema: *For there is no other name under heaven given to men, whereby we must be saved.* Whence that voice: *Behold the lamb of God, behold him who taketh away the sins of the world;* and that other: *As many as have been baptized, have put on Christ.*

DECREE ON JUSTIFICATION

. . . No one, moreover, so long as he is in this mortal life, ought so far to presume as regards the secret mystery of divine predestination, as to determine for certain that he is assuredly in the number of the predestinate; as if it were true, that he that is justified, either cannot sin any more, or, if he do sin, that he ought to promise himself an assured repentance; for except by special revelation, it cannot be known whom God hath chosen unto Himself. . . .

DECREE ON THE SACRAMENTS IN GENERAL

Canon I.—If any one saith, that the sacraments of the New Law were not all instituted by Jesus Christ, our Lord; or, that they are more, or less, than seven, to wit, Baptism, Confirmation, the Eucharist, Penance, Extreme Unction, Order, and Matrimony; or even that any one of these seven is not truly and properly a sacrament; let him be anathema.

Canon IV.—If any one saith, that the sacraments of the New Law are not necessary unto salvation, but superfluous; and that, without them, or without the desire thereof, men obtain of God, through faith alone, the grace of justification;—though all (the sacraments) are not indeed necessary for every individual; let him be anathema.

Canon V.—If any one saith, that these sacraments were instituted for the sake of nourishing faith alone; let him be anathema.

Canon VI.—If any one saith, that the sacraments of the New Law do not contain the grace which they signify; or, that they do not confer that grace on those who do not place an obstacle thereunto; as though they were merely outward signs of grace or justice received through faith, and certain marks of the Christian profession, whereby believers are distinguished amongst men from unbelievers; let him be anathema.

Canon VII.—If any one saith, that grace, as far as God's part is concerned, is not given through the said sacraments, always, and to all men, even though they receive them rightly, but (only) sometimes, and to some persons; let him be anathema.

Canon VIII.—If any one saith, that by the said sacraments of the New Law grace is not conferred through the act performed, but that faith alone in the divine promise suffices for the otbaining of grace; let him be anathema.

Canon IX.—If any one saith, that, in the three sacraments, Baptism, to wit, Confirmation, and Order, there is not imprinted in the soul a character, that is, a certain spiritual and indelible sign, on account of which they cannot be repeated; let him be anathema.

Canon X.—If any one saith, that all Christians have power to administer the word, and all the sacraments; let him be anathema.

Canon XI.—If any one saith, that, in ministers, when they effect, and confer the sacraments, there is not required the intention at least of doing what the Church does; let him be anathema.

Canon XII.—If any one saith, that a minister, being in mortal sin,—if so be that he observe all the essentials which belong to the effecting, or conferring of, the sacrament,—neither effects, nor confers the sacrament; let him be anathema. . . .

DECREE CONCERNING THE MOST HOLY SACRAMENT OF THE EUCHARIST

. . . And because that Christ, our Redeemer, declared that which He offered under the species of bread to be truly His own body, therefore has it ever been a firm belief in the Church of God, and this holy Synod doth now declare it anew, that, by the consecration of the bread and of the wine, a conversion is made of the whole substance of the bread into the substance of the body of Christ our Lord, and of the whole substance of the wine into the substance of His blood; which conversion is, by the holy Catholic Church, suitably and properly called Transubstantiation.

ON THE MOST HOLY SACRAMENT OF THE EUCHARIST

Canon I.—If any one denieth, that, in the sacrament of the most holy Eucharist, are contained truly, really, and substantially, the body and blood together with the soul and divinity of our Lord Jesus Christ, and consequently the whole Christ; but saith that He is only therein as in a sign, or in figure, or virtue; let him be anathema.

Canon II.—If any one saith, that, in the sacred and holy sacrament of the Eucharist, the substance of the bread and wine remains conjointly with the body and blood of our Lord Jesus Christ, and denieth that wonderful and singular conversion of the whole substance of the bread into the Body, and of the whole substance of the wine into the Blood—the species only of the bread and wine remaining—which conversion indeed the Catholic Church most aptly calls Transubstantiation; let him be anathema.

Canon III.—If any one denieth, that, in the venerable sacrament of the Eucharist, the whole Christ is contained under each species, and under every part of each species, when separated; let him be anathema.

Canon IV.—If any one saith, that, after the consecration is completed, the body and blood of our Lord Jesus Christ are not in the admirable sacrament of the Eucharist, but (are there) only during the use, whilst it is being taken, and not either before or after; and that, in the hosts, or consecrated particles, which are reserved or which remain after communion, the true Body of the Lord remaineth not; let him be anathema.

Canon V.—If any one saith, either that the principal fruit of the most holy Eucharist is the remission of sins, or, that other effects do not result therefrom; let him be anathema.

Canon VI.—If any one saith, that, in the holy sacrament of the Eucharist, Christ, the only-begotten Son of God, is not to be adored with the worship, even external of latria; and is, consequently, neither to be venerated with a special festive solemnity, nor to be solemnly borne about in processions, according to the laudable and universal rite and custom of holy church; or, is not to be proposed publicly to the people to be adored, and that the adorers thereof are idolaters; let him be anathema.

Canon VII.—If any one saith, that it is not lawful for the sacred Eucharist to be reserved in the *sacrarium*, but that, immediately after consecration, it must necessarily be distributed amongst those present; or, that it is not lawful that it be carried with honour to the sick; let him be anathema.

Canon VIII.—If any one saith, that Christ, given in the Eucharist, is eaten spiritually only, and not also sacramentally and really; let him be anathema.

Canon IX.—If any one denieth, that all and each of Christ's faithful of both sexes are bound, when they have attained to years of discretion, to communicate every year, at least at Easter, in accordance with the precept of holy Mother Church; let him be anathema.

Canon X.—If any one saith, that it is not lawful for the celebrating priest to communicate himself; let him be anathema.

Canon XI.—If any one saith, that faith alone is a sufficient preparation for receiving the sacrament of the most holy Eucharist; let him be anathema. And for fear lest so great a sacrament may be received unworthily, and so unto death and condemnation, this holy Synod ordains and declares, that sacramental confession, when a confessor may be had, is of necessity to be made beforehand, by those whose conscience is burthened with mortal sin, how contrite even soever they may think themselves. But if any one shall presume to teach, preach,

or obstinately to assert, or even in public disputation to defend the contrary, he shall be thereupon excommunicated.

DECREE ON REFORMATION

. . . And forasmuch as, though the habit does not make the monk, it is nevertheless needful that clerics always wear a dress suitable to their proper order, that by the decency of their outward apparel they may show forth the inward correctness of their morals; but to such a pitch, in these days, have the contempt of religion and the rashness of some grown, as that, making but little account of their own dignity, and of the clerical honour, they even wear in public the dress of laymen—setting their feet in different paths, one of God, the other of the flesh;—for this cause, all ecclesiastical persons, howsoever exempted, who are either in sacred orders or in possession of any manner of dignities, personates, or other offices, or benefices ecclesiastical; if, after having been admonished by their own bishop, even by a public edict, they shall not wear a becoming clerical dress, suitable to their order and dignity, and in conformity with the ordinance and mandate of the said bishop, they may, and ought to be, compelled thereunto, by suspension from their orders, office, benefice, and from the fruits, revenues, and proceeds of the said benefices; and also, if, after having been once rebuked, they offend again herein (they are to be coerced) even by deprivation of the said offices and benefices. . . .

Whereas too, *he who has killed his neighbour on set purpose and by lying in wait for him, is to be taken away from the altar,* because he has voluntarily committed a homicide; even though that crime have neither been proved by ordinary process of law, nor be otherwise public, but is secret, such an one can never be promoted to sacred orders; nor shall it be lawful to confer upon him any ecclesiastical benefices, even though they have no cure of souls; but he shall be for ever excluded from every ecclesiastical order, benefice, and office. . . .

ON THE SACRIFICE OF THE MASS

. . . Canon I.—If any one saith, that in the mass a true and proper sacrifice is not offered to God; or, that to be offered is nothing else but that Christ is given us to eat; let him be anathema.

Canon II.—If any one saith, that by those words, *Do this for the commemoration of me, . . .* Christ did not institute the apostles priests; or, did not ordain that they, and other priests should offer His own body and blood; let him be anathema.

Canon III.—If any one saith, that the sacrifice of the mass is only a sacrifice of praise and of thanksgiving; or, that it is a bare commemoration of the sacrifice consummated on the cross, but not a propitiatory sacrifice; or, that it profits him only who receives; and that it ought not to be offered for the living and the dead for sins, pains, satisfactions, and other necessities; let him be anathema.

DECREE ON REFORMATION

. . . There is nothing that continually *instructs others unto piety,* and the service of God, more than the life and example of those who have dedicated themselves to the divine ministry. For as they are seen to be raised to a higher position, above the things of this world, others fix their eyes upon them as upon a mirror, and derive from them what they are to imitate. Wherefore clerics called to have the Lord for their portion, ought by all means so to regulate their whole life and conversation, as that in their dress, comportment, gait, discourse, and all things else, nothing appear but what is grave, regulated, and replete with religiousness; avoiding even slight faults, which in them would be most grievous; that so their actions may impress all with veneration. Whereas, therefore, the more useful and decorous these things are for the Church of God, the more carefully also are they to be attended to; the holy Synod ordains, that those things which have been heretofore copiously and wholesomely enacted by sovereign pontiffs and sacred councils,—relative to the life, propriety of conduct, dress, and learning of clerics, and also touching the luxuriousness, feastings, dances, gambling, sports, and all sorts of crime whatever, as also the secular employments, to be by them shunned,—the same shall be henceforth observed, under the same penalties, or

greater, to be imposed at the discretion of the Ordinary; nor shall any appeal suspend the execution hereof, as relating to the correction of manners. But if anything of the above shall be found to have fallen into desuetude, they shall make it their care that it be brought again into use as soon as possible, and be accurately observed by all; any customs to the contrary notwithstanding; lest they themselves may have, God being the avenger, to pay the penalty deserved by their neglect of the correction of those subject to them. . . .

ON THE SACRAMENT OF ORDER

Canon I.—If any one saith, that there is not in the New Testament a visible and external priesthood; or that there is not any power of consecrating and offering the true body and blood of the Lord, and of forgiving and retaining sins; but only an office and bare ministry of preaching the Gospel; or, that those who do not preach are not priests at all; let him be anathema.

Canon II.—If any one saith, that, besides the priesthood, there are not in the Catholic Church other orders, both greater and minor, by which, as by certain steps, advance is made unto the priesthood; let him be anathema.

Canon III.—If any one saith, that order, or sacred ordination, is not truly and properly a sacrament instituted by Christ the Lord; or, that it is a kind of human figment devised by men unskilled in ecclesiastical matters; or, that it is only a kind of rite for choosing ministers of the word of God and of the sacraments; let him be anathema.

Canon IV.—If any one saith, that, by sacred ordination, the Holy Ghost is not given; and that vainly therefore do the bishops say, *Receive ye the Holy Ghost;* or, that a character is not imprinted by that ordination; or, that he who has once been a priest, can again become a layman; let him be anathema.

Canon V.—If any one saith, that the sacred unction which the Church uses in holy ordination, is not only not required, but is to be despised and is pernicious, as likewise are the other ceremonies of Order; let him be anathema.

Canon VI.—If any one saith, that, in the

Catholic Church there is not a hierarchy by divine ordination instituted, consisting of bishops, priests, and ministers; let him be anathema.

Canon VII.—If any one saith, that bishops are not superior to priests; or, that they have not the power of confirming and ordaining; or, that the power which they possess is common to them and to priests; or, that orders, conferred by them, without the consent, or vocation of the people, or of the secular power, are invalid; or, that those who have neither been rightly ordained, nor sent, by ecclesiastical and canonical power, but come from elsewhere, are lawful ministers of the word and of the sacraments; let him be anathema.

Canon VIII.—If any one saith, that the bishops, who are assumed by authority of the Roman Pontiff, are not legitimate and true bishops, but are a human figment; let him be anathema.

ON THE SACRAMENT OF MATRIMONY

Canon IX.—If any one saith, that clerics constituted in sacred orders, or Regulars, who have solemnly professed chastity, are able to contract marriage, and that being contracted it is valid, notwithstanding the ecclesiastical law, or vow; and that the contrary is nothing else than to condemn marriage; and, that all who do not feel that they have the gift of chastity, even though they have made a vow thereof, may contract marriage; let him be anathema: seeing that God refuses not that gift to those who ask for it rightly, neither does *He suffer us to be tempted above that which we are able.*

ON THE INVOCATION, VENERATION, AND RELICS, OF SAINTS, AND ON SACRED IMAGES

The holy Synod enjoins on all bishops, and others who sustain the office and charge of teaching, that, agreeably to the usage of the Catholic and Apostolic Church, received from the primitive times of the Christian religion, and agreeably to the consent of the holy Fathers, and to the decrees of sacred Councils, they especially instruct the faithful diligently concerning the intercession and invocation of saints; the honour (paid) to relics; and the legitimate use of images: teaching them, that the saints, who reign together with Christ, offer up their own prayers to God for men; that it is good and useful suppliantly to invoke them, and to have recourse to their prayers, aid, (and) help for obtaining benefits from God, through His Son, Jesus Christ our Lord, who is our alone Redeemer and Saviour; but that they think impiously, who deny that the saints, who enjoy eternal happiness in heaven, are to be invocated; or who assert either that they do not pray for men; or, that the invocation of them to pray for each of us even in particular, is idolatry; or, that it is repugnant to the word of God; and is opposed to the honour of the *one mediator of God and men, Christ Jesus;* or, that it is foolish to supplicate, vocally, or mentally, those who reign in heaven. Also, that the holy bodies of holy martyrs, and of others now living with Christ,—which bodies were the living members of Christ, and *the temple of the Holy Ghost,* and which are by Him to be raised unto eternal life, and to be glorified, —are to be venerated by the faithful; through which (bodies) many benefits are bestowed by God on men; so that they who affirm that veneration and honour are not due to the relics of saints; or, that these, and other sacred monuments, are uselessly honoured by the faithful; and that the places dedicated to the memories of the saints are in vain visited with the view of obtaining their aid; are wholly to be condemned, as the Church has already long since condemned, and now also condemns them.

Moreover, that the images of Christ, of the Virgin Mother of God, and of the other saints, are to be had and retained particularly in temples, and that due honour and veneration are to be given them; not that any divinity, or virtue, is believed to be in them, on account of which they are to be worshipped; or that anything is to be asked of them; or, that trust is to be reposed in images, as was of old done by the Gentiles who placed their hope in idols; but because the honour which is shown them is referred to the prototypes which those images represent; in such wise that by the images which we kiss, and before which we uncover the head, and prostrate ourselves, we adore Christ; and we venerate the saints, whose similitude they bear: as, by the decrees of Councils, and especially of the second Synod of Nicaea, has been defined against the opponents of images. . . .

ON REFORMATION

. . . How shameful a thing, and how unworthy it is of the name of clerics who have devoted themselves to the service of God, to live in the filth of impurity, and unclean bondage, the thing itself doth testify, in the common scandal of all the faithful, and the extreme disgrace entailed on the clerical order. To the end, therefore, that the ministers of the Church may be recalled to that continency and integrity of life which becomes them; and that the people may hence learn to reverence them the more, that they know them to be more pure of life: the holy Synod forbids all clerics whatsoever to dare to keep concubines, or any other woman of whom any suspicion can exist, either in their own houses, or elsewhere, or to presume to have any intercourse with them: otherwise they shall be punished with the penalties imposed by the sacred canons, or by the statutes of the (several) churches. But if, after being admonished by their superiors, they shall not abstain from these women, they shall be *ipso facto* deprived of the third part of the fruits, rents, and proceeds of all their benefices whatsoever, and pensions; which third part shall be applied to the fabric of the church, or to some other pious place, at the discretion of the bishop. If, however, persisting in the same crime, with the same or some other woman, they shall not even yet have obeyed upon a second admonition, not only shall they thereupon forfeit all the fruits and proceeds of their benefices and pensions, which shall be applied to the places aforesaid, but they shall also be suspended from the administration of the benefices themselves, for as long a period as shall seem fit to the Ordinary, even as the delegate of the Apostolic See. And if, having been thus suspended, they nevertheless shall not put away those women, or, even if they shall have intercourse with them, then shall they be for ever deprived of their ecclesiastical benefices,

portions, offices, and pensions of whatsoever kind, and be rendered thenceforth incapable and unworthy of any manner of honours, dignities, benefices and offices, until, after a manifest amendment of life, it shall seem good to their superiors, for a cause, to grant them a dispensation. But if, after having once put them away, they shall have dared to renew the interrupted connexion, or to take to themselves other scandalous women of this sort, they shall, in addition to the penalties aforesaid, be smitten with the sword of excommunication. Nor shall any appeal, or exemption, hinder or suspend the execution of the aforesaid; and the cognizance of all the matters above-named shall not belong to archdeacons, or deans, or other inferiors, but to the bishops themselves, who may proceed without the noise and the formalities of justice, and by the sole investigation of the truth of the fact. . . .

DECREE CONCERNING INDULGENCES

Whereas the power of conferring indulgences was granted by Christ to the Church; and she has, even in the most ancient times, used the said power, delivered unto her of God; the sacred holy Synod teaches, and enjoins, that the use of Indulgences, for the Christian people most salutary, and approved of by the authority of sacred Councils, is to be retained in the Church; and It condemns with anathema those who either assert, that they are useless; or who deny that there is in the Church the power of granting them. In granting them, however, It desires that, in accordance with the ancient and approved custom in the Church, moderation be observed; lest, by excessive facility, ecclesiastical discipline be enervated. And being desirous that the abuses which have crept therein, and by occasion of which this honourable name of Indulgences is blasphemed by heretics, be amended and corrected, It ordains generally by this decree, that all evil gains for the obtaining thereof,— whence a most prolific cause of abuses amongst the Christian people has been derived,—be wholly abolished. But as regards the other abuses. . . . [they should be reported and referred to Rome for action.]

Civilization in the Seventeenth and Eighteenth Centuries

By 1600, overseas economic and colonial expansion had given new wealth to the monarchs of Europe, and they were finding it increasingly possible to establish their independence from both the feudal nobility and the Christian hierarchy. As the power of the sovereigns and their states grew, political theorists wrote of new doctrines to justify their absolutism. When this control of authority was in turn challenged by the new mercantile classes, produced by the expansion of trade, other writers sought to justify parliamentary and even democratic control of the state. Culturally, these centuries were marked by a variety of trends, some of them reflecting the influence of the dynastic court life, and others the remarkable advances made in the realm of science. The stimulus to investigation and observation of nature which had come with the Renaissance continued to influence men, and with the epoch-making work of Isaac Newton a new era of science was initiated. In the eighteenth century, reason and the study of nature penetrated into nearly all phases of culture resulting in the Age of the Enlightenment, of which Voltaire was a leading exponent.

Jacques Bénigne Bossuet

Jacques Bénigne Bossuet (1627–1704) was a Frenchman in the age of Louis XIV. He became a distinguished cleric and scholar and was selected in 1670 to be the tutor of the young dauphin, the only child of Louis XIV. While serving in this capacity, Bossuet wrote his Political Economy Drawn from Holy Scripture. He undertook this work as part of his task of instructing the royal heir. In it he set forth one of the best-known statements of the divine right of kings to govern. He drew his conclusions from Holy Scripture in an age when the leaders of the Protestant revolt were emphasizing the importance of the Bible in religious matters. Thus he hoped to strengthen both the political and the religious unity of France by meeting the Protestants on their own ground. Throughout the book Bossuet sought to rationalize the absolutism of Louis XIV. In reading the translation from this work note (1) the sources to which Bossuet referred his young charge, (2) the characteristics of royal authority, (3) the relationship between monarchs and God, (4) the origins of kingship, (5) the nature of the royal person, (6) the responsibility of subjects to their rulers, and (7) the limitations placed upon royal authority.

From: POLITICAL ECONOMY DRAWN FROM HOLY SCRIPTURE

Monseigneur le Dauphin: God is the king of kings; it belongs to Him to instruct and direct them as His ministers. Heed then, Monseigneur, the lessons which He gives them in his Scriptures, and learn from Him the rules and the examples on which they ought to form their conduct.

In addition to the other advantages of the Scriptures, they have also this, that they trace the history of the world from its beginnings and reveal to us by this means, better than all other histories, the basic principles which have formed empires. No history better reveals what is good and what is evil in the human heart, what sustains and what overthrows kingdoms, what religion can do to establish them, what impiety can do toward destroying them. . . .

THIRD BOOK: THE NATURE OF ROYAL AUTHORITY

First Article: The essential characteristics. SINGLE PROPOSITION: There are four essential characteristics or qualities to royal authority: (1) royal authority is sacred; (2) it is paternal; (3) it is absolute; (4) it is subject to reason.

Second Article: Royal authority is sacred. FIRST PROPOSITION: God established kings as His ministers, and reigns through them over the peoples.—We have already seen that all power comes from God. The prince, adds Saint Paul, "is a minister of God to thee for good. But if thou do that which is evil, be afraid; for he beareth not the sword in vain; for he is a minister of God, an avenger for wrath to him that doeth evil."

The princes act therefore as ministers of God and as His lieutenants on earth. It is by them that He exercises His sway. "And now ye think to withstand the kingdom of Jehovah in the hand of the sons of David?"

For such a reason the royal throne is not the throne of a man, but the throne of God Himself. "God hath chosen Solomon my son to sit upon the throne of the kingdom of Jehovah over Israel." And further, "Then Solomon sat on the throne of Jehovah as king."

And in order that no one should think this

Reprinted from History 11, *History of Western Civilization, A Syllabus,* Stanford University Press, Stanford University, 1940, 34–35, with the permission of the author and of the publishers, Stanford University Press.

peculiar to the Israelites to have kings established by God, here is what the Book of Ecclesiastes says: "God gives to each people its governor; and Israel is manifestly reserved to Him." He therefore governs all peoples and gives them all their kings, although He governs Israel in a more special and declared manner

SECOND PROPOSITION: The person of kings is sacred.—It follows from all this that the person of kings is sacred, and that any attack on them is a sacrilege. God causes them to be anointed by his prophets with a sacred ointment, just as he causes the pontiffs and his altars to be anointed.

But even without the external application of this ointment, they are sacred by their charge, as being representatives of the divine majesty, deputed by His providence for the execution of His designs. "Thus saith Jehovah to his anointed, to Cyrus, whose right hand I have holden, to subdue nations before him."

The title of Christ is given to kings; one sees them everywhere called christs, or the anointed of the Lord. Under this venerable name, even the prophets revered them, and looked upon them as associated with the sovereign sway of God, for whom they exercise authority over the people. . . .

One must guard kings as sacred things; and he who neglects to guard them is worthy of death. "As Jehovah liveth," said David to the captains of Saul, "ye are worthy to die, because ye have not kept watch over your Lord, Jehovah's anointed.". . .

THIRD PROPOSITION: One should obey the prince on grounds of religion and of conscience. Saint Paul, after having said that the prince is the minister of God, concluded thus: "Wherefore ye must needs be in subjection, not only because of the wrath, but also for conscience's sake."

That is why it is necessary "to be obedient unto them that according to the flesh are your masters, with fear and trembling, in singleness of your heart, as unto Christ; not in the way of eyeservice, as men-pleasers; but as servants of Christ, doing the will of God from the heart.". . .

That is why Saint Peter said, "Be subject to every ordinance of man for the Lord's sake: whether to the king, as supreme; or unto governors, as sent by him for vengeance on evildoers and for praise to them that do well.". . .

FOURTH BOOK: FURTHER CONCERNING THE CHARACTER OF ROYALTY

First Article: Royal authority is absolute. FIRST PROPOSITION: The prince owes an explanation to no one for what he orders. "Keep the king's command, and that in regard of the oath of God. Be not hasty to go out of his presence; persist not in an evil thing: for he doeth whatsoever pleaseth him. For the king's word hath power; and who may say unto him, What doest thou? Whoso keepeth the commandment shall know no evil thing."

SECOND PROPOSITION: When the prince has judged, there is no other judgment—Sovereign judgments are attributed to God himself. When Jehosaphat established judges to judge the people he said, "Consider what ye do: for ye judge not for man, but for Jehovah: and he is with you in the judgment."

It is necessary to obey princes as justice itself, without which there is neither order nor an end to affairs. They are gods [that is, princes and rulers are gods] and participate in some manner in the divine independence. "I said, ye are gods, and all of you sons of the Most High. . . ."

Thomas Hobbes

Thomas Hobbes (1588–1679) was one of the earliest political philosophers to write in support of the modern sovereign state. He lived most of his life in an England at war, either foreign or civil, and inevitably he came to long for the peace and security of a strong government. To him absolute monarchy seemed to offer the best assurance of a stable society. He also had a deep interest in mathematics and its application to the forces of nature, an interest which he developed while traveling on the continent where he came into contact with the theories of Galileo and Descartes. Following the execution of Charles I in 1649, advocacy of absolute monarchy needed a stronger support than an appeal to divine right. The natural order and natural law, soon to be used with great effectiveness by Newton and others, offered possibilities to Hobbes and other writers to whom divine right appeared as a shaky and faltering buttress. In The Leviathan (1651) Hobbes brought together his theories of government and his study of natural law and formulated a justification for absolutism. His basic thesis in this work was the assumption that the first law of man's nature was to seek peace. In the following selections from The Leviathan note (1) the discussion of human nature and its theoretical results, (2) the forces influencing mankind to seek peace, (3) the principal cause for the formation of commonwealths, (4) the method by which the commonwealth was contracted, (5) the responsibility of the contracting groups toward the sovereignty thereby established, (6) the authority and responsibility of the sovereignty, (7) the three types of sovereignty that may be established over the commonwealth, and (8) the advantages listed for absolute monarchy.

From: THE LEVIATHAN

OF THE NATURAL CONDITION OF MANKIND AS CONCERNING THEIR FELICITY AND MISERY

Nature hath made men so equal, in the faculties of the body and mind; as that though there be found one man sometimes manifestly stronger in body, or of quicker mind than another, yet when all is reckoned together, the difference between man and man, is not so considerable, as that one man can thereupon claim to himself any benefit, to which another may not pretend, as well as he. For as to the strength of body, the weakest has strength enough to kill the strongest, either by secret machination, or by confederacy with others, that are in the same danger with himself.

And as to the faculties of the mind, setting aside the arts grounded upon words, and especially that skill of proceeding upon general and infallible rules, called science; which very few have, and but in few things; as being not a native faculty, born with us; nor attained, as prudence, while we look after somewhat else, I find yet a greater equality amongst men than that of strength. For prudence is but experience; which equal time, equally bestows on all men, in those things they equally apply themselves unto. That which may perhaps make such equality incredible, is but a vain conceit of one's own wisdom, which almost all men think they have in a greater degree than the vulgar; that is, than all men but themselves, and a few others, whom by fame or for concurring with themselves, they approve. For such is the nature of men, that howsoever they may acknowledge many others to be more witty, or more eloquent, or more learned; yet they will hardly believe there be many so wise as themselves; for they see their own wit at

Thomas Hobbes, *The Leviathan, or the Matter, Form and Power of a Commonwealth, Ecclesiastical and Civil,* London, n.d., 63–65; 82–88.

hand, and other men's at a distance. But this proveth rather that men are in that point equal, than unequal. For there is not ordinarily a greater sign of the equal distribution of anything, than that every man is contented with his share.

From this equality of ability, ariseth equality of hope in the attaining of our ends. And therefore if any two men desire the same thing, which nevertheless they cannot both enjoy, they become enemies; and in the way to their end, which is principally their own conservation, and sometimes their delectation only, endeavour to destroy or subdue one another. And from hence it comes to pass, that where an invader hath no more to fear than another man's single power; if one plant, sow, build, or possess a convenient seat, others may probably be expected to come prepared with forces united, to dispossess and deprive him, not only of the fruit of his labour, but also of his life or liberty. And the invader again is in the like danger of another.

And from this diffidence of one another, there is no way for any man to secure himself, so reasonable, as anticipation; that is, by force, or wiles, to master the persons of all men he can, so long, till he see no other power great enough to endanger him: and this is no more than his own conservation requireth, and is generally allowed. Also because there be some, that taking pleasure in contemplating their own power in the acts of conquest, which they pursue farther than their security requires; if others, that otherwise would be glad to be at ease within modest bounds, should not by invasion increase their power, they would not be able, long time, by standing only on their defence, to subsist. And by consequence, such augmentation of dominion over men being necessary to a man's conservation, it ought to be allowed him.

Again, men have no pleasure, but on the contrary a great deal of grief, in keeping company, where there is no power able to overawe them all. For every man looketh that his companion should value him, at the same rate he sets upon himself: and upon all signs of contempt, or undervaluing, naturally endeavours, as far as he dares (which amongst them that have no common power to keep them in quiet,

is far enough to make them destroy each other), to extort a greater value from his contemners, by damage; and from others, by the example.

So that in the nature of man, we find three principal causes of quarrel. First, competition; secondly, diffidence; thirdly, glory.

The first, maketh men invade for gain; the second, for safety; and the third, for reputation. The first use violence, to make themselves masters of other men's persons, wives, children, and cattle; the second, to defend them; the third, for trifles, as a word, a smile, a different opinion, and any other sign of undervalue, either direct in their persons, or by reflection in their kindred, their friends, their nation, their profession, or their name.

Hereby it is manifest, that during the time men live without a common power to keep them all in awe, they are in that condition which is called war; and such a war, as is of every man, against every man. For "war" consisteth not in battle only, or the act of fighting; but in a tract of time, wherein the will to contend by battle is sufficiently known: and therefore the notion of "time" is to be considered in the nature of war, as it is in the nature of weather. For as the nature of foul weather lieth not in a shower or two of rain, but in an inclination thereto of many days together; so the nature of war consisteth not in actual fighting, but in the known disposition thereto during all the time there is no assurance to the contrary. All other time is "peace."

Whatsoever therefore is consequent to a time of war, where every man is enemy to every man, the same is consequent to the time wherein men live without other security than what their own strength and their own invention shall furnish them withal. In such condition there is no place for industry, because the fruit thereof is uncertain, and consequently no culture of the earth; no navigation, nor use of the commodities that may be imported by sea; no commodious building; no instruments of moving and removing such things as require much force; no knowledge of the face of the earth; no account of time; no arts; no letters; no society; and, which is worst of all, continual fear and danger of violent death; and the life of man, solitary, poor, nasty, brutish, and short.

It may seem strange to some man, that has not well weighed these things, that Nature should thus dissociate, and render men apt to invade and destroy one another; and he may therefore, not trusting to this inference made from the passions, desire perhaps to have the same confirmed by experience. Let him therefore consider with himself, when taking a journey, he arms himself, and seeks to go well accompanied; when going to sleep, he locks his doors; when even in his house, he locks his chests; and this when he knows there be laws, and public officers, armed, to revenge all injuries shall be done him; what opinion he has of his fellow-subjects, when he rides armed; of his fellow-citizens, when he locks his doors; and of his children and servants, when he locks his chests. Does he not there as much accuse mankind by his actions as I do by my words? But neither of us accuse man's nature in it. The desires and other passions of man are in themselves no sin. No more are the actions that proceed from those passions, till they know a law that forbids them; which till laws be made they cannot know, nor can any law be made till they have agreed upon the person that shall make it.

It may peradventure be thought there was never such a time nor condition of war as this; and I believe it was never generally so, over all the world, but there are many places where they live so now. For the savage people in many places of America, except the government of small families, the concord whereof dependeth on natural lust, have no government at all, and live at this day in that brutish manner, as I said before. Howsoever, it may be perceived what manner of life there would be, where there were no common power to fear, by the manner of life which men that have formerly lived under a peaceful government, use to degenerate into a civil war.

But though there had never been any time, wherein particular men were in a condition of war one against another; yet in all times, kings, and persons of sovereign authority, because of their independency, are in continual jealousies, and in the state and posture of gladiators; having their weapons pointing, and their eyes fixed on one another; that is, their forts, garrisons, and guns upon the frontiers of their king-

doms; and continual spies upon their neighbours; which is a posture of war. But because they uphold thereby the industry of their subjects; there does not follow from it that misery which accompanies the liberty of particular men.

To this war of every man, against every man, this also is consequent; that nothing can be unjust. The notions of right and wrong, justice and injustice, have there no place. Where there is no common power, there is no law: where no law, no injustice. Force and fraud, are in war the two cardinal virtues. Justice and injustice are none of the faculties neither of the body nor mind. If they were, they might be in a man that were alone in the world, as well as his senses, and passions. They are qualities that relate to men in society, not in solitude. It is consequent also to the same condition, that there be no propriety, no dominion, no "mine" and "thine" distinct; but only that to be every man's, that he can get; and for so long, as he can keep it. And thus much for the ill condition, which man by mere nature is actually placed in; though with a possibility to come out of it, consisting partly in the passions, partly in his reason.

The passions that incline men to peace, are fear of death; desire of such things as are necessary to commodious living; and a hope by their industry to obtain them. And reason suggesteth convenient articles of peace, upon which men may be drawn to agreement. These articles are they which otherwise are called the Laws of Nature. . . .

OF THE CAUSES, AND DEFINITION OF A COMMONWEALTH

The final cause, end, or design of men, who naturally love liberty, and dominion over others, in the introduction of that restraint upon themselves, in which we see them live in commonwealths, is the foresight of their own preservation, and of a more contented life thereby; that is to say, of getting themselves out from that miserable condition of war, which is necessarily consequent, as hath been shown [above] . . . to the natural passions of men, when there is no visible power to keep them in awe, and tie them by fear of punishment to the performance of their covenants, and observation of those laws of Nature. . . .

For the laws of Nature, as "justice," "equity," "modesty," "mercy," and, in sum, "doing to others, as we would be done to," of themselves, without the terror of some power, to cause them to be observed, are contrary to our natural passions, that carry us to partiality, pride, revenge, and the like. And covenants, without the sword, are but words, and of no strength to secure a man at all. Therefore notwithstanding the laws of Nature, which every one hath then kept, when he has the will to keep them, when he can do it safely, if there be no power erected, or not great enough for our security; every man will, and may lawfully rely on his own strength and art, for caution against all other men. And in all places, where men have lived by small families, to rob and spoil one another, has been a trade, and so far from being reputed against the law of Nature, that the greater spoils they gained, the greater was their honour; and men observed no other laws therein, but the laws of honour; that is, to abstain from cruelty, leaving to men their lives, and instruments of husbandry. And as small families did then; so now do cities and kingdoms, which are but greater families, for their own security, enlarge their dominions, upon all pretences of danger, and fear of invasion, or assistance that may be given to invaders, and endeavour as much as they can, to subdue, or weaken their neighbours, by open force and secret arts, for want of other caution, justly; and are remembered for it in after ages with honour.

Nor is it the joining together of a small number of men, that gives them this security; because in small numbers, small additions on the one side or the other, make the advantage of strength so great, as is sufficient to carry the victory; and therefore gives encouragement to an invasion. The multitude sufficient to confide in for our security, is not determined by any certain number, but by comparison with the enemy we fear; and is then sufficient, when the odds of the enemy is not of so visible and conspicuous moment, to determine the event of war, as to move him to attempt.

And be there never so great a multitude; yet if their actions be directed according to their particular judgments and particular appetites, they can expect thereby no defence, nor protection, neither against a common enemy, nor against the injuries of one another. For being distracted in opinions concerning the best use and application of their strength, they do not help but hinder one another; and reduce their strength by mutual opposition to nothing: whereby they are easily, not only subdued by a very few that agree together; but also when there is no common enemy, they make war upon each other, for their particular interests. For if we could suppose a great multitude of men to consent in the observation of justice, and other laws of Nature, without a common power to keep them all in awe; we might as well suppose all mankind to do the same; and then there neither would be, nor need to be any civil government or commonwealth at all; because there would be peace without subjection.

Nor is it enough for the security, which men desire should last all the time of their life, that they be governed and directed by one judgment, for a limited time: as in one battle, or one war. For though they obtain a victory by their unanimous endeavour against a foreign enemy; yet afterwards, when either they have no common enemy, or he that by one part is held for an enemy, is by another part held for a friend, they must needs by the difference of their interests dissolve, and fall again into a war amongst themselves.

It is true that certain living creatures, as bees and ants, live sociably one with another, which are therefore by Aristotle numbered amongst political creatures; and yet have no other direction, than their particular judgments and appetites; nor speech, whereby one of them can signify to another, what he thinks expedient for the common benefit: and therefore some man may perhaps desire to know, why mankind cannot do the same. To which I answer,

First, that men are continually in competition for honour and dignity, which these creatures are not; and consequently amongst men there ariseth on that ground, envy and hatred, and finally war; but amongst these not so.

Secondly, that amongst these creatures, the common good differeth not from the private;

and being by nature inclined to their private, they procure thereby the common benefit. But man, whose joy consisteth in comparing himself with other men, can relish nothing but what is eminent.

Thirdly, that these creatures, having not, as man, the use of reason, do not see, nor think they see any fault, in the administration of their common business; whereas amongst men, there are very many that think themselves wiser, and abler to govern the public, better than the rest; and these strive to reform and innovate, one this way, another that way; and thereby bring it into distraction and civil war.

Fourthly, that these creatures, though they have some use of voice, in making known to one another their desires and other affections; yet they want that art of words, by which some men can represent to others that which is good in the likeness of evil; and evil in the likeness of good; and augment or diminish the apparent greatness of good and evil; discontenting men, and troubling their peace at their pleasure.

Fifthly, irrational creatures cannot distinguish between "injury" and "damage;" and therefore as long as they be at ease, they are not offended with their fellows: whereas man is then most troublesome, when he is most at ease; for then it is that he loves to show his wisdom, and control the actions of them that govern the commonwealth.

Lastly, the agreement of these creatures is natural; that of men is by covenant only, which is artificial: and therefore it is no wonder if there be somewhat else required, besides covenant, to make their agreement constant and lasting; which is a common power, to keep them in awe, and to direct their actions to the common benefit.

The only way to erect such a common power, as may be able to defend them from the invasion of foreigners, and the injuries of one another, and thereby to secure them in such sort, as that by their own industry, and by the fruits of the earth, they may nourish themselves and live contentedly, is, to confer all their power and strength upon one man, or upon one assembly of men, that may reduce all their wills, by plurality of voices, unto one will: which is as much as to say, to appoint one man, or assembly of men, to bear their person; and

every one to own, and acknowledge himself to be author of whatsoever he that so beareth their person, shall act, or cause to be acted, in those things which concern the common peace and safety; and therein to submit their wills, every one to his will, and their judgments, to his judgment. This is more than consent, or concord; it is a real unity of them all, in one and the same person, made by covenant of every man with every man, in such manner, as if every man should say to every man, "I authorize and give up my right of governing myself, to this man, or to this assembly of men, on this condition, that thou give up thy right to him, and authorize all his actions in like manner." This done, the multitude so united in one person is called a "commonwealth," in Latin *civitas*. This is the generation of that great "leviathan," or rather, to speak more reverently, of that "mortal god," to which we owe under the "immortal God," our peace and defence. For by this authority, given him by every particular man in the commonwealth, he hath the use of so much power and strength conferred on him, that by terror thereof, he is enabled to perform the wills of them all, to peace at home, and mutual aid against their enemies abroad. And in him consisteth the essence of the commonwealth; which, to define it, is "one person, of whose acts a great multitude, by mutual covenants one with another, have made themselves every one the author, to the end he may use the strength and means of them all, as he shall think expedient, for their peace and common defence."

And he that carrieth this person is called "sovereign," and said to have "sovereign power"; and every one besides, his "subject."

The attaining to this sovereign power is by two ways. One, by natural force; as when a man maketh his children to submit themselves, and their children, to his government, as being able to destroy them if they refuse; or by war subdueth his enemies to his will, giving them their lives on that condition. The other is, when men agree amongst themselves to submit to some man, or assembly of men, voluntarily, on confidence to be protected by him against all others. This latter may be called a political commonwealth, or commonwealth by "institution"; and the former, a commonwealth by "acquisition." And first, I shall speak of a commonwealth by institution.

OF THE RIGHTS OF SOVEREIGNS BY INSTITUTION

A "COMMONWEALTH" is said to be "instituted," when a "multitude" of men do agree, and "covenant, every one, with every one," that to whatsoever "man," or "assembly of men," shall be given by the major part, the "right" to "present" the person of them all, that is to say, to be their "representative"; every one, as well he that "voted for it," as he that "voted against it," shall "authorize" all the actions and judgments, of that man, or assembly of men, in the same manner, as if they were his own, to the end, to live peaceably amongst themselves, and be protected against other men.

From this institution of a commonwealth are derived all the "rights" and "faculties" of him, or them, on whom sovereign power is conferred by the consent of the people assembled.

First, because they covenant, it is to be understood, they are not obliged by former covenant to anything repugnant hereunto. And consequently they that have already instituted a commonwealth, being thereby bound by covenant, to own the actions and judgments of one, cannot lawfully make a new covenant, amongst themselves, to be obedient to any other, in anything whatsoever, without his permission. And therefore, they that are subjects to a monarch, cannot without his leave cast off monarchy, and return to the confusion of a disunited multitude; nor transfer their person from him that beareth it, to another man, or other assembly of men: for they are bound, every man to every man, to own, and be reputed author of all, that he that already is their sovereign, shall do, and judge fit to be done: so that one man dissenting, all the rest should break their covenant made to that man, which is injustice: and they have also every man given the sovereignty to him that beareth their person; and therefore if they depose him, they take from him that which is his own, and so again it is injustice. Besides, if he that attempteth to depose his sovereign, be killed, or punished by him for such attempt, he is author

of his own punishment, as being by the institution, author of all his sovereign shall do: and because it is injustice for a man to do anything for which he may be punished by his own authority, he is also upon that title unjust. And whereas some men have pretended for their disobedience to their sovereign, a new covenant, made not with men, but with God; this also is unjust: for there is no covenant with God but by mediation of somebody that representeth God's person; which none doth but God's lieutenant, who hath the sovereignty under God. But this pretence of covenant with God, is so evident a lie, even in the pretenders' own consciences, that it is not only an act of an unjust, but also of a vile and unmanly disposition.

Secondly, because the right of bearing the person of them all, is given to him they make sovereign, by covenant only of one to another, and not of him to any of them; there can happen no breach of covenant on the part of the sovereign: and consequently none of his subjects, by any pretence of forfeiture, can be freed from his subjection. That he which is made sovereign maketh no covenant with his subjects beforehand, is manifest; because either he must make it with the whole multitude, as one party to the covenant; or he must make a several covenant with every man. With the whole, as one party, it is impossible; because as yet they are not one person; and if he make so many several covenants as there be men, those covenants after he hath the sovereignty are void; because what act soever can be pretended by any one of them for breach thereof, is the act both of himself and of all the rest, because done in the person and by the right of every one of them in particular. Besides, if any one or more of them, pretend a breach of the covenant made by the sovereign at his institution; and others, or one other of his subjects, or himself alone, pretend there was no such breach, there is in this case no judge to decide the controversy; it returns therefore to the sword again; and every man recovereth the right of protecting himself by his own strength, contrary to the design they had in the institution. It is therefore in vain to grant sovereignty by way of precedent covenant. The opinion that any monarch receiveth his power by covenant, that is to say, on condition, proceedeth from want of understanding this easy truth, that covenants being but words and breath, have no force to oblige, contain, constrain, or protect any man, but what it has from the public sword; that is, from the united hands of that man, or assembly of men that hath the sovereignty, and whose actions are avouched by them all, and performed by the strength of them all, in him united. But when an assembly of men is made sovereign; then no man imagineth any such covenant to have passed in the institution; for no man is so dull as to say, for example, the people of Rome made a covenant with the Romans, to hold the sovereignty on such or such conditions; which not performed, the Romans might lawfully depose the Roman people. That men see not the reason to be alike in a monarchy, and in a popular government, proceedeth from the ambition of some, that are kinder to the government of an assembly, whereof they may hope to participate, than of monarchy, which they despair to enjoy.

Thirdly, because the major part hath by consenting voices declared a sovereign; he that dissented must now consent with the rest; that is, be contented to avow all the actions he shall do, or else justly be destroyed by the rest. For if he voluntarily entered into the congregation of them that were assembled, he sufficiently declared thereby his will, and therefore tacitly covenanted to stand to what the major part should ordain: and therefore if he refuse to stand thereto, or make protestation against any of their decrees, he does contrary to his covenant, and therefore unjustly. And whether he be of the congregation or not; and whether his consent be asked or not, he must either submit to their decrees, or be left in the condition of war he was in before; wherein he might without injustice be destroyed by any man whatsoever.

Fourthly, because every subject is by this institution author of all the actions and judgments of the sovereign instituted, it follows, that whatsoever he doth it can be no injury to any of his subjects, nor ought he to be by any of them accused of injustice. For he that doth anything by authority from another doth therein no injury to him by whose authority he acteth: but by this institution of a common-wealth every particular man is author of all the sovereign doth; and consequently, he that complaineth of injury from his sovereign complaineth of that whereof he himself is author, and therefore ought not to accuse any man but himself; no, nor himself of injury; because to do injury to one's self is impossible. It is true that they that have sovereign power may commit iniquity, but not injustice or injury in the proper signification.

Fifthly, and consequently to that which was said last, no man that hath sovereign power can justly be put to death, or otherwise in any manner by his subjects punished. For seeing every subject is author of the actions of his sovereign, he punisheth another for the actions committed by himself.

And because the end of this institution is the peace and defence of them all; and whosoever has right to the end has right to the means; it belongeth of right to whatsoever man or assembly that hath the sovereignty to be judge both of the means of peace and defence, and also of the hindrances and disturbances of the same, and to do whatsoever he shall think necessary to be done, both beforehand, for the preserving of peace and security, by prevention of discord at home and hostility from abroad; and, when peace and security are lost, for the recovery of the same. And therefore,

Sixthly, it is annexed to the sovereignty to be judge of what opinions and doctrines are averse and what conducing to peace; and consequently, on what occasions, how far, and what men are to be trusted withal, in speaking to multitudes of people, and who shall examine the doctrines of all books before they be published. For the actions of men proceed from their opinions, and in the well-governing of opinions consisteth the well-governing of men's actions, in order to their peace and concord. And though in matter of doctrine nothing ought to be regarded but the truth; yet this is not repugnant to regulating the same by peace. For doctrine repugnant to peace can be no more true than peace and concord can be against the law of Nature. It is true that in a commonwealth, where, by the negligence or unskilfulness of governors and teachers, false doctrines are by time generally received; the contrary truths may be generally offensive. Yet the most sudden and rough bursting in of a new truth that can be, does never break the peace, but only sometimes awakes the war. For those men that are so remissly governed, that they dare take up arms to defend or introduce an opinion, are still in war; and their condition not peace, but only a cessation of arms for fear of one another; and they live, as it were, in the precincts of battle continually. It belongeth therefore to him that hath the sovereign power to be judge, or constitute all judges of opinions and doctrines, as a thing necessary to peace, thereby to prevent discord and civil war.

Seventhly, is annexed to the sovereignty, the whole power of prescribing the rules, whereby every man may know what goods he may enjoy, and what actions he may do, without being molested by any of his fellow subjects; and this is it men call "propriety." For before constitution of sovereign power, as hath already been shown, all men had right to all things, which necessarily causeth war: and therefore this propriety, being necessary to peace, and depending on sovereign power, is the act of that power, in order to the public peace. These rules of propriety, or *meum* and *tuum,* and of "good," "evil," "lawful," and "unlawful" in the actions of subjects, are the civil laws; that is to say, the laws of each commonwealth in particular; though the name of civil law be now restrained to the ancient civil laws of the city of Rome, which being the head of a great part of the world, her laws at that time were in these parts the civil law.

Eighthly, is annexed to the sovereignty, the right of judicature; that is to say, of hearing and deciding all controversies, which may arise concerning law, either civil or natural, or concerning fact. For without the decision of controversies, there is no protection of one subject against the injuries of another; the laws concerning *meum* and *tuum* are in vain, and to every man remaineth, from the natural and necessary appetite of his own conservation, the right of protecting himself by his private strength, which is the condition of war, and contrary to the end for which every commonwealth is instituted.

Ninthly, is annexed to the sovereignty, the right of making war and peace with other nations and commonwealths; that is to say, of judging when it is for the public good, and how great forces are to be assembled, armed, and paid for that end; and to levy money upon the subjects to defray the expenses thereof. For the power by which the people are to be defended consisteth in their armies, and the strength of an army, in the union of their strength under one command, which command the sovereign instituted, therefore hath; because the command of the "militia," without other institution, maketh him that hath it sovereign. And therefore whosoever is made general of an army, he that hath the sovereign power is always generalissimo.

Tenthly, is annexed to the sovereignty, the choosing of all counsellors, ministers, magistrates, and officers, both in peace and war. For seeing the sovereign is charged with the end, which is the common peace and defence, he is understood to have power to use such means as he shall think most fit for his discharge.

Eleventhly, to the sovereign is committed the power of rewarding with riches or honour, and of punishing with corporal or pecuniary punishment, or with ignominy, every subject according to the law he hath formerly made; or if there be no law made, according as he shall judge most to conduce to the encouraging of men to serve the commonwealth, or deterring of them from doing disservice to the same.

Lastly, considering what value men are naturally apt to set upon themselves; what respect they look for from others; and how little they value other men; from whence continually arise amongst them, emulation, quarrels, factions, and at last war, to the destroying of one another, and diminution of their strength against a common enemy; it is necessary that there be laws of honour, and a public rate of the worth of such men as have deserved, or are able to deserve well of the commonwealth; and that there be force in the hands of some or other, to put those laws in execution. But it hath already been shown, that not only the whole "militia," or forces of the commonwealth; but also the judicature of all controversies, is annexed to the sovereignty. To the sovereign therefore it belongeth also to give titles of honour; and to appoint what order of place and dignity each man shall hold; and what signs of respect, in public or private meetings, they shall give to one another. . . .

OF THE SEVERAL KINDS OF COMMONWEALTH BY INSTITUTION, AND OF SUCCESSION TO THE SOVEREIGN POWER

The difference of commonwealths consisteth in the difference of the sovereign, or the person representative of all and every one of the multitude. And because the sovereignty is either in one man, or in an assembly of more than one; and into that assembly either every man hath right to enter, or not every one, but certain men distinguished from the rest; it is manifest, there can be but three kinds of commonwealth. For the representative must needs be one man, or more: and if more, then it is the assembly of all, or but of a part. When the representative is one man, then is the commonwealth a "monarchy": when an assembly of all that will come together, then it is a "democracy," or popular commonwealth: when an assembly of a part only, then it is called an "aristocracy." Other kind of commonwealth there can be none: for either one or more, or all, must have the sovereign power, which I have shown to be indivisible, entire.

There be other names of government in the histories and books of policy, as "tyranny," and "oligarchy": but they are not the names of other forms of government, but of the same forms misliked. For they that are discontented under "monarchy," call it "tyranny"; and they that are displeased with "aristocracy," call it "oligarchy": so also they which find themselves grieved under a "democracy," call it "anarchy," which signifies want of government; and yet I think no man believes that want of government is any new kind of government: nor by the same reason ought they to believe that the government is of one kind when they like it, and another when they dislike it, or are oppressed by the governors.

It is manifest, that men who are in absolute liberty may, if they please, give authority to one man to represent them every one; as well as give such authority to any assembly of men whatsoever; and consequently may subject themselves, if they think good, to a monarch as absolutely as to any other representative. Therefore, where there is already erected a sovereign power, there can be no other representative of the same people, but only to certain particular ends, by the sovereign limited. For that were to erect two sovereigns; and every man to have his person represented by two actors, that by opposing one another, must needs divide that power, which, if men will live in peace, is indivisible, and thereby reduce the multitude into the condition of war, contrary to the end for which all sovereignty is instituted. And therefore as it is absurd to think that a sovereign assembly, inviting the people of their dominion to send up their deputies, with power to make known their advice, or desires, should therefore hold such deputies rather than themselves, for the absolute representatives of the people: so it is absurd also to think the same in a monarchy. And I know not how this so manifest a truth should of late be so little observed; that in a monarchy, he that had the sovereignty from a descent of six hundred years, was alone called sovereign, had the title of Majesty from every one of his subjects, and was unquestionably taken by them for their king, was notwithstanding never considered as their representative; the name without contradiction passing for the title of those men, which at his command were sent up by the people to carry their petitions, and give him, if he permitted it, their advice. Which may serve as an admonition, for those that are the true and absolute representative of a people, to instruct men in the nature of that office, and to take heed how they admit of any other general representation upon any occasion whatsoever, if they mean to discharge the trust committed to them.

The difference between these three kinds of commonwealth, consisteth not in the difference of power; but in the difference of convenience, or aptitude to produce the peace and security of the people; for which end they were instituted. And to compare monarchy with the other two, we may observe; first, that whosoever beareth the person of the people, or is one of that assembly that bears it, beareth also his own natural person. And though he be careful in his politic person to procure the common interest; yet he is more or no less careful to procure the private good of himself, his family, kindred, and friends; and for the most part, if the public interest chance to cross the private, he prefers the private: for the passions of men are commonly more potent than their reason. From whence it follows, that where the public and private interest are most closely united, there is the public most advanced. Now in monarchy, the private interest is the same with the public. The riches, power, and honour of a monarch, arise only from the riches, strength, and reputation of his subjects. For no king can be rich, nor glorious, nor secure, whose subjects are either poor, or contemptible, or too weak through want or dissension, to maintain a war against their enemies: whereas in a democracy, or aristocracy, the public prosperity confers not so much to the private fortune of one that is corrupt, or ambitious, as doth many times a perfidious advice, a treacherous action, or a civil war.

Secondly, that a monarch receiveth counsel of whom, when, and where he pleaseth; and consequently may hear the opinion of men versed in the matter about which he deliberates, of what rank or quality soever, and as long before the time of action, and with as much secrecy, as he will. But when a sovereign assembly has need of counsel, none are admitted but such as have a right thereto from the beginning; which for the most part are of those who have been versed more in the acquisition of wealth than of knowledge; and are to give their advice in long discourses, which may and do commonly excite men to action, but not govern them in it. For the "understanding" is by the flame of the passions, never enlightened, but dazzled. Nor is there any place, or time, wherein an assembly can receive counsel with secrecy, because of their own multitude.

Thirdly, that the resolutions of a monarch, are subject to no other inconstancy, than that of human nature; but in assemblies, besides that of Nature, there ariseth an inconstancy from the number. For the absence of a few, that would have the resolution once taken, continue firm, which may happen by security, negligence, or private impediments, or the diligent appearance of a few of the contrary opinion, undoes to-day all that was concluded yesterday.

Fourthly, that a monarch cannot disagree with himself, out of envy or interest; but an assembly may; and that to such a height, as may produce a civil war.

Fifthly, that in monarchy there is this inconvenience; that any subject, by the power of one man, for the enriching of a favourite or flatterer, may be deprived of all he possesseth; which I confess is a great and inevitable inconvenience.

But the same may as well happen, where the sovereign power is an assembly: for their power is the same; and they are as subject to evil counsel, and to be seduced by orators, as a monarch by flatterers; and becoming one another's flatterers, serve one another's covetousness and ambition by turns. And whereas the favourites of monarchs are few, and they have none else to advance but their own kindred; the favourites of an assembly are many; and the kindred much more numerous than of any monarch. Besides there is no favourite of a monarch, which cannot as well succour his friends as hurt his enemies; but orators, that is to say, favourites of sovereign assemblies, though they have great power to hurt, have little to save. For to accuse, requires less eloquence, such is man's nature, than to excuse; and condemnation, than absolution more resembles justice. . . .

John Locke

The great English scholar, John Locke (1632–1704), was born less than 50 years after Hobbes, but during that time England had undergone a rapid political development. In 1689, by the so-called Glorious Revolution, the English destroyed the principle of royal absolutism and established parliamentary supremacy. In the Second Treatise of Government, which appeared in 1690, Locke used Hobbes' contract theory to justify this political upheaval, although Hobbes, in The Leviathan, had specifically condemned revolution. Locke stressed the necessity of limiting power as well as of distributing power among different branches of government. In reading the selection, note (1) Locke's description of the origins of the state, (2) the objects of government, (3) the forms of government, (4) the limits of government, (5) the principal obligation of government to its citizens, (6) his definition of tyranny, (7) his distinction between the dissolution of society and the dissolution of government, (8) his answer to the charge that he advocated frequent revolution, (9) the final umpire between the king and the legislature, (10) the method advocated for deciding ultimate disputes, and (11) when power might revert to individuals.

From: THE SECOND TREATISE ON GOVERNMENT

OF THE STATE OF NATURE

To understand political power aright, and derive it from its original, we must consider what estate all men are naturally in, and that is, a *state of perfect freedom* to order their actions, and dispose of their possessions and persons as they think fit, within the bounds of the law of nature, without asking leave or depending upon the will of any other man.

A *state* also *of equality*, wherein all the power and jurisdiction is reciprocal, no one having more than another, there being nothing more evident than that creatures of the same species and rank, promiscuously born to all the same advantages of nature, and the use of the same faculties, should also be equal one amongst another without subordination or subjection, unless the lord and master of them all should, by any manifest declaration of his will, set one above another, and confer on him, by an evident and clear appointment, an undoubted right to dominion and sovereignty. . . .

But though this be *a state of liberty*, yet *it is not a state of license;* though man in that state have an uncontrollable liberty to dispose of his person or possessions, yet he has not liberty to destroy himself, or so much as any creature in his possession, but where some nobler use than its bare preservation calls for it. The *state of nature* has a law of nature to govern it, which obliges every one, and reason, which is that law, teaches all mankind who will but consult it, that being all *equal and independent*, no one ought to harm another in his life, health, liberty or possessions: for men being all the workmanship of one omnipotent and infinitely wise Maker; all the servants of one sovereign Master, sent into the world by His order and about His business; they are His property, whose workmanship they are made to last during His, not one another's pleasure. And, being furnished with like faculties, sharing all in one community of nature, there cannot be supposed any such *subordination* among us that may authorize us to destroy one another, as if we were made for one another's uses, as the inferior ranks of creatures are for ours. Every one as he is *bound to preserve himself*, and not to quit his station wilfully, so by the like reason, when his own preservation comes not in competition, ought he as much as he can, to *preserve the rest of mankind*, and not unless it be to do justice on an offender, take away, or impair the life, or

John Locke, *The Second Treatise on Government*, in *Selections from John Locke's Second Treatise of Government, 1690, Old South Leaflets,* no. 208. Courtesy of the Old South Association.

what tends to the preservation of the life, the liberty, health, limb, or goods of another. . . .

OF SLAVERY

The *natural liberty* of man is to be free from any superior power on earth, and not to be under the will or legislative authority of man, but to have only the law of nature for his rule.

The *liberty of man in society* is to be under no other legislative power but that established by consent in the commonwealth; nor under the dominion of any will, or restraint of any law, but what that legislative shall enact according to the trust put in it. Freedom, then, is not what Sir Robert Filmer tells us: "A liberty for every one to do what he lists, to live as he pleases, and not to be tied by any laws"; but *freedom of men under government* is to have a *standing rule* to live by, common to every one of that society, and made by the *legislative power* erected in it; a liberty to follow my own will in all things where that rule prescribes not, not to be subject to the inconstant, uncertain, unknown, arbitrary will of another man. . . .

OF THE BEGINNING OF POLITICAL SOCIETIES

Men being, as has been said, by nature all free, equal, and independent, no one can be put out of this estate and subjected to the political power of another without his own consent. The only way whereby anyone divests himself of his natural liberty and puts on the bonds of civil society, is by agreeing with other men, to join and unite into a community for their comfortable, safe and peaceable living one amongst another, in a secure enjoyment of their properties, and a greater security against any that are not of it. This any number of men may do, because it injures not the freedom of the rest; they are left, as they were, in the liberty of the state of nature. When any number of men have so *consented to make one community or government*, they are thereby presently incorporated, and make *one body politic*, wherein the *majority* have a right to act and conclude the rest. . . .

And thus every man, by consenting with others to make one body politic under one government, puts himself under an obligation to every one of that society to submit to the determination of the *majority*, and to be concluded by it; or else this *original compact*, whereby he with others incorporates into *one society*, would signify nothing. . . .

For if *the consent of the majority* shall not, in reason, be received as *the act of the whole*, and conclude every individual; nothing but the consent of every individual can make anything to be the act of the whole; but such a consent it is next to impossible ever to be had. . . .

OF THE ENDS OF POLITICAL SOCIETY AND GOVERNMENT

If man in the state of nature be so free as has been said, if he be absolute lord of his own person and possessions, equal to the greatest and subject to nobody, why will he part with his freedom? Why will he give up this empire, and subject himself to the dominion and control of any other power? To which it is obvious to answer, that though in the state of nature he hath such a right, yet the enjoyment of it is very uncertain and constantly exposed to the invasion of others; for all being kings as much as he, every man his equal, and the greater part no strict observers of equity and justice, the enjoyment of the property he has in this state is very unsafe, very insecure. This makes him willing to quit this condition which, however free, is full of fears and continual dangers; and it is not without reason that he seeks out and is willing to join in society with others who are already united, or have a mind to unite *for the mutual preservation of their lives, liberties and estates*, which I call by the general name—*property*.

The great and *chief end*, therefore, of men uniting into commonwealths, and putting themselves under government, *is the preservation of their property*; to which in the state of nature there are many things wanting.

First. There wants an *established*, settled, known *law*, received and allowed by common consent to be the standard of right and wrong, and the common measure to decide all controversies between them. For though the law of nature be plain and intelligible to all rational creatures, yet men, being biased by their interest, as well as ignorant for want of study of it, are not apt to allow of it as a law binding to them in the application of it to their particular cases.

Secondly. In the state of nature there wants a *known and indifferent judge,* with authority to determine all differences according to the established law. For every one in that state being both judge and executioner of the law of nature, men being partial to themselves, passion and revenge is very apt to carry them too far, and with too much heat in their own cases, as well as negligence and unconcernedness, make them too remiss in other men's.

Thirdly. In the state of nature there often wants *power* to back and support the sentence when right, and to *give* it due *execution.* They who by any injustice offend will seldom fail where they are able by force to make good their injustice. Such resistance many times makes the punishment dangerous, and frequently destructive to those who attempt it.

Thus mankind, notwithstanding all the privileges of the state of nature, being but in an ill condition while they remain in it, are quickly driven into society. Hence it comes to pass, that we seldom find any number of men live any time together in this state. The inconveniencies that they are therein exposed to by the irregular and uncertain exercise of the power every man has of punishing the transgressions of others, make them take sanctuary under the established laws of government, and therein seek *the preservation of their property.* It is this makes them so willingly give up every one his single power of punishing to be exercised by such alone as shall be appointed to it amongst them, and by such rules as the community, or those authorized by them to that purpose, shall agree on. And in this we have the original *right and rise of both the legislative and executive power* as well as of the governments and societies themselves.

For in the state of nature . . . a man has two powers. The first is to do whatsoever he thinks fit for the preservation of himself and others within the permission of the *law* of nature. . . . The other is the *power to punish the crimes* committed against that law. Both these he gives up when he joins in a private, if I may so call it, or particular political society, and incorporates into any commonwealth separate from the rest of mankind.

The first *power*—viz., *of doing whatsoever he thought fit for the preservation of himself* and the rest of mankind, *he gives up* to be regulated by laws made by the society, so far forth as the preservation of himself and the rest of that society shall require; which laws of the society in many things confine the liberty he had by the law of nature.

Secondly. The *power of punishing he wholly gives up,* and engages his natural force (which he might before employ in the execution of the law of nature, by his own single authority, as he thought fit), to assist the executive power of the society as the law thereof shall require. For being now in a new state, wherein he is to enjoy many conveniences from the labor, assistance, and society of others in the same community, as well as protection from its whole strength, he is to part also with as much of his natural liberty, in providing for himself, as the good, prosperity, and safety of the society shall require, which is not only necessary but just, since the other members of the society do the like.

But though men when they enter into society give up the equality, liberty, and executive power they had in the state of nature into the hands of the society, to be so far disposed of by the legislative as the good of the society shall require, yet it being only with an intention in every one the better to preserve himself, his liberty and property (for no rational creature can be supposed to change his condition with an intention to be worse), the power of the society or *legislative* constituted by them can *never be supposed to extend farther than the common good,* but is obliged to secure every one's property by providing against those three defects above mentioned that made the state of nature so unsafe and uneasy. And so, whoever has the legislative or supreme power of any commonwealth, is bound to govern by established *standing laws,* promulgated and known to the people, and not by extemporary decrees; by *indifferent* and upright *judges,* who are to decide controversies by those laws; and to employ the force of the community at home *only in the execution of such laws,* or abroad to prevent or redress foreign injuries and secure the community from inroads and invasion. And all this to be directed to no other *end* but the *peace, safety,* and *public good* of the people.

OF THE FORMS OF A COMMONWEALTH

The majority having, as has been showed, upon men's first uniting into society, the whole power of the community naturally in them, may employ all that power in making laws for the community from time to time, and executing those laws by officers of their own appointing, and then the *form* of the government is a perfect *democracy:* or else may put the power of making laws into the hands of a few select men, and their heirs or successors, and then it is an *oligarchy;* or else into the hands of one man, and then it is a *monarchy;* if to him and his heirs, it is a *hereditary monarchy;* if to him only for life, but upon his death the power only of nominating a successor, to return to them, an *elective monarchy.* And so accordingly of these make compounded and mixed forms of government, as they think good. And if the legislative power be at first given by the majority to one or more persons only for their lives, or any limited time, and then the supreme power to revert to them again, when it is so reverted the community may dispose of it again anew into what hands they please, and so constitute a new form of government: for the *form of government depending upon the placing the supreme power,* which is the *legislative,* it being impossible to conceive that an inferior power should prescribe to a superior, or any but the supreme make laws, according as the power of making laws is placed, such is the *form of the commonwealth.*

By *commonwealth* I must be understood all along to mean not a democracy, or any *form* of government, but *any independent community,* which the Latins signified by the word *civitas,* to which the word which best answers in our language is *commonwealth.*

OF THE EXTENT OF THE LEGISLATIVE POWER

The great end of men's entering into society being the enjoyment of their properties in peace and safety, and the great instrument and means of that being the laws established in that society, the *first and fundamental positive law* of all commonwealths is the *establishing of the legislative power.* . . . This *legislative* is not only the *supreme power* of the commonwealth, but sacred and unalterable in the hands where the community have once placed it. Nor can any edict of anybody else, in what form soever conceived, or by what power soever backed, have the force and obligation of a *law* which has not its *sanction* from that legislative which the public has chosen and appointed. . . . Nor can any oaths to any foreign power whatsoever, or any domestic subordinate power, discharge any member of the society from his *obedience to the legislative,* acting pursuant to their trust, nor oblige him to any obedience contrary to the laws so enacted or farther than they do allow, it being ridiculous to imagine one can be tied ultimately to *obey* any *power* in the society which is not the *supreme.*

Though the legislative . . . be the *supreme* power in every commonwealth; yet,

First, it is *not,* nor can possibly be, absolutely *arbitrary* over the lives and fortunes of the people. . . . For nobody can transfer to another more power than he has in himself, and nobody has an absolute arbitrary power over himself, or over any other, to destroy his own life, or take away the life or property of another. A man, as has been proved, cannot subject himself to the arbitrary power of another; and having, in the state of nature, no arbitrary power over the life, liberty, or possession of another, but only so much as the law of nature gave him for the preservation of himself and the rest of mankind, this is all he doth, or can give up to the commonwealth, and by it to the legislative power; so that the legislative can have no more than this. Their power in the utmost bounds of it is *limited to the public good of the society.* It is a power that hath no other end but preservation, and therefore can never have a right to destroy, enslave, or designedly to impoverish the subjects. The obligations of the law of nature cease not in society, but only in many cases are drawn closer, and have, by human laws, known penalties annexed to them to enforce their observation. Thus the law of nature stands as an eternal rule to all men, *legislators* as well as others. The rules that they make for other men's actions must, as well as their own and other men's actions, be conformable to the law of nature—*i.e.*, to the will of God, of which that is a declaration, and the fundamental law of nature being the preservation of mankind, no human sanction can be good or valid against it.

Secondly, the *legislative* or supreme authority cannot assume to itself a power to rule by extemporary arbitrary decrees, but *is bound to dispense justice* and decide the rights of the subject by *promulgated standing laws, and known authorized judges*. For the law of nature being unwritten, and so nowhere to be found but in the minds of men, they who, through passion or interest, shall miscite or misapply it, cannot so easily be convinced of their mistake where there is no established judge. To avoid these inconveniences which disorder men's properties in the state of nature, men unite into societies that they may have the united strength of the whole society to secure and defend their properties, and may have *standing rules* to bound it by which every one may know what is his. To this end it is that men give up all their natural power to the society they enter into, and the community put the legislative power into such hands as they think fit, with this trust, that they shall be governed by *declared laws*, or else their peace, quiet, and property will still be at the same uncertainty as it was in the state of nature.

Absolute arbitrary power, or governing without *settled standing laws*, can neither of them consist with the ends of society and government. . . . It cannot be supposed that [men] should intend, had they a power so to do, to give any one or more an *absolute arbitrary power* over their persons and estates, and put a force into the magistrate's hand to execute his unlimited will arbitrarily upon them;

this were to put themselves into a worse condition than the state of nature, wherein they had a liberty to defend their right against the injuries of others, and were upon equal terms of force to maintain it, whether invaded by a single man or many in combination. Whereas by supposing they have given up themselves to the absolute arbitrary power and will of a legislator, they have disarmed themselves, and armed him to make a prey of them when he pleases; he being in a much worse condition that is exposed to the arbitrary power of one man who has the command of a hundred thousand than he that is exposed to the arbitrary power of a hundred thousand single men. . . . And, therefore, whatever form the commonwealth is under, the ruling power ought to govern by *declared* and *received* laws, and not by extemporary dictates and undetermined resolutions. . . . For all the power the government has, being only for the good of the society, as it ought not to be *arbitrary* and at pleasure, so it ought to be exercised by *established and promulgated laws*, that both the people may know their duty, and be safe and secure within the limits of the law, and the rulers, too, kept within their due bounds, and not be tempted by the power they have in their hands to employ it to purposes, and by such measures as they would not have known, and own not willingly.

Thirdly, the supreme power cannot take from any man any part of his *property* without his own consent. For the preservation of property being the end of government, and that for which men enter into society, it necessarily supposes and requires that the people should *have property*, without which they must be supposed to lose that by entering into society, which was the end for which they entered into it; too gross an absurdity for any man to own. Men, therefore, in society having property, they have such a right to the goods, which by the law of the community are theirs, that nobody hath a right to take them, or any part of them, from them without their own consent; without this they have no *property* at all. For I have truly no property in that which another can by right take from me when he pleases against my consent. Hence it is a mistake to think that the *supreme or legislative power* of any commonwealth can do what it will, and dispose of the estates of the subject arbitrarily, or take any part of them at pleasure. This is not much to be feared in governments where the legislative consists wholly or in part in assemblies which are variable, whose members upon the dissolution of the assembly are subjects under the common laws of their country, equally with the rest. But in governments where the legislative is in one lasting assembly, always in being or in one man as in absolute monarchies, there is danger still, that they will think themselves to have a distinct interest from the rest of the community, and so will be apt to increase their own riches and power by taking what they think fit from the people. For a man's *property* is not at all secure, though there be good and equitable laws to set the bounds of it between him and his fellow-subjects, if he who commands those subjects have power to take from any private man what part he pleases of his *property*, and use and dispose of it as he thinks good.

But government into whosesoever hands it is put, being as I have before showed, entrusted with this condition, and *for this end,* that men might have and secure their properties, the prince or senate, however it may have power to make laws for the *regulating of property* between the subjects one amongst another, yet can never have a power to take to themselves the whole, or any part of the subjects' *property*, without their own consent; for this would be in effect to leave them no property at all. And to let us see that even absolute power, where it is necessary, is not arbitrary by being absolute, but is still limited by that reason, and confined to those ends which required it in some cases to be absolute, we need look no farther than the common practice of martial discipline. For the preservation of the army, and in it of the whole commonwealth, requires an absolute obedience to the command of every superior officer, and it is justly death to disobey or dispute the most dangerous or unreasonable of them; but yet we see that neither the sergeant that could command a soldier to march up to the mouth of a cannon, or stand in a breach where he is almost sure to perish, can command that soldier to give him one penny of his money; nor the general that can condemn him to death for deserting his post, or not obeying the most desperate orders, cannot yet with all his absolute power of life and death dispose of one farthing of that soldier's estate, or seize one jot of his goods; whom yet he can command anything, and hang for the least disobedience. Because such a blind obedience is necessary to that end for which the commander has his power—viz., the preservation of the rest, but the disposing of his goods has nothing to do with it.

It is true governments cannot be supported without great charge, and it is fit every one who enjoys his share of the protection should pay out of his estate his proportion for the maintenance of it. But still it must be with his own consent—*i.e.*, the consent of the majority, giving it either by themselves or their representatives chosen by them; for if any one shall claim a *power to lay and levy taxes* on the people by his *own authority*, and without such consent of the people, he thereby invades the *fundamental law of property*, and subverts the end of government. For what property have I in that which another may by right take when he pleases to himself?

Fourthly. The legislative *cannot transfer the power of making laws* to any other hands, for it being but a delegated power from the people, they who have it cannot pass it over to others. The people alone can appoint the form of the commonwealth, which is by constituting the legislative, and appointing in whose hands that shall be. And when the people have said, "We will submit, and be governed by *laws* made by such men, and in such forms," nobody else can say other men shall make laws for them; nor can they be bound by any laws but such as are enacted by those whom they have chosen and authorized to make laws for them. . . .

These are the bounds which the trust that is put in them by the society and the law of God and nature have *set to the legislative power* of every commonwealth, in all forms of government.

First: They are to govern by *promulgated established laws,* not to be varied in particular cases, but to have one rule for rich and poor, for the favorite at court, and the countryman at plough.

Secondly: These laws also ought to be designed for no other end ultimately but the *good of the people.*

Thirdly: They must not raise taxes on the property of the people *without the consent of the people* given by themselves or their deputies. . . .

Fourthly: The legislative neither must nor can *transfer the power of making laws* to anybody else, or place it anywhere but where the people have.

OF THE LEGISLATIVE, EXECUTIVE, AND FEDERATIVE POWER OF THE COMMONWEALTH

The *legislative* power is that which has a right *to direct how the force of the commonwealth* shall be employed for preserving the community and the members of it. Because those laws which are constantly to be executed, and whose force is always to continue, may be made in a little time; therefore there is no need that the *legislative* should be always in being, not having always business to do. And because it may be too great temptation to human frailty, apt to grasp at power, for the same persons who have the power of making laws to have also in their hands the power to execute them; . . . therefore in well-ordered commonwealths . . . the *legislative* power is put into the hands of divers persons who, duly assembled, have by themselves, or jointly with others, a power to make laws, which when they have done, being separated again, they are themselves subject to the laws they have made; which is a new and near tie upon them to take care that they make them for the public good.

But because the laws that are at once, and in a short time made, have a constant and lasting force, and need a *perpetual execution,* or an attendance thereunto, therefore it is necessary there should be a *power always in being* which should see to the *execution* of the laws that are made, and remain in force. And thus the *legislative* and *executive power* come often to be *separated.* . . .

OF THE SUBORDINATION OF THE POWERS OF THE COMMONWEALTH

Though in a constituted commonwealth . . . there can be but *one supreme power,* which is the legislative, to which all the rest are and must be subordinate, yet the legislative being only a fiduciary power to act for certain ends, there remains still *in the people a supreme power to remove or alter the legislative,* when they find the legislative act contrary to the trust reposed in them. For all *power given with trust* for the attaining an *end* being limited by that end; whenever that end is manifestly neglected or opposed, the *trust* must necessarily be *forfeited,* and the power devolve into the hands of those that gave it, who may place it anew where they shall think best for their safety and security. And thus the *community* perpetually *retains a supreme power* of saving themselves from the attempts and designs of anybody, even of their legislators, whenever they shall be so foolish or so wicked as to lay and carry on designs against the liberties and properties of the subject. For no man or society of men having a power to deliver up their preservation, or consequently the means of it, to the absolute will and arbitrary dominion of another, whenever any one shall go about to bring them into such a slavish condition, they will always have a right to preserve what they have not a power to part with, and to rid thmeselves of those who invade this fundamental, sacred, and unalterable law of *self-preservation* for which they entered into society. And thus the *community* may be said in this respect to be *always the supreme power,* but not as considered under any form of government, because this power of the people can never take place till the government be dissolved.

In all cases *whilst the government subsists, the legislative is the supreme power.* For what can give laws to another must needs be superior to him. . . .

It may be demanded here, what if the executive power, being possessed of the force of the commonwealth, shall make use of that force to hinder the *meeting* and *acting of the legislative,* when the original constitution or the public exigencies require it? I say, using force upon the people, without authority, and contrary to the trust put in him that does so, is a state of war with the people, who have a right to *reinstate* their *legislative in the exercise of* their power. . . . In all states and conditions the true remedy of *force* without authority is to oppose *force* to it. The use of force without authority always puts him that uses it into a *state of war* as the aggressor, and renders him liable to be treated accordingly. . . .

OF TYRANNY

As usurpation is the exercise of power which another hath a right to, so *tyranny is the exercise of power beyond right,* which nobody can have a right to; and this is making use of the power any one has in his hands, not for the good of those who are under it, but for his own private, separate advantage. When the governor, however entitled, makes not the law, but his will, the rule, and his commands and actions are not directed to the preservation of the properties of his people, but the satisfaction of his own ambition, revenge, covetousness, or any other irregular passion. . . .

It is a mistake to think this fault is proper only to monarchies. Other forms of government are liable to it as well as that; for wherever the power that is put in any hands for the government of the people and the preservation of their properties is applied to other ends, and made use of to impoverish, harass, or subdue them to the arbitrary and irregular commands of those that have it, there it presently becomes tyranny, whether those that thus use it are one or many. Thus we read of the thirty tyrants at *Athens,* as well as one at *Syracuse;* and the intolerable dominion of the *Decemviri* at *Rome* was nothing better.

Wherever law ends, tyranny begins, if the law be transgressed to another's harm; and whosoever in authority exceeds the power given him by the law, and makes use of the force he has under his command to compass that upon the subject which the law allows not, ceases in that to be a magistrate, and acting without authority may be opposed, as any other man who by force invades the right of another. This is acknowledged in subordinate magistrates. He that hath authority to seize my person in the street may be opposed as a thief and a robber if he endeavors to break into my house to execute a writ, notwithstanding that I know he has such a warrant and such a legal authority as will empower him to arrest me abroad. And why this should not hold in the highest, as well as in the most inferior magistrate, I would gladly be informed. Is it reasonable that the eldest brother, because he has the greatest part of his father's estate, should thereby have a right to take away any of his younger brothers' portions? Or, that a rich man, who possessed a whole country, should from thence have a right to seize, when he pleased, the cottage and garden of his poor neighbor? The being rightfully possessed of great power and riches, exceedingly beyond the greatest part of the sons of Adam, is so far from being an excuse, much less a reason for rapine and oppression, which the endamaging another without authority is, that it is a great aggravation of it. For the exceeding the bounds of authority is no more a right in a great than a petty officer, no more justifiable in a king than a constable. . . .

May the *commands,* then, *of a prince be opposed?* May he be resisted, as often as anyone shall find himself aggrieved, and but imagine he has not right done him? This will unhinge and overturn all polities, and instead of government and order, leave nothing but anarchy and confusion.

To this I answer: That *force* is to be opposed to nothing but to *unjust and unlawful force.* Whoever makes any opposition in any other case draws on himself a just condemnation, both from God and man; and so no such danger or confusion will follow, as is often suggested. . . .

OF THE DISSOLUTION
OF GOVERNMENTS

He that will, with any clearness, speak of the *dissolution of government,* ought in the first place to distinguish between the dissolution of the *society* and the dissolution of the *government.* That which makes the community, and brings men out of the loose state of nature into *one politic society,* is the agreement which every one has with the rest to incorporate and act as one body, and so be one distinct commonwealth. The usual, and almost only way whereby *this union is dissolved,* is the inroad of foreign force making a conquest upon them. . . . The world is too well instructed in, and too forward to allow of this way of dissolving of governments, to need any more to be said of it. . . .

There is, therefore, secondly, another way

whereby *governments are dissolved,* and that is, when the legislative, or the prince, either of them act contrary to their trust.

First: the *legislative acts against the trust* reposed in them when they endeavor to invade the property of the subject, and to make themselves, or any part of the community, masters or arbitrary disposers of the lives, liberties, or fortunes of the people.

. . . Whensoever, therefore, the legislative shall transgress this fundamental rule of society, and either by ambition, fear, folly, or corruption, *endeavor to grasp themselves,* or *put into the hands of any other, an absolute power* over the lives, liberties, and estates of the people; by this breach of trust they *forfeit the power* the people had put into their hands for quite contrary ends; and it devolves to the people, who have a right to resume their original liberty, and by the establishment of a new legislative (such as they shall think fit), provide for their own safety and security, which is the end for which they are in society. What I have said here concerning the legislative in general holds true also concerning the supreme executor, who having a double trust put in him, both to have a part in the legislative and the supreme execution of the law, acts against both, when he goes about to set up his own arbitrary will as the law of the society. He acts also *contrary to his trust* when he employs the force, treasure, and offices of the society to *corrupt the representatives,* and gain them to his purposes, when he openly pre-engages the electors, and prescribes, to their choice, such whom he has, by solicitation, threats, promises, or otherwise, won to his designs, and employs them to bring in such who have promised beforehand what to vote and what to enact. Thus to regulate candidates and electors, and new model the ways of election, what is it but to cut up the government by the roots, and poison the very fountain of public security? . . .

To this, perhaps, it will be said that the people being ignorant and always discontented, to lay the foundation of government in the unsteady opinion and uncertain humor of the people, is to expose it to certain ruin; and *no government will be able long to subsist* if the people may set up a new legislative whenever they take offence at the old one. To this I answer, quite the contrary. People are not so easily got out of their old forms as some are apt to suggest. They are hardly to be prevailed with to amend the acknowledged faults in the frame they have been accustomed to. And if there be any original defects, or adventitious ones introduced by time or corruption, it is not an easy thing to get them changed, even when all the world sees there is an opportunity for it. This slowness and aversion in the people to quit their old constitutions has in the many revolutions that have been seen in this kingdom, in this and former ages, still kept us (or after some interval of fruitless attempts, still brought us back again) to our old legislative of kings, lords and commons; and whatever provocations have made the crown be taken from some of our princes' heads, they never carried the people so far as to place it in another line.

But it will be said this *hypothesis* lays a *ferment* for frequent *rebellion.* To which I answer:

First: no more than any other hypothesis. For when the people are made miserable, and find themselves *exposed to the ill usage or arbitrary power,* cry up their governors as much as you will for sons of Jupiter, let them be sacred and divine, descended or authorized from Heaven; give them out for whom or what you please, the same will happen. *The people generally ill treated,* and contrary to right, will be ready upon any occasion to ease themselves of a burden that sits heavy upon them. They will wish and seek for the opportunity, which in the change, weakness, and accidents of human affairs, seldom delays long to offer itself. He must have lived but a little while in the world, who has not seen examples of this in his time; and he must have read very little who cannot produce examples of it in all sorts of governments in the world.

Secondly: I answer, such *revolutions happen* not upon every little mismanagement in public affairs. *Great mistakes* in the ruling part, many wrong and inconvenient laws, and all the slips of human frailty will be *borne by the people* without mutiny or murmur. But if a *long train of abuses,* prevarications, and artifices, all tending the same way, make the design visible to the people, and they cannot but feel what they lie under, and see whither they are going, it is not to be wondered that they should then rouse themselves, and endeavor to put the rule into such hands which may secure to them the ends for which government was at first erected, and without which, ancient names and specious forms are so far from being better, that they are much worse than the state of nature or pure anarchy; the inconveniences being all as great and as near, but the remedy farther off and more difficult.

Thirdly: I answer, that this . . . power in the people of providing for their safety anew by a new legislative when their legislators have acted contrary to their trust by invading their property, is the *best fence against rebellion,* and the probablest means to hinder it. For rebellion being an opposition, not to persons, but authority, which is founded only in the constitutions and laws of the government; those, whoever they be, who by force break through, and by force justify their violation of them, are truly and properly *rebels.* For when men, by entering into society and civil government, have excluded force, and introduced laws for the preservation of property, peace, and unity amongst themselves, those who set up force again in opposition to the laws, do *rebellare—* that is, bring back again the state of war, and are properly rebels, which they who are in power (by the pretence they have to authority, the temptation of force they have in their hands, and the flattery of those about them), being likeliest to do, the properest way to prevent the evil is to show them the danger and injustice of it who are under the greatest temptation to run into it. . . .

But if they who say *it lays a foundation for rebellion* mean that it may occasion civil wars or intestine broils to tell the people they are absolved from obedience when illegal attempts are made upon their liberties or properties, and may oppose the unlawful violence of those who were their magistrates when they invade their properties, contrary to the trust put in them, and that, therefore, this doctrine is not to be allowed, being so destructive to the peace of the world; they may as well say, upon the same ground, that honest men may not oppose robbers or pirates, because this may occasion disorder or bloodshed. If any mischief come in such cases, it is not to be charged upon him who defends his own right, but on *him that invades his neighbor's.* If the innocent honest man must quietly quit all he has for peace's sake to him who will lay violent hands upon it, I desire it may be considered what a kind of peace there will be in the world which consists only in violence and rapine, and which is to be maintained only for the benefit of robbers and oppressors. Who would not think it an admirable peace betwixt the mighty and the mean, when the lamb, without resistance, yielded his throat to be torn by the imperious wolf? *Polyphemus's* den gives us a perfect pattern of such a peace. Such a government wherein *Ulysses* and his companions had nothing to do but quietly to suffer themselves to be devoured. And no doubt *Ulysses*, who was a prudent man, preached up *passive obedience,* and exhorted them to a quiet submission by representing to them of what concernment peace was to mankind, and by showing the inconveniences [that] might happen if they should offer to resist *Polyphemus*, who had now the power over them.

The end of government is the good of mankind; and which is *best for mankind,* that the people should be always exposed to the boundless will of tyranny, or that the rulers should be sometimes liable to be opposed when they grow exorbitant in the use of their power, and employ it for the destruction, and not the preservation, of the properties of their people?

Nor let any one say that mischief can arise from hence as often as it shall please a busy head or turbulent spirit to desire the alteration of the government. It is true such men may stir whenever they please, but it will be only to their own just ruin and perdition. For till the mischief be grown general, and the ill designs of the rulers become visible, or their attempts sensible to the greater part, the people, who are more disposed to suffer than right themselves by resistance, are not apt to stir. The examples of particular injustice or oppression of here and there an unfortunate man moves them not. But if they universally have a persuasion grounded upon manifest evidence that designs are carrying on against their liberties, and the general course and tendency of things cannot but give them strong suspicions of the evil intention of their governors, who is to be blamed for it? Who can help it if they, who might avoid it, bring themselves into this suspicion? Are the people to be blamed if they have the sense of rational creatures, and can think of things no otherwise than as they find and feel them? And is it not rather *their fault* who put things in such a posture that they would not have them thought as they are? I grant that the pride, ambition, and turbulency of private men have sometimes caused great disorders in commonwealths, and factions have been fatal to states and kingdoms. But whether the mischief hath oftener begun in the *people's wantoness,* and a desire to cast off the lawful authority of their rulers, or in the *rulers' insolence* and endeavors to get and exercise an arbitrary power over their people, whether oppression or disobedience gave the first rise to the disorder, I leave it to impartial history to determine. This I am sure, whoever, either ruler or subject, by force goes about to invade the rights of either prince or people, and lays the foundation for *overturning* the constitution and frame of any *just government,* he is guilty of the greatest crime I think a man is capable of, being to answer for all those mischiefs of blood, rapine, and desolation, which the breaking to pieces of governments bring on a country; and he who does it is justly to be esteemed the common enemy and pest of mankind, and is to be treated accordingly. . . .

Here, it is like, the common question will be made, *Who shall be judge* whether the prince or legislative act contrary to their trust? . . . To this I reply, *The people shall be judge;* for who shall be *judge* whether his trustee or deputy acts well and according to the trust reposed in him, but he who deputes him and must, by having deputed him, have still a power to discard him when he fails in his trust? If this be reasonable in particular cases of private men, why should it be otherwise in that of the greatest moment, where the welfare of millions is concerned and also where the evil, if not prevented, is greater, and the redress very difficult, dear, and dangerous? . . .

If a controversy arise betwixt a prince and some of the people in a matter where the law is silent or doubtful, and the thing be of great consequence, I should think the proper *umpire* in such a case should be the *body of the people.* For in cases where the prince hath a trust reposed in him, and is dispensed from the common, ordinary rules of the law, there, if any men find themselves aggrieved, and think the prince acts contrary to, or beyond that trust, who so proper to *judge* as the *body of the people* (who at first lodged that trust in him) how far they meant it should extend? But if the prince, or whoever they be in the administration, decline that way of determination, the appeal then lies nowhere but to Heaven. Force between either persons who have no known superior on earth, or which permits no appeal to a judge on earth, being properly a state of war, wherein the appeal lies only to Heaven; and in that state the injured party must judge for himself when he will think fit to make use of that appeal and put himself upon it.

To conclude: The *power that every individual gave the society* when he entered into it can never revert to the individuals again, as long as the society lasts, but will always remain in the community; because without this there can be no community—no commonwealth, which is contrary to the original agreement; so also when the society hath placed the legislative in any assembly of men, to continue in them and their successors, with direction and authority for providing such successors, *the legislative can never revert to the people whilst that government lasts;* because, having provided a legislative with power to continue for ever, they have given up their political power to the legislative, and cannot resume it. But if they have set limits to the duration of their legislative, and made this supreme power in any person or assembly only temporary; or else, when, by the miscarriages of those in authority, it is forfeited; upon the forfeiture of their rulers, or at the determination of the time set, *it reverts to the society,* and the people have a right to act as supreme, and continue the legislative in themselves or place it in a new form, or new hands, as they think good.

Jean-Jacques Rousseau

Jean-Jacques Rousseau (1712–1778), a French intellectual of the Enlightenment, adapted the theory of the social contract to the growing concept of popular sovereignty. Influenced by his age, with its emphasis upon natural law and the idea of progress, he conceived of a society which, if it followed its natural capacity for development, could achieve the ultimate in human freedom. To him the social contract was between all the individuals composing the state but did not include the government. The latter existed only to carry out the expressed will of the people. For Rousseau the ultimate human freedom consisted of the voluntary submission by the individual to the general will. Thus in his writings there existed the seeds both of revolution against constituted government whenever it ceased to perform its functions dutifully, and of the present-day concept of complete democratic sovereignty with the will of the majority becoming the will of all. In reading the following selections from Rousseau's great book, The Social Contract, note (1) Rousseau's justification for undertaking this work, (2) the discussion of "right" and "might" and their relationship to the exercise of authority in government, (3) the fundamental human problem that the social contract solved, (4) the identity of interest between the sovereign and its subjects, (5) the distinction made between the individual will and the general will, (6) the need for force in making an individual free, (7) the balance sheet of gains and losses in forming the social contract, (8) how the general will may be corrupted, (9) how the sovereign power is limited, and (10) the methods by which government may be prevented from usurping power.

From: THE SOCIAL CONTRACT

I propose to inquire if, in the civil order, there can be any certain and legitimate administration, men being what they are and the laws what they might be. In this investigation I shall always try to combine right sanctions with what interest prescribes, so that justice and utility in no case may be divided.

I begin my task without proving the importance of the subject. I shall be asked if I am a ruler or a legislator, to write about politics. I answer that I am neither, and that is why I write. If I were a ruler or a legislator, I should not waste time saying what needs doing; I should do it, or keep quiet.

As I was born a citizen of a free State, and a member of the Sovereign, I feel that, however weak my influence on public affairs, the right of voting makes it my duty to study them; and I am happy, when I reflect upon governments, to discover that my inquiries always provide me with new reasons for loving that of my own country.

As translated by the editors from Jean-Jacques Rousseau, *Du Contrat Social*, Paris, 1903, 105–107; 113–114; 125–137; 150–162; 271–274.

SUBJECT OF THE FIRST BOOK

Man is born free; and everywhere he is in chains. One believes himself the master of others, yet remains a greater slave than they. How did this change occur? I do not know. What can render it legitimate? I think I can answer that question.

If I considered only force, and the effects derived therefrom, I should say: "As long as a people is forced to obey, and it obeys, it does well; as soon as it can shake off the yoke, and it shakes it off, it does still better; for, in recovering its liberty by the same right by which it was removed, either it is justified in regaining it, or there was no justification for those who took it away." But the social order is a sacred right which is the basis of all the others. Nevertheless, this right does not come from nature; it is founded on conventions. . . .

THE RIGHT OF THE STRONGEST

The strongest is never strong enough always to be the master, if he fails to transform strength into right, and obedience into duty. Hence the right of the strongest, which right, though to all appearances meant ironically, is really established as a principle. But are we never to have an explanation of this phrase? Might is physical power; I cannot see what moral effects it can have. To yield to might is an act of necessity, not of will; at the most, it is an act of prudence. In what sense can it be a duty?

Suppose for a moment the existence of this so-called right. I say that the only result is inexplicable nonsense; for, if might makes right, the effect changes with the cause; every force that is greater than the first succeeds to its right. As soon as it is possible to disobey with impunity, one does so legitimately; and, the strongest always being in the right, needs only to act so as to become the strongest. But what kind of right is that which perishes when might fails? If we must obey by force, there is no need to obey because we ought; and if we are not forced to obey, we are not obliged to do so. Clearly, the word *right* adds nothing to force; here, it means absolutely nothing.

Obey the powers that be. If this means: yield to force, the precept is good, but superflous; I reply that it will never be violated. All power comes from God, I admit; so does all sickness. Does that mean that we are forbidden to call the doctor? A robber surprises me at the edge of a forest: must I not merely give up my purse on compulsion; but, even if I could keep it, am I in conscience obliged to give it up? Certainly the pistol he holds is also a power.

Let us then admit that might does not create right, and that we are only obliged to obey legitimate powers. In that case, my original question recurs. . . .

THE SOCIAL COMPACT

I suppose men to have reached that point where the obstacles to their preservation in the state of nature reveal their resistance to be greater than the resources available to each individual for his maintenance in that state. Then that primitive condition can subsist no longer; and the human race would perish unless it changed its way of being.

But, as men cannot engender new forces, but only unite and direct existing ones, they have no other means of preserving themselves, save the formation, by aggregation, of a sum of forces great enough to overcome the resistance; these they must initiate by means of a single motive power, and cause to act in concert.

This sum of forces can arise only when several persons come together; but, since the force and the liberty of each man constitute the principal instruments of his self-preservation, how can he pledge them without hurting his own interests and neglecting the care which he owes himself? This difficulty, in its bearing on my subject, may be stated in these terms:

"Find a form of association which defends and protects with the whole force of the community the person and the goods of each associate, and in which each, while uniting with all, may still obey himself alone, and remain as free as before." This is the fundamental problem of which the *Social Contract* offers the solution.

The clauses of this contract are so determined by the nature of the act, that the slightest modification would render them vain and of no effect; so that, although they have perhaps never been formally announced, they are always the same and everywhere tacitly admitted and recognized, and, when the social compact is violated, each regains his original rights and regains his natural liberty while losing the conventional liberty for which he renounced it.

These clauses, properly understood, may be reduced to a single one—the total alienation of each associate with all his rights to the whole community; for, in the first place, as each gives himself entirely, the conditions are equal for all, and, the condition being equal for all, no one has an interest in making them burdensome to the others.

Moreover, the alienation being without reserve, the union is as perfect as it can be, and no associate has anything to demand: for, if the individuals retained certain rights in particular, as there would be no common superior to decide between them and the public, each, being on one point his own judge, would ask to be so on all; the state of nature would continue, and the association would necessarily become tyrannical or useless.

Finally, each in giving himself to all, gives himself to no one; and as there is no associate over whom he does not gain the same right as he grants to others over himself, he gains the equivalent for all that he loses, and a greater force for the conservation of what he has.

If then we discard from the social compact what is not of its essence, we shall find that it reduces itself to the following terms:

"Each of us puts his person and all his power in common under the supreme direction of the general will, and as in a body, we receive each member as an indivisible part of the whole."

At once, in place of the individual personality of each contracting party, this act of association produces a moral and collective body, composed of as many members as the assembly contains votes, and which receives from this same act its unity, its common identity, its life and its will. This public person, so formed by the union of all the others, formerly took the name of *city,* and now takes that of *Republic,* or *body politic.* It is called by its members,

State, when it is passive; *Sovereign,* when it is active; and *Power,* when compared with others like itself. Respecting the associates, they take collectively the name of *people,* and are called *citizens,* as participating in the sovereign power, and *subjects,* as being under the laws of the State. But these terms are often confused and taken the one for the other; it is sufficient to know how to distinguish them when they are used with precision. . . .

THE SOVEREIGN

We see by this formula that the act of association comprises a reciprocal undertaking between the public and individuals, and that each individual, contracting as it were, with himself, is bound in a double capacity: as a member of the Sovereign he is bound to the individuals, and as a member of the State, to the Sovereign. But we do not apply here the maxim of civil right that no one is bound by undertakings made to himself; for there is a great difference between undertaking an obligation to one's self and incurring one to a whole of which one is a part.

It is further necessary to call attention to the fact that public deliberation, while able to bind all the subjects to the Sovereign, because of the two different capacities in which each of them may be regarded, cannot, for the opposite reason, bind the Sovereign to itself; and that consequently it is against the nature of the body politic for the Sovereign to impose on itself a law which it cannot infringe. Being able to consider itself in only one capacity, it is in the position of an individual contracting with himself; thus one sees that there neither is nor can be a kind of fundamental law binding the body of the people—not even the social contract itself. This does not mean that the body politic cannot enter into undertakings with others, provided there is no infringement of the terms of the contract; for regarding what is external to it, it becomes a simple being, an individual.

But the body politic or the Sovereign, drawing its being only from the sanctity of the contract, can never bind itself, even to an outsider, to do anything derogatory to the original act, that is, to alienate any part of itself, or to submit to another Sovereign. Violation of the act by which it exists would be self-annihilation; and that which is itself nothing, can create nothing.

As soon as this multitude is thus united in one body, it cannot offend one of the members without attacking the whole, and still more to offend against the body without the members resenting it. Thus duty and interest equally oblige the two contracting parties mutually to aid each other; and the same men should seek to combine, in their double capacity, all the advantages dependent upon that capacity.

Again, the Sovereign, being formed entirely of the individuals comprising it, neither has nor can have any interest contrary to theirs; consequently the sovereign power need give no guarantee to its subjects, because it is impossible for the body to will to injure all its members. And we shall also see later on that it cannot hurt any in particular. The Sovereign, because of what it is, is always what it should be.

But this is not the case with the relation of the subjects to the Sovereign, which, in spite of the common interest, lacks a guarantee of fulfilment of their undertakings, unless it found means to assure itself of their fidelity.

In fact, each individual, as a man, may have a particular will contrary or dissimilar to the general will which he possesses as a citizen. His particular interest may speak to him quite differently from that of the common interest; his sole existence and natural independence, may make him look upon that which he owes to the common cause as a free contribution, the loss of which will do less harm to the others than the payment of it is onerous to himself; and concerning the moral person which constitutes the State as an imaginary being, because not a man, he may wish to enjoy the rights of citizenship without being willing to fulfil the duties of a subject. The continuance of such an injustice could not but prove the ruin of the body politic.

So that the social compact may not be an empty formula, it tacitly includes that undertaking, which alone can give force to the others, that whoever refuses to obey the general will shall be forced to do so by the whole body. This means nothing less than that he will be compelled to be free; for this is the condition which, by giving each citizen to his country, it guarantees him against all personal dependence. This condition permits the smooth operation of the political machine, and this alone renders civil undertakings legitimate, which, without it, would be absurd, tyrannical, and subject to the most enormous abuses.

THE CIVIL STATE

The passage from the state of nature to the civil state produces in man a very remarkable change, by substituting in his conduct justice for instinct, and giving his actions the morality they had formerly lacked. It is then only that the voice of duty supplants physical impulses and the right of appetite, and man, who so far had regarded himself only, finds that he is compelled to act on different principles, and to consult his reason before listening to his inclinations. Being in this state, he deprives himself of several advantages which he held from nature, but in return he receives others so great, his faculties are so stimulated and developed, his ideas so extended, his feelings so ennobled, and his whole soul so elevated, that, did not the abuses of this new condition often degrade him below that which he left, he must bless continually the happy hour which took him from it forever, and which, instead of a stupid and unimaginative animal, made him an intelligent being and a man.

Let us balance the whole in easily commensurable terms. That which man loses by the social contract is his natural liberty and an unlimited right to everything he attempts to get and succeeds in getting; that which he gains is civil liberty and the proprietorship of all he possesses. To avoid error in evaluating one against the other, we must clearly distinguish natural liberty, which is limited only by the strength of the individual, from civil liberty, which is limited by the general will; and possession, which is merely the effect of might or the right of the first occupant, from property, which can be founded only on a positive title.

We might, moreover, add moral liberty to what man acquires in the civil state, which alone renders him truly master of himself; for the mere impulse of appetite is slavery, while obedience to a law which we prescribe for ourselves is liberty. But I have already said too much about this, and the philosophical sense of the word *liberty* does not here concern me. . . .

WHETHER THE GENERAL WILL IS FALLIBLE

It follows from what has been said that the general will is always right and always tends to the public advantage; but it does not follow that the deliberations of the people are always equally right. Our will is always for our good, but we do not always recognize what that is; the people is never corrupted, but often deceived, and only on such occasions does it seem to will that which is bad.

There is often considerable difference between the will of all and the general will; the latter only regards the common interest, while the former considers private interest, and is only a sum of particular wills; but take away from these same wills the pluses and minuses that cancel one another, and the sum of the differences constitutes the general will.

If, when the people, having sufficient information, deliberate, the citizens lacked communication one with another, the grand total of the small differences would always represent the general will, and the decision would always be good. But when factions arise, and partial associations are formed at the expense of the great association, the will of each of these associations becomes general in relation to its members, and particular in relation to the State; one may then say that there are no longer as many votes as men, but only as many as there are associations. The differences become less numerous and give a less general result. Finally, when one of these associations is so great as to prevail over all the rest, you no longer have a sum of small differences, but a single difference; then there is no longer a general will, and the opinion which prevails is a purely particular opinion.

It is therefore essential, if the general will is to express itself, that there should be no partial society within the State, and that each citizen should think only his own thoughts; such

was indeed the unique and sublime system instituted by the great Lycurgus. But if there are partial societies, it is best to multiply the number and to prevent them from being unequal, as was done by Solon, Numa, and Servius. These precautions are the only guarantees that the general will shall always be enlightened, and that the people shall not deceive itself.

THE LIMITS OF THE SOVEREIGN POWER

If the State or the City is only a moral person whose life consists in the union of its members, and if the most important of its concerns is the care for its proper preservation, it must have a universal and compulsive force to move and dispose each part to the greatest advantage for the whole. As nature gives each man absolute power over all his members, so the social compact gives to the body politic absolute power over all its members; and it is this power which, under the direction of the general will, bears, as I have said, the name of Sovereignty.

But, besides the public person, we have to consider the private persons who compose it, and whose life and liberty are naturally independent of it. We must then clearly distinguish between the respective rights of the citizens and of the Sovereign, and between the duties the former are to fulfil as subjects, and the natural rights which they should enjoy in their capacity as men.

By the social compact each man alienates such part of his powers, goods, and liberty as it is important for the community to control; but it must be granted also that the Sovereign is alone judge of what is important.

All of the services that a citizen can render the State, he ought to render as soon as the Sovereign demands them; but the Sovereign, for its part, cannot impose upon its subjects any fetters that are useless to the community: nor can it even wish to do so; for, under the law of reason, nothing occurs without a cause, no more than under the law of nature.

The undertakings binding us to the social body are obligatory only because they are mutual; and their nature is such that in fulfilling them we cannot work for others without working for ourselves. Why is it that the general will is always right, and why does it seek continually to will the happiness of each one, unless it is because there is no man who does not think of *each* as meaning him, and who considers himself in voting for all? This proves that equality of rights and the notion of justice which such equality produces derives from the preference each man gives to himself, and consequently in the very nature of man. [It proves] that the general will, to be truly such, must be [general] in its object as well as in its essence; that it must proceed from all as well as apply to all; and that it loses its natural rectitude when it tends to some particular and determinate object, because in such a case we judge of something foreign to us, and we have no true principle of equity to guide us.

In effect, as soon as a question of fact or of a particular right arises on a point not regulated previously by a general convention, the matter becomes contentious. It is a process where the interested individuals are one party, and the public the other, but where I can see neither the law that ought to be followed nor the judge who ought to render the decision. It would be ridiculous to wish in that case to refer it to an express decision of the general will, which could only be the conclusion of one of the parties, and which consequently for the other party, would be only an external and particular will, inclined on this occasion to injustice and subject to error. Thus, just as a particular will cannot represent the general will, the general will, in turn, changes its nature, having a particular object, and cannot, as general, pronounce on a man or a fact. When, for example, the people of Athens nominated or displaced its rulers, decreed honors to one, and imposed penalties on another, and, by a multitude of particular decrees, exercised indiscriminately all the functions of government, it no longer had in such cases a general will properly speaking; it was acting no longer as Sovereign, but as magistrate. This will seem contrary to common views; but I must be given time to expound my own.

One can see from the foregoing that what makes the will general is less the number of voters than the common interest which unites them; for, under this institution, each necessarily submits to the conditions he imposes on the others: this admirable agreement between interest and justice, gives to the common deliberations an equitable character which at once vanishes in the discussion of any particular question, in the absence of a common interest which unites and identifies the ruling of the judge with that of the party.

From whatever side we approach our principle, we arrive at the same conclusion; that the social compact establishes among the citizens such an equality, that they all bind themselves to observe the same conditions and should all enjoy the same rights. Thus, from the very nature of the compact, every act of Sovereignty, that is to say every authentic act of the general will, binds or favours equally all the citizens; so that the Sovereign recognizes only the body of the nation, and draws no distinctions between those of whom it is composed. What, then, properly speaking is an act of Sovereignty? It is not a convention between a superior and an inferior, but a convention between the body with each of its members: a legitimate convention, because it is based on the social contract; equitable, because common to all; useful, because it can have no other object than the general good; and stable, because guaranteed by the public force and the supreme power. So long as the subjects have to submit only to conventions of this sort, they obey no one, but only their own will; and to ask how far the respective rights of the Sovereign and the citizens extend, is to ask to what point the latter can contract with themselves, each with all, and all with each.

We see from this that the sovereign power, entirely absolute, wholly sacred and inviolable as it is, does not and cannot exceed the limits of general conventions, and that every man may fully dispose of such goods and liberty as these conventions leave him; so that the Sovereign never has a right to charge one subject more than another, because, in that case, the issue becomes particular, and ceases to be within its competency.

When one once admits these distinctions, it is seen to be so untrue that there is, in the social contract, any genuine renunciation on the part of the individuals; so that their position, as a result of the contract, is truly preferable to that in which they were before. Instead of an alienation they have made an advantageous exchange; instead of an uncertain and precarious manner of living, they have one that is better and more secure; instead of natural independence, they have liberty; instead of the power to harm others, security for themselves; and instead of their might, which others might overcome, a right which social union makes invincible. Their very life, which they have devoted to the State, is by it constantly protected; and when they risk it in its defence, what more are they doing than giving back what they have received from it? What are they doing that they would not do more often and with greater danger in the state of nature, in which they would fight inevitable battles at the peril of their lives, to preserve the means of their preservation? All have indeed to fight when their country needs them; but then no one has ever to fight for himself. Do we not gain something by running, for that which gives us our security, only some of the risks we should have to run for ourselves, as soon as we lost it?

THE MEANS OF PREVENTING THE USURPATIONS OF GOVERNMENT

What we have just said . . . makes it clear that the institution of government is not a contract, but a law; that the repositories of the executive power are not the people's masters, but its officers; that it can set them up and pull them down when it pleases; that for them there is no question of contract, but of obedience; and that in undertaking the functions the State imposes on them, they are merely fulfilling their duty as citizens, without having the remotest right to dispute about the conditions.

When therefore the people establish a hereditary government, whether it be monarchical within one family, or aristocratic of one class of citizens, it is not an undertaking that it enters: a provisional form is given the administration, until the people choose to order it otherwise.

It is true that these changes are always dangerous, and that the established government should never be touched except when it becomes incompatible with the public good; but this circumspection is a maxim of policy, and not a rule of right; and the State is no more bound to leave civil authority to its rulers than military authority to its generals.

It is also true that it is impossible, in such cases to observe, with too much care, all the formalities required to distinguish a regular and legitimate act from a seditious tumult, and the will of a whole people from the clamour of a faction. It is here, above all, that no further concession should be made to the untoward possibility that cannot, strictly speaking, be refused it. And it is also from this obligation that the prince derives a great advantage in preserving his power despite the people, without it being possible to say that he has usurped it; for, appearing to avail himself only of his rights, he finds it very easy to extend them, and to prevent, under the pretext of keeping the peace, assemblies that are destined to re-establish good order; with the result that he takes advantage of a silence he does not permit to be broken, or of irregularities he causes to be committed, to assume that he has the support of those whom fear prevents from speaking, and to punish those who dare to speak. Thus it was that the Decemvirs, having been elected for one year and then kept on in office for another year, tried to retain their power in perpetuity by forbidding the Comitia to assemble; and by this easy method every government in the world, once clothed with the public power, sooner or later usurps the sovereign authority.

The periodical assemblies of which I have spoken are designed especially to prevent or postpone this evil, above all when they need no formal convocation; for then, the prince cannot stop them without openly declaring himself a breaker of the laws and an enemy of the State.

The opening of these assemblies, whose only object is the maintenance of the social treaty, should always take the form of making two propositions that may never be suppressed, which should be voted on separately by the voters.

First: "Does it please the Sovereign to preserve the present form of government?"

Second: "Does it please the people to leave its administration in the hands of those actually in charge of it?"

I assume here what I believe I have demonstrated, namely, that there is in the State no fundamental law that cannot be revoked, not excluding the social compact itself; for if all the citizens assembled of one accord to break the compact, one cannot doubt that it would be very legitimately broken. Grotius even thinks that each man can renounce the State of which he is a member and recover his natural liberty and his goods on leaving the country. It would truly be absurd if all the citizens together could not do what each can do by himself.

Daniel Defoe

Daniel Defoe (about 1659–1731) was an outstanding English literary figure during the last decades of the Stuart dynasty and the first years of the Hanoverian. In many ways he personified the rising commercial middle class which, in these decades, was achieving both social and political prestige alongside the cavalier society of the period. He was born into a nonconformist family of some means, and for a time he followed a commercial career which included participation in the import trade. The wide variety of topics on which he wrote made of his works an excellent reflection of the historical trends of the time. Thus the rise of parliament was reflected in The Original Power of the Collective Body of the People of England Examined and Asserted; the religious conflict was revealed in Shortest Way with Dissenters; the interest in discovery and exploration in Robinson Crusoe and A New Voyage Around the World; and the rise of commercial capitalism in The Complete English Tradesman, which appeared in 1726. In the following selections from the latter work note (1) the evidences of national pride, (2) the social position of tradesmen, (3) the services this class rendered to the nation, (4) the comparison he made between the gentry and tradesmen, (5) his explanation for England's greatness, and (6) the significance of trade to America.

From: THE COMPLETE ENGLISH TRADESMAN

Of the dignity of trade in England, more than in other countries. That England is the greatest trading country in the world; that our climate is the best to live in; that our men are the stoutest and best; that the tradesmen in England are not of the meanest of the people; that the wealth of the nation lies chiefly among them; that trade is a continual fund for supplying the decays in the rank of gentry; that an ordinary trader can spend more than a gentleman of 500 £. a year; that an estate is a pond, but trade a spring; that the descendants of tradesmen here, for gallantry of spirit and greatness of soul, are not inferior to the descendants of the best families. Further hints to the ladies whose pride will not let them stoop to marry a tradesman. To trade, and not to conquest, is owing the present grandeur of the English nation. How much the landed interest owes to trade.

Daniel Defoe, *The Complete English Tradesman*, vols. **17–18** of *The Novels and Miscellaneous Works of Daniel De Foe.* . . . Oxford, 1840–1841, chapter 25.

The instances which we have given in the last chapter, abundantly make for the honour of the British traders; and we may venture to say, at the same time, are very far from doing dishonour to the nobility who have from time to time entered into alliance with them; for it is very well known, that besides the benefit which we reap by being a trading nation, which is our principal glory, trade is a very different thing in England than it is in many other countries, and is carried on by persons who, both in their education and descent, are far from being the dregs of the people.

King Charles II, who was perhaps the prince of all the kings that ever reigned in England, who best understood the country and the people he governed, used to say, that the tradesmen were the only gentry in England. His majesty spoke it merrily, but it had a happy signification in it, such as was peculiar to the bright genius of that prince, who, though he was not the best governor, was the best acquainted with the world of all the princes of his age, if not of all the men in it; and I make no scruple to advance these three points in honour of our country; viz.—

1. That we are the greatest trading country in the world, because we have the greatest exportation of the growth and product of our land, and of the manufacture and labour of our people; and the greatest importation and consumption of the growth, product, and manufactures of other countries from abroad, of any nation in the world.

2. That our climate is the best and most agreeable to live in, because a man can be more out of doors in England than in other countries.

3. That our men are the stoutest and best, because, strip them naked from the waist upwards, and give them no weapons at all but their hands and heels, and turn them into a room or stage, and lock them in with the like number of other men of any nation, man for man, and they shall beat the best men you shall find in the world.

And so many of our noble and wealthy families, as we have shown, are raised by and derived from trade, so it is true, and indeed it cannot well be otherwise, that many of the younger branches of our gentry, and even of the nobility itself, have descended again into the spring from whence they flowed, and have become tradesmen; and thence it is that, as I said above, our tradesmen in England are not, as it generally is in other countries, always of the meanest of our people. Nor is trade itself in England, as it generally is in other countries, the meanest thing that men can turn their hand to; but, on the contrary, trade is the readiest way for men to raise their fortunes and families; and therefore it is a field for men of figure and of good families to enter upon.

N. B. By trade we must be understood to include navigation and foreign discoveries; because they are, generally speaking, all promoted and carried on by trade, and even by tradesmen, as well as merchants; and the tradesmen, as owners, are at this time as much concerned in shipping as the merchants, only the latter may be said to be the chief employers of the shipping.

Having thus done a particular piece of justice to ourselves, in the value we put upon trade and tradesmen in England, it reflects very much upon the understandings of those refined heads who pretend to depreciate that part of the nation which is so infinitely superior in wealth to the families who call themselves gentry, and so infinitely more numerous.

As to the wealth of the nation, that undoubtedly lies chiefly among the trading part of the people; and though there are a great many families raised within few years, in the late war, by great employments and by great actions abroad, to the honour of the English gentry, yet how many more families among the tradesmen have been raised to immense estates, even during the same time, by the attending circumstances of the war; such as the clothing, the paying, the victualling and furnishing, &c., both army and navy. And by whom have the prodigious taxes been paid, the loans supplied, and money advanced upon all occasions? By whom are the banks and companies carried on, and on whom are the customs and excises levied? Have not the trade and tradesmen borne the burden of the war? And do they not still pay four millions a year interest for the public debts. On whom are the funds levied, and by whom the public credit supported? Is not trade the inexhausted fund of all funds, and upon which all the rest depend?

As is the trade, so in proportion are the tradesmen; and how wealthy are tradesmen in almost all the several parts of England, as well as in London? How common is it to see a tradesman go off the stage, even but from mere shopkeeping, with from ten to forty thousand pounds' estate to divide among his family! when, on the contrary, take the gentry in England, from one end to the other, except a few here and there, what with excessive high living, which is of late grown so much into a disease, and the other ordinary circumstances of families, we find few families of the lower gentry, that is to say from six or seven hundred a year downwards, but they are in debt, and in necessitous circumstances, and a great many of greater estates also.

On the other hand, let any one who is acquainted with England, look but abroad into the several counties, especially near London, or within fifty miles of it; how are the ancient families worn out by time and family misfortunes, and the estates possessed by a new race of tradesmen, grown up into families of gentry, and established by the immense wealth gained, as I may say, behind the counter; that is, in the shop, the warehouse, and the counting-house.

How many noble seats, superior to the palaces of sovereign princes, in some countries, do we see erected within few miles of this city by tradesmen, or the sons of tradesmen, while the seats and castles of the ancient gentry, like their families, look worn out and fallen into decay! witness the noble house of sir John Eyles, himself a merchant, at Giddyhall, near Romford; sir Gregory Page, on Blackheath, the son of a brewer; sir Nathanael Mead, near Weal-green, his father a linen draper, with many others, too long to repeat; and, to crown all, the lord Castlemain's, now earl of Tilney, at Wanstead, his father, sir Josiah Child, originally a tradesman.

Again; in how superior a port or figure (as we now call it) do our tradesmen live, to what the middling gentry either do or can support! An ordinary tradesman now, not in the city only, but in the country, shall spend more money by the year, than a gentleman of four

or five hundred pounds a year can do, and shall increase and lay up every year too; whereas the gentleman shall at the best stand stock still just where he began, nay, perhaps, decline: and as for the lower gentry, from a hundred pounds a year to three hundred, or thereabouts, though they are often as proud and high in their appearance as the other; as to them, I say, a shoemaker in London shall keep a better house, spend more money, clothe his family better, and yet grow rich too. It is evident where the difference lies; an estate's a pond, but trade's a spring: the first, if it keeps full, and the water wholesome, by the ordinary supplies and drains from the neighbouring grounds, it is well, and it is all that is expected; but the other is an inexhausted current, which not only fills the pond, and keeps it full, but is continually running over, and fills all the lower ponds and places about it.

This being the case in England, and our trade being so vastly great, it is no wonder that the tradesmen in England fill the lists of our nobility and gentry; no wonder that the gentlemen of the best families marry tradesmen's daughters, and put their younger sons apprentices to tradesmen; and how often do these younger sons come to buy the elder sons' estates, and restore the family, when the elder and head of the house, proving rakish and extravagant, has wasted his patrimony, and is obliged to make out the blessing of Israel's family, where the younger son bought the birthright, and the elder was doomed to serve him!

Trade is so far here from being inconsistent with a gentleman, that, in short, trade in England makes gentlemen, and has peopled this nation with gentlemen; for, after a generation or two, the tradesman's children, or at least their grandchildren, come to be as good gentlemen, statesmen, parliamentmen, privy-counsellors, judges, bishops, and noblemen, as those of the highest birth and the most ancient families; as we have shown. Nor do we find any defect either in the genius or capacities of the posterity of tradesmen, arising from any remains of mechanic blood, which, it is pretended, should influence them; but all the gallantry of spirit, greatness of soul, and all the generous principles that can be found in any of the ancient families, whose blood is the most untainted, as they call it, with the low mixtures of a mechanic race, are found in these; and, as is said before, they generally go beyond them in knowledge of the world, which is the best education.

We see the tradesmen of England, as they grow wealthy, coming every day to the herald's office to search for the coats of arms of their ancestors, in order to paint them upon their coaches, and engrave them upon their plate, embroider them upon their furniture, or carve them upon the pediments of their new houses; and how often do we see them trace the registers of their families up to the prime nobility, or the most ancient gentry of the kingdom!

In this search we find them often qualified to raise new families, if they do not descend from old; as was said of a certain tradesman of London, that if he could not find the ancient race of gentlemen, from which he came, he would begin a new race, who should be as good gentlemen as any that went before him.

Thus, in the late wars between England and France, how was our army full of excellent officers, who went from the shop, and behind the counter, into the camp, and who distinguished themselves there by their merits and gallant behaviour! And several such came to command regiments, and even to be general officers, and to gain as much reputation in the service as any; as colonel Pierce, Wood, Richards, and several others that may be named.

All this confirms what I have said before, viz., that trade in England neither is or ought to be levelled with what it is in other countries; or the tradesmen depreciated as they are abroad, and as some of our gentry would pretend to do in England; but that as many of our best families rose from trade, so many branches of the best families in England, under the nobility, have stooped so low as to be put apprentices to tradesmen in London, and to set up and follow those trades when they have come out of their times, and have thought it no dishonour to their blood.

To bring this once more home to the ladies, who are scandalized at that mean step, which they call it, of marrying a tradesman, it may be told them, for their humiliation, that, however they think fit to act, sometimes those tradesmen come of better families than their own; and oftentimes, when they have refused them to their loss, those very tradesmen have married ladies of superior fortune to them, and have raised families of their own, who, in one generation, have been superior to those nice ladies both in dignity and estate; and have, to their great mortification, been ranked above them upon all public occasions.

The word "tradesmen," in England, does not sound so harsh as it does in other countries; and to say a gentleman-tradesman, is not so much nonsense as some people would persuade us to reckon it; and, indeed, the very name of an English tradesman, will and does already obtain in the world; and as our soldiers, by the late war, gained the reputation of being some of the best troops in the world; and our seamen are at this day, and very justly too, esteemed the best sailors in the world; so the English tradesman may be allowed to rank with the best gentlemen in Europe. . . .

And hence it is natural to ask, whence comes all this to be so? How is it produced? War has not done it; no, nor so much as helped or assisted to it; it is not by any martial exploits; we have made no conquests abroad, added no new kingdoms to the British empire, reduced no neighbouring nations, or extended the possession of our monarchs into the properties of others; we have gained nothing by war and encroachment; we are butted and bounded just where we were in queen Elizabeth's time; the Dutch, the Flemings, the French, are in view of us, just as they were then; we have subjected no new provinces or people to our government; and, with few or no exceptions, we are almost, for dominion, where king Edward I. left us: nay, we have lost all the dominions which our ancient kings for some hundreds of years held in France; such as the rich and powerful provinces of Normandy, Poictou, Gascoigne, Bretagne, and Aquitaine; and, instead of being enriched by war and victory, on the contrary, we have been torn in pieces by civil wars and rebellions, as well in Ireland as in England, and that several times, to the ruin of our richest families, and the slaughter of our nobility and gentry; nay, to the destruction even of monarchy itself, as in the long bloody wars between the houses of Lancaster and

York, the many rebellions of the Irish, as well in queen Elizabeth's time, as in king Charles I time; and the fatal massacre, and almost extirpation of the English name in that kingdom; and, at last, the late rebellion in England, in which the monarch fell a sacrifice to the fury of the people, and monarchy itself gave way to tyranny and usurpation, for almost twenty years.

These things prove abundantly that the greatness of the British nation is not owing to war and conquests, to enlarging its dominions by the sword, or subjecting the people of other countries to our power; but it is all owing to trade, to the increase of our commerce at home, and the extending it abroad.

It is owing to trade, that new discoveries have been made in lands unknown, and new settlements and plantations made, new colonies planted, and new governments formed, in the uninhabited islands, and the uncultivated continent of America; and those plantings and settlements have again enlarged and increased the trade, and thereby the wealth and power of the nation by whom they were discovered and planted; we have not increased our power, or the number of our subjects, by subduing the nations which possess those countries, and incorporating them into our own; but have entirely planted our colonies, and peopled the countries with our own subjects, natives of this island; and, excepting the negroes, which we transport from Africa to America, as slaves to work in the sugar and tobacco plantations, all our colonies, as well in the islands, as on the continent of America, are entirely peopled from Great Britain and Ireland, and chiefly the former; the natives having either removed further up into the country, or, by their own folly and treachery raising war against us, been destroyed and cut off.

As trade has thus extended our colonies abroad [Defoe here refers primarily to the colonies in the New World], so it has (except those colonies) kept our people at home, where they are multiplied to that prodigious degree, and do still continue to multiply in such a manner, that, if it goes on so, time may come that all the lands in England will do little more than serve for gardens for them and to feed their cows, and their corn and cattle be supplied from Scotland and Ireland. . . .

Pierre Corneille

*P*ierre Corneille (1606–1684) was one of the great dramatists of seventeenth-century France. He helped to establish modern French drama with the production of his most famous play, Le Cid. In his writing, he reflected the brilliant civilization which flourished during the absolutism of Louis XIV. Displaying an interest in classical drama, Corneille created a tragedy based upon what were thought to be the classic rules of the theater. He made use of the so-called classical unities of time, space, and action, thereby harmonizing his plays with the insistence of the period upon the role of reason in life. In Cinna, which perhaps was his greatest work, he told the story of the reign of Augustus. Writing in a century when absolutism was supreme in his native land, it was perhaps natural that he should stress the stability of absolutism and the evils of popular government. In reading this selection from the second act of Cinna note (1) the proposition which Augustus has just made to his friends, Cinna and Maximus, (2) Cinna's reply in which he analyzed the value of liberty to Rome, (3) his comments on rule by the people, (4) his estimate of Rome under the rule

of Augustus, (5) the influence he thought Augustus could
have on the unity of Rome, (6) the decision which Augustus made, and (7) the significant rewards he gave to his
faithful friends for their counsel.

From: CINNA

SCENE ONE

Augustus, Cinna, Maximus,
Group of courtiers.

Augustus

Let everyone retire; let no one enter;
Only you, Cinna and Maximus, remain.

*All retire, except Augustus, Cinna, and Maxi-
mus*

This empire o'er the land and o'er the sea,
This sovereign power that's mine o'er all the
world
This grandeur without bounds, illustrious rank,
Which cost so much of pain, so much of blood,
In short, all that's admired in my high fortune
By importunate courtiers in this flattering
court,
Is only a beauty whose surface brilliance daz-
zles,
Which loses its attraction, once enjoyed.
Ambition cools when it has had its way
And some contrary passion takes its place,
And, as our spirit toward some fond desire
Forever pushing to the peak of strife,
Recoils, without another way to turn,
Having reached this peak, would fain descend.
I longed for empire; now the empire's mine;
But while I wished I knew not what it was.
Now, having it, I find in it no charms,
But only heavy cares, eternal fear,
A thousand secret fears, death everywhere,
No pleasure without trouble, no repose.
Sulla preceded me in this high rank;
Great Julius, my Father, had it, too.
But with what different eyes these two re-
garded it!
One gave it up, the other would have stayed;
One, cruel, barbarous, died in peace, belovèd,
Like some good citizen within his town;

The other, good, upon the Senate floor
Saw his days cut off by the assassins' daggers.
Examples that might sufficiently instruct me,
If by example only one might learn:
For the one I'd follow; the other inspires fear.
But example's only a deceptive mirror,
And the plan of fate that so disturbs our
thoughts
Is written not, nor clearly, in things past.
Sometimes one man is broken, one preserved;
What crushes one, another often saves.

Behold, my dearest friends, what troubles
me.
You, who for me are Agrippa and Maecenas,
To resolve this problem I with them debated,
Take, o'er my spirit, the power they have had.
Consider not this grandeur that is mine,
Hateful to Romans, weighing on myself;
Treat me as friend, and not as sovereign.
Rome, the State—all is in your hands.
Europe, Asia, Africa, you shall place
Beneath the laws of monarch or republic;
Your counsel is my law, by this device
Emperor I become—or simple citizen.

Cinna

Despite surprise and insufficiency,
I shall obey you, Sire, against my will,
Suppress the reverence that might forbid me
To oppose this plan toward which you seem in-
clined.
Indulge a spirit jealous for your glory,
That you will darken with a blot too deep
By opening your soul to these impressions
Which dare condemn your every imperial ac-
tion.
One does not renounce one's rightful grandeur.
One justly holds what one acquired by right;
The nobler, grander be the prize surrendered,

Reprinted from Maxwell H. Savelle, editor, History 11, *History of Western Civilization, A Syllabus*, Stanford University Press, Stanford University, 1942, 31–33, with the permission of the editor and of the publishers, Stanford University Press

The more he who abandons seems to deem it
Badly won. Mark not with this impression
Those virtues rare by which you won your
    crown;
Your title's just; for without the stain of crime
You changed the framework of the Roman
    State.
Rome obeys your laws by the right of war
That brought the world beneath the laws of
    Rome.
Your arms have conquered Rome, and con-
    querors,
Though called usurpers, tyrants never are.
When under their arms they've brought the
    provinces,
Governing justly, they become just princes:
Thus did Caesar; we today must do
As Caesar did, or condemn his memory.
If Augustus repudiates the sovereign power,
Caesar was tyrant, his execution just,
And to the gods you stand accountable
For all the blood with which you avenged him
To climb to his exalted imperial station.
Fear not, my Lord, an unhappy end;
A spirit far more powerful guards your years.
Ten times vain men have sought to end your
    life:
Who would destroy has only strengthened you.
Many attempt, but no one e'er succeeds;
Many assassins are there, but no Brutus;
In short, if regicide we must expect,
How great to die master of the universe!
These are the few small words I dare to speak,
Believing Maximus agrees with me.

Maximus

Yes, I agree, Augustus has the right
To rule the empire his own virtue's won;
That at the price of his own blood, and peril
Of his head, his conquest of the state
Is just; without disgrace he cannot drop
The burden that his hand grows tired of carry-
    ing.
That he by that accuses Caesar of tyranny,
Or approves great Caesar's death, that I deny.
    Rome is yours, my Lord, the empire yours
And freely one disposes of his own:
Freely he retains, or puts away.
Can you alone not do what common men
So freely do? Have you who conquered all
Become the slave of the grandeur you have
    won?

Possess it, Sire, let it not possess you;
Far from enslaving you, make it obey;
Bring men at last highly to know that you
Can rise above the power of rank and glory.
'Twas Rome, in years gone by, that gave you
    birth;
Now you'd return to Rome your sovereign
    power.
And Cinna imputes to you as mortal crime
Your generous impulse toward your native
    land!
He calls remorse your love of fatherland!
By highest virtue glory now is withered,
Become an object meriting our scorn,
Since glory's highest act is known as infamy!
No! I would say a gesture great as this
Would give to Rome more than you hold from
    her;
Does one commit a crime beyond our pardon
When restitution's richer than the gift?
Hear, hear, my Lord, the heaven who inspires
    you;
Your glory doubles when you renounce the
    empire,
And men will know your fame through all
    posterity,
Less for conquest than for renunciation.
Happy fate may lead to supreme power,
But to renounce it calls for purest virtue,
Few are so generous, nobly to disdain,
Once the scepter's won, the joys of sovereignty.
Consider, besides, that you are ruling Rome,
Where, whatever be the fashion of your nam-
    ing,
Men hate all monarchy; and the name of em-
    peror,
Concealing that of king, is no less horrible.
They take for tyrant who makes himself their
    master,
Who serves him for a slave, who loves him,
    traitor;
Who endures him has a craven heart, soft,
    cowardly;
And all that's done for freedom is thought
    virtuous.
Of that, my Lord, the proof is all too sure:
Ten times against you hands were raised in
    vain;
Mayhap the eleventh is ready to burst upon
    you;
Mayhap this foreboding mood that darkly
    moves you

Is but the secret warning sent from heaven,
Who, for your salvation, has no other way.
Expose yourself no more to evil fortune;
'Tis good to die a ruler of the universe,
But the sweetest death but saddens the memory
Of one who might have lived to greater glory.

Cinna

If love of country should determine us,
'Tis the country's good alone you should desire;
This liberty which Rome esteems so dear
Is nothing, Sire, but an imagined good,
More troublesome than useful, in no wise rivalling
The benefit a good prince brings the state.
  With order and reason he dispenses honors;
Evenly he punishes and rewards;
Of everything disposes as possessor,
Nor is he hurried by fear of his successor.
When the people rule, all action is by tumult,
The voice of reason never can be heard,
Honors are sold for a price to the ambitious,
Authority to traitors to the state.
These petty sovereigns, their one year given power,
Seeing by time so short their power bounded,
To abortive fruitage rush their dark designs,
For fear that those who follow them might reap.
As they have little stake in what they govern
They harvest richly in the public field,
Assured each one of easy public pardon,
Since every citizen desires the same himself.
Of all state forms the popular state is worst.

Augustus

And yet the only kind that Rome will have.
This hate of kings that these five hundred years
Rome's children suckle with their mother's milk,
Cannot now be uprooted from their hearts.

Maximus

In this dear vice Rome, Sire, is obstinate;
Her people, who enjoy it, flee its cure;
Her custom rules her, not dictate of reason;
And this old error that Cinna would erase,
She worships as the happiest of errors,
By which the world entire, beneath her sway,

Has seen her tread upon a thousand thrones,
Her treasury grow rich upon their spoil.
What more could the best of princes give to Rome?
  I dare, my Lord, to say that every clime
May not enjoy all systems of the state:
To each people its own, according to its nature,
A form not altered without injury:
Such is the law of heaven, whose wise justice
Sows in the world this wise diversity.
The Macedonians love their monarchy,
The rest of Greece prefers its liberty;
The Parthians and the Persians keep their despots;
The consulate alone is meet for Rome.

Cinna

'Tis true, indeed, that heaven's infinite wisdom,
Assigns each people a genius of its own;
Yet no less true that under heaven's guidance
This order changes according to place and time.
From kings Rome had her walls and her beginnings,
She holds from consuls all her growth to power,
And now receives from your imperial bounty
The highest reaches of prosperity.
The state's no longer victim of its armies,
The gates of Janus by your hands are closed,
Which under the consuls never once was true,
Nor in the ages since Rome's second king.

Maximus

The changes in the state that are of heaven
Come not at cost of blood, nor bring they ill.

Cinna

It is a rule of heaven, never broken,
That the blessings sold to men are dearly bought:
E'en Tarquin's exile bathed our land in blood,
And our first consuls cost us many wars.

Maximus

Thus your grandfather, Pompey, resisted heaven
When he was struggling for our liberty!

Cinna

Had heaven wished that Rome might lose her freedom,
By the hands of Pompey Rome had been defended;

Nay, by his death heaven chose to mark more
    worthily,
With a sign eternal, this eternal change;
Heaven owed this glory to the shade of such
    a man,
That it carry with it the liberty of Rome.
For long, Rome's name serves but the world
    to dazzle;
Its very grandeur works against enjoyment.
Since Rome herself made mistress of the world,
Since wealth mounts high within the Roman
    walls,
And since her breast, fruitful of great deeds,
Rears citizens more powerful than kings,
The great, to fix their power, buy votes of
    citizens,
And pompously hold their masters in their pay,
Who meekly with gilded iron accept enchain-
    ment,
To receive from them the laws they thought to
    give.
Envious men, they govern by intrigue
That their ambition turns to bloody plots.
Thus Marius stirred the jealousy of Sulla;
My grandfather, that of Caesar, you of An-
    thony;
Thus liberty no longer use retains,
Except to stir the fires of civil war,
When, amid disorder fatal to the universe,
One wants no master, another wants no peer.
   Rome, my Lord, to be saved, must be united
In the rule of some good chief whom all obey.
If you still wish to serve her well and truly,
Take from her the means for further strife.
Sulla, quitting the place he had usurped,
Opened the field to Caesar and to Pompey,
Which the evil of the time had hid from us,
Had he but fixed his power in his family.
What did the cruel murder of great Caesar
But raise against you Anthony and Lepidus,
Who never had destroyed Rome by the Romans
Had Caesar left the empire in your hands?
Again you'll plunge her, quitting the empire
    thus,
Into those ills from which she suffers still,
And of that little blood that yet remains,
New civil war will drain her to her death.
   Let love of country, let sweet pity, touch
    you,

On bended knee Rome prays to you through
    me.
Consider well the price that you have cost
    her—
Nor that she thinks you were too dearly
    bought:
For the ills that she has suffered, she's repaid;
But one just fear now holds her terrified.
If, jealous of her good, and tired of govern-
    ing,
You return to her a power she cannot keep,
At this price another she must buy,
If you prefer your welfare to her good,
This fatal gift must bring her to despair;
I dare not tell here what I dare forsee.
Sire, save yourself, a master under whom
Rome's happiness begins to be reborn;
And, the better to assure the common good,
Name a successor who will be worthy of you.

Augustus

Let's speak no more; pity has won the day.
Repose to me is dear, but Rome is stronger,
And, whatever evil fate await me now,
I am resigned, if so I may save Rome.
In vain my heart sighs for tranquility;
For by your counsel, Cinna, I retain
The empire; yet I keep it but to share
The rule with you. I see full well that your
Two hearts wear no disguise for me, or guile,
And each of you, in the counsel that he gives,
Thinks only of the state and my best good:
It is your love makes this conflict of counsel,
And both of you shall have a fit reward.
You, Maximus, be governor of Sicily.
Go, give my laws to this good and fertile land;
Remember 'tis for me that you are governing;
I'll be responsible for what you do.
On you, Cinna, Amelia I bestow
For wife. You know she holds the place of Julia,
And that, if grim necessity, now past,
Forced me to treat her father with severity,
My generous bounty, opened in her favor,
Has sought to assuage the bitterness of that
    loss.
See her for me; go, and try to win her,
You're not the sort of man she might disdain;
By the offer of your troth she will be charmed.
Adieu. I go to bear the news to Livia.

Isaac Newton

Isaac Newton (1642–1727) was an English intellectual who contributed much to the rise of science and to the era of modern rationalism. When only 23 years of age he worked out the fundamentals of calculus; but this represented only the beginning of his contribution to knowledge. Newton achieved his greatest fame in the field of astrophysics when he worked out the principles of gravitation. Relying upon the work of his predecessors as well as upon his own labors, Newton brought together the laws of planetary motion as developed by Kepler and Galileo's laws of falling bodies into a synthesis that at once related occurrences among the heavenly bodies with action upon the surface of the Earth. The Mathematical Principles of Natural Philosophy, embodying this universal synthesis, became the guiding light of scientists for more than two centuries and brought to Newton the reputation of the lawgiver for the natural universe. The following selection is from one of the prefaces which Newton wrote for his Principles, and in reading it note (1) the degree of complexity which the philosopher should attribute to nature, (2) how Newton extended the law of cause and effect, (3) the importance of the senses in the work of the philosopher, (4) the method by which the character of the heavenly bodies might be determined, (5) how he arrived at his conclusion that the principle of mutual gravitation applied to all heavenly bodies, and (6) the warning he gave to those who would inject hypotheses into experimental philosophy.

From: THE MATHEMATICAL PRINCIPLES OF NATURAL PHILOSOPHY

NEWTON'S RULES OF REASONING IN PHILOSOPHY

RULE I

We are to admit no more causes of natural things than such as are both true and sufficient to explain their appearances.

To this purpose the philosophers say that Nature does nothing in vain, and more is in vain when less will serve; for Nature is pleased with simplicity, and affects not the pomp of superfluous causes.

RULE II

Therefore to the same natural effects we must, as far as possible, assign the same causes.

As to respiration in a man and in a beast; the descent of stones in Europe and in America; the light of our culinary fire and of the sun; the reflection of light on the earth, and in the planets.

RULE III

The qualities of bodies, which admit neither intension nor remission of degrees, and which are found to belong to all bodies within the reach of our experiments, are to be esteemed the universal qualities of all bodies whatsoever.

For since the qualities of bodies are only known to us by experiments, we are to hold for universal all such as universally agree with experiments and such as are not liable to

Isaac Newton, *The Mathematical Principles of Natural Philosophy*, 2 vols., London, 1803, II, 160–162.

diminution can never be quite taken away. We are certainly not to relinquish the evidence of experiments for the sake of dreams and vain fictions of our own devising; nor are we to recede from the analogy of Nature, which uses to be simple, and always consonant to itself. We no other way know the extension of bodies than by our senses, nor do these reach it in all bodies; but because we perceive extension in all that are sensible, therefore we ascribe it universally to all others also. That abundance of bodies are hard, we learn by experience; and because the hardness of the whole arises from the hardness of the parts, we therefore justly infer the hardness of the undivided particles not only of the bodies we feel but of all others. That all bodies are impenetrable, we gather not from reason, but from sensation. The bodies which we handle we find impenetrable, and thence conclude impenetrability to be an universal property of all bodies whatsoever. That all bodies are moveable, and endowed with certain powers (which we call the *vires inertiae*) of persevering in their motion, or in their rest, we only infer the like properties observed in the bodies which we have seen. The extension, hardness, impenetrability, mobility, and *vis inertiae* of the whole, result from the extension, hardness, impenetrability, mobility, and *vires inertiae* of the parts; and thence we conclude the least particles of all bodies to be also all extended, and hard, and impenetrable, and moveable, and endowed with their proper *vires inertiae*. And this is the foundation of all philosophy. Moreover, that the divided but contiguous particles of bodies may be separated from one another, is matter of observation; and, in the particles that remain undivided, our minds are able to distinguish yet lesser parts, as is mathematically demonstated. But whether the parts so distinguished, and not yet divided, may, by the powers of Nature, be actually divided and separated from one

another, we cannot certainly determine. Yet, had we the proof of but one experiment that any undivided particle, in breaking a hard and solid body, suffered a division, we might by virtue of this rule conclude that the undivided as well as the divided particles may be divided and actually separated to infinity.

Lastly, if it universally appears, by experiments and astronomical observations, that all bodies about the earth gravitate towards the earth, and that in proportion to the quantity of matter which they severally contain; that the moon likewise, according to the quantity of its matter, gravitates towards the earth; that, on the other hand, our sea gravitates towards the moon; and all the planets mutually one towards another; and the comets in like manner towards the sun; we must, in consequence of this rule, universally allow that all bodies whatsoever are endowed with a principle of mutual gravitation. For the argument from the appearances concludes with more force for the universal gravitation of all bodies than for their impenetrability; of which, among those in the celestial regions, we have no experiments, nor any manner of observation. Not that I affirm gravity to be essential to bodies: by their *vis infita* I mean nothing but their *vis inertiae*. This is immutable. Their gravity is diminished as they recede from the earth.

RULE IV

In experimental philosophy we are to look upon propositions collected by general induction from phaenomena as accurately or very nearly true, notwithstanding any contrary hypotheses that may be imagined, till such time as other phaenomena occur, by which they may either be made more accurate, or liable to exceptions.

This rule must follow, that the argument of induction may not be evaded by hypotheses.

John Locke

John Locke is well known for his ideas on political theory (see p. 420), but his greatest work was done in the field of philosophy. In 1690 he published An Essay Concerning Human Understanding, in which he made a definitive study of the entire problem of knowledge. In keeping with the scientific and rational spirit of the seventeenth century, Locke rejected Plato's theory of innate ideas and insisted that the mind at birth was a tabula rasa, and that all knowledge was acquired empirically. In reading the following selections from this great work note (1) the product which thinking produced in the mind, (2) the two sources of all ideas which the mind possessed, (3) how knowledge is formed from these ideas, (4) the character of intuitive knowledge, (5) the additional process required in demonstrative knowledge, (6) the situations to which Locke applied the term "sensitive" knowledge, and (7) why clear ideas did not always result in comparably clear knowledge.

From: AN ESSAY CONCERNING HUMAN UNDERSTANDING

OF IDEAS IN GENERAL, AND THEIR ORIGINAL

1. *Idea is the object of thinking.* —Every man being conscious to himself, that he thinks, and that which his mind is applied about, whilst thinking, being the ideas that are there, it is past doubt that men have in their mind several ideas, such as are those expressed by the words, "whiteness, hardness, sweetness, thinking, motion, man, elephant, army, drunkenness," and others. It is in the first place then to be inquired, How he comes by them? I know it is a received doctrine, that men have native ideas and original characters stamped upon their minds in their very first being. This opinion I have at large examined already; and, I suppose, what I have said in the foregoing book will be much more easily admitted, when I have shown whence the understanding may get all the ideas it has, and by what ways and degrees they may come into the mind; for which I shall appeal to every one's own observation and experience.

2. *All ideas come from sensation or reflection.* —Let us then suppose the mind to be, as we say, white paper, void of all characters, without any ideas; how comes it to be furnished? Whence comes it by that vast store, which the busy and boundless fancy of man has painted on it with an almost endless variety? Whence has it all the materials of reason and knowledge? To this I answer, in one word, From experience: in that all our knowledge is founded, and from that it ultimately derives itself. Our observation, employed either about external sensible objects, or about the internal operations of our minds, perceived and reflected on by ourselves, is that which supplies our understandings with all the materials of thinking. These two are the fountains of knowledge, from whence all the ideas we have, or can naturally have, do spring.

3. *The object of sensation one source of ideas.* —First. Our senses, conversant about particular sensible objects, do convey into the mind several distinct perceptions of things, according to those various ways wherein those objects do affect them; and thus we come by those ideas we have of yellow, white, heat, cold, soft, hard, bitter, sweet, and all those which we call sensible qualities; which when I say the senses convey into the mind, I mean, they from external objects convey into the mind what produces there those perceptions. This great source of most of the ideas we have, depending wholly upon our senses, and derived by them to the understanding, I call "sensation."

4. *The operations of our minds the other source of them.* —Secondly. The other fountain, from which experience furnisheth the understanding with ideas, is the perception of the operations of our own minds within us, as it is employed about the ideas it has got; which operations, when the soul comes to reflect on

John Locke, *An Essay Concerning the Human Understanding*, London, 1881, 59–61; 424; 433–434; 438–439.

and consider, do furnish the understanding with another set of ideas which could not be had from things without; and such are perception, thinking, doubting, believing, reasoning, knowing, willing, and all the different actings of our own minds; which we, being conscious of, and observing in ourselves, do from these receive into our understanding as distinct ideas, as we do from bodies affecting our senses. This source of ideas every man has wholly in himself; and though it be not sense as having nothing to do with external objects, yet it is very like it, and might properly enough be called "internal sense." But as I call the other "sensation," so I call this "reflection," the ideas it affords being such only as the mind gets by reflecting on its own operations within itself. By reflection, then, in the following part of this discourse, I would be understood to mean that notice which the mind takes of its own operations, and the manner of them, by reason whereof there come to be ideas of these operations in the understanding. These two, I say, viz., external material things as the objects of sensation, and the operations of our own minds within as the objects of reflection, are, to me, the only originals from whence all our ideas take their beginnings. The term "operations" here, I use in a large sense, as comprehending not barely the actions of the mind about its ideas, but some sort of passions arising sometimes from them, such as is the satisfaction or uneasiness arising from any thought.

5. *All our ideas are of the one or the other of these.* —The understanding seems to me not to have the least glimmering of any ideas which it doth not receive from one of these two. External objects furnish the mind with the ideas of sensible qualities, which are all those different perceptions they produce in us; and the mind furnishes the understanding with ideas of its own operations.

These, when we have taken a full survey of them, and their several modes, combinations, and relations, we shall find to contain all our whole stock of ideas; and that we have nothing in our minds which did not come in one of these two ways. Let any one examine his own thoughts, and thoroughly search into his understanding, and then let him tell me, whether all the original ideas he has there, are any

other than of the objects of his senses, or of the operations of his mind considered as objects of his reflection; and how great a mass of knowledge soever he imagines to be lodged there, he will, upon taking a strict view, see that he has not any idea in his mind but what one of these two hath imprinted, though perhaps with infinite variety compounded and enlarged by the understanding, as we shall see hereafter. . . .

OF KNOWLEDGE IN GENERAL

1. *Our knowledge conversant about our ideas.* —Since the mind, in all its thoughts and reasonings, hath no other immediate object but its own ideas, which it alone does or can contemplate, it is evident that our knowledge is only conversant about them.

2. *Knowledge is the perception of the agreement or disagreement of two ideas.* —Knowledge then seems to me to be nothing but the perception of the connection and agreement, or disagreement and repugnancy, of any of our ideas. In this alone it consists. Where this perception is, there is knowledge; and where it is not, there, though we may fancy, guess, or believe, yet we always come short of knowledge. For, when we know that white is not black, what do we else but perceive that these two ideas do not agree? When we possess ourselves with the utmost security of the demonstration that the three angles of a triangle are equal to two right ones, what do we more but perceive, that equality to two right ones does necessarily agree to, and is inseparable from the three angles of a triangle?

3. *This agreement fourfold.* —But, to understand a little more distinctly, wherein this agreement or disagreement consists, I think we may reduce it all to these four sorts: (1.) Identity, or diversity. (2.) Relation. (3.) Coexistence, or necessary connection. (4.) Real existence. . . .

OF THE DEGREES OF OUR KNOWLEDGE

1. *Intuitive.* —All our knowledge consisting, as I have said, in the view the mind has of its own ideas, which is the utmost light and great-

est certainty we, with our faculties and in our way of knowledge, are capable of, it may not be amiss to consider a little the degrees of its evidence. The different clearness of our knowledge seems to me to lie in the different way of perception the mind has of the agreement or disagreement of any of its ideas. For if we will reflect on our own ways of thinking, we shall find that sometimes the mind perceives the agreement or disagreement of two ideas immediately by themselves, without the intervention of any other: and this, I think, we may call "intuitive knowledge." For in this the mind is at no pains of proving or examining, but perceives the truth, as the eye doth light, only by being directed towards it. Thus the mind perceives that white is not black, that a circle is not a triangle, that three are more than two, and equal to one and two. Such kind of truths the mind perceives at the first sight of the ideas together, by bare intuition, without the intervention of any other idea; and this kind of knowledge is the clearest and most certain that human frailty is capable of. This part of knowledge is irresistible, and, like bright sunshine, forces itself immediately to be perceived as soon as ever the mind turns its view that way; and leaves no room for hesitation, doubt, or examination, but the mind is presently filled with the clear light of it. It is on this intuition that depends all the certainty and evidence of all our knowledge, which certainty every one finds to be so great that he cannot imagine, and therefore not require, a greater: for a man cannot conceive himself capable of a greater certainty, than to know that any idea in his mind is such as he perceives it to be; and that two ideas, wherein he perceives a difference, are different, and not precisely the same. He that demands a greater certainty than this demands he knows not what, and shows only that he has a mind to be a sceptic without being able to be so. Certainty depends so wholly on this intuition, that in the next degree of knowledge, which I call "demonstrative," this intuition is necessary in all the connexions of the intermediate ideas, without which we cannot attain knowledge and certainty.

2. *Demonstrative.* —The next degree of knowledge is, where the mind perceives the agreement or disagreement of any ideas, but not immediately. Though wherever the mind perceives the agreement or disagreement of any of its ideas, there be certain knowledge; yet it does not always happen that the mind sees that agreement or disagreement which there is between them, even where it is discoverable; and in that case remains in ignorance, and at most gets no farther than a probable conjecture. The reason why the mind cannot always perceive presently the agreement or disagreement of two ideas, is, because those ideas concerning whose agreement or disagreement the inquiry is made, cannot by the mind be so put together as to show it. In this case then, when the mind cannot so bring its ideas together as, by their immediate comparison and, as it were, juxtaposition or application one to another, to perceive their agreement or disagreement, it is fain, by the intervention of other ideas (one or more, as it happens), to discover the agreement or disagreement which it searches; and this is that which we call "reasoning." Thus the mind, being willing to know the agreement or disagreement in bigness between the three angles of a triangle and two right ones, cannot, by an immediate view and comparing them, do it: because the three angles of a triangle cannot be brought at once, and be compared with any one or two angles; and so of this the mind has no immediate, no intuitive knowledge. In this case the mind is fain to find out some other angles, to which the three angles of a triangle have an equality; and finding those equal to two right ones, comes to know their equality to two right ones.

3. *Depends on proofs.* —Those intervening ideas which serve to show the agreement of any two others, are called "proofs"; and where the agreement or disagreement is by this means plainly and clearly perceived, it is called "demonstration," it being shown to the understanding, and the mind made to see that it is so. A quickness in the mind to find out these intermediate ideas (that shall discover the agreement or disagreement of any other) and to apply them right, is, I suppose, that which is called "sagacity."

4. *But not so easy.*—This knowledge by intervening proofs, though it be certain, yet the

evidence of it is not altogether so clear and bright, nor the assent so ready, as in intuitive knowledge. For though in demonstration the mind does at last perceive the agreement or disagreement of the ideas it considers, yet it is not without pains and attention; there must be more than one transient view to find it. . . .

14. *Sensitive knowledge of particular existence.* —These two, viz., intuition and demonstration, are the degrees of our knowledge; whatever comes short of one of these, with what assurance soever embraced, is but faith or opinion, but not knowledge, at least in all general truths. There is, indeed, another perception of the mind employed about the particular existence of finite beings without us; which going beyond bare probability, and yet not reaching perfectly to either of the foregoing degrees of certainty, passes under the name of "knowledge." There can be nothing more certain, than that the idea we receive from an external object is in our minds; this is intuitive knowledge. But whether there be any thing more than barely that idea in our minds, whether we can hence certainly infer the existence of any thing without us which corresponds to that idea, is that whereof some men think there may be a question made; because men may have such ideas in their minds when no such thing exists, no such object affects their senses. But yet here, I think, we are provided with an evidence that puts us past doubting; for I ask any one, whether he be not invincibly conscious to himself of a different perception when he looks on the sun by day, and thinks on it by night; when he actually tastes wormwood, or smells a rose, or only thinks on that savour or odour? We as plainly find the difference there is between any idea revived in our minds by our own memory, and actually coming into our minds by our senses, as we do between any two distinct ideas. If any one say, "A dream may do the same thing, and all these ideas may be produced in us without any external objects;" he may please to dream that I make him this answer: (1.) That it is no great matter whether I remove his scruple or no: where all is but dream, reasoning and arguments are of no use, truth and knowledge nothing. (2.) That I believe he will allow a very

manifest difference between dreaming of being in the fire, and being actually in it. But yet if he be resolved to appear so sceptical as to maintain, that what I call "being actually in the fire" is nothing but a dream; and that we cannot thereby certainly know that any such thing as fire actually exists without us; I answer, that we certainly find that pleasure or pain follows upon the application of certain objects to us, whose existence we perceive, or dream that we perceive, by our senses: this certainty is as great as our happiness or misery, beyond which we have no concernment to know or to be. So that, I think, we may add to the two former sorts of knowledge this also, of the existence of particular external objects by that perception and consciousness we have of the actual entrance of ideas from them, and allow these three degrees of knowledge, viz., intuitive, demonstrative, and sensitive: in each of which there are different degrees and ways of evidence and certainty.

15. *Knowledge not always clear, where the ideas are so.* —But since our knowledge is founded on and employed about our ideas only, will it not follow from thence that it is conformable to our ideas; and that where our ideas are clear and distinct, or obscure and confused, our knowledge will be so too? To which I answer, No; for our knowledge consisting in the perception of the agreement or disagreement of any two ideas, its clearness or obscurity consists in the clearness or obscurity of that perception, and not in the clearness or obscurity of the ideas themselves; v. g., a man that has as clear ideas of the angles of a triangle, and of equality to two right ones, as any mathematician in the world, may yet have but a very obscure perception of their agreement, and so have but a very obscure knowledge of it. But ideas which by reason of their obscurity or otherwise are confused, cannot produce any clear or distinct knowledge; because as far as any ideas are confused, so far the mind cannot perceive clearly whether they agree or disagree. Or, to express the same thing in a way less apt to be misunderstood, he that hath not determined the ideas to the words he uses cannot make propositions of them, of whose truth he can be certain.

Alexander Pope

Alexander Pope (1688–1744) was born of a good family in London, where his father was a substantial merchant. Never physically strong, he early devoted himself to literature as a principal interest. At the age of twenty he published his Essay on Criticism and four years later he brought out his Rape of the Lock. Many more poems and essays poured from his prolific pen. In 1729 he turned to a moral and philosophical subject which resulted in An Essay on Man, from which the following selection is taken. In this poem Pope gave popular expression to the glowing faith displayed by the Age of Reason in the simple harmony of nature revealed by Newton. Pope had sung:

> Nature and Nature's laws lay hid in night:
> God said, Let Newton be! and all was Light.

In addition to voicing the veneration of nature and of Newton, Pope phrased into familiar maxims (universal laws) the moral and intellectual convictions of his day. His style likewise reflected his age, for he evidenced a strong dependence upon nature, reason, common sense, and classicism. In reading this passage note (1) Pope's stated objective in writing the essay, (2) the sources of our information about man, (3) man's relationship to the rest of nature, (4) upon what man's happiness depends, (5) the causes of man's unhappiness, (6) the results of pride in man, (7) the unreasonableness of man's complaints against providence, (8) the ranking of man's attributes and the place of reason in this scale, (9) the interrelationships sustained by man with nature, (10) the character of the universe as a whole and Pope's worship of the perfection of nature, and (11) the natural rhythm in which he cast his verses.

From: AN ESSAY ON MAN

Epistle I

Awake, my St. John! leave all meaner things
To low ambition and the pride of kings,
Let us (since life can little more supply
Than just to look about us and to die)
Expatiate free o'er all this scene of Man;
A mighty maze! but not without a plan;
A wild, where weeds and flowers promiscuous
    shoot;
Or garden, tempting with forbidden fruit.
Together let us beat this ample field,

Try what the open, what the covert yield;
The latent tracts, the giddy heights, explore,
Of all who blindly creep, or sightless soar;
Eye Nature's walks, shoot Folly as it flies,
And catch the Manners living as they rise;
Laugh where we must, be candid where we
    can;
But vindicate the ways of God to Man.

I.

Say first of God above or Man below,
What can we reason but from what we know?

Alexander Pope, An Essay on Man, London, 1815, 43–57.

Of man, what see we but his station here,
From which to reason, or to which refer?
Through worlds unnumber'd tho' the God be
    known,
'Tis ours to trace him only in our own.
He, who through vast immensity can pierce,
See worlds on worlds compose one universe,
Observe how system into system runs,
What other planets circle other suns,
What vary'd being peoples every star,
May tell why heaven has made us as we are.
But of this frame, the bearings, and the ties,
The strong connections, nice dependencies,
Gradations just; has thy pervading soul
Look'd through? or can a part contain the
    whole?
Is the great chain, that draws all to agree,
And drawn supports, upheld by God, or thee?

II.

    Presumptuous man! the reason wouldst thou
        find,
Why form'd so weak, so little and so blind?
First, if thou canst, the harder reason guess,
Why form'd no weaker, blinder, and no less.
Ask of thy mother earth, why oaks are made
Taller or stronger than the weeds they shade?
Or ask of yonder argent fields above,
Why Jove's satellites are less than Jove?
    Of systems possible, if 'tis confest
That wisdom infinite must form the best,
Where all must fall or not coherent be,
And all that rises, rise in due degree;
Then, in the scale of reas'ning life, 'tis plain,
There must be, somewhere, such a rank as
    man:
And all the question (wrangle e'er so long)
Is only this, if God has plac'd him wrong?
    Respecting man, whatever wrong we call,
Nay, must be right, as relative to all.
In human works, tho' labour'd on with pain,
A thousand movements scarce one purpose
    gain;
In God's one single can its end produce;
Yet serves to second too some other use.
So man, who here seems principal alone,
Perhaps acts second to some sphere unknown;
Touches some wheel, or verges to some goal;
'Tis but a part we see, and not the whole.
    When the proud steed shall know why man
        retains

His fiery course, or drives him o'er the plains;
When the dull ox, why now he breaks the
    clod,
Is now a victim, and now Ægypt's God:
Then shall man's pride and dulness compre-
    hend
His actions', passions', being's, use and end;
Why doing, suff'ring, check'd, impell'd; and
    why
This hour a slave, the next a deity.
    Then say not man's imperfect, Heaven in
        fault;
Say rather man's as perfect as he ought;
His knowledge measur'd to his state and place;
His time a moment, and a point his space.
If to be perfect in a certain sphere,
What matter, soon or late, or here or there?
The blest to-day is as completely so,
As who began a thousand years ago.

III.

    Heaven from all creatures hides the book of
        fate,
All but the page prescrib'd, their present state·
From brutes what men, from men what spirits
    know;
Or who could suffer being here below?
The lamb thy riot dooms to bleed to-day,
Had he thy reason, would he skip and play?
Pleas'd to the last he crops the flow'ry food,
And licks the hand just rais'd to shed his blood.
O blindness to the future! kindly given,
That each may fill the circle mark'd by heaven!
Who sees with equal eye, as God of all,
A hero perish, or a sparrow fall;
Atoms or systems into ruin hurl'd,
And now a bubble burst, and now a world.
    Hope humbly then; with trembling pinions
        soar;
Wait the great teacher Death; and God adore.
What future bliss, he gives not thee to know,
But gives that hope to be thy blessing now.
Hope springs eternal in the human breast;
Man never is, but always *to be* blest:
The soul, uneasy and confin'd from home,
Rests and expatiates in a life to come.
    Lo, the poor Indian! whose untutor'd mind
Sees God in clouds, or hears him in the wind;
His soul, proud science never taught to stray,
Far as the solar walk or milky way;
Yet simple Nature to his hope has giv'n

Behind the cloud-top hill, an humbler heav'n;
Some safer world in depth of woods embrac'd,
Some happier island in the wat'ry waste,
Where slaves once more their native land behold,
No fiends torment, no Christians thirst for gold.
To be content's his natural desire,
He asks no angel's wing, no seraph's fire;
But thinks admitted to that equal sky,
His faithful dog shall bear him company.

IV.

Go, wiser thou! and, in thy scale of sense,
Weigh thy opinions against providence;
Call imperfection what thou fancy'st such,
Say here he gives too little, there too much;
Destroy all creatures for thy sport or gust,
Yet cry, if man's unhappy, God's unjust;
If man alone engross not Heaven's high care,
Alone made perfect here, immortal there:
Snatch from his hand the balance and the rod,
Re-judge his justice, be the God of God.
In pride, in reas'ning pride, our error lies;
All quit their sphere and rush into the skies.
Pride still is aiming at the blest abodes,
Men would be angels, angels would be gods.
Aspiring to be gods, if angels fell,
Aspiring to be angels, men rebel:
And who but wishes to invert the laws
Of Order, sins against the eternal cause.

V.

Ask for what end the heavenly bodies shine,
Earth for whose use? Pride answers, " 'Tis for mine.
For me kind nature wakes her genial power,
Suckles every herb, and spreads out ev'ry flower;
Annual for me, the grape, the rose renew
The juice nectareous, and the balmy dew;
For me, the mine a thousand treasures brings;
For me, health gushes from a thousand springs;
Seas roll to waft me, suns to light me rise;
My footstool earth, my canopy the skies."
But errs not Nature from this gracious end,
From burning suns when livid deaths descend,
When earthquakes swallow, or when tempests sweep
Towns to one grave, whole nations to the deep?
"No ('tis reply'd,) the first Almighty Cause
Acts not by partial, but by gen'ral laws;
The exceptions few; some change since all began;
And what created perfect?"—Why then man?
If the great end be human happiness,
Then Nature deviates; and can man do less?
As much that end a constant course requires,
Of showers and sunshine, as of man's desires:
As much eternal springs and cloudless skies,
As men for ever temperate, calm, and wise.
If plagues or earthquakes break not heaven's design,
Why then a Borgia or a Cataline?
Who knows but he whose hand the lightning forms,
Who heaves old ocean, and wings the storms;
Pours fierce ambition in a Caesar's mind,
Or turns young Ammon loose to scourge mankind?
From pride, from pride, our very reas'ning springs;
Account for moral, as for natural things:
Why charge we heaven in those, in these acquit?
In both, to reason right is to submit.
Better for us, perhaps, it might appear,
Were there all harmony, all virtue here;
That never air or ocean felt the wind;
That never passion discompos'd the mind.
But ALL subsists by elemental strife;
And passions are the elements of life.
The gen'ral ORDER since the whole began,
Is kept in nature, and is kept in man.

VI.

What would this man? now upward will he soar,
And little less than angel, would be more;
Now looking downwards, just as griev'd appears
To want the strength of bulls, the fur of bears.
Made for his use, all creatures, if he call,
Say what their use, had he the powers of all?
Nature to these, without profusion kind,
The proper organs proper powers assign'd;
Each seeming want compensated of course,
Here with degrees of swiftness, there of force:
All in exact proportion to the state;
Nothing to add, and nothing to abate.
Each beast, each insect, happy in its own;

Is heaven unkind to man, and man alone?
Shall he alone, whom rational we call,
Be pleas'd with nothing, if not pleas'd with all?
  The bliss of man (could pride that blessing
    find)
Is not to act or think beyond mankind;
No powers of body or of soul to share,
But what his nature and his state can bear.
Why has not man a microscopic eye?
For this plain reason, man is not a fly.
Say what the use, were finer optics given,
T' inspect a mite, not comprehend the heaven?
Or touch, if tremblingly alive all o'er,
To smart and agonize at every pore?
Or quick effluvia darting through the brain,
Die of a rose in aromatic pain?
If Nature thunder'd in his op'ning ears,
And stunn'd him with the music of the spheres,
How would he wish that heaven had left him
    still
The whisp'ring zephyr and the purling rill?
Who finds not Providence all good and wise,
Alike in what it gives, and what denies?

VII.

  Far as creation's ample range extends,
The scale of sensual, mental power ascends:
Mark how it mounts, to man's imperial race,
From the green myriads in the peopled grass:
What modes of sight betwixt each wide ex-
    treme,
The mole's dim curtain, and the lynx's beam!
Of smell, the headlong lioness between,
And hound sagacious on the tainted green!
Of hearing, from the life that fills the flood,
To that which warbles through the vernal
    wood!
The spider's touch, how exquisitely fine!
Feels at each thread, and lives along the line:
In the nice bee, what sense so subtilely true,
From pois'nous herbs extracts the healing dew!
How instinct varies in the grov'ling swine,
Compar'd, half reas'ning elephant, with thine!
'Twixt that and reason, what a nice barrier!
For ever separate, yet for ever near!
Remembrance and reflection how ally'd!
What thin partitions sense from thought di-
    vide!
And middle natures, how they long to join,
Yet never pass the insuperable line!

Without this just gradation could they be
Subjected, these to those, or all to thee?
The powers of all subdu'd by thee alone,
Is not thy reason all these powers in one?

VIII.

  See through this air, this ocean, and this
    earth,
All matter quick, and bursting into birth.
Above, how high, progressive life may go!
Around how wide! how deep extend below!
Vast chain of being! which from God began,
Natures aethereal, human, angel, man,
Beast, bird, fish, insect, what no eye can see,
No glass can reach; from infinite to thee;
From thee to nothing. On superior powers
Were we to press, inferior might on our's:
Or in the full creation leave a void,
Where, one step broken, the great scale's de-
    stroy'd:
From Nature's chain, whatever link you strike,
Tenth, or ten thousandth, breaks the chain
    alike.
  And, if each system in gradation roll
Alike essential to th' amazing whole,
The least confusion but in one, not all
That system only, but the whole must fall.
Let earth, unbalanc'd from her orbit fly,
Planets and suns run lawless through the sky;
Let ruling angels from their spheres be hurl'd,
Being on being wreck'd, and world on world;
Heaven's whole foundations to their centre
    nod,
And Nature tremble to the throne of God.
All this dread Order break—for whom? for
    thee?
Vile worm! ah madness! pride! impiety!

IX.

  What if the foot, ordain'd the dust to tread,
Or hand, to toil, aspir'd to be the head?
What if the head, the eye, or ear repin'd
To serve mere engines to the ruling mind?
Just as absurd for any part to claim
To be another, in this gen'ral frame:
Just as absurd to mourn the tasks or pains
The great directing Mind of All ordains.
  All are but parts of one stupendous whole,
Whose body Nature is, and God the soul:
That chang'd through all, and yet in all the
    same:

Great in the earth, as in th' aethereal frame;
Warms in the sun, refreshes in the breeze,
Glows in the stars, and blossoms in the trees;
Lives through all life, extends through all extent,
Spreads undivided, operates unspent;
Breathes in our soul, informs our mortal part,
As full, as perfect, in a hair as heart;
As full, as perfect, in vile man that mourns,
As the rapt seraph that adores and burns:
To him no high, no low, no great, no small;
He fills, he bounds, connects, and equals all.

X.

Cease then, nor Order imperfection name;
Our proper bliss depends on what we blame.

Know thy own point: this kind, this due degree
Of blindness, weakness, Heaven bestows on thee.
Submit. In this, or any other sphere,
Secure to be as blest as thou canst bear:
Safe in the hand of one disposing Power,
Or in the natal, or the mortal hour.
All nature is but art, unknown to thee;
All chance, direction, which thou canst not see;
All discord, harmony not understood;
All partial evil, universal good:
And, spite of Pride, in erring Reason's spite,
One truth is clear, WHATEVER IS, IS RIGHT.

Voltaire

François Marie Arouet de Voltaire (1694–1778) was a French writer and philosopher who personified the rationalism of the eighteenth-century Enlightenment. Living in a France still dominated by Bourbon absolutism, he nevertheless daringly espoused the cause of tolerance, progress, and cosmopolitanism while at the same time attacking orthodoxy, both political and religious. In 1759, he wrote Candide, taking only three days to write this famous satire. Four years earlier the city of Lisbon, Portugal, had been badly damaged by one of the great forces of nature, an earthquake. Voltaire used this incident in Candide as one of the means of ridiculing the excessive and complacent optimism which had been reflected by some of the intellectuals of his day. He directed his satire particularly at the German philosopher, Leibnitz (1646–1716). Voltaire also used Candide to uphold some of the ideals of the Enlightenment. In reading the following passage [Part One] from this great work, note (1) evidence of Voltaire's attitude toward the belief in the perfection of nature, (2) his position regarding the extreme emphasis which the Enlightenment placed on reason, (3) the fun he poked at those who try to express everything in terms of mathematics, (4) his position in regard to nationalism and war, (5) the attitude he expressed toward the clergy and organized Christianity, (6) the opposition he displayed toward tyrannical government, (7) evidences of Voltaire's belief in social equality, and (8) how he believed morality could best be obtained.

Voltaire, *Candide*, The Modern Library, New York, 1930, 3–149. Courtesy of Random House, Inc.

From: CANDIDE

HOW CANDIDE WAS BROUGHT UP IN A NOBLE CASTLE AND HOW HE WAS EXPELLED FROM THE SAME

In the castle of Baron Thunder-ten-tronckh in Westphalia there lived a youth, endowed by Nature with the most gentle character. His face was the expression of his soul. His judgment was quite honest and he was extremely simple-minded; and this was the reason, I think, that he was named Candide. Old servants in the house suspected that he was the son of the Baron's sister and a decent honest gentleman of the neighbourhood, whom this young lady would never marry because he could only prove seventy-one quarterings, and the rest of his genealogical tree was lost, owing to the injuries of time. The Baron was one of the most powerful lords in Westphalia, for his castle possessed a door and windows. His Great Hall was even decorated with a piece of tapestry. The dogs in his stable-yards formed a pack of hounds when necessary; his grooms were his huntsmen; the village curate was his Grand Almoner. They all called him "My Lord," and laughed heartily at his stories. The Baroness weighed about three hundred and fifty pounds, was therefore greatly respected, and did the honours of the house with a dignity which rendered her still more respectable. Her daughter Cunegonde, aged seventeen, was rosy-cheeked, fresh, plump and tempting. The Baron's son appeared in every respect worthy of his father. The tutor Pangloss was the oracle of the house, and little Candide followed his lessons with all the candour of his age and character. Pangloss taught metaphysico-theologo-cosmolonigology. He proved admirably that there is no effect without a cause and that in this best of all possible worlds, My Lord the Baron's castle was the best of castles and his wife the best of all possible Baronesses. " 'Tis demonstrated," said he, "that things cannot be otherwise; for, since everything is made for an end, everything is necessarily for the best end. Observe that noses were made to wear spectacles; and so we have spectacles. Legs were visibly instituted to

be breeched, and we have breeches. Stones were formed to be quarried and to build castles; and My Lord has a very noble castle; the greatest Baron in the province should have the best house; and as pigs were made to be eaten, we eat pork all the year round; consequently, those who have asserted that all is well talk nonsense; they ought to have said that all is for the best." Candide listened attentively and believed innocently; for he thought Mademoiselle Cunegonde extremely beautiful, although he was never bold enough to tell her so. He decided that after the happiness of being born Baron of Thunder-ten-tronckh, the second degree of happiness was to be Mademoiselle Cunegonde; the third, to see her every day; and the fourth, to listen to Doctor Pangloss, the greatest philosopher of the province and therefore of the whole world. One day when Cunegonde was walking near the castle, in a little wood which was called The Park, she observed Doctor Pangloss in the bushes, giving a lesson in experimental physics to her mother's waiting-maid, a very pretty and docile brunette. Mademoiselle Cunegonde had a great inclination for science and watched breathlessly the reiterated experiments she witnessed; she observed clearly the Doctor's sufficient reason, the effects and the causes, and returned home very much excited, pensive, filled with the desire of learning, reflecting that she might be the sufficient reason of young Candide and that he might be hers. On her way back to the castle she met Candide and blushed; Candide also blushed. She bade him good-morning in a hesitating voice; Candide replied without knowing what he was saying. Next day, when they left the table after dinner, Cunegonde and Candide found themselves behind a screen; Cunegonde dropped her handkerchief, Candide picked it up; she innocently held his hand; the young man innocently kissed the young lady's hand with remarkable vivacity, tenderness and grace; their lips met, their eyes sparkled, their knees trembled, their hands wandered. Baron Thunder-ten-tronckh passed near the screen, and, observing this cause and effect, expelled Candide from the castle by kicking him in the backside frequently and hard. Cunegonde swooned; when she recovered her senses, the Baroness slapped her in the face; and all was in consternation in the noblest and most agreeable of all possible castles.

WHAT HAPPENED TO CANDIDE AMONG THE BULGARIANS

Candide, expelled from the earthly paradise, wandered for a long time without knowing where he was going, turning up his eyes to Heaven, gazing back frequently at the noblest of castles which held the most beautiful of young Baronesses; he lay down to sleep supperless between two furrows in the open fields; it snowed heavily in large flakes. The next morning the shivering Candide, penniless, dying of cold and exhaustion, dragged himself towards the neighbouring town, which was called Waldberghoff-trarbk-dikdorff. He halted sadly at the door of an inn. Two men dressed in blue noticed him. "Comrade," said one, "there's a well-built young man of the right height." They went up to Candide and very civilly invited him to dinner. "Gentlemen," said Candide with charming modesty, "you do me a great honour, but I have no money to pay my share." "Ah, sir," said one of the men in blue, "persons of your figure and merit never pay anything; are you not five feet five tall?" "Yes, gentlemen," said he, bowing, "that is my height." "Ah, sir, come to table; we will not only pay your expenses, we will never allow a man like you to be short of money; men were only made to help each other." "You are in the right," said Candide, "that is what Doctor Pangloss was always telling me, and I see that everything is for the best." They begged him to accept a few crowns, he took them and wished to give them an IOU; they refused to take it and all sat down to table. "Do you not love tenderly . . ." "Oh, yes," said he. "I love Mademoiselle Cunegonde tenderly." "No," said one of the gentlemen. "We were asking if you do not tenderly love the King of the Bulgarians." "Not a bit," said he, "for I have never seen him." "What! He is the most charming of Kings, and you must drink his health." "Oh, gladly, gentlemen." And he drank. "That is

sufficient," he was told. "You are now the support, the aid, the defender, the hero of the Bulgarians; your fortune is made and your glory assured." They immediately put irons on his legs and took him to a regiment. He was made to turn to the right and left, to raise the ramrod and return the ramrod, to take aim, to fire, to double up, and he was given thirty strokes with a stick; the next day he drilled not quite so badly, and received only twenty strokes; the day after, he only had ten and was looked on as a prodigy by his comrades. Candide was completely mystified and could not make out how he was a hero. One fine spring day he thought he would take a walk, going straight ahead, in the belief that to use his legs as he pleased was a privilege of the human species as well as of animals. He had not gone two leagues when four other heroes, each six feet tall, fell upon him, bound him and dragged him back to a cell. He was asked by his judges whether he would rather be thrashed thirty-six times by the whole regiment or receive a dozen lead bullets at once in his brain. Although he protested that men's wills are free and that he wanted neither one nor the other, he had to make a choice; by virtue of that gift of God which is called *liberty*, he determined to run the gauntlet thirty-six times and actually did so twice. There were two thousand men in the regiment. That made four thousand strokes which laid bare the muscles and nerves from his neck to his backside. As they were about to proceed to a third turn, Candide, utterly exhausted, begged as a favour that they would be so kind as to smash his head; he obtained this favour; they bound his eyes and he was made to kneel down. At that moment the King of the Bulgarians came by and inquired the victim's crime; and as this King was possessed of a vast genius, he perceived from what he learned about Candide that he was a young metaphysician very ignorant in worldly matters, and therefore pardoned him with a clemency which will be praised in all newspapers and all ages. An honest surgeon healed Candide in three weeks with the ointments recommended by Dioscorides. He had already regained a little skin and could walk when the King of the Bulgarians went to war with the King of the Abares.

HOW CANDIDE ESCAPED FROM THE BULGARIANS AND WHAT BECAME OF HIM

Nothing could be smarter, more splendid, more brilliant, better drawn up than the two armies. Trumpets, fifes, hautboys, drums, cannons, formed a harmony such as has never been heard even in hell. The cannons first of all laid flat about six thousand men on each side; then the musketry removed from the best of worlds some nine or ten thousand blackguards who infested its surface. The bayonet also was the sufficient reason for the death of some thousands of men. The whole might amount to thirty thousand souls. Candide, who trembled like a philosopher, hid himself as well as he could during this heroic butchery. At last, while the two Kings each commanded a Te Deum in his camp, Candide decided to go elsewhere to reason about effects and causes. He clambered over heaps of dead and dying men and reached a neighbouring village, which was in ashes; it was an Abare village which the Bulgarians had burned in accordance with international law. Here, old men dazed with blows watched the dying agonies of their murdered wives who clutched their children to their bleeding breasts; there, disembowelled girls who had been made to satisfy the natural appetites of heroes gasped their last sighs; others, half-burned, begged to be put to death. Brains were scattered on the ground among dismembered arms and legs. Candide fled to another village as fast as he could; it belonged to the Bulgarians, and Abarian heroes had treated it in the same way. Candide, stumbling over quivering limbs or across ruins, at last escaped from the theatre of war, carrying a little food in his knapsack, and never forgetting Mademoiselle Cunegonde. His provisions were all gone when he reached Holland; but, having heard that everyone in that country was rich and a Christian, he had no doubt at all but that he would be as well treated as he had been in the Baron's castle before he had been expelled on account of Mademoiselle Cunegonde's pretty eyes. He asked an alms of several grave persons, who all replied that if he continued in that way he would be shut up in a house of correction to teach him how to live. He then addressed himself to a man who had been discoursing on charity in a large assembly for an hour on end. This orator, glancing at him askance, said: "What are you doing here? Are you for the good cause?" "There is no effect without a cause," said Candide modestly. "Everything is necessarily linked up and arranged for the best. It was necessary that I should be expelled from the company of Mademoiselle Cunegonde, that I ran the gauntlet, and that I beg my bread until I can earn it; all this could not have happened differently." "My friend," said the orator, "do you believe that the Pope is Anti-Christ?" "I had never heard so before," said Candide, "but whether he is or isn't, I am starving." "You don't deserve to eat," said the other. "Hence, rascal; hence, you wretch; and never come near me again." The orator's wife thrust her head out of the window and seeing a man who did not believe that the Pope was Anti-Christ, she poured on his head a full . . . O Heavens! To what excess religious zeal is carried by ladies! A man who had not been baptized, an honest Anabaptist named Jacques, saw the cruel and ignominious treatment of one of his brothers, a featherless two-legged creature with a soul; he took him home, cleaned him up, gave him bread and beer, presented him with two florins, and even offered to teach him to work at the manufacture of Persian stuffs which are made in Holland. Candide threw himself at the man's feet, exclaiming: "Doctor Pangloss was right in telling me that all is for the best in this world, for I am vastly more touched by your extreme generosity than by the harshness of the gentleman in the black cloak and his good lady." The next day when he walked out he met a beggar covered with sores, dull-eyed, with the end of his nose fallen away, his mouth awry, his teeth black, who talked huskily, was tormented with a violent cough and spat out a tooth at every cough.

HOW CANDIDE MET HIS OLD MASTER IN PHILOSOPHY, DOCTOR PANGLOSS, AND WHAT HAPPENED

Candide, moved even more by compassion than by horror, gave this horrible beggar the two florins he had received from the honest Anabaptist, Jacques. The phantom gazed fixedly at him, shed tears and threw its arms round his neck. Candide recoiled in terror. "Alas!" said the wretch to the other wretch, "don't you recognise your dear Pangloss?" "What do I hear? You, my dear master! You, in this horrible state! What misfortune has happened to you? Why are you no longer in the noblest of castles? What has become of Mademoiselle Cunegonde, the pearl of young ladies, the masterpiece of Nature?" "I am exhausted," said Pangloss. Candide immediately took him to the Anabaptist's stable where he gave him a little bread to eat; and when Pangloss had recovered: "Well!" said he, "Cunegonde?" "Dead," replied the other. At this word Candide swooned; his friend restored him to his senses with a little bad vinegar which happened to be in the stable. Candide opened his eyes. "Cunegonde dead! Ah! best of worlds, where are you? But what illness did she die of? Was it because she saw me kicked out of her father's noble castle?" "No," said Pangloss. "She was disembowelled by Bulgarian soldiers, after having been raped to the limit of possibility; they broke the Baron's head when he tried to defend her; the Baroness was cut to pieces; my poor pupil was treated exactly like his sister; and as to the castle, there is not one stone standing on another, not a barn, not a sheep, not a duck, not a tree; but we were well avenged, for the Abares did exactly the same to a neighbouring barony which belonged to a Bulgarian Lord." At this, Candide swooned again; but, having recovered and having said all that he ought to say, he inquired the cause and effect, the sufficient reason which had reduced Pangloss to so piteous a state. "Alas!" said Pangloss, " 'tis love; love, the consoler of the human race, the preserver of the universe, the soul of all tender creatures, gentle love." "Alas!" said Candide, "I am acquainted with this love, this sovereign of hearts, this soul of our soul; it has never brought me anything but one kiss and twenty kicks in the backside. How could this beautiful cause produce in you so abominable an effect?" Pangloss replied as follows: "My dear Candide! You remember Paquette, the maid-servant of our august Baroness; in her arms I enjoyed the delights of Paradise which have produced the tortures of Hell by which you see I am devoured; she was infected and perhaps is dead. Paquette received this present from a most learned monk, who had it from the source; for he received it from an old countess, who had it from a cavalry captain, who owed it to a marchioness, who derived it from a page, who had received it from a Jesuit, who, when a novice, had it in a direct line from one of the companions of Christopher Columbus. For my part, I shall not give it to anyone, for I am dying." "O Pangloss!" exclaimed Candide, "this is a strange genealogy! Wasn't the devil at the root of it?" "Not at all," replied that great man. "It was something indispensable in this best of worlds, a necessary ingredient; for, if Columbus in an island of America had not caught this disease, which poisons the source of generation, and often indeed prevents generation, we should not have chocolate and cochineal; it must also be noticed that hitherto in our continent this disease is peculiar to us, like theological disputes. The Turks, the Indians, the Persians, the Chinese, the Siamese and the Japanese are not yet familiar with it; but there is a sufficient reason why they in their turn should become familiar with it in a few centuries. Meanwhile, it has made marvellous progress among us, and especially in those large armies composed of honest, well-bred stipendiaries who decide the destiny of States; it may be asserted that when thirty thousand men fight a pitched battle against an equal number of troops, there are about twenty thousand with the pox on either side." "Admirable!" said Candide. "But you must get cured." "How can I?" said Pangloss. "I haven't a sou, my friend, and in the whole extent of this globe, you cannot be bled or receive an enema without paying or without someone paying for you." This last speech determined Candide; he went and threw himself at the feet of his charitable Anabaptist, Jacques, and drew so touching a picture of the state to which his friend was reduced that the good easy man did not hesitate to succour Pangloss; he had him cured at his own expense. In this cure Pangloss only lost one eye and one ear. He could write well and knew arithmetic perfectly. The Anabaptist made him his book-keeper. At the end of two months he was compelled to go to Lisbon on business and took his two philosophers on the boat with him. Pangloss explained to him how everything was for the best. Jacques was not of this opinion. "Men," said he, "must have corrupted nature a little, for they were not born wolves, and they have become wolves. God did not give them twenty-four-pounder cannons or bayonets, and they have made bayonets and cannons to destroy each other. I might bring bankruptcies into the account and Justice which seizes the goods of bankrupts in order to deprive the creditors of them." "It was all indispensable," replied the one-eyed doctor," and private misfortunes make the public good, so that the more private misfortunes there are, the more everything is well." While he was reasoning, the air grew dark, the winds blew from the four quarters of the globe and the ship was attacked by the most horrible tempest in sight of the port of Lisbon.

STORM, SHIPWRECK, EARTHQUAKE, AND WHAT HAPPENED TO DR. PANGLOSS, TO CANDIDE AND THE ANABAPTIST JACQUES

Half the enfeebled passengers, suffering from that inconceivable anguish which the rolling of a ship causes in the nerves and in all the humours of bodies shaken in contrary directions, did not retain strength enough even to trouble about the danger. The other half screamed and prayed; the sails were torn, the masts broken, the vessel leaking. Those worked who could, no one co-operated, no one commanded. The Anabaptist tried to help the crew a little; he was on the main-deck; a furious sailor struck him violently and stretched him on the deck; but the blow he delivered gave him so violent a shock that he fell head-first out of the ship. He remained hanging and clinging to part of the broken mast. The good Jacques ran to his aid, helped him to climb back, and from the effort he made was flung into the sea in full view of the sailor, who allowed him to drown without condescending even to look at him. Candide came up, saw his benefactor reappear for a moment and then be engulfed for ever. He tried to throw himself after him into the sea; he was prevented by the philosopher Pangloss, who proved to him that the Lisbon roads had been expressly created for the Anabaptist to be drowned in them. While he was proving this a priori, the vessel sank, and every one perished except Pangloss, Candide and the brutal sailor who had drowned the virtuous Anabaptist; the blackguard swam successfully to the shore and Pangloss and Candide were carried there on a plank. When they had recovered a little, they walked toward Lisbon; they had a little money by the help of which they hoped to be saved from hunger after having escaped the storm. Weeping the death of their benefactor, they had scarcely set foot in the town when they felt the earth tremble under their feet; the sea rose in foaming masses in the port and smashed the ships which rode at anchor. Whirlwinds of flame and ashes covered the streets and squares; the houses collapsed, the roofs were thrown upon the foundations, and the foundations were scattered; thirty thousand inhabitants of every age and both sexes were crushed under the ruins. Whistling and swearing, the sailor said: "There'll be something to pick up here." "What can be the sufficient reason for this phenomenon?" said Pangloss. "It is the last day!" cried Candide. The sailor immediately ran among the debris, dared death to find money, found it, seized it, got drunk, and having slept off his wine, purchased the favours of the first woman of goodwill he met on the ruins of the houses and among the dead and dying. Pangloss, however, pulled him by the sleeve. "My friend," said he, "this is not well, you are disregarding universal reason, you choose the wrong time." "Blood and 'ounds!" he retorted, "I am a sailor and I was born in Batavia; four times have I stamped on the crucifix during four voyages to Japan; you have found the right man for your universal reason!" Candide had been hurt by some falling stones; he lay in the street covered with debris. He said to Pangloss: "Alas! Get me a little wine and oil; I am dying." "This earthquake is not a new thing," replied Pangloss. "The town of Lima felt the same shocks in America last year; similar causes produce similar effects; there must certainly be a train of sulphur underground from Lima to Lisbon." "Nothing is more probable," replied Candide; "but, for God's sake, a little oil and wine."

"What do you mean, probable?" replied the philosopher; "I maintain that it is proved." Candide lost consciousness, and Pangloss brought him a little water from a neighbouring fountain. Next day they found a little food as they wandered among the ruins and regained a little strength. Afterwards they worked like others to help the inhabitants who had escaped death. Some citizens they had assisted gave them as good a dinner as could be expected in such a disaster; true, it was a dreary meal; the hosts watered their bread with their tears, but Pangloss consoled them by assuring them that things could not be otherwise. "For," said he, "all this is for the best; for, if there is a volcano at Lisbon, it cannot be anywhere else; for it is impossible that things should not be where they are; for all is well." A little, dark man, a familiar of the Inquisition, who sat beside him, politely took up the conversation, and said: "Apparently, you do not believe in original sin; for, if everything is for the best, there was neither fall nor punishment." "I most humbly beg your excellency's pardon," replied Pangloss still more politely, "for the fall of man and the curse necessarily entered into the best of all possible worlds." "Then you do not believe in free-will?" said the familiar. "Your excellency will pardon me," said Pangloss; "free-will can exist with absolute necessity; for it was necessary that we should be free; for in short, limited will . . ." Pangloss was in the middle of his phrase when the familiar nodded to his armed attendant who was pouring out port or Oporto wine for him.

HOW A SPLENDID AUTO-DA-FÉ WAS HELD TO PREVENT EARTHQUAKES, AND HOW CANDIDE WAS FLOGGED

After the earthquake which destroyed three-quarters of Lisbon, the wise men of that country could discover no more efficacious way of preventing a total ruin than by giving the people a splendid *auto-da-fé*. It was decided by the university of Coimbre that the sight of several persons being slowly burned in great ceremony is an infallible secret for preventing earthquakes. Consequently they had arrested a Biscayan convicted of having married his fellow-godmother, and two Portuguese who,

when eating a chicken, had thrown away the bacon; after dinner they came and bound Dr. Pangloss and his disciple Candide, one because he had spoken and the other because he had listened with an air of approbation; they were both carried separately to extremely cool apartments, where there was never any discomfort from the sun; a week afterwards each was dressed in a sanbenito and their heads were ornamented with paper mitres; Candide's mitre and sanbenito were painted with flames upside down and with devils who had neither tails nor claws; but Pangloss's devils had claws and tails, and his flames were upright. Dressed in this manner they marched in procession and listened to a most pathetic sermon, followed by lovely plain-song music. Candide was flogged in time to the music, while the singing went on; the Biscayan and the two men who had not wanted to eat bacon were burned, and Pangloss was hanged, although this is not the custom. The very same day, the earth shook again with a terrible clamour. Candide, terrified, dumbfounded, bewildered, covered with blood, quivering from head to foot, said to himself: "If this is the best of all possible worlds, what are the others? Let it pass that I was flogged, for I was flogged by the Bulgarians, but, O my dear Pangloss! The greatest of philosophers! Must I see you hanged without knowing why! O my dear Anabaptist! The best of men! Was it necessary that you should be drowned in port! O Mademoiselle Cunegonde! The pearl of women! Was it necessary that your belly should be slit!" He was returning, scarcely able to support himself, preached at, flogged, absolved and blessed, when an old woman accosted him and said: "Courage, my son, follow me."

HOW AN OLD WOMAN TOOK CARE OF CANDIDE AND HOW HE REGAINED THAT WHICH HE LOVED

Candide did not take courage, but he followed the old woman to a hovel; she gave him a pot of ointment to rub on, and left him food and drink; she pointed out a fairly clean bed; near the bed there was a suit of clothes. "Eat, drink, sleep," said she, "and may our Lady of Atocha, my Lord Saint Anthony of Padua and my Lord Saint James of Compostella take care of you; I shall come back tomorrow." Candide, still amazed by all he had seen, by all he had suffered, and still more by the old woman's charity, tried to kiss her hand. " 'Tis not my hand you should kiss," said the old woman, "I shall come back to-morrow. Rub on the ointment, eat and sleep." In spite of all his misfortune, Candide ate and went to sleep. Next day the old woman brought him breakfast, examined his back and smeared him with another ointment; later she brought him dinner, and returned in the evening with supper. The next day she went through the same ceremony. "Who are you?" Candide kept asking her. "Who has inspired you with so much kindness? How can I thank you?" The good woman never made any reply; she returned in the evening without any supper. "Come with me," said she, "and do not speak a word." She took him by the arm and walked into the country with him for about a quarter of a mile; they came to an isolated house, surrounded with gardens and canals. The old woman knocked at a little door. It was opened; she led Candide up a back stairway into a gilded apartment, left him on a brocaded sofa, shut the door and went away. Candide thought he was dreaming, and felt that his whole life was a bad dream and the present moment an agreeable dream. The old woman soon reappeared; she was supporting with some difficulty a trembling woman of majestic stature, glittering with precious stones and covered with a veil. "Remove the veil," said the old woman to Candide. The young man advanced and lifted the veil with a timid hand. What a moment! What a surprise! He thought he saw Mademoiselle Cunegonde, in fact he was looking at her, it was she herself. His strength failed him, he could not utter a word and fell at her feet. Cunegonde fell on the sofa. The old woman dosed them with distilled waters; they recovered their senses and began to speak: at first they uttered only broken words, questions and answers at cross purposes, sighs, tears, exclamations. The old woman advised them to make less noise and left them alone. "What! Is it you?" said Candide. "You are alive, and I find you here in Portugal! Then you were not raped? Your belly was not slit, as the philosopher Pangloss assured me?" "Yes, indeed," said the fair Cunegonde; "but those two accidents are not always fatal." "But your father and mother were killed?" " 'Tis only too true," said Cunegonde, weeping. "And your brother?" "My brother was killed too." "And why are you in Portugal? And how did you know I was here? And by what strange adventure have you brought me to this house?" "I will tell you everything," replied the lady, "but first of all you must tell me everything that has happened to you since the innocent kiss you gave me and the kicks you received." Candide obeyed with profound respect; and, although he was bewildered, although his voice was weak and trembling, although his back was still a little painful, he related in the most natural manner all he had endured since the moment of their separation. Cunegonde raised her eyes to heaven; she shed tears at the death of the good Anabaptist and Pangloss, after which she spoke as follows to Candide, who did not miss a word and devoured her with his eyes.

CUNEGONDE'S STORY

I was fast asleep in bed when it pleased Heaven to send the Bulgarians to our noble castle of Thunder-ten-tronckh; they murdered my father and brother and cut my mother to pieces. A large Bulgarian six feet tall, seeing that I had swooned at the spectacle, began to rape me; this brought me to, I recovered my senses, I screamed, I struggled, I bit, I scratched, I tried to tear out the big Bulgarian's eyes, not knowing that what was happening in my father's castle was a matter of custom; the brute stabbed me with a knife in the left side where I still have the scar." "Alas! I hope I shall see it," said the naïf Candide. "You shall see it," said Cunegonde, "but let me go on." "Go on," said Candide. She took up the thread of her story as follows: "A Bulgarian captain came in, saw me covered with blood, and the soldier did not disturb himself. The captain was angry at the brute's lack of respect to him, and killed him on my body. Afterwards, he had me bandaged and took me to his billet as a prisoner of war. I washed the few shirts he had and did the cooking; I must admit he thought me very pretty; and I will not deny that he was very well built and that his skin was white and soft; otherwise he had little wit and little philosophy; it was plain that he had not been brought up by Dr. Pangloss. At the end of three months he lost all his money and got tired of me; he sold me to a Jew named Don Issachar, who traded in Holland and Portugal and had a passion for women. This Jew devoted himself to my person but he could not triumph over it; I resisted him better than the Bulgarian soldier; a lady of honour may be raped once, but it strengthens her virtue. In order to subdue me, the Jew brought me to this country house. Up till then I believed that there was nothing on earth so splendid as the castle of Thunder-ten-tronckh; I was undeceived. One day the Grand Inquisitor noticed me at Mass; he ogled me continually and sent a message that he wished to speak to me on secret affairs. I was taken to his palace; I informed him of my birth; he pointed out how much it was beneath my rank to belong to an Israelite. A proposition was made on his behalf to Don Issachar to give me up to His Lordship. Don Issachar, who is the court banker and a man of influence, would not agree. The Inquisitor threatened him with an *auto-da-fé*. At last the Jew was frightened and made a bargain whereby the house and I belong to both in common. The Jew has Mondays, Wednesdays and the Sabbath day, and the Inquisitor has the other days of the week. This arrangement has lasted for six months. It has not been without quarrels; for it has often been debated whether the night between Saturday and Sunday belonged to the old law or the new. For my part, I have hitherto resisted them both; and I think that is the reason why they still love me. At last My Lord the Inquisitor was pleased to arrange an *auto-da-fé* to remove the scourge of earthquakes and to intimidate Don Issachar. He honoured me with an invitation. I had an excellent seat; and refreshments were served to the ladies between the Mass and the execution. I was indeed horror-stricken when I saw the burning of the two Jews and the honest Biscayan who had married his fellow-godmother; but what was my surprise, my terror, my anguish, when I saw in a sanbenito and under a mitre a face which resembled Pangloss's! I rubbed my eyes, I looked carefully, I saw him hanged; and I fainted. I had scarcely recovered my senses when I saw you stripped

naked; that was the height of horror, of consternation, of grief and despair. I will frankly tell you that your skin is even whiter and of a more perfect tint than that of my Bulgarian captain. This spectacle redoubled all the feelings which crushed and devoured me. I exclaimed, I tried to say: 'Stop, Barbarians!' but my voice failed and my cries would have been useless. When you had been well flogged, I said to myself: 'How does it happen that the charming Candide and the wise Pangloss are in Lisbon, the one to receive a hundred lashes, and the other to be hanged, by order of My Lord the Inquisitor, whose darling I am? Pangloss deceived me cruelly when he said that all is for the best in the world.' I was agitated, distracted, sometimes beside myself and sometimes ready to die of faintness, and my head was filled with the massacre of my father, of my mother, of my brother, the insolence of my horrid Bulgarian soldier, the gash he gave me, my slavery, my life as a kitchen-wench, my Bulgarian captain, my horrid Don Issachar, my abominable Inquisitor, the hanging of Dr. Pangloss, that long plain-song *miserere* during which you were flogged, and above all the kiss I gave you behind the screen that day when I saw you for the last time. I praised God for bringing you back to me through so many trials, I ordered my old woman to take care of you and to bring you here as soon as she could. She has carried out my commission very well; I have enjoyed the inexpressible pleasure of seeing you again, of listening to you, and of speaking to you. You must be very hungry; I have a good appetite; let us begin by having supper." Both sat down to supper; and after supper they returned to the handsome sofa we have already mentioned; they were still there when Signor Don Issachar, one of the masters of the house, arrived. It was the day of the Sabbath. He came to enjoy his rights and to express his tender love.

WHAT HAPPENED TO CUNEGONDE, TO CANDIDE, TO THE GRAND INQUISITOR AND TO A JEW

This Issachar was the most choleric Hebrew who had been seen in Israel since the Babylonian captivity. "What!" said he. "Bitch of a Galilean, isn't it enough to have the Inquisitor? Must this scoundrel share with me too? So saying, he drew a long dagger which he always carried and, thinking that his adversary was unarmed, threw himself upon Candide; but our good Westphalian had received an excellent sword from the old woman along with his suit of clothes. He drew his sword, and although he had a most gentle character, laid the Israelite stone-dead on the floor at the feet of the fair Cunegonde. "Holy Virgin!" she exclaimed, "what will become of us? A man killed in my house! If the police come we are lost." "If Pangloss had not been hanged," said Candide, "he would have given us good advice in this extremity, for he was a great philosopher. In default of him, let us consult the old woman." She was extremely prudent and was beginning to give her advice when another little door opened. It was an hour after midnight, and Sunday was beginning. This day belonged to My Lord the Inquisitor. He came in and saw the flogged Candide sword in hand, a corpse lying on the ground, Cunegonde in terror, and the old woman giving advice. At this moment, here is what happened in Candide's soul and the manner of his reasoning: "If this holy man calls for help, he will infallibly have me burned; he might do as much to Cunegonde; he had me pitilessly lashed; he is my rival; I am in the mood to kill, there is no room for hesitation." His reasoning was clear and swift; and, without giving the Inquisitor time to recover from his surprise, he pierced him through and through and cast him beside the Jew. "Here's another," said Cunegonde, "there is no chance of mercy; we are excommunicated, our last hour has come. How does it happen that you, who were born so mild, should kill a Jew and a prelate in two minutes?" "My dear young lady," replied Candide, "when a man is in love, jealous, and has been flogged by the Inquisition, he is beside himself." The old woman then spoke up and said: "In the stable are three Andalusian horses, with their saddles and bridles; let the brave Candide prepare them; mademoiselle has moidores and diamonds; let us mount quickly, although I can only sit on one buttock, and go to Cadiz; the weather is beautifully fine, and it is most pleas-

ant to travel in the coolness of the night." Candide immediately saddled the three horses. Cunegonde, the old woman and he rode thirty miles without stopping. While they were riding away, the Holy Hermandad arrived at the house; My Lord was buried in a splendid church and Issachar was thrown into a sewer. Candide, Cunegonde and the old woman had already reached the little town of Avacena in the midst of the mountains of the Sierra Morena; and they talked in their inn as follows

HOW CANDIDE, CUNEGONDE AND THE OLD WOMAN ARRIVED AT CADIZ IN GREAT DISTRESS, AND HOW THEY EMBARKED

"Who can have stolen my pistoles and my diamonds?" said Cunegonde, weeping. "How shall we live? What shall we do? Where shall we find Inquisitors and Jews to give me others?" "Alas!" said the old woman, "I strongly suspect a reverend Franciscan father who slept in the same inn at Badajoz with us; Heaven forbid that I should judge rashly! But he twice came into our room and left long before we did." "Alas!" said Candide, "the good Pangloss often proved to me that this world's goods are common to all men and that every one has an equal right to them. According to these principles the monk should have left us enough to continue our journey. Have you nothing left then, my fair Cunegonde?" "Not a maravedi," said she. "What are we to do?" said Candide. "Sell one of the horses," said the old woman. "I will ride postillion behind Mademoiselle Cunegonde, although I can only sit on one buttock, and we will get to Cadiz." In the same hotel there was a Benedictine friar. He bought the horse very cheap. Candide, Cunegonde and the old woman passed through Lucena, Chillas, Lebrixa, and at last reached Cadiz. A fleet was there being equipped and troops were being raised to bring to reason the reverend Jesuit fathers of Paraguay, who were accused of causing the revolt of one of their tribes against the kings of Spain and Portugal near the town of Sacramento. Candide, having served with the Bulgarians, went through the Bulgarian drill before the general of the little army with so much grace, celerity, skill, pride and agility, that he was given the command of an infantry company. He was now a captain; he embarked with Mademoiselle Cunegonde, the old woman, two servants, and the two Andalusian horses which had belonged to the Grand Inquisitor of Portugal. During the voyage they had many discussions about the philosophy of poor Pangloss. "We are going to a new world," said Candide, "and no doubt it is there that everything is for the best; for it must be admitted that one might lament a little over the physical and moral happenings in our own world." "I love you with all my heart," said Cunegonde, "but my soul is still shocked by what I have seen and undergone." "All will be well," replied Candide; "the sea in this new world already is better than the seas of our Europe; it is calmer and the winds are more constant. It is certainly the new world which is the best of all possible worlds." "God grant it!" said Cunegonde, "but I have been so horribly unhappy in mine that my heart is nearly closed to hope." "You complain," said the old woman to them. "Alas! you have not endured such misfortunes as mine." Cunegonde almost laughed and thought it most amusing of the old woman to assert that she was more unfortunate. "Alas! my dear," said she, "unless you have been raped by two Bulgarians, stabbed twice in the belly, have had two castles destroyed, two fathers and mothers murdered before your eyes, and have seen two of your lovers flogged in an *auto-da-fé*, I do not see how you can surpass me; moreover, I was born a Baroness with seventy-two quarterings and I have been a kitchen wench." "You do not know my birth," said the old woman, "and if I showed you my backside you would not talk as you do and you would suspend your judgment." This speech aroused intense curiosity in the minds of Cunegonde and Candide. And the old woman spoke as follows.

THE OLD WOMAN'S STORY

"My eyes were not always bloodshot and red-rimmed; my nose did not always touch my chin and I was not always a servant. I am the daughter of Pope Urban X and the Princess of Palestrina. Until I was fourteen I was brought up in a palace to which all the castles of your German Barons would not have served as stables; and one of my dresses cost more than all the magnificence of Westphalia. I increased in beauty, in grace, in talents, among pleasures, respect and hopes; already I inspired love, my breasts were forming; and what breasts! White, firm, carved like those of the Venus de' Medici. And what eyes! What eyelids! What black eyebrows! What fire shone from my two eye-balls, and dimmed the glitter of the stars, as the local poets pointed out to me. The women who dressed and undressed me fell into ecstasy when they beheld me in front and behind; and all the men would have liked to be in their place. I was betrothed to a ruling prince of Massa-Carrara. What a prince! As beautiful as I was, formed of gentleness and charms, brilliantly witty and burning with love; I loved him with a first love, idolatrously and extravagantly. The marriage ceremonies were arranged with unheard-of pomp and magnificence; there were continual fêtes, revels and comic operas; all Italy wrote sonnets for me and not a good one among them. I touched the moment of my happiness when an old marchioness who had been my prince's mistress invited him to take chocolate with her; less than two hours afterwards he died in horrible convulsions; but that is only a trifle. My mother was in despair, though less distressed than I, and wished to absent herself for a time from a place so disastrous. She had a most beautiful estate near Gaeta; we embarked on a galley, gilded like the altar of St. Peter's at Rome. A Salle pirate swooped down and boarded us; our soldiers defended us like soldiers of the Pope; they threw down their arms, fell on their knees and asked the pirates for absolution *in articulo mortis*. They were immediately stripped as naked as monkeys and my mother, our ladies of honour and myself as well. The diligence with which these gentlemen strip people is truly admirable; but I was still more surprised by their inserting a finger in a place belonging to all of us where we women usually only allow the end of a syringe. This appeared to me a very strange ceremony; but that is how we judge everything when we leave our own country. I soon learned that it was to find out if we had hidden any diamonds there; 'tis a custom established from time immemorial among the civilized nations who roam the seas. I have learned that the religious Knights of Malta never fail in it when they capture Turks and Turkish women; this is an international law which has never been broken. I will not tell you how hard it is for a young princess to be taken with her mother as a slave to Morocco; you will also guess all we had to endure in the pirates' ship. My mother was still very beautiful; our ladies of honour, even our waiting-maids possessed more charms than could be found in all Africa; and I was ravishing, I was beauty, grace itself, and I was a virgin; I did not remain so long; the flower which had been reserved for the handsome prince of Massa Carrara was ravished from me by a pirate captain; he was an abominable negro who thought he was doing me a great honour. The Princess of Palestrina and I must indeed have been strong to bear up against all we endured before our arrival in Morocco! But let that pass; these things are so common that they are not worth mentioning. Morocco was swimming in blood when we arrived. The fifty sons of the Emperor Muley Ismael had each a faction; and this produced fifty civil wars, of blacks against blacks, browns against browns, mulattoes against mulattoes. There was continual carnage throughout the whole extent of the empire. Scarcely had we landed when the blacks of a party hostile to that of my pirate arrived with the purpose of depriving him of his booty. After the diamonds and the gold, we were the most valuable possessions. I witnessed a fight such as is never seen in your European climates. The blood of the northern peoples is not sufficiently ardent; their madness for women does not reach the point which is common in Africa. The Europeans seem to have milk in their veins; but vitriol and fire flow in the veins of the inhabitants of Mount Atlas and the neighbouring countries. They fought with the fury of the lions, tigers and serpents of the country to determine who should have us. A Moor grasped my mother by the right arm, my captain's lieutenant held her by the left arm; a Moorish soldier held one leg and one of our pirates seized the other. In a moment nearly all our women were seized in the same way by four soldiers. My captain kept me hidden be-hind him; he had a scimitar in his hand and killed everybody who opposed his fury. I saw my mother and all our Italian women torn in pieces, gashed, massacred by the monsters who disputed them. The prisoners, my companions, those who had captured them, soldiers, sailors, blacks, browns, whites, mulattoes and finally my captain were all killed and I remained ex-piring on a heap of corpses. As every one knows, such scenes go on in an area of more than three hundred square leagues and yet no one ever fails to recite the five daily prayers ordered by Mahomet. With great difficulty I extricated myself from the bloody heaps of corpses and dragged myself to the foot of a large orange-tree on the bank of a stream; there I fell down with terror, weariness, horror, despair and hunger. Soon afterwards, my ex-hausted senses fell into a sleep which was more like a swoon than repose. I was in this state of weakness and insensibility between life and death when I felt myself oppressed by some-thing which moved on my body. I opened my eyes and saw a white man of good appearance who was sighing and muttering between his teeth: O che sciagura d'essere senza coglioni!

CONTINUATION OF THE OLD WOMAN'S MISFORTUNES

"Amazed and delighted to hear my native language, and not less surprised at the words spoken by this man, I replied that there were greater misfortunes than that of which he com-plained. In a few words I informed him of the horrors I had undergone and then swooned again. He carried me to a neighbouring house, had me put to bed, gave me food, waited on me, consoled me, flattered me, told me he had never seen anyone so beautiful as I, and that he had never so much regretted that which no one could give back to him. 'I was born at Naples,' he said, 'and every year they make two or three thousand children there into capons; some die of it, others acquire voices more beautiful than women's, and others be-come the governors of States. This operation was performed upon me with very great suc-cess and I was a musician in the chapel of the Princess of Palestrina!' 'Of my mother,' I ex-claimed. 'Of your mother!' cried he, weeping.

'What! Are you that young princess I brought up to the age of six and who even then gave promise of being as beautiful as you are?' 'I am! my mother is four hundred yards from here, cut into quarters under a heap of corpses. . . .' I related all that had happened to me; he also told me his adventures and informed me how he had been sent to the King of Morocco by a Christian power to make a treaty with that monarch whereby he was supplied with powder, cannons and ships to help to exterminate the commerce of other Christians. 'My mission is accomplished,' said this honest eunuch, 'I am about to embark at Ceuta and I will take you back to Italy. Ma che sciagura d'essere senza coglioni!' I thanked him with tears of gratitude; and instead of taking me back to Italy he conducted me to Algiers and sold me to the Dey. I had scarcely been sold when the plague which had gone through Africa, Asia and Europe, broke out furiously in Algiers. You have seen earthquakes; but have you ever seen the plague?" "Never," replied the Baroness. "If you had," replied the old woman, "you would admit that it is much worse than an earthquake. It is very common in Africa; I caught it. Imagine the situation of a Pope's daughter aged fifteen, who in three months had undergone poverty and slavery, had been raped nearly every day, had seen her mother cut into four pieces, had undergone hunger and war, and was now dying of the plague in Algiers. However, I did not die; but my eunuch and the Dey and almost all the seraglio of Algiers perished. When the first ravages of this frightful plague were over, the Dey's slaves were sold. A merchant bought me and carried me to Tunis; he sold me to another merchant who re-sold me at Tripoli; from Tripoli I was re-sold to Alexandria, from Alexandria re-sold to Smyrna, from Smyrna to Constantinople. I was finally bought by an Aga of the Janizaries, who was soon ordered to defend Azov against the Russians who were besieging it. The Aga, who was a man of great gallantry, took his whole seraglio with him, and lodged us in a little fort on the Islands of Palus-Maeotis, guarded by two black eunuchs and twenty soldiers. He killed a prodigious number of Russians but they returned the compliment as well. Azov was given up to fire and blood, neither sex nor age was pardoned; only our little fort remained; and the enemy tried to reduce it by starving us. The twenty Janizaries had sworn never to surrender us. The extremities of hunger to which they were reduced forced them to eat our two eunuchs for fear of breaking their oath. Some days later they resolved to eat the women. We had with us a most pious and compassionate Imam who delivered a fine sermon to them by which he persuaded them not to kill us altogether. 'Cut,' said he, 'only one buttock from each of these ladies and you will make very good cheer; if you have to return, there will still be as much left in a few days; Heaven will be pleased at so charitable an action and you will be saved.' He was very eloquent and persuaded them. This horrible operation was performed upon us; the Imam anointed us with the same balm that is used for children who have just been circumcised; we were all at the point of death. Scarcely had the Janizaries finished the meal we had supplied when the Russians arrived in flat-bottomed boats; not a Janizary escaped. The Russians paid no attention to the state we were in. There are French doctors everywhere; one of them, who was very skilful, took care of us; he healed us and I shall remember all my life that, when my wounds were cured, he made propositions to me. For the rest, he told us all to cheer up; he told us that the same thing had happened in several sieges and that it was a law of war. As soon as my companions could walk they were sent to Moscow. I fell to the lot of a Boyar who made me his gardener and gave me twenty lashes a day. But at the end of two years this lord was broken on the wheel with thirty other Boyars owing to some court disturbance, and I profited by this adventure; I fled; I crossed all Russia; for a long time I was servant in an inn at Riga, then at Rostock, at Wismar, at Leipzig, at Cassel, at Utrecht, at Leyden, at the Hague, at Rotterdam; I have grown old in misery and in shame, with only half a backside, always remembering that I was the daughter of a Pope; a hundred times I wanted to kill myself, but I still loved life. This ridiculous weakness is perhaps the most disastrous of our inclinations; for is there anything sillier than to desire to bear continually a burden one always wishes to [discard]? . . .

CONCLUSION

[Following more experiences (involving separations from Cunegonde) and after collecting new associates, the principal characters were reunited at Constantinople.

At the bottom of his heart Candide had not the least wish to marry Cunegonde. But the Baron's extreme impertinence determined him to complete the marriage, and Cunegonde urged it so warmly that he could not retract. He consulted Pangloss, Martin, and the faithful Cacambo. Pangloss wrote an excellent memorandum by which he proved that the Baron had no rights over his sister and that by all the laws of the empire she could make a left-handed marriage with Candide. . . .

This was thought to be very good advice; the old woman approved it; they said nothing to the sister; the plan was carried out with the aid of a little money and they had the pleasure of duping a Jesuit and punishing the pride of a German Baron. It would be natural to suppose that when, after so many disasters, Candide was married to his mistress, and living with the philosopher Pangloss, the philosopher Martin, the prudent Cacambo and the old woman, having brought back so many diamonds from the country of the ancient Incas, he would lead the most pleasant life imaginable. But he was so cheated by the Jews that he had nothing left but his little farm; his wife, growing uglier every day, became shrewish and unendurable; the old woman was ailing and even more bad-tempered than Cunegonde. Cacambo, who worked in the garden and then went to Constantinople to sell vegetables, was overworked and cursed his fate. Pangloss was in despair because he did not shine in some German university. As for Martin, he was firmly convinced that people are equally uncomfortable everywhere; he accepted things patiently. Candide, Martin and Pangloss sometimes argued about metaphysics and morals. From the windows of the farm they often watched the ships going by, filled with effendis, pashas, and cadis, who were being exiled to Lemnos, to Mitylene and Erzerum. They saw other cadis, other pashas and other effendis coming back to take the place of the exiles and to be exiled in their turn. They saw the

neatly impaled heads which were taken to the Sublime Porte. These sights redoubled their discussions; and when they were not arguing, the boredom was so excessive that one day the old woman dared to say to them: "I should like to know which is worse, to be raped a hundred times by negro pirates, to have a buttock cut off, to run the gauntlet among the Bulgarians, to be whipped and flogged in an *auto-da-fé*, to be dissected, to row in a galley, in short, to endure all the miseries through which we have passed, or to remain here doing nothing?" "'Tis a great question," said Candide. These remarks led to new reflections, and Martin especially concluded that man was born to live in the convulsions of distress or in the lethargy of boredom. Candide did not agree, but he asserted nothing. Pangloss confessed that he had always suffered horribly; but, having once maintained that everything was for the best, he had continued to maintain it without believing it. One thing confirmed Martin in his detestable principles, made Candide hesitate more than ever, and embarrassed Pangloss. And it was this. One day there came to their farm Paquette and Friar Giroflée, who were in the most extreme misery; they had soon wasted their three thousand piastres, had left each other, made it up, quarrelled again, been put in prison, escaped, and finally Friar Giroflée had turned Turk. Paquette continued her occupation everywhere and now earned nothing by it. "I foresaw," said Martin to Candide, "that your gifts would soon be wasted and would only make them the more miserable. You and Cacambo were once bloated with millions of piastres and you are no happier than Friar Giroflée and Paquette." "Ah! Ha!" said Pangloss to Paquette, "so Heaven brings you back to us, my dear child? Do you know that you cost me the end of my nose, an eye and an ear! What a plight you are in! Ah! What a world this is!" This new occurrence caused them to philosophise more than ever. In the neighbourhood there lived a very famous Dervish, who was supposed to be the best philosopher in Turkey; they went to consult him; Pangloss was the spokesman and said: "Master, we have come to beg you to tell us why so strange an animal as man was ever created." "What has it to do with you?" said the Dervish. "Is it your business?" "But, reverend father," said Candide, "there is a horrible amount of evil in the world." "What does it matter," said the Dervish, "whether there is evil or good? When his highness sends a ship to Egypt, does he worry about the comfort or discomfort of the rats in the ship?" "Then what should we do?" said Pangloss. "Hold your tongue," said the Dervish. "I flattered myself," said Pangloss, "that I should discuss with you effects and causes, this best of all possible worlds, the origin of evil, the nature of the soul and pre-established harmony." At these words the Dervish slammed the door in their faces. During this conversation the news went round that at Constantinople two viziers and the mufti had been strangled and several of their friends impaled. This catastrophe made a prodigious noise everywhere for several hours. As Pangloss, Candide and Martin were returning to their little farm, they came upon an old man who was taking the air under a bower of orange-trees at his door. Pangloss, who was as curious as he was argumentative, asked him what was the name of the mufti who had just been strangled. "I do not know," replied the old man. "I have never known the name of any mufti or of any vizier. I am entirely ignorant of the occurrence you mention; I presume that in general those who meddle with public affairs sometimes perish miserably and that they deserve it; but I never inquire what is going on in Constantinople; I content myself with sending there for sale the produce of the garden I cultivate." Having spoken thus, he took the strangers into his house. His two daughters and his two sons presented them with several kinds of sherbet which they made themselves, caymac flavoured with candied citron peel, oranges, lemons, limes, pine-apples, dates, pistachios and Mocha coffee which had not been mixed with the bad coffee of Batavia and the Isles. After which this good Mussulman's two daughters perfumed the beards of Candide, Pangloss, and Martin. "You must have a vast and magnificent estate?" said Candide to the Turk. "I have only twenty acres," replied the Turk. "I cultivate them with my children; and work keeps at bay three great evils: boredom, vice, and need." As Candide returned to his farm he reflected deeply on the Turk's re-

marks. He said to Pangloss and Martin: "That good old man seems to me to have chosen an existence preferable by far to that of the six kings with whom we had the honour to sup." "Exalted rank," said Pangloss, "is very dangerous, according to the testimony of all philosophers; for Eglon, King of the Moabites, was murdered by Ehud; Absalom was hanged by the hair and pierced by three darts; King Nadab, son of Jeroboam, was killed by Baasha; King Elah, by Zimri; Ahaziah, by Jehu; Athaliah, by Jehoiada; the Kings Jehoiakim, Jeconiah and Zedekiah were made slaves. You know in what manner died Croesus, Astyages, Darius, Denys of Syracuse, Pyrrhus, Perseus, Hannibal, Jugurtha, Ariovistus, Caesar, Pompey, Nero, Otho, Vitellius, Domitian, Richard II of England, Edward II, Henry VI, Richard III, Mary Stuart, Charles I, the three Henrys of France, the Emperor Henry IV. You know . . ." "I also know," said Candide, "that we should cultivate our gardens." "You are right," said Pangloss, "for, when man was placed in the Garden of Eden, he was placed there *ut operaretur eum,* to dress it and to keep it; which proves that man was not born for idleness." "Let us work without theorizing," said Martin; " 'tis the only way to make life endurable." The whole small fraternity entered into this praiseworthy plan, and each started to make use of his talents. The little farm yielded well. Cunegonde was indeed very ugly, but she became an excellent pastry-cook; Paquette embroidered; the old woman took care of the linen. Even Friar Giroflée performed some service; he was a very good carpenter and even became a man of honour; and Pangloss sometimes said to Candide: "All events are linked up in this best of all possible worlds; for, if you had not been expelled from the noble castle, by hard kicks in your backside for love of Mademoiselle Cunegonde, if you had not been clapped into the Inquisition, if you had not wandered about America on foot, if you had not stuck your sword in the Baron, if you had not lost all your sheep from the land of Eldorado, you would not be eating candied citrons and pistachios here." " 'Tis well said," replied Candide, "but we must cultivate our gardens."

Condorcet

Marie-Jean-Antoine-Nicolas Caritat, Marquis de Condorcet (1743–1794), was born in Picardy, France, of a noble family and was educated at the Jesuit Collège de Navarre. An able mathematician and scientist, he quickly established his competence and became Secretary of the Académie des sciences in 1781. Condorcet became a member of that famous group of 18th century philosophers and reformers that clustered around Voltaire. An apostle of scientific enlightenment and social reform, Condorcet participated in the French Revolution, but because of his moderation he fell out with the Jacobins when they came to power. He was arrested and imprisoned at Paris; he died the day following his incarceration, apparently a suicide. The Progress of the Human Mind is merely a sketch of a major work which Condorcet hoped eventually to write. A great monument of liberal thought, it is a summary of the major ideas of the Enlightenment, ideas that have exerted a dominating influence on Western thought in the 19th and 20th centuries. In reading the selections, note (1) the psychological foundations of Condorcet's thought, (2) his faith in the illimitable perfectability of humanity, (3) his trust in science as the method of progress and his proposals for the application of science to other aspects of human endeavor, (4) his view of the function of history, (5) the social achievements he anticipated for the future, (6) his expectations concerning the spread of liberalism, (7) his convictions regarding colonialism and war, (8) his faith in the rule of reason, and (9) the radical program he presents for the remaking of society.

From: THE PROGRESS OF THE HUMAN MIND

INTRODUCTION

Man is born with the ability to receive sensations; to perceive them and to distinguish between the various simple sensations of which they are composed; to remember, recognize and combine them; to compare these combinations; to apprehend what they have in common and the ways in which they differ; to attach signs to them all in order to recognize them more easily and to allow for the ready production of new combinations.

This faculty is developed in him through the action of external objects, that is to say, by the occurrence of certain composite sensations whose constancy or coherence in change are independent of him; through communication with other beings like himself; and finally through various artificial methods which these first developments have led him to invent.

Sensations are attended by pleasure or pain; and man for his part has the capacity to trans-

As translated by June Barraclough in *Antoine-Nicolas De Condorcet, Sketch for a Historical Picture of the Progress of the Human Mind*, London: Weidenfeld and Nicolson. 1955, 3–5; 7; 136–137; 147–151; 160–189; 194–199; 201–202.

form such momentary impressions into permanent feelings of an agreeable or disagreeable character, and then to experience these feelings when he either observes or recollects the pleasures and pains of other sentient beings.

Finally, as a consequence of this capacity and of his ability to form and combine ideas, there arise between him and his fellow-creatures ties of interest and duty, to which nature herself has wished to attach the most precious portion of our happiness and the most painful of our ills.

If one confines oneself to the study and observation of the general facts and laws about the development of these faculties, considering only what is common to all human beings, this science is called metaphysics. But if one studies this development as it manifests itself in the inhabitants of a certain area at a certain period of time and then traces it on from generation to generation, one has the picture of the progress of the human mind. This progress is subject to the same general laws that can be observed in the development of the faculties of the individual, and it is indeed no more than the sum of that development realized in a large number of individuals joined together in society. What happens at any particular moment is the result of what has happened at all previous moments, and itself has an influence on what will happen in the future.

So such a picture is historical, since it is a record of change and is based on the observation of human societies throughout the different stages of their development. It ought to reveal the order of this change and the influence that each moment exerts upon the subsequent moment, and so ought also to show, in the modifications that the human species has undergone, ceaselessly renewing itself through the immensity of the centuries, the path that it has followed, the steps that it has made towards truth or happiness.

Such observations upon what man has been and what he is today, will instruct us about the means we should employ to make certain and rapid the further progress that his nature allows him still to hope for.

Such is the aim of the work that I have undertaken, and its result will be to show by appeal to reason and fact that nature has set no term to the perfection of human faculties; that the perfectibility of man is truly indefinite; and that the progress of this perfectibility, from now onwards independent of any power that might wish to halt it, has no other limit than the duration of the globe upon which nature has cast us. This progress will doubtless vary in speed, but it will never be reversed as long as the earth occupies its present place in the system of the universe, and as long as the general laws of this system produce neither a general cataclysm nor such changes as will deprive the human race of its present faculties and its present resources. . . .

The history of man from the time when alphabetical writing was known in Greece to the condition of the human race at the present day in the most enlightened countries of Europe is linked by an uninterrupted chain of facts and observations; and so at this point the picture of the march and progress of the human mind becomes truly historical. Philosophy has nothing more to guess, no more hypothetical surmises to make; it is enough to assemble and order the facts and to show the useful truths that can be derived from their connections and from their totality.

When we have shown all this, there will remain one last picture for us to sketch: that of our hopes, and of the progress reserved for future generations, which the constancy of the laws of nature seems to assure them. It will be necessary to indicate by what stages what must appear to us today a fantastic hope ought in time to become possible, and even likely; to show why, in spite of the transitory successes of prejudice and the support that it receives from the corruption of governments or peoples, truth alone will obtain a lasting victory; we shall demonstrate how nature has joined together indissolubly the progress of knowledge and that of liberty, virtue and respect for the natural rights of man; and how these, the only real goods that we possess, though so often separated that they have even been held to be incompatible, must on the contrary become inseparable from the moment when enlightenment has attained a certain level in a number of nations, and has penetrated throughout the whole mass of a great people whose language is universally known and whose commercial relations embrace the whole area of the globe. Once such a close accord had been established between all enlightened men, from then onwards all will be the friends of humanity, all will work together for its perfection and its happiness. . . . Everything tells us that we are now close upon one of the great revolutions of the human race. . . .

THE NINTH STAGE

Up till now we have shown the progress of philosophy only in the men who have cultivated, deepened and perfected it. It remains for us to show what have been its effects on public opinion; how reason, while it learnt to safeguard itself against the errors into which the imagination and respect for authority had so often led it, at last found a sure method of discovering and recognizing truth; and how at the same time it destroyed the prejudices of the masses which had for so long afflicted and corrupted the human race.

At last man could proclaim aloud his right, which for so long had been ignored, to submit all opinions to his own reason and to use in the search for truth the only instrument for its recognition that he has been given. Every man learnt with a sort of pride that nature had not for ever condemned him to base his beliefs on the opinions of others; the superstitions of antiquity and the abasement of reason before the transports of supernatural religion disappeared from society as from philosophy.

Soon there was formed in Europe a class of men who were concerned less with the discovery or development of the truth than with its propagation, men who whilst devoting themselves to the tracking down of prejudices in the hiding places where the priests, the schools, the governments and all long-established institutions had gathered and protected them, made it their life-work to destroy popular errors rather than to drive back the frontiers of human knowledge—an indirect way of aiding its progress which was not less fraught with peril, nor less useful.

In England Collins and Bolingbroke, in France Bayle, Fontenelle, Voltaire, Montesquieu and the schools founded by these famous men, fought on the side of truth, using in turn all the weapons with which learning, philosophy, wit and literary talent can furnish reason; using every mood from humour to pathos, every literary form from the vast erudite encyclopaedia to the novel or the broadsheet of the day; covering truth with a veil that spared weaker eyes and excited one to guess what lay beyond it; skilfully flattering prejudices so as to attack them the better; seldom threatening them, and then always either only one in its entirety or several partially; sometimes conciliating the enemies of reason by seeming to wish only for a half-tolerance in religious matters, only for a half freedom in politics; sparing despotism when tilting against the absurdities of religion, and religion when abusing tyranny; yet always attacking the principles of these two scourges even when they seemed to be against only their more revolting or ridiculous abuses, and laying their axes to the very roots of these sinister trees when they appeared to be lopping off a few stray branches; sometimes teaching the friends of liberty that superstition is the invincible shield behind which despotism shelters and should therefore be the first victim to be sacrificed, the first chain to be broken, and sometimes denouncing it to the despots as the real enemy of their power, and frightening them with stories of its secret machinations and its bloody persecutions; never ceasing to demand the independence of reason and the freedom of the press as the right and the salvation of mankind; protesting with indefatigable energy against all the crimes of fanaticism and tyranny; pursuing, in all matters of religion, administration, morals and law, anything that bore the marks of tyranny, harshness or barbarism; invoking the name of nature to bid kings, captains, magistrates and priests to show respect for human life; laying to their charge, with vehemence and severity, the blood their policy or their indifference still spilled on the battlefield or on the scaffold; and finally, taking for their battle cry—*reason, tolerance, humanity.* . . .

Not only did the application of algebra to geometry become a fruitful source of discoveries in these two sciences, but in proving by this great example how in general the methods of calculating magnitudes could be extended to all questions that were concerned with the measuring of extension, Descartes announced in advance that they would be applied with equal success to all the objects whose relations are capable of precision; and this great discovery, showing for the first time this final objective of the sciences, which is to subject all truths to the rigour of calculation, gave hope of reaching it and afforded a glimpse of the means towards that end.

Soon this discovery was followed by the discovery of a new calculus, showing how to find the rate of increase or decrease of a variable quantity, or to rediscover the quantity itself from the knowledge of this rate, regardless of whether one imputes a finite magnitude to this increase, or whether the rate is to be determined for a given instant—that is, when the increase is nil; a method which, as it applies to all combinations of variable magnitudes and to all hypotheses concerning their variations, also allows us to determine, for all objects whose changes are capable of precise measurement, either the relations between the elements when only those between the objects are known, or the relations between the objects when only those between the elements are known.

We owe to Newton and to Leibniz the invention of these calculi for which the work of the geometers of the previous generation had prepared the way. Their continuous progress for more than a century has been the work of several men of genius whose glory they made. They present to the eyes of the philosopher who can observe them even without being able to follow them, an imposing monument to the power of the human intelligence.

When we come to describe the formation and the principles of the language of algebra, the only really exact and analytical language yet in existence, the nature of the technical methods of this science and how they compare with the natural workings of the human understanding, we shall show that even though this method is by itself only an instrument pertaining to the science of quantities, it contains within it the principles of a universal instrument, applicable to all combinations of ideas.

Rational mechanics soon became an extensive and profound science. The true laws of the collision of bodies about which Descartes had been mistaken finally became known.

Huyghens discovered the laws of circular motion. At the same time he furnished the method of determining to what circle each element of any curve ought to belong. By combining these two theories Newton discovered the theory of curvilinear motion and applied it to those laws which Kepler had found to be followed by the planets in their elliptical orbits.

It was discovered that a planet, imagined to be projected into space at a certain moment with a certain speed and in a predetermined direction, described an ellipse round the sun by reason of a force acting upon it and inversely proportional to the square of the distance. The same force keeps the satellites in their orbits round the principal planet. And it extends to the entire system of heavenly bodies and acts reciprocally between all the elements composing them.

The regularity of planetary ellipses is disturbed by this force and the calculus explains in detail these perturbations. It acts upon the comets for which the same theory holds, and determines their orbits and predicts their return. The movements we notice in the axes of rotation of the earth and of the moon prove once again the existence of this universal force. It is finally the cause of the weight of bodies on the earth, in which it appears to be constant because we cannot observe them at sufficiently varied distances from the centre of action.

Thus man at last discovered one of the physical laws of the universe; a law that has hitherto remained unique, like the glory of the man who revealed it.

A hundred years of labour have confirmed that law which appears to govern all celestial phenomena to a degree that is, so to say, miraculous. Every time that a phenomenon appears not to come under that law, this uncertainty soon becomes the occasion of a new triumph.

Philosophy is nearly always obliged to look into the writings of a man of genius in order to find the secret thread that guided him; but in this case, interest, inspired by admiration, has discovered and preserved some precious stories which enable us to follow Newton's progress step by step. These will be useful to us in showing how the happy conjunctions of chance combined with the efforts of genius to lead to a great discovery, and how less favourable conjunctions might have retarded them or reserved them for other hands.

But Newton perhaps did more for the progress of the human mind than discover this general law of nature; he taught men to admit in physics only precise and mathematical theories, which account not merely for the existence of a certain phenomenon but also for its quantity and extension. Nevertheless he was accused of reviving the occult qualities of the Ancients because he confined himself to locating the general cause of celestial phenomena in one simple fact, whose incontestable reality was proved by observation. And this accusation itself proves how much the methods of science still stood in need of enlightenment from philosophy.

A host of problems of statics and dynamics had been successively formulated and solved when D'Alembert discovered a general principle, which alone was enough to determine the movement of any number of particles urged by any number of forces, and related to each other by certain conditions. Soon he extended this same principle to finite bodies of a determinate figure, to those which, being elastic or flexible, could change their figure according to certain laws whilst still preserving certain relations between their parts. Finally he extended it to fluids themselves whether of a constant density or in a state of expansion. A new calculus was required for the solution of these latter questions. It could not escape his genius, and consequently mechanics was transformed into a pure calculus.

These discoveries belong to the mathematical sciences. But the nature of the law of universal gravitation and of the principles of mechanics and their consequences in so far as they reflect on the eternal order of the universe are within the province of philosophy. It was learnt that all bodies are subject to necessary laws which tend by themselves to produce or maintain equilibrium and create or preserve regularity of motion. . . .

The existing applications of the calculus of probability foretell how they can aid the progress of the other sciences. In some cases they can determine the probability of unusual facts and inform us whether they should be rejected or whether they deserve to be verified. In other cases they can determine the probability of the constant recurrence of those facts which often present themselves in the practice of the arts and which are not by themselves linked to an order already regarded as a general law: as, for example, in medicine the salutary results of certain remedies and the success of certain preservatives. Other applications show us what is the probability of a class of phenomena being the result of the intention of an intelligent being or of their being dependent on other preceding or coexisting phenomena; the probability too that must be attributed to that necessary and unknown cause which we call chance, a word whose true meaning can be determined only by the study of this calculus.

These applications have also taught us to recognize the different degrees of certainty that we can hope to attain; the degree of likelihood an opinion must possess before we can adopt it and use it in argument, without infringing the rights of reason or the principles of conduct, without sacrificing prudence or offending justice. They show us the advantages and disadvantages of the different systems of voting and the different ways of deciding an issue by a majority vote; the different degrees of probability that these methods produce, and for any question the degree that the public interest may rightly demand. They tell us how to determine the degree of probability with virtual certainty in cases where a decision is not necessary or where the disadvantages of the two possible courses of action are discrepant and so one of them should not be adopted as long as its chances of success remain below this degree of probability; or alternatively how to determine the degree of probability in advance and with complete certainty in cases where a decision is necessary and where even the slightest likelihood of its being right justifies its adoption. We may number amongst these applications the examination of the probability of facts for those who cannot base their beliefs on their own observations—a probability which arises either from the reliability of witnesses or from the relation of the facts in question to others that have been directly observed.

The knowledge of physical man, medicine and public economy are bound to benefit from the researches about the duration of human life and the way this is influenced by differences in sex, temperature, climate, profession, government and ordinary habits; about the dependence of the death-rate on various illnesses; about changes in population, and the extent to which they depend on the action of various causes; about the distribution of population in the various countries according to age, sex and occupation.

And how useful to public economy has been the application of these same calculi in the organization of life annuities, tontines, private savings banks, benefit schemes and insurance policies of every kind! Ought not the application of the calculus of probability to be applied to that part of public economy which includes the theory of measures, money, banking, financial operations, as well as taxation, its legal distribution, its actual distribution which so often contradicts the law, and its consequences for all sections of the social system?

How many important questions in this same science have been resolved only by the aid of our knowledge of natural history, agriculture, the physical constitution of plants and the mechanical or chemical arts!

Such, in a word, has been the general progress of the sciences that there is not really one of them whose principles and details can be fully developed without the help of all the others. In presenting our picture of the new truths with which each of the sciences has been enriched and of how much each owes to the application of theories or methods that seem to belong more particularly to other systems of knowledge, we shall investigate the nature and limits of the truths to which observation, experiment, and meditation can lead us in each science. We shall also inquire what precisely constitutes, for each one of them, the talent of invention, that primary faculty of the human intelligence which has been given the name *genius;* by which means the mind can make the discoveries that it seeks or sometimes be led to those which it did not seek and could not even have foreseen. We shall point out how the methods which lead us to discoveries can be exhausted so that science is somehow forced to stop, unless new methods appear to provide genius with a new instrument, or to facilitate the use of those which, it seemed, could no longer be employed without waste of time and energy.

If we were to confine ourselves to showing the benefits that we have derived from the sciences in their immediate uses or in their applications to the arts, either for the well-being of individuals or for the prosperity of nations, we should display only a very small portion of their blessings.

The most important of these, perhaps, is to have destroyed prejudices and to have redirected the human intelligence, which had been obliged to follow the false directions imposed on it by the absurd beliefs that were implanted in each generation in infancy with the terrors of superstition and the fear of tyranny.

All errors in politics and morals are based on philosophical errors and these in turn are connected with scientific errors. There is not a religious system nor a supernatural extravagance that is not founded on ignorance of the laws of nature. The inventors, the defenders of these absurdities could not foresee the successive perfection of the human mind. Convinced that men in their day knew everything that they could ever know and would always believe what they then believed, they confidently supported their idle dreams on the current opinions of their country and their age.

Advances in the physical sciences are all the more fatal to these errors in that they often destroy them without appearing to attack them [and that they can shower on those who defend them so obstinately the humiliating taunt of ignorance].

At the same time the habit of correct reasoning about the objects of these sciences, the precise ideas gained by their methods, and the means of recognizing or proving the truth of a belief should naturally lead us to compare the sentiment that forces us to accept well founded opinions credible for good reasons, with that which ties us to habitual prejudices or forces us to submit to authority. Such a comparison is enough to teach us to mistrust opinions of the latter kind, to convince us that we do not really believe them even when we boast of believing them, even when we profess them with the purest sincerity. This secret, once discovered, makes their destruction immediate and certain.

Finally this progress of the physical sciences which neither the passions nor self-interest can disturb, in which neither birth, nor profession, nor position are thought to confer on one the right to judge what one is not in a condition to understand, this inexorable progress cannot be contemplated by men of enlightenment without their wishing to make the other sciences follow the same path. It offers them at every step a model to emulate and one by which they may judge of their own efforts, recognize the false roads on which they may have set out, and preserve themselves equally from pyrrhonism, from credulity, from extreme diffidence, and from a too great submission even to the authority of learning and fame.

Admittedly, metaphysical analysis led to the same results but it gave only abstract principles, while now these same abstract principles, put into practice, are illuminated by example and fortified by success.

Up to this stage, the sciences had been the birthright of very few; they were now becoming common property and the time was at hand when their elements, their principles, and their simpler methods would become truly popular. For it was then, at last, that their application to the arts and their influence on men's judgment would become of truly universal utility.

We shall follow the progress of European nations in the education both of children and of adults. This progress may appear to have been slow, if one considers only the philosophical foundations on which education has been based, for it is still in the grip of scholastic superstition: but it appears swift enough if one considers the nature and the extent of the subjects taught, for these are now confined almost completely to genuine inquiries, and include the elements of nearly all the sciences; while dictionaries, abstracts, and periodicals provide men of all ages with the information they require—even if this does not always appear in an unadulterated form. We shall examine the utility of combining oral instruction in the sciences with the immediate instruction to be acquired from books and private study, and we shall also examine whether any advantage has accrued from the development of compila-

tion into an accredited profession in whose practice a man may hope to earn a livelihood; a development that has augmented the number of indifferent books in circulation, but has also increased the roads to knowledge open to men of little education. We shall give an account of the influence exercised by learned societies, for these will long remain a useful bulwark against charlatanry and false scholarship. Finally we shall unfold the story of the encouragement given by certain governments to the progress of knowledge, and also of the obstacles that were laid in its path often enough by these same governments, at the same time, in the same country. We shall expose, on the one hand, the prejudices and Machiavellian principles that have directed these governments in their opposition to men's progress towards the truth, and on the other, the political opinions originating either from self-interest or even from a genuine concern for the public good, that have guided them when they have seemed interested in accelerating and protecting it.

The spectacle presented by the fine arts has no less brilliant results to show. Music has become almost a new art, and, at the same time, its theory has been illuminated by the application of numerical calculation to the vibration of resonating bodies and the oscillation of the air. The graphic arts, which had already passed from Italy to Flanders, Spain, and France, rose in the latter country to the heights they had attained in Italy during the preceding stage, and there shone with even greater brilliance than in Italy itself. The art of our painters is still the art of Raphael and the Carracci. Their methods, so far from dying out, have not only been kept alive in the schools, but have been more widely diffused. Nevertheless, too much time has elapsed without the appearance of a genius comparable to Raphael for us to attribute so long a period of sterility to chance alone. It is not that the methods of the art have been exhausted, although major achievements in it have become more difficult: it is not that nature has denied us faculties as perfect as those of the Italians of the sixteenth century; it is solely to changes in politics and in manners that we must attribute, not indeed the decadence of the art, but the feebleness of its products.

The art of letters, which, though in no way decadent in Italy, is cultivated there with less success, has made such progress in the French language that it has earned for it the honour of becoming the all but universal language of Europe. In the hands of Corneille, of Racine, of Voltaire, tragedy has risen step by step to a hitherto unknown perfection; and, in the hands of Molière, comedy has risen even more rapidly to heights as yet unattained in any other nation.

At the beginning of this period, the English language was brought to perfection, and so, more recently was the German. Both in England and in Germany, the arts of poetry and prose learned to accept, if with less docility than in France, the yoke of those universal rules of reason and of Nature which ought to be their guide. These rules are true for all languages and all peoples, although until now only very few have been capable of understanding them and of attaining that justice and certainty of taste which is merely a feeling for these rules, which presided over the works of Sophocles and Virgil as over those of Pope and Voltaire, which taught the Greeks and the Romans, as later the English and the French, to be delighted by the same beauties and to be shocked by the same faults.

We shall show what factors have favoured or impeded the progress of the arts in each nation, the reasons for the so unequal degrees of excellence attained in each nation by the various kinds of poetry and prose, and the way in which the literary rules can be modified, with no infraction of the universal principles on which they are based, by the manners and the opinions of the nation in which a given *genre* is practised, and by the use for which it is destined. So, for example, tragedy intended to be spoken in daily performance, before a small audience in a room of moderate size, cannot have the same practical rules as tragedy intended to be sung in an immense theatre, as part of solemn festivities to which a whole nation is convened. We shall endeavour to prove that the rules of taste have the same universality and . . . constancy as the other laws of the . . . universe, but are susceptible to the same kind of modification as they are when it is a question of their application. . . .

We shall show how the printing press multiplies and spreads abroad even those works primarily intended to be performed or read aloud in public, and so allows them to reach incomparably more people as readers than they ever could as mere listeners; we shall show how, as a consequence of the way that any important decision taken in a large assembly is now determined by what the members of that assembly have learnt through the written word, a new art of persuasion has arisen amongst the moderns, different from that practised by the ancients, a difference that is analogous to the differences in the effects produced, in the means employed between this modern art and that of the ancients; and, finally, we shall show how in those branches of literature where even the ancients confined themselves to the written word, such as history or philosophy, the invention of printing makes it so much easier for the author to expand and develop his ideas, that here again it has inevitably modified those rules.

The progress of philosophy and the sciences has favoured and extended the progress of letters, and this in turn has served to make the study of the sciences easier, and that of philosophy more popular. The sciences and the arts have assisted one another despite the efforts of the ignorant and the foolish to separate them and make them enemies. Scholarship, which seemed doomed by its respect for the past and its deference towards authority always to lend its support to harmful superstitions, has nevertheless contributed to their eradication, for it was able to borrow the torch of a sounder criticism from philosophy and the sciences. It already knew how to weigh up authorities and compare them; it now learned how to bring every authority before the bar of Reason. It had already discounted prodigies, fantastic anecdotes, facts contrary to all probability; but after attacking the evidence on which such absurdities relied, it now learned that all extraordinary facts must always be rejected, however impressive the evidence in their favour, unless this can truly turn the scale against the weight of their physical or moral probability.

Thus all the intellectual activities of **man**, however different they may be in their **aims**, their methods, or the qualities of mind they exact, have combined to further the progress of human reason. Indeed, the whole system of human labour is like a well-made machine, whose several parts have been systematically distinguished but none the less, being intimately bound together, form a single whole and work towards a single end.

Turning now our attention to the human race in general, we shall show how the discovery of the correct method of procedure in the sciences, the growth of scientific theories, their application to every part of the natural world, to the subject of every human need, the lines of communication established between one science and another, the great number of men who cultivate the sciences, and most important of all, the spread of printing, how together all these advances ensure that no science will ever fall below the point it has reached. We shall point out that the principles of philosophy, the slogans of liberty, the recognition of the true rights of man and his real interests, have spread through far too great a number of nations, and now direct in each of them the opinions of far too great a number of enlightened men, for us to fear that they will ever be allowed to relapse into oblivion. And indeed what reason could we have for fear, when we consider that the languages most widely spoken are the languages of the two peoples who enjoy liberty to the fullest extent and who best understand its principles, and that no league of tyrants, no political intrigues, could prevent the resolute defence, in these two languages, of the rights of reason and of liberty?

But although everything tells us that the human race will never relapse into its former state of barbarism, although everything combines to reassure us against that corrupt and cowardly political theory which would condemn it to oscillate forever between truth and error, liberty and servitude, nevertheless we still see the forces of enlightenment in possession of no more than a very small portion of the globe, and the truly enlightened vastly outnumbered by the great mass of men who are still given over to ignorance and prejudice. We still see vast areas in which men groan in slavery, vast areas offering the spectacle of nations either degraded by the vices of a civilization whose progress is impeded by corruption, or still vegetating in the infant condition of early times. We observe that the labours of recent ages have done much for the progress of the human mind, but little for the perfection of the human race; that they have done much for the honour of man, something for his liberty, but so far almost nothing for his happiness. At a few points our eyes are dazzled with a brilliant light; but thick darkness still covers an immense stretch of the horizon. There are a few circumstances from which the philosopher can take consolation; but he is still afflicted by the spectacle of the stupidity, slavery, barbarism, and extravagance of mankind; and the friend of humanity can find unmixed pleasure only in tasting the sweet delights of hope for the future.

Such are the subjects that ought to enter into a historical sketch of the progress of the human mind. In presenting it, we shall endeavour above all to exhibit the influence of this progress on the opinions and the welfare of the great mass of the people, in the different nations, at the different stages of their political existence. We shall endeavour to exhibit the truths they have learnt, the errors from which they have been freed, the habits of virtue they have contracted, and the developments in their capacities that have established a more fortunate relation between their wants and these capacities; and, then by way of contrast, the prejudices that have enslaved them, the political or religious superstitions with which they have been infected, the vices with which they have been corrupted by ignorance or tyranny, and the misery to which they have been subjected either by force or by their own degradation.

Up till now, the history of politics, like that of philosophy or of science, has been the history of only a few individuals: that which really constitutes the human race, the vast mass of families living for the most part on the fruits of their labour, has been forgotten, and even of those who follow public professions, and work not for themselves but for society, who are engaged in teaching, ruling, protecting or healing others, it is only the leaders who have held the eye of the historian.

In writing the history of individuals, it is enough to collect facts; but the history of a group of men must be supported by observations; and to select these observations and to fasten upon their essential features enlightenment is necessary, and, to use them to good effect, philosophy in the same measure.

Moreover, these observations relate to quite ordinary matters, which lie open to every eye, and which anyone who so desires can find out about by himself. Consequently almost all the observations that have been collected have been made by travellers or foreigners; for facts that are regarded as common-place in their own country become for them objects of curiosity. But unfortunately travellers are nearly always inaccurate observers; they observe things too hastily, through the prejudices of their own country or of that in which they are travelling; they discuss them with those into whose company chance has thrown them, and what they are told is nearly always dictated by self interest, by the spirit of party, by patriotic pride, or merely by the mood of the moment.

Thus it is not only to the servility of historians, as has been said with justice about the official historians of monarchs, that we must attribute the scarcity of records that would allow us to follow this, the most important chapter in the history of man.

These records we can supplement, but only imperfectly, by a study of legal systems, of the practical principles of politics and public economy, and of religion and superstition in general. For there can be such a vast discrepancy between the law in writing and the law applied, between the principles of rulers and their practice as modified by the will of their subjects, between a social institution in the minds of those who conceive it and the same institution when its provisions are realized in practice, between the religion of books and the religion of the people, between the apparently universal acceptance of a superstition and the support which it can in fact command, that the actual effects may bear no relation whatever to their apparent and generally accepted causes as studied by the historian.

It is this most obscure and neglected chapter of the history of the human race, for which we can gather so little material from records, that must occupy the foreground of our picture; and whether we are concerned with a discovery, an important theory, a new legal system, or a political revolution, we shall endeavour to determine its consequences for the majority in each society. For it is there that one finds the true subject matter of philosophy, for all intermediate consequences may be ignored except in so far as they eventually influence the greater mass of the human race.

It is only when we come to this final link in the chain that our contemplation of historical events and the reflections that occur to us are of true utility. Only then can we appreciate men's true claims to fame, and can take real pleasure in the progress of their reason; only then can we truly judge the perfection of the human race.

The idea that everything must be considered in relation to this single point of reference is dictated both by justice and by reason. Nevertheless one might be tempted to regard it as fantastic. But one would be wrong. To show this is so, we have only to cite two striking examples.

The man who tills our soil owes his enjoyment of the commonest goods, which plentifully supply his needs, to the long-continued labours of industry assisted by science: and his enjoyment of these goods can be traced even further back, to the victory of Salamis, but for which the shadows of Oriental despotism threatened to engulf the earth. Similarly, the mariner who is preserved from shipwreck by precise observations of longitude, owes his life to a theory which can be traced back, through a chain of truths, to discoveries made in the school of Plato, and thereafter buried for twenty centuries in total disuse.

THE TENTH STAGE: THE FUTURE PROGRESS OF THE HUMAN MIND

If man can, with almost complete assurance, predict phenomena when he knows their laws, and if, even when he does not, he can still, with great expectation of success, forecast the future on the basis of his experience of the past, why, then, should it be regarded as a fantastic undertaking to sketch, with some pretence to truth, the future destiny of man on the basis of his history? The sole foundation for belief in the natural sciences is this idea, that the general laws directing the phenomena of the universe, known or unknown, are necessary and constant. Why should this principle be any less true for the development of the intellectual and moral faculties of man than for the other operations of nature? Since beliefs founded on past experience of like conditions provide the only rule of conduct for the wisest of men, why should the philosopher be forbidden to base his conjectures on these same foundations, so long as he does not attribute to them a certainty superior to that warranted by the number, the constancy, and the accuracy of his observations?

Our hopes for the future condition of the human race can be subsumed under three important heads: the abolition of inequality between nations, the progress of equality within each nation, and the true perfection of mankind. Will all nations one day attain that state of civilization which the most enlightened, the freest, and the least burdened by prejudices, such as the French and the Anglo-Americans, have attained already? Will the vast gulf that separates these peoples from the slavery of nations under the rule of monarchs, from the barbarism of African tribes, from the ignorance of savages, little by little disappear?

Is there on the face of the earth a nation whose inhabitants have been debarred by nature herself from the enjoyment of freedom and the exercise of reason?

Are those differences which have hitherto been seen in every civilized country in respect of the enlightenment, the resources, and the wealth enjoyed by the different classes into which it is divided, is that inequality between men which was aggravated or perhaps produced by the earliest progress of society, are these part of civilization itself, or are they due to the present imperfections of the social art? Will they necessarily decrease and ultimately make way for a real equality, the final end of the social art, in which even the effects of the natural differences between men will be mitigated and the only kind of inequality to persist will be that which is in the interests of all and which favours the progress of civilization, of education, and of industry, without entailing either poverty, humiliation, or dependence? In other words, will men approach a condition in which everyone will have the knowledge neces-

sary to conduct himself in the ordinary affairs of life, according to the light of his own reason, to preserve his mind free from prejudice, to understand his rights and to exercise them in accordance with his conscience and his creed; in which everyone will become able, through the development of his faculties, to find the means of providing for his needs; and in which at last misery and folly will be the exception, and no longer the habitual lot of a section of society?

Is the human race to better itself, either by discoveries in the sciences and the arts, and so in the means to individual welfare and general prosperity; or by progress in the principles of conduct or practical morality; or by a true perfection of the intellectual, moral, or physical faculties of man, an improvement which may result from a perfection either of the instruments used to heighten the intensity of these faculties and to direct their use or of the natural constitution of man?

In answering these three questions we shall find in the experience of the past, in the observation of the progress that the sciences and civilization have already made, in the analysis of the progress of the human mind and of the development of its faculties, the strongest reasons for believing that nature has set no limit to the realization of our hopes. . . .

As we move from nation to nation, we can see in each what special obstacles impede this revolution and what attitudes of mind favour it. We can distinguish the nations where we may expect it to be introduced gently by the perhaps belated wisdom of their governments, and those nations where its violence intensified by their resistance must involve all alike in a swift and terrible convulsion.

Can we doubt that either common sense or the senseless discords of European nations will add to the effects of the slow but inexorable progress of their colonies, and will soon bring about the independence of the New World? And then will not the European population in these colonies, spreading rapidly over that enormous land, either civilize or peacefully remove the savage nations who still inhabit vast tracts of its land?

Survey the history of our settlements and commercial undertakings in Africa or in Asia, and you will see how our trade monopolies, our treachery, our murderous contempt for men of another colour or creed, the insolence of our usurpations, the intrigues or the exaggerated proselytic zeal of our priests, have destroyed the respect and goodwill that the superiority of our knowledge and the benefits of our commerce at first won for us in the eyes of the inhabitants. But doubtless the moment approaches when, no longer presenting ourselves as always either tyrants or corrupters, we shall become for them the beneficent instruments of their freedom. . . .

So the peoples of Europe, confining themselves to free trade, understanding their own rights too well to show contempt for those of other peoples, will respect this independence, which until now they have so insolently violated. Their settlements, no longer filled with government hirelings hastening, under the cloak of place or privilege, to amass treasure by brigandry and deceit, so as to be able to return to Europe and purchase titles and honour, will now be peopled with men of industrious habit, seeking in these propitious climates the wealth that eluded them at home. The love of freedom will retain them there, ambition will no longer recall them, and what have been no better than the counting-houses of brigands will become colonies of citizens propagating throughout Africa and Asia the principles and the practice of liberty, knowledge, and reason, that they have brought from Europe. We shall see the monks who brought only shameful superstition to these peoples and aroused their antagonism by the threat of yet another tyranny, replaced by men occupied in propagating amongst them the truths that will promote their happiness and in teaching them about their interests and their rights. Zeal for the truth is also one of the passions, and it will turn its efforts to distant lands once there are no longer at home any crass prejudices to combat, any shameful errors to dissipate.

These vast lands are inhabited partly by large tribes who need only assistance from us to become civilized, who wait only to find brothers amongst the European nations to become their friends and pupils; partly by races oppressed by sacred despots or dull-witted conquerors, and who for so many centuries have cried out to be liberated; partly by tribes living in a condition of almost total savagery in a climate whose harshness repels the sweet blessings of civilization and deters those who would teach them its benefits; and finally, by conquering hordes who know no other law but force, no other profession but piracy. The progress of these two last classes of people will be slower and stormier; and perhaps it will even be that, reduced in number as they are driven back by civilized nations, they will finally disappear imperceptibly before them or merge into them. . . .

The progress of these peoples is likely to be more rapid and certain than our own because they can receive from us everything that we have had to find out for ourselves, and in order to understand those simple truths and infallible methods which we have acquired only after long error, all that they need to do is to follow the expositions and proofs that appear in our speeches and writings. If the progress of the Greeks was lost to later nations, this was because of the absence of any form of communication between the different peoples, and for this we must blame the tyrannical domination of the Romans. But when mutual needs have brought all men together, and the great powers have established equality between societies as well as between individuals and have raised respect for the independence of weak states and sympathy for ignorance and misery to the rank of political principles, when maxims that favour action and energy have ousted those which would compress the province of human faculties, will it then be possible to fear that there are still places in the world inaccessible to enlightenment, or that despotism in its pride can raise barriers against truth that are insurmountable for long?

The time will therefore come when the sun will shine only on free men who know no other master but their reason; when tyrants and slaves, priests and their stupid or hypocritical instruments, will exist only in works of history and on the stage; and when we shall think of them only to pity their victims and their dupes; to maintain ourselves in a state of vigilance by thinking on their excesses; and to learn how to recognize and so to destroy, by force of reason, the first seeds of tyranny and superstition, should they ever dare to reappear amongst us.

In looking at the history of societies we shall have had occasion to observe that there is often a great difference between the rights that the law allows its citizens and the rights that they actually enjoy, and, again, between the equality established by political codes and that which in fact exists amongst individuals: and we shall have noticed that these differences were one of the principal causes of the destruction of freedom in the Ancient republics, of the storms that troubled them, and of the weakness that delivered them over to foreign tyrants.

These differences have three main causes: inequality in wealth; inequality in status between the man whose means of subsistence are hereditary and the man whose means are dependent on the length of his life, or, rather, on that part of his life in which he is capable of work; and, finally, inequality in education.

We therefore need to show that these three sorts of real inequality must constantly diminish without however disappearing altogether: for they are the result of natural and necessary causes which it would be foolish and dangerous to wish to eradicate; and one could not even attempt to bring about the entire disappearance of their effects without introducing even more fecund sources of inequality, without striking more direct and more fatal blows at the rights of man.

It is easy to prove that wealth has a natural tendency to equality, and that any excessive disproportion could not exist or at least would rapidly disappear if civil laws did not provide artificial ways of perpetuating and uniting fortunes; if free trade and industry were allowed to remove the advantages that accrued wealth derives from any restrictive law or fiscal privilege; if taxes on covenants, the restrictions placed on their free employment, their subjection to tiresome formalities and the uncertainty and inevitable expense involved in implementing them did not hamper the activity of the poor man and swallow up his meagre capital; if the administration of the country did not afford some men ways of making their fortune that were closed to other citizens; if prejudice and avarice, so common in old age, did not preside over the making of marriages; and if, in a society enjoying simpler manners and more sensible institutions, wealth ceased to be a means of satisfying vanity and ambition, and if the equally misguided notions of austerity, which condemn spending money in the cultivation of the more delicate pleasures, no longer insisted on the hoarding of all one's earnings.

Let us turn to the enlightened nations of Europe, and observe the size of their present populations in relation to the size of their territories. Let us consider, in agriculture and industry, the proportion that holds between labour and the means of subsistence, and we shall see that it would be impossible for those means to be kept at their present level and consequently for the population to be kept at its present size if a great number of individuals were not almost entirely dependent for the maintenance of themselves and their family either on their own labour or on the interest from capital invested so as to make their labour more productive. Now both these sources of income depend on the life and even on the health of the head of the family. They provide what is rather like a life annuity, save that it is more dependent on chance; and in consequence there is a very real difference between people living like this and those whose resources are not at all subject to the same risks, who live either on revenue from land, or on the interest on capital which is almost independent of their own labour.

Here then is a necessary cause of inequality, of dependence and even of misery, which ceaselessly threatens the most numerous and most active class in our society.

We shall point out how it can be in great part eradicated by guaranteeing people in old age a means of livelihood produced partly by their own savings and partly by the savings of others who make the same outlay, but who die before they need to reap the reward; or, again, on the same principle of compensation, by securing for widows and orphans an income which is the same and costs the same for those families which suffer an early loss and for those which suffer it later; or again by providing all children with the capital necessary for the full use of their labour, available at the age when they start work and found a family, a capital which increases at the expense of those whom premature death prevents from reaching this age. It is to the application of the calculus to the probabilities of life and the investment of money that we owe the idea of these methods which have already been successful, although they have not been applied in a sufficiently comprehensive and exhaustive fashion to render them really useful, not merely to a few individuals, but to society as a whole, by making it possible to prevent those periodic disasters which strike at so many families and which are such a recurrent source of misery and suffering.

We shall point out that schemes of this nature, which can be organized in the name of the social authority and become one of its greatest benefits, can also be the work of private associations, which will be formed without any real risk, once the principles for the proper working of these schemes have been widely diffused and the mistakes which have been the undoing of a large number of these associations no longer hold terrors for us.

[We shall reveal other methods of ensuring this equality, either by seeing that credit is no longer the exclusive privilege of great wealth, but that it has another and no less sound foundation; or by making industrial progress and commercial activity more independent of the existence of the great capitalists. And once again, it is to the application of the calculus that we shall be indebted for such methods.]

The degree of equality in education that we can reasonably hope to attain, but that should be adequate, is that which excludes all dependence, either forced or voluntary. We shall show how this condition can be easily attained in the present state of human knowledge even by those who can study only for a small number of years in childhood, and then during the rest of their life in their few hours of leisure. We shall prove that, by a suitable choice of syllabus and methods of education, we can teach the citizen everything that he needs to know in order to be able to manage his household, administer his affairs, and employ his labour and his faculties in freedom; to know his rights and to be able to exercise them; to be acquainted with his duties and fulfil them satisfactorily; to judge his own and other men's actions according to his own lights and to be a stranger to none of the high and delicate feelings which honour human nature; not to be

in a state of blind dependence upon those to whom he must entrust his affairs or the exercise of his rights; to be in a proper condition to choose and supervise them; to be no longer the dupe of those popular errors which torment man with superstitious fears and chimerical hopes; to defend himself against prejudice by the strength of his reason alone; and, finally, to escape the deceits of charlatans who would lay snares for his fortune, his health, his freedom of thought and his conscience under the pretext of granting him health, wealth, and salvation.

From such time onwards the inhabitants of a single country will no longer be distinguished by their use of a crude or refined language; they will be able to govern themselves according to their own knowledge; they will no longer be limited to a mechanical knowledge of the procedures of the arts or of professional routine; they will no longer depend for every trivial piece of business, every insignificant matter of instruction, on clever men who rule over them in virtue of their necessary superiority; and so they will attain a real equality, since differences in enlightenment or talent can no longer raise a barrier between men who understand each other's feelings, ideas, and language, some of whom may wish to be taught by others but, to do so, will have no need to be controlled by them, or who may wish to confide the care of government to the ablest of their number but will not be compelled to yield them absolute power in a spirit of blind confidence.

This kind of supervision has advantages even for those who do not exercise it, since it is employed for them and not against them. Natural differences of ability between men whose understanding has not been cultivated give rise, even in savage tribes, to charlatans and dupes, to clever men and men readily deceived. These same differences are truly universal, but now they are differences only between men of learning and upright men who know the value of learning without being dazzled by it; or between talent or genius and the common sense which can appreciate and benefit from them; so that even if these natural differences were greater, and more extensive than they are, they would be only the more influential in improving the relations between men and promoting what is advantageous for their independence and happiness.

These various causes of equality do not act in isolation; they unite, combine, and support each other and so their cumulative effects are stronger, surer, and more constant. With greater equality of education there will be greater equality in industry and so in wealth; equality in wealth necessarily leads to equality in education: and equality between the nations and equality within a single nation are mutually dependent.

So we might say that a well directed system of education rectifies natural inequality in ability instead of strengthening it, just as good laws remedy natural inequality in the means of subsistence, and just as in societies where laws have brought about this same equality, liberty, though subject to a regular constitution, will be more widespread, more complete than in the total independence of savage life. Then the social art will have fulfilled its aim, that of assuring and extending to all men enjoyment of the common rights to which they are called by nature.

The real advantages that should result from this progress, of which we can entertain a hope that is almost a certainty, can have no other term than that of the absolute perfection of the human race; since, as the various kinds of equality come to work in its favour by producing ampler sources of supply, more extensive education, more complete liberty, so equality will be more real and will embrace everything which is really of importance for the happiness of human beings.

It is therefore only by examining the progress and the laws of this perfection that we shall be able to understand the extent or the limits of our hopes.

No one has ever believed that the mind can gain knowledge of all the facts of nature or attain the ultimate means of precision in the measurement, or in the analysis of the facts of nature, the relations between objects and all the possible combinations of ideas. Even the relations between magnitudes, the mere notion of quantity or extension, taken in its fullest comprehension, gives rise to a system so vast that it will never be mastered by the human mind in its entirety, that there will always be a part of

it, always indeed the larger part of it that will remain for ever unknown. People have believed that man can never know more than a part of the objects that the nature of his intelligence allows him to understand, and that he must in the end arrive at a point where the number and complexity of the objects that he already knows have absorbed all his strength so that any further progress must be completely impossible.

But since, as the number of known facts increases, the human mind learns how to classify them and to subsume them under more general facts, and, at the same time, the instruments and methods employed in their observation and their exact measurement acquire a new precision; since, as more relations between various objects become known, man is able to reduce them to more general relations, to express them more simply, and to present them in such a way that it is possible to grasp a greater number of them with the same degree of intellectual ability and the same amount of application; since, as the mind learns to understand more complicated combinations of ideas, simpler formulae soon reduce their complexity; so truths that were discovered only by great effort, that could at first only be understood by men capable of profound thought, are soon developed and proved by methods that are not beyond the reach of common intelligence. If the methods which have led to these new combinations of ideas are ever exhausted, if their application to hitherto unsolved questions should demand exertions greater than either the time or the capacity of the learned would permit, some method of a greater generality or simplicity will be found so that genius can continue undisturbed on its path. The strength and the limits of man's intelligence may remain unaltered; and yet the instruments that he uses will increase and improve, the language that fixes and determines his ideas will acquire greater breadth and precision and, unlike mechanics where an increase of force means a decrease of speed, the methods that lead genius to the discovery of truth increase at once the force and the speed of its operations.

Therefore, since these developments are themselves the necessary consequences of progress in detailed knowledge, and since the need for new methods in fact only arises in circumstances that give rise to new methods, it is evident that, within the body of the sciences of observation, calculation, and experiment, the actual number of truths may always increase, and that every part of this body may develop, and yet man's faculties be of the same strength, activity, and extent.

If we apply these general reflections to the various sciences, we can find in each of them examples of progressive improvement that will remove any doubts about what we may expect for the future. We shall point out in particular the progress that is both likely and imminent in those sciences which prejudice regards as all but exhausted. We shall give examples of the manner and extent of the precision and unity which could accrue to the whole system of human knowledge as the result of a more general and philosophical application of the sciences of calculation to the various branches of knowledge. We shall show how favourable to our hopes would be a more universal system of education by giving a greater number of people the elementary knowledge which could awaken their interest in a particular branch of study, and by providing conditions favourable to their progress in it; and how these hopes would be further raised, if more men possessed the means to devote themselves to these studies, for at present even in the most enlightened countries scarcely one in fifty of the people who have natural talents, receives the necessary education to develop them; and how, if this were done there would be a proportionate increase in the number of men destined by their discoveries to extend the boundaries of science.

We shall show how this equality in education and the equality which will come about between the different nations would accelerate the advance of these sciences whose progress depends on repeated observations over a large area; what benefits would thereby accrue to mineralogy, botany, zoology, and meteorology; and what a vast disproportion holds in all these sciences between the poverty of existing methods which have nevertheless led to useful and important new truths, and the wealth of those methods which man would then be able to employ.

We shall show how even the sciences in which discovery is the fruit of solitary medita-

tion would benefit from being studied by a greater number of people, in the matter of those improvements in detail which do not demand the intellectual energy of an inventor but suggest themselves to mere reflection.

If we turn now to the arts, whose theory depends on these same sciences, we shall find that their progress depending as it does on that of theory, can have no other limits; that the procedures of the different arts can be perfected and simplified in the same way as the methods of the sciences; new instruments, machines, and looms can add to man's strength and can improve at once the quality and the accuracy of his productions, and can diminish the time and labour that has to be expended on them. The obstacles still in the way of this progress will disappear, accidents will be foreseen and prevented, the insanitary conditions that are due either to the work itself or to the climate will be eliminated.

A very small amount of ground will be able to produce a great quantity of supplies of greater utility or higher quality; more goods will be obtained for a smaller outlay; the manufacture of articles will be achieved with less wastage in raw materials and will make better use of them. Every type of soil will produce those things which satisfy the greatest number of needs; of several alternative ways of satisfying needs of the same order, that will be chosen which satisfies the greatest number of people and which requires least labour and least expenditure. So, without the need for sacrifice, methods of preservation and economy in expenditure will improve in the wake of progress in the arts of producing and preparing supplies and making articles from them.

So not only will the same amount of ground support more people, but everyone will have less work to do, will produce more, and satisfy his wants more fully.

With all this progress in industry and welfare which establishes a happier proportion between men's talents and their needs, each successive generation will have larger possessions, either as a result of this progress or through the preservation of the products of industry; and so, as a consequence of the physical constitution of the human race, the number of people will increase. Might there not then come a moment when these necessary laws begin to work in a contrary direction; when, the number of people in the world finally exceeding the means of subsistence, there will in consequence ensue a continual diminution of happiness and population, a true retrogression, or at best an oscillation between good and bad? In societies that have reached this stage will not this oscillation be a perennial source of more or less periodic disaster? Will it not show that a point has been attained beyond which all further improvement is impossible, that the perfectibility of the human race has after long years arrived at a term beyond which it may never go?

There is doubtless no one who does not think that such a time is still very far from us; but will it ever arrive? It is impossible to pronounce about the likelihood of an event that will occur only when the human species will have necessarily acquired a degree of knowledge of which we can have no inkling. And who would take it upon himself to predict the condition to which the art of converting the elements to the use of man may in time be brought?

But even if we agree that the limit will one day arrive, nothing follows from it that is in the least alarming as far as either the happiness of the human race or its indefinite perfectibility is concerned; if we consider that, before all this comes to pass, the progress of reason will have kept pace with that of the sciences, and that the absurd prejudices of superstition will have ceased to corrupt and degrade the moral code by its harsh doctrines instead of purifying and elevating it, we can assume that by then men will know that, if they have a duty towards those who are not yet born, that duty is not to give them existence but to give them happiness; their aim should be to promote the general welfare of the human race or of the society in which they live or of the family to which they belong, rather than foolishly to encumber the world with useless and wretched beings. It is, then, possible that there should be a limit to the amount of food that can be produced, and, consequently, to the size of the population of the world, without this involving that untimely destruction of some of those creatures who have been given life, which is so contrary to nature and to social prosperity. . . .

Nations will learn that they cannot conquer other nations without losing their own liberty; that permanent confederations are their only means of preserving their independence; and that they should seek not power but security. Gradually mercantile prejudices will fade away: and a false sense of commercial interest will lose the fearful power it once had of drenching the earth in blood and of ruining nations under pretext of enriching them. When at last the nations come to agree on the principles of politics and morality, when in their own better interests they invite foreigners to share equally in all the benefits men enjoy either through the bounty of nature or by their own industry, then all the causes that produce and perpetuate national animosities and poison national relations will disappear one by one; and nothing will remain to encourage or even to arouse the fury of war.

Organizations more intelligently conceived than those projects of eternal peace which have filled the leisure and consoled the hearts of certain philosophers, will hasten the progress of the brotherhood of nations, and wars between countries will rank with assassinations as freakish atrocities, humiliating and vile in the eyes of nature and staining with indelible opprobrium the country or the age whose annals record them. . . .

The progress of the sciences ensures the progress of the art of education which in turn advances that of the sciences. This reciprocal influence, whose activity is ceaselessly renewed, deserves to be seen as one of the most powerful and active causes working for the perfection of mankind. At the present time a young man on leaving school may know more of the principles of mathematics than Newton ever learnt in years of study or discovered by dint of genius, and he may use the calculus with a facility then unknown. The same observation, with certain reservations, applies to all the sciences. As each advances, the methods of expressing a large number of proofs in a more economical fashion and so of making their comprehension an easier matter, advance with it. So, in spite of the progress of science, not only do men of the same ability find themselves at the same age on a level with the existing state of science, but with every generation, that which can be acquired in a certain time with a certain degree of intelligence and a certain amount of concentration will be permanently on the increase, and, as the elementary part of each science to which all men may attain grows and grows, it will more and more include all the knowledge necessary for each man to know for the conduct of the ordinary events of his life, and will support him in the free and independent exercise of his reason.

In the political sciences there are some truths that, with free people (that is to say, with certain generations in all countries) can be of use only if they are widely known and acknowledged. So the influence of these sciences upon the freedom and prosperity of nations must in some degree be measured by the number of truths that, as a result of elementary instruction, are common knowledge; the swelling progress of elementary instruction, connected with the necessary progress of these sciences promises us an improvement in the destiny of the human race, which may be regarded as indefinite, since it can have no other limits than that of this same progress.

We have still to consider two other general methods which will influence both the perfection of education and that of the sciences. One is the more extensive and less imperfect use of what we might call technical methods; the other is the setting up of a universal language.

I mean by technical methods the art of arranging a large number of subjects in a system so that we may straightway grasp their relations, quickly perceive their combinations, and readily form new combinations out of them.

We shall develop the principles and examine the utility of this art, which is still in its infancy, and which, as it improves, will enable us, within the compass of a small chart, to set out what could possibly not be expressed so well in a whole book, or, what is still more valuable, to present isolated facts in such a way as to allow us to deduce their general consequences. We shall see how by means of a small number of these charts, whose use can easily be learned, men who have not been sufficiently educated to be able to absorb details useful to them in ordinary

life, may now be able to master them when the need arises; and how these methods may likewise be of benefit to elementary education itself in all those branches where it is concerned either with a regular system of truths or with a series of observations and facts. . . .

All the causes that contribute to the perfection of the human race, all the means that ensure it must by their very nature exercise a perpetual influence and always increase their sphere of action. The proofs of this we have given and in the great work they will derive additional force from elaboration. We may conclude then that the perfectibility of man is indefinite. Meanwhile we have considered him as possessing the natural faculties and organization that he has at present. How much greater would be the certainty, how much vaster the scheme of our hopes if we could believe that these natural faculties themselves and this organization could also be improved? This is the last question that remains for us to ask ourselves.

These are the questions with which we shall conclude this final stage. How consoling for the philosopher who laments the errors, the crimes, the injustices which still pollute the earth and of which he is often the victim is this view of the human race, emancipated from its shackles, released from the empire of fate and from that of the enemies of its progress, advancing with a firm and sure step along the path of truth, virtue and happiness! It is the contemplation of this prospect that rewards him for all his efforts to assist the progress of reason and the defence of liberty. He dares to regard these strivings as part of the eternal chain of human destiny; and in this persuasion he is filled with the true delight of virtue and the pleasure of having done some lasting good which fate can never destroy by a sinister stroke of revenge, by calling back the rein of slavery and prejudice. Such contemplation is for him an asylum, in which the memory of his persecutors cannot pursue him; there he lives in thought with man restored to his natural rights and dignity, forgets man tormented and corrupted by greed, fear, or envy; there he lives with his peers in an Elysium created by reason and graced by the purest pleasures known to the love of mankind.

The Revolutionary Era and the Conservative Reaction

Beginning in the seventeenth century the English made a notable contribution to the expansion of European civilization when they established a colonial empire in North America. Gradually these British subjects, living in a new environment and exploiting their extensive natural resources, developed political and social points of view and economic interests that not only differed from those of the mother country but actually conflicted with them. Independence became the inevitable result of of this deviation, and in the eighteenth century the leaders of the thirteen colonies turned to the principles of the Enlightenment to justify the revolution they were embarking upon. Shortly thereafter, France, laboring under the political and social encumbrances of the Old Regime, followed a similar trend toward revolution in order to obtain more enlightened government. On both sides of the Atlantic the initial liberal impulse of the revolution was eventually diverted into more conservative channels. In the new world this reaction found expression in the constitutional convention of 1787 and the federal union, while in the old it came about through the career of Napoleon. Political conservatism found its literary exponents who sought to justify it on such grounds as the value of historical experience and the concept of the organic growth of the State. This trend in political thought was paralleled in literature and the arts by the romantic movement. Poets and authors wrote in strongly emotional terms of man and his feelings of love, romance, sentiment, and passion. Painters gave expression to their feelings by painting romantic scenes from the past in warm colors and with much movement and linear contrast.

Michel-Guillaume Jean de Crèvecoeur

Michel-Guillaume Jean de Crèvecoeur (1735–1813) was a Frenchman who migrated to Canada, where he fought under Montcalm at Quebec and later explored in the Great Lakes region. In 1759 he went south to the English colonies, and, following the pattern set by other immigrants, became naturalized, married an American, and became a successful farmer. In 1782 he published a series of essays under the title of Letters From an American Farmer. This work, written as it was by a recent arrival who saw America as a new land and Americans as a new race, is a valuable social document illustrating the transit of European society and civilization across the Atlantic. In reading the letter "What Is an American" from Crèvecoeur's writings note (1) what he had to say about class distinctions in American society, (2) the extent of American resources, (3) the general description of the countryside, (4) the effect of the American environment upon the downtrodden of Europe, (5) the emergence of the American, (6) the influence environment had had on Americans in different parts of the country, (7) the description of the crudeness of life on the frontier, (8) the foreign group he found most successful and his explanation for it, and (9) the note of gratitude on which he concluded the essay.

From: LETTERS FROM AN AMERICAN FARMER

I wish I could be acquainted with the feelings and thoughts which must agitate the heart and present themselves to the mind of an enlightened Englishman, when he first lands on this continent. He must greatly rejoice, that he lived at a time to see this fair country discovered and settled; he must necessarily feel a share of national pride, when he views the chain of settlements which embellishes these extended shores. When he says to himself, this is the work of my countrymen, who, when convulsed by factions, afflicted by a variety of miseries and wants, restless and impatient, took refuge here. They brought along with them their national genius, to which they principally owe what liberty they enjoy, and what substance they possess. Here he sees the industry of his native country, displayed in a new manner, and traces in their works the embrios of all the arts, sciences, and ingenuity which flourish in Europe. Here he beholds fair cities, substantial villages, extensive fields, an immense country filled with decent houses, good roads, orchards, meadows, and bridges, where an hundred years ago all was wild, woody, and uncultivated!

What a train of pleasing ideas this fair spectacle must suggest! it is a prospect which must inspire a good citizen with the most heartfelt pleasure. The difficulty consists in the manner of viewing so extensive a scene. He is arrived on a new continent; a modern society offers itself to his contemplation, different from what he had hitherto seen. It is not composed, as in Europe, of great lords who possess every thing, and of a herd of people who have nothing. Here are no aristocratical families, no courts, no kings, no bishops, no ecclesiastical dominion, no invisible power giving to a few a very visible one; no great manufactures employing thousands, no great refinements of luxury. The rich and the poor are not so far removed from each other as they are in Europe.

Some few towns excepted, we are all tillers

J. Hector St. John, A Farmer in Pennsylvania, *Letters from an American Farmer* . . . , London, 1782, 45–87.

of the earth, from Nova Scotia to West Florida. We are a people of cultivators, scattered over an immense territory, communicating with each other by means of good roads and navigable rivers, united by the silken bands of mild government, all respecting the laws without dreading their power, because they are equitable. We are all animated with the spirit of industry, which is unfettered, and unrestrained, because each person works for himself. If he travels through our rural districts, he views not the hostile castle, and the haughty mansion, contrasted with the clay-built hut and miserable cabbin, where cattle and men help to keep each other warm, and dwell in meanness, smoke and indigence. A pleasing uniformity of decent competence appears throughout our habitations. The meanest of our log-houses is a dry and comfortable habitation. Lawyer or merchant are the fairest titles our towns afford; that of a farmer is the only appellation of the rural inhabitants of our country. It must take some time ere he can reconcile himself to our dictionary, which is but short in words of dignity, and names of honour. There, on a Sunday, he sees a congregation of respectable farmers and their wives, all clad in neat homespun, well mounted, or riding in their own humble waggons. There is not among them an esquire, saving the unlettered magistrate. There he sees a parson as simple as his flock, a farmer who does not riot on the labour of others. We have no princes, for whom we toil, starve, and bleed: we are the most perfect society now existing in the world. Here man is free as he ought to be; nor is this pleasing equality so transitory as many others are. Many ages will not see the shores of our great lakes replenished with inland nations, nor the unknown bounds of North America entirely peopled. Who can tell how far it extends? Who can tell the millions of men whom it will feed and contain? for no European foot has as yet travelled half the extent of this mighty continent!

The next wish of this traveller will be to know whence came all these people? they are a mixture of English, Scotch, Irish, French, Dutch, Germans, and Swedes. From this promiscuous breed, that race now called Americans have arisen. The eastern provinces must indeed be excepted, as being the unmixed descendants of Englishmen. I have heard many wish they had been more intermixed also: for my part, I am no wisher; and think it much better as it has happened. They exhibit a most conspicuous figure in this great and variegated picture; they too enter for a great share in the pleasing perspective displayed in these thirteen provinces. I know it is fashionable to reflect on them; but I respect them for what they have done; for the accuracy and wisdom with which they have settled their territory; for the decency of their manners; for their early love of letters; their ancient college, the first in this hemisphere; for their industry, which to me, who am but a farmer, is the criterion of every thing. There never was a people, situated as they are, who, with so ungrateful a soil, have done more in so short a time. Do you think that the monarchial ingredients which are more prevalent in other governments, have purged them from all foul stains? Their histories assert the contrary.

In this great American asylum, the poor of Europe have by some means met together, and in consequence of various causes; to what purpose should they ask one another, what countrymen they are? Alas, two thirds of them had no country. Can a wretch who wanders about, who works and starves, whose life is a continual scene of sore affliction or pinching penury; can that man call England or any other kingdom his country? A country that had no bread for him, whose fields procured him no harvest, who met with nothing but the frowns of the rich, the severity of the laws, with jails and punishments; who owned not a single foot of the extensive surface of this planet? No! urged by a variety of motives, here they came. Every thing has tended to regenerate them; new laws, a new mode of living, a new social system; here they are become men: in Europe they were as so many useless plants, wanting vegetative mould, and refreshing showers; they withered, and were mowed down by want, hunger, and war: but now, by the power of transplantation, like all other plants, they have taken root and flourished! Formerly they were not numbered in any civil list of their country, except in those of the poor; here they rank as citizens. By what invisible power has this surprizing metamorphosis been performed? By that of the laws and that of their industry. The laws, the indulgent laws, protect them as they arrive, stamping on them the symbol of adoption; they receive ample rewards for their labours; these accumulated rewards procure them lands; those lands confer on them the title of freemen; and to that title every benefit is affixed which men can possibly require. This is the great operation daily performed by our laws. From whence proceed these laws? From our government. Whence that government? It is derived from the original genius and strong desire of the people, ratified and confirmed by government. This is the great chain which links us all, this is the picture which every province exhibits, Nova Scotia excepted. There the crown has done all; either there were no people who had genius, or it was not much attended to: the consequence is, that the province is very thinly inhabited indeed; the power of the crown, in conjunction with the musketos, has prevented men from settling there. Yet some part of it flourished once, and it contained a mild harmless set of people. But for the fault of a few leaders the whole were banished. The greatest political error the crown ever committed in America, was to cut off men from a country which wanted nothing but men.

What attachment can a poor European emigrant have for a country where he had nothing? The knowledge of the language, the love of a few kindred as poor as himself, were the only cords that tied him: his country is now that which gives him land, bread, protection, and consequence: *Ubi panis ibi patria,* is the motto of all emigrants. What then is the American, this new man? He is either an European, or the descendant of an European; hence that strange mixture of blood, which you will find in no other country. I could point out to you a man, whose grandfather was an Englishman, whose wife was Dutch, whose son married a French woman, and whose present four sons have now four wives of different nations. *He* is an American, who, leaving behind him all his ancient prejudices and manners, receives new ones from the new mode of life he has embraced, the new government he obeys, and the new rank he holds. He becomes an American by being received in the broad lap of our great *Alma Mater.*

Here individuals of all nations are melted into a new race of men, whose labours and posterity will one day cause great change in the world. Americans are the western pilgrims, who are carrying along with them that great mass of arts, sciences, vigour, and industry, which began long since in the east; they will finish the great circle. The Americans were once scattered all over Europe; here they are incorporated into one of the finest systems of population which has ever appeared, and which will hereafter become distinct by the power of the different climates they inhabit. The American ought, therefore, to love this country much better than that wherein either he or his forefathers were born. Here the rewards of his industry follow with equal steps the progress of his labour; his labour is founded on the basis of nature, *self-interest;* can it want a stronger allurement? Wives and children, who before in vain demanded of him a morsel of bread, now, fat and frolicsome, gladly help their father to clear those fields whence exuberant crops are to arise to feed and to clothe them all; without any part being claimed, either by a despotic prince, a rich abbot, or a mighty lord. Here religion demands but little of him; a small voluntary salary to the minister, and gratitude to God; can he refuse these? The American is a new man, who acts upon new principles; he must therefore entertain new ideas, and form new opinions. From involuntary idleness, servile dependance, penury, and useless labour, he has passed to toils of a very different nature, rewarded by ample subsistence.—This is an American.

North America is divided into many provinces, forming a large association, scattered along a coast 1,500 miles extent and about 200 wide. This society I would fain examine, at least such as it appears in the middle provinces; if it does not afford that variety of tinges and gradations which may be observed in Europe, we have colours peculiar to ourselves. For instance, it is natural to conceive that those who live near the sea, must be very different from those who live in the woods; the intermediate space will afford a separate and distinct class.

Men are like plants; the goodness and flavour of the fruit proceed from the peculiar soil and exposition in which they grow. We are nothing but what we derive from the air we breathe, the climate we inhabit, the government we obey, the system of religion we profess, and the nature of our employment. Here you will find but few crimes; these have acquired as yet no root among us. I wish I were able to trace all my ideas; if my ignorance prevents me from describing them properly, I hope I shall be able to delineate a few of the outlines, which are all I propose.

Those who live near the sea, feed more on fish than on flesh, and often encounter that boisterous element. This renders them more bold and enterprising; this leads them to neglect the confined occupations of the land. They see and converse with a variety of people; their intercourse with mankind becomes extensive. The sea inspires them with a love of traffic, a desire of transporting produce from one place to another; leads them to a variety of resources, which supply the place of labour. Those who inhabit the middle settlements, by far the most numerous, must be very different; the simple cultivation of the earth purifies them; but the indulgences of the government, the soft remonstrances of religion, the rank of independent freeholders, must necessarily inspire them with sentiments, very little known in Europe among people of the same class. What do I say? Europe has no such class of man; the early knowledge they acquire, the early bargains they make, give them a great degree of sagacity. As freemen, they will be litigious; pride and obstinacy are often the cause of law suits; the nature of our laws and governments may be another. As citizens, it is easy to imagine, that they will carefully read the newspapers, enter into every political disquisition, freely blame or censure governors and others. As farmers, they will be careful and anxious to get as much as they can, because what they get is their own. As northern men, they will love the cheerful cup. As christians, religion curbs them not in their opinions; the general indulgence leaves every one to think for himself in spiritual matters; the laws inspect our actions; our thoughts are left to God. Industry, good living, selfishness, litigiousness, country politics, the pride of freemen, religious indifference, are their characteristics. If you recede

still farther from the sea, you will come into more modern settlements; they exhibit the same strong lineaments, in a ruder appearance. Religion seems to have still less influence, and their manners are less improved.

Now we arrive near the great woods, near the last inhabited districts; there men seem to be placed still farther beyond the reach of government, which in some measure leaves them to themselves. How can it pervade every corner? as they were driven there by misfortunes, necessity of beginnings, desire of acquiring large tracts of land, idleness, frequent want of economy, ancient debts; the reunion of such people does not afford a very pleasing spectacle. When discord, want of unity and friendship—when either drunkenness or idleness prevail in such remote districts—contention, inactivity, and wretchedness must ensue. There are not the same remedies to these evils as in a long established community. The few magistrates they have are in general little better than the rest; they are often in a perfect state of war; that of man against man, sometimes decided by blows, sometimes by means of the law; that of man against every wild inhabitant of these venerable woods, of which they are come to dispossess them. There men appear to be no better than carnivorous animals of a superior rank, living on the flesh of wild animals when they can catch them; and when they are not able, they subsist on the grain.

He who would wish to see America in its proper light, and have a true idea of its feeble beginnings and barbarous rudiments, must visit our extended line of frontiers where the last settlers dwell, and where he may see the first labours of settlement, the mode of clearing the earth, in all their different appearances; where men are wholly left dependent on their native tempers, and on the spur of uncertain industry, which often fails, when not sanctified by the efficacy of a few moral rules. There, remote from the power of example, and check of shame, many families exhibit the most hideous parts of our society. They are a kind of forlorn hope, preceding by ten or twelve years the most respectable army of veterans which come after them. In that space, prosperity will polish some, vice and the law will drive off the rest, who uniting again with others like themselves will recede still farther; making room for more industrious people, who will finish their improvements, convert the log-house into a convenient habitation, and rejoicing that the first heavy labours are finished, will change in a few years that hitherto barbarous country into a fine, fertile, well regulated district.

Such is our progress, such is the march of the Europeans toward the interior parts of this continent. In all societies there are off-casts; this impure part serves as our precursors or pioneers; my father himself was one of that class; but he came upon honest principles, and was therefore one of the few who held fast; by good conduct and temperance, he transmitted to me his fair inheritance, when not above one in fourteen of his contemporaries had the same good fortune.

Forty years ago, this smiling country was thus inhabited; it is now purged, a general decency of manners prevails throughout; and such has been the fate of our best countries.

Exclusive of those general characteristics, each province has its own, founded on the government, climate, mode of husbandry, customs, and peculiarity of circumstances. Europeans submit insensibly to these great powers, and become in the course of a few generations, not only Americans in general, but either Pennsylvanians, Virginians, or provincials under some other name. Whoever traverses the continent, must easily observe those strong differences, which will grow more evident in time. The inhabitants of Canada, Massachusetts, the middle provinces, the southern ones will be as different as their climates; their only points of unity will be those of religion and language.

. . . . Europe contains hardly any other distinctions but lords and tenants; this fair country alone is settled by freeholders, the possessors of the soil they cultivate, members of the government they obey, and the framers of their own laws, by means of their representatives. This is a thought which you have taught me to cherish; our distance from Europe, far from diminishing, rather adds to our usefulness and consequence as men and subjects. Had our forefathers remained there, they would only have crouded it, and perhaps prolonged those convulsions which had shook it so long. Every industrious European who transports

himself here, may be compared to a sprout growing at the foot of a great tree; it enjoys and draws but a little portion of sap; wrench it from the parent roots, transplant it, and it will become a tree bearing fruit also. Colonists are therefore intitled to the consideration due to the most useful subjects; a hundred families, barely existing in some parts of Scotland, will here in six years, cause an annual exportation of 10,000 bushels of wheat: 100 bushels being but a common quantity for an industrious family to sell, if they cultivate good land. It is here, then, that the idle may be employed, the useless become useful, and the poor become rich: but by riches I do not mean gold and silver; we have but little of those metals; I mean a better sort of wealth, cleared lands, cattle, good houses, good clothes, and an increase of people to enjoy them.

There is no wonder that this country has so many charms, and presents to Europeans so many temptations to remain in it. A traveller in Europe becomes a stranger as soon as he quits his own kingdom; but it is otherwise here. We know, properly speaking, no strangers; this is every person's country; the variety of our soils, situations, climates, governments, and produce, hath something which must please every body. No sooner does an European arrive, no matter of what condition, than his eyes are opened upon the fair prospects; he hears his language spoke, he retraces many of his own country manners, he perpetually hears the names of families and towns with which he is acquainted; he sees happiness and prosperity in all places disseminated; he meets with hospitality, kindness, and plenty every where: he beholds hardly any poor, he seldom hears of punishments and executions; and he wonders at the elegance of our towns, those miracles of industry and freedom. He cannot admire enough our rural districts, our convenient roads, good taverns, and our many accommodations; he involuntarily loves a country where every thing is so lovely. When in England, he was a mere Englishman; here he stands on a larger portion of the globe, not less than its fourth part, and may see the productions of the north, in iron and naval stores; the provisions of Ireland, the grain of Egypt, the indigo, the rice of China. He does not find, as in Europe, a crouded society, where every place is over-stocked; he does not feel that perpetual collision of parties, that difficulty of beginning, that contention which oversets so many.

There is room for every body in America: has he any particular talent, or industry? he exerts it in order to procure a livelihood, and it succeeds. Is he a merchant? the avenues of trade are infinite; is he eminent in any respect? he will be employed and respected. Does he love a country life? pleasant farms present themselves; he may purchase what he wants, and thereby become an American farmer. Is he a labourer, sober and industrious; he need not go many miles, nor receive many informations before he will be hired, well fed at the table of his employer, and paid four or five times more than he can get in Europe. Does he want uncultivated lands? thousands of acres present themselves, which he may purchase cheap. Whatever be his talents or inclinations, if they are moderate, he may satisfy them. I do not mean, that every one who comes will grow rich in a little time; no, but he may procure an easy, decent maintenance, by his industry. Instead of starving, he will be fed; instead of being idle, he will have employment; and these are riches enough for such men as come over here. The rich stay in Europe; it is only the middling and poor that emigrate. Would you wish to travel in independent idleness, from north to south, you will find easy access, and the most chearful reception at every house; society without ostentation, good cheer without pride, and every decent diversion which the country affords, with little expense. It is no wonder that the European who has lived here a few years is desirous to remain; Europe, with all its pomp, is not to be compared to this continent, for men of middle stations or labourers.

An European, when he first arrives, seems limited in his intentions, as well as in his views; but he very suddenly alters his scale; two hundred miles formerly appeared a very great distance; it is now but a trifle; he no sooner breathes our air than he forms schemes, and embarks in designs he never would have thought of in his own country. There the plentitude of society confines many useful ideas, and often extinguishes the most laudable schemes which here ripen into maturity. Thus Europeans become Americans.

But how is this accomplished in that croud of low, indigent people, who flock here every year from all parts of Europe? I will tell you; they no sooner arrive than they immediately feel the good effects of that plenty of provisions we possess: they fare on our best food, and are kindly entertained; their talents, character, and peculiar industry are immediately enquired into; they find countrymen every where disseminated, let them come from whatever part of Europe.

Let me select one as an epitome of the rest; he is hired, he goes to work, and works moderately; instead of being employed by a haughty person, he finds himself with his equal, placed at the substantial table of the farmer, or else at an inferior one as good; his wages are high, his bed is not like that bed of sorrow on which he used to lie: if he behaves with propriety, and is faithful, he is caressed, and becomes, as it were, a member of the family. He begins to feel the effects of a sort of resurrection; hitherto he had not lived, but simply vegetated; he now feels himself a man, because he is treated as such; the laws of his own country had overlooked him in his insignificancy; the laws of this cover him with their mantle. Judge what an alteration there must arise in the mind and thoughts of this man; he begins to forget his former servitude and dependence; his heart involuntarily swells and glows; this first swell inspires him with those new thoughts which constitute an American. What love can he entertain for a country where his existence was a burden to him! if he is a generous good man, the love of his new adoptive parent, will sink deep into his heart. He looks around, and sees many a prosperous person, who but a few years before was as poor as himself. This encourages him much; he begins to form some little scheme, the first, alas, he ever formed in his life. If he is wise, he thus spends two or three years, in which time he acquires knowledge, the use of tools, the modes of working the lands, felling trees, &c. This prepares the foundation of a good name, the most useful acquisition he can make. He is encouraged; he has gained friends; he is advised and directed; he feels bold; he purchases some land; he gives all the money he has brought over, as well as what he has earned, and trusts to the God of harvests for the discharge of the rest. His good name procures him credit; he is now possessed of the deed, conveying to him and his posterity the fee simple, and absolute property of two hundred acres of land, situated on such a river. What an epocha in this man's life! He is become a freeholder, from perhaps a German boor—he is now an American, a Pennsylvanian. He is naturalized; his name is enrolled with those of the other citizens of the province. Instead of being a vagrant, he has a place of residence; he is called the inhabitant of such a county, or of such a district, and for the first time in his life counts for something; for hitherto he had been a cypher. I only repeat what I have heard many say, and no wonder their hearts should glow, and be agitated with a multitude of feelings, not easy to describe. From nothing to start into being; from a servant to the rank of master; from being the slave of some despotic prince, to become a free man, invested with lands, to which every municipal blessing is annexed! What a change indeed! It is in consequence of that change, that he becomes an American.

This great metamorphosis has a double effect; it extinguishes all his European prejudices; he forgets that mechanism of subordination, that servility of disposition which poverty had taught him; and sometimes he is apt to forget it too much, often passing from one extreme to the other. If he is a good man, he forms schemes of future prosperity; he proposes to educate his children better than he has been educated himself; he thinks of future modes of conduct, feels an ardour to labour he never felt before. Pride steps in, and leads him to every thing that the laws do not forbid: he respects them; with a heart-felt gratitude he looks toward that government from whose wisdom all his new felicity is derived, and under whose wings and protection he now lives. These reflexions constitute him the good man and the good subject.

Ye poor Europeans, ye, who sweat and work for the great—ye, who are obliged to give so many sheaves to the church, so many to your lords, so many to your government, and have hardly any left for yourselves—ye, who are held in less estimation than favourite hunters or useless lap-dogs—ye, who only breathe the air of nature, because it cannot be withheld from you; it is here that ye can conceive the possibility of those feelings I have been describing; it is here the laws of naturalization invite every one to partake of our great labours and felicity, to till unrented, untaxed lands!

Many, corrupted beyond the power of amendment, have brought with them all their vices, and, disregarding the advantages held out to them, have gone on in their former career of iniquity, until they have been overtaken and punished by our laws. It is not every emigrant who succeeds; no, it is only the sober, the honest, and industrious: happy those, to whom this transition has served as a powerful spur to labour, to prosperity, and to the good establishment of children, born in the days of their poverty: and who had no other portion to expect, but the rags of their parents, had it not been for their happy emigration. Others again, have been led astray by this enchanting scene; their new pride, instead of leading them to the fields, has kept them in idleness; the idea of possessing lands is all that satisfies them—though surrounded with fertility, they have mouldered away their time in inactivity, misinformed husbandry, and ineffectual endeavours. How much wiser, in general, the honest Germans than almost all other Europeans; they hire themselves to some of their wealthy landsmen, and in that apprenticeship learn every thing that is necessary. They attentively consider the prosperous industry of others, which imprints on their minds a strong desire of possessing the same advantages. This forcible idea never quits them; they launch forth, and by dint of sobriety, rigid parsimony, and the most persevering industry, they commonly succeed. Their astonishment at their first arrival from Germany is very great; it is to them a dream; the contrast must be very powerful indeed; they observe their countrymen flourishing in every place; they travel through whole counties where not a word of English is spoken; and in the names and the language of the people they retrace Germany. They have been an useful acquisition to this continent, and to Pennsylvania in particular; to them it owes some share of its prosperity; to their mechanical knowledge and patience, it owes the finest mills in all America, the best teams of horses, and many other advantages. The recollection of their former poverty and slavery never quits them as long as they live.

The Scotch and the Irish might have lived in their own country perhaps as poor; but enjoying more civil advantages, the effects of their new situation do not strike them so forcibly, nor has it so lasting an effect. From whence the difference arises, I know not; but out of twelve families of emigrants of each country, generally seven Scotch will succeed, nine German, and four Irish. The Scotch are frugal and laborious; but their wives cannot work so hard as the German women, who, on the contrary, vie with their husbands, and often share with them the most severe toils of the field, which they understand better. They have therefore nothing to struggle against, but the common casualties of nature. The Irish do not prosper so well; they love to drink and to quarrel; they are litigious, and soon take to the gun, which is the ruin of every thing; they seem, beside, to labour under a greater degree of ignorance in husbandry than the others; perhaps it is that their industry had less scope, and was less exercised at home. I have heard many relate, how the land was parcelled out in that kingdom; their ancient conquest has been a great detriment to them, by over-setting their landed property. The lands, possessed by a few, are leased down *ad infinitum;* and the occupiers often pay five guineas an acre. The poor are worse lodged there than any where else in Europe; their potatoes, which are easily raised, are perhaps an inducement to laziness: their wages are too low, and their whiskey too cheap.

There is no tracing observations of this kind, without making at the same time very great

allowances; as there are everywhere to be found a great many exceptions. The Irish themselves, from different parts of that kingdom are very different. It is difficult to account for this surprising locality; one would think on so small an island all Irishmen must be alike; yet it is not so; they are different in their aptitude to, and in their love of labour.

The Scotch, on the contrary, are all industrious and saving; they want nothing more than a field to exert themselves in; and they are commonly sure of succeeding. The only difficulty they labour under is, that technical American knowledge, which requires some time to obtain; it is not easy for those who seldom saw a tree, to conceive how it is to be felled, cut up, and split into rails and posts.

. . . After a foreigner from any part of Europe is arrived, and become a citizen; let him devoutly listen to the voice of our great parent, which says to him, "Welcome to my shores, distressed European; bless the hour in which thou didst see my verdant fields, my fair navigable rivers, and my green mountains!— If thou wilt work, I have bread for thee; if thou wilt be honest, sober and industrious, I have greater rewards to confer on thee—ease and independence. I will give thee fields to feed and clothe thee; a comfortable fire-side to sit by, and tell thy children by what means thou hast prospered; and a decent bed to repose on. I shall endow thee, beside, with the immunities of a freeman. If thou wilt carefully educate thy children, teach them gratitude to God, and reverence to that government, that philanthropic government, which has collected here so many men and made them happy, I will also provide for thy progeny: and to every good man this ought to be the most holy, the most powerful, the most earnest wish he can possibly form, as well as the most consolatory prospect when he dies.

"Go thou, and work and till; thou shalt prosper, provided thou be just, grateful and industrious."

Benjamin Franklin

Benjamin Franklin (1706–1790) is remembered by most Americans as a statesman, scientist, and philanthropist, but it should also be noted that he was a true son of the Enlightenment and practiced nearly all the ideals of that age. He endeavored to use reason at all times; he had a passion for progress; his humanitarian deeds were legion; and he was as cosmopolitan as any figure of his century, equally at home in Philadelphia, London, and Paris. For superstition and tradition he had little sympathy, while on the other hand, he was an ardent supporter of experimentation and change. In 1771, Franklin began his famous Autobiography as a helpful guide to his son, but he did not complete it until many years later, and then only shortly before his death in 1790. This work is not only considered to be one of the best of all autobiographies, but it is also highly regarded as an excellent personal documentation of the American version of the Age of the Enlightenment. In reading the following selections from Franklin's Autobiography note (1) the clear and readable style with which he wrote, (2) the discourse on his ancestry, (3) the great works which he read as a boy, (4) men of the Enlightenment who influenced him, (5) the nature of his early religious training and subsequent religious beliefs, (6) his numerous efforts to improve society, (7) the method Franklin used to achieve his own moral perfection, (8) the devices he used to instruct society, (9) his humanitarian interests, (10) his use of the scientific method and the contributions he made to the advance of scientific knowledge, and (11) evidences of Franklin's cosmopolitanism.

From: THE AUTOBIOGRAPHY

Twyford, at the Bishop of St. Asaph's, 1771.

Dear Son: I have ever had pleasure in obtaining any little anecdotes of my ancestors. You may remember the inquiries I made among the remains of my relations when you were with me in England, and the journey I undertook for that purpose. Imagining it may be equally agreeable to you to know the circumstances of my life, many of which you are yet unacquainted with, and expecting the enjoyment of a week's uninterrupted leisure in my present country retirement, I sit down to write them for you. To which I have besides some other inducements. Having emerged from the poverty and obscurity in which I was born and bred, to a state of affluence and some degree of reputation in the world, and having gone so far through life with a considerable share of felicity, the conducing means I made use of, which with the blessing of God so well succeeded, my posterity may like to know, as they may find some of them suitable to their own situations, and therefore fit to be imitated.

That felicity, when I reflected on it, has induced me sometimes to say, that were it offered to my choice, I should have no objection to a

Adapted from Benjamin Franklin, *Memoirs of Benjamin Franklin*, 2 vols., Philadelphia, 1840, I, 1–3; 5; 7; 23–24; 26–28; 32–39; 41–44; 46–48; 50–51; 62–63.

repetition of the same life from its beginning, only asking the advantages authors have in a second edition to correct some faults of the first. So I might, besides correcting the faults, change some sinister accidents and events of it for others more favourable. But though this were denied, I should still accept the offer. Since such a repetition is not to be expected, the next thing most like living one's life over again seems to be a recollection of that life, and to make that recollection as durable as possible by putting it down in writing.

Hereby, too, I shall indulge the inclination so natural in old men, to be talking of themselves and their own past actions; and I shall indulge it without being tiresome to others, who, through respect to age, might conceive themselves obliged to give a hearing, since this may be read or not as any one pleases. And, lastly (I may as well confess it, since my denial of it will be believed by nobody), perhaps I shall a good deal gratify my own *vanity*. Indeed, I scarce ever heard or saw the introductory words, *"Without vanity I may say,"* etc., but some vain thing immediately followed. Most people dislike vanity in others, whatever share they have of it themselves; but I give it fair quarter wherever I meet with it, being persuaded that it is often productive of good to the possessor, and to others that are within his sphere of action; and therefore, in many cases, it would not be altogether absurd if a man were to thank God for his vanity among the other comforts of life.

And now I speak of thanking God, I desire with all humility to acknowledge that I owe the mentioned happiness of my past life to His kind providence, which lead me to the means I used and gave them success. My belief of this induces me to *hope*, though I must not *presume*, that the same goodness will still be exercised toward me, in continuing that happiness, or enabling me to bear a fatal reverse, which I may experience as others have done; the complexion of my future fortune being known to Him only in whose power it is to bless to us even our afflictions.

The notes one of my uncles (who had the same kind of curiosity in collecting family anecdotes) once put into my hands, furnished me with several particulars relating to our ances-

tors. From these notes I learned that the family had lived in the same village, Ecton, in Northamptonshire, for three hundred years, and how much longer he knew not (perhaps from the time when the name of Franklin, that before was the name of an order of people, was assumed by them as a surname when others took surnames all over the kingdom), on a free-hold of about thirty acres, aided by the smith's business, which had continued in the family till his time, the eldest son being always bred to that business; a custom which he and my father followed as to their eldest sons. When I searched the registers at Ecton, I found an account of their births, marriages and burials from the year 1555 only, there being no registers kept in that parish at any time preceding. By that register I perceived that I was the youngest son of the youngest son for five generations back. My grandfather Thomas, who was born in 1598, lived at Ecton till he grew too old to follow business longer, when he went to live with his son John, a dyer at Banbury, in Oxfordshire, with whom my father served an apprenticeship. There my grandfather died and lies buried. We saw his gravestone in 1758. His eldest son Thomas lived in the house at Ecton, and left it with the land to his only child, a daughter, who, with her husband, one Fisher, of Wellingborough, sold it to Mr. Isted, now lord of the manor there. My grandfather had four sons that grew up, viz.: Thomas, John, Benjamin, and Josiah. . . .

Josiah, my father, married young, and carried his wife with three children into New England, about 1682. The conventicles having been forbidden by law, and frequently disturbed, induced some considerable men of his acquaintance to remove to that country, and he was prevailed with to accompany them thither, where they expected to enjoy their mode of religion with freedom. By the same wife he had four children more born there, and by a second wife ten more, in all seventeen; of which I remember thirteen sitting at one time at his table, who all grew up to be men and women, and married; I was the youngest son, and the youngest child but two, and was born in Boston, New England. My mother, the second wife, was Abiah Folger, daughter of Peter

Folger, one of the first settlers of New England, of whom honourable mention is made by Cotton Mather, in his church history of that country, entitled *Magnalia Christi Americana*, as "*A godly, learned Englishman*," if I remember the words rightly. I have heard that he wrote sundry small occasional pieces, but only one of them was printed, which I saw now many years since. It was written in 1675, in the home-spun verse of that time and people, and addressed to those then concerned in the government there. It was in favor of liberty of conscience, and in behalf of the Baptists, Quakers, and other sectaries that had been under persecution, ascribing the Indian wars, and other distresses that had befallen the country, to that persecution, as so many judgments of God to punish so heinous an offense, and exhorting a repeal of those uncharitable laws. The whole appeared to me as written with a good deal of decent plainness and manly freedom. The six concluding lines I remember, though I have forgotten the two first of the stanza; but the purport of them was, that his censures proceeded from good-will, and, therefore, he would be known to be the author.

"Because to be a libeller (says he)
 I hate it with my heart;
From Sherburne town, where now I dwell
 My name I do put here;
Without offense your real friend,
 It is Peter Folgier."

. . . .

From a child I was fond of reading, and all the little money that came into my hands was ever laid out in books. Pleased with the *Pilgrim's Progress*, my first collection was of John Bunyan's words in separate little volumes. I afterward sold them to enable me to buy R. Burton's *Historical Collections;* they were small chapmen's books, and cheap, 40 or 50 in all. My father's little library consisted chiefly of books in polemic divinity, most of which I read, and have since often regretted that, at a time when I had such a thirst for knowledge, more proper books had not fallen in my way, since it was now resolved I should not be a clergyman. Plutarch's *Lives* there was in which I read abundantly, and I still think that time spent to great advantage. There was also a book of De Foe's, called an *Essay on Projects*, and another of Dr. Mather's called *Essays to do Good,* which perhaps gave me a turn of thinking that had an influence on some of the principal future events of my life. . . .

And now it was that, being on some occasion made asham'd of my ignorance in figures, which I had twice failed in learning when at school, I took Cocker's book of Arthimetick, and went through the whole by myself with great ease. I also read Seller's and Shermy's books of Navigation, and became acquainted with the little geometry they contain; but never proceeded far in that science. And I read about this time Locke *On Human Understanding,* and the *Art of Thinking*, by Messrs. du Port Royal.

While I was intent on improving my language, I met with an English grammar (I think it was Greenwood's), at the end of which there were two little sketches of the arts of rhetoric and logic, the latter finishing with a specimen of a dispute in the Socratic method; and soon after I procur'd Xenophon's *Memorable Things of Socrates*, wherein there are many instances of the same method. I was charm'd with it, adopted it, dropt my abrupt contradiction and positive argumentation, and put on the humble inquirer and doubter. And being then, from reading Shaftesbury and Collins, become a real doubter in many points of our religious doctrine, I found this method safest for myself and very embarrassing to those against whom I used it; therefore I took a delight in it, practis'd it continually, and grew very artful and expert in drawing people, even of superior knowledge, into concessions, the consequences of which they did not foresee, entangling them in difficulties out of which they could not extricate themselves, and so obtaining victories that neither myself nor my cause always deserved. I continu'd this method some few years, but gradually left it, retaining only the habit of expressing myself in terms of modest diffidence; never using, when I advanced anything that may possibly be disputed, the words *certainly, undoubtedly,* or any others that gave the air of positiveness to an opinion; but rather say, I conceive or apprehend a thing to be so and so; it appears to me, or I *should think it so or so,* for such and such reasons; or *I imagine it to be so,* or *it is so, if I am not mistaken.* This habit, I believe, has been of great advantage to me when I have had occasion to inculcate my opinions, and persuade men into measures that I have been from time to time engag'd in promoting; and, as the chief ends of conversation are to *inform* or to be *informed,* to *please* or to *persuade,* I wish well-meaning, sensible men would not lessen their power of doing good by a positive, assuming manner, that seldom fails to disgust, tends to create opposition, and to defeat everyone of those purposes for which speech was given to us, to wit, giving or receiving information or pleasure. For, if you would inform, a positive and dogmatical manner in advancing your sentiments may provoke contradiction and prevent a candid attention. If you wish information and improvement from the knowledge of others, and yet at the same time express yourself as firmly fix'd in your present opinions, modest, sensible men, who do not love disputation, will probably leave you undisturbed in the possession of your error. And by such a manner, you can seldom hope to recommend yourself in *pleasing* your hearers, or to persuade those whose concurrence you desire. . . .

Before I enter upon my public appearance in business, it may be well to let you know the then state of my mind with regard to my principles and morals, that you may see how far those influenc'd the future events of my life. My parents had early given me religious impressions, and brought me through my childhood piously in the Dissenting way. But I was scarce fifteen, when, after doubting by turns of several points, as I found them disputed in the different books I read, I began to doubt of Revelation itself. Some books against Deism fell into my hands; they were said to be the substance of sermons preached at Boyle's Lectures. It happened that they wrought an effect on me quite contrary to what was intended by them; for the arguments of the Deists, which were quoted to be refuted, appeared to me much stronger than the refutations; in short, I soon became a thorough Deist. My arguments perverted some others, particularly Collins and Ralph; but, each of them having

afterwards wrong'd me greatly without the least compunction, and recollecting Keith's conduct towards me (who was another free-thinker), and my own towards Vernon and Miss Read, which at times gave me great trouble, I began to suspect that this doctrine, tho' it might be true, was not very useful. My London pamphlet, which had for its motto these lines of Dryden:

"Whatever is is right. Though purblind man
See but a part o' the chain, the nearest link:
His eyes not carrying to the equal beam,
That poises all above;"

and from the attributes of God, his infinite wisdom, goodness and power, concluded that nothing could possibly be wrong in the world, and that vice and virtue were empty distinctions, no such things existing, appear'd now not so clever a performance as I once thought it; and I doubted whether some error had not insinuated itself unperceiv'd into my argument, so as to infect all that follow'd, as is common in metaphysical reasonings.

I grew convinc'd that *truth, sincerity* and *integrity* in dealings between man and man were of the utmost importance to the felicity of life; and I form'd written resolutions, which still remain in my journal book, to practice them ever while I lived. Revelation had indeed no weight with me, as such; but I entertain'd an opinion that, though certain actions might not be bad *because* they were forbidden by it, or good *because* it commanded them, yet probably these actions might be forbidden *because* they were bad for us, or commanded *because* they were beneficial to us, in their own natures, all the circumstances of things considered. And this persuasion, with the kind hand of Providence, or some guardian angel, or accidental favorable circumstances and situations, or all together, preserved me, thro' this dangerous time of youth, and the hazardous situations I was sometimes in among strangers, remote from the eye and advice of my father, without any willful gross immorality or injustice, that might have been expected from my want of religion. I say willful, because the instances I have mentioned had something of *necessity* in them, from my youth, inexperience, and the knavery of others. I had therefore a tolerable character to begin the world with; I value it properly, and determin'd to preserve it. . . .

About this time [1729] there was a cry among the people for more paper money, only fifteen thousand pounds being extant in the province, and that soon to be sunk. The wealthy inhabitants oppos'd any addition, being against all paper currency, from an apprehension that it would depreciate, as it had done in New England, to the prejudice of all creditors. We had discuss'd this point in our Junto, where I was on the side of an addition, being persuaded that the first small sum struck in 1723 had done much good by increasing the trade, employment, and number of inhabitants in the province, since I now saw all the old houses inhabited, and many new ones building: whereas I remembered well, that when I first walk'd about the streets of Philadelphia, eating my roll, I saw most of the houses in Walnut Street, between Second and Front streets, with bills on their doors, "To be let"; and many likewise in Chestnut Street and other streets, which made me then think the inhabitants of the city were deserting it one after another.

Our debates possess'd me so fully of the subject, that I wrote and printed an anonymous pamphlet on it, entitled *"The Nature and Necessity of a Paper Currency."* It was well receiv'd by the common people in general; but the rich men dislik'd it, for it increas'd and strengthen'd the clamour for more money, and they happening to have no writers among them that were able to answer it, their opposition slacken'd, and the point was carried by a majority in the House. My friends there, who conceiv'd I had been of some service, thought fit to reward me by employing me in printing the money; a very profitable jobb and a great help to me. This was another advantage gain'd by my being able to write.

The utility of this currency became by time and experience so evident as never afterwards to be much disputed; so that it grew soon to fifty-five thousand pounds, and in 1739 to eighty thousand pounds, since which it arose during war to upwards of three hundred and fifty thousand pounds, trade, building, and inhabitants all the while increasing, tho' I now

think there are limits beyond which the quantity may be hurtful.

I soon after obtain'd, thro' my friend Hamilton, the printing of the Newcastle paper money, another profitable jobb as I then thought it; small things appearing great to those in small circumstances; and these, to me, were really great advantages, as they were great encouragements. He procured for me, also, the printing of the laws and notes of that government, which continu'd in my hands as long as I follow'd the business.

I now open'd a little stationer's shop. I had in it blanks of all sorts, the correctest that ever appear'd among us, being assisted in that by my friend Breintnal. I had also paper, parchment, chapmen's books, etc. One Whitemash, a compositor I had known in London, an excellent workman, now came to me, and work'd with me constantly and diligently; and I took an apprentice, the son of Aquila Rose.

I began now gradually to pay off the debt I was under for the printing-house. In order to secure my credit and character as a tradesman, I took care not only to be in *reality* industrious and frugal, but to avoid all appearances to the contrary. I drest plainly; I was seen at no places of idle diversion. I never went out a fishing or shooting; a book, indeed, sometimes debauch'd me from my work, but that was seldom, snug, and gave no scandal; and, to show that I was not above my business, I sometimes brought home the paper I purchas'd at the stores thro' the streets on a wheelbarrow. Thus being esteem'd an industrious, thriving young man, and paying duly for what I bought, the merchants who imported stationery solicited my custom; others proposed supplying me with books, and I went on swimmingly. In the mean time, Keimer's credit and business declining daily, he was at last forc'd to sell his printing-house to satisfy his creditors. He went to Barbadoes, and there lived some years in very poor circumstances. . . .

I had hitherto continu'd to board with Godfrey, who lived in part of my house with his wife and children, and had one side of the shop for his glazier's business, tho' he worked little, being always absorbed in his mathematics. Mrs. Godfrey projected a match for me with a relation's daughter, took opportunities of bringing us often together, till a serious courtship on my part ensu'd, the girl being in herself very deserving. The old folks encourag'd me by continual invitations to supper, and by leaving us together, till at length it was time to explain. Mrs. Godfrey manag'd our little treaty. I let her know that I expected as much money with their daughter as would pay off my remaining debt for the printing-house, which I believe was not then above a hundred pounds. She brought me word they had no such sum to spare; I said they might mortgage their house in the loan-office. The answer to this, after some days, was, that they did not approve the match; that, on inquiry of Bradford, they had been informed the printing business was not a profitable one; the types would soon be worn out, and more wanted; that S. Keimer and D. Harry had failed one after the other, and I should probably soon follow them; and, therefore, I was forbidden the house, and the daughter shut up.

Whether this was a real change of sentiment or only artifice, on a supposition of our being too far engaged in affection to retract, and therefore that we should steal a marriage, which would leave them at liberty to give or withhold what they pleas'd, I know not; but I suspected the latter, resented it, and went no more. Mrs. Godfrey brought me afterward some more favorable accounts of their disposition, and would have drawn me on again; but I declared absolutely my resolution to have nothing more to do with that family. This was resented by the Godfrey's; we differ'd, and they removed, leaving me the whole house, and I resolved to take no more inmates.

But this affair having turned my thoughts to marriage, I look'd around me and made overtures of acquaintance in other places; but soon found that, the business of a printer being generally thought a poor one, I was not to expect money with a wife, unless with such a one as I should not otherwise think agreeable. In the meantime, that hard-to-be-governed passion of youth hurried me frequently into intrigues with low women that fell in my way, which were attended with some expense and great inconvenience, besides a continual risque to my health by a distemper which of all things

I dreaded, though by great good luck I escaped it. A friendly correspondence as neighbors and old acquaintances had continued between me and Mrs. Read's family, who all had a regard for me from the time of my first lodging in their house. I was often invited there and consulted in their affairs, wherein I sometimes was of service. I piti'd poor Miss Read's unfortunate situation, who was generally dejected, seldom cheerful, and avoided company. I considered my giddiness and inconstancy when in London as in a great degree the cause of her unhappiness, tho' the mother was good enough to think the fault more her own than mine, as she had prevented our marrying before I went thither, and persuaded the other match in my absence. Our mutual affection was revived, but there were now great objections to our union. The match was indeed looked upon as invalid, a preceding wife being said to be living in England; but this could not easily be prov'd, because of the distance; and, tho' there was a report of his death, it was not certain. Then, tho' it should be true, he had left many debts, which his successor might be call'd upon to pay. We ventured, however, over all these difficulties, and I took her to wife, September 1st, 1730. None of the inconveniences happened that we had apprehended; she proved a good and faithful helpmate, assisted me much by attending the shop; we throve together, and have ever mutually endeavor'd to make each other happy. Thus I corrected that great *erratum* as well as I could.

About this time, our club meeting, not at a tavern, but in a little room of Mr. Grace's, set apart for that purpose, a proposition was made by me, that, since our books were often referr'd to in our disquisitions upon the queries, it might be convenient to us to have them altogether where we met, that upon occasion they might be consulted; and by thus clubbing our books to a common library, we should, while we lik'd to keep them together, have each of us the advantage of using the books of all the other members, which would be nearly as beneficial as if each owned the whole.

It was lik'd and agreed to, and we fill'd one end of the room with such books as we could best spare. The number was not so great as we expected; and tho' they had been of great use, yet some inconveniences occurring for want of due care of them, the collection, after about a year, was separated, and each took his books home again.

And now I set on foot my first project of a public nature, that for a subscription library. I drew up the proposals, got them put into form by our great scrivener, Brockden, and, by the help of my friends in the Junto, procured fifty subscribers of forty shillings each to begin with, and ten shillings a year for fifty years, the term our company was to continue. We afterwards obtain'd a charter, the company being increased to one hundred: this was the mother of all the North American subscription libraries, now so numerous. It is become a great thing itself, and continually increasing. These libraries have improved the general conversation of the Americans, made the common tradesmen and farmers as intelligent as most gentlemen from other countries, and perhaps have contributed in some degree to the stand so generally made throughout the colonies in defence of their privileges. . . .

This library afforded me the means of improvement by constant study, for which I set apart an hour or two each day, and thus repair'd in some degree the loss of the learned education my father once intended for me. Reading was the only amusement I allow'd myself. I spent no time in taverns, games, or frolicks of any kind; and my industry in my business continu'd as indefatigable as it was necessary. I was indebted for my printing-house; I had a young family coming on to be educated, and I had to contend with for business two printers, who were established in the place before me. My circumstances, however, grew daily easier. My original habits of frugality continuing, and my father having, among his instructions to me when a boy, frequently repeated a proverb of Solomon, "Seest thou a man diligent in his calling, he shall stand before kings, he shall not stand before mean men," I from thence considered industry as a means of obtaining wealth and distinction, which encourag'd me, tho' I did not think that I should ever literally *stand before kings*, which, however, has since happened; for I have stood before *five*, and even had the honour of sitting down with one, the King of Denmark, to dinner.

We have an English proverb that says, "*He that would thrive, must ask his wife.*" It was lucky for me that I had one as much dispos'd to industry and frugality as myself. She assisted me cheerfully in my business, folding and stitching pamphlets, tending shop, purchasing old linen rags for the paper-makers, etc., etc. We kept no idle servants, our table was plain and simple, our furniture of the cheapest. For instance, my breakfast was a long time bread and milk (no tea), and I ate it out of a twopenny earthen porringer, with a pewter spoon. But mark how luxury will enter families, and make a progress, in spite of principle: being call'd one morning to breakfast, I found it in a China bowl, with a spoon of silver! They had been bought for me without my knowledge by my wife, and had cost her the enormous sum of three-and-twenty shillings, for which she had no other excuse or apology to make, but that she thought *her* husband deserv'd a silver spoon and China bowl as well as any of his neighbors. This was the first appearance of plate and China in our house, which afterward, in a course of years, as our wealth increas'd, augmented gradually to several hundred pounds in value.

I had been religiously educated as a Presbyterian; and tho' some of the dogmas of that persuasion, such as *the eternal decrees of God, election, reprobation, etc.,* appeared to me unintelligible, others doubtful, and I early absented myself from the public assemblies of the sect, Sunday being my studying day, I never was without some religious principles. I never doubted, for instance, the existence of the Deity; that he made the world, and govern'd it by his Providence; that the most acceptable service of God was the doing good to man; that our souls are immortal; and that all crime will be punished, and virtue rewarded, either here or hereafter. These I esteem'd the essentials of every religion; and, being to be found in all the religions we had in our country, I respected them all, tho' with different degrees of respect, as I found them more or less mix'd with other articles, which, without any tendency to inspire, promote, or confirm morality, serv'd principally to divide us, and make us unfriendly to one another. This respect to all, with an opinion that the worst had some good effects, induc'd me to avoid all discourse that might tend to lessen the good opinion another might have of his own religion; and as our province increas'd in people, and new places of worship were continually wanted, and generally erected by voluntary contribution, my mite for such purpose, whatever might be the sect, was never refused.

Tho' I seldom attended any public worship, I had still an opinion of its propriety, and of its utility when rightly conducted, and I regularly paid my annual subscription for the support of the only Presbyterian minister or meeting we had in Philadelphia. He us'd to visit me sometimes as a friend, and admonish me to attend his administrations, and I was now and then prevail'd on to do so, once for five Sundays successively. Had he been in my opinion a good preacher, perhaps I might have continued, notwithstanding the occasion I had for the Sunday's leisure in my course of study; but his discourses were chiefly either polemic arguments, or explications of the peculiar doctrines of our sect, and were all to me very dry, uninteresting, and unedifying, since not a single moral principle was inculcated or enforc'd, their aim seeming to be rather to make us Presbyterians than good citizens.

At length he took for his text that verse of the fourth chapter of Philippians, *"Finally, brethren, whatsoever things are true, honest, just, pure, lovely, or of good report, if there be any virtue, or any praise, think on these things."* And I imagin'd, in a sermon on such a text, we could not miss of having some morality. But he confin'd himself to five points only, as meant by the apostle, viz.: 1. Keeping holy the Sabbath day. 2. Being diligent in reading the holy Scriptures. 3. Attending duly the publick worship. 4. Partaking of the Sacrament. 5. Paying a due respect to God's ministers. These might be all good things; but, as they were not the kind of good things that I expected from that text, I despaired of ever meeting with them from any other, was disgusted and attended his preaching no more. I had some years before compos'd a little Liturgy, or form of prayer, for my own private use (viz., in 1728), entitled, *Articles of Belief and Acts of Religion.* I re-

turn'd to the use of this, and went no more to the public assemblies. My conduct might be blameable, but I leave it, without attempting further to excuse it; my present purpose being to relate facts, and not to make apologies for them.

It was about this time I conceiv'd the bold and arduous project of arriving at moral perfection. I wish'd to live without committing any fault at any time; I would conquer all that either natural inclination, custom, or company might lead me into. As I knew, or thought I knew, what was right and wrong, I did not see why I might not always do the one and avoid the other. But I soon found I had undertaken a task of more difficulty than I had imagined. While my care was employ'd in guarding against one fault, I was often surprised by another; habit took the advantage of inattention; inclination was sometimes too strong for reason. I concluded, at length, that the mere speculative conviction that it was our interest to be completely virtuous, was not sufficient to prevent our slipping; and that the contrary habits must be broken, and good ones acquired and established, before we can have any dependence on a steady, uniform rectitude of conduct. For this purpose I therefore contrived the following method.

In the various enumerations of the moral virtues I had met with in my reading, I found the catalogue more or less numerous, as different writers included more or fewer ideas under the same name. Temperance, for example, was by some confined to eating and drinking, while by others it was extended to mean the moderating every other pleasure, appetite, inclination, or passion, bodily or mental, even to our avarice and ambition. I propos'd to myself, for the sake of clearness, to use rather more names, with fewer ideas annex'd to each, than a few names with more ideas; and I included under thirteen names of virtues all that at that time occurr'd to me as necessary or desirable, and annexed to each a short precept, which fully express'd the extent I gave to its meaning. These names of virtues, with their precepts, were:

1. TEMPERANCE.
Eat not to dulness; drink not to elevation.

2. SILENCE.

Speak not but what may benefit others or yourself; avoid trifling conversation.

3. ORDER.

Let all your things have their places; let each part of your business have its time.

4. RESOLUTION.

Resolve to perform what you ought; perform without fail what you resolve.

5. FRUGALITY.

Make no expense but to do good to others or yourself; *i.e.*, waste nothing.

6. INDUSTRY.

Lose no time; be always employ'd in something useful; cut off all unnecessary actions.

7. SINCERITY.

Use no hurtful deceit; think innocently and justly, and, if you speak, speak accordingly.

8. JUSTICE.

Wrong none by doing injuries, or omitting the benefits that are your duty.

9. MODERATION.

Avoid extreams; forbear resenting injuries so much as you think they deserve.

10. CLEANLINESS.

Tolerate no uncleanliness in body, cloaths, or habitation.

11. TRANQUILLITY.

Be not disturbed at trifles, or at accidents common or unavoidable.

12. CHASTITY.

Rarely use venery but for health or offspring, never to dulness, weakness, or the injury of your own or another's peace or reputation.

13. HUMILITY.

Imitate Jesus and Socrates.

My intention being to acquire the *habitude* of all these virtues, I judg'd it would be well not to distract my attention by attempting the whole at once, but to fix it on one of them at a time; and, when I should be master of that, then to proceed to another, and so on, till I should have gone thro' the thirteen; and, as the previous acquisition of some might facili-

tate the acquisition of certain others, I arrang'd them with that view, as they stand above. *Temperance* first, as it tends to procure that coolness and clearness of head, which is so necessary where constant vigilance was to be kept up, and guard maintained against the unremitting attraction of ancient habits, and the force of perpetual temptations. This being acquir'd and establish'd, *Silence* would be more easy; and my desire being to gain knowledge at the same time that I improv'd in virtue, and considering that in conversation it was obtain'd rather by the use of the ears than of the tongue, and therefore wishing to break a habit I was getting into of prattling, punning, and joking, which only made me acceptable to trifling company, I gave *Silence* the second place. This and the next, *Order,* I expected would allow me more time for attending to my project and my studies. *Resolution,* once become habitual, would keep me firm in my endeavors to obtain all the subsequent virtues; *Frugality* and *Industry* freeing me from my remaining debt, and producing affluence and independence, would make more easy the practice of *Sincerity* and *Justice,* etc., etc. Conceiving then, that, agreeably to the advice of Pythagoras in his Golden Verses, daily examination would be necessary, I contrived the following method for conducting that examination.

Form of the pages.

TEMPERANCE						
EAT NOT TO DULNESS; DRINK NOT TO ELEVATION.						
	S.	M.	T.	W.	T.	F.	S.
T.							
S.	*	*		*		*	
O.	**	*	*		*	*	*
R.			*			*	
F.		*			*		
I.			*				
S.							
J.							
M.							
C.							
T.							
C.							
H.							

I made a little book, in which I allotted a page for each of the virtues. I ruled each page with red ink, so as to have seven columns, one for each day of the week, marking each column with a letter for the day. I cross'd these columns with thirteen red lines, marking the beginning of each line with the first letter of one of the virtues, on which line, and in its proper column, I might mark, by a little black spot, every fault I found upon examination to have been committed respecting that virtue upon that day.

I determined to give a week's strict attention to each of the virtues successively. Thus, in the first week, my great guard was to avoid ever the least offence against *Temperance*, leaving the other virtues to their ordinary chance, only marking every evening the faults of the day. Thus, if in the first week I could keep my first line, marked T, clear of spots, I suppos'd the habit of that virtue so much strengthen'd, and its opposite weaken'd, that I might venture extending my attention to include the next, and for the following week keep both lines clear of spots. Proceeding thus to the last, I could go thro' a course compleat in thirteen weeks, and four courses in a year. And like him, who, having a garden to weed, does not attempt to eradicate all the bad herbs at once, which would exceed his reach and his strength, but works on one of the beds at a time, and, having accomplish'd the first, proceeds to a second, so I should have, I hoped, the encouraging pleasure of seeing on my pages the progress I made in virtue, by clearing successively my lines of their spots, till in the end, by a number of courses, I should be happy in viewing a clean book, after a thirteen weeks' daily examination.

This my little book had for its motto these lines from Addison's *Cato:*

"Here will I hold. If there's a power above us
(And that there is, all nature cries aloud
Thro' all her works), He must delight in virtue;
And that which he delights in must be happy."

Another from Cicero,

"O vitae Philosophia dux! O virtutum indagatrix expultrixque vitiorum! Unus dies, bene et ex praeceptis tuis actus, peccanti immortalitati est anteponendus."

Another from the Proverbs of Solomon, speaking of wisdom or virtue:

"Length of days is in her right hand, and in her left hand riches and honour. Her ways are ways of pleasantness, and all her paths are peace." III. 16, 17.

And conceiving God to be the fountain of wisdom, I thought it right and necessary to solicit his assistance for obtaining it; to this end I formed the following little prayer, which was prefix'd to my tables of examination, for daily use.

"O Powerful Goodness! bountiful Father! merciful Guide! Increase in me that wisdom which discovers my truest interest. Strengthen my resolutions to perform what that wisdom dictates. Accept my kind offices to thy other children as the only return in my power for thy continual favours to me."

I used also sometimes a little prayer which I took from Thomson's Poems, viz.:

"Father of light and life, thou Good Supreme!
O teach me what is good; teach me Thyself!
Save me from folly, vanity, and vice,
From every low pursuit; and fill my soul
With knowledge, conscious peace, and virtue
    pure;
Sacred, substantial, never-fading bliss!"

The precept of *Order* requiring that *every part of my business should have its allotted time,* one page in my little book contain'd the following scheme of employment for the twenty-four hours of a natural day.

THE MORNING. *Question.* What good shall I do this day?	5 6 7	Rise, wash and address *Powerful Goodness!* Contrive day's business, and take the resolution of the day; prosecute the present study, and breakfast.
	8 9 10 11	Work.

NOON.	$\left\{\begin{array}{c} 12 \\ 1 \end{array}\right\}$	Read, or over-look my ac-counts, and dine.
	$\left.\begin{array}{c} 2 \\ 3 \\ 4 \\ 5 \end{array}\right\}$	Work.

EVENING.	$\left\{\begin{array}{c} \\ 6 \\ 7 \\ 8 \\ 9 \\ \end{array}\right.$	Put things in their places. Sup-per. Music or di-version, or con-versation. Exami-nation of the day.

Question. What good have I done to-day?

NIGHT.	$\left\{\begin{array}{c} 10 \\ 11 \\ 12 \\ 1 \\ 2 \\ 3 \\ 4 \end{array}\right\}$	Sleep.

I enter'd upon the execution of this plan for self-examination, and continu'd it with occa-sional intermissions for some time. I was sur-pris'd to find myself so much fuller of faults than I had imagined; but I had the satisfaction of seeing them diminish. To avoid the trouble of renewing now and then my little book, which, by scraping out the marks on the paper of old faults to make room for new ones in a new course, became full of holes, I transferr'd my tables and precepts to the ivory leaves of a memorandum book, on which the lines were drawn with red ink, that made a durable stain, and on those lines I mark'd my faults with a black-lead pencil, which marks I could easily wipe out with a wet sponge. After a while I went thro' one course only in a year, and after-ward only one in several years, till at length I omitted them entirely, being employ'd in voy-ages and business abroad, with a multiplicity of affairs that interfered; but I always carried my little book with me.

My scheme of ORDER gave me the most trouble; and I found that, tho' it might be prac-ticable where a man's business was such as to leave him the disposition of his time, that of a journeyman printer, for instance, it was not

possible to be exactly observed by a master, who must mix with the world, and often re-ceive people of business at their own hours. *Order,* too, with regard to places for things, papers, etc., I found extreamly difficult to ac-quire. I had not been early accustomed to it, and, having an exceeding good memory, I was not so sensible of the inconvenience attending want of method. This article, therefore, cost me so much painful attention, and my faults in it vexed me so much, and I made so little prog-ress in amendment, and had such frequent re-lapses, that I was almost ready to give up the attempt, and content myself with a faulty char-acter in that respect, like the man who, in buy-ing an ax of a smith, my neighbour, desired to have the whole of its surface as bright as the edge. The smith consented to grind it bright for him if he would turn the wheel; he turn'd, while the smith press'd the broad face of the ax hard and heavily on the stone, which made the turning of it very fatiguing. The man came every now and then from the wheel to see how the work went on, and at length would take his ax as it was, without farther grinding. "No," said the smith, "turn on, turn on; we shall have it bright by-and-by; as yet, it is only speckled." "Yes," says the man, *"but I think I like a speck-led ax best."* And I believe this may have been the case with many, who, having, for want of some such means as I employ'd, found the dif-ficulty of obtaining good and breaking bad habits in other points of vice and virtue, have given up the struggle, and concluded that *"a speckled ax was best";* for something, that pre-tended to be reason, was every now and then suggesting to me that such extream nicety as I exacted of myself might be a kind of foppery in morals, which, if it were known, would make me ridiculous; that a perfect character might be attended with the inconvenience of being envied and hated; and that a benevolent man should allow a few faults in himself, to keep his friends in countenance.

In truth, I found myself incorrigible with re-spect to *Order;* and now I am grown old, and my memory bad, I feel very sensibly the want of it. But, on the whole, tho' I never arrived at the perfection I had been so ambitious of ob-taining, but fell far short of it, yet I was, by the endeavour, a better and a happier man than I otherwise should have been if I had not attempted it; as those who aim at perfect writing by imitating the engraved copies, tho' they never reach the wish'd-for excellence of those copies, their hand is mended by the endeavour, and is tolerable while it continues fair and legible.

It may be well my posterity should be informed that to this little artifice, with the blessing of God, their ancestor ow'd the constant felicity of his life, down to his 79th year, in which this is written. What reverses may attend the remainder is in the hand of Providence; but, if they arrive, the reflection on past happiness enjoy'd ought to help his bearing them with more resignation. To Temperance he ascribes his long-continued health, and what is still left to him of a good constitution; to Industry and Frugality, the early easiness of his circumstances and acquisition of his fortune, with all that knowledge that enabled him to be a useful citizen, and obtained for him some degree of reputation among the learned; to Sincerity and Justice, the confidence of his country, and the honorable employs it conferred upon him; and to the joint influence of the whole mass of the virtues, even in the imperfect state he was able to acquire them, all that evenness of temper, and that cheerfulness in conversation, which makes his company still sought for, and agreeable even to his younger acquaintance. I hope, therefore, that some of my descendants may follow the example and reap the benefit.

It will be remark'd that, tho' my scheme was not wholly without religion, there was in it no mark of any of the distinguishing tenets of any particular sect. I had purposely avoided them; for, being fully persuaded of the utility and excellency of my method, and that it might be serviceable to people in all religions, and intending some time or other to publish it, I would not have anything in it that should prejudice any one, of any sect, against it. I purposed writing a little comment on each virtue, in which I would have shown the advantages of possessing it, and the mischiefs attending its opposite vice; and I should have called my book THE ART OF VIRTUE, because it would have shown the means and manner of obtaining virtue, which would have distinguished it from the mere exhortation to be good, that does not instruct and indicate the

means, but is like the apostle's man of verbal charity, who only without showing to the naked and hungry how or where they might get clothes or victuals, exhorted them to be fed and clothed.—James II. 15, 16.

But it so happened that my intention of writing and publishing this comment was never fulfilled. I did, indeed, from time to time, put down short hints of the sentiments, reasonings, etc., to be made use of in it, some of which I have still by me; but the necessary close attention to private business in the earlier part of my life, and public business since, have occasioned my postponing it; for, it being connected in my mind with *a great and extensive project*, that required the whole man to execute, and which an unforeseen succession of employs prevented my attending to, it has hitherto remain'd unfinish'd.

In this piece it was my design to explain and enforce this doctrine, that vicious actions are not hurtful because they are forbidden, but forbidden because they are hurtful, the nature of man alone considered; that it was, therefore, every one's interest to be virtuous who wish'd to be happy even in this world; and I should, from this circumstance (there being always in the world a number of rich merchants, nobility, states, and princes, who have need of honest instruments for the management of their affairs, and such being so rare), have endeavored to convince young persons that no qualities were so likely to make a poor man's fortune as those of probity and integrity.

My list of virtues contain'd at first but twelve; but a Quaker friend having kindly informed me that I was generally thought proud; that my pride show'd itself frequently in conversation; that I was not content with being in the right when discussing any point, but was overbearing, and rather insolent, of which he convinc'd me by mentioning several instances; I determined endeavouring to cure myself, if I could, of this vice or folly among the rest, and I added *Humility* to my list, giving an extensive meaning to the word. . . .

In reality, there is, perhaps, no one of our national passions so hard to subdue as pride. Disguise it, struggle with it, beat it down, stifle it, mortify it as much as one pleases, it is still alive, and will every now and then peep out and show itself; you will see it, perhaps, often in this history; for, even if I could conceive that I had compleatly overcome it, I should probably be proud of my humility.

HAVING mentioned *a great and extensive project* which I had conceiv'd, it seems proper that some account should be here given of that project and its object. Its first rise in my mind appears in the following little paper, accidentally preserv'd, viz:

Observations on my reading history, in Library, May 19th, 1731.

"That the great affairs of the world, the wars, revolutions, etc., are carried on and affected by parties.

"That the view of these parties is their present general interest, or what they take to be such.

"That the different views of these different parties occasion all confusion.

"That while a party is carrying on a general design, each man has his particular private interest in view.

"That as soon as a party has gain'd its general point, each member becomes intent upon his particular interest; which, thwarting others, breaks that party into divisions, and occasions more confusion.

"That few in public affairs act from a meer view of the good of their country, whatever they may pretend; and, tho' their actings bring real good to their country, yet men primarily considered that their own and their country's interest was united, and did not act from a principle of benevolence.

"That fewer still, in public affairs, act with a view to the good of mankind.

"There seems to me at present to be great occasion for raising a United Party for Virtue, by forming the virtuous and good men of all nations into a regular body, to be govern'd by suitable good and wise rules, which good and wise men may probably be more unanimous in their obedience to, than common people are to common laws.

"I at present think that whoever attempts this aright, and is well qualified, can not fail of pleasing God, and of meeting with success.
B. F."

Resolving this project in my mind, as to be undertaken hereafter, when my circumstances should afford me the necessary leisure, I put down from time to time, on pieces of paper, such thoughts as occurr'd to me respecting it. Most of these are lost; but I find one purporting to be the substance of an intended creed, containing, as I thought, the essentials of every known religion, and being free of every thing that might shock the professor of any religion. It is express'd in these words, viz.:

"That there is one God, who made all things.

"That he governs the world by his providence.

"That he ought to be worshiped by adoration, prayer, and thanksgiving.

"But that the most acceptable service of God is doing good to man.

"That the soul is immortal.

"And that God will certainly reward virtue and punish vice, either here or hereafter."

My ideas at that time were, that the sect should be begun and spread at first among young and single men only; that each person to be initiated should not only declare his assent to such creed, but should have exercised himself with the thirteen weeks' examination and practice of the virtues, as in the before-mention'd model; that the existence of such a society should be kept a secret, till it was become considerable, to prevent solicitations for the admission of improper persons, but that the members should each of them search among his acquaintance for ingenuous, well-disposed youths, to whom, with prudent caution, the scheme should be gradually communicated; that the members should engage to afford their advice, assistance, and support to each other in promoting one another's interests, business, and advancement in life; that, for distinction, we should be call'd *The Society of the Free and Easy:* free, as being, by the general practice and habit of the virtues, free from the dominion of vice; and particularly by the practice of industry and frugality, free from debt, which exposes a man to confinement, and a species of slavery to his creditors.

This is as much as I can now recollect of the project, except that I communicated it in part to two young men, who adopted it with some enthusiasm; but my then narrow circumstances, and the necessity I was under of sticking close to my business, occasion'd my postponing the further prosecution of it at that time; and my multifarious occupations, public and private, induc'd me to continue postponing, so that it has been omitted till I have no longer strength or activity left sufficient for such an enterprise; tho' I am still of opinion that it was a practicable scheme, and might have been very useful, by forming a great number of good citizens; and I was not discourag'd by the seeming magnitude of the undertaking, as I have always thought that one man of tolerable abilities may work great changes, and accomplish great affairs among mankind, if he first forms a good plan, and, cutting off all amusements or other employments that would divert his attention, makes the execution of that same plan his sole study and business.

In 1732 I first publish'd my Almanack, under the name of *Richard Saunders;* it was continu'd by me about twenty-five years, commonly call'd *Poor Richard's Almanack.* I endeavor'd to make it both entertaining and useful, and it accordingly came to be in such demand, that I reap'd considerable profit from it, vending annually near ten thousand. And observing that it was generally read, scarce any neighborhood in the province being without it, I consider'd it as a proper vehicle for conveying instruction among the common people, who bought scarcely any other books; I therefore filled all the little spaces that occurr'd between the remarkable days in the calandar with proverbial sentences, chiefly such as inculcated industry and frugality, as the means of procuring wealth, and thereby securing virtue; it being more difficult for a man in want, to act always honestly, as, to use here one of those proverbs, *it is hard for an empty sack to stand upright.*

These proverbs, which contained the wisdom of many ages and nations, I assembled and form'd into a connected discourse prefix'd to the Almanack of 1757, as the harangue of a wise old man to the people attending an auction. The bringing all these scatter'd counsels thus into a focus enabled them to make greater impression. The piece, being universally approved, was copied in all the newspapers of the Continent; reprinted in Britain on a broad side, to be stuck up in houses; two translations were made of it in French, and great numbers bought by the clergy and gentry, to distribute gratis among their poor parishioners and tenants. In Pennsylvania, as it discouraged useless expense in foreign superfluities, some thought it had its share of influence in producing that growing plenty of money which was observable for several years after its publication.

I considered my newspaper, also, as another means of communicating instruction, and in that view frequently reprinted in it extracts from the Spectator, and other moral writers; and sometimes publish'd little pieces of my own, which had been first compos'd for reading in our Junto. Of these are a Socratic dialogue, tending to prove that, whatever might be his parts and abilities, a vicious man could not properly be called a man of sense; and a discourse on self-denial, showing that virtue was not secure till its practice became a habitude, and was free from the opposition of contrary inclinations. These may be found in the papers about the beginning of 1735.

In the conduct of my newspaper, I carefully excluded all libelling and personal abuse, which is of late years become so disgraceful to our country. Whenever I was solicited to insert any thing of that kind, and the writers pleaded, as they generally did, the liberty of the press, and that a newspaper was like a stage-coach, in which any one who would pay had a right to a place, my answer was, that I would print the piece separately if desired, and the author might have as many copies as he pleased to distribute himself, but that I would not take upon me to spread his detraction; and that, having contracted with my subscribers to furnish them with what might be either useful or entertaining, I could not fill their papers with private altercation, in which they had no concern, without doing them manifest injustice. Now, many of our printers make no scruple of gratifying the malice of individuals by false accusations of the fairest characters among ourselves, augmenting animosity even to the producing of duels; and are, moreover, so indiscreet as to print scurrilous reflections on the government of neighboring states, and even on the conduct of our best national allies, which may be attended with the most pernicious consequences. These things I mention as a caution to young printers, and that they may be encouraged not to pollute their presses and disgrace their profession by such infamous practices, but refuse steadily, as they may see by my example that such a course of conduct will not, on the whole, be injurious to their interests.

I began now to turn my thoughts a little to public affairs, beginning, however, with small matters. The city watch was one of the first things that I conceiv'd to want regulation. It was managed by the constables of the respective wards in turn; the constable warned a number of housekeepers to attend him for the night. Those who chose never to attend, paid him six shillings a year to be excus'd, which was suppos'd to be for hiring substitutes, but was, in reality, much more than was necessary for that purpose, and made the constableship a place of profit; and the constable, for a little drink, often got such ragamuffins about him as a watch, that respectable housekeepers did not choose to mix with. Walking the rounds, too, was often neglected, and most of the nights spent in tippling. I thereupon wrote a paper to be read in Junto, representing these irregularities, but insisting more particularly on the inequality of this six-shilling tax of the constables, respecting the circumstances of those who paid it, since a poor widow housekeeper, all whose property to be guarded by the watch did not perhaps exceed the value of fifty pounds, paid as much as the wealthiest merchant, who had thousands of pounds' worth of goods in his stores.

On the whole, I proposed as a more effectual watch, the hiring of proper men to serve constantly in that business; and as a more equitable way of supporting the charge, the levying a tax that should be proportion'd to the property. This idea, being approv'd by the Junto, was communicated to the other clubs, but as arising in each of them; and though the plan was not immediately carried into execution, yet, by preparing the minds of people for the change, it paved the way for the law obtained a few years after, when the members of our clubs were grown into more influence.

About this time I wrote a paper (first to be read in Junto, but it was afterward publish'd) on the different accidents and carelessnesses by which houses were set on fire, with cautions against them, and means proposed of avoiding them. This was much spoken of as a useful piece, and gave rise to a project, which soon followed it, of forming a company for the more ready extinguishing of fires, and mutual assistance in removing and securing of goods when in danger. Associates in this scheme were presently found, amounting to thirty. Our articles of agreement oblig'd every member to keep always in good order, and fit for use, a certain number of leather buckets, with strong bags and baskets (for packing and transporting of goods), which were to be brought to every fire; and we agreed to meet once a month to spend a social evening together, in discoursing and communicating such ideas as occurred to us upon the subject of fires, as might be useful in our conduct on such occasions.

The utility of this institution soon appeared, and many more desiring to be admitted than we thought convenient for one company, they were advised to form another, which was accordingly done; and this went on, one new company being formed after another, till they became so numerous as to include most of the inhabitants who were men of property; and now, at the time of my writing this, tho' upward of fifty years since its establishment, that which I first formed, called the Union Fire Company, still subsists and flourishes, tho' the first members are all deceas'd but myself and one, who is older by a year than I am. The small fines that have been paid by members for absence at the monthly meetings have been apply'd to the purchase of fire-engines, ladders, fire-hooks, and other useful implements for each company, so that I question whether there is a city in the world better provided with the means of putting a stop to beginning conflagrations; and, in fact, since these institutions, the city has never lost by fire more than one or two houses at a time, and the flames have often been extinguished before the house in which they began has been half consumed.

In 1739 arrived among us from Ireland the Reverend Mr. Whitefield, who had made himself remarkable there as an itinerant preacher. He was at first permitted to preach in some of our churches; but the clergy, taking a dislike to him, soon refus'd him their pulpits, and he was oblig'd to preach in the fields. The multitudes of all sects and denominations that attended his sermons were enormous, and it was matter of speculation to me, who was one of the number, to observe the extraordinary influence of his oratory on his hearers, and how much they admir'd and respected him, notwithstanding his common abuse of them, by assuring them they were naturally *half beasts and half devils*. It was wonderful to see the change soon made in the manners of our inhabitants. From being thoughtless or indifferent about religion, it seem'd as if all the world were growing religious, so that one could not walk thro' the town in an evening without hearing psalms sung in different families of every street.

And it being found inconvenient to assemble in the open air, subject to its inclemencies, the building of a house to meet in was no sooner propos'd, and persons appointed to receive contributions, but sufficient sums were soon received to procure the ground and erect the building, which was one hundred feet long and seventy broad, about the size of Westminster Hall; and the work was carried on with such spirit as to be finished in a much shorter time than could have been expected. Both house and ground were vested in trustees, expressly for the use of any preacher of any religious persuasion who might desire to say something to the people at Philadelphia; the design in building not being to accommodate any particular sect, but the inhabitants in general; so that even if the Mufti of Constantinople were to send a missionary to preach Mohammedanism to us, he would find a pulpit at his service.

Mr. Whitefield, in leaving us, went preaching all the way thro' the colonies to Georgia. The settlement of that province had lately been begun, but, instead of being made with hardy, industrious husbandmen, accustomed to labor, the only people fit for such an enterprise, it was with families of broken shop-keepers and other insolvent debtors, many of indolent and idle habits, taken out of the jails, who, being set down in the woods, unqualified for clearing land, and unable to endure the hardships of a new settlement, perished in numbers, leaving many helpless children unprovided for. The sight of their miserable situation inspir'd the benevolent heart of Mr. Whitefield with the idea of building an Orphan House there, in which they might be supported and educated. Returning northward, he preach'd up this char-

ity, and made large collections, for his eloquence had a wonderful power over the hearts and purses of his hearers, of which I myself was an instance.

I did not disapprove of the design, but, as Georgia was then destitute of materials and workmen, and it was proposed to send them from Philadelphia at a great expense, I thought it would have been better to have built the house there, and brought the children to it. This I advis'd; but he was resolute in his first project, rejected my counsel, and I therefor refus'd to contribute. I happened soon after to attend one of his sermons, in the course of which I perceived he intended to finish with a collection, and I silently resolved he should get nothing from me. I had in my pocket a handful of copper money, three or four silver dollars, and five pistoles in gold. As he proceeded I began to soften, and concluded to give the coppers. Another stroke of his oratory made me asham'd of that, and determin'd me to give the silver; and he finish'd so admirably, that I empty'd my pocket wholly into the collector's dish, gold and all. At this sermon there was also one of our club, who, being of my sentiments respecting the building in Georgia, and suspecting a collection might be intended, had, by precaution, emptied his pockets before he came from home. Towards the conclusion of the discourse, however, he felt a strong desire to give, and apply'd to a neighbour, who stood near him, to borrow some money for the purpose. The application was unfortunately [made] to perhaps the only man in the company who had the firmness not to be affected by the preacher. His answer was, "*At any other time, Friend Hopkinson, I would lend to thee freely; but not now, for thee seems to be out of thy right senses.*"

Some of Mr. Whitefield's enemies affected to suppose that he would apply these collections to his own private emolument; but I, who was intimately acquainted with him (being employed in printing his Sermons and Journals, etc.), never had the least suspicion of his integrity, but am to this day decidedly of opinion that he was in all his conduct a perfectly *honest man*; and methinks my testimony in his favour ought to have the more weight, as we had no religious connection. He us'd, indeed, sometimes to pray for my conversion, but never had the satisfaction of believing that his prayers were heard. Ours was a mere civil friendship, sincere on both sides, and lasted to his death. . . .

I had, on the whole, abundant reason to be satisfied with my being established in Pennsylvania. There were, however, two things that I regretted, there being no provision for defense, nor for a compleat education of youth; no militia, nor any college. I therefore, in 1743, drew up a proposal for establishing an academy; and at that time, thinking the Reverend Mr. Peters, who was out of employ, a fit person to superintend such an institution, I communicated the project to him; but he, having more profitable views in the service of the proprietaries, which succeeded, declin'd the undertaking; and, not knowing another at that time suitable for such a trust, I let the scheme lie a while dormant. I succeeded better the next year, 1744, in proposing and establishing a Philosophical Society. The paper I wrote for that purpose will be found among my writings, when collected.

With respect to defense, Spain having been several years at war against Great Britain, and being at length join'd by France, which brought us into great danger; and the laboured and long-continued endeavour of our governor, Thomas, to prevail with our Quaker Assembly to pass a militia law, and make other provisions for the security of the province, having proved abortive, I determined to try what might be done by a voluntary association of the people. To promote this, I first wrote and published a pamphlet, entitled PLAIN TRUTH, in which I stated our defenceless situation in strong lights, with the necessity of union and discipline for our defense, and promis'd to propose in a few days an association, to be generally signed for that purpose. The pamphlet had a sudden and surprising effect. I was call'd upon for the instrument of association, and having settled the draft of it with a few friends, I appointed a meeting of the citizens in the large building before mentioned. The house was pretty full; I had prepared a number of printed copies, and provided pens and ink dispers'd all over the room. I harangued them a little on the subject, read the paper, and explained it, and then distributed the copies, which were eagerly signed, not the least objection being made. . . .

My being many years in the Assembly, the majority of which were constantly Quakers, gave me frequent opportunities of seeing the embarrassment given them by their principle against war, whenever application was made to them, by order of the crown, to grant aids for military purposes. They were unwilling to offend government, on the one hand, by a direct refusal; and their friends, the body of the Quakers, on the other, by a compliance contrary to their principles; hence a variety of evasions to avoid complying, and modes of disguising the compliance when it became unavoidable. The common mode at last was, to grant money under the phrase of its being *"for the king's use,"* and never to inquire how it was applied.

But, if the demand was not directly from the crown, that phrase was found not so proper, and some other was to be invented. As, when powder was wanting (I think it was for the garrison at Louisburg), and the government of New England solicited a grant of some from Pennsylvania, which was much urg'd on the House by Governor Thomas, they could not grant money to buy powder, because that was an ingredient of war; but they voted an aid to New England of three thousand pounds, to be put into the hands of the governor, and appropriated it for the purchasing of bread, flour, wheat, or *other grain.* Some of the council, desirous of giving the House still further embarrassment, advis'd the governor not to accept provision, as not being the thing he had demanded; but he reply'd, "I shall take the money, for I understand very well their meaning; other grain is gunpowder," which he accordingly bought, and they never objected to it. . . .

In order of time, I should have mentioned before, that having, in 1742, invented an open stove for the better warming of rooms, and at the same time saving fuel, as the fresh air admitted was warmed in entering, I made a present of the model to Mr. Robert Grace, one of my early friends, who, having an iron-furnace, found the casting of the plates for these stoves a profitable thing, as they were growing in demand. To promote that demand, I wrote and published a pamphlet, entitled *"An Account of the new-invented Pennsylvania Fireplaces; wherein their Construction and Manner of Operation is particularly explained; their Advantages above every other Method of warming Rooms demonstrated; and all Objections that have been raised against the Use of them answered and obviated,"* etc. This pamphlet had a good effect. Gov'r. Thomas was so pleas'd with the construction of this stove, as described in it, that he offered to give me a patent for the sole vending of them for a term of years; but I declin'd it from a principle which has ever weighed with me on such occasions, viz., *That, as we enjoy great advantages from the inventions of others, we should be glad of an opportunity to serve others by any invention of ours; and this we should do freely and generously.* . . .

Peace being concluded, and the association business therefore at an end, I turn'd my thoughts again to the affair of establishing an academy. The first step I took was to associate in the design a number of active friends, of whom the Junto furnished a good part; the next was to write and publish a pamphlet, entitled *Proposals Relating to the Education of Youth in Pennsylvania.* This I distributed among the principal inhabitants gratis; and as soon as I could suppose their minds a little prepared by the perusal of it, I set on foot a subscription for opening and supporting an academy; it was to be paid in quotas yearly for five years; by so dividing it, I judg'd the subscription might be larger, and I believed it was so, amounting to no less, if I remember right, than five thousand pounds. . . .

The trustees of the academy, after a while, were incorporated by a charter from the governor; their funds were increas'd by contributions in Britain and grants of land from the proprietaries, to which the Assembly has since made considerable addition; and thus was established the present University of Philadelphia. I have been continued one of its trustees from the beginning, now near forty years, and have had the very great pleasure of seeing a number of the youth who have receiv'd their education in it, distinguish'd by their improv'd abilities, serviceable in public stations, and ornaments to their country. . . .

After some time I drew a bill for paving the city, and brought it into the Assembly. It was just before I went to England, in 1757, and did not pass till I was gone, and then with an alteration in the mode of assessment, which I thought for the better, but with an additional provision for lighting as well as paving the streets, which was a great improvement. It was by a private person, the late Mr. John Clifton, his giving a sample of the utility of lamps, by placing one at his door, that the people were first impress'd with the idea of enlighting all the city. The honour of this public benefit has also been ascrib'd to me, but it belongs truly to that gentleman. I did but follow his example, and have only some merit to claim respecting the form of our lamps, as differing from the globe lamps we were at first supply'd with from London. Those we found inconvenient in these respects: they admitted no air below; the smoke, therefore, did not readily go out above, but circulated in the globe, lodg'd on its inside, and soon obstructed the light they were intended to afford; giving, besides the daily trouble of wiping them clean; and an accidental stroke on one of them would demolish it, and render it totally useless. I therefore suggested the composing them of four flat panes, with a long funnel above to draw up the smoke, and crevices admitting air below, to facilitate the ascent of the smoke; by this means they were kept clean, and did not grow dark in a few hours, as the London lamps do, but continu'd bright till morning, and an accidental stroke would generally break but a single pane, easily repaired. . . .

It may not be amiss here to give some account of the rise and progress of my philosophical reputation.

In 1746, being in Boston, I met there with a Dr. Spence, who was lately arrived from Scotland, and show'd me some electric experiments. They were imperfectly perform'd, as he was not very expert; but, being on a subject quite new to me, they equally surpris'd and pleased me.

Soon after my return to Philadelphia, our library company receiv'd from Mr. P. Collinson, Fellow of the Royal Society of London, a present of a glass tube, with some account of the use of it in making such experiments. I eagerly seized the opportunity of repeating what I had seen at Boston; and, by much practice, acquir'd great readiness in performing those, also, which we had an account of from England, adding a number of new ones. I say much practice, for my house was continually full, for some time, with people who came to see these new wonders.

To divide a little this incumbrance among my friends, I caused a number of similar tubes to be blown at our glass-house, with which they furnish'd themselves, so that we had at length several performers. Among these, the principal was Mr. Kinnersley, an ingenious neighbor, who, being out of business, I encouraged to undertake showing the experiments for money, and drew up for him two lectures, in which the experiments were rang'd in such order, and accompanied with such explanations in such method, as that the foregoing should assist in comprehending the following. He procur'd an elegant apparatus for the purpose, in which all the little machines that I had roughly made for myself were nicely form'd by instrument-makers. His lectures were well attended, and gave great satisfaction; and after some time he went thro' the colonies, exhibiting them in every capital town, and pick'd up some money. In the West India islands, indeed, it was with difficulty the experiments could be made, from the general moisture of the air.

Oblig'd as we were to Mr. Collinson for his present of the tube, etc., I thought it right he should be inform'd of our success in using it, and wrote him several letters containing accounts of our experiments. He got them read in the Royal Society, where they were not at first thought worth so much notice as to be printed in their Transactions. One paper, which I wrote for Mr. Kinnersley, on the sameness of lightning with electricity, I sent to Dr. Mitchel, an acquaintance of mine, and one of the members also of that society, who wrote me word that it had been read, but was laughed at by the connoisseurs. The papers, however, being

shown to Dr. Fothergill, he thought them of too much value to be stifled, and advis'd the printing of them. Mr. Collinson then gave them to *Cave* for publication in his Gentleman's Magazine; but he chose to print them separately in a pamphlet, and Dr. Fothergill wrote the preface. Cave, it seems, judged rightly for his profit, for by the additions that arrived afterward they swell'd, to a quarto volume, which has had five editions, and cost him nothing for copy-money.

It was, however, some time before those papers were much taken notice of in England. A copy of them happening to fall into the hands of the Count de Buffon, a philosopher deservedly of great reputation in France, and, indeed, all over Europe, he prevailed with M. Dalibard to translate them into French, and they were printed at Paris. The publication offended the Abbé Nollet, preceptor in Natural Philosophy to the royal family, and an able experimenter, who had form'd and publish'd a theory of electricity, which then had the general vogue. He could not at first believe that such a work came from America, and said it must have been fabricated by his enemies at Paris, to decry his system. Afterwards, having been assur'd that there really existed such a person as Franklin at Philadelphia, which he had doubted, he wrote and published a volume of Letters, chiefly address'd to me, defending his theory, and denying the verity of my experiments, and of the positions deduc'd from them.

I once purpos'd answering the abbé, and actually began the answer; but, on consideration that my writings contain'd a description of experiments which any one might repeat and verify, and if not to be verifi'd, could not be defended; or of observations offer'd as conjectures, and not delivered dogmatically, therefore not laying me under any obligation to defend them; and reflecting that a dispute between two persons, writing in different languages, might be lengthened greatly by mistranslations, and thence misconceptions of one another's meaning, much of one of the abbé's letters being founded on an error in the translation, I concluded to let my papers shift for themselves, believing it was better to spend what time I could spare from public business in making new experiments, than in disputing about those already made. I therefore never answered M. Nollet, and the event gave me no cause to repent my silence; for my friend M. le Roy, of the Royal Academy of Sciences, took up my cause and refuted him; my book was translated into the Italian, German, and Latin languages; and the doctrine it contain'd was by degrees universally adopted by the philosophers of Europe, in preference to that of the abbé; so that he lived to see himself the last of his sect, except Monsieur B——, of Paris, his *élève* and immediate disciple.

What gave my book the more sudden and general celebrity, was the success of one of its proposed experiments, made by Messrs. Dalibard and De Lor at Marly, for drawing lightning from the clouds. This engag'd the public attention every where. M. de Lor, who had an apparatus for experimental philosophy, and lectur'd in that branch of sicence, undertook to repeat what he called the *Philadelphia Experiments;* and, after they were performed before the king and court, all the curious of Paris flocked to see them. I will not swell this narrative with an account of that capital experiment, nor of the infinite pleasure I received in the success of a similar one I made soon after with a kite at Philadelphia, as both are to be found in the histories of electricity.

Dr. Wright, an English physician, when at Paris, wrote to a friend, who was of the Royal Society, an account of the high esteem my experiments were in among the learned abroad, and of their wonder that my writings had been so little noticed in England. The society, on this, resum'd the consideration of the letters that had been read to them; and the celebrated Dr. Watson drew up a summary account of them, and of all I had afterwards sent to England on the subject, which he accompanied with some praise of the writer. This summary was then printed in their Transactions; and some members of the society in London, particularly the very ingenious Mr. Canton, having verified the experiment of procuring lightning from the clouds by a pointed rod, and acquainting them with the success, they soon made me more than amends for the slight with which they had before treated me. Without my having made any application for that honor, they chose me a member, and voted that 1 should be excus'd the customary payments, which would have amounted to twenty-five guineas; and ever since have given me their Transactions gratis. They also presented me with the gold medal of Sir Godfrey Copley for the year 1753, the delivery of which was accompanied by a very handsome speech of the president, Lord Macclesfield, wherein I was highly honoured.

Second Continental Congress

The Declaration of American Independence was written to justify a resolution of independence adopted by the Second Continental Congress on July 2, 1776. It was largely the work of Thomas Jefferson, an American who was representative of the Enlightenment. As a consequence, this famous document naturally reflected certain political theories which had already been expressed by others and widely accepted. John Locke, in particular, should be noted in this regard. In reading the Declaration note (1) the appeal in the preamble to the laws of nature and of nature's God, (2) the secular purposes for which governments were formed, (3) evidences of the social contract, (4) the appeal to the "right" of revolution, (5) the branch of the English government against which the principal charges were made, (6) the political abuses cited, (7) the evidences of economic discontent contained in the charges,

(8) *the references to tyranny in a neighboring province,* (9) *the charge that the Indians were being incited to destroy civilized communities,* (10) *evidences that the writers already looked upon themselves as a people independent of the English, and* (11) *the conclusion reached.*

THE DECLARATION OF AMERICAN INDEPENDENCE

In Congress, July 4, 1776

The Unanimous Declaration of the Thirteen United States of America

When, in the course of human events, it becomes necessary for one people to dissolve the political bands which have connected them with another, and to assume among the powers of the earth the separate and equal station to which the laws of nature and of nature's God entitle them, a decent respect to the opinions of mankind requires that they should declare the causes which impel them to the separation.

We hold these truths to be self-evident: That all men are created equal; that they are endowed by their Creator with certain unalienable rights; that among these are life, liberty, and the pursuit of happiness; that, to secure these rights, governments are instituted among men, deriving their just powers from the consent of the governed; that whenever any form of government becomes destructive of these ends, it is the right of the people to alter or to abolish it and to institute a new government, laying its foundation on such principles, and organizing its powers in such form, as to them shall seem most likely to effect their safety and happiness. Prudence, indeed, will dictate that governments long established should not be changed for light and transient causes; and, accordingly, all experience hath shown that mankind are more disposed to suffer while evils are sufferable, than to right themselves by abolishing the forms to which they are accustomed. But when a long train of abuses and usurpations, pursuing invariably the same object, evinces a design to reduce them under absolute despotism, it is their right, it is their duty, to throw off such government and to provide new guards for their future security. Such

has been the patient sufferance of these colonies; and such is now the necessity which constrains them to alter their former systems of government.

The history of the present King of Great Britain is a history of repeated injuries and usurpations, all having in direct object the establishment of an absolute tyranny over these States. To prove this, let facts be submitted to a candid world:

He has refused his assent to laws, the most wholesome and necessary for the public good.

He has forbidden his Governors to pass laws of immediate and pressing importance, unless suspended in their operation till his assent should be obtained; and, when so suspended, he has utterly neglected to attend to them.

He has refused to pass other laws for the accommodation of large districts of people, unless those people would relinquish the right of representation in the Legislature, a right inestimable to them and formidable to tyrants only.

He has called together legislative bodies at places unusual, uncomfortable, and distant from the depository of their public records, for the sole purpose of fatiguing them into compliance with his measures.

He has dissolved representative Houses repeatedly for opposing with manly firmness his invasions on the rights of the people.

He has refused for a long time after such dissolutions to cause others to be elected; whereby the legislative powers, incapable of annihilation, have returned to the people at large for their exercise; the State remaining, in the meantime, exposed to all the dangers of invasions from without and convulsions within.

He has endeavored to prevent the population of these States; for that purpose obstruct-

Adapted from a photograph of the original document now in the Library of Congress.

ing the laws for naturalization of foreigners, refusing to pass others to encourage their migration hither, and raising the conditions of new appropriations of lands.

He has obstructed the administration of justice by refusing his assent to laws for establishing judiciary powers.

He has made judges dependent on his will alone for the tenure of their offices and the amount and payment of their salaries.

He has erected a multitude of new offices, and sent hither swarms of officers to harass our people and eat out their substance.

He has kept among us, in times of peace, standing armies, without the consent of our Legislatures.

He has affected to render the military independent of, and superior to, the civil power.

He has combined with others to subject us to a jurisdiction foreign to our Constitution and unacknowledged by our laws, giving his assent to their acts of pretended legislation:

For quartering large bodies of armed troops among us;

For protecting them, by a mock trial, from punishment for any murders which they should commit on the inhabitants of these States;

For cutting off our trade with all parts of the world;

For imposing taxes on us without our consent;

For depriving us, in many cases, of the benefits of trial by jury;

For transporting us beyond seas to be tried for pretended offenses;

For abolishing the free system of English laws in a neighboring province, establishing therein an arbitrary government, and enlarging its boundaries so as to render it at once an example and fit instrument for introducing the same absolute rule into these colonies;

For taking away our charters, abolishing our most valuable laws, and altering fundamentally the forms of our governments;

For suspending our own Legislatures, and declaring themselves invested with power to legislate for us in all cases whatsoever.

He has abdicated government here by declaring us out of his protection and waging war against us.

He has plundered our seas, ravaged our coasts, burnt our towns, and destroyed the lives of our people.

He is at this time transporting large armies of foreign mercenaries to complete the works of death, desolation, and tyranny, already begun with circumstances of cruelty and perfidy scarcely paralleled in the most barbarous ages, and totally unworthy the head of a civilized nation.

He has constrained our fellow citizens, taken captive on the high seas, to bear arms against their country, to become the executioners of their friends and brethren, or to fall themselves by their hands.

He has excited domestic insurrections amongst us, and has endeavored to bring on the inhabitants of our frontiers the merciless Indian savages, whose known rule of warfare is an undistinguished destruction of all ages, sexes, and conditions.

In every stage of these oppressions we have petitioned for redress in the most humble terms: our repeated petitions have been answered only by repeated injury. A prince, whose character is thus marked by every act which may define a tyrant, is unfit to be the ruler of a free people.

Nor have we been wanting in attentions to our British brethren. We have warned them from time to time of attempts by their Legislature to extend an unwarrantable jurisdiction over us. We have reminded them of the circumstances of our emigration and settlement here. We have appealed to their native justice and magnanimity, and we have conjured them by the ties of our common kindred to disavow these usurpations which would inevitably interrupt our connections and correspondence. They, too, have been deaf to the voice of justice and of consanguinity. We must, therefore, acquiesce in the necessity which denounces our separation, and hold them, as we hold the rest of mankind, enemies in war; in peace, friends.

WE, THEREFORE, THE REPRESENTATIVES OF THE UNITED STATES OF AMERICA, in General Congress assembled, appealing to the Supreme

Judge of the world for the rectitude of our intentions, do, in the name and by the authority of the good people of these colonies, solemnly publish and declare that these United Colonies are, and of right ought to be, FREE AND INDEPENDENT STATES; that they are absolved from all allegiance to the British Crown, and that all political connection between them and the State of Great Britain is, and ought to be, totally dissolved; and that as free and independent states they have full power to levy war, conclude peace, contract alliances, establish commerce, and to do all other acts and things which independent States may of right do. And for the support of this declaration, with a firm reliance on the protection of Divine Providence, we mutually pledge to each other our lives, our fortunes, and our sacred honor.

James Madison

James Madison (1751–1836) was born in the tidewater section of Virginia. He graduated from the College of New Jersey (Princeton) in 1771, studied law, then entered upon a long career in the service of his country. In 1787 Madison associated himself with Alexander Hamilton and John Jay in writing a series of letters to the New York press during the debate over the ratification of the Constitution of the United States in an effort to influence opinion in support of the Federal Constitution. Its framers aimed to place effective checks upon democratic government in America, and they achieved signal success in the document submitted to the states for ratification in 1787. Madison approached the problem of government in a coldly realistic and non-romantic fashion and defended the new instrument of government on the grounds that it would protect not only the majority against a minority, but also would protect a minority against the majority. The following was the tenth in the series of papers written in 1787 to the people of the state of New York. In reading it note (1) what Madison regarded as one of the major vices confronting popular governments, (2) his definition of faction, (3) available remedies for curing the evils of faction, (4) where Madison found the latent causes of faction, (5) what he saw as the most common source of factions, (6) what he conceived the principal tasks of government to be, (7) how he arrived at the conclusion that relief from faction could only be sought in controlling its effects, (8) the bases for his argument that a republic promises the best cure for the effects of faction, (9) his differentiation between democracy and a republic, and (10) his reasons for defending a republic as against a democracy.

THE FEDERALIST, NO. 10

Among the numerous advantages promised by a well-constructed union, none deserves to be more accurately developed than its tendency to break and control the violence of faction. The friend of popular governments never finds himself so much alarmed for their charac-

Adapted from Alexander Hamilton, Jay and Madison, *The Federalist* . . . , Philadelphia, 1892, 104–112.

ter and fate as when he contemplates their propensity to this dangerous vice. He will not fail, therefore, to set a due value on any plan which, without violating the principles to which he is attached, provides a proper cure for it. The instability, injustice, and confusion introduced into the public councils have, in truth, been the mortal diseases under which popular governments have everywhere perished; as they continue to be the favorite and fruitful topics from which the adversaries to liberty derive their most specious declamations. The valuable improvements made by the American constitutions on the popular models, both ancient and modern, cannot certainly be too much admired; but it would be an unwarrantable partiality, to contend that they have as effectually obviated the danger on this side as was wished and expected. Complaints are everywhere heard from our most considerate and virtuous citizens, equally the friends of public and private faith and of public and personal liberty, that our governments are too unstable; that the public good is disregarded in the conflicts of rival parties; and that measures are too often decided, not according to the rules of justice, and the rights of the minor party, but by the superior force of an interested and overbearing majority. However anxiously we may wish that these complaints had no foundation, the evidence of known facts will not permit us to deny that they are in some degree true. It will be found, indeed, on a candid review of our situation, that some of the distresses under which we labor have been erroneously charged on the operation of our governments; but it will be found, at the same time, that other causes will not alone account for many of our heaviest misfortunes; and, particularly, for that prevailing and increasing distrust of public engagements, and alarm for private rights, which are echoed from one end of the continent to the other. These must be chiefly, if not wholly, effects of the unsteadiness and injustice with which a factious spirit has tainted our public administrations.

By a faction, I understand a number of citizens, whether amounting to a majority or minority of the whole, who are united and actuated by some common impulse of passion, or of interest, adverse to the rights of other citizens or to the permanent and aggregate interests of the community.

There are two methods of curing the mischiefs of faction: the one, by removing its causes; the other, by controlling its effects.

There are again two methods of removing the causes of faction: the one, by destroying the liberty which is essential to its existence; the other, by giving to every citizen the same opinions, the same passions, and the same interests.

It could never be more truly said than of the first remedy, that it was worse than the disease. Liberty is to faction what air is to fire, an ailment without which it instantly expires. But it could not be less folly to abolish liberty, which is essential to political life, because it nourishes faction, than it would be to wish the annihilation of air, which is essential to animal life, because it imparts to fire its destructive agency.

The second expedient is as impracticable as the first would be unwise. As long as the reason of man continues fallible, and he is at liberty to exercise it, different opinions will be formed. As long as the connection subsists between his reason and his self-love, his opinions and his passions will have a reciprocal influence on each other; and the former will be objects to which the latter will attach themselves. The diversity in the faculties of men, from which the rights of property originate, is not less an insuperable obstacle to a uniformity of interests. The protection of these faculties is the first object of government. From the protection of different and unequal faculties of acquiring property, the possession of different degrees and kinds of property immediately results; and from the influence of these on the sentiments and views of the respective proprietors ensues a division of the society into different interests and parties.

The latent causes of faction are thus sown in the nature of man; and we see them everywhere brought into different degrees of activity, according to the different circumstances of civil society. A zeal for different opinions concerning religion, concerning government and many other points, as well as speculation as of practice; an attachment to different leaders ambitiously contending for pre-eminence and power, or to persons of other descriptions whose fortunes have been interesting to the human passions, have, in turn, divided mankind into parties, inflamed them with mutual animosity, and rendered them much more disposed to vex and oppress each other, than to co-operate for their common good. So strong is this propensity of mankind to fall into mutual animosities, that where no substantial occasion presents itself, the most frivolous and fanciful distinctions have been sufficient to kindle their unfriendly passions and excite their most violent conflicts. But the most common and durable source of factions has been the various and unequal distribution of property. Those who hold and those who are without property have ever formed distinct interests in society. Those who are creditors and those who are debtors fall under a like discrimination. A landed interest, a manufacturing interest, a mercantile interest, a moneyed interest, with many lesser interests, grow up of necessity in civilized nations, and divide them into different classes, actuated by different sentiments and views. The regulation of these various and interfering interests forms the principal task of modern legislation, and involves the spirit of party and faction in the necessary and ordinary operations of the government.

No man is allowed to be a judge in his own cause; because his interest would certainly bias his judgment and, not improbably, corrupt his integrity. With equal, nay, with greater reason, a body of men are unfit to be both judges and parties at the same time; yet what are many of the most important acts of legislation, but so many judicial determinations, not indeed concerning the rights of single persons, but concerning the rights of large bodies of citizens? and what are the different classes of legislators, but advocates and parties to the causes which they determine? Is a law proposed concerning private debts?—it is a question to which the creditors are parties on one side, and the debtors on the other. Justice ought to hold the balance between them. Yet the parties are, and must be, themselves the judges; and the most numerous party, or, in other words, the most powerful faction, must be expected to prevail. Shall domestic manufactures be encouraged, and in what degree by

restrictions on foreign manufactures? are questions which would be differently decided by the landed and the manufacturing classes, and probably by neither with a sole regard to justice and the public good. The apportionment of taxes on the various descriptions of property is an act which seems to require the most exact impartiality; yet there is, perhaps, no legislative act in which greater opportunity and temptation are given to a predominant party, to trample on the rules of justice. Every shilling with which they overburden the inferior number is a shilling saved to their own pockets.

It is in vain to say that enlightened statesmen will be able to adjust these clashing interests and render them all subservient to the public good. Enlightened statesmen will not always be at the helm; nor, in many cases, can such an adjustment be made at all, without taking into view indirect and remote considerations, which will rarely prevail over the immediate interest which one party may find in disregarding the rights of another or the good of the whole.

The inference to which we are brought is that the causes of faction cannot be removed, and that relief is only to be sought in the means of controlling its effects.

If a faction consists of less than a majority, relief is supplied by the republican principle, which enables the majority to defeat its sinister views by regular vote. It may clog the administration, it may convulse the society; but it will be unable to execute and mask its violence under the forms of the Constitution. When a majority is included in a faction, the form of popular government, on the other hand, enables it to sacrifice to its ruling passion or interest both the public good and the rights of other citizens. To secure the public good, and private rights, against the danger of such a faction, and at the same time to preserve the spirit and the form of popular government, is then the great object to which our inquiries are directed. Let me add that it is the great *desideratum*, by which alone this form of government can be rescued from the opprobrium under which it has so long labored, and be recommended to the esteem and adoption of mankind.

By what means is this object attainable?

Evidently by one of two only. Either the existence of the same passion or interest in a majority, at the same time, must be prevented; or the majority, having such coexistent passion or interest, must be rendered, by their number and local situation, unable to concert and carry into effect schemes of oppression. If the impulse and the opportunity be suffered to coincide, we well know that neither moral nor religious motives can be relied on as an adequate control. They are not found to be such on the injustice and violence of individuals, and lose their efficacy in proportion to the number combined together; that is, in proportion as their efficacy becomes needful.

From this view of the subject it may be concluded that a pure democracy, by which I mean a society consisting of a small number of citizens, who assemble and administer the government in person, can admit of no cure for the mischiefs of faction. A common passion or interest will, in almost every case, be felt by a majority of the whole; a communication and concert results from the form of government itself; and there is nothing to check the inducements to sacrifice the weaker party or an obnoxious individual. Hence it is that such democracies have ever been spectacles of turbulence and contention; have ever been found incompatible with personal security, or the rights of property, and have in general been as short in their lives as they have been violent in their deaths. Theoretic politicians, who have patronized this species of government, have erroneously supposed that by reducing mankind to a perfect equality in their political rights, they would at the same time be perfectly equalized and assimilated in their possessions, their opinions, and their passions.

A republic, by which I mean a government in which the scheme of representation takes place, opens a different prospect, and promises the cure for which we are seeking. Let us examine the points in which it varies from pure democracy, and we shall comprehend both the nature of the cure and the efficacy which it must derive from the union.

The two great points of difference between a democracy and a republic are: First, the delegation of the government, in the latter, to a small number of citizens elected by the rest; secondly, the greater number of citizens, and greater sphere of country, over which the latter may be extended.

The effect of the first difference is, on the one hand, to refine and enlarge the public views, by passing them through the medium of a chosen body of citizens, whose wisdom may best discern the true interest of their country, and whose patriotism and love of justice will be least likely to sacrifice it to temporary or partial considerations. Under such a regulation, it may well happen that the public voice, pronounced by the representatives of the people, will be more consonant to the public good than if pronounced by the people themselves, convened for the purpose. On the other hand, the effect may be inverted. Men of factious tempers, of local prejudices, or of sinister designs, may by intrigue, by corruption, or by other means, first obtain the suffrages, and then betray the interests of the people. The question resulting is, whether small or extensive republics are most favorable to the election of proper guardians of the public weal; and it is clearly decided in favor of the latter by two obvious considerations.

In the first place, it is to be remarked that, however small the republic may be, the representatives must be raised to a certain number, in order to guard against the cabals of a few; and that, however large it may be, they must be limited to a certain number, in order to guard against the confusion of a multitude. Hence, the number of representatives in the two cases not being in proportion to that of the constituents, and being proportionally greatest in the small republic, it follows that if the proportion of fit characters be not less in the large than in the small republic, the former will present a greater option, and consequently a greater probability of a fit choice.

In the next place, as each representative will be chosen by a greater number of citizens in the large than in the small republic, it will be more difficult for unworthy candidates to practise with success the vicious arts, by which elections are too often carried; and the suffrages of the people, being more free, will be more likely to centre in men who possess the most attractive merit and the most diffusive and established characters.

It must be confessed that in this as in most other cases, there is a mean, on both sides of which inconveniences will be found to lie. By enlarging too much the number of electors, you render the representative too little acquainted with all their local circumstances and lesser interests; as by reducing it too much, you render him unduly attached to these, and too little fit to comprehend and pursue great and national objects. The federal Constitution forms a happy combination in this respect; the great and aggregate interests being referred to the national, the local and particular to the State, legislatures.

The other point of difference is, the greater number of citizens and extent of territory which may be brought within the compass of republican than of democratic government; and it is this circumstance principally which renders factious combinations less to be dreaded in the former, than in the latter. The smaller the society, the fewer probably will be the distinct parties and interests composing it; the fewer the distinct parties and interests, the more frequently will a majority be found of the same party; and the smaller the number of individuals composing a majority, and the smaller the compass within which they are placed, the more easily will they concert and execute their plans of oppression. Extend the sphere, and you take in a greater variety of parties and interests; you make it less probable that a majority of the whole will have a common motive to invade the rights of other citizens; or if such a common motive exists, it will be more difficult for all who feel it to discover their own strength, and to act in unison with each other. Besides other impediments, it may be remarked that where there is a consciousness of unjust or dishonorable purposes, communication is always checked by distrust, in proportion to the number whose concurrence is necessary.

Hence it clearly appears that the same advantage which a republic has over a democracy, in controlling the effects of faction, is enjoyed by a large over a small republic—is enjoyed by the Union over the States composing it. Does the advantage consist in the substitution of representatives, whose enlightened views and virtuous sentiments render them superior to local prejudices, and to schemes of injustice? It will not be denied that the representation of the Union will be most likely to possess these requisite endowments. Does it consist in the greater security afforded by a greater variety of parties, against the event of any one party being able to outnumber and oppress the rest? In an equal degree does the increased variety of parties, comprised within the Union, increase this security. Does it, in fine, consist in the greater obstacles opposed to the concert and accomplishment of the secret wishes of an unjust and interested majority? Here, again, the extent of the Union gives it the most palpable advantage.

The influence of factious leaders may kindle a flame within their particular States, but will be unable to spread a general conflagration through the other States. A religious sect may degenerate into a political faction in a part of the confederacy; but the variety of sects dispersed over the entire face of it must secure the national councils against any danger from that source. A rage for paper money, for an abolition of debts, for an equal division of property, or for any other improper and wicked project will be less apt to pervade the whole body of the union than a particular member of it; in the same proportion as such a malady is more likely to taint a particular county or district than an entire State.

In the extent and proper structure of the Union, therefore, we behold a republican remedy for the diseases most incident to republican government. And according to the degree of pleasure and pride we feel in being republicans, ought to be our zeal in cherishing the spirit and supporting the character of federalists.

PUBLIUS [Madison]

French National Assembly

In 1789 the Bourbon dynasty in France faced a financial crisis growing out of the excesses of the Old Regime. In a last desperate effort to raise money Louis XVI convened the almost forgotten Estates General, and its meeting provided an opportunity for those leaders bent on reforming the French government. The members of the Third Estate quickly formed a national assembly and began writing a constitution for France. Following the example set by the English in 1689, and the Americans in the 1770's, they drew up, as the first part of the new instrument of government, a bill of rights which is known as The Declaration of the Rights of Man and Citizen. It reflected the essentially middle-class character of the revolution in its early stages in that it stressed laissez-faire principles and property rights. In addition to its influence on the French reform movement, The Declaration of the Rights of Man served as a pattern for liberal constitutions drawn up in other European countries during the nineteenth century. In reading the Declaration, note (1) the authors' motives in issuing the Declaration, (2) their views concerning the primary aims of government, (3) premonitions of nationalism, (4) the evidence of Rousseau's ideas, (5) the freedom claimed for each citizen, (6) the abuses of the Old Regime, (7) the provisions for taxation, (8) the stress placed upon specific laws to regulate each power of government, and (9) the emphasis given to property rights.

DECLARATION OF THE RIGHTS OF MAN AND CITIZEN

The representatives of the French people, organized in National Assembly, considering that ignorance, forgetfulness or contempt of the rights of man are the sole causes of the public miseries and of the corruption of governments, have resolved to set forth in a solemn declaration the natural, inalienable, and sacred rights of man, in order that this declaration, being ever present to all the members of the social body, may unceasingly remind them of their rights and their duties: in order that the acts of the legislative power and those of the executive power may be each moment compared with the aim of every political institution and thereby may be more respected; and in order that the demands of the citizens, grounded henceforth upon simple and incon-testable principles, may always take the direction of maintaining the constitution and the welfare of all.

In consequence, the National Assembly recognizes and declares, in the presence and under the auspices of the Supreme Being, the following rights of man and citizen.

1. Men are born and remain free and equal in rights. Social distinctions can be based only upon public utility.

2. The aim of every political association is the preservation of the natural and impre-scriptible rights of man. These rights are liberty, property, security, and resistance to oppression.

3. The source of all sovereignty is essen-

Frank Maloy Anderson, *The Constitutions and other Select Documents Illustrative of the History of France 1789–1901*, Minneapolis, 1904, 58–60. Courtesy of Frank Maloy Anderson.

tially in the nation; no body, no individual can exercise authority that does not proceed from it in plain terms.

4. Liberty consists in the power to do anything that does not injure others; accordingly, the exercise of the natural rights of each man has for its only limits those that secure to the other members of society the enjoyment of these same rights. These limits can be determined only by law.

5. The law has the right to forbid only such actions as are injurious to society. Nothing can be forbidden that is not interdicted by the law and no one can be constrained to do that which it does not order.

6. Law is the expression of the general will. All citizens have the right to take part personally or by their representatives in its formation. It must be the same for all, whether it protects or punishes. All citizens being equal in its eyes, are equally eligible to all public dignities, places, and employments, according to their capacities, and without other distinction than that of their virtues and their talents.

7. No man can be accused, arrested, or detained except in the cases determined by the law and according to the forms that it has prescribed. Those who procure, expedite, execute, or cause to be executed arbitrary orders ought to be punished: but every citizen summoned or seized in virtue of the law ought to render instant obedience; he makes himself guilty by resistance.

8. The law ought to establish only penalties that are strictly and obviously necessary and no one can be punished except in virtue of a law established and promulgated prior to the offence and legally applied.

9. Every man being presumed innocent until he has been pronounced guilty, if it is thought indispensable to arrest him, all severity that may not be necessary to secure his person ought to be strictly suppressed by law.

10. No one ought to be disturbed on account of his opinions, even religious, provided their manifestation does not derange the public order established by law.

11. The free communication of ideas and opinions is one of the most precious of the rights of man; every citizen then can freely speak, write, and print, subject to responsibility for the abuse of this freedom in the cases determined by law.

12. The guarantee of the rights of man and citizen requires a public force; this force then is instituted for the advantage of all and not for the personal benefit of those to whom it is entrusted.

13. For the maintenance of the public force and for the expenses of administration a general tax is indispensable; it ought to be equally apportioned among all the citizens according to their means.

14. All the citizens have the right to ascertain, by themselves or by their representatives, the necessity of the public tax, to consent to it freely, to follow the employment of it, and to determine the quota, the assessment, the collection, and the duration of it.

15. Society has the right to call for an account from every public agent of its administration.

16. Any society in which the guarantee of the rights is not secured or the separation of powers not determined has no constitution at all.

17. Property being a sacred and inviolable right, no one can be deprived of it unless a legally established public necessity evidently demands it, under the condition of a just and prior indemnity.

Maximilien Robespierre

In 1792 the French Revolution entered a second and more radical stage. The lower classes rather than the bourgeoisie came to dominate the government, and a republic replaced the limited monarchy. Violence became the order of the day, and the lives of those who opposed radicalism were in constant danger. A national convention was elected to draft a new constitution for France. This body completed its task, but the results were never put into operation because of the disorder and violence. Maximilien Robespierre (1758–1794) was a leader of the radical movement and a member of the convention. In 1793 he presented a draft of the Proposed Declaration of Rights for the republican constitution. It was not adopted, but its clauses revealed some of the rational ideals held by its author, and which he put into effect as president of the national convention. In reading the document, note (1) the contrast between Robespierre's objectives and those of the 1789 Declaration, (2) the purpose Robespierre ascribes to governments, (3) his definition of liberty in contrast to that of the 1789 Declaration, (4) his definition of property and the restrictions he would impose upon its owners, (5) evidence of Robespierre's ideas of social security and social justice, (6) his views on taxation, (7) influences of Rousseau on Robespierre, (8) Robespierre's position respecting insurrection and revolution, and (9) his attitudes towards the peoples and rulers of other nations.

PROPOSED DECLARATION OF RIGHTS

The representatives of the French people, met in National Convention, recognizing that human laws which do not flow from the eternal laws of justice and reason are only the outrages of ignorance and despotism upon humanity; convinced that neglect and contempt of the natural rights of man are the sole causes of the crimes and misfortunes of the world; have resolved to set forth in a solemn declaration these sacred and inalienable rights, in order that all citizens, being enabled to compare constantly the acts of the government with the purpose of every social institution, may never permit themselves to be oppressed and disgraced by tyranny; and in order that the people may always have before their eyes the foundations of their liberty and their welfare; the magistrate, the rule of his duties; the legislator, the purpose of his mission.

In consequence, the National Convention proclaims in the face of the world and under the eyes of the Immortal Legislator the following declaration of the rights of man and citizen.

1. The purpose of every political association is the maintenance of the natural and imprescriptible rights of man and the development of all his faculties.

2. The principal rights of man are those of providing for the preservation of his existence and his liberty.

3. These rights belong equally to all men, whatever may be the difference of their physical and mental powers.

4. Equality of rights is established by nature: society, far from impairing it, exists only to guarantee it against the abuse of power which renders it illusory.

5. Liberty is the power which belongs to man to exercise at his will all his faculties; it has justice for rule, the rights of others for limits, nature for principle, and the law for safeguard.

6. The right to assemble peaceably, the right to express one's opinions, either by means of the press or in any other manner, are such necessary consequences of the principle of the liberty of man, that the necessity to enunciate them supposes either the presence or the fresh recollection of despotism.

7. The law can forbid only that which is injurious to society; it can order only that which is useful.

8. Every law which violates the imprescriptible rights of man is essentially unjust and tyrannical; it is not a law.

Frank Maloy Anderson, *The Constitutions and other Select Documents Illustrative of the History of France 1789–1901*, Minneapolis, 1904, 160–164. Courtesy of Frank Maloy Anderson.

9. Property is the right which each citizen has, to enjoy and dispose of the portion of goods which the law guarantees to him.

10. The right of property is restricted, as are all the others, by the obligation to respect the possessions of others.

11. It cannot prejudice the security, nor the liberty, nor the existence, nor the property of our fellow creatures.

12. All traffic which violates this principle is essentially illicit and immoral.

13. Society is under obligation to provide for the support of all its members either by procuring work for them or by assuring the means of existence to those who are not in condition to work.

14. The relief indispensable for those who lack the necessities of life is a debt of those who possess a superfluity; it belongs to the law to determine the manner in which this debt must be discharged.

15. The citizens whose incomes do not exceed what is necessary for their subsistence are exempted from contributing to the public expenses; the others shall support them progressively, according to the extent of their fortunes.

16. Society ought to favor with all its power the progress of public reason and to put instruction at the door of all the citizens.

17. Law is the free and solemn expression of the will of the people.

18. The people are the sovereign, the government is their creation, the public functionaries are their agents; the people can, when they please, change their government and recall their mandatories.

19. No portion of the people can exercise the power of the entire people; but the opinion which it expresses shall be respected as the opinion of a portion of the people who ought to participate in the formation of the general will. Each section of the assembled sovereign ought to enjoy the right to express its will with entire liberty; it is essentially independent of all the constituted authorities and is capable of regulating its police and its deliberations.

20. The law ought to be equal for all.

21. All citizens are admissible to all public offices, without any other distinctions than those of their virtues and talents and without any other title than the confidence of the people.

22. All citizens have an equal right to participate in the selection of the mandatories of the people and in the formation of the law.

23. In order that these rights may not be illusory and the equality chimerical, society ought to give salaries to the public functionaries and to provide so that all the citizens who live by their labor can be present in the public assemblies to which the law calls them, without compromising their existence or that of their families.

24. Every citizen ought to obey religiously the magistrates and the agents of the government, when they are the organs or the executors of the law.

25. But every act against the liberty, security, or property of a man, committed by anyone whomsoever, even in the name of the law outside of the cases determined by it and the forms which it prescribes, is arbitrary and void; respect for the law even forbids submission to it; and if an attempt is made to execute it by violence, it is permissible to repel it by force.

26. The right to present petitions to the depositories of the public authority belongs to every person. Those to whom they are addressed ought to pass upon the points which are the object thereof; but they can never interdict, nor restrain, nor condemn their use.

27. Resistance to oppression is a consequence of the other rights of man and citizen.

28. There is oppression against the social body when one of its members is oppressed. There is oppression against each member of the social body when the social body shall be oppressed.

29. When the government violates the rights of the people, insurrection is for the people and for each portion of the people the most sacred of rights and the most indispensable of duties.

30. When the social guarantee is lacking to a citizen he re-enters into the natural right to defend all his rights himself.

31. In either case, to tie down to legal forms resistance to oppression is the last refinement of tyranny. In every free State the law ought especially to defend public and personal liberty against the abuse of the authority of those who govern: every institution which is not based upon the assumption that the people

are good and the magistrate is corruptible is vicious.

32. The public offices cannot be considered as distinctions, nor as rewards, but only as duties.

33. The offences of the mandatories of the people ought to be severely and quickly punished. No one has the right to claim for himself more inviolability than other citizens. The people have the right to know all the transactions of their mandatories: these ought to render to them a faithful account of their own administration and to submit to their judgment with respect.

34. Men of all countries are brothers and

the different peoples ought to aid one another, according to their power, as if citizens of the same State.

35. The one who oppresses a single nation declares himself the enemy of all.

36. Those who make war on a people in order to arrest the progress of liberty and to destroy the rights of man ought to be pursued by all, not as ordinary enemies, but as assassins and rebellious brigands.

37. Kings, aristocrats, and tyrants, whoever they may be, are slaves in rebellion against the sovereign of the earth, which is mankind, and against the legislator of the universe, which is nature.

Napoleon Bonaparte

In 1795 the French Revolution entered a reactionary third phase, during which a small group known as the Directory largely controlled the government. Its rule was characterized by four years of corruption and greed, and a general neglect of the reforms enacted in the earlier stages. The masses suffered untold hardships, and everywhere there was despair and disillusion. Meanwhile, Napoleon Bonaparte (1769–1821) had been leading French troops to victory over the coalitions formed by the monarchs of Europe to check the revolution. To most Frenchmen Napoleon seemed to be the only person who could restore order at home and win victory abroad. Only the extreme Jacobin radicals remained unfriendly, but their opposition was not sufficient to prevent him from staging a coup d'état at St. Cloud in November, 1799. The two councils (Elders and Five Hundred) quickly granted the executive power to Napoleon and two others, and the revolution was over. On the following day Napoleon issued a proclamation, explaining his part in the affair. It was typical of the arguments generally advanced by dictators and should be read in order to understand (1) the situation Napoleon found when he returned to France, (2) the reason why he guarded the Council of Elders, (3) the acts he performed in the Council of Elders and the Council of Five Hundred, (4) the position he claimed for himself in regard to the law and the councils, (5) his characterization of those who used force to outlaw him, and (6) his closing profession of zeal for liberty and the republic.

James Harvey Robinson and Charles A. Beard, *Readings in Modern European History* . . . , 2 vols., Ginn and Company, Boston, 1908, I, 322–323. Courtesy of Ginn and Company.

PROCLAMATION 19TH BRUMAIRE

PROCLAMATION

19th Brumaire, 11 o'clock P.M.

To the People:

Frenchmen, on my return to France I found division reigning among all the authorities. They agreed only on this single point, that the constitution was half destroyed and was unable to protect liberty.

Each party in turn came to me, confided to me their designs, imparted their secrets, and requested my support. But I refused to be the man of any party.

The Council of Elders appealed to me. I answered their appeal. A plan of general restoration had been conspired at by men whom the nation has been accustomed to regard as the defenders of liberty, equality, and property. This plan required calm deliberation, free from all influence and all fear. The Elders therefore resolved upon the removal of the legislative bodies to St. Cloud. They placed at my disposal the force necessary to secure their independence. I was bound, in duty to my fellow-citizens, to the soldiers perishing in our armies, and to the national glory acquired at the cost of so much blood, to accept the command.

The Council assembled at St. Cloud. Republican troops guaranteed their safety from without, but assassins created terror within. Many deputies in the Council of Five Hundred, armed with stilettos and pistols, spread the menace of death around them.

The plans which ought to have been developed were withheld. The majority of the Council was disorganized, the boldest orators were disconcerted, and the futility of submitting any salutary proposition was quite evident.

I proceeded, filled with indignation and chagrin, to the Council of the Elders. I besought them to carry their noble designs into execution. I directed their attention to the evils of the nation, which were their motives for conceiving those designs. They concurred in giving me new proofs of their unanimous good will.

I presented myself before the Council of the Five Hundred alone, unarmed, my head uncovered, just as the Elders had received and applauded me. My object was to restore to the majority the expression of its will and to secure to it its power.

The stilettos which had menaced the deputies were instantly raised against their deliverer. Twenty assassins rushed upon me and aimed at my breast. The grenadiers of the legislative body, whom I had left at the door of the hall, ran forward and placed themselves between me and the assassins. One of these brave grenadiers had his clothes pierced by a stiletto. They bore me out.

At the same moment cries of "Outlaw him!" were raised against the defender of the law. It was the horrid cry of assassins against the power destined to repress them. They crowded around the president, uttering threats. With arms in their hands, they commanded him to declare me outlawed. I was informed of this. I ordered him to be rescued from their fury, and six grenadiers of the legislative body brought him out. Immediately afterwards some grenadiers of the legislative body charged the hall and cleared it.

The seditious, thus intimidated, dispersed and fled. The majority, freed from their assailants, returned freely and peaceably into the hall, listened to the propositions for the public safety, deliberated, and drew up the salutary resolution which will become the new and provisional law of the republic.

Frenchmen, you will doubtless recognize in this conduct the zeal of a soldier of liberty, of a citizen devoted to the republic. Conservative, judicial, and liberal ideas resumed their sway upon the dispersion of those seditious persons who had domineered in the councils and who proved themselves the most odious and contemptible of men.

BONAPARTE

Edmund Burke

Edmund Burke (1729–1797) was an English intellectual and politician who was deeply concerned with some of the political theories produced by the Age of the Enlightenment. He did not adhere to the view that reason could construct a new and better society, nor did he accept Rousseau's view of popular sovereignty. He also looked with apprehension upon Locke's social contract with its implication that society could form governments and destroy them. Burke maintained that society was an organic whole, experiencing gradual growth, and that sudden, violent change was detrimental and might even destroy it. Thus Burke was reverting back to the medieval Christian concept of society and was attempting to conserve for England those ideals of government and of liberty which had been the product of historical growth. To him the French Revolution was a catastrophe from which he wished to spare England. He wrote his Reflections on the Revolution in France in 1790 as a warning to his countrymen, some of whom were expressing sympathy with the events occurring across the channel. He approached the problem on the philosophical level, and his calm, clear analysis not only accomplished Burke's immediate purpose, but it has persisted as one of the best defenses of conservatism ever written. The Reflections were written in the form of a correspondence to a resident of Paris, a fact which helps to explain the terminology. In reading the following excerpts from this work note (1) the immediate incident motivating Burke to write this essay, (2) his answer to the assertion that the English king was chosen by the people, (3) the appeal to history to illustrate the evolution of the English constitution, (4) the reasons he gave why governments could not be constructed à priori, (5) the colorful passage in which he ridiculed the extreme emphasis of the reformers on the use of reason and the rights of man, (6) the criticism of the French intellectuals and politicians who condemned all that was old and admired anything new, (7) his answer to the French assertion that they were following the English example, (8) the attitude he recommended for all reformers when considering the defects of government, and (9) Burke's interpretation of society as a contract.

From: REFLECTIONS ON THE REVOLUTION IN FRANCE

On the forenoon of the 4th of November last, Doctor Richard Price, a non-conforming minister of eminence, preached at the dissenting meeting-house of the Old Jewry, to his club or society, a very extraordinary miscellaneous sermon, in which there are some good

Edmund Burke, *Reflections on the Revolution in France*, 3 vols., New York, 1836, I, 459–461; 469–470; 482; 493–494.

moral and religious sentiments, and not ill expressed, mixed up in a sort of porridge of various political opinions and reflections; but the Revolution in France is the grand ingredient in the cauldron. I consider the address transmitted by the Revolution Society to the National Assembly, through Earl Stanhope, as originating in the principles of the sermon, and as a corollary from them. It was moved by the preacher of that discourse. It was passed by those who came reeking from the effect of the sermon, without any censure or qualification, expressed or implied. If, however, any of the gentlemen concerned shall wish to separate the sermon from the resolution, they know how to acknowledge the one, and to disavow the other. They may do it: I cannot.

For my part, I looked on that sermon as the public declaration of a man much connected with literary caballers, and intriguing philosophers; with political theologians, and theological politicians, both at home and abroad. I know they set him up as a sort of oracle; because, with the best intentions in the world, he naturally *philippizes,* and chants his prophetic song in exact unison with their designs. . . .

He tells the Revolution Society in this political sermon, that his Majesty "is almost the *only* lawful king in the world, because the *only* one who owes his crown to the *choice of his people.*" As to the kings of *the world,* all of whom (except one) this archpontiff of the *rights of men,* with all the plenitude, and with more than the boldness, of the papal deposing power in its meridian fervour of the twelfth century, puts into one sweeping clause of ban and anathema, and proclaims usurpers by circles of longitude and latitude, over the whole globe, it behoves them to consider how they admit into their territories these apostolic missionaries, who are to tell their subjects they are not lawful kings. That is their concern. It is ours, as a domestic interest of some moment, seriously to consider the solidity of the *only* principle upon which these gentlemen acknowledge a king of Great Britain to be entitled to their allegiance.

This doctrine, as applied to the prince now on the British throne, either is nonsense, and therefore neither true nor false, or it affirms a most unfounded, dangerous, illegal, and unconstitutional position. According to this spiritual doctor of politics, if his Majesty does not owe his crown to the choice of his people, he is no *lawful king.* Now nothing can be more untrue than that the crown of this kingdom is so held by his Majesty. Therefore if you follow their rule, the king of Great Britain, who most certainly does not owe his high office to any form of popular election, is in no respect better than the rest of the gang of usurpers, who reign, or rather rob, all over the face of this our miserable world, without any sort of right or title to the allegiance of their people. The policy of this general doctrine, so qualified, is evident enough. The propagators of this political gospel are in hopes that their abstract principle (their principle that a popular choice is necessary to the legal existence of the sovereign magistracy) would be overlooked, whilst the king of Great Britain was not affected by it. In the mean time the ears of their congregations would be gradually habituated to it, as if it were a first principle admitted without dispute. For the present it would only operate as a theory, pickled in the preserving juices of pulpit eloquence, and laid by for future use. *Condo et compono quae mox depromere possim.* By this policy, whilst our government is soothed with a reservation in its favour, to which it has no claim, the security, which it has in common with all governments, so far as opinion is security, is taken away.

Thus these politicians proceed, whilst little notice is taken of their doctrines; but when they come to be examined upon the plain meaning of their words, and the direct tendency of their doctrines, then equivocations and slippery constructions come into play. When they say the king owes his crown to the choice of his people, and is therefore the only lawful sovereign in the world, they will perhaps tell us they mean to say no more than that some of the king's predecessors have been called to the throne by some sort of choice; and therefore he owes his crown to the choice of his people. Thus, by a miserable subterfuge, they hope to render their proposition safe, by rendering it nugatory. They are welcome to the asylum they seek for their offence, since they take refuge in their folly. For, if you admit this interpretation, how does their idea of election differ from our idea of inheritance? And how does the settlement of the crown in the Brunswick line derived from James the First come to legalize our monarchy, rather than that of any of the neighbouring countries? At some time or other, to be sure, all the beginners of dynasties were chosen by those who called them to govern. There is ground enough for the opinion that all the kingdoms of Europe were, at a remote period, elective, with more or fewer limitations in the objects of choice. But whatever kings might have been here, or elsewhere, a thousand years ago, or in whatever manner the ruling dynasties of England or France may have begun, the king of Great Britain is, at this day, king by a fixed rule of succession, according to the laws of his country; and whilst the legal conditions of the compact of sovereignty are performed by him (as they are performed), he holds his crown in contempt of the choice of the Revolution Society, who have not a single vote for a king amongst them, either individually or collectively; though I make no doubt they would soon erect themselves into an electoral college, if things were ripe to give effect to their claim. His Majesty's heirs and successors, each in his time and order, will come to the crown with the same contempt of their choice with which his Majesty has succeeded to that he wears. . . .

You will observe, that from Magna Charta to the Declaration of Right, it has been the uniform policy of our constitution to claim and assert our liberties, as an *entailed inheritance* derived to us from our forefathers, and to be transmitted to our posterity; as an estate specially belonging to the people of this kingdom, without any reference whatever to any other more general or prior right. By this means our constitution preserves a unity in so great a diversity of its parts. We have an inheritable crown; an inheritable peerage; and a House of Commons and a people inheriting privileges, franchises, and liberties, from a long line of ancestors.

This policy appears to me to be the result of profound reflection; or rather the happy effect of following nature, which is wisdom without reflection, and above it. A spirit of innovation is generally the result of a selfish temper and confined views. People will not look forward to posterity, who never look backward to their ancestors. Besides, the people of England well know, that the idea of inheritance furnishes a sure principle of conservation and a sure principle of transmission; without at all excluding a principle of improvement. It leaves acquisition free; but it secures what it acquires. Whatever advantages are obtained by a state proceeding on these maxims, are locked fast as in a sort of family settlement; grasped as in a kind of mortmain for ever. By a constitutional policy, working after the pattern of nature, we receive, we hold, we transmit our government and our privileges, in the same manner in which we enjoy and transmit our property and our lives. The institutions of policy, the goods of fortune, the gifts of providence, are handed down to us, and from us, in the same course and order. Our political system is placed in a just correspondence and symmetry with the order of the world, and with the mode of existence decreed to a permanent body composed of transitory parts; wherein, by the disposition of a stupendous wisdom, moulding together the great mysterious incorporation of the human race, the whole, at one time, is never old, or middle-aged, or young, but, in a condition of unchangeable constancy, moves on through the varied tenor of perpetual decay, fall, renovation, and progression. Thus, by preserving the method of nature in the conduct of the state, in what we improve, we are never wholly new; in what we retain, we are never wholly obsolete. By adhering in this manner and on those principles to our forefathers, we are guided not by the superstition of antiquarians, but by the spirit of philosophic analogy. In this choice of inheritance we have given to our frame of polity the image of a relation in blood; binding up the constitution of our country with our dearest domestic ties; adopting our fundamental laws into the bosom of our family affections; keeping inseparable, and cherishing with the warmth of all their combined and mutually reflected charities, our state, our hearths, our sepulchres, and our altars. . . .

The science of constructing a commonwealth, or renovating it, or reforming it, is, like every other experimental science, not to be taught *à priori*. Nor is it a short experience that can instruct us in that practical science; because the real effects of moral causes are not always immediate; but that which in the first instance is prejudicial may be excellent in its remoter operation; and its excellence may arise even from the ill effects it produces in the beginning. The reverse also happens: and very plausible schemes, with very pleasing commencements, have often shameful and lamentable conclusions. In states there are often some obscure and almost latent causes, things which appear at first view of little moment, on which a very great part of its prosperity or adversity may most essentially depend. The science of government being therefore so practical in itself, and intended for such practical purposes, a matter which requires experience, and even more experience than any person can gain in his whole life, however sagacious and observing he may be, it is with infinite caution that any man ought to venture upon pulling down an edifice, which has answered in any tolerable degree for ages the common purposes of society, or on building it up again, without having models and patterns of approved utility before his eyes. . . .

Thanks to our sullen resistance to innovation, thanks to the cold sluggishness of our national character, we still bear the stamp of our forefathers. We have not (as I conceive) lost the generosity and dignity of thinking of the fourteenth century; nor as yet have we subtilized ourselves into savages. We are not the converts of Rousseau; we are not the disciples of Voltaire; Helvetius has made no progress amongst us. Atheists are not our preachers; madmen are not our lawgivers. We know that *we* have made no discoveries, and we think that no discoveries are to be made, in morality; nor many in the great principles of government, nor in the ideas of liberty, which were understood long before we were born, altogether as well as they will be after the grave has heaped its mould upon our presumption, and the silent tomb shall have imposed its law on our pert loquacity. In England we have not yet been completely embowelled of our natural entrails; we still feel within us, and we cherish and cultivate, those inbred sentiments which are the faithful guardians, the active monitors of our duty, the true supporters of all liberal and manly morals. We have not been drawn and trussed, in order that

we may be filled, like stuffed birds in a museum, with chaff and rags and paltry blurred shreds of paper about the rights of man. We preserve the whole of our feelings still native and entire, unsophisticated by pedantry and infidelity. We have real hearts of flesh and blood beating in our bosoms. We fear God; we look up with awe to kings; with affection to parliaments; with duty to magistrates; with reverence to priests; with respect to nobility. Why? Because when such ideas are brought before our minds, it is *natural* to be so affected; because all other feelings are false and spurious, and tend to corrupt our minds, to vitiate our primary morals, to render us unfit for rational liberty; and by teaching us a servile, licentious, and abandoned insolence, to be our low sport for a few holidays, to make us perfectly fit for, and justly deserving of, slavery, through the whole course of our lives.

You see, Sir, that in this enlightened age I am bold enough to confess, that we are generally men of untaught feelings; that instead of casting away all our old prejudices, we cherish them to a very considerable degree, and, to take more shame to ourselves, we cherish them because they are prejudices; and the longer they have lasted, and the more generally they have prevailed, the more we cherish them. We are afraid to put men to live and trade each on his own private stock of reason; because we suspect that this stock in each man is small, and that the individuals would do better to avail themselves of the general bank and capital of nations and of ages. Many of our men of speculation, instead of exploding general prejudices, employ their sagacity to discover the latent wisdom which prevails in them. If they find what they seek, and they seldom fail, they think it more wise to continue the prejudice, with the reason involved, than to cast away the coat of prejudice, and to leave nothing but the naked reason; because prejudice, with its reason, has a motive to give action to that reason, and an affection which will give it permanence. Prejudice is of ready application in the emergency; it previously engages the mind in a steady course of wisdom and virtue, and does not leave the man hesitating in the moment of decision, sceptical, puzzled, and unresolved. Prejudice renders a man's virtue his habit; and not a series of unconnected acts. Through just prejudice, his duty becomes a part of his nature.

Your literary men, and your politicians, and so do the whole clan of the enlightened among us, essentially differ in these points. They have no respect for the wisdom of others; but they pay it off by a very full measure of confidence in their own. With them it is a sufficient motive to destroy an old scheme of things, because it is an old one. As to the new, they are in no sort of fear with regard to the duration of a building run up in haste; because duration is no object to those who think little or nothing has been done before their time, and who place all their hopes in discovery. They conceive, very systematically, that all things which give perpetuity are mischievous, and therefore they are at inexpiable war with all establishments. They think that government may vary like modes of dress, and with as little ill effect: that there needs no principle of attachment, except a sense of present conveniency, to any constitution of the state. They always speak as if they were of opinion that there is a singular species of compact between them and their magistrates, which binds the magistrate, but which has nothing reciprocal in it, but that the majesty of the people has a right to dissolve it without any reason, but its will. Their attachment to their country itself is only so far as it agrees with some of their fleeting projects; it begins and ends with that scheme of polity which falls in with their momentary opinion.

These doctrines, or rather sentiments, seem prevalent with your new statesmen. But they are wholly different from those on which we have always acted in this country.

I hear it is sometimes given out in France, that what is doing among you is after the example of England. I beg leave to affirm, that scarcely anything done with you has originated from the practice or the prevalent opinions of this people, either in the act or in the spirit of the proceeding. Let me add, that we are as unwilling to learn these lessons from France, as we are sure that we never taught them to that nation. The cabals here, who take a sort of share in your transactions, as yet consist of but a handful of people. If unfortunately by their intrigues, their sermons, their publica-

tions, and by a confidence derived from an expected union with the counsels and forces of the French nation, they should draw considerable numbers into their faction, and in consequence should seriously attempt anything here in imitation of what has been done with you, the event, I dare venture to prophesy, will be, that, with some trouble to their country, they will soon accomplish their own destruction. This people refused to change their law in remote ages from respect to the infallibility of popes; and they will not now alter it from a pious implicit faith in the dogmatism of philosophers; though the former was armed with the anathema and crusade, and though the latter should act with the libel and the lamp-iron.

Formerly your affairs were your own concern only. We felt for them as men; but we kept aloof from them, because we were not citizens of France. But when we see the model held up to ourselves, we must feel as Englishmen, and feeling, we must provide as Englishmen. Your affairs, in spite of us, are made a part of our interest; so far at least as to keep at a distance your panacea, or your plague. If it be a panacea, we do not want it. We know the consequences of unnecessary physic. If it be a plague, it is such a plague that the precautions of the most severe quarantine ought to be established against it. . . .

To avoid therefore the evils of inconstancy and versatility, ten thousand times worse than those of obstinacy and the blindest prejudice, we have consecrated the state, that no man should approach to look into its defects or corruptions but with due caution; that he should never dream of beginning its reformation by its subversion; that he should approach to the faults of the state as to the wounds of a father, with pious awe and trembling solicitude. By this wise prejudice we are taught to look with horror on those children of their country, who are prompt rashly to hack that aged parent in pieces, and put him into the kettle of magicians, in hopes that by their poisonous weeds, and wild incantations, they may regenerate the paternal constitution, and renovate their father's life.

Society is indeed a contract. Subordinate contracts for objects of mere occasional interest may be dissolved at pleasure—but the state ought not to be considered as nothing better than a partnership agreement in a trade of pepper and coffee, calico or tobacco, or some other such low concern, to be taken up for a little temporary interest, and to be dissolved by the fancy of the parties. It is to be looked on with other reverence; because it is not a partnership in things subservient only to the gross animal existence of a temporary and perishable nature. It is a partnership in all science; a partnership in all art; a partnership in every virtue, and in all perfection. As the ends of such a partnership cannot be obtained in many generations, it becomes a partnership not only between those who are living, but between those who are living, those who are dead, and those who are to be born. Each contract of each particular state is but a clause in the great primaeval contract of eternal society, linking the lower with the higher natures, connecting the visible and invisible world, according to a fixed compact sanctioned by the inviolable oath which holds all physical and all moral natures, each in their appointed place. This law is not subject to the will of those, who by an obligation above them, and infinitely superior, are bound to submit their will to that law. The municipal corporations of that universal kingdom are not morally at liberty at their pleasure, and on their speculations of a contingent improvement, wholly to separate and tear asunder the bands of their subordinate community, and to dissolve it into an unsocial, uncivil, unconnected chaos of elementary principles. It is the first and supreme necessity only, a necessity that is not chosen, but chooses, a necessity paramount to deliberation, that admits no discussion, and demands no evidence, which alone can justify a resort to anarchy. This necessity is no exception to the rule; because this necessity itself is a part too of that moral and physical disposition of things, to which man must be obedient by consent or force: but if that which is only submission to necessity should be made the object of choice, the law is broken, nature is disobeyed, and the rebellious are outlawed, cast forth, and exiled, from this world of reason, and order, and peace, and virtue, and fruitful penitence, into the antagonist world of madness, discord, vice, confusion, and unavailing sorrow. . . .

William Wordsworth

William Wordsworth (1770–1850) was an English poet who lived his early years in a world shaken by the French Revolution, and reached maturity during the conservative reaction to that epoch-making event. In the realm of culture he was familiar as a young man with the last period of the Enlightenment and its emphasis on nature and natural law; but he wrote some of his best known works in the decades when the romantic movement was emerging as a protest against the extremes of the Age of Reason. In his poetry he reflected some of the interest of the leaders of the Enlightenment in nature, but to Wordsworth nature was more than a source of law—it was a manifestation of the all-pervading spirit which unites all mankind. Thus by communing with the beauties of the natural world one could become aware of the universal brotherhood of man and the true meaning of life. It was this mystical idealization of nature that gave to Wordsworth's poetry its romantic character. The two following selections were written by him in 1798. "The Tables Turned" reflected his interest in nature as a source of inspiration for the guidance of men, while in "We Are Seven" he has

given us in the form of the maiden's devotion to her family
an indication of the unity of all life. In reading the first
selection note (1) Wordsworth's attitude toward the study
of books, (2) the role he assigned to nature, (3) his com-
parison of the relative value of impulses and the teaching
of the learned, (4) the effect intellect has on the beauties
of nature, and (5) the part played by the heart in under-
standing nature. In "We Are Seven" note (1) the descrip-
tion of the child, (2) her simple response to the writer's
query, (3) the argument that developed between them,
(4) the child's devotion to the two in the church-yard,
(5) the spiritual unity of her family, and (6) the beautiful
simplicity of Wordsworth's lines.

THE TABLES TURNED and WE ARE SEVEN

THE TABLES TURNED

An Evening Scene . . . [Alfoxden, 1798?].

Up, up! my Friend, and quit your books;
Or surely you'll grow double:
Up, up! my Friend, and clear your looks;
Why all this toil and trouble?

The sun, above the mountain's head,
A freshening lustre mellow
Through all the long green fields has spread,
His first sweet evening yellow.

Books! 'tis a dull and endless strife:
Come, hear the woodland linnet,
How sweet his music! on my life,
There's more of wisdom in it.

And hark! how blithe the throstle sings!
He, too, is no mean preacher:
Come forth into the light of things,
Let Nature be your teacher.

She has a world of ready wealth,
Our minds and hearts to bless—
Spontaneous wisdom breathed by health,
Truth breathed by cheerfulness.

One impulse from a vernal wood
May teach you more of man,
Of moral evil and of good,
Than all the sages can.

Sweet is the lore which Nature brings;
Our meddling intellect
Mis-shapes the beauteous forms of things:—
We murder to dissect.

Enough of Science and of Art;
Close up those barren leaves;
Come forth, and bring with you a heart
That watches and receives.

WE ARE SEVEN

—A simple Child,
That lightly draws its breath,
And feels its life in every limb,
What should it know of death?

I met a little cottage Girl:
She was eight years old, she said;
Her hair was thick with many a curl
That clustered round her head.

She had a rustic, woodland air,
And she was wildly clad:
Her eyes were fair, and very fair;
—Her beauty made me glad.

"Sisters and brothers, little Maid,
How many may you be?"
"How many? Seven in all," she said,
And wondering looked at me.

Ernest Rhys, ed., *The Lyric Poems of William Wordsworth*, London, n.d., 119–120; 126–129.

"And where are they? I pray you tell."
She answered, "Seven are we;
And two of us at Conway dwell,
And two are gone to sea.

"Two of us in the church-yard lie,
My sister and my brother;
And, in the church-yard cottage, I
Dwell near them with my mother."

"You say that two at Conway dwell,
And two are gone to sea,
Yet ye are seven!—I pray you tell,
Sweet Maid, how this may be."

Then did the little Maid reply,
"Seven boys and girls are we;
Two of us in the church-yard lie,
Beneath the church-yard tree."

"You run about, my little Maid,
Your limbs they are alive;
If two are in the church-yard laid,
Then ye are only five."

"Their graves are green, they may be seen,"
The little Maid replied,
"Twelve steps or more from my mother's door,
And they are side by side.

"My stockings there I often knit,
My kerchief there I hem;

And there upon the ground I sit,
And sing a song to them.

"And often after sunset, Sir,
When it is light and fair,
I take my little porringer,
And eat my supper there.

"The first that died was sister Jane;
In bed she moaning lay,
Till God released her of her pain;
And then she went away.

"So in the church-yard she was laid;
And, when the grass was dry,
Together round her grave we played,
My brother John and I.

"And when the ground was white with snow,
And I could run and slide,
My brother John was forced to go,
And he lies by her side."

"How many are you, then," said I,
"If they two are in heaven?"
Quick was the little Maid's reply,
"O Master! we are seven."

"But they are dead; those two are dead!
Their spirits are in heaven!"
'Twas throwing words away; for still
The little Maid would have her will,
And said, "Nay, we are seven!"

Thomas Malthus

Thomas Robert Malthus (1766–1834) was a clergyman and professor of history and political economy at Haileybury College, near London. He became interested in the doctrine of human perfectibility through his reading of William Godwin and J. A. N. Condorcet. Malthus, who lived his mature life during the period of the romantic reaction against the Age of Reason, rejected the belief in man's ability indefinitely to extend the world's food supply and refused to abandon a morality that would operate to control population growth. As a counter to the easy optimistic notion of human perfectibility, Malthus proposed the idea that man endured the conflict with evil and that this conflict enobled the race. He first published his study in 1798, later republishing it several times. The selection given here is chapter one taken from the first edition. In it

> Malthus presented a succinct account of his leading princi-
> ples. In reading it note (1) Malthus's statement of the
> great issue confronting men, (2) his description of the po-
> sition of the two advocates in the contest and the limita-
> tions under which each suffered, (3) the two postulates he
> advanced, (4) his treatment of the argument of the opposi-
> tion, (5) the ratios of increase of population and food sup-
> ply, (6) the new problem involved in the inequality of the
> two powers, (7) the implication for population control,
> (8) his description of the law of nature respecting popula-
> tion and production, and of its consequences, and (9) his
> conclusions.

From: AN ESSAY ON POPULATION

OUTLINE OF THE PRINCIPAL ARGUMENT OF THE ESSAY

The great and unlooked for discoveries that have taken place of late years in natural philosophy; the increasing diffusion of general knowledge from the extension of the art of printing; the ardent and unshackled spirit of inquiry that prevails throughout the lettered, and even unlettered, world; the new and extraordinary lights that have been thrown on political subjects, which dazzle and astonish the understanding; and particularly that tremendous phenomenon in the political horizon, the French Revolution, which, like a blazing comet, seems destined either to inspire with fresh life and vigour, or to scorch up and destroy the thinking inhabitants of the earth, have all concurred to lead able men into the opinion, that we are touching upon a period big with the most important changes, changes that would in some measure be decisive of the future fate of mankind.

It has been said, that the great question is now at issue, whether man shall henceforth start forwards with accelerated velocity towards illimitable, and hitherto unconceived improvement; or be condemned to a perpetual oscillation between happiness and misery, and after every effort remain still at an immeasurable distance from the wished-for goal.

Yet, anxiously as every friend of mankind must look forwards to the termination of this painful suspense; and, eagerly as the inquiring mind would hail every ray of light that might assist its view into futurity, it is much to be lamented, that the writers on each side of this momentous question still keep far aloof from each other. Their mutual arguments do not meet with a candid examination. The question is not brought to rest on fewer points; and even in theory scarcely seems to be approaching to a decision.

The advocate for the present order of things, is apt to treat the sect of speculative philosophers, either as a set of artful and designing knaves, who preach up ardent benevolence, and draw captivating pictures of a happier state of society, only the better to enable them to destroy the present establishments, and to forward their own deep-laid schemes of ambition: or, as wild and mad-headed enthusiasts, whose silly speculations, and absurd paradoxes, are not worthy the attention of any reasonable man.

The advocate for the perfectibility of man, and of society, retorts on the defender of establishments a more than equal contempt. He brands him as the slave of the most miserable and narrow prejudices; or, as the defender of the abuses of civil society, only because he profits by them. He paints him either as a character who prostitutes his understanding to his interest; or as one whose powers of mind are not of a size to grasp anything great and noble; who cannot see above five yards before him;

Thomas Robert Malthus, *An Essay on the Principles of Population as it Affects the Future Improvement of Society* . . . , London, 1798, chapter 1.

and who must therefore be utterly unable to take in the views of the enlightened benefactor of mankind.

In this unamicable contest, the cause of truth cannot but suffer. The really good arguments on each side of the question are not allowed to have their proper weight. Each pursues his own theory, little solicitous to correct, or improve it, by an attention to what is advanced by his opponents.

The friend of the present order of things condemns all political speculations in the gross. He will not even condescend to examine the grounds from which the perfectibility of society is inferred. Much less will he give himself the trouble in a fair and candid manner to attempt an exposition of their fallacy.

The speculative philosopher equally offends against the cause of truth. With eyes fixed on a happier state of society, the blessings of which he paints in the most captivating colours, he allows himself to indulge in the most bitter invectives against every present establishment, without applying his talents to consider the best and safest means of removing abuses, and without seeming to be aware of the tremendous obstacles that threaten, even in theory, to oppose the progress of man towards perfection.

It is an acknowledged truth in philosophy, that a just theory will always be confirmed by experiment. Yet so much friction, and so many minute circumstances occur in practice, which it is next to impossible for the most enlarged and penetrating mind to foresee, that on few subjects can any theory be pronounced just, that has not stood the test of experience. But an untried theory cannot be advanced as probable, much less as just, till all the arguments against it have been maturely weighed, and clearly and consistently confuted.

I have read some of the speculations on the perfectibility of man and of society with great pleasure. I have been warmed and delighted with the enchanting picture which they hold forth. I ardently wish for such happy improvements. But I see great, and, to my understanding, unconquerable difficulties in the way to them. These difficulties it is my present purpose to state; declaring, at the same time, that so far from exulting in them, as a cause of tri-

umphing over the friends of innovation, nothing would give me greater pleasure than to see them completely removed.

The most important argument that I shall adduce is certainly not new. The principles on which it depends have been explained in part by Hume, and more at large by Dr. Adam Smith. It has been advanced and applied to the present subject, though not with its proper weight, or in the most forcible point of view, by Mr. Wallace: and it may probably have been stated by many writers that I have never met with. I should certainly, therefore, not think of advancing it again, though I mean to place it in a point of view in some degree different from any that I have hitherto seen, if it had ever been fairly and satisfactorily answered.

The cause of this neglect on the part of the advocates for the perfectibility of mankind is not easily accounted for. I cannot doubt the talents of such men as Godwin and Condorcet. I am unwilling to doubt their candour. To my understanding, and probably to that of most others, the difficulty appears insurmountable. Yet these men of acknowledged ability and penetration, scarcely deign to notice it, and hold on their course in such speculations, with unabated ardour and undiminished confidence. I have certainly no right to say that they purposely shut their eyes to such arguments. I ought rather to doubt the validity of them, when neglected by such men, however forcibly their truth may strike my own mind. Yet in this respect it must be acknowledged that we are all of us too prone to err. If I saw a glass of wine repeatedly presented to a man, and he took no notice of it, I should be apt to think that he was blind or uncivil. A juster philosophy might teach me rather to think that my eyes deceived me, and that the offer was not really what I conceived it to be.

In entering upon the argument I must premise that I put out of the question, at present, all mere conjectures; that is, all suppositions, the probable realization of which cannot be inferred upon any just philosophical grounds. A writer may tell me that he thinks man will ultimately become an ostrich. I cannot properly contradict him. But before he can expect to bring any reasonable person over to his opinion, he ought to show that the necks of mankind have been gradually elongating; that the lips have grown harder, and more prominent; that the legs and feet are daily altering their shape; and that the hair is beginning to change into stubs of feathers. And till the probability of so wonderful a conversion can be shown, it is surely lost time and lost eloquence to expatiate on the happiness of man in such a state; to describe his powers, both of running and flying; to paint him in a condition where all narrow luxuries would be contemned; where he would be employed, only in collecting the necessaries of life; and where, consequently, each man's share of labour would be light, and his portion of leisure ample.

I think I may fairly make two postulata.

First, That food is necessary to the existence of man.

Secondly, That the passion between the sexes is necessary, and will remain nearly in its present state.

These two laws, ever since we have had any knowledge of mankind, appear to have been fixed laws of our nature; and, as we have not hitherto seen any alteration in them, we have no right to conclude that they will ever cease to be what they are now, without an immediate act of power in that Being who first arranged the system of the universe; and for the advantage of his creatures, still executes, according to fixed laws, all its various operations.

I do not know that any writer has supposed that on this earth man will ultimately be able to live without food. But Mr. Godwin has conjectured that the passion between the sexes may in time be extinguished. As, however, he calls this part of his work, a deviation into the land of conjecture, I will not dwell longer upon it at present, than to say, that the best arguments for the perfectibility of man are drawn from a contemplation of the great progress that he has already made from the savage state, and the difficulty of saying where he is to stop. But towards the extinction of the passion between the sexes, no progress whatever has hitherto been made. It appears to exist in as much force at present as it did two thousand, or four thousand years ago. There are individual exceptions now as there always have been. But, as these exceptions do not appear to increase in number, it would surely be a very unphilosophical mode of arguing, to infer merely from the existence of an exception, that the exception would, in time, become the rule, and the rule the exception.

Assuming, then, my postulata as granted, I say, that the power of population is indefinitely greater than the power in the earth to produce subsistence for man.

Population, when unchecked, increases in a geometrical ratio. Subsistence only increases in an arithmetical ratio. A slight acquaintance with numbers will show the immensity of the first power in comparison of the second.

By that law of our nature which makes food necessary to the life of man, the effects of these two unequal powers must be kept equal.

This implies a strong and constantly operating check on population from the difficulty of subsistence. This difficulty must fall some where; and must necessarily be severely felt by a large portion of mankind.

Through the animal and vegetable kingdoms, nature has scattered the seeds of life abroad with the most profuse and liberal hand. She has been comparatively sparing in the room, and the nourishment necessary to rear them. The germs of existence contained in this spot of earth, with ample food, and ample room to expand it, would fill millions of worlds in the course of a few thousand years. Necessity, that imperious, all-pervading law of nature, restrains them within the prescribed bounds. The race of plants, and the race of animals shrink under this great restrictive law. And the race of man cannot, by any efforts of reason, escape from it. Among plants and animals its effects are waste of seed, sickness, and premature death. Among mankind, misery and vice. The former, misery, is an absolutely necessary consequence of it. Vice is a highly probable consequence, and we therefore see it abundantly prevail; but it ought not, perhaps, to be called an absolutely necessary consequence. The ordeal of virtue is to resist all temptation to evil.

This natural inequality of the two powers of population, and of production in the earth, and that great law of our nature which must constantly keep their effects equal, form the great difficulty that to me appears insurmountable **in** the way to perfectibility of society. All other arguments are of slight and subordinate consideration in comparison of this. I see no way by which man can escape from the weight of this law which pervades all animated nature. No fancied equality, no agrarian regulations in their utmost extent, could remove the pressure of it even for a single century. And it appears, therefore, to be decisive against the possible existence of a society, all the members of which should live in ease, happiness, and comparative leisure; and feel no anxiety about providing the means of subsistence for themselves and families.

Consequently, if the premises are just, the argument is conclusive against the perfectibility of the mass of mankind.

I have thus sketched the general outline of the argument; but I will examine it more particularly; and I think it will be found that experience, the true source and foundation of all knowledge, invariably confirms its truth.

Johann Wolfgang von Goethe

Johann Wolfgang von Goethe (1749–1832) was one of the outstanding German literary figures who, in the late eighteenth and early nineteenth centuries, endeavored to free German culture from its artificial imitation of foreign, and particularly French, patterns. He and his contemporaries, Gottfried Lessing and Friedrich Schiller, used both legend and history as the subject matter for romantic novels, plays, and poems in order to stir the latent spirit of the German people. Goethe's greatest work was the drama, Faust, the first part of which he completed in 1808, and the second in 1831. Based upon a sixteenth-century German legend, it tells the story of the scholarly Faust who, restless for knowledge about the supernatural, bargained with the Devil (Mephistopheles), and risked his soul as the possible cost. In the character of Faust, Goethe personified the romantic individualism of the nineteenth century, the emotional restlessness and striving so characteristic of the romantic reaction to the rationalism of the Enlightenment. Thus this drama, one of the great literary masterpieces of all time, not only symbolized the stirring of German national feeling, but it stands as one of the signposts marking the end of the culture of the Enlightenment. In reading the prologue, Faust's opening soliloquy, and the scene between Faust and Mephistopheles note (1) the fluent and glowing description of the universe made by the three archangels, (2) the contrasting humor and sarcasm in the words of Mephistopheles, (3) his implied criticism of the extremes to which man had carried reason, (4) the Lord's query about earthly conditions, (5) their discussion of Faust and the Devil's description of the Faust spirit, (6) the agreement which they made concerning Faust's soul, (7) the romantic gratitude expressed by the Devil for God's conversation with him, (8) Faust's restless lamentation over the futility of learning, and his willingness to resort to the mystical to find that which he was seeking and *could not find through study, (9) Faust's moving description of the longing in his breast, (10) Mephistopheles' offer to guide Faust, (11) Faust's insistence on establishing the terms of the agreement, and the manner in which Mephistopheles wanted the contract sealed, and (12) Mephistopheles' triumphant musing over his victim.*

From: FAUST

PROLOGUE IN HEAVEN

The Lord.   The Heavenly Hosts.   *Afterwards*
Mephistopheles
(*The* Three Archangels *come forward.*)

Raphael

The sun-orb sings, in emulation,
'Mid brother-spheres, his ancient round:
His path predestined through Creation
He ends with step of thunder-sound.
The angels from his visage splendid
Draw power, whose measure none can say;
The lofty works, uncomprehended,
Are bright as on the earliest day.

Gabriel

And swift, and swift beyond conceiving,
The splendor of the world goes round,
Day's Edenbrightness still relieving
The awful Night's intense profound:
The ocean-tides in foam are breaking,
Against the rocks' deep bases hurled,
And both, the spheric race partaking,
Eternal, swift, are onward whirled!

Michael

And rival storms abroad are surging
From sea to land, from land to sea.
A chain of deepest action forging
Round all, in wrathful energy.
There flames a desolation, blazing
Before the Thunder's crashing way:
Yet, Lord, Thy messengers are praising
The gentle movement of Thy Day.

The Three

Though still by them uncomprehended,
From these the angels draw their power,
And all Thy works, sublime and splendid,
Are bright as in Creation's hour.

Mephistopheles

Since Thou, O Lord, deign'st to approach again
And ask us how we do, in manner kindest,
And heretofore to meet myself wert fain,
Among Thy menials, now, my face Thou find-
est.
Pardon, this troop I cannot follow after
With lofty speech, though by them scorned
and spurned,
My pathos certainly would move Thy laughter,
If Thou hadst not all merriment unlearned.
Of suns and worlds I've nothing to be quoted;
How men torment themselves, is all I've noted.
The little god o' the world sticks to the same
old way,
And is as whimsical as on Creation's day.
Life somewhat better might content him,
But for the gleam of heavenly light which
Thou hast lent him:
He calls it Reason—thence his power's in-
creased,
To be far beastlier than any beast.
Saving Thy Gracious Presence, he to me
A long-legged grasshopper appears to be,
That springing flies, and flying springs,
And in the grass the same old ditty sings.
Would he still lay among the grass he grows in!
Each bit of dung he seeks, to stick his nose in.

The Lord

Hast thou, then, nothing more to mention?
Com'st ever, thus, with ill intention?
Find'st nothing right on earth, eternally?

Mephistopheles

No, Lord! I find things, there, still bad as they
can be.

As translated by Bayard Taylor in Johann Wolfgang von Goethe, *Faust, A Tragedy*, Boston, 1871, 13–24; 85–103.

Man's misery even to pity moves my nature;
I've scarce the heart to plague the wretched
creature.

The Lord

Know'st Faust?

Mephistopheles

The Doctor Faust?

The Lord

My servant, he!

Mephistopheles

Forsooth! He serves you after strange devices:
No earthly meat or drink the fool suffices:
His spirit's ferment far aspireth;
Half conscious of his frenzied, crazed unrest,
The fairest stars from Heaven he requireth,
From Earth the highest raptures and the best,
And all the Near and Far that he desireth
Fails to subdue the tumult of his breast.

The Lord

Though still confused his service unto Me,
I soon shall lead him to a clearer morning.
Sees not the gardener, even while buds his
tree,
Both flower and fruit the future years adorn-
ing?

Mephistopheles

What will you bet? There's still a chance to
gain him,
If unto me full leave you give,
Gently upon *my* road to train him!

The Lord

As long as he on earth shall live,
So long I make no prohibition.
While Man's desires and aspirations stir,
He cannot choose but err.

Mephistopheles

My thanks! I find the dead no acquisition,
And never cared to have them in my keeping.
I much prefer the cheeks where ruddy blood
is leaping,
And when a corpse approaches, close my
house:
It goes with me, as with the cat the mouse.

The Lord

Enough! What thou hast asked is granted.
Turn off this spirit from his fountain-head;
To trap him, let thy snares be planted,
And him, with thee, be downward led;
Then stand abashed, when thou art forced to
say:
A good man, through obscurest aspiration,
Has still an instinct of the one true way.

Mephistopheles

Agreed! But 't is a short probation.
About my bet I feel no trepidation.
If I fulfil my expectation,
You'll let me triumph with a swelling breast:
Dust shall he eat, and with a zest,
As did a certain snake, my near relation.

The Lord

Therein thou 'rt free, according to thy merits;
The like of thee have never moved My hate.
Of all the bold, denying Spirits,
The waggish knave least trouble doth create.
Man's active nature, flagging, seeks too soon
the level;
Unqualified repose he learns to crave;
Whence, willingly, the comrade him I gave,
Who works, excites, and must create, as Devil.
But ye, God's sons in love and duty,
Enjoy the rich, the ever-living Beauty!
Creative Power, that works eternal schemes,
Clasp you in bonds of love, relaxing never,
And what in wavering apparition gleams
Fix in its place with thoughts that stand for-
ever!

(*Heaven closes: the* Archangels *separate.*)

Mephistopheles (solus)

I like, at times, to hear The Ancient's word,
And have a care to be most civil:
It's really kind of such a noble Lord
So humanly to gossip with the Devil!

FIRST PART OF THE TRAGEDY
I
Night

(*A lofty-arched, narrow, Gothic chamber.*
Faust, *in a chair at his desk, restless.*)

Faust

I've studied now Philosophy
And jurisprudence, Medicine,—

And even, alas! Theology,—
From end to end, with labor keen;
And here, poor fool! with all my lore
I stand, no wiser than before:
I'm Magister—yea, Doctor—hight,
And straight or cross-wise, wrong or right,
These ten years long, with many woes,
I've led my scholars by the nose,—
And see, that nothing can be known!
That knowledge cuts me to the bone.
I'm cleverer, true, than those fops of teachers,
Doctors and Magisters, Scribes and Preach-
ers;
Neither scruples nor doubts come now to
smite me,
Nor Hell nor Devil can longer affright me.
For this, all pleasure am I foregoing;
I do not pretend to aught worth knowing,
I do not pretend I could be a teacher
To help or convert a fellow-creature.
Then, too, I've neither lands nor gold,
Nor the world's least pomp or honor hold—
No dog would endure such a curst existence!
Wherefore, from Magic I seek assistance,
That many a secret perchance I reach
Through spirit-power and spirit-speech,
And thus the bitter task forego
Of saying the things I do not know,—
That I may detect the inmost force
Which binds the world, and guides its course;
Its germs, productive powers explore,
And rummage in empty words no more!

O full and splendid Moon, whom I
Have, from this desk, seen climb the sky
So many a midnight,—would thy glow
For the last time beheld my woe!
Ever thine eye, most mournful friend,
O'er books and papers saw me bend;
But would that I, on mountains grand,
Amid thy blessed light could stand,
With spirits through mountain-caverns hover,
Float in thy twilight the meadows over,
And, freed from the fumes of lore that swathe
me,
To health in thy dewy fountains bathe me!

Ah, me! this dungeon still I see,
This drear, accursed masonry,
Where even the welcome daylight strains
But duskly through the painted panes.

Hemmed in by many a toppling heap
Of books worm-eaten, gray with dust,
Which to the vaulted ceiling creep,
Against the smoky papers thrust,—
With glasses, boxes, round me stacked,
And instruments together hurled,
Ancestral lumber, stuffed and packed—
Such is my world: and what a world!

And do I ask, wherefore my heart
Falters, oppressed with unknown needs?
Why some inexplicable smart
All movement of my life impedes?
Alas! in living Nature's stead,
Where God His human creature set,
In smoke and mould the fleshless dead
And bones of beasts surround me yet!

Fly! Up, and seek the broad, free land!
And this one Book of Mystery
From Nostradamus' very hand,
Is 't not sufficient company?
When I the starry courses know,
And Nature's wise instruction seek,
With light of power my soul shall glow,
As when to spirits spirits speak.
'T is vain, this empty brooding here,
Though guessed the holy symbols be:
Ye, Spirits, come—ye hover near—
Oh, if you hear me, answer me! . . .

IV

THE STUDY

Faust. Mephistopheles.

Faust

A knock? Come in! Again my quiet broken?

Mephistopheles

'T is I!

Faust

    Come in!

Mephistopheles

    Thrice must the words be spoken.

Faust

Come in, then!

Mephistopheles

    Thus thou pleasest me.
I hope we'll suit each other well;

For now, thy vapors to dispel,
I come, a squire of high degree,
In scarlet coat, with golden trimming,
A cloak in silken lustre swimming,
A tall cock's-feather in my hat,
A long, sharp sword for show or quarrel,—
And I advise thee, brief and flat,
To don the self-same gay apparel,
That, from this den released, and free,
Life be at last revealed to thee!

Faust

This life of earth, whatever my attire,
Would pain me in its wonted fashion.
Too old am I to play with passion;
Too young, to be without desire.
What from the world have I to gain?
Thou shalt abstain—renounce—refrain!
Such is the everlasting song
That in the ears of all men rings,—
That unrelieved, our whole life long,
Each hour, in passing, hoarsely sings.
In very terror I at morn awake,
Upon the verge of bitter weeping,
To see the day of disappointment break,
To no one hope of mine—not one—its promise
    keeping:—
That even each joy's presentiment
With wilful cavil would diminish,
With grinning masks of life prevent
My mind its fairest work to finish!
Then, too, when night descends, how anxiously
Upon my couch of sleep I lay me:
There, also, comes no rest to me,
But some wild dream is sent to fray me.
The God that in my breast is owned
Can deeply stir the inner sources;
The God, above my powers enthroned,
He cannot change external forces.
So, by the burden of my days oppressed,
Death is desired, and Life a thing unblest!

Mephistopheles

And yet is never Death a wholly welcome
    guest.

Faust

O fortunate, for whom, when victory glances,
The bloody laurels on the brow he bindeth!
Whom, after rapid, maddening dances,
In clasping maiden-arms he findeth!

O would that I, before that spirit-power,
Ravished and rapt from life, had sunken!

Mephistopheles

And yet, by some one, in that nightly hour,
A certain liquid was not drunken.

Faust

Eavesdropping, ha! thy pleasure seems to be.

Mephistopheles

Omniscient am I not; yet much is known to me.

Faust

Though some familiar tone, retrieving
My thoughts from torment, led me on,
And sweet, clear echoes came, deceiving
A faith bequeathed from Childhood's dawn,
Yet now I curse whate'er entices
And snares the soul with visions vain;
With dazzling cheats and dear devices
Confines it in this cave of pain!
Cursed be, at once, the high ambition
Wherewith the mind itself deludes!
Cursed be the glare of apparition
That on the finer sense intrudes!
Cursed be the lying dream's impression
Of name, and fame, and laurelled brow!
Cursed, all that flatters as possession,
As wife and child, as knave and plow!
Cursed Mammon be, when he with treasures
To restless action spurs our fate!
Cursed when, for soft, indulgent leisures,
He lays for us the pillows straight!
Cursed be the vine's transcendent nectar,—
The highest favor Love lets fall!
Cursed, also, Hope!—cursed Faith, the spec-
    tre!
And cursed be Patience most of all!

Chorus of Spirits (invisible)

Woe! woe!
Thou hast it destroyed,
The beautiful world,
With powerful fist:
In ruin 't is hurled,
By the blow of a demigod shattered!
The scattered
Fragments into the Void we carry,
Deploring
The beauty perished beyond restoring.

Mightier
For the children of men,
Brightlier
Build it again,
In thine own bosom build it anew!
Bid the new career
Commence,
With clearer sense,
And the new songs of cheer
Be sung thereto!

Mephistopheles

These are the small dependants
Who give me attendance.
Hear them, to deeds and passion
Counsel in shrewd old-fashion!
Into the world of strife,
Out of this lonely life,
That of senses and sap has betrayed thee,
They would persuade thee.
This nursing of the pain forego thee,
That, like a vulture, feeds upon thy breast!
The worst society thou find'st will show thee
Thou art a man among the rest.
But 't is not meant to thrust
Thee into the mob thou hatest!
I am not one of the greatest,
Yet, wilt thou to me entrust
Thy steps through life, I'll guide thee,—
Will willingly walk beside thee,—
Will serve thee at once and forever
With best endeavor,
And, if thou art satisfied,
Will as servant, slave, with thee abide.

Faust

And what shall be my counter-service therefor?

Mephistopheles

The time is long: thou need'st not now insist.

Faust

No—no! The Devil is an egotist,
And is not apt, without a why or wherefore,
"For God's sake," others to assist.
Speak thy conditions plain and clear!
With such a servant danger comes, I fear.

Mephistopheles

Here, an unwearied slave, I'll wear thy tether,
And to thine every nod obedient be:

When *There* again we come together,
Then shalt thou do the same for me.

Faust

The *There* my scruples naught increases.
When thou hast dashed this world to pieces,
The other, then, its place may fill.
Here, on this earth, my pleasures have their
sources;
Yon sun beholds my sorrows in his courses;
And when from these my life itself divorces,
Let happen all that can or will!
I'll hear no more: 't is vain to ponder
If there we cherish love or hate,
Or, in the spheres we dream of yonder,
A High and Low our souls await.

Mephistopheles

In this sense, even, canst thou venture.
Come, bind thyself by prompt indenture,
And thou mine arts with joy shalt see:
What no man ever saw, I'll give to thee.

Faust

Canst thou, poor Devil, give me whatsoever?
When was a human soul, in its supreme en-
deavor,
E'er understood by such as thou?
Yet, hast thou food which never satiates,
now,—
The restless, ruddy gold hast thou,
That runs, quicksilver-like, one's fingers
through,—
A game whose winnings no man ever knew,—
A maid, that, even from my breast,
Beckons my neighbor with her wanton glances,
And Honor's godlike zest,
The meteor that a moment dances,—
Show me the fruits that, ere they're gathered,
rot,
And trees that daily with new leafage clothe
them!

Mephistopheles

Such a demand alarms me not:
Such treasures have I, and can show them.
But still the time may reach us, good my friend,
When peace we crave and more luxurious diet.

Faust

When on an idler's bed I stretch myself in
quiet,

There let, at once, my record end!
Canst thou with lying flattery rule me,
Until, self-pleased, myself I see,—
Canst thou with rich enjoyment fool me,
Let that day be the last for me!
The bet I offer.

Mephistopheles
Done!

Faust
And heartily!
When thus I hail the Moment flying:
"Ah, still delay—thou art so fair!"
Then bind me in thy bonds undying,
My final ruin then declare!
Then let the death-bell chime the token,
Then art thou from thy service free!
The clock may stop, the hand be broken,
Then Time be finished unto me!

Mephistopheles
Consider well: my memory good is rated.

Faust
Thou hast a perfect right thereto.
My powers I have not rashly estimated:
A slave am I, whate'er I do—
If thine, or whose? 'tis needless to debate it.

Mephistopheles
Then at the Doctors'-banquet I, to-day,
Will as a servant wait behind thee.
But one thing more! Beyond all risk to bind
thee,
Give me a line or two, I pray.

Faust
Demand'st thou, Pedant, too, a document?
Hast never known a man, nor proved his word's
intent?
Is 't not enough, that what I speak to-day
Shall stand, with all my future days agreeing?
In all its tides sweeps not the world away,
And shall a promise bind my being?
Yet this delusion in our hearts we bear:
Who would himself therefrom deliver?
Blest he, whose bosom Truth makes pure and
fair!
No sacrifice shall he repent of ever.
Nathless a parchment, writ and stamped with
care,

A spectre is, which all to shun endeavor.
The word, alas! dies even in the pen,
And wax and leather keep the lordship then.
What wilt from me, Base Spirit, say?—
Brass, marble, parchment, paper, clay?
The terms with graver, quill, or chisel, stated?
I freely leave the choice to thee.

Mephistopheles
Why heat thyself, thus instantly,
With eloquence exaggerated?
Each leaf for such a pact is good;
And to subscribe thy name thou 'lt take a drop
of blood.

Faust
If thou therewith art fully satisfied,
So let us by the farce abide.

Mephistopheles
Blood is a juice of rarest quality.

Faust
Fear not that I this pact shall seek to sever!
The promise that I make to thee
Is just the sum of my endeavor.
I have myself inflated all too high;
My proper place is thy estate:
The Mighty Spirit deigns me no reply,
And Nature shuts on me her gate.
The thread of Thought at last is broken,
And knowledge brings disgust unspoken.
Let us the sensual deeps explore,
To quench the fervors of glowing passion!
Let every marvel take form and fashion
Through the impervious veil it wore!
Plunge we in Time's tumultuous dance,
In the rush and roll of Circumstance!
Then may delight and distress,
And worry and success,
Alternately follow, as best they can:
Restless activity proves the man!

Mephistopheles
For you no bound, no term is set.
Whether you everywhere be trying,
Or snatch a rapid bliss in flying,
May it agree with you, what you get!
Only fall to, and show no timid balking.

Faust
But thou hast heard, 't is not of joy we're talking.

I take the wildering whirl, enjoyment's keenest
  pain,
Enamored hate, exhilarant disdain.
My bosom, of its thirst for knowledge sated,
Shall not, henceforth, from any pang be
  wrested,
And all of life for all mankind created
Shall be within mine inmost being tested:
The highest, lowest forms my soul shall bor-
  row,
Shall heap upon itself their bliss and sorrow,
And thus, my own sole self to all their selves
  expanded
I too, at last, shall with them all be stranded!

Mephistopheles

Believe me, who for many a thousand year
The same tough meat have chewed and tested,
That from the cradle to the bier
No man the ancient leaven has digested!
Trust one of us, this Whole supernal
Is made but for a God's delight!
He dwells in splendor single and eternal,
But *us* he thrusts in darkness, out of sight,
And *you* he dowers with Day and Night.

Faust

Nay, but I will!

Mephistopheles

            A good reply!
One only fear still needs repeating:
The art is long, the time is fleeting.
Then let thyself be taught, say I!
Go, league thyself with a poet,
Give the rein to his imagination,
Then wear the crown, and show it,
Of the qualities of his creation,—
The courage of the lion's breed.
The wild stag's speed,
The Italian's fiery blood,
The North's firm fortitude!
Let him find for thee the secret tether
That binds the Noble and Mean together,
And teach thy pulses of youth and pleasure
To love by rule, and hate by measure!
I'd like, myself, such a one to see:
Sir Microcosm his name should be.

Faust

What am I, then, if 't is denied my part
The crown of all humanity to win me,
Whereto yearns every sense within me?

Mephistopheles

Why, on the whole, thou 'rt—what thou art.
Set wigs of million curls upon thy head, to
  raise thee,
Wear shoes an ell in height,—the truth betrays
  thee,
And thou remainest—what thou art.

Faust

I feel, indeed, that I have made the treasure
Of human thought and knowledge mine, in
  vain;
And if I now sit down in restful leisure,
No fount of newer strength is in my brain:
I am no hair's-breadth more in height,
Nor nearer to the Infinite.

Mephistopheles

Good Sir, you see the facts precisely
As they are seen by each and all.
We must arrange them now, more wisely,
Before the joys of life shall pall.
Why, Zounds! Both hands and feet are, truly—
And head and virile forces—thine:
Yet all that I indulge in newly,
Is 't thence less wholly mine?
If I've six stallions in my stall,
Are not their forces also lent me?
I speed along, completest man of all,
As though my legs were four-and-twenty.
Take hold, then! let reflection rest,
And plunge into the world with zest!
I say to thee, a speculative wight
Is like a beast on moorlands lean,
That round and round some fiend misleads to
  evil plight,
While all about lie pastures fresh and green.

Faust

Then how shall we begin?

Mephistopheles

              We'll try a wider sphere.
What place of martyrdom is here!
Is 't life, I ask, is 't even prudence,
To bore thyself and bore the students?
Let Neighbor Paunch to that attend!
Why plague thyself with threshing straw for-
  ever?
The best thou learnest, in the end
Thou dar'st not tell the youngsters—never!
I hear one's footsteps, hither steering.

Faust

To see him now I have no heart.

Mephistopheles

So long the poor boy waits a hearing,
He must not unconsoled depart.
Thy cap and mantle straightway lend me!
I'll play the comedy with art.
                    (*He disguises himself.*)
My wits, be certain, will befriend me.
But fifteen minutes' time is all I need;
For our fine trip, meanwhile, prepare thyself
    with speed!

                                    [*Exit* Faust

Mephistopheles

                    (*In* Faust's *long mantle.*)
Reason and Knowledge only thou despise,
The highest strength in man that lies!
Let but the Lying Spirit bind thee

With magic works and shows that blind thee,
And I shall have thee fast and sure!
Fate such a bold, untrammelled spirit gave
    him,
As forwards, onwards, ever must endure;
Whose over-hasty impulse drave him
Past earthly joys he might secure.
Dragged through the wildest life, will I enslave
    him,
Through flat and stale indifference;
With struggling, chilling, checking, so deprave
    him
That, to his hot, insatiate sense,
The dream of drink shall mock, but never lave
    him:
Refreshment shall his lips in vain implore—
Had he not made himself the Devil's, naught
    could save him,
Still were he lost forevermore! . . .

Clemens Metternich

The Austrian statesman, Clemens Metternich (1773–1859) dominated the European political scene from the Congress of Vienna in 1815 to the liberal revolutions of 1848. He led the conservative reaction which swept over Europe following the close of the revolutionary and Napoleonic eras. In an effort to restore Austria to its former strategic position he espoused the principles of restoration, legitimacy, and absolutism, and sought in every possible way to beat down the rising tide of liberalism and nationalism. The Confession of Faith which follows was written by him in 1820, and in it he summarized his political and social philosophy. In reading it note (1) the events which prompted Metternich to write his Confession, (2) the evil which he believed threatened to destroy civilization, (3) the cause for this evil, (4) his attitude toward secret societies, (5) his characterization of the great mass of the people, (6) the class from which the discontented were largely drawn, (7) his attitude toward the past, and (8) the various proposals he offered to monarchs to correct the evil.

CONFESSION OF FAITH

SECRET MEMORANDUM TO THE EMPEROR ALEXANDER

"*L'Europe,*" a celebrated writer has recently said, "*fait aujourd'hui pitié à l'homme d'esprit et horreur à l'homme vertueux.*"

It would be difficult to comprise in a few words a more exact picture of the situation at the time we are writing these lines!

Kings have to calculate the chances of their very existence in the immediate future; passions are let loose, and league together to over-

As translated by Mrs. Alexander Napier in *Memoirs of Prince Metternich,* edited by Prince Richard Metternich, 5 vols., London, 1880–1882, III, 454–476.

throw everything which society respects as the basis of its existence; religion, public morality, laws, customs, rights, and duties, all are attacked, confounded, overthrown, or called in question. The great mass of the people are tranquil spectators of these attacks and revolutions, and of the absolute want of all means of defence. A few are carried off by the torrent, but the wishes of the immense majority are to maintain a repose which exists no longer, and of which even the first elements seem to be lost.

What is the cause of all these evils? By what methods has this evil established itself, and how is it that it penetrates into every vein of the social body?

Do remedies still exist to arrest the progress of this evil, and what are they?

These are doubtless questions worthy of the solicitude of every good man who is a true friend to order and public peace—two elements inseparable in principle, and which are at once the first needs and the first blessings of humanity.

Has there never been offered to the world an institution really worthy of the name? Has truth been always confounded with error ever since society has believed itself able to distinguish one from the other? Have the experiences bought at the price of so many sacrifices, and repeated at intervals, and in so many different places, been all in error? Will a flood of light be shed upon society at one stroke? Will knowledge come by inspiration? If one could believe in such phenomena it would not be the less necessary, first of all, to assure oneself of their reality. Of all things, nothing is so fatal as error; and it is neither our wish nor our intention ever to give ourselves up to it. Let us examine the matter!

THE SOURCE OF THE EVIL

Man's nature is immutable. The first needs of society are and remain the same, and the differences which they seem to offer find their explanation in the diversity of influences, acting on the different races by natural causes, such as the diversity of climate, barrenness or richness of soil, insular or continental position, &c. &c. These local differences no doubt pro-

duce effects which extend far beyond purely physical necessities; they create and determine particular needs in a more elevated sphere; finally, they determine the laws, and exercise an influence even on religions.

It is, on the other hand, with institutions as with everything else. Vague in their origin, they pass through periods of development and perfection, to arrive in time at their decadence; and, conforming to the laws of man's nature, they have, like him, their infancy, their youth, their age of strength and reason, and their age of decay.

Two elements alone remain in all their strength, and never cease to exercise their indestructible influence with equal power. These are the precepts of morality, religious as well as social, and the necessities created by locality. From the time that men attempt to swerve from these bases, to become rebels against these sovereign arbiters of their destinies, society suffers from a *malaise* which sooner or later will lead to a state of convulsion. The history of every country, in relating the consequences of such errors, contains many pages stained with blood; but we dare to say, without fear of contradiction, one seeks in vain for an epoch when an evil of this nature has extended its ravages over such a vast area as it has done at the present time. The causes are natural.

History embraces but a very limited space of time. It did not begin to deserve the name of history until long after the fall of great empires. There, where it seems to conduct us to the cradle of civilisation, it really conducts us to ruins. We see republics arise and prosper, struggle, and then submit to the rule of one fortunate soldier. We see one of these republics pass through all the phases common to society, and end in an almost universal monarchy—that is to say, subjugating the scattered portions of the then civilised world. We see this monarchy suffer the fate of all political bodies: we see its first springs become enfeebled, and finally decay.

Centuries of darkness followed the irruption of the barbarians. The world, however, could not return to barbarism. The Christian religion had appeared; imperishable in its essence, its very existence was sufficient to disperse the darkness and establish civilisation on new foundations, applicable to all times and all places, satisfying all needs, and establishing the most important of all on the basis of a pure and eternal law! To the formation of new Christian States succeeded the Crusades, a curious mixture of good and evil.

A decisive influence was shortly exercised on the progress of civilisation by three discoveries —the invention of printing, that of gunpowder, and the discovery of the New World. Still later came the Reformation—another event which had incalculable effects, on account of its influence on the moral world. From that time the face of the world was changed.

The facilitation of the communication of thoughts by printing; the total change in the means of attack and defence brought about by the invention of gunpowder; the difference suddenly produced in the value of property by the quantity of metals which the discovery of America put in circulation; the spirit of adventure provoked by the chances of fortune opened in a new hemisphere; the modifications in the relations of society caused by so many and such important changes, all became more developed, and were in some sort crowned by the revolution which the Reformation worked in the moral world.

The progress of the human mind has been extremely rapid in the course of the last three centuries. This progress having been accelerated more rapidly than the growth of wisdom (the only counterpoise to passions and to error); a revolution prepared by the false systems, the fatal errors into which many of the most illustrious sovereigns of the last half of the eighteenth century fell, has at last broken out in a country advanced in knowledge, and enervated by pleasure, in a country inhabited by a people whom one can only regard as frivolous, from the facility with which they comprehend and the difficulty they experience in judging calmly.

Having now thrown a rapid glance over the first causes of the present state of society, it is necessary to point out in a more particular manner the evil which threatens to deprive it, at one blow, of the real blessings, the fruits of genuine civilisation, and to disturb it in the midst of its enjoyments. This evil may be described in one word—presumption; the natural effect of the rapid progression of the human mind towards the perfecting of so many things. This it is which at the present day leads so many individuals astray, for it has become an almost universal sentiment.

Religion, morality, legislation, economy, politics, administration, all have become common and accessible to everyone. Knowledge seems to come by inspiration; experience has no value for the presumptuous man; faith is nothing to him; he substitutes for it a pretended individual conviction, and to arrive at this conviction dispenses with all inquiry and with all study; for these means appear too trivial to a mind which believes itself strong enough to embrace at one glance all questions and all facts. Laws have no value for him, because he has not contributed to make them, and it would be beneath a man of his parts to recognise the limits traced by rude and ignorant generations. Power resides in himself; why should he submit himself to that which was only useful for the man deprived of light and knowledge? That which, according to him, was required in an age of weakness cannot be suitable in an age of reason and vigour, amounting to universal perfection, which the German innovators designate by the idea, absurd in itself, of the Emancipation of the People! Morality itself he does not attack openly, for without it he could not be sure for a single instant of his own existence; but he interprets its essence after his own fashion, and allows every other person to do so likewise, provided that other person neither kills nor robs him.

In thus tracing the character of the presumptuous man, we believe we have traced that of the society of the day, composed of like elements, if the denomination of society is applicable to an order of things which only tends in principle towards individualising all the elements of which society is composed. Presumption makes every man the guide of his own belief, the arbiter of laws according to which he is pleased to govern himself, or to allow some one else to govern him and his neighbours; it makes him, in short, the sole judge of his own faith, his own actions, and the principles according to which he guides them.

Is it necessary to give a proof of this last fact? We think we have furnished it in remarking that one of the sentiments most natural to man, that of nationality, is erased from the Liberal catechism, and that where the word is still employed, it is used by the heads of the party as a pretext to enchain Governments, or as a lever to bring about destruction. The real aim of the idealists of the party is religious and political fusion, and this being analysed is nothing else but creating in favour of each individual an existence entirely independent of all authority, or of any other will than his own, an idea absurd and contrary to the nature of man, and incompatible with the needs of human society.

THE COURSE WHICH THE EVIL HAS FOLLOWED AND STILL FOLLOWS

The causes of the deplorable intensity with which this evil weighs on society appear to us to be of two kinds. The first are so connected with the nature of things that no human foresight could have prevented them. The second should be subdivided into two classes, however similar they may appear in their effects.

Of these causes, the first are negative, the others positive. We will place among the first the feebleness and the inertia of Governments.

It is sufficient to cast a glance on the course which the Governments followed during the eighteenth century, to be convinced that not one among them was ignorant of the evil or of the crisis towards which the social body was tending. There were, however, some men, unhappily endowed with great talents, who felt their own strength, and were not slow to appraise the progressive course of their influence, taking into account the weakness or the inertia of their adversaries; and who had the art to prepare and conduct men's minds to the triumph of their detestable enterprise—an enterprise all the more odious as it was pursued without regard to results, simply abandoning themselves to the one feeling of hatred of God and of His immutable moral laws.

France had the misfortune to produce the greatest number of these men. It is in her midst that religion and all that she holds sacred, that morality and authority, and all connected with them, have been attacked with a steady and systematic animosity, and it is

there that the weapon of ridicule has been used with the most ease and success.

Drag through the mud the name of God and the powers instituted by His divine decrees, and the revolution will be prepared! Speak of a social contract, and the revolution is accomplished! The revolution was already completed in the palaces of Kings, in the drawing-rooms and boudoirs of certain cities, while among the great mass of the people it was still only in a state of preparation.

It would be difficult not to pause here to consider the influence which the example of England had for a long time exercised on France. England is herself placed in such a peculiar situation that we believe we may safely say that not one of the forms possible to that State, not one of its customs or institutions, would suit any Continental State, and that where we might wish to take them for models, we should only obtain inconvenience and danger, without securing a single one of the advantages which accompany them.

According to the bent of minds in France, at the time of the convocation of the *notables*, and in consequence of the direction which public opinion had received for more than fifty years—a direction which, latterly, had been strengthened and in some sort adapted to France by the imprudent help which her Government had given to the American revolution —all reform in France touching the very foundations of the monarchy was soon transformed into a revolution. What might have been foreseen, and what had been foretold by everybody, the Government alone excepted, was realised but too soon. The French Revolution broke out, and has gone through a complete revolutionary cycle in a very short period, which could only have appeared long to its victims and to its contemporaries.

The scenes of horror which accompanied the first phases of the French Revolution prevented the rapid propagation of its subversive principles beyond the frontiers of France, and the wars of conquest which succeeded them gave to the public mind a direction little favourable to revolutionary principles. Thus the Jacobin propaganda failed entirely to realise criminal hopes.

Nevertheless the revolutionary seed had penetrated into every country and spread more or less. It was greatly developed under the *régime* of the military despotism of Bonaparte. His conquests displaced a number of laws, institutions, and customs; broke through bonds sacred among all nations, strong enough to resist time itself; which is more than can be said of certain benefits conferred by these innovators. From these perturbations it followed that the revolutionary spirit could in Germany, Italy, and later on in Spain, easily hide itself under the veil of patriotism.

Prussia committed a grave fault in calling to her aid such dangerous weapons as secret associations always will be: a fault which could not be justified even by the deplorable situation in which that Power then found itself. This it was that first gave a strong impulse to the revolutionary spirit in her States, and this spirit made rapid progress, supported as it was in the rest of Germany by the system of foreign despotism which since 1806 has been there developed. Many Princes of the Rhenish Confederation were secretly auxiliaries and accomplices of this system, to which they sacrificed the institutions which in their country from time immemorial had served as a protection against despotism and democracy.

The war of the Allies, by putting bounds to the predominance of France, was vigorously supported in Germany by the same men whose hatred of France was in reality nothing but hatred of the military despotism of Bonaparte, and also of the legitimate power of their own masters. With wisdom in the Governments and firmness in principles, the end of the war in 1814 might nevertheless have insured to the world the most peaceful and happy future. Great experiences had been gained and great lessons, which might have been usefully applied. But fate had decided otherwise.

The return of the usurped to France, and the completely false steps taken by the French Government from 1815 to 1820, accumulated a mass of new dangers and great calamities for the whole civilised world. It is to the first of these misfortunes that is partly due the critical state in which France and the whole social body is placed. Bonaparte destroyed in a hundred days the work of the fourteen years during which he had exercised his authority. He set free the revolution which he came to France to subdue; he brought back men's minds, not to the epoch of the 18th Brumaire, but to the principles which the National Assembly had adopted in its deplorable blindness.

What Bonaparte had thus done to the detriment of France and Europe, the grave errors which the French Government have since committed, and to which other Governments have yielded—all these unhappy influences weigh heavily on the world of to-day; they threaten with total ruin the work of restoration, the fruit of so many glorious efforts, and of a harmony between the greatest monarchs unparalleled in the records of history, and they give rise to fears of indescribable calamities to society.

In this memoir we have not yet touched on one of the most active and at the same time most dangerous instruments used by the revolutionists of all countries, with a success which is no longer doubtful. I refer to the secret societies, a real power, all the more dangerous as it works in the dark, undermining all parts of the social body, and depositing everywhere the seeds of a moral gangrene which is not slow to develop and increase. This plague is one of the worst which those Governments who are lovers of peace and of their people have to watch and fight against.

DO REMEDIES FOR THIS EVIL EXIST, AND WHAT ARE THEY?

We look upon it as a fundamental truth, that for every disease there is a remedy, and that the knowledge of the real nature of the one should lead to the discovery of the other. Few men, however, stop thoroughly to examine a disease which they intend to combat. There are hardly any who are not subject to the influence of passion, or held under the yoke of prejudice; there are a great many who err in a way more perilous still, on account of its flattering and often brilliant appearance: we speak of *l'esprit de système;* that spirit always false, but indefatigable, audacious and irrepressible, is satisfactory to men imbued with it (for they live in and govern a world created by themselves), but it is so much the more dangerous for the inhabitants of the real world, so different from that created by *l'esprit de système.*

There is another class of men who, judging of a disease by its outward appearance, confound the accessory manifestations with the root of the disease, and, instead of directing their efforts to the source of the evil, content themselves with subduing some passing symptoms.

It is our duty to try and avoid both of these dangers.

The evil exists and it is enormous. We do not think we can better define it and its cause at all times and in all places than we have already done by the word "presumption" [that inseparable companion of the half-educated, that spring of an unmeasured ambition, and yet easy to satisfy in times of trouble and confusion].

It is principally the middle classes of society which this moral gangrene has affected, and it is only among them that the real heads of the party are found.

For the great mass of the people it has no attraction and can have none. The labours to which this class—the real people—are obliged to devote themselves, are too continuous and too positive to allow them to throw themselves into vague abstractions and ambitions. The people know what is the happiest thing for them: namely, to be able to count on the morrow, for it is the morrow which will repay them for the cares and sorrows of to-day. The laws which afford a just protection to individuals, to families, and to property, are quite simple in their essence. The people dread any movement which injures industry and brings new burdens in its train.

Men in the higher classes of society who join the revolution are either falsely ambitious men or, in the widest acceptation of the word, lost spirits. Their career, moreover, is generally short! They are the first victims of political reforms, and the part played by the small number among them who survive is mostly that of courtiers despised by upstarts, their inferiors, promoted to the first dignities of the State; and of this France, Germany, Italy, and Spain furnish a number of living examples.

We do not believe that fresh disorders with a directly revolutionary end—not even revolutions in the palace and the highest places in the Government—are to be feared at present in France, because of the decided aversion of the people to anything which might disturb the peace they are now enjoying after so many troubles and disasters.

In Germany, as in Spain and Italy, the people ask only for peace and quiet.

In all four countries the agitated classes are principally composed of wealthy men—real cosmopolitans, securing their personal advantage at the expense of any order of things whatever—paid State officials, men of letters, lawyers, and the individuals charged with the public education.

To these classes may be added that of the falsely ambitious, whose number is never considerable among the lower orders, but is larger in the higher ranks of society.

There is besides scarcely any epoch which does not offer a rallying cry to some particular faction. This cry, since 1815, has been *Constitution*. But do not let us deceive ourselves: this word, susceptible of great latitude of interpretation, would be but imperfectly understood if we supposed that the factions attached quite the same meaning to it under the different *régimes*. Such is certainly not the case. In pure monarchies it is qualified by the name of "national representation." In countries which have lately been brought under the representative *régime* it is called "development," and promises charters and fundamental laws. In the only State which possesses an ancient national representation it takes "reform" as its object. Everywhere it means change and trouble.

In pure monarchies it may be paraphrased thus:—"The level of equality shall pass over your heads; your fortunes shall pass into other hands; your ambitions, which have been satisfied for centuries, shall now give place to our ambitions, which have been hitherto repressed."

In the States under a new *régime* they say:—"The ambitions satisfied yesterday must give place to those of the morrow, and this is the morrow for us."

Lastly, in England, the only place in the third class, the rallying cry—that of Reform—combines the two meanings.

Europe thus presents itself to the impartial observer under an aspect at the same time deplorable and peculiar. We find everywhere the people praying for the maintenance of peace and tranquillity, faithful to God and their Princes, remaining proof against the efforts and seductions of the factions who call themselves friends of the people and wish to lead them to an agitation which the people themselves do not desire!

The Governments, having lost their balance, are frightened, intimidated, and thrown into confusion by the cries of the intermediary class of society, which, placed between the Kings and their subjects, breaks the sceptre of the monarch, and usurps the cry of the people— that class so often disowned by the people, and nevertheless too much listened to, caressed and feared by those who could with one word reduce it again to nothingness.

We see this intermediary class abandon itself with a blind fury and animosity which proves much more its own fears than any confidence in the success of its enterprises, to all the means which seem proper to assuage its thirst for power, applying itself to the task of persuading Kings that their rights are confined to sitting upon a throne, while those of the people are to govern, and to attack all that centuries have bequeathed as holy and worthy of man's respect—denying, in fact, the value of the past, and declaring themselves the masters of the future. We see this class take all sorts of disguises, uniting and subdividing as occasion offers, helping each other in the hour of danger, and the next day depriving each other of all their conquests. It takes possession of the press, and employs it to promote impiety, disobedience to the laws of religion and the State, and goes so far as to preach murder as a duty for those who desire what is good.

One of its leaders in Germany defined public opinion as "the will of the strong man in the spirit of the party"—a maxim too often put in practice, and too seldom understood by those whose right and duty it is to save society from its own errors, its own weaknesses, and the crimes which the factious commit while pretending to act in its interests.

The evil is plain; the means used by the faction which causes these disorders are so blameable in principle, so criminal in their application, and expose the faction itself to so many dangers, that what men of narrow views (whose head and heart are broken by circumstances stronger than their calculations or their courage) regard as the end of society may become the first step towards a better order of things. These weak men would be right unless men stronger than they are come forward to close their ranks and determine the victory.

We are convinced that society can no longer be saved without strong and vigorous resolutions on the part of the Governments still free in their opinions and actions.

We are also convinced that this may yet be, if the Governments face the truth, if they free themselves from all illusion, if they join their ranks and take their stand on a line of correct, unambiguous, and frankly announced principles.

By this course the monarchs will fulfil the duties imposed upon them by Him who, by entrusting them with power, has charged them to watch over the maintenance of justice, and the rights of all, to avoid the paths of error, and tread firmly in the way of truth. Placed beyond the passions which agitate society, it is in days of trial chiefly that they are called upon to despoil realities of their false appearances, and to show themselves as they are, fathers invested with the authority belonging by right to the heads of families, to prove that in days of mourning, they know how to be just, wise, and therefore strong, and that they will not abandon the people whom they ought to govern to be the sport of factions, to error and its consequences, which must involve the loss of society. The moment in which we are putting our thoughts on paper is one of these critical moments. The crisis is great; it will be decisive according to the part we take or do not take.

There is a rule of conduct common to individuals and to States, established by the experience of centuries as by that of everyday life. This rule declares "that one must not dream of reformation while agitated by passion; wisdom directs that at such moments we should limit ourselves to maintaining."

Let the monarchs vigorously adopt this principle; let all their resolutions bear the impression of it. Let their actions, their measures, and even their words announce and prove to the world this determination—they will find allies everywhere. The Governments, in establishing the principle of *stability*, will in no wise exclude the development of what is good, for stability is not immobility. But it is for those who are burdened with the heavy task of government to augment the well-being of their people! It is for Governments to regulate it according to necessity and to suit the times. It is not by concessions, which the factions strive to force from legitimate power, and which they have neither the right to claim nor the faculty of keeping within just bounds, that wise reforms can be carried out. That all the good possible should be done is our most ardent wish; but that which is not good must never be confounded with that which is, and even real good should be done only by those who unite to the right of authority the means of enforcing it. Such should be also the sincere wish of the people, who know by sad experience the value of certain phrases and the nature of certain caresses.

Respect for all that is; liberty for every Government to watch over the well-being of its own people; a league between all Governments against factions in all States; contempt for the meaningless words which have become the rallying cry of the factions; respect for the progressive development of institutions in lawful ways; refusal on the part of every monarch to aid or succour partisans under any mask whatever—such are happily the ideas of the great monarchs: the world will be saved if they bring them into action—it is lost if they do not.

Union between the monarchs is the basis of the policy which must now be followed to save society from total ruin.

What is the particular object towards which this policy should be directed? The more important this question is, the more necessary it is to solve it. A principle is something, but it acquires real value only in its application.

The first sources of the evil which is crushing the world have been indicated by us in a paper which has no pretension to be anything more than a mere sketch. Its further causes have also there been pointed out, if, with respect to individuals, it may be defined by the word *presumption*, in applying it to society,

taken as a whole, we believe we can best describe the existing evil as the *confusion of ideas*, to which too much generalisation constantly leads. This is what now troubles society. Everything which up to this time has been considered as fixed in principle is attacked and overthrown.

In religious matters criticism and inquiry are to take the place of faith, Christian morality is to replace the Law of Christ as it is interpreted by Christian authorities.

In the Catholic Church, the Jansenists and a number of isolated sectarians, who wish for a religion without a Church, have devoted themselves to this enterprise with ardent zeal: among the Protestant sects, the Methodists, sub-divided into almost as many sects as there are individuals; then the enlightened promoters of the Bible Societies and the Unitarians—the promoters of the fusion of Lutherans and Calvinists in one Evangelical community—all pursue the same end.

The object which these men have in common, to whatever religion they may ostensibly belong, is simply to overthrow all authority Put on moral grounds, they wish *to enfranchise souls* in the same way as some of the political revolutionists who were not actuated by motives of personal ambition wished to *enfranchise the people.*

If the same elements of destruction which are now throwing society into convulsion have existed in all ages—for every age has seen immoral and ambitious men, hypocrites, men of heated imaginations, wrong motives, and wild projects—yet ours, by the single fact of the liberty of the press, possesses more than any preceding age the means of contact, seduction, and attraction whereby to act on these different classes of men.

We are certainly not alone in questioning if society can exist with the liberty of the press, a scourge unknown to the world before the latter half of the seventeenth century, and restrained until the end of the eighteenth, with scarcely any exceptions but England—a part of Europe separated from the continent by the sea, as well as by her language and by her peculiar manners.

The first principle to be followed by the

monarchs, united as they are by the coincidence of their desires and opinions, should be that of maintaining the stability of political institutions against the disorganised excitement which has taken possession of men's minds; the immutability of principles against the madness of their interpretation; and respect for laws actually in force against a desire for their destruction.

The hostile faction is divided into two very distinct parties. One is that of the Levellers; the other, that of the Doctrinaires. United in times of confusion, these men are divided in times of inaction. It is for the Governments to understand and estimate them at their just value.

In the class of Levellers there are found men of strong will and determination. The Doctrinaires can count none such among their ranks. If the first are more to be feared in action, the second are more dangerous in that time of deceitful calm which precedes it; as with physical storms, so with those of social order. Given up to abstract ideas inapplicable to real wants, and generally in contradiction to those very wants, men of this class unceasingly agitate the people by their imaginary or simulated fears, and disturb Governments in order to make them deviate from the right path. The world desires to be governed by facts and according to justice, not by phrases and theories; the first need of society is to be maintained by strong authority (no authority without real strength deserves the name) and not to govern itself. In comparing the number of contests between parties in mixed Governments, and that of just complaints caused by aberrations of power in a Christian State, the comparison would not be in favour of the new doctrines. The first and greatest concern for the immense majority of every nation is the stability of the laws, and their uninterrupted action—never their change. Therefore let the Governments govern, let them maintain the groundwork of their institutions, both ancient and modern; for if it is at all times dangerous to touch them, it certainly would not now, in the general confusion, be wise to do so.

Let them announce this determination to their people, and demonstrate it by facts. Let them reduce the Doctrinaires to silence within their States, and show their contempt for them abroad. Let them not encourage by their attitude or actions the suspicion of being favourable or indifferent to error: let them not allow it to be believed that experience has lost all its rights to make way for experiments which at the least are dangerous. Let them be precise and clear in all their words, and not seek by concessions to gain over those parties who aim at the destruction of all power but their own, whom concessions will never gain over, but only further embolden in their pretensions to power.

Let them in these troublous times be more than usually cautious in attempting real ameliorations, not imperatively claimed by the needs of the moment, to the end that good itself may not turn against them—which is the case whenever a Government measure seems to be inspired by fear.

Let them not confound concessions made to parties with the good they ought to do for their people, in modifying, according to their recognised needs, such branches of the administration as require it.

Let them give minute attention to the financial state of their kingdoms, so that their people may enjoy, by the reduction of public burdens, the real, not imaginary, benefits of a state of peace.

Let them be just, but strong; beneficent, but strict.

Let them maintain religious principles in all their purity, and not allow the faith to be attacked and morality interpreted according to the *social contract* or the visions of foolish sectarians.

Let them suppress Secret Societies, that gangrene of society.

In short, let the great monarchs strengthen their union, and prove to the world that if it exists, it is beneficent, and ensures the political peace of Europe: that it is powerful only for the maintenance of tranquillity at a time when so many attacks are directed against it; that the principles which they profess are paternal and protective, menacing only the disturbers of public tranquillity.

The Governments of the second order will

see in such a union the anchor of their salvation, and they will be anxious to connect themselves with it. The people will take confidence and courage, and the most profound and salutary peace which the history of any time can show will have been effected. This peace will first act on countries still in a good state, but will not be without a very decided influence on the fate of those threatened with destruction, and even assist the restoration of those which have already passed under the scourge of revolution.

To every great State determined to survive the storm there still remain many chances of salvation, and a strong union between the States on the principles we have announced will overcome the storm itself.

Industrialism, Liberalism, and Democracy in the Nineteenth Century

Beginning in the late eighteenth century and continuing through the nineteenth, a series of important developments occurred in the production system of Western Europe and the United States. These changes have been given the name Industrial Revolution, and in the sense that they profoundly altered the economic and social phases of Western Civilization, this is an accurate term. The introduction of machinery in production and its concentration in factories located in cities induced large sections of the population to adopt a new way of life. Factory workers found themselves victims of poor working and living conditions, and efforts to improve their condition were frowned upon as contrary to the liberal principles of the period. Economic liberalism stressed the importance of free enterprise and free trade together with a laissez-faire attitude on the part of government, while political liberalism looked with favor upon the least government possible. As the nineteenth century advanced, however, a new political phenomenon began to emerge in the form of democracy. It developed most rapidly in the United States where the frontier environment helped to foster it, but Europeans, too, were attracted by its principles; some came to the United States to observe democracy in action. Gradually, its principles began to take root in Europe, and a new force was thus developing through which the social and economic evils of industrialism could be attacked.

Industrialism, Liberalism, and Democracy in the Nineteenth Century

Parliamentary Committee

During the latter part of the eighteenth century Western Civilization experienced the beginnings of a tremendous change in its method of producing goods. The various events associated with this important development are known as the Industrial Revolution. For a variety of reasons, some economic and social, others political and geographic, Great Britain was the first country to experience these advances. Two of the products of the Industrial Revolution, the factory system and the mill towns, presented England with some unfortunate social results. The laissez-faire doctrine, exalting free enterprise and frowning upon mercantilism and state control, dominated the political thought of the era, thereby intensifying these evils. In the decade of the 1830's a group of reformers, which included Michael Sadler, began agitating for some governmental controls, and in 1832 a Parliamentary committee was appointed, with Sadler as chairman, to investigate the abuses of child labor in English factories. As a consequence of this investigation, Parliament passed the Factory Act of 1833. This measure marked the end of unrestricted laissez faire in England. The following selections are from the evidence presented before the committee. In reading them note (1) the working and health conditions the witnesses described, (2) the length of hours children worked, (3) the reasons given for working, (4) why the workers did not quit their jobs as a protest, (5) the amount of pay given for overtime work, (6) evidence of pressure brought to bear upon mill workers to prevent them from testifying, (7) why workers did not join unions, (8) the comparison made with slave labor in the West Indies, and (9) the humanitarianism expressed by the doctor.

From: THE SADLER REPORT

MINUTES OF EVIDENCE

Jovis, 12° *die Aprilis*, 1832
Michael Thomas Sadler, Esquire, in the Chair.
William Cooper called in; and Examined.

What is your business? —I follow the cloth-dressing at present.

What is your age? —I was eight-and-twenty last February.

When did you first begin to work in mills or factories? —When I was about 10 years of age.

With whom did you first work? —At Mr. Benyon's flax mills, in Meadow's-lane, Leeds.

What were your usual hours of working? —We began at five, and gave over at nine; at five o'clock in the morning.

And you gave over at nine o'clock? —At nine at night.

At what distance might you have lived from the mill? —About a mile and a half.

At what time had you to get up in the morning to attend to your labour? —I had to be up soon after four o'clock.

Every morning? —Every morning.

What intermissions had you for meals? —When we began at five in the morning, we went on until noon, and then we had 40 minutes for dinner.

Great Britain, *Sessional Papers*, 1833, vol. 123, cd. 706, pp. 5–11; 158–164; 428–430; 598–602.

Had you no time for breakfast? —No, we got it as we could, while we were working.

Had you any time for an afternoon refreshment, or what is called in Yorkshire your "drinking"? —No; when we began at noon, we went on till night; there was only one stoppage, the 40 minutes for dinner.

Then as you had to get your breakfast, and what is called "drinking" in that manner, you had to put it on one side? —Yes, we had to put it on one side; and when we got our frames doffed, we ate two or three mouthfuls, and then put it by again.

Is there not considerable dust in a flax mill? —A flax mill is very dusty indeed.

Was not your food therefore frequently spoiled? —Yes, at times with the dust; sometimes we could not eat it, when it had got a lot of dust on.

What were you when you were ten years old? —What is called a bobbin-doffer; when the frames are quite full, we have to doff them.

Then as you lived so far from home, you took your dinner to the mill? —We took all our meals with us, living so far off.

During the 40 minutes which you were allowed for dinner, had you ever to employ that time in your turn in cleaning the machinery? —At times we had to stop to clean the machinery, and then we got our dinner as well as we could; they paid us for that.

At these times you had no resting at all? —No.

How much had you for cleaning the machinery? —I cannot exactly say what they gave us, as I never took any notice of it.

Did you ever work even later than the time you have mentioned? —I cannot say that I worked later there. I had a sister who worked upstairs, and she worked till 11 at night, in what they call the card-room.

At what time in the morning did she begin to work? —At the same time as myself.

And they kept her there till 11 at night? —Till 11 at night.

You say that your sister was in the card-room? —Yes.

Is not that a very dusty department? —Yes, very dusty indeed.

She had to be at the mill at five, and was kept at work till eleven at night? —Yes.

During the whole time she was there? —During the whole time; there was only 40 minutes allowed at dinner out of that.

To keep you at your work for such a length of time, and especially towards the termination of such a day's labour as that, what means were taken to keep you awake and attentive? —They strapped us at times, when we were not quite ready to be doffing the frame when it was full.

Were you frequently strapped? —At times we were frequently strapped.

What sort of strap was it? —About this length [*describing it*].

What was it made of? —Of leather.

Were you occasionally very considerably hurt with the strap? —Sometimes it hurt us very much, and sometimes they did not lay on so hard as they did at others.

Were the girls strapped in that sort of way? —They did not strap what they called the grown-up women.

Were any of the female children strapped? —Yes; they were strapped in the same way as the lesser boys.

What were your wages at 10 years old at Mr. Benyon's? —I think it was 4 *s.* a week.

When you left Mr. Benyon, to what mill did you then go? —To Mr. Clayton's; that was a flax mill.

What age were you when you went there? —I was at Mr. Benyon's nearly a year and a half.

Then you were eleven years and a half old? —Yes.

What were your hours of work at Mr. Clayton's? —We started at five in the morning, and worked till ten minutes past eight at night.

That is 15 hours and 10 minutes? —Yes; and we had only 40 minutes out of that for dinner.

You assembled at five in the morning? —From five in the morning until ten minutes past eight at night.

Had you any time allowed for breakfast or drinking at that mill? —No, it was just the same as the other, with only 40 minutes for dinner.

So that, in point of fact, you had to be attending to your work on your legs for that length of time, with the short intermission of

40 minutes? —Yes, we had to get our meals as we could get them, all but our dinner.

Were your punishments the same in that mill as in the other? —Yes, they used the strap the same there.

How long did you work in that mill? —Five years.

And how did it agree with your health? —I was sometimes well, and sometimes not very well.

Did it affect your breathing at all? —Yes; sometimes we were stuffed.

When your hours were so long, you had not any time to attend to a day-school? —We had no time to go to a day-school, only to a Sunday-school; and then with working such long hours we wanted to have a bit of rest, so that I slept till the afternoon, sometimes till dinner, and sometimes after.

Did you attend a place of worship? —I should have gone to a place of worship many times, but I was in the habit of falling asleep, and that kept me away; I did not like to go for fear of being asleep.

Do you mean that you could not prevent yourself from falling asleep, in consequence of the fatigue of the preceding week? —Yes.

Did you work in any other flax mill? —In no other flax mill.

Did you afterwards work in a woollen mill? —I worked in what they call a cloth-dressing mill.

In whose mill did you next work? —I went to Mr. Pearson's.

What were your hours there? —I think it was from six to eight.

What time was allowed there for meals? —Half an hour for breakfast, an hour at dinner, and half an hour at drinking.

That was 12 hours at the woollen mill? —Yes.

When you left that mill, where did you go to next? —I went to Mr. Wilks's, in Meadow's-lane; that is a cloth mill.

Were your hours the same there? —No; there were short hours there.

Did you find the short hours working suit your health better? —It did a great deal better with me.

Where did you go to then? —To Mr. Giles, in Bowman-lane; that is a cloth mill.

What hours did you work there? —From six to eight, and from six to nine.

With the same intermissions? —Yes, with the same intermissions.

What was the next mill you worked at? —Then I went to Mr. Chorley's.

Were your hours the same there? —Not quite so long there; they were from six to seven.

With the same intervals for meals? —Yes.

You have already stated that your health was better when the labour was shorter? —It was a deal better when only working these hours.

Where did you go then? —To Mr. James Brown's.

What were you at Mr. James Brown's? —I was a gigger and a boiler.

When did you go there? —I should think I must be about 20 years of age when I went there.

Were you a gigger and a boiler when you first went to Mr. Brown's? —I was a gigger when I went to Mr. Brown's; I was a boiler a good while after.

State what was your usual work when you were only a gigger. —When I was only a gigger I went at five o'clock on a Monday morning, and had half an hour at breakfast and an hour at dinner, and half an hour at drinking; then went on till nine on Monday evening, and stopped half an hour; then went on to twelve at midnight, and stopped an hour; then went on to half-past four on Tuesday morning, and stopped half an hour; then went on again from five to eight, and stopped half an hour; then went on till twelve, and stopped an hour; then went on again from one to five, and stopped half an hour; then went on again to nine o'clock at night, when we went home.

What did you do on the Wednesday? —Went again at five o'clock in the morning.

What time did you close at night? —At nine.

What did you do on the Thursday? —Went again on Thursday morning at five, and returned at nine at night. On Friday morning we went at five; worked all Friday, Friday night, and till Saturday evening at five, with the same time for meals as before.

When you became a boiler, will you state the number of hours you had to labour at the same mill? —When I was a boiler, I began **work at one o'clock on the Monday morning;**

went on till five, and stopped half an hour; then went on to eight, and stopped half an hour; then went on to twelve, and stopped an hour; then went on to five, and stopped half an hour; then went on to nine, and stopped half an hour; then went on to twelve, and stopped an hour; then began again, and went on to half-past four on Tuesday morning, and stopped half an hour; then went on to eight, and stopped half an hour; then went on to twelve, and stopped an hour; then went on to five, and stopped half an hour; then went on to nine, and then gave over on the Tuesday night. On Wednesday morning we went at five, and stopped half an hour at breakfast; then went on to twelve, and stopped an hour; then went on to five, and stopped half an hour; then went on to nine, and then gave over. Thursday was the same as Wednesday. On Friday morning we went at five, and stopped half an hour at breakfast; then we went on to twelve, and stopped an hour; then we went on to five, and stopped half an hour; then we went on to nine, and stopped half an hour; then we went on to twelve at midnight, and stopped an hour; then we went on to half-past four, and stopped half an hour; then we went on to eight, and stopped half an hour; then we went on to twelve, and stopped an hour; then we went on to five o'clock on Saturday night, and gave over.

Then in the whole week you had only four nights' rest, exclusive of Sunday night? —No.

And that rest was after nine o'clock, and before five? —Yes.

As I calculate, you laboured as a boiler 44 hours running, from Monday morning till Tuesday night, having 10 intervals, amounting altogether to only six hours and a half, and never going to bed? —You cannot go to bed.

And 36 hours of labour from Friday morning till you were let loose on Saturday evening, including five hours and an half for meals? —Yes.

On Wednesday and Thursday you had, from five till nine, 16 hours of labour, including meals? —Yes.

Then on Monday and Friday nights you had no rest? —No rest.

What was the effect of this excessive labour upon you? —We all felt unwell, and were stiff, and could not make proper use of our limbs

till we had worked a little, when it went off.

Had this a serious effect on your health? —Yes, it had a great deal of effect on our health.

But as to yourself personally? —Yes.

After working at a mill to this excess, how did you find your health at last? —I found it very bad indeed; I found illness coming on me a long time before I fell down.

Did you at length become so ill as to be unable to pursue your work? —I was obliged to give it up entirely.

How long were you ill? —For six months.

Who attended? —Mr. Metcalf and Mr. Freeman.

What were you told by your medical attendants was the reason of your illness? —Nothing but hard labour, and working long hours; and they gave me up, and said no good could be done for me, that I must go into the country.

Did this excessive labour not only weaken you, but destroy your appetite? —It destroyed the appetite, and I became so feeble, that I could not cross the floor unless I had a stick to go with; I was in great pain, and could find ease in no posture.

You could drink in the meantime, if you could not eat? —Yes, I could drink.

But you found that [did] not improve your health? —No.

Has it been remarked that your excessive labour from early life has greatly diminished your growth? —A number of persons have said that such was the case, and that I was the same as if I had been made of iron or stone.

What height are you? —About five feet. It is that that has hindered me of my growth.

When you were somewhat recovered, did you apply for labour? —I applied for my work again, but the overlooker said I was not fit to work; he was sure of that, and he would not let me have it. I was then obliged to throw myself on the parish.

Have you subsisted on the parish ever since? —Yes.

Have you been always willing and anxious to work? —I was always willing and anxious to work from my infancy.

Have you been on the parish since your severe illness? —Yes. . . .

When did you first begin to receive wages yourself? —Ever since I began to work; I gave them to my parents.

How old were you then? —Ten years.

How soon did you begin to work on your own account and make your own bargain with your master for wages? —I always bargained for my wages ever since I began to work for wages; always; my parents never bargained for me. I always bargained for myself.

Not when you were 10 years old? —Yes.

Do you know anything, of your own knowledge, of the hours of working at present in Mr. Benyon's and Mr. Clayton's flax-mills? —Mr. Clayton's flax-mill is not going; Mr. Benyon's is going; but I do not know what hours they are working now.

Is not trade rather slack in that part of the country just now? —It is very slack at present.

While you were with Mr. Pearson, Mr. Giles and Mr. Chorley, you were in a better state of health? —Yes.

How old were you when you became a boiler in Mr. Brown's mill? —I believe I was about 20 years of age when I went to Mr. Brown.

You said you were a gigger at first? —That is, what I mean, when I became a boiler, I was somewhere about between 25 and 26.

You received 18 *s.* a week wages? —Yes.

Was that the regular wages without the extra hours, or did you receive more than 18 *s.* a week when you worked all these extra hours? —Yes.

How much did you ever receive? —I received 18 *s.* and over-hours; about 26 *s.* or 27 *s.* and sometimes 28 *s.*

At a regular charge of 3 *d.* an hour? —No, at 18 *s.* a week; it is 3½ *d.* for all the hours over.

If you had not worked these over-hours, you would not have been kept in your employment? —No, I should not have been kept in employ if I had not worked them.

Did not you and others choose to undergo this excessive labor, rather than incur the disgrace of throwing yourselves on the parish? —Yes.

You attended at the mill at five in the morning; was that both winter and summer? —It has been, for two years back, winter and summer, working at Mr. Brown's.

Were you able to be punctual in your attendance at five o'clock? —I was always there at five o'clock; if we were too late they took us off what we call bating; if we were a quarter of an hour too late in the morning they took off a penny.

Are they ever turned away for being too late? —If they are what is called "bad comers," they turn them off and get fresh ones.

Are they ever strapped for being too late? —They did not strap them at the room that I was in.

How did you contrive to be awake so soon in the morning? —My father always used to call me up.

Did he get up so early as that for his own business? —He got up on purpose to call me.

How many hours did he work in a day at his own business? —Sometimes from five in the morning till eight at night.

You say he was a shoemaker? —Yes.

Then, according to this, he worked more hours than you did? —I think not so long.

Did your father take his regular intervals for his meals? —I should think so.

And walked about to market for his family; had he not many pauses in his labour? —He worked at home, and therefore could do as he pleased.

After you worked a month at these long hours, could you not get back into lighter employment? —I do not know whether you could get back or not.

You said that you were about 17 when you first went from the flax-spinning mills into the cloth-mills? —Yes.

Was that before the Act of Parliament made to regulate the hours? —I know nothing about that.

How often did these extra hours come about? —Very often.

Describe to us a period in which you have worked the greatest possible number of hours; how many weeks running have you worked? —I have gone on for a year round.

Working all the Monday night and Friday night? —Yes; always working long hours.

Is your sister older or younger than yourself? —There is a year and a half between us; I am the elder.

Has your health improved since you left off working long hours? —I am a deal better than

I was; but I believe that if I could have got work, and have had something to support me, I should have recruited my health better. I have been very poorly kept for these last six months, having been out of work. I have only half a crown a week allowed from the parish for my wife and myself.

When you were working the long hours, were there any people in the same employment, when you were a gigger, for instance, who were working the short hours? —Yes; some mills were working short hours in the same line; there were none in the same room that worked less hours than I did.

[*Joseph Hebergam examined.*] What particular department of the mill had you to attend to? —I attended what are called the throstle machines.

How long did you continue in that mill? —I attended the throstles two years and a half, and then I went to the steam looms for half a year.

Were there many children in that mill? —Yes, I believe there were about fifty, of about the same age that I was.

State to the Committee how this excessive labour agreed with the health of these children so employed? —They were often sick and poorly; there were always, perhaps, half a dozen regularly that were ill.

From excessive labour? —Yes.

Did you consider the work to be hard work? —It was not very hard, but having to work so very many hours made it worse; it was rather hard of itself, but it would have been better if we had not had so long to stand.

Did you not become very drowsy and sleepy towards the end of the day, and feel much fatigued? —Yes; that began about 3 o'clock, and grew worse and worse, and it came to be very bad towards 6 and 7.

And still you had to labour on? —Yes.

What means were taken to keep you at your work so long? —There were three overlookers; there was a head overlooker, and then there was one man kept to grease the machines, and then there was one kept on purpose to strap.

Was the main business of one of the overlookers that of strapping the children up to this excessive labour? —Yes, the same as strapping an old restive horse that has fallen down and will not get up.

Was that the constant practice? —Yes, day by day.

Were there straps regularly provided for that purpose? —Yes, he is continually walking up and down with it in his hand.

And his office is to strap you on to your labour? —Yes.

Do you think the children could be kept so long to labour as you have stated, if they were not so treated? —No, they could not; they are obliged to do it.

Was it not reckoned by the children to be very bad usage, and did they not conceive themselves to be very unfortunate in being subject to such a course of labour as this? —Yes; and towards the end of the day the flies of the machines would burst their knuckles.

Did you meet with frequent accidents? —Yes.

So that you were not capable of performing the labour that was exacted from you without this perpetual cruelty? —No.

Had you any brothers or sisters similarly occupied? —I had at that time a brother and a sister; they called him John, and my sister Charlotte.

What ages were they when they began working at the mills? —I cannot say how old my sister Charlotte was, but my brother John was 7.

How did it suit their health? —It did not suit it at all; they were often sick.

Where is your brother John working now? —He died three years ago.

What age was he when he died? —Sixteen years and eight months.

To what was his death attributed by your mother and the medical attendants? —It was attributed to this, that he died from working such long hours, and that it had been brought on by the factory. They have to stop the flies with their knees, because they go so swift they cannot stop them with their hands; he got a bruise on the shin by a spindle-board, and it went on to that degree that it burst; the surgeon cured that, then he was better; then he went to work again; but when he had worked about two months more his spine became affected, and he died.

Was the labour continued for an equal length of time? —Yes, the same hours, from 5 in the morning till 8 at night.

Did you ever work later than 8? —When trade was brisk, I have worked from 5 in the morning to 9 at night.

In that department were you also strapped? —Yes.

When you have worked an hour additional, did you get any more wages? —We worked two summers, and during that time my master had a strong order, and we worked for six months, all the summer, beginning at the spring and ending in August, and we had only 10½ *d.* a piece, big and little, for the whole time.

For what hours? —From 5 in the morning till 9 at night.

And for this additional hour for six months you had only 10½ *d.*? —Only 10½ *d.*

A week? —No, for the whole time.

Need you have worked that additional hour without you chose? —Yes, we were forced to work it.

Should you not have been discharged if you had refused to work that extra hour? —Yes.

Were you still chastised in that department of the mill? —When we worked at the bobbin work, we were not used so cruelly.

Was it when you were a bobbin-winder that you worked all those hours, and received only 10½ *d.*? —No, it was when I worked at the throstles.

What was your chastisement at the bobbin-winding? —There was no strap; only the over-looker was a very savage man, and he used to strike them under the ribs, till it took their wind away, and they fell on the floor, and perhaps lay there for two minutes.

That was not the same man you spoke of before? —No, not the same.

Are all the overlookers in the habit of treating children with this severity? —Yes.

And does the master know of it? —Yes, they put them up to it, because they could not get the quantity of work done they wanted, unless they were to beat them.

When you left that mill, to what place did you go? —I went to Mr. Brooks's woollen manufactory, Upper Mill, Huddersfield.

What were your usual hours of labour there? —Our regular hours were 12 hours a day. We worked from 6 in the morning till 8 at night; we had half an hour to breakfast, an hour at noon, and half an hour at drinking time.

Making altogether twelve hours of actual labour? —Yes.

Was that too much for you? —Yes, we could not stand it.

What age were you at that time? —I was 10 when I went there first.

How long did you stay there? —Nearly four years.

What department of the business was it you worked at? —At the Lewis machine, in the dressing department.

You have stated the regular hours of working; mention to the Committee how long you were required to work when trade was particularly brisk? —I was obliged to work from 5 in the morning till half-past 10, sometimes till 11, and once all night, for four months together.

What was your additional wages for that extra labour? —I had 5 *s.* a week, and they gave us a shilling for over-hours.

And again you had no option; you must either have worked those over-hours or have left your place? —Yes; and if we had left it, it was the same in other places when trade was good. If we had left and gone to another place, we should perhaps, in the course of a fortnight, have had to work till 10 at night there.

Was it easy to get a new place in those times? —No, it was not easy to get a place, because there are so many boys; there is always somebody out of work.

You found that labour to be very distressing to you? —Yes.

And did it increase the pain in your limbs? —Very much.

Did it also increase the deformity which came upon you? —Yes, and I have had to drop it several times for a fortnight together.

Were you beaten up to that degree of labour in that mill? —Yes; they used not to strap them; they used to strike them with their fist, and kick them with their foot. During the time I worked there I wished many times they would have sent me for a West India slave. . . .

You had heard the condition of the slaves in the West Indies described to you? —Yes, I had.

Did you feel yourself very much overworked, with insufficient rest, and very much injured by that length of labour? —Yes.

Did that render you very miserable in your mind? —Yes, it did; and I thought there could be nothing worse, and that there could not be worse slaves than those who worked in factories.

To what department were you then removed? —To the Davis's machines.

What were your hours there? —I have worked the same hours, from 5 in the morning till 10 at night, and half-past 10.

Did you ever work all Friday, Friday night, and Saturday, when you were working at the Davis's machines? —Yes, one night I worked all night at the Davis's machines.

Did you leave that situation? —Yes; one morning I was between ten minutes and a quarter of an hour too late, and the overlooker met me, and he gave me a knock on the head and sent my head against a step, and caused a great bump to rise; he said he would turn me off, "a young devil, for being too late;" he followed me up the steps, but he could not catch me; I ran round the steps to get away from him, and I left that place.

How old were you then? —Near 14.

So that he beat you and kicked you to that degree for being too late? —Yes.

Do they stop your wages also for being too late? —Yes, they do sometimes; they would bate a man 6 d. for being a quarter of an hour too late; but I do not think they did that at Mr. Brooks's.

Did they stop the children's wages also? —Yes, 1 d., and 2 d. at another mill; but it was not a regular rule there.

Does the Committee understand you to state that to be a regular thing at the other mills? —Yes.

State the scale of forfeiture you have known at any mill? —I left that mill, and I went to Mr. William Firth's, Greenhead, Huddersfield, and they began this rule,—they bated the boys 1½ d. for six minutes, and a man 3 d.; and when it got to sixteen minutes they doubled it, 6 d. for a man and 3 d. for a boy, and it was dou-

bled again when it got up to thirty-one minutes.

What was the forfeiture for thirty-one minutes for a boy? —Four-pence halfpenny.

And what was a boy's daily wages? —Ten-pence, a shilling, and so on.

Who took the fines, the master or the overlooker? —I do not know whether the overlooker kept the fines or not; he used to take them when he paid the wages.

Were you beaten for being too late, as well as fined? —Yes.

Was it a general system in that mill to beat the children as well as stop their wages? —They did not beat them so cruelly; but at times they would beat them, not with straps, but with their fists.

Do you think the regulation of stopping their wages for being too late prevented so much beating as you had at other mills? —Yes, it prevents beating.

Does it not entirely do it away? —No, it does not do it away; but they were beat the more where they did not pay the fines.

How many hours did you work at Mr. Firth's? —The longest hours I worked there were from 5 in the morning till 9 at night.

What intervals had you for refreshment? —Two hours.

So that you had fourteen hours of actual labours? —Yes.

Why did you leave that employment? —I left it because I could stand it no longer; the weakness was so bad in my knees and ankles, I was obliged totally to give up work.

Had your health been very much injured also? —I believe I should have died if I had not given up; the doctors have nearly cured me.

Under whose medical treatment did your mother place you? —Dr. Walker's, of the Huddersfield Infirmary.

Was you an in-patient or an out-patient? —An out-patient.

Why did they not take you into the house? —They could only take in twenty at once, because there are not subscribers enough to enable them to take more, and there are so many accidents that they are obliged to take in; they would have taken me in if they could; they have twenty-two in sometimes, but twenty is the regular rule.

So that there was no room for you, on account of the accidents from the factories, to which they must pay instant attention? —Yes.

Has that been established long? —No, it is a new place.

Who sent you to the Infirmary? —My mother got a recommendation from Mr. Bradley Clay.

Did you leave your work to go to the Infirmary? —Yes; it is near eleven weeks since I dropped work.

Where did you go to when you left the Huddersfield Infirmary? —Mr. Oastler got me into Leeds Infirmary, as an in-patient.

Under whose care? —Mr. Hey.

Did Mr. Hey examine you? —He did; and he said it was come on with the factory system. He said, he thought he could have done me good if he had had me a few years ago; there would have been means of bringing me straight; he said it was all from the factory system, working so long, and standing so many hours.

Did he give you any hopes of recovering your limbs? —No; he said there were poor hopes of me. Dr. Walker says I never shall be right any more.

Have you got worse since you were 14 years of age? —It was continuing on all along, but I have got rather worse since.

Are you capable of walking? —I cannot walk above thirty yards before my legs begin aching very bad, and then I cannot walk at all.

Had you any opportunity of learning to read and write while you went to the factory? —No; only a little bit on the Sabbath-day.

Are you learning to write a little now? —Yes, I have tried within this last ten or eleven weeks.

You could not previously write? —No; I did not know how to hold my pen.

What proportion of the children in the factories in which you have worked can write? —I do not think there is above one in a hundred that can write.

You said you were an in-patient of the Leeds Infirmary; are there any cases similar to yours there, that have been brought on by this excess

labour in the factories? —Yes, there is one boy; he is weak in the knees, the same as I am, but not quite so far gone; he is under Mr. Smith, I think, a surgeon; and there is another boy in the same ward as I am, he was struck by a slubber with a billy-roller on his hip; there is another boy who was kicked by an overlooker with his foot, and his body is the same as if it was taken off and set on behind him; his body is twisted, and he goes upon crutches.

How long have you been in the Leeds Infirmary? —A week last Saturday night; if I had been this week at Leeds I should have been a fortnight next Saturday.

Have any cases of accidents in mills or factories been brought into the Infirmary since you were there? —Yes, last Tuesday but one there was a boy brought in about 5 or 6 o'clock in the evening from a mill; he had got catched with the shaft, and he had both his thighs broke, and from his knee to his hip the flesh was ripped up the same as if it had been cut by a knife, his head was bruised, his eyes were nearly torn out, and his arms broken. His sister, who ran to pull him off, got both her arms broke and her head bruised, and she is bruised all over her body. The boy died last Thursday night but one, about 8 o'clock; I do not know whether the girl is dead, but she was not expected to live.

Did that accident occur in consequence of the shaft not being sheathed? —Yes.

Do not you happen to know that the shafts of mills could be sheathed at comparatively very small expense? —Yes, all could be boxed off for a very little expense. In the mill I worked at last I do not think it would take above 10 s. to box them all off; and a man has had his two fingers cut off for want of its being done.

Something has been said about the fear of giving evidence regarding this factory question; do you know whether any threats have ever been used on that account? —Yes; Dr. Walker ordered me to wear irons from the ankle to the thigh; my mother was not able to get them, and he said he would write a note, and she might go to some gentlemen in the town, and give them that note, and see if they would not give her something towards them;

and so she did, and I have got the bare irons made; and I was coming into the yard where I live; and there was a man who worked at the same place that I did, asked me to let him look at them; I told him I could not get money to line them with, and he said, "I will tell you where there is a gentleman who will give you the money;" he told me of Mr. Oastler, and he said, "I will go and see if he is at home, that you may not lose your trouble." Mr. Oastler was at home, and said I was to be there at 8 o'clock in the morning, because he wanted to go off on a journey; I got there about half-past 8. Mr. Wood of Bradford gave me a sovereign, and Mr. Oastler gave me 3 *s.* 6 *d.*, and so I had them made. He asked me questions what my lameness came on with, and I told him, and he happened to mention it at the County Meeting at York; my master saw it in the newspaper; I think it was in Mr. Baines's newspaper, of Leeds; he is an enemy to the Ten Hours' Bill, and he happened to see it in the paper, and he sent the foreman on to our house where I lived; he had not patience to read it, and he said to my mother, "I suppose it is owing to our place that your Joseph got the use of his limbs taken away?" and my mother said he was informed wrong, that he had it before he went to that factory; but he said, "If he has said anything about our factory, we shall certainly turn him off, and both his brothers." I have two little brothers working at the same place.

Did the foreman say this to you? —To my mother and me; he said he did not know exactly how it was, but he would go back and see the paper himself, and if he found out that we said anything about the factory system, that we should be turned off.

Have you been turned off? —I have not, but my master will not speak to me or look at me: I do not know whether he will let me start again or not.

You have been unwell? —Yes.

Have your brothers been turned off? —No.

You are able to work now? —I cannot work, because I have not strength in my legs.

When you left the mill, could that machine at which you worked be worked without you? —No, they have another boy working in the place.

Then the machine could not go on without another boy being put in your place? —No; there is often a boy kept in case any one falls poorly.

You never met with any accident in your limbs? —Yes, I have got one of my arms broken.

Are you sure the injury you suffered was entirely owing to working in factories? —Yes, and standing so many hours.

When did you begin to feel the weakness in your limbs? —When I had worked about half a year.

Did you not say that at 14 you ran away from the over-looker? —I said he turned me away; it is generally their way to beat them out of the place; so I got up the stairs before him, and ran round the machine, and he could not catch me.

Then your limbs were not much injured then? —I had just been lying up at home a fortnight, a little before.

Does it hurt you to walk now? —Yes, a great deal.

Did you not state that you met with an accident in the mill? —Yes, I had one of my arms broke.

What were you doing when that occurred? —I was working at what is called a brushing mill; there is a pin they put into the roller to make it run round, and the pin catched my sleeve, and twisted my arm round and broke it, and another boy has had his arm broken in the same way.

Is there any way of avoiding such accidents? —Yes; at Mr. Brooks's mill they cannot break their arms by that part of the machine, owing to a different arrangement. There was a boy who, to fettle the machine, was kneeling down, and a strap catched him about his ankles, and carried him round the wheel, and dashed his brains out on the floor.

Do you think these accidents usually happen at the latter end of the day, when the children get tired? —Yes, that boy got killed at a quarter past 7 at night.

Do you think it is possible for the children to be so active and nimble as to avoid the danger of the machinery when they are so over-worked and fatigued? —No, because they are sleepy.

It appears you have worked, in all, ten years in these mills? —Yes.

Have you found that in all those mills you have been required to labour longer than your strength could bear? —Yes, I have.

And have you found that, on the whole, you have been rendered ill, deformed and miserable, by the factory system, as at present pursued? —Yes; oh! if I had a thousand pounds, I would give them to have the use of my limbs again.

Would not you and the rest of the children be very happy to avail yourselves of an opportunity of learning the rudiments of a decent education, if leisure were afforded you after your day's toil? —I have tried to read after I have come home at 9 o'clock, but I have fallen asleep directly, with my book open.

When you were so long worked, you could not avail yourselves of the Sunday-school very profitably, on account of the fatigue you endured? —No; when we worked so long, I could not get to school at all on the Sabbath-day.

Though you have been required to work so long at a particular period of the year, have there not been other parts of the year in which you had not full employment? —We have worked during the summer all those hours at Brooks's mill; and in winter, perhaps, we have not had four days' work in the week.

You stated that you found it your duty to go to those mills, in order to maintain your mother, who is a widow, and very poor? —Yes.

Veneris, 6° die Julii, 1832

Michael Thomas Sadler, Esquire, in the Chair.
William Longston, called in; and Examined

Where do you reside? —At Stockport.

What is your age? —Between 40 and 41.

Have you had considerable experience in the spinning of cotton, and in other operations connected with that trade? —Some little in the spinning, but more in the previous preperations.

Have you known the operatives in the manufacture of cotton from your youth up? —Not without intervals; for about six years in my youth, and in maturer years as a manager.

Is it a subject, on the whole, to which you have paid much and serious attention,—the management of the cotton factories of this country? —Yes, my attention has been very frequently called to it in disputed and difficult matters.

Are the hours of labour more now than they were when you were a boy? —I should think they are fully as short now as then.

Have the laws, then, already enacted, diminished the hours of labour, or have they had a tendency to do so? —I should think, in the general struggle of competition, if it had not been for the enactment of some restrictive law, that the hours must have been now longer.

But, in point of fact, in consequence of such restrictive laws, they have somewhat abated? —I think not abated, but I think they may have had this tendency, that occasional convictions for working young persons too long hours may have operated as a salutary check, and have prevented them from working as long as they otherwise would have done. In country places they work even longer than they do at Stockport; and in Manchester the hours are not so long as they are usually at Stockport and the country places; not being under the eyes of those who might be likely to inform, they take liberties and work longer hours; and from this I infer that those checks have a good tendency in preventing the owners from working so long as they otherwise would.

So that at all events, it is your impression, that legislative interference has been beneficial, though not to the extent that it is desirable it should be carried? —Yes, that is my opinion.

You have already stated that, in country places, the law is evaded to a considerable extent; I would ask whether you think that any legal provisions can be so constructed as to become effectual? —Yes, I think they might, in case the penalties were made adequate to the offence and the restriction; if they were made such that a large capitalist would regard them; at present I think them insignificant; and if they can be evaded 500 times, one penalty may be considered trifling, in comparison with the profit which might arise from transgressing the law.

Is it your opinion, that personal punishment ought to await those who habitually and intentionally evade the law made to protect the infant and rising generation; I am meaning now to allude to the incarceration of offenders? —The question is indeed a delicate one to be answered, but in conscience I should think that masters who set to their workmen the example of transgressing the law, and so diminish that respect that ought to be maintained in them for the laws, I think, and must say, that their criminality is augmented by that circumstance, and that (as you term it) personal punishment, and (as you explained it) incarceration, I really think would be a punishment not more than adequate to the criminality.

Do the operatives connive at the violations of laws which have been enacted for their own express protection? —Yes, almost universally.

State why and how they do so? —If they do not connive, they must be brought forward as witnesses against the masters; but, being brought forward as a witness against the master, if the person be a voluntary witness, it is ten to one if they can obtain employment anywhere in the district where they are known, and where their name could be sent, so that their persons could be in anywise identified; I think this explanation will show and prove that employment would be exceedingly improbable for them anywhere, as employers would never deem themselves safe where they had in employ one who had been a voluntary witness against them.

So that the operatives themselves, in such cases, are obliged to become parties to a breach of the law enacted for their own protection? —There are other reasons; for instance, in the case of a spinner; a spinner has piecers; they (the piecers) are universally persons who are under the age limited by the law for protection; in case the piecers are taken away from the spinner, he finds then a difficulty in turning off the quantity which is required; and even were it not so, a wish to do as much as they can, causes them to keep the piecers more than the law prescribes; the spinners in general (though some of them are well-meaning people), I think deserve, at the very least, censure for their eagerness to keep those little piecers in the factory so many hours.

You mean by that, to keep them in longer than the law allows? —To keep them in at work as long as they are kept in in general.

You spoke as to the difficulty of finding employment, in case any operative employed in a mill or factory should be a party to asking redress by legal means, for a breach of that law which has been enacted for his protection; is that difficulty so general as to operate upon the minds of the working people in mills and factories, so as to deter them from seeking redress by such legal means? —It may be thought that there have not occurred instances sufficiently numerous to justify the assertion which I have made; but, for example, there was an arbitration law enacted, amended and extended in 1824, and made applicable to persons of all trades or employments; and yet, since the enactment of that law, none of the operatives of Stockport have dared to avail themselves of it, when their wages have been arbitrarily abated. I allude to fines; the law is this, that if the parties complaining do not wish the matter in dispute to go before a magistrate, it is legal to refer it to persons who understand it, and their decision is legally binding upon the parties complaining and those complained of.

So that you think that, in a case in which the operative has either to inform against his employer, or to be a principal witness to sustain some other information for breaches of an Act passed for his protection, that in those cases the interference of any such operative would be very highly to his disadvantage, and that he would find it difficult to obtain his employment there, or anywhere else? —Yes, and I saw an instance of it, perhaps four or five months ago; a manufacturer in the town of Stockport was brought before the magistrates for overworking children, and the decision was in the manufacturer's favour; curiosity caused me to go, and I do not think he was guilty; I think it was one of the cases wherein the manufacturer really was wronged; the decision, however, was in his favour; but the persons who came as witnesses against him I saw in the streets afterwards, and they told me that they could not get employment.

Neither with their actual master nor with any other person? —Nowhere; they told me they had applied at various places, but that their having become witnesses, occasioned them to be refused employment wherever they applied.

Then you presume that there is a combination among the masters, to exclude from work those individuals who give information upon the infraction of the law? —I am not aware that there is any combination, I have judged it rather to be a tacit consent, or a general practice, than a combination.

Perhaps you have known of instances, since you speak so fully upon this subject, in which employers have dictated terms of the employed, which interfere with their rights as workmen? —Yes, I have known a great many instances of that kind; but one or two I remember which seemed extraordinary.

Will you state them? —There was a contention between the employers and the employed at Stockport, in the beginning of 1829, about wages; and of this contest a strike was the consequence; and the masters of Hyde thought proper to interfere, and that interference it may be necessary to give in their own words, as published and placarded. They say—

"We, the undersigned Spinners and Power-loom Manufacturers of Hyde, Staley, Bridge, Dukenfield, and the neighbourhood,

Having observed with regret the self-inflicted and continuing distress of the operatives of Stockport, instigated by evil-designing persons to turn out against their masters, and being informed that this distress is prolonged by assistance being rendered by our work-people to the turn-outs in that town, do hereby agree to abate ten per cent, every fortnight from the wages of such of our piece-work hands who shall refuse to sign a declaration, that they will not remain or become members of any combination, interfering with the free exercise of individual labour; or directly or indirectly contribute to the support of any turn-outs, on pain of forfeiting a fortnight's wages, should they be found so doing."

Were any other steps taken to prevent the free-agency of the work-people on that occasion? —It appears that there had been a combination; for immediately afterwards, as is seen by that placard on the walls of Stockport, a written requirement, called an agreement, was offered by the masters for the operatives to sign, which was a *sine quâ non* of employment; the operatives were to sign the following words, or not be employed; and thousands of them did so, and were obliged to do so.

[*The following Document was then put in, and read:*]

"We, the undersigned, agree with Messrs. ———, that we will work for them on the following terms:

"We declare that we do not belong to the society called the 'Union,' or any other society for the support of turn-outs, or which has for its object any interference with the rules laid down for the government of mills or manufactories.

"We agree with our said masters, that we will not become members of, or be connected with, any such society, while we remain in our present employ.

"That we will not, directly or indirectly, subscribe or contribute to any such society, or to any turn-out hands whatsoever.

"That we will give a fortnight's notice previous to leaving our employ; and we will observe all the other rules of this mill, and all special agreements that we may enter into with our masters.

"And if we are discovered to act contrary to the above agreement, each of us so offending will forfeit a sum equal to a fortnight's wages; and our masters shall have power to deduct the same from our wages, or discharge us from their employ without any notice, at their own option."

I may observe, that by the wording of this document, they say they would not directly or indirectly support any turn-out hands whatsoever; that they were liable to the penalty here announced, in case they supported a son, or even gave anything, directly or indirectly, to a starving daughter or other relative.

Do not the operatives of that town and neighbourhood consider themselves not only exceedingly interfered with in their lawful rights, but entirely degraded by conditions of that sort being imposed upon them when they were entering into employment, or were already in it? —They did consider themselves exceedingly degraded; and a Member of Parliament, in the presence of several operatives, said that any person of spirit would rather be reduced to the necessity of eating cabbage-stalks than sign such a document. That is the same document which Mr. Edward Davenport so strongly reprobated upon presenting a petition to the House of Commons, of which I hold a copy in my hand.

Do not those facts impress you more strongly with the conviction of the necessity of the legislative interference in regard to the labour of the children and young persons in the employ of the owners of mills and factories? —Yes, those and other facts convince me that the legislative protection is necessary; that the operatives are perfectly powerless in fixing the hours of their own labour; that it is a mistake in legislators to think that they are such free agents as the hand-loom weavers who work at home, or tailors or others who are employed in domestic employment, and who certainly can fix the hours of their own labour; but an instance of those employed in a cotton-mill fixing the hours of their own labour never was known, and therefore I consider that legislative protection is as necessary for them as it is for persons liable to be overwrought abroad.

Did you not say that the hours of labour now are about the same as when you were a boy? —I think they are.

Is the intensity of application and of labour altered, either against or in favour of the operative and of the children employed in mills and factories? —I was a great number of years out of any factory, but those who were my acquaintances during my boyhood have often conversed with me, and they very frequently say that it cannot be less than double in intensity and exertion of physical application. . . .

Martis, 7° die Augusti, 1832
Michael Thomas Sadler, Esquire, in the Chair.
John Richard Farre, Esq., M.D., called in; and Examined

What is your profession? —That of a physician.

Have you had considerable experience in this city in attending to the diseases of the poor, whether in hospitals or in private practice? —The whole period of my medical study and experience in all the branches of the profession, for the purposes of a consulting physician, has extended to forty-two years.

Do you not regard it as an established principle in your profession, that moderate exercise, with due intervals for rest and for meals, are necessary for the preservation of health? —So essential that without it medical treatment is unavailing.

It is found, on the contrary, that excessive labour, exertion or employment, so as to produce weariness of body and mind, and without due intervals for meals and refreshment, must in ordinary cases be extremely prejudicial to the human constitution? —Man can do no more than he is allowed or permitted to do by nature, and in attempting to transgress the bounds Providence has pointed out for him, he abridges his life in the exact proportion in which he transgresses the laws of nature and the Divine command.

You would think that one of those violations of the laws of nature is excessive labour, excessive both as to its length and the fatigue which it induces, and that it is more prejudicial to young persons than to those advanced to full maturity? —In exact proportion to their feebleness.

Do you conceive that the ordinary limits of a day's labour, as already settled by universal custom, whether in agriculture or mechanical pursuits, namely, about twelve hours a day, with due intermission, is, generally speaking, as much as the human constitution is capable of sustaining without injury? —It depends upon the kind and degree of exertion, for the human being is the creature of a day, and it is possible for the most athletic man under the highest conflicts of body or mind, and especially of both, to exhaust in one hour the whole of his nervous energy provided for that day, so as to be reduced, even in that short space of time, to a state of extreme torpor, confounded with apoplexy, resembling and sometimes terminating in death.

Would labour, too long continued, of a less strenuous nature, but becoming very wearisome both to body and mind, be prejudicial if persevered in? —The injury is in proportion to the exhaustion of the sensorial power. Let me take the life of a day to make myself clearly understood. It consists of alternate action and repose, and repose is not sufficient without sleep. The alternation of the day and the night is a beautiful provision in the order of Providence for the healing of man, so that the night repairs the waste of the day; and he is thereby fitted for the labour of the ensuing day. If he attempt to live two days in one, or to give only one night and two days' labour, he abridges his life in the same, or rather in a greater proportion, for as his days are, so will his years be.

Upon the whole, then, recurring to the question, should not you think that a day's labour, consisting of twelve hours, pursued for a continuance, would, in ordinary cases, be as much as a human being could endure with impunity? —I think that twelve hours' labour is too much for a very large majority of human beings. If I am to state the precise quantity, in my experience, as tending to give the longest and the most vigorous life, I should take it, even in the adult, at eight hours' active exertion, eight hours' sleep, and eight hours allowed for recreation and meals. Those are the divisions of the day which would procure the happiest and the most vigorous life, and which would, I think, yield the greatest sum of labour; but the child requires a greater proportion of sleep than the adult; for sleep is not simply repose, but it is a restorative process.

You are aware that a much greater duration of labour is required than that to which you have alluded, as the most consistent with health; have you seen the effect of forced labour upon the human body? —In the course of my medical life I have seen it extensively; the first part of my medical education was conducted in the West Indies, where I had an opportunity of observing the effects of slavery, and the diseases produced by slavery.

Were you engaged in medical practice as well as medical studies in the West Indies? —I was.

Will you state to this Committee whether, when human beings are regarded as mere property, it is not found necessary, with a view to the preservation of that property, to limit the duration of their labour, and more particularly the labour of young persons? —It has been found necessary to diminish that labour, especially in regard to the young, insomuch that the young are never accounted fit for labour; their employment is always of the lightest kind.

Until what age? —The exact time for employing them in the field varies with their growth. In the West Indies, human life is often precocious: in the island in which my observations were made, namely, the island of Barbadoes, the oldest established colony, a colony in which there is the hardest work, for it is a hill country, and the whole production of that island is the effect of manual labour, as it is a rocky, and often an artificial soil, through the greater part of the island: it affords therefore a fair specimen of the effect of the fullest labour on the human constitution, and the returns of the increase in the slave population in that island would be a fair criterion to enable the Committee to judge of the effect of that labour, and whether proper provisions were used to render it less injurious. I have reason to believe, it would be found that the population has been for a great many years considerably on the increase, notwithstanding that labour.

Have the regulations recommended by medical authorities in that island been adopted with a view to the preservation of the youth of that colony; and if so, what is their nature? —Each plantation has its regular medical superintendent; but there is a number of highly educated gentlemen in that island; and to my knowledge, an agricultural society was established about a quarter of a century ago, for the express purpose of improving the condition of the slaves, without reference at all to the proceedings on that subject which have occurred in this country. Medical gentlemen, I say, of the highest education were members of that society, and to my certain knowledge, took the two main questions of labour and feeding into their consideration, and communicated papers to that society for their guidance respecting the management of the slaves, both old and young, as to labour and as to food, and as to the proper labour and rest; and I know that extraordinary care was taken, both in regard to regulating the labour of the young and in feeding them, to make them a vigorous race and fit for the work.

What were the regulations in respect of the labour of the children and young persons? —As far as I am acquainted with them, they consisted in not employing them in field labour, in digging or in carrying manure, but in exercising them in gathering the green crops for the stock. The plan of working them lightly in the open air and feeding them, not trusting to the food provided by the parents' care, but by the care of the master, had the most beneficial effect in improving their condition. When I contributed to superintend the negro population, I never knew the young over-worked. I observed that their diseases were more frequently the effect of improper feeding.

Supposing that the employment of children in the factories of this country is spread over twelve or fourteen hours a day, and often with but very short intervals for the taking of their meals; is there any thing equal to that sort of labour imposed upon the children of the slaves in that island? —Nothing of the kind; even the adult, in the most vigorous condition of body, is not subjected to labour of that duration.

Do you happen to know whether the owners of those slaves, alluding to the children, attempt to make a profit by their labour before they arrive at that period of life when they are capable of rendering it? —Never; I have always, as a medical observer, considered that their employment was used only as a training for health and for future occupation.

So that you consider that the limitation of the length and degree of the labour of the children and young persons in Barbadoes is eminently advantageous to the planter himself, with a view merely to his own interest and future advantage? —Certainly; it is necessary. In English factories, every thing which is valuable in manhood is sacrificed to an inferior advantage in childhood. You purchase your advantage at the price of infanticide; the profit thus gained is death to the child. Looking at its effects, I should suppose it was a system directly intended to diminish population.

What have been the provisions to guard against the ill effects of excessive labour? —The provisions consist in the proper management of the youth, in not sacrificing them, and in exercising them in the open air.

Do you consider that labour in the open air, at a given high temperature, is less pernicious than labour performed in a confined atmosphere artificially heated to the same degree of temperature? —There is only a certain portion of labour which any human being can bear in a day, but that labour is better accomplished in a pure atmosphere than in a confined and impure one, because air is vital food, and the relative value of a pure air to the blood is to the grosser aliments which supply blood, as one minute to fourteen days; and it admits of this demonstration, that if a human being, by malformation, disease, or the accidents of life, be deprived of the grosser aliments of bread, flesh and water, he dies in a period of from eleven to nineteen days, and the ordinary period may be taken at fourteen; if he be *completely* deprived of air, he dies in one minute. The relative value therefore of food through the organs of supply, to sanguinification effected in the lungs by pure atmospheric air, is as the value of one minute to fourteen days, according to my estimate. And the deterioration of the atmosphere in which human beings are working produces a deleterious effect in proportion to that deterioration. Supposing that in a place where human beings are congregated, and the air, for want of ventilation and from having been breathed, is impaired, the blood is immediately deteriorated; it passes from its red or vital state to black blood, and the vitality of the being is lowered; it gives a pallid or livid expression, according to its degree; it destroys the appetite, diminishes the action of the heart and arteries, lowers gradually the whole vigour of the system, and produces premature death. This is the inevitable effect of continued labour in a confined, heated and foul atmosphere.

Are the children in the West Indies ever employed in night-work? —I never knew an instance of that.

None are employed in night-work but those who are called the strong gang? —It is only a privileged and higher class, often the most valuable persons on the property, who are employed during a part of the night in the manufacture of sugar in Barbadoes. . . .

None but persons in the full enjoyment of strength are employed in night-work? . . .

It appears, from an official document presented to this Committee, that a greater proportion of mortality exists wherever this system of long and irksome labour is allowed; would you be prepared for such results from the principles you have stated? —I think that the result is so inevitable, that I view it as a species of infanticide, and a very cruel, because lingering, species of infanticide, resulting from the overextension of a principle in itself good, the principle of cheap production demanding overlabour; and that the only safeguard to the state consists in opposing this principle of political economy by the medical voice, whenever it trenches on vital economy.

You think that political economy, supposing it were made manifest that the system would produce national wealth, ought not to be suffered to interfere with vital economy? —It ought not to be suffered to trench on vital economy, because if it does, it is guilty of homicide. I have no hesitation in affirming that the voice of the profession would maintain this truth, and never assent to life being balanced against wealth. That the life is more than the meat, is a divine maxim which we are bound to obey.

So that it is your settled conviction, that what you have denominated, very properly, the forcing system, injures the present generation, and threatens the most injurious effects regarding the future? —The vigour of the animal life depends upon the perfection of the blood, and the balance preserved between the pulmonary and aortic circulation; but in the aortic circulation there is also a balance between the arterial and the venous systems, and the heart is the regulating organ of the whole. Now if the arterial circulation be too much exhausted, an accumulation necessarily takes place on the venous side, and the blood is deteriorated, and organic diseases, which abridge life, are produced. It would carry me too far to investigate this point; I only state the fact which can be demonstrated; but there is another and a higher effect; for man is to be

considered as something vastly better than an animal; and the effect of diminishing the power of the heart and arteries by over-labour in a confined atmosphere is to deteriorate the blood, and to excite, in the *animal* part of the mind, gloomy and discontented trains of thought, which disturb and destroy human happiness, and lead to habits of over-stimulation. The reflecting or spiritual mind gradually becomes debased; and unless education interpose to meet the difficulties of the case, the being is necessarily ruined, both for present and for future life.

Are there any countervailing means which suggest themselves to your mind, which would render this continued labour less injurious to present health and happiness, and more conducive to the prosperity of future life? —Ventilation, exercise, and diminished exertion, are the most obvious means of meeting the difficulties of the case, joined to the change of ideas resulting from an education adapted to the spiritual nature of man.

So that you think it would be eminently beneficial if the hours of labour were somewhat abated during the day, so as to afford an opportunity for the change of mental exertion, and to direct that exertion to the purposes of education? —It would be a positive gain to the child, which not only mercy, but justice demands; and I think, also, it would be beneficial to the state.

It appears in evidence before this Committee, that the labour in mills and factories undergone by children and young persons of both sexes, is rarely less than fourteen hours a day, including the time allowed for meals; and that in many instances it greatly exceeds that term, and extends sometimes to eighteen or twenty hours, or upwards; during your residence in the West Indies, was there any system of labour imposed upon any of the children and young persons at all equal to that? —Never in the slightest degree approaching to it.

It is in evidence, that the children and young persons employed in factories have often to be roused from their lethargy induced by exertions too long continued, and to be stimulated to their labour (their strength being exhausted) by constant whippings, beatings, or other means of a like nature; are the children of the slaves in the West Indies more hardly worked or more cruelly treated than this state of things implies? —In the colony of which I have spoken, I never saw nor heard of such inhumanity.

Assuming that the children of this country are not free agents, can you have any doubt whatever, the slightest hesitation upon your mind, that they demand protection equally with the child of the West Indian slave? —I think the word "demand" is a very proper mode of putting the question; for I myself consider that the nation is responsible for it, and, as a medical man, I assert that if you deem it a part of your duty to make laws against mur-

der, I consider that legislation is equally necessary for the prevention of death in any mode in which it can be prematurely inflicted; and certainly this must be viewed as a most cruel mode of inflicting it.

You have no hesitation then, in saying that whether considered as a medical, or a political question, a remission of the hours of labour imposed upon the children and young persons of this country would be essentially beneficial? —I view it not only as a benefit, but as a duty; and I would say, not only as a physician, a Christian, and a parent, but also from the common sympathies of a man, that you are bound to afford it.

Adam Smith

Adam Smith (1723–1790) was a Scottish educator and economist who deeply affected the thinking of the nineteenth century. He himself lived in the Age of Enlightenment and was strongly influenced by the emphasis which some of his contemporaries placed upon natural law and the advantage of achieving the natural order unrestricted by man-made regulations. It was this phase of his thinking that appealed to the economic liberals of the nineteenth century and which was used by them to support their doctrine of laissez faire. Like the mercantilists of an earlier day, Smith was interested in increasing the prosperity of the nation, but unlike them he found the answer, not in a favorable trade balance, but in the production of goods which would have the greatest exchange value in the world's markets. This advantage could be achieved, according to Smith, by permitting each individual the freedom to follow his natural self-interest in both production and trade. Thus, the state should remove restrictions on all economic pursuits. In 1776, Smith published his great work, An Inquiry into the Nature and Causes of the Wealth of Nations, in which he summarized his theories. In reading the following selections from it note (1) the importance which Smith attached to labor in the production of wealth, (2) the advantages of division of labor, (3) the three factors contributing to increased output through division of labor, (4) the natural human quality to which Smith attributed the division of labor, (5) his implied estimate of human nature, (6) the importance of the size of the market to the division of labor, (7) the effect of import duties upon the division of labor, (8) the relative ability of the individual *and the lawgiver to determine what was to the individual's self-interest, (9) his analysis of the infant-industry argument, (10) the cases in which protective duties might be advantageous, (11) the problem of retaliatory duties, (12) his consideration of humanitarianism in removing duties, and (13) the vested interests and political lobbies resulting from protection.*

From: AN INQUIRY INTO THE NATURE AND CAUSES OF THE WEALTH OF NATIONS

INTRODUCTION

The annual labour of every nation is the fund which originally supplies it with all the necessaries and conveniences of life which it annually consumes, and which consist always either in the immediate produce of that labour, or in what is purchased with that produce from other nations.

According, therefore, as this produce, or what is purchased with it, bears a greater or smaller proportion to the number of those who are to consume it, the nation will be better or worse supplied with all the necessaries and conveniences for which it has occasion.

But this proportion must in every nation be regulated by two different circumstances: first, by the skill, dexterity, and judgment with which its labour is generally aplied; and, secondly, by the proportion between the number of those who are employed in useful labour, and that of those who are not so employed. Whatever be the soil, climate, or extent of territory of any particular nation, the abundance or scantiness of its annual supply must, in that particular situation, depend upon those two circumstances.

The abundance or scantiness of this supply, too, seems to depend more upon the former of those two circumstances than upon the latter. Among the savage nations of hunters and fishers, every individual who is able to work is more or less employed in useful labour, and endeavours to provide, as well as he can, the necessaries and conveniences of life, for himself, and such of his family or tribe as are either too old, or too young, or too infirm, to go a-hunting and fishing. Such nations, however, are so miserably poor, that, from mere want, they are frequently reduced, or at least think themselves reduced, to the necessity sometimes of directly destroying, and sometimes of abandoning, their infants, their old people, and those afflicted with lingering diseases, to perish with hunger, or to be devoured by wild beasts. Among civilised and thriving nations, on the contrary, though a great number of people do not labour at all, many of whom consume the produce of ten times, frequently of a hundred times, more labour than the greater part of those who work; yet the produce of the whole labour of the society is so great, that all are often abundantly supplied; and a workman, even of the lowest and poorest order, if he is frugal and industrious, may enjoy a greater share of the necessaries and conveniences of life than it is possible for any savage to acquire.

The causes of this improvement in the productive powers of labour, and the order according to which its produce is naturally distributed among the different ranks and conditions of men in the society, make the subject of the first book of this Inquiry. . . .

The greatest improvements in the productive powers of labour, and the greater part of the skill, dexterity, and judgment, with which it is anywhere directed, or applied, seem to have been the effects of the division of labour.

The effects of the division of labour, in the general business of society, will be more easily understood, by considering in what manner it operates in some particular manufactures. It is commonly supposed to be carried furthest in some very trifling ones; not perhaps that it

Adam Smith, *An Inquiry into the Nature and Causes of the Wealth of Nations,* London, 1870, 1; 3–8; 183–191.

really is carried further in them than in others of more importance: but in those trifling manufactures which are destined to supply the small wants of but a small number of people, the whole number of workmen must necessarily be small; and those employed in every different branch of the work can often be collected into the same workhouse, and placed at once under the view of the spectator. In those great manufactures, on the contrary, which are destined to supply the great wants of the great body of the people, every different branch of the work employs so great a number of workmen, that it is impossible to collect them all into the same workhouse. We can seldom see more, at one time, than those employed in one single branch. Though in such manufactures, therefore, the work may really be divided into a much greater number of parts, than in those of a more trifling nature, the division is not near so obvious, and has accordingly been much less observed.

To take an example, therefore, from a very trifling manufacture, but one in which the division of labour has been very often taken notice of, the trade of a pinmaker: a workman not educated to this business (which the division of labour has rendered a distinct trade), nor acquainted with the use of the machinery employed in it (to the invention of which the same division of labour has probably given occasion), could scarce, perhaps, with his utmost industry, make one pin in a day, and certainly could not make twenty. But in the way in which this business is now carried on, not only the whole work is a peculiar trade, but it is divided into a number of branches, of which the greater part are likewise peculiar trades. One man draws out the wire; another straights it; a third cuts it; a fourth points it; a fifth grinds it at the top for receiving the head; to make the head requires two or three distinct operations; to put it on is a peculiar business; to whiten the pins is another, it is even a trade by itself to put them into the paper; and the important business of making a pin is, in this manner, divided into about eighteen distinct operations, which, in some manufactories, are all performed by distinct hands, though in others the same man will sometimes perform two or three of them. I have seen a small manufactory of this kind, where ten men only were employed, and where some of them consequently performed two or three distinct operations. But though they were very poor, and therefore but indifferently accommodated with the necessary machinery, they could, when they exerted themselves, make among them about twelve pounds of pins in a day. There are in a pound upwards of four thousand pins of a middling size. Those ten persons, therefore, could make among them upwards of forty-eight thousand pins in a day. Each person, therefore, making a tenth part of forty-eight thousand pins, might be considered as making four thousand eight hundred pins in a day. But if they had all wrought separately and independently, and without any of them having been educated to this peculiar business, they certainly could not each of them have made twenty, perhaps not one pin in a day; that is, certainly, not the two hundred and fortieth, perhaps not the four thousand eight hundredth, part of what they are at present capable of performing, in consequence of a proper division and combination of their different operations.

In every other art and manufacture, the effects of the division of labour are similar to what they are in this very trifling one, though, in many of them, the labour can neither be so much subdivided, nor reduced to so great a simplicity of operation. The division of labour, however, so far as it can be introduced, occasions, in every art, a proportionable increase of the productive powers of labour. The separation of different trades and employments from one another, seems to have taken place in consequence of this advantage. This separation, too, is generally carried furthest in those countries which enjoy the highest degree of industry and improvement; what is the work of one man, in a rude state of society, being generally that of several in an improved one. In every improved society, the farmer is generally nothing but a farmer; the manufacturer, nothing but a manufacturer. The labour, too, which is necessary to produce any one complete manufacture, is almost always divided among a great number of hands. How many different trades are employed in each branch of the linen and woollen manufactures, from the growers of the flax and the wool, to the bleachers and smoothers of the linen, or to the dyers and dressers of the cloth! The nature of agriculture, indeed, does not admit of so many subdivisions of labour, nor of so complete a separation of one business from another, as manufactures. It is impossible to separate so entirely the business of the grazier from that of the corn-farmer, as the trade of the carpenter is commonly separated from that of the smith. The spinner is almost always a distinct person from the weaver; but the ploughman, the harrower, the sower of the seed, and the reaper of the corn, are often the same. The occasions for those different sorts of labour returning with the different seasons of the year, it is impossible that one man should be constantly employed in any one of them. This impossibility of making so complete and entire a separation of all the different branches of labour employed in agriculture, is perhaps the reason why the improvement of the productive powers of labour, in this art, does not always keep pace with their improvement in manufactures. The most opulent nations, indeed, generally excel all their neighbours in agriculture as well as in manufactures; but they are commonly more distinguished by their superiority in the latter than in the former. . . .

This great increase in the quantity of work, which, in consequence of the division of labour, the same number of people are capable of performing, is owing to three different circumstances; first, to the increase of dexterity in every particular workman; secondly, to the saving of the time which is commonly lost in passing from one species of work to another; and, lastly, to the invention of a great number of machines which facilitate and abridge labour, and enable one man to do the work of many. . . .

It is the great multiplication of the productions of all the different arts, in consequence of the division of labour, which occasions, in a well-governed society, that universal opulence which extends itself to the lowest ranks of the people. Every workman has a great quantity of his own work to dispose of beyond what he himself has occasion for; and every

other workman being exactly in the same situation, he is enabled to exchange a great quantity of his own goods for a great quantity, or, what comes to the same thing, for the price of a great quantity of theirs. He supplies them abundantly with what they have occasion for, and they accommodate him as amply with what he has occasion for, and a general plenty diffuses itself through all the different ranks of the society.

Observe the accommodation of the most common artificer or day-labourer in a civilised and thriving country, and you will perceive that the number of people, of whose industry a part, though but a small part, has been employed in procuring him this accommodation, exceeds all computation. The woollen coat, for example, which covers the day-labourer, as coarse and rough as it may appear, is the produce of the joint labour of a great multitude of workmen. The shepherd, the sorter of the wool, the wool-comber or carder, the dyer, the scribbler, the spinner, the weaver, the fuller, the dresser, with many others, must all join their different arts in order to complete even this homely production. How many merchants and carriers, besides, must have been employed in transporting the materials from some of those workmen to others who often live in a very distant part of the country? How much commerce and navigation in particular, how many ship-builders, sailors, sail-makers, rope-makers, must have been employed in order to bring together the different drugs made use of by the dyer, which often come from the remotest corners of the world? . . .

. . . If we examine, I say, all these things, and consider what a variety of labour is employed about each of them, we shall be sensible that, without the assistance and co-operation of many thousands, the very meanest person in a civilised country could not be provided, even according to, what we very falsely imagine, the easy and simple manner in which he is commonly accommodated. Compared, indeed, with the more extravagant luxury of the great, his accommodation must no doubt appear extremely simple and easy; and yet it may be true, perhaps, that the accommodation of an European prince does not always so much exceed that of an industrious and frugal peasant, as the accommodation of the latter exceeds that of many an African king, the absolute masters of the lives and liberties of ten thousand naked savages.

OF THE PRINCIPLE WHICH GIVES OCCASION TO THE DIVISION OF LABOUR

This division of labour, from which so many advantages are derived, is not originally the effect of any human wisdom, which foresees and intends that general opulence to which it gives occasion. It is the necessary, though very slow and gradual, consequence of a certain propensity in human nature, which has in view no such extensive utility; the propensity to truck, barter, and exchange one thing for another.

Whether this propensity be one of those original principles in human nature, of which no further account can be given, or whether, as seems more probable, it be the necessary consequence of the faculties of reason and speech, it belongs not to our present subject to inquire. It is common to all men, and to be found in no other race of animals, which seem to know neither this nor any other species of contracts. Two greyhounds, in running down the same hare, have sometimes the appearance of acting in some sort of concert. Each turns her towards his companion, or endeavours to intercept her when his companion turns her toward himself. This, however, is not the effect of any contract, but of the accidental concurrence of their passions in the same object at that particular time. Nobody ever saw a dog make a fair and deliberate exchange of one bone for another with another dog. Nobody ever saw one animal, by its gestures and natural cries, signify to another, this is mine, that yours; I am willing to give this for that. When an animal wants to obtain something either of a man, or of another animal, it has no other means of persuasion, but to gain the favour of those whose service it requires. A puppy fawns upon its dam, and a spaniel endeavours, by a thousand attractions, to engage the attention of its master who is at dinner, when it wants to be fed by him. Man sometimes uses the same arts with his brethren, and when he has no other means of engaging them to act according to his inclinations, endeavours by every servile and fawning attention to obtain their good will. He has not time, however, to do this upon every occasion. In civilised society he stands at all times in need of the co-operation and assistance of great multitudes, while his whole life is scarce sufficient to gain the friendship of a few persons. In almost every other race of animals, each individual, when it is grown up to maturity, is entirely independent, and in its natural state has occasion for the assistance of no other living creature. But man has almost constant occasion for the help of his brethren, and it is in vain for him to expect it from their benevolence only. He will be more likely to prevail if he can interest their self-love in his favour, and show them that it is for their own advantage to do for him what he requires of them. Whoever offers to another a bargain of any kind, proposes to do this. Give me that which I want, and you shall have this which you want, is the meaning of every such offer; and it is in this manner that we obtain from one another the far greater part of those good offices which we stand in need of. It is not from the benevolence of the butcher, the brewer, or the baker, that we expect our dinner, but from their regard to their own interest. We address ourselves, not to their humanity, but to their self-love, and never talk to them of our own necessities, but of their advantages. Nobody but a beggar chooses to depend chiefly upon the benevolence of his fellow-citizens. Even a beggar does not depend upon it entirely. The charity of well-disposed people, indeed, supplies him with the whole fund of his subsistence. But though this principle ultimately provides him with all the necessaries of life which he has occasion for, it neither does nor can provide him with them as he has occasion for them. The greater part of his occasional wants are supplied in the same manner as those of other people, by treaty, by barter, and by purchase. With the money which one man gives him he purchases food. The old clothes which another bestows upon him he exchanges for other clothes which suit him better, or for lodging, or for food, or for money, with which he can buy either food, clothes, or lodging, as he has occasion.

As it is by treaty, by barter, and by purchase, that we obtain from one another the greater part of those mutual good offices which we stand in need of, so it is this same trucking disposition which originally gives occasion to the division of labour. In a tribe of hunters or shepherds, a particular person makes bows and arrows, for example, with more readiness and dexterity than any other. He frequently exchanges them for cattle or for venison, with his companions; and he finds at last that he can, in this manner, get more cattle and venison, than if he himself went to the field to catch them. From a regard to his own interest, therefore, the making of bows and arrows grows to be his chief business, and he becomes a sort of armourer. Another excels in making the frames and covers of their little huts or moveable houses. He is accustomed to be of use in this way to his neighbours, who reward him in the same manner with cattle and with venison, till at last he finds it his interest to dedicate himself entirely to this employment, and to become a sort of house-carpenter. In the same manner a third becomes a smith or a brazier; a fourth, a tanner or dresser of hides or skins, the principal part of the clothing of savages. And thus the certainty of being able to exchange all that surplus part of the produce of his own labour, which is over and above his own consumption, for such parts of the produce of other men's labour as he may have occasion for, encourages every man to apply himself to a particular occupation, and to cultivate and bring to perfection whatever talent of genius he may possess for that particular species of business.

The difference of natural talents in different men, is, in reality, much less than we are aware of; and the very different genius which appears to distinguish men of different professions, when grown up to maturity, is not upon many occasions so much the cause, as the effect of the division of labour. The difference between the most dissimilar characters, between a philosopher and a common street porter, for example, seems to arise not so much from nature, as from habit, custom, and education. When they came into the world, and for the first six or eight years of their existence, they were, perhaps, very much alike, and neither their parents nor playfellows could perceive any remarkable difference. About that age, or soon after, they come to be employed in very different occupations. The difference of talents comes then to be taken notice of, and widens by degrees till at last the vanity of the philosopher is willing to acknowledge scarce any resemblance. But without the disposition to truck, barter, and exchange, every man must have procured to himself every necessary and conveniency of life which he wanted. All must have had the same duties to perform, and the same work to do, and there could have been no such difference of employment as could alone give occasion to any great difference of talents.

As it is this disposition which forms that difference of talents, so remarkable among men of different professions, so it is this same disposition which renders that difference useful. Many tribes of animals, acknowledged to be all of the same species, derive from nature a much more remarkable distinction of genius, than what, antecedent to custom and education, appears to take place among men. By nature a philosopher is not in genius and disposition half so different from a street porter, as a mastiff is from a greyhound, or a greyhound from a spaniel, or this last from a shepherd's dog. Those different tribes of animals, however, though all of the same species, are of scarce any use to one another. The strength of the mastiff is not in the least supported either by the swiftness of the greyhound, or by the sagacity of the spaniel, or by the docility of the shepherd's dog. The effects of those different geniuses and talents, for want of the power or disposition to barter and exchange, cannot be brought into a common stock, and do not in the least contribute to the better accommodation and conveniency of the species. Each animal is still obliged to support and defend itself, separately and independently, and derives no sort of advantage from that variety of talents with which nature has distinguished its fellows. Among men, on the contrary, the most dissimilar geniuses are of use to one another; the different produces of their respective talents, by the general disposition to truck, barter, and exchange, being brought, as it were, into a common stock, where every man may purchase whatever part of the produce of other men's talent he has occasion for.

THAT THE DIVISION OF LABOUR IS LIMITED BY THE EXTENT OF THE MARKET

As it is the power of exchanging that gives occasion to the division of labour, so the extent of this division must always be limited by the extent of the market. When the market is very small, no person can have any encouragement to dedicate himself entirely to one employment, for want of the power to exchange all that surplus part of the produce of his own labour, which is over and above his own consumption, for such parts of the produce of other men's labour as he has occasion for.

There are some sorts of industry, even of the lowest kind, which can be carried on nowhere but in a great town. A porter, for example, can find employment and subsistence in no other place. A village is by much too narrow a sphere for him; even an ordinary market-town is scarce large enough to afford him constant occupation. In the lone houses and very small villages which are scattered about in so desert a country as the highlands of Scotland, every farmer must be butcher, baker, and brewer, for his own family. In such situations we can scarce expect to find even a smith, a carpenter, or a mason, within less than twenty miles of another of the same trade. The scattered families that live at eight or ten miles distance from the nearest of them, must learn to perform themselves a great number of little pieces of work, for which, in more populous countries, they would call in the assistance of those workmen. Country workmen are almost everywhere obliged to apply themselves to all the different branches of industry that have so much affinity to one another as to be employed about the same sort of materials. A country carpenter deals in every sort of work that is made of wood; a country smith in every sort of work that is made of iron. The former is not only a carpenter, but a joiner, a cabinet-maker, and even a carver in wood, as well as a wheelwright, a plough-wright, a cart and waggon-maker. The employments of the latter are still more various. It is impossible that there should be such a trade as even that of a nailer in the remote and inland parts of the highlands of Scotland. Such a workman at the rate of a thousand nails a-day, and three hundred working days in the year, will make three hundred thousand nails in the year. But in such a situation it would be impossible to dispose of one thousand, that is, of one day's work in the year.

As by means of water-carriage, a more extensive market is opened to every sort of industry than what land-carriage alone can afford it, so it is upon the seacoast, and along the banks of navigable rivers, that industry of every kind naturally begins to subdivide and improve itself, and it is frequently not till a long time after that those improvements extend themselves to the inland parts of the country. A broad-wheeled waggon, attended by two men, and drawn by eight horses, in about six weeks' time, carries and brings back between London and Edinburgh near four ton weight of goods. In about the same time a ship navigated by six or eight men, and sailing between the ports of London and Leith, frequently carries and brings back two hundred ton weight of goods. Six or eight men, therefore, by the help of water-carriage, can carry and bring back, in the same time, the same quantity of goods between London and Edinburgh as fifty broad-wheeled waggons, attended by a hundred men, and drawn by four hundred horses. Upon two hundred tons of goods, therefore, carried by the cheapest land-carriage from London to Edinburgh, there must be charged the maintenance of a hundred men for three weeks, and both the maintenance and what is nearly equal to maintenance the wear and tear of four hundred horses, as well as of fifty great waggons. Whereas, upon the same quantity of goods carried by water, there is to be charged only the maintenance of six or eight men, and the wear and tear of a ship of two hundred tons burthen, together with the value of the superior risk, or the difference of the insurance between land and water-carriage. Were there no other communication between those two places, therefore, but by land-carriage, as no goods could be transported from the one to the other, except such whose price was very considerable in proportion to their weight, they could carry on but a small part of that commerce which at present subsists between them, and consequently could give but a small part of that encouragement which they at present mutually afford to each other's industry. There could be little or no commerce of any kind between the distant parts of the world. What goods could bear the expense of land-carriage between London and Calcutta? Or if there were any so precious as to be able to support this expense, with what safety could they be transported through the territories of so many barbarous nations? Those two cities, however, at present carry on a very considerable commerce with each other, and by mutually affording a market, give a good deal of encouragement to each other's industry. . . .

OF RESTRAINTS UPON IMPORTATION FROM FOREIGN COUNTRIES OF SUCH GOODS AS CAN BE PRODUCED AT HOME

By restraining, either by high duties, or by absolute prohibitions, the importations of such goods from foreign countries as can be produced at home, the monopoly of the home market is more or less secured to the domestic industry employed in producing them. Thus the prohibition of importing either live cattle or salt provisions from foreign countries, secures to the graziers of Great Britain the monopoly of the home market for butcher's meat. The high duties upon the importation of corn, which in times of moderate plenty, amount to a prohibition, give a like advantage to the growers of that commodity. The prohibition of the importation of foreign woollens is equally favourable to the woollen manufacturers. The silk manufacture, though altogether employed upon foreign materials, has lately obtained the same advantage. The linen manufacture has not yet obtained it, but is making great strides towards it. Many other sorts of manufactures have, in the same manner obtained in Great Britain, either altogether, or very nearly, a monopoly against their countrymen. The va-

riety of goods, of which the importation into Great Britain is prohibited, either absolutely, or under certain circumstances, greatly exceeds what can easily be suspected by those who are not well acquainted with the laws of the customs.

That this monopoly of the home market frequently gives great encouragement to that particular species of industry which enjoys it, and frequently turns towards that employment a greater share of both the labour and stock of the society than would otherwise have gone to it, cannot be doubted. But whether it tends either to increase the general industry or the society, or to give it the most advantageous direction, is not, perhaps, altogether so evident.

The general industry of the society can never exceed what the capital of the society can employ. As the number of workmen that can be kept in employment by any particular person must bear a certain proportion to his capital, so the number of those that can be continually employed by all the members of a great society must bear a certain proportion to the whole capital of the society, and never can exceed that proportion. No regulation of commerce can increase the quantity of industry in any society beyond what its capital can maintain. It can only divert a part of it into a direction into which it might not otherwise have gone; and it is by no means certain that this artificial direction is likely to be more advantageous to the society than that into which it would have gone of its own accord.

Every individual is continually exerting himself to find out the most advantageous employment for whatever capital he can command. It is his own advantage, indeed, and not that of the society, which he has in view. But the study of his own advantage naturally, or rather necessarily, leads him to prefer that employment which is most advantageous to the society. . . .

The produce of industry is what it adds to the subject or materials upon which it is employed. In proportion as the value of this produce is great or small, so will likewise be the profits of the employer. But it is only for the sake of profit that any man employs a capital in the support of industry; and he will always, therefore, endeavour to employ it in the support of that industry of which the produce is likely to be of the greatest value, or to exchange for the greatest quantity either of money or of other goods.

But the annual revenue of every society is always precisely equal to the exchangeable value of the whole annual produce of its industry, or rather is precisely the same thing with that exchangeable value. As every individual, therefore, endeavours as much as he can, both to employ his capital in the support of domestic industry, and so to direct that industry that its produce may be of the greatest value, every individual necessarily labours to render the annual revenue of the society as great as he can. He generally, indeed, neither intends to promote the public interest, nor knows how much he is promoting it. By preferring the support of domestic to that of foreign industry, he intends only his own security; and by directing that industry in such a manner as its produce may be of the greatest value, he intends only his own gain; and he is in this, as in many other cases, led by an invisible hand to promote an end which was no part of his intention. Nor is it always the worse for the society that it was no part of it. By pursuing his own interest, he frequently promotes that of the society more effectually than when he really intends to promote it. I have never known much good done by those who affected to trade for the public good. It is an affectation, indeed, not very common among merchants, and very few words need be employed in dissuading them from it.

What is the species of domestic industry which his capital can employ, and of which the produce is likely to be of the greatest value, every individual, it is evident, can in his local situation judge much better than any statesman or lawgiver can do for him. The statesman, who should attempt to direct private people in what manner they ought to employ their capitals, would not only load himself with a most unnecessary attention, but assume an authority which could safely be trusted, not only to no single person, but to no council or senate whatever, and which would nowhere be so dangerous as in the hands of a man who had folly and presumption enough to fancy himself fit to exercise it.

To give the monopoly of the home market to the produce of domestic industry, in any particular art or manufacture, is in some measure to direct private people in what manner they ought to employ their capitals, and must in almost all cases be either a useless or a hurtful regulation. If the produce of domestic can be brought there as cheap as that of foreign industry, the regulation is evidently useless. If it cannot, it must generally be hurtful. It is the maxim of every prudent master of a family, never to attempt to make at home what it will cost him more to make than to buy. The tailor does not attempt to make his own shoes, but buys them of the shoemaker. The shoemaker does not attempt to make his own clothes, but employs a tailor. The farmer attempts to make neither the one nor the other, but employs those different artificers. All of them find it for their interest to employ their whole industry in a way in which they have some advantage over their neighbours, and to purchase with a part of its produce, or, what is the same thing, with the price of a part of it, whatever else they have occasion for.

What is prudence in the conduct of every private family, can scarcely be folly in that of a great kingdom. If a foreign country can supply us with a commodity cheaper than we ourselves can make it, better buy it of them with some part of the produce of our own industry, employed in a way in which we have some advantage. The general industry of the country being always in proportion to the capital which employs it, will not thereby be diminished, no more than that of the above-mentioned artificers; but only left to find out the way in which it can be employed with the greatest advantage. It is certainly not employed to the greatest advantage, when it is thus directed towards an object which it can buy cheaper than it can make. The value of its annual produce is certainly more or less diminished, when it is thus turned away from producing commodities evidently of more value than the commodity which it is directed to produce. According to the supposition, that commodity could be purchased from foreign countries cheaper than it can be made at home; it could therefore have been purchased with a part only of the commodities, or, what is the same thing, with a part only of the price of the commodities, which the industry employed by an equal capital would have produced at home, had it been left to follow its natural course. The industry of the country, therefore, is thus turned away from a more to a less advantageous employment; and the exchangeable value of its annual produce, instead of being increased, according to the intention of the lawgiver, must necessarily be diminished by every such regulation.

By means of such regulations, indeed, a particular manufacture may sometimes be acquired sooner than it could have been otherwise, and after a certain time may be made at home as cheap, or cheaper, than in the foreign country. But though the industry of the society may be thus carried with advantage into a particular channel sooner than it could have been otherwise, it will by no means follow that the sum total, either of its industry, or of its revenue, can ever be augmented by any such regulation. The industry of the society can augment only in proportion as its capital augments, and its capital can augment only in proportion to what can be gradually saved out of its revenue. But the immediate effect of every such regulation is to diminish its revenue; and what diminishes its revenue is certainly not very likely to augment its capital faster than it would have augmented of its own accord, had both capital and industry been left to find out their natural employments.

Though, for want of such regulations, the society should never acquire the proposed manufacture, it would not upon that account necessarily be the poorer in any one period of its duration. In every period of its duration its whole capital and industry might still have been employed, though upon different objects, in the manner that was most advantageous at the time. In every period its revenue might have been the greatest which its capital could afford, and both capital and revenue might have been augmented with the greatest possible rapidity.

The natural advantages which one country has over another, in producing particular commodities, are sometimes so great, that it is acknowledged by all the world to be in vain to struggle with them. By means of glasses, hot-beds, and hot-walls, very good grapes can be raised in Scotland, and very good wine, too, can be made of them, at about thirty times the expense for which at least equally good can be brought from foreign countries. Would it be a reasonable law to prohibit the importation of all foreign wines, merely to encourage the making of claret and Burgundy in Scotland? But if there would be a manifest absurdity in turning towards any employment thirty times more of the capital and industry of the country than would be necessary to purchase from foreign countries an equal quantity of the commodities wanted, there must be an absurdity, though not altogether so glaring, yet exactly of the same kind, in turning towards any such employment a thirtieth, or even a three hundredth part more of either. Whether the advantages which one country has over another be natural or acquired, is in this respect of no consequence. As long as the one country has those advantages, and the other wants them, it will always be more advantageous for the latter rather to buy of the former than to make. It is an acquired advantage only, which one artificer has over his neighbour, who exercises another trade; and yet they both find it more advantageous to buy of one another, than to make what does not belong to their particular trades. . . .

There seem, however, to be two cases, in which it will generally be advantageous to lay some burden upon foreign, for the encouragement of domestic industry.

The first is, when some particular sort of industry is necessary for the defence of the country. The defence of Great Britain, for example, depends very much upon the number of its sailors and shipping. The act of navigation, therefore, very properly endeavours to give the sailors and shipping of Great Britain the monopoly of the trade of their own country, in some cases, by absolute prohibitions, and in others, by heavy burdens upon the shipping of foreign countries. . . .

The second case, in which it will generally be advantageous to lay some burden upon foreign for the encouragement of domestic industry, is when some tax is imposed at home upon the produce of the latter. In this case, it seems reasonable that an equal tax should be imposed upon the like produce of the former. This would not give the monopoly of the home market to domestic industry, nor turn towards a particular employment a greater share of the stock and labour of the country, than what would naturally go to it. It would only hinder any part of what would naturally go to it from being turned away by the tax into a less natural direction, and would leave the competition between foreign and domestic industry, after the tax, as nearly as possible upon the same footing as before it. In Great Britain, when any such tax is laid upon the produce of domestic industry, it is usual, at the same time, in order to stop the clamorous complaints of our merchants and manufacturers, that they will be undersold at home, to lay a much heavier duty upon the importation of all foreign goods of the same kind. . . .

As there are two cases in which it will generally be advantageous to lay some burden upon foreign for the encouragement of domestic industry, so there are two others in which it may sometimes be a matter of deliberation, in the one, how far it is proper to continue the free importation of certain foreign goods; and, in the other, how far, or in what manner, it may be proper to restore that free importation, after it has been for some time interrupted.

The case in which it may sometimes be a matter of deliberation how far it is proper to continue the free importation of certain foreign goods, is when some foreign nation restrains, by high duties or prohibitions, the importation of some of our manufactures into their country. Revenge, in this case, naturally dictates retaliation, and that we should impose the like duties and prohibitions upon the importation of some or all of their manufactures into ours. Nations, accordingly, seldom fail to retaliate in this manner. The French have been particularly forward to favour their own manufactures, by restraining the importation of such foreign goods as could come into competition with them. . . .

There may be good policy in retaliations of this kind when there is a probability that they will procure the repeal of the high duties or prohibitions complained of. The recovery of a great foreign market will generally more than compensate the transitory inconveniency of paying dearer during a short time for some sorts of goods. To judge whether such retaliations are likely to produce such an effect, does not, perhaps, belong so much to the science of a legislator, whose deliberations ought to be governed by general principles, which are always the same, as to the skill of that insidious and crafty animal vulgarly called a statesman or politician, whose councils are directed by the momentary fluctuations of affairs. When there is no probability that any such repeal can be procured, it seems a bad method of compensating the injury done to certain classes of our people, to do another injury ourselves, not only to those classes, but to almost all the other classes of them. When our neighbours prohibit some manufacture of ours, we generally prohibit, not only the same, for that alone would seldom affect them considerably, but some other manufacture of theirs. This may, no doubt, give encouragement to some particular class of workmen among ourselves, and, by excluding some of their rivals, may enable them to raise their price in the home market. Those workmen, however, who suffered by our neighbours prohibition, will not be benefited by ours. On the contrary, they, and almost all the other classes of our citizens, will thereby be obliged to pay dearer than before for certain goods. Every such law, therefore, imposes a real tax upon the whole country, not in favour of that particular class of workmen who were injured by our neighbours' prohibitions, but of some other class.

The case in which it may sometimes be a matter of deliberation, how far, or in what manner, it is proper to restore the free importation of foreign goods, after it has been for some time interrupted, is when particular manufactures, by means of high duties or prohibitions upon all foreign goods which can come into competition with them, have been so far extended as to employ a great multitude of hands. Humanity may in this case require that the freedom of trade should be restored only by slow gradations, and with a good deal of reserve and circumspection. Were those high duties and prohibitions taken away all at once, cheaper foreign goods of the same kind might be poured so fast into the home market, as to deprive all at once many thousands of our people of their ordinary employment and means of subsistence. The disorder which this would occasion might no doubt be very considerable. . . .

To expect, indeed, that the freedom of trade should ever be entirely restored in Great Britain, is as absurd as to expect that an Oceana or Utopia should ever be established in it. Not only the prejudices of the public, but, what is much more unconquerable, the private interests of many individuals, irresistibly oppose it. Were the officers of the army to oppose, with the same zeal and unanimity, any reduction in the number of forces, with which master manufacturers set themselves against every law that is likely to increase the number of their rivals in the home market; were the former to animate the soldiers, in the same manner as the latter inflame their workmen, to attack with violence and outrage the proposers of any such regulation; to attempt to reduce the army would be as dangerous as it has now become to attempt to diminish, in any respect, the monopoly which our manufacturers have obtained against us. This monopoly has so much increased the number of some particular tribes of them, that like an overgrown standing army, they have become formidable to the government, and, upon many occasions, intimidate the legislature. The member of parliament who supports every proposal for strengthening this monopoly, is sure to acquire not only the reputation of understanding trade, but great popularity and influence with an order of men whose numbers and wealth render them of great importance. If he opposes them, on the contrary, and still more, if he has authority enough to be able to thwart them, neither the most acknowledged probity, nor the highest rank, nor the greatest public services, can protect him from the most infamous abuse and detraction, from personal insults, nor sometimes from real danger, arising from the insolent outrage of furious and disappointed monopolists.

The undertaker of a great manufacture, who, by the home markets being suddenly laid open to the competition of foreigners, should be obliged to abandon his trade, would no doubt suffer very considerably. That part of his capital which had usually been employed in purchasing materials, and in paying his workmen, might, without much difficulty, perhaps, find another employment; but that part of it which was fixed in workhouses, and in the instruments of trade, could scarce be disposed of without considerable loss. The equitable regard, therefore, to his interest, requires that changes of this kind should never be introduced suddenly, but slowly, gradually, and after a very long warning. The legislature, were it possible that its deliberations could be always directed, not by the clamorous importunity of partial interests, but by an extensive view of the general good, ought, upon this very account, perhaps, to be particularly careful, neither to establish any new monopolies of this kind, nor to extend further those which are already established. Every such regulation introduces some degree of real disorder into the constitution of the state, which it will be difficult afterwards to cure without occasioning another disorder.

Thomas Jefferson

Thomas Jefferson (1743–1826), third president of the United States, was the first occupant of that office to hold distinctly liberal political views in the nineteenth-century meaning of the term. He was an apostle of the Enlightenment in America, and like many intellectuals of his time, believed in the worth of the individual, and in certain natural rights from which he should not be alienated. The aim of government, therefore, should be to assure the liberty or freedom of the individual to enjoy these rights, and leave him otherwise unmolested. Political liberalism meant, therefore, a minimum of governmental *functions. The administrations of George Washington and John Adams had been characterized by conservatism and a paternalistic attitude toward the citizenry, but with Jefferson's election the entire tone of American political life changed. A forecast of what was to come was given by him in his "First Inaugural Address," delivered March 4, 1801. In reading it note (1) his attitude toward the majority and the minority, (2) the advantages which Americans as a people had, (3) his description of what good government was, (4) the goal which he hoped to achieve for all, and (5) Jefferson's illustrations of the ideals of the Enlightenment.*

JEFFERSON'S FIRST INAUGURAL ADDRESS

Friends and Fellow-Citizens:

Called upon to undertake the duties of the first executive office of our country, I avail myself of the presence of that portion of my fellow-citizens which is here assembled to express my grateful thanks for the favor with which they have been pleased to look toward me, to declare a sincere consciousness that the task is above my talents, and that I approach it with those anxious and awful presentiments which the greatness of the charge and the weakness of my powers so justly inspire. A rising nation, spread over a wide and fruitful land, traversing all the seas with the rich productions of their industry, engaged in commerce with nations who feel power and forget right, advancing rapidly to destinies beyond the reach of mortal eye—when I contemplate these transcendent objects, and see the honor, the happiness, and the hopes of this beloved country committed to the issue and the auspices of this day, I shrink from the contemplation, and humble myself before the magnitude of the undertaking. Utterly, indeed, should I despair did not the presence of many whom I here see remind me that in the other high authorities provided by our Constitution I shall find resources of wisdom, of virtue, and of zeal on which to rely under all difficulties. To you, then, gentlemen, who are charged with the sovereign functions of legislation, and to those associated with you, I look with encouragement for that guidance and support which

may enable us to steer with safety the vessel in which we are all embarked amidst the conflicting elements of a troubled world.

During the contest of opinion through which we have passed the animation of discussions and of exertions has sometimes worn an aspect which might impose on strangers unused to think freely and to speak and to write what they think; but this being now decided by the voice of the nation, announced according to the rules of the Constitution, all will, of course, arrange themselves under the will of the law, and unite in common efforts for the common good. All, too, will bear in mind this sacred principle, that though the will of the majority is in all cases to prevail, that will to be rightful must be reasonable; that the minority possess their equal rights, which equal law must protect, and to violate would be oppression. Let us, then, fellow-citizens, unite with one heart and one mind. Let us restore to social intercourse that harmony and affection without which liberty and even life itself are but dreary things. And let us reflect that, having banished from our land that religious intolerance under which mankind so long bled and suffered, we have yet gained little if we countenance a political intolerance as despotic, as wicked, and capable of as bitter and bloody persecutions. During the throes and convulsions of the ancient world, during the agonizing spasms of infuriated man, seeking through blood and slaughter his long-lost liberty, it was not won-

Thomas Jefferson, "Inaugural Address," in United States, *Journal of the Executive Proceedings of the Senate of the United States of America.* . . . , Washington, 1828, I, 392–395.

derful that the agitation of the billows should reach even this distant and peaceful shore; that this should be more felt and feared by some and less by others, and should divide opinions as to measures of safety. But every difference of opinion is not a difference of principle. We have called by different names brethren of the same principle. We are all Republicans, we are all Federalists. If there be any among us who would wish to dissolve this Union or to change its republican form, let them stand undisturbed as monuments of the safety with which error of opinion may be tolerated where reason is left free to combat it. I know, indeed, that some honest men fear that a republican government cannot be strong, that this Government is not strong enough; but would the honest patriot, in the full tide of successful experiment, abandon a government which has so far kept us free and firm on the theoretic and visionary fear that this Government, the world's best hope, may by possibility want energy to preserve itself? I trust not. I believe this, on the contrary, the strongest Government on earth. I believe it the only one where every man, at the call of the law, would fly to the standard of the law, and would meet invasions of the public order as his own personal concern. Sometimes it is said that man cannot be trusted with the government of himself. Can he, then, be trusted with the government of others? Or have we found angels in the forms of kings to govern him? Let history answer this question.

Let us, then, with courage and confidence pursue our own Federal and Republican principles, our attachment to union and representative government. Kindly separated by nature and a wide ocean from the exterminating havoc of one quarter of the globe; too high-minded to endure the degradations of the others; possessing a chosen country, with room enough for our descendants to the thousandth and thousandth generation; entertaining a due sense of our equal right to the use of our own faculties, to the acquisitions of our own industry, to honor and confidence from our fellow-citizens, resulting not from birth, but from our actions and their sense of them; enlightened by a benign religion, professed, indeed, and practiced in various forms, yet all of them inculcating honesty, truth, temperance, gratitude, and the love of man; acknowledging and adoring an overruling Providence, which by all its dispensations proves that it delights in the happiness of man here and his greater happiness hereafter—with all these blessings, what more is necessary to make us a happy and a prosperous people? Still one thing more, fellow-citizens—a wise and frugal Government, which shall restrain men from injuring one another, shall leave them otherwise free to regulate their own pursuits of industry and improvement, and shall not take from the mouth of labor the bread it has earned. This is the sum of good government, and this is necessary to close the circle of our felicities.

About to enter, fellow-citizens, on the exercise of duties which comprehend everything dear and valuable to you, it is proper you should understand what I deem the essential principles of our Government, and consequently those which ought to shape its Administration. I will compress them within the narrowest compass they will bear, stating the general principle, but not all its limitations. Equal and exact justice to all men, of whatever state or persuasion, religious or political; peace, commerce, and honest friendship with all nations, entangling alliances with none; the support of the State governments in all their rights, as the most competent administrations for our domestic concerns and the surest bulwarks against antirepublican tendencies; the preservation of the General Government in its whole constitutional vigor, as the sheet anchor of our peace at home and safety abroad; a jealous care of the right of election by the people—a mild and safe corrective of abuses which are lopped by the sword of revolution where peaceable remedies are unprovided; absolute acquiescence in the decisions of the majority, the vital principle of republics, from which is no appeal but to force, the vital principle and immediate parent of despotism; a well-disciplined militia, our best reliance in peace and for the first moments of war, till regulars may relieve them; the supremacy of the civil over the military authority; economy in the public expense, that labor may be lightly burthened; the honest payment of our debts and sacred preservation of the public faith;

encouragement of agriculture, and of commerce as its handmaid; the diffusion of information and arraignment of all abuses at the bar of the public reason; freedom of religion; freedom of the press, and freedom of person under the protection of the habeas corpus, and trial by juries impartially selected. These principles form the bright constellation which has gone before us and guided our steps through an age of revolution and reformation. The wisdom of our sages and blood of our heroes have been devoted to their attainment. They should be the creed of our political faith, the text of civic instruction, the touchstone by which to try the services of those we trust; and should we wander from them in moments of error or of alarm, let us hasten to retrace our steps and to regain the road which alone leads to peace, liberty, and safety.

I repair, then, fellow-citizens, to the post you have assigned me. With experience enough in subordinate offices to have seen the difficulties of this the greatest of all, I have learnt to expect that it will rarely fall to the lot of imperfect man to retire from this station with the reputation and the favor which bring him into it. Without pretensions to that high confidence you reposed in our first and greatest revolutionary character, whose preëminent services

had entitled him to the first place in his country's love and destined for him the fairest page in the volume of faithful history, I ask so much confidence only as may give firmness and effect to the legal administration of your affairs. I shall often go wrong through defect of judgment. When right, I shall often be thought wrong by those whose positions will not command a view of the whole ground. I ask your indulgence for my own errors, which will never be intentional, and your support against the errors of others, who may condemn what they would not if seen in all its parts. The approbation implied by your suffrage is a great consolation to me for the past, and my future solicitude will be to retain the good opinion of those who have bestowed it in advance, to conciliate that of others by doing them all the good in my power, and to be instrumental to the happiness and freedom of all.

Relying, then, on the patronage of your good will, I advance with obedience to the work, ready to retire from it whenever you become sensible how much better choice it is in your power to make. And may that Infinite Power which rules the destinies of the universe lead our councils to what is best, and give them a favorable issue for your peace and prosperity.

John Stuart Mill

John Stuart Mill (1806–1873), English economist, philosopher, and political figure, was the son of James Mill, the famous utilitarian. Educated in the classical tradition by his father, it was only natural that the younger Mill should accept some of the elder's principles, particularly in philosophy. In politics he was a Liberal and sat in Parliament as a member of the Liberal Party. He did not agree with some of his colleagues in regard to the extreme laissez-faire policy, however, and he was one of the first to advocate some governmental regulation in the interest of individual freedom, a cause for which he fought unceasingly. In 1859 he wrote his great essay, On Liberty, selections from which follow. In reading them note (1) his discussion of the tyranny of the majority, (2) the one principle that should determine society's interference with an individual's actions, (3) the evil involved in suppressing freedom of expression, (4) the utilitarian value of freedom of individual action, (5) the relationship between individual development and the Will of God, (6) where the limits of society's control over the individual should be set, (7) the only pressure society might use against an individual when his acts injure only himself, (8) the examples he cited to illustrate his principles, and (9) Mill's typically Liberal objections to governmental action even when it did not involve the liberty of its citizens.

From: ON LIBERTY

The subject of this Essay is not the so-called Liberty of the Will, so unfortunately opposed to the misnamed doctrine of Philosophical Necessity; but Civil, or Social Liberty: the nature and limits of the power which can be legitimately exercised by society over the individual: a question seldom stated, and hardly ever discussed, in general terms, but which profoundly influences the practical controversies of the age by its latent presence and is likely soon to make itself recognized as the vital question of the future. It is so far from being new, that, in a certain sense, it has divided mankind almost from the remotest ages; but in the stage of progress into which the more civilised portions of the species have now entered, it presents itself under new conditions, and requires a different and more fundamental treatment.

The struggle between Liberty and Authority is the most conspicuous feature in the portions of history with which we are earliest familiar, particularly in that of Greece, Rome, and England. But in old times this contest was between subjects, or some classes of subjects, and the Government. By liberty, was meant protection against the tyranny of the political rulers. The rulers were conceived (except in some of the popular governments of Greece) as in a necessarily antagonistic position to the people whom they ruled. They consisted of a governing One, or a governing tribe or caste, who derived their authority from inheritance or conquest, who, at all events, did not hold it at the pleasure of the governed, and whose supremacy men did not venture, perhaps did not desire, to contest, whatever precautions might be taken against its oppressive exercise. Their power was regarded as necessary, but

also as highly dangerous; as a weapon which they would attempt to use against their subjects, no less than against external enemies. To prevent the weaker members of the community from being preyed upon by innumerable vultures, it was needful that there should be an animal of prey stronger than the rest, commissioned to keep them down. But as the king of the vultures would be no less bent upon preying on the flock than any of the minor harpies, it was indispensable to be in a perpetual attitude of defence against his beak and claws. The aim, therefore, of patriots was to set limits to the power which the ruler should be suffered to exercise over the community; and this limitation was what they meant by liberty. It was attempted in two ways. First, by obtaining a recognition of certain immunities, called political liberties or rights, which it was to be regarded as a breach of duty in the ruler to infringe, and which if he did infringe, specific resistance, or general rebellion, was held to be justifiable. A second, and generally a later expedient, was the establishment of constitutional checks, by which the consent of the community, or of a body of some sort, supposed to represent its interests, was made a necessary condition to some of the more important acts of the governing power. To the first of these modes of limitation, the ruling power, in most European countries, was compelled, more or less, to submit. It was not so with the second; and, to attain this or, when already in some degree possessed, to attain it more completely, became everywhere the principal object of the lovers of liberty. And so long as mankind were content to combat one enemy by another, and to be ruled by a master, on condition of being guaranteed more or

John Stuart Mill, On Liberty, London, 1870, 1–6; 9–10; 30–37; 44–46; 64–68.

less efficaciously against his tyranny, they did not carry their aspirations beyond this point.

A time, however, came, in the progress of human affairs, when men ceased to think it a necessity of nature that their governors should be an independent power, opposed in interest to themselves. It appeared to them much better that the various magistrates of the State should be their tenants or delegates, revocable at their pleasure. In that way alone, it seemed, could they have complete security that the powers of government would never be abused to their disadvantage. By degrees this new demand for elective and temporary rulers became the prominent object of the exertions of the popular party, wherever any such party existed; and superseded, to a considerable extent, the previous efforts to limit the power of rulers. As the struggle proceeded for making the ruling power emanate from the periodical choice of the ruled, some persons began to think that too much importance had been attached to the limitation of the power itself. *That* (it might seem) was a resource against rulers whose interests were habitually opposed to those of the people. What was now wanted was, that the rulers should be identified with the people; that their interest and will should be the interest and will of the nation. The nation did not need to be protected against its own will. There was no fear of its tyrannising over itself. Let the rulers be effectually responsible to it, promptly removable by it, and it could afford to trust them with power of which it could itself dictate the use to be made. Their power was but the nation's own power, concentrated, and in a form convenient for exercise. This mode of thought, or rather perhaps of feeling, was common among the last generation of European liberalism, in the Continental section of which it still apparently predominates. Those who admit any limit to what a government may do, except in the case of such governments as they think ought not to exist, stand out as brilliant exceptions among the political thinkers of the Continent. A similar tone of sentiment might by this time have been prevalent in our own country, if the circumstances which for a time encouraged it, had continued unaltered.

But in political and philosophical theories, as well as in persons, success discloses faults and infirmities which failure might have concealed from observation. The notion that the people have no need to limit their power over themselves might seem axiomatic, when popular government was a thing only dreamed about, or read of as having existed at some distant period of the past. Neither was that notion necessarily disturbed by such temporary aberrations as those of the French Revolution, the worst of which were the work of a usurping few, and which, in any case, belonged, not to the permanent working of popular institutions, but to a sudden and convulsive outbreak against monarchical and aristocratic despotism. In time, however, a democratic republic came to occupy a large portion of the earth's surface, and made itself felt as one of the most powerful members of the community of nations; and elective and responsible government became subject to the observations and criticisms which wait upon a great existing fact. It was now perceived that such phrases as "self-government," and "the power of the people over themselves," do not express the true state of the case. "The people" who exercise the power are not always the same people with those over whom it is exercised; and the "self-government" spoken of is not the government of each by himself, but of each by all the rest. The will of the people, moreover, practically means the will of the most numerous or the most active *part* of the people—the majority, or those who succeed in making themselves accepted as the majority; the people, consequently, *may* desire to oppress a part of their number; and precautions are as much needed against this as against any other abuse of power. The limitation, therefore, of the power of government over individuals loses none of its importance when the holders of power are regularly accountable to the community; that is, to the strongest party therein. This view of things, recommending itself equally to the intelligence of thinkers and to the inclination of those important classes in European society to whose real or supposed interests democracy is adverse, has had no difficulty in establishing itself; and in political speculations, "the tyr-

anny of the majority" is now generally included among the evils against which society
requires to be on its guard.

Like other tyrannies, the tyranny of the majority was at first, and is still vulgarly, held in
dread, chiefly as operating through the acts of
the public authorities. But reflecting persons
perceived that when society is itself the tyrant
—society collectively over the separate individuals who compose it—its means of tyrannising are not restricted to the acts which it
may do by the hands of its political functionaries. Society can and does execute its own
mandates; and if it issues wrong mandates instead of right, or any mandates at all in things
with which it ought not to meddle, it practises
a social tyranny more formidable than many
kinds of political oppression; since, though not
usually upheld by such extreme penalties, it
leaves fewer means of escape, penetrating
much more deeply into the details of life, and
enslaving the soul itself. Protection, therefore,
against the tyranny of the magistrate is not
enough: there needs protection also against the
tyranny of the prevailing opinion and feeling;
against the tendency of society to impose, by
other means than civil penalties, its own ideas
and practises as rules of conduct on those who
dissent from them; to fetter the development,
and, if possible, prevent the formation, of any
individuality not in harmony with its ways,
and to compel all characters to fashion themselves upon the model of its own. There is a
limit to the legitimate interference of collective
opinion with individual independence: and to
find that limit, and maintain it against encroachment, is as indispensable to a good condition of human affairs, as protection against
political despotism.

But though this proposition is not likely to
be contested in general terms, the practical
question, where to place the limit,—how to
make the fitting adjustment between individual
independence and social control,—is a subject
on which nearly everything remains to be
done. All that makes existence valuable to
anyone depends on the enforcement of restraints upon the actions of other people.
Some rules of conduct, therefore, must be imposed, by law in the first place, and by opinion

on many things which are not fit subjects for
the operation of law. What these rules should
be is the principal question in human affairs;
but if we except a few of the most obvious
cases, it is one of those which least progress
has been made in resolving. No two ages, and
scarcely any two countries, have decided it
alike; and the decision of one age or country
is a wonder to another. Yet the people of any
given age and country no more suspect any
difficulty in it, than if it were a subject on
which mankind had always been agreed. The
rules which obtain among themselves appear
to them self-evident and self-justifying. This
all but universal illusion is one of the examples
of the magical influence of custom, which is
not only, as the proverb says, a second nature,
but is continually mistaken for the first. The
effect of custom, in preventing any misgiving
respecting the rules of conduct which mankind impose on one another, is all the more
complete because the subject is one on which
it is not generally considered necessary that
reasons should be given, either by one person
to others or by each to himself. People are accustomed to believe, and have been encouraged in the belief by some who aspire to the
character of philosophers, that their feelings,
on subjects of this nature, are better than reasons, and render reasons unnecessary. The
practical principle which guides them to their
opinions on the regulation of human conduct
is the feeling in each person's mind that
everybody should be required to act as he,
and those with whom he sympathises, would
like them to act. No one, indeed, acknowledges to himself that his standard of judgment is his own liking; but an opinion on a
point of conduct, not supported by reasons,
can only count as one person's preference; and
if the reasons, when given, are a mere appeal
to a similar preference felt by other people, it
is still only many people's liking instead of one.
To an ordinary man, however, his own preference, thus supported, is not only a perfectly
satisfactory reason, but the only one he generally has for any of his notions of morality,
taste, or propriety, which are not expressly
written in his religious creed; and his chief
guide in the interpretation even of that. Men's

opinions, accordingly, on what is laudable or blamable, are affected by all the multifarious causes which influence their wishes in regard to the conduct of others, and which are as numerous as those which determine their wishes on any other subject. Sometimes their reason—at other times their prejudices or superstitions: often their social affections, not seldom their antisocial ones, their envy or jealousy, their arrogance or contemptuousness: but most commonly their desires or fears for themselves—their legitimate or illegitimate self-interest. Wherever there is an ascendant class, a large portion of the morality of the country emanates from its class interests, and its feelings of class superiority. The morality between Spartans and Helots, between planters and negroes, between princes and subjects, between nobles and roturiers, between men and women, has been for the most part the creation of these class interests and feelings: and the sentiments thus generated react in turn upon the moral feelings of the members of the ascendant class, in their relations among themselves. Where, on the other hand, a class, formerly ascendant, has lost its ascendancy, or where its ascendancy is unpopular, the prevailing moral sentiments frequently bear the impress of an impatient dislike of superiority. Another grand determining principle of the rules of conduct, both in act and forbearance, which have been enforced by law or opinion, has been the servility of mankind towards the supposed preferences or aversions of their temporal masters or of their gods. This servility, though essentially selfish, is not hypocrisy: it gives rise to perfectly genuine sentiments of abhorrence; it made men burn magicians and heretics. Among so many baser influences, the general and obvious interests of society have of course had a share, and a large one, in the direction of the moral sentiments: less, however, as a matter of reason and on their own account, than as a consequence of the sympathies and antipathies which grew out of them: and sympathies and antipathies which had little or nothing to do with the interests of society have made themselves felt in the establishment of moralities with quite as great force.

The likings and dislikings of society, or of some powerful portion of it, are thus the main thing which has practically determined the rules laid down for general observance, under the penalties of law or opinion. And, in general, those who have been in advance of society in thought and feeling have left this condition of things unassailed in principle, however they may have come into conflict with it in some of its details. They have occupied themselves rather in inquiring what things society ought to like or dislike, than in questioning whether its likings or dislikings should be a law to individuals. They preferred endeavouring to alter the feelings of mankind on the particular points on which they were themselves heretical, rather than make common cause, in defence of freedom, with heretics generally. The only case in which the higher ground has been taken on principle and maintained with consistency, by any but an individual here and there, is that of religious belief: a case instructive in many ways, and not least so as forming a most striking instance of the fallibility of what is called the moral sense: for the *odium theologicum*, in a sincere bigot, is one of the most unequivocal cases of moral feeling. Those who first broke the yoke of what called itself the Universal Church were, in general, as little willing to permit difference of religious opinion as that church itself. But when the heat of the conflict was over, without giving a complete victory to any party, and each church or sect was reduced to limit its hopes to retaining possession of the ground it already occupied, minorities—seeing that they had no chance of becoming majorities—were under the necessity of pleading to those whom they could not convert for permission to differ. It is accordingly on this battlefield, almost solely, that the rights of the individual against society have been asserted on broad grounds of principle, and the claim of society to exercise authority over dissentients openly controverted. The great writers to whom the world owes what religious liberty it possesses, have mostly asserted freedom of conscience as an indefeasible right, and denied absolutely that a human being is accountable to others for his religious belief. Yet so natural to mankind is intolerance in whatever they really care about, that religious freedom has hardly anywhere been practically realised, except where religious indifference, which dislikes to have its peace disturbed by theological quarrels, has added its weight to the scale. In the minds of almost all religious persons, even in the most tolerant countries, the duty of toleration is admitted with tacit reserves. One person will bear with dissent in matters of church government, but not of dogma; another can tolerate everybody, short of a Papist or a Unitarian; another everyone who believes in revealed religion; a few extend their charity a little further, but stop at the belief in a God and in a future state. Wherever the sentiment of the majority is still genuine and intense, it is found to have abated little of its claim to be obeyed.

In England, from the peculiar circumstances of our political history, though the yoke of opinion is perhaps heavier, that of law is lighter than in most other countries of Europe; and there is considerable jealousy of direct interference, by the legislative or the executive power, with private conduct; not so much from any just regard for the independence of the individual, as from the still subsisting habit of looking on the government as representing an opposite interest to the public. The majority have not yet learnt to feel the power of the government their power, or its opinions their opinions. When they do so, individual liberty will probably be as much exposed to invasion from the government, as it already is from public opinion. But, as yet, there is a considerable amount of feeling ready to be called forth against any attempt of the law to control individuals in things in which they have not hitherto been accustomed to be controlled by it; and this with very little discrimination as to whether the matter is, or is not, within the legitimate sphere of legal control; insomuch that the feeling, highly salutary on the whole, is perhaps quite as often misplaced as well grounded in the particular instances of its application. There is, in fact, no recognised principle by which the propriety or impropriety of government interference is customarily tested. People decide according to their personal preferences. Some, whenever they see any good to be done, or evil to be remedied, would willingly instigate the government to undertake the business; while others prefer to bear almost any amount of social evil rather than add one to the departments of human interests amenable to governmental control. And men range themselves on one or the other side in any particular case according to this general direction of their sentiments; or according to the degree of interest which they feel in the particular thing which it is proposed that the government should do; or according to the belief they entertain that the government would, or would not, do it in the manner they prefer; but very rarely on account of any opinion to which they consistently adhere, as to what things are fit to be done by a government. And it seems to me that, in consequence of this absence of rule or principle, one side is at present as often wrong as the other; the interference of government is, with about equal frequency, improperly invoked and improperly condemned.

The object of this Essay is to assert one very simple principle, as entitled to govern absolutely the dealings of society with the individual in the way of compulsion and control, whether the means used be physical force in the form of legal penalties, or the moral coercion of public opinion. That principle is, that the sole end for which mankind are warranted, individually or collectively, in interfering with the liberty of action of any of their number, is self-protection. That the only purpose for which power can be rightfully exercised over any member of a civilised community, against his will, is to prevent harm to others. His own good, either physical or moral, is not a sufficient warrant. He cannot rightfully be compelled to do or to forbear because it will be better for him to do so, because it will make him happier, because, in the opinions of others, to do so would be wise, or even right. These are good reasons for remonstrating with him, or reasoning with him, or persuading him, or entreating him, but not for compelling him, or visiting him with any evil in case he do otherwise. To justify that, the conduct from which it is desired to deter him must be calculated to produce evil to someone else. The only part of the conduct of anyone, for which he is amenable to society, is that which concerns others.

In the part which merely concerns himself, his independence is, of right, absolute. Over himself, over his own body and mind, the individual is sovereign. . . .

OF THE LIBERTY OF THOUGHT AND DISCUSSION

The time, it is to be hoped, is gone by, when any defence would be necessary of the "liberty of the press" as one of the securities against corrupt or tyrannical government. No argument, we may suppose, can now be needed, against permitting a legislature or an executive, not identified in interest with the people, to prescribe opinions to them and determine what doctrines or what arguments they shall be allowed to hear. This aspect of the question, besides, has been so often and so triumphantly enforced by preceding writers, that it needs not be specially insisted on in this place. Though the law of England, on the subject of the press, is as servile to this day as it was in the time of the Tudors, there is little danger of its being actually put in force against political discussion, except during some temporary panic, when fear of insurrection drives ministers and judges from their propriety; and, speaking generally, it is not, in constitutional countries, to be apprehended, that the government, whether completely responsible to the people or not, will often attempt to control the expression of opinion, except when in doing so it makes itself the organ of the general intolerance of the public. Let us suppose, therefore, that the government is entirely at one with the people, and never thinks of exerting any power of coercion unless in agreement with what it conceives to be their voice. But I deny the right of the people to exercise such coercion, either by themselves or by their government. The power itself is illegitimate. The best government has no more title to it than the worst. It is as noxious, or more noxious, when exerted in accordance with public opinion, than when in opposition to it. If all mankind minus one were of one opinion, and only one person were of the contrary opinion, mankind would be no more justified in silencing that one person, than he, if he had the power, would be

justified in silencing mankind. Were an opinion a personal possession of no value except to the owner; if to be obstructed in the enjoyment of it were simply a private injury, it would make some difference whether the injury was inflicted only on a few persons or on many. But the peculiar evil of silencing the expression of an opinion is, that it is robbing the human race: posterity as well as the existing generation; those who dissent from the opinion still more than those who hold it. If the opinion is right, they are deprived of the opportunity of exchanging error for truth; if wrong, they lose, what is almost as great a benefit, the clearer perception and livelier impression of truth, produced by its collision with error. . . .

We have now recognised the necessity to the mental well-being of mankind (on which all their other well-being depends) of freedom of opinion, and freedom of the expression of opinion, on four distinct grounds; which we will now briefly recapitulate.

First, if any opinion is compelled to silence, that opinion may, for aught we can certainly know, be true. To deny this is to assume our own infallibility.

Secondly, though the silenced opinion be an error, it may, and very commonly does, contain a portion of truth; and since the general or prevailing opinion on any subject is rarely or never the whole truth, it is only by the collision of adverse opinions that the remainder of the truth has any chance of being supplied.

Thirdly, even if the received opinion be not only true, but the whole truth; unless it is suffered to be, and actually is, vigorously and earnestly contested, it will, by most of those who receive it, be held in the manner of a prejudice, with little comprehension or feeling of its rational grounds. And not only this, but, fourthly, the meaning of the doctrine itself will be in danger of being lost, or enfeebled, and deprived of its vital effect on the character and conduct: the dogma becoming a mere formal profession, inefficacious for good, but cumbering the ground, and preventing the growth of any real and heartfelt conviction, from reason or personal experience.

Before quitting the subject of freedom of opinion, it is fit to take some notice of those who say that the free expression of all opinions should be permitted, on condition that the manner be temperate, and do not pass the bounds of fair discussion. Much might be said on the impossibility of fixing where these supposed bounds are to be placed; for if the test be offence to those whose opinions are attacked, I think experience testifies that this offence is given whenever the attack is telling and powerful, and that every opponent who pushes them hard, and whom they find it difficult to answer, appears to them, if he shows any strong feeling on the subject, an intemperate opponent. But this, though an important consideration in a practical point of view, merges in a more fundamental objection. Undoubtedly the manner of asserting an opinion, even though it be a true one, may be very objectionable, and may justly incur severe censure. But the principal offences of the kind are such as it is mostly impossible, unless by accidental self-betrayal, to bring home to conviction. The gravest of them is, to argue sophistically, to suppress facts or arguments, to misstate the elements of the case, or misrepresent the opposite opinion. But all this, even to the most aggravated degree, is so continually done in perfect good faith, by persons who are not considered, and in many other respects may not deserve to be considered, ignorant or incompetent, that it is rarely possible, on adequate grounds, conscientiously to stamp the misrepresentation as morally culpable; and still less could law presume to interfere with this kind of controversial misconduct. With regard to what is commonly meant by intemperate discussion, namely invective, sarcasm, personality, and the like, the denunciation of these weapons would deserve more sympathy if it were ever proposed to interdict them equally to both sides; but it is only desired to restrain the employment of them against the prevailing opinion: against the unprevailing they may not only be used without general disapproval, but will be likely to obtain for him who uses them the praise of honest zeal and righteous indignation. Yet whatever mischief arises from their use is greatest when they are employed against the comparatively defenceless; and whatever unfair advantage can be derived by any opinion from this mode

of asserting it, accrues almost exclusively to received opinions. The worst offence of this kind which can be committed by a polemic is to stigmatise those who hold the contrary opinion as bad and immoral men. To calumny of this sort, those who hold any unpopular opinion are peculiarly exposed, because they are in general few and uninfluential, and nobody but themselves feels much interested in seeing justice done them; but this weapon is, from the nature of the case, denied to those who attack a prevailing opinion: they can neither use it with safety to themselves, nor, if they could, would it do anything but recoil on their own cause. In general, opinions contrary to those commonly received can only obtain a hearing by studied moderation of language, and the most cautious avoidance of unnecessary offence, from which they hardly ever deviate even in a slight degree without losing ground: while unmeasured vituperation employed on the side of the prevailing opinion really does deter people from professing contrary opinions, and from listening to those who profess them. For the interest, therefore, of truth and justice, it is far more important to restrain this employment of vituperative language than the other; and, for example, if it were necessary to choose, there would be much more need to discourage offensive attacks on infidelity than on religion. It is, however, obvious that law and authority have no business with restraining either, while opinion ought, in every instance, to determine its verdict by the circumstances of the individual case; condemning everyone, on whichever side of the argument he places himself, in whose mode of advocacy either want of candour, or malignity, bigotry, or intolerance of feeling manifest themselves; but not inferring these vices from the side which a person takes, though it be the contrary side of the question to our own; and giving merited honour to everyone, whatever opinion he may hold, who has calmness to see and honesty to state what his opponents and their opinions really are, exaggerating nothing to their discredit, keeping nothing back which tells, or can be supposed to tell, in their favour. This is the real morality of public discussion; and if often violated, I am happy to think that there are many controversialists who to a great extent observe it, and a still greater number who conscientiously strive towards it.

OF INDIVIDUALITY, AS ONE OF THE ELEMENTS OF WELL-BEING

Such being the reasons which make it imperative that human beings should be free to form opinions, and to express their opinions without reserve; and such the baneful consequences to the intellectual and, through that, to the moral nature of man, unless this liberty is either conceded, or asserted in spite of prohibition, let us next examine whether the same reasons do not require that men should be free to act upon their opinions—to carry these out in their lives, without hindrance, either physical or moral, from their fellow men, so long as it is at their own risk and peril. This last proviso is of course indispensable. No one pretends that actions should be as free as opinions. On the contrary even opinions lose their immunity when the circumstances in which they are expressed are such as to constitute their expression a positive instigation to some mischievous act. An opinion that corn-dealers are starvers of the poor, or that private property is robbery, ought to be unmolested when simply circulated through the press, but may justly incur punishment when delivered orally to an excited mob assembled before the house of a corn-dealer, or when handed about among the same mob in the form of a placard. Acts, of whatever kind, which, without justifiable cause, do harm to others, may be, and in the more important cases absolutely require to be, controlled by the unfavourable sentiments, and, when needful, by the active interference, of mankind. The liberty of the individual must be thus far limited: he must not make himself a nuisance to other people. But if he refrains from molesting others in what concerns them, and merely acts according to his own inclination and judgment in things which concern himself, the same reasons which show that opinion should be free prove also that he should be allowed, without molestation, to carry his opinions into practise at his own cost. That mankind are not infallible; that their truths, for the most part, are only half-truths; that unity of opinion, unless resulting from the fullest and freest comparison of opposite opinions, is not desirable, and diversity not an evil, but a good, until mankind are much more capable than at present of recognising all sides of the truth, are principles applicable to men's modes of action, not less than to their opinions. As it is useful that while mankind are imperfect there should be different opinions, so it is that there should be different experiments of living; that free scope should be given to varieties of character, short of injury to others; and that the worth of different modes of life should be proved practically, when anyone thinks fit to try them. It is desirable, in short, that in things which do not primarily concern others, individuality should assert itself. Where, not the person's own character, but the traditions or customs of other people, are the rule of conduct, there is wanting one of the principal ingredients of human happiness, and quite the chief ingredient of individual and social progress.

In maintaining this principle, the greatest difficulty to be encountered does not lie in the appreciation of means towards an acknowledged end, but in the indifference of persons in general to the end itself. If it were felt that the free development of individuality is one of the leading essentials of well-being; that it is not only a coördinate element with all that is designated by the terms civilisation, instruction, education, culture, but is itself a necessary part and condition of all those things, there would be no danger that liberty should be undervalued, and the adjustment of the boundaries between it and social control would present no extraordinary difficulty. But the evil is, that individual spontaneity is hardly recognised by the common modes of thinking as having any intrinsic worth, or deserving any regard on its own account. The majority, being satisfied with the ways of mankind as they now are (for it is they who make them what they are), cannot comprehend why those ways should not be good enough for everybody; and, what is more, spontaneity forms no part of the ideal of the majority of moral and social reformers, but is rather looked on with jealousy, as a troublesome and perhaps rebellious obstruction to the general acceptance of what these reformers, in their own judgment, think would be best for mankind. Few persons, out of Germany, even comprehend the meaning of the doctrine which Wilhelm von Humboldt, so eminent both as a *savant* and as a politician, made the text of a treatise—that "the end of man, or that which is prescribed by the eternal or immutable dictates of reason, and not suggested by vague and transient desires, is the highest and most harmonious development of his powers to a complete and consistent whole"; that, therefore, the object "towards which every human being must ceaselessly direct his efforts, and on which especially those who design to influence their fellow men must ever keep their eyes, is the individuality of power and development"; that for this there are two requisites, "freedom, and variety of situations"; and that from the union of these arise "individual vigour and manifold diversity," which combine themselves in "originality."

Little, however, as people are accustomed to a doctrine like that of von Humboldt, and surprising as it may be to them to find so high a value attached to individuality, the question, one must nevertheless think, can only be one of degree. No one's idea of excellence in conduct is that people should do absolutely nothing but copy one another. No one would assert that people ought not to put into their mode of life, and into the conduct of their concerns, any impress whatever of their own judgment, or of their own individual character. On the other hand, it would be absurd to pretend that people ought to live as if nothing whatever had been known in the world before they came into it; as if experience had as yet done nothing towards showing that one mode of existence, or of conduct, is preferable to another. Nobody denies that people should be so taught and trained in youth as to know and benefit by the ascertained results of human experience. But it is the privilege and proper condition of a human being, arrived at the maturity of his faculties, to use and interpret experience in his own way. It is for him to find out what part of recorded experience is properly applicable to his own circumstances and character. The traditions and customs of other people are, to a certain extent, evidence of what their experience has taught *them*—presumptive evidence, and as such, have a claim to his deference: but, in the first place, their experience may be too narrow, or they may not have interpreted it rightly. Secondly, their interpretation of experience may be correct, but unsuitable to him. Customs are made for customary circumstances and customary characters; and his circumstances or his character may be uncustomary. Thirdly, though the customs be both good as customs, and suitable to him, yet to conform to custom, merely *as* custom, does not educate or develop in him any of the qualities which are the distinctive endowment of a human being. The human faculties of perception, judgment, discriminative feeling, mental activity, and even moral preference, are exercised only in making a choice. He who does anything because it is the custom makes no choice. He gains no practise either in discerning or in desiring what is best. The mental and moral, like the muscular powers, are improved only by being used. The faculties are called into no exercise by doing a thing merely because others do it, no more than by believing a thing only because others believe it. If the grounds of an opinion are not conclusive to the person's own reason, his reason cannot be strengthened, but is likely to be weakened, by his adopting it: and if the inducements to an act are not such as are consentaneous to his own feelings and character (where affection, or the rights of others, are not concerned), it is so much done towards rendering his feelings and character inert and torpid, instead of active and energetic.

He who lets the world, or his own portion of it, choose his plan of life for him, has no need of any other faculty than the ape-like one of imitation. He who chooses his plan for himself, employs all his faculties. He must use observation to see, reasoning and judgment to foresee, activity to gather materials for decision, discrimination to decide, and, when he has decided, firmness and self-control to hold to his deliberate decision. And these qualities he requires and exercises exactly in proportion as the part of his conduct which he determines according to his own judgment and feelings is a large one. It is possible that he might be guided in some good path, and kept out of harm's way, without any of these things. But what will be his comparative worth as a human being? It really is of importance, not only what men do, but also what manner of men they are that do it. Among the works of man, which human life is rightly employed in perfecting and beautifying, the first in importance surely is man himself. Supposing it were possible to get houses built, corn grown, battles fought, causes tried, and even churches erected and prayers said, by machinery,—by automatons in human form,—it would be a considerable loss to exchange for these automatons even the men and women who at present inhabit the more civilised parts of the world, and who assuredly are but starved specimens of what nature can and will produce. Human nature is not a machine to be built after a model, and set to do exactly the work prescribed for it, but a tree, which requires to grow and develop itself on all sides, according to the tendency of the inward forces which make it a living thing.

It will probably be conceded that it is desirable people should exercise their understandings, and that an intelligent following of custom, or even occasionally an intelligent deviation from custom, is better than a blind and simply mechanical adhesion to it. To a certain extent it is admitted that our understanding should be our own: but there is not the same willingness to admit that our desires and impulses should be our own likewise; or that to possess impulses of our own, and of any strength, is anything but a peril and a snare. Yet desires and impulses are as much a part of a perfect human being as beliefs and restraints; and strong impulses are only perilous when not properly balanced; when one set of aims and inclinations is developed into strength, while others, which ought to co-exist with them, remain weak and inactive. It is not because men's desires are strong that they act ill; it is because their consciences are weak. There is no natural connection between strong impulses and a weak conscience. The natural connection is the other way. To say that one person's desires and feelings are

stronger and more various than those of another, is merely to say that he has more of the raw material of human nature, and is therefore capable, perhaps, of more evil, but certainly of more good. Strong impulses are but another name for energy. Energy may be turned to bad uses; but more good may always be made of an energetic nature, than of an indolent and impassive one. Those who have most natural feeling are always those whose cultivated feelings may be made the strongest. The same strong susceptibilities which make the personal impulses vivid and powerful, are also the source from whence are generated the most passionate love of virtue, and the sternest self-control. It is through the cultivation of these that society both does its duty and protects its interests: not by rejecting the stuff of which heroes are made, because it knows not how to make them. A person whose desires and impulses are his own—are the expression of his own nature, as it has been developed and modified by his own culture—is said to have a character. One whose desires and impulses are not his own has no character, no more than a steam-engine has a character. If, in addition to being his own, his impulses are strong, and are under the government of a strong will, he has an energetic character. Whoever thinks that individuality of desires and impulses should not be encouraged to unfold itself must maintain that society has no need of strong natures—is not the better for containing many persons who have much character—and that a high general average of energy is not desirable.

In some early states of society, these forces might be, and were, too much ahead of the power which society then possessed of disciplining and controlling them. There has been a time when the element of spontaneity and individuality was in excess, and the social principle had a hard struggle with it. The difficulty then was to induce men of strong bodies or minds to pay obedience to any rules which required them to control their impulses. To overcome this difficulty, law and discipline, like the Popes struggling against the Emperors, asserted a power over the whole man, claiming to control all his life in order to control his character—which society had not found any other sufficient means of binding. But society has now fairly got the better of individuality; and the danger which threatens human nature is not the excess, but the deficiency, of personal impulses and preferences. Things are vastly changed since the passions of those who were strong by station or by personal endowment were in a state of habitual rebellion against laws and ordinances, and required to be rigorously chained up to enable the persons within their reach to enjoy any particle of security. In our times, from the highest class of society down to the lowest, everyone lives as under the eye of a hostile and dreaded censorship. Not only in what concerns others, but in what concerns only themselves, the individual or the family do not ask themselves—what do I prefer? or, what would suit my character and disposition? or, what would allow the best and highest in me to have fair play, and enable it to grow and thrive? They ask themselves, what is suitable to my position? what is usually done by persons of my station and pecuniary circumstances? or (worse still) what is usually done by persons of a station and circumstances superior to mine? I do not mean that they choose what is customary in preference to what suits their own inclination. It does not occur to them to have any inclination, except for what is customary. Thus the mind itself is bowed to the yoke: even in what people do for pleasure, conformity is the first thing thought of; they like in crowds; they exercise choice only among things commonly done: peculiarity of taste, eccentricity of conduct, are shunned equally with crimes: until, by dint of not following their own nature, they have no nature to follow; their human capacities are withered and starved; they become incapable of any strong wishes or native pleasures, and are generally without either opinions or feelings of home growth, or properly their own. Now is this, or is it not, the desirable condition of human nature?

It is so, on the Calvinistic theory. According to that, the one great offence of man is self-will. All the good of which humanity is capable is comprised in obedience. You have no choice; thus you must do, and no otherwise; "whatever is not a duty, is a sin." Human nature being radically corrupt, there is no redemption for anyone until human nature is killed within him. To one holding this theory of life, crushing out any of the human faculties, capacities, and susceptibilities, is no evil: man needs no capacity but that of surrendering himself to the will of God: and if he uses any of his faculties for any other purpose but to do that supposed will more effectually, he is better without them. This is the theory of Calvinism; and it is held, in a mitigated form, by many who do not consider themselves Calvinists; the mitigation consisting in giving a less ascetic interpretation to the alleged will of God; asserting it to be his will that mankind should gratify some of their inclinations; of course, not in the manner they themselves prefer, but in the way of obedience, that is, in a way prescribed to them by authority; and, therefore, by the necessary condition of the case, the same for all.

In some such insidious form there is at present a strong tendency to this narrow theory of life, and to the pinched and hidebound type of human character which it patronises. Many persons, no doubt, sincerely think that human beings thus cramped and dwarfed are as their Maker designed them to be; just as many have thought that trees are a much finer thing when clipped into pollards, or cut out into figures of animals, than as nature made them. But if it be any part of religion to believe that man was made by a good Being, it is more consistent with that faith to believe that this Being gave all human faculties that they might be cultivated and unfolded, not rooted out and consumed, and that he takes delight in every nearer approach made by his creatures to the ideal conception embodied in them, every increase in any of their capabilities of comprehension, of action, or of enjoyment. There is a different type of human excellence from the Calvinistic: a conception of humanity as having its nature bestowed on it for other purposes than merely to be abnegated. "Pagan self-assertion" is one of the elements of human worth, as well as "Christian self-denial." There is a Greek ideal of self-development, which the Platonic and Christian ideal of self-government blends with, but does not supersede. It may be **better** to be a John Knox than an Alcibiades, but it is better to be a Pericles than either; nor would a Pericles, if we had one in these days, be without anything good which belonged to John Knox.

It is not by wearing down unto uniformity all that is individual in themselves, but by cultivating it, and calling it forth, within the limits imposed by the rights and interests of others, that human beings become a noble and beautiful object of contemplation; and as the works partake the character of those who do them, by the same process human life also becomes rich, diversified, and animating, furnishing more abundant aliment to high thoughts and elevating feelings, and strengthening the tie which binds every individual to the race, by making the race infinitely better worth belonging to. In proportion to the development of his individuality, each person becomes more valuable to himself, and is therefore capable of being more valuable to others. There is a greater fulness of life about his own existence, and when there is more life in the units there is more in the mass which is composed of them. As much compression as is necessary to prevent the stronger specimens of human nature from encroaching on the rights of others cannot be dispensed with; but for this there is ample compensation, even in the point of view of human development. The means of development which the individual loses by being prevented from gratifying his inclinations to the injury of others, are chiefly obtained at the expense of the development of other people. And even to himself there is a full equivalent in the better development of the social part of his nature, rendered possible by the restraint put upon the selfish part. To be held to rigid rules of justice for the sake of others develops the feelings and capacities which have the good of others for their object. But to be restrained in things not affecting their good, by their mere displeasure, develops nothing valuable, except such force of character as may unfold itself in resisting the restraint. If acquiesced in, it dulls and blunts the whole nature. To give any fair play to the nature of each, it is essential that different persons should be allowed to lead different lives. In proportion as this latitude has been exercised in any age, has that age been noteworthy

to posterity. Even despotism does not produce its worst effects so long as individuality exists under it; and whatever crushes individuality is despotism, by whatever name it may be called, and whether it professes to be enforcing the will of God or the injunctions of men. . . .

OF THE LIMITS TO THE AUTHORITY OF SOCIETY OVER THE INDIVIDUAL

What, then, is the rightful limit to the sovereignty of the individual over himself? Where does the authority of society begin? How much of human life should be assigned to individuality, and how much to society?

Each will receive its proper share, if each has that which more particularly concerns it. To individuality should belong the part of life in which it is chiefly the individual that is interested; to society, the part which chiefly interests society.

Though society is not founded on a contract, and though no good purpose is answered by inventing a contract in order to deduce social obligations from it, everyone who receives the protection of society owes a return for the benefit, and the fact of living in society renders it indispensable that each should be bound to observe a certain line of conduct towards the rest. This conduct consists, first, in not injuring the interests of one another; or rather certain interests, which, either by express legal provision or by tacit understanding, ought to be considered as rights; and secondly, in each person's bearing his share (to be fixed on some equitable principle) of the labours and sacrifices incurred for defending the society or its members from injury and molestation. These conditions society is justified in enforcing, at all costs to those who endeavour to withhold fulfilment. Nor is this all that society may do. The acts of an individual may be hurtful to others, or wanting in due consideration for their welfare, without going to the length of violating any of their constituted rights. The offender may then be justly punished by opinion, though not by law. As soon as any part of a person's conduct affects prejudicially the interests of others, society has jurisdiction over it, and the question whether the general welfare will or will not be promoted by interfering with it becomes open to discussion. But there is no room for entertaining any such question when a person's conduct affects the interests of no persons beside himself, or needs not affect them unless they like (all the persons concerned being of full age, and the ordinary amount of understanding). In all such cases, there should be perfect freedom, legal and social, to do the action and stand the consequences.

It would be a great misunderstanding of this doctrine to suppose that it is one of selfish indifference, which pretends that human beings have no business with each other's conduct in life, and that they should not concern themselves about the well-doing or well-being of one another, unless their own interest is involved. Instead of any diminution, there is need of a great increase of disinterested exertion to promote the good of others. But disinterested benevolence can find other instruments to persuade people to their good than whips and scourges, either of the literal or the metaphorical sort. I am the last person to undervalue the self-regarding virtues; they are only second in importance, if even second, to the social. It is equally the business of education to cultivate both. But even education works by conviction and persuasion as well as by compulsion, and it is by the former only that, when the period of education is passed, the self-regarding virtues should be inculcated. Human beings owe to each other help to distinguish the better from the worse, and encouragement to choose the former and avoid the latter. They should be for ever stimulating each other to increased exercise of their higher faculties, and increased direction of their feelings and aims towards wise instead of foolish, elevating instead of degrading, objects and contemplations. But neither one person, nor any number of persons, is warranted in saying to another human creature of ripe years, that he shall not do with his life for his own benefit what he chooses to do with it. He is the person most interested in his own well-being: the interest which any other person, except in cases of strong personal attachment, can have in it, is trifling, compared with that which he himself has; the interest which society has in him individually (except as to his conduct to others) is fractional, and altogether indirect; while

with respect to his own feelings and circumstances, the most ordinary man or woman has means of knowledge immeasurably surpassing those that can be possessed by anyone else. The interference of society to overrule his judgment and purposes in what only regards himself must be grounded on general presumptions, which may be altogether wrong, and, even if right, are as likely as not to be misapplied to individual cases, by persons no better acquainted with the circumstances of such cases than those are who look at them merely from without. In this department, therefore, of human affairs, Individuality has its proper field of action. In the conduct of human beings towards one another it is necessary that general rules should for the most part be observed, in order that people may know what they have to expect: but in each person's own concerns his individual spontaneity is entitled to free exercise. Considerations to aid his judgment, exhortations to strengthen his will, may be offered to him, even obtruded on him, by others; but he himself is the final judge. All errors which he is likely to commit against advice and warning are far outweighed by the evil of allowing others to constrain him to what they deem his good.

I do not mean that the feelings with which a person is regarded by others ought not to be in any way affected by his self-regarding qualities or deficiencies. This is neither possible nor desirable. If he is eminent in any of the qualities which conduce to his own good, he is, so far, a proper object of admiration. He is so much the nearer to the ideal perfection of human nature. If he is grossly deficient in those qualities, a sentiment the opposite of admiration will follow. There is a degree of folly, and a degree of what may be called (though the phrase is not unobjectionable) lowness or depravation of taste, which, though it cannot justify doing harm to the person who manifests it, renders him necessarily and properly a subject of distaste, or, in extreme cases, even of contempt; a person could not have the opposite qualities in due strength without entertaining these feelings. Though doing no wrong to anyone, a person may so act as to compel us to judge him, and feel to him, as a fool, or as a being of an inferior order: and since this judgment and feeling are a fact which he would prefer to avoid, it is doing him a service to warn him of it beforehand, as of any other disagreeable consequence to which he exposes himself. It would be well, indeed, if this good office were much more freely rendered than the common notions of politeness at present permit, and if one person could honestly point out to another that he thinks him in fault, without being considered unmannerly or presuming. We have a right, also, in various ways, to act upon our unfavourable opinion of anyone, not to the oppression of his individuality, but in the exercise of ours. We are not bound, for example, to seek his society; we have a right to avoid it (though not to parade the avoidance), for we have a right to choose the society most acceptable to us. We have a right, and it may be our duty, to caution others against him, if we think his example or conversation likely to have a pernicious effect on those with whom he associates. We may give others a preference over him in optional good offices, except those which tend to his improvement. In these various modes a person may suffer very severe penalties at the hands of others for faults which directly concern only himself; but he suffers these penalties only in so far as they are the natural and, as it were, the spontaneous consequences of the faults themselves, not because they are purposely inflicted on him for the sake of punishment. A person who shows rashness, obstinacy, self-conceit—who cannot live within moderate means—who cannot restrain himself from hurtful indulgences—who pursues animal pleasures at the expense of those of feeling and intellect —must expect to be lowered in the opinion of others, and to have a less share of their favourble sentiments; but of this he has no right to complain, unless he has merited their favour by special excellence in his social relations, and has thus established a title to their good offices, which is not affected by his demerits toward himself.

What I contend for is, that the inconveniences which are strictly inseparable from the unfavourable judgment of others are the only ones to which a person should ever be subjected for that portion of his conduct and character which concerns his own good, but which does not affect the interest of others in their relations with him. Acts injurious to others require a totally different treatment. Encroachment on their rights; infliction on them of any loss or damage not justified by his own rights; falsehood or duplicity in dealing with them; unfair or ungenerous use of advantages over them; even selfish abstinence from defending them against injury—these are fit objects of moral reprobation, and, in grave cases, of moral retribution and punishment. And not only these acts, but the dispositions which lead to them are properly immoral, and fit subjects of disapprobation which may rise to abhorrence. Cruelty of disposition; malice and ill-nature; that most anti-social and odious of all passions, envy; dissimulation and insincerity; irascibility on insufficient cause, and resentment disproportioned to the provocation; the love of domineering over others; the desire to engross more than one's share of advantages . . . ; the pride which derives gratification from the abasement of others; the egotism which thinks self and its concerns more important than everything else, and decides all doubtful questions in its own favour—these are moral vices, and constitute a bad and odious moral character; unlike the self-regarding faults previously mentioned, which are not properly immoralities, and, to whatever pitch they may be carried, do not constitute wickedness. They may be proofs of any amount of folly, or want of personal dignity and self-respect; but they are only a subject of moral reprobation when they involve a breach of duty to others, for whose sake the individual is bound to have care for himself. What are called duties to ourselves are not socially obligatory, unless circumstances render them at the same time duties to others. The term duty to oneself, when it means anything more than prudence, means self-respect or self-development, and for none of these is anyone accountable to his fellow-creatures, because for none of them is it for the good of mankind that he be held accountable to them. . . .

APPLICATIONS

The principles asserted in these pages must be more generally admitted as the basis for discussion of details, before a consistent application of them to all the various departments of government and morals can be attempted with any prospect of advantage. The few observations I propose to make on questions of detail are designed to illustrate the principles, rather than to follow them out to their consequences. I offer, not so much applications, as specimens of application; which may serve to bring into greater clearness the meaning and limits of the two maxims which together form the entire doctrine of this Essay, and to assist the judgment in holding the balance between them, in the cases where it appears doubtful which of them is applicable to the case.

The maxims are, first, that the individual is not accountable to society for his actions, in so far as these concern the interests of no person but himself. Advice, instruction, persuasion, and avoidance by other people, if thought necessary by them for their own good, are the only measures by which society can justifiably express its dislike or disapprobation of his conduct. Secondly, that for such actions as are prejudicial to the interests of others, the individual is accountable, and may be subjected either to social or to legal punishment, if society is of opinion that the one or the other is requisite for its protection.

In the first place, it must by no means be supposed, because damage, or probability of damage, to the interests of others, can alone justify the interference of society, that therefore it always does justify such interference. In many cases, an individual, in pursuing a legitimate object, necessarily and therefore legitimately causes pain or loss to others, or intercepts a good which they had a reasonable hope of obtaining. Such oppositions of interest between individuals often arise from bad social institutions, but are unavoidable while those institutions last; and some would be unavoidable under any institutions. Whoever succeeds in an overcrowded profession, or in a competitive examination; whoever is preferred to another in any contest for an object which both desire, reaps benefit from the loss of others, from their wasted exertion and their disappointment. But it is, by common admission, better for the general interest of mankind, that persons should pursue their objects undeterred by this sort of consequences. In other words, so-

ciety admits no right, either legal or moral, in the disappointed competitors to immunity from this kind of suffering; and feels called on to interfere, only when means of success have been employed which it is contrary to the general interest to permit—namely, fraud or treachery, and force.

Again, trade is a social act. Whoever undertakes to sell any description of goods to the public does what affects the interest of other persons, and of society in general; and thus his conduct, in principle, comes within the jurisdiction of society: accordingly, it was once held to be the duty of governments, in all cases which were considered of importance, to fix prices, and regulate the processes of manufacture. But it is now recognised, though not till after a long struggle, that both the cheapness and the good quality of commodities are most effectually provided for by leaving the producers and sellers perfectly free, under the sole check of equal freedom to the buyers for supplying themselves elsewhere. This is the so-called doctrine of Free Trade, which rests on grounds different from, though equally solid with, the principle of individual liberty asserted in this Essay. Restrictions on trade, or on production for purposes of trade, are indeed restraints; and all restraint, *quâ* restraint, is an evil: but the restraints in question affect only that part of conduct which society is competent to restrain, and are wrong solely because they do not really produce the results which it is desired to produce by them. As the principle of individual liberty is not involved in the doctrine of Free Trade, so neither is it in most of the questions which arise respecting the limits of that doctrine; as, for example, what amount of public control is admissible for the prevention of fraud by adulteration; how far sanitary precautions, or arrangements to protect workpeople employed in dangerous occupations, should be enforced on employers. Such questions involve considerations of liberty, only in so far as leaving people to themselves is always better, *caeteris paribus*, than controlling them: but that they may be legitimately controlled for these ends is in principle undeniable. On the other hand, there are questions relating to interference with trade which are essentially questions of liberty; such as the Maine Law [prohibition of liquor], already touched upon; the prohibition of the importation of opium into China; the restriction of the sale of poisons; all cases, in short, where the object of the interference is to make it impossible or difficult to obtain a particular commodity. These interferences are objectionable, not as infringements on the liberty of the producer or seller, but on that of the buyer.

One of these examples, that of the sale of poisons, opens a new question: the proper limits of what may be called the functions of police; how far liberty may legitimately be invaded for the prevention of crime, or of accident. It is one of the undisputed functions of government to take precautions against crime before it has been committed, as well as to detect and punish it afterwards. The preventive function of government, however, is far more liable to be abused, to the prejudice of liberty, than the punitory function; for there is hardly any part of the legitimate freedom of action of a human being which would not admit of being represented, and fairly too, as increasing the facilities for some form or other of delinquency. Nevertheless, if a public authority, or even a private person, sees anyone evidently preparing to commit a crime, they are not bound to look on inactive until the crime is committed, but may interfere to prevent it. If poisons were never bought or used for any purpose except the commission of murder, it would be right to prohibit their manufacture and sale. They may, however, be wanted not only for innocent but for useful purposes, and restrictions cannot be imposed in the one case without operating in the other. Again, it is a proper office of public authority to guard against accidents. If either a public officer or anyone else saw a person attempting to cross a bridge which had been ascertained to be unsafe, and there were no time to warn him of his danger, they might seize him and turn him back, without any real infringement of his liberty; for liberty consists in doing what one desires, and he does not desire to fall into the river. Nevertheless, when there is not a certainty, but only a danger of mischief, no one but the person himself can judge of the sufficiency of the motive which may prompt him to incur the risk: in this case, therefore (unless he is a

child, or delirious, or in some state of excitement or absorption incompatible with the full use of the reflecting faculty), he ought, I conceive, to be only warned of the danger; not forcibly prevented from exposing himself to it. Similar considerations, applied to such a question as the sale of poisons, may enable us to decide which among the possible modes of regulation are or are not contrary to principle. Such a precaution, for example, as that of labelling the drug with some word expressive of its dangerous character, may be enforced without violation of liberty: the buyer cannot wish not to know that the thing he possesses has poisonous qualities. But to require in all cases the certificate of a medical practitioner would make it sometimes impossible, always expensive, to obtain the article for legitimate uses. The only mode apparent to me in which difficulties may be thrown in the way of crime committed through this means, without any infringement worth taking into account upon the liberty of those who desire the poisonous substance for other purposes, consists in providing what, in the apt language of Bentham, is called "preappointed evidence." This provision is familiar to everyone in the case of contracts. It is usual and right that the law, when a contract is entered into, should require as the condition of its enforcing performance, that certain formalities should be observed, such as signatures, attestation of witnesses, and the like, in order that in case of subsequent dispute there may be evidence to prove that the contract was really entered into, and that there was nothing in the circumstances to render it legally invalid; the effect being to throw great obstacles in the way of fictitious contracts, or contracts made in circumstances which, if known, would destroy their validity. Precautions of a similar nature might be enforced in the sale of articles adapted to be instruments of crime. The seller, for example, might be required to enter in a register the exact time of the transaction, the name and address of the buyer, the precise quality and quantity sold; to ask the purpose for which it was wanted, and record the answer he received. When there was no medical prescription, the presence of some third person might be required, to bring home the fact to the purchaser, in case there should afterwards be reason to believe that the article had been applied to criminal purposes. Such regulations would in general be no material impediment to obtaining the article, but a very considerable one to making an improper use of it without detection.

The right, inherent in society, to ward off crimes against itself by antecedent precautions, suggests the obvious limitations to the maxim that purely self-regarding misconduct cannot properly be meddled with in the way of prevention or punishment. Drunkenness, for example, in ordinary cases, is not a fit subject for legislative interference; but I should deem it perfectly legitimate that a person, who had once been convicted of any act of violence to others under the influence of drink, should be placed under a special legal restriction, personal to himself; that if he were afterwards found drunk, he should be liable to a penalty; and that if, when in that state, he committed another offence, the punishment to which he would be liable for that other offence should be increased in severity. The making himself drunk, in a person whom drunkenness excites to do harm to others, is a crime against others. So, again, idleness, except in a person receiving support from the public, or except when it constitutes a breach of contract, cannot without tyranny be made a subject of legal punishment; but if, either from idleness or from any other avoidable cause, a man fails to perform his legal duties to others, as for instance to support his children, it is no tyranny to force him to fulfil that obligation, by compulsory labour, if no other means are available.

Again, there are many acts which, being directly injurious only to the agents themselves, ought not to be legally interdicted, but which, if done publicly, are a violation of good manners and, coming thus within the category of offences against others, may rightly be prohibited. Of this kind are offences against decency; on which it is unnecessary to dwell, the rather as they are connected only indirectly with our subject, the objection to publicity being equally strong in the case of many actions not in themselves condemnable, nor supposed to be so. . . .

I have reserved for the last place a large class of questions respecting the limits of government interference, which, though closely connected with the subject of this Essay, do not, in strictness, belong to it. These are cases in which the reasons against interference do not turn upon the principle of liberty: the question is not about restraining the actions of individuals, but about helping them; it is asked whether the government should do, or cause to be done, something for their benefit, instead of leaving it to be done by themselves, individually or in voluntary combination.

The objections to government interference, when it is not such as to involve infringement of liberty, may be of three kinds.

The first is, when the thing to be done is likely to be better done by individuals than by the government. Speaking generally, there is no one so fit to conduct any business, or to determine how or by whom it shall be conducted, as those who are personally interested in it. This principle condemns the interferences, once so common, of the legislature, or the officers of government, with the ordinary processes of industry. But this part of the subject has been sufficiently enlarged upon by political economists, and is not particularly related to the principles of this Essay.

The second objection is more nearly allied to our subject. In many cases, though individuals may not do the particular thing so well, on the average, as the officers of government, it is nevertheless desirable that it should be done by them, rather than by the government, as a means to their own mental education—a mode of strengthening their active faculties, exercising their judgment, and giving them a familiar knowledge of the subjects with which they are thus left to deal. This is a principal, though not the sole, recommendation of jury trial (in cases not political); of free and popular local and municipal institutions; of the conduct of industrial and philanthropic enterprises by voluntary associations. These are not questions of liberty, and are connected with that subject only by remote tendencies; but they are questions of development. It belongs to a different occasion from the present to dwell on these things as parts of national education; as being, in truth, the peculiar training of a citizen, the practical part of the political education of a free people, taking them out of the narrow cir-

cle of personal and family selfishness, and ac-
customing them to the comprehension of joint
interests, the management of joint concerns—
habituating them to act from public or semi-
public motives, and guide their conduct by
aims which unite instead of isolating them from
one another. Without these habits and powers,
a free constitution can neither be worked nor
preserved; as is exemplified by the too-often
transitory nature of political freedom in countries where it does not rest upon a sufficient
basis of local liberties. The management of
purely local business by the localities, and of
the great enterprises of industry by the union
of those who voluntarily supply the pecuniary
means, is further recommended by all the advantages which have been set forth in this Essay as belonging to individuality of development, and diversity of modes of action. Government operations tend to be everywhere
alike. With individuals and voluntary associations, on the contrary, there are varied experiments, and endless diversity of experience.
What the State can usefully do is to make itself
a central depository, and active circulator and
diffuser, of the experience resulting from many
trials. Its business is to enable each experimen-
talist to benefit by the experiments of others,
instead of tolerating no experiments but its
own.

The third and most cogent reason for restricting the interference of government is the
great evil of adding unnecessarily to its power.
Every function superadded to those already exercised by the government causes its influence
over hopes and fears to be more widely diffused, and converts, more and more, the active
and ambitious part of the public into hang-
ers-on of the government, or of some party
which aims at becoming the government. If
the roads, the railways, the banks, the insurance offices, the great joint-stock companies,
the universities, and the public charities, were
all of them branches of the government; if, in
addition, the municipal corporations and local
boards, with all that now devolves on them,
became departments of the central administration; if the employees of all these different enterprises were appointed and paid by the government, and looked to the government for

every rise in life; not all the freedom of the
press and popular constitution of the legislature
would make this or any other country free
otherwise than in name. And the evil would be
greater, the more efficiently and scientifically
the administrative machinery was constructed
—the more skilful the arrangements for obtaining the best qualified hands and heads
with which to work it.

In England it has of late been proposed that
all the members of the civil service of government should be selected by competitive examination, to obtain for these employments the
most intelligent and instructed persons procur-
able; and much has been said and written for
and against this proposal. One of the arguments
most insisted on by its opponents is that the
occupation of a permanent official servant of
the State does not hold out sufficient prospects
of emolument and importance to attract the
highest talents, which will always be able to
find a more inviting career in the professions,
or in the service of companies and other public
bodies. One would not have been surprised if
this argument had been used by the friends of
the proposition, as an answer to its principal
difficulty. Coming from the opponents it is
strange enough. What is urged as an objection
is the safety-valve of the proposed system. If
indeed all the high talent of the country *could*
be drawn into the service of the government,
a proposal tending to bring about that result
might well inspire uneasiness. If every part of
the business of society which required organised concert, or large and comprehensive views,
were in the hands of the government, and if
government offices were universally filled by
the ablest men, all the enlarged culture and
practised intelligence in the country, except
the purely speculative, would be concentrated
in a numerous bureaucracy, to whom alone the
rest of the community would look for all
things: the multitude for direction and dictation in all they had to do; the able and aspiring
for personal advancement. To be admitted into
the ranks of this bureaucracy, and when admitted, to rise therein, would be the sole objects of ambition. Under this *régime*, not only
is the outside public ill qualified, for want of
practical experience, to criticise or check the

mode of operation of the bureaucracy, but even if the accidents of despotic or the natural working of popular institutions occasionally raise to the summit a ruler or rulers of reforming inclinations, no reform can be effected which is contrary to the interest of the bureaucracy. Such is the melancholy condition of the Russian empire, as shown in the accounts of those who have had sufficient opportunity of observation. The Czar himself is powerless against the bureaucratic body; he can send any one of them to Siberia, but he cannot govern without them, or against their will. On every decree of his they have a tacit veto, by merely refraining from carrying it into effect. In countries of more advanced civilisation and of a more insurrectionary spirit, the public, accustomed to expect everything to be done for them by the State, or at least to do nothing for themselves without asking from the State not only leave to do it, but even how it is to be done, naturally hold the State responsible for all evil which befalls them; and when the evil exceeds their amount of patience, they rise against the government, and make what is called a revolution; whereupon somebody else, with or without legitimate authority from the nation, vaults into the seat, issues his orders to the bureaucracy, and everything goes on much as it did before, the bureaucracy being unchanged, and nobody else being capable of taking their place.

A very different spectacle is exhibited among a people accustomed to transact their own business. In France, a large part of the people having been engaged in military service, many of whom have held at least the rank of non-commissioned officers, there are in every popular insurrection several persons competent to take the lead, and improvise some tolerable plan of action. What the French are in military affairs, the Americans are in every kind of civil business: let them be left without a government, every body of Americans is able to improvise one, and to carry on that or any other public business with a sufficient amount of intelligence, order, and decision. This is what every free people ought to be: and a people capable of this is certain to be free; it will never let itself be enslaved by any man or body of men because these are able to seize and pull the reins of the central administration. No bureaucracy can hope to make such a people as this do or undergo anything that they do not like. But where everything is done through the bureaucracy, nothing to which the bureaucracy is really adverse can be done at all. The constitution of such countries is an organisation of the experience and practical ability of the nation into a disciplined body for the purpose of governing the rest; and the more perfect that organisation is in itself, the more successful in drawing to itself and educating for itself the persons of greatest capacity from all ranks of the community, the more complete is the bondage of all, the members of the bureaucracy included. For the governors are as much the slaves of their organisation and discipline as the governed are of the governors. A Chinese mandarin is as much the tool and creature of a despotism as the humblest cultivator. An individual Jesuit is to the utmost degree of abasement the slave of his order, though the order itself exists for the collective power and importance of its members.

It is not, also, to be forgotten, that the absorption of all the principal ability of the country into the governing body is fatal, sooner or later, to the mental activity and progressiveness of the body itself. Banded together as they are, —working a system which, like all systems, necessarily proceeds in a great measure by fixed rules—the official body are under the constant temptation of sinking into indolent routine; or, if they now and then desert that mill-horse round, of rushing into some half-examined crudity which has struck the fancy of some leading member of the corps; and the sole check to these closely allied, though seemingly opposite, tendencies, the only stimulus which can keep the ability of the body itself up to a high standard, is liability to the watchful criticism of equal ability outside the body. It is indispensable, therefore, that the means should exist, independently of the government, of forming such ability, and furnishing it with the opportunities and experience necessary for a correct judgment of great practical affairs. If we would possess permanently a skilful and efficient body of functionaries—above all, a body able to originate and willing to adopt improvements; if we would not have our bureaucracy degenerate into a pedantocracy, this body must not engross all the occupations which form and cultivate the faculties required for the government of mankind.

To determine the point at which evils, so formidable to human freedom and advancement, begin, or rather at which they begin to predominate over the benefits attending the collective application of the force of society, under its recognised chiefs, for the removal of the obstacles which stand in the way of its well-being; to secure as much of the advantages of centralised power and intelligence as can be had without turning into governmental channels too great a proportion of the general activity—is one of the most difficult and complicated questions in the art of government. It is, in a great measure, a question of detail, in which many and various considerations must be kept in view, and no absolute rule can be laid down. But I believe that the practical principle in which safety resides, the ideal to be kept in view, the standard by which to test all arrangements intended for overcoming the difficulty, may be conveyed in these words: the greatest dissemination of power consistent with efficiency; but the greatest possible centralisation of information, and diffusion of it from the centre. Thus, in municipal administration, there would be, as in the New England States, a very minute division among separate officers, chosen by the localities, of all business which is not better left to the persons directly interested; but besides this, there would be, in each department of local affairs, a central superintendence, forming a branch of the general government. The organ of this superintendence would concentrate, as in a focus, the variety of information and experience derived from the conduct of that branch of public business in all the localities, from everything analogous which is done in foreign countries, and from the general principles of political science. This central organ should have a right to know all that is done, and its special duty should be that of making the knowledge acquired in one place available for others. Emancipated from the petty prejudices and narrow views of a locality by its elevated position and comprehensive sphere of observation, its advice would naturally carry much authority; but its actual power, as a permanent institution, should, I conceive, be limited to compelling the local officers to obey the laws laid down for their guidance. In all things not provided for by general rules, those officers should be left to their own judgment, under responsibility to their constituents. For the violation of rules, they should be responsible to law, and the rules themselves should be laid down by the legislature; the central administrative authority only watching over their execution, and, if they were not properly carried into effect, appealing, according to the nature of the case, to the tribunals to enforce the law, or to the constituencies to dismiss the functionaries who had not executed it according to its spirit. Such, in its general conception, is the central superintendence which the Poor Law Board is intended to exercise over the administrators of the Poor Rate throughout the country. Whatever powers the Board exercises beyond this limit were right and necessary in that peculiar case, for the cure of rooted habits of maladministration in matters deeply affecting not the localities merely, but the whole community; since no locality has a moral right to make itself by mismanagement a nest of pauperism, necessarily overflowing into other localities, and impairing the moral and physical condition of the whole labouring community. The powers of administrative coercion and subordinate legislation possessed by the Poor Law Board (but which, owing to the state of opinion on the subject, are very scantily exercised by them), though perfectly justifiable in a case of first-rate national interest, would be wholly out of place in the superintendence of interests purely local. But a central organ of information and instruction for all the localities would be equally valuable in all departments of administration. A government cannot have too much of the kind of activity which does not impede, but aids and stimulates, individual exertion and development. The mischief begins when, instead of calling forth the activity and powers of individuals and bodies, it substitutes its own activity for theirs; when, instead of informing, advising, and, upon occasion, denouncing, it makes them work in fetters, or bids them stand aside and does their work instead of them.

The worth of a State, in the long run, is the worth of the individuals composing it; and a State which postpones the interests of *their* mental expansion and elevation to a little more of administrative skill, or of that semblance of it which practice gives, in the details of business; a State which dwarfs its men, in order that they may be more docile instruments in its hands even for beneficial purposes, will find that with small men no great thing can really be accomplished; and that the perfection of machinery to which it has sacrificed everything will in the end avail it nothing, for want of the vital power which, in order that the machine might work more smoothly, it has preferred to banish.

Alexis de Tocqueville

Alexis de Tocqueville (1805–1859) was a French aristocrat who became deeply concerned with the problem of liberty. He was trained for the magistracy and served for a time in that capacity. Subsequently he entered the French Chamber of Deputies and, after the Liberal revolution of 1848, served in the government as minister of foreign affairs. In 1830 he came to the United States ostensibly to study the American penal system, but in reality to study American life generally. He returned to Europe deeply impressed with what he had seen of democracy in action. He was particularly concerned about the future of individual liberty under this form of government. In 1835 he published his Democracy in America, which was the first comprehensive analysis written on the American political experiment. The book received widespread attention throughout Europe and helped to inspire the democratic movement on the continent. Thus de Tocqueville was a force in the backward flow of Western Civilization from America to Europe. In reading the following selections from this work note (1) the similar situation in Europe and the United States which influenced de Tocqueville to write Democracy in America, (2) the extent to which popular sovereignty had developed in America, (3) why he thought the people there truly governed, (4) the pragmatic character of American philosophy, (5) the tendency for popular opinion to supersede thought, (6) the effect of equalitarianism on American concepts of human perfectibility, (7) the effect of democracy upon the arts, (8) de Tocqueville's discussion of freedom and equality and which of these democratic communities preferred, (9) the methods by which Americans successfully combatted the dangers of equality, (10) the possibility of democratic America producing an industrial autocracy, (11) the threat of despotic government emerging over a people socially equal, and (12) the means by which he believed democratic nations could preserve personal freedom.

As translated by Henry Reeves in Alexis de Tocqueville, *The Republic of the United States of America, and its Political Institutions, Reviewed and Examined*, 2 vols. in 1, New York, 1856, I, 1; 57; 59; 184–185; II, 1–3; 9–11; 33–34; 49–53; 99–103; 110–113; 169–172; 343–344; 346; 347–351.

618 · ALEXIS DE TOCQUEVILLE

From: DEMOCRACY IN AMERICA

Among the novel objects that attracted my attention during my stay in the United States, nothing struck me more forcibly than the general equality of conditions. I readily discovered the prodigious influence which this primary fact exercises on the whole course of society, by giving a certain direction to public opinion, and a certain tenor to the laws; by imparting new maxims to the governing powers, and peculiar habits to the governed.

I speedily perceived that the influence of this fact extends far beyond the political character and the laws of the country, and that it has no less empire over civil society than over the government; it creates opinions, engenders sentiments, suggests the ordinary practices of life, and modifies whatever it does not produce.

The more I advanced in the study of American society, the more I perceived that the equality of conditions is the fundamental fact from which all others seem to be derived, and the central point at which all my observations constantly terminated.

I then turned my thoughts to our own hemisphere, where I imagined that I discerned something analogous to the spectacle which the New World presented to me. I observed that the equality of conditions is daily advancing toward those extreme limits which it seems to have reached in the United States; and that the democracy which governs the American communities, appears to be rapidly rising into power in Europe.

I hence conceived the idea of the book which is now before the reader. . . .

THE PRINCIPLE OF THE SOVEREIGNTY OF THE PEOPLE IN AMERICA

Whenever the political laws of the United States are to be discussed, it is with the doctrine of the sovereignty of the people that we must begin.

The principle of the sovereignty of the people, which is to be found, more or less, at the bottom of almost all human institutions, generally remains concealed from view. It is obeyed without being recognised, or if for a moment it be brought to light, it is hastily cast back into the gloom of the sanctuary.

"The will of the nation" is one of those expressions which have been most profusely abused by the wily and the despotic of every age. To the eyes of some it has been represented by the venal suffrages of a few of the satellites of power; to others, by the votes of a timid or an interested minority; and some have even discovered it in the silence of a people, on the supposition that the fact of submission established the right of command.

In America, the principle of the sovereignty of the people is not either barren or concealed, as it is with some other nations; it is recognised by the customs and proclaimed by the laws; it spreads freely, and arrives without impediment at its most remote consequences. If there be a country in the world where the doctrine of the sovereignty of the people can be fairly appreciated, where it can be studied in its application to the affairs of society, and where its dangers and its advantages may be foreseen, that country is assuredly America. . . .

At the present day the principle of the sovereignty of the people has acquired, in the United States, all the practical development which the imagination can conceive. It is unencumbered by those fictions which have been thrown over it in other countries, and it appears in every possible form according to the exigency of the occasion. Sometimes the laws are made by the people in a body, as at Athens; and sometimes its representatives, chosen by universal suffrage, transact business in its name, and almost under its immediate control.

In some countries a power exists which, though it is in a degree foreign to the social body, directs it, and forces it to pursue a certain track. In others the ruling force is divided, being partly within and partly without the ranks of the people. But nothing of the kind is to be seen in the United States; there society governs itself for itself. All power centres in its bosom; and scarcely an individual is to be met with who would venture to conceive, or, still more, to express, the idea of seeking it elsewhere. The nation participates in the making of its laws by the choice of its legislators, and in the execution of them by the choice of the agents of the executive government; it may almost be said to govern itself, so feeble and so restricted is the share left to the administration, so little do the authorities forget their popular origin and the power from which they emanate. . . .

WHY THE PEOPLE MAY STRICTLY BE SAID TO GOVERN IN THE UNITED STATES

In America the people appoints the legislative and the executive power, and furnishes the jurors who punish all offences against the laws. The American institutions are democratic, not only in their principle but in all their consequences; and the people elects its representatives *directly*, and for the most part *annually*, in order to ensure their dependance. The people is therefore the real directing power; and although the form of government is representative, it is evident that the opinions, the prejudices, the interests, and even the passions of the community are hindered by no durable obstacles from exercising a perpetual influence on society. In the United States the majority governs in the name of the people, as is the case in all the countries in which the people is supreme. This majority is principally composed of peaceable citizens, who, either by inclination or by interest, are sincerely desirous of the welfare of their country. But they are surrounded by the incessant agitation of parties, which attempt to gain their co-operation and to avail themselves of their support. . . .

PHILOSOPHICAL METHOD AMONG THE AMERICANS

I think that in no country in the civilized world is less attention paid to philosophy than in the United States. The Americans have no philosophical school of their own; and they care but little for all the schools into which Europe is divided, the very names of which are scarcely known to them.

Nevertheless it is easy to perceive that almost all the inhabitants of the United States conduct their understanding in the same manner, and govern it by the same rules; that is to say, that without ever having taken the trouble to define the rules of a philosophical method, they are in possession of one, common to the whole people.

To evade the bondage of system and habit, of family-maxims, class-opinions, and, in some degree, of national prejudices; to accept tradition only as a means of information, and existing facts only as a lesson used in doing otherwise and doing better; to seek the reason of things for oneself, and in oneself alone; to tend to results without being bound to means, and to aim at the substance through the form;—such are the principal characteristics of what I shall call the philosophical method of the Americans.

But if I go further, and if I seek among these characteristics that which predominates over and includes almost all the rest, I discover, that in most of the operations of the mind, each American appeals to the individual exercise of his own understanding alone.

America is therefore one of the countries in the world where philosophy is least studied, and where the precepts of Descartes are best applied. Nor is this surprising. The Americans do not read the works of Descartes, because their social condition deters them from speculative studies; but they follow his maxims, because this very social condition naturally disposes their understanding to adopt them.

In the midst of the continual movement which agitates a democratic community, the tie which unites one generation to another is relaxed or broken; every man readily loses the trace of the ideas of his forefathers or takes no care about them.

Nor can men living in this state of society derive their belief from the opinions of the class to which they belong; for, so to speak, there are no longer any classes, or those which still exist are composed of such mobile elements, that their body can never exercise a real control over its members.

As to the influence which the intelligence of one man has on that of another, it must necessarily be very limited in a country where the citizens, placed on the footing of a general similitude, are all closely seen by each other;

and where, as no signs of incontestable greatness or superiority are perceived in any one of them, they are constantly brought back to their own reason as the most obvious and proximate source of truth. It is not only confidence in this or that man which is then destroyed, but the taste for trusting the *ipse dixit* of any man whatsoever. Every one shuts himself up in his own breast, and affects from that point to judge the world.

The practice which obtains among the Americans of fixing the standard of their judgement in themselves alone, leads them to other habits of mind. As they perceive that they succeed in resolving without assistance all the little difficulties which their practical life presents, they readily conclude that every thing in the world may be explained, and that nothing in it transcends the limits of the understanding. Thus they fall to denying what they cannot comprehend; which leaves them but little faith for whatever is extraordinary, and an almost insurmountable distaste for whatever is supernatural. As it is on their own testimony that they are accustomed to rely, they like to discern the object which engages their attention with extreme clearness; they therefore strip off as much as possible all that covers it, they rid themselves of whatever separates them from it, they remove whatever conceals it from sight, in order to view it more closely and in the broad light of day. This disposition of the mind soon leads them to contemn forms, which they regard as useless and inconvenient veils placed between them and the truth.

The Americans then have not required to extract their philosophical method from books; they have found it in themselves. The same thing may be remarked in what has taken place in Europe.

This same method has only been established and made popular in Europe in proportion as the condition of society has become more equal, and men have grown more like each other. . . .

OF THE PRINCIPAL SOURCE OF BELIEF AMONG DEMOCRATIC NATIONS

. . . When the ranks of society are unequal, and men unlike each other in condition, there are some individuals invested with all the power of superior intelligence, learning, and enlightenment, while the multitude is sunk in ignorance and prejudice. Men living at these aristocratic periods are therefore naturally induced to shape their opinions by the superior standard of a person or a class of persons, while they are averse to recognise the infallibility of the mass of the people.

The contrary takes place in ages of equality. The nearer the citizens are drawn to the common level of an equal and similar condition, the less prone does each man become to place implicit faith in a certain man or a certain class of men. But his readiness to believe the multitude increases, and opinion is more than ever mistress of the world. Not only is common opinion the only guide which private judgement retains among a democratic people, but among such a people it possesses a power infinitely beyond what it has elsewhere. At periods of equality men have no faith in one another, by reason of their common resemblance; but this very resemblance gives them almost unbounded confidence in the judgement of the public; for it would not seem probable, as they are all endowed with equal means of judging, but that the greater truth should go with the greater number.

When the inhabitant of a democratic country compares himself individually with all those about him, he feels with pride that he is the equal of any one of them; but when he comes to survey the totality of his fellows, and to place himself in contrast to so huge a body, he is instantly overwhelmed by the sense of his own insignificance and weakness.

The same equality which renders him independent of each of his fellow-citizens, taken severally, exposes him alone and unprotected to the influence of the greater number.

The public has therefore among a democratic people a singular power, of which aristocratic nations could never so much as conceive an idea; for it does not persuade to certain opinions, but it enforces them, and infuses them into the faculties by a sort of enormous pressure of the minds of all upon the reason of each.

In the United States the majority undertakes to supply a multitude of ready-made opinions for the use of individuals, who are thus relieved from the necessity of forming opinions of their own. Everybody there adopts great numbers of theories on philosophy, morals, and politics, without inquiry, upon public trust; and if we look to it very narrowly, it will be perceived that religion herself holds her sway there, much less as a doctrine of revelation than as a commonly received opinion.

The fact that the political laws of the Americans are such that the majority rules the community with sovereign sway, materially increases the power which that majority naturally exercises over the mind. For nothing is more customary in man than to recognise superior wisdom in the person of his oppressor. This political omnipotence of the majority in the United States doubtless augments the influence which public opinion would obtain without it over the mind of each member of the community; but the foundations of that influence do not rest upon it. They must be sought for in the principle of equality itself, not in the more or less popular institutions which men living under that condition may give themselves. The intellectual dominion of the greater number would probably be less absolute among a democratic people governed by a king than in the sphere of a pure democracy, but it will always be extremely absolute; and by whatever political laws men are governed in the ages of equality, it may be foreseen that faith in public opinion will become a species of religion there, and the majority its ministering prophet.

Thus intellectual authority will be different, but it will not be diminished; and far from thinking that it will disappear, I augur that it may readily acquire too much preponderance, and confine the action of private judgement within narrower limits than are suited either to the greatness or the happiness of the human race. In the principle of equality I very clearly discern two tendencies; the one leading the mind of every man to untried thoughts, the other inclined to prohibit him from thinking at all. And I perceive how, under the dominion of certain laws, democracy would extinguish that liberty of the mind to which a democratic social condition is favorable; so that, after having broken all the bondage once imposed on it by ranks or by men, the human mind would be closely fettered to the general will of the greatest number.

If the absolute power of a majority were to be substituted by democratic nations, for all the different powers which checked or retarded overmuch the energy of individual minds, the evil would only have changed its symptoms. Men would not have found the means of independent life; they would simply have invented (no easy task) a new dress for servitude. There is—and I cannot repeat it too often—there is in this matter for profound reflection for those who look on freedom as a holy thing, and who hate not only the despot, but despotism. For myself, when I feel the hand of power lie heavy on my brow, I care but little to know who oppresses me; and I am not the more disposed to pass beneath the yoke, because it is held out to me by the arms of a million men. . . .

THE PRINCIPLE OF EQUALITY SUGGESTS TO THE AMERICANS THE IDEA OF THE INDEFINITE PERFECTIBILITY OF MAN

Equality suggests to the human mind several ideas which would not have originated from any other source, and it modifies almost all those previously entertained. I take as an example the idea of human perfectibility, because it is one of the principal notions that the intellect can conceive, and because it constitutes of itself a great philosophical theory, which is every instant to be traced by its consequences in the practice of human affairs.

Although man has many points of resemblance with the brute creation, one characteristic is peculiar to himself—he improves; they are incapable of improvement. Mankind could not fail to discover this difference from its earliest period. The idea of perfectibility is therefore as old as the world: equality did not give birth to it, although it has imparted to it a novel character.

When the citizens of a community are classed according to their rank, their profession or their birth, and when all men are constrained to follow the career which happens to open before them, every one thinks that the utmost limits of human power are to be discerned in proximity to himself, and none seeks any longer to resist the inevitable law of his destiny. Not indeed that an aristocratic people absolutely contests man's faculty of self-improvement, but they do not hold it to be indefinite; amelioration they conceive, but not change: they imagine that the future condition of society may be better, but not essentially different; and while they admit that mankind has made vast strides in improvement, and may still have some to make, they assign to it beforehand certain impassable limits.

Thus they do not presume that they have arrived at the supreme good or at absolute truth (what people or what man was ever wild enough to imagine it?), but they cherish a persuasion that they have pretty nearly reached that degree of greatness and knowledge which our imperfect nature admits of; and, as nothing moves about them, they are willing to fancy that every thing is in its fit place. Then it is that the legislator affects to lay down eternal laws; that kings and nations will raise none but imperishable monuments; and that the present generation undertakes to spare generations to come the care of regulating their destinies.

In proportion as castes disappear and the classes of society approximate—as manners, customs and laws vary, from the tumultuous intercourse of men—as new facts arise—as new truths are brought to light—as ancient opinions are dissipated and others take their place—the image of an ideal perfection, for ever on the wing, presents itself to the human mind. Continual changes are then every instant occurring under the observation of every man: the position of some is rendered worse; and he learns but too well, that no people and no individual, how enlightened soever they may be, can lay claim to infallibility;—the condition of others is improved; whence he infers that man is endowed with an indefinite faculty of improvement. His reverses teach him that none may hope to have discovered absolute good—his success stimulates him to the never-ending pursuit of it. Thus, for ever seeking—for ever falling, to rise again—often disappointed, but not discouraged—he tends unceasingly toward that unmeasured greatness so indistinctly visible at the end of the long track which humanity has yet to tread.

It can hardly be believed how many facts naturally flow from the philosophical theory of the indefinite perfectibility of man, or how strong an influence it exercises even on men who, living entirely for the purposes of action and not of thought, seem to conform their actions to it, without knowing anything about it.

I accost an American sailor, and I inquire why the ships of his country are built so as to last but for a short time; he answers without hesitation that the art of navigation is every day making such rapid progress, that the finest vessel would become almost useless if it lasted beyond a certain number of years. In these words, which fell accidentally and on a particular subject from a man of rude attainments, I recognise the general and systematic idea upon which a great people directs all its concerns.

Aristocratic nations are naturally too apt to narrow the scope of human perfectibility; democratic nations to expand it beyond compass. . . .

CONCERNING THE SPIRIT IN WHICH THE AMERICANS CULTIVATE THE ARTS

It would be to waste the time of my readers and my own, if I strove to demonstrate how the general mediocrity of fortunes, the absence of superfluous wealth, the universal desire of comfort, and the constant efforts by which every one attempts to procure it, make the taste for the useful predominate over the love of the beautiful in the heart of man. Democratic nations, among which all these things exist, will therefore cultivate the arts which serve to render life easy, in preference to those whose object is to adorn it. They will habitually prefer the useful to the beautiful, and they will require that the beautiful should be useful.

But I propose to go further; and after having pointed out this first feature, to sketch several others.

It commonly happens that in the ages of privilege the practice of almost all the arts becomes a privilege; and that every profession is a separate walk upon which it is not allowable for every one to enter. Even when productive industry is free, the fixed character which belongs to aristocratic nations gradually segregates all the persons who practise the same art, till they form a distinct class, always composed of the same families, whose members are all known to each other, and among whom a public opinion of their own, and a species of corporate pride soon spring up. In a class or guild of this kind, each artisan has not only his fortune to make, but his reputation to preserve. He is not exclusively swayed by his own interest, or even by that of his customer, but by that of the body to which he belongs; and the interest of that body is, that each artisan should produce the best possible workmanship. In aristocratic ages, the object of the arts is therefore to manufacture as well as possible—not with the greatest dispatch, or at the lowest rate.

When, on the contrary, every profession is open to all—when a multitude of persons are constantly embracing and abandoning it—and when its several members are strangers to each other, indifferent and from their numbers hardly seen among themselves; the social tie is destroyed, and each workman, standing alone, endeavours simply to gain the greatest possible quantity of money at the least possible cost. The will of the customer is then his only limit. But at the same time a corresponding revolution takes place in the customer also. In countries in which riches as well as power are concentrated and retained in the hands of the few, the use of the greater part of this world's goods belongs to a small number of individuals, who are always the same. Necessity, public opinion, or moderate desires exclude all others from the enjoyment of them. As this aristocratic class remains fixed at the pinnacle of greatness on which it stands, without diminution or increase, it is always acted upon by the same wants and affected by them in the same manner. The men of whom it is composed naturally derive from their superior and hereditary position a taste for what is extremely well-made and lasting. This affects the general way of thinking of the nation in relation to the arts. It often occurs, among such a people, that even the peasant will rather go without the objects he covets, than procure them in a state of imperfection. In aristocracies, then, the handicraftsmen work for only a limited number of very fastidious customers: the profit they hope to make depends principally on the perfection of their workmanship.

Such is no longer the case when, all privileges being abolished, ranks are intermingled, and men are for ever rising or sinking upon the ladder of society. Among a democratic people a number of citizens always exist whose patrimony is divided and decreasing. They have contracted, under more prosperous circumstances, certain wants, which remain after the means of satisfying such wants are gone; and they are anxiously looking out for some surreptitious method of providing for them. On the other hand, there are always in democracies a large number of men whose fortune is upon the increase, but whose desires grow much faster than their fortunes; and who gloat upon the gifts of wealth in anticipation, long before they have means to command them. Such men are eager to find some short cut to these gratifications, already almost within their reach. From the combination of these two causes the result is, that in democracies there are always a multitude of individuals whose wants are above their means, and who are very willing to take up with imperfect satisfaction, rather than abandon the object of their desires.

The artisan readily understands these passions, for he himself partakes in them: in an aristocracy he would seek to sell his workmanship at a high price to the few; he now conceives that the more expeditious way of getting rich is to sell them at a low price to all. But there are only two ways of lowering the price of commodities. The first is to discover some better, shorter, and more ingenious method of producing them: the second is to manufacture a larger quantity of goods, nearly similar, but of less value. Among a democratic population, all the intellectual faculties of the workman are directed to these two objects: he strives to invent methods which may enable him not only to work better, but quicker and cheaper; or, if he cannot succeed in that, to diminish the intrinsic qualities of the thing he makes, without rendering it wholly unfit for the use for which it is intended. When none but the wealthy had watches, they were almost all very good ones: few are now made which are worth much, but every body has one in his pocket. Thus the democratic principle not only tends to direct the human mind to the useful arts, but it induces the artisan to produce with great rapidity a quantity of imperfect commodities, and the consumer to content himself with these commodities.

Not that in democracies the arts are incapable of producing very commendable works, if such be required. This may occasionally be the case, if customers appear who are ready to pay for time and trouble. In this rivalry of every kind of industry—in the midst of this immense competition and these countless experiments, some excellent workmen are formed who reach the utmost limits of their craft. But they have rarely an opportunity of displaying what they can do; they are scrupulously sparing of their powers; they remain in a state of accomplished mediocrity, which condemns itself, and, though it be very well able to shoot beyond the mark before it, aims only at what it hits. In aristocracies, on the contrary, workmen always do all they can; and when they stop, it is because they have reached the limit of their attainments.

When I arrive in a country where I find some of the finest productions of the arts, I learn from this fact nothing of the social condition or of the political constitution of the country. But if I perceive that the productions of the arts are generally of an inferior quality, very abundant and very cheap, I am convinced that, among the people where this occurs, privilege is on the decline, and that ranks are beginning to intermingle and will soon be confounded together.

The handicraftsmen of democratic ages endeavour not only to bring their useful productions within the reach of the whole community, but they strive to give to all their commodities attractive qualities which they do not in reality possess. In the confusion of all ranks every one hopes to appear what he is not, and makes great exertions to succeed in this object. This sentiment indeed, which is but too natural to the heart of man, does not originate in the democratic principle; but that principle applies it to material objects. To mimic virtue is of every age; but the hypocrisy of luxury belongs more particularly to the ages of democracy.

To satisfy these new cravings of human vanity, the arts have recourse to every species of imposture: and these devices sometimes go so far as to defeat their own purpose. Imitation

diamonds are now made which may be easily mistaken for real ones; as soon as the art of fabricating false diamonds shall have reached so high a degree of perfection that they cannot be distinguished from real ones, it is probable that both one and the other will be abandoned, and become mere pebbles again.

This leads me to speak of those arts which are called the fine arts, by way of distinction. I do not believe that it is a necessary effect of a democratic social condition and of democratic institutions to diminish the number of men who cultivate the fine arts; but these causes exert a very powerful influence on the manner in which these arts are cultivated. Many of those who had already contracted a taste for the fine arts are impoverished; on the other hand, many of those who are not yet rich begin to conceive that taste, at least by imitation; and the number of consumers increases, but opulent and fastidious consumers become more scarce. Something analogous to what I have already pointed out in the useful arts then takes place in the fine arts; the productions of artists are more numerous, but the merit of each production is diminished. No longer able to soar to what is great, they cultivate what is pretty and elegant; and appearance is more attended to than reality.

In aristocracies a few great pictures are produced; in democratic countries, a vast number of insignificant ones. In the former, statues are raised of bronze; in the latter, they are modelled in plaster.

When I arrived for the first time at New York, by that part of the Atlantic Ocean which is called the Narrows, I was surprised to perceive along the shore, at some distance from the city, a considerable number of little palaces of white marble, several of which were built after the models of ancient architecture. When I went the next day to inspect more closely the buildings which had particularly attracted my notice, I found that its walls were of whitewashed brick, and its columns of painted wood. All the edifices which I had admired the night before were of the same kind.

The social condition and the institutions of democracy impart, moreover, certain peculiar tendencies to all the imitative arts which it is easy to point out. They frequently withdraw them from the delineation of the soul to fix them exclusively on that of the body: and they substitute the representation of motion and sensation for that of sentiment and thought: in a word, they put the Real in the place of the Ideal. . . .

WHY DEMOCRATIC NATIONS SHOW A MORE ARDENT AND ENDURING LOVE OF EQUALITY THAN OF LIBERTY

The first and most intense passion which is engendered by the equality of conditions is, I need hardly say, the love of that same equality. My readers will therefore not be surprised that I speak of it before all others.

Everybody has remarked, that in our time, and especially in France, this passion for equality is every day gaining ground in the human heart. It has been said a hundred times that our contemporaries are far more ardently and tenaciously attached to equality than to freedom; but, as I do not find that the causes of the fact have been sufficiently analyzed, I shall endeavour to point them out.

It is possible to imagine an extreme point at which freedom and equality would meet and be confounded together. Let us suppose that all the members of the community take a part in the government, and that each one of them has an equal right to take a part in it. As none is different from his fellows, none can exercise a tyrannical power: men will be perfectly free, because they will all be entirely equal; and they will all be perfectly equal, because they will be entirely free. To this ideal state democratic nations tend. Such is the completest form that equality can assume upon earth; but there are a thousand others which, without being equally perfect, are not less cherished by those nations.

The principle of equality may be established in civil society, without prevailing in the political world. Equal rights may exist of indulging in the same pleasures, of entering the same professions, of frequenting the same places—in a word, of living in the same manner and seeking wealth by the same means, although all men do not take an equal share in the government.

A kind of equality may even be established in the political world, though there should be no political freedom there. A man may be the equal of all his countrymen save one, who is the master of all without distinction, and who selects equally from among them all the agents of his power.

Several other combinations might be easily imagined, by which very great equality would be united to institutions more or less free, or even to institutions wholly without freedom.

Although men cannot become absolutely equal unless they be entirely free, and consequently equality, pushed to its furthest extent, may be confounded with freedom, yet there is good reason for distinguishing the one from the other. The taste which men have for liberty, and that which they feel for equality, are, in fact, two different things; and I am not afraid to add, that, among democratic nations, they are two unequal things.

Upon close inspection, it will be seen that there is in every age some peculiar and preponderating fact with which all others are connected; this fact almost always gives birth to some pregnant idea or some ruling passion, which attracts to itself, and bears away in its course, all the feelings and opinions of the time: it is like a great stream, toward which each of the surrounding rivulets seem to flow.

Freedom has appeared in the world at different times and under various forms; it has not been exclusively bound to any social condition, and it is not confined to democracies. Freedom cannot, therefore, form the distinguishing characteristic of democratic ages. The peculiar and preponderating fact which marks those ages as its own is the equality of conditions; the ruling passion of men in those periods is the love of this equality. Ask not what singular charm the men of democratic ages find in being equal, or what special reasons they may have for clinging so tenaciously to equality rather than to the other advantages which society holds out to them: equality is the distinguishing characteristic of the age they live in; that, of itself, is enough to explain that they prefer it to all the rest.

But independently of this reason there are several others, which will at all times habitually lead men to prefer equality to freedom.

If a people could ever succeed in destroying, or even in diminishing, the equality which prevails in its own body, this could only be accomplished by long and laborious efforts. Its social condition must be modified, its laws abolished, its opinions superseded, its habits changed, its manners corrupted. But political liberty is more easily lost; to neglect to hold it fast, is to allow it to escape.

Men therefore not only cling to equality because it is dear to them; they also adhere to it because they think it will last for ever.

That political freedom may compromise in its excesses the tranquillity, the property, the lives of individuals, is obvious to the narrowest and most unthinking minds. But, on the contrary, none but attentive and clear-sighted men perceive the perils with which equality threatens us, and they commonly avoid pointing them out. They know that the calamities they apprehend are remote, and flatter themselves that they will only fall upon future generations, for which the present generation takes but little thought. The evils which freedom sometimes brings with it are immediate; they are apparent to all, and all are more or less affected by them. The evils which extreme equality may produce are slowly disclosed; they creep gradually into the social frame; they are only seen at intervals, and at the moment at which they become most violent, habit already causes them to be no longer felt.

The advantages which freedom brings are only shown by length of time; and it is always easy to mistake the cause in which they originate. The advantages of equality are instantaneous, and they may constantly be traced from their source.

Political liberty bestows exalted pleasures, from time to time, upon a certain number of citizens. Equality every day confers a number of small enjoyments on every man. The charms of equality are every instant felt, and are within the reach of all: the noblest hearts are not insensible to them, and the most vulgar souls exult in them. The passion which equality engenders must therefore be at once strong and general. Men cannot enjoy political liberty unpurchased by some sacrifices, and they never obtain it without great exertions. But the pleasures of equality are self-proffered: each of the petty incidents of life seems to occasion them, and in order to taste them nothing is required but to live.

Democratic nations are at all times fond of equality, but there are certain epochs at which the passion they entertain for it swells to the height of fury. This occurs at the moment when the old social system, long menaced, completes its own destruction after a last intestine struggle, and when the barriers of rank are at length thrown down. At such times men pounce upon equality as their booty, and they cling to it as to some precious treasure which they fear to lose. The passion for equality penetrates on every side into men's hearts, expands there, and fills them entirely. Tell them not that by this blind surrender of themselves to an exclusive passion, they risk their dearest interests: they are deaf. Show them not freedom escaping from their grasp, while they are looking another way: they are blind—or rather, they can discern but one sole object to be desired in the universe.

What I have said is applicable to all democratic nations: what I am about to say concerns the French alone. Among most modern nations, and especially among all those of the continent of Europe, the taste and the idea of freedom only began to exist and to extend itself at the time when social conditions were tending to equality, and as a consequence of that very equality. Absolute kings were the most efficient levellers of ranks among their subjects. Among these nations equality preceded freedom: equality was therefore a fact of some standing, when freedom was still a novelty: the one had already created customs, opinions, and laws belonging to it, when the other, alone and for the first time, came into actual existence. Thus the latter was still only an affair of opinion and of taste, while the former had already crept into the habits of the people, possessed itself of their manners, and given a particular turn to the smallest actions in their lives. Can it be wondered that the men of our own time prefer the one to the other?

I think that democratic communities have a natural taste for freedom: left to themselves, they will seek it, cherish it, and view any privation of it with regret. But for equality, their passion is ardent, insatiable, incessant, invincible: they call for equality in freedom; if they cannot obtain that, they still call for equality in slavery. They will endure poverty, servitude, barbarism—but they will not endure aristocracy.

This is true at all times, and especially true in our own. All men and all powers seeking to cope with this irresistible passion, will be overthrown and destroyed by it. In our age, freedom cannot be established without it, and despotism itself cannot reign without its support. . . .

THAT THE AMERICANS COMBAT THE EFFECTS OF INDIVIDUALISM BY FREE INSTITUTIONS

. . . The Americans have combated by free institutions the tendency of equality to keep men asunder, and they have subdued it. The legislators of America did not suppose that a general representation of the whole nation would suffice to ward off a disorder at once so natural to the frame of democratic society, and so fatal: they also thought that it would be well to infuse political life into each portion of the territory, in order to multiply to an infinite extent opportunities of acting in concert, for all the members of the community, and to make them constantly feel their mutual dependance on each other. The plan was a wise one. The general affairs of a country only engage the attention of leading politicians, who assemble from time to time in the same places; and as they often lose sight of each other afterward, no lasting ties are established between them. But if the object be to have the local affairs of a district conducted by the men who reside there, the same persons are always in contact, and they are, in a manner, forced to be acquainted, and to adapt themselves to one another.

It is difficult to draw a man out of his own circle to interest him in the destiny of the state, because he does not clearly undestand what influence the destiny of the state can have upon his own lot. But if it be proposed to make a road cross the end of his estate, he will see at a glance that there is a connexion between this small public affair and his greatest private affairs; and he will discover, without its being

shown to him, the close tie which unites private to general interest. Thus, far more may be done by entrusting to the citizens the administration of minor affairs than by surrendering to them the control of important ones, toward interesting them in the public welfare, and convincing them that they constantly stand in need one of the other in order to provide for it. A brilliant achievement may win for you the favour of a people at one stroke; but to earn the love and respect of the population which surrounds you, a long succession of little services rendered and of obscure good deeds—a constant habit of kindness, and an established reputation for disinterestedness—will be required. Local freedom, then, which leads a great number of citizens to value the affection of their neighbours and of their kindred, perpetually brings men together, and forces them to help one another, in spite of the propensities which sever them.

In the United States the more opulent citizens take great care not to stand aloof from the people; on the contrary, they constantly keep on easy terms with the lower classes: they listen to them, they speak to them every day. They know that the rich in democracies always stand in need of the poor; and that in democratic ages you attach a poor man to you more by your manner than by benefits conferred. The magnitude of such benefits, which sets off the difference of conditions, causes a secret irritation to those who reap advantage from them; but the charm of simplicity of manners is almost irresistible: their affability carries men away, and even their want of polish is not always displeasing. This truth does not take root at once in the minds of the rich. They generally resist it as long as the democratic revolution lasts, and they do not acknowledge it immediately after that revolution is accomplished. They are very ready to do good to the people, but they still choose to keep them at arm's length; they think that is sufficient, but they are mistaken. They might spend fortunes thus without warming the hearts of the population around them;—that population does not ask them for the sacrifice of their money, but of their pride.

It would seem as if every imagination in the United States were upon the stretch to invent means of increasing the wealth and satisfying the wants of the public. The best informed inhabitants of each district constantly use their information to discover new truths which may augment the general prosperity; and, if they have made any such discoveries, they eagerly surrender them to the mass of the people.

When the vices and weaknesses, frequently exhibited by those who govern in America, are closely examined, the prosperity of the people occasions—but improperly occasions—surprise. Elected magistrates do not make the American democracy flourish; it flourishes because the magistrates are elective.

It would be unjust to suppose that the patriotism and the zeal which every American displays for the welfare of his fellow-citizens are wholly insincere. Although private interest directs the greater part of human actions in the United States, as well as elsewhere, it does not regulate them all. I must say that I have often seen Americans make great and real sacrifices to the public welfare; and I have remarked a hundred instances in which they hardly ever failed to lend faithful support to each other. The free institutions which the inhabitants of the United States possess, and the political rights of which they make so much use, remind every citizen, and in a thousand ways, that he lives in society. They every instant impress upon his mind the notion that it is the duty as well as the interest of men to make themselves useful to their fellow-creatures; and as he sees no particular ground of animosity to them, since he is never either their master or their slave, his heart readily leans to the side of kindness. Men attend to the interests of the public, first by necessity, afterward by choice: what was intentional becomes an instinct; and by dint of working for the good of one's fellow-citizens, the habit and the taste for serving them is at length acquired.

Many people in France consider equality of conditions as one evil, and political freedom as a second. When they are obliged to yield to the former, they strive at least to escape from the latter. But I contend, that in order to combat the evils which equality may produce, there is only one effectual remedy—namely, political freedom. . . .

THAT ARISTOCRACY MAY BE ENGENDERED BY MANUFACTURES

I have shown that democracy is favourable to the growth of manufactures, and that it increases without limit the numbers of the manufacturing classes: we shall now see by what side-road manufactures may possibly in their turn bring men back to aristocracy.

It is acknowledged, that when a workman is engaged every day upon the same detail, the whole commodity is produced with greater ease, promptitude, and economy. It is likewise acknowledged, that the cost of the production of manufactured goods is diminished by the extent of the establishment in which they are made, and by the amount of capital employed or of credit. These truths had long been imperfectly discerned, but in our time they have been demonstrated. They have been already applied to many very important kinds of manufactures, and the humblest will gradually be governed by them. I know of nothing in politics which deserves to fix the attention of the legislator more closely than these two new axioms of the science of manufactures.

When a workman is unceasingly and exclusively engaged in the fabrication of one thing, he ultimately does his work with singular dexterity; but at the same time he loses the general faculty of applying his mind to the direction of the work. He every day becomes more adroit and less industrious; so that it may be said of him, that in proportion as the workman improves the man is degraded. What can be expected of a man who has spent twenty years of his life in making heads for pins? and to what can that mighty human intelligence, which has so often stirred the world, be applied to him, except it be to investigate the best method of making pins' heads? When a workman has spent a considerable portion of his existence in this manner, his thoughts are for ever set upon the object of his daily toil: his body has contracted certain fixed habits, which it can never shake off: in a word, he no longer belongs to himself, but to the calling which he has chosen. It is in vain that laws and manners have been at the pains to level all barriers round such a man, and to open to him on every side a thousand different paths to fortune; a theory of manufactures more powerful than manners and laws binds him to a craft, and frequently to a spot, which he cannot leave: it assigns to him a certain place in society, beyond which he cannot go: in the midst of universal movement, it has rendered him stationary.

In proportion as the principle of the division of labour is more extensively applied, the workman becomes more weak, more narrow-minded and more dependant. The art advances, the artisan recedes. On the other hand, in proportion as it becomes more manifest that the productions of manufactures are by so much the cheaper and better as the manufacture is larger and the amount of capital employed more considerable, wealthy and educated men come forward to embark in manufactures which were heretofore abandoned to poor or ignorant handicraftsmen. The magnitude of the efforts required, and the importance of the results to be obtained, attract them. Thus, at the very time at which the science of manufactures lowers the class of workmen, it raises the class of masters.

Whereas the workman concentrates his faculties more and more upon the study of a single detail, the master surveys a more extensive whole, and the mind of the latter is enlarged in proportion as that of the former is narrowed. In a short time the one will require nothing but physical strength without intelligence; the other stands in need of science, and almost of genius, to ensure success. This man resembles more and more the administrator of a vast empire—that man, a brute.

The master and the workman have then here no similarity, and their differences increase every day. They are only connected as the two rings at the extremities of a long chain. Each of them fills the station which is made for him, and out of which he does not get: the one is continually, closely, and necessarily dependant upon the other, and seems as much born to obey as that other is to command. What is this but aristocracy?

As the conditions of men constituting the nation become more and more equal, the demand for manufactured commodities becomes more general and more extensive; and the cheapness which places these objects within the reach of slender fortunes becomes a great element of success. Hence there are every day more men of great opulence and education who devote their wealth and knowledge to manufactures; and who seek, by opening large establishments, and by a strict division of labour, to meet the fresh demands which are made on all sides. Thus, in proportion as the mass of the nation turns to democracy, that particular class which is engaged in manufactures becomes more aristocratic. Men grow more alike in the one—more different in the other; and inequality increases in the less numerous class, in the same ratio in which it decreases in the community.

Hence it would appear, on searching to the bottom, that aristocracy should naturally spring out of the bosom of democracy.

But this kind of aristocracy by no means resembles those kinds which preceded it. It will be observed at once, that, as it applies exclusively to manufactures and to some manufacturing callings, it is a monstrous exception in the general aspect of society. The small aristocratic societies which are formed by some manufacturers in the midst of the immense democracy of our age, contain, like the great aristocratic societies of former ages, some men who are very opulent, and a multitude who are wretchedly poor. The poor have few means of escaping from their condition and becoming rich; but the rich are constantly becoming poor, or they give up business when they have realized a fortune. Thus the elements of which the class of the poor is composed are fixed; but the elements of which the class of the rich is composed are not so. To say the truth, though there are rich men, the class of rich men does not exist; for these rich individuals have no feelings or purposes in common, no mutual traditions or mutual hopes: there are therefore members, but no body.

Not only are the rich not compactly united among themselves, but there is no real bond between them and the poor. Their relative position is not a permanent one; they are constantly drawn together or separated by their interests. The workman is generally dependant on the master, but not on any particular master; these two men meet in the factory, but know not each other elsewhere; and while they come into contact on one point, they stand very wide apart on all others. The manufacturer asks nothing of the workman but his labour; the workman expects nothing from him but his wages. The one contracts no obligation to protect, nor the other to defend; and they are not permanently connected either by habit or by duty.

The aristocracy created by business rarely settles in the midst of the manufacturing population which it directs: the object is not to govern that population, but to use it. An aristocracy thus constituted can have no great hold upon those whom it employs; and even if it succeed in retaining them at one moment, they escape the next: it knows not how to will, and it cannot act.

The territorial aristocracy of former ages was either bound by law, or thought itself bound by usage, to come to the relief of its serving-men, and to succour their distresses. But the manufacturing aristocracy of our age first impoverishes and debases the men who serve it, and then abandons them to be supported by the charity of the public. This is a natural consequence of what has been said before. Between the workman and the master there are frequent relations, but no real partnership.

I am of opinion, upon the whole, that the manufacturing aristocracy which is growing up under our eyes, is one of the harshest which ever existed in the world; but at the same time it is one of the most confined and least dangerous. Nevertheless the friends of democracy should keep their eyes anxiously fixed in this direction; for if ever a permanent inequality of conditions and aristocracy again penetrate into the world, it may be predicted that this is the channel by which they will enter. . . .

DESPOTISM IN A SOCIETY PRACTICING EQUALITY

I believe that it is easier to establish an absolute and despotic government among a people in which the conditions of society are equal, than among any other; and I think that if such a government were once established among

such a people, it would not only oppress men, but would eventually strip each of them of several of the highest qualities of humanity. Despotism therefore appears to me peculiarly to be dreaded in democratic ages. I should have loved freedom, I believe, at all times, but in the time in which we live I am ready to worship it.

On the other hand, I am persuaded that all who shall attempt, in the ages upon which we are entering, to base freedom upon aristocratic privilege, will fail;—that all who shall attempt to draw and to retain authority within a single class, will fail. At the present day no ruler is skilful or strong enough to found a despotism, by re-establishing permanent distinctions of rank among his subjects: no legislator is wise or powerful enough to preserve free institutions, if he does not take equality for his first principle and his watchword. All those of our contemporaries who would establish or secure the independence and the dignity of their fellowmen, must show themselves the friends of equality; and the only worthy means of showing themselves as such, is to be so: upon this depends the success of their holy enterprise. Thus the question is not how to reconstruct aristocratic society, but how to make liberty proceed out of that democratic state of society in which God has placed us.

These two truths appear to me simple, clear, and fertile in consequences; and they naturally lead me to consider what kind of free government can be established among a people in which social conditions are equal.

It results from the very constitution of democratic nations and from their necessities, that the power of government among them must be more uniform, more centralized, more extensive, more searching, and more efficient than in other countries. Society at large is naturally stronger and more active, individuals more subordinate and weak; the former does more, the latter less; and this is inevitably the case.

It is not therefore to be expected that the range of private independence will ever be as extensive in democratic as in aristocratic countries—nor is this to be desired; for, among aristocratic nations, the mass is often sacrificed to the individual, and the prosperity of the greater number to the greatness of the few. It is both necessary and desirable that the government of a democratic people should be active and powerful: and our object should not be to render it weak or indolent, but solely to prevent it from abusing its aptitude and its strength. . . .

I think that men living in aristocracies may, strictly speaking, do without the liberty of the press: but such is not the case with those who live in democratic countries. To protect their personal independence I trust not to great political assemblies, to parliamentary privilege, nor to the assertion of popular sovereignty. All these things may, to a certain extent, be reconciled with personal servitude—but that servitude cannot be complete if the press is free: the press is the chiefest democratic instrument of freedom.

Something analogous may be said of the judicial power. It is a part of the essence of judicial power to attend to private interests, and to fix itself with predilection on minute objects submitted to its observation: another essential quality of judicial power is never to volunteer its assistance to the oppressed, but always to be at the disposal of the humblest of those who solicit it; their complaint, however feeble they may themselves be, will force itself upon the ear of justice and claim redress, for this is inherent in the very constitution of the courts of justice.

A power of this kind is therefore peculiarly adapted to the wants of freedom, at a time when the eye and finger of the government are constantly intruding into the minutest details of human actions, and when private persons are at once too weak to protect themselves, and too much isolated for them to reckon upon the assistance of their fellows. The strength of the courts of law has ever been the greatest security which can be offered to personal independence; but this is more especially the case in democratic ages: private rights and interests are in constant danger, if the judicial power does not grow more extensive and more strong to keep pace with the growing equality of conditions. . . .

Another tendency, which is extremely natural to democratic nations and extremely dangerous, is that which leads them to despise and undervalue the rights of private persons. The attachment which men feel to a right, and the respect which they display for it, is generally proportioned to its importance, or to the length of time during which they have enjoyed it. The rights of private persons among democratic nations are commonly of small importance, of recent growth, and extremely precarious—the consequence is that they are often sacrificed without regret, and almost always violated without remorse.

But it happens that at the same period and among the same nations in which men conceive a natural contempt for the rights of private persons, the rights of society at large are naturally extended and consolidated: in other words, men become less attached to private rights at the very time at which it would be most necessary to retain and to defend what little remains of them. It is therefore most especially in the present democratic ages, that the true friends of the liberty and the greatness of man ought constantly to be on the alert to prevent the power of government from lightly sacrificing the private rights of individuals to the general execution of its designs. At such times no citizen is so obscure that it is not very dangerous to allow him to be oppressed—no private rights are so unimportant that they can be surrendered with impunity to the caprices of a government. The reason is plain:—if the private right of an individual is violated at a time when the human mind is fully impressed with the importance and the sanctity of such rights, the injury is confined to the individual whose right is infringed; but to violate such a right, at the present day, is deeply to corrupt the manners of the nation and to put the whole community in jeopardy, because the very notion of this kind of right constantly tends among us to be impaired and lost. . . .

I shall conclude by one general idea, which comprises not only all the particular ideas which have been expressed in the present chapter, but also most of those which it is the object of this book to treat of. In the ages of aristocracy which preceded our own, there were private persons of great power, and a social authority of extreme weakness. The outline of society itself was not easily discernible, and constantly confounded with the different powers by which the community was ruled. The principal efforts of the men of those times were required to strengthen, aggrandize, and secure the supreme power; and on the other hand, to circumscribe individual independence within narrower limits, and to subject private interests to the interests of the public. Other perils and other cares await the men of our age. Among the greater part of modern nations, the government, whatever may be its origin, its constitution, or its name, has become almost omnipotent, and private persons are falling, more and more, into the lowest stage of weakness and dependance.

In olden society everything was different: unity and uniformity were nowhere to be met with. In modern society everything threatens to become so much alike, that the peculiar characteristics of each individual will soon be entirely lost in the general aspect of the world. Our forefathers were ever prone to make an improper use of the notion that private rights ought to be respected; and we are naturally prone on the other hand to exaggerate the idea that the interest of a private individual ought always to bend to the interest of the many.

The political world is metamorphosed: new remedies must henceforth be sought for new disorders. To lay down extensive, but distinct and settled limits, to the action of the government; to confer certain rights on private persons, and to secure to them the undisputed enjoyment of those rights; to enable individual man to maintain whatever independence, strength, and original power he still possesses; to raise him by the side of society at large, and uphold him in that position—these appear to me the main objects of legislators in the ages upon which we are now entering.

It would seem as if the rulers of our time sought only to use men in order to make things great; I wish that they would try a little more to make great men; that they would set less value on the work, and more upon the workman; that they would never forget that a nation cannot long remain strong when every man belonging to it is individually weak, and that no form or combination of social polity has yet been devised, to make an energetic people out of a community of pusillanimous and enfeebled citizens.

I trace among our contemporaries two contrary notions which are equally injurious. One set of men can perceive nothing in the principle of equality but the anarchical tendencies which it engenders: they dread their own free agency —they fear themselves. Other thinkers, less numerous but more enlightened, take a different view: beside that track which starts from the principle of equality to terminate in anarchy, they have at last discovered the road which seems to lead men to inevitable servitude. They shape their souls beforehand to this necessary condition; and, despairing of remaining free, they already do obeisance in their hearts to the master who is soon to appear. The former abandon freedom, because they think it dangerous; the latter, because they hold it to be impossible.

If I had entertained the latter conviction, I should not have written this book, but I should have confined myself to deploring in secret the destiny of mankind. I have sought to point out the dangers to which the principle of equality exposes the independence of man, because I firmly believe that these dangers are the most formidable, as well as the least foreseen, of all those which futurity holds in store; but I do not think that they are insurmountable.

The men who live in the democratic ages upon which we are entering have naturally a taste for independence: they are naturally impatient of regulation, and they are wearied by the permanence even of the condition they themselves prefer. They are fond of power; but they are prone to despise and hate those who wield it, and they easily elude its grasp by their own mobility and insignificance.

These propensities will always manifest themselves, because they originate in the groundwork of society, which will undergo no change: for a long time they will prevent the establishment of any despotism, and they will furnish fresh weapons to each succeeding generation which shall struggle in favour of the liberty of mankind. Let us then look forward to the future with that salutary fear which makes men keep watch and ward for freedom, not with that faint and idle terror which depresses and enervates the heart.

Frederick Jackson Turner

Frederick Jackson Turner (1861–1932), born at Portage, on the northern fringe of agricultural Wisconsin, revolutionized historical thinking in the United States by calling attention to the significance of the frontier in the development of American life. In this historical essay, which he read at a meeting held at the Chicago World's Fair in 1893, Turner emphasized the role of the American West in the emergence of democracy in the United States and Europe. Since that day Turner's paper has become a classic and his interpretation of American history affected an entire generation of teachers and scholars. Turner and his disciples argued that the presence of free land in large quantities in North America shaped democracy not only in America but in Europe by making it possible for men and women to achieve economic independence which they saw as a prelude to political independence and popular participation in government. The impact of this American West upon the older regions of the United States and of Europe served to liberalize political and social as well as economic relationships. In reading the essay, note (1) the author's basic thesis, (2) his environmentalism, (3) the stages of frontier advance, (4) the types of frontiersmen, (5) the nationalizing force of the frontier, (6) the impact of the frontier on the nation's economy and on legislation, (7) differing attitudes toward land, (8) the influences of the frontier on democracy, (9) efforts to regulate the frontier, and (10) traits associated with the frontier.

From: THE SIGNIFICANCE OF THE FRONTIER IN AMERICAN HISTORY

In a recent bulletin of the Superintendent of the Census for 1890 appear these significant words: "Up to and including 1880 the country had a frontier of settlement, but at present the unsettled area has been so broken into by isolated bodies of settlement that there can hardly be said to be a frontier line. In the discussion of its extent, its westward movement, etc., it can not, therefore, any longer have a place in the census reports." This brief official statement marks the closing of a great historic movement. Up to our own day American history has been in a large degree the history of the colonization of the Great West. The existence of an area of free land, its continuous recession, and the advance of American settlement westward, explain American development.

Behind institutions, behind constitutional forms and modifications, lie the vital forces that call these organs into life and shape them to meet changing conditions. The peculiarity of American institutions is, the fact that they have been compelled to adapt themselves to the changes of an expanding people—to the changes involved in crossing a continent, in winning a wilderness, and in developing at each area of this progress out of the primitive economic and political conditions of the frontier

Frederick J. Turner, "The Significance of the Frontier in American History," American Historical Association, *Annual Report*, 1893, 199–227.

into the complexity of city life. Said Calhoun in 1817, "We are great, and rapidly—I was about to say fearfully—growing!" So saying, he touched the distinguishing feature of American life. All peoples show development; the germ theory of politics has been sufficiently emphasized. In the case of most nations, however, the development has occurred in a limited area; and if the nation has expanded, it has met other growing peoples whom it has conquered. But in the case of the United States we have a different phenomenon. Limiting our attention to the Atlantic coast, we have the familiar phenomenon of the evolution of institutions in a limited area, such as the rise of representative government; the differentiation of simple colonial governments into complex organs; the progress from primitive industrial society, without division of labor, up to manufacturing civilization. But we have in addition to this a recurrence of the process of evolution in each western area reached in the process of expansion. Thus American development has exhibited not merely advance along a single line, but a return to primitive conditions on a continually advancing frontier line, and a new development for that area. American social development has been continually beginning over again on the frontier. This perennial rebirth, this fluidity of American life, this expansion westward with its new opportunities, its continuous touch with the simplicity of primitive society, furnish the forces dominating American character. The true point of view in the history of this nation is not the Atlantic coast, it is the Great West. Even the slavery struggle, which is made so exclusive an object of attention by writers like Professor von Holst, occupies its important place in American history because of its relation to westward expansion.

In this advance, the frontier is the outer edge of the wave—the meeting point between savagery and civilization. Much has been written about the frontier from the point of view of border warfare and the chase, but as a field for the serious study of the economist and the historian it has been neglected.

The American frontier is sharply distinguished from the European frontier—a fortified boundary line running through dense populations. The most significant thing about the American frontier is, that it lies at the hither edge of free land. In the census reports it is treated as the margin of that settlement which has a density of two or more to the square mile. The term is an elastic one, and for our purposes does not need sharp definition. We shall consider the whole frontier belt, including the Indian country and the outer margin of the "settled area" of the census reports. This paper will make no attempt to treat the subject exhaustively; its aim is simply to call attention to the frontier as a fertile field for investigation, and to suggest some of the problems which arise in connection with it.

In the settlement of America we have to observe how European life entered the continent, and how America modified and developed that life and reacted on Europe. Our early history is the study of European germs developing in an American environment. Too exclusive attention has been paid by institutional students to the Germanic origins, too little to the American factors. The frontier is the line of most rapid and effective Americanization. The wilderness masters the colonist. It finds him a European in dress, industries, tools, modes of travel, and thought. It takes him from the railroad car and puts him in the birch canoe. It strips off the garments of civilization and arrays him in the hunting shirt and the moccasin. It puts him in the log cabin of the Cherokee and Iroquois and runs an Indian palisade around him. Before long he has gone to planting Indian corn and plowing with a sharp stick; he shouts the war cry and takes the scalp in orthodox Indian fashion. In short, at the frontier the environment is at first too strong for the man. He must accept the conditions which it furnishes, or perish, and so he fits himself into the Indian clearings and follows the Indian trails. Little by little he transforms the wilderness, but the outcome is not the old Europe, not simply the development of Germanic germs, any more than the first phenomenon was a case of reversion to the Germanic mark. The fact is, that here is a new product that is American. At first, the frontier was the Atlantic coast. It was the frontier of Europe in a very real sense. Moving westward, the frontier became more and more American. As successive terminal moraines result from successive glaciations, so each frontier leaves its traces behind it, and when it becomes a settled area the region still partakes of the frontier characteristics. Thus the advance of the frontier has meant a steady movement away from the influence of Europe, a steady growth of independence on American lines. And to study this advance, the men who grew up under these conditions, and the political, economic, and social results of it, is to study the really American part of our history.

In the course of the seventeenth century the frontier was advanced up the Atlantic river courses, just beyond the "fall line," and the tidewater region became the settled area. In the first half of the eighteenth century another advance occurred. Traders followed the Delaware and Shawnese Indians to the Ohio as early as the end of the first quarter of the century. Gov. Spotswood, of Virginia, made an expedition in 1714 across the Blue Ridge. The end of the first quarter of the century saw the advance of the Scotch-Irish and the Palatine Germans up the Shenandoah Valley into the western part of Virginia, and along the Piedmont region of the Carolinas. The Germans in New York pushed the frontier of settlement up the Mohawk to German Flats. In Pennsylvania the town of Bedford indicates the line of settlement. Settlements had begun on New River, a branch of the Kanawha, and on the sources of the Yadkin and French Broad. The King attempted to arrest the advance by his proclamation of 1763, forbidding settlements beyond the sources of the rivers flowing into the Atlantic; but in vain. In the period of the Revolution the frontier crossed the Alleghanies into Kentucky and Tennessee, and the upper waters of the Ohio were settled. When the first census was taken in 1790, the continuous settled area was bounded by a line which ran near the coast of Maine, and included New England except a portion of Vermont and New Hampshire, New York along the Hudson and up the Mohawk about Schenectady, eastern and southern Pennsylvania, Virginia well across the Shenandoah Valley, and the Carolinas and eastern Georgia. Beyond this region of continuous settlement were the small settled areas of Kentucky and Tennessee, and the Ohio, with the mountains intervening between them and the Atlantic area, thus giving a new and important character to the frontier. The isolation of the region increased its peculiarly American tendencies, and the need of transportation facilities to connect it with the East called out important schemes of internal improvement, which will be noted farther on. The "West," as a self-conscious section, began to evolve.

From decade to decade distinct advances of the frontier occurred. By the census of 1820 the settled area included Ohio, southern Indiana and Illinois, southeastern Missouri, and about one-half of Louisiana. This settled area had surrounded Indian areas, and the management of these tribes became an object of political concern. The frontier region of the time lay along the Great Lakes, where Astor's American Fur Company operated in the Indian trade, and beyond the Mississippi, where Indian traders extended their activity even to the Rocky Mountains; Florida also furnished frontier conditions. The Mississippi River region was the scene of typical frontier settlements.

The rising steam navigation on western waters, the opening of the Erie Canal, and the westward extension of cotton culture added five frontier states to the Union in this period. Grund, writing in 1836, declares: "It appears then that the universal disposition of Americans to emigrate to the western wilderness, in order to enlarge their dominion over inanimate nature, is the actual result of an expansive power which is inherent in them, and which by continually agitating all classes of society is constantly throwing a large portion of the whole population on the extreme confines of the State, in order to gain space for its development. Hardly is a new State or Territory formed before the same principle manifests itself again and gives rise to a further emigration; and so is it destined to go on until a physical barrier must finally obstruct its progress."

In the middle of this century the line indicated by the present eastern boundary of Indian Territory, Nebraska, and Kansas marked the frontier of the Indian country. Minnesota and Wisconsin still exhibited frontier conditions, but the distinctive frontier of the period is found in California, where the gold discoveries had sent a sudden tide of adventurous miners, and in Oregon, and the settlements in Utah. As the frontier had leaped over the Alleghanies, so now it skipped the Great Plains and the Rocky Mountains; and in the same way that the advance of the frontiersmen beyond the Alleghanies had caused the rise of important questions of transportation and internal improvement, so now the settlers beyond the Rocky Mountains needed means of communication with the East, and in the furnishing of these arose the settlement of the Great Plains and the development of still another kind of frontier life. Railroads, fostered by land grants, sent an increasing tide of immigrants into the Far West. The United States Army fought a series of Indian wars in Minnesota, Dakota, and the Indian Territory.

By 1880 the settled area had been pushed into northern Michigan, Wisconsin, and Minnesota, along Dakota rivers, and in the Black Hills region, and was ascending the rivers of Kansas and Nebraska. The development of mines in Colorado had drawn isolated frontier settlements into that region, and Montana and Idaho were receiving settlers. The frontier was found in these mining camps and the ranches of the Great Plains. The superintendent of the census for 1890 reports, as previously stated, that the settlements of the West lie so scattered over the region that there can no longer be said to be a frontier line.

In these successive frontiers we find natural boundary lines which have served to mark and to affect the characteristics of the frontiers, namely: the "fall line;" the Alleghany Mountains; the Mississippi; the Missouri where its direction approximates north and south; the line of the arid lands, approximately the ninety-ninth meridian; and the Rocky Mountains. The fall line marked the frontier of the seventeenth century; the Alleghanies that of the eighteenth; the Mississippi that of the first quarter of the nineteenth; the Missouri that of the middle of this century (omitting the California movement); and the belt of the Rocky Mountains and the arid tract, the present frontier. Each was won by a series of Indian wars.

At the Atlantic frontier one can study the germs of processes repeated at each successive frontier. We have the complex European life sharply precipitated by the wilderness into the simplicity of primitive conditions. The first frontier had to meet its Indian question, its question of the disposition of the public domain, of the means of intercourse with older settlements, of the extension of political organization, of religious and educational activity. And the settlement of these and similar questions for one frontier served as a guide for the next. The American student needs not to go to the "prim little townships of Sleswick" for illustrations of the law of continuity and development. For example, he may study the origin of our land policies in the colonial land policy; he may see how the system grew by adapting the statutes to the customs of the successive frontiers. He may see how the mining experience in the lead regions of Wisconsin, Illinois, and Iowa was applied to the mining laws of the Sierras, and how our Indian policy has been a series of experimentations on successive frontiers. Each tier of new States has found in the older ones material for its constitutions. Each frontier has made similar contributions to American character, as will be discussed farther on.

But with all these similarities there are essential differences, due to the place element and the time element. It is evident that the farming frontier of the Mississippi Valley presents different conditions from the mining frontier of the Rocky Mountains. The frontier reached by the Pacific Railroad, surveyed into rectangles, guarded by the United States Army, and recruited by the daily immigrant ship, moves forward at a swifter pace and in a different way than the frontier reached by the birch canoe or the pack horse. The geologist traces patiently the shores of ancient seas, maps their areas, and compares the older and the newer. It would be a work worth the historian's labors to mark these various frontiers and in detail compare one with another. Not only would there result a more adequate conception of American development and characteristics, but invaluable additions would be made to the history of society.

Loria, the Italian economist, has urged the study of colonial life as an aid in understanding the stages of European development, affirming that colonial settlement is for economic science what the mountain is for geology, bringing to light primitive stratifications. "America," he says, "has the key to the historical enigma which Europe has sought for centuries in vain, and the land which has no history reveals luminously the course of universal history." There is much truth in this. The United States lies like a huge page in the history of society. Line by line as we read this continental page from West to East we find the record of social evolution. It begins with the Indian and the hunter; it goes on to tell of the disintegration of savagery by the entrance of the trader, the pathfinder of civilization; we read the annals of the pastoral stage in ranch life; the exploitation of the soil by the raising of unrotated crops of corn and wheat in sparsely settled farming communities; the intensive culture of the denser farm settlement; and finally the manufacturing organization with city and factory system. This page is familiar to the student of census statistics, but how little of it has been used by our historians. Particularly in eastern States this page is a palimpsest. What is now a manufacturing State was in an earlier decade an area of intensive farming. Earlier yet it had been a wheat area, and still earlier the "range" had attracted the cattleherder. Thus Wisconsin, now developing manufacture, is a State with varied agricultural interests. But earlier it was given over to almost exclusive grain-raising, like North Dakota at the present time.

Each of these areas has had an influence in our economic and political history; the evolution of each into a higher stage has worked political transformations. But what constitutional historian has made any adequate attempt to interpret political facts by the light of these social areas and changes?

The Atlantic frontier was compounded of fisherman, fur-trader, miner, cattle-raiser, and farmer. Excepting the fisherman, each type of industry was on the march toward the West, impelled by an irresistible attraction. Each passed in successive waves across the continent. Stand at Cumberland Gap and watch the procession of civilization, marching single file— the buffalo following the trail to the salt springs, the Indian, the fur-trader and hunter, the cattle-raiser, the pioneer farmer—and the frontier has passed by. Stand at South Pass in the Rockies a century later and see the same procession with wider intervals between. The unequal rate of advance compels us to distinguish the frontier into the trader's frontier, the ranch-er's frontier, or the miner's frontier, and the farmer's frontier. When the mines and the cow pens were still near the fall line the traders' pack trains were tinkling across the Alleghanies, and the French on the Great Lakes were fortifying their posts, alarmed by the British trad-er's birch canoe. When the trappers scaled the Rockies, the farmer was still near the mouth of the Missouri.

Why was it that the Indian trader passed so rapidly across the continent? What effects followed from the trader's frontier? The trade was coeval with American discovery. . . . The explanation of the rapidity of this advance is connected with the effects of the trader on the Indian. The trading post left the unarmed tribes at the mercy of those that had purchased firearms—a truth which the Iroquois Indians wrote in blood, and so the remote and un-visited tribes gave eager welcome to the trader. "The savages," wrote La Salle, "take better care of us French than of their own children; from us only can they get guns and goods." This accounts for the trader's power and the rapidity of his advance. Thus the disintegrating forces of civilization entered the wilderness. Every river valley and Indian trail became a fissure in Indian society, and so that society became honey combed. Long before the pioneer farmer appeared on the scene, primitive Indian life had passed away. The farmers met Indians armed with guns. The trading frontier, while steadily undermining Indian power by making the tribes ultimately dependent on the whites, yet, through its sale of guns, gave to the Indian increased power of resistance to the farming frontier. French colonization was dominated by its trading frontier; English colonization by its farming frontier. There was an antagonism between the two frontiers as between the two nations.

And yet, in spite of this opposition of the interests of the trader and the farmer, the Indian trade pioneered the way for civilization. The buffalo trail became the Indian trail, and this became the trader's "trace;" the trails widened into roads, and the roads into turnpikes, and these in turn were transformed into railroads. The same origin can be shown for the railroads of the South, the Far West, and the Dominion of Canada. The trading posts reached by these trails were on the sites of Indian villages which had been placed in positions suggested by nature; and these trading posts, situated so as to command the water systems of the country, have grown into such cities as Albany, Pittsburgh, Detroit, Chicago, St. Louis, Council Bluffs, and Kansas City. Thus civilization in America has followed the arteries made by geology, pouring an ever richer tide through them, until at last the slender paths of aboriginal intercourse have been broadened and interwoven into the complex mazes of modern commercial lines; the wilderness has been interpenetrated by lines of civilization growing ever more numerous. It is like the steady growth of a complex nervous system for the originally simple, inert continent. If one would understand why we are to-day one nation, rather than a collection of isolated states, he must study this economic and social consolidation of the country. In this progress from savage conditions lie topics for the evolutionist.

The effect of the Indian frontier as a consolidating agent in our history is important. From the close of the seventeenth century various intercolonial congresses have been called to treat with Indians and establish common measures of defense. Particularism was strongest in colonies with no Indian frontier. This frontier stretched along the western border like a cord of union. The Indian was a common danger, demanding united action. . . .

The exploitation of the beasts took hunter and trader to the west, the exploitation of the grasses took the rancher west, and the exploitation of the virgin soil of the river valleys and prairies attracted the farmer. Good soils have been the most continuous attraction to the farmer's frontier. The land hunger of the Virginians drew them down the rivers into Carolina, in early colonial days; the search for soils took the Massachusetts men to Pennsylvania and to New York. As the eastern lands were taken up migration flowed across them to the west. Daniel Boone, the great backwoodsman, who combined the occupations of hunter, trader, cattle-raiser, farmer, and surveyor— learning, probably from the traders, of the fertility of the lands of the upper Yadkin, where the traders were wont to rest as they took their way to the Indians, left his Pennsylvania home with his father, and passed down the Great

Valley road to that stream. Learning from a trader whose posts were on the Red River in Kentucky of its game and rich pastures, he pioneered the way for the farmers to that region. Thence he passed to the frontier of Missouri, where his settlement was long a landmark on the frontier. Here again he helped to open the way for civilization, finding salt licks, and trails, and land. His son was among the earliest trappers in the passes of the Rocky Mountains, and his party are said to have been the first to camp on the present site of Denver. His grandson, Col. A. J. Boone, of Colorado, was a power among the Indians of the Rocky Mountains, and was appointed an agent by the government. Kit Carson's mother was a Boone. Thus this family epitomizes the backwoodsman's advance across the continent. . . .

Omitting those of the pioneer farmers who move from the love of adventure, the advance of the more steady farmer is easy to understand. Obviously the immigrant was attracted by the cheap lands of the frontier, and even the native farmer felt their influence strongly. Year by year the farmers who lived on soil whose returns were diminished by unrotated crops were offered the virgin soil of the frontier at nominal prices. Their growing families demanded more lands, and these were dear. The competition of the unexhausted, cheap, and easily tilled prairie lands compelled the farmer either to go west and continue the exhaustion of the soil on a new frontier, or to adopt intensive culture. Thus the census of 1890 shows, in the Northwest, many counties in which there is an absolute or a relative decrease of population. These States have been sending farmers to advance the frontier on the plains, and have themselves begun to turn to intensive farming and to manufacture. A decade before this, Ohio had shown the same transition stage. Thus the demand for land and the love of wilderness freedom drew the frontier ever onward.

Having now roughly outlined the various kinds of frontiers, and their modes of advance, chiefly from the point of view of the frontier itself, we may next inquire what were the influences on the East and on the Old World. A rapid enumeration of some of the more noteworthy effects is all that I have time for.

First, we note that the frontier promoted the formation of a composite nationality for the

American people. The coast was preponderantly English, but the later tides of continental immigration flowed across to the free lands. This was the case from the early colonial days. The Scotch-Irish and the Palatine Germans, or "Pennsylvania Dutch," furnished the dominant element in the stock of the colonial frontier. With these peoples were also the freed indented servants, or redemptioners, who at the expiration of their time of service passed to the frontier. Governor Spotswood of Virginia writes in 1717, "The inhabitants of our frontiers are composed generally of such as have been transported hither as servants, and, being out of their time, settle themselves where land is to be taken up and that will produce the necessarys of life with little labour." Very generally these redemptioners were of non-English stock. In the crucible of the frontier the immigrants were Americanized, liberated, and fused into a mixed race, English in neither nationality nor characteristics. The process has gone on from the early days to our own. Burke and other writers in the middle of the eighteenth century believed that Pennsylvania was "threatened with the danger of being wholly foreign in language, manners, and perhaps even inclinations." The German and Scotch-Irish elements in the frontier of the South were only less great. In the middle of the present century the German element in Wisconsin was already so considerable that leading publicists looked to the creation of a German state out of the commonwealth by concentrating their colonization. Such examples teach us to beware of misinterpreting the fact that there is a common English speech in America into a belief that the stock is also English.

In another way the advance of the frontier decreased our dependence on England. The coast, particularly of the South, lacked diversified industries, and was dependent on England for the bulk of its supplies. In the South there was even a dependence on the Northern colonies for articles of food. Governor Glenn, of South Carolina, writes in the middle of the eighteenth century: "Our trade with New York and Philadelphia was of this sort, draining us of all the little money and bills we could gather from other places for their bread, flour, beer, hams, bacon, and other things of their produce, all which, except beer, our new townships begin to supply us with, which are settled with very industrious and thriving Germans. This no doubt diminishes the number of shipping and the appearance of our trade, but it is far from being a detriment to us." Before long the frontier created a demand for merchants. As it retreated from the coast it became less and less possible for England to bring her supplies directly to the consumer's wharfs, and carry away staple crops, and staple crops began to give way to diversified agriculture for a time. The effect of this phase of the frontier action upon the northern section is perceived when we realize how the advance of the frontier aroused seaboard cities like Boston, New York, and Baltimore, to engage in rivalry for what Washington called "the extensive and valuable trade of a rising empire."

The legislation which most developed the powers of the national government, and played the largest part in its activity, was conditioned on the frontier. Writers have discussed the subjects of tariff, land, and internal improvement, as subsidiary to the slavery question. But when American history comes to be rightly viewed it will be seen that the slavery question is an incident. In the period from the end of the first half of the present century to the close of the Civil War slavery rose to primary, but far from exclusive, importance. But this does not justify Dr. von Holst (to take an example) in treating our constitutional history in its formative period down to 1828 in a single volume, giving six volumes chiefly to the history of slavery from 1828 to 1861, under the title "Constitutional History of the United States." The growth of nationalism and the evolution of American political institutions were dependent on the advance of the frontier. Even so recent a writer as Rhodes, in his *History of the United States since the Compromise of 1850*, has treated the legislation called out by the western advance as incidental to the slavery struggle.

This is a wrong perspective. The pioneer needed the goods of the coast, and so the grand series of internal improvement and railroad legislation began, with potent nationalizing effects. Over internal improvements occurred great debates, in which grave constitutional questions were discussed. Sectional groupings appear in the votes, profoundly significant for the historian. Loose construction increased as the nation marched westward. But the West was not content with bringing the farm to the factory. Under the lead of Clay—"Harry of the West"—protective tariffs were passed, with the cry of bringing the factory to the farm. The disposition of the public lands was a third important subject of national legislation influenced by the frontier.

The public domain has been a force of profound importance in the nationalization and development of the Government. The effects of the struggle of the landed and the landless States, and of the Ordinance of 1787, need no discussion. Administratively the frontier called out some of the highest and most vitalizing activities of the general government. The purchase of Louisiana was perhaps the constitutional turning point in the history of the Republic, inasmuch as it afforded both a new area for national legislation and the occasion of the downfall of the policy of strict construction. But the purchase of Louisiana was called out by frontier needs and demands. As frontier States accrued to the Union the national power grew. In a speech on the dedication of the Calhoun monument Mr. Lamar explained: "In 1789 the States were the creators of the Federal Government; in 1861 the Federal Government was the creator of a large majority of the States."

When we consider the public domain from the point of view of the sale and disposal of the public lands we are again brought face to face with the frontier. The policy of the United States in dealing with its lands is in sharp contrast with the European system of scientific administration. Efforts to make this domain a source of revenue, and to withhold it from emigrants in order that settlement might be compact, were in vain. The jealousy and the fears of the East were powerless in the face of the demands of the frontiersmen. John Quincy Adams was obliged to confess: "My own system of administration, which was to make the national domain the inexhaustible fund for progressive and unceasing internal improvement, has failed." The reason is obvious; a system of administration was not what the West demanded; it wanted land. Adams states the situation as follows: "The slaveholders of the South have bought the cooperation of the western country by the bribe of the western lands,

abandoning to the new Western States their own proportion of the public property and aiding them in the design of grasping all the lands into their own hands. Thomas H. Benton was the author of this system, which he brought forward as a substitute for the American system of Mr. Clay, and to supplant him as the leading statesman of the West. Mr. Clay, by his tariff compromise with Mr. Calhoun, abandoned his own American system. At the same time he brought forward a plan for distributing among all the States of the Union the proceeds of the sales of the public lands. His bill for that purpose passed both Houses of Congress, but was vetoed by President Jackson, who, in his annual message of December, 1832, formally recommended that all public lands should be gratuitously given away to individual adventurers and to the States in which the lands are situated."

"No subject," said Henry Clay, "which has presented itself to the present, or perhaps any preceding, Congress, is of greater magnitude than that of the public lands." When we consider the far-reaching effects of the government's land policy upon political, economic, and social aspects of American life, we are disposed to agree with him. But this legislation was framed under frontier influences, and under the lead of Western statesmen like Benton and Jackson. Said Senator Scott of Indiana in 1841: "I consider the pre-emption law merely declaratory of the custom or common law of the settlers."

It is safe to say that the legislation with regard to land, tariff, and internal improvements—the American system of the nationalizing Whig party—was conditioned on frontier ideas and needs. But it was not merely in legislative action that the frontier worked against the sectionalism of the coast. The economic and social characteristics of the frontier worked against sectionalism. The men of the frontier had closer resemblances to the Middle region than to either of the other sections. Pennsylvania had been the seed-plot of frontier emigration, and, although she passed on her settlers along the Great Valley into the west of Virginia and the Carolinas, yet the industrial society of these Southern frontiersmen was always more like that of the Middle region than like that of the tide-water portion of the South, which later came to spread its industrial type throughout the South.

The middle region, entered by New York harbor, was an open door to all Europe. The tide-water part of the South represented typical Englishmen, modified by a warm climate and servile labor, and living in baronial fashion on great plantations; New England stood for a special English movement—Puritanism. The Middle region was less English than the other sections. It had a wide mixture of nationalities, a varied society, the mixed town and county system of local government, a varied economic life, many religious sects. In short, it was a region mediating between New England and the South, and the East and the West. It represented that composite nationality which the contemporary United States exhibits, that juxtaposition of non-English groups, occupying a valley or a little settlement, and presenting reflections of the map of Europe in their variety. It was democratic and nonsectional, if not national; "easy, tolerant, and contented;" rooted strongly in material prosperity. It was typical of the modern United States. It was least sectional, not only because it lay between North and South, but also because with no barriers to shut out its frontiers from its settled region, and with a system of connecting waterways, the Middle region mediated between East and West as well as between North and South. Thus it became the typically American region. Even the New Englander, who was shut out from the frontier by the Middle region, tarrying in New York or Pennsylvania on his Westward march, lost the acuteness of his sectionalism on the way.

The spread of cotton culture into the interior of the South finally broke down the contrast between the "tide-water" region and the rest of the State, and based Southern interests on slavery. Before this process revealed its results the western portion of the South, which was akin to Pennsylvania in stock, society, and industry, showed tendencies to fall away from the faith of the fathers into internal improvement legislation and nationalism. In the Virginia convention of 1829–30, called to revise the constitution, Mr. Leigh, of Chesterfield, one of the tide-water counties, declared:

One of the main causes of discontent which led to this convention, that which had the strongest influence in overcoming our veneration for the work of our fathers, which taught us to contemn the sentiments of Henry and Mason and Pendleton, which weaned us from our reverence for the constituted authorities of the State, was an overweening passion for internal improvement. I say this with perfect knowledge, for it has been avowed to me by gentlemen from the West over and over again. And let me tell the gentleman from Albemarle (Mr. Gordon) that it has been another principal object of those who set this ball of revolution in motion, to overturn the doctrine of State rights, of which Virginia has been the very pillar, and to remove the barrier she has interposed to the interference of the Federal Government in that same work of internal improvement, by so reorganizing the legislature that Virginia, too, may be hitched to the Federal car.

It was this nationalizing tendency of the West that transformed the democracy of Jefferson into the national republicanism of Monroe and the democracy of Andrew Jackson. The West of the war of 1812, the West of Clay, and Benton and Harrison, and Andrew Jackson, shut off by the Middle States and the mountains from the coast sections, had a solidarity of its own with national tendencies. On the tide of the Father of Waters, North and South met and mingled into a nation. Interstate migration went steadily on—a process of cross-fertilization of ideas and institutions. The fierce struggle of the sections over slavery on the western frontier does not diminish the truth of this statement; it proves the truth of it. Slavery was a sectional trait that would not down, but in the West it could not remain sectional. It was the greatest of frontiersmen who declared: "I believe this Government can not endure permanently half slave and half free. It will become all of one thing or all of the other." Nothing works for nationalism like intercourse within the nation. Mobility of population is death to localism, and the western frontier worked irresistibly in unsettling population. The effects reached back from the frontier and affected profoundly the Atlantic coast and even the Old World.

But the most important effect of the frontier has been in the promotion of democracy here and in Europe. As has been indicated, the frontier is productive of individualism. Complex society is precipitated by the wilderness into a kind of primitive organization based on the family. The tendency is anti-social. It produces antipathy to control, and particularly to any direct control. The tax-gatherer is viewed as a representative of oppression. Prof. Osgood, in an able article, has pointed out that the frontier conditions prevalent in the colonies are important factors in the explanation of the American Revolution, where individual liberty was sometimes confused with absence of all effective government. The same conditions aid in explaining the difficulty of instituting a strong government in the period of the confederacy. The frontier individualism has from the beginning promoted democracy.

The frontier States that came into the Union in the first quarter of a century of its existence came in with democratic suffrage provisions, and had reactive effects of the highest importance upon the older States whose peoples were being attracted there. An extension of the franchise became essential. It was *western* New York that forced an extension of suffrage in the constitutional convention of that State in 1821; and it was *western* Virginia that compelled the tide-water region to put a more liberal suffrage provision in the constitution framed in 1830, and to give to the frontier region a more nearly proportionate representation with the tide-water aristocracy. The rise of democracy as an effective force in the nation came in with western preponderance under Jackson and William Henry Harrison, and it meant the triumph of the frontier—with all of its good and with all of its evil elements. An interesting illustration of the tone of frontier democracy in 1830 comes from the same debates in the Virginia convention already referred to. A representative from Western Virginia declared:

But, sir, it is not the increase of population in the West which this gentleman ought to fear. It is the energy which the mountain breeze and western habits impart to those emigrants. They are regenerated, politically I mean, sir. They soon become *working politicians;* and the difference, sir, between a *talking* and a *working* politician is immense. The Old Dominion has long been celebrated for producing great orators; the ablest metaphysicians in policy; men that can split hairs in all abstruse questions of political economy. But at home, or when they return from Congress, they have negroes to fan them asleep. But a Pennsylvania, a New York, an Ohio, or a western Virginia statesman, though far inferior in logic, metaphysics, and rhetoric to an old Virginia statesman, has this advantage, that when he returns home he takes off his coat and takes hold of the plow. This gives him bone and muscle, sir, and preserves his republican principles pure and uncontaminated.

So long as free land exists, the opportunity for a competency exists, and economic power secures political power. But the democracy born of free land, strong in selfishness and individualism, intolerant of administrative experience and education, and pressing individual liberty beyond its proper bounds, has its dangers as well as its benefits. Individualism in America has allowed a laxity in regard to governmental affairs which has rendered possible the spoils system and all the manifest evils that follow from the lack of a highly developed civic spirit. In this connection may be noted also the influence of frontier conditions in permitting lax business honor, inflated paper currency, and wild-cat banking. The colonial and revolutionary frontier was the region whence emanated many of the worst forms of an evil currency. The West in the War of 1812 repeated the phenomenon on the frontier of that day, while the speculation and wild-cat banking of the period of the crisis of 1837 occurred on the new frontier belt of the next tier of States. Thus each one of the periods of lax financial integrity coincides with periods when a new set of frontier communities had arisen, and coincides in area with these successive frontiers, for the most part. The recent Populist agitation is a case in point. Many a State that now declines any connection with the tenets of the Populists, itself adhered to such ideas in an earlier stage of the development of the State. A primitive society can hardly be expected to show the intelligent appreciation of the complexity of business interests in a developed society. The continual recurrence of these areas of paper-money agitation is another evidence that the frontier can be isolated and studied as a factor in American history of the highest importance.

The East has always feared the result of an unregulated advance of the frontier, and has tried to check and guide it. The English authorities would have checked settlement at the headwaters of the Atlantic tributaries and allowed the "savages to enjoy their deserts in quiet lest the peltry trade should decrease." This called out Burke's splendid protest:

If you stopped your grants, what would be the consequence? The people would occupy without grants. They have already so occupied in many places. You can not station garrisons in every part of these deserts. If you drive the people from one place, they will carry on their annual tillage and remove with their flocks and herds to another. Many of the people in the back settlements are already little attached to particular situations. Already they have topped the Appalachian Mountains. From whence they behold before them an immense plain, one vast, rich, level meadow; a square of five hundred miles. Over this they would wander without a possibility of restraint; they would change their manners with their habits of life; would soon forget a government by which they were disowned; would become hordes of English Tartars; and, pouring down upon your unfortified frontiers a fierce and irresistible cavalry, become masters of your governors and your counselers, your collectors and comptrollers, and of all the slaves that adhered to them. Such would, and in no long time must, be the effect of attempting to forbid as a crime and to suppress as an evil the command and blessing of Providence, "Increase and multiply." Such would be the happy result of an endeavor to keep as a lair of wild beasts that earth which God, by an express charter, has given to the children of men.

But the English Government was not alone in its desire to limit the advance of the frontier and guide its destinies. Tide-water Virginia and South Carolina gerrymandered those colonies to insure the dominance of the coast in their legislatures. Washington desired to settle a State at a time in the Northwest; Jefferson would reserve from settlement the territory of his Louisiana Purchase north of the thirty-second parallel, in order to offer it to the Indians in exchange for their settlements east of the Mississippi. "When we shall be full on this side," he writes, "we may lay off a range of States on the western bank from the head to the mouth, and so range after range, advancing compactly as we multiply." Madison went so far as to argue to the French minister that the United States had no interest in seeing population extend itself on the right bank of the Mississippi, but should rather fear it. When the Oregon question was under debate, in 1824, Smyth, of Virginia, would draw an unchangeable line for the limits of the United States at the outer limit of two tiers of States beyond the Mississippi, complaining that the seaboard States were being drained of the flower of their population by the bringing of too much land into market. Even Thomas Benton, the man of widest views of the destiny of the West, at this stage of his career declared that along the ridge of the Rocky mountains "the western limits of the Republic should be drawn, and the statue of the fabled god Terminus should be raised upon its highest peak, never to be thrown down." But the attempts to limit the boundaries, to restrict land sales and settlement, and to deprive the West of its share of political power were all in vain. Steadily the frontier of settlement advanced and carried with it individualism, democracy, and nationalism, and powerfully affected the East and the Old World.

The most effective efforts of the East to regulate the frontier came through its educational and religious activity, exerted by interstate migration and by organized societies. Speaking in 1835, Dr. Lyman Beecher declared: "It is equally plain that the religious and political destiny of our nation is to be decided in the West," and he pointed out that the population of the West "is assembled from all the States of the Union and from all the nations of Europe, and is rushing in like the waters of the flood, demanding for its moral preservation the immediate and universal action of those institutions which discipline the mind and arm the conscience and the heart. And so various are the opinions and habits, and so recent and imperfect is the acquaintance, and so sparse are the settlements of the West, that no homogeneous public sentiment can be formed to legislate immediately into being the requisite institutions. And yet they are all needed immediately in their utmost perfection and power. A nation is being 'born in a day.' . . . But what will become of the West if her prosperity rushes up to such a majesty of power, while those great institutions linger which are necessary to form the mind and the conscience and the heart of that vast world. It must not be permitted. . . . Let no man at the East quiet himself and dream of liberty, whatever may become of the West. . . . Her destiny is our destiny."

With the appeal to the conscience of New England, he adds appeals to her fears lest other religious sects anticipate her own. The New England preacher and school-teacher left their mark on the West. The dread of Western emancipation from New England's political and economic control was paralleled by her fears lest the West cut loose from her religion. Commenting in 1850 on reports that settlement was rapidly extending northward in Wisconsin, the editor of the *Home Missionary* writes: "We scarcely know whether to rejoice or mourn over this extension of our settlements. While we sympathize in whatever tends to increase the physical resources and prosperity of our country, we can not forget that with all these dispersions into remote and still remoter corners of the land the supply of the means of grace is becoming relatively less and less." Acting in accordance with such ideas, home missions were established and Western colleges were erected. As seaboard cities like Philadelphia, New York, and Baltimore strove for the mastery of Western trade, so the various denominations strove for the possession of the West. Thus an intellectual stream from New England sources fertilized the West. Other sections sent their missionaries; but the real struggle was between sects. The contest for power and the expansive tendency furnished to the various sects by the existence of a moving frontier must have had important results on the character of religious organization in the United States. The multiplication of rival churches in the little frontier towns had deep and lasting social effects. The religious aspects of the frontier make a chapter in our history which needs study.

From the conditions of frontier life came intellectual traits of profound importance. The works of travelers along each frontier from colonial days onward describe certain common traits, and these traits have, while softening down, still persisted as survivals in the place of their origin, even when a higher social organization succeeded. The result is that to the frontier the American intellect owes its striking characteristics. That coarseness and strength combined with acuteness and inquisitiveness; that practical, inventive turn of mind, quick to find expedients; that masterful grasp of material things, lacking in the artistic but powerful to effect great ends; that restless, nervous energy; that dominant individualism, working for good and for evil, and withal that buoyancy and exuberance which comes with freedom—these are traits of the frontier, or traits called out elsewhere because of the existence of the frontier. Since the days when the fleet of Columbus sailed into the waters of the New World, America has been another name for opportunity, and the people of the United States have taken their tone from the incessant expansion which has not only been open but has even been forced upon them. He would be a rash prophet who should assert that the expansive character of American life has now entirely ceased. Movement has been its dominant fact, and, unless this training has no effect upon a people, the American energy will continually demand a wider field for its exercise. But never again will such gifts of free land offer themselves. For a moment, at the frontier, the bonds of custom are broken and unrestraint is triumphant. There is not *tabula rasa*. The stubborn American environment is there with its imperious summons to accept its conditions; the inherited ways of doing things are also there; and yet, in spite of environment, and in spite of custom, each frontier did indeed furnish a new field of opportunity, a gate of escape from the bondage of the past; and freshness, and confidence, and scorn of older society, impatience of its restraints and its ideas, and indifference to its lessons, have accompanied the frontier. What the Mediterranean Sea was to the Greeks, breaking the bond of custom, offering new experiences, calling out new institutions and activities, that, and more, the ever retreating frontier has been to the United States directly, and to the nations of Europe more remotely. And now, four centuries from the discovery of America, at the end of a hundred years of life under the Constitution, the frontier has gone, and with its going has closed the first period of American history.

Social and Cultural Trends in the Nineteenth Century

The social evils resulting from the Industrial Revolution became an object of concern to many groups, and during the nineteenth century numerous programs of social reform were advanced. Prominent among these was socialism, which assumed a variety of forms including revolutionary socialism at one extreme and moderate Fabian socialism at the other. In the United States the trend was generally in the direction of collective bargaining for better working conditions with labor organized into unions for this purpose. Others, including leaders in the Catholic Church, stressed the teachings of Christ as the solution for the social ills of the modern world. Germany, after it achieved unification, favored state socialism, a policy of paternalism on the part of the State toward its subjects. Culturally the nineteenth century produced a variety of trends, but the principal influence stemmed from the new scientific theory of evolution. This idea modified scientific principles generally, but it also made an impact upon literature and philosophy as well. Inevitably, there were reactions away from the dominant mood, and in some instances these took the form of highly individualized literary expression, while in others it resulted in distorted applications of the theory of evolution. Generally, however, nineteenth-century culture strongly reflected the scientific and social changes of the time, while realism characterized both the method of producing it and the results attained.

Karl Marx and Friedrich Engels

Karl Marx (1818–1883) was a German intellectual who came under the influence of the Hegelian philosophy while a student at the University of Berlin. He had intended to enter the teaching profession, but was unable to do so because of his unorthodox political views. For a time he worked on the staff of a radical newspaper, first as a writer and then as editor. In 1843 he went to Paris, at that time the center for intellectuals interested in socialism and working-class movements. There he met another German, Friedrich Engels (1820–1895), and the two became active associates in the Communist League. In 1848 they issued the Communist Manifesto, which appeared shortly before the revolutions of that year. In this work they traced the history of the working-class movement, which they interpreted as a series of class struggles. In developing this thesis Marx reflected both the early training he had received in Hegelian idealism and the nineteenth-century concept of evolutionary growth resulting from struggle and survival. In place of Hegel's concept of the evolutionary development of society out of the conflict of ideas, however, Marx substituted a materialistic conflict of classes centering around the mode of economic production and exchange of goods prevailing in each historical epoch. The survival of the proletariat in the last of these struggles was the inevitable conclusion of Marx's historical materialism. The worldwide popularity which the Communist Manifesto has achieved among certain groups of intellectuals and of the working class is largely the result of the way in which it placed communism in the stream of history and made its final triumph seem inevitable. In reading the selections from this work note (1) why the Manifesto was written, (2) the authors' description of how classes have been formed by the various historical systems of production, (3) the explanation as to how the bourgeoisie rose to power, (4) how the authors distinguished the bourgeois epoch from all earlier ones, (5) the influences they saw of bourgeois capitalism on imperialism and urban development, (6) their description of the weapons which the bourgeoisie have forged and which will destroy them, (7) the analysis of the growing degradation of the proletariat, (8) the process by which the proletariat constantly gained recruits, (9) how the authors integrated the proletarian movement into the stream of history, both past and future, (10) the relationship between the Communists and the other members of the working class, (11) the writers' clarification of the communist stand on the abolition of property, (12) their analysis of capital, (13) the authors' answers to the various objections raised against communism, (14) how the relationship of ideas to the system of material production was analyzed, (15) the steps they described for the revolution, including the use of the state by the workers as a *means of gaining their ends, (16) the destruction of classes by destroying the basis on which they exist, (17) the decline of the state as a political force when its reason for existence is thus destroyed, and (18) any points made by the authors that have not been realized in the course of history since their time.*

From: THE COMMUNIST MANIFESTO

A spectre is haunting Europe—the spectre of Communism. All the powers of old Europe have entered into a holy alliance to exorcise this spectre: Pope and Czar, Metternich and Guizot, French Radicals and German police-spies.

Where is the party in opposition that has not been decried as communistic by its opponents in power? Where the Opposition that has not hurled back the branding reproach of Communism, against the more advanced opposition parties, as well as against its reactionary adversaries?

Two things result from this fact:

I. Communism is already acknowledged by all European powers to be itself a power.

II. It is high time that Communists should openly, in the face of the whole world, publish their views, their aims, their tendencies, and meet this nursery tale of the spectre of Communism with a manifesto of the party itself.

To this end, Communists of various nationalities have assembled in London, and sketched the following manifesto, to be published in the English, French, German, Italian, Flemish, and Danish languages.

BOURGEOIS AND PROLETARIANS

The history of all hitherto existing society is the history of class struggles.

Freeman and slave, patrician and plebeian, lord and serf, guild-master and journeyman, in a word, oppressor and oppressed, stood in constant opposition to one another, carried on an uninterrupted, now hidden, now open fight, a fight that each time ended, either in a revolutionary reconstitution of society at large, or in the common ruin of the contending classes.

In the earlier epochs of history, we find almost everywhere a complicated arrangement of society into various orders, a manifold gradation of social rank. In ancient Rome we have patricians, knights, plebeians, slaves; in the Middle Ages, feudal lords, vassals, guildmasters, journeymen, apprentices, serfs; in almost all of these classes, again, subordinate gradations.

The modern bourgeois society that has sprouted from the ruins of feudal society, has not done away with class antagonisms. It has but established new classes, new conditions of oppression, new forms of struggle in place of the old ones.

Our epoch, the epoch of the bourgeoisie, possesses, however, this distinctive feature: It has simplified the class antagonisms. Society as a whole is more and more splitting up into two great hostile camps, into two great classes directly facing each other—bourgeoisie and proletariat.

From the serfs of the Middle Ages sprang the chartered burghers of the earliest towns. From these burgesses the first elements of the bourgeoisie were developed.

The discovery of America, the rounding of the Cape, opened up fresh ground for the rising bourgeoisie. The East-Indian and Chinese markets, the colonisation of America, trade with the colonies, the increase in the means of exchange and in commodities generally, gave to commerce, to navigation, to industry, an impulse never before known, and thereby, to the revolutionary element in the tottering feudal society, a rapid development.

The feudal system of industry, in which industrial production was monopolised by closed guilds, now no longer sufficed for the growing

Karl Marx and Friedich Engels, *Manifesto of the Communist Party,* International Publishers, New York, 1932, 3–31. Courtesy of International Publishers.

wants of the new markets. The manufacturing system took its place. The guild-masters were pushed aside by the manufacturing middle class; division of labour between the different corporate guilds vanished in the face of division of labour in each single workshop.

Meantime the markets kept ever growing, the demand ever rising. Even manufacture no longer sufficed. Thereupon, steam and machinery revolutionised industrial production. The place of manufacture was taken by the giant, modern industry, the place of the industrial middle class, by industrial millionaires—the leaders of whole industrial armies, the modern bourgeois.

Modern industry has established the world market, for which the discovery of America paved the way. This market has given an immense development to commerce, to navigation, to communication by land. This development has, in its turn, reacted on the extension of industry; and in proportion as industry, commerce, navigation, railways extended, in the same proportion the bourgeoisie developed, increased its capital, and pushed into the background every class handed down from the Middle Ages.

We see, therefore, how the modern bourgeoisie is itself the product of a long course of development, of a series of revolutions in the modes of production and of exchange.

Each step in the development of the bourgeoisie was accompanied by a corresponding political advance of that class. An oppressed class under the sway of the feudal nobility, it became an armed and self-governing association in the mediaeval commune; here independent urban republic (as in Italy and Germany), there taxable "third estate" of the monarchy (as in France); afterwards, in the period of manufacture proper, serving either the semi-feudal or the absolute monarchy as a counterpoise against the nobility, and, in fact, corner-stone of the great monarchies in general—the bourgeoisie has at last, since the establishment of modern industry and of the world market, conquered for itself, in the modern representative state, exclusive political sway. The executive of the modern state is but a committee for managing the common affairs of the whole bourgeoisie.

The bourgeoisie has played a most revolutionary rôle in history.

The bourgeoisie, wherever it has got the upper hand, has put an end to all feudal, patriarchal, idyllic relations. It has pitilessly torn asunder the motley feudal ties that bound man to his "natural superiors," and has left no other bond between man and man than naked self-interest, than callous "cash payment." It has drowned the most heavenly ecstasies of religious fervour, of chivalrous enthusiasm, of philistine sentimentalism, in the icy water of egotistical calculation. It has resolved personal worth into exchange value, and in place of the numberless indefeasible chartered freedoms, has set up that single, unconscionable freedom—Free Trade. In one word, for exploitation, veiled by religious and political illusions, it has substituted naked, shameless, direct, brutal exploitation.

The bourgeoisie has stripped of its halo every occupation hitherto honoured and looked up to with reverent awe. It has converted the physician, the lawyer, the priest, the poet, the man of science, into its paid wage-labourers.

The bourgeoisie has torn away from the family its sentimental veil, and has reduced the family relation to a mere money relation.

The bourgeoisie has disclosed how it came to pass that the brutal display of vigour in the Middle Ages, which reactionaries so much admire, found its fitting complement in the most slothful indolence. It has been the first to show what man's activity can bring about. It has accomplished wonders far surpassing Egyptian pyramids, Roman aqueducts, and Gothic cathedrals; it has conducted expeditions that put in the shade all former migrations of nations and crusades.

The bourgeoisie cannot exist without constantly revolutionising the instruments of production, and thereby the relations of production, and with them the whole relations of society. Conservation of the old modes of production in unaltered form, was, on the contrary, the first condition of existence for all earlier industrial classes. Constant revolutionising of production, uninterrupted disturbance of all social conditions, everlasting uncertainty and agitation distinguish the bourgeois epoch from all earlier ones. All fixed, fast-frozen relations, with their train of ancient and venerable prejudices and opinions, are swept away, all new-formed ones become antiquated before they can ossify. All that is solid melts into air, all that is holy is profaned, and man is at last compelled to face with sober senses his real conditions of life and his relations with his kind.

The need of a constantly expanding market for its products chases the bourgeoisie over the whole surface of the globe. It must nestle everywhere, settle everywhere, establish connections everywhere.

The bourgeoisie has through its exploitation of the world market given a cosmopolitan character to production and consumption in every country. To the great chagrin of reactionaries, it has drawn from under the feet of industry the national ground on which it stood. All old-established national industries have been destroyed or are daily being destroyed. They are dislodged by new industries, whose introduction becomes a life and death question for all civilised nations, by industries that no longer work up indigenous raw material, but raw material drawn from the remotest zones; industries whose products are consumed, not only at home, but in every quarter of the globe. In place of the old wants, satisfied by the production of the country, we find new wants, requiring for their satisfaction the products of distant lands and climes. In place of the old local and national seclusion and self-sufficiency, we have intercourse in every direction, universal inter-dependence of nations. And as in material, so also in intellectual production. The intellectual creations of individual nations become common property. National one-sidedness and narrow-mindedness become more and more impossible, and from the numerous national and local literatures there arises a world literature.

The bourgeoisie, by the rapid improvement of all instruments of production, by the immensely facilitated means of communication, draws all nations, even the most barbarian, into civilisation. The cheap prices of its commodities are the heavy artillery with which it batters down all Chinese walls, with which it forces the barbarians' intensely obstinate hatred of foreigners to capitulate. It compels all nations, on pain of extinction, to adopt the bourgeois mode of production; it compels them to introduce what it calls civilisation into their midst, i.e., to become bourgeois themselves. In a word, it creates a world after its own image.

The bourgeoisie has subjected the country to the rule of the towns. It has created enormous cities, has greatly increased the urban population as compared with the rural, and has thus rescued a considerable part of the population from the idiocy of rural life. Just as it has made the country dependent on the towns, so it has made barbarian and semi-barbarian countries dependent on the civilised ones, nations of peasants on nations of bourgeois, the East on the West.

More and more the bourgeoisie keeps doing away with the scattered state of the population, of the means of production, and of property. It has agglomerated population, centralised means of production, and has concentrated property in a few hands. The necessary consequence of this was political centralisation. Independent, or but loosely connected provinces, with separate interests, laws, governments and systems of taxation, became lumped together into one nation, with one government, one code of laws, one national class interest, one frontier and one customs tariff.

The bourgeoisie, during its rule of scarce one hundred years, has created more massive and more colossal productive forces than have all preceding generations together. Subjection of nature's forces to man, machinery, application of chemistry to industry and agriculture, steam-navigation, railways, electric telegraphs, clearing of whole continents for cultivation, canalisation of rivers, whole populations conjured out of the ground—what earlier century had even a presentiment that such productive forces slumbered in the lap of social labour?

We see then that the means of production and of exchange, which served as the foundation for the growth of the bourgeoisie, were generated in feudal society. At a certain stage in the development of these means of production and of exchange, the conditions under which feudal society produced and exchanged, the feudal organisation of agriculture and manufacturing industry, in a word, the feudal relations of property became no longer compatible with the already developed productive forces; they became so many fetters. They had to be burst asunder; they were burst asunder.

Into their place stepped free competition, accompanied by a social and political constitution adapted to it, and by the economic and political sway of the bourgeois class.

A similar movement is going on before our own eyes. Modern bourgeois society with its relations of production, of exchange and of property, a society that has conjured up such gigantic means of production and of exchange, is like the sorcerer who is no longer able to control the powers of the nether world whom he has called up by his spells. For many a decade past, the history of industry and commerce is but the history of the revolt of modern productive forces against modern conditions of production, against the property relations that are the conditions for the existence of the bourgeoisie and of its rule. It is enough to mention the commercial crises that by their periodical return put the existence of the entire bourgeois society on trial, each time more threateningly. In these crises a great part not only of the existing products, but also of the previously created productive forces, are periodically destroyed. In these crises there breaks out an epidemic that, in all earlier epochs, would have seemed an absurdity—the epidemic of over-production. Society suddenly finds itself put back into a state of momentary barbarism; it appears as if a famine, a universal war of devastation had cut off the supply of every means of subsistence; industry and commerce seem to be destroyed. And why? Because there is too much civilisation, too much means of subsistence, too much industry, too much commerce. The productive forces at the disposal of society no longer tend to further the development of the conditions of bourgeois property; on the contrary, they have become too powerful for these conditions, by which they are fettered, and no sooner do they overcome these fetters than they bring disorder into the whole of bourgeois society, endanger the existence of bourgeois property. The conditions of bourgeois society are too narrow to comprise the wealth created by them. And how does the bourgeoisie get over these crises? On the one hand by enforced de-

struction of a mass of productive forces; on the other, by the conquest of new markets, and by the more thorough exploitation of the old ones. That is to say, by paving the way for more extensive and more destructive crises, and by diminishing the means whereby crises are prevented.

The weapons with which the bourgeoisie felled feudalism to the ground are now turned against the bourgeoisie itself.

But not only has the bourgeoisie forged the weapons that bring death to itself; it has also called into existence the men who are to wield those weapons—the modern working class— the proletarians.

In proportion as the bourgeoisie, i.e., capital, is developed, in the same proportion is the proletariat, the modern working class, developed—a class of labourers, who live only so long as they find work, and who find work only so long as their labour increases capital. These labourers, who must sell themselves piecemeal, are a commodity, like every other article of commerce, and are consequently exposed to all the vicissitudes of competition, to all the fluctuations of the market.

Owing to the extensive use of machinery and to division of labour, the work of the proletarians has lost all individual character, and, consequently, all charm for the workman. He becomes an appendage of the machine, and it is only the most simple, most monotonous, and most easily acquired knack, that is required of him. Hence, the cost of production of a workman is restricted, almost entirely, to the means of subsistence that he requires for his maintenance, and for the propagation of his race. But the price of a commodity, and therefore also of labour, is equal to its cost of production. In proportion, therefore, as the repulsiveness of the work increases, the wage decreases. Nay more, in proportion as the use of machinery and division of labour increases, in the same proportion the burden of toil also increases, whether by prolongation of the working hours, by increase of the work exacted in a given time, or by increased speed of the machinery, etc.

Modern industry has converted the little workshop of the patriarchal master into the great factory of the industrial capitalist. Masses of labourers, crowded into the factory, are organised like soldiers. As privates of the industrial army they are placed under the command of a perfect hierarchy of officers and sergeants. Not only are they slaves of the bourgeois class, and of the bourgeois state; they are daily and hourly enslaved by the machine, by the overlooker, and, above all, by the individual bourgeois manufacturer himself. The more openly this despotism proclaims gain to be its end and aim, the more petty, the more hateful and the more embittering it is.

The less the skill and exertion of strength implied in manual labour, in other words, the more modern industry develops, the more is the labour of men superseded by that of women. Differences of age and sex have no longer any distinctive social validity for the working class. All are instruments of labour, more or less expensive to use, according to their age and sex.

No sooner has the labourer received his wages in cash, for the moment escaping exploitation by the manufacturer, than he is set upon by the other portions of the bourgeoisie, the landlord, the shopkeeper, the pawnbroker, etc.

The lower strata of the middle class—the small tradespeople, shopkeepers, and retired tradesmen generally, the handicraftsmen and peasants—all these sink gradually into the proletariat, partly because their diminutive capital does not suffice for the scale on which modern industry is carried on, and is swamped in the competition with the large capitalists, partly because their specialised skill is rendered worthless by new methods of production. Thus the proletariat is recruited from all classes of the population.

The proletariat goes through various stages of development. With its birth begins its struggle with the bourgeoisie. At first the contest is carried on by individual labourers, then by the work people of a factory, then by the operatives of one trade, in one locality, against the individual bourgeois who directly exploits them. They direct their attacks not against the bourgeois conditions of production, but against the instruments of production themselves; they destroy imported wares that compete with their labour, they smash machinery to pieces, they set factories ablaze, they seek to restore by force the vanished status of the workman of the Middle Ages.

At this stage the labourers still form an incoherent mass scattered over the whole country, and broken up by their mutual competition. If anywhere they unite to form more compact bodies, this is not yet the consequence of their own active union, but of the union of the bourgeoisie, which class, in order to attain its own political ends, is compelled to set the whole proletariat in motion, and is moreover still able to do so for a time. At this stage, therefore, the proletarians do not fight their enemies, but the enemies of their enemies, the remnants of absolute monarchy, the landowners, the nonindustrial bourgeois, the petty bourgeoisie. Thus the whole historical movement is concentrated in the hands of the bourgeoisie; every victory so obtained is a victory for the bourgeoisie.

But with the development of industry the proletariat not only increases in number; it becomes concentrated in greater masses, its strength grows, and it feels that strength more. The various interests and conditions of life within the ranks of the proletariat are more and more equalised, in proportion as machinery obliterates all distinctions of labour and nearly everywhere reduces wages to the same low level. The growing competition among the bourgeois, and the resulting commercial crises, make the wages of the workers ever more fluctuating. The unceasing improvement of machinery, ever more rapidly developing, makes their livelihood more and more precarious; the collisions between individual workmen and individual bourgeois take more and more the character of collisions between two classes. Thereupon the workers begin to form combinations (trade unions) against the bourgeoisie; they club together in order to keep up the rate of wages; they found permanent associations in order to make provision beforehand for these occasional revolts. Here and there the contest breaks out into riots.

Now and then the workers are victorious, but only for a time. The real fruit of their battles lies, not in the immediate result, but in the ever expanding union of the workers. This union is furthered by the improved means of communication which are created by modern industry, and which place the workers of different localities in contact with one another. It was just this contact that was needed to centralise the numerous local struggles, all of the same character, into one national struggle between classes. But every class struggle is a political struggle. And that union, to attain which the burghers of the Middle Ages, with their miserable highways, required centuries, the modern proletarians, thanks to railways, achieve in a few years.

This organisation of the proletarians into a class, and consequently into a political party, is continually being upset again by the competition between the workers themselves. But it ever rises up again, stronger, firmer, mightier. It compels legislative recognition of particular interests of the workers, by taking advantage of the divisions among the bourgeoisie itself. Thus the ten-hour bill in England was carried.

Altogether, collisions between the classes of the old society further the course of development of the proletariat in many ways. The bourgeoisie finds itself involved in a constant battle. At first with the aristocracy; later on, with those portions of the bourgeoisie itself whose interests have become antagonistic to the progress of industry; at all times with the bourgeoisie of foreign countries. In all these battles it sees itself compelled to appeal to the proletariat, to ask for its help, and thus, to drag it into the political arena. The bourgeoisie itself, therefore, supplies the proletariat with its own elements of political and general education, in other words, it furnishes the proletariat with weapons for fighting the bourgeoisie.

Further, as we have already seen, entire sections of the ruling classes are, by the advance of industry, precipitated into the proletariat, or are at least threatened in their conditions of existence. These also supply the proletariat with fresh elements of enlightenment and progress.

Finally, in times when the class struggle nears the decisive hour, the process of dissolution going on within the ruling class, in fact within the whole range of old society, assumes such a violent, glaring character, that a small section of the ruling class cuts itself adrift, and joins the revolutionary class, the class that holds the future in its hands. Just as, therefore, at an earlier period, a section of the nobility went over to the bourgeoisie, so now a portion of the bourgeoisie goes over to the proletariat, and in particular, a portion of the bourgeois ideologists, who have raised themselves to the level of comprehending theoretically the historical movement as a whole.

Of all the classes that stand face to face with the bourgeoisie today, the proletariat alone is a really revolutionary class. The other classes decay and finally disappear in the face of modern industry; the proletariat is its special and essential product.

The lower middle class, the small manufacturer, the shopkeeper, the artisan, the peasant, all these fight against the bourgeoisie, to save from extinction their existence as fractions of the middle class. They are therefore not revolutionary, but conservative. Nay more, they are reactionary, for they try to roll back the wheel of history. If by chance they are revolutionary, they are so only in view of their impending transfer into the proletariat; they thus defend not their present, but their future interests; they desert their own standpoint to adopt that of the proletariat.

The "dangerous class," the social scum (*Lumpenproletariat*), that passively rotting mass thrown off by the lowest layers of old society, may, here and there, be swept into the movement by a proletarian revolution; its conditions of life, however, prepare it far more for the part of a bribed tool of reactionary intrigue.

The social conditions of the old society no longer exist for the proletariat. The proletarian is without property; his relation to his wife and children has no longer anything in common with bourgeois family relations; modern industrial labour, modern subjection to capital, the same in England as in France, in America as in Germany, has stripped him of every trace of national character. Law, morality, religion, are to him so many bourgeois prejudices, behind which lurk in ambush just as many bourgeois interests.

All the preceding classes that got the upper hand, sought to fortify their already acquired status by subjecting society at large to their conditions of appropriation. The proletarians cannot become masters of the productive forces of society, except by abolishing their own previous mode of appropriation, and thereby also every other previous mode of appropriation. They have nothing of their own to secure and to fortify; their mission is to destroy all previous securities for, and insurances of, individual property.

All previous historical movements were movements of minorities, or in the interest of minorities. The proletarian movement is the self-conscious, independent movement of the immense majority, in the interest of the immense majority. The proletariat, the lowest stratum of our present society, cannot stir, cannot raise itself up, without the whole super-incumbent strata of official society being sprung into the air.

Though not in substance, yet in form, the struggle of the proletariat with the bourgeoisie is at first a national struggle. The proletariat of each country must, of course, first of all settle matters with its own bourgeoisie.

In depicting the most general phases of the development of the proletariat, we traced the more or less veiled civil war, raging within existing society, up to the point where that war breaks out into open revolution, and where the violent overthrow of the bourgeoisie lays the foundation for the sway of the proletariat.

Hitherto, every form of society has been based, as we have already seen, on the antagonism of oppressing and oppressed classes. But in order to oppress a class, certain conditions must be assured to it under which it can, at least, continue its slavish existence. The serf, in the period of serfdom, raised himself to membership in the commune, just as the petty bourgeois, under the yoke of feudal absolutism, managed to develop into a bourgeois. The modern labourer, on the contrary, instead of rising with the progress of industry, sinks deeper and deeper below the conditions of existence of his own class. He becomes a pauper, and pauperism develops more rapidly than population and wealth. And here it becomes evident, that the bourgeoisie is unfit any longer to be the ruling class in society, and to impose its conditions of existence upon society as an over-riding law. It is unfit to rule because it is incompetent to assure an existence to its slave within his slavery, because it cannot help letting him sink into such a state, that it has to feed him, instead of being fed by him. Society can no longer live under this bourgeoisie, in other words, its existence is no longer compatible with society.

The essential condition for the existence and sway of the bourgeois class, is the formation and augmentation of capital; the condition for capital is wage-labour. Wage-labour rests exclusively on competition between the labourers. The advance of industry, whose involuntary promoter is the bourgeoisie, replaces the isolation of the labourers, due to competition, by their revolutionary combination, due to association. The development of modern industry, therefore, cuts from under its feet the very foundation on which the bourgeoisie produces and appropriates products. What the bourgeoisie therefore produces, above all, are its own grave-diggers. Its fall and the victory of the proletariat are equally inevitable.

PROLETARIANS AND COMMUNISTS

In what relation do the Communists stand to the proletarians as a whole?

The Communists do not form a separate party opposed to other working class parties.

They have no interests separate and apart from those of the proletariat as a whole.

They do not set up any sectarian principles of their own, by which to shape and mould the proletarian movement.

The Communists are distinguished from the other working class parties by this only: 1. In the national struggles of the proletarians of the different countries, they point out and bring to the front the common interests of the entire proletariat, independently of all nationality. 2. In the various stages of development which the struggle of the working class against the bourgeoisie has to pass through, they always and everywhere represent the interests of the movement as a whole.

The Communists, therefore, are on the one hand, practically, the most advanced and resolute section of the working class parties of every country, that section which pushes forward all others; on the other hand, theoretically, they have over the great mass of the proletariat the advantage of clearly understanding the line of march, the conditions, and the ultimate general results of the proletarian movement.

The immediate aim of the Communists is the same as that of all the other proletarian parties: formation of the proletariat into a class, overthrow of bourgeois supremacy, conquest of political power by the proletariat.

The theoretical conclusions of the Communists are in no way based on ideas or principles that have been invented, or discovered, by this or that would-be universal reformer.

They merely express, in general terms, actual relations springing from an existing class struggle, from a historical movement going on under our very eyes. The abolition of existing property relations is not at all a distinctive feature of Communism.

All property relations in the past have continually been subject to historical change consequent upon the change in historical conditions.

The French Revolution, for example, abolished feudal property in favour of bourgeois property.

The distinguishing feature of Communism is not the abolition of property generally, but the abolition of bourgeois property. But modern bourgeois private property is the final and most complete expression of the system of producing and appropriating products that is based on class antagonisms, on the exploitation of the many by the few.

In this sense, the theory of the Communists may be summed up in the single sentence: Abolition of private property.

We Communists have been reproached with the desire of abolishing the right of personally acquiring property as the fruit of a man's own labour, which property is alleged to be the groundwork of all personal freedom, activity, and independence.

Hard-won, self-acquired, self-earned property! Do you mean the property of the petty artisan and of the small peasant, a form of property that preceded the bourgeois form? There is no need to abolish that; the development of industry has to a great extent already destroyed it, and is still destroying it daily.

Or do you mean modern bourgeois private property?

But does wage-labour create any property for the labourer? Not a bit. It creates capital, i.e., that kind of property which exploits wage-labour, and which cannot increase except upon condition of begetting a new supply of wage-labour for fresh exploitation. Property, in its present form, is based on the antagonism of capital and wage-labour. Let us examine both sides of this antagonism.

To be a capitalist, is to have not only a purely personal, but a social *status* in production. Capital is a collective product, and only by the united action of many members, nay, in the last resort, only by the united action of all members of society, can it be set in motion.

Capital is therefore not a personal, it is a social, power.

When, therefore, capital is converted into common property, into the property of all members of society, personal property is not thereby transformed into social property. It is only the social character of the property that is changed. It loses its class character.

Let us now take wage-labour.

The average price of wage-labour is the minimum wage, i.e., that quantum of the means of subsistence which is absolutely requisite to keep the labourer in bare existence as a labourer. What, therefore, the wage-labourer appropriates by means of his labour, merely suffices to prolong and reproduce a bare existence. We by no means intend to abolish this personal appropriation of the products of labour, an appropriation that is made for the maintenance and reproduction of human life, and that leaves no surplus wherewith to command the labour of others. All that we want to do away with is the miserable character of this appropriation, under which the labourer lives merely to increase capital, and is allowed to live only insofar as the interest of the ruling class requires it.

In bourgeois society, living labour is but a

means to increase accumulated labour. In Communist society, accumulated labour is but a means to widen, to enrich, to promote the existence of the labourer.

In bourgeois society, therefore, the past dominates the present; in Communist society, the present dominates the past. In bourgeois society capital is independent and has individuality, while the living person is dependent and has no individuality.

And the abolition of this state of things is called by the bourgeois, abolition of individuality and freedom! And rightly so. The abolition of bourgeois individuality, bourgeois independence, and bourgeois freedom is undoubtedly aimed at.

By freedom is meant, under the present bourgeois conditions of production, free trade, free selling and buying.

But if selling and buying disappears, free selling and buying disappears also. This talk about free selling and buying, and all the other "brave words" of our bourgeoisie about freedom in general, have a meaning, if any, only in contrast with restricted selling and buying, with the fettered traders of the Middle Ages, but have no meaning when opposed to the Communist abolition of buying and selling, of the bourgeois conditions of production, and of the bourgeoisie itself.

You are horrified at our intending to do away with private property. But in your existing society, private property is already done away with for nine-tenths of the population; its existence for the few is solely due to its nonexistence in the hands of those nine-tenths. You reproach us, therefore, with intending to do away with a form of property, the necessary condition for whose existence is the nonexistence of any property for the immense majority of society.

In a word, you reproach us with intending to do away with your property. Precisely so; that is just what we intend.

From the moment when labour can no longer be converted into capital, money, or rent, into a social power capable of being monopolised, i.e., from the moment when individual property can no longer be transformed into bourgeois property, into capital, from that moment, you say, individuality vanishes.

You must, therefore, confess that by "individual" you mean no other person than the bourgeois, than the middle-class owner of property. This person must, indeed, be swept out of the way, and made impossible.

Communism deprives no man of the power to appropriate the products of society; all that it does is to deprive him of the power to subjugate the labour of others by means of such appropriation.

It has been objected, that upon the abolition of private property all work will cease, and universal laziness will overtake us.

According to this, bourgeois society ought long ago to have gone to the dogs through sheer idleness; for those of its members who work, acquire nothing, and those who acquire anything, do not work. The whole of this objection is but another expression of the tautology: There can no longer be any wage-labour when there is no longer any capital.

All objections urged against the Communist mode of producing and appropriating material products, have, in the same way, been urged against the Communist modes of producing and appropriating intellectual products. Just as, to the bourgeois, the disappearance of class property is the disappearance of production itself, so the disappearance of class culture is to him identical with the disappearance of all culture.

That culture, the loss of which he laments, is, for the enormous majority, a mere training to act as a machine.

But don't wrangle with us so long as you apply, to our intended abolition of bourgeois property, the standard of your bourgeois notions of freedom, culture, law, etc. Your very ideas are but the outgrowth of the conditions of your bourgeois production and bourgeois property, just as your jurisprudence is but the will of your class made into a law for all, a will whose essential character and direction are determined by the economic conditions of existence of your class.

The selfish misconception that induces you to transform into eternal laws of nature and of reason, the social forms springing from your present mode of production and form of property—historical relations that rise and disappear in the progress of production—this misconception you share with every ruling class that has preceded you. What you see clearly in the case of ancient property, what you admit in the case of feudal property, you are of course forbidden to admit in the case of your own bourgeois form of property.

Abolition of the family! Even the most radical flare up at this infamous proposal of the Communists.

On what foundation is the present family, the bourgeois family, based? On capital, on private gain. In its completely developed form this family exists only among the bourgeoisie. But this state of things finds its complement in the practical absence of the family among the proletarians, and in public prostitution.

The bourgeois family will vanish as a matter of course when its complement vanishes, and both will vanish with the vanishing of capital.

Do you charge us with wanting to stop the exploitation of children by their parents? To this crime we plead guilty.

But, you will say, we destroy the most hallowed of relations, when we replace home education by social.

And your education! Is not that also social, and determined by the social conditions under which you educate, by the intervention of society, direct or indirect, by means of schools, etc.? The Communists have not invented the intervention of society in education; they do but seek to alter the character of that intervention, and to rescue education from the influence of the ruling class.

The bourgeois claptrap about the family and education, about the hallowed co-relation of parent and child, becomes all the more disgusting, the more, by the action of modern industry, all family ties among the proletarians are torn asunder, and their children transformed into simple articles of commerce and instruments of labour.

But you Communists would introduce community of women, screams the whole bourgeoisie in chorus.

The bourgeois sees in his wife a mere instrument of production. He hears that the instruments of production are to be exploited in common, and, naturally, can come to no other conclusion than that the lot of being common to all will likewise fall to the women.

He has not even a suspicion that the real point aimed at is to do away with the status of women as mere instruments of production.

For the rest, nothing is more ridiculous than the virtuous indignation of our bourgeois at the community of women which, they pretend, is to be openly and officially established by the Communists. The Communists have no need to introduce community of women; it has existed almost from time immemorial.

Our bourgeois, not content with having the wives and daughters of their proletarians at their disposal, not to speak of common prostitutes, take the greatest pleasure in seducing each other's wives.

Bourgeois marriage is in reality a system of wives in common and thus, at the most, what the Communists might possibly be reproached with is that they desire to introduce, in substitution for a hypocritically concealed, an openly legalised community of women. For the rest, it is self-evident, that the abolition of the present system of production must bring with it the abolition of the community of women springing from that system, i.e., of prostitution both public and private.

The Communists are further reproached with desiring to abolish countries and nationality.

The workingmen have no country. We cannot take from them what they have not got. Since the proletariat must first of all acquire political supremacy, must rise to be the leading class of the nation, must constitute itself *the* nation, it is, so far, itself national, though not in the bourgeois sense of the word.

National differences and antagonisms between peoples are vanishing gradually from day to day, owing to the development of the bourgeoisie, to freedom of commerce, to the world market, to uniformity in the mode of production and in the conditions of life corresponding thereto.

The supremacy of the proletariat will cause them to vanish still faster. United action, of the leading civilised countries at least, is one of the first conditions for the emancipation of the proletariat.

In proportion as the exploitation of one individual by another is put an end to, the exploitation of one nation by another will also be put an end to. In proportion as the antagonism between classes within the nation vanishes, the hostility of one nation to another will come to an end.

The charges against Communism made from a religious, a philosophical, and, generally, from an ideological standpoint, are not deserving of serious examination.

Does it require deep intuition to comprehend that man's ideas, views, and conceptions, in one word, man's consciousness, changes with every change in the conditions of his material existence, in his social relations, and in his social life?

What else does the history of ideas prove, than that intellectual production changes its character in proportion as material production is changed? The ruling ideas of each age have ever been the ideas of its ruling class.

When people speak of ideas that revolutionise society, they do but express the fact that within the old society the elements of a new one have been created, and that the dissolution of the old ideas keeps even pace with the dissolution of the old conditions of existence.

When the ancient world was in its last throes, the ancient religions were overcome by Christianity. When Christian ideas succumbed in the 18th century to rationalist ideas, feudal society fought its death-battle with the then revolutionary bourgeoisie. The ideas of religious liberty and freedom of conscience, merely gave expression to the sway of free competition within the domain of knowledge.

"Undoubtedly," it will be said, "religion, moral, philosophical and juridical ideas have been modified in the course of historical development. But religion, morality, philosophy, political science, and law, constantly survived this change.

"There are, besides, eternal truths, such as Freedom, Justice, etc., that are common to all states of society. But Communism abolishes eternal truths, it abolishes all religion, and all morality, instead of constituting them on a new basis; it therefore acts in contradiction to all past historical experience."

What does this accusation reduce itself to? The history of all past society has consisted in the development of class antagonisms, antagonisms that assumed different forms at different epochs.

But whatever form they may have taken, one fact is common to all past ages, viz., the exploitation of one part of society by the other. No wonder, then, that the social consciousness of past ages, despite all the multiplicity and variety it displays, moves within certain common forms, or general ideas, which cannot completely vanish except with the total disappearance of class antagonisms.

The Communist revolution is the most radical rupture with traditional property relations; no wonder that its development involves the most radical rupture with traditional ideas.

But let us have done with the bourgeois objections to Communism.

We have seen above, that the first step in the revolution by the working class, is to raise the proletariat to the position of ruling class, to establish democracy.

The proletariat will use its political supremacy to wrest, by degrees, all capital from the bourgeoisie, to centralise all instruments of production in the hands of the state, i.e., of the proletariat organised as the ruling class; and to increase the total of productive forces as rapidly as possible.

Of course, in the beginning, this cannot be effected except by means of despotic inroads on the rights of property, and on the conditions of bourgeois production; by means of measures, therefore, which appear economically insufficient and untenable, but which, in the course of the movement, outstrip themselves, necessitate further inroads upon the old social order, and are unavoidable as a means of entirely revolutionising the mode of production.

These measures will of course be different in different countries.

Nevertheless in the most advanced countries, the following will be pretty generally applicable.

1. Abolition of property in land and application of all rents of land to public purposes.

2. A heavy progressive or graduated income tax.

3. Abolition of all right of inheritance.

4. Confiscation of the property of all emigrants and rebels.

5. Centralisation of credit in the hands of the state, by means of a national bank with state capital and an exclusive monopoly.

6. Centralisation of the means of communication and transport in the hands of the state.

7. Extension of factories and instruments of production owned by the state; the bringing into cultivation of waste lands, and the improvement of the soil generally in accordance with a common plan.

8. Equal obligation of all to work. Establishment of industrial armies, especially for agriculture.

9. Combination of agriculture with manufacturing industries; gradual abolition of the distinction between town and country, by a more equable distribution of the population over the country.

10. Free education for all children in public schools. Abolition of child factory labour in its present form. Combination of education with industrial production, etc.

When, in the course of development, class distinctions have disappeared, and all production has been concentrated in the hands of a vast association of the whole nation, the public power will lose its political character. Political power, properly so called, is merely the organised power of one class for oppressing another. If the proletariat during its contest with the bourgeoisie is compelled, by the force of circumstances, to organise itself as a class; if, by means of a revolution, it makes itself the ruling class, and, as such, sweeps away by force the old conditions of production, then it will, along with these conditions, have swept away the conditions for the existence of class antagonisms, and of classes generally, and will thereby have abolished its own supremacy as a class.

In place of the old bourgeois society, with its classes and class antagonisms, we shall have an association, in which the free development of each is the condition for the free development of all. [The text concludes with a description of the types of socialism and their literature.]

Peter Kropotkin

Peter Kropotkin (1842–1921), a Russian prince who had been trained for the army, became a prominent figure in the proletarian movement of the nineteenth and early twentieth centuries. His first association with workers occurred in 1872 when he joined the International Workingmen's Association at Geneva. This group was not radical enough to fit in with Kropotkin's ideals, however, and he finally associated himself with the anarchist movement. Originally, this group had favored the immediate destruction of the state and the substitution for it of entirely free co-operation among individuals, groups, and areas. Under the influence of Marxian or "scientific socialism," however, anarchism moved gradually in the direction of a communistic society. It was with this trend that Kropotkin associated himself. He believed that a new society could be constructed on the ruins of the state—a society composed of the community voluntarily co-operating on a high moral level and for the common good of all. In 1896 he published his concepts in Anarchism, Its Philosophy and Ideal. In reading the following excerpts from this work note (1) the emphasis he placed on individual development under

anarchism, (2) the widespread development of the principle of voluntary federation existing in Europe during the
Middle Ages, (3) how these groups carried on voluntarily
the functions of the state, (4) the groups who found mutual insurance in the state, (5) the relationship between
the rise and fall of the moral level of society, and the rise
and fall of governments, (6) his description of society under communism and how it will evolve from smaller into
larger units, (7) how he harmonized communism and anarchism, and (8) the evils which governments have produced.

From: ANARCHISM, ITS PHILOSOPHY AND IDEAL

Under the name Anarchy, a new interpretation of the past and present life of society
arises, giving at the same time a forecast as
regards its future. . . . It seeks the most complete development of individuality combined
with the highest development of voluntary association in all its aspects, in all possible degrees, for all imaginable aims; ever changing,
ever modified associations which carry in
themselves the elements of their durability and
constantly assume new forms, which answer
best to the multiple aspirations of all. . . .

This conception and ideal of society is certainly not new. On the contrary, when we analyse the history of popular institutions—the
clan, the village community, the guild and
even the urban commune of the Middle Ages
in their first stages,—we find the same popular
tendency to constitute a society according to
this idea; a tendency, however, always tram-
melled by domineering minorities. . . .

It was only in the sixteenth century that a
mortal blow was dealt to ideas of local independence, to free union and organisation, to
federation of all degrees among sovereign
groups, possessing all functions now seized
upon by the State. It was only then that the
alliance between Church and the nascent
power of Royalty put an end to an organisation, based on the principle of federation,
which had existed from the ninth to the fifteenth century, and which had produced in
Europe the great period of free cities of the
Middle Ages. . . .

It is now hardly thirty or forty years ago

that we began to reconquer by struggle, by
revolt, the first steps of the right of association,
that was freely practised by the artisans and
the tillers of the soil through the whole of the
Middle Ages.

And, already now, Europe is covered by
thousands of voluntary associations for study
and teaching, for industry, commerce, science,
art, literature, exploitation, resistance to exploitation, amusement, serious work, gratification, and self-denial, for all that makes up the
life of an active and thinking being. . . .
These societies already begin to encroach
everywhere on the functions of the State, and
strive to substitute free action of volunteers
for that of a centralised State. . . .

And when we mark the progress already accomplished in that direction, in spite of and
against the State, which tries by all means to
maintain its supremacy of recent origin; when
we see how voluntary societies invade everything and are only impeded in their development by the State, we are forced to recognise
a powerful *tendency*, a latent force in modern
society. And we ask ourselves this question:
If, five, ten, or twenty years hence—it matters
little—the workers succeed by revolt in destroying the said mutual insurance society of
landlords, bankers, priests, judges, and soldiers; if the people become masters of their
destiny for a few months, and lay hands on the
riches they have created, and which belong to
them by right—will they really begin to reconstitute that blood-sucker, the State? Or will
they not rather try to organise from the simple

Peter Kropotkin, *Anarchism, Its Philosophy and Ideal, Freedom Pamphlets*, no. 10, n.p., 1896.

to the complex, according to mutual agreement and to the infinitely varied, ever-changing needs of each locality, in order to secure the possession of those riches for themselves, to mutually guarantee one another's life, and to produce what will be found necessary for life?

Will they follow the dominant tendency of the century, towards decentralisation, home rule, and free agreement; or will they march contrary to this tendency and strive to reconstitute demolished authority? . . .

It is often said that Anarchists live in a world of dreams to come, and do not see the things which happen today. . . .

Far from living in a world of visions and imagining men better than they are, we see them as they are; and that is why we affirm that the best of men is made essentially bad by the exercise of authority. . . .

Oh, the beautiful utopia, the lovely Christmas dream we can make as soon as we admit that those who govern represent a superior caste, and have hardly any or no knowledge of simple mortals' weaknesses! . . . All the science of government, imagined by those who govern, is imbibed with these utopias. But we know men too well to dream such dreams. We have not two measures for the virtues of the governed and those of the governors; we know that we ourselves are not without faults and that the best of us would soon be corrupted by the exercise of power. We take men for what they are worth—and that is why we hate the government of man by man, and that we work with all our might— perhaps not strong enough—to put an end to it.

But it is not enough to destroy. We must also know how to build, and it is owing to not having thought about it that the masses have always been led astray in all their revolutions. After having demolished they abandoned the care of reconstruction to the middle-class people, who possessed a more or less precise conception of what they wished to realise, and who consequently reconstituted authority to their own advantage.

That is why Anarchy, when it works to destroy authority in all its aspects, when it demands that abrogation of laws and the aboli-

tion of the mechanism that serves to impose them, when it refuses all hierarchical organisation and preaches free agreement—at the same time strives to maintain and enlarge the precious kernel of social customs without which no human or animal society can exist. Only, instead of demanding that those social customs should be maintained through the authority of a few, it demands it from the continued action of all.

Communist customs and institutions are of absolute necessity for society, not only to solve economic difficulties, but also to maintain and develop social customs that bring men in contact with one another; they must be looked to for establishing such relations between men that the interest of each should be the interest of all; and this alone can unite men instead of dividing them. . . .

As to the impotence of repression—it is sufficiently demonstrated by the disorder of present society and by the necessity of a revolution that we all desire or feel inevitable. . . .

All that was an element of progress in the past or an instrument of moral and intellectual improvement of the human race is due *to the practice of mutual aid,* to the customs that recognised the equality of men and brought them to ally, to unite, to associate for the purpose of producing and consuming, to unite for purposes of defence, to federate and to recognise no other judges in fighting out their differences than the arbitrators they took from their own midst.

Each time these institutions, issued from popular genius, when it had reconquered its liberty for a moment,—each time these institutions developed in a new direction, the moral level of society, its material well-being, its liberty, its intellectual progress, and the affirmation of individual originality made a step in advance. And, on the contrary, each time that in the course of history, whether following upon a foreign conquest, or whether by developing authoritarian prejudices men become more and more divided into governors and governed, exploiters and exploited, the moral level fell, the well-being of the masses decreased in order to insure riches to a few, and the spirit of the age declined.

History teaches us this, and from this lesson

we have learned to have confidence in free Communist institutions to raise the moral level of societies, debased by the practice of authority.

Today we live side by side without knowing one another. We come together at meetings on an election day; we listen to the lying or fanciful professions of faith of a candidate, and we return home. The State has the care of all questions of public interest; the State alone has the function of seeing that we do not harm the interests of our neighbour, and, if it fails in this, of punishing us in order to repair the evil. . . .

In a Communist society such estrangement, such confidence in an outside force, could not exist. Communist organisation cannot be left to be constructed by legislative bodies called parliaments, municipal or communal councils. It must be the work of all, a natural growth, a product of the constructive genius of the great mass. Communism cannot be imposed from above; it could not live even for a few months if the constant and daily co-operation of all did not uphold it. It must be free.

It cannot exist without creating a continual contact between all for the thousands and thousands of common transactions; it cannot exist without creating local life, independent in the smallest unities—the block of houses, the street, the district, the commune. It would not answer its purpose if it did not cover society with a network of thousands of associations to satisfy its thousand needs: the necessaries of life, articles of luxury, of study, enjoyment, amusements. And such associations cannot remain narrow and local; they must necessarily tend (as is already the case with learned societies, cyclist clubs, humanitarian societies, and the like) to become international. . . .

This, then, is the form—sociable institution —of which we ask the development of the spirit of harmony that Church and State had undertaken to impose on us—with the sad result we know only too well. And these remarks contain our answer to those who affirm that Communism and Anarchy cannot go together. They are, you see, a necessary complement to one another. The most powerful development of individuality of individual

originality—as one of our comrades has so well said,—can be produced only when the first needs of food and shelter are satisfied; when the struggle for existence against the forces of nature has been simplified; when man's time is no longer taken up entirely by the meaner side of daily subsistence,—then, only, his intelligence, his artistic taste, his inventive spirit, his genius, can develop freely and ever strive to greater achievements.

Communism is the best basis for individual development and freedom; not that individualism which drives man to the war of each against all—this is the only one known up till now—but that which represents the full expansion of man's faculties, the superior development of what is original in him, the greatest fruitfulness of intelligence, feeling and will.

Such being our ideal, what does it matter to us that it cannot be realised at once! . . .

It is evident that so profound a revolution producing itself in people's minds cannot be confined to the domain of ideas without expanding to the sphere of action. . . . Consequently, the new ideas have provoked a multitude of acts of revolt in all countries, under all possible conditions: first, individual revolt against Capital and State; then collective revolt—strikes and working-class insurrections —both preparing, in men's minds as in actions, a revolt of the masses, a revolution. . . .

And, during this same period, massacres, wholesale and retail, organised by *governments,* follow their regular course. . . . What a terrible indictment the balance-sheet of the sufferings endured by workers and their friends, during this last quarter of a century, would be! What a multitude of horrible details that are unknown to the public at large! . . .

As long as society accepts the law of retaliation, as long as religion and law, the barrack and the law-courts, the prison and industrial penal servitude, the press and the school continue to teach supreme contempt for the life of the individual,—do not ask the rebels against that society to respect it. It would be exacting a degree of gentleness and magnanimity from them infinitely superior to that of the whole of society.

If you wish, like us, that the entire liberty of the individual and, consequently, his life be respected, you are necessarily brought to repudiate the government of man by man, whatever shape it assumes; you are forced to accept the principles of Anarchy that you have spurned so long. You must then search with us the forms of society that can best realise that ideal and put an end to all the violence that arouses your indignation.

George Bernard Shaw

In 1883 a group of English intellectuals who were interested in socialism founded the Fabian Society. They were not, however, sympathetic with the assertion of Marxian socialists that class conflict and violence were inevitable prerequisites to the triumph of socialism, but rather they believed that by parliamentary procedure and through evolutionary growth the transition from capitalism to socialism could be made. At the outset they sought to educate the public through lectures and pamphlets, but in the early part of the twentieth century they turned to the working classes for organized support. Thus, when the English Labour Party was formed in 1906, the Fabian Society became a constituent member. However, the Fabians never emphasized their program in terms of a class movement, and as a consequence the English Labour Party has been able to attract support from all classes in British society. In 1884 the British playright George Bernard Shaw (1856–1950) joined the society; he wrote the following report in 1896. In reading it note (1) the object of the Fabian Society, (2) the methods it advocated in achieving its objective, (3) its attitude toward those who expected a great historical crisis in the socialist movement, (4) what the Fabians meant by socialism, (5) their attitude toward individualism and individual enterprise, and (6) the ideas which Shaw specifically repudiated.

From: REPORT ON THE FABIAN POLICY

I. THE MISSION OF THE FABIANS

The object of the Fabian Society is to persuade the English people to make their political constitution thoroughly democratic and so to socialize their industries as to make the livelihood of the people entirely independent of private capitalism.

The Fabian Society endeavors to pursue its Socialist and Democratic objects with complete singleness of aim. For example:

It has no distinctive opinions on the Marriage Question, Religion, Art, abstract Economics, historic Evolution, Currency, or any other subject than its own special business of practical Democracy and Socialism.

It brings all the pressure and persuasion in its power to bear on existing forces, caring nothing by what name any party calls itself, or what principles, Socialist or other, it professes, but having regard solely to the tendency of its actions, supporting those which

Report on Fabian Policy and Resolutions Presented by the Fabian Society to the . . . [Second International], 1896, Fabian Tract no. 70 in The Fabian Society, *Fabian Tracts. . . .* London, n.d. (1900?).

make for Socialism and Democracy, and opposing those which are reactionary.

It does not propose that the practical steps towards Social-Democracy should be carried out by itself, or by any other specially organized society or party.

It does not ask the English people to join the Fabian Society.

II. FABIAN ELECTORAL TACTICS

The Fabian Society does not claim to be the people of England, or even the Socialist party, and therefore does not seek direct political representation by putting forward Fabian candidates at elections. But it loses no opportunity of influencing elections and inducing constituencies to select Socialists as their candidates. . . .

III. FABIAN TOLERATION

The Fabian Society, far from holding aloof from other bodies, urges its members to lose no opportunity of joining them and permeating them with Fabian ideas as far as possible. Almost all organizations and movements contain elements making for Socialism, no matter how remote the sympathies and intentions of their founders may be from those of the Socialists. On the other hand, unintentionally reactionary proposals are constantly being brought forward in Socialist bodies. Fabians are therefore encouraged to join all other organizations, Socialist or non-Socialist, in which Fabian work can be done.

IV. FABIAN CONSTITUTIONALISM

The Fabian Society is perfectly constitutional in its attitude; and its methods are those usual in political life in England.

The Fabian Society accepts the conditions imposed on it by human nature and by the national character and political circumstances of the English people. It sympathizes with the ordinary citizen's desire for gradual, peaceful changes, as against revolution, conflict with the army and police, and martyrdom. It recognizes the fact that Social-Democracy is not the whole of the working-class program, and that every separate measure towards the socialization of industry will have to compete for precedence with numbers of other reforms. It therefore does not believe that the moment will ever come when the whole of Socialism will be staked on the issue of a single General Election or a single Bill in the House of Commons, as between the proletariat on one side and the proprietariat on the other. Each installment of Social-Democracy will only be a measure among other measures, and will have to be kept to the front by an energetic Socialist section. The Fabian Society therefore begs those Socialists who are looking forward to a sensational historical crisis, to join some other Society.

V. FABIAN DEMOCRACY

Democracy, as understood by the Fabian Society, means simply the control of the administration by freely elected representatives of the people. The Fabian Society energetically repudiates all conceptions of Democracy as a system by which the technical work of government administration, and the appointment of public officials, shall be carried on by referendum or any other form of direct popular decision. Such arrangements may be practical in a village community, but not in the complicated industrial civilizations which are ripening for Social-Democracy. When the House of Commons is freed from the veto of the House of Lords and thrown open to candidates from all classes by an effective system of Payment of Representatives and a more rational method of election, the British parliamentary system will be, in the opinion of the Fabian Society, a first-rate practical instrument of democratic government.

Democracy, as understood by the Fabian Society, makes no political distinction between men and women.

VI. FABIAN COMPROMISE

The Fabian Society, having learnt from experience that Socialists cannot have their own way in everything any more than other people, recognizes that in a Democratic community Compromise is a necessary condition of political progress.

VII. FABIAN SOCIALISM

Socialism, as understood by the Fabian Society, means the organization and conduct of the necessary industries of the country, and the appropriation of all forms of economic rent of land and capital by the nation as a whole, through the most suitable public authorities, parochial, municipal, provincial, or central.

The Socialism advocated by the Fabian Society is State Socialism exclusively. The foreign friends of the Fabian Society must interpret this declaration in view of the fact that since England now possesses an elaborate democratic State machinery, graduated from the Parish Council or Vestry up to the central Parliament, and elected under a franchise which enables the working-class vote to overwhelm all others, the opposition which exists in the Continental monarchies between the State and the people does not hamper English Socialists. For example, the distinction made between State Socialism and Social-Democracy in Germany, where the municipalities and other local bodies are closed against the working classes, has no meaning in England. The difficulty in England is not to secure more political power for the people, but to persuade them to make any sensible use of the power they already have.

VIII. FABIAN INDIVIDUALISM

The Fabian Society does not suggest that the State should monopolize industry as against private enterprise or individual initiative further than may be necessary to make the livelihood of the people and their access to the sources of production completely independent of both. The freedom of individuals to test the social value of new inventions; to initiate improved methods of production; to anticipate and lead public enterprise in catering for new social wants; to practise all arts, crafts, and professions independently; in short, to complete the social organization by adding the resources of private activity and judgment to those of public routine, is, subject to the above conditions, as highly valued by the Fabian Society as Freedom of Speech, Freedom of the Press, or any other article in the charter of popular liberties.

IX. FABIAN FREEDOM OF THOUGHT

The Fabian Society strenuously maintains its freedom of thought and speech with regard to the errors of Socialist authors, economists, leaders, and parties, no less than to those of its opponents. For instance, it insists on the necessity of maintaining as critical an attitude towards Marx and Lassalle, some of whose views must by this time be discarded as erroneous or obsolete, as these eminent Socialists themselves maintained towards their predecessors, St. Simon and Robert Owen. . . .

XII. FABIAN NATURAL PHILOSOPHY

The Fabian Society endeavors to rouse social compunction by making the public conscious of the evil condition of society under the present system. This it does by the collection and publication of authentic and impartial statistical tracts, compiled, not from the works of Socialists, but from official sources. The first volume of Karl Marx's *Das Kapital*, which contains an immense mass of carefully verified facts concerning modern capitalistic civilization, and practically nothing about Socialism, is probably the most successful propagandist work ever published. The Fabian Society, in its endeavors to continue the work of Marx in this direction, has found that the guesses made by Socialists at the condition of the people almost invariably flatter the existing system instead of, as might be suspected, exaggerating its evils. The Fabian Society therefore concludes that in the natural philosophy of Socialism, light is a more important factor than heat.

XIII. FABIAN REPUDIATIONS

The Fabian Society discards such phrases as "the abolition of the wage system," which can only mislead the public as to the aims of Socialism. Socialism does not involve the abolition of wages, but the establishment of standard allowances for the maintenance of all workers by the community in its own service, as an alternative to wages fixed by the competition of destitute men and women for private employment, as well as to commercial profits, commissions, and all other speculative and competitive forms of remuneration. In short, the Fabian Society, far from desiring to abolish wages, wishes to secure them for everybody.

The Fabian Society resolutely opposes all pretensions to hamper the socialization of industry with equal wages, equal hours of labor, equal official status, or equal authority for everyone. Such conditions are not only impracticable, but incompatible with the equality of subordination to the common interest which is fundamental in modern Socialism.

The Fabian Society steadfastly discountenances all schemes for securing to any person, or any group of persons, "the entire product of their labor." It recognizes that wealth is social in its origin and must be social in its distribution, since the evolution of industry has made it impossible to distinguish the particular contribution that each person makes to the common product, or to ascertain its value.

The Fabian Society desires to offer to all projectors and founders of Utopian communities in South America, Africa, and other remote localities, its apologies for its impatience of such adventures. To such projectors, and all patrons of schemes for starting similar settlements and workshops at home, the Society announces emphatically that it does not believe in the establishment of Socialism by private enterprise.

XIV. FINALLY

The Fabian Society does not put Socialism forward as a panacea for the ills of human society, but only for those produced by defective organization of industry and by a radically bad distribution of wealth.

American Labor Leaders

S ince medieval times employers throughout Europe had been successful in influencing the state to prohibit the organization of workers for collective action. Labor was forced to submit to these restrictions until the beginning of the nineteenth century, but with the tremendous increase in their numbers resulting from the Industrial Revolution, the workers gradually succeeded in having this handicap removed. The earliest combinations of laborers took the form of trade unions and were formed primarily for economic rather than for political aims. It was this pattern that was followed by labor in the United States where local trade unions were first formed in the early years of the last century. In 1850 American printers formed the first national trade union and their example was quickly followed by other trades. In the eighties these unions formed the American Federation of Labor which has consistently adhered to the original policy of trade unionism regarding political action. In reading the following selections from statements by prominent American labor leaders note (1) the attitude expressed toward capital, (2) the program which unions support, (3) Samuel Gompers' position on industrial as opposed to trade unions, (4) his warning to labor in its use of the sympathetic strike, (5) wherein the strength of labor lies, and (6) the issue of political partisanship within the American Federation of Labor.

Reprinted from David Harris and Easton Rothwell, eds., *Selected Documents of Social Reform and Revolution*, Stanford University Press, Stanford University, 1939, 21–25, with the permission of the editors and of the publishers.

STATEMENTS FROM AMERICAN LABOR LEADERS

THE PURPOSE OF UNIONS: SELECTIONS FROM JOHN MITCHELL, ORGANIZED LABOR, ITS PROBLEMS, PURPOSES, AND IDEALS, 1903

The average wage earner has made up his mind that he must remain a wage earner. He has given up the hope of a kingdom to come, where he himself will be a capitalist, and he asks that the reward for his work be given to him as a workingman. Singly, he has been too weak to enforce his just demands and he has sought strength in union and has associated himself into labor organizations.

Labor unions are *for* the workman, but *against* no one. They are not hostile to employers, not inimical to the interests of the general public. They are for a class, because that class exists and has class interests, but the unions did not create and do not perpetuate the class or its interests and do not seek to evoke a class conflict.

There is no necessary hostility between labor and capital. Neither can do without the other; each has evolved from the other. Capital is labor saved and materialized; the power to labor is in itself a form of capital. There is not even a necessary, fundamental antagonism between the laborer and the capitalist. Both are men, with the virtues and vices of men, and each wishes at times more than his fair share. Yet, broadly considered, the interest of the one is the interest of the other, and the prosperity of the one is the prosperity of the other. . . .

The trade unions stand for the principle of united action and for the policy of a living wage earned under fair living conditions. In union there is strength, justice, and moderation; in disunion, nothing but an alternating humility and insolence, a state of industrial despotism tempered by futile and passing revolutions. Unions stand for the right of association, self-government, and free speech, for the dignity and self-respect of the workman, for the mutual esteem of capitalist and wage earner, and for a wide, far-seeing, open-minded, democratic conduct of industry. . . .

PRESIDENT GOMPERS ON INDUSTRIAL UNIONISM, 1903

The attempt to force the trade unions into what has been termed industrial organization is perversive to the history of the labor movement, runs counter to the best conceptions of the toilers' interests now, and is sure to lead to the confusion which precedes dissolution and disruption. It is time for the American Federation of Labor solemnly to call a halt. . . .

The advocates of the so-called industrial system of labor organizations urge that an effective strike can be conducted only when all workmen, regardless of trade, calling, or occupation, are affected.

That this is not borne out by the history of strikes in the whole labor movement is easily demonstrable. Though here and there such strikes have been temporarily successful, in the main they have been fraught with injury to all. The so-called industrial system of organization implies sympathetic strikes, and these time and experience have demonstrated as a general proposition should be discarded, while strikes of particular trades or callings have had the largest number of successes and the minimum of defeats. Quite apart from these considerations, however, are the splendid advantages obtained by the trade unions without the necessity of strikes or the interruption of industry. No one will attempt to say that a sympathetic strike shall under no circumstances occur. Under certain conditions it may be not only justifiable but practical and successful, even if only as an emphatic protest against a great injustice or wrong; but generally and normally considered, such strikes cannot be of advantage.

One feature in connection with a system of industrial organization and its concomitant, the sympathetic strike, has been overlooked. By its methods any one of our international organizations could be financially drained and actually ruined in a very brief period in an effort to sustain the members involved; while, on the other hand, in a well-formulated trade union movement, a large number of men of different crafts, belonging to their own international trade unions, could be indefinitely sustained financially and victory achieved. At least the organizations could be maintained, not only to continue that battle, but to take up the cudgels in defense of their members elsewhere.

THE VALUE OF ECONOMIC ORGANIZATION: REPORT OF THE EXECUTIVE COUNCIL, AMERICAN FEDERATION OF LABOR PROCEEDINGS, 1914

The principle that has directed and controlled all policies of the A. F. of L. is that organization in industry is the key to the betterment of conditions for the workers. Organization for the purpose of making united effort to remedy wrongs that affect the work and the lives of all has been the instrumentality that has brought cheer and hope and betterment to the workers.

Economic organization gives power—power to protect the workers against industrial exploitation and injustice; power to secure for them opportunities for development; power to secure for them things that will make life sane, whole, and good; power to bring into their lives something of beauty and pleasure; power to secure political representation for their ideals and recognition of their demands in legislation. The influence of organization in industry and its infinite number of contacts with other organizations constitute an intricate force that is the most powerful single force in society. The power of Labor is commensurate with its unity, solidarity and federation.

Economic organization is that upon which we justly concentrate our thought and effort. When economic organization is achieved, every other good thing becomes possible for the workers. But because of the great power attaching to this agency, many other movements or forces seek to destroy or to use them. For this reason, the A. F. of L. early adopted the policy of avoiding entangling alliances. This policy has been consistently pursued during all these years. But with great success and increased growth come additional power. Many and tempting will be the avenues for activity and the associations open to the A. F. of L. Increasingly difficult will it be to distinguish the things which are most important

and vital for the continuous development of the Federation—the things which make for life rather than mere power. Ever must be held up the policy, the organization—federation, that is the thing.

POLITICAL NON-PARTISANSHIP: FROM AN A. F. OF L. PAMPHLET, FORTY YEARS OF ACTION

The partisanship of Labor is a partisanship of principle. The American Federation of Labor is not partisan to a political party, it is partisan to a principle, the principle of equal rights and human freedom. We, therefore, repeat: Stand faithfully by our friends and *elect* them. Oppose our enemies and *defeat* them; whether they be candidates for President, for Congress, or for other offices; whether Executive, Legislative, or Judicial.

The experiences and results attained through the non-partisan political policy of the American Federation of Labor cover a generation. They indicate that through its application the workers of America have secured a much larger measure of fundamental legislation, establishing their rights, safeguarding their interests, protecting their welfare and opening the doors of opportunity than have been secured by the workers of any other country. . . .

In these nearly forty years of actively taking part in the making of the economic and political history of this nation our Federation has witnessed the birth, the struggle for life, and the passing away of all sorts of political movements designed to save the republic from varying degrees of destruction; it has been coddled and mauled, petted and cajoled by the cohorts of particular brands of Liberty; it has been assailed by isms and ologies without number; it has been baited with sugared doses for economic chills and political fevers; it has heard the dirge and attended the last sad rites over many a promising political corpse. It has been courted by all the allurements of the partisan politician; all of the thralling visions of the emotional enthusiast have been pictured for its enticement; all the arts of the crafty self-seeker have been practiced to tempt it. But, despite all these, the American Federation of Labor has never been swerved from its non-partisan political course. . . .

Pope Leo XIII

Pope Leo XIII (1810–1903) became the supreme head of the Roman Catholic Church in 1878, at a time when the problems created for labor by the Industrial Revolution were attracting the attention of the church and the state, as well as of men like Marx and Engels. In 1891 Leo issued his encyclical, Rerum Novarum, written to relate Catholic principles to the political and social problems of his day. The relatively liberal position taken by Leo XIII on these matters earned for him the title of the "working-men's pope." In reading the following selections from this encyclical, note (1) the problem which Leo proposed to resolve, (2) the church's attitude toward private property, (3) the importance of private property to the family relationship, (4) the position taken on the issue of the class conflict and on the distribution of wealth, (5) the part the church played in remedying the problem, (6) the role the state should take in regulating economic problems, and (7) the authorities whom Leo cited.

From: RERUM NOVARUM

Once the passion for revolutionary change was aroused—a passion long disturbing governments—it was bound to follow sooner or later that eagerness for change would pass from the political sphere over into the related field of economics. In fact, new developments in industry, new techniques striking out on new paths, changed relations of employer and employee, abounding wealth among a very small number and destitution among the masses, increased self-reliance on the part of workers as well as a closer bond of union with one another, and, in addition to all this, a decline in morals have caused conflict to break forth.

The momentous nature of the questions involved in this conflict is evident from the fact that it keeps men's minds in anxious expectation, occupying the talents of the learned, the discussions of the wise and experienced, the assemblies of the people, the judgment of lawmakers, and the deliberations of rulers, so that now no topic more strongly holds men's interests.

Therefore, Venerable Brethren, with the cause of the Church and the common welfare before Us, We have thought it advisable, following Our custom on other occasions when We issued to you the Encyclicals On Political Power, On Human Liberty, On the Christian Constitution of States, and others of similar nature, which seemed opportune to refute erroneous opinions, that We ought to do the same now, and for the same reasons, On the Condition of Workers. We have on occasion touched more than once upon this subject. In this Encyclical, however, consciousness of Our Apostolic office admonishes Us to treat the entire question thoroughly, in order that the principles may stand out in clear light, and the conflict may thereby be brought to an end as required by truth and equity.

The problem is difficult to resolve and is not free from dangers. It is hard indeed to fix the boundaries of the rights and duties within which the rich and the proletariat—those who furnish material things and those who furnish work—ought to be restricted in relation to each other. The controversy is truly dangerous, for in various places it is being twisted by

Pope Leo XIII, *Rerum Novarum: Encyclical Letter on the Condition of Labor,* Washington, D. C., n.d., 5–7; 8–9; 10–15; 17–18; 21–27.

turbulent and crafty men to pervert judgment as to truth and seditiously to incite the masses.

In any event, We see clearly, and all are agreed that the poor must be speedily and fittingly cared for, since the great majority of them live undeservedly in miserable and wretched conditions.

After the old trade guilds had been destroyed in the last century, and no protection was substituted in their place, and when public institutions and legislation had cast off traditional religious teaching, it gradually came about that the present age handed over the workers, each alone and defenseless, to the inhumanity of employers and the unbridled greed of competitors. A devouring usury, although often condemned by the Church, but practiced nevertheless under another form by avaricious and grasping men, has increased the evil; and in addition the whole process of production as well as trade in every kind of goods has been brought almost entirely under the power of a few, so that a very few rich and exceedingly rich men have laid a yoke almost of slavery on the unnumbered masses of non-owning workers.

To cure this evil, the Socialists, exciting the envy of the poor toward the rich, contend that it is necessary to do away with private possession of goods and in its place to make the goods of individuals common to all, and that the men who preside over a municipality or who direct the entire State should act as administrators of these goods. They hold that, by such a transfer of private goods from private individuals to the community, they can cure the present evil through dividing wealth and benefits equally among the citizens.

But their program is so unsuited for terminating the conflict that it actually injures the workers themselves. Moreover, it is highly unjust, because it violates the rights of lawful owners, perverts the functions of the State, and throws governments into utter confusion.

Clearly the essential reason why those who engage in any gainful occupation undertake labor, and at the same time the end to which workers immediately look, is to procure property for themselves and to retain it by individual right as theirs and as their very own.

When the worker places his energy and his labor at the disposal of another, he does so for the purpose of getting the means necessary for livelihood. He seeks in return for the work done, accordingly, a true and full right not only to demand his wage but to dispose of it as he sees fit. Therefore, if he saves something by restricting expenditures and invests his savings in a piece of land in order to keep the fruit of his thrift more safe, a holding of this kind is certainly nothing else than his wage under a different form; and on this account land which the worker thus buys is necessarily under his full control as much as the wage which he earned by his labor. But, as is obvious, it is clearly in this that the ownership of movable and immovable goods consists. Therefore, inasmuch as the Socialists seek to transfer the goods of private persons to the community at large, they make the lot of all wage earners worse, because in abolishing the freedom to dispose of wages they take away from them by this very act the hope and the opportunity of increasing their property and of securing advantages for themselves.

But, what is of more vital concern, they propose a remedy openly in conflict with justice, inasmuch as nature confers on man the right to possess things privately as his own. . . .

The fact that God gave the whole human race the earth to use and enjoy cannot indeed in any manner serve as an objection against private possessions. For God is said to have given the earth to mankind in common, not because He intended indiscriminate ownership of it by all, but because He assigned no part to anyone in ownership, leaving the limits of private possessions to be fixed by the industry of men and the institutions of peoples. Yet, however the earth may be apportioned among private owners, it does not cease to serve the common interest of all, inasmuch as no living being is sustained except by what the fields bring forth. Those who lack resources supply labor, so that it can be truly affirmed that the entire scheme of securing a livelihood consists in the labor which a person expends either on his own land or in some working occupation, the compensation for which is drawn ultimately from no other source than from the varied products of the earth and is exchanged for them.

For this reason it also follows that private possessions are clearly in accord with nature. The earth indeed produces in great abundance the things to preserve and, especially, to perfect life, but of itself it could not produce them without human cultivation and care. Moreover, since man expends his mental energy and his bodily strength in procuring the goods of nature, by this very act he appropriates that part of physical nature to himself which he has cultivated. On it he leaves impressed, as it were, a kind of image of his person, so that it must be altogether just that he should possess that part as his very own and that no one in any way should be permitted to violate his right. . . .

It is a most sacred law of nature that the father of a family see that his offspring are provided with all the necessities of life, and nature even prompts him to desire to provide and to furnish his children, who, in fact reflect and in a sense continue his person, with the means of decently protecting themselves against harsh fortune in the uncertainties of life. He can do this surely in no other way than by owning fruitful goods to transmit by inheritance to his children. As already noted, the family like the State is by the same token a society in the strictest sense of the term, and it is governed by its own proper authority, namely, by that of the father. Wherefore, assuming, of course, that those limits be observed which are fixed by its immediate purpose, the family assuredly possesses rights, at least equal with those of civil society, in respect to choosing and employing the things necessary for its protection and its just liberty. We say "at least equal" because, inasmuch as domestic living together is prior both in thought and in fact to uniting into a polity, it follows that its rights and duties are also prior and more in conformity with nature. But if citizens, if families, after becoming participants in common life and society, were to experience injury in a commonwealth instead of help, impairment of their rights instead of protection, society would be something to be repudiated rather than to be sought for.

To desire, therefore, that the civil power should enter arbitrarily into the privacy of homes is a great and pernicious error. If a family perchance is in such extreme difficulty and is so completely without plans that it is entirely unable to help itself, it is right that the distress be remedied by public aid, for each individual family is a part of the community. Similarly, if anywhere there is a grave violation of mutual rights within the family walls, public authority shall restore to each his right: for this is not usurping the rights of citizens, but protecting and confirming them with just and due care. Those in charge of public affairs, however, must stop here: nature does not permit them to go beyond these limits. Paternal authority is such that it can be neither abolished nor absorbed by the State, because it has the same origin in common with that of man's own life. "Children are a part of their father," and, as it were, a kind of extension of the father's person; and, strictly speaking, not through themselves, but through the medium of the family society in which they are begotten, they enter into and participate in civil society. And for the very reason that children "are by nature part of their father . . . before they have the use of free will, they are kept under the care of their parents." Inasmuch as the Socialists, therefore, disregard care by parents and in its place introduce care by the State, they act *against natural justice* and dissolve the structure of the home.

And apart from the injustice involved, it is also only too evident what turmoil and disorder would obtain among all classes; and what a harsh and odious enslavement of citizens would result! The door would be open to mutual envy, detraction, and dissension. If incentives to ingenuity and skill in individual persons were to be abolished, the very fountains of wealth would necessarily dry up; and the equality conjured up by the Socialist imagination would, in reality, be nothing but uniform wretchedness and meanness for one and all, without distinction.

From all these considerations, it is perceived that the fundamental principle of Socialism which would make all possessions public property is to be utterly rejected because it injures the very ones whom it seeks to help, contravenes the natural rights of individual persons, and throws the functions of the State and public peace into confusion. Let it be regarded, therefore, as established that in seeking help for the masses this principle before all is to be considered as basic, namely, that private ownership must be preserved inviolate. . . .

It is a capital evil with respect to the question We are discussing to take for granted that the one class of society is of itself hostile to the other, as if nature had set rich and poor against each other to fight fiercely in implacable war. This is so abhorrent to reason and truth that the exact opposite is true; for just as in the human body the different members harmonize with one another, whence arises that disposition of parts and proportion in the human figure rightly called symmetry, so likewise nature has commanded in the case of the State that the two classes mentioned should agree harmoniously and should properly form equally balanced counterparts to each other. Each needs the other completely: neither capital can do without labor, nor labor without capital. Concord begets beauty and order in things. Conversely, from perpetual strife there must arise disorder accompanied by bestial cruelty. But for putting an end to conflict and for cutting away its very roots, there is wondrous and multiple power in Christian institutions.

And first and foremost, the entire body of religious teaching and practice, of which the Church is the interpreter and guardian, can pre-eminently bring together and unite the rich and the poor by recalling the two classes of society to their mutual duties, and in particular to those duties which derive from justice.

Among these duties the following concern the poor and the workers: To perform entirely and conscientiously whatever work has been voluntarily and equitably agreed upon; not in any way to injure the property or to harm the person of employers; in protecting their own interests, to refrain from violence and never to engage in rioting; not to associate with vicious men who craftily hold out exaggerated hopes and make huge promises, a course usually ending in vain regrets and in the destruction of wealth.

The following duties, on the other hand, concern rich men and employers: Workers are not to be treated as slaves; justice demands that the dignity of human personality be respected in them, ennobled as it has been through what we call the Christian character. If we hearken to natural reason and to Christian philosophy, gainful occupations are not a mark of shame to man, but rather of respect, as they provide him with an honorable means of supporting life. It is shameful and inhuman, however, to use men as things for gain and to put no more value on them than what they are worth in muscle and energy. Likewise it is enjoined that the religious interests and the spiritual well-being of the workers receive proper consideration. Wherefore, it is the duty of employers to see that the worker is free for adequate periods to attend to his religious obligations; not to expose anyone to corrupting influences or the enticements of sin, and in no way to alienate him from care for his family and the practice of thrift. Likewise, more work is not to be imposed than strength can endure, nor that kind of work which is unsuited to a worker's age or sex.

Among the most important duties of employers the principal one is to give every worker what is justly due him. Assuredly, to establish a rule of pay in accord with justice, many factors must be taken into account. But, in general, the rich and employers should remember that no laws, either human or divine, permit them for their own profit to oppress the needy and the wretched or to seek gain from another's want. To defraud anyone of the wage due him is a great crime that calls down avenging wrath from Heaven. "Behold, the wages of the laborers . . . which have been kept back by you unjustly, cry out: and their cry has entered into the ears of the Lord of Hosts." Finally, the rich must religiously avoid harming in any way the savings of the workers either by coercion, or by fraud, or by the arts of usury; and the more for this reason, that the workers are not sufficiently protected against injustices and violence, and their property, being so meagre, ought to be regarded as all the more sacred. Could not the observance alone of the foregoing laws remove the bitterness and the causes of conflict? . . .

Those who lack fortune's goods are taught by the Church that, before God as Judge, poverty is no disgrace, and that no one should be ashamed because he makes his living by toil. And Jesus Christ has confirmed this by fact and by deed, Who for the salvation of men, "being rich, became poor;" and although He was the Son of God and God Himself, yet He willed to seem and to be thought the son of a carpenter; nay, He even did not disdain to spend a great part of his life at the work of a carpenter. "Is not this the carpenter, the Son of Mary?" Those who contemplate this Divine example will more easily understand these truths: True dignity and excellence in men resides in moral living, that is, in virtue; virtue is the common inheritance of man, attainable equally by the humblest and the mightiest, by the rich and the poor; and the reward of eternal happiness will follow upon virtue and merit alone, regardless of the person in whom they may be found. Nay, rather the favor of God Himself seems to incline more toward the unfortunate as a class; for Jesus Christ calls the poor blessed, and He invites most lovingly all who are in labor or sorrow to come to Him for solace, embracing with special love the lowly and those harassed by injustice. At the realization of these things the proud spirit of the rich is easily brought down, and the downcast heart of the afflicted is lifted up; the former are moved toward kindness, the latter, toward reasonableness in their demands. Thus the distance between the classes which pride seeks is reduced, and it will easily be brought to pass that the two classes, with hands clasped in friendship, will be united in heart.

Yet, if they obey Christian teachings, not merely friendship but brotherly love also will bind them to each other. They will feel and understand that all men indeed have been created by God, their common Father; that all strive for the same object of good, which is God Himself, Who alone can communicate to both men and angels perfect and absolute happiness; that all equally have been redeemed by the grace of Jesus Christ and restored to the dignity of the sons of God, so that they are clearly united by the bonds of brotherhood not only with one another but also with Christ the Lord, "the firstborn among many brethren," and further, that the goods of nature and the gifts of divine grace belong in common and without distinction to all human kind, and that no one, unless he is unworthy, will be deprived of the inheritance of Heaven. "But if we are sons, we are also heirs: heirs indeed of God and joint heirs with Christ."

Such is the economy of duties and rights according to Christian philosophy. Would it not seem that all conflict would soon cease wherever this economy were to prevail in civil society?

Finally, the Church does not consider it enough to point out the way of finding the cure, but she administers the remedy herself. For she occupies herself fully in training and forming men according to discipline and doctrine; and through the agency of bishops and clergy, she causes the health-giving streams of this doctrine to be diffused as widely as possible. Furthermore, she strives to enter into men's minds and to bend their wills so that they may suffer themselves to be ruled and governed by the discipline of the divine precepts. And in this field, which is of first and greatest importance because in it the whole substance and matter of benefits consists, the Church indeed has a power that is especially unique. For the instruments which she uses to move souls were given her for this very purpose by Jesus Christ, and they have an efficacy implanted in them by God. Such instruments alone can properly penetrate the inner recesses of the heart and lead man to obedience to duty, to govern the activities of his self-seeking mind, to love God and his neighbors with a special and sovereign love, and to overcome courageously all things that impede the path of virtue. . . .

But it is now in order to inquire what portion of the remedy should be expected from the State. By State here We understand not the form of government which this or that people has, but rather that form which right reason in accordance with nature requires and the teachings of Divine wisdom approve, matters that We have explained specifically in Our Encyclical *On the Christian Constitution of States.*

Therefore those governing the State ought primarily to devote themselves to the service of individual groups and of the whole commonwealth, and through the entire scheme of laws and institutions to cause both public and individual well-being to develop spontaneously out of the very structure and administration of the State. For this is the duty of wise statesmanship and the essential office of those in charge of the State. Now, States are made prosperous especially by wholesome morality, properly ordered family life, protection of religion and justice, moderate imposition and equitable distribution of public burdens, progressive development of industry and trade, thriving agriculture, and by all other things of this nature, which the more actively they are promoted, the better and happier the life of the citizens is destined to be. Therefore, by virtue of these things, it is within the competence of the rulers of the State that, as they benefit other groups, they also improve in particular the condition of the workers. Furthermore, they do this with full right and without laying themselves open to any charge of unwarranted interference. For the State is bound by the very law of its office to serve the common interest. And the richer the benefits which come from this general providence on the part of the State, the less necessary it will be to experiment with other measures for the well-being of workers.

This ought to be considered, as it touches the question more deeply, namely, that the State has one basic purpose for existence, which embraces in common the highest and the lowest of its members. Non-owning workers are unquestionably citizens by nature in virtue of the same right as the rich, that is, true and vital parts whence, through the medium of families, the body of the State is constituted; and it hardly need be added that they are by far the greatest number in every urban area. Since it would be quite absurd to look out for one portion of the citizens and to neglect another, it follows that public authority ought to exercise due care in safeguarding the well-being and the interests of non-owning workers. Unless this is done, justice, which commands that everyone be given his own, will be violated. Wherefore St. Thomas says wisely: "Even as part and whole are in a certain way the same, so too that which pertains to the whole pertains in a certain way to the part also." Consequently, among the numerous and weighty duties of rulers who would serve their people well, this is first and foremost, namely, that they protect equitably each and every class of citizens, maintaining inviolate that justice especially which is called *distributive.*

Although all citizens, without exception, are obliged to contribute something to the sum-total common goods, some share of which naturally goes back to each individual, yet all can by no means contribute the same amount and in equal degree. Whatever the vicissitudes that occur in the forms of government, there will always be those differences in the condition of citizens without which society could neither exist nor be conceived. It is altogether necessary that there be some who dedicate themselves to the service of the State, who make laws, who dispense justice, and finally, by whose counsel and authority civil and military affairs are administered. These men, as is clear, play the chief role in the State, and among every people are to be regarded as occupying first place, because they work for the common good most directly and preeminently. On the other hand, those engaged in some calling benefit the State, but not in the same way as the men just mentioned, nor by performing the same duties; yet they, too, in a high degree, although less directly, serve the public weal. Assuredly, since social good must be of such a character that men through its acquisition are made better, it must necessarily be founded chiefly on virtue.

Nevertheless, an abundance of corporeal and external goods is likewise a characteristic of a well constituted State, "the use of which goods is necessary for the practice of virtue." To produce these goods the labor of the workers, whether they expend their skill and strength on farms or in factories, is most efficacious and necessary. Nay, in this respect, their energy and effectiveness are so important that it is incontestable that the wealth of nations originates from no other source than from the labor of workers. Equity therefore commands that public authority show proper concern for the worker so that from what he contributes to the common good he may receive what will enable him, housed, clothed, and secure, to live his life without hardship. Whence, it follows that all those measures ought to be favored which seem in any way capable of benefiting the condition of workers. Such solicitude is so far from injuring anyone, that it is destined rather to benefit all, because it is of absolute interest to the State that those citizens should not be miserable in every respect from whom such necessary goods proceed.

It is not right, as We have said, for either the citizen or the family to be absorbed by the State; it is proper that the individual and the family should be permitted to retain their freedom of action, so far as this is possible without jeopardizing the common good and without injuring anyone. Nevertheless, those who govern must see to it that they protect the community and its constituent parts: the community, because nature has entrusted its safeguarding to the sovereign power in the State to such an extent that the protection of the public welfare is not only the supreme law, but is the entire cause and reason for sovereignty; and the constituent parts, because philosophy and Christian faith agree that the administration of the State has from nature as its purpose, not the benefit of those to whom it has been entrusted, but the benefit of those who have been entrusted to it. And since the power of governing comes from God and is a participation, as it were, in His supreme sovereignty, it ought to be administered according to the example of the Divine power, which looks with paternal care to the welfare of individual creatures as well as to that of all creation. If, therefore, any injury has been done to or threatens either the common good or the interests of individual groups, which injury cannot in any other way be repaired or prevented, it is necessary for public authority to intervene.

It is vitally important to public as well as to private welfare that there be peace and good order; likewise, that the whole regime of family life be directed according to the ordinances of God and the principles of nature, that religion be observed and cultivated, that sound morals flourish in private and public life, that justice be kept sacred and that no one be wronged with impunity by another, and that strong citizens grow up, capable of supporting, and, if necessary, of protecting the State. Wherefore, if at any time disorder should threaten because of strikes or concerted stoppages of work, if the natural bonds of family life should be relaxed among the poor, if religion among the workers should be outraged by failure to provide sufficient opportunity for performing religious duties, if in factories danger should assail the integrity of morals through the mixing of the sexes or other pernicious incitements to sin, or if the employer class should oppress the working class with unjust burdens or should degrade them with conditions inimical to human personality or to human dignity, if health should be injured by immoderate work and such as is not suited to sex or age—in all these cases, the power and authority of the law, but of course within certain limits, manifestly ought to be employed. And these limits are determined by the same reason which demands the aid of the law, that is, the law ought not undertake more, nor it go farther, than the remedy of evils or the removal of danger requires.

Rights indeed, by whomsoever possessed, must be religiously protected; and public authority, in warding off injuries and punishing wrongs, ought to see to it that individuals may have and hold what belongs to them. In protecting the rights of private individuals, however, special consideration must be given to the weak and the poor. For the nation, as it were, of the rich, is guarded by its own defences and is in less need of governmental protection, whereas the suffering multitude, without the means to protect itself, relies especially on the protection of the State. Wherefore, since wage workers are numbered among the great mass of the needy, the State must include them under its special care and foresight.

But it will be well to touch here expressly on certain matters of special importance. The capital point is this, that private property ought to be safeguarded by the sovereign power of the State and through the bulwark of its laws. And especially, in view of such a great flaming up of passion at the present time, the masses ought to be kept within the bounds of their moral obligations. For while justice does not oppose our striving for better things, on the other hand, it does forbid any-one to take from another what is his and, in the name of a certain absurd equality, to seize forcibly the property of others; nor does the interest of the common good itself permit this. Certainly, the great majority of working people prefer to secure better conditions by honest toil, without doing wrong to anyone. Nevertheless, not a few individuals are found who, imbued with evil ideas and eager for revolution, use every means to stir up disorder and incite to violence. The authority of the State, therefore, should intervene and, by put-ting restraint upon such disturbers, protect the morals of workers from their corrupting arts and lawful owners from the danger of spolia-tion.

Labor which is too long and too hard and the belief that pay is inadequate not infre-quently give workers cause to strike and be-come voluntarily idle. This evil, which is fre-quent and serious, ought to be remedied by public authority, because such interruption of work inflicts damage not only upon employers and upon the workers themselves, but also injures trade and commerce and the general interests of the State; and, since it is usually not far removed from violence and rioting, it very frequently jeopardizes public peace. In this matter it is more effective and salutary that the authority of the law anticipate and completely prevent the evil from breaking out by removing early the causes from which it would seem that conflict between employers and workers is bound to arise.

And in like manner, in the case of the worker, there are many things which the power of the State should protect; and, first of all, the goods of his soul. For however good and desirable mortal life be, yet it is not the ulti-mate goal for which we are born, but a road

only and a means for perfecting, through knowledge of truth and love of good, the life of the soul. The soul bears the express image and likeness of God, and there resides in it that sovereignty through the medium of which man has been bidden to rule all created na-ture below him and to make all lands and all seas serve his interests. "Fill the earth and subdue it, and rule over the fishes of the sea and the fowls of the air and all living creatures that move upon the earth." In this respect all men are equal, and there is no difference be-tween rich and poor, between masters and servants, between rulers and subjects: "For there is the same Lord of all." No one may with impunity outrage the dignity of man, which God Himself treats with great reverence, nor impede his course to that level of perfec-tion which accords with eternal life in heaven. Nay, more, in this connection a man cannot even by his own free choice allow himself to be treated in a way inconsistent with his na-ture, and suffer his soul to be enslaved; for there is no question here of rights belonging to man, but of duties owed to God, which are to be religiously observed.

Hence follows necessary cessation from toil and work on Sundays and Holy Days of Ob-ligation. Let no one, however, understand this in the sense of greater indulgence of idle lei-sure, and much less in the sense of that kind of cessation from work, such as many desire, which encourages vice and promotes wasteful spending of money, but solely in the sense of a repose from labor made sacred by religion. Rest combined with religion calls man away from toil and the business of daily life to admonish him to ponder on heavenly goods and to pay his just and due homage to the Eternal Deity. This is especially the nature, and this the cause, of the rest to be taken on Sundays and Holy Days of Obligation, and God has sanctioned the same in the Old Testament by a special law: "Remember thou keep holy the Sabbath Day," and He Himself taught it by His own action: namely the mystical rest taken immediately after He had created man: "He rested on the seventh day from all His work which He had done."

Now as concerns the protection of corporeal and physical goods, the oppressed workers, above all, ought to be liberated from the savagery of greedy men, who inordinately use human beings as things of gain. Assuredly, neither justice nor humanity can countenance the exaction of so much work that the spirit is dulled from excessive toil and that along with it the body sinks crushed from exhaustion. The working energy of a man, like his entire nature, is circumscribed by definite limits beyond which it cannot go. It is developed indeed by exercise and use, but only on condition that a man cease from work at regular intervals and rest. With respect to daily work, therefore, care ought to be taken not to extend it beyond the hours that human strength warrants. The length of rest intervals ought to be decided on the basis of the varying nature of the work, of the circumstances of time and place, and of the physical condition of the workers themselves. Since the labor of those who quarry stone from the earth, or who mine iron, copper, and other underground materials, is much more severe and harmful to health, the working period for such men ought to be correspondingly shortened. The seasons of the year also must be taken into account; for often a given kind of work is easy to endure in one season but cannot be endured at all in another, or not without the greatest difficulty.

Finally, it is not right to demand of a woman or a child what a strong adult man is capable of doing or would be willing to do. Nay, as regards children, special care ought to be taken that the factory does not get hold of them before age has sufficiently matured their physical, intellectual, and moral powers. For budding strength in childhood, like greening verdure in spring, is crushed by premature harsh treatment; and under such circumstances all education of the child must needs be foregone. Certain occupations likewise are less fitted for women, who are intended by nature for work of the home—work indeed which especially protects modesty in women and accords by nature with the education of children and the well-being of the family. Let it be the rule everywhere that workers be given as much leisure as will compensate for the energy consumed by toil, for rest from work is necessary to restore strength consumed by use. In every obligation which is mutually contracted between employers and workers, this condition, either written or tacit, is always present, that both kinds of rest be provided for; nor would it be equitable to make an agreement otherwise, because no one has the right to demand of, or to make an agreement with anyone to neglect those duties which bind a man to God or to himself. . . .

Otto von Bismarck

While Marx and Engels were still prediciting the withering away of the state, and while the Fabians were only beginning to propagandize for democratic socialism through the state, Prince Otto von Bismarck (1815–1898), chancellor of Germany, was already using the state to improve the condition of the German working classes. As the leading political figure in the new German Empire, he sponsored various acts designed, not only to strengthen his country socially and economically, but also to halt the growth of Marxian socialism within her frontiers. Prussia, the largest state in the Empire, had a long tradition of royal paternalism, and it was only natural, therefore, that Germany should take the lead in the movement away from the laissez-faire policy of the mid-nineteenth century, and toward the goal of state socialism. The following excerpts are from various speeches made by Bismarck on the subject of state reform and state socialism. In reading them note

(1) Bismarck's attitude toward those groups who opposed state intervention, (2) his feeling for the poor, (3) his position on capital and capitalism, (4) the distinction he made between urban and rural landowners, (5) the program he advocated for social security, (6) the goal he hoped to achieve by such a program, (7) the responsibility of the state to provide work for its citizens, and (8) his reaction to the term "socialism."

From: THE SPEECHES OF CHANCELLOR BISMARCK

Herr Richter has called attention to the responsibility of the State for what it does. But it is my opinion that the State can also be responsible for what it does not do. I do not think that doctrines like those of *"Laissez-faire, laissez-aller,"* "Pure Manchesterdom in politics," *"Jeder sehe, wie er's treibe, Jeder sehe, wo er bleibe,"* "He who is not strong enough to stand must be knocked down, and trodden to the ground," "To him that hath shall be given, and from him that hath not shall be taken away even that which he hath" —that doctrines like these should be applied in the State, and especially in a monarchically, paternally governed State. On the other hand, I believe that those who profess horror at the intervention of the State for the protection of the weak lay themselves open to the suspicion that they are desirous of using their strength —be it that of capital, that of rhetoric, or whatever it be—for the benefit of a section, for the oppression of the rest, for the introduction of party domination, and that they will be chagrined as soon as this design is disturbed by any action of the government.

I ask you what right had I to close the way to the throne against these people? The kings of Prussia have never been by preference kings of the rich. Frederick the Great said when Crown Prince: *"Quand je serai roi, je serai un vrai roi des gueux."* He undertook to be the protector of the poor, and this principle has been followed by our later kings. At their throne suffering has always found a refuge and a hearing. . . .

Our kings have secured the emancipation of the serfs, they have created a thriving peas-antry, and they may possibly be successful— the earnest endeavour exists, at any rate—in improving the condition of the working classes somewhat. To have refused access to the throne to the complaints of these operatives would not have been the right course to pursue, and it was, moreover, not my business to do it. The question would afterwards have been asked: "How rich must a deputation be in order to insure its reception by the King?". . . .

I am not antagonistic to the rightful claims of capital; I am far from wanting to flourish a hostile flag; but I am of opinion that the masses, too, have rights which should be considered.

I wish we could immediately create a few hundred millionaires. They would expend their money in the country, and this expenditure would act fruitfully on labour all round. They could not eat their money themselves; they would have to spend the interest on it. Be glad, then, when people become rich with us. The community at large, and not only the tax authority, is sure to benefit.

The large land-owner who lives in the country is not the worst evil; the worst is the large land-owner who lives in the town, be it Paris, Rome, or Berlin, and who only requires money from his estates and agents, who does not represent his estates in the Reichstag or Landtag, and does not even know how it fares with them. Therein lies the evil of large estates. Large estates whose owners live in the country are under certain circumstances a great blessing, and very useful. . . . I regard the large land-owners who are really farmers, and

William H. Dawson, *Bismarck and State Socialism: An Exposition of the Social and Economic Legislation of Germany Since 1870*, London, 1891, 29; 31–35; 53–64; 118–119.

buy land from a predilection for this industry, as a blessing for our country, and especially for the provinces where I live. And if you succeed in destroying this race, you would see the result in the palsying of our entire economic and political life. . . . But so long as God is still minded to preserve the German Empire and the Kingdom of Prussia, this war of yours against landed proprietorship will not succeed, however many allies you may obtain.

Give the working-man the right to work as long as he is healthy; assure him care when he is sick; assure him maintenance when he is old. If you do that, and do not fear the sacrifice, or cry out at State Socialism directly the words "provision for old age" are uttered,—if the State will show a little more Christian solicitude for the working-man, then I believe that the gentlemen of the Wyden [Social-Democratic] programme will sound their bird-call in vain, and that the thronging to them will cease as soon as working-men see that the Government and legislative bodies are earnestly concerned for their welfare.

Yes, I acknowledge unconditionally a right to work, and I will stand up for it as long as I am in this place. But here I do not stand upon the ground of Socialism, which is said to have only begun with the Bismarck Ministry, but on that of the Prussian common law. . . . Was not the right to work openly proclaimed at the time of the publication of the common law? Is it not established in all our social arrangements that the man who comes before his fellow-citizens and says, "I am healthy, I desire to work, but can find no work," is entitled to say also, "Give me work," and that the State is bound to give him work?

I will further every endeavour which positively aims at improving the condition of the working classes. . . . As soon as a positive proposal came from the Socialists for fashioning the future in a sensible way, in order that the lot of the working-man might be improved, I would not at any rate refuse to examine it favourably, and I would not even shrink from the idea of State help for the people who would help themselves.

The establishment of the freedom of the peasantry was Socialistic; Socialistic, too, is every expropriation in favour of railways; Socialistic to the utmost extent is the aggregation of estates—the law exists in many provinces—taking from one and giving to another, simply because this other can cultivate the land more conveniently; Socialistic is expropriation under the Water Legislation, on account of irrigation, etc., where a man's land is taken away from him because another can farm it better; Socialistic is our entire poor relief, compulsory school attendance, compulsory construction of roads, so that I am bound to maintain a road upon my lands for travellers. That is all Socialistic, and I could extend the register further; but if you believe that you can frighten any one or call up spectres with the word "Socialism," you take a standpoint which I abandoned long ago, and the abandonment of which is absolutely necessary for our entire imperial legislation.

The whole matter centres in the question, Is it the duty of the State, or is it not, to provide for its helpless citizens? I maintain that it is its duty, that it is the duty not only of the "*Christian* State". . . but of every State. It would be foolish for a corporation to undertake matters which the individual can attend to alone. . . . But there are purposes which only the State as a whole can fulfil. To these belong national defence, the general system of communications, and . . . the help of the necessitous and the removal of those just complaints which provide Social Democracy with really effective material for agitation. This is a duty of the State, a duty which the State cannot permanently disregard. . . .

If an establishment employing twenty thousand or more workpeople were to be ruined . . . we could not allow these men to hunger. We should have to resort to real State Socialism and find work for them, and this is what we do in every case of distress. If the objection were right that we should shun State Socialism as we would an infectious disease, how do we come to organise works . . . which we would not undertake if the labourers had employment and wages? In such cases we build railways whose profitableness is questionable; we carry out improvements which otherwise would be left to private initiative. If that is Communism, I have no objection at all to it. . . .

Walt Whitman

W alt Whitman (1819–1892), American poet, lived
most of his life in and near his beloved Manhattan.
An office boy, printer's devil, country school teacher, editor
of newspapers, war nurse, traveler, and observer of and
prophet for American democracy, Whitman celebrated in
his writings the common man and everyday things. He
sang a mystic internationalism based upon universal brotherhood and at the same time expressed a fervent love for
the whole of America. He believed his native land to be
the natural home of the ordinary man and looked for the
emergence of a new race fashioned from the many people
seeking asylum upon the American continent. In reading
the selections from Song of Myself note (1) Whitman's
emphasis upon the universal character of all life and spirit,
(2) his expression of the brotherhood of all men, (3) his
identification of himself with individual men, women, and
children as well as with all mankind, and (4) the freedom
from conventionality in the subject matter as well as the
form of his poetry.

From: SONG OF MYSELF

1

I celebrate myself, and sing myself,
And what I assume you shall assume,
For every atom belonging to me as good belongs to you.

I loafe and invite my soul,
I lean and loafe at my ease observing a spear of summer grass.

My tongue, every atom of my blood, form'd from this soil, this air,
Born here of parents born here from parents the same, and their parents the same,
I, now thirty-seven years old in perfect health begin,
Hoping to cease not till death.

Creeds and schools in abeyance,
Retiring back a while sufficed at what they are, but never forgotten,
I harbor for good or bad, I permit to speak at every hazard,
Nature without check with original energy.

. . . .

3

I have heard what the talkers were talking, the talk of the beginning and the end,
But I do not talk of the beginning or the end.

Walt Whitman, *Leaves of Grass*, Philadelphia, 1883, 29–33; 34–43; 48–50; 55–61.

There was never any more inception than there is now,
Nor any more youth or age than there is now,
And will never be any more perfection than there is now,
Nor any more heaven or hell than there is now.

Urge and urge and urge,
Always the procreant urge of the world.
Out of the dimness opposite equals advance, always substance and increase, always sex,
Always a knit of identity, always distinction, always a breed of life.

To elaborate is no avail, learn'd and unlearn'd feel that it is so.
Sure as the most certain sure, plumb in the uprights, well entretied, braced in the beams,
Stout as a horse, affectionate, haughty, electrical,
I and this mystery here we stand.

Clear and sweet is my soul, and clear and sweet is all that is not my soul.

Lack one lacks both, and the unseen is proved by the seen,
Till that becomes unseen and receives proof in its turn.

Showing the best and dividing it from the worst age vexes age,
Knowing the perfect fitness and equanimity of things, while they discuss I am silent, and go
     bathe and admire myself.

Welcome is every organ and attribute of me, and of any man hearty and clean,
Not an inch nor a particle of an inch is vile, and none shall be less familiar than the rest.

I am satisfied—I see, dance, laugh, sing;
As the hugging and loving bed-fellow sleeps at my side through the night, and withdraws at
     the peep of the day with stealthy tread,
Leaving me baskets cover'd with white towels swelling the house with their plenty.
Shall I postpone my acceptation and realization and scream at my eyes,
That they turn from gazing after and down the road,
And forthwith cipher and show me to a cent,
Exactly the value of one and exactly the value of two, and which is ahead?

· · · ·

5

I believe in you my soul, the other I am must not abase itself to you,
And you must not be abased to the other.

Loafe with me on the grass, loose the stop from your throat,
Not words, not music or rhyme I want, not custom or lecture, not even the best,
Only the lull I like, the hum of your valvèd voice.

I mind how once we lay such a transparent summer morning,
How you settled your head athwart my hips and gently turn'd over upon me,
And parted the shirt from my bosom-bone, and plunged your tongue to my bare-stript heart,
And reach'd till you felt my beard, and reach'd till you held my feet.

Swiftly arose and spread around me the peace and knowledge that pass all the argument of
    the earth,
And I know that the hand of God is the promise of my own,
And I know that the spirit of God is the brother of my own,
And that all the men ever born are also my brothers, and the women my sisters and lovers,
And that a kelson of the creation is love,
And limitless are leaves stiff or drooping in the fields,
And brown ants in the little wells beneath them,
And mossy scabs of the worm fence, heap'd stones, elder, mullein and poke-weed.

. . . .

7

Has any one supposed it lucky to be born?
I hasten to inform him or her it is just as lucky to die, and I know it.

I pass death with the dying and birth with the new-wash'd babe, and am not contain'd between
    my hat and boots,
And peruse manifold objects, no two alike and every one good,
The earth good and the stars good, and their adjuncts all good.

I am not an earth nor an adjunct of an earth,
I am the mate and companion of people, all just as immortal and fathomless as myself,
(They do not know how immortal, but I know.)

Every kind for itself and its own, for me mine male and female,
For me those that have been boys and that love women,
For me the man that is proud and feels how it stings to be slighted,
For me the sweet-heart and the old maid, for me mothers and mothers of mothers,
For me lips that have smiled, eyes that have shed tears,
For me children and the begetters of children.
Undrape! you are not guilty to me, nor stale nor discarded,
I see through the broadcloth and gingham whether or no,
And am around, tenacious, acquisitive, tireless, and cannot be shaken away.

8

The little one sleeps in its cradle,
I lift the gauze and look a long time, and silently brush away flies with my hand.
The youngster and the red-faced girl turn aside up the bushy hill,
I peeringly view them from the top.
The suicide sprawls on the bloody floor of the bedroom,
I witness the corpse with its dabbled hair, I note where the pistol has fallen.

The blab of the pave, tires of carts, sluff of boot-soles, talk of the promenaders,
The heavy omnibus, the driver with his interrogating thumb, the clank of the shod horses on
    the granite floor,
The snow-sleighs, clinking, shouted jokes, pelts of snow-balls,
The hurrahs for popular favorites, the fury of rous'd mobs,

The flap of the curtain'd litter, a sick man inside borne to the hospital,
The meeting of enemies, the sudden oath, the blows and fall,
The excited crowd, the policeman with his star quickly working his passage to the centre of the crowd,
The impassive stones that receive and return so many echoes,
What groans of over-fed or half-starv'd who fall sunstruck or in fits,
What exclamations of women taken suddenly who hurry home and give birth to babes,
What living and buried speech is always vibrating here, what howls restrain'd by decorum,
Arrests of criminals, slights, adulterous offers made, acceptances, rejections with convex lips,
I mind them or the show or resonance of them—I come and I depart.

9

The big doors of the country barn stand open and ready,
The dried grass of the harvest-time loads the slow-drawn wagon,
The clear light plays on the brown gray and green intertinged,
The armfuls are pack'd to the sagging mow.

I am there, I help, I came stretch'd atop of the load,
I felt its soft jolts, one leg reclined on the other,
I jump from the cross-beams and seize the clover and timothy,
And roll head over heels and tangle my hair full of wisps.

10

Alone far in the wilds and mountains I hunt,
Wandering amazed at my own lightness and glee,
In the late afternoon choosing a safe spot to pass the night,
Kindling a fire and broiling the fresh-kill'd game,
Falling asleep on the gather'd leaves with my dog and gun by my side.

The Yankee clipper is under her sky-sails, she cuts the sparkle and scud,
My eyes settle the land, I bend at her prow or shout joyously from the deck.

The boatmen and clam-diggers arose early and stopt for me,
I tuck'd my trowser-ends in my boots and went and had a good time;
You should have been with us that day round the chowder-kettle.

I saw the marriage of the trapper in the open air in the far west, the bride was a red girl,
Her father and his friends sat near cross-legged and dumbly smoking, they had moccasins to their feet and large thick blankets hanging from their shoulders,
On a bank lounged the trapper, he was drest mostly in skins, his luxuriant beard and curls protected his neck, he held his bride by the hand,
She had long eyelashes, her head was bare, her coarse straight locks descended upon her voluptuous limbs and reach'd to her feet.
The runaway slave came to my house and stopt outside,
I heard his motions crackling the twigs of the woodpile,
Through the swung half-door of the kitchen I saw him limpsy and weak,
And went where he sat on a log and led him in and assured him,

And brought water and fill'd a tub for his sweated body and bruis'd feet,
And gave him a room that enter'd from my own, and gave him some coarse clean clothes,
And remember perfectly well his revolving eyes and his awkwardness,
And remember putting plasters on the galls of his neck and ankles;
He staid with me a week before he was recuperated and pass'd north,
I had him sit next me at table, my fire-lock lean'd in the corner.

11

Twenty-eight young men bathe by the shore,
Twenty-eight young men and all so friendly;
Twenty-eight years of womanly life and all so lonesome.

She owns the fine house by the rise of the bank,
She hides handsome and richly drest aft the blinds of the window.

Which of the young men does she like the best?
Ah the homeliest of them is beautiful to her.

Where are you off to, lady? for I see you,
You splash in the water there, yet stay stock still in your room.

Dancing and laughing along the beach came the twenty-ninth bather,
The rest did not see her, but she saw them and loved them.
The beards of the young men glisten'd with wet, it ran from their long hair,
Little streams pass'd all over their bodies.

An unseen hand also pass'd over their bodies.
It descended tremblingly from their temples and ribs.

The young men float on their backs, their white bellies bulge to the sun, they do not ask who
    seizes fast to them,
They do not know who puffs and declines with pendant and bending arch,
They do not think whom they souse with spray.

12

The butcher-boy puts off his killing-clothes, or sharpens his knife at the stall in the market,
I loiter enjoying his repartee and his shuffle and break-down.

Blacksmiths with grimed and hairy chests environ the anvil,
Each has his main-sledge, they are all out, there is a great heat in the fire.

From the cinder-strew'd threshold I follow their movements,
The lithe sheer of their waists plays even with their massive arms,
Overhand the hammers swing, overhand so slow, overhand so sure,
They do not hasten, each man hits in his place.

13

The negro holds firmly the reins of his four horses, the block swags underneath on its tied-over chain,
The negro that drives the long dray of the stone-yard, steady and tall he stands pois'd on one leg on the string-piece,
His blue shirt exposes his ample neck and breast and loosens over his hip-band,
His glance is calm and commanding, he tosses the slouch of his hat away from his forehead,
The sun falls on his crispy hair and mustache, falls on the black of his polish'd and perfect limbs.

I behold the picturesque giant and love him, and I do not stop there,
I go with the team also.

In me the caresser of life wherever moving, backward as well as forward sluing,
To niches aside and junior bending, not a person or object missing,
Absorbing all to myself and for this song.

Oxen that rattle the yoke and chain or halt in the leafy shade, what is that you express in your eyes?
It seems to me more than all the print I have read in my life.

My tread scares the wood-drake and wood-duck on my distant and day-long ramble,
They rise together, they slowly circle around.

I believe in those wing'd purposes,
And acknowledge red, yellow, white, playing within me,
And consider green and violet and the tufted crown intentional,
And do not call the tortoise unworthy because she is not something else,
And the jay in the woods never studied the gamut, yet trills pretty well to me,
And the look of the bay mare shames silliness out of me.

14

The wild gander leads his flock through the cool night,
Ya-honk he says, and sounds it down to me like an invitation,
The pert may suppose it meaningless, but I listening close,
Find its purpose and place up there toward the wintry sky.

The sharp-hoof'd moose of the north, the cat on the house-sill, the chickadee, the prairie-dog,
The litter of the grunting sow as they tug at her teats,
The brood of the turkey-hen and she with her half-spread wings,
I see in them and myself the same old law.

The press of my foot to the earth springs a hundred affections,
They scorn the best I can do to relate them.

I am enamour'd of growing out-doors,
Of men that live among cattle or taste of the ocean or woods,
Of the builders and steerers of ships and the wielders of axes and mauls, and the drivers of horses,
I can eat and sleep with them week in and week out.

What is commonest, cheapest, nearest, easiest, is Me,
Me going in for my chances, spending for vast returns,
Adorning myself to bestow myself on the first that will take me,
Not asking the sky to come down to my good will,
Scattering it freely forever.

15

The pure contralto sings in the organ loft,
The carpenter dresses his plank, the tongue of his foreplane whistles its wild ascending lisp,
The married and unmarried children ride home to their Thanksgiving dinner,
The pilot seizes the king-pin, he heaves down with a strong arm,
The mate stands braced in the whale-boat, lance and harpoon are ready,
The duck-shooter walks by silent and cautious stretches,
The deacons are ordain'd with cross'd hands at the altar,
The spinning-girl retreats and advances to the hum of the big wheel,
The farmer stops by the bars as he walks on a First-day loafe and looks at the oats and rye,
The lunatic is carried at last to the asylum a confirm'd case,
(He will never sleep any more as he did in the cot in his mother's bed-room;)
The jour printer with gray head and gaunt jaws works at his case,
He turns his quid of tobacco while his eyes blurr with the manuscript;
The malform'd limbs are tied to the surgeon's table,
What is removed drops horribly in a pail;
The quadroon girl is sold at the auction-stand, the drunkard nods by the bar-room stove,
The machinist rolls up his sleeves, the policeman travels his beat, the gate-keeper marks who pass,
The young fellow drives the express-wagon, (I love him, though I do not know him;)
The half-breed straps on his light boots to compete in the race,
The western turkey-shooting draws old and young, some lean on their rifles, some sit on logs,
Out from the crowd steps the marksman, takes his position, levels his piece;
The groups of newly-come immigrants cover the wharf or levee,
As the woolly-pates hoe in the sugar-field, the overseer views them from his saddle,
The bugle calls in the ball-room, the gentlemen run for their partners, the dancers bow to each other,
The youth lies awake in the cedar-roof'd garret and harks to the musical rain,
The Wolverine sets traps on the creek that helps fill the Huron,
The squaw wrapt in her yellow-hemm'd cloth is offering moccasins and bead-bags for sale,
The connoisseur peers along the exhibition-gallery with half-shut eyes bent sideways,
As the deck-hands make fast the steamboat the plank is thrown for the shore-going passengers,
The young sister holds out the skein while the elder sister winds it off in a ball, and stops now and then for the knots,
The one-year wife is recovering and happy having a week ago borne her first child,
The clean-hair'd Yankee girl works with her sewing-machine or in the factory or mill,
The paving-man leans on his two-handed rammer, the reporter's lead flies swiftly over the note-book, the sign-painter is lettering with blue and gold,
The canal boy trots on the tow-path, the bookkeeper counts at his desk, the shoemaker waxes his thread,
The conductor beats time for the band and all the performers follow him,
The child is baptized, the convert is making his first professions,
The regatta is spread on the bay, the race is begun, (how the white sails sparkle!)
The drover watching his drove sings out to them that would stray,

The pedler sweats with his pack on his back, (the purchaser higgling about the odd cent;)
The bride unrumples her white dress, the minute-hand of the clock moves slowly,
The opium-eater reclines with rigid head and just-open'd lips,
The prostitute draggles her shawl, her bonnet bobs on her tipsy and pimpled neck,
The crowd laugh at her blackguard oaths, the men jeer and wink to each other,
(Miserable! I do not laugh at your oaths nor jeer you;)
The President holding a cabinet council is surrounded by the great Secretaries,
On the piazza walk three matrons stately and friendly with twined arms,
The crew of the fish-smack pack repeated layers of halibut in the hold,
The Missourian crosses the plains toting his wares and his cattle,
As the fare-collector goes through the train he gives notice by the jingling of loose change,
The floor-men are laying the floor, the tinners are tinning the roof, the masons are calling for
    mortar,
In single file each shouldering his hod pass onward the laborers;
Seasons pursuing each other the indescribable crowd is gather'd, it is the fourth of Seventh-
    month, (what salutes of cannon and small arms!)
Seasons pursuing each other the plougher ploughs, the mower mows, and the winter-grain falls
    in the ground;
Off on the lakes the pike-fisher watches and waits by the hole in the frozen surface,
The stumps stand thick round the clearing, the squatter strikes deep with his axe,
Flatboatmen make fast towards dusk near the cotton-wood or pecan-trees,
Coon-seekers go through the regions of the Red river or through those drain'd by the Tennessee,
    or through those of the Arkansas,
Torches shine in the dark that hangs on the Chattahooche or Altamahaw,
Patriarchs sit at supper with sons and grandsons and great-grandsons around them,
In walls of adobie, in canvas tents, rest hunters and trappers after their day's sport,
The city sleeps and the country sleeps,
The living sleep for their time, the dead sleep for their time,
The old husband sleeps by his wife and the young husband sleeps by his wife;
And these tend inward to me, and I tend outward to them,
And such as it is to be of these more or less I am,
And of these one and all I weave the song of myself.

16

I am of old and young, of the foolish as much as the wise,
Regardless of others, ever regardful of others,
Maternal as well as paternal, a child as well as a man,
Stuff'd with the stuff that is coarse and stuff'd with the stuff that is fine,
One of the Nation of many nations, the smallest the same and the largest the same,
A Southerner soon as a Northerner, a planter nonchalant and hospitable down by the Oconee I
    live,
A Yankee bound my own way ready for trade, my joints the limberest joints on earth and the
    sternest joints on earth,
A Kentuckian walking the vale of the Elkhorn in my deer-skin leggings, a Louisianian or
    Georgian,
A boatman over lakes or bays or along coasts, a Hoosier, Badger, Buckeye;
At home on Kanadian snow-shoes or up in the bush, or with fishermen off Newfoundland,
At home in the fleet of ice-boats, sailing with the rest and tacking,
At home on the hills of Vermont or in the woods of Maine, or the Texan ranch,

Comrade of Californians, comrade of free North Westerners, (loving their big proportions,)
Comrade of raftsmen and coalmen, comrade of all who shake hands and welcome to drink and
    meat,
A learner with the simplest, a teacher of the thoughtfullest,
A novice beginning yet experient of myriads of seasons,
Of every hue and caste am I, of every rank and religion,
A farmer, mechanic, artist, gentleman, sailor, quaker,
Prisoner, fancy-man, rowdy, lawyer, physician, priest.

I resist any thing better than my own diversity,
Breathe the air but leave plenty after me,
And am not stuck up, and am in my place.

(The moth and the fish-eggs are in their place,
The bright suns I see and the dark suns I cannot see are in their place,
The palpable is in its place and the impalpable is in its place.)

17

These are really the thoughts of all men in all ages and lands, they are not original with me,
If they are not yours as much as mine they are nothing, or next to nothing,
If they are not the riddle and the untying of the riddle they are nothing,
If they are not just as close as they are distant they are nothing.

This is the grass that grows wherever the land is and the water is,
This the common air that bathes the globe.

. . . .

24

Walt Whitman, a kosmos, of Manhattan the son,
Turbulent, fleshy, sensual, eating, drinking and breeding,
No sentimentalist, no stander above men and women or apart from them,
No more modest than immodest.

Unscrew the locks from the doors!
Unscrew the doors themselves from their jambs!

Whoever degrades another degrades me,
And whatever is done or said returns at last to me.

Through me the afflatus surging and surging, through me the current and index.

I speak the pass-word primeval, I give the sign of democracy,
By God! I will accept nothing which all cannot have their counterpart of on the same terms.

Through me many long dumb voices,
Voices of the interminable generations of prisoners and slaves,

Voices of the diseas'd and despairing and of thieves and dwarfs,
Voices of cycles of preparation and accretion,
And of the threads that connect the stars, and of wombs and of the father-stuff,

And of the rights of them the others are down upon,
Of the deform'd, trivial, flat, foolish, despised,
Fog in the air, beetles rolling balls of dung.

Through me forbidden voices,
Voices of sexes and lusts, voices veil'd and I remove the veil,
Voices indecent by me clarified and transfigur'd.
I do not press my fingers across my mouth,
I keep as delicate around the bowels as around the head and heart,
Copulation is no more rank to me than death is.

I believe in the flesh and the appetites,
Seeing, hearing, feeling, are miracles, and each part and tag of me is a miracle.
Divine am I inside and out, and I make holy whatever I touch or am touch'd from.
The scent of these arm-pits aroma finer than prayer,
This head more than churches, bibles, and all the creeds.

If I worship one thing more than another it shall be the spread of my own body, or any part of it,
Translucent mould of me it shall be you!
Shaded ledges and rests it shall be you!
Firm masculine colter it shall be you!
Whatever goes to the tilth of me it shall be you!
You my rich blood! your milky stream pale strippings of my life!
Breast that presses against other breasts it shall be you!
My brain it shall be your occult convolutions!
Root of wash'd sweet flag! timorous pond-snipe! nest of guarded duplicate eggs! it shall be you!
Mix'd tussled hay of head, beard, brawn, it shall be you!
Trickling sap of maple, fibre of manly wheat, it shall be you!
Sun so generous it shall be you!
Vapors lighting and shading my face it shall be you!
You sweaty brooks and dews it shall be you!
Winds whose soft-tickling genitals rub against me it shall be you!
Broad muscular fields, branches of live oak, loving lounger in my winding paths, it shall be you!
Hands I have taken, face I have kiss'd, mortal I have ever touch'd, it shall be you.

I dote on myself, there is that lot of me and all so luscious,
Each moment and whatever happens thrills me with joy,
I cannot tell how my ankles bend, nor whence the cause of my faintest wish,
Nor the cause of the friendship I emit, nor the cause of the friendship I take again.

That I walk up my stoop, I pause to consider if it really be,
A morning-glory at my window satisfies me more than the metaphysics of books.

To behold the day-break!
The little light fades the immense and diaphanous shadows,
The air tastes good to my palate.
Hefts of the moving world at innocent gambols silently rising, freshly exuding,
Scooting obliquely high and low.

Something I cannot see puts upward libidinous prongs,
Seas of bright juice suffuse heaven.
The earth by the sky staid with, the daily close of their junction,
The heav'd challenge from the east that moment over my head,
The mocking taunt, See then whether you shall be master!

. . . .

33

Space and Time! now I see it is true, what I guess'd at,
What I guess'd when I loaf'd on the grass,
What I guess'd while I lay alone in my bed,
And again as I walk'd the beach under the paling stars of the morning.
My ties and ballasts leave me, my elbows rest in sea-gaps,
I skirt sierras, my palms cover continents,
I am afoot with my vision.

. . . .

I ascend to the foretruck,
I take my place late at night in the crow's-nest,
We sail the arctic sea, it is plenty light enough,
Through the clear atmosphere I stretch around on the wonderful beauty,
The enormous masses of ice pass me and I pass them, the scenery is plain in all directions,
The white-topt mountains show in the distance, I fling out my fancies toward them,
We are approaching some great battle-field in which we are soon to be engaged,
We pass the colossal outposts of the encampment, we pass with still feet and caution,
Or we are entering by the suburbs some vast and ruin'd city,
The blocks and fallen architecture more than all the living cities of the globe.

I am a free companion, I bivouac by invading watchfires,
I turn the bridegroom out of bed and stay with the bride myself,
I tighten her all night to my thighs and lips.

My voice is the wife's voice, the screech by the rail of the stairs,
They fetch my man's body up dripping and drown'd.

I understand the large hearts of heroes,
The courage of present times and all times,
How the skipper saw the crowded and rudderless wreck of the steam-ship, and Death chasing it
    up and down the storm,
How he knuckled tight and gave not back an inch, and was faithful of days and faithful of
    nights,
And chalk'd in large letters on a board, *Be of good cheer, we will not desert you;*
How he follow'd with them and tack'd with them three days and would not give it up,
How he saved the drifting company at last,
How the lank loose-gown'd women look'd when boated from the side of their prepared graves,
How the silent old-faced infants and the lifted sick, and the sharp-lipp'd unshaven men;
All this I swallow, it tastes good, I like it well, it becomes mine,
I am the man, I suffer'd, I was there.

The disdain and calmness of martyrs,
The mother of old, condemn'd for a witch, burnt with dry wood, her children gazing on,
The hounded slave that flags in the race, leans by the fence, blowing, cover'd with sweat.
The twinges that sting like needles his legs and neck, the murderous buckshot and the bullets
All these I feel or am.

I am the hounded slave, I wince at the bite of the dogs,
Hell and despair are upon me, crack and again crack the marksmen,
I clutch the rails of the fence, my gore drips, thinn'd with the ooze of my skin,
I fall on the weeds and stones,
The riders spur their unwilling horses, haul close,
Taunt my dizzy ears and beat me violently over the head with whip-stocks.

Agonies are one of my changes of garments,
I do not ask the wounded person how he feels, I myself become the wounded person,
My hurts turn livid upon me as I lean on a cane and observe.

I am the mash'd fireman with breast-bone broken,
Tumbling walls buried me in their debris,
Heat and smoke I inspired, I heard the yelling shouts of my comrades,
I heard the distant click of their picks and shovels,
They have clear'd the beams away, they tenderly lift me forth.
I lie in the night air in my red shirt, the pervading hush is for my sake,
Painless after all I lie exhausted but not so unhappy,
White and beautiful are the faces around me, the heads are bared of their fire-caps,
The kneeling crowd fades with the light of the torches.

Distant and dead resuscitate,
They show as the dial or move as the hands of me, I am the clock myself.

I am an old artillerist, I tell of my fort's bombardment,
I am there again.

Again the long roll of the drummers,
Again the attacking cannon, mortars,
Again to my listening ears the cannon responsive.
I take part, I see and hear the whole,
The cries, curses, roar, the plaudits for well-aim'd shots,
The ambulanza slowly passing trailing its red drip,
Workmen searching after damages, making indispensable repairs,
The fall of grenades through the rent roof, the fan-shaped explosion,
The whizz of limbs, heads, stone, wood, iron, high in the air.
Again gurgles the mouth of my dying general, he furiously waves with his hand,
He gasps through the clot *Mind not me—mind—the entrenchments.*

· · · ·

Charles Darwin

Charles Darwin (1809–1882) was a member of an English family noted for its intellectual accomplish-
ments. From an early age he displayed a remarkable interest in nature and its ramifications. In 1831 Darwin left
Cambridge University to serve as naturalist on a scientific
surveying expedition aboard the Beagle to South America
and the southern hemisphere. The voyage lasted five years
and gave him the opportunity of observing in great detail
the immense variation in, and distribution of, the organic
beings in South America, as well as the geological relations
of the existing to the past inhabitants of that continent. In
1832 he read the thought-provoking essay by Malthus on
population with its emphasis on the struggle for existence,
and this essay helped to confirm Darwin's theory of the
survival of those variants possessing characteristics favorable
to life in their particular environment. In 1859 he published
The Origin of Species, in which he summarized his views
of organic evolution by means of variation, natural selection, and survival of the fittest. The following selection is
from the recapitulation and conclusion of this momentous
work. In reading it note (1) Darwin's summary of his
theory, (2) his reply to those who objected to his views on
religious grounds, (3) what he considered the chief cause
of men's unwillingness to accept his theory, (4) his argument for refuting the idea of special creations for each species, (5) the evidence he presented to substantiate the idea
that all animals and plants are descended from one prototype, (6) the possibility of using organic change as a measure of time, (7) Darwin's argument that organic evolution
is an enobling act on the part of the Creator, and (8) his
illustration, in the final paragraph of the selection, of the
various phases of his theory.

From: THE ORIGIN OF SPECIES

I have now recapitulated the facts and considerations which have thoroughly convinced
me that species have been modified, during a
long course of descent. This has been effected
chiefly through the natural selection of numerous successive, slight, favourable variations;
aided in an important manner by the inherited
effects of the use and disuse of parts; and in
an unimportant manner, that is in relation to
adaptive structures, whether past or present,
by the direct action of external conditions, and
by variations which seem to us in our ignorance
to arise spontaneously. It appears that I formerly underrated the frequency and value of
these latter forms of variation, as leading to
permanent modifications of structure independently of natural selection. But as my conclusions have lately been much misrepresented,
and it has been stated that I attribute the modification of species exclusively to natural selec-

Charles Darwin, The Origin of Species by Means of Natural Selection or the Preservation of Favored Races in the Struggle for Life, 6th ed., New York, n.d., 465–474.

tion, I may be permitted to remark that in the first edition of this work, and subsequently, I placed in a most conspicuous position—namely, at the close of the Introduction—the following words: "I am convinced that natural selection has been the main but not the exclusive means of modification." This has been of no avail. Great is the power of steady misrepresentation; but the history of science shows that fortunately this power does not long endure.

It can hardly be supposed that a false theory would explain, in so satisfactory a manner as does the theory of natural selection, the several large classes of facts above specified. It has recently been objected that this is an unsafe method of arguing; but it is a method used in judging of the common events of life, and has often been used by the greatest natural philosophers. The undulatory theory of light has thus been arrived at; and the belief in the revolution of the earth on its axis was until lately supported by hardly any direct evidence. It is no valid objection that science as yet throws no light on the far higher problem of the essence or origin of life. Who can explain what is the essence of the attraction of gravity? No one now objects to following out the results consequent on this unknown element of attraction; notwithstanding that Leibnitz formerly accused Newton of introducing "occult qualities and miracles into philosophy."

I see no good reason why the views given in this volume should shock the religious feelings of any one. It is satisfactory, as showing how transient such impressions are, to remember that the greatest discovery ever made by man, namely, the law of the attraction of gravity, was also attacked by Leibnitz, "as subversive of natural, and inferentially of revealed, religion." A celebrated author and divine has written to me that "he has gradually learnt to see that it is just as noble a conception of the Deity to believe that He created a few original forms capable of self-development into other and needful forms, as to believe that He required a fresh act of creation to supply the voids caused by the action of His laws."

Why, it may be asked, until recently did nearly all the most eminent living naturalists and geologists disbelieve in the mutability of species. It cannot be asserted that organic beings in a state of nature are subject to no variation; it cannot be proved that the amount of variation in the course of long ages is a limited quantity; no clear distinction has been, or can be, drawn between species and well-marked varieties. It cannot be maintained that species when intercrossed are invariably sterile, and varieties invariably fertile; or that sterility is a special endowment and sign of creation. The belief that species were immutable productions was almost unavoidable as long as the history of the world was thought to be of short duration; and now that we have acquired some idea of the lapse of time, we are too apt to assume, without proof, that the geological record is so perfect that it would have afforded us plain evidence of the mutation of species, if they had undergone mutation.

But the chief cause of our natural unwillingness to admit that one species has given birth to other and distinct species, is that we are always slow in admitting great changes of which we do not see the steps. The difficulty is the same as that felt by so many geologists, when Lyell first insisted that long lines of inland cliffs had been formed, and great valleys excavated, by the agencies which we see still at work. The mind cannot possibly grasp the full meaning of the term of even a million years; it cannot add up and perceive the full effects of many slight variations, accumulated during an almost infinite number of generations.

Although I am fully convinced of the truth of the views given in this volume under the form of an abstract, I by no means expect to convince experienced naturalists whose minds are stocked with a multitude of facts all viewed, during a long course of years, from a point of view directly opposite to mine. It is so easy to hide our ignorance under such expressions as the "plan of creation," "unity of design," etc., and to think that we give an explanation when we only restate a fact. Any one whose disposition leads him to attach more weight to unexplained difficulties than to the explanation of a certain number of facts will certainly reject the theory. A few naturalists, endowed with much flexibility of mind, and who have already begun to doubt the immutability of species, may be influenced by this volume; but I look with confidence to the future, to young and rising naturalists, who will be able to view both sides of the question with impartiality. Whoever is led to believe that species are mutable will do good service by conscientiously expressing his conviction; for thus only can the load of prejudice by which this subject is overwhelmed be removed.

Several eminent naturalists have of late published their belief that a multitude of reputed species in each genus are not real species; but that other species are real, that is, have been independently created. This seems to me a strange conclusion to arrive at. They admit that a multitude of forms, which till lately they themselves thought were special creations, and which are still thus looked at by the majority of naturalists, and which consequently have all the external characteristic features of true species,—they admit that these have been produced by variation, but they refuse to extend the same view to other and slightly different forms. Nevertheless they do not pretend that they can define, or even conjecture, which are the created forms of life, and which are those produced by secondary laws. They admit variation as a *vera causa* in one case, they arbitrarily reject it in another, without assigning any distinction in the two cases. The day will come when this will be given as a curious illustration of the blindness of preconceived opinion. These authors seem no more startled at a miraculous act of creation than at an ordinary birth. But do they really believe that at innumerable periods in the earth's history certain elemental atoms have been commanded suddenly to flash into living tissues? Do they believe that at each supposed act of creation one individual or many were produced? Were all the infinitely numerous kinds of animals and plants created as egg or seed, or as full grown? and in the case of mammals, were they created bearing the false marks of nourishment from the mother's womb? Undoubtedly some of these same questions cannot be answered by those who believe in the appearance or creation of only a few forms of life, or of some one form alone. It has been maintained by several authors that it is as easy to believe in the creation of a million beings as of one; but Maupertuis'

philosophical axiom "of least action" leads the mind more willingly to admit the smaller number; and certainly we ought not to believe that innumerable beings within each great class have been created with plain, but deceptive, marks of descent from a single parent.

As a record of a former state of things, I have retained in the foregoing paragraphs, and elsewhere, several sentences which imply that naturalists believe in the separate creation of each species; and I have been much censured for having thus expressed myself. But undoubtedly this was the general belief when the first edition of the present work appeared. I formerly spoke to very many naturalists on the subject of evolution, and never once met with any sympathetic agreement. It is probable that some did then believe in evolution, but they were either silent, or expressed themselves so ambiguously that it was not easy to understand their meaning. Now, things are wholly changed, and almost every naturalist admits the great principle of evolution. There are, however, some who still think that species have suddenly given birth, through quite unexplained means, to new and totally different forms: but, as I have attempted to show, weighty evidence can be opposed to the admission of great and abrupt modifications. Under a scientific point of view, and as leading to further investigation, but little advantage is gained by believing that new forms are suddenly developed in an inexplicable manner from old and widely different forms, over the old belief in the creation of species from the dust of the earth.

It may be asked how far I extend the doctrine of the modification of species. The question is difficult to answer, because the more distinct the forms are which we consider, by so much the arguments in favour of community of descent become fewer in number and less in force. But some arguments of the greatest weight extend very far. All the members of whole classes are connected together by a chain of affinities, and all can be classed on the same principle, in groups subordinate to groups. Fossil remains sometimes tend to fill up very wide intervals between existing orders.

Organs in a rudimentary condition plainly show that an early progenitor had the organ in a fully developed condition; and this in some cases implies an enormous amount of modification in the descendants. Throughout whole classes various structures are formed on the same pattern, and at a very early age the embryos closely resemble each other. Therefore I cannot doubt that the theory of descent with modification embraces all the members of the same great class or kingdom. I believe that animals are descended from at most only four or five progenitors, and plants from an equal or lesser number.

Analogy would lead me one step farther, namely, to the belief that all animals and plants are descended from some one prototype. But analogy may be a deceitful guide. Nevertheless all living things have much in common, in their chemical composition, their cellular structure, their laws of growth, and their liability to injurious influences. We see this even in so trifling a fact as that the same poison often similarly affects plants and animals; or that the poison secreted by the gallfly produces monstrous growths on the wild rose or oak tree. With all organic beings, excepting perhaps some of the very lowest, sexual reproduction seems to be essentially similar. With all, as far as is at present known, the germinal vesicle is the same; so that all organisms start from a common origin. If we look even to the two main divisions—namely, to the animal and vegetable kingdoms—certain low forms are so far intermediate in character that naturalists have disputed to which kingdom they should be referred. As Professor Asa Gray has remarked, "the spores and other reproductive bodies of many of the lower algae may claim to have first a characteristically animal, and then an unequivocal vegetable, existence." Therefore, on the principle of natural selection with divergence of character, it does not seem incredible that, from some such low and intermediate form, both animals and plants may have been developed; and, if we admit this, we must likewise admit that all the organic beings which have ever lived on this earth may be descended from some one primordial form. But this inference is chiefly grounded on analogy, and it is immaterial whether or not it be accepted. No doubt it is possible, as Mr. G. H. Lewes has urged, that at the first commencement of life many different forms were evolved; but if so, we may conclude that only a very few have left modified descendants. For, as I have recently remarked in regard to the members of each great kingdom, such as the Vertebrata, Articulata, etc., we have distinct evidence in their embryological, homologous, and rudimentary structures, that within each kingdom all the members are descended from a single progenitor.

When the views advanced by me in this volume, and by Mr. Wallace, or when analogous views on the origin of species are generally admitted, we can dimly forsee that there will be a considerable revolution in natural history. Systematists will be able to pursue their labours as at present; but they will not be incessantly haunted by the shadowy doubt whether this or that form be a true species. This, I feel sure and I speak after experience, will be no slight relief. The endless disputes whether or not some fifty species of British brambles are good species will cease. Systematists will have only to decide (not that this will be easy) whether any form be sufficiently constant and distinct from other forms, to be capable of definition; and if definable, whether the differences be sufficiently important to deserve a specific name. This latter point will become a far more essential consideration than it is at present; for differences, however slight, between any two forms, if not blended by intermediate gradations, are looked at by most naturalists as sufficient to raise both forms to the rank of species.

Hereafter we shall be compelled to acknowledge that the only distinction between species and well-marked varieties is, that the latter are known, or believed, to be connected at the present day by intermediate gradations whereas species were formerly thus connected. Hence, without rejecting the consideration of the present existence of intermediate gradations between any two forms, we shall be led to weigh more carefully and to value higher the actual amount of difference between them. It is quite possible that forms now generally acknowledged to be merely varieties may hereafter be thought worthy of specific names; and in this case scientific and common language will come into accordance. In short, we shall have to treat species in the same manner as those naturalists treat genera, who admit that genera are merely artificial combinations made for convenience. This may not be a cheering prospect; but we shall at least be freed from the vain search for the undiscovered and undiscoverable essence of the term species.

The other and more general departments of natural history will rise greatly in interest. The terms used by naturalists, of affinity, relationship, community of type, paternity, morphology, adaptive characters, rudimentary and aborted organs, etc., will cease to be metaphorical, and will have a plain signification. When we no longer look at an organic being as a savage looks at a ship, as something wholly beyond his comprehension; when we regard every production of nature as one which has had a long history; when we contemplate every complex structure and instinct as the summing up of many contrivances, each useful to the possessor, in the same way as any great mechanical invention is the summing up of the labour, the experience, the reason, and even the blunders of numerous workmen; when we thus view each organic being, how far more interesting—I speak from experience—does the study of natural history become!

A grand and almost untrodden field of inquiry will be opened, on the causes and laws of variation, on correlation, on the effects of use and disuse, on the direct action of external conditions, and so forth. The study of domestic productions will rise immensely in value. A new variety raised by man will be a more important and interesting subject for study than one more species added to the infinitude of already recorded species. Our classifications will come to be, as far as they can be so made, genealogies; and will then truly give what may be called the plan of creation. The rules for classifying will no doubt become simpler when we have a definite object in view. We possess no pedigrees or amorial bearings; and we have to discover and trace the many diverging lines of descent in our natural genealogies, by characters of any kind which have long been inherited. Rudimentary organs will speak infallibly with respect to the nature of long-lost structures. Species and groups of species which are called aberrant, and which may fancifully

be called living fossils, will aid us in forming a picture of the ancient forms of life. Embryology will often reveal to us the structure, in some degree obscured, of the prototypes of each great class.

When we can feel assured that all the individuals of the same species, and all the closely allied species of most genera, have, within a not very remote period descended from one parent, and have migrated from some one birth-place; and when we better know the many means of migration, then, by the light which geology now throws, and will continue to throw, on former changes of climate and of the level of the land, we shall surely be enabled to trace in an admirable manner the former migrations of the inhabitants of the whole world. Even at present, by comparing the differences between the inhabitants of the sea on the opposites sides of a continent, and the nature of the various inhabitants on that continent in relation to their apparent means of immigration, some light can be thrown on ancient geography.

The noble science of Geology loses glory from the extreme imperfection of the record. The crust of the earth with its imbedded remains must not be looked at as a well-filled museum, but as a poor collection made at hazard and at rare intervals. The accumulation of each great fossiliferous formation will be recognised as having depended on an unusual concurrence of favourable circumstances, and the blank intervals between the successive stages as having been of vast duration. But we shall be able to gauge with some security the duration of these intervals by a comparison of the preceding and succeeding organic forms. We must be cautious in attempting to correlate as strictly contemporaneous two formations, which do not include many identical species, by the general succession of the forms of life. As species are produced and exterminated by slowly acting and still existing causes, and not by miraculous acts of creation; and as the most important of all cause of organic change is one which is almost independent of altered and perhaps suddenly altered physical conditions, namely, the mutual relation of organism to organism,—the improvement of one organism entailing the improvement or the extermination of others; it follows, that the amount of organic change in the fossils of consecutive formations probably serves as a fair measure of the relative, though not actual lapse of time. A number of species, however, keeping in a body might remain for a long period unchanged, whilst within the same period, several of these species by migrating into new countries and coming into competition with foreign associates, might become modified; so that we must not overrate the accuracy of organic change as a measure of time.

In the future I see open fields for far more important researches. Psychology will be securely based on the foundation already well laid by Mr. Herbert Spencer, that of the necessary acquirement of each mental power and capacity by gradation. Much light will be thrown on the origin of man and his history.

Authors of the highest eminence seem to be fully satisfied with the view that each species has been independently created. To my mind it accords better with what we know of the laws impressed on matter by the Creator, that the production and extinction of the past and present inhabitants of the world should have been due to secondary causes, like those determining the birth and death of the individual. When I view all beings not as special creations, but as the lineal descendants of some few beings which lived long before the first bed of the Cambrian system was deposited, they seem to me to become ennobled. Judging from the past, we may safely infer that not one living species will transmit its unaltered likeness to a distant futurity. And of the species now living very few will transmit progeny of any kind to a far distant futurity; for the manner in which all organic beings are grouped, shows that the greater number of species in each genus, and all the species in many genera, have left no descendants, but have become utterly extinct.

We can so far take a prophetic glance into futurity as to foretell that it will be the common and widely spread species, belonging to the larger and dominant groups within each class, which will ultimately prevail and procreate new and dominant species. As all the living forms of life are the lineal descendants of those which lived long before the Cambrian epoch, we may feel certain that the ordinary succession by generation has never once been broken, and that no cataclysm has desolated the whole world. Hence we may look with some confidence to a secure future of great length. And as natural selection works solely by and for the good of each being, all corporeal and mental endowments will tend to progress towards perfection.

It is interesting to contemplate a tangled bank, clothed with many plants of many kinds, with birds singing on the bushes, with various insects flitting about, and with worms crawling through the damp earth, and to reflect that these elaborately constructed forms, so different from each other, and dependent upon each other in so complex a manner, have all been produced by laws acting around us. These laws, taken in the largest sense, being Growth with Reproduction; Inheritance which is almost implied by reproduction; Variability from the indirect and direct action of the conditions of life, and from use and disuse: a Ratio of Increase so high as to lead to a Struggle for Life, and as a consequence to Natural Selection, entailing Divergence of Character and the Extinction of less improved forms. Thus, from the war of nature, from famine and death, the most exalted object which we are capable of conceiving, namely, the production of the higher animals, directly follows. There is grandeur in this view of life, with its several powers, having been originally breathed by the Creator into a few forms or into one; and that, whilst this planet has gone cycling on according to the fixed law of gravity, from so simple a beginning endless forms most beautiful and most wonderful have been, and are being, evolved.

John Stuart Mill

J ohn Stuart Mill (1806–1873), in addition to his interest
in the nature and scope of governmental authority (see
p. 608), was vitally concerned with the whole problem of
human knowledge and morality. His philosophic position,
similar to that of Jeremy Bentham, was known as utilitarianism. In 1863 he published an essay on Utilitarianism, selections from which follow. In reading them note (1) the two
opinions regarding moral standards described by Mill, (2)
the one he upheld in this essay, (3) his definition of utilitarianism, (4) how moral standards were determined by
this philosophy, (5) his discussion of happiness and how it
differed from "animal" pleasure, (6) the forces impelling
man to chose the "higher" rather than the "lower" pleasures, (7) the social consciousness implicit in the utilitarian
concept of happiness, (8) the external and internal sanctions which generally enforce moral standards, and (9) the
extent to which these were effective in the utilitarian concept of morality.

From: UTILITARIANISM

GENERAL REMARKS

There are few circumstances among those
which make up the present condition of human
knowledge, more unlike what might have been
expected, or more significant of the backward
state in which speculation on the most important subjects still lingers, than the little progress which has been made in the decision of
the controversy respecting the criterion of
right and wrong. From the dawn of philosophy,
the question concerning the *summum bonum*,
or, what is the same thing, concerning the foundation of morality, has been accounted the
main problem in speculative thought, has occupied the most gifted intellects, and divided
them into sects and schools, carrying on a vigorous warfare against one another. And after
more than two thousand years the same discussions continue, philosophers are still ranged
under the same contending banners, and neither thinkers nor mankind at large seem nearer
to being unanimous on the subject, than when
the youth Socrates listened to the old Pro-

tagoras, and asserted (if Plato's dialogue be
grounded on a real conversation) the theory of
utilitarianism against the popular morality of
the so-called sophist.

It is true that similar confusion and uncertainty, and in some cases similar discordance,
exist respecting the first principles of all the
sciences, not excepting that which is deemed
the most certain of them, mathematics; without
much impairing, generally indeed without impairing at all, the trustworthiness of the conclusions of those sciences. An apparent anomaly, the explanation of which is, that the detailed doctrines of a science are not usually
deduced from, nor depend for their evidence
upon, what are called its first principles. Were
it not so, there would be no science more precarious, or whose conclusions were more in-
sufficiently made out, than algebra; which derives none of its certainty from what are commonly taught to learners as its elements, since
these, as laid down by some of its most eminent
teachers, are as full of fictions as English law,
and of mysteries as theology. The truths which

John Stuart Mill, "Utilitarianism," in *Fraser's Magazine*, LXIV (October, November, 1861), 391–397; 526–530.

are ultimately accepted as the first principles of a science, are really the last results of metaphysical analysis, practised on the elementary notions with which the science is conversant; and their relation to the science is not that of foundations to an edifice, but of roots to a tree, which may perform their office equally well though they be never dug down to and exposed to light. But though in science the particular truths precede the general theory, the contrary might be expected to be the case with a practical art, such as morals or legislation. All action is for the sake of some end, and rules of action, it seems natural to suppose, must take their whole character and colour from the end to which they are subservient. When we engage in a pursuit, a clear and precise conception of what we are pursuing would seem to be the first thing we need, instead of the last we are to look forward to. A test of right and wrong must be the means, one would think, of ascertaining what is right or wrong, and not a consequence of having already ascertained it.

The difficulty is not avoided by having recourse to the popular theory of a natural faculty, a sense or instinct, informing us of right and wrong. For—besides that the existence of such a moral instinct is itself one of the matters in dispute—those believers in it who have any pretensions to philosophy, have been obliged to abandon the idea that it discerns what is right or wrong in the particular case in hand, as our other senses discern the sight or sound actually present. Our moral faculty, according to all those of its interpreters who are entitled to the name of thinkers, supplies us only with the general principles of moral judgments; it is a branch of our reason, not of our sensitive faculty; and must be looked to for the abstract doctrines of morality, not for perception of it in the concrete. The intuitive, no less than what may be termed the inductive, school of ethics, insists on the necessity of general laws. They both agree that the morality of an individual action is not a question of direct perception, but of the application of a law to an individual case. They recognise also, to a great extent, the same moral laws; but differ as to their evidence, and the source from which they derive their authority. According to the one opinion, the principles of morals are evident à priori, requiring nothing to command assent, except that the meaning of the terms be understood. According to the other doctrine, right and wrong, as well as truth and falsehood, are questions of observation and experience. But both hold equally that morality must be deduced from principles; and the intuitive school affirm as strongly as the inductive, that there is a science of morals. Yet they seldom attempt to make out a list of the à priori principles which are to serve as the premises of the science; still more rarely do they make any effort to reduce those various principles to one first principle, or common ground of obligation. They either assume the ordinary precepts of morals as of à priori authority, or they lay down as the common groundwork of those maxims, some generality much less obviously authoritative than the maxims themselves, and which has never succeeded in gaining popular acceptance. Yet to support their pretensions there ought either to be some one fundamental principle or law, at the root of all morality, or if there be several, there would be a determinate order of precedence among them; and the one principle, or the rule for deciding between the various principles when they conflict, ought to be self-evident.

To inquire how far the bad effects of this deficiency have been mitigated in practice, or to what extent the moral beliefs of mankind have been vitiated or made uncertain by the absence of any distinct recognition of an ultimate standard, would imply a complete survey and criticism of past and present ethical doctrine. It would, however, be easy to show that whatever steadiness or consistency these moral beliefs have attained, has been mainly due to the tacit influence of a standard not recognised. Although the non-existence of an acknowledged first principle has made ethics not so much a guide as a consecration of men's actual sentiments, still, as men's sentiments, both of favour and of aversion, are greatly influenced by what they suppose to be the effects of things upon their happiness, the principle of utility, or as Bentham latterly called it, the greatest happiness principle, has had a large share in forming the moral doctrines even of those who most scornfully reject its authority. Nor is there any school of thought which refuses to admit that the influence of actions on happiness is a most material and even predominant consideration in many of the details of morals, however unwilling to acknowledge it as the fundamental principle of morality, and the source of moral obligation. I might go much further, and say that to all those *à priori* moralists who deem it necessary to argue at all, utilitarian arguments are indispensable. It is not my present purpose to criticise these thinkers; but I cannot help referring, for illustration, to a systematic treatise by one of the most illustrious of them, the *Metaphysics of Ethics* by Kant. This remarkable man, whose system of thought will long remain one of the landmarks in the history of philosophical speculation, does, in the treatise in question, lay down a universal first principle as the origin and ground of moral obligation; it is this:—"So act, that the rule on which thou actest would admit of being adopted as a law by all rational beings." But when he begins to deduce from this precept any of the actual duties of morality, he fails, almost grotesquely, to show that there would be any contradiction, any logical (not to say physical) impossibility, in the adoption by all rational beings of the most outrageously immoral rules of conduct. All he shows is that the *consequences* of their universal adoption would be such as no one would choose to incur.

On the present occasion, I shall, without further discussion of the other theories, attempt to contribute something towards the understanding and appreciation of the Utilitarian or Happiness theory, and towards such proof as it is susceptible of. It is evident that this cannot be proof in the ordinary and popular meaning of the term. Questions of ultimate ends are not amenable to direct proof. Whatever can be proved to be good, must be so by being shown to be a means to something admitted to be good without proof. The medical art is proved to be good by its conducing to health; but how is it possible to prove that health is good? The art of music is good, for the reason, among others, that it produces pleasure; but what proof is it possible to give that pleasure is good? If, then, it is asserted that there is a comprehensive formula, including all things which are in themselves good, and whatever else is good,

is not so as an end, but as a mean, the formula may be accepted or rejected, but is not a subject of what is commonly understood by proof. We are not, however, to infer that its acceptance or rejection must depend on blind impulse, or arbitrary choice. There is a larger meaning of the word proof, in which this question is as amenable to it as any other of the disputed questions of philosophy. The subject is within the cognisance of the rational faculty; and neither does that faculty deal with it solely in the way of intuition. Considerations may be presented capable of determining the intellect either to give or withhold its assent to the doctrine; and this is equivalent to proof.

We shall examine presently of what nature are these considerations; in what manner they apply to the case, and what rational grounds, therefore, can be given for accepting or rejecting the utilitarian formula. But it is a preliminary condition of rational acceptance or rejection, that the formula should be correctly understood. I believe that the very imperfect notion ordinarily formed of its meaning, is the chief obstacle which impedes its reception; and that could it be cleared, even from only the grosser misconceptions, the question would be greatly simplified, and a large proportion of its difficulties removed. Before, therefore, I attempt to enter into the philosophical grounds which can be given for assenting to the utilitarian standard, I shall offer some illustrations of the doctrine itself; with the view of showing more clearly what it is, distinguishing it from what it is not, and disposing of such of the practical objections to it as either originate in, or are closely connected with, mistaken interpretations of its meaning. Having thus prepared the ground, I shall afterwards endeavour to throw such light as I can upon the question, considered as one of philosophical theory.

WHAT UTILITARIANISM IS

A passing remark is all that needs be given to the ignorant blunder of supposing that those who stand up for utility as the test of right and wrong, use the term in that restricted and merely colloquial sense in which utility is opposed to pleasure. An apology is due to the philosophical opponents of utilitarianism, for even the momentary appearance of confounding them with any one capable of so absurd a misconception; which is the more extraordinary, inasmuch as the contrary accusation, of referring everything to pleasure, and that too in its grossest form, is another of the common charges against utilitarianism: and, as has been pointedly remarked by an able writer, the same sort of persons, and often the very same persons, denounce the theory "as impracticably dry when the word utility precedes the word pleasure, and as too practicably voluptuous when the word pleasure precedes the word utility." Those who know anything about the matter are aware that every writer, from Epicurus to Bentham, who maintained the theory of utility, meant by it, not something to be contradistinguished from pleasure, but pleasure itself, together with exemption from pain; and instead of opposing the useful to the agreeable or the ornamental, have always declared that the useful means these, among other things. Yet the common herd, including the herd of writers, not only in newspapers and periodicals, but in books of weight and pretension, are perpetually falling into this shallow mistake. Having caught up the word utilitarian, while knowing nothing whatever about it but its sound, they habitually express by it the rejection, or the neglect, of pleasure in some of its forms; of beauty, of ornament, or of amusement. Nor is the term thus ignorantly misapplied solely in disparagement, but occasionally in compliment; as though it implied superiority to frivolity and the mere pleasures of the moment. And this perverted use is the only one in which the word is popularly known, and the one from which the new generation are acquiring their sole notion of its meaning. Those who introduced the word, but who had for many years discontinued it as a distinctive appellation, may well feel themselves called upon to resume it, if by doing so they can hope to contribute anything towards rescuing it from this utter degradation.

The creed which accepts as the foundation of morals, Utility, or the Greatest Happiness Principle, holds that actions are right in proportion as they tend to promote happiness, wrong as they tend to produce the reverse of happiness. By happiness is intended pleasure, and the absence of pain; by unhappiness, pain, and the privation of pleasure. To give a clear view of the moral standard set up by the theory, much more requires to be said; in particular, what things it includes in the ideas of pain and pleasure; and to what extent this is left an open question. But these supplementary explanations do not affect the theory of life on which this theory of morality is grounded—namely, that pleasure, and freedom from pain, are the only things desirable as ends; and that all desirable things (which are as numerous in the utilitarian as in any other scheme) are desirable either for the pleasure inherent in themselves, or as means to the promotion of pleasure and the prevention of pain.

Now, such a theory of life excites in many minds, and among them in some of the most estimable in feeling and purpose, inveterate dislike. To suppose that life has (as they express it) no higher end than pleasure—no better and nobler object of desire and pursuit—they designate as utterly mean and grovelling; as a doctrine worthy only of swine, to whom the followers of Epicurus were, at a very early period, contemptuously likened; and modern holders of the doctrine are occasionally made the subject of equally polite comparisons by its German, French, and English assailants.

When thus attacked, the Epicureans have always answered, that it is not they, but their accusers, who represent human nature in a degrading light; since the accusation supposes human beings to be capable of no pleasures except those of which swine are capable. If this supposition were true, the charge could not be gainsaid, but would then be no longer an imputation; for if the sources of pleasure were precisely the same to human beings and to swine, the rule of life which is good enough for the one would be good enough for the other. The comparison of the Epicurean life to that of beasts is felt as degrading, precisely because a beast's pleasures do not satisfy a human being's conceptions of happiness. Human beings have faculties more elevated than the animal appetites, and when once made conscious of them, do not regard anything as happiness which does not include their gratification. I do not, indeed, consider the Epicureans to have been by any means faultless in drawing out their scheme of consequences from the utilitarian principle. To do this in any sufficient manner, many Stoic, as well as Christian elements require to be included. But there is no known Epicurean theory of life which does not assign to the pleasures of the intellect, of the feelings and imagination, and of the moral sentiments, a much higher value as pleasures than to those of mere sensation. It must be admitted, however, that utilitarian writers in general have placed the superiority of mental over bodily pleasures chiefly in the greater permanency, safety, uncostliness, etc., of the former—that is, in their circumstantial advantages rather than in their intrinsic nature. And on all these points utilitarians have fully proved their case; but they might have taken the other, and, as it may be called, higher ground, with entire consistency. It is quite compatible with the principle of utility to recognise the fact, that some *kinds* of pleasure are more desirable and more valuable than others. It would be absurd that while, in estimating all other things, quality is considered as well as quantity, the estimation of pleasures should be supposed to depend on quantity alone.

If I am asked, what I mean by difference of quality in pleasures, or what makes one pleasure more valuable than another, merely as a pleasure, except its being greater in amount, there is but one possible answer. Of two pleasures, if there be one to which all or almost all who have experience of both give a decided preference, irrespective of any feeling of moral obligation to prefer it, that is the more desirable pleasure. If one of the two is, by those who are competently acquainted with both, placed so far above the other that they prefer it, even though knowing it to be attended with a greater amount of discontent, and would not resign it for any quantity of the other pleasure which their nature is capable of, we are justified in ascribing to the preferred enjoyment a superiority in quality, so far out-weighing quantity as to render it, in comparison, of small account.

Now it is an unquestionable fact that those who are equally acquainted with, and equally capable of appreciating and enjoying, both, do give a most marked preference to the manner of existence which employs their higher faculties. Few human creatures would consent to be changed into any of the lower animals, for a promise of the fullest allowance of a beast's pleasures; no intelligent human being would consent to be a fool, no instructed person would be an ignoramus, no person of feeling and conscience would be selfish and base, even though they should be persuaded that the fool, the dunce, or the rascal is better satisfied with his lot than they are with theirs. They would not resign what they possess more than he for the most complete satisfaction of all the desires which they have in common with him. If they ever fancy they would, it is only in cases of unhappiness so extreme, that to escape from it they would exchange their lot for almost any other, however undesirable in their own eyes. A being of higher faculties requires more to make him happy, is capable probably of more acute suffering, and certainly accessible to it at more points, than one of an inferior type; but in spite of these liabilities, he can never really wish to sink into what he feels to be a lower grade of existence. We may give what explanation we please of this unwillingness; we may attribute it to pride, a name which is given indiscriminately to some of the most and to some of the least estimable feelings of which mankind are capable: we may refer it to the love of liberty and personal independence, an appeal to which was with the Stoics one of the most effective means for the inculcation of it; to the love of power, or to the love of excitement, both of which do really enter into and contribute to it: but its most appropriate appellation is a sense of dignity, which all human beings possess in one form or other, and in some, though by no means in exact, proportion to their higher faculties, and which is so essential a part of the happiness of those in whom it is strong, that nothing which conflicts with it could be, otherwise than momentarily, an object of desire to them. Whoever supposes that this preference takes place at a sacrifice of happiness—that the superior being, in anything like equal circumstances, is not happier than the inferior—confounds the two very different ideas, of happiness, and content. It is indisputable that the being whose capacities of enjoyment are low, has the greatest chance of having them fully satisfied; and a highly endowed being will always feel that any happiness which he can look for, as the world is constituted, is imperfect. But he can learn to bear its imperfections, if they are at all bearable; and they will not make him envy the being who is indeed unconscious of the imperfections, but only because he feels not at all the good which those imperfections qualify. It is better to be a human being dissatisfied than a pig satisfied; better to be Socrates dissatisfied than a fool satisfied. And if the fool, or the pig, are of a different opinion, it is because they only know their own side of the question. The other party to the comparison knows both sides.

It may be objected, that many who are capable of the higher pleasures, occasionally, under the influence of temptation, postpone them to the lower. But this is quite compatible with a full appreciation of the intrinsic superiority of the higher. Men often, from infirmity of character, make their election for the nearer good, though they know it to be the less valuable; and this no less when the choice is between two bodily pleasures, than when it is between bodily and mental. They pursue sensual indulgences to the injury of health, though perfectly aware that health is the greater good. It may be further objected, that many who begin with youthful enthusiasm for everything noble, as they advance in years sink into indolence and selfishness. But I do not believe that those who undergo this very common change, voluntarily choose the lower description of pleasures in preference to the higher. I believe that before they devote themselves exclusively to the one, they have already become incapable of the other. Capacity for the nobler feelings is in most natures a very tender plant, easily killed, not only by hostile influences, but by mere want of sustenance; and in the majority of young persons it speedily dies away if the occupations to which their position in life has devoted them, and the society into which it has thrown them, are not favourable to keeping that higher capacity in exercise. Men lose their high aspirations as they lose their intellectual tastes, because they have not time or opportunity for indulging them; and they addict themselves to inferior pleasures, not because they deliberately prefer them, but because they are either the only ones to which they have access, or the only ones which they are any longer capable of enjoying. It may be questioned whether any one who has remained equally susceptible to both classes of pleasures, ever knowingly and calmly preferred the lower; though many, in all ages, have broken down in an ineffectual attempt to combine both.

From this verdict of the only competent judges, I apprehend there can be no appeal. On a question which is the best worth having of two pleasures, or which of two modes of existence is the most grateful to the feelings, apart from its moral attributes and from its consequences, the judgment of those who are qualified by knowledge of both, or, if they differ, that of the majority among them, must be admitted as final. And there needs be the less hesitation to accept this judgment respecting the quality of pleasures, since there is no other tribunal to be referred to even on the question of quantity. What means are there of determining which is the acutest of two pains, or the intensest of two pleasurable sensations, except the general suffrage of those who are familiar with both? Neither pains nor pleasures are homogeneous, and pain is always heterogeneous with pleasure. What is there to decide whether a particular pleasure is worth purchasing at the cost of a particular pain, except the feelings and judgment of the experienced? When, therefore, those feelings and judgment declare the pleasures derived from the higher faculties to be preferable *in kind*, apart from the question of intensity, to those of which the animal nature, disjoined from the higher faculties, is suspectible, they are entitled on this subject to the same regard.

I have dwelt on this point, as being a necessary part of a perfectly just conception of Utility or Happiness, considered as the directive rule of human conduct. But it is by no means an indispensable condition to the acceptance of the utilitarian standard; for that standard is not the agent's own greatest happiness, but the greatest amount of happiness altogether; and if it may possibly be doubted whether a noble character is always the happier for its nobleness, there can be no doubt that it makes other people happier, and that the world in general is immensely a gainer by it. Utilitarianism, therefore, could only attain its end by the general cultivation of nobleness of character, even if each individual were only benefited by the nobleness of others, and his own, so far as happiness is concerned, were a sheer deduction from the benefit. But the bare enunciation of such an absurdity as this last, renders refutation superfluous. . . .

OF THE ULTIMATE SANCTION OF THE PRINCIPLE OF UTILITY

The question is often asked, and properly so, in regard to any supposed moral standard—What is its sanction? what are the motives to obey it? or more specifically, what is the source of its obligation? whence does it derive its binding force? It is a necessary part of moral philosophy to provide the answer to this question; which, though frequently assuming the shape of an objection to the utilitarian morality, as if it had some special applicability to that above others, really arises in regard to all standards. It arises, in fact, whenever a person is called on to *adopt* a standard, or refer morality to any basis on which he has not been accustomed to rest it. For the customary morality, that which education and opinion have consecrated, is the only one which presents itself to the mind with the feeling of being *in itself* obligatory; and when a person is asked to believe that this morality *derives* its obligation from some general principle round which custom has not thrown the same halo, the assertion is to him a paradox; the supposed corollaries seem to have a more binding force than the original theorem; the super-structure seems to stand better without, than with, what is represented as its foundation. He says to himself, I feel that I am bound not to rob or murder, betray or deceive; but why am I bound to promote the general happiness? If my own happiness lies in something else, why may I not give that the preference?

If the view adopted by the utilitarian philosophy of the nature of the moral sense be correct, this difficulty will always present itself, until the influences which form moral character have taken the same hold of the principle which they have taken of some of the consequences—until, by the improvement of education, the feeling of unity with our fellow-crea-

tures shall be (what it cannot be denied that Christ intended it to be) as deeply rooted in our character, and to our own consciousness as completely a part of our nature, as the horror of crime is in an ordinarily well brought up young person. In the meantime, however, the difficulty has no peculiar application to the doctrine of utility, but is inherent in every attempt to analyse morality and reduce it to principles; which, unless the principle is already in men's minds invested with as much sacredness as any of its applications, always seems to divest them of a part of their sanctity.

The principle of utility either has, or there is no reason why it might not have, all the sanctions which belong to any other system of morals. Those sanctions are either external or internal. Of the external sanctions it is not necessary to speak at any length. They are, the hope of favour and the fear of displeasure, from our fellow-creatures or from the Ruler of the Universe, along with whatever we may have of sympathy or affection for them, or of love and awe of Him, inclining us to do his will independently of selfish consquences. There is evidently no reason why all these motives for observance should not attach themselves to the utilitarian morality, as completely and as powerfully as to any other. Indeed, those of them which refer to our fellow-creatures are sure to do so, in proportion to the amount of general intelligence; for whether there be any other ground of moral obligation than the general happiness or not, men do desire happiness; and however imperfect may be their own practice, they desire and commend all conduct in others towards themselves, by which they think their happiness is promoted. With regard to the religious motive, if men believe, as most profess to do, in the goodness of God, those who think that conduciveness to the general happiness is the essence, or even only the criterion of good, must necessarily believe that it is also that which God approves. The whole force therefore of external reward and punishment, whether physical or moral, and whether proceeding from God or from our fellow men, together with all that the capacities of human nature admit of disinterested devotion to either, become available to enforce the utilitarian morality, in proportion as that morality is recognised; and the more powerfully, the more the appliances of education and general cultivation are bent to the purpose.

So far as to external sanctions. The internal sanction of duty, whatever our standard of duty may be, is one and the same—a feeling in our own mind; a pain, more or less intense, attendant on violation of duty, which in properly cultivated moral natures rises, in the more serious cases, into shrinking from it as an impossibility. This feeling, when disinterested, and connecting itself with the pure idea of duty, and not with some particular form of it, or with any of the merely accessory circumstances, is the essence of Conscience; though in that complex phenomenon as it actually exists, the simple fact is in general all encrusted over with collateral associations, derived from sympathy, from love, and still more from fear; from all the forms of religious feeling; from the recollections of childhood and of all our past life; from self-esteem, desire of the esteem of others, and occasionally even self-abasement. This extreme complication is, I apprehend, the origin of the sort of mystical character, which, by a tendency of the human mind of which there are many other examples, is apt to be attributed to the idea of moral obligation, and which leads people to believe that the idea cannot possibly attach itself to any other objects than those which, by a supposed mysterious law, are found in our present experience to excite it. Its binding force, however, consists in the existence of a mass of feeling which must be broken through in order to do what violates our standard of right, and which, if we do nevertheless violate that standard, will probably have to be encountered afterwards in the form of remorse. Whatever theory we have of the nature or origin of conscience, this is what essentially constitutes it.

The ultimate sanction, therefore, of all morality (external motives apart) being a subjective feeling in our own minds, I see nothing embarrassing to those whose standard is utility, in the question, what is the sanction of that particular standard? We may answer, the same as of all other moral standards—the conscientious feelings of mankind. Undoubtedly this sanction has no binding efficacy on those who do not possess the feelings it appeals to; but

neither will these persons be more obedient to any other moral principle than to the utilitarian one. On them morality of any kind has no hold but through the external sanctions. Meanwhile the feelings exist, a fact in human nature, the reality of which, and the great power with which they are capable of acting on those in whom they have been duly cultivated, are proved by experience. No reason has ever been shown why they may not be cultivated to as great intensity in connection with the utilitarian, as with any other rule of morals.

There is, I am aware, a disposition to believe that a person who sees in moral obligation a transcendental fact, an objective reality belonging to the province of "Things in themselves," is likely to be more obedient to it than one who believes it to be entirely subjective, having its seat in human consciousness only. But whatever a person's opinion may be on this point of Ontology, the force he is really urged by is his own subjective feeling, and is exactly measured by its strength. No one's belief that duty is an objective reality is stronger than the belief that God is so; yet the belief in God, apart from the expectation of actual reward and punishment, only operates on conduct through, and in proportion to, the subjective religious feeling. The sanction, so far as it is disinterested, is always in the mind itself; and the notion therefore of the transcendental moralists must be, that this sanction will not exist *in* the mind unless it is believed to have its root out of the mind; and that if a person is able to say to himself, This which is restraining me, and which is called my conscience, is only a feeling in my own mind, he may possibly draw the conclusion that when the feeling ceases the obligation ceases, and that if he find the feeling inconvenient, he may disregard it, and endeavour to get rid of it. But is this danger confined to the utilitarian morality? Does the belief that moral obligation has its seat outside the mind make the feeling of it too strong to be got rid of? The fact is so far otherwise, that all moralists admit and lament the ease with which, in the generality of minds, conscience can be silenced or stifled. The question, Need I obey my conscience? is quite as often put to themselves by persons who never heard of the principle of utility, as by its adherents. Those whose conscientious feelings are so weak as to allow of their asking this question, if they answer it affirmatively, will not do so because they believe in the transcendental theory, but because of the external sanctions.

It is not necessary, for the present purpose, to decide whether the feeling of duty is innate or implanted. Assuming it to be innate, it is an open question to what objects it naturally attaches itself; for the philosophic supporters of that theory are now agreed that the intuitive perception is of principles of morality and not of the details. If there be anything innate in the matter, I see no reason why the feeling which is innate should not be that of regard to the pleasures and pains of others. If there is any principle of morals which is intuitively obligatory, I should say it must be that. If so, the intuitive ethics would coincide with the utilitarian, and there would be no further quarrel between them. Even as it is, the intuitive moralists, though they believe that there are other intuitive moral obligations, do already believe this to be one; for they unanimously hold that a large *portion* of morality turns upon the consideration due to the interests of our fellow-creatures. Therefore, if the belief in the transcendental origin of moral obligation gives any additional efficacy to the internal sanction, it appears to me that the utilitarian principle has already the benefit of it.

On the other hand, if, as is my own belief, the moral feelings are not innate, but acquired, they are not for that reason the less natural. It is natural to man to speak, to reason, to build cities, to cultivate the ground, though these are acquired faculties. The moral feelings are not indeed a part of our nature, in the sense of being in any perceptible degree present in all of us; but this, unhappily, is a fact admitted by those who believe the most strenuously in their transcendental origin. Like the other acquired capacities above referred to, the moral faculty, if not a part of our nature, is a natural outgrowth from it; capable, like them, in a certain small degree, of springing up spontaneously; and susceptible of being brought by cultivation to a high degree of development. Unhappily it is also susceptible, by a sufficient use of the external sanctions and of the force of early impressions, of being cultivated in almost any direction: so that there is hardly anything so absurd or so mischievous that it may not, by means of these influences, be made to act on the human mind with all the authority of conscience. To doubt that the same potency might be given by the same means to the principle of utility, even if it had no foundation in human nature, would be flying in the face of all experience.

But moral associations which are wholly of artificial creation, when intellectual culture goes on, yield by degrees to the dissolving force of analysis: and if the feeling of duty, when associated with utility, would appear equally arbitrary; if there were no leading department of our nature, no powerful class of sentiments, with which that association would harmonise, which would make us feel it congenial, and incline us not only to foster it in others (for which we have abundant interested motives), but also to cherish it in ourselves; if there were not, in short, a natural basis of sentiment for utilitarian morality, it might well happen that this association also, even after it had been implanted by education, might be analysed away.

But there *is* this basis of powerful natural sentiment; and this it is which, when once the general happiness is recognised as the ethical standard, will constitute the strength of the utilitarian morality. This firm foundation is that of the social feelings of mankind; the desire to be in unity with our fellow creatures, which is already a powerful principle in human nature, and happily one of those which tend to become stronger, even without express inculcation, from the influences of advancing civilisation. The social state is at once so natural, so necessary, and so habitual to man, that, except in some unusual circumstances or by an effort of voluntary abstraction, he never conceives himself otherwise than as a member of a body; and this association is riveted more and more, as mankind are further removed from the state of savage independence. Any condition, therefore, which is essential to a state of society, becomes more and more an inseparable part of every person's conception of the state of things which he is born into, and which is the destiny of a human being. Now, society between human beings, except in the relation of master and slave, is manifestly impossible on any other footing than that the interests of all are to be consulted. Society between equals can only exist on the understanding that the interests of all are to be regarded equally. And since in all states of civilisation, every person, except an absolute monarch, has equals, every one is obliged to live on these terms with somebody; and in every age some advance is made towards a state in which it will be impossible to live permanently on other terms with anybody. In this way people grow up unable to conceive as possible to them a state of total disregard of other people's interests. They are under a necessity of conceiving themselves as at least abstaining from all the grosser injuries, and (if only for their own protection) living in a state of constant protest against them. They are also familiar with the fact of co-operating with others and proposing to themselves a collective, not an individual interest as the aim (at least for the time being) of their actions. So long as they are co-operating, their ends are identified with those of others; there is at least a temporary feeling that the interests of others are their own interests. Not only does all strengthening of social ties, and all healthy growth of society, give to each individual a stronger personal interest in practically consulting the welfare of others; it also leads him to identify his *feelings* more and more with their good, or at least with an even greater degree of practical consideration for it. He comes, as though instinctively, to be conscious of himself as a being who *of course* pays regard to others. The good of others becomes to him a thing naturally and necessarily to be attended to, like any of the physical conditions of our existence. Now, whatever amount of this feeling a person has, he is urged by the strongest motives both of interest and of sympathy to demonstrate it, and to the utmost of his power encourage it in others; and even if he has none of it himself, he is as greatly interested as any one else that others should have it. Consequently the smallest germs of the feeling are laid hold of and nourished by the contagion of sympathy and the influences of education; and a complete web of corroborative association is woven round it, by the powerful agency of the external sanctions. This mode of conceiving ourselves and human life, as civilisation goes on, is felt to be more and more natural. Every

step in political improvement renders it more so, by removing the sources of opposition of interest, and levelling those inequalities of legal privilege between individuals or classes, owing to which there are large portions of mankind whose happiness it is still practicable to disregard. In an improving state of the human mind, the influences are constantly on the increase, which tend to generate in each individual a feeling of unity with all the rest; which, if perfect, would make him never think of, or desire, any beneficial condition for himself, in the benefits of which they are not included. If we now suppose this feeling of unity to be taught as a religion, and the whole force of education, of institutions, and of opinion, directed, as it once was in the case of religion, to make every person grow up from infancy surrounded on all sides both by the profession and the practice of it, I think that no one, who can realise this conception, will feel any misgiving about the sufficiency of the ultimate sanction for the Happiness morality. To any ethical student who finds the realisation difficult, I recommend, as a means of facilitating it, the second of M. Comte's two principal works, the *Traité de Politique Positive*. I entertain the strongest objections to the system of politics and morals set forth in that treatise; but I think it has superabundantly shown the possibility of giving to the service of humanity, even without the aid of belief in a Providence, both the psychological power and the social efficacy of a religion; making it take hold of human life, and colour all thought, feeling, and action, in a manner of which the greatest ascendancy ever exercised by any religion may be but a type and foretaste; and of which the danger is, not that it should be insufficient, but that it should be so excessive as to interfere unduly with human freedom and individuality.

Neither is it necessary to the feeling which constitutes the binding force of the utilitarian morality on those who recognise it, to wait for those social influences which would make its obligation felt by mankind at large. In the comparatively early state of human advancement in which we now live, a person cannot indeed feel that entireness of sympathy with all others, which would make any real discordance in the general direction of their conduct in life impossible; but already a person in whom the social feeling is at all developed, cannot bring himself to think of the rest of his fellow-creatures as struggling rivals with him for the means of happiness, whom he must desire to see defeated in their object in order that he may succeed in his. The deeply rooted conception which every individual even now has of himself as a social being, tends to make him feel it one of his natural wants that there should be harmony between his feelings and aims and those of his fellow-creatures. If differences of opinion and of mental culture make it impossible for him to share many of their actual feelings—perhaps make him denounce and defy those feelings—he still needs to be conscious that his real aim and theirs do not conflict; that he is not opposing himself to what they really wish for, namely their own good, but is, on the contrary, promoting it. This feeling in most individuals is much inferior in strength to their selfish feelings, and is often wanting altogether. But to those who have it, it possesses all the characters of a natural feeling. It does not present itself to their minds as a superstition of education, or a law despotically imposed by the power of society, but as an attribute which it would not be well for them to be without. This conviction is the ultimate sanction of the greatest happiness morality. This it is which makes any mind, of well-developed feelings, work with, and not against, the outward motives to care for others, afforded by what I have called the external sanctions; and when those sanctions are wanting, or act in an opposite direction, constitutes in itself a powerful internal binding force, in proportion to the sensitiveness and thoughtfulness of the character; since few but those whose mind is a moral blank, could bear to lay out their course of life on the plan of paying no regard to others except so far as their own private interest compels. . . .

Friedrich Nietzsche

Friedrich Nietzsche (1844–1900), a German educator and philosopher, reacted rather violently to some of the prevailing intellectual trends of the nineteenth century. In his later years he developed a mental and emotional instability that finally resulted in complete insanity. This tragic climax to his life undoubtedly helped to explain the character of Nietzsche's thought. He studied the Darwinian theory and became convinced that natural selection, as applied to human reproduction, was being circumvented by the Christian ethical insistence on protection of the weak. Thus he advocated a new and "nobler" morality for those with the will to achieve power, and through them a superrace would evolve. He also rejected the democratic notion of equality, a concept he regarded as contrary to natural reality. The fateful importance of Nietzsche's emphasis upon the decadence of Christianity and democracy, upon the Will to Power, and upon the emergence of the Superman is only too apparent in the recent history of his unhappy native land. In 1886 he wrote Beyond Good and Evil, which is characteristic of his rambling style and which presents the essence of his ethics. In reading the following selections from this work note (1) the importance of slavery in the advance of the type "man," (2) the attitude a "good" aristocracy should assume toward the suppressed classes, (3) Nietzsche's definition of life and its relationship to the Will to Power, (4) his rejection of Marxian

doctrine concerning exploitation, (5) the dual morality
that he described, (6) the subjective character of the master-morality, (7) the utilitarian nature of the slave-morality,
(8) his attitude toward the Christian Church, (9) the position of women in his thinking, (10) his interpretation of
the struggle for existence and the part mediocrity plays in
it, and (11) Nietzsche's emphasis upon rank.

From: BEYOND GOOD AND EVIL

WHAT IS NOBLE?

Every elevation of the type "man," has
hitherto been the work of an aristocratic society
—and so will it always be—a society believing
in a long scale of gradations of rank and differences of worth among human beings, and requiring slavery in some form or other. Without
the *pathos of distance,* such as grows out of the
incarnated difference of classes, out of the constant outlooking and downlooking of the ruling
caste on subordinates and instruments, and out
of their equally constant practice of obeying
and commanding, of keeping down and keeping at a distance—that other more mysterious
pathos could never have arisen, the longing for
an ever new widening of distance within the
soul itself, the formation of ever higher, rarer,
further, more extended, more comprehensive
states, in short, just the elevation of the type
"man," the continued "self-surmounting of
man," to use a moral formula in a supermoral
sense. To be sure, one must not resign oneself
to any humanitarian illusions about the history
of the origin of an aristocratic society (that is
to say, of the preliminary condition for the elevation of the type "man"): the truth is hard.
Let us acknowledge unprejudicedly how every
higher civilisation hitherto has *originated!* Men
with a still natural nature, barbarians in every
terrible sense of the word, men of prey, still in
possession of unbroken strength of will and desire for power, threw themselves upon weaker,
more moral, more peaceful races (perhaps
trading or cattle-rearing communities), or upon
old mellow civilisations in which the final vital
force was flickering out in brilliant fireworks of
wit and depravity. At the commencement, the
noble caste was always the barbarian caste:
their superiority did not consist first of all in
their physical, but in their psychical power—
they were more *complete* men (which at every
point also implies the same as "more complete
beasts").

Corruption—as the indication that anarchy
threatens to break out among the instincts, and
that the foundation of the emotions, called
"life," is convulsed—is something radically different according to the organisation in which
it manifests itself. When, for instance, an aristocracy like that of France at the beginning of
the Revolution, flung away its privileges with
sublime disgust and sacrificed itself to an excess of its moral sentiments, it was corruption:
—it was really only the closing act of the corruption which had existed for centuries, by
virtue of which that aristocracy had abdicated
step by step its lordly prerogatives and lowered
itself to a *function* of royalty (in the end even
to its decoration and parade-dress). The essential thing, however, in a good and healthy aristocracy is that it should *not* regard itself as a
function either of the kingship or the commonwealth, but as the *significance* and highest
justification thereof—that it should therefore
accept with a good conscience the sacrifice of
a legion of individuals, who, *for its sake,* must
be suppressed and reduced to imperfect men,
to slaves and instruments. Its fundamental belief must be precisely that society is *not* allowed to exist for its own sake, but only as a
foundation and scaffolding, by means of which
a select class of beings may be able to elevate
themselves to their higher duties, and in general to a higher *existence:* like those sun-seek-
ing climbing plants in Java—they are called

As translated by Helen Zimmern in Friedrich Nietzsche, *Beyond Good and Evil, Prelude to a Philosophy of the Future,*
T. N. Foulis, Edinburgh, 1911, 223–239. Courtesy of Peter Davies, Ltd.

Sipo Matador,—which encircle an oak so long and so often with their arms, until at last, high above it, but supported by it, they can unfold their tops in the open light, and exhibit their happiness.

To refrain mutually from injury, from violence, from exploitation, and put one's will on a par with that of others: this may result in a certain rough sense in good conduct among individuals when the necessary conditions are given (namely, the actual similarity of the individuals in amount of force and degree of worth, and their co-relation within one organisation). As soon, however, as one wished to take this principle more generally, and if possible even as *the fundamental principle of society,* it would immediately disclose what it really is—namely, a Will to the *denial* of life, a principle of dissolution and decay. Here one must think profoundly to the very basis and resist all sentimental weakness: life itself is *essentially* appropriation, injury, conquest of the strange and weak, suppression, severity, obtrusion of peculiar forms, incorporation, and at the least, putting it mildest, exploitation;—but why should one for ever use precisely these words on which for ages a disparaging purpose has been stamped? Even the organisation within which, as was previously supposed, the individuals treat each other as equal—it takes place in every healthy aristocracy—must itself, if it be a living and not a dying organisation, do all that towards other bodies, which the individuals within it refrain from doing to each other: it will have to be the incarnated Will to Power, it will endeavour to grow, to gain ground, attract to itself and acquire ascendency—not owing to any morality or immorality, but because it *lives,* and because life *is* precisely Will to Power. On no point, however, is the ordinary consciousness of Europeans more unwilling to be corrected than on this matter; people now rave everywhere, even under the guise of science, about coming conditions of society in which "the exploiting character" is to be absent:—that sounds to my ears as if they promised to invent a mode of life which should refrain from all organic functions. "Exploitation" does not belong to a depraved, or imperfect and primitive society; it belongs to the *nature* of the living being as a primary organic func-

tion; it is a consequence of the intrinsic Will to Power, which is precisely the Will to Life.—Granting that as a theory this is a novelty—as a reality it is the *fundamental fact* of all history: let us be so far honest towards ourselves!

In a tour through the many finer and coarser moralities which have hitherto prevailed or still prevail on the earth, I found certain traits recurring regularly together, and connected with one another, until finally two primary types revealed themselves to me, and a radical distinction was brought to light. There is *master-morality* and *slave-morality;*—I would at once add, however, that in all higher and mixed civilisations, there are also attempts at the reconciliation of the two moralities; but one finds still oftener the confusion and mutual misunderstanding of them, indeed, sometimes their close juxtaposition—even in the same man, within one soul. The distinctions of moral values have either originated in a ruling caste, pleasantly conscious of being different from the ruled—or among the ruled class, the slaves and dependents of all sorts. In the first case, when it is the rulers who determine the conception "good," it is the exalted, proud disposition which is regarded as the distinguishing feature, and that which determines the order of rank. The noble type of man separates from himself the beings in whom the opposite of this exalted, proud disposition displays itself: he despises them. Let it at once be noted that in this first kind of morality the antithesis "good" and "bad" means practically the same as "noble" and "despicable";—the antithesis "good" and "*evil*" is of a different origin. The cowardly, the timid, the insignificant, and those thinking merely of narrow utility are despised; moreover, also, the distrustful, with their constrained glances, the self-abasing, the dog-like kind of men who let themselves be abused, the mendicant flatterers, and above all the liars:—it is a fundamental belief of all aristocrats that the common people are untruthful. "We truthful ones"—the nobility in ancient Greece called themselves. It is obvious that everywhere the designations of moral value were at first applied to *men,* and were only derivatively and at a later period applied to *actions;* it is a gross mistake, therefore, when historians of morals start with questions like, "Why have sympathetic actions been praised?" The noble type of man regards *himself* as a determiner of values; he does not require to be approved of; he passes the judgment: "What is injurious to me is injurious in itself"; he knows that it is he himself only who confers honour on things; he is a *creator of values.* He honours whatever he recognises in himself: such morality is self-glorification. In the foreground there is the feeling of plenitude, of power, which seeks to overflow, the happiness of high tension, the consciousness of a wealth which would fain give and bestow:—the noble man also helps the unfortunate, but not—or scarcely—out of pity, but rather from an impulse generated by the superabundance of power. The noble man honours in himself the powerful one, him also who has power over himself, who knows how to speak and how to keep silence, who takes pleasure in subjecting himself to severity and hardness, and has reverence for all that is severe and hard. "Wotan placed a hard heart in my breast," says an old Scandinavian Saga: it is thus rightly expressed from the soul of a proud Viking. Such a type of man is even proud of *not* being made for sympathy; the hero of the Saga therefore adds warningly: "He who has not a hard heart when young, will never have one." The noble and brave who think thus are the furthest removed from the morality which sees precisely in sympathy, or in acting for the good of others, or in *désintéressement,* the characteristic of the moral; faith in oneself, pride in oneself, a radical enmity and irony towards "selflessness," belong as definitely to noble morality, as do a careless scorn and precaution in presence of sympathy and the "warm heart." —It is the powerful who *know* how to honour, it is their art, their domain for invention. The profound reverence for age and for tradition—all law rests on this double reverence,—the belief and prejudice in favour of ancestors and unfavourable to newcomers, is typical in the morality of the powerful; and if, reversely, men of "modern ideas" believe almost instinctively in "progress" and the "future," and are more and more lacking in respect for old age, the ignoble origin of these "ideas" has complacently betrayed itself thereby. A morality of the ruling class, however, is more especially foreign and irritating to present-day taste in the sternness of its principle that one has duties only to one's equals; that one may act towards beings of a lower rank, towards all that is foreign, just as seems good to one, or "as the heart desires," and in any case "beyond good and evil": it is here that sympathy and similar sentiments can have a place. The ability and obligation to exercise prolonged gratitude and prolonged revenge—both only within the circle of equals,—artfulness in retaliation, *raffinement* of the idea in friendship, a certain necessity to have enemies (as outlets for the emotions of envy, quarrelsomeness, arrogance—in fact, in order to be a good *friend*): all these are typical characteristics of the noble morality, which, as has been pointed out, is not the morality of "modern ideas," and is therefore at present difficult to realise, and also to unearth and disclose. —It is otherwise with the second type of morality, *slave-morality.* Supposing that the abused, the oppressed, the suffering, the unemancipated, the weary, and those uncertain of themselves, should moralise, what will be the common element in their moral estimates? Probably a pessimistic suspicion with regard to the entire situation of man will find expression, perhaps a condemnation of man, together with his situation. The slave has an unfavourable eye for the virtues of the powerful; he has a scepticism and distrust, a *refinement* of distrust of everything "good" that is there honoured—he would fain persuade himself that the very happiness there is not genuine. On the other hand, *those* qualities which serve to alleviate the existence of sufferers are brought into prominence and flooded with light; it is here that sympathy, the kind, helping hand, the warm heart, patience, diligence, humility, and friendliness attain to honour; for here these are the most useful qualities, and almost the only means of supporting the burden of existence. Slave-morality is essentially the morality of utility. Here is the seat of the origin of the famous antithesis "good" and "evil":—power and dangerousness are assumed to reside in the evil, a certain dreadfulness, subtlety, and strength, which do not admit of being despised. According to slave-morality, therefore, the "evil" man arouses fear; according to master-morality, it is precisely the "good" man who arouses fear and seeks to arouse it, while the bad man is regarded as the despicable being. The contrast attains its maximum when, in accordance with the logical consequences of slave-morality, a shade of depreciation—it may be slight and well-intentioned—at last attaches itself even to the "good" man of this morality; because, according to the servile mode of thought, the good man must in any case be the *safe* man: he is good-natured, easily deceived, perhaps a little stupid, *un bonhomme.* Everywhere that slave-morality gains the ascendency, language shows a tendency to approximate the significations of the words "good" and "stupid." —A last fundamental difference: the desire for *freedom,* the instinct for happiness and the refinements of the feeling of liberty belong as necessarily to slave-morals and morality, as artifice and enthusiasm in reverence and devotion are the regular symptoms of an aristocratic mode of thinking and estimating. —Hence we can understand without further detail why love *as a passion*—it is our European speciality—must absolutely be of noble origin; as is well known, its invention is due to the Provençal poet-cavaliers, those brilliant ingenious men of the *"gai saber,"* to whom Europe owes so much, and almost owes itself.

Vanity is one of the things which are perhaps most difficult for a noble man to understand: he will be tempted to deny it, where another kind of man thinks he sees it self-evidently. The problem for him is to represent to his mind beings who seek to arouse a good opinion of themselves which they themselves do not possess—and consequently also do not "deserve,"—and who yet *believe* in this good opinion afterwards. This seems to him on the one hand such bad taste and so self-disrespectful, and on the other hand so grotesquely unreasonable, that he would like to consider vanity an exception, and is doubtful about it in most cases when it is spoken of. He will say, for instance: "I may be mistaken about my value, and on the other hand may nevertheless demand that my value should be acknowledged by others precisely as I rate it:—that, however, is not vanity (but self-conceit, or, in most cases, that which is called 'humility,' and also 'modesty')." Or he will even say: "For

many reasons I can delight in the good opinion of others, perhaps because I love and honour them, and rejoice in all their joys, perhaps also because their good opinion endorses and strengthens my belief in my own good opinion, perhaps because the good opinion of others, even in cases where I do not share it, is useful to me, or gives promise of usefulness:—all this, however, is not vanity." The man of noble character must first bring it home forcibly to his mind, especially with the aid of history, that, from time immemorial, in all social strata in any way dependent, the ordinary man *was* only that which he *passed for:*—not being at all accustomed to fix values, he did not assign even to himself any other value than that which his master assigned to him (it is the peculiar *right of masters* to create values). It may be looked upon as the result of an extraordinary atavism, that the ordinary man, even at present, is still always *waiting* for an opinion about himself, and then instinctively submitting himself to it; yet by no means only to a "good" opinion, but also to a bad and unjust one (think, for instance, of the greater part of the self-appreciations and self-depreciations which believing women learn from their confessors, and which in general the believing Christian learns from his Church). In fact, conformably to the slow rise of the democratic social order (and its cause, the blending of the blood of masters and slaves), the originally noble and rare impulse of the masters to assign a value to themselves and to "think well" of themselves, will now be more and more encouraged and extended; but it has at all times an older, ampler, and more radically ingrained propensity opposed to it—and in the phenomenon of "vanity" this older propensity overmasters the younger. The vain person rejoices over *every* good opinion which he hears about himself (quite apart from the point of view of its usefulness, and equally regardless of its truth or falsehood), just as he suffers from every bad opinion: for he subjects himself to both, he *feels* himself subjected to both, by that oldest instinct of subjection which breaks forth in him. —It is "the slave" in the vain man's blood, the remains of the slave's craftiness—and how much of the "slave" is still left in woman, for instance!—which seeks to *se-*

duce to good opinions of itself; it is the slave, too, who immediately afterwards falls prostrate himself before these opinions, as though he had not called them forth. —And to repeat it again: vanity is an atavism.

A *species* originates, and a type becomes established and strong in the long struggle with essentially constant *unfavourable* conditions. On the other hand, it is known by the experience of breeders that species which receive superabundant nourishment, and in general a surplus of protection and care, immediately tend in the most marked way to develop variations, and are fertile in prodigies and monstrosities (also in monstrous vices). Now look at an aristocratic commonwealth, say an ancient Greek *polis*, or Venice, as a voluntary or involuntary contrivance for the purpose of *rearing* human beings; there are there men beside one another, thrown upon their own resources, who want to make their species prevail, chiefly because they *must* prevail, or else run the terrible danger of being exterminated. The favour, the superabundance, the protection are there lacking under which variations are fostered; the species needs itself as species, as something which, precisely by virtue of its hardness, its uniformity, and simplicity of structure, can in general prevail and make itself permanent in constant struggle with its neighbours, or with rebellious or rebellion-threatening vassals. The most varied experience teaches it what are the qualities to which it principally owes the fact that it still exists, in spite of all Gods and men, and has hitherto been victorious: these qualities it calls virtues, and these virtues alone it develops to maturity. It does so with severity, indeed it desires severity; every aristocratic morality is intolerant in the education of youth, in the control of women, in the marriage customs, in the relations of old and young, in the penal laws (which have an eye only for the degenerating): it counts intolerance itself among the virtues, under the name of "justice." A type with few, but very marked features, a species of severe, warlike, wisely silent, reserved and reticent men (and as such, with the most delicate sensibility for the charm and *nuances* of society) is thus established, unaffected by the vicissitudes of generations; the constant struggle with uni-

form *unfavourable* conditions is, as already remarked, the cause of a type becoming stable and hard. Finally, however, a happy state of things results, the enormous tension is relaxed; there are perhaps no more enemies among the neighbouring peoples, and the means of life, even of the enjoyment of life, are present in superabundance. With one stroke the bond and constraint of the old discipline severs: it is no longer regarded as necessary, as a condition of existence—if it would continue, it can only do so as a form of *luxury*, as an archaïsing *taste*. Variations, whether they be deviations (into the higher, finer, and rarer), or deteriorations and monstrosities, appear suddenly on the scene in the greatest exuberance and splendour; the individual dares to be individual and detach himself. At this turning-point of history there manifest themselves, side by side, and often mixed and entangled together, a magnificent, manifold, virgin-forest-like up-growth and up-striving, a kind of *tropical tempo* in the rivalry of growth, and an extraordinary decay and self-destruction, owing to the savagely opposing and seemingly exploding egoisms, which strive with one another "for sun and light," and can no longer assign any limit, restraint, or forbearance for themselves by means of the hitherto existing morality. It was this morality itself which piled up the strength so enormously, which bent the bow in so threatening a manner:—it is now "out of date," it is getting "out of date." The dangerous and disquieting point has been reached when the greater, more manifold, more comprehensive life *is lived beyond* the old morality; the "individual" stands out, and is obliged to have recourse to his own law-giving, his own arts and artifices for self-preservation, self-elevation, and self-deliverance. Nothing but new "Whys," nothing but new "Hows," no common formulas any longer, misunderstanding and disregard in league with each other, decay, deterioration, and the loftiest desires frightfully entangled, the genius of the race overflowing from all the cornucopias of good and bad, a portentous simultaneousness of Spring and Autumn, full of new charms and mysteries peculiar to the fresh, still inexhausted, still unwearied corruption. Danger is again present, the mother of morality, great danger; this time shifted into the individual, into the neighbour and friend, into the street, into their own child, into their own heart, into all the most personal and secret recesses of their desires and volitions. What will the moral philosophers who appear at this time have to preach? They discover, these sharp onlookers and loafers, that the end is quickly approaching, that everything around them decays and produces decay, that nothing will endure until the day after to-morrow, except one species of man, the incurably *medio-cre*. The mediocre alone have a prospect of continuing and propagating themselves—they will be the men of the future, the sole survivors; "be like them! become mediocre!" is now the only morality which has still a significance, which still obtains a hearing. —But it is difficult to preach this morality of mediocrity! it can never avow what it is and what it desires! it has to talk of moderation and dignity and duty and brotherly love—it will have difficulty *in concealing its irony!*

There is an *instinct for rank,* which more than anything else is already the sign of a *high* rank; there is a *delight* in the *nuances* of reverence which leads one to infer noble origin and habits. The refinement, goodness, and loftiness of a soul are put to a perilous test when something passes by that is of the highest rank, but is not yet protected by the awe of authority from obtrusive touches and incivilities: something that goes its way like a living touchstone, undistinguished, undiscovered, and tentative, perhaps voluntarily veiled and disguised. He whose task and practice it is to investigate souls, will avail himself of many varieties of this very art to determine the ultimate value of a soul, the unalterable, innate order of rank to which it belongs: he will test it by its *in-stinct for reverence. Différence engendre haine:* the vulgarity of many a nature spurts up suddenly like dirty water, when any holy vessel, any jewel from closed shrines, any book bearing the marks of great destiny, is brought before it; while on the other hand, there is an involuntary silence, a hesitation of the eye, a cessation of all gestures, by which it is indicated that a soul *feels* the nearness of what is worthiest of respect. The way in which, on the whole, the reverence for the *Bible* has hitherto been maintained in Europe, is perhaps the best example of discipline and refinement of manners which Europe owes to Christianity: books of such profoundness and supreme significance require for their protection an external tyranny of authority, in order to acquire the *period* of thousands of years which is necessary to exhaust and unriddle them. Much has been achieved when the sentiment has been at last instilled into the masses (the shallow-pates and the boobies of every kind) that they are not allowed to touch everything, that there are holy experiences before which they must take off their shoes and keep away the unclean hand—it is almost their highest advance towards humanity.

On the contrary, in the so-called cultured classes, the believers in "modern ideas," nothing is perhaps so repulsive as their lack of shame, the easy insolence of eye and hand with which they touch, taste, and finger everything; and it is possible that even yet there is more *relative* nobility of taste, and more tact for reverence among the people, among the lower classes of the people, especially among peasants, than among the newspaper-reading *demimonde* of intellect, the cultured class. . . .

William James

William James (1842–1910) was born in New York City and educated in America and Europe. He trained in art, science, and medicine, but developed a professional career in psychology and philosophy. His sensitive humanist nature was affronted by the materialism and determinism of his day yet he was strongly attracted to the sciences which he had studied. James picked up an old doctrine that stated that the meaning of an idea consists *in the particular consequences to which it leads and elaborated it and popularized it in a very appealing way. Bitter critics as well as staunch defenders of James's pragmatism appeared on both sides of the Atlantic Ocean. To his supporters James seemed to have resolved the controversy between the religionists and the scientists recently sharpened by the outbursts engendered by the publication of Darwin's The Origin of Species. James offered a philosophy particularly attuned to the dynamic, on-going, progressive age of the dawning 20th century. In reading the selection note (1) James's emphasis upon practicality, (2) what he meant by the pragmatic method, (3) his rejection of traditional rationalist philosophies and his reasons therefor, (4) the meaning of his pragmatic theory of truth, (5) the meaning of instrumentalism, (6) the relationship he envisioned between old and new ideas, (7) the difference between rationalist philosophies and pragmatism, (8) his method of reconciling empiricist ways of thinking with religious demands, (9) his reconciliation of abstractions with the pragmatists' concern with facts, (10) his discussion of the good, and (11) his grounds for believing that pragmatism is democratic.*

From: PRAGMATISM: A NEW NAME FOR SOME OLD WAYS OF THINKING

WHAT PRAGMATISM MEANS

Some years ago, being with a camping party in the mountains, I returned from a solitary ramble to find every one engaged in a ferocious metaphysical dispute. The *corpus* of the dispute was a squirrel—a live squirrel supposed to be clinging to one side of a tree-trunk; while over against the tree's opposite side a human being was imagined to stand. This human witness tries to get sight of the squirrel by moving rapidly round the tree, but no matter how fast he goes, the squirrel moves as fast in the opposite direction, and always keeps the tree between himself and the man, so that never a glimpse of him is caught. The resultant metaphysical problem now is this: *Does the man go round the squirrel or not?* He goes round the tree, sure enough, and the squirrel is on the tree; but does he go round the squirrel? In the unlimited leisure of the wilderness, discussion

had been worn threadbare. Everyone had taken sides, and was obstinate; and the numbers on both sides were even. Each side, when I appeared therefore appealed to me to make it a majority. Mindful of the scholastic adage that whenever you meet a contradiction you must make a distinction, I immediately sought and found one, as follows: "Which party is right," I said, "depends on what you *practically mean* by 'going round' the squirrel. If you mean passing from the north of him to the east, then to the south, then to the west, and then to the north of him again, obviously the man does go round him, for he occupies these successive positions. But if on the contrary you mean being first in front of him, then on the right of him, then behind him, then on his left, and finally in front again, it is quite as obvious that the man fails to go round him, for by the compensating movements the squirrel makes, he keeps his belly turned towards the man all the time, and his

William James, *Pragmatism: A New Name for Some Old Ways of Thinking; Popular Lectures on Philosophy*, New York: Longmans, Green, and Co., 1907, 43–81.

back turned away. Make the distinction, and there is no occasion for any farther dispute. You are both right and both wrong according as you conceive the verb 'to go round' in one practical fashion or the other."

Although one or two of the hotter disputants called my speech a shuffling evasion, saying they wanted no quibbling or scholastic hair-splitting, but meant just plain honest English 'round,' the majority seemed to think that the distinction had assuaged the dispute.

I tell this trivial anecdote because it is a peculiarly simple example of what I wish now to speak of as *the pragmatic method*. The pragmatic method is primarily a method of settling metaphysical disputes that otherwise might be interminable. Is the world one or many?—fated or free?—material or spiritual?—here are notions either of which may or may not hold good of the world; and disputes over such notions are unending. The pragmatic method in such cases is to try to interpret each notion by tracing its respective practical consequences. What difference would it practically make to any one if this notion rather than that notion were true? If no practical difference whatever can be traced, then the alternatives mean practically the same thing, and all dispute is idle. Whenever a dispute is serious, we ought to be able to show some practical difference that must follow from one side or the other's being right.

A glance at the history of the idea will show you still better what pragmatism means. The term is derived from the same Greek word, πράγμα, meaning action, from which our words 'practice' and 'practical' come. It was first introduced into philosophy by Mr. Charles Peirce in 1878. In an article entitled 'How to Make Our Ideas Clear,' in the *Popular Science Monthly* for January of that year Mr. Peirce, after pointing out that our beliefs are really rules for action, said that, to develop a thought's meaning, we need only determine what conduct it is fitted to produce: that conduct is for us its sole significance. And the tangible fact at the root of all our thought-distinctions, however subtle, is that there is no one of them so fine as to consist in anything but a possible difference of practice. To attain perfect clearness in our thoughts of an object, then, we

need only consider what conceivable effects of a practical kind the object may involve—what sensations we are to expect from it, and what reactions we must prepare. Our conception of these effects, whether immediate or remote, is then for us the whole of our conception of the object, so far as that conception has positive significance at all.

This is the principle of Peirce, the principle of pragmatism. It lay entirely unnoticed by any one for twenty years, until I, in an address before Professor Howison's philosophical union at the University of California, brought it forward again and made a special application of it to religion. By that date (1898) the times seemed ripe for its reception. The word 'pragmatism' spread, and at present it fairly spots the pages of the philosophic journals. On all hands we find the 'pragmatic movement' spoken of, sometimes with respect, sometimes with contumely, seldom with clear understanding. It is evident that the term applies itself conveniently to a number of tendencies that hitherto have lacked a collective name, and that it has 'come to stay.'

To take in the importance of Peirce's principle, one must get accustomed to applying it to concrete cases. I found a few years ago that Ostwald, the illustrious Leipzig chemist, had been making perfectly distinct use of the principle of pragmatism in his lectures on the philosophy of science, though he had not called it by that name.

"All realities influence our practice," he wrote me, "and that influence is their meaning for us. I am accustomed to put questions to my classes in this way: In what respects would the world be different if this alternative or that were true? If I can find nothing that would become different, then the alternative has no sense."

That is, the rival views mean practically the same thing, and meaning, other than practical, there is for us none. Ostwald in a published lecture gives this example of what he means. Chemists have long wrangled over the inner constitution of certain bodies called 'tautomerous.' Their properties seemed equally consistent with the notion that an instable hydrogen atom oscillates inside of them, or that they are instable mixtures of two bodies. Controversy raged, but never was decided. "It would never have begun," says Ostwald, "if the combatants had asked themselves what particular experimental fact could have been made different by one or the other view being correct. For it would then have appeared that no difference of fact could possibly ensue; and the quarrel was as unreal as if, theorizing in primitive times about the raising of dough by yeast, one party should have invoked a 'brownie,' while another insisted on an 'elf' as the true cause of the phenomenon."

It is astonishing to see how many philosophical disputes collapse into insignificance the moment you subject them to this simple test of tracing a concrete consequence. There can *be* no difference anywhere that doesn't *make* a difference elsewhere—no difference in abstract truth that doesn't express itself in a difference in concrete fact and in conduct consequent upon that fact, imposed on somebody, somehow, somewhere, and somewhen. The whole function of philosophy ought to be to find out what definite difference it will make to you and me, at definite instants of our life, if this world-formula or that world-formula be the true one.

There is absolutely nothing new in the pragmatic method. Socrates was an adept at it. Aristotle used it methodically. Locke, Berkeley, and Hume made momentous contributions to truth by its means. Shadworth Hodgson keeps insisting that realities are only what they are 'known as.' But these forerunners of pragmatism used it in fragments: they were a prelude only. Not until in our time has it generalized itself, become conscious of a universal mission, pretended to a conquering destiny. I believe in that destiny, and I hope I may end by inspiring you with my belief.

Pragmatism represents a perfectly familiar attitude in philosophy, the empiricist attitude, but it represents it, as it seems to me, both in a more radical and in a less objectionable form that it has ever yet assumed. A pragmatist turns his back resolutely and once for all upon a lot of inveterate habits dear to professional philosophers. He turns away from abstraction and insufficiency, from verbal solutions, from bad *a priori* reasons, from fixed principles, closed systems, and pretended absolutes and origins. He turns towards concreteness and adequacy, towards facts, towards action and

towards power. That means the empiricist temper regnant and the rationalist temper sincerely given up. It means the open air and possibilities of nature, as against dogma, artificiality, and the pretence of finality in truth.

At the same time it does not stand for any special results. It is a method only. But the general triumph of that method would mean an enormous change in what I called in my last lecture the 'temperament' of philosophy. Teachers of the ultra-rationalistic type would be frozen out, much as the courtier type is frozen out in republics, as the ultramontane type of priest is frozen out in Protestant lands. Science and metaphysics would come much nearer together, would in fact work absolutely hand in hand.

Metaphysics has usually followed a very primitive kind of quest. You know how men have always hankered after unlawful magic, and you know what a great part in magic *words* have always played. If you have his name, or the formula of incantation that binds him, you can control the spirit, genie, afrit, or whatever the power may be. Solomon knew the names of all the spirits, and having their names, he held them subject to his will. So the universe has always appeared to the natural mind as a kind of enigma, of which the key must be sought in the shape of some illuminating or power-bringing word or name. That word names the universe's *principle,* and to possess it is after a fashion to possess the universe itself. 'God,' 'Matter,' 'Reason,' 'the Absolute,' 'Energy,' are so many solving names. You can rest when you have them. You are at the end of your metaphysical quest.

But if you follow the pragmatic method, you cannot look on any such word as closing your quest. You must bring out of each word its practical cash-value, set it at work within the stream of your experience. It appears less as a solution, then, than as a program for more work, and more particularly as an indication of the ways in which existing realities may be *changed.*

Theories thus become instruments, not answers to enigmas, in which we can rest. We don't lie back upon them, we move forward, and, on occasion, make nature over again by their aid. Pragmatism unstiffens all our theories, limbers them up, and sets each one at work. Being nothing essentially new, it harmonizes with many ancient philosophic tendencies. It agrees with nominalism for instance, in always appealing to particulars; with utilitarianism in emphasizing practical aspects; with positivism in its disdain for verbal solutions, useless questions, and metaphysical abstractions.

All these, you see, are *anti-intellectualist* tendencies. Against rationalism as a pretension and a method pragmatism is fully armed and militant. But, at the outset, at least, it stands for no particular results. It has no dogmas, and no doctrines save its method. As the young Italian pragmatist Papini has well said, it lies in the midst of our theories, like a corridor in a hotel. Innumerable chambers open out of it. In one you may find a man writing an atheistic volume; in the next some one on his knees praying for faith and strength; in a third a chemist investigating a body's properties. In a fourth a system of idealistic metaphysics is being excogitated; in a fifth the impossibility of metaphysics is being shown. But they all own the corridor, and all must pass through it if they want a practicable way of getting into or out of their respective rooms.

No particular results then, so far, but only an attitude of orientation, is what the pragmatic method means. *The attitude of looking away from first things, principles, 'categories,' supposed necessities; and of looking towards last things, fruits, consequences, facts.*

So much for the pragmatic method! You may say that I have been praising it rather than explaining it to you, but I shall presently explain it abundantly enough by showing how it works on some familiar problems. Meanwhile the word pragmatism has come to be used in a still wider sense, as meaning also a certain *theory of truth.* I mean to give a whole lecture to the statement of that theory, after first paving the way, so I can be very brief now. But brevity is hard to follow, so I ask for your redoubled attention for a quarter of an hour. If much remains obscure, I hope to make it clearer in the later lectures.

One of the most successfully cultivated branches of philosophy in our time is what is called inductive logic, the study of the conditions under which our sciences have evolved. Writers on this subject have begun to show a singular unanimity as to what the laws of nature and elements of fact mean, when formulated by mathematicians, physicists, and chemists. When the first mathematical, logical, and natural uniformities, the first *laws,* were discovered, men were so carried away by the clearness, beauty and simplification that resulted, that they believed themselves to have deciphered authentically the eternal thoughts of the Almighty. His mind also thundered and reverberated in syllogisms. He also thought in conic sections, squares and roots and ratios, and geometrized like Euclid. He made Kepler's laws for the planets to follow; he made velocity increase proportionally to the time in falling bodies; he made the law of the sines for light to obey when refracted; he established the classes, orders, families and genera of plants and animals, and fixed the distances between them. He thought the archetypes of all things, and devised their variations; and when we rediscover any one of these his wondrous institutions, we seize his mind in its very literal intention.

But as the sciences have developed farther, the notion has gained ground that most, perhaps all, of our laws are only approximations. The laws themselves, moreover, have grown so numerous that there is no counting them; and so many rival formulations are proposed in all the branches of science that investigators have become accustomed to the notion that no theory is absolutely a transcript of reality, but that any one of them may from some point of view be useful. Their great use is to summarize old facts and to lead to new ones. They are only a man-made language, a conceptual shorthand, as some one calls them, in which we write our reports of nature; and languages, as is well known, tolerate much choice of expression and many dialects.

Thus human arbitrariness has driven divine necessity from scientific logic. If I mention the names of Sigwart, Mach, Ostwald, Pearson, Milhaud, Poincaré, Duhem, Heymans, those of you who are students will easily identify the tendency I speak of, and will think of additional names.

Riding now on the front of this wave of scientific logic Messrs. Schiller and Dewey appear with their pragmatistic account of what truth everywhere signifies. Everywhere, these teachers say, 'truth' in our ideas and beliefs means the same thing that it means in science. It means, they say, nothing but this, *that ideas (which themselves are but parts of our experience) become true just in so far as they help us to get into satisfactory relation with other parts of our experience,* to summarize them and get about among them by conceptual short-cuts instead of following the interminable succession of particular phenomena. Any idea upon which we can ride, so to speak; any idea that will carry us prosperously from any one part of our experience to any other part, linking things satisfactorily, working securely, simplifying, saving labor; is true for just so much, true in so far forth, true *instrumentally.* This is the 'instrumental' view of truth taught so successfully at Chicago, the view that truth in our ideas means their power to 'work,' promulgated so brilliantly at Oxford.

Messrs. Dewey, Schiller and their allies, in reaching this general conception of all truth, have only followed the example of geologists, biologists, and philologists. In the establishment of these other sciences, the successful stroke was always to take some simple process actually observable in operation—as denudation by weather, say, or variation from parental type, or change of dialect by incorporation of new words and pronunciations—and then to generalize it, making it apply to all times, and produce great results by summating its effects through the ages.

The observable process which Schiller and Dewey particularly singled out for generalization is the familiar one by which any individual settles into *new opinions.* The process here is always the same. The individual has a stock of old opinions already, but he meets a new experience that puts them to a strain. Somebody contradicts them; or in a reflective moment he discovers that they contradict each other; or he hears of facts with which they are incompatible; or desires arise in him which they cease to satisfy. The result is an inward trouble to which his mind till then had been a stranger, and from which he seeks to escape by modifying his previous mass of opinions. He saves as

much of it as he can, for in this matter of belief we are all extreme conservatives. So he tries to change first this opinion, and then that (for they resist change very variously), until at last some new idea comes up which he can graft upon the ancient stock with a minimum of disturbance of the latter, some idea that mediates between the stock and the new experience and runs them into one another most felicitously and expediently.

This new idea is then adopted as the true one. It preserves the older stock of truths with a minimum of modification, stretching them just enough to make them admit the novelty, but conceiving that in ways as familiar as the case leaves possible. An *outrée* explanation, violating all our preconceptions, would never pass for a true account of a novelty. We should scratch round industriously till we found something less excentric. The most violent revolutions in an individual's beliefs leave most of his old order standing. Time and space, cause and effect, nature and history, and one's own biography remain untouched. New truth is always a go-between, a smoother-over of transitions. It marries old opinion to new fact so as ever to show a minimum of jolt, a maximum of continuity. We hold a theory true just in proportion to its success in solving this 'problem of maxima and minima.' But success in solving this problem is eminently a matter of approximation. We say this theory solves it on the whole more satisfactorily than that theory; but that means more satisfactorily to ourselves, and individuals will emphasize their points of satisfaction differently. To a certain degree, therefore, everything here is plastic.

The point I now urge you to observe particularly is the part played by the older truths. Failure to take account of it is the source of much of the unjust criticism levelled against pragmatism. Their influence is absolutely controlling. Loyalty to them is the first principle—in most cases it is the only principle; for by far the most usual way of handling phenomena so novel that they would make for a serious rearrangement of our preconception is to ignore them altogether, or to abuse those who bear witness for them.

You doubtless wish examples of this process of truth's growth, and the only trouble is their superabundance. The simplest case of new truth is of course the mere numerical addition of new kinds of facts, or of new single facts of old kinds, to our experience—an addition that involves no alteration in the old beliefs. Day follows day, and its contents are simply added. The new contents themselves are not true, they simply *come* and *are*. Truth is *what we say about* them, and when we say that they have come, truth is satisfied by the plain additive formula.

But often the day's contents oblige a rearrangement. If I should now utter piercing shrieks and act like a maniac on this platform, it would make many of you revise your ideas as to the probable worth of my philosophy. 'Radium' came the other day as part of the day's content, and seemed for a moment to contradict our ideas of the whole order of nature, that order having come to be identified with what is called the conservation of energy. The mere sight of radium paying heat away indefinitely out of its own pocket seemed to violate that conservation. What to think? If the radiations from it were nothing but an escape of unsuspected 'potential' energy, pre-existent inside of the atoms, the principle of conservation would be saved. The discovery of 'helium' as the radiation's outcome, opened a way to this belief. So Ramsay's view is generally held to be true, because, although it extends our old ideas of energy, it causes a minimum of alteration in their nature.

I need not multiply instances. A new opinion counts as 'true' just in proportion as it gratifies the individual's desire to assimilate the novel in his experience to his beliefs in stock. It must both lean on old truth and grasp new fact; and its success (as I said a moment ago) in doing this, is a matter for the individual's appreciation. When old truth grows, then, by new truth's addition, it is for subjective reasons. We are in the process and obey the reasons. That new idea is truest which performs most felicitously its function of satisfying our double urgency. It makes itself true, gets itself classed as true, by the way it works; grafting itself then upon the ancient body of truth, which thus grows much as a tree grows by the activity of a new layer of cambium.

Now Dewey and Schiller proceed to generalize this observation and to apply it to the most ancient parts of truth. They also once were plastic. They also were called true for human reasons. They also mediated between still earlier truths and what in those days were novel observations. Purely objective truth, truth in whose establishment the function of giving human satisfaction in marrying previous parts of experience with newer parts played no rôle whatever, is nowhere to be found. The reasons why we call things true is the reason why they *are* true, for 'to be true' *means* only to perform this marriage-function.

The trail of the human serpent is thus over everything. Truth independent; truth that we *find* merely; truth no longer malleable to human need; truth incorrigible, in a word; such truth exists indeed superabundantly—or is supposed to exist by rationalistically minded thinkers; but then it means only the dead heart of the living tree, and its being there means only that truth also has its paleontology, and its 'prescription,' and may grow stiff with years of veteran service and petrified in men's regard by sheer antiquity. But how plastic even the oldest truths nevertheless really are has been vividly shown in our day by the transformation of logical and mathematical ideas, a transformation which seems even to be invading physics. The ancient formulas are reinterpreted as special expressions of much wider principles, principles that our ancestors never got a glimpse of in their present shape and formulation.

Mr. Schiller still gives to all this view of truth the name of 'Humanism,' but, for this doctrine too, the name of pragmatism seems fairly to be in the ascendant, so I will treat it under the name of pragmatism in these lectures.

Such then would be the scope of pragmatism—first, a method; and second, a genetic theory of what is meant by truth. And these two things must be our future topics.

What I have said of the theory of truth will, I am sure, have appeared obscure and unsatisfactory to most of you by reason of its brevity. I shall make amends for that hereafter. In a lecture on 'common sense' I shall try to show what I mean by truths grown petrified by antiquity. In another lecture I shall expatiate on the idea that our thoughts become true in proportion as they successfully exert their go-between function. In a third I shall show how hard it is to discriminate subjective from objective factors in Truth's development. You may not follow me wholly in these lectures; and if you do, you may not wholly agree with me. But you will, I know, regard me at least as serious, and treat my effort with respectful consideration.

You will probably be surprised to learn, then, that Messrs. Schiller's and Dewey's theories have suffered a hailstorm of contempt and ridicule. All rationalism has risen against them. In influential quarters Mr. Schiller, in particular, has been treated like an impudent schoolboy who deserves a spanking. I should not mention this, but for the fact that it throws so much sidelight upon that rationalistic temper to which I have opposed the temper of pragmatism. Pragmatism is uncomfortable away from facts. Rationalism is comfortable only in the presence of abstractions. This pragmatist talk about truths in the plural, about their utility and satisfactoriness, about the success with which they 'work,' etc., suggests to the typical intellectualist mind a sort of coarse lame second-rate makeshift article of truth. Such truths are not real truth. Such tests are merely subjective. As against this, objective truth must be something non-utilitarian, haughty, refined, remote, august, exalted. It must be an absolute correspondence of our thoughts with an equally absolute reality. It must be what we *ought* to think unconditionally. The conditioned ways in which we *do* think are so much irrelevance and matter for psychology. Down with psychology, up with logic, in all this question!

See the exquisite contrast of the types of mind! The pragmatist clings to facts and concreteness, observes truth at its work in particular cases, and generalizes. Truth, for him, becomes a class-name for all sorts of definite working-values in experience. For the rationalist it remains a pure abstraction, to the bare name of which we must defer. When the pragmatist undertakes to show in detail just *why* we must defer, the rationalist is unable to recognize the concretes from which his own abstraction is taken. He accuses us of *denying* truth; whereas we have only sought to trace exactly why people follow it and always ought to follow it. Your typical ultra-abstractionist fairly shudders at concreteness: other things equal, he positively prefers the pale and spectral. If the two universes were offered, he would always choose the skinny outline rather than the rich thicket of reality. It is so much purer, clearer, nobler.

I hope that as these lectures go on, the concreteness and closeness to facts of the pragmatism which they advocate may be what approves itself to you as its most satisfactory peculiarity. It only follows here the example of the sister-sciences, interpreting the unobserved by the observed. It brings old and new harmoniously together. It converts the absolutely empty notion of a static relation of 'correspondence' (what that may mean we must ask later) between our minds and reality, into that of a rich and active commerce (that any one may follow in detail and understand) between particular thoughts of ours, and the great universe of other experiences in which they play their parts and have their uses.

But enough of this at present! The justification of what I say must be postponed. I wish now to add a word in further explanation of the claim I made at our last meeting, that pragmatism may be a happy harmonizer of empiricist ways of thinking with the more religious demands of human beings.

Men who are strongly of the fact-loving temperament, you may remember me to have said, are liable to be kept at a distance by the small sympathy with facts which that philosophy from the present-day fashion of idealism offers them. It is far too intellectualistic. Old fashioned theism was bad enough, with its notion of God as an exalted monarch, made up of a lot of unintelligible or preposterous 'attributes'; but, so long as it held strongly by the argument from design, it kept some touch with concrete realities. Since, however, Darwinism has once for all displaced design from the minds of the 'scientific,' theism has lost that foothold; and some kind of an immanent or pantheistic deity working *in* things rather than above them is, if any, the kind recommended to our contemporary imagination. Aspirants to a philosophic religion turn, . . . towards . . . pantheism than towards the older dualistic theism, in spite of the fact that the latter still counts able defenders.

But, as I said in my first lecture, the brand of pantheism offered is hard for them to assimilate if they are lovers of facts, or empirically minded. It is the absolutistic brand, spurning the dust and reared upon pure logic. It keeps no connexion whatever with concreteness. Affirming the Absolute Mind, which is its substitute for God, to be the rational presupposition of all particulars of fact, whatever they may be, it remains supremely indifferent to what the particular facts in our world actually are. Be they what they may, the Absolute will father them. Like the sick lion in Aesop's fable, all footprints lead into his den, but *nulla vestigia retrorsum.* You cannot redescend into the world of particulars by the Absolute's aid, or deduce any necessary consequences of detail important for your life from your idea of his nature. He gives you indeed the assurance that all is well with *Him,* and for his eternal way of thinking; but thereupon he leaves you to be finitely saved by your own temporal devices.

Far be it from me to deny the majesty of this conception, or its capacity to yield religious comfort to a most respectable class of minds. But from the human point of view, no one can pretend that it doesn't suffer from the faults of remoteness and abstractness. It is eminently a product of what I have ventured to call the rationalistic temper. It disdains empiricism's needs. It substitutes a pallid outline for the real world's richness. It is dapper, it is noble in the bad sense, in the sense in which to be noble is to be inapt for humble service. In this real world of sweat and dirt, it seems to me that when a view of things is 'noble,' that ought to count as a presumption against its truth, and as a philosophic disqualification. The prince of darkness may be a gentleman, as we are told he is, but whatever the God of earth and heaven is, he can surely be no gentleman. His menial services are needed in the dust of our human trials, even more than his dignity is needed in the empyrean.

Now pragmatism, devoted though she be to facts, has no such materialistic bias as ordinary empiricism labors under. Moreover, she has no objection whatever to the realizing of abstractions, so long as you get about among particulars with their aid and they actually carry you somewhere. Interested in no conclusions but those which our minds and our experiences work out together, she has no *a priori* prejudices against theology. *If theological ideas prove to have a value for concrete life, they will be true, for pragmatism, in the sense of being good for so much. For how much more they are true, will depend entirely on their relations to the other truths that also have to be acknowledged.*

What I said just now about the Absolute, of transcendental idealism, is a case in point. First, I called it majestic and said it yielded religious comfort to a class of minds, and then I accused it of remoteness and sterility. But so far as it affords such comfort, it surely is not sterile; it has that amount of value; it performs a concrete function. As a good pragmatist, I myself ought to call the Absolute true 'in so far forth,' then; and I unhesitatingly now do so.

But what does *true in so far forth* mean in this case? To answer, we need only apply the pragmatic method. What do believers in the Absolute mean by saying that their belief affords them comfort? They mean that since, in the Absolute finite evil is 'overruled' already, we may, therefore, whenever we wish, treat the temporal as if it were potentially the eternal, be sure that we can trust its outcome, and, without sin, dismiss our fear and drop the worry of our finite responsibility. In short, they mean that we have a right ever and anon to take a moral holiday, to let the world wag in its own way, feeling that its issues are in better hands than ours and are none of our business.

The universe is a system of which the individual members may relax their anxieties occasionally, in which the don't-care mood is also right for men, and moral holidays in order—that, if I mistake not, is part, at least, of what the Absolute is 'known-as,' that is the great difference in our particular experiences which his being true makes, for us, that is his cash-value when he is pragmatically interpreted. Farther than that the ordinary lay-reader in philosophy who thinks favorably of absolute idealism does not venture to sharpen his conceptions. He can use the Absolute for so much, . . . He is pained at hearing you speak incredulously of the Absolute . . . and disregards your criticisms because they deal with aspects of the conception that he fails to follow.

If the Absolute means this, and means no more than this, who can possibly deny the truth of it? To deny it would be to insist that men should never relax, and that holidays are never in order.

I am well aware how odd it must seem to some of you to hear me say that an idea is 'true' so long as to believe it is profitable to our lives. That it is *good,* for as much as it profits, you will gladly admit. If what we do by its aid is good, you will allow the idea itself to be good in so far forth, for we are the better for possessing it. But is it not a strange misuse of the word 'truth,' you will say, to call ideas also 'true' for this reason?

To answer this difficulty fully is impossible at this stage of my account. You touch here upon the very central point of Messrs. Schiller's, Dewey's, and my own doctrine of truth, which I can not discuss with detail until my sixth lecture. Let me now say only this, that truth is *one species of good,* and not, as is usually supposed, a category distinct from good, and co-ordinate with it. *The true is the name of whatever proves itself to be good in the way of belief, and good, too, for definite, assignable reasons.* Surely you must admit this, that if there were *no* good for life in true ideas, or if the knowledge of them were positively disadvantageous and false ideas the only useful ones, then the current notion that truth is divine and precious, and its pursuit a duty, could never have grown up and become a dogma. In a world like that, our duty would be to *shun* truth, rather. But in this world, just as certain foods are not only agreeable to our taste, but good for our teeth, our stomach, and our tissues; so certain ideas are not only agreeable to think about, or agreeable as supporting other ideas that we are fond of, but they are also helpful in life's practical struggles. If there be any life that it is really better we should lead, and if there be any idea which, if believed in, would help us to lead that life, then it would be really *better for us* to believe in that idea, *unless, indeed, belief in it incidentally clashed with other greater vital benefits.*

'What would be better for us to believe'! This sounds very like a definition of truth. It comes very near to saying 'what we *ought* to believe': and in *that* definition none of you would find

any oddity. Ought we ever not to believe what it is *better for us* to believe? And can we then keep the notion of what is better for us, and what is true for us, permanently apart?

Pragmatism says no, and I fully agree with her. Probably you also agree, so far as the abstract statement goes, but with a suspicion that if we practically did believe everything that made for good in our own personal lives, we should be found indulging all kinds of fancies about this world's affairs, and all kinds of sentimental superstitions about a world hereafter. Your suspicion here is undoubtedly well founded, and it is evident that something happens when you pass from the abstract to the concrete that complicates the situation.

I said just now that what is better for us to believe is true *unless the belief incidentally clashes with some other vital benefit.* Now in real life what vital benefits is any particular belief of ours most liable to clash with? What indeed except the vital benefits yielded by *other beliefs* when these prove incompatible with the first ones? In other words, the greatest enemy of any one of our truths may be the rest of our truths. Truths have once for all this desperate instinct of self-preservation and of desire to extinguish whatever contradicts them. My belief in the Absolute, based on the good it does me, must run the gauntlet of all my other beliefs. Grant that it may be true in giving me a moral holiday. Nevertheless, as I conceive it—and let me speak now confidentially, as it were, and merely in my own private person—it clashes with other truths of mine whose benefits I hate to give up on its account. It happens to be associated with a kind of logic of which I am the enemy, I find that it entangles me in metaphysical paradoxes that are inacceptable, etc., etc. But as I have enough trouble in life already without adding the trouble of carrying these intellectual inconsistencies, I personally just give up the Absolute. I just *take* my moral holidays; or else as a professional philosopher, I try to justify them by some other principle.

If I could restrict my notion of the Absolute to its bare holiday-giving value, it wouldn't clash with my other truths. But we can not easily thus restrict our hypotheses. They carry supernumerary features, and these it is that clash so. My disbelief in the Absolute means, then, disbelief in those other supernumerary features, for I fully believe in the legitimacy of taking moral holidays.

You see by this what I meant when I called pragmatism a mediator and reconciler and said, borrowing the word from Papini, that she 'unstiffens' our theories. She has in fact no prejudices whatever, no obstructive dogmas, no rigid canons of what shall count as proof. She is completely genial. She will entertain any hypothesis, she will consider any evidence. It follows that in the religious field she is at a great advantage both over positivistic empiricism, with its anti-theological bias, and over religious rationalism, with its exclusive interest in the remote, the noble, the simple, and the abstract in the way of conception.

In short, she widens the field of search for God. Rationalism sticks to logic and the empyrean. Empiricism sticks to the external senses. Pragmatism is willing to take anything, to follow either logic or the senses and to count the humblest and most personal experiences. She will count mystical experiences if they have practical consequences. She will take a God who lives in the very dirt of private fact—if that should seem a likely place to find him.

Her only test of probable truth is what works best in the way of leading us, what fits every part of life best and combines with the collectivity of experience's demands, nothing being omitted. If theological ideas should do this, if the notion of God, in particular, should prove to do it, how could pragmatism possibly deny God's existence? She could see no meaning in treating as 'not true' a notion that was pragmatically so successful. What other kind of truth could there be, for her, than all this agreement with concrete reality?

In my last lecture I shall return again to the relations of pragmatism with religion. But you see already how democratic she is. Her manners are as various and flexible, her resources as rich and endless, and her conclusions as friendly as those of mother nature.

Nationalism, Imperialism, and the War of 1914-1918

During the nineteenth century, Western Civilization felt the impact of the growing spirit of nationalism which permeated various ethnic groups in Europe and elsewhere throughout the world. A variety of factors, some stemming from the French Revolution and others from recent industrial and economic changes, contributed to the growth of this emotional feeling. Prominent among the fruits of this development were the political unification of the German and Italian peoples, and the intensification of national pride in countries already unified. Another result was the growth of militarism as a guaranty of national security. In the last quarter of the century nationalism combined with the expanding industrial activity of the time to bring about another phenomenon of the nineteenth century—imperialism. Colonies were sought as sources of raw materials, as outlets for manufactured products, and as areas for profitable investment of surplus capital; there ensued an intensive race to appropriate the backward areas of the world. This imperial rivalry, together with the rising spirit of nationalism, resulted in frequent international incidents, and it became increasingly evident, as Western Civilization entered the twentieth century, that a major war was inevitable. It finally came in 1914, and four years of bitter combat followed, with each of the major belligerents insisting that it was fighting a defensive war with no idea of furthering its colonial holdings. Secret treaties entered into during the course of the war contradicted these professions of altruism. The war, with its heavy expenditure of blood and treasure, rudely shocked the civilized world, which had come to believe that progress in time would outmode such conflicts. It was in the hope that war, imperialism, and intrigue might be forever removed from society that the leading statesmen drew up a covenant for a league of nations in order to further international cooperation and to outlaw aggressive warfare.

Giuseppe Mazzini

Giuseppe Mazzini (1805–1872), Italian patriot and writer, helped to inspire the spirit of liberal nationalism that emerged among the various European groups suppressed by the Congress of Vienna in 1815. His ideals were largely determined by his education, which was concentrated in the fields of history and theology. From the former he derived his romanticism, his interest in republican governmental forms, and his intense feeling for the Italian nation, while from the latter he acquired his high idealism, a belief in human liberty, and his interest in Humanity and a united mankind. He urged his countrymen to liberate themselves from foreign domination by uniting politically, and to free themselves from domestic tyranny by replacing monarchies with a republic. Only when national groups were organized into liberal political units could they participate in a larger movement to unite Humanity, which, to Mazzini, was God's ultimate plan. He wrote The Duties of Man as a series of essays to be read by the Italian working class, and they were published between 1844 and 1858. In reading the following, entitled "Duties toward Your Company" note (1) Mazzini's concept of the first duty of Italians, (2) the means God gave them of accomplishing this duty, (3) those who have disfigured God's design, (4) his appeal to all the factors producing a national feeling, (5) his comparison of Humanity with an army and of the nation as a family, (6) his definition of a country, (7) the form of government essential to a true country, (8) the stress he placed on Italy's history as a unifying force in Europe, and (9) the emotional tone characterizing the entire essay.

From: THE DUTIES OF MAN

Your first Duties—first, at least, in importance—are, as I have told you, to Humanity. You are *men* before you are *citizens* or *fathers*. If you do not embrace the whole human family in your love, if you do not confess your faith in its unity—consequent on the unity of God—and in the brotherhood of the Peoples who are appointed to reduce that unity to fact—if wherever one of your fellowmen groans, wherever the dignity of human nature is violated by falsehood or tyranny, you are not prompt, being able, to succour that wretched one, or do not feel yourself called, being able, to fight for the purpose of relieving the deceived or oppressed—you disobey your law of life, or do not comprehend the religion which will bless the future.

But what can *each* of you, with his isolated powers, *do* for the moral improvement, for the progress of Humanity? You can, from time to time, give sterile expression to your belief; you may, on some rare occasion, perform an act of *charity* to a brother not belonging to your own land, no more. Now, *charity* is not the watchword of the future faith. The watchword of the future faith is *association*, fraternal co-opera-

As translated by Thomas Okey in *Essays by Joseph Mazzini*, London, 1894, and reprinted in Joseph Mazzini, *The Duties of Man and Other Essays*, Everyman's Library, J. M. Dent and Sons, Ltd., London and Toronto, E. P. Dutton and Company. New York, 1915, 51–59. Courtesy of E. P. Dutton and Company, Inc.

tion towards a common aim, and this is as much superior to *charity* as the work of many uniting to raise with one accord a building for the habitation of all together would be superior to that which you would accomplish by raising a separate hut each for himself, and only helping one another by exchanging stones and bricks and mortar. But divided as you are in language, tendencies, habits, and capacities, you cannot attempt this common work. The *individual* is too weak, and Humanity too vast. *My God,* prays the Breton mariner as he puts out to sea, *protect me, my ship is so little, and Thy ocean so great!* And this prayer sums up the condition of each of you, if no means is found of multiplying your forces and your powers of action indefinitely. But God gave you this means when he gave you a Country, when, like a wise overseer of labour, who distributes the different parts of the work according to the capacity of the workmen, he divided Humanity into distinct groups upon the face of our globe, and thus planted the seeds of nations. Bad governments have disfigured the design of God, which you may see clearly marked out, as far, at least, as regards Europe, by the courses of the great rivers, by the lines of the lofty mountains, and by other geographical conditions; they have disfigured it by conquest, by greed, by jealousy of the just sovereignty of others; disfigured it so much that to-day there is perhaps no nation except England and France whose confines correspond to this design. They did not, and they do not, recognise any country except their own families and dynasties, the egoism of caste. But the divine design will infallibly be fulfilled. Natural divisions, the innate spontaneous tendencies of the peoples will replace the arbitrary divisions sanctioned by bad governments. The map of Europe will be remade. The Countries of the People will rise, defined by the voice of the free, upon the ruins of the Countries of Kings and privileged castes. Between these Countries there will be harmony and brotherhood. And then the work of Humanity for the general amelioration, for the discovery and application of the real law of life, carried on in association and distributed according to local capacities, will be accomplished by peaceful and progressive development; then each of

you, strong in the affections and in the aid of many millions of men speaking the same language, endowed with the same tendencies, and educated by the same historic tradition, may hope by your personal effort to benefit the whole of Humanity.

To you, who have been born in Italy, God has allotted, as if favouring you specially, the best-defined country in Europe. In other lands, marked by more uncertain or more interrupted limits, questions may arise which the pacific vote of all will one day solve, but which have cost, and will yet perhaps cost, tears and blood; in yours, no. God has stretched round you sublime and indisputable boundaries; on one side the highest mountains of Europe, the Alps; on the other the sea, the immeasurable sea. Take a map of Europe and place one point of a pair of compasses in the north of Italy on Parma; point the other to the mouth of the Var, and describe a semicircle with it in the direction of the Alps; this point, which will fall, when the semicircle is completed, upon the mouth of the Isonzo, will have marked the frontier which God has given you. As far as this frontier your language is spoken and understood; beyond this you have no rights. Sicily, Sardinia, Corsica, and the smaller islands between them and the mainland of Italy belong undeniably to you. Brute force may for a little while contest these frontiers with you, but they have been recognised from of old by the tacit general consent of the peoples; and the day when, rising with one accord for the final trial, you plant your tricoloured flag upon that frontier, the whole of Europe will acclaim re-risen Italy, and receive her into the community of the nations. To this final trial all your efforts must be directed.

Without Country you have neither name, token, voice, nor rights, no admission as brothers into the fellowship of the Peoples. You are the bastards of Humanity. Soldiers without a banner, Israelites among the nations, you will find neither faith nor protection; none will be sureties for you. Do not beguile yourselves with the hope of emancipation from unjust social conditions if you do not first conquer a Country for yourselves; where there is no Country there is no common agreement to which you can appeal; the egoism of self-interest rules alone, and he who has the upper hand keeps it, since there is no common safeguard for the interests of all. Do not be led away by the idea of improving your material conditions without first solving the national question. You cannot do it. Your industrial associations and mutual help societies are useful as a means of educating and disciplining yourselves; as an economic fact they will remain barren until you have an Italy. The economic problem demands, first and foremost, an increase of capital and production; and while your Country is dismembered into separate fragments—while shut off by the barrier of customs and artificial difficulties of every sort, you have only restricted markets open to you—you cannot hope for this increase. To-day—do not delude yourselves—you are not the working-class of Italy; you are only fractions of that class; powerless, unequal to the great task which you propose to yourselves. Your emancipation can have no practical beginning until a National Government, understanding the signs of the times, shall, seated in Rome, formulate a Declaration of Principles to be the guide for Italian progress, and shall insert into it these words, *Labour is sacred, and is the source of the wealth of Italy.*

Do not be led astray, then, by hopes of material progress which in your present conditions can only be illusions. Your Country alone, the vast and rich Italian Country, which stretches from the Alps to the farthest limit of Sicily, can fulfil these hopes. You cannot obtain your *rights* except by obeying the commands of *Duty.* Be worthy of them, and you will have them. O my Brothers! love your Country. Our Country is our home, the home which God has given us, placing therein a numerous family which we love and are loved by, and with which we have a more intimate and quicker communion of feeling and thought than with others; a family which by its concentration upon a given spot, and by the homogeneous nature of its elements, is destined for a special kind of activity. Our Country is our field of labour; the products of our activity must go forth from it for the benefit of the whole earth; but the instruments of labour which we can use best and most effectively

exist in it, and we may not reject them without being unfaithful to God's purpose and diminishing our own strength. In labouring according to true principles for our Country we are labouring for Humanity; our Country is the fulcrum of the lever which we have to wield for the common good. If we give up this fulcrum we run the risk of becoming useless to our Country and to Humanity. Before *associating* ourselves with the Nations which compose Humanity we must exist as a Nation. There can be no association except among equals; and you have no recognised collective existence.

Humanity is a great army moving to the conquest of unknown lands, against powerful and wary enemies. The Peoples are the different corps and divisions of that army. Each has a post entrusted to it; each a special operation to perform; and the common victory depends on the exactness with which the different operations are carried out. Do not disturb the order of the battle. Do not abandon the banner which God has given you. Wherever you may be, into the midst of whatever people circumstances may have driven you, fight for the liberty of that people if the moment calls for it; but fight as Italians, so that the blood which you shed may win honour and love, not for you only, but for your Country. And may the constant thought of your soul be for Italy, may all the acts of your life be worthy of her, and may the standard beneath which you range yourselves to work for Humanity be Italy's. Do not say *I;* say *we.* Be every one of you an incarnation of your Country, and feel himself and make himself responsible for his fellow-countrymen; let each one of you learn to act in such a way that in him men shall respect and love his Country.

Your Country is one and indivisible. As the members of a family cannot rejoice at the common table if one of their number is far away, snatched from the affection of his brothers, so you should have no joy or repose as long as a portion of the territory upon which your language is spoken is separated from the Nation.

Your Country is the token of the mission which God has given you to fulfil in Humanity. The faculties, the strength of *all* its sons should be united for the accomplishment of this mission. A certain number of common duties and rights belong to every man who answers to the *Who are you?* of the other peoples, *I am an Italian.* Those duties and those rights cannot be represented except by one *single* authority resulting from your votes. A Country must have, then, a single government. The politicians who call themselves federalists, and who would make Italy into a brotherhood of different states, would dismember the Country, not understanding the idea of Unity. The States into which Italy is divided to-day are not the creation of our own people; they are the result of the ambitions and calculations of princes or of foreign conquerors, and serve no purpose but to flatter the vanity of local aristocracies for which a narrower sphere than a great Country is necessary. What you, the people, have created, beautified, and consecrated with your affections, with your joys, with your sorrows, and with your blood, is the City and the Commune, not the Province or the State. In the City, in the Commune, where your fathers sleep and where your children will live, where you exercise your faculties and your personal rights, you live out your lives as *individuals.* It is of your City that each of you can say what the Venetians say of theirs: "Venice is our own: we have made her." In your City you have need of *liberty* as in your Country you have need of *association.* The Liberty of the Commune and the Unity of the Country—let that, then, be your faith. Do not say Rome and Tuscany, Rome and Lombardy, Rome and Sicily; say Rome and Florence, Rome and Siena, Rome and Leghorn, and so through all the Communes of Italy. Rome for all that represents Italian life; your Commune for whatever represents the *individual* life. All the other divisions are artificial, and are not confirmed by your national tradition.

A Country is a fellowship of free and equal men bound together in a brotherly concord of labour towards a single end. You must make it and maintain it such. A Country is not an aggregation, it is an *association.* There is no true Country without a uniform right. There is no true Country where the uniformity of that right is violated by the existence of caste, privilege, and inequality—where the powers and faculties of a large number of individuals are sup-

pressed or dormant—where there is no common principle accepted, recognised, and developed by all. In such a state of things there can be no Nation, no People, but only a multitude, a fortuitous agglomeration of men whom circumstances have brought together and different circumstances will separate. In the name of your love for your Country you must combat without truce the existence of every privilege, every inequality, upon the soil which has given you birth. One privilege only is lawful—the privilege of Genius when Genius reveals itself in brotherhood with Virtue; but it is a privilege conceded by God and not by men, and when you acknowledge it and follow its inspirations, you acknowledge it freely by the exercise of your own reason and your own choice. Whatever privilege claims your submission in virtue of force or heredity, or any right which is not a common right, is a usurpation and a tyranny, and you ought to combat it and annihilate it. Your Country should be your Temple. God at the summit, a People of equals at the base. Do not accept any other formula, any other moral law, if you do not want to dishonour your Country and yourselves. Let the secondary laws for the gradual regulation of your existence be the progressive application of this supreme law.

And in order that they should be so, it is necessary that *all* should contribute to the making of them. The laws made by one fraction of the citizens only can never by the nature of things and men do otherwise than reflect the thoughts and aspirations and desires of that fraction; they represent, not the whole country, but a third, a fourth part, a class, a zone of the country. The law must express the general aspiration, promote the good of all, respond to a beat of the nation's heart. The whole nation therefore should be, directly or indirectly, the legislator. By yielding this mission to a few men, you put the egoism of one class in the place of the Country, which is the union of *all* the classes.

A Country is not a mere territory; the particular territory is only its foundation. The Country is the idea which rises upon that foundation; it is the sentiment of love, the sense of fellowship which binds together all the sons of that territory. So long as a single one of your brothers is not represented by his own vote in the development of the national life—so long as a single one vegetates uneducated among the educated—so long as a single one able and willing to work languishes in poverty for want of work—you have not got a Country such as it ought to be, the Country of all and for all. *Votes, education, work* are the three main pillars of the nation; do not rest until your hands have solidly erected them.

And when they have been erected—when you have secured for every one of you food for both body and soul—when freely united, entwining your right hands like brothers round a beloved mother, you advance in beautiful and holy concord towards the development of your faculties and the fulfilment of the Italian mission—remember that that mission is the moral unity of Europe; remember the immense duties which it imposes upon you. Italy is the only land that has twice uttered the great word of unification to the disjoined nations. Twice Rome has been the metropolis, the temple, of the European world; the first time when our conquering eagles traversed the known world from end to end and prepared it for union by introducing civilised institutions; the second time when, after the Northern conquerors had themselves been subdued by the potency of Nature, of great memories and of religious inspiration, the genius of Italy incarnated itself in the Papacy and undertook the solemn mission—abandoned four centuries ago—of preaching the union of souls to the peoples of the Christian world. To-day a third mission is dawning for our Italy; as much vaster than those of old as the Italian People, the free and united Country which you are going to found, will be greater and more powerful than Caesars or Popes. The presentiment of this mission agitates Europe and keeps the eye and the thought of the nations chained to Italy.

Your duties to your Country are proportioned to the loftiness of this mission. You have to keep it pure from egoism, uncontaminated by falsehood and by the arts of that political Jesuitism which they call diplomacy.

The government of the country will be based through your labours upon the worship of principles, not upon the idolatrous worship of interests and of opportunity. There are countries in Europe where Liberty is sacred within, but is systematically violated without; peoples who say, *Truth is one thing, utility another: theory is one thing, practice another.* Those countries will have inevitably to expiate their guilt in long isolation, oppression, and anarchy. But you know the mission of our Country, and will pursue another path. Through you Italy will have, with one only God in the heavens, one only truth, one only faith, one only rule of political life upon earth. Upon the edifice, sublimer than Capitol or Vatican, which the people of Italy will raise, you will plant the banner of Liberty and of Association, so that it shines in the sight of all the nations, nor will you lower it ever for terror of despots or lust for the gains of a day. You will have boldness as you have faith. You will speak out aloud to the world, and to those who call themselves the lords of the world, the thought which thrills in the heart of Italy. You will never deny the sister nations. The life of the Country shall grow through you in beauty and in strength, free from servile fears and the hesitations of doubt, keeping as its *foundation* the people, as its *rule* the consequences of its principles logically deduced and energetically applied, as its *strength* the strength of all, as its *outcome* the amelioration of all, as its *end* the fulfilment of the mission which God has given it. And because you will be ready to die for Humanity, the life of your Country will be immortal.

Heinrich von Treitschke

Heinrich von Treitschke (1834–1896), *historian and political writer, was born in Dresden, the son of a Saxon army officer. Educated at Leipzig and Bonn, he held teaching posts at Freiburg, Kiel, and Heidelberg before becoming a professor at the University of Berlin. Treitschke* *represents a curious blend of liberalism, romanticism, and realism. Very popular with students, he helped to mold the minds of the younger generation of Germans coming to maturity at the end of the nineteenth century. He displayed an extreme spirit of partisanship in his teaching and writing and sought to advance the cause of German nationalism. Not daunted by opposition, he violently attacked all opinions and parties which appeared in any way to hamper the emergence of a powerful German state. The selections that follow are from lectures on political subjects published after his death. They reveal a man passionately devoted to German unification under the Prussian aegis by means of Bismarck's policy of blood and iron. In reading the selections note (1) Treitschke's definition of, and romantic conception of, the state, (2) his regard for the social contract and natural law school of political theory, (3) the nature of the state's personality, (4) the primary obligations of the state, (5) his view of international treaties, (6) the tests of sovereignty, (7) the advantages of large states, (8) the aims of the state, (9) to what extent a state should be regarded as a means to private ends, (10) the functions of a state, (11) the function and significance of war, and (12) Treitschke's views concerning the ultimate duties and responsibilities of the state.*

From: POLITICS

THE STATE IDEA

The State is the people, legally united as an independent entity. By the word "people" we understand briefly a number of families permanently living side by side. This definition implies that the State is primordial and necessary, that it is as enduring as history, and no less essential to mankind than speech. . . .

Moreover, we must take into consideration that the idea of stateless humanity is not only without historical warrant, but also contradicts the general laws of reason. If the State were a machine—as Justus Möser still took it to be— artificially created and developed—it might equally well not have arisen at all. We can imagine humanity without a number of important attributes; but humanity without government is simply unthinkable, for it would then be humanity without reason. Man is driven by his political instinct to construct a constitution as inevitably as he constructs a language. . . .

If, then, political capacity is innate in man, and is to be further developed, it is quite inaccurate to call the State a necessary evil. We have to deal with it as a lofty necessity of Nature. Even as the possibility of building up a civilization is dependent upon the limitation of our powers combined with the gift of reason, so also the State depends upon our inability to live alone. This Aristotle has already demonstrated. The State, says he, arose in order to make life possible; it endured to make good life possible.

This natural necessity of a constituted order is further displayed by the fact that the political institutions of a people, broadly speaking, appear to be the external forms which are the inevitable outcome of its inner life. Just as its

As translated by Blanche Dugdale and Torben De Bille in Heinrich von Treitschke, *Politics,* New York: The Macmillan Company, 1916, I, 3–7; 10; 12–17; 19–37; 60–68; 71; 74; 81; 94–99; 104–106.

language is not the product of caprice but the immediate expression of its most deep-rooted attitude towards the world, so also its political institutions regarded as a whole, and the whole spirit of its jurisprudence, are the symbols of its political genius and of the outside destinies which have helped to shape the gifts which Nature bestowed. . . .

Nothing can be more inverted than the opinion that constitutional laws were artificially evolved in opposition to the conception of a Natural Law. Ultramontanes and Jacobins both start with the assumption that the legislation of a modern State is the work of sinful man. They thus display their total lack of reverence for the objectively revealed Will of God, as unfolded in the life of the State.

When we assert the evolution of the State to be something inherently necessary, we do not thereby deny the power of genius or of creative Will in history. For it is of the essence of political genius to be national. There has never been an example of the contrary. The summit of historical fame was never attained by Wallenstein because he was never a national hero, but a Czech who played the German for the sake of expediency. He was, like Napoleon, a splendid adventurer of history. The truly great maker of history always stands upon a national basis. This applies equally to men of letters. He only is a great writer who so writes that all his countrymen respond, "Thus it must be. Thus we all feel,"—who is in fact a microcosm of his nation.

If we have grasped that the State is the people legally constituted we thereby imply that it aims at establishing a permanent tradition throughout the ages. A people does not only comprise the individuals living side by side, but also the successive generations of the same stock. This is one of the truths which Materialists dismiss as a mystical doctrine, and yet it is an obvious truth. Only the continuity of human history makes man a political animal. He alone stands upon the achievements of his forbears, and deliberately continues their work in order to transmit it more perfect to his children and children's children. Only a creature like man, needing aid and endowed with reason, can have a history, and it is one of the ineptitudes of the Materialists to speak of ani-

mal States. It is just a play upon words to talk of a bee State. Beasts merely reproduce unconsciously what has been from all time, and none but human beings can possess a form of government which is calculated to endure. There never was a form of Constitution without a law of inheritance. The rational basis for this is obvious, for by far the largest part of a nation's wealth was not created by the contemporary generation. The continuous legalized intention of the past, exemplified in the law of inheritance, must remain a factor in the distribution of property amongst posterity. In a nation's continuity with bygone generations lies the specific dignity of the State. It is consequently a contradiction to say that a distribution of property should be regulated by the deserts of the existing generation. Who would respect the banners of a State if the power of memory had fled? There are cases when the shadows of the past are invoked against the perverted will of the present, and prove more potent. . . . Genuine patriotism is the consciousness of co-operating with the body-politic, of being rooted in ancestral achievements and of transmitting them to descendants. Fichte has finely said, "Individual man sees in his country the realisation of his earthly immortality."

This involves that the State has a personality, primarily in the juridical, and secondly in the politico-moral sense. Every man who is able to exercise his will in law has a legal personality. Now it is quite clear that the State possesses this deliberate will; nay more, that it has the juridical personality in the most complete sense. In State treaties it is the will of the State which is expressed, not the personal desires of the individuals who conclude them, and the treaty is binding as long as the contracting State exists. When a State is incapable of enforcing its will, or of maintaining law and order at home and prestige abroad, it becomes an anomaly and falls a prey either to anarchy or a foreign enemy. . . .

The State, then, has from all time been a legal person. It appears to be so still more clearly in the historico-moral sense. States must be conceived as the great collective personalities of history, thoroughly capable of bearing responsibility and blame. We may even speak of their legal guilt, and still more accurately of their individuality. Even as certain people have certain traits, which they cannot alter however much they try, so also the State has characteristics which cannot be obliterated. . . .

Treat the State as a person, and the necessary and rational multiplicity of States follows. Just as in individual life the ego implies the existence of the non-ego, so it does in the State. The State is power, precisely in order to assert itself as against other equally independent powers. War and the administration of justice are the chief tasks of even the most barbaric States. But these tasks are only conceivable where a plurality of States are found existing side by side. Thus the idea of one universal empire is odious—the ideal of a State co-extensive with humanity is no ideal at all. In a single State the whole range of culture could never be fully spanned; no single people could unite the virtues of aristocracy and democracy. All nations, like all individuals, have their limitations, but it is exactly in the abundance of these limited qualities that the genius of humanity is exhibited. The rays of the Divine light are manifested, broken by countless facets among the separate peoples, each one exhibiting another picture and another idea of the whole. Every people has a right to believe that certain attributes of the Divine reason are exhibited in it to their fullest perfection. No people ever attains to national consciousness without overrating itself. The Germans are always in danger of enervating their nationality through possessing too little of this rugged pride. The average German has very little political pride; but even our Philistines generally revel in the intellectual boast of the freedom and universality of the German spirit, and this is well, for such a sentiment is necessary if a people is to maintain and assert itself. . . .

Brave peoples alone have an existence, an evolution or a future; the weak and cowardly perish, and perish justly. The grandeur of history lies in the perpetual conflict of nations, and it is simply foolish to desire the suppression of their rivalry. Mankind has ever found it to be so. . . .

The rational task of a legally constituted people, conscious of a destiny, is to assert its rank in the world's hierarchy and in its measure to participate in the great civilizing mission of mankind.

Further, if we examine our definition of the State as "the people legally united as an independent entity," we find that it can be more briefly put thus: "The State is the public force for Offence and Defence." It is, above all, Power which makes its will to prevail, it is not the totality of the people as Hegel assumes in his deification of it. The nation is not entirely comprised in the State, but the State protects and embraces the people's life, regulating its external aspects on every side. It does not ask primarily for opinion, but demands obedience, and its laws must be obeyed, whether willingly or no.

A step forward has been taken when the mute obedience of the citizens is transformed into a rational inward assent, but it cannot be said that this is absolutely necessary. Powerful, highly-developed Empires have stood for centuries without its aid. Submission is what the State primarily requires; it insists upon acquiescence; its very essence is the accomplishment of its will. . . . A State which can no longer carry out its purpose collapses in anarchy. . . .

The State is not an Academy of Arts. If it neglects its strength in order to promote the idealistic aspirations of man, it repudiates its own nature and perishes. This is in truth for the State equivalent to the sin against the Holy Ghost, for it is indeed a mortal error in the State to subordinate itself for sentimental reasons to a foreign Power, as we Germans have often done to England.

Therefore the power of ideas in the life of the State is only limited. It is undoubtedly very great, but ideas by themselves do not move political forces. If they are to influence public life effectively they must find support in the vital economic interests of the people. The *ancien régime* was not shattered by the ideas of the French Philosophers, but by the mutual interaction of various classes which resulted from the spread of these ideas. . . .

We have described the State as an independent force. This pregnant theory of independence implies first so absolute a moral supremacy that the State cannot legitimately tolerate any power above its own, and secondly a temporal freedom entailing a variety of material resources adequate to its protection against hostile influences. Legal sovereignty, the State's complete independence of any other earthly power, is so rooted in its nature that it may be said to be its very standard and criterion. . . .

Human communities do exist which in their own fashion pursue aims no less lofty than those of the State, but which must be legally subject to it in their outward relations with the world. It is obvious that contradictions must arise, and that two such authorities, morally but not legally equal, must sometimes collide with each other. Nor is it to be wished that the conflicts between Church and State should wholly cease, for if they did one party or the other would be soulless and dead, like the Russian Church for example. Sovereignty, however, which is the peculiar attribute of the State, is of necessity supreme, and it is a ridiculous inconsistency to speak of a superior and inferior authority within it. The truth remains that the essence of the State consists in its incompatibility with any power over it. . . .

The notion of sovereignty must not be rigid, but flexible and relative, like all political conceptions. Every State, in treaty making, will limit its power in certain directions for its own sake. States which conclude treaties with each other thereby curtail their absolute authority to some extent. . . . No State can pledge its future to another. It knows no arbiter, and draws up all its treaties with this implied reservation. This is supported by the axiom that so long as international law exists all treaties lose their force at the very moment when war is declared between the contracting parties; moreover, every sovereign State has the undoubted right to declare war at its pleasure, and is consequently entitled to repudiate its treaties. Upon this constantly recurring alteration of treaties the progress of history depends; every State must take care that its treaties do not survive their effective value, lest another Power should denounce them by a declaration of war; for antiquated treaties must necessarily be denounced and replaced by others more consonant with circumstances.

It is clear that the international agreements which limit the power of a State are not absolute, but voluntary self-restrictions. Hence,

it follows that the establishment of a permanent international Arbitration Court is incompatible with the nature of the State, which could at all events only accept the decision of such a tribunal in cases of second- or third-rate importance. When a nation's existence is at stake there is no outside Power whose impartiality can be trusted. Were we to commit the folly of treating the Alsace-Lorraine problem as an open question, by submitting it to arbitration, who would seriously believe that the award could be impartial? It is, moreover, a point of honour for a State to solve such difficulties for itself. International treaties may indeed become more frequent, but a finally decisive tribunal of the nations is an impossibility. The appeal to arms will be valid until the end of history, and therein lies the sacredness of war.

However flexible the conception of Sovereignty may be we are not to infer from that any self-contradiction, but rather a necessity to establish in what its pith and kernel consists. Legally it lies in the competence to define the limits of its own authority, and politically in the appeal to arms. An unarmed State, incapable of drawing the sword when it sees fit, is subject to one which wields the power of declaring war. . . .

This, then, is the only real criterion. The right of arms distinguishes the State from all other forms of corporate life, and those who cannot take up arms for themselves may not be regarded as States, but only as members of a federated constellation of States. The difference between the Prussian Monarchy and the other German States is here apparent, namely, that the King of Prussia himself wields the supreme command, and therefore Prussia, unlike the others, has not lost its sovereignty.

The other test of sovereignty is the right to determine independently the limits of its power, and herein lies the difference between a federation of States and a Federal State. In the latter the central power is sovereign and can extend its competence according to its judgment, whereas in the former, every individual State is sovereign. . . .

Over and above these two essential factors of the State's sovereignty there belongs to the nature of its independence what Aristotle called "αὐτάρκεια," i.e. the capacity to be self-sufficing.

This involves, first that it should consist of a large enough number of families to secure the continuance of the race, and secondly, a certain geographical area. A ship an inch long, as Aristotle truly observes, is not a ship at all, because it is impossible to row it. Again, the State must possess such material resources as put it in a position to vindicate its theoretic independence by force of arms. Here everything depends upon the form of the community to which the State in question belongs. One cannot reckon its quality by its mileage, it must be judged by its proportionate strength compared with other States. The City State of Athens was not a petty State, but stood in the first rank in the hierarchy of nations of antiquity; the same is true of Sparta, and of Florence and Milan in the Middle Ages. But any political community not in a position to assert its native strength as against any given group of neighbours will always be on the verge of losing its characteristics as a State. This has always been the case. Great changes in the art of war have destroyed numberless States. It is because an army of 20,000 men can only be reckoned to-day as a weak army corps that the small States of Central Europe cannot maintain themselves in the long run. . . .

The entire development of European polity tends unmistakeably to drive the second-rate Powers into the background, and this raises issues of immeasurable gravity for the German nation, in the world outside Europe. Up to the present, Germany has always had too small a share of the spoils in the partition of non-European territories among the Powers of Europe, and yet our existence as a State of the first rank is vitally affected by the question whether we can become a power beyond the seas. If not, there remains the appalling prospect of England and Russia dividing the world between them, and in such a case it is hard to say whether the Russian knout or the English money bags would be the worst alternative.

On close examination then, it becomes clear that if the State is power, only that State which has power realizes its own idea, and this accounts for the undeniably ridiculous element which we discern in the existence of a small State. Weakness is not itself ridiculous, except when masquerading as strength. In small States

that puling spirit is hatched, which judges the State by the taxes it levies, and does not perceive that if the State may not enclose and repress like an egg-shell, neither can it protect. Such thinkers fail to understand that the moral benefits for which we are indebted to the State are above all price. It is by generating this form of materialism that small States have so deleterious an effect upon their citizens. . . .

Everything considered, therefore, we reach the conclusion that the large State is the nobler type. This is more especially true of its fundamental functions, such as wielding the sword in defence of the hearth and of justice. Both are better protected by a large State than a small one. The latter cannot wage war with any prospect of success. . . .

The economic superiority of big countries is patent. A splendid security springs from the mere largeness of their scale. They can overcome economic crises far more easily. Famine, for instance, can hardly attack every part of them at once, and only in them can that truly national pride arise which is a sign of the moral stamina of a people. Their citizens' outlook upon the world will be freer and greater. The command of the sea more especially promotes it. The poet's saying is true indeed that "wide horizons liberate the mind." The time may come when no State will be counted great unless it can boast of territories beyond the seas.

Another essential for the State is a capital city to form a pivot for its culture. No great nation can endure for long without a centre in which its political, intellectual, and material life is concentrated, and its people can feel themselves united. . . . Such capitals are necessary, their sins and their crimes not withstanding. . . .

Examining closely, we find that culture in general, and in the widest sense of the word, matures more happily in the broader conditions of powerful countries than within the narrow limits of a little State. . . . It must be obvious that the material resources favourable to Art and Science are more abundant in a large State; and if we inquire of history whether at any time the fairest fruit of human culture has ripened in a genuine petty State, the answer must be that in the normal course of a people's development the zenith of its political power coincides with that of its literary excellence. . . .

THE AIM OF THE STATE

When we begin to consider the aim of the State we are immediately confronted with the old vexed question which has needlessly fretted both the learned and the ignorant, namely —Should we look upon it as a means towards the private ends for which its citizens strive, or are those citizens means towards the great national ends of the State? The severely political outlook of the ancient world favoured the second alternative; the first is maintained by the modern social conception of the State, and the eighteenth century believed itself to have discovered in it the theory that the State should be treated only as an instrument to promote the aims of its citizens. . . .

When we conceive the State as a personality, we see clearly that it must seek its own goal within itself. This truth was first pointed out at the beginning of the nineteenth century by Adam Müller and the Romantic School of political thinkers. It is impossible to discover what the ultimate aim of any living personality should be, without putting the further question, What is the moral task of that personality? Let us in the same way ask the State what is its appointed work in the civilized world,—and, first, what are the natural boundaries of its activity? . . .

Theoretically, therefore, no limit can be set to the functions of a State. It will attempt to dominate the outer life of its members as far as it is able to do so. A more fruitful subject for speculation will be to fix the theoretic minimum for its activity, and decide what functions it must at the least fulfil before it can be given the name of State. When we have set this minimum we shall come to the further question of how far beyond it the State may reasonably extend its action. We then see at once that since its first duty, as we have already said, is the double one of maintaining power without, and law within, its primary obligations must be the care of its Army and its Jurisprudence, in order to protect and to restrain the community of its citizens. The fulfillment of these two functions is attained by

certain material means; therefore some form of fiscal system must exist, even in the most primitive of States, in order to provide these means.

No State can endure which can no longer fulfill these elementary duties. It is only in abnormal circumstances that we find any exception to this rule, as when an artificial balance of power protects the smaller States which can no longer protect themselves.

The functions of the State in maintaining its own internal administration of justice are manifold. It must firstly, in civil law, place the prescribed limit upon the individual will. It will nevertheless proportionately restrict its own activity in this sphere, since no individual is compelled to exercise his own legal rights. Here the State will issue no direct commands, but merely act as mediator, leaving the carrying out of its decrees to the free will of the contracting parties. . . .

The next essential function of the State is the conduct of war. The long oblivion into which this principle had fallen is a proof of how effeminate the science of government had become in civilian hands. In our century this sentimentality was dissipated by Clausewitz, but a one-sided materialism arose in its place, after the fashion of the Manchester school, seeing in man a biped, whose destiny lies in buying cheap and selling dear. It is obvious that this idea is not compatible with war, and it is only since the last war that a sounder theory arose of the State and its military power.

Without war no State could be. All those we know of arose through war, and the protection of their members by armed force remains their primary and essential task. War, therefore, will endure to the end of history, as long as there is multiplicity of States. The laws of human thought and of human nature forbid any alternative, neither is one to be wished for. The blind worshipper of an eternal peace falls into the error of isolating the State, or dreams of one which is universal, which we have already seen to be at variance with reason.

Even as it is impossible to conceive of a tribunal above the State, which we have recognized as sovereign in its very essence, so it is likewise impossible to banish the idea of war from the world. It is a favorite fashion of our time to instance England as particularly ready for peace. But England is perpetually at war; there is hardly an instant in her recent history in which she has not been obliged to be fighting somewhere. The great strides which civilization makes against barbarism and unreason are only made actual by the sword. Between civilized nations also war is the form of litigation by which States make their claims valid. The arguments brought forward in these terrible law suits of the nations compel as no argument in civil suits can ever do. Often as we have tried by theory to convince the small States that Prussia alone can be the leader in Germany, we had to produce the final proof upon the battlefields of Bohemia and the Main.

Moreover war is a uniting as well as a dividing element among nations; it does not draw them together in enmity only, for through its means they learn to know and to respect each other's peculiar qualities. . . .

The grandeur of war lies in the utter annihilation of puny man in the great conception of the State, and it brings out the full magnificence of the sacrifice of fellow-countrymen for one another. In war the chaff is winnowed from the wheat. Those who have lived through 1870 cannot fail to understand Niebuhr's description of his feelings in 1813, when he speaks of how no one who has entered into the joy of being bound by a common tie to all his compatriots, gentle and simple alike, can ever forget how he was uplifted by the love, the friendliness, and the strength of that mutual sentiment.

It is war which fosters the political idealism which the materialist rejects. What a disaster for civilization it would be if mankind blotted its heroes from memory. The heroes of a nation are the figures which rejoice and inspire the spirit of its youth, and the writers whose words ring like trumpet blasts become the idols of our boyhood and our early manhood. He who feels no answering thrill is unworthy to bear arms for his country. To appeal from this judgment to Christianity would be sheer perversity, for does not the Bible distinctly say that the ruler shall rule by the sword, and again that greater love hath no man than to lay down his life for his friend? To Aryan races, who are before all things courageous, the foolish preaching of everlasting peace has always been in

vain. They have always been men enough to maintain with the sword what they have attained through the spirit. . . .

The historian who moves in the world of the real Will sees at once that the demand for eternal peace is purely reactionary. He sees that all movement and all growth would disappear with war, and that only the exhausted, spiritless, degenerate periods of history have toyed with the idea. . . .

The modern theory of individualism, decked with its various titles, stands as the poles asunder from these conceptions of antiquity. From it the doctrine emanates that the State should content itself with protection of life and property, and with wings thus clipped be pompously dubbed a Constitutional State.

This teaching is the legitimate child of the old doctrine of Natural Law. According to it the State can only exist as a means for the individual's ends. The more ideal the view adopted of human life, the more certain does it seem that the State should content itself with the purely exterior protective functions. . . .

The State is a moral community called to positive labours for the improvement of the human race, and its ultimate aim is to build up real national character through and within itself, for this is the highest moral duty of nations as well as individuals. When we have taken this to our hearts we are able to perceive that the Germans are far from having accomplished these great national tasks. National character is exactly what they lack in comparison with their neighbours, for their unity is so young. A sure and certain national instinct is not a universal quality with us, as it is with the French people. . . .

THE STATE IN RELATION TO THE MORAL LAW

If we conceive the State to be a moral community, bound to take its appointed part in the education of the human race, it must indubitably also be subject to the universal moral law. Nevertheless we constantly hear of the conflict between politics and morals, which shows at once that the relation of the two is not perfectly simple and clear. . . .

It is necessary then to choose between public

and private morality, and since the State is power its duties must rank differently from those of the individual. Many which are incumbent upon him have no claim upon it. The injunction to assert itself remains always absolute. Weakness must always be condemned as the most disastrous and despicable of crimes, the unforgivable sin of politics. Some weaknesses of character are excusable in private life, but never in the State. It is power, and cannot be too hardly judged if it belies its essence. . . . It is equally part of the essence of the State to uphold and impose its will within its own borders. A State which permits the slightest doubt about the firmness of its purpose and the enforcement of its decrees, shatters respect for law. . . .

It is a further consequence of the essential sovereignty of the State that it can acknowledge no arbiter above it, and must ultimately submit its legal obligations to its own verdict. We must beware of judging a great crisis from the advocates' philistine standpoint. When Prussia broke the Treaty of Tilsit the civil law would have pronounced her wrong, but who would dare assert that she was guilty now? Not the French themselves. This applies to international treaties less devoid of all morality than that which Prussia was compelled to conclude with France. Every State reserves to itself the right to be judge of its own treaties, and the historian must not condemn, without searching deeper to discover whether it is fulfilling its unqualified duty of self-maintenance. . . .

The maintenance of its power then is a task of incomparable grandeur for the State, but lest it should contradict its own nature the goals it strives after must be moral ones. . . .

We recognize now that the world-capturing policy of our old German Empire was likewise a colossal blunder. It accumulated provinces whose nature forbade their complete embodiment in the National State. We have been punished for this crime by centuries of passive cosmopolitanism. Likewise it is both unpolitical and immoral for the State to interfere forcibly and oppressively in the religious life of its subjects, for here it trespasses upon their rights. By persecuting and expelling so many of the best of her German subjects during the wars of religion, Austria inflicted a blow upon the Germanic element within her State from which it has never recovered.

Thus the State cannot disregard with impunity the law to which its moral being is subject. . . .

Up to this point there will scarcely be any conflict of serious opinion, but the most difficult question arises when we come to consider the extent to which the State, to attain political ends which for it are moral, may employ means which everyday life would reject. No one can deny that the well-known Jesuit proverb contains a modicum of truth, although its expression is too crude and uncompromising. In public, as in private life, there are unfortunately too many cases where it is not possible only to have recourse to means which are absolutely above reproach. Whenever it is possible to attain an end which is moral in itself by methods which are also moral these should be preferred, even when they lead more slowly and more circuitously towards the goal. . . .

One more question arises naturally in this context. How far is the individual responsible for the morality of the State to which he belongs? Here the Natural Law, which defines the State as nothing but a collection of small individualities, goes seriously astray. We have already recognized that *la volonté générale* is not the same thing as *la volonté de tous*. The pure individualism of the Natural Law teaching came to the preposterous conclusion that the citizen has the right to desert the State if it declares a war which he holds to be unjust. But since his first duty is obedience, such unfettered power cannot be granted to his individual conscience. For me, the upholding of the mother country is a moral duty. The machinery of the political world would cease to revolve if every man made bold to say "the State should not; therefore I will not." We know of wars which have proved to be absolutely necessary, which have nevertheless been repudiated by the nation and its spokesmen. We have therefore no assurance that the subjective judgment of the individual citizen is nearer the truth than that of the King or the Minister responsible, who command so much wider a political horizon. I cannot be held responsible for a war which I personally do not approve of, but I am still under the obligation to serve my country if it breaks out. . . .

The individual should feel himself a member of his State, and as such have courage to take its errors upon him. There must be no question of subjects having the right to oppose a sovereignty which in their opinion is not moral. Cases may arise when the State's action touches the foundation of the moral life, namely, religious feeling. When the Huguenots in France had their religion proscribed, and were commanded to worship their God under forms which their deepest conviction held to be unchristian, conscience drove them out from their fatherland, but we must not praise the fine temper of these martyrs for religion from the standpoint of the theologian without recog-

nizing the degree of tragic guilt which is always blended with such moral compulsion. The Huguenots who left their homes were gallant men, no doubt, but each of them had a bitter conflict to fight out within himself before he placed his love for the Heidelberg Catechism above his hereditary love for his country and his king. In modern times there have been radical parties who have in their vanity imagined themselves faced with a similar struggle, which had in fact only a subjective existence in their own exalted imagination. This was the reason why a number of the German-Americans forsook their fatherland. It is foolish to admire them for this. We must always maintain the principle that the State is in itself an ethical force and a high moral good.

Joseph Chamberlain

Joseph Chamberlain (1836–1914), British industrialist and statesman, entered Parliament in 1876 as a representative of a Birmingham constituency. For a variety of reasons the countries of Europe were manifesting a new interest in colonial expansion during the last quarter of the nineteenth century, and Chamberlain rapidly developed into an outstanding exponent of British imperialism in Africa and elsewhere. In the eighties English and German business interests were penetrating into Uganda, and the British East Africa Company undertook the construction of a railroad from the coast into Uganda in order to gain control of its trade. In 1890, however, the two rivals reached an agreement whereby Uganda was placed in the British sphere of influence and Heligoland was ceded to the Germans. Shortly thereafter the company experienced financial difficulties and appealed to the British government for monetary aid. In 1893 the issue came before Parliament and a portion of the debate is reproduced below. Mr. Storey, as an anti-imperialist radical, spoke against the loan, while Chamberlain argued for it as an aid to imperialism. In reading the debate, note (1) the domestic social reform advocated by Mr. Storey, (2) Chamberlain's appeal to history as a justification for colonial expansion, (3) his references to the colonizing ability of the Anglo-Saxon race, (4) the discussion of the "white man's burden," (5) his description of the pax Britannica, (6) the moral obligation which he believed the government had in Uganda, (7) the economic motives mentioned for the development of Uganda, and (8) Chamberlain's humanitarian justification for the construction of the railroad.

From: A PARLIAMENTARY DEBATE ON UGANDA

MR. STOREY: He would ask right hon. Gentlemen on the Treasury Bench, and the Radicals who were in the last House of Commons, if the late Government had done this thing what would have been the attitude that they (the Radicals) would have assumed? They would have condemned such a thing as wrong, and they would have said, and with immense force, to the then Government, "You may wish to spend British money, and expend British lives in Uganda, but if you have got millions to spare, and time at your command, we would ask you to use those millions first for the good of our own country." As a Radical he should hold himself for ever disgraced if, on a matter like this—when he lived in a country which called itself Christian, but in which, at this time, millions of people were living under shameful and insanitary conditions, and which yet permitted hundreds of poor men and women to die in the workhouse wearing pauper garb—the Government should come and say they would expend these millions of money, annex a territory in Central Africa, where they were not wanted, separated by 700 miles of desert through which they would have to build a railway, he did not at once protest. If that Government came to him and proposed such a wild scheme as that, he would have said to them, "Your business is first at home, and if you have got millions to spare spend them here.". . .

MR. JOSEPH CHAMBERLAIN: He [Mr. Storey] is opposed to expansion of the Empire and to any expense, on the ground, as I understand, that we have enough to do at home. Now, suppose this view which he puts before the Committee, and which I suppose will not be accepted even to-day by the majority of the Committee, had been put 50 or 100 years ago, and suppose it had been accepted by the Parliament of that day, I ask myself what would now be the position of this country, what would be the position of persons in the slums for whom my hon. Friend has so much sympathy and feeling? Does my hon. Friend believe, if it were not for the gigantic foreign trade that has been created by the policy of expansion, that we could subsist in this country in any kind of way—I do not say in luxury, but in the condition in which at present a great part of our population live? Does he think that we could support 40,000,000 of people in these small islands? Is it not the fact that the great proportion of the 40,000,000 people of this country earns its livelihood by the trade brought to the country in consequence of the action of our ancestors 50 or 100 years ago who did not shrink from making sacrifices, and who were not ashamed—if I may borrow the expression which has been referred to more than once to-night—to peg our claims for posterity? We are the posterity who enjoy the result of that policy; and are we to be meaner and more selfish than those who preceded us? Are we to do nothing for those who come after us? Are we to sacrifice that which those who went before have gained for us? Why, if this idea of closing all the doors through which all new trade is to come to us is to be accepted by this House, we must adopt some means or other by which our population can be kept stationary. And I venture to say that when our ancestors pegged out claims for us, as they did in many parts of the world, they were not at the time more promising than the claims which are now under consideration. Well, what is it we are asked to do to-night? This is not a question of Uganda only; but we are asked to reverse the whole policy of this country—a policy undertaken, I believe, with the consent of the vast majority of the people of this country. We are asked to give up all the advantages which have been secured by the surrender of Heligoland, and by the Treaties and arrangements made with foreign Powers. My hon. Friend does not take into account any advantages. At any rate, we have made sacrifices. We gave up territory with the full consent of the majority of our people in the belief that we were getting a *quid pro quo.* Parliament is now asked to sacrifice the *quid*

Great Britain, *The Parliamentary Debates,* 4th series, 2nd Sess., 25th Parl., 57 Victoriae, X, 14 March–10 April 1893, cols. 559; 593–595; 597–599; 601–604.

pro quo which this country obtained. We are asked to give up all part and share in what has been called the partition of Africa. I am bound to do my hon. Friend this justice—to point out that he always speaks in the first person singular; therefore, I do not suppose that he claims to speak for more than himself. He will be in a minority in the House to-day. I believe he will be in a small minority in the House, and I believe that in the country he is in a still smaller minority. I believe that the people of this country have decided this matter in their minds, and have determined that they will take their full share in the disposition of these new lands and in the work of civilisation they have to carry out there. I think they are justified in that determination—justified by the spirit of the past, justified by that spirit which has shown that the spirit of travel and adventure and enterprise distinguishing the Anglo-Saxon race has made us peculiarly fit to carry out the work of colonisation. It is a curious fact, and one which I have never been able to explain, that of all the nations of the world we are the only one able to carry out this work without absolute cost to ourselves. Take, for instance, the case of France, which has been for a long time ruling in Algeria. Up to this moment, although French rule there has been beneficent, Algeria costs to the French Exchequer large sums every year. The same is the case with regard to Tunis, and the German possessions with regard to Italy in Abyssinia, and also with the foreign possessions of Portugal. There is no other country in the world except Spain, in the early days of America and Holland up to comparatively recent times, which has been able permanently to carry out a policy of colonisation without imposing burdens on its subjects. I say that all these facts should lead us to be hopeful in undertaking this new work of colonisation, which does not differ in any respect from the work we have carried out successfully in the past. If we are not going to give up this mission—to use a word I do not much like, but it has been previously employed—let us look the matter courageously in the face, and be prepared, if need be, for sacrifice of life and money, which, in the first instance, we may have to make in order to carry it out. We have come to the point

at which we do not consider life so sacred that it may not be sacrificed to save life. For my own part, I hold that, both in matters of life and money, we may sacrifice both, if we see before us a prospect of good and a satisfaction for the sacrifice we may make. The people of this country, in my opinion, have by large majorities declared that it is our duty to take our share in the work of civilisation in Africa. I do not believe they are at all prepared to sympathise with my hon. Friend below me. They know that an omelette cannot be made without breaking eggs, and I do not believe that they are prepared to count the cost. They think that in the long run any expenditure they may have incurred will prove to have been well expended. . . .

What have we done there? By a Charter we gave to a Company certain powers. Not only was the Company entrusted with discretion, but distinct and definite pressure was put upon it to go forward and to prevent other countries from coming in and taking possession of territories which were within the sphere of British influence. Rightly or wrongly, the Company yielded to the pressure of public opinion; they went forward in Uganda; they broke up such government as there was in Uganda. I am told the hon. Member for Dumfries has said, in an excellent and powerful speech, which I had not the advantage of hearing, that the normal condition there was one of massacre. But, of course, there was a Government there—such a Government as you may expect in those countries. But after all, suppose we have no business there whatever, and no responsibility, and never intend to take any, we had better have left those people to work out their own salvation for themselves, be it by massacre or in any other way. However, as a matter of fact we did not do so. We broke up the authority of those who were held to be chiefs and rulers in Uganda. We came in at a cost which to my mind was trifling in comparison with the results achieved. We have secured for Uganda the *pax Britannica* which has been so beneficial in India. I heard the Prime Minister to-night—and I confess I was delighted to hear him—I heard him talk about the sad and deplorable occurrence in Uganda. I think he spoke of those occurrences as constituting massacre.

There was no massacre at all. What existed in Uganda at that time were anarchy and civil war of the worst kind. If we had not been there thousands and perhaps hundreds of thousands of people would have been cruelly massacred; and after the victory of one party or the other what remained of the minority would have been cruelly tortured to death. Captain Lugard was on the spot. Let me say in passing that I sometimes feel we do not do justice to our bravest and noblest citizens. Of Captain Lugard I know no more than any Member of the House may know—I know him only through reading his works. He was, I believe, an Indian officer who was sent to Uganda under the orders of the Company. He undertook a work of the highest responsibility and the greatest importance, and I say that anyone who reads his accounts impartially will agree with me to this extent, that he was, at all events, a man of extraordinary power and capacity, tact, discretion, and courage. Courage is a common virtue, but he has shown it in no common way, and he has exhibited a modesty which is beyond all praise. I say it is something for England, for the United Kingdom, to glory in that we can still boast such servants as these. I was saying that Captain Lugard was present in Uganda when this state of things arose. He took his measures, and as a matter of fact in all the confusion which followed, 400 lives at the outside—he himself puts the number at considerably less—were killed. It was deplorable, no doubt; but that sacrifice cheaply purchased the peace, the pacification, and temporary civilisation which followed; and at all events, long before now the people of that great country would have been at each other's throats but for the presence of the English. You have taken this responsibility through the Company to whom you gave a Charter; you have never disavowed them; and now you cannot leave that country whatever it cost you. Even if, as the hon. Member for Northampton said, it cost you another expedition, you are bound at all costs to fulfil the obligations of this country to maintain the faith of this country to the people to whom it is pledged. What would happen if you left? Would not the Protestants, Catholics, and Mahomedans be at one another's throats, and would there not be a

massacre almost unparalleled even in the history of Africa? And who would suffer most? Those who have been our allies. They are the people whom we have disarmed and who would now fall an easy prey to their enemies. I do not think my hon. Friend contemplated such an abandonment as that. I am quite ready to protest against any further extension of the Empire. But we are dealing now with what has taken place and cannot be recalled; and I say it would be a greater disgrace than ever befell England if you were to retire from a country whose prosperity and the lives of whose people depended absolutely upon your continuance of the hold you have upon them. . . .

As to the commerce of Uganda, the late Mr. Mackay, the missionary, who was universally respected, said that the climate of Uganda was excellent, that the country would produce almost anything, and that the only difficulty was the want of transport and of British enterprise, but that once those two things were secured there was no reason whatever why Uganda should not be a most prosperous, even a wealthy, country. Of course, Uganda, 600 miles from the coast, in such a position that everything brought there from the coast or taken to the coast from there costs £200 per ton in transport, is not likely to have a very brisk trade at present. But I would ask hon. Gentlemen what they would have said about the cost of carriage to the North-West of Canada 100 years ago? Until the Canadian Pacific Railway was constructed there was scarcely any trade in those great dominions of the British Crown. I say that the prospects of Uganda at this moment are quite equal to those of the North-West of Canada 50 years ago. This is what Lord Rosebery means by pegging out claims for prosperity. Lord Rosebery is sensible that our returns cannot be immediate, but, on the other hand, a return at some time or another is almost certain. . . .

I firmly believe that the railway will pay in the end, and will prove a good investment. If you spend this £1,500,000 or £3,000,000, the working classes of this country, and the people in the slums, for whom the hon. Member for Sunderland is so anxious, will benefit, for the whole of the work will, of course, be done in this country, and the line will be engineered by natives of this country. Even in the hon. Member's view, therefore, the money will not be wholly thrown away. I believe that the chances of this railway are every bit as good as the railways which this country made 30 years ago in the Peninsular of India, and which are now bringing in a good revenue. This railway will bring us into contact with 12,000,000 of people, as, besides the people of Uganda, there is the population of the countries conterminous with the Victoria Lake and the other great lakes to be considered, and whatever may be said of Uganda, nobody will deny that the neighbouring countries, like Unyoro and Usoga, are countries of enormous natural wealth. I believe that just as soon as you make porterage possible, we shall have a very large commerce. We shall get from this country gum and rubber, and perhaps even wheat, and in return we shall send out large quantities of our manufactures. One thing I must say in confirmation of this. I think it is a most remarkable fact that since we created this Company and this sphere of influence, the British and the general trade of Zanzibar has been increasing at a perfectly marvellous rate. In one year—the last year for which we have Returns—it nearly doubled, increasing from 72,000 to 131,000 tons. If that is done in the green tree, what will be done in the dry? I have no hesitation in saying, therefore, that the investment is one which a rich country can wisely undertake. The hon. Member for Sunderland says he does feel a certain amount of obligation in connection with the suppression of the Slave Trade, though to his mind it is inferior to the obligation we have to the inhabitants of the slums. Well, I say with regard to the Slave Trade, that the railway will do more to suppress that abominable traffic than can be accomplished by any other expenditure of the same sum. What is the Slave Trade, and what is the cause of it? People do not make slaves through love of cruelty or mischief, but they do so because they made their livelihood by it. Tribes are enslaved, are taken as slaves, in order to carry burdens to the coast, and when

they have done that they are sold for what they will fetch. If you could give to the slave-raiding Arabs, who at the present moment are the most barbarous and brutal people on the face of the earth, peaceful means of making an honest livelihood, do you mean to say that they enjoy war so much that they will not accept these means? If you say so, I think all history and experience is against you. You have never found a case where it has been made profitable to a nation or tribe to keep the peace that they have not done so. Take an illustration. In the old days we had to fight with the Punjabees, and when we had conquered them they supplied us with our best soldiers in India. But now that we established peace, and the country is more prosperous than it ever was before, and people, who were once the most warlike race in India, are settling down, or I should say, rising up, into agriculturalists and peasants, and we cannot get from them an adequate number of recruits for our Army. We have to go farther afield. What happened in India will happen in Africa. Make it the interest of the Arab slave traders to give up the Slave Trade, and you will see the end of that traffic. It costs at present between £200 and £300 to carry a ton of merchandise to Uganda. Construct your railway, and increase the means of traffic, and you will take away three-fourths, almost the whole, of the temptation to carry on the Slave Trade. I ask the Committee, and I should like to put it to the country: Are they in earnest in this matter of the Slave Trade? Is the hereditary sentiment of the British people still existent amongst us? Do we hold it to be one of our prime duties, as Lord Rosebery said, and great glories, to take a prominent part in suppressing this trade? If we do, let us look boldly in the face the necessities of the situation and let us spend our money wisely and direct it to this purpose. We are spending £200,000 a year for a squadron on the East Coast, as I said just now, which I am afraid, has too often increased indirectly the horrors and sufferings in connection with the trade. . . .

Albert J. Beveridge

Albert J. Beveridge (1862–1927) was an American politician, lawyer, historian, and orator who served two terms (1899–1911) as a United States Senator from Indiana. He became associated toward the close of the century with a group of young men actively interested in American imperialism. In 1898 he favored the war against Spain, and in the congressional elections of that year, he warmly defended the peace terms demanded of Spain by the McKinley administration. In thus supporting the Republicans and opposing the free silver Democrats, Beveridge revealed himself as an ardent imperialist, advocating American expansion both in the Pacific and in the Caribbean area. At times his speeches had a decided jingoistic tinge, as, for example, "The March of the Flag" address given in Indianapolis during the campaign. In reading the following selections from this speech note (1) the references Beveridge made to Divine participation in American progress, (2) the size and nature of the issue before the voters, (3) what he considered to be the fruits of victory, (4) the manner in which he related the deeds of McKinley with those of earlier Americans, (5) his reply to those who opposed colonial expansion on grounds of democratic principles, (6) how he refuted the opposition's "contiguous territory" argument, (7) the economic arguments he advanced for the annexation of the new territories, (8) the importance of a sound financial system to a trading nation, (9) his emphasis upon America's manifest destiny, and (10) the similarities between his arguments and those of Joseph Chamberlain.

From: THE MARCH OF THE FLAG

Fellow-Citizens—It is a noble land that God has given us; a land that can feed and clothe the world: a land whose coast lines would inclose half the countries of Europe; a land set like a sentinel between the two imperial oceans of the globe; a greater England with a nobler destiny. It is a mighty people that He has planted on this soil; a people sprung from the most masterful blood of history; a people perpetually revitalized by the virile workingfolk of all the earth; a people imperial by virtue of their power, by right of their institutions, by authority of their heaven-directed purposes, the propagandists and not the misers of liberty. It is a glorious history our God has bestowed upon His chosen people; a history whose keynote was struck by Liberty Bell; a history heroic with faith in our mission and our future; a history of statesmen, who flung the boundaries of the Republic out into unexplored lands and savage wildernesses; a history of soldiers, who carried the flag across blazing deserts and through the ranks of hostile mountains, even to the gates of sunset: a history of a multiplying people, who overran a continent in half a century; a history divinely logical, in the process of whose tremendous reasoning we find ourselves to-day.

Therefore, in this campaign the question is larger than a party question. It is an American question. It is a world question. Shall the American people continue their resistless march toward the commercial supremacy of the world? Shall free institutions broaden their blessed reign as the children of liberty wax in strength until the empire of our principles is established over the hearts of all mankind? Have we no mission to perform—no duty to discharge to our fellow-man? Has the Almighty Father endowed us with gifts beyond our deserts, and marked us as the people of His peculiar favor, merely to rot in our own selfishness, as men and nations must who take cowardice for their companion and self for their deity—as China has, as India has, as Egypt has? Shall we be as the man who had one talent and hid it, or as he who had ten talents and used them until they grew to riches. And shall we reap the reward that waits on the discharge of our high duty as the sovereign power of earth; shall we occupy new markets for what our farmers raise, new markets for what our factories make, new markets for what our merchants sell,—aye, and please God, new markets for what our ships shall carry? Shall we avail ourselves of new sources of supply of what we do not raise or make, so that what are luxuries to-day shall be necessities to-morrow? Shall we conduct the mightiest commerce of history with the best money known to man or shall we use the pauper money of Mexico, China and the Chicago [Democratic Party] platform? Shall we be worthy of our mighty past of progress, brushing aside, as we have always done, the spider webs of technicality, and march ever onward upon the highway of development, to the doing of real deeds, the achievement of real things, and the winning of real victories?

In a sentence, shall the American people endorse at the polls the American administration of William McKinley, which, under the guidance of Divine Providence, has started the Republic on its noblest career of prosperity, duty and glory; or shall the American people rebuke that administration, reverse the wheels of history, halt the career of the flag and turn to that purposeless horde of criticism and carping that is assailing the government at Washington? Shall it be McKinley, sound money and a world-conquering commerce, or Bryan, Bailey, Bland, and Blackburn, a bastard currency and a policy of commercial retreat? In the only foreign war that this Nation has had in two generations, will you, the voters of this Republic and the guardians of its good repute, give the other nations of the world to understand that the American people do not approve and indorse the administration that conducted it? These are the questions that you must answer at the polls, and I well know how you will answer them. The thunder of American guns at Santiago and Manila will find its answer in the approval of the voters of the Republic. For the administration of William McKinley, in both peace and war, will receive the mightiest endorsement of a grateful people ever registered. In both peace and war, for we rely on the new birth of national prosperity as well as on the new birth of national glory. Think of both! Think of our country two years ago, and think of it to-day! . . .

For William McKinley is continuing the policy that Jefferson began, Monroe continued, Seward advanced, Grant promoted, Harrison championed. Hawaii is ours; Porto Rico is to be ours; at the prayer of its people Cuba will finally be ours; in the islands of the East, even to the gates of Asia, coaling stations are to be ours; at the very least the flag of a liberal government is to float over the Philippines, and it will be the stars and stripes of glory. And the burning question of this campaign is whether the American people will accept the gifts of events; whether they will rise, as lifts their soaring destiny; whether they will proceed along the lines of national development surveyed by the statesmen of our past; or whether, for the first time, the American people doubt their mission, question their fate, prove apostate to the spirit of their race, and halt the ceaseless march of free institutions?

The opposition tells us that we ought not to govern a people without their consent. I answer, the rule of liberty that all just government derives its authority from the consent of the governed, applies only to those who are capable of self-government. We govern the

Indians without their consent; we govern our Territories without their consent; we govern our children without their consent. I answer, would not the natives of the Philippines prefer the just, humane, civilizing government of this Republic to the savage, bloody rule of pillage and extortion from which we have rescued them? Do not the blazing fires of joy and the ringing bells of gladness in Porto Rico prove the welcome of our flag? And regardless of this formula of words made only for enlightened, self-governing peoples, do we owe no duty to the world? Shall we turn these peoples back to the reeking hands from which we have taken them? Shall we save them from those nations, to give them to a self-rule of tragedy? It would be like giving a razor to a babe and telling it to shave itself. It would be like giving a typewriter to an Esquimau and telling him to publish one of the great dailies of the world. . . .

Distance and oceans are no longer arguments. The fact that all the territory our fathers bought and seized is contiguous is no longer an argument. In 1819 Florida was further from New York than Porto Rico is from Chicago today; Texas further from Washington in 1845 than Hawaii is from Boston in 1898; California more inaccessible in 1847 than the Philippines are now. Gibraltar is further from London than Havana is from Washington; Melbourne is further from Liverpool than Manila is from San Francisco. The ocean does not separate us from the lands of our duty and desire—the ocean to join us, a river never to be dredged, a canal never to be repaired. Steam joins us; electricity joins us—the very elements are in league with our destiny. Cuba not contiguous! Porto Rico not contiguous! Hawaii and the Philippines not contiguous! Our navy will make them contiguous. Dewey and Sampson and Schley have made them contiguous and American speed, American guns, American heart and brain and nerve will keep them contiguous forever.

But there is a difference. We did not need the western Mississippi valley when we acquired it, nor Florida, nor Texas, nor California, nor the royal provinces of the far Northwest. We had no emigrants to people this vast wilderness, no money to develop it, even no

highways to cover it. No trade awaited us in its savage fastnesses. Our productions were not greater than our internal trade. There was not one reason for the land lust of our statesmen from Jefferson to Harrison other than the prophet and the Saxon within them. But today, we are raising more than we can consume. Today, we are making more than we can use. Therefore, we must find new markets for our produce, new occupation for our capital, new work for our labor. And so, while we did not need the territory taken during the past century at the time it was acquired, we do need what we have taken in 1898, and we need it now. Think of the thousands of Americans who will pour into Hawaii and Porto Rico when the Republic's laws cover those islands with justice and safety. Think of the tens of thousands of Americans who will invade the Philippines when a liberal government shall establish order and equity there. Think of the hundreds of thousands of Americans who will build a soap-and-water, common school civilization of energy and industry in Cuba, when a government of law replaces the double reign of anarchy and tyranny. Think of the prosperous millions that empress of islands will support when, obedient to the law of political gravitation, her people ask for the highest honor liberty can bestow—the sacred order of the stars and stripes, the citizenship of the great Republic!

What does all this mean for every one of us? First of all, it means opportunity for all the glorious young manhood of the Republic. It means that the resources and the commerce of those immensely rich dominions will be increased as much as American energy is greater than Spanish sloth; for Americans, henceforth, will monopolize those resources and that commerce. In Cuba, alone, there are 15,000,000 acres of forest unacquainted with the ax. There are exhaustless mines of iron. There are priceless deposits of manganese. There are millions of acres yet unexplored. The resources of Porto Rico have only been trifled with. The resources of the Philippines have hardly been touched by the finger tips of modern methods. And they produce what we cannot, and they consume what we produce—the very predestination of reciprocity. And William McKinley intends that their trade shall be ours. It means an opportunity for the rich man to do something with his money, besides hoarding it or lending it. It means occupation for every workingman in the country at wages which the development of new resources, the launching of new enterprises, the monopoly of new markets always brings. Cuba is as large as Pennsylvania, and is the richest spot on all the globe. Hawaii is as large as New Jersey; Porto Rico half as large as Hawaii; the Philippines larger than all New England, New York, New Jersey and Delaware. The trade of these islands, developed as we will develop it, will set every reaper in the Republic singing, every furnace spouting the flames of industry. . . .

Now on the threshold of our career as the first power of earth, is the time to permanently adjust our system of finance. The American people have the most tremendous tasks of history to perform. They have the mightiest commerce of the world to conduct. They cannot halt their progress of wealth and power to unsettle their money system at the command of ignorance. Think of Great Britain becoming the commercial monarch of the world with her financial system periodically assailed! Think of Holland or Germany or France yet sending their flag in every sea, with their money at the mercy of politicians seeking for an issue! Sixteen to one is passed in our career. Why go back to it, like the victim of opium to his deadly pipe? Now, when new rivers of gold are pouring through the fields of business, the foundation of all silver-standard argument that there is not enough gold, is swept away. Why mumble the meaningless phrases of a tale that is told when the golden future is before us, the world calls us, its wealth awaits us and God's command is on us? There are so many real things to be done—canals to be dug, railways to be laid, forests to be felled, cities to be builded, unviolated fields to be tilled, priceless markets to be won, ships to be launched, peoples to be saved, civilization to be proclaimed and the flag of liberty flung to the eager air of every sea. Is this an hour to waste upon triflers with Nature's laws? Is this a season to give our destiny over to word mongers and prosperity wreckers? No! It is an hour to remember your duty to the home. It is a moment to realize the opportunities Fate has opened to this favored people and to you. It is a time to bethink you of your Nation and its sovereignty of the seas. It is a time to remember that the God of our fathers is our God and that the gifts and the duties He gave to them, enriched and multiplied, He renews to us, their children. It is a time to sustain that devoted man, servant of the people and of the most high God, who is guiding the Republic out into the ocean of infinite possibilities. It is a time to cheer the beloved President of God's chosen people, till the whole world is vocal with American loyalty to the American government and William McKinley, its head and chief.

Fellow-Americans, we are God's chosen people. Yonder at Bunker Hill and Yorktown His providence was above us. At New Orleans and on ensanguined seas His hand sustained us. Abraham Lincoln was His minister, and His was the altar of freedom the boys in blue set up on a hundred smoking battlefields. His power directed Dewey in the east, and He delivered the Spanish fleet into our hands on Liberty's natal day as He delivered the elder Armada into the hands of our English sires two centuries ago. His great purposes are revealed in the progress of the flag, which surpasses the intentions of Congresses and Cabinets, and leads us, like a holier pillar of cloud by day and pillar of fire by night, into situations unforeseen by finite wisdom and duties unexpected by the unprophetic heart of selfishness. The American people cannot use a dishonest medium of exchange; it is ours to set the world its example of right and honor. We cannot fly from our world duties; it is ours to execute the purposes of a fate that has driven us to be greater than our small intentions. We cannot retreat from any soil where Providence has unfurled our banner; it is ours to save that soil for liberty and civilization. For liberty and civilization and God's promises fulfilled, the flag must henceforth be the symbol and the sign to all mankind.

William II, Poincaré, Nicholas II, and Asquith

On June 28, 1914 the Archduke, Franz Ferdinand, was assassinated in the Bosnian capital of Sarajevo as the result of a Serbian nationalist plot. One month later, on July 28, the Austro-Hungarian government declared war on Serbia with the intention of punishing her for this fatal attack on the heir to the Habsburg throne and of removing the Serbian threat to the empire of the dual monarchy. Immediately, the system of alliances which had divided Europe into two hostile groups, began to function, and within a week five of the six major European powers were at war. In the first days of the struggle the governmental heads of the belligerent nations issued statements to their peoples to justify their action and to arouse popular feeling in support of the struggle ahead. In reading these statements compare them on such points as (1) which nations were waging defensive war, (2) the emphasis each placed on national honor, (3) the appeals to Divine assistance, (4) their concern for conquest, (5) the efforts made to preserve peace, and (6) the references made to obligations to support alliances.

STATEMENTS MADE AT THE OUTBREAK OF WORLD WAR I

GERMAN STATEMENTS

*Speech of Emperor William II
from the balcony of the Imperial Palace,
31 July 1914*

A momentous hour has struck for Germany. Envious rivals everywhere drive us to legitimate defense. The sword has been forced into our hand. I hope that, if my endeavors up to the very last moment should not succeed in bringing the adversaries to reason and in preserving peace, we may wield the sword, with God's help, so that we may sheathe it again with honor. War would demand enormous sacrifices from the German people, but we would show the enemy what it means to attack

Germany. And so I commend you to God. Go now into the churches, kneel before God, and implore His help for our brave army.

*Emperor William's Speech from the Throne,
4 August 1914*

Honored gentlemen, at a time of such importance I have assembled the elected representatives of the German people about me. For nearly half a century we have been allowed to follow the ways of peace. The attempts to attribute to Germany warlike intentions and to hedge in her position in the world have often sorely tried the patience of my people. Undeterred, my Government has pursued the development of our moral, spiritual,

Speech of the Emperor William II, 31 July 1914, from Ralph Haswell Lutz, *Fall of the German Empire, 1914–1918*, Stanford University Press, Stanford University, 1932, I, 4; statement of the Emperor William II, 4 August 1914, from *ibid.*, I, 8–9. Courtesy of the Stanford University Press. Manifesto of Tsar Nicholas II, 2 August 1914, from Frank Alfred Golder, *Documents of Russian History, 1914–1917*, The Century Company, New York, 1927, 29–30. Courtesy of Appleton-Century-Crofts, Inc. Message, President Poincaré, Chamber of Deputies, 4 August 1914, translated by the editors from France, *Assemblée nationale, Annales de la Chambre des deputes, 1914*, sess. ord. et ext., II, 907–910. Prime Minister Asquith, House of Commons, 6 August 1914 from Great Britain, *The Parliamentary Debates*, 5th series, Commons, 1914, LXV, cols. 2078–2079.

and economic strength as its highest aim, with all frankness, even under provocative circumstances. The world has been witness that during the last years, under all pressure and confusion, we have stood in the first rank in saving the nations of Europe from a war between the great powers.

The most serious dangers to which the events in the Balkans had given rise seemed to have been overcome—then suddenly an abyss was opened through the murder of my friend the Archduke Franz Ferdinand. My lofty ally, the Emperor and King Franz Josef, was forced to take up arms to defend the security of his empire against dangerous machinations from a neighboring state. The Russian Empire stepped in to hinder the allied monarchy from following out her just interests. Not only does our duty as ally call us to the side of Austria-Hungary, but it is our great task to protect our own position and the old community of culture between the two Empires against the attack of hostile forces. . . .

The present situation is the result of an ill will which has been active for many years against the power and the prosperity of the German Empire.

No lust of conquest drives us on; we are inspired by the unalterable will to protect the place in which God has set us for ourselves and all coming generations. From the documents which have been submitted to you, you will see how my Government, and especially my Chancellor, have endeavored even to the last moment to stave off the inevitable. In a defensive war that has been forced upon us, with a clear conscience and a clean hand we take up the sword. . . .

FRENCH STATEMENT

Message of President Poincaré to the Chamber of Deputies, 4 August 1914

Gentlemen of the Chamber of Deputies, France has become the object of a brutal and premeditated aggression which is an insolent defiance of international law. Before a declaration of war was addressed to us, before even the German ambassador had asked for his passport, our territory was invaded. . . .

For more than forty years the French, in a sincere love of peace, have stifled the desire for legitimate reparation. They have given to the world the example of a great nation which, definitively resurrected from defeat by strength of will, by patience and work, has used its renewed and revived force only in the interest of progress and for the good of humanity.

Since the Austrian crisis opened up a situation threatening to the whole of Europe, France has set herself to follow and to recommend everywhere a policy of prudence, wisdom, and moderation. No one can charge her with an act, with a gesture, with a word which has not been peaceful and conciliating. In this hour of the first combats, she has the right to credit herself with the fact that she made supreme efforts up until the last moment to avoid this war which has just broken out and for which Germany will bear before history the crushing responsibility. . . .

In the war which has begun, France will have on her side that right whose eternal moral force no people, no individual can defy with impunity. She will be heroically defended by her sons whose sacred unity before the enemy nothing can break and who are today joined in the same indignation against the aggressor and in the same patriotic faith. She is faithfully seconded by Russia, her ally; she is supported by the loyal friendship of England.

Already from all parts of the civilized world come to her expressions of sympathy and good wishes. Because she represents again today before the universe liberty, justice, and reason.

Haut les coeurs et vive la France!

RUSSIAN STATEMENT

Manifesto of Tsar Nicholas II, 2 August 1914

By the Grace of God, We, Nicholas II, Emperor and Autocrat of all Russia, Tsar of Poland, Grand Duke of Finland, etc., etc., etc., proclaim to all Our loyal subjects:

Following her historical traditions, Russia, united in faith and blood with the Slav nations, has never regarded their fate with indifference. The unanimous fraternal sentiments of the Russian people for the Slavs have been aroused to special intensity in the past few days, when Austria-Hungary presented to Serbia demands which she foresaw would be unacceptable to a Sovereign State.

Having disregarded the conciliatory and peaceable reply of the Serbian Government, and having declined Russia's well-intentioned mediation, Austria hastened to launch an armed attack in a bombardment of unprotected Belgrad.

Compelled, by the force of circumstances thus created, to adopt the necessary measures of precaution, We commanded that the army and the navy be put on a war footing, but, at the same time, holding the blood and the treasure of Our subjects dear, We made every effort to obtain a peaceable issue of the negotiations that had been started.

In the midst of friendly communications, Austria's Ally, Germany, contrary to Our trust in century-old relations of neighborliness, and paying no heed to Our assurances that the measures We had adopted implied no hostile aims whatever, insisted upon their immediate abandonment, and, meeting with a rejection of this demand, suddenly declared war on Russia.

We have now to intercede not only for a related country, unjustly attacked, but also to safeguard the honor, dignity, and integrity of Russia, and her position among the Great Powers. We firmly believe that all Our loyal subjects will rally self-sacrificingly and with one accord to the defense of the Russian soil.

At this hour of threatening danger, let domestic strife be forgotten. Let the union between the Tsar and His people be stronger than ever, and let Russia, rising like one man, repel the insolent assault of the enemy.

With a profound faith in the justice of Our cause, and trusting humbly in Almighty Providence, We invoke prayerfully the Divine blessing for Holy Russia and Our valiant troops. . . .

BRITISH STATEMENT

Statement by Prime Minister Asquith in the House of Commons, 6 August 1914

. . . I am entitled to say, and I do so on behalf of this country—I speak not for a party, I speak for the country as a whole—that we made every effort any Government could possibly make for peace. But this war has been forced upon us. What is it we are fighting for? Everyone knows, and no one knows better than the Government, the terrible, incalculable suffering, economic, social, personal, and political, which war, and especially a war between the Great Powers of the world, must entail. There is no man amongst us sitting upon this bench in these trying days—more trying perhaps than any body of statesmen for a hundred years have had to pass through—there is not a man amongst us who has not, during the whole of that time, had clearly before his vision the almost unequalled suffering which war, even in a just cause, must bring about, not only to the peoples who are for the moment living in this country and in other countries of the world, but to posterity and to the whole prospects of European civilisation. Every step we took we took with that vision before our eyes, and with a sense of responsibility which it is impossible to describe. . . .

If I am asked what we are fighting for I reply in two sentences. In the first place, to fulfil a solemn international obligation, an obligation which, if it had been entered into between private persons in the ordinary concerns of life, would have been regarded as an obligation not only of law but of honour, which no self-respecting man could possibly have repudiated. I say, secondly, we are fighting to vindicate the principle which, in these days when force, material force, sometimes seems to be the dominant influence and factor in the development of mankind, we are fighting to vindicate the principle that small nationalities are not to be crushed, in defiance of international good faith, by the arbitrary will of a strong and overmastering Power.

I do not believe that any nation ever entered into a great controversy—and this is one of the greatest history will ever know—with a clearer conscience and a stronger conviction that it is fighting, not for aggression, not for the maintenance even of its own selfish interest, but that it is fighting in defence of principles the maintenance of which is vital to the civilisation of the world. With a full conviction, not only of the wisdom and justice, but of the obligations which lay upon us to challenge this great issue, we are entering into the struggle. . . .

Entente Diplomacy

For generations the Russian ambition to control Constantinople and the adjacent straits leading to the Mediterranean had been opposed by the British. On October 28, 1914, Turkey entered the war on the side of the Central Powers and the Czarist government was not slow in pressing its claims for Turkish territory upon Great Britain and France. Naturally, the British assent was given more reluctantly than that of the French, a fact which was revealed by the memorandums exchanged among the three powers in March, 1915. The British and French replies to the Russian demands are significant in that they prepared the way for the partition of the Turkish Empire among the members of the Entente. In reading them note (1) the description of the territory demanded by the Russian Minister of Foreign Affairs, (2) the importance attached to the demand by the British Embassy in Petrograd, (3) the statement by the British on how their assent fitted in with their traditional policy, (4) the British request for future concessions in the ceded area, (5) the reservations regarding Moslem holy places, (6) why the British wanted the understanding kept secret, and (7) the statement in the memorandum to the Russian ambassador in Paris of the political aspirations of England.

From: THE SECRET AGREEMENT OF MARCH, 1915

MEMORANDUM OF THE RUSSIAN FOREIGN OFFICE

On February 19 (March 4), 1915, the Minister of Foreign Affairs handed to the French and British Ambassadors a Memorandum which set forth the desire to add the following territories to Russia as the result of the present war:

The town of Constantinople, the western coast of the Bosphorus, the Sea of Marmora, and the Dardanelles; Southern Thrace, as far as the Enos-Media line; the coast of Asia Minor between the Bosphorus and the River Sakaria, and a point on the Gulf of Ismid to be defined later; the islands in the Sea of Marmora, and the Islands of Imbros and Tenedos. The special

rights of France and England in the above territories were to remain inviolate.

MEMORANDUM OF THE BRITISH EMBASSY IN PETROGRAD, 12 MARCH 1915

. . . The claim made by the Imperial [Russian] Government in their Aide-Mémoire of February 19—March 4, 1915 considerably exceeds the desiderata which were foreshadowed by M. Sasonow as probable a few weeks ago. Before His Majesty's Government have had time to take into consideration what their own desiderata elsewhere would be in the final terms of peace, Russia is asking for a definite promise that her wishes shall be satisfied with

Memorandum of the Russian Foreign Office, March 1915, from F. Seymour Cocks, *The Secret Treaties and Understandings*, London, 1918, 19–24. Memorandum of the British Embassy in Petrograd, 12 March 1915, from Frank A Golder, *Documents of Russian History, 1914–1917*, The Century Company, New York, 1927, 60–62. Courtesy of Appleton-Century-Crofts, Inc. Russian Minister of Foreign Affairs to Russian Ambassador, Paris, 5/18 March 1915, from F. Seymour Cocks, *op. cit.*, 17–18.

regard to what is in fact the richest prize of the entire war. Sir Edward Grey accordingly hopes that M. Sasonow will realize that it is not in the power of His Majesty's Government to give a greater proof of friendship than that which is afforded by the terms of the above-mentioned Aide-Mémoire. That document involves a complete reversal of the traditional policy of His Majesty's Government and is in direct opposition to the opinions and sentiment at one time universally held in England and which have still by no means died out. Sir Edward Grey therefore trusts that the Imperial Government will recognize that the recent general assurances given to M. Sasonow have been most loyally and amply fulfilled. In presenting the Aide-Mémoire now, His Majesty's Government believe and hope that a lasting friendship between Russia and Great Britain will be assured as soon as the proposed settlement is realized.

From the British Aide-Mémoire it follows that the desiderata of His Majesty's Government, however important they may be to British interests in other parts of the world, will contain no condition which could impair Russia's control over the territories described in the Russian Aide-Mémoire of February 19—March 4, 1915.

In view of the fact that Constantinople will always remain a trade entrepôt for South-Eastern Europe and Asia Minor, His Majesty's Government will ask that Russia shall, when she comes in the possession of it, arrange for a free port for goods in transit to and from non-Russian territory. His Majesty's Government will also ask that there shall be commercial freedom for merchant ships passing through the Straits, as M. Sasonow has already promised. . . .

Sir E. Grey points out that it will obviously be necessary to take into consideration the whole question of the future interests of France and Great Britain in what is now Asiatic Turkey; and, in formulating the desiderata of His Majesty's Government with regard to the Ottoman Empire, he must consult the French as well as the Russian Government. As soon, however, as it becomes known that Russia is to have Constantinople at the conclusion of the war, Sir E. Grey will wish to state that,

throughout the negotiations, His Majesty's Government have stipulated that the Mussulman Holy Places and Arabia shall under all circumstances remain under independent Mussulman dominion.

Sir E. Grey is as yet unable to make any definitive proposal on any point of the British desiderata; but one of the points of the latter will be the revision of the Persian portion of the Anglo-Russian Agreement of 1907, so as to recognize the present neutral sphere as a British sphere.

Until the Allies are in a position to give to the Balkan States, and especially to Bulgaria and Rumania, some satisfactory assurance as to their prospects and general position with regard to the territories contiguous to their frontiers, to the possession of which they are known to aspire; and until a more advanced stage of the agreement as to the French and British desiderata in the final peace terms is reached, Sir E. Gray points out that it is most desirable that the understanding now arrived at between the Russian, French, and British Governments should remain secret.

THE RUSSIAN MINISTER OF FOREIGN AFFAIRS TO THE RUSSIAN AMBASSADOR IN PARIS, 5/18 MARCH 1915

On February 23 (March 8) the French Ambassador, on behalf of his Government, announced to me that France was prepared to take up a most favourable attitude in the matter of realisation of our desires as set out in my telegram to you, No. 937, in respect of the Straits and Constantinople, for which I charged you to tender Delcassé my gratitude.

In his conversations with you, Delcassé had previously more than once given his assurance that we could rely on the sympathy of France, and only referred to the need of elucidating the question of the attitude of England, from whom he feared some objections, before he could give us a more definite assurance in the above sense. Now the British Government has given its complete consent in writing to the annexation by Russia of the Straits and Constantinople within the limits indicated by us, and only demanded security for its economic interests and a similar benevolent attitude on our part towards the political aspirations of England in other parts.

For me, personally, filled as I am with most complete confidence in Delcassé, the assurance received from him is quite sufficient, but the Imperial Government would desire a more definite pronouncement of France's assent to the complete satisfaction of our desires, similar to that made by the British Government.

The Governments of France, Russia, Great Britain, and Italy

When the war broke out in August, 1914, Italy, despite her membership in the Triple Alliance, remained neutral. She claimed that Germany and Austria were waging an offensive war and that, therefore, the terms of their alliance, which were defensive in character, did not apply. In May, 1915, Italy joined the Entente against the Central Powers. Subsequently, it has been revealed that France, Russia, and Great Britain signed a secret treaty with Italy in London on April 26, 1915, the terms of which are given below. Undoubtedly, the agreement influenced Italy's decision to enter the war. Note, in reading (1) the obligation Russia assumed, (2) the extent of Italian military aid promised, (3) the naval agreement entered into by France and Great Britain, (4) the Austrian areas promised to Italy, (5) the terms reached regarding Albania, (6) the projected division of the Turkish Empire, and (7) evidences of Anglo-French imperialistic plans in Africa and elsewhere.

From: THE SECRET TREATY OF LONDON, 1915

Article 1. A military convention shall be immediately concluded between the General Staffs of France, Great Britain, Italy and Russia. This convention shall settle the minimum number of military forces to be employed by Russia against Austria-Hungary in order to prevent that Power from concentrating all its strength against Italy, in the event of Russia deciding to direct her principal effort against Germany.

This military convention shall settle the question of armistices, which necessarily comes within the scope of the Commanders-in-Chief of the Armies.

Article 2. On her part, Italy undertakes to use her entire resources for the purpose of waging war jointly with France, Great Britain and Russia against all their enemies.

Article 3. The French and British fleets shall

render active and permanent assistance to Italy until such time as the Austro-Hungarian fleet shall have been destroyed or until peace shall have been concluded.

A naval convention shall be immediately concluded to this effect between France, Great Britain and Italy.

Article 4. Under the Treaty of Peace, Italy shall obtain the Trentino, Cisalpine Tyrol with its geographical and natural frontier (the Brenner frontier), as well as Trieste, the counties of Gorizia and Gradisca, all Istria as far as the Quarnero and including Volosca and the Istrian islands of Cherso and Lussin, as well as the small islands. . . .

Article 5. Italy shall also be given the province of Dalmatia within its present administrative boundaries. . . .

Article 6. Italy shall receive full sovereignty

Great Britain, *Parliamentary Papers,* 1920, LI, Cmd. 671.

over Valona, the island of Saseno and surrounding territory of sufficient extent to assure defence of these points (from the Voïussa to the north and east, approximately to the northern boundary of the district of Chimara on the south).

Article 7. Should Italy obtain the Trentino and Istria in accordance with the provisions of Article 4, together with Dalmatia and the Adriatic islands within the limits specified in Article 5, and the Bay of Valona (Article 6), and if the central portion of Albania is reserved for the establishment of a small autonomous neutralised State, Italy shall not oppose the division of Northern and Southern Albania between Montenegro, Serbia and Greece, should France, Great Britain and Russia so desire. The coast from the southern boundary . . . of Valona . . . to Cape Stylos shall be neutralised.

Italy shall be charged with the representation of the State of Albania in its relations with foreign Powers. . . .

Article 8. Italy shall receive entire sovereignty over the Dodecanese Islands which she is at present occupying.

Article 9. Generally speaking, France, Great Britain and Russia recognise that Italy is interested in the maintenance of the balance of power in the Mediterranean and that, in the event of the total or partial partition of Turkey in Asia, she ought to obtain a just share of the Mediterranean region adjacent to the province of Adalia, where Italy has already acquired rights and interests which formed the subject of an Italo-British convention. The zone which shall eventually be allotted to Italy shall be delimited, at the proper time, due account being taken of the existing interests of France and Great Britain.

The interests of Italy shall also be taken into consideration in the event of the territorial integrity of the Turkish Empire being maintained and of alterations being made in the zones of interest of the Powers.

If France, Great Britain and Russia occupy any territories in Turkey in Asia during the course of the war, the Mediterranean region bordering on the Province of Adalia within the limits indicated above shall be reserved to Italy, who shall be entitled to occupy it.

Article 10. All rights and privileges in Libya at present belonging to the Sultan by virtue of the Treaty of Lausanne are transferred to Italy.

Article 11. Italy shall receive a share of any eventual war indemnity corresponding to her efforts and her sacrifices.

Article 12. Italy declares that she associates herself in the declaration made by France, Great Britain and Russia to the effect that Arabia and the Moslem Holy Places in Arabia shall be left under the authority of an independent Moslem Power.

Article 13. In the event of France and Great Britain increasing their colonial territories in Africa at the expense of Germany, those two Powers agree in principle that Italy may claim some equitable compensation, particularly as regards the settlement in her favour of the questions relative to the frontiers of the Italian colonies of Eritrea, Somaliland and Libya and the neighbouring colonies belonging to France and Great Britain.

Article 14. Great Britain undertakes to facilitate the immediate conclusion, under equitable conditions, of a loan of at least £ 50,000,000 to be issued on the London market.

Article 15. France, Great Britain and Russia shall support such opposition as Italy may make to any proposal in the direction of introducing a representative of the Holy See in any peace negotiations or negotiations for the settlement of questions raised by the present war.

Article 16. The present arrangement shall be held secret. The adherence of Italy to the Declaration of the 5th September, 1914, shall alone be made public, immediately upon declaration of war by or against Italy.

John Maynard Keynes

John Maynard Keynes (1883–1946), British economist and leading critic of orthodox economics, was born at Cambridge. He was educated at Eton and Cambridge and in 1908 accepted the post of lecturer at his alma mater which position he occupied until his death. He was holding a civil service appointment at the time World War I ended, and the British Treasury sent him to Paris as its principal representative at the peace conference. During the negotiations at Paris he became convinced that the reparation clauses of the treaty made impossible demands upon Germany; moreover, following further study of the document, he doubted the wisdom of many of the treaty's economic provisions. He resigned his post in order to write The Economic Consequences of the Peace, a damning indictment of the treaty which was published in 1919 shortly after the peace conference adjourned. The selections reveal a liberal's disappointment with the Paris settlement which President Wilson had hoped to fashion into a "peace of justice, sympathy, fair play, and goodwill." Vindictiveness, greed, and a determination to destroy the political and economic power of Germany prevailed at Versailles which rendered the war to make the world safe for democracy a mockery. In reading the selections note (1) Keynes's estimate of the treaty's impact upon Germany's overseas commerce, (2) his view of the treatment of German nationals within former German colonies and territory, (3) his discussion of the institution of private property in the light of the treaty's demands, (4) his estimate of the consequences for Germany of the provisions relating to coal and iron deposits, (5) the contrast he notes between the treaty and pre-conference Allied statements of intent, (6) the effects of the settlement upon Germany's foreign exchange supplies, (7) the impact of the Versailles treaty upon Germany's transportation system, (8) his judgment of the reparations provisions, (9) his description of the influence of the British election upon the writing of the pact, (10) his reasons for believing that an indemnity was wrong and what the victors ought to do to rehabilitate Europe, and (11) why he thought the treaty unwise.

From: THE ECONOMIC CONSEQUENCES OF THE PEACE

The German economic system as it existed before the war depended on three main factors:

I. Overseas commerce as represented by her mercantile marine, her colonies, her foreign

John Maynard Keynes, *The Economic Consequences of the Peace*, New York: Harcourt, Brace and Howe, 1920, 65–72; 81–89; 101–110; 113; 135–137; 139; 141–143; 145–148; 226–228; 255–256; 295–297.

investments, her exports, and the overseas connections of her merchants; II. The exploitation of her coal and iron and the industries built upon them; III. Her transport and tariff system. Of these the first, while not the least important, was certainly the most vulnerable. The Treaty aims at the systematic destruction of all three, but principally of the first two.

I

(1) Germany has ceded to the Allies *all* the vessels of her mercantile marine exceeding 1,600 tons gross, half the vessels between 1,000 tons and 1,600 tons, and one quarter of her trawlers and other fishing boats. The cession is comprehensive, including not only vessels flying the German flag, but also all vessels owned by Germans but flying other flags, and all vessels under construction as well as those afloat. Further, Germany undertakes, if required, to build for the Allies such types of ships as they may specify up to 200,000 tons annually for five years, the value of these ships being credited to Germany against what is due from her for Reparation.

Thus the German mercantile marine is swept from the seas and cannot be restored for many years to come on a scale adequate to meet the requirements of her own commerce. For the present, no lines will run from Hamburg, except such as foreign nations may find it worth while to establish out of their surplus tonnage. Germany will have to pay to foreigners for the carriage of her trade such charges as they may be able to exact, and will receive only such conveniences as it may suit them to give her. The prosperity of German ports and commerce can only revive, it would seem, in proportion as she succeeds in bringing under her effective influence the merchant marines of Scandinavia and of Holland.

(2) Germany has ceded to the Allies "all her rights and titles over her oversea possessions." This cession not only applies to sovereignty but extends on unfavorable terms to Government property, all of which, including railways, must be surrendered without payment, while, on the other hand, the German Government remains liable for any debt which may have been incurred for the purchase or construction of this property, or for the development of the colonies generally.

In distinction from the practice ruling in the case of most similar cessions in recent history, the property and persons of private German nationals, as distinct from their Government, are also injuriously affected. The Allied Government exercising authority in any former German colony "may make such provisions as it thinks fit with reference to the repatriation from them of German nationals and to the conditions upon which German subjects of European origin shall, or shall not, be allowed to reside, hold property, trade or exercise a profession in them." All contracts and agreements in favor of German nationals for the construction or exploitation of public works lapse to the Allied Governments as part of the payment due for Reparation.

But these terms are unimportant compared with the more comprehensive provision by which "the Allied and Associated Powers reserve the right to retain and liquidate *all* property, rights, and interests belonging at the date of the coming into force of the present Treaty to German nationals, or companies controlled by them," within the former German colonies. This wholesale expropriation of private property is to take place without the Allies affording any compensation to the individuals expropriated, and the proceeds will be employed, first, to meet private debts due to Allied nationals from any German nationals, and second, to meet claims due from Austrian, Hungarian, Bulgarian, or Turkish nationals. Any balance may either be returned by the liquidating Power direct to Germany, or retained by them. If retained, the proceeds must be transferred to the Reparation Commission for Germany's credit in the Reparation account.

In short, not only are German sovereignty and German influence extirpated from the whole of her former oversea possessions, but the persons and property of her nationals resident or owning property in those parts are deprived of legal status and legal security.

(3) The provisions just outlined in regard to the private property of Germans in the ex-German colonies apply equally to private German property in Alsace-Lorraine, except in so far as the French Government may choose to grant

exceptions. This is of much greater practical importance than the similar expropriation overseas because of the far higher value of the property involved and the closer interconnection, resulting from the great development of the mineral wealth of these provinces since 1871, of German economic interests there with those in Germany itself. Alsace-Lorraine has been part of the German Empire for nearly fifty years— a considerable majority of its population is German-speaking—and it has been the scene of some of Germany's most important economic enterprises. Nevertheless, the property of those Germans who reside there, or who have invested in its industries, is now entirely at the disposal of the French Government without compensation, except insofar as the German Government itself may choose to afford it. The French Government is entitled to expropriate without compensation the personal property of private German citizens and German companies resident or situated within Alsace-Lorraine, the proceeds being credited in part satisfaction of various French claims. The severity of this provision is only mitigated to the extent that the French Government may expressly permit German nationals to continue to reside, in which case the above provision is not applicable. Government, State, and Municipal property, on the other hand, is to be ceded to France without any credit being given for it. This includes the railway system of the two provinces, together with its rolling-stock. But while the property is taken over, liabilities contracted in respect of it in the form of public debts of any kind remain the liability of Germany. The provinces also return to French sovereignty free and quit of their share of German war or pre-war dead-weight debt; nor does Germany receive a credit on this account in respect of Reparation.

(4) The expropriation of German private property is not limited, however, to the ex-German colonies and Alsace-Lorraine. The treatment of such property forms, indeed, a very significant and material section of the Treaty, which has not received as much attention as it merits, although it was the subject of exceptionally violent objection on the part of the German delegates at Versailles. So far as I know, there is no precedent in any peace treaty of recent history for the treatment of private property set forth below, and the German representatives urged that the precedent now established strikes a dangerous and immoral blow at the security of private property everywhere. This is an exaggeration, and the sharp distinction, approved by custom and convention during the past two centuries, between the property and rights of a State and the property and rights of its nationals is an artificial one, which is being rapidly put out of date by many other influences than the Peace Treaty, and is inappropriate to modern socialistic conceptions of the relations between the State and its citizens. It is true, however, that the Treaty strikes a destructive blow at a conception which lies at the root of much of so-called international law, as this has been expounded hitherto. . . .

The provisions relating to coal and iron are more important in respect of their ultimate consequences on Germany's internal industrial economy than for the money value immediately involved. The German Empire has been built more truly on coal and iron than on blood and iron. The skilled exploitation of the great coal-fields of the Ruhr, Upper Silesia, and the Saar, alone made possible the development of the steel, chemical, and electrical industries which established her as the first industrial nation of continental Europe. One-third of Germany's population lives in towns of more than 20,000 inhabitants, an industrial concentration which is only possible on a foundation of coal and iron. In striking, therefore, at her coal supply, the French politicians were not mistaking their target. It is only the extreme immoderation, and indeed technical impossibility, of the Treaty's demands which may save the situation in the long-run.

(1) The Treaty strikes at Germany's coal supply in four ways:—

(i.) "As compensation for the destruction of the coal-mines in the north of France, and as part payment towards the total reparation due from Germany for the damage resulting from the war, Germany cedes to France in full and absolute possession, with exclusive rights of exploitation, unencumbered, and free from all debts and charges of any kind, the coal-mines situated in the Saar Basin." While the administration of this district is vested for fifteen years in the League of Nations, it is to be observed that the mines are ceded to France absolutely. Fifteen years hence the population of the district will be called upon to indicate by plebiscite their desires as to the future sovereignty of the territory; and, in the event of their electing for union with Germany, Germany is to be entitled to repurchase the mines at a price payable in gold.

The judgment of the world has already recognized the transaction of the Saar as an act of spoliation and insincerity. So far as compensation for the destruction of French coal-mines is concerned, this is provided for, as we shall see in a moment, elsewhere in the Treaty. "There is no industrial region in Germany," the German representatives have said without contradiction, "the population of which is so permanent, so homogeneous, and so little complex as that of the Saar district. Among more than 650,000 inhabitants, there were in 1918 less than 100 French. The Saar district has been German for more than 1,000 years. Temporary occupation as a result of warlike operations on the part of the French always terminated in a short time in the restoration of the country upon the conclusion of peace. During a period of 1,048 years France has possessed the country for not quite 68 years in all. When, on the occasion of the first Treaty of Paris in 1814, a small portion of the territory now coveted was retained for France, the population raised the most energetic opposition and demanded 'reunion with their German fatherland,' to which they were 'related by language, customs, and religion.' After an occupation of one year and a quarter, this desire was taken into account in the second Treaty of Paris in 1815. Since then the country has remained uninterruptedly attached to Germany, and owes its economic development to that connection."

The French wanted the coal for the purpose of working the ironfields of Lorraine, and in the spirit of Bismarck they have taken it. Not precedent, but the verbal professions of the Allies, have rendered it indefensible.

(ii.) Upper Silesia, a district without large towns, in which, however, lies one of the major coalfields of Germany with a production of about 23 per cent of the total German output of hard coal, is, subject to a plebiscite, to be ceded to Poland. Upper Silesia was never part of historic Poland; but its population is mixed Polish, German, and Czecho-Slovakian, the precise proportions of which are disputed. Economically it is intensely German; the industries of Eastern Germany depend upon it for their coal; and its loss would be a destructive blow at the economic structure of the German State.

With the loss of the fields of Upper Silesia and the Saar, the coal supplies of Germany are diminished by not far short of one-third.

(iii.) Out of the coal that remains to her, Germany is obliged to make good year by year the estimated loss which France has incurred by the destruction and damage of war in the coal-fields of her nothern Provinces. In para. 2 of Annex V. to the Reparation Chapter, "Germany undertakes to deliver to France annually, for a period not exceeding ten years, an amount of coal equal to the difference between the annual production before the war of the coal-mines of the Nord and Pas de Calais, destroyed as a result of the war, and the production of the mines of the same area during the year in question: such delivery not to exceed 20,000,000 tons in any one year of the first five years, and 8,000,000 tons in any one year of the succeeding five years."

This is a reasonable provision if it stood by itself, and one which Germany should be able to fulfil if she were left her other resources to do it with.

(iv.) The final provision relating to coal is part of the general scheme of the Reparation Chapter by which the sums due for Reparation are to be partly paid in kind instead of in cash. As a part of the payment due for Reparation, Germany is to make the following deliveries of coal or its equivalent in coke (the deliveries to France being wholly additional to the amounts available by the cession of the Saar or in compensation for destruction in Northern France):—

(i.) To France 7,000,000 tons annually for ten years;

(ii.) To Belgium 8,000,000 tons annually for ten years;

(iii.) To Italy an annual quantity, rising by annual increments from 4,500,000 tons in 1919–1920 to 8,500,000 tons in each of the six years, 1923–1924 to 1928–1929;

(iv.) To Luxemburg, if required, a quantity

of coal equal to the pre-war annual consumption of German coal in Luxemburg.

This amounts in all to an annual average of about 25,000,000 tons.

These figures have to be examined in relation to Germany's probable output. The maximum pre-war figure was reached in 1913 with a total of 191,500,000 tons. Of this, 19,000,000 tons were consumed at the mines, and on balance (*i.e.*, exports less imports) 33,500,000 tons were exported, leaving 139,000,000 tons for domestic consumption. It is estimated that this total was employed as follows:—

Railways	18,000,000	tons
Gas, water, and electricity .	12,500,000	"
Bunkers	6,500,000	"
House-fuel, small industry and agriculture . . .	24,000,000	"
Industry	78,000,000	"
	139,000,000	"

The diminution of production due to loss of territory is:—

Alsace-Lorraine. . . .	3,800,000	tons
Saar Basin	13,200,000	"
Upper Silesia	43,800,000	"
	60,800,000	"

There would remain, therefore, on the basis of the 1913 output, 130,700,000 tons, or, deducting consumption at the mines themselves, (say) 118,000,000 tons. For some years there must be sent out of this supply upwards of 20,000,000 tons to France as compensation for damage done to French mines, and 25,000,000 tons to France, Belgium, Italy, and Luxemburg; as the former figure is a maximum, and the latter figure is to be slightly less in the earliest years, we may take the total export to Allied countries which Germany has undertaken to provide as 40,000,000 tons, leaving, on the above basis, 78,000,000 tons for her own use as against a pre-war consumption of 139,000,000 tons. . . .

There remain those Treaty provisions which relate to the transport and the tariff systems of Germany. These parts of the Treaty have not nearly the importance and the significance of those discussed hitherto. They are pin-pricks, interferences and vexations, not so much objectionable for their solid consequences, as dishonorable to the Allies in the light of their professions. Let the reader consider what follows in the light of the assurances already quoted, in reliance on which Germany laid down her arms.

(i.) The miscellaneous Economic Clauses commence with a number of provisions which would be in accordance with the spirit of the third of the Fourteen Points,—if they were reciprocal. Both for imports and exports, and as regards tariffs, regulations, and prohibitions, Germany binds herself for five years to accord most-favored-nation treatment to the Allied and Associated States. But she is not entitled herself to receive such treatment.

For five years Alsace-Lorraine shall be free to export into Germany, without payment of customs duty, up to the average amount sent annually into Germany from 1911 to 1913. But there is no similar provision for German exports into Alsace-Lorraine.

For three years Polish exports to Germany, and for five years Luxemburg's exports to Germany, are to have a similar privilege,—but not German exports to Poland or to Luxemburg. Luxemburg also, which for many years has enjoyed the benefits of inclusion within the German Customs Union, is permanently excluded from it henceforward.

For six months after the Treaty has come into force Germany may not impose duties on imports from the Allied and Associated States higher than the most favorable duties prevalent before the war; and for a further two years and a half (making three years in all) this prohibition continues to apply to certain commodities, notably to some of those as to which special agreements existed before the war, and also to wine, to vegetable oils, to artificial silk, and to washed or scoured wool. This is a ridiculous and injurious provision, by which Germany is prevented from taking those steps necessary to conserve her limited resources for the purchase of necessaries and the discharge of Reparation. As a result of the existing distribution of wealth in Germany, and of financial wantonness amongst individuals, the offspring of uncertainty, Germany is threatened with a deluge of luxuries and semi-luxuries from abroad, of which she has been starved for years, which would exhaust or diminish her small supplies of foreign exchange. These provisions strike at the authority of the German Government to ensure economy in such consumption, or to raise taxation during a critical period. What an example of senseless greed overreaching itself, to introduce, after taking from Germany what liquid wealth she has and demanding impossible payments for the future, a special and particularized injunction that she must allow as readily as in the days of her prosperity the import of champagne and of silk!

One other Article affects the Customs Régime of Germany which, if it was applied, would be serious and extensive in its consequences. The Allies have reserved the right to apply a special customs régime to the occupied area on the left bank of the Rhine, "in the event of such a measure being necessary in their opinion in order to safeguard the economic interests of the population of these territories." This provision was probably introduced as a possibly useful adjunct to the French policy of somehow detaching the left bank provinces from Germany during the years of their occupation. The project of establishing an independent Republic under French clerical auspices, which would act as a buffer state and realize the French ambition of driving Germany proper beyond the Rhine, has not yet been abandoned. Some believe that much may be accomplished by a régime of threats, bribes, and cajolery extended over a period of fifteen years or longer. If this Article is acted upon, and the economic system of the left bank of the Rhine is effectively severed from the rest of Germany, the effect would be far-reaching. But the dreams of designing diplomats do not always prosper, and we must trust the future.

(ii.) The clauses relating to Railways, as originally presented to Germany, were substantially modified in the final Treaty, and are now limited to a provision by which goods coming from Allied territory to Germany, or in transit through Germany, shall receive the most favored treatment as regards rail freight rates, applied to goods of the same kind carried on *any* German lines "under similar conditions of transport, for example, as regards length of route." As a nonreciprocal provision this is an act of interference in internal arrangements which it is difficult to justify, but the practical effect of this, and of an analogous provision relating to passenger traffic, will much depend on the interpretation of the phrase, "similar conditions of transport."

For the time being, Germany's transport system will be much more seriously disordered by the provisions relating to the cession of rolling-stock. Under paragraph 7 of the Armistice conditions, Germany was called on to surrender 5,000 locomotives and 150,000 wagons, "in good working order, with all necessary spare parts and fittings." Under the Treaty, Germany is required to confirm this surrender and to recognize the title of the Allies to the material. She is further required, in the case of railway systems in ceded territory, to hand over these systems complete with their full complement of rolling-stock "in a normal state of upkeep" as shown in the last inventory before November 11, 1918. That is to say, ceded railway systems are not to bear any share in the general depletion and deterioration of the German rolling-stock as a whole.

This is a loss which in course of time can doubtless be made good. But lack of lubricating oils and the prodigious wear and tear of the war, not compensated by normal repairs, had already reduced the German railway system to a low state of efficiency. The further heavy losses under the Treaty will confirm this state of affairs for some time to come, and are a substantial aggravation of the difficulties of the coal problem and of export industry generally.

(iii.) There remain the clauses relating to the river system of Germany. These are largely unnecessary and are so little related to the supposed aims of the Allies that their purport is generally unknown. Yet they constitute an unprecedented interference with a country's domestic arrangements, and are capable of being so operated as to take from Germany all effective control over her own transport system. In their present form they are incapable of justification; but some simple changes might transform them into a reasonable instrument.

Most of the principal rivers of Germany have their source or their outlet in non-German territory. The Rhine, rising in Switzerland, is now a frontier river for a part of its course, and finds the sea in Holland; the Danube rises in Germany but flows over its greater length elsewhere; the Elbe rises in the mountains of Bohemia, now called Czecho-Slovakia; the Oder traverses Lower Silesia; and the Niemen now bounds the frontier of East Prussia and has its source in Russia. Of these, the Rhine and the Niemen are frontier rivers; the Elbe is primarily German, but in its upper reaches has much importance for Bohemia; the Danube, in its German parts, appears to have little concern for any country but Germany; and the Oder is an almost purely German river unless the result of the plebiscite is to detach all Upper Silesia.

Rivers which, in the words of the Treaty, "naturally provide more than one State with access to the sea," properly require some measure of international regulation and adequate guarantees against discrimination. This principle has long been recognized in the International Commissions which regulate the Rhine and the Danube. But on such Commissions the States concerned should be represented more or less in proportion to their interests. The Treaty, however, has made the international character of these rivers a pretext for taking the river system of Germany out of German control.

After certain Articles which provide suitably against discrimination and interference with freedom of transit, the Treaty proceeds to hand over the administration of the Elbe, the Oder, the Danube, and the Rhine to International Commissions. The ultimate powers of these Commissions are to be determined by "a General Convention drawn up by the Allied and Associated Powers, and approved by the League of Nations." In the meantime the Commissions are to draw up their own constitutions and are apparently to enjoy powers of the most extensive description, "particularly in regard to the execution of works of maintenance, control, and improvement on the river system, the financial régime, the fixing and collection of charges, and regulations for navigation."

So far there is much to be said for the Treaty. Freedom of through transit is a not unimportant part of good international practice and should be established everywhere. The objectionable feature of the Commissions lies in their membership. In each case the voting is so weighted as to place Germany in a clear minority. On the Elbe Commission Germany has four votes out of ten; on the Oder Commission three out of nine; on the Rhine Commission four out of nineteen;

on the Danube Commission, which is not yet definitely constituted, she will be apparently in a small minority. On the government of all these rivers France and Great Britain are represented; and on the Elbe for some undiscoverable reason there are also representatives of Italy and Belgium.

Thus the great waterways of Germany are handed over to foreign bodies with the widest powers; and much of the local and domestic business of Hamburg, Magdeburg, Dresden, Stettin, Frankfurt, Breslau, and Ulm will be subject to a foreign jurisdiction. It is almost as though the Powers of Continental Europe were to be placed in a majority on the Thames Conservancy or the Port of London. . . .

The categories of damage in respect of which the Allies were entitled to ask for Reparation are governed by the relevant passages in President Wilson's Fourteen Points of January 8, 1918, as modified by the Allied Governments in their qualifying Note, the text of which the President formally communicated to the German Government as the basis of peace on November 5, 1918. These passages have been quoted in full at the beginning of Chapter IV [omitted]. That is to say, "compensation will be made by Germany for all damage done to the civilian population of the Allies and to their property by the aggression of Germany by land, by sea, and from the air." The limiting quality of this sentence is reinforced by the passage in the President's speech before Congress on February 11, 1918 (the terms of this speech being an express part of the contract with the enemy), that there shall be "no contributions" and "no punitive damages.". . .

I believe that it would have been a wise and just act to have asked the German Government at the Peace Negotiations to agree to a sum of $10,000,000,000 in final settlement, without further examination of particulars. This would have provided an immediate and certain solution, and would have required from Germany a sum which, if she were granted certain indulgences, it might not have proved entirely impossible for her to pay. This sum should have been divided up amongst the Allies themselves on a basis of need and general equity.

But the question was not settled on its merits.

THE CONFERENCE AND THE TERMS OF THE TREATY

I do not believe that, at the date of the Armistice, responsible authorities in the Allied countries expected any indemnity from Germany beyond the cost of reparation for the direct material damage which had resulted from the invasion of Allied territory and from the submarine campaign. At that time there were serious doubts as to whether Germany intended to accept our terms, which in other respects were inevitably very severe. It would have been thought an unstatesmanlike act to risk a continuance of the war by demanding a money payment which Allied opinion was not then anticipating and which probably could not be secured in any case. The French, I think, never quite accepted this point of view; but it was certainly the British attitude; and in this atmosphere the pre-Armistice conditions were framed.

A month later the atmosphere had changed completely. We had discovered how hopeless the German position really was, a discovery which some, though not all, had anticipated, but which no one had dared reckon on as a certainty. It was evident that we could have secured unconditional surrender if we had determined to get it.

But there was another new factor in the situation which was of greater local importance. The British Prime Minister had perceived that the conclusion of hostilities might soon bring with it the break-up of the political *bloc* upon which he was depending for his personal ascendancy, and that the domestic difficulties which would be attendant on demobilization, the turn-over of industry from war to peace conditions, the financial situation, and the general psychological reactions of men's minds, would provide his enemies with powerful weapons, if he were to leave them time to mature. The best chance, therefore, of consolidating his power which was personal, and exercised as such independently of party or principle to an extent unusual in British politics, evidently lay in active hostilities before the prestige of victory had abated, and in an attempt, to found on the emotions of the moment a new basis of power which might outlast the inevitable reactions of

the near future. Within a brief period, therefore, after the Armistice, the popular victor, at the height of his influence and his authority, decreed a General Election. It was widely recognized at the time as an act of political immorality. There were no grounds of public interest which did not call for a short delay until the issues of the new age had a little defined themselves and until the country had something more specific before it on which to declare its mind and to instruct its new representatives. But the claims of private ambition determined otherwise. . . .

The progress of the General Election of 1918 affords a sad, dramatic history of the essential weakness of one who draws his chief inspiration not from his own true impulses, but from the grosser effluxions of the atmosphere which momentarily surrounds him. . . .

On December 6, the Prime Minister issued a statement of policy and aims in which he stated, with significant emphasis on the word *European*, that "All the European Allies have accepted the principle that the Central Powers must pay the cost of the war up to the limit of their capacity.". . .

On December 9, at the Queen's Hall, the Prime Minister avoided the subject. But fron now on, the debauchery of thought and speech progressed hour by hour. The grossest spectacle was provided by Sir Eric Geddes in the Guildhall at Cambridge. An earlier speech in which, in a moment of injudicious candor, he had cast doubts on the possibility of extracting from Germany the whole cost of the war had been the object of serious suspicion, and he had therefore a reputation to regain. "We will get out of her all you can squeeze out of a lemon and a bit more," the penitent shouted, "I will squeeze her until you can hear the pips squeak"; his policy was to take every bit of property belonging to Germans in neutral and Allied countries, and all her gold and silver and her jewels, and the contents of her picture-galleries and libraries, to sell the proceeds for the Allies' benefit. "I would strip Germany," he cried, "as she has stripped Belgium."

By December 11 the Prime Minister had capitulated. His Final Manifesto . . . furnishes a melancholy comparison with his program of three weeks earlier. I quote it in full:

"1. Trial of the Kaiser.
2. Punishment of those responsible for atrocities.
3. Fullest Indemnities from Germany.
4. Britain for the British, socially and industrially.
5. Rehabilitation of those broken in the war.
6. A happier country for all."

Here is food for the cynic. To this concoction of greed and sentiment, prejudice and deception, three weeks of the platform had reduced the powerful governors of England, who but a little while before had spoken not ignobly of Disarmament and a League of Nations and of a just and lasting peace which should establish the foundations of a new Europe. . . .

This was the atmosphere in which the Prime Minister left for Paris, and these the entanglements he had made for himself. He had pledged himself and his Government to make demands of a helpless enemy inconsistent with solemn engagements on our part, on the faith of which this enemy had laid down his arms. There are few episodes in history which posterity will have less reason to condone,—a war ostensibly waged in defense of the sanctity of international engagements ending in a definite breach of one of the most sacred possible of such engagements on the part of the victorious champions of these ideals. (Only after the most painful consideration have I written these words. The almost complete absence of protest from the leading Statesmen of England makes one feel that one must have made some mistake. But I believe that I know all the facts, and I can discover no such mistake. . . .)

Apart from other aspects of the transaction, I believe that the campaign for securing out of Germany the general costs of the war was one of the most serious acts of political unwisdom for which our statesmen have ever been responsible. To what a different future Europe might have looked forward if either Mr. Lloyd George or Mr. Wilson had apprehended that the most serious of the problems which claimed their attention were not political or territorial but financial and economic, and that the perils of the future lay not in frontiers or sovereignties but in food, coal, and transport. Neither of them paid adequate attention to these problems at any stage of the Conference. But in any event the atmosphere for the wise and reasonable consideration of them was hopelessly befogged by the commitments of the British delegation on the question of Indemnities. The hopes to which the Prime Minister had given rise not only compelled him to advocate an unjust and unworkable economic basis to the Treaty with Germany, but set him at variance with the President, and on the other hand with competing interests to those of France and Belgium. The clearer it became that but little could be expected from Germany, the more necessary it was to exercise patriotic greed and "sacred egotism" and snatch the bone from the juster claims and greater need of France or the well-founded expectations of Belgium. Yet the financial problems which were about to exercise Europe could not be solved by greed. The possibility of *their* cure lay in magnanimity.

Europe, if she is to survive her troubles, will need so much magnanimity from America, that she must herself practice it. It is useless for the Allies, hot from stripping Germany and one another, to turn for help to the United States to put the States of Europe, including Germany, on to their feet again. If the General Election of December, 1918, had been fought on lines of prudent generosity instead of imbecile greed, how much better the financial prospect of Europe might now be. I still believe that before the main Conference, or very early in its proceedings, the representatives of Great Britain should have entered deeply, with those of the United States, into the economic and financial situation as a whole, and that the former should have been authorized to make concrete proposals on the general lines (1) that all interallied indebtedness be canceled outright; (2) that the sum to be paid by Germany be fixed at $10,000,000,000; (3) that Great Britain renounce all claim to participation in this sum and that any share to which she proves entitled be placed at the disposal of the Conference for the purpose of aiding the finances of the New States about to be established; (4) that in order to make some basis of credit immediately available an appropriate proportion of the German obligations representing the sum to be paid by her should be guaranteed by all parties to the Treaty; and (5) that the ex-enemy

Powers should also be allowed, with a view to their economic restoration, to issue a moderate amount of bonds carrying a similar guarantee. Such proposals involved an appeal to the generosity of the United States. But that was inevitable; and, in view of her far less financial sacrifices, it was an appeal which could fairly have been made to her. Such proposals would have been practicable. There is nothing in them quixotic or Utopian. And they would have opened up for Europe some prospect of financial stability and reconstruction. . . .

This chapter must be one of pessimism. The Treaty includes no provisions for the economic rehabilitation of Europe,—nothing to make the defeated Central Empires into good neighbors, nothing to stabilize the new States of Europe, nothing to reclaim Russia; nor does it promote in any way a compact of economic solidarity amongst the Allies themselves; no arrangement was reached at Paris for restoring the disordered finances of France and Italy, or to adjust the systems of the Old World and the New.

The Council of Four paid no attention to these issues, being preoccupied with others,—Clemenceau to crush the economic life of his enemy, Lloyd George to do a deal and bring home something which would pass muster for a week, the President to do nothing that was not just and right. It is an extraordinary fact that the fundamental economic problems of a Europe starving and disintegrating before their eyes, was the one question in which it was impossible to arouse the interest of the Four. Reparation was their main excursion into the economic field, and they settled it as a problem of theology, of politics, of electoral chicane, from every point of view except that of the economic future of the States whose destiny they were handling.

I leave, from this point onwards, Paris, the Conference, and the Treaty, briefly to consider the present situation of Europe, as the War and the Peace have made it; and it will no longer be part of my purpose to distinguish between the inevitable fruits of the War and the avoidable misfortunes of the Peace.

The essential facts of the situation, as I see them, are expressed simply. Europe consists of the densest aggregation of population in the history of the world. This population is accustomed to a relatively high standard of life, in which, even now, some sections of it anticipate improvement rather than deterioration. In relation to other continents Europe is not self-sufficient; in particular it cannot feed itself. Internally the population is not evenly distributed, but much of it is crowded into a relatively small number of dense industrial centers. This population secured for itself a livelihood before the war, without much margin of surplus, by means of a delicate and immensely complicated organization, of which the foundations were supported by coal, iron, transport, and an unbroken supply of imported food and raw materials from other continents. By the destruction of this organization and the interruption of the stream of supplies, a part of this population is deprived of its means of livelihood. Emigration is not open to the redundant surplus. For it would take years to transport them overseas, even, which is not the case, if countries could be found which were ready to receive them. The danger confronting us, therefore, is the rapid depression of the standard of life of the European populations to a point which will mean actual starvation for some (a point already reached in Russia and approximately reached in Austria). Men will not always die quietly. For starvation, which brings to some lethargy and a helpless despair, drives other temperaments to the nervous instability of hysteria and to a mad despair. And these in their distress may overturn the remnants of organization, and submerge civilization itself in their attempts to satisfy desperately the overwhelming needs of the individual. This is the danger against which all our resources and courage and idealism must now co-operate. . . .

What then is to be done? The tentative suggestions of this chapter may appear to the reader inadequate. But the opportunity was missed at Paris during the six months which followed the Armistice, and nothing we can do now can repair the mischief wrought at that time. Great privation and great risks to society have become unavoidable. All that is now open to us is to redirect, . . . the fundamental economic tendencies which underlie the events of the hour, so that they promote the reestablishment of prosperity and order, instead of leading us deeper into misfortune.

We must first escape from the atmosphere and the methods of Paris. Those who controlled the Conference may bow before the gusts of popular opinion, but they will never lead us out of our troubles. It is hardly to be supposed that the Council of Four can retrace their steps, even if they wished to do so. The replacement of the existing Governments of Europe is, therefore, an almost indispensable preliminary. . . .

I see few signs of sudden or dramatic developments anywhere. Riots and revolutions there may be, but not such, at present, as to have fundamental significance. Against political tyranny and injustice Revolution is a weapon. But what counsels of hope can Revolution offer to sufferers from economic privation, which does not arise out of the injustices of distribution but is general? The only safeguard against Revolution in Central Europe is indeed the fact that, even to the minds of men who are desperate, Revolution offers no prospect of improvement whatever. There may, therefore, be ahead of us a long, silent process of semi-starvation, and of a gradual, steady lowering of the standards of life and comfort. The bankruptcy and decay of Europe, if we allow it to proceed, will affect every one in the long-run, but perhaps not in a way that is striking or immediate.

This has one fortunate side. We may still have time to reconsider our courses and to view the world with new eyes. For the immediate future events are taking charge, and the near destiny of Europe is no longer in the hands of any man. The events of the coming year will not be shaped by the deliberate acts of statesmen, but by the hidden currents, flowing continually beneath the surface of political history, of which no one can predict the outcome. In one way only can we influence these hidden currents,— by setting in motion those forces of instruction and imagination which change *opinion*. The assertion of truth, the unveiling of illusion, the dissipation of hate, the enlargement and instruction of men's hearts and minds, must be the means.

In this autumn of 1919, in which I write, we are at the dead season of our fortunes. The reaction from the exertions, the fears, and the sufferings of the past five years is at its height. Our power of feeling or caring beyond the immediate questions of our own material well-being is temporarily eclipsed. The greatest events outside our own direct experience and the most dreadful anticipations cannot move us. . . .

We have been moved already beyond endurance, and need rest. Never in the lifetime of men now living has the universal element in the soul of man burnt so dimly.

Economic, Social, and Political Changes in the Twentieth Century

In the twentieth century steady progress has been made in improving the techniques of industrial production, thereby making it possible to manufacture an ever-growing volume of goods. Profits, too, have increased, giving rise to concentrations of wealth which have enabled small minorities to dominate the industrial and financial life of large areas. Industrialists have sponsored research which has produced new processes for saving labor, thus creating instabilities within the social order. Even before 1914, statesmen in the western democracies recognized the problem and began to lead their governments away from laissez-faire principles and toward the assumption by the states of greater responsibility for the welfare of their citizens. Governments were elected with popular mandates to impose regulations on the large corporations, while, with the other hand, extending various forms of social security to the workers. Following the 1914–1918 war and the great depression of 1929, the trend was accelerated on both sides of the Atlantic. Russia, after a revolution in 1917, which took her out of the war then raging, turned to communism as a means of improving the social and economic condition of the masses. Italy and Germany experienced serious economic maladjustment following the 1918 armistice, and in the postwar period attempted to build up national morale and to restore economic prosperity by accepting the totalitarian programs advocated by fascist groups. Thus, by 1939 the countries of Western Civilization were struggling to improve the lives of their citizens, but by methods so different as to make any peaceful understanding between them extremely difficult.

Louis Brandeis

L ouis D. Brandeis (1856–1941) was an American lawyer and jurist who served as counsel in many freight-rate, wage-hour, and public utility cases. His experiences in these investigations gave him an unparalleled insight into the financial and industrial developments which transformed American economic life in the early years of the twentieth century. He was particularly conversant with the methods used by financial interests to gain control of industrial production, the development which President Wilson considered to be the greatest problem of American democracy. In 1916 Wilson appointed Brandeis to the Supreme Court, but prior to that event, this eminent American jurist wrote Other People's Money, a chapter from which is given below. In reading "Big Men and Little Business" note (1) the relation between the great banking houses and the growth of American industry, (2) the method by which the large corporations had been created, (3) the number of activities in which J. P. Morgan & Co. had been a participant, (4) the extent to which the great banking houses had arrested the industrial development of America, (5) the concentration of wealth made possible by stock exchange transactions, (6) the practices of the General Electric Company carried on through subsidiaries, and (7) the recommendations made by Mr. Brandeis for checking these practices.

From: OTHER PEOPLE'S MONEY

J. P. Morgan & Co. declare, in their letter to the Pujo Committee, that "practically all the railroad and industrial development of this country has taken place initially through the medium of the great banking houses." That statement is entirely unfounded in fact. On the contrary, nearly every such contribution to our comfort and prosperity was "initiated" *without* their aid. The "great banking houses" came into relation with these enterprises, either after success had been attained, or upon "reorganization" after the possibility of success had been demonstrated, but the funds of the hardy pioneers, who had risked their all, were exhausted.

This is true of our early railroads, of our early street railways, and of the automobile; of the telegraph, the telephone and the wireless; of gas and oil; of harvesting machinery, and of our steel industry; of the textile, paper and shoe industries; and of nearly every other important branch of manufacture. The *initiation* of each of these enterprises may properly be characterized as "great transactions"; and the men who contributed the financial aid and business management necessary for their introduction are entitled to share, equally with inventors, in our gratitude for what has been accomplished. But the instances are extremely rare where the original financing of such enterprises was undertaken by investment bankers, great or small. It was usually done by some common business man, accustomed to taking risks; or by some well-to-do friend of the inventor or pioneer, who was influenced largely by considerations other than money-getting. Here and there you will find that banker-aid was given; but usually in those

Louis D. Brandeis, *Other People's Money and How the Bankers Use It*, new edition, Frederick A. Stokes Company New York, 1932, 135–161. Courtesy of Mrs. Susan Brandeis Gilbert.

cases it was a small local banking concern, not a "great banking house" which helped to "initiate" the undertaking.

RAILROADS

We have come to associate the great bankers with railroads. But their part was not conspicuous in the early history of the Eastern railroads; and in the Middle West the experience was, to some extent, similar. The Boston & Maine Railroad owns and leases 2,215 miles of line; but it is a composite of about 166 separate railroad companies. The New Haven Railroad owns and leases 1,996 miles of line; but it is a composite of 112 separate railroad companies. The necessary capital to build these little roads was gathered together, partly through state, county or municipal aid; partly from business men or landholders who sought to advance their special interests; partly from investors; and partly from well-to-do public-spirited men, who wished to promote the welfare of their particular communities. About seventy-five years after the first of these railroads was built, J. P. Morgan & Co. became fiscal agent for all of them by creating the New Haven-Boston & Maine monopoly.

STEAMSHIPS

The history of our steamship lines is similar. In 1807, Robert Fulton, with the financial aid of Robert R. Livingston, a judge and statesman—not a banker—demonstrated with the *Claremont*, that it was practicable to propel boats by steam. In 1833 the three Cunard brothers of Halifax and 232 other persons—stockholders of the Quebec and Halifax Steam Navigation Company—joined in supplying about $80,000 to build the *Royal William*—the first steamer to cross the Atlantic. In 1902, many years after individual enterprises had developed practically all the great ocean lines, J. P. Morgan & Co. floated the International Mercantile Marine with its $52,744,000 of 4½ bonds, now selling at about 60, and $100,-000,000 of stock (preferred and common) on which no dividend has ever been paid. It was just sixty-two years after the first regular line

of transatlantic steamers—The Cunard—was founded that Mr. Morgan organized the Shipping Trust.

TELEGRAPH

The story of the telegraph is similar. The money for developing Morse's invention was supplied by his partner and co-worker, Alfred Vail. The initial line (from Washington to Baltimore) was built with an appropriation of $30,000 made by Congress in 1843. Sixty-six years later J. P. Morgan & Co. became bankers for the Western Union through financing its purchase by the American Telephone & Telegraph Company.

HARVESTING MACHINERY

Next to railroads and steamships, harvesting machinery has probably been the most potent factor in the development of America; and most important of the harvesting machines was Cyrus H. McCormick's reaper. That made it possible to increase the grain harvest twenty- or thirty-fold. No investment banker had any part in introducing this great businessman's invention.

McCormick was without means; but William Butler Ogden, a railroad builder, ex-Mayor and leading citizen of Chicago, supplied $25,-000 with which the first factory was built there in 1847. Fifty-five years later, J. P. Morgan & Co. performed the service of combining the five great harvester companies, and received a commission of $3,000,000. The concerns then consolidated as the International Harvester Company, with a capital stock of $120,000,-000, had, despite their huge assets and earning power, been previously capitalized, in the aggregate, at only $10,500,000—strong evidence that in all the preceding years no investment banker had financed them. Indeed, McCormick was as able in business as in mechanical invention. Two years after Ogden paid him $25,000 for a half interest in the business, McCormick bought it back for $50,-000; and thereafter, until his death in 1884, no one but members of the McCormick family had any interest in the business.

THE BANKER ERA

It may be urged that railroads and steamships, the telegraph and harvesting machinery were introduced before the accumulation of investment capital had developed the investment banker, and before America's "great banking houses" had been established; and that, consequently, it would be fairer to inquire what services bankers had rendered in connection with later industrial development. The firm of J. P. Morgan & Co. is fifty-five years old; Kuhn, Loeb & Co. fifty-six years old; Lee, Higginson & Co. over fifty years; and Kidder, Peabody & Co. forty-eight years; and yet the investment banker seems to have had almost as little part in "initiating" the great improvements of the last half century, as did bankers in the earlier period.

STEEL

The modern steel industry of America is forty-five years old. The "great bankers" had no part in initiating it. Andrew Carnegie, then already a man of large means, introduced the Bessemer process in 1868. In the next thirty years our steel and iron industry increased greatly. By 1898 we had far outstripped all competitors. America's production about equalled the aggregate of England and Germany. We had also reduced costs so much that Europe talked of the "American Peril." It was 1898, when J. P. Morgan & Co. took their first step in forming the Steel Trust, by organizing the Federal Steel Company. Then followed the combination of the tube mills into an $80,000,-000 corporation, J. P. Morgan & Co. taking for their syndicate services $20,000,000 of common stock. About the same time the consolidation of the bridge and structural works, the tin plate, the sheet steel, the hoop and other mills followed; and finally, in 1901, the Steel Trust was formed, with a capitalization of $1,402,-000,000. These combinations came thirty years after the steel industry had been "initiated."

THE TELEPHONE

The telephone industry is less than forty years old. It is probably America's greatest contribution to industrial development. The bankers had no part in "initiating" it. The glory belongs to a simple, enthusiastic, warm-hearted, business man of Haverhill, Massachusetts, who was willing to risk *his own* money. H. N. Casson tells of this, most interestingly, in his "History of the Telephone":

"The only man who had money and dared to stake it on the future of the telephone was Thomas Sanders, and he did this not mainly for business reasons. Both he and Hubbard were attached to Bell primarily by sentiment, as Bell had removed the blight of dumbness from Sanders' little son, and was soon to marry Hubbard's daughter. Also, Sanders had no expectation, at first, that so much money would be needed. He was not rich. His entire business, which was that of cutting out soles for shoe manufacturers, was not at any time worth more than thirty-five thousand dollars. Yet, from 1874 to 1878, he had advanced nine-tenths of the money that was spent on the telephone. The first five thousand telephones, and more, were made with his money. And so many long, expensive months dragged by before any relief came to Sanders, that he was compelled, much against his will and his business judgment, to stretch his credit within an inch of the breaking-point to help Bell and the telephone. Desperately he signed note after note until he faced a total of one hundred and ten thousand dollars. If the new 'scientific toy' succeeded, which he often doubted, he would be the richest citizen in Haverhill; and if it failed, which he sorely feared, he would be a bankrupt. Sanders and Hubbard were leasing telephones two by two, to business men who previously had been using the private lines of the Western Union Telegraph Company. This great corporation was at this time their natural and inevitable enemy. It had swallowed most of its competitors, and was reaching out to monopolize all methods of communication by wire. The rosiest hope that shone in front of Sanders and Hubbard was that the Western Union might conclude to buy the Bell patents, just as it had already bought many others. In one moment of discouragement they had offered the telephone to President Orton, of the Western Union, for $100,000; and Orton had refused it. 'What use,' he asked pleasantly, 'could this company make of an electrical toy?'

"But besides the operation of its own wires, the Western Union was supplying customers with various kinds of printing-telegraphs and dial-telegraphs, some of which could transmit sixty words a minute. These accurate instruments, it believed, could never be displaced by such a scientific oddity as the telephone, and it continued to believe this until one of its subsidiary companies—the Gold and Stock —reported that several of its machines had been superseded by telephones.

"At once the Western Union awoke from its indifference. Even this tiny nibbling at its business must be stopped. It took action quickly, and organized the 'American Speaking-Telephone Company,' and with $300,000 capital, and with three electrical inventors, Edison, Gray, and Dolbear, on its staff. With all the bulk of its great wealth and prestige, it swept down upon Bell and his little body-guard. It trampled upon Bell's patent with as little concern as an elephant can have when he tramples upon an ant's nest. To the complete bewilderment of Bell, it coolly announced that it had the only original telephone, and that it was ready to supply superior telephones with all the latest improvements made by the original inventors—Dolbear, Gray, and Edison.

"The result was strange and unexpected. The Bell group, instead of being driven from the field, were at once lifted to a higher level in the business world. And the Western Union, in the endeavor to protect its private lines, became involuntarily a 'bell-wether' to lead capitalists in the direction of the telephone."

Even then, when financial aid came to the Bell enterprise, it was from capitalists, not from bankers, and among these capitalists was William H. Forbes (son of the builder of the Burlington) who became the first President of the Bell Telephone Company. That was in 1878. More than twenty years later, after the telephone had spread over the world, the great house of Morgan came into financial control of the property. The American Telephone & Telegraph Company was formed. The process of combination became active. Since January, 1900, its stock has increased from $25,886,300 to $344,606,400. In six years (1906 to 1912),

the Morgan associates marketed about $300,-000,000 bonds of that company or its subsidiaries. In that period the volume of business done by the telephone companies had, of course, grown greatly, and the plant had to be constantly increased; but the proceeds of these huge security issues were used, to a large extent, in effecting combinations; that is, in buying out telephone competitors; in buying control of the Western Union Telegraph Company; and in buying up outstanding stock interests in semi-independent Bell companies. It is these combinations which have led to the investigation of the Telephone Company by the Department of Justice; and they are, in large part, responsible for the movement to have the government take over the telephone business.

ELECTRICAL MACHINERY

The business of manufacturing electrical machinery and apparatus is only a little over thirty years old. J. P. Morgan & Co. became interested early in one branch of it; but their dominance of the business today is due, not to their "initiating" it, but to their effecting a combination, and organizing the General Electric Company in 1892. There were then three large electrical companies, the Thomson-Houston, the Edison, and the Westinghouse, besides some small ones. The Thomson-Houston of Lynn, Massachusetts, was in many respects the leader, having been formed to introduce, among other things, important inventions of Prof. Elihu Thomson and Prof. Houston. Lynn is one of the principal shoe-manufacturing centers of America. It is within ten miles of State Street, Boston; but Thomson's early financial support came not from Boston bankers, but mainly from Lynn business men and investors; men active, energetic, and used to taking risks with *their own* money. Prominent among them was Charles A. Coffin, a shoe manufacturer, who became connected with the Thomson-Houston Company upon its organization and president of the General Electric when Mr. Morgan formed that company in 1892, by combining the Thomson-Houston and the Edison. To his continued service, supported by other Thomson-Houston men in high positions, the great prosperity of the company is, in large part, due. The two companies so combined controlled probably one-half of all electrical patents then existing in America; and certainly more than half of those which had any considerable value.

In 1896 the General Electric pooled its patents with the Westinghouse, and thus competition was further restricted. In 1903 the General Electric absorbed the Stanley Electric Company, its other large competitor; and became the largest manufacturer of electric apparatus and machinery in the world. In 1912 the resources of the Company were $131,942,-144. It billed sales to the amount of $89,182,-185. It employed directly over 60,000 persons, —more than a fourth as many as the Steel Trust. And it is protected against "undue" competition; for one of the Morgan partners has been a director, since 1909, in the Westinghouse—the only other large electrical machinery company in America.

THE AUTOMOBILE

The automobile industry is about twenty years old. It is now America's most prosperous business. When Henry B. Joy, President of the Packard Motor Car Company, was asked to what extent the bankers aided in "initiating" the automobile, he replied:

"It is the observable facts of history, it is also my experience of thirty years as a business man, banker, etc., that first the seer conceives an opportunity. He has faith in his almost second sight. He believes he can do something—develop a business—construct an industry—build a railroad—or Niagara Falls Power Company, —and make it pay!

"Now the human measure is not the actual physical construction, but the 'make it pay'!

"A man raised the money in the late '90s and built a beet sugar factory in Michigan. Wiseacres said it was nonsense. He gathered together the money from his friends who would take a chance with him. He not only built the sugar factory (and there was never any doubt of his ability to do that) but he made it pay. The next year two more sugar factories were built, and were financially successful. These were built by private individuals of wealth, taking chances in the face of cries of doubting bankers and trust companies.

"Once demonstrated that the industry was a sound one financially and *then* bankers and trust companies would lend the new sugar companies which were speedily organized a large part of the necessary funds to construct and operate.

"The motor-car business was the same.

"When a few gentlemen followed me in my vision of the possibilities of the business, the banks and older business men (who in the main were the banks) said, 'fools and their money soon to be parted'—etc., etc.

"Private capital at first establishes an industry, backs it through its troubles, and, if possible, wins financial success when banks would not lend a dollar of aid.

"The business once having proved to be practicable and financially successful, then do the banks lend aid to its needs."

Such also was the experience of the greatest of the many financial successes in the automobile industry—the Ford Motor Company.

HOW BANKERS ARREST DEVELOPMENT

But "great banking houses" have not merely failed to initiate industrial development: they have definitely arrested development because to them the creation of the trusts is largely due. The recital in the Memorial addressed to the President by the Investors' Guild in November, 1911, is significant:

"It is a well-known fact that modern trade combinations tend strongly toward constancy of process and products, and by their very nature are opposed to new processes and new products originated by independent inventors, and hence tend to restrain competition in the development and sale of patents and patent rights; and consequently tend to discourage independent inventive thought, to the great detriment of the nation, and with injustice to inventors whom the Constitution especially intended to encourage and protect in their rights."

And more specific was the testimony of the *Engineering News:*

"We are today something like five years behind Germany in iron and steel metallurgy, and such innovations as are being introduced by our iron and steel manufacturers are most of them merely following the lead set by foreigners years ago.

"We do not believe this is because American engineers are any less ingenious or original than those of Europe, though they may indeed be deficient in training and scientific education compared with those of Germany. We believe the main cause is the wholesale consolidation which has taken place in American industry. A huge organization is too clumsy to take up the development of an original idea. With the market closely controlled and profits certain by following standard methods, those who control our trusts do not want the bother of developing anything new.

"We instance metallurgy only by way of illustration. There are plenty of other fields of industry where exactly the same condition exists. We are building the same machines and using the same methods as a dozen years ago, and the real advances in the art are being made by European inventors and manufacturers."

To which President Wilson's statement may be added:

"I am not saying that all invention had been stopped by the growth of trusts, but I think it is perfectly clear that invention in many fields has been discouraged, that inventors have been prevented from reaping the full fruits of their ingenuity and industry, and that mankind has been deprived of many comforts and conveniences, as well as the opportunity of buying at lower prices.

"Do you know, have you had occasion to learn, that there is no hospitality for invention, now-a-days?"

TRUSTS AND FINANCIAL CONCENTRATION

The fact that industrial monopolies arrest development is more serious even than the direct burden imposed through extortionate prices. But the most harm-bearing incident of the trusts is their promotion of financial concentration. Industrial trusts feed the money trust.

Practically every trust created has destroyed the financial independence of some communities and of many properties; for it has centered the financing of a large part of whole lines of business in New York, and this usually with one of a few banking houses. This is well illustrated by the Steel Trust, which is a trust of trusts; that is, the Steel Trust combines in one huge holding company the trusts previously formed in the different branches of the steel business. Thus the Tube Trust combined 17 tube mills, located in 16 different cities, scattered over 5 states and owned by 13 different companies. The wire trust combined 19 mills; the sheet steel trust 26; the bridge and structural trust 27; and the tin plate trust 36; all scattered similarly over many states. Finally these and other companies were formed into the United States Steel Corporation, combining 228 companies in all, located in 127 cities and towns, scattered over 18 states. Before the combinations were effected, nearly every one of these companies was owned largely by those who managed it, and had been financed, to a large extent, in the place, or in the state, in which it was located. When the Steel Trust was formed all these concerns came under one management. Thereafter, the financing of each of these 228 corporations (and some which were later acquired) had to be done through or with the consent of J. P. Morgan & Co. *That was the greatest step in financial concentration ever taken.*

STOCK EXCHANGE INCIDENTS

The organization of trusts has served in another way to increase the power of the Money Trust. Few of the independent concerns out of which the trusts have been formed, were listed on the New York Stock Exchange; and few of them had financial offices in New York. Promoters of large corporations, whose stock is to be held by the public, and also investors, desire to have their securities listed on the New York Stock Exchange. Under the rules of the Exchange, no security can be so listed unless the corporation has a transfer agent and registrar in New York City. Furthermore, banker-directorships have contributed largely to the establishment of the financial offices of the trusts in New York City. That alone would tend to financial concentration. But the listing of the stock enhances the power of the Money Trust in another way. An industrial stock, once listed, frequently becomes the subject of active speculation; and speculation feeds the Money Trust indirectly in many ways. It draws the money of the country to New York. The New York bankers handle the loans of other people's money on the Stock Exchange; and members of the Stock Exchange receive large amounts from commissions. For instance: There are 5,084,952 shares of United States Steel common stock outstanding. But in the five years ending December 31, 1912, speculation in that stock was so extensive that there were sold on the Exchange an average of 29,380,888 shares a year; or nearly six times as much as there is Steel common in existence. Except where the transactions are by or for the brokers, sales on the Exchange involve the payment of twenty-five cents in commission for each share of stock sold; that is, twelve and one-half cents by the seller and twelve and one-half cents by the buyer. Thus the commission from the Steel common alone afforded a revenue averaging many millions a year. The Steel preferred stock is also much traded in; and there are 138 other industrials, largely trusts, listed on the New York Stock Exchange.

TRUST RAMIFICATIONS

But the potency of trusts as a factor in financial concentration is manifested in still other ways; notably through their ramifying operations. This is illustrated forcibly by the General Electric Company's control of water-power companies which has now been disclosed in an able report of the United States Bureau of Corporations:

"The extent of the General Electric influence is not fully revealed by its consolidated balance sheet. A very large number of corporations are connected with it through its subsidiaries and through corporations controlled by these subsidiaries or affiliated with them. There is a still wider circle of influence due to the fact that officers and directors of the General Electric Company and its subsidiaries are also officers or directors of many other corporations,

some of whose securities are owned by the General Electric Company.

"The General Electric Company holds in the first place all the common stock in three security holding companies: the United Electric Securities Co., the Electrical Securities Corporation, and the Electric Bond and Share Co. Directly and through these corporations and their officers the General Electric controls a large part of the water power of the United States. . . .

"The water-power companies in the General Electric group are found in 18 States. These 18 States have 2,325,757 commercial horsepower developed or under construction, and of this total the General Electric group includes 939,115 h. p. or 40.4 per cent. The greatest amount of power controlled by the companies in the General Electric group in any State is found in Washington. This is followed by New York, Pennsylvania, California, Montana, Iowa, Oregon, and Colorado. In five of the States shown in the table the water-power companies included in the General Electric group control more than 50 per cent of the commercial power, developed and under construction. The percentage of power in the States included in the General Electric group ranges from a little less than 2 per cent in Michigan to nearly 80 per cent in Pennsylvania. In Colorado they control 72 per cent; in New Hampshire 61 per cent; in Oregon 58 per cent; and in Washington 55 per cent.

Besides the power developed and under construction water-power concerns included in the General Electric group own in the States shown in the table 641,600 h. p. undeveloped."

This water-power control enables the General Electric group to control other public service corporations:

"The water-power companies subject to General Electric influence control the street railways in at least 16 cities and towns; the electric-light plants in 78 cities and towns; gas plants in 19 cities and towns; and are affiliated with the electric light and gas plants in other towns. Though many of these communities, particularly those served with light only, are small, several of them are the most important in the States where these water-power companies operate. The water-power companies in the General Electric group own, control, or are closely affiliated with, the street railways in Portland and Salem, Ore.; Spokane, Wash.; Great Falls, Mont.; St. Louis, Mo.; Winona, Minn.; Milwaukee and Racine, Wis.; Elmira, N. Y.; Asheville and Raleigh, N. C., and other relatively less important towns. The towns in which the lighting plants (electric or gas) are owned or controlled include Portland, Salem, Astoria, and other towns in Oregon; Bellingham and other towns in Washington; Butte, Great Falls, Bozeman and other towns in Montana; Leadville and Colorado Springs in Colorado; St. Louis, Mo.; Milwaukee, Racine and several small towns in Wisconsin; Hudson and Rensselaer, N. Y.; Detroit, Mich.; Asheville and Raleigh, N. C.; and in fact one or more towns in practically every community where developed water power is controlled by this group. In addition to the public-service corporations thus controlled by the water-power companies subject to General Electric influence, there are numerous public-service corporations in other municipalities that purchase power from the hydroelectric developments controlled by or affiliated with the General Electric Co. This is true of Denver, Colo., which has already been discussed. In Baltimore, Md., a water-power concern in the General Electric group, namely, the Pennsylvania Water & Power Co., sells 20,000 h. p. to the Consolidated Gas, Electric Light & Power Co., which controls the entire light and power business of that city. The power to operate all the electric street railway systems of Buffalo, N. Y., and vicinity, involving a trackage of approximately 375 miles, is supplied through a subsidiary of the Niagara Falls Power Co."

And the General Electric Company, through the financing of public service companies, exercises a like influence in communities where there is no water power:

"It, or its subsidiaries, has acquired control of or an interest in the public-service corporations of numerous cities where there is no water-power connection, and it is affiliated with still others by virtue of common directors. . . . This vast network of relationship between hydro-electric corporations through prominent officers and directors of the largest manufacturer of electrical machinery and supplies in the United States is highly significant. . . .

"It is possible that this relationship to such a large number of strong financial concerns, through common officers and directors, affords the General Electric Company an advantage that may place rivals at a corresponding disadvantage. Whether or not this great financial power has been used to the particular disadvantage of any rival water-power concern is not so important as the fact that such power exists and that it might be so used at any time."

THE SHERMAN LAW

The Money Trust cannot be broken, if we allow its power to be constantly augmented. To break the Money Trust, we must stop that power at its source. The industrial trusts are among its most effective feeders. Those which are illegal should be dissolved. The creation of new ones should be prevented. To this end the Sherman Law should be supplemented both by providing more efficient judicial machinery, and by creating a commission with administrative functions to aid in enforcing the law. When that is done, another step will have been taken toward securing the New Freedom. But restrictive legislation alone will not suffice. We should bear in mind the admonition with which the Commissioner of Corporations closes his review of our water-power development:

"There is . . . presented such a situation in water powers and other public utilities as might bring about at any time under a single management the control of a majority of the developed water power in the United States and similar control over the public utilities in a vast number of cities and towns, including some of the most important in the country."

We should conserve all rights which the Federal Government and the States now have in our natural resources, and there should be a complete separation of our industries from railroads and public utilities.

Sherwood Anderson

Sherwood Anderson (1876–1941) was an American industrialist who in his fortieth year left the business
world and turned to writing. He quickly moved into a position of prominence among American literary figures, reflecting in his work the new emphasis on realism and insisting that the fundamental truths of human existence should
be revealed. Like Theodore Dreiser and Eugene O'Neill,
Anderson was in revolt against the great illusion built up in
the mind of America that its civilization was the ultimate in
man's progress. Quite naturally he drew upon his earlier experiences for his material and criticized in his novels and
essays the technical progress which had transformed American production during the second and third industrial
revolutions. To Anderson modern machinery was invading
and destroying the pioneer American civilization built by
earlier generations. In the short essay Lift Up Thine Eyes
Anderson condemned the modern factory and its influence
upon the workers. In reading it note (1) the importance of
salesmanship in modern economic life, (2) the description
and characterization of "the belt," (3) the element of
competition employed in modern production, (4) how
Anderson related the title of the essay to the process he was
describing, and (5) how he used his literary style to enhance "the speed-up" theme he was describing.

LIFT UP THINE EYES

In verses twenty-three to twenty-seven of
the third chapter of Deuteronomy, Moses
speaks these words to his people in the wilderness:

And I besought the Lord at that time, saying,
O Lord God, thou hast begun to shew thy
servant thy greatness, and thy mighty hand:
for what God is there in heaven or earth, that
can do according to thy works, and according
to thy might?

I pray thee, let me go over, and see the good
land that is beyond Jordan, that goodly mountain, and Lebanon.

But the Lord was wroth with me for your
sakes, and would not hear me: and the Lord
said unto me, Let it suffice thee; speak no more
unto me of this matter.

Get thee up into the top of Pisgah, and lift
up thine eyes westward, and northward, and
southward, and eastward, and behold it with
thine eyes: for thou shalt not go over this
Jordan.

It is a big assembling plant in a city of the
Northwest. They assemble there the Bogel car.
It is a car that sells in large numbers and at a
low price. The parts are made in one great
central plant and shipped to the places where
they are to be assembled. There is little or no
manufacturing done in the assembling plant
itself. The parts come in. These great companies have learned to use the railroad cars for
storage.

At the central plant everything is done on
schedule. As soon as the parts are made they

Sherwood Anderson, "Lift Up Thine Eyes," in *The Nation*, 28 May 1930. Courtesy of *The Nation*.

go into railroad cars. They are on their way to the assembling plants scattered all over the United States and they arrive on schedule.

The assembling plant assembles cars for a certain territory. A careful survey has been made. This territory can afford to buy so and so many cars per day.

"But suppose the people do not want the cars?"

"What has that to do with it?"

People, American people, no longer buy cars. They do not buy newspapers, books, foods, pictures, clothes. Things are sold to people now. If a territory can take so and so many Bogel cars, find men who can make them take the cars. That is the way things are done now.

In the assembling plant everyone works "on the belt." This is a big steel conveyor, a kind of moving sidewalk, waist-high. It is a great river running down through the plant. Various tributary streams come into the main stream, the main belt. They bring tires, they bring headlights, horns, bumpers for cars. They flow into the main stream. The main stream has its source at the freight cars, where the parts are unloaded, and it flows out to the other end of the factory and into other freight cars.

The finished automobiles go into the freight cars at the delivery end of the belt. The assembly plant is a place of peculiar tension. You feel it when you go in. It never lets up. Men here work always on tension. There is no let-up to the tension. If you can't stand it get out.

It is the belt. The belt is boss. It moves always forward. Now the chassis goes on the belt. A hoist lifts it up and places it just so. There is a man at each corner. The chassis is deposited on the belt and it begins to move. Not too rapidly. There are things to be done.

How nicely everything is calculated. Scientific men have done this. They have watched men work. They have stood looking, watch in hand. There is care taken about everything. Look up. Lift up thine eyes. Hoists are bringing engines, bodies, wheels, fenders. These come out of side streams flowing into the main stream. They move at a pace very nicely calculated. They will arrive at the main stream at just a certain place at just a certain time.

In this shop there is no question of wages to be wrangled about. The men work but eight hours a day and are well paid. They are, almost without exception, young, strong men. It is, however, possible that eight hours a day in this place may be much longer than twelve or even sixteen hours in the old carelessly run plants.

They can get better pay here than at any other shop in town. Although I am a man wanting a good many minor comforts in life, I could live well enough on the wages made by the workers in this place. Sixty cents an hour to begin and then, after a probation period of sixty days, if I can stand the pace, seventy cents or more.

To stand the pace is the real test. Special skill is not required. It is all perfectly timed, perfectly calculated. If you are a body upholsterer, so many tacks driven per second. Not too many. If a man hurries too much too many tacks drop on the floor. If a man gets too hurried he is not efficient. Let an expert take a month, two months, to find out just how many tacks the average good man can drive per second.

There must be a certain standard maintained in the finished product. Remember that. It must pass inspection after inspection.

Do not crowd too hard.

Crowd all you can.

Keep crowding.

There are fifteen, twenty, thirty, perhaps fifty such assembling plants, all over the country, each serving its own section. Wires pass back and forth daily. The central office—from which all the parts come—at Jointville is the nerve center. Wires come in and go out of Jointville. In so and so many hours Williamsburg, with so and so many men, produced so and so many cars.

Now Burkesville is ahead. It stays ahead. What is up at Burkesville? An expert flies there.

The man at Burkesville was a major in the army. He is the manager there. He is a cold, rather severe, rather formal man. He has found out something. He is a real Bogel man, an ideal Bogel man. There is no foolishness about him. He watches the belt. He does not say foolishly to himself, "I am the boss here." He knows the belt is boss.

He says there is a lot of foolishness talked about the belt. The experts are too expert, he says. He has found out that the belt can be made to move just a little faster than the experts say. He has tried it. He knows. Go and look for yourself. There are the men out there on the belt, swarming along the belt, each in his place. They are all right, aren't they?

Can you see anything wrong?

Just a trifle more speed in every man. Shove the pace up just a little, not much. With the same number of men, in the same number of hours, six more cars a day.

That's the way a major gets to be a colonel, a colonel to a general. Watch that fellow at Burkesville, the man with the military stride, the cold steady voice. He'll go far.

Everything is nicely, perfectly calculated in all the Bogel assembling plants. There are white marks on the floor everywhere. Everything is immaculately clean. No one smokes, no one chews tobacco, no one spits. There are white banks on the cement floor along which the men walk. As they work, sweepers follow them. Tacks dropped on the floor are at once swept up. You can tell by the sweepings in a plant where there is too much waste, too much carelessness. Sweep everything carefully and frequently. Weigh the sweepings. Have an expert examine the sweepings. Report to Jointville.

Jointville says: "Too many upholsterers' tacks wasted in the plant at Port Smith. Belleville produced one hundred and eleven cars a day, with seven hundred and forty-nine men, wasting only nine hundred and six tacks."

It is a good thing to go through the plant now and then, select one man from all the others, give him a new and bigger job, just like that, offhand. If he doesn't make good, fire him.

It is a good thing to go through the plant occasionally, pick out some man, working apparently as the others are, fire him.

If he asks why, just say to him, "You know."

He'll know all right. He'll imagine why.

The thing is to build up Jointville. This country needs a religion. You have got to build up the sense of a mysterious central thing, a thing working outside your knowledge.

Let the notion grow and grow that there is something superhuman at the core of all this.

Lift up thine eyes, lift up thine eyes.

The central office reaches down into your secret thoughts. It knows, it knows.

Jointville knows.

Do not ask questions of Jointville. Keep up the pace.

Get the cars out.

Get the cars out.

Get the cars out.

The pace can be accelerated a little this year. The men have all got tuned into the old pace now.

Step it up a little, just a little.

They have got a special policeman in all the Bogel assembling plants. They have got a special doctor there. A man hurts his finger a little. It bleeds a little, a mere scratch. The doctor reaches down for him. The finger is fixed. Jointville wants no blood poisonings, no infections.

The doctor puts men who want jobs through a physical examination, as in the army. Try his nerve reactions. We want only the best men here, the youngest, the fastest.

Why not?

We pay the best wages, don't we?

The policeman in the plant has a special job. That's queer. It is like this. Now and then the big boss passes through. He selects a man off the belt.

"You're fired."

"Why?"

"You know."

Now and then a man goes off his nut. He goes fantoed. He howls and shouts. He grabs up a hammer.

A stream of crazy profanity comes from his lips.

There is Jointville. That is the central thing. That controls the belt.

The belt controls me.

It moves.

It moves.

It moves.

I've tried to keep up.

I tell you I have been keeping up.

Jointville is God.

Jointville controls the belt.

The belt is God.

God has rejected me.

You're fired.

Sometimes a man, fired like that, goes nutty. He gets dangerous. A strong policeman on hand knocks him down, takes him out.

You walk within certain definite white lines.

It is calculated that a man, rubbing automobile bodies with pumice, makes thirty thousand and twenty-one arm strokes per day. The difference between thirty thousand and twenty-one and twenty-eight thousand and four will tell a vital story of profits or loss at Jointville.

Do you think things are settled at Jointville, or at the assembling plants of the Bogel car scattered all over America? Do you think men know how fast the belt can be made to move, what the ultimate, the final pace will be, can be?

Certainly not.

There are experts studying the nerves of men, the movements of men. They are watching, watching. Calculations are always going on. The thing is to produce goods and more goods at less cost. Keep the standard up. Increase the pace a little.

Stop waste.

Calculate everything.

A man walking to and from his work between white lines saves steps. There is a tremendous science of lost motion not perfectly calculated yet.

More goods at less cost.

Increase the pace.

Keep up standards.

It is so you advance civilization.

In the Bogel assembling plants, as at Jointville itself, there isn't any laughter. No one stops work to play. No one fools around or throws things, as they used to do in the old factories. That is why Bogel is able to put the old-fashioned factories, one by one, out of business.

It is all a matter of calculation. You feel it when you go in. You feel rigid lines. You feel movement. You feel a strange tension in the air. There is a quiet terrible intensity.

The belt moves. It keeps moving. The day I was there a number of young boys had come in. They had been sent by a Bogel car dealer, away back somewhere in the country. They had driven in during the night and were to drive Bogel cars back over the country roads to some dealer. A good many Bogel cars go out to dealers from the assembling plants, driven out by boys like that.

Such boys, driving all night, fooling along the road, getting no sleep.

They have a place for them to wait for the cars in the Bogel assembling plants. You have been at dog shows and have seen how prize dogs are exhibited, each in his nice clean cage. They have nice clean cages like that for country boys who drive in to Bogel assembling plants to get cars.

The boys come in. There is a place to lie down in there. It is clean. After the boy goes into his cage a gate is closed. He is fastened in.

If a country boy, sleepy like that, waiting for his car, wandered about in a plant he might get hurt.

There might be damage suits, all sorts of things.

Better to calculate everything. Be careful. Be exact.

Jointville thought of that. Jointville thinks of everything. It is the center of power, the new mystery.

Every year in America Jointville comes nearer and nearer being the new center. Men nowadays do not look to Washington. They look to Jointville.

Lift up thine eyes, lift up thine eyes.

Stuart Chase

Stuart Chase (1888–   ) is an American writer trained as a public accountant. He has been associated with various government agencies for many years and has participated in numerous investigations of business and industrial practices. He is the author of a long series of books and articles analyzing and criticizing the American economic structure. In particular he has been concerned about machine production and its implications, both actual and potential, for human labor. In 1930, Chase wrote an article for Fortune entitled "Danger at the A. O. Smith Corporation," an analytical study of trends in industrial production. In reading it note (1) Chase's reply to those who feared industrial workers were becoming robots, (2) the innovation developed at the Smith plant, (3) what had become the chief business of the company, (4) the vivid description of the "dragon," (5) the contrast between the old and the new mills, (6) what Chase considered the danger at the A. O. Smith Corporation to be, and (7) the ultimate utopia which might emerge from this development.

DANGER AT THE A. O. SMITH CORPORATION

Jeremiahs of monumental profundity wring their hands and tear their beards lamenting the conversion of men into robots in the age of the machine. They adduce no figures, but the impression given is a wholesale operation, affecting nearly all of us. Elsewhere I have sought to verify, quantitively, the strength of this indictment. With the Census of Occupations as a base, I found that of 42,000,000 Americans gainfully employed, not more than 10,000,000 spent their working hours in close contact with machinery. Further analysis discloses that only about 5,000,000 can properly be called robots at all in that they surrender their personalities to the machine.

The other 5,000,000 either are handicraft men and other helpers about factories who have little to do with machinery, or—and this is important—they themselves *dominate* the mechanism, and thus let some of its energy into their own veins. Air pilots are not robots by any stretch of the imagination, and neither are operators of motor cars, locomotive engineers, or structural steel workers. Lastly, of those who might be termed robots—some 12 per cent of the gainfully employed—the number is actually declining, and for two reasons. Due to technical improvements in output per man, factory employees are growing fewer. Second, the automatic function in industry is steadily gaining around, displacing machine-feeders and nut-screwers by skilled designers, inspectors, dial-watchers. A large number of so-called robots give way to a small number of workers with reasonably intelligent and independent jobs.

In order that the Jeremiahs may see exactly what I mean, I take pleasure in presenting in some detail the most advanced single exhibit of the automatic function in the world. The honor belongs beyond peradventure to the mill which makes automobile frames practically by itself on the premises of the A. O. Smith Corporation in the city of Milwaukee. And I take pleasure in presenting one or two additional aspects of this extraordinary company which ought to give the machine age philosophers, both gloomy and cheerio, enough to reflect on for quite a while to come. This plant not only threatens to end the scourge of the robot; it threatens to end industry itself—in the form that we have hitherto known it. There is a mixture brewing here which if it explodes, will make Milwaukee more famous than ever did its beer.

The company was founded over half a century ago with the commendable purpose of fabricating baby carriages. In due time, babies were abandoned for bicycle riders. About 1900, Mr. A. O. Smith, the son of the founder, gave the first recorded example of that policy to which the company now dedicates itself. He

Stuart Chase, "Danger at the A. O. Smith Corporation," in *Fortune*, November, 1930. Courtesy of Stuart Chase and of *Fortune*.

had been following the early flounderings of the automobile. Bankers and other sensible folk knew it for what it was—a crazy, impracticable contraption. Not so Mr. Smith. He was convinced that the motor car had a future. Some day it would be made in large quantities. It would need a frame on which its engine would rest. That frame might be made of wood, iron, or pressed steel. He pondered over these three alternatives as the one-lungers gurgled, back-fired, and frightened live stock out of its wits. He concluded his ruminations in favor of pressed steel. With a group of men from the bicycle shop, he proceeded to design and erect special machinery for making steel frames, *a full year before there was any call for them, or indeed any evidence that America would take to making automobiles in a determined way at all!* He had thought out his problem, designed and set up his equipment in advance of the world's recognition that there was a problem. This is the sort of thinking which is coming out of Milwaukee to-day.

In 1902, the orders—more or less on schedule—began to arrive, the machines were put at productive labor, and the first frames shipped out. They came from the shop at the rate of ten per day, and Mr. Smith offered a house and lot to the foreman who could get out twelve. (Now they are coming at 10,000 a day.) It was hand and machine work, much of it robot work, if you please. The business prospered. The grandson of the founder Mr. L. R. Smith, took the helm his father laid down. He looked at the rows of men handling heavy steel side bars, performing a single operation. "It's stupid," he thought, "and wasteful. It costs too much; it's bad for the men. Men have too much innate ability to be condemned to such work as this." He turned to his engineers, a growing corps and one upon which he came more and more to depend. (He is himself an engineer.) "Could we design a machine to do this whole job automatically, a machine as big as a factory, to pick up the raw steel and throw these things out at four or five thousand a day? I know it is a crazy idea, but can we do it?" His engineers had learned to expect anything from this man. The T-squares spanked and the drawing boards groaned. Ten times the plant

was built on paper, and the cost of the crazy idea had mounted to $1,500,000.

Finally, after incredible labor and some of the boldest mechanical thinking ever done on this planet, a plan was evolved which looked as though, by the grace of God, it might work. Bankers were called in and their advice asked. The rosy-gilled fraternity was petrified, and advised, whatever it was, not to do it. They were thanked politely, and the metamorphosis of paper into concrete and steel promptly begun. Fortunately, money in the home stocking was still available.

Beyond the technical incredibility of the project was the whole question of the potential market. Suppose the plant could be built, who was to buy frames in lots of 7,000 each and every day; 2,000,000 frames a year? Competitors were in the field, and in 1916 only 1,500,000 motor cars were manufactured the country over. The blueprints called for more frames than there were engines to mount on them. But even as his father had sensed the beginning of an industry in 1900, the son sensed the postwar automotive boom. "We were aiming at million-lot machinery, million-lot production, and million-lot costs," and lo! the market came to meet this million-lot expectancy. The plant was built in 1920. Soon afterward the roaring twenties, building 3,000,000, 4,000,000, 5,000,000 motor cars a year, were in full swing and demanding Smith frames.

By the time the mill was built, $6,000,000 had been sunk in it, including the drawing paper. Would the damn thing work? The blueprints were optimistic, but how about Madame Nature? Here were 552 separate operations to be performed on every frame. If any one of them went wrong, the whole gigantic mechanism might jam.

I will never forget that moment when it became necessary for me or an associate to throw on the power. Both of us were stalling, one waiting for the other. Neither can remember clearly which one threw the switch. But for an hour and fifty-seven minutes, the unit functioned without a hitch. Then it shut down for want of raw material!

The damn thing would work. It has been working ever since. And, of course, for all the palpitations when the first switch was thrown, Mr. Smith and his engineers *knew* it would work. Too much sound research had already gone in to permit of failure. It was no miracle nor are the subsequent achievements miracles, spectacular as they appear. It is the sort of thing to be expected when engineering takes the place of rule of thumb, and its possibilities developed *to the limit*. In due time production was stepped up from 7,000 frames a day to 10,000—and the end is not yet.

One goes through a guarded gate into the great enclosure upon which the company's property stands: a company which sells $60,-000,000 of tonnage products a year, moving out on 30,000 freight cars. The buildings are not huge but squat and grim, full of noise and full of power. There is an air of spaciousness and cleanliness, but no hint of lawns, flowers and the tra la la la school of mill design. Clean, muscled, and stripped to the waist is the dominant note. But stop a moment. What is this partly finished building of peculiar steel construction with black granite base and fluted aluminum creeping up over the stanchions? It is the new Research Building, equipped to house 1,000 engineers. It could have been built for $400,000 but is costing $1,500,000. And why, pray, the extra $1,000,000? It is expended to make as just and lovely a temple to the god of science as devoted hands have reared to other gods in other ages. Engineering research is the chief business of this company. Frames for motor cars, pipes for oil fields, pressure vessels—these are by-products.

We enter a door in one of the squat mills and are suddenly drowned in sound. We are in a room perhaps 300 feet long and 200 wide, with walls of glass. Its floor is one solid mass of glittering steel, a thousand shapes which rush and stop, rise and fall, advance and retreat, dancing to some gigantic rhythm, yet to a counterpoint which sets up no vibration. One quadrille offsets the other, leaving the building without a tremor. The multiplicity of moving shapes confuses us, but as we mount a platform, a sense of discipline, of patterned harmony, becomes apparent. Wide, clean aisles separate the moving groups. There are no towering mechanisms, no belts; the whole upper part of the building is clear. The largest single shape is near the door by which we entered. It is also the noisiest. With drum-shattering gasps it is solemnly picking up pieces of steel, fitting them to a pattern, dropping the unit down for some attention (the seat of the noise apparently), raising it up, placing it on a little carriage of delicate steel rods . . . carriage after carriage, which rush and stop, rush and stop, rush and stop, in our direction.

Comprehension dawns. Upon each carriage is obviously a motor car frame; the hissing mechanism has assembled the various side bars and cross bars which compose it, and the dropping motion—our guide assists us here—is the automatic insertion of 100 rivets into their waiting holes. The assembled frame moves toward us for the job of heading the rivets and so locking the parts finally together.

As the frames advance and stop, two batteries of steel dragons, with jaws like those of stone Aztec serpents, move forward upon them, one from either side. Their round metal eyes glitter, their jaws are distended to cavernous proportions, they nuzzle into their victim's vitals, select each a sought-for rivet, then slowly, relentlessly, even softly, the great jaws close. The final crunch of 40,000 pounds upon the rivet head is effortless. Gently the jaw opens; gently and solemnly both batteries retreat. The frame moves on to another group of monsters, where the process is repeated with a second set of rivets. One hundred rivets require about 100 dragons, and only about six can operate comfortably at one "station."

Sometimes, if you please, the beast opens its mouth to bite, thinks better of it, retires, rears up into a more ferocious position, and then comes dreadfully down. It is reported that Mr. Otto Kahn could not be budged from his entranced survey of this deliberate animal. "I have seen many ingenious machines," he said, "but this is the first that ever I saw which started to do a job, stopped, spit on its hands, hitched up its overalls, and then went to work!" This is a good story—but dragons, my dear Mr. Kahn, really, dragons do not spit on their hands.

There are nine units in the total process. In each unit are a number of stations—connecting a single operation. What I have described is but the operation of several stations on unit No. 6, the general assembly line. As we walk along our platform which runs the length of the building, each unit is identified between its dividing aisles, and its general function if not its bewildering detail, made plain. A little table tells the story.

Unit	Function
No. 1.—	Picks up the raw steel strips, examines them, throws out those which do not meet the required standards of length, breadth, and thickness.
No. 2.—	Douses the admitted strips into baths of pickle for cleaning.
No. 3.—	Fabricates the longer strips into right and left side bars—bending them, turning up their edges, punching holes for future rivets.
No. 4.—	Fabricates the shorter strips into cross bars.
No. 5.—	Assembles the various parts of the side bars.
No. 6.—	Assembles the whole frame, inserts and drives home the rivets—by virtue of monsters altogether fabulous, as we have seen.
No. 7.—	General inspection of the assembled frame, a partly human job.
No. 8.—	Automatic washing, painting, and drying.
No. 9.—	The snatching of the painted, dried, completed frame by the left hind leg, as it were, and bearing it, like a hog in a packing house, to a vast overhead storage space. There it hangs, in carload lots, until a man in a little underslung crane, which crawls like a busy beetle among these towering heights, drops it, kerplunk, into a waiting freight car.

One hour and a half from raw steel to suspension by the hind leg, and a minute or two more to freight car if there is any rush. Every eight seconds a completed frame goes swinging into storage, 420 an hour, 10,000 a day. Frames for Pontiac, Chrysler, Chevrolet, Buick. For each type of frame, the great dance stops for a few hours. Skilled mechanics swarm out from the tool shop at the end of the building and reset the dragons' jaws and the other mechanisms to take care of the new size. Given an over-all length and width, any variety—past, present, or future—of frame can be made. About thirty different styles are now fabricated, but the total variety is virtually limitless. The goal of standardization with *flexibility* has been won. In nine years of operation no automobile maker has ever had to shut down his assembly line for lack of frames, this in spite of eleventh-hour increases in orders on the part of customers.

Are the Jeremiahs answered? Academically no. Practically yes, if this sort of thing is to expand. Mr. Smith admits his mill to be an engineering failure though a huge commercial success. He set out to build a machine that would make frames without men. He did not quite succeed. At one or two stations, men touch the frame with their hands, thus breaking 100 per cent performance, though this is still the goal. The Jeremiahs, I among them, find other objections in the thought of ex-robots walking the streets. As technological unemployment advances, a technological solution must be found. I was glad to hear Mr. Smith say that shorter hours offered one remedy from the long swing point of view.

But consider the tangible achievement. Not a stone's throw away is the old "hand" mill. I went through it, and the contrast was staggering. Here are 2,000 men in long assembly lines, drilling holes, driving bolts, twisting shapes, conveying the growing frame by hand from process to process. Yet work as they may, they can make no more frames a day than can the automatic mill with a scant 200 men, not more than fifty of whom actually touch the product. Two thousand dreary jobs against 200 amusing ones, for an identical output! Ponder this well, ye Jeremiahs. The cost of the automatic frame to the hand frames is as two to three (and rather less in total than a good pair of shoes), with a very large absorption of development overhead. Some day when this overhead cost is all absorbed, the automatic cost will fall into the subcellar. . . .

Few men ever voluntarily leave the automatic mill. There is a long waiting list. They appreciate it as "something different"; they appreciate the boldness of the boss in designing it, and their jobs are certainly far more independent and interesting than those in the hand mill. One man sits in a little tower, the control switches of a whole unit under his hand; another resets the gape of the dragon's jaws; another adjusts the "nailing machine," the automatic riveter which shoots by compressed air a hundred tiny bars of steel at once. (To skilled technicians this is the supreme mechanical achievement of the mill and the engine of which Mr. Smith is himself the proudest.) Skill varies; some jobs can be taught in a few days, others require months and months of intensive training, while in design, erection, and repair we have as skilled a group of crafts as this, or any other age, has ever glimpsed. The whole building is one vast integrated machine. Another major job remains, however, before the Jeremiahs are completely routed. There is, I believe, too much noise in that place for human ears to stand indefinitely without injury.

I asked Mr. Smith if the process were applicable to other industries. "Yes," he said, "almost everywhere when the demand is great enough to warrant 'million-lots.' Even automobiles could be assembled automatically if we were sure of their general style long enough to spend the time and money."

All the eggs of the A. O. Smith Corporation are not in one basket. Far from it. Frame-making is depressed at the present time due to the slump in motor cars (90 per cent of the frame makers retain their jobs at shorter hours), but the pipe business is roaring as never before. Nor is the demand for pressure vessels in the doldrums, due to its close association with the developing chemical industry. . . .

One last field observation before we move to general principles. In a rambling wing I found the very efficient safety department and the department of preventive medicine equipped for as complete a physical examination as the best hospital can give. This is said to be the most thorough-going medical study of *normal* persons ever conducted. As the records grow and the years go by, it will be profoundly helpful in telling the well person what he must do to keep well. . . . There are scientists of steel

in this company and scientists of flesh and blood.

The Smith dynasty has a guiding star. It employs seven salesmen—I counted them—and not far from 600 engineers. Presently the new research building will house 1,000 engineers in quarters equipped with facilities beyond their wildest dreams. Their work is not primarily to keep the present output increasingly efficient, but to develop new varieties of output, and totally new processes for fabricating them. A program of industrial depth bombs, but geared to three basic principles:

I.—The product must lie in the field of mass production, with an established market, or one which the economic research staff knows can be established.

II.—A product to be made so much better and cheaper than anything else in the field that it will sell itself on its engineering merits alone, with no outlays for high pressure salesmanship or advertising.

III.—A product profitable enough to liquidate its fixed investment in not longer than a year or two. (The success of this principle hitherto is reflected in the company's luxuriant profit and loss accounts. I speak as a sometime C. P. A.)

The product having been determined according to these principles, it is put through three stages, or stations as Mr. Smith calls them. First comes the "pencil sketch" station. It may die there. But if the figures look sound, it goes to the "test tube" station, of laboratory analysis. If it survives this manhandling, it goes to the "pilot plant" station—a miniature factory where it is actually produced under normal operating conditions, and its performance, and particularly its costs per unit, accurately determined. The pilot plant answers the question: can it be made in the expected quantities at the calculated costs and how big must the real operating plant be? This delimits the design of the proposed plant and makes its construction practically automatic, with everything accounted for in advance. If the answer is in the negative, whatever the time and money spent upon the idea, it goes down the trap door. "I can get out of a business faster than anyone in the country," says Mr. Smith— an art which few executives have learned. . . .

Certain by-products of profound industrial significance arise from this program. The production of a given article under these principles of engineering research, automatic fabrication, low costs, tends to insure high quality. If the mill is not to jam, every incoming piece of raw material—as we saw in the frame plant —must pass rigid tests of inspection. The delicate controls demand an absolutely uniform product, without flaw or break. Engineering and its handmaiden, mathematics, are sciences to which the word "elegance" has been frequently applied. In full control of the job, other things being equal, the output will share that perfection and that elegance. Mr. Lewis Mumford, the distinguished architectural critic, has been hinting at this for a long time. I am glad to supply him with concrete evidence of the soundness of his stand.

A second philosophical by-product—and not so exclusively philosophical either—is the factor of obsolescence. The Smith policy is ruthlessly to scrap anything which is not a jump or two ahead of the rest of the world; to scrap indeed when it *is* ahead, if the research staff has developed a better process. Certain great corporations buy up, or develop, improvements and file them in their safes. Mr. Smith puts them to work instanter; ground for the new plant is broken before the signature of the patent office is dry. "I grant it is wasteful, I grant the overhead cost is enormous, but it is far more wasteful to burn up men and materials in the old way when a better way has been found."

It all boils down, of course, to the margin of economy in the new way. If the margin is de-monstrably greater than the cost of installing the method, it is cheaper to the company and to society to scrap the old; aye, to throw uncounted millions of investment on the dump heap. The only trouble is in locating the marginal point. Aging boards of corporate directors have some difficulty in the premises, but to a stripped, flexible organization with every executive ready to go through hell and out again with Mr. Smith, and 1,000 engineers supplying the facts, the point is easier to determine. Nine times out of ten an organization like this will succeed, where the ordinary manufacturer, regarding engineers as so many expensive plumbers, will fail if he attempts to flirt with the ballistics of obsolescence. "How can you afford to spend so much for engineers?" these gentlemen ask our hero. "I can't afford not to," says a lean, brown man in the upper forties, with a face like a Yankee skipper's.

I regard Milwaukee as the most dangerous area in the U. S. It promises, in the persons of the Smith dynasty, to deal American industry a wallop beside which the late stock market crash was a chuck under the chin. Any determined adoption of its principles will turn the economic structure upside down and inside out, scrap billions of dollars of investment, shatter the nerves of untold bankers, and set the exalted profession of high-pressure salesmanship in a roadside ditch.

But when the hurricane is over, we may find a world where poverty has disappeared, where robots are unheard of, where working hours have been cut in two, where waste is at a minimum, and where the era of the salesman has given way to the era of the engineer.

Woodrow Wilson

Woodrow Wilson (1856–1924) forsook his chosen profession of education in order to enter public life as a defender of democratic principles against the growing power of monopolies. He was convinced that the freedom of the individual, which in Jefferson's day had to be protected from too much government power, could in the twentieth century only be preserved from the encroachment of big business by that same power of government. He campaigned for, and won, the presidency in 1912 on a platform designed to control corporations, to lower tariffs, and to levy income taxes to pay the cost of increased government functions. During his two terms in the White House, Wilson was largely successful in bringing about a silent revolution from the old liberalism of Jefferson's day to the "New Freedom" of his own. In 1913 he published The New Freedom, a book of speeches delivered during the 1912 presidential campaign. The first chapter is entitled "The Old Order Changeth"; in reading it note (1) what Wilson meant by the "old order," (2) the relationship of existing laws to the "new order," (3) why there existed a labor question, (4) how Americans were unintentionally victimized by corporations, (5) what had happened to freedom of economic enterprise, (6) what he considered the country needed above everything else, (7) where the treasured strength of America lay, (8) his analysis of Jefferson's ideal of government, (9) the duties the government must assume in the "new order," (10) the intolerable relationship existing between government and business, and (11) the nature and purpose of the revolution which Wilson believed was about to sweep America.

From: THE NEW FREEDOM

There is one great basic fact which underlies all the questions that are discussed on the political platform at the present moment. That singular fact is that nothing is done in this country as it was done twenty years ago.

We are in the presence of a new organization of society. Our life has broken away from the past. The life of America is not the life that it was twenty years ago. We have changed our economic conditions, absolutely, from top to bottom; and, with our economic society, the organization of our life. The old political formulas do not fit the present problems; they read now like documents taken out of a forgotten age. The older cries sound as if they belonged to a past age which men have almost forgotten. Things which used to be put into the party platforms of ten years ago would sound antiquated if put into a platform now. We are facing the necessity of fitting a new social organization, as we did once fit the old organization, to the happiness and prosperity of the great body of citizens; for we are conscious that the new order of society has not been made to fit and provide the convenience or prosperity of the average man. The life of the nation has grown infinitely varied. It does not centre now upon questions of governmental structure or of the distribution of governmental powers. It centres upon questions of the very structure and operation of society itself, of which government is only the instrument. Our development has run so fast and so far along the lines sketched in the earlier day of constitutional definition, has so crossed and interlaced those lines, has piled upon them such novel structures of trust and combination, has elaborated within them a life so manifold, so full of forces which transcend the boundaries of the country itself and fill the eyes of the world, that a new nation seems to have been created which the old formulas do not fit or afford a vital interpretation of.

We have come upon a very different age from any that preceded us. We have come upon an age when we do not do business in the way in which we used to do business,—when we do not carry on any of the operations

Woodrow Wilson, *The New Freedom: A Call for the Emancipation of the Generous Energies of a People*, Doubleday, Doran and Company, Inc., Garden City, 1933, 3–32. Copyright 1913 by Doubleday and Company, Inc. Courtesy of Doubleday and Company, Inc.

of manufacture, sale, transportation, or communication as men used to carry them on. There is a sense in which in our day the individual has been submerged. In most parts of our country men work, not for themselves, not as partners in the old way in which they used to work, but generally as employees,—in a higher or lower grade,—of great corporations. There was a time when corporations played a very minor part in our business affairs, but now they play the chief part, and most men are the servants of corporations.

You know what happens when you are the servant of a corporation. You have in no instance access to the men who are really determining the policy of the corporation. If the corporation is doing the things that it ought not to do, you really have no voice in the matter and must obey the orders, and you have oftentimes with deep mortification to co-operate in the doing of things which you know are against the public interest. Your individuality is swallowed up in the individuality and purpose of a great organization.

It is true that, while most men are thus submerged in the corporation, a few, a very few, are exalted to a power which as individuals they could never have wielded. Through the great organizations of which they are the heads, a few are enabled to play a part unprecedented by anything in history in the control of the business operations of the country and in the determination of the happiness of great numbers of people.

Yesterday, and ever since history began, men were related to one another as individuals. To be sure there were the family, the Church, and the State, institutions which associated men in certain wide circles of relationship. But in the ordinary concerns of life, in the ordinary work, in the daily round, men dealt freely and directly with one another. To-day, the everyday relationships of men are largely with great impersonal concerns, with organizations, not with other individual men.

Now this is nothing short of a new social age, a new era of human relationships, a new stage-setting for the drama of life.

In this new age we find, for instance, that our laws with regard to the relations of employer and employee are in many respects wholly antiquated and impossible. They were framed for another age, which nobody now living remembers, which is, indeed, so remote from our life that it would be difficult for many of us to understand it if it were described to us. The employer is now generally a corporation or a huge company of some kind; the employee is one of hundreds or of thousands brought together, not by individual masters whom they know and with whom they have personal relations, but by agents of one sort or another. Workingmen are marshaled in great numbers for the performance of a multitude of particular tasks under a common discipline. They generally use dangerous and powerful machinery, over whose repair and renewal they have no control. New rules must be devised with regard to their obligations and their rights, their obligations to their employers and their responsibilities to one another. Rules must be devised for their protection, for their compensation when injured, for their support when disabled.

There is something very new and very big and very complex about these new relations of capital and labor. A new economic society has sprung up, and we must effect a new set of adjustments. We must not pit power against weakness. The employer is generally, in our day, as I have said, not an individual, but a powerful group; and yet the workingman when dealing with his employer is still, under our existing law, an individual.

Why is it that we have a labor question at all? It is for the simple and very sufficient reason that the laboring man and the employer are not intimate associates now as they used to be in time past. Most of our laws were formed in the age when employer and employees knew each other, knew each other's characters, were associates with each other, dealt with each other as man with man. That is no longer the case. You not only do not come into personal contact with the men who have the supreme command in those corporations, but it would be out of the question for you to do it. Our modern corporations employ thousands, and in some instances hundreds of thousands, of men. The only persons whom you see or deal with are local superintendents or local representatives of a vast organization, which is not like anything that the workingmen of the time in which our laws were framed knew anything about. A little group of workingmen, seeing their employer every day, dealing with him in a personal way, is one thing, and the modern body of labor engaged as employees of the huge enterprises that spread all over the country, dealing with men of whom they can form no personal conception, is another thing. A very different thing. You never saw a corporation, any more than you ever saw a government. Many a workingman to-day never saw the body of men who are conducting the industry in which he is employed. And they never saw him. What they know about him is written in ledgers and books and letters, in the correspondence of the office, in the reports of the superintendents. He is a long way off from them.

So what we have to discuss is, not wrongs which individuals intentionally do,—I do not believe there are a great many of those,—but the wrongs of a system. I want to record my protest against any discussion of this matter which would seem to indicate that there are bodies of our fellow-citizens who are trying to grind us down and do us injustice. There are some men of that sort. I don't know how they sleep o' nights, but there are men of that kind. Thank God, they are not numerous. The truth is, we are all caught in a great economic system which is heartless. The modern corporation is not engaged in business as an individual. When we deal with it, we deal with an impersonal element, an immaterial piece of society. A modern corporation is a means of co-operation in the conduct of an enterprise which is so big that no one man can conduct it, and which the resources of no one man are sufficient to finance. A company is formed; that company puts out a prospectus; the promoters expect to raise a certain fund as capital stock. Well, how are they going to raise it? They are going to raise it from the public in general, some of whom will buy their stock. The moment that begins, there is formed—what? A joint stock corporation. Men begin to pool their earnings, little piles, big piles. A certain number of men are elected by the stockholders to be directors, and these directors elect a president. This president is the head of the undertaking, and the directors are its managers.

Now, do the workingmen employed by that stock corporation deal with that president and those directors? Not at all. Does the public deal with that president and that board of directors? It does not. Can anybody bring them to account? It is next to impossible to do so. If you undertake it you will find it a game of hide and seek, with the objects of your search taking refuge now behind the tree of their individual personality, now behind that of their corporate irresponsibility.

And do our laws take note of this curious state of things? Do they even attempt to distinguish between a man's act as a corporation director and as an individual? They do not. Our laws still deal with us on the basis of the old system. The law is still living in the dead past which we have left behind. This is evident, for instance, with regard to the matter of employers' liability for workingmen's injuries. Suppose that a superintendent wants a workman to use a certain piece of machinery which it is not safe for him to use, and that the workman is injured by that piece of machinery. Some of our courts have held that the superintendent is a fellow-servant, or, as the law states it, a fellow-employee, and that, therefore, the man cannot recover damages for his injury. The superintendent who probably engaged the man is not his employer. Who is his employer? And whose negligence could conceivably come in there? The board of directors did not tell the employee to use that piece of machinery; and the president of the corporation did not tell him to use that piece of machinery. And so forth. Don't you see by that theory that a man never can get redress for negligence on the part of the employer? When I hear judges reason upon the analogy of the relationships that used to exist between workmen and their employers a generation ago, I wonder if they have not opened their eyes to the modern world. You know, we have a right to expect that judges will have their eyes open, even though the law which they administer hasn't awakened.

Yet that is but a single small detail illustrative of the difficulties we are in because we have not adjusted the law to the facts of the new order.

Since I entered politics, I have chiefly had

men's views confided to me privately. Some of the biggest men in the United States, in the field of commerce and manufacture, are afraid of somebody, are afraid of something. They know that there is a power somewhere so organized, so subtle, so watchful, so interlocked, so complete, so pervasive, that they had better not speak above their breath when they speak in condemnation of it.

They know that America is not a place of which it can be said, as it used to be, that a man may choose his own calling and pursue it just as far as his abilities enable him to pursue it; because to-day, if he enters certain fields, there are organizations which will use means against him that will prevent his building up a business which they do not want to have built up; organizations that will see to it that the ground is cut from under him and the markets shut against him. For if he begins to sell to certain retail dealers, to any retail dealers, the monopoly will refuse to sell to those dealers, and those dealers, afraid, will not buy the new man's wares.

And this is the country which has lifted to the admiration of the world its ideals of absolutely free opportunity, where no man is supposed to be under any limitation except the limitations of his character and of his mind; where there is supposed to be no distinction of class, no distinction of blood, no distinction of social status, but where men win or lose on their merits.

I lay it very close to my own conscience as a public man whether we can any longer stand at our doors and welcome all newcomers upon those terms. American industry is not free, as once it was free; American enterprise is not free; the man with only a little capital is finding it harder to get into the field, more and more impossible to compete with the big fellow. Why? Because the laws of this country do not prevent the strong from crushing the weak. That is the reason, and because the strong have crushed the weak, the strong dominate the industry and the economic life of this country. No man can deny that the lines of endeavor have more and more narrowed and stiffened; no man who knows anything about the development of industry in this country

can have failed to observe that the larger kinds of credit are more and more difficult to obtain, unless you obtain them upon the terms of uniting your efforts with those who already control the industries of the country; and nobody can fail to observe that any man who tries to set himself up in competition with any process of manufacture which has been taken under the control of large combinations of capital will presently find himself either squeezed out or obliged to sell and allow himself to be absorbed.

There is a great deal that needs reconstruction in the United States. I should like to take a census of the business men,—I mean the rank and file of the business men,—as to whether they think that business conditions in this country, or rather whether the organization of business in this country, is satisfactory or not. I know what they would say if they dared. If they could vote secretly they would vote overwhelmingly that the present organization of business was meant for the big fellows and was not meant for the little fellows; that it was meant for those who are at the top and was meant to exclude those who were at the bottom; that it was meant to shut out beginners, to prevent new entries in the race, to prevent the building up of competitive enterprises that would interfere with the monopolies which the great trusts have built up.

What this country needs above everything else is a body of laws which will look after the men who are on the make rather than the men who are already made. Because the men who are already made are not going to live indefinitely, and they are not always kind enough to leave sons as able and as honest as they are.

The originative part of America, the part of America that makes new enterprises, the part into which the ambitious and gifted working-man makes his way up, the class that saves, that plans, that organizes, that presently spreads its enterprises until they have a national scope and character,—that middle class is being more and more squeezed out by the processes which we have been taught to call processes of prosperity. Its members are sharing prosperity, no doubt; but what alarms me is that they are not *originating* prosperity. No country can afford to have its prosperity originated by a small controlling class. The treasury of America does not lie in the brains of the small body of men now in control of the great enterprises that have been concentrated under the direction of a very small number of persons. The treasury of America lies in those ambitions, those energies, that cannot be restricted to a special favored class. It depends upon the inventions of unknown men, upon the originations of unknown men, upon the ambitions of unknown men. Every country is renewed out of the ranks of the unknown, not out of the ranks of those already famous and powerful and in control.

There has come over the land that un-American set of conditions which enables a small number of men who control the government to get favors from the government; by those favors to exclude their fellows from equal business opportunity; by those favors to extend a network of control that will presently dominate every industry in the country, and so make men forget the ancient time when America lay in every hamlet, when America was to be seen in every fair valley, when America displayed her great forces on the broad prairies, ran her fine fires of enterprise up over the mountainsides and down into the bowels of the earth, and eager men were everywhere captains of industry, not employees; not looking to a distant city to find out what they might do, but looking about among their neighbors, finding credit according to their character, not according to their connections, finding credit in proportion to what was known to be in them and behind them, not in proportion to the securities they held that were approved where they were not known. In order to start an enterprise now, you have to be authenticated, in a perfectly impersonal way, not according to yourself, but according to what you own that somebody else approves of your owning. You cannot begin such an enterprise as those that have made America until you are so authenticated, until you have succeeded in obtaining the good-will of large allied capitalists. Is that freedom? That is dependence, not freedom.

We used to think in the old-fashioned days when life was very simple that all that government had to do was to put on a policeman's uniform, and say, "Now don't anybody hurt anybody else." We used to say that the ideal of government was for every man to be left alone and not interfered with, except when he interfered with somebody else; and that the best government was the government that did as little governing as possible. That was the idea that obtained in Jefferson's time. But we are coming now to realize that life is so complicated that we are not dealing with the old conditions, and that the law has to step in and create new conditions under which we may live, the conditions which will make it tolerable for us to live. . . .

One of the most alarming phenomena of the time,—or rather it would be alarming if the nation had not awakened to it and shown its determination to control it,—one of the most significant signs of the new social era is the degree to which government has become associated with business. I speak, for the moment, of the control over the government exercised by Big Business. Behind the whole subject, of course, is the truth that, in the new order, government and business must be associated closely. But that association is at present of a nature absolutely intolerable; the precedence is wrong, the association is upside down. Our government has been for the past few years under the control of heads of great allied corporations with special interests. It has not controlled these interests and assigned them a proper place in the whole system of business; it has submitted itself to their control. As a result, there have grown up vicious systems and schemes of governmental favoritism (the most obvious being the extravagant tariff), far-reaching in effect upon the whole fabric of life, touching to his injury every inhabitant of the land, laying unfair and impossible handicaps upon competitors, imposing taxes in every direction, stifling everywhere the free spirit of American enterprise.

Now this has come about naturally; as we go on we shall see how very naturally. It is no use denouncing anybody, or anything, except human nature. Nevertheless, it is an intolerable thing that the government of the republic should have got so far out of the hands of the people; should have been captured by interests which are special and not general. In the train of this capture follow the troops of scandals, wrongs, indecencies, with which our politics swarm.

There are cities in America of whose government we are ashamed. There are cities everywhere, in every part of the land, in which we feel that, not the interests of the public, but the interests of special privileges, of selfish men, are served; where contracts take precedence over public interest. Not only in big cities is this the case. Have you not noticed the growth of socialistic sentiment in the smaller towns? Not many months ago I stopped at a little town in Nebraska, and while my train lingered I met on the platform a very engaging young fellow dressed in overalls who introduced himself to me as the mayor of the town, and added that he was a Socialist. I said, "What does that mean? Does that mean that this town is socialistic?" "No, sir," he said; "I have not deceived myself; the vote by which I was elected was about 20 per cent socialistic and 80 per cent protest." It was protest against the treachery to the people of those who led both the other parties of that town.

All over the Union people are coming to feel that they have no control over the course of affairs. I live in one of the greatest States in the union, which was at one time in slavery. Until two years ago we had witnessed with increasing concern the growth in New Jersey of a spirit of almost cynical despair. Men said: "We vote; we are offered the platform we want; we elect the men who stand on that platform, and we get absolutely nothing." So they began to ask: "What is the use of voting? We know that the machines of both parties are subsidized by the same persons, and therefore it is useless to turn in either direction."

This is not confined to some of the state governments and those of some of the towns and cities. We know that something intervenes between the people of the United States and the control of their own affairs at Washington. It is not the people who have been ruling there of late.

Why are we in the presence, why are we at the threshold, of a revolution? Because we are profoundly disturbed by the influences which we see reigning in the determination of our public life and our public policy. There was a time when America was blithe with self-confidence. She boasted that she, and she alone, knew the processes of popular government; but now she sees her sky overcast; she sees that there are at work forces which she did not dream of in her hopeful youth.

Don't you know that some man with eloquent tongue, without conscience, who did not care for the nation, could put this whole country into a flame? Don't you know that this country from one end to the other believes that something is wrong? What an opportunity it would be for some man without conscience to spring up and say: "This is the way. Follow me!" —and lead in paths of destruction!

The old order changeth—changeth under our very eyes, not quietly and equably, but swiftly and with the noise and heat and tumult of reconstruction.

I suppose that all struggle for law has been conscious, that very little of it has been blind or merely instinctive. It is the fashion to say, as if with superior knowledge of affairs and of human weakness, that every age has been an age of transition, and that no age is more full of change than another; yet in very few ages of the world can the struggle for change have been so widespread, so deliberate, or upon so great a scale as in this in which we are taking part.

The transition we are witnessing is no equable transition of growth and normal alteration; no silent, unconscious unfolding of one age into another, its natural heir and successor. Society is looking itself over, in our day, from top to bottom; is making fresh and critical analysis of its very elements; is questioning its oldest practices as freely as its newest, scrutinizing every arrangement and motive of its life; and it stands ready to attempt nothing less than a radical reconstruction, which only frank and honest counsels and the forces of generous co-operation can hold back from becoming a revolution. We are in a temper to reconstruct economic society, as we were once in a temper to reconstruct political society, and political society may itself undergo a radical modification in the process. I doubt if any age was ever more conscious of its task or more unanimously desirous of radical and extended changes in its economic and political practice.

We stand in the presence of a revolution,—not a bloody revolution; America is not given to the spilling of blood,—but a silent revolution, whereby America will insist upon recovering in practice those ideals which she has always professed, upon securing a government devoted to the general interest and not to special interests.

We are upon the eve of a great reconstruction. It calls for creative statesmanship as no age has done since that great age in which we set up the government under which we live, that government which was the admiration of the world until it suffered wrongs to grow up under it which have made many of our own compatriots question the freedom of our institutions and preach revolution against them. I do not fear revolution. I have unshaken faith in the power of America to keep its self-possession. Revolution will come in peaceful guise, as it came when we put aside the crude gov-ernment of the Confederation and created the great Federal Union which governs individuals, not States, and which has been these hundred and thirty years our vehicle of progress. Some radical changes we must make in our law and practice. Some reconstructions we must push forward, which a new age and new circumstances impose upon us. But we can do it all in calm and sober fashion, like statesmen and patriots.

I do not speak of these things in apprehension, because all is open and above-board. This is not a day in which great forces rally in secret. The whole stupendous program must be publicly planned and canvassed. Good temper, the wisdom that comes of sober counsel, the energy of thoughtful and unselfish men, the habit of co-operation and of compromise which has been bred in us by long years of free government, in which reason rather than passion has been made to prevail by the sheer virtue of candid and universal debate, will enable us to win through to still another great age without violence.

Franklin Delano Roosevelt

Franklin Delano Roosevelt (1882–1945), thirty-second President of the United States, rose to political prominence during the great depression of the 1930's. A consummate politician who enjoyed the great game of politics, he sensed the opportunity that the depression presented. In the presidential campaigns of the 1930's and 1940's he swept all opposition aside. With his commanding presence and ingratiating voice he spoke of a New Deal for reconstructing a stricken nation, of plans for "the forgotten, the unorganized but indispensable units of economic power," of measures that "build from the bottom up and not from the top down, that put their faith once more in the forgotten man at the foot of the economic pyramid." People were instinctively drawn to him and trusted him to find the means of accommodating inherited American institutions to the demands of a twentieth-century industrial society without following the iron-clad "new orders" of the communists, the fascists, or the nazis. One searches in vain for a blueprint or program for the New Deal. It was not based upon a well-wrought plan; it was constructed out of trial and error—improvisation was its principal characteristic. The two addresses that follow suggest the underlying assumptions of the New Deal as well as the spirit that permeated it. In reading them note (1) Roosevelt's basic assumption concerning the nature of twentieth-century economic development, (2) the parallel he draws between political power and economic power, (3) his ambition to achieve a balance between competing economic groups and the reasons therefor, (4) his reinterpretation of the Declaration of Independence and what this implied, (5) the spirit of dedication manifest in his inaugural address, (6) his description of the state of the nation and his diagnosis of its ills, (7) his prescription for the restoration of economic well being, (8) specific remedies which he proposed, (9) his plea for unity and submission to leadership, (10) his profession of faith in American ideals, and (11) comparisons and contrasts with Soviet communism, Italian fascism, and German nazism (see pp. 797–824).

From: NEW CONDITIONS IMPOSE NEW REQUIREMENTS UPON GOVERNMENT AND THOSE WHO CONDUCT GOVERNMENT

Campaign Address on Progressive Government

Our task now is not discovery or exploitation of natural resources, or necessarily producing more goods. It is the soberer, less dramatic business of administering resources and plants already in hand, of seeking to reestablish foreign markets for our surplus production, of meeting the problem of underconsumption, of adjusting production to consumption, of distributing wealth and products more equitably, of adapting existing economic organizations to the service of the people. The day of enlightened administration has come.

Just as in older times the central Government was first a haven of refuge, and then a threat, so now in a closer economic system the central and ambitious financial unit is no longer a servant of national desire, but a danger. I would draw the parallel one step farther. We did not think because national Government had become a threat in the eighteenth century that therefore we should abandon the principle of national Government. Nor today should we abandon the principle of strong economic units called corporations, merely because their power is susceptible of easy abuse. In other times we dealt with the problem of an unduly ambitious central Government by modifying it gradually into a constitutional democratic Government. So today we are modifying and controlling our economic units.

As I see it, the task of Government in its relation to business is to assist the development of an economic declaration of rights, an economic constitutional order. This is the common task of statesman and business man. It is the minimum requirement of a more permanently safe order of things.

Happily, the times indicate that to create such an order not only is the proper policy of Government, but it is the only line of safety for

Franklin Delano Roosevelt, "New Conditions Impose New Requirements upon Government and Those Who Conduct Government," San Francisco, California, September 23, 1932, in *The Public Papers and Addresses of Franklin D. Roosevelt*, New York: Random House, 1938, I, 751–55. Franklin Delano Roosevelt, "Inaugural Address," March 4, 1933, New York *Times*, March 5, 1933, 1:5–6.

our economic structures as well. We know, now, that these economic units cannot exist unless prosperity is uniform, that is, unless purchasing power is well distributed throughout every group in the Nation. That is why even the most selfish of corporations for its own interest would be glad to see wages restored and unemployment ended and to bring the Western farmer back to his accustomed level of prosperity and to assure a permanent safety to both groups. That is why some enlightened industries themselves endeavor to limit the freedom of action of each man and business group within the industry in the common interest of all; why business men everywhere are asking a form of organization which will bring the scheme of things into balance, even though it may in some measure qualify the freedom of action of individual units within the business. . . .

The Declaration of Independence discusses the problem of Government in terms of a contract. Government is a relation of give and take, a contract, perforce, if we would follow the thinking out of which it grew. Under such a contract rulers were accorded power, and the people consented to that power on consideration that they be accorded certain rights. The task of statesmanship has always been the redefinition of these rights in terms of a changing and growing social order. New conditions impose new requirements upon Government and those who conduct Government. . . .

I feel that we are coming to a view through the drift of our legislation and our public thinking in the past quarter century that private economic power is, to enlarge an old phrase, a public trust as well. I hold that continued enjoyment of that power by any individual or group must depend upon the fulfillment of that trust. The men who have reached the summit of American business life know this best; happily, many of these urge the binding quality of this greater social contract.

The terms of that contract are as old as the Republic, and as new as the new economic order.

Every man has a right to life; and this means that he has also a right to make a comfortable living. He may by sloth or crime decline to exercise that right; but it may not be denied him. We have no actual famine or dearth; our industrial and agricultural mechanism can produce enough and to spare. Our Government, formal and informal, political and economic, owes to everyone an avenue to possess himself of a portion of that plenty sufficient for his needs, through his own work.

Every man has a right to his own property; which means a right to be assured, to the fullest extent attainable, in the safety of his savings. By no other means can men carry the burdens of those parts of life which, in the nature of things, afford no chance of labor; childhood, sickness, old age. In all thought of property, this right is paramount; all other property rights must yield to it. If, in accord with this principle, we must restrict the operations of the speculator, the manipulator, even the financier, I believe we must accept the restriction as needful, not to hamper individualism but to protect it.

These two requirements must be satisfied, in the main, by the individuals who claim and hold control of the great industrial and financial combinations which dominate so large a part of our industrial life. They have undertaken to be, not business men, but princes of property. I am not prepared to say that the system which produces them is wrong. I am very clear that they must fearlessly and competently assume the responsibility which goes with the power. So many enlightened business men know this that the statement would be little more than a platitude, were it not for an added implication. . . .

The final term of the high contract was for liberty and the pursuit of happiness. We have learned a great deal of both in the past century. We know that individual liberty and individual happiness mean nothing unless both are ordered in the sense that one man's meat is not another man's poison. We know that the old "rights of personal competency," the right to read, to think, to speak, to choose and live a mode of life, must be respected at all hazards. We know that liberty to do anything which deprives others of those elemental rights is outside the protection of any compact; and that Government in this regard is the maintenance of a balance, within which every individual may find safety if he wishes it; in which every individual may attain such power as his ability permits, consistent with his assuming the accompanying responsibility.

From: *FIRST INAUGURAL ADDRESS*

This is a day of national consecration, and I am certain that my fellow-Americans expect that on my induction into the Presidency I will address them with a candor and a decision which the present situation of our nation impels.

This is pre-eminently the time to speak the truth, the whole truth, frankly and boldly. Nor need we shrink from honestly facing conditions in our country today. This great nation will endure as it has endured, will revive and will prosper.

So first of all let me assert my firm belief that the only thing we have to fear is fear itself—nameless, unreasoning, unjustified terror which paralyzes needed efforts to convert retreat into advance. . . .

In such a spirit on my part and on yours we face our common difficulties. They concern, thank God, only material things. Values have shrunken to fantastic levels; taxes have risen; our ability to pay has fallen, government of all kinds is faced by serious curtailment of income; the means of exchange are frozen in the currents of trade; the withered leaves of industrial enterprise lie on every side; farmers find no markets for their produce; the savings of many years in thousands of families are gone.

More important, a host of unemployed citizens face the grim problem of existence, and an equally great number toil with little return. Only a foolish optimist can deny the dark realities of the moment.

Yet our distress comes from no failure of substance. We are stricken by no plague of locusts. Compared with the perils which our forefathers conquered because they believed and were not afraid, we have still much to be thankful for. Nature still offers her bounty and human efforts have multiplied it. Plenty is at our doorstep, but a generous use of its languishes in the very sight of the supply.

Primarily, this is because the rulers of the exchange of mankind's goods have failed through their own stubbornness and their own incompetence, have admitted their failure and abdicated. . . .

They have no vision, and when there is no vision the people perish. . . .

The measure of the restoration lies in the extent to which we apply social values more noble than mere monetary profit.

Happiness lies not in the mere possession of money; it lies in the joy of achievement, in the thrill of creative effort. . . .

Our greatest primary task is to put people to work. This is no unsolvable problem if we face it wisely and courageously.

It can be accomplished in part by direct recruiting by the government itself, treating the task as we would treat the emergency of a war, but at the same time, through this employment, accomplishing greatly needed projects to stimulate and reorganize the use of our natural resources.

Hand in hand with this, we must frankly recognize the overbalance of population in our industrial centers and, by engaging on a national scale in the redistribution, endeavor to provide a better use of the land for those best fitted for the land.

The task can be helped by definite efforts to raise the values of agricultural products and with this the power to purchase the output of our cities. . . .

The basic thought that guides these specific means of national recovery is not narrowly nationalistic. . . .

It is the insistence, as a first consideration, upon the interdependence of the various elements in, and parts of, the United States—a recognition of the old and permanently important manifestation of the American spirit of the pioneer. . . .

In the field of world policy I would dedicate this nation to the policy of the good neighbor—the neighbor who resolutely respects himself and, because he does so, respects the rights of others—the neighbor who respects his obligations and respects the sanctity of his agreements in and with a world of neighbors.

If I read the temper of our people correctly, we now realize as we have never before, our interdependence on each other; that we cannot merely take, but we must give as well; that if we are to go forward we must move as a trained and loyal army willing to sacrifice for the good of a common discipline, because, without such discipline, no progress is made, no leadership becomes effective.

We are, I know, ready and willing to submit our lives and property to such discipline because it makes possible a leadership which aims at a larger good.

This I propose to offer, pledging that the larger purposes will bind upon us all as a sacred obligation with a unity of duty hitherto evoked only in time of armed strife.

With this pledge taken, I assume unhesitatingly the leadership of this great army of our people, dedicated to a disciplined attack upon our common problems. . . .

I am prepared under my constitutional duty to recommend the measures that a stricken nation in the midst of a stricken world may require.

These measures, or such other measures as the Congress may build out of its experience and wisdom, I shall seek, within my constitutional authority, to bring to speedy adoption.

But in the event that the Congress shall fail to take one of these two courses, and in the event that the national emergency is still critical, I shall not evade the clear course of duty that will then confront me.

I shall ask the Congress for the one remaining instrument to meet the crisis—broad executive power to wage a war against the emergency as great as the power that would be given me if we were in fact invaded by a foreign foe. . . .

We face the arduous days that lie before us in the warm courage of national unity; with the clear consciousness of seeking old and precious moral values; with the clear satisfaction that comes from the stern performance of duty by old and young alike. . . .

We do not distrust the future of essential democracy. The people of the United States have not failed. In their need they have registered a mandate that they want direct, vigorous action. . . .

In this dedication of a nation we humbly ask the blessing of God. May He protect each and every one of us! May He guide me in the days to come!

Lenin

Vladimir Ilich Lenin (1870–1924) was a Russian revolutionary who devoted his life to bringing about the destruction of the Czarist regime and the establishment of Marxian socialism in Russia. He participated in the abortive revolution of 1905, and then, of necessity, lived in exile, first in Germany and England, and later in Switzerland. He devoted his time to study, writing, and propagandist activities until 1917, when the Russian effort in the First World War collapsed and internal revolution broke out. With the help of the Germans, who sent him across Central Europe in a sealed car, Lenin returned to Russia to become a participant in the civil strife and later to be the first leader of Soviet Russia. Between the March and November revolutions of 1917, Lenin was forced into hiding because of the hostility of the provisional government toward him. During this period he wrote State and Revolution, largely as a reply to the revisionist socialists of Europe who, according to him, were distorting the teachings of Marx and Engels in regard to the "withering away of the state." His interpretation of Marx has provided one of the principal ideological supports for Russian Soviet Communism. In reading the following selections from this work note (1) Lenin's method of dependence upon authority, (2) what he asserted the bourgeoisie were doing to Marxism, (3) Lenin's description of the Marxian characterization of the state, (4) his view of the essential power of the state, (5) the special privileges Lenin accorded to the police force, (6) what Marxism proposed the proletariat should do in regard to the state, (7) the author's explanation of what Marx meant by the state "withering away," (8) how, according to Lenin, this concept had been shorn of its revolutionary implications, (9) his analysis of the exact time when the state "becomes dormant," (10) what he meant by the evolutionary nature of the "withering away" process, (11) the "scientific" character of communism's evolution from capitalism, (12) Lenin's explanation of how the "dictatorship" of the proletariat fitted into the evolutionary development of communism, (13) Lenin's description of capitalist democracy, and (14) his characterization of the transitional "state."

From: STATE AND REVOLUTION

What is now happening to Marx's doctrine has, in the course of history, often happened to the doctrines of other revolutionary thinkers and leaders of oppressed classes struggling for emancipation. During the lifetime of great revolutionaries, the oppressing classes have visited relentless persecution on them and received their teaching with the most savage hostility, the most furious hatred, the most ruthless campaign of lies and slanders. After their death, attempts are made to turn them into harmless icons, canonise them, and surround their *names* with a certain halo for the "consolation" of the oppressed classes and with the object of duping them, while at the same time emasculating and vulgarising the *real essence* of their revolutionary theories and blunting their revolutionary edge. At the present time, the bourgeoisie and the opportunists within the labour movement are co-operating in this work of adulterating Marxism. They omit, obliterate, and distort the revolutionary side of its teaching, its revolutionary soul. They push to the foreground and extol what is, or seems, acceptable to the bourgeoisie. All the social-chauvinists are now "Marxists"—joking aside! And more and more do German bourgeois professors,

erstwhile specialists in the demolition of Marx, speak now of the "national-German" Marx, who, they aver, has educated the labour unions which are so splendidly organised for conducting the present predatory war!

In such circumstances, the distortion of Marxism being so widespread, it is our first task to *resuscitate* the real teachings of Marx on the state. For this purpose it will be necessary to quote at length from the works of Marx and Engels themselves. . . .

Let us begin with the most popular of Engels' works, *Der Ursprung der Familie, des Privateigentums und des Staats,* the sixth edition of which was published in Stuttgart as far back as 1894. We must translate the quotations from the German originals, as the Russian translations, although very numerous, are for the most part either incomplete or very unsatisfactory.

Summarising his historical analysis Engels says:

The state is therefore by no means a power imposed on society from the outside; just as little is it "the reality of the moral idea," "the image and reality of reason," as Hegel asserted. Rather, it is a product of society at a certain stage of development; it is the admission that this society has be-

Vladimir Ilich Lenin, *State and Revolution,* International Publishers, New York, 1932, 7–10; 12–13; 15–17; 69–75. Courtesy of International Publishers.

come entangled in an insoluble contradiction with itself, that it is cleft into irreconcilable antagonisms which it is powerless to dispel. But in order that these antagonisms, classes with conflicting economic interests, may not consume themselves and society in sterile struggle, a power apparently standing above society becomes necessary, whose purpose is to moderate the conflict and keep it within the bounds of "order"; and this power arising out of society, but placing itself above it, and increasingly separating itself from it, is the state.

Here we have, expressed in all its clearness, the basic idea of Marxism on the question of the historical rôle and meaning of the state. The state is the product and the manifestation of the *irreconcilability* of class antagonisms. The state arises when, where, and to the extent that the class antagonisms *cannot* be objectively reconciled. And, conversely, the existence of the state proves that the class antagonisms *are* irreconcilable.

It is precisely on this most important and fundamental point that distortions of Marxism arise along two main lines.

On the one hand, the bourgeois, and particularly the petty-bourgeois, ideologists, compelled under the pressure of indisputable historical facts to admit that the state only exists where there are class antagonisms and the class struggle, "correct" Marx in such a way as to make it appear that the state is an organ for *reconciling* the classes. According to Marx, the state could neither arise nor maintain itself if a reconciliation of classes were possible. But with the petty-bourgeois and philistine professors and publicists, the state—and this frequently on the strength of benevolent references to Marx!—becomes a conciliator of the classes. According to Marx, the state is an organ of class *domination,* an organ of *oppression* of one class by another; its aim is the creation of "order" which legalises and perpetuates this oppression by moderating the collisions between the classes. But in the opinion of the petty-bourgeois politicians, order means reconciliation of the classes, and not oppression of one class by another; to moderate collisions does not mean, they say, to deprive the oppressed classes of certain definite means and methods of struggle for overthrowing the oppressors, but to practice reconciliation. . . .

Engels develops the conception of that "power" which is termed the state—a power arising from society, but placing itself above it and becoming more and more separated from it. What does this power mainly consist of? It consists of special bodies of armed men who have at their disposal prisons, etc.

We are justified in speaking of special bodies of armed men, because the public power peculiar to every state is not "absolutely identical" with the armed population, with its "self-acting armed organisation.". . .

For the maintenance of a special public force standing above society, taxes and state loans are needed.

Having at their disposal the public force and the right to exact taxes, the officials now stand as organs of society *above* society. The free, voluntary respect which was accorded to the organs of the gentilic form of government does not satisfy them, even if they could have it. . . .

Special laws are enacted regarding the sanctity and the inviolability of the officials. "The shabbiest police servant . . . has more authority" than the representative of the clan, but even the head of the military power of a civilised state "may well envy the least among the chiefs of the clan the unconstrained and uncontested respect which is paid to him.". . .

Engels' words regarding the "withering away" of the state enjoy such popularity, they are so often quoted, and they show so clearly the essence of the usual adulteration by means of which Marxism is made to look like opportunism, that we must dwell on them in detail. Let us quote the whole passage from which they are taken.

The proletariat seizes state power, and then transforms the means of production into state property. But in doing this, it puts an end to itself as the proletariat, it puts an end to all class differences and class antagonisms, it puts an end also to the state as the state. Former society, moving in class antagonisms, had need of the state, that is, an organisation of the exploiting class at each period for the maintenance of its external conditions of production; therefore, in particular, for the forcible holding down of the exploited class in the conditions of oppression (slavery, bondage or serfdom, wage-labour) determined by the existing mode of production. The state was the official representative of society as a whole, its embodiment in a visible corporate body; but it was this only in so far as it was the state of that class which itself, in its epoch, represented society as a whole: in ancient times, the state of the slave-owning citizens; in the Middle Ages, of the feudal nobility; in our epoch, of the bourgeoisie. When ultimately it becomes really representative of society as a whole, it makes itself superfluous. As soon as there is no longer any class of society to be held in subjection; as soon as, along with class domination and the struggle for individual existence based on the former anarchy of production, the collisions and excesses arising from these have also been abolished, there is nothing more to be repressed, and a special repressive force, a state, is no longer necessary. The first act in which the state really comes forward as the representative of society as a whole—the seizure of the means of production in the name of society—is at the same time its last independent act as a state. The interference of a state power in social relations becomes superfluous in one sphere after another, and then becomes dormant of itself. Government over persons is replaced by the administration of things and the direction of the processes of production. The state is not "abolished," *it withers away*. It is from this standpoint that we must appraise the phrase "people's free state"—both its justification at times for agitational purposes, and its ultimate scientific inadequacy—and also the demand of the so-called Anarchists that the state should be abolished overnight.

Without fear of committing an error, it may be said that of this argument by Engels so singularly rich in ideas, only one point has become an integral part of Socialist thought among modern Socialist parties, namely, that, unlike the Anarchist doctrine of the "abolition" of the state, according to Marx the state "withers away." To emasculate Marxism in such a manner is to reduce it to opportunism, for such an "interpretation" only leaves the hazy conception of a slow, even, gradual change, free from leaps and storms, free from revolution. The current popular conception, if one may say so, of the "withering away" of the state undoubtedly means a slurring over, if not a negation, of revolution.

Yet, such an "interpretation" is the crudest distortion of Marxism, which is advantageous only to the bourgeoisie; in point of theory, it is based on a disregard for the most important

circumstances and considerations pointed out in the very passage summarising Engels' ideas, which we have just quoted in full.

In the first place, Engels at the very outset of his argument says that, in assuming state power, the proletariat by that very act "puts an end to the state as the state." One is "not accustomed" to reflect on what this really means. Generally, it is either ignored altogether, or it is considered as a piece of "Hegelian weakness" on Engels' part. As a matter of fact, however, these words express succinctly the experience of one of the greatest proletarian revolutions—the Paris Commune of 1871, of which we shall speak in greater detail in its proper place. As a matter of fact, Engels speaks here of the destruction of the bourgeois state by the proletarian revolution, while the words about its withering away refer to the remains of *proletarian* statehood *after* the Socialist revolution. The bourgeois state does not "wither away," according to Engels, but is "put an end to" by the proletariat in the course of the revolution. What withers away after the revolution is the proletarian state or semi-state.

Secondly, the state is a "special repressive force." This splendid and extremely profound definition of Engels' is given by him here with complete lucidity. It follows from this that the "special repressive force" of the bourgeoisie for the suppression of the proletariat, of the millions of workers by a handful of the rich, must be replaced by a "special repressive force" of the proletariat for the suppression of the bourgeoisie (the dictatorship of the proletariat). It is just this that constitutes the destruction of "the state as the state." It is just this that constitutes the "act" of "the seizure of the means of production in the name of society." And it is obvious that such a substitution of one (proletarian) "special repressive force" for another (bourgeois) "special repressive force" can in no way take place in the form of a "withering away."

Thirdly, as to the "withering away" or, more expressively and colourfully, as to the state "becoming dormant," Engels refers quite clearly and definitely to the period *after* "the seizure of the means of production [by the state] in the name of society," that is *after* the Socialist revolution. We all know that the political form of the "state" at that time is complete democracy. But it never enters the head of any of the opportunists who shamelessly distort Marx that when Engels speaks here of the state "withering away," or "becoming dormant," he speaks of *democracy*. At first sight this seems very strange. But it is "unintelligible" only to one who has not reflected on the fact that democracy is *also* a state and that, consequently, democracy will *also* disappear when the state disappears. The bourgeois state can only be "put an end to" by a revolution. The state in general, *i.e.*, most complete democracy, can only "wither away.". . .

It is clear that there can be no question of defining the exact moment of the *future* withering away—the more so as it must obviously be a rather lengthy process. . . .

The whole theory of Marx is an application of the theory of evolution—in its most consistent, complete, well considered and fruitful form—to modern capitalism. It was natural for Marx to raise the question of applying this theory both to the *coming* collapse of capitalism and to the *future* evolution of *future* Communism.

On the basis of what *data* can the future evolution of future Communism be considered?

On the basis of the fact that *it has its origin* in capitalism, that it develops historically from capitalism, that it is the result of the action of a social force to which capitalism *has given birth*. There is no shadow of an attempt on Marx's part to conjure up a Utopia, to make idle guesses about that which cannot be known. Marx treats the question of Communism in the same way as a naturalist would treat the question of the evolution of, say, a new biological species, if he knew that such and such was its origin, and such and such the direction in which it changed. . . .

The first fact that has been established with complete exactness by the whole theory of evolution, by science as a whole—a fact which the Utopians forgot, and which is forgotten by the present-day opportunists who are afraid of the Socialist revolution—is that, historically, there

must undoubtedly be a special stage or epoch of *transition* from capitalism to Communism.

Between capitalist and Communist society— Marx continues—lies the period of the revolutionary transformation of the former into the latter. To this also corresponds a political transition period, in which the state can be no other than *the revolutionary dictatorship of the proletariat.*

This conclusion Marx bases on an analysis of the rôle played by the proletariat in modern capitalist society, on the data concerning the evolution of this society, and on the irreconcilability of the opposing interests of the proletariat and the bourgeoisie

Earlier the question was put thus: to attain its emancipation, the proletariat must overthrow the bourgeoisie, conquer political power and establish its own revolutionary dictatorship.

Now the question is put somewhat differently: the transition from capitalist society, developing towards Communism, towards a Communist society, is impossible without a "political transition period," and the state in this period can only be the revolutionary dictatorship of the proletariat.

What, then, is the relation of this dictatorship to democracy?

We have seen that the *Communist Manifesto* simply places side by side the two ideas; the "transformation of the proletariat into the ruling class" and the "establishment of democracy." On the basis of all that has been said above, one can define more exactly how democracy changes in the transition from capitalism to Communism.

In capitalist society, under the conditions most favourable to its development, we have more or less complete democracy in the democratic republic. But this democracy is always bound by the narrow framework of capitalist exploitation, and consequently always remains, in reality, a democracy for the minority, only for the possessing classes, only for the rich. Freedom in capitalist society always remains just about the same as it was in the ancient Greek republics: freedom for the slave-owners. The modern wage-slaves, owing to the conditions of capitalist exploitation, are so much crushed by want and poverty that "democracy is nothing to them," "politics is nothing to them"; that, in the ordinary peaceful course of events, the majority of the population is debarred from participating in social and political life.

The correctness of this statement is perhaps most clearly proved by Germany, just because in this state constitutional legality lasted and remained stable for a remarkably long time—for nearly half a century (1871–1914)—and because Social-Democracy in Germany during that time was able to achieve far more than in other countries in "utilising legality," and was able to organise into a political party a larger proportion of the working class than anywhere else in the world.

What, then, is this largest proportion of politically conscious and active wage-slaves that has so far been observed in capitalist society? One million members of the Social-Democratic Party—out of fifteen million wage-workers! Three million organised in trade unions—out of fifteen million!

Democracy for an insignificant minority, democracy for the rich—that is the democracy of capitalist society. If we look more closely into the mechanism of capitalist democracy, everywhere, both in the "petty"—so-called petty—details of the suffrage (residential qualification, exclusion of women, etc.), and in the technique of the representative institutions, in the actual obstacles to the right of assembly (public buildings are not for "beggars"!), in the purely capitalist organisation of the daily press, etc., etc.—on all sides we see restriction after restriction upon democracy. These restrictions, exceptions, exclusions, obstacles for the poor, seem slight, especially in the eyes of one who has himself never known want and has never been in close contact with the oppressed classes in their mass life (and nine-tenths, if not ninety-nine hundredths, of the bourgeois publicists and politicians are of this class), but in their sum total these restrictions exclude and squeeze out the poor from politics and from an active share in democracy.

Marx splendidly grasped this *essence* of capitalist democracy, when, in analysing the experience of the Commune, he said that the oppressed were allowed, once every few years, to decide which particular representatives of the oppressing class should be in parliament to represent and repress them!

But from this capitalist democracy—inevitably narrow, subtly rejecting the poor, and therefore hypocritical and false to the core—progress does not march onward, simply, smoothly and directly, to "greater and greater democracy," as the liberal professors and petty-bourgeois opportunists would have us believe. No, progress marches onward, *i.e.*, towards Communism, through the dictatorship of the proletariat; it cannot do otherwise, for there is no one else and no other way to *break the resistance* of the capitalist exploiters.

But the dictatorship of the proletariat—*i.e.*, the organisation of the vanguard of the oppressed as the ruling class for the purpose of crushing the oppressors—cannot produce merely an expansion of democracy. *Together* with an immense expansion of democracy which *for the first time* becomes democracy for the poor, democracy for the people, and not democracy for the rich folk, the dictatorship of the proletariat produces a series of restrictions of liberty in the case of the oppressors, the exploiters, the capitalists. We must crush them in order to free humanity from wage-slavery; their resistance must be broken by force; it is clear that where there is suppression there is also violence, there is no liberty, no democracy.

Engels expressed this splendidly in his letter to Bebel when he said, as the reader will remember, that "as long as the proletariat still *needs* the state, it needs it not in the interests of freedom, but for the purpose of crushing its antagonists; and as soon as it becomes possible to speak of freedom, then the state, as such, ceases to exist."

Democracy for the vast majority of the people, and suppression by force, *i.e.*, exclusion from democracy, of the exploiters and oppressors of the people—this is the modification of democracy during the *transition* from capitalism to Communism.

Only in Communist society, when the resistance of the capitalists has been completely broken, when the capitalists have disappeared, when there are no classes (*i.e.*, there is no difference between the members of society in their relation to the social means of production), *only then* "the state ceases to exist," and *"it becomes possible to speak of freedom."* Only then a really full democracy, a democracy without any exceptions, will be possible and will be realised. And only then will democracy itself begin to *wither away* due to the simple fact that, freed from capitalist slavery, from the untold horrors, savagery, absurdities and infamies of capitalist exploitation, people will gradually *become accustomed* to the observance of the elementary rules of social life that have been known for centuries and repeated for thousands of years in all school books; they will become accustomed to observing them without force, without compulsion, without subordination, without the *special apparatus* for compulsion which is called the state.

The expression "the state *withers away,*" is very well chosen, for it indicates both the gradual and the elemental nature of the process. Only habit can, and undoubtedly will, have such an effect; for we see around us millions of times how readily people get accustomed to observe the necessary rules of life in common, if there is no exploitation, if there is nothing that causes indignation, that calls forth protest and revolt and has to be *suppressed.*

Thus, in capitalist society, we have a democracy that is curtailed, poor, false; a democracy only for the rich, for the minority. The dictatorship of the proletariat, the period of transition to Communism, will, for the first time, produce democracy for the people, for the majority, side by side with the necessary suppression of the minority—the exploiters. Communism alone is capable of giving a really complete democracy, and the more complete it is the more quickly will it become unnecessary and wither away of itself.

In other words: under capitalism we have a state in the proper sense of the word, that is, special machinery for the suppression of one class by another, and of the majority by the minority at that. Naturally, for the successful discharge of such a task as the systematic suppression by the exploiting minority of the exploited majority, the greatest ferocity and savagery of suppression are required, seas of blood are required, through which mankind is marching in slavery, serfdom, and wage-labour.

Again, during the *transition* from capitalism to Communism, suppression is *still* necessary; but it is the suppression of the minority of exploiters by the majority of exploited. A special apparatus, special machinery for suppression, the "state," is *still* necessary, but this is now a transitional state, no longer a state in the usual sense, for the suppression of the minority of exploiters, by the majority of the wage slaves *of yesterday,* is a matter comparatively so easy, simple and natural that it will cost far less bloodshed than the suppression of the risings of slaves, serfs or wage labourers, and will cost mankind far less. This is compatible with the diffusion of democracy among such an overwhelming majority of the population, that the need for *special machinery* of suppression will begin to disappear. The exploiters are, naturally, unable to suppress the people without a most complex machinery for performing this task; but *the people* can suppress the exploiters even with very simple "machinery," almost without any "machinery," without any special apparatus, by the simple *organisation of the armed masses* (such as the Soviets of Workers' and Soldiers' Deputies, we may remark, anticipating a little).

Finally, only Communism renders the state absolutely unnecessary, for there is *no one* to be suppressed—"no one" in the sense of a *class,* in the sense of a systematic struggle with a definite section of the population. We are not Utopians, and we do not in the least deny the possibility and inevitability of excesses on the part of *individual persons,* nor the need to suppress *such* excesses. But, in the first place, no special machinery, no special apparatus of repression is needed for this; this will be done by the armed people itself, as simply and as readily as any crowd of civilised people, even in modern society, parts a pair of combatants or does not allow a woman to be outraged. And, secondly, we know that the fundamental social cause of excesses which consist in violating the rules of social life is the exploitation of the masses, their want and their poverty. With the removal of this chief cause, excesses will inevitably begin to *"wither away."* We do not know how quickly and in what succession, but we know that they will wither away. With their withering away, the state will also *wither away.* . . .

Government of the Soviet Union

Distinct limitations were placed upon the political liberties of those considered unfriendly to communism in the constitutions of 1918 and 1924. These constitutions established the "dictatorship of the proletariat"; industrial workers enjoyed marked advantages since they had been the most oppressed by the old order and displayed the most enthusiasm for the new. In 1936, as a result of the success of social planning, those in control of Russian affairs decided that sufficient progress had been made toward socialism and the classless society to warrant the adoption of a more liberal constitution. It was designed partially to ease internal discontent and partially to serve as a propaganda instrument abroad. It was made definitely flexible in character in order to serve the immediate purposes of the communist authorities. After 1945 the constitution of 1936 served as the model for the Russian satellite governments that emerged out of the chaos of war. In reading the following selections from the Soviet Constitution of December 6, 1936, note (1) the social and economic foundations of the USSR, (2) the extent to which private economy and ownership was permitted, (3) the nature of the political organization of the USSR, (4) the "rights" included in the civil liberties of Russians, (5) the facilities provided to ensure these rights, (6) the provisions regarding the Communist Party, (7) evidences of nationalism, (8) the provisions regarding voting and elections, and (9) the responsibilities of the elected deputy.

From: THE SOVIET CONSTITUTION OF 1936

SOCIAL ORGANIZATION

Article 1. The Union of Soviet Socialist Republics (USSR) is a socialist state of workers and peasants.

Article 2. The political foundation of the USSR is formed by the Soviets of toilers' deputies which have grown and become strong as a result of the overthrow of the power of the landlords and capitalists and the conquests of the dictatorship of the proletariat.

Article 3. All power in the USSR belongs to the toilers of the town and village in the form of Soviets of toilers' deputies.

Article 4. The economic foundation of the USSR consists in the socialist system of economy and socialist ownership of the implements and means of production, firmly established as a result of the liquidation of the capitalist system of economy, the abolition of private ownership of the implements and means of production and the abolition of exploitation of man by man.

Article 5. Socialist ownership in the USSR has either the form of state ownership (public property) or the form of co-operative and collective-farm ownership (property of individual collective farms, property of co-operative associations).

Article 6. The land, its deposits, waters, for-

Sir Bernard Pares, ed., "Text of the New Constitution of the U.S.S.R.," in *International Conciliation*, February, 1937, no. 327, Articles 1–13; 118–142. Courtesy of the Carnegie Endowment for International Peace.

ests, mills, factories, mines, railway, water and air transport, banks, means of communication, large agricultural enterprises organized by the state (state farms, machine-tractor stations, and so on), as well as communal enterprises and the essential part of housing in the cities and industrial centers, are state property, that is, public property.

Article 7. Public enterprises in collective farms and co-operative organizations, with their livestock and implements, products produced by the collective farms and co-operative organizations as well as their public buildings, constitute the public, socialist property of the collective farms and co-operative organizations.

Each collective farm household, in addition to the basic income from the socialized collective-farm economy, has for its own use a plot of land attached to the household and, as individual property, subsidiary establishments on the land attached to the household, a house, productive livestock and poultry, and minor agricultural implements—in accordance with the statutes of the agricultural *artel*.

Article 8. The land occupied by collective farms is secured to them for use without payment and time limit, that is, in perpetuity.

Article 9. Alongside the socialist system of economy, which is the dominant form of economy in the USSR, the law allows small private economy of individual peasants and handicraftsmen based on individual labor and excluding the exploitation of the labor of others.

Article 10. The right of personal ownership by citizens of their income from work and savings, home and auxiliary household economy, of objects of domestic and household economy, of objects of personal use and comfort, as well as the right of inheritance of the personal property of citizens—is protected by law.

Article 11. The economic life of the USSR is determined and directed by the national economic state plan for the purposes of increasing public wealth, of a steady rise in the material and cultural level of the toilers, of strengthening the independence of the USSR and its defense capacity.

Article 12. Work in the USSR is the obligation and matter of honor of each citizen capable of working, according to the principle: "He who does not work shall not eat." In the USSR

the principle of socialism is being realized: "From each according to his ability, to each according to his work."

STATE ORGANIZATION

Article 13. The USSR is a federal state, formed on the basis of the voluntary association of the Soviet Socialist Republics with equal rights:

Russian Soviet Federated Socialist Republic
Ukrainian Soviet Socialist Republic
White-Russian Soviet Socialist Republic
Azerbaizhan Soviet Socialist Republic
Georgian Soviet Socialist Republic
Armenian Soviet Socialist Republic
Turkmenian Soviet Socialist Republic
Uzbek Soviet Socialist Republic
Tadzhik Soviet Socialist Republic
Kazakh Soviet Socialist Republic
Kirghiz Soviet Socialist Republic

BASIC RIGHTS AND OBLIGATIONS OF CITIZENS

Article 118. Citizens of the USSR have the right to work, that is the right to receive guaranteed work with payment for their work in accordance with its quantity and quality.

The right to work is ensured by the socialist organization of national economy, the steady growth of the productive forces of Soviet society, the absence of economic crises, and the abolition of unemployment.

Article 119. Citizens of the USSR have the right to rest.

The right to rest is ensured by the reduction of the working day to seven hours for the overwhelming majority of the workers, establishment of annual vacations with pay for workers and employees, and provision for a wide network of sanatoria, rest-homes and clubs for the accommodation of the toilers.

Article 120. Citizens of the USSR have the right to material security in old age as well as in the event of sickness and loss of capacity to work.

This right is ensured by the wide development of social insurance of workers and employees at the expense of the state, free medical aid, and the provision of a wide network of health resorts for the use of the toilers.

Article 121. Citizens of the USSR have the right to education.

This right is ensured by universal compulsory elementary education, free of charge, including higher education, by the system of state stipends for the overwhelming majority of students in higher schools, instruction in schools in the native language, and organization of free industrial, technical and agronomic education for the toilers at the factories, state farms, machine-tractor stations, and collective farms.

Article 122. Women in the USSR are accorded equal rights with men in all fields of economic, state, cultural, social, and political life.

The possibility of realizing these rights of women is ensured by affording women equally with men the right to work, payment for work, rest, social insurance and education, state protection of the interests of mother and child, granting pregnancy leave with pay, and the provision for a wide network of maternity homes, nurseries and kindergartens.

Article 123. The equality of the rights of citizens of the USSR, irrespective of their nationality or race, in all fields of economic, state, cultural, social and political life, is an irrevocable law.

Any direct or indirect restriction of these rights, or conversely, the establishment of direct or indirect privileges for citizens on account of the race or nationality to which they belong, as well as any propagation of racial or national exceptionalism or hatred and contempt, is punishable by law.

Article 124. To ensure to citizens freedom of conscience the church in the USSR is separated from the state and the school from the church. Freedom to perform religious rites and freedom of anti-religious propaganda is recognized for all citizens.

Article 125. In accordance with the interests of the toilers and for the purpose of strengthening the socialist system, the citizens of the USSR are guaranteed:

(a) Freedom of speech;
(b) Freedom of the press;
(c) Freedom of assembly and meetings;
(d) Freedom of street processions and demonstrations.

These rights of the citizens are ensured by placing at the disposal of the toilers and their organizations printing presses, supplies of paper, public buildings, streets, means of communication and other material conditions necessary for their realization.

Article 126. In accordance with the interests of the toilers and for the purpose of developing the organizational self-expression and political activity of the masses of the people, citizens of the USSR are ensured the right of combining in public organizations: trade unions, co-operative associations, youth organizations, sport and defense organizations, cultural, technical and scientific societies, and for the most active and conscientious citizens from the ranks of the working class and other strata of the toilers, of uniting in the All-Union Communist Party (of Bolsheviks), which is the vanguard of the toilers in their struggle for strengthening and developing the socialist system and which represents the leading nucleus of all organizations of the toilers, both public and state.

Article 127. The citizens of the USSR are ensured the inviolability of the person. No one may be subjected to arrest except upon the decision of a court or with the sanction of the prosecutor.

Article 128. The inviolability of the homes of citizens and the secrecy of correspondence are protected by law.

Article 129. The USSR grants the right of asylum to foreign citizens persecuted for defending the interests of the toilers or for their scientific activity or for their struggle for national liberation.

Article 130. Every citizen of the USSR is obliged to observe the constitution of the Union of Soviet Socialist Republics, to carry out the laws, observe labor discipline, honestly fulfill his social duties, and respect the rules of the socialist community.

Article 131. Every citizen of the USSR is obliged to safeguard and consolidate public, socialist property as the sacred and inviolable foundation of the Soviet system, as the source of wealth and might of the fatherland, as the source of the prosperous cultural life of all the toilers. Persons attempting to violate public socialist property are enemies of the people.

Article 132. Universal military service is the law.

Military service in the Workers' and Peasants' Red Army represents the honorable duty of the citizens of the USSR.

Article 133. The defense of the fatherland is the sacred duty of every citizen of the USSR. Treason to the fatherland: violation of oath, desertion to the enemy, impairing the military might of the state, espionage—is punishable with the full severity of the law as the most heinous crime.

ELECTORAL SYSTEM

Article 134. Deputies to all Soviets of toilers' deputies, the Supreme Council of the USSR, Supreme Councils of the Union republics, territorial and provincial Soviets of toilers' deputies, Supreme Councils of autonomous republics, Soviets of toilers' deputies of autonomous provinces, regional, district, city and village Soviets of toilers' deputies (including stanitsas, villages, khutors, kishlaks, auls), are elected by the electors on the basis of universal, equal and direct suffrage by secret ballot.

Article 135. Elections of the deputies are universal: all citizens of the USSR who have reached the age of 18, irrespective of race or nationality, religion, educational qualifications, residential qualifications, social origin, property status and past activity, have the right to participate in elections of deputies and to be elected, with the exception of the mentally deficient and persons deprived of electoral rights by the courts.

Article 136. Elections of deputies are equal: every citizen has one vote; all citizens participate in the elections on equal terms.

Article 137. Women have the right to elect and be elected on equal terms with men.

Article 138. Citizens serving in the ranks of the Red Army have the right to elect and be elected on equal terms with all other citizens.

Article 139. Elections of deputies are direct: elections to all Soviets of toilers' deputies from the village and city Soviets of toilers' deputies up to the Supreme Council of the USSR are affected by the citizens voting directly.

Article 140. Voting at elections of deputies is secret.

Article 141. Candidates are put forward for election according to electoral districts.

The right to put forward candidates is granted to social organizations and societies of the toilers: Communist Party organizations, trade unions, co-operatives, youth organizations and cultural societies.

Article 142. Every deputy is obliged to render account to the electors of his work and the work of the Soviet of toilers' deputies, and may at any time be recalled in the manner established by law on the decision of a majority of the electors.

Benito Mussolini

B enito Mussolini (1883–1945) was an Italian editor and political leader who spent most of his early life working for radical political movements. While still a young man he became interested in socialism, and it was because of its principles that he left his native land in 1902 in order to avoid military service. He spent some years in Switzerland, studying and participating in various working-class activities, but in 1904 he returned to Italy and for several years served on the editorial staff of various left-wing periodicals. In 1912 he established his own newspaper, Il Popolo d'Italia, which he used, strangely enough, to agitate for Italy's entrance into the First World War on the allied side. When she did, he served for two years in the army before returning to his editorial duties. In 1919 he formed a group of war veterans to oppose the Versailles treaty, which Mussolini characterized as a fraud perpetrated against the Italian people. This organization developed into the Fascist

Party, which in 1922 took advantage of the postwar economic and political unrest to seize control of the government in Rome. Thus began the fascist regime in Italy, and
with it the gradual development of fascist doctrine. In
1932, Mussolini contributed to the Enciclopedia Italiana
an article in which he described the philosophic basis of
fascism. In reading this article note (1) Mussolini's description of his doctrine in 1919, (2) under what circumstances
fascist doctrine emerged, (3) its attitude toward peace and
war, (4) the Machiavellian attitude fascism assumed toward
neighboring nations, (5) Mussolini's views on Marxian socialism, (6) his refutation of democracy, (7) the historical
analysis he made of liberalism, (8) the eclectic and pragmatic aspects of fascism, (9) the foundation of fascism in
the state, (10) the organic character of the fascist state,
(11) the relation of the individual to the state, (12) fascist
position on religion, and (13) the importance of imperialism to the strength of the fascist state.

From: THE POLITICAL AND SOCIAL DOCTRINE OF FASCISM

When, in the now distant March of 1919, I
summoned a meeting at Milan through the
columns of the *Popolo d'Italia* of the surviving
members of the Interventionist Party who had
themselves been in action, and who had followed me since the creation of the Fascist Revolutionary Party (which took place in the January of 1915), I had no specific doctrinal attitude in my mind. I had a living experience of
one doctrine only—that of Socialism, from
1903–4 to the winter of 1914—that is to say,
about a decade: and from Socialism itself, even
though I had taken part in the movement first
as a member of the rank and file and then later
as a leader, yet I had no experience of its doctrine in practice. My own doctrine, even in this
period, had always been a doctrine of action.
A unanimous, universally accepted theory of
Socialism did not exist after 1905, when the
revisionist movement began in Germany under
the leadership of Bernstein, while under pressure of the tendencies of the time, a Left
Revolutionary movement also appeared, which
though never getting further than talk in Italy,
in Russian Socialistic circles laid the foundations of Bolshevism. Reformation, Revolution,

Centralization—already the echoes of these
terms are spent—while in the great stream of
Fascism are to be found ideas which began
with Sorel, Peguy, with Lagerdelle in the
"Mouvement Socialiste," and with the Italian
trades-union movement which throughout the
period 1904–14 was sounding a new note in
Italian Socialist circles (already weakened by
the betrayal of Giolitti) through Olivetti's *Pa-
gine Libre*, Orano's *La Lupa*, and Enrico Le-
one's *Divenire Sociale*.

After the War, in 1919, Socialism was already dead as a doctrine: it existed only as a
hatred. There remained to it only one possibility of action, especially in Italy, reprisals
against those who had desired the War and
who must now be made to "expiate" its results.
The *Popolo d'Italia* was then given the sub-
title of "The newspaper of ex-servicemen and
producers," and the word producers was already the expression of a mental attitude. Fascism was not the nursling of a doctrine worked
out beforehand with detailed elaboration; it
was born of the need for action and it was itself
from the beginning practical rather than theoretical; it was not merely another political

Benito Mussolini, "The Political and Social Doctrine of Fascism," in *International Conciliation*, January, 1935, no.
306, 5–17. Courtesy of the Hogarth Press, Ltd. and the Division of Intercourse and Education of the Carnegie Endowment for International Peace.

party but, even in the first two years, in opposition to all political parties as such, and itself a living movement. The name which I then gave to the organization fixed its character. And yet, if one were to re-read, in the now dusty columns of that date, the report of the meeting in which the *Fasci Italiana di combattimento* were constituted, one would there find no ordered expression of doctrine, but a series of aphorisms, anticipations, and aspirations which, when refined by time from the original ore, were destined after some years to develop into an ordered series of doctrinal concepts, forming the Fascists political doctrine—different from all others either of the past or the present day.

"If the bourgeoisie," I said then, "think that they will find lightning-conductors in us, they are the more deceived; we must start work at once. . . . We want to accustom the working-class to real and effectual leadership, and also to convince them that it is no easy thing to direct an industry or a commercial enterprise successfully. . . . We shall combat every retrograde idea, technical or spiritual. . . . When the succession to the seat of government is open, we must not be unwilling to fight for it. We must make haste; when the present régime breaks down, we must be ready at once to take its place. It is we who have the right to the succession, because it was we who forced the country into the War, and led her to victory. The present method of political representation cannot suffice, we must have a representation direct from the individuals concerned. It may be objected against this program that it is a return to the conception of the corporation, but that is no matter. . . . Therefore, I desire that this assembly shall accept the revindication of national trades-unionism from the economic point of view. . . ."

Now is it not a singular thing that even on this first day in the Piazza San Sepolcro that word "corporation" arose, which later, in the course of the Revolution, came to express one of the creations of social legislation at the very foundation of the régime?

The years which preceded the march to Rome were years of great difficulty, during which the necessity for action did not permit of research or any complete elaboration of doctrine. The battle had to be fought in the towns and villages. There was much discussion, but—what was more important and more sacred—men died. They knew how to die. Doctrine, beautifully defined and carefully elucidated, with headlines and paragraphs, might be lacking; but there was to take its place something more decisive—Faith. Even so, anyone who can recall the events of the time through the aid of books, articles, votes of congresses, and speeches of great and minor importance—anyone who knows how to research and weigh evidence—will find that the fundamentals of doctrine were cast during the years of conflict. It was precisely in those years that Fascist thought armed itself, was refined, and began the great task of organization. The problem of the relation between the individual citizen and the State; the allied problems of authority and liberty; political and social problems as well as those specifically national—a solution was being sought for all these while at the same time the struggle against Liberalism, Democracy, Socialism, and the Masonic bodies was being carried on, contemporaneously with the "punitive expedition." But, since there was inevitably some lack of system, the adversaries of Fascism have disingenuously denied that it had any capacity to produce a doctrine of its own, though that doctrine was growing and taking shape under their very eyes, even though tumultuously; first, as happens to all ideas in their beginnings, in the aspect of a violent and dogmatic negation, and then in the aspect of positive construction which has found its realization in the laws and institutions of the régime as enacted successively in the years 1926, 1927, and 1928.

Fascism is now a completely individual thing, not only as a régime but as a doctrine. And this means that today Fascism, exercising its critical sense upon itself and upon others, has formed its own distinct and peculiar point of view, to which it can refer and upon which, therefore, it can act in the face of all problems, practical or intellectual, which confront the world.

And above all, Fascism, the more it considers and observes the future and the development of humanity quite apart from political considerations of the moment, believes neither in the possibility nor the utility of perpetual peace. It thus repudiates the doctrine of Pacifism—born of a renunciation of the struggle and an act of cowardice in the face of sacrifice. War alone brings up to its highest tension all human energy and puts the stamp of nobility upon the peoples who have the courage to meet it. All other trials are substitutes, which never really put men into the position where they have to make the great decision—the alternative of life or death. Thus a doctrine which is founded upon this harmful postulate of peace is hostile to Fascism. And thus hostile to the spirit of Fascism, though accepted for what use they can be in dealing with particular political situations, are all the international leagues and societies which, as history will show, can be scattered to the winds when once strong national feeling is aroused by any motive—sentimental, ideal, or practical. This antipacifist spirit is carried by Fascism even into the life of the individual; the proud motto of the *Squadrista,* "Me ne frego," written on the bandage of the wound, is an act of philosophy not only stoic, the summary of a doctrine not only political—it is the education to combat, the acceptation of the risks which combat implies, and a new way of life for Italy. Thus the Fascist accepts life and loves it, knowing nothing of and despising suicide: he rather conceives of life as duty and struggle and conquest, life which should be high and full, lived for oneself, but above all for others—those who are at hand and those who are far distant, contemporaries, and those who will come after.

This "demographic" policy of the régime is the result of the above premise. Thus the Fascist loves in actual fact his neighbor, but this "neighbor" is not merely a vague and undefined concept, this love for one's neighbor puts no obstacle in the way of necessary educational severity, and still less to differentiation of status and to physical distance. Fascism repudiates any universal embrace, and in order to live worthily in the community of civilised peoples watches its contemporaries with vigilant eyes, takes good note of their state of mind and, in the changing trend of their interests, does not allow itself to be deceived by temporary and fallacious appearances.

Such a conception of life makes Fascism the complete opposite of that doctrine, the base of so-called scientific and Marxian Socialism, the materialist conception of history; according to which the history of human civilization can be explained simply through the conflict of interests among the various social groups and by the change and development in the means and instruments of production. That the changes in the economic field—new discoveries of raw materials, new methods of working them, and the inventions of science—have their importance no one can deny; but that these factors are sufficient to explain the history of humanity excluding all others is an absurd delusion. Fascism, now and always, believes in holiness and in heroism; that is to say, in actions influenced by no economic motive, direct or indirect. And if the economic conception of history be denied, according to which theory men are no more than puppets, carried to and fro by the waves of chance, while the real directing forces are quite out of their control, it follows that the existence of an unchangeable and unchanging class-war is also denied—the natural progeny of the economic conception of history. And above all Fascism denies that class-war can be the preponderant force in the transformation of society. These two fundamental concepts of Socialism being thus refuted, nothing is left of it but the sentimental aspiration—as old as humanity itself—towards a social convention in which the sorrows and sufferings of the humblest shall be alleviated. But here again Fascism repudiates the conception of "economic" happiness, to be realized by Socialism and, as it were, at a given moment in economic evolution to assure to everyone the maximum of well-being. Fascism denies the materialist conception of happiness as a possibility, and abandons it to its inventors, the economists of the first half of the nineteenth century: that is to say, Fascism denies the validity of the equation, well-being–happiness, which would reduce men to the level of animals, caring for one thing only—to be fat and well-fed—and would thus degrade humanity to a purely physical existence.

After Socialism, Fascism combats the whole complex system of democratic ideology, and repudiates it, whether in its theoretical premises or in its practical application. Fascism denies that the majority, by the simple fact that it is a majority, can direct human society; it denies that numbers alone can govern by means of a periodical consultation, and it affirms the immutable, beneficial, and fruitful inequality of mankind, which can never be permanently leveled through the mere operation of a mechanical process such as universal suffrage. The democratic régime may be defined as from time to time giving the people the illusion of sovereignty, while the real effective sovereignty lies in the hands of other concealed and irresponsible forces. Democracy is a régime nominally without a king, but it is ruled by many kings—more absolute, tyrannical, and ruinous than one sole king, even though a tyrant. This explains why Fascism, having first in 1922 (for reasons of expediency) assumed an attitude tending towards republicanism, renounced this point of view before the march to Rome; being convinced that the question of political form is not today of prime importance, and after having studied the examples of monarchies and republics past and present reached the conclusion that monarchy or republicanism are not to be judged, as it were, by an absolute standard; but that they represent forms in which the evolution—political, historical, traditional, or psychological—of a particular country has expressed itself. . . .

Fascism has taken up an attitude of complete opposition to the doctrines of Liberalism, both in the political field and the field of economics. There should be no undue exaggeration (simply with the object of immediate success in controversy) of the importance of Liberalism in the last century, nor should what was but one among many theories which appeared in that period be put forward as a religion for humanity for all time, present and to come. Liberalism only flourished for half a century. It was born in 1830 in reaction against the Holy Alliance, which had been formed with the object of diverting the destinies of Europe back to the period before 1789, and the highest point of its success was the year 1848, when even Pius IX was a Liberal. Immediately after that date it began to decay, for if the year 1848 was a year of light and hope, the following year, 1849, was a year of darkness and tragedy. The Republic of Rome

was dealt a mortal blow by a sister republic—that of France—and in the same year Marx launched the gospel of the Socialist religion, the famous Communist Manifesto. In 1851 Napoleon III carried out his far from Liberal *coup d'état* and reigned in France until 1870, when he was deposed by a popular movement as the consequence of a military defeat which must be counted as one of the most decisive in history. The victor was Bismarck, who knew nothing of the religion of liberty, or the prophets by which that faith was revealed. And it is symptomatic that such a highly civilized people as the Germans were completely ignorant of the religion of liberty during the whole of the nineteenth century. It was nothing but a parenthesis, represented by that body which has been called "The ridiculous Parliament of Frankfort," which lasted only for a short period. Germany attained her national unity quite outside the doctrines of Liberalism—a doctrine which seems entirely foreign to the German mind, a mind essentially monarchic—while Liberalism is the logical and, indeed, historical forerunner of anarchy. The stages in the achievement of German unity are the three wars of '64, '66, and '70, which were guided by such "Liberals" as Von Moltke and Bismarck. As for Italian unity, its debt to Liberalism is completely inferior in contrast to that which it owes to the work of Mazzini and Garibaldi, who were not Liberals. Had it not been for the intervention of the anti-Liberal Napoleon, we should not have gained Lombardy; and without the help of the again anti-Liberal Bismarck at Sadowa and Sedan it is very probable that we should never have gained the province of Venice in '66, or been able to enter Rome in '70. From 1870 to 1914 a period began during which even the very high priests of the religion themselves had to recognize the gathering twilight of their faith —defeated as it was by the decadence of literature and atavism in practice—that is to say, Nationalism, Futurism, Fascism. The era of Liberalism, after having accumulated an infinity of Gordian knots, tried to untie them in the slaughter of the World War—and never has any religion demanded of its votaries such a monstrous sacrifice. Perhaps the Liberal Gods were athirst for blood? But now, today, the

Liberal faith must shut the doors of its deserted temples, deserted because the peoples of the world realize that its worship—agnostic in the field of economics and indifferent in the field of politics and morals—will lead, as it has already led, to certain ruin. In addition to this, let it be pointed out that all the political hopes of the present day are anti-Liberal, and it is therefore supremely ridiculous to try to classify this sole creed as outside the judgment of history, as though history were a hunting ground reserved for the professors of Liberalism alone—as though Liberalism were the final unalterable verdict of civilization.

But the Fascist negation of Socialism, Democracy, and Liberalism must not be taken to mean that Fascism desires to lead the world back to the state of affairs before 1789, the date which seems to be indicated as the opening years of the succeeding semi-Liberal century: we do not desire to turn back; Fascism has not chosen De Maistre for its high-priest. Absolute monarchy has been and can never return, any more than blind acceptance of ecclesiastical authority.

So, too, the privileges of the feudal system "have been," and the division of society into castes impenetrable from outside, and with no intercommunication among themselves: the Fascist conception of authority has nothing to do with such a polity. A party which entirely governs a nation is a fact entirely new to history, there are no possible references or parallels. Fascism uses in its construction whatever elements in the Liberal, Social, or Democratic doctrines still have a living value; it maintains what may be called the certainties which we owe to history, but it rejects all the rest—that is to say, the conception that there can be any doctrine of unquestioned efficacy for all times and all peoples. Given that the nineteenth century was the century of Socialism, of Liberalism, and of Democracy, it does not necessarily follow that the twentieth century must also be a century of Socialism, Liberalism, and Democracy: political doctrines pass, but humanity remains; and it may rather be expected that this will be a century of authority, a century of the Left, a century of Fascism. For if the nineteenth century was a century of individualism (Liberalism always signifying individualism)

it may be expected that this will be the century of collectivism, and hence the century of the State. It is a perfectly logical deduction that a new doctrine can utilize all the still vital elements of previous doctrines.

No doctrine has ever been born completely new, completely defined and owing nothing to the past; no doctrine can boast a character of complete originality; it must always derive, if only historically, from the doctrines which have preceded it and develop into further doctrines which will follow. Thus the scientific Socialism of Marx is the heir of the Utopian Socialism of Fourier, of the Owens and of Saint-Simon; thus again the Liberalism of the eighteenth century is linked with all the advanced thought of the seventeenth century, and thus the doctrines of Democracy are the heirs of the Encyclopedists. Every doctrine tends to direct human activity towards a determined objective; but the action of men also reacts upon the doctrine, transforms it, adapts it to new needs, or supersedes it with something else. A doctrine then must be no mere exercise in words, but a living act; and thus the value of Fascism lies in the fact that it is veined with pragmatism, but at the same time has a will to exist and a will to power, a firm front in face of the reality of "violence."

The foundation of Fascism is the conception of the State, its character, its duty, and its aim. Fascism conceives of the State as an absolute, in comparison with which all individuals or groups are relative, only to be conceived of in their relation to the State. The conception of the Liberal State is not that of a directing force, guiding the play and development, both material and spiritual, of a collective body, but merely a force limited to the function of recording results: on the other hand, the Fascist State is itself conscious, and has itself a will and a personality—thus it may be called the "ethic" State. In 1929, at the first five-yearly assembly of the Fascist régime, I said:

"For us Fascists, the State is not merely a guardian, preoccupied solely with the duty of assuring the personal safety of the citizens; nor is it an organization with purely material aims, such as to guarantee a certain level of well-being and peaceful conditions of life; for a mere council of administration would be sufficient to realize such objects. Nor is it a purely political creation, divorced from all contact with the complex material reality which makes up the life of the individual and the life of the people as a whole. The State, as conceived of and as created by Fascism, is a spiritual and moral fact in itself, since its political, juridical, and economic organization of the nation is a concrete thing: and such an organization must be in its origins and development a manifestation of the spirit. The State is the guarantor of security both internal and external, but it is also the custodian and transmitter of the spirit of the people, as it has grown up through the centuries in language, in customs, and in faith. And the State is not only a living reality of the present, it is also linked with the past and above all with the future, and thus transcending the brief limits of individual life, it represents the immanent spirit of the nation. The forms in which States express themselves may change, but the necessity for such forms is eternal. It is the State which educates its citizens in civic virtue, gives them a consciousness of their mission and welds them into unity; harmonizing their various interests through justice, and transmitting to future generations the mental conquests of science, of art, of law and the solidarity of humanity. It leads men from primitive tribal life to that highest expression of human power which is Empire: it links up through the centuries the names of those of its members who have died for its existence and in obedience to its laws, it holds up the memory of the leaders who have increased its territory and the geniuses who have illumined it with glory as an example to be followed by future generations. When the conception of the State declines, and disunifying and centrifugal tendencies prevail, whether of individuals or of particular groups, the nations where such phenomena appear are in their decline."

From 1929 until today, evolution, both political and economic, has everywhere gone to prove the validity of these doctrinal premises. Of such gigantic importance is the State. It is the force which alone can provide a solution to the dramatic contradictions of capitalism, and that state of affairs which we call the crisis can only be dealt with by the State, as between other States. . . . Fascism desires the State to be a strong and organic body, at the same time reposing upon broad and popular support. The Fascist State has drawn into itself even the economic activities of the nation, and, through the corporative social and educational institutions created by it, its influence reaches every aspect of the national life and includes, framed in their respective organizations, all the political, economic and spiritual forces of the nation. A State which reposes upon the support of millions of individuals who recognize its authority, are continually conscious of its power and are ready at once to serve it, is not the old tyrannical State of the medieval lord nor has it any thing in common with the absolute governments either before or after 1789. The individual in the Fascist State is not annulled but rather multiplied, just in the same way that a soldier in a regiment is not diminished but rather increased by the number of his comrades. The Fascist State organizes the nation, but leaves a sufficient margin of liberty to the individual; the latter is deprived of all useless and possibly harmful freedom, but retains what is essential; the deciding power in this question cannot be the individual, but the State alone.

The Fascist State is not indifferent to the fact of religion in general, or to that particular and positive faith which is Italian Catholicism. The State professes no theology, but a morality, and in the Fascist State religion is considered as one of the deepest manifestations of the spirit of man, thus it is not only respected but defended and protected. The Fascist State has never tried to create its own God, as at one moment Robespierre and the wildest extremists of the Convention tried to do; nor does it vainly seek to obliterate religion from the hearts of men as does Bolshevism: Fascism respects the God of the ascetics, the saints and heroes, and equally, God as He is perceived and worshipped by simple people.

The Fascist State is an embodied will to power and government: the Roman tradition is here an ideal of force in action. According to Fascism, government is not so much a thing to be expressed in territorial or military terms as in terms of morality and the spirit. It must be thought of as an empire—that is to say, a nation which directly or indirectly rules other nations, without the need for conquering a single square yard of territory. For Fascism, the growth of empire, that is to say the expansion of the nation, is an essential manifestation of vitality, and its opposite a sign of decadence. Peoples which are rising, or rising again after a period of decadence, are always imperialist; any renunciation is a sign of decay and of death.

Fascism is the doctrine best adapted to represent the tendencies and the aspirations of a people, like the people of Italy, who are rising again after many centuries of abasement and foreign servitude. But empire demands discipline, the co-ordination of all forces and a deeply felt sense of duty and sacrifice: this fact explains many aspects of the practical working of the régime, the character of many forces in the State, and the necessarily severe measures which must be taken against those

who would oppose this spontaneous and inevitable movement of Italy in the twentieth century, and would oppose it by recalling the outworn ideology of the nineteenth century—repudiated wheresoever there has been the courage to undertake great experiments of social and political transformation: for never before has the nation stood more in need of authority, of direction, and of order. If every age has its own characteristic doctrine, there are a thousand signs which point to Fascism as the characteristic doctrine of our time. For if a doctrine must be a living thing, this is proved by the fact that Fascism has created a living faith; and that this faith is very powerful in the minds of men, is demonstrated by those who have suffered and died for it.

Fascism has henceforth in the world the universality of all those doctrines which, in realizing themselves, have represented a stage in the history of the human spirit.

National Socialism

The National Socialist Party was organized by Adolf Hitler (1889–1945) and six other German nationalists in 1919. The Nazi movement, like that of the Italian Fascists, was directed against the Treaty of Versailles and toward the strengthening of the nation state. For ten years the Nazi's made little headway; following the world-wide economic collapse of 1929, however, the Nazi cause gained rapidly in popular support, and in 1933 Von Hindenburg, President of the Republic, appointed Hitler Chancellor of the German Reich. The Nazis quickly launched their revolution, and by 1939 Germany's revival as a great nation was so far accomplished that Hitler defied the Western democracies and initiated World War II. Nazi ideology grew and developed during the years prior to and after the party came to power. No single document, such as Mussolini's article on fascism, provides a succinct statement of Nazi ideology. The selections that follow are from a United States Department of State study prepared from a variety of sources, principally National Socialist in origin. In reading them note (1) the three basic concepts upon which the Nazi state rested, (2) what was meant by the Volk and what its relation to the state was, (3) the relation of the Volk to race, (4) the romantic views of the Volk and of the state reminiscent of Treitschke, (5) Nazi doctrines of racial supremacy, (6) what was meant by the Führer principle and how the Führer was related to the Volk and *to the state, (7) the role of the party and its relationship to the Volk and to the state, (8) the qualifications and duties of party members, (9) the means used to establish a totalitarian state, and (10) the nature and function of propaganda.*

From: NATIONAL SOCIALISM

THE VOLK

Ernst Rudolf Huber, in his basic work *Verfassungsrecht des grossdeutschen Reiches* (*Constitutional Law of the Greater German Reich*), published in 1939, states:

The new constitution of the German Reich . . . is not a constitution in the formal sense such as was typical of the nineteenth century. The new Reich has no written constitutional declaration, but its constitution exists in the unwritten basic political order of the Reich. One recognizes it in the spiritual powers which fill our people, in the real authority in which our political life is grounded, and in the basic laws regarding the structure of the state which have been proclaimed so far. The advantage of such an unwritten constitution over the formal constitution is that the basic principles do not become rigid but remain in a constant, living movement. Not dead institutions but living principles determine the nature of the new constitutional order.

In developing his thesis Huber points out that the National Socialist state rests on three basic concepts, the *Volk* or people, the Führer, and the movement or party. With reference to the first element, the *Volk*, he argues that the democracies develop their concept of the people from the wrong approach: They start with the concept of the state and its functions and consider the people as being made up of all the elements which fall within the borders or under the jurisdiction of the state. National Socialism, on the other hand, starts with the concept of the people, which forms a political unity, and builds the state upon this foundation.

There is no people without an objective unity, but there is also none without a common conscious-

ness of unity. A people is determined by a number of different factors: by racial derivation and by the character of its land, by language and other forms of life, by religion and history, but also by the common consciousness of its solidarity and by its common will to unity. For the concrete concept of a people, as represented by the various peoples of the earth, it is of decisive significance which of these various factors they regard as determinants for the nature of the people. The new German Reich proceeds from the concept of the political people, determined by the natural characteristics and by the historical idea of a closed community. The political people is formed through the uniformity of its natural characteristics. Race is the natural basis of the people. . . . As a political people the natural community becomes conscious of its solidarity and strives to form itself, to develop itself, to defend itself, to realize itself. "Nationalism" is essentially this striving of a people which has become conscious of itself toward self-direction and self-realization, toward a deepening and renewing of its natural qualities.

This consciousness of self, springing from the consciousness of a historical idea, awakens in a people its will to historical formation: the will to action. The political people is no passive, sluggish mass, no mere object for the efforts of the state at government or protective welfare work. . . . The great misconception of the democracies is that they can see the active participation of the people only in the form of plebiscites according to the principle of majority. In a democracy the people does not act as a unit but as a complex of unrelated individuals who form themselves into parties. . . . The new Reich is based on the principle that real action of a self-determining people is only possible according to the principle of leadership and following.

According to Huber, geographical considerations play a large part in the shaping of a people:

Raymond E. Murphy and others, eds., *National Socialism*. . . . Washington: US Government Printing Office, 1943, 23–25; 28–36; 39; 41–45; 47–48; 59–62.

The people stands in a double relation, to its lands; it settles and develops the land, but the land also stamps and determines the people. . . . That a certain territory belongs to a certain people is not justified by state authority alone but it is also determined objectively by its historical, political position. Territory is not merely a field for the exercise of state control but it determines the nature of a people and thereby the historical purpose of the state's activity. England's island position, Italy's Mediterranean position, and Germany's central position between east and west are such historical conditions, which unchangeably form the character of the people.

But the new Germany is based upon a "unity and entirety of the people" which does not stop at geographical boundaries:

The German people forms a closed community which recognizes no national borders. It is evident that a people has not exhausted its possibilities simply in the formation of a national state but that it represents an independent community which reaches beyond such limits.

The state justifies itself only so far as it helps the people to develop itself more fully. In the words of Hitler, quoted by Huber from *Mein Kampf*, " 'It is a basic principle, therefore, that the state represents not an end but a means. It is a condition for advanced human culture, but not the cause of it. . . . Its purpose is in the maintenance and advancement of a community of human beings with common physical and spiritual characteristics.' "

Huber continues:

In the theory of the folk-Reich [*völkisches Reich*], people and state are conceived as an inseparable unity. The people is the prerequisite for the entire political order; the state does not form the people but the people moulds the state out of itself as the form in which it achieves historical permanence. . . .

"The state is a function of the people, but it is not therefore a subordinate, secondary machine which can be used or laid aside at will. It is the form in which the people attains to historical reality. It is the bearer of the historical continuity of the people, which remains the same in the center of its being in spite of all changes, revolutions, and transformations." . . .

Some of the most striking expressions of the race concept are found in *Die Erziehung im dritten Reich* (*Education in the Third Reich*),

by Friedrich Alfred Beck, which was published in 1936. It is worthy of note that the tendency which may be observed in Huber . . . and Neesse to associate the ideas of *Volk* and race is very marked with Beck. "All life, whether natural or spiritual, all historical progress, all state forms, and all cultivation by education are in the last analysis based upon the racial make-up of the people in question." *Race* finds its expression in human life through the phenomenon of the *people:*

Race and *people* belong together. National Socialism has restored the concept of the people from its modern shallowness and sees in the people something different from and appreciably greater than a chance social community of men, a grouping of men who have the same external interests. By *people* we understand an entire living body which is racially uniform and which is held together by common history, common fate, a common mission, and common tasks. Through such an interpretation the people takes on a significance which is only attributed to it in times of great historical importance and which makes it the center, the content, and the goal of all human work. Only that race still possesses vital energy which can still bring its unity to expression in the totality of the people. The people is the space in which race can develop its strength. Race is the vital law of arrangement which gives the people its distinctive form. In the course of time the people undergoes historical transformations, but race prevents the loss of the people's own nature in the course of these transformations. Without the people the race has no life; without race the people has no permanence. . . . Education, from the standpoint of race and people, is the creation of a form of life in which the racial unity will be preserved through the totality of the people.

Beck describes the politically spiritual National Socialist personality which National Socialist education seeks to develop, in the following terms:

Socialism is the direction of personal life through dependence on the community, consciousness of the community, feeling for the community, and action in the community; nationalism is the elevation of individual life to a unique (microcosmic) expression of the community in the unity of the personality.

National Socialist education must stress the heroic life and teach German youth the importance of fulfilling their duty to the *Volk*.

Heroism is that force and that conviction which consecrates its whole life to the service of an idea, a faith, a task, or a duty even when it knows that the destruction of its own life is certain. . . . German life, according to the laws of its ideology, is heroic life. . . . All German life, every person belonging to the community of Germans must bear heroic character within himself. Heroic life fulfils itself in the daily work of the miner, the farmer, the clerk, the statesman, and the serving self-sacrifice of the mother. Wherever a life is devoted with an all-embracing faith and with its full powers to the service of some value, there is true heroism. . . . Education to the heroic life is education to the fulfilment of duty. . . . One must have experienced it repeatedly that the inner fruition of a work in one's own life has nothing to do with material or economic considerations, that man keeps all of his faculties alive through his obligation to his work and his devotion to his duty, and that he uses them in the service of an idea without any regard for practical considerations, before one recognizes the difference between this world of heroic self-sacrifice and the liberalistic world of barter. Because the younger generation has been brought up in this heroic spirit it is no longer understood by the representatives of the former era who judge the values of life according to material advantage. . . . German life is heroic life. Germany is not a mere community of existence and of interests whose only function is to insure the material and cultural needs of its members, but it also represents an elemental obligation on the part of the members. The eternal Germany cannot be drawn in on the map; it does not consist of the constitution or the laws of the state. This Germany is the community of those who are solemnly bound together and who experience and realize these eternal national values. This Germany is our eternal mission, our most sacred law. . . . The developing personality must be submerged in the living reality of the people and the nation from earliest youth on, must take an active and a suffering part in it. Furthermore the heroic life demands a recognition and experiencing of the highest value of life which man must serve with all his powers. This value can perhaps be recognized and presented theoretically in the schools but it can only be directly comprehended and personally experienced in the community of the people. Therefore all education must preserve this *direct connection with the community of the people* and school education must derive from it the form and substance of its instruction.

This nationalism, which is based upon the laws of life, has nothing in common with the weak and presumptuous patriotism of the liberalistic world; it is not a gift or a favor, not a possession or a privilege, but it is the form of national life which we have won in hard battle and which suits our Nordic-German racial and spiritual heritage. In the nationalistic personality the powers and values which have been established in the socialistic personality will be purposefully exerted for the perfection of the temporal and eternal idea of life. . . .

Such indeed is the supreme goal of all National Socialist education: to make each individual an expression of "the eternal German":

Whoever wishes fully to realize himself, whoever wishes to experience and embody the eternal German ideal within himself must lift his eyes from everyday life and must listen to the beat of his blood and his conscience. . . . He must be capable of that superhuman greatness which is ready to cast aside all temporal bonds in the battle for German eternity. . . . National Socialist education raises the eternal German character into the light of our consciousness. . . . National Socialism is the eternal law of our German life; the development of the eternal German is the transcendental task of National Socialist education.

RACIAL SUPREMACY

The theory of the racial supremacy of the Nordic, *i.e.* the German, which was developed by Wagner and Stewart Chamberlain reaches its culmination in the writings of Alfred Rosenberg, the high priest of Nazi racial theory and herald of the *Herrenvolk* (master race). Rosenberg developed his ideas in the obscure phraseology of *Der Mythus des 20. Jahrhunderts* (*The Myth of the Twentieth Century*). "The 'meaning of world history,'" he wrote, "has radiated out from the north over the whole world, borne by a blue-eyed blond race which in several great waves determined the spiritual face of the world. . . . These wander-periods were the legendary migration of the Atlantides across north Africa, the migration of the Aryans into India and Persia; the migration of the Dorians, Macedonians, Latins; the migration of the Germanic tribes; the colonization of the world by the Germanic occident." He discusses at length Indian, Persian, Greek, Roman, and European cultures; in each case, he concludes, the culture is created by the ruling Nordic element and declines through the racial decay of the Nordics resulting from their intermixture with inferior races.

It has long been accepted, Rosenberg claims, that all the states of the West and their creative values have been generated by Germans; and it follows that if the Germanic blood were to vanish away completely in Europe all Western culture would also fall to ruin.

Rosenberg acclaims the new faith of the blood which is to replace the non-German religion of Christianity. "A *new* faith is arising today: the myth of the blood, the faith to defend with the blood the divine essence of man. The faith, embodied in clearest knowledge, that the Nordic blood represents that *mysterium* which has replaced and overcome the old sacraments."

Rosenberg accepts the classic German view of the *Volk*, which he relates closely to the concept of race.

The state is nowadays no longer an independent idol, before which everything must bow down; the state is not even an end but is only a means for the preservation of the folk. . . . Forms of the state change, and laws of the state pass away; the folk remains. From this alone follows that the nation is the first and *last*, that to which everything else has to be subordinated. . . . The new thought puts folk and race higher than the state and its forms. It declares protection of the folk more important than protection of a religious denomination, a class, the monarchy, or the republic; it sees in treason against the folk a greater crime than high treason against the state.

The essence of Rosenberg's racial ideas was incorporated in point 4 of the program of the Nazi Party, which reads as follows: "None but members of the nation [*Volk*] may be citizens of the State. None but those of German blood, whatever their creed, may be members of the nation. No Jew, therefore, may be a member of the nation." After the Nazis came to power, this concept was made the basis of the German citizenship law of September 15, 1935.

Commenting upon point 4 of the Nazi program in his pamphlet, *Nature, Principles, and Aims of the NSDAP*, Rosenberg wrote:

An indispensable differentiation must be made sometime in the German *Volk* consciousness: The right of nationality should not represent something which is received in the cradle as a gift, but should be regarded as a good which must be earned. Although every German is a subject of the state, the rights of nationality should only be received when at the age of twenty or twenty-two he has completed his education or his military service or has finished the labor service which he owes to the state and after having given evidence of honorable conduct. The right to nationality, which must be earned, must become an opportunity for every German to strive for complete humanity and achievement in the service of the *Volk*. This consciousness, which must always be kept alive, will cause him to regard this earned good quite differently from the way it was regarded in the past and today more than ever.

The prevailing concept of state nationality completely ignores the idea of race. According to it, whoever has a German passport is a German, whoever has Czech documents is a Czech, although he may have not a single drop of Czech blood in his veins. . . .

National Socialism also sees in the nature of the structure and leadership of the state an outflowing of a definite character in the *Volk*. If one permits a wholly foreign race—subject to other impulses—to participate therein, the purity of the organic expression is falsified and the existence of the *Volk* is crippled. . . .

This whole concept of the state [parliamentary democracy] is replaced by National Socialism with a basically different concept. National Socialism recognizes that, although the individual racial strains in German-speaking territory differ, they nevertheless belong to closely related races, and that many mixtures among the members of these different branches have produced new and vital strains, among them the complex but still *German* man, but that a mixture with the Jewish enemy race, which in its whole spiritual and physical structure is basically different and antagonistic and has strong resemblances to the peoples of the Near East, can only result in bastardization.

True to the tradition of German imperialism, Rosenberg does not confine his ideas of racial supremacy to the Germans in the Reich alone. He even extends them to the United States, where he envisages the day when the awakening German element will realize its destiny in this country. In *Der Mythus des 20. Jahrhunderts*, for example, he writes,

After throwing off the worn-out idea upon which it was founded . . . *i.e.*, after the destruction of the idea represented by New York, the

United States of North America has the great task . . . of setting out with youthful energy to put into force the new racial-state idea which a few awakened Americans have already foreseen.

This idea was developed at length by the German geopolitician, Colin Ross. In his book *Unser Amerika (Our America)* published in 1936, Ross develops the thesis that the German element in the United States has contributed all that is best in American life and civilization and urges it to become conscious of its racial heritage and to prepare for the day when it may take over complete control of the country.

Reference was made in the preceding section to Beck's *Education in the Third Reich.* On the subject of racial supremacy Beck points out that certain new branches of learning have been introduced into the National Socialist schools and certain old ones have been given a new emphasis. The most important of these are the science of race and the cultivation of race (*Rassenkunde und Rassenpflege*), which teach the pupil to recognize and develop those racial powers which alone make possible the fullest self-realization in the national community. An awakening of a true racial consciousness in the people should lead to a "qualitative and quantitative" racial refinement of the German people by inducing a procreative process of selection which would reduce the strains of foreign blood in the national body.

German racial consciousness must have pride in the Nordic race as its first condition. It must be a feeling of the highest personal pride to belong to the Nordic race and to have the possibility and the obligation to work within the German community for the advancement of the Nordic race. Beck points out that pupils must be made to realize that the downfall of the Nordic race would mean the collapse of the national tradition, the disintegration of the living community and the destruction of the individual.

Under the influence of war developments, which have given the Nazis a chance to apply their racial theories in occupied territories, their spokesmen have become increasingly open with regard to the political implications of the folk concept. In an article on "The Structure and Order of the Reich," published late in 1941, Ernst Rudolf Huber wrote,

this folk principle has found its full confirmation for the first time in the events of this war, in which the unity of the folk has been realized to an extent undreamed of through the return to the homeland of territories which had been torn from it and the resettlement of German folk-groups. Thus the awakening of Germandom to become a political folk has had a twofold result: the unity of the folk-community has risen superior to differences of birth or wealth, of class, rank, or denomination; and the unity of Germandom above all state boundaries has been consciously experienced in the European livingspace [*Siedlungsraum*].

THE FÜHRER PRINCIPLE

The second pillar of the Nazi state is the Führer, the infallible leader, to whom his followers owe absolute obedience. The Führer principle envisages government of the state by a hierarchy of leaders, each of whom owes unconditional allegiance to his immediate superior and at the same time is the absolute leader in his own particular sphere of jurisdiction.

One of the best expositions of the Nazi concept of the Führer principle is given by Huber in his *Constitutional Law of the Greater German Reich:*

The Führer-Reich of the [German] people is founded on the recognition that the true will of the people cannot be disclosed through parliamentary votes and plebiscites but that the will of the people in its pure and uncorrupted form can only be expressed through the Führer. Thus a distinction must be drawn between the supposed will of the people in a parliamentary democracy, which merely reflects the conflict of the various social interests, and the true will of the people in the Führer-state, in which the collective will of the real political unit is manifested. . . .

The Führer is the bearer of the people's will; he is independent of all groups, associations, and interests, but he is bound by laws which are inherent in the nature of his people. In this twofold condition: independence of all factional interests but unconditional dependence on the people, is reflected the true nature of the Führer principle. Thus the Führer has nothing in common with the functionary, the agent, or the exponent who exercises a mandate delegated to him and who is bound to the will of those who appoint him. The Führer is no 'representative' of a particular group whose wishes he must carry out. He is no "organ" of the state in the sense of a mere executive agent. He is rather himself the bearer of the collective will of the people. In his will the will of the people is realized. He transforms the mere feelings of the people into a conscious will. . . . Thus it is possible for him, in the name of the true will of the people which he serves, to go against the subjective opinions and convictions of single individuals within the people if these are not in accord with the objective destiny of the people. . . . He shapes the collective will of the people within himself and he embodies the political unity and entirety of the people in opposition to individual interests. . . .

But the Führer, even as the bearer of the people's will, is not arbitrary and free of all responsibility. His will is not the subjective, individual will of a single man, but the collective national will is embodied within him in all its objective, historical greatness. . . . Such a collective will is not a fiction, as is the collective will of the democracies, but it is a political reality which finds its expression in the Führer. The people's collective will has its foundation in the political idea which is given to a people. It is present in the people, but the Führer raises it to consciousness and discloses it. . . .

In the Führer are manifested also the natural laws inherent in the people: It is he who makes them into a code governing all national activity. In disclosing these natural laws he sets up the great ends which are to be attained and draws up the plans for the utilization of all national powers in the achievement of the common goals. Through his planning and directing he gives the national life its true purpose and value. This directing and planning activity is especially manifested in the lawgiving power which lies in the Führer's hand. The great change in significance which the law has undergone is characterized therein that it no longer sets up the limits of social life, as in liberalistic times, but that it drafts the plans and the aims of the nation's actions. . . .

The Führer principle rests upon unlimited authority but not upon mere outward force. It has often been said, but it must constantly be repeated, that the Führer principle has nothing in common with arbitrary bureaucracy and represents no system of brutal force, but that it can only be maintained by mutual loyalty which must find its expression in a free relation. The Führer-order depends upon the responsibility of the following, just as it counts on the responsibility and loyalty of the Führer to his mission and to his following. . . . There is no greater responsibility than that upon which the Führer principle is grounded.

The nature of the plebiscites which are held from time to time in a National Socialist state, Huber points out, cannot be understood from a democratic standpoint. Their purpose is not to give the people an opportunity to decide some issue but rather to express their unity behind a decision which the Führer, in his capacity as the bearer of the people's will, has already made:

That the will of the people is embodied in the Führer does not exclude the possibility that the Führer can summon all members of the people to a plebiscite on a certain question. In this "asking of the people" the Führer does not, of course, surrender his decisive power to the voters. The purpose of the plebiscite is not to let the people act in the Führer's place or to replace the Führer's decision with the result of the plebiscite. Its purpose is rather to give the whole people an opportunity to demonstrate and proclaim its support of an aim announced by the Führer. It is intended to solidify the unity and agreement between the objective people's will embodied in the Führer and the living, subjective conviction of the people as it exists in the individual members. . . . This approval of the Führer's decision is even more clear and effective if the plebiscite is concerned with an aim which has already been realized rather than with a mere intention.

Huber states that the Reichstag elections in the Third Reich have the same character as the plebiscites. The list of delegates is made up by the Führer and its approval by the people represents an expression of renewed and continued faith in him. The Reichstag no longer has any governing or lawgiving powers but acts merely as a sounding board for the Führer. . . .

Great emphasis is placed by the Nazi leaders on the infallibility of the Führer and the duty of obedience of the German people. In a speech on June 12, 1935, for instance, Robert Ley, director of the party organization, said, "Germany must obey like a well-trained soldier: the Führer, Adolf Hitler, is always right." Developing the same idea, Ley wrote in an article in the *Angriff* on April 9, 1942: "Right is what serves my people; wrong is what damages it. I am born a German and have, therefore, only one holy mission: work for my people and take care of it." And with reference to the position of Hitler, Ley wrote:

The National Socialist Party is Hitler, and Hitler is the party. The National Socialists believe in Hitler, who embodies their will. Therefore our conscience is clearly and exactly defined. Only what Adolf Hitler, our Führer, commands, allows, or does not allow is our conscience. *We have no understanding for him who hides behind an anonymous conscience, behind God, whom everybody conceives according to his own wishes.*

These ideas of the Führer's infallibility and the duty of obedience are so fundamental in fact that they are incorporated as the first two commandments for party members. These are set forth in the *Organisationsbuch der NSDAP* (*Nazi Party Organization Book*) for 1940. The first commandment is "The Führer is always right!" and the second is "Never go against discipline!". . .

THE PARTY: LEADERSHIP BY AN ELITE CLASS

Functions of the Party

The third pillar of the Nazi state, the link between *Volk* and Führer, is the Nazi Party. According to Nazi ideology, all authority within the nation is derived ultimately from the people, but it is the party through which the people expresses itself. In *Rechtseinrichtungen und Rechtsaufgaben der Bewegung* (*Legal Organization and Legal Functions of the Movement*), published in 1939, Otto Gauweiler states:

The will of the German people finds its expression in the party as the political organization of the people. It represents the political conception, the political conscience, and the political will. It is the expression and the organ of the people's creative will to life. It comprises a select part of the German people for "only the best Germans should be party members.". . . The inner organization of the party must therefore bring the national life which is concentrated within itself to manifestation and development in all the fields of national endeavor in which the party is represented.

Gauweiler defines the relationship of the party to the state in the following terms:

The party stands above and beside the state as the wielder of an authority derived from the people with its own sovereign powers and its own sphere of sovereignty. . . . The legal position of the party is therefore that of a completely sovereign authority whose legal supremacy and self-sufficiency rest upon the original independent political authority which the Führer and the movement have attained as a result of their historical achievements. . . .

The educational tasks of the party are stressed by Beck, who develops the idea that the *Volk* can be divided into three main groups, "a supporting, a leading, and a creative class." It is the duty of the leading class, that is, the party, from which the creative class of leaders is drawn, to provide for the education of the supporting class.

Every member of the body of the people must belong to the politically supporting class, that is, each one who bears within himself the basic racial, spiritual, and mental values of the people. . . . Here no sort of leading or creative activity is demanded but only a recognition of the leading and creative will. . . . Only those are called to leadership in political life who have recognized the community-bound law of all human life in purest clarity and in the all-embracing extent of its validity and who will place all the powers of their personal lives with the help of a politically moral character in the service of the formation of community life. . . . From the politically leading class arise the politically creative personalities. These are the mysterious elemental forces which are beyond all explanation by human reason and which through their action and by means of the living idea within them give to the community of the people an expression which is fresh, young, and eternal. Here is the fulfilment of the highest and purest political humanity. . . . The education of the socialistic personality is essentially the forming of the politically supporting class within the German people and the encouragement of those political tendencies which make a man a political leader. To educate to political creativeness is just as impossible as to educate to genius. Education can only furnish the spiritual atmosphere, can only prepare the spiritual living-space for the politically creative personality by forming a uniform political consciousness in the socialistic personality, and in the development of politically creative personalities it can at the most give special attention to those values of character and spirit which are of decisive importance for the development of this personality.

Goebbels in *The Nature and Form of National Socialism* emphasizes the responsibility of the party for the leadership of the state:

The party must always continue to represent the hierarchy of National Socialist leadership. This minority must always insist upon its prerogative to control the state. It must keep the way open for the German youth which wishes to take its place in this hierarchy. In reality the hierarchy has fewer rights than duties! It is responsible for the leadership of the state, and it solemnly relieves the people of this responsibility. It has the duty to control the state in the best interests and to the general welfare of the nation. . . .

To Dr. Ley, the party is identical with the Führer. As he wrote in the *Angriff* on April 9, 1942, "The National Socialist Party is Hitler, and Hitler is the party.". . .

Party Membership

Details concerning the qualifications and duties of party members are contained in the *Party Organization Book* for 1940.

Membership is finally confirmed by the issuance of a membership card or a membership book. Anyone who becomes a party member does not merely join an organization but he becomes a soldier in the German freedom movement and that means much more than just paying his dues and attending the members' meetings. He obligates himself to subordinate his own ego and to place everything he has in the service of the people's cause. Only he who is capable of doing this should become a party member. A selection must be made in accordance with this idea.

Readiness to fight, readiness to sacrifice, and strength of character are the requirements for a good National Socialist. Small blemishes, such as a false step which someone has made in his youth, should be overlooked; the contribution in the struggle for Germany should alone be decisive. The healthy will naturally prevail over the bad if the will to health finds sufficient support in leadership and achievement. Admission to the party should not be controlled by the old bourgeois point of view. The party must always represent the elite of the people.

German blood is one of the prerequisites for party membership. The *Party Organization Book* for 1940 . . . states, "Only those racial comrades who possess German citizenship are eligible for admission."

Party members shall not exceed 10 percent of the German population of the region. "The ideal proportion of the number of party members to the number of racial comrades is set at 10 percent. This proportion is to apply also to the individual Province [Gau].". . .

THE TOTALITARIAN STATE

The Weimar Constitution, although never formally abrogated by the Nazis, was rendered totally ineffectual by two basic laws, promulgated within two months after the seizure of power by the party. The first of these was the "Decree of the Reich's President for the Protection of the People and State," issued February 28, 1933, the day after the Reichstag was burned down. It suspended "until further notice" articles of the Weimar Constitution guaranteeing essential democratic rights of the individual. Thus, according to article 1 of this decree,

restrictions on personal liberty, on the right of free expression of opinion, including freedom of the press, on the right of assembly and the right of association, and violations of the privacy of postal, telegraphic, and telephonic communications, and warrants for house-searches, orders for confiscations as well as restrictions on property, are also permissible beyond the legal limits otherwise prescribed.

The abrogation by the Nazis of these fundamental rights of democracy has never been repealed or amended. In fact, this decree represents the presupposition and confirmation of the police sway established throughout Germany by the Nazis.

The second basic law, known as the "Enabling Act," the "Law To Remove the Distress of People and State," of March 24, 1933, swept away parliamentary government entirely. By abrogating the pertinent articles of the Weimar Constitution, it enabled the Nazi Cabinet under Hitler's chancelorship to appropriate money and legislate without any responsibility to the Reichstag or any obligation to respect the Constitution.

The dissolution of democracy in Germany was sealed by the unification of the authoritarian Nazi Party with the German state. Soon after the party came to power in 1933, steps were taken to effect and secure this unity. . . .

INTERNAL PROPAGANDA

Within Germany the notorious propaganda machine of Dr. Goebbels, together with a systematic terrorization of oppositionist elements, has been the principle support of the rise and triumph of the Nazi movement. . . .

The character and quality of Nazi propaganda was fully presaged in *Mein Kampf*. Here Hitler paid a striking tribute to the power of lies, commenting on—

the very correct principle that the size of the lie always involves a certain factor of credibility, since the great mass of a people will be more spoiled in the innermost depths of its heart, rather than consciously and deliberately bad. Consequently, in view of the primitive simplicity of its mind it is more readily captivated by a big lie than by a small one, since it itself often uses small lies but would be, nevertheless, too ashamed to make use of big lies. Such an untruth will not even occur to it, and it will not even believe that others are capable of the enormous insolence of the most vile distortions. Why, even when enlightened, it will still vacillate and be in doubt about the matter and will nevertheless accept as true at least some cause or other. Consequently, even from the most impudent lie something will always stick. . . .

A number of other passages display Hitler's low opinion of the intellectual capacities and critical faculties of the masses:

All propaganda has to appeal to the people and its intellectual level has to be set in accordance with the receptive capacities of the most-limited persons among those to whom it intends to address itself. The larger the mass of men to be reached, the lower its purely intellectual level will have to be set.

The receptive capacity of the great masses is very restricted, its understanding small. On the other hand, however, its forgetfulness is great. On account of these facts all effective propaganda must restrict itself to very few points and impress these by slogans, until even the last person is able to bring to mind what is meant by such a word.

The task of propaganda is, for instance, not to evaluate diverse rights but to emphasize exclusively the single right of that which it is representing. It does not have to investigate objectively the truth, so far as this is favorable to the others, in order then to present it to the masses in strict honesty, but rather to serve its own side ceaselessly.

If one's own propaganda even once accords just the shimmer of right to the other side, then the basis is therewith laid for doubt regarding one's own cause. The masses are not able to distinguish where the error of the other side ends and the error of one's own side begins.

But all talent in presentation of propaganda will lead to no success if a fundamental principle is not always strictly followed. Propaganda has to restrict itself to a few matters and to repeat these eternally. Persistence is here, as with so many other things in the world, the first and most important presupposition for success.

In view of their slowness of mind, they [the masses] require always, however, a certain period before they are ready even to take cognizance of a matter, and only after a thousandfold repetition of the most simple concept will they finally retain it.

In all cases in which there is a question of the fulfilment of apparently impossible demands or tasks, the entire attention of a people must be concentrated only on this one question, in such a way as if being or non-being actually depends on its solution. . . .

The great mass of the people can never see the entire way before them, without tiring and doubting the task.

In general the art of all truly great popular leaders at all times consists primarily in not scattering the attention of a people but rather in concentrating it always on one single opponent. The more unified this use of the fighting will of a people, the greater will be the magnetic attractive force of a movement and the more powerful the force of its push. It is a part of the genius of a great leader to make even quite different opponents appear as if they belonged only to one category, because the recognition of different enemies leads weak and unsure persons only too readily to begin doubting their own cause.

When the vacillating masses see themselves fighting against too many enemies, objectivity at once sets in and raises the question whether really all the others are wrong and only one's own people or one's own movement is right.

It has been the aim of Nazi propaganda, then, to unite the masses of the people in hatred of certain enemies, designated by such conveniently broad and simple terms as "Jews," "democrats," "plutocrats," "bolshevists," or "Anglo-Saxons," which so far as possible were to be identified with one another in the public mind. The Germans were represented to themselves, on the other hand, as a racial folk of industrious workers. It then became possible to plunge the people into a war on a wave of emotional hatred against those nations which were pictured as combining to keep Germany from attaining her rightful place in the sun.

The important role which propaganda would have to play in the coming war was fully recognized by Ewald Banse, an ardent Nazi military theorist of the geopolitical school and professor of military science at Brunswick Military College. In his book *Raum und Volk im Weltkrieg* (*Space and People in the World War*) which appeared in 1932 [an English translation by Alan Harris was published under the title *Germany Prepares for War* (New York: Harcourt, Brace and Co., 1934)], he stated:

Preparation for future wars must not stop at the creation, equipment and training of an efficient army, but must go on to train the minds of the whole people for the war and must employ all the resources of science to master the conditions governing the war itself and the possibility of endurance. In 1914 we had a first-class army, but our scientific mobilization was bad, and the mobilization of men's minds a thing undreamed of. The unveiling of war memorials, parades of war veterans, flag-waggings, fiery speeches and guard-mounting are not of themselves enough to prepare a nation's mind for the dangers that threaten. Conviction is always more lasting than enthusiasm. . . .

Such teaching is necessary at a time and in a world in which countries are no longer represented by monarchs or a small aristocracy or by a specialist army, but in which the whole nation, from the commander-in-chief to the man in the ranks, from the loftiest thought to the simplest wish, from corn to coal, from the treasury vaults to the last trouser-button, must be permeated through and through with the idea of national defense, if it is to preserve its national identity and political independence. The science of national defense is not the same as military science; it does not teach generals how to win battles or company commanders how to train recruits. Its lessons are addressed first and foremost to the whole people. It seeks to train the popular mind to heroism and war and to implant in it an understanding of the nature and prerequisite conditions of modern warfare. It teaches us about countries and peoples, especially our own country and its neighbors, their territories and economic capacity, their communications and their mentality—all for the purpose of creating the best possible conditions for waging future wars in defense of the national existence.

World War II and Its Aftermath

Germany, by 1939, had moved so far along the path of national regeneration within the framework of national socialism, that it was ready to defy the other nations of Europe and seek to impose its will upon the continent. The democracies of the Western World, facing, as they thought, the alternative of war or eventual domination of their nations by Hilter, chose to fight. For the second time within a generation the world was plunged into a bloody conflict. Before the struggle ended, mankind was introduced to atomic warfare, and thus sharply confronted with the implications of twentieth-century science unchecked by an adequate system of ethics and an effective international organization. Before the war's end, the nations who had united in the common effort to defeat Germany, Japan, and their allies met in San Francisco and drew up a charter for a new world organization to assure more certain international cooperation in the post-war era. Despite these efforts to provide an atmosphere devoid of conflict in which to proceed with the individual and collective affairs of life, the nations of the world realigned themselves into three major blocs: the communist nations led by the Soviet Union; the capitalist "free world" led by the United States; and a group of "new" nations, for the most part underdeveloped (by Western standards) and often recently emergent from a colonial status in which their peoples had been dominated politically or economically or both by Western Nations. The capitalist and communist blocs meanwhile have engaged in a bitter contest for supremacy over men's minds which is destined to continue during the ensuing decades. The communist leadership is determined, ruthless, and aggressive. Although faith in capitalism and democracy have suffered deflation in the modern world, defenders have appeared to remind the peoples of the world that there are some generalities that still glitter and that the means for a reinvigoration of liberalism and democracy can be found in the democratic process itself.

Adolf Hitler

Adolf Hitler (see p. 814) sent his mechanized hosts rolling into Poland on September 1, 1939, and within a
month had brought that nation to its knees. England, after
demanding a cessation of the Polish campaign, entered into
war with Germany on September 3. Other nations quickly
followed England and a second world war within a generation began. The fate of Danzig, a German city surrounded
by Poland, served as the immediate cause of the war. On
September 19, Hitler came to Danzig to receive the city
back into the German Empire. The selection given here is
from his speech to the people of Danzig and represents, in
a measure, Hitler's explanation of Germany's attack upon
Poland. In reading this selection note (1) Hitler's description of World War I and the Peace of Versailles, (2) his
statement of Poland's maltreatment of Germans, (3) Hitler's review of his efforts to avoid conflict, (4) his explanation of Russia's attack upon Poland, (5) his renunciation
of other territorial claims, (6) his review of overtures to
Italy, France, and England, and (7) his prophecy for the
future.

From: HITLER'S SPEECH TO THE PEOPLE OF DANZIG

My District Leader, My Dear Danzigers: . . .

The fate of this city, this beautiful land, is
the fate of entire Germany. The World War,
which was the most senseless struggle of all
times, made also this city a victim; this World
War which left neither victors nor vanquished;
this World War which, after its finish, left all
with the conviction that a similar fate should
not be repeated, but which, alas, apparently
has been forgotten by those who were the main
agitators and main profiteers of this slaughter.

When this sanguinary struggle—into which
Germany entered without any objective—was
over, a peace was to be given to mankind that
should be a renaissance of justice and abolition
of all misery. This peace was given to our
people at Versailles not through discussions, on
an equal plane, but was imposed upon us by
dictation. The authors of this peace saw in it
the end of the German nation—at any rate, the
beginning for new disturbances.

In one respect the authors of this peace
erred, however; this peace did not solve problems but created numerous new ones, and it
was only a question of time that the German
nation would arise to bring about a solution
of these problems. Because the most essential
problem was then overlooked, namely, the
fact that nations live and exist whether or not
one or another of the warmongers likes it. The
fact remains that 82,000,000 Germans are
united in this Lebensraum, and these 82,000,-
000 want to live, and shall live, even if warmongers again do not like it.

The Versailles peace did the greatest injustice to Germany. If today a foreign statesman
believes he may state that he has no confidence
in the word of German statesmen or German
people, then we Germans, above all, are entitled to say that we have no confidence whatsoever in the assurances of those who then
broke their most solemn assurances.

I do not want to hear talk about the injustice
of Versailles. The worst in the life of the nation
is perhaps not this injustice but the senseless-
ness and stupidity wherewith peace was then
imposed upon a world which disregarded all
historical, economic, ethnographical and political facts.

Then settlements were made, and it actually

Adolf Hitler, "Speech to the People of Danzig," from the New York *Times*, 20 September 1939.

may be doubted whether the men who made them really had their senses. Without any knowledge whatsoever of historical developments of these Lebensraume and without any consideration for economic necessities did these men tear apart estates in Europe, separate countries, oppress peoples and destroy cultures. . . .

The world, which immediately sheds tears when Germany expels a Polish Jew who only a few decades ago came to Germany, remained dumb and deaf toward the misery of those who, numbering not thousands but millions, were forced to leave their home country on account of Versailles—that is, if these unfortunates were Germans.

What was for us and also for me most depressing was the fact that we had to suffer all this from a State which was far inferior to us; for, after all, Germany is a great power, even though mad men believed the vital rights of a great nation could be wiped out by a crazy treaty or by dictation.

Germany was a big power and had to look on while a far inferior people of a far inferior State maltreated these Germans. There were two especially unbearable conditions: First, this city whose German character nobody could deny was not only prevented from returning to the Reich but in addition an attempt was made to Polonize it by all kinds of devices; second, the province [East Prussia] severed from the German Reich had no direct contact with the Reich, but traffic with this province was dependent upon all kinds of chicanery or upon the good-will of this Polish State.

No power on earth would have borne this condition as long as Germany. I do not know what England would have said about a similar "peace solution" at its expense or how America or France would have accepted it. I attempted to find a solution—a tolerable solution —even for this problem. I submitted this attempt to the Polish rulers in the form of verbal proposals. You know these proposals. They were more than moderate.

I attempted to find a solution between our desire to restore connection between East Prussia and the Reich and the Poles' wish to retain access to the sea. I attempted, above all, to find a synthesis between the German-character of the city of Danzig with its will to return to the Reich and Poland's economic demands.

I believe I may say that I was more than modest and that there were moments when I reviewed and thought over the question as to whether I would be able to justify before my own people my having made such proposals for the solution of the Polish question.

I did this only because I wanted to spare the German people and the Polish people the suffering of another conflict. I repeated this proposal early this year in the most concrete form: Danzig was to return to the German Reich, an extraterritorial road was to be built to East Prussia, of course, at our expense— Poland was to get free extraterritorial harbor rights in Danzig and the same extraterritorial access. I was ready to offer even to guarantee borders which were hardly tolerable for us, and lastly to offer Poland participation in the security of Slovakia.

I do not know what mental condition the Polish Government was in when it refused these proposals. I knew, however, that millions of Germans sighed with relief, since they felt I had gone too far. As an answer, Poland gave the order for the first mobilization. Thereupon wild terror was initiated, and my request to the Polish Foreign Minister to visit me in Berlin once more to discuss these questions was refused. Instead of going to Berlin, he went to London. For the next weeks and months there were heightened threats, threats which were hardly bearable for a small State but which were impossible for a great power to bear for any length of time. . . .

So, we have beaten Poland within eighteen days and thus created a situation which perhaps makes it possible one day to speak to representatives of the Polish people calmly and reasonably.

Meantime, Russia felt moved, on its part, to march in for the protection of the interests of the White Russian and Ukrainian people in Poland. We realize now that in England and France this German and Russian co-operation is considered a terrible crime. An Englishman even wrote that it is perfidious—well, the English ought to know. I believe England thinks this co-operation perfidious because the co-operation of democratic England with Bolshevist

Russia failed, while National Socialist Germany's attempt with Soviet Russia succeeded.

I want to give here an explanation: Russia remains what she is; Germany also remains what she is. About only one thing are both regimes clear: neither the German nor the Russian regime wants to sacrifice a single man for the interest of the western democracies. A lesson of four years was sufficient for both peoples. We know only too well that alternately, now one, then the other, would be granted the honor to fill the breach for the ideals of the western democracies.

We therefore thank both peoples and both States for this task. We intend henceforth to look after our interests ourselves, and we have found that we best have been able to look after them when two of the largest peoples and States reconcile each other. And this is made simpler by the fact that the British assertion as to the unlimited character of German foreign policy is a lie. I am happy now to be able to refute this lie for British statesmen. British statesmen, who continually maintain that Germany intends to dominate Europe to the Urals now will be pleased to learn the limits of German political intentions. I believe this will deprive them of a reason for war because they profess to have to fight against the present regime because it today pursues unlimited political goals. . . .

Firstly, Germany, by extensive yielding and renunciation in the west and south of the Reich, has accepted definite boundaries. Germany tried by these renunciations to attain lasting pacification. And we believe we would have succeeded were it not that certain warmongers could be interested in disturbing the European peace.

I have neither toward England nor France any war claims, nor has the German nation since I assumed power. I tried gradually to establish confidence between Germany and especially its former war enemies. I attempted to eliminate all tensions which once existed between Germany and Italy, and I may state with satisfaction that I fully succeeded.

That ever-closer and more cordial relations were established was due also to personal and human relations between Il Duce and myself. I went still further. I tried to achieve the same between Germany and France. Immediately after the settlement of the Saar question I solemnly renounced all further frontier revisions, not only in theory but in practice. I harnessed all German propaganda to this end in order to eliminate everything which might lead to doubt or anxiety in Paris.

You know of my offers to England. I had only in mind the goal of attaining the sincere friendship of the British people. Since this now has been repulsed, and since England today thinks it must wage war against Germany, I would like to answer thus: . . .

If peoples go to pieces it will not be the German people, who are fighting for justice, who have no war aims and who were attacked. . . .

England's goal is not "a fight against the régime" but a fight against the German people, women and children. Our reaction will be compatible, and one thing will be certain: This Germany does not capitulate. We know too well what fate would be in store for Germany. . . . A second Versailles, only worse. . . .

I was determined to come to Danzig only as a liberator. I now take Danzig into the great German community with a firm determination never to allow her to be taken away. Generations will come and generations will go. They all will look back on our twenty years of absence from this city as a sad period in our history. They not only will remember the year 1918, but will remember with pride the time of the resurrection and rise of the German Reich, that Reich which welds all real Germans together, which created unity, and which we are determined to defend to our last breath. . . .

All hail our Great German Reich.

Benito Mussolini

Benito Mussolini (see p. 807), *after the rise to power of Adolf Hitler in Germany, tended to follow a more thoroughly chauvinist foreign policy than he had pursued in the 1920's. In July, 1936, Mussolini and Hitler announced the formation of the Rome-Berlin axis, which served as a mutual assistance pact against other powers. Italy failed to join the European war until June, 1940; by that time Hitler's mechanized forces were about to enter Paris in triumph. On June 10, 1940, Italy declared war against France and England, and the same day Mussolini spoke in Rome to his people, explaining Italy's action. In reading this selection note (1) Mussolini's description of Italy's enemies, (2) his statement of what was needed to avoid war, (3) his justification for entering the conflict, (4) how Mussolini placed the war in a larger setting, (5) Mussolini's declaration of intent concerning Italy's neighbors, (6) his order to the people of Italy, and (7) his prophecy for the future.*

MUSSOLINI'S SPEECH, JUNE 10, 1940

Fighters of land, sea and air, Blackshirts of the revolution and of the legions, men and women of Italy, of the empire and of the Kingdom of Albania, listen!

The hour destined by fate is sounding for us. The hour of irrevocable decision has come. A declaration of war already has been handed to the Ambassadors of Great Britain and France.

We take the field against the plutocratic and reactionary democracies who always have blocked the march and frequently plotted against the existence of the Italian people.

Several decades of recent history may be summarized in these words: Phrases, promises, threats of blackmail, and finally, crowning that ignoble edifice, the League of Nations of fifty-two nations.

Our conscience is absolutely clear.

With you, the entire world is witness that the Italy of fascism has done everything humanly possible to avoid the tempest that envelops Europe, but all in vain.

It would have sufficed to revise treaties to adapt them to changing requirements vital to nations and not consider them untouchable for eternity.

It would have sufficed not to begin the stupid policy of guarantees, which proved particularly deadly for those who accepted them.

It would have sufficed not to reject the proposal the Fuehrer made last October 6 after the campaign in Poland ended.

Now all that belongs to the past.

If today we have decided to take the risks and sacrifices of war, it is because the honor, interests, and future firmly impose it since a great people is truly such if it considers its obligations sacred and does not avoid the supreme trials that determine the course of history.

We are taking up arms, after having solved the problem of our continental frontiers, to solve our maritime frontiers. We want to break the territorial and military chains that confine us in our sea because a country of 45,000,000 souls is not truly free if it has not free access to the ocean.

This gigantic conflict is only a phase of the logical development of our revolution. It is the conflict of poor, numerous peoples who labor against starvers who ferociously cling to a monopoly of all riches and all gold on earth.

Benito Mussolini, Speech, Rome, 10 June 1940, from the New York *Times,* 11 June 1940

It is a conflict of fruitful, useful peoples against peoples who are in a decline. It is a conflict between two ages, two ideas.

Now the die is cast and our will has burned our ships behind us.

I solemnly declare that Italy does not intend to drag other peoples bordering on her by sea or land into the conflict. Switzerland, Yugoslavia, Greece, Turkey and Egypt, take note of these words of mine. It depends on them and only on them if these words are rigorously confirmed or not.

Italians, in a memorable mass meeting in Berlin, I said that according to the rules of Fascist morals when one has a friend one marches with him to the end. This we have done and will continue to do with Germany, her people and her victorious armed forces.

On this eve of an event of import for centuries, we turn our thoughts to His Majesty, the King and Emperor, who always has understood the thought of the country.

Lastly, we salute the new Fuehrer, the chief of great allied Germany.

Proletarian, Fascist Italy has arisen for the third time, strong, proud, compact as never before.

There is only one order. It is categorical and obligatory for every one. It already wings over and enflames hearts from the Alps to the Indian Ocean: Conquer!

And we will conquer in order, finally, to give a new world of peace with justice to Italy, to Europe and to the universe.

Italian people, rush to arms and show your tenacity, your courage, your valor.

Winston Churchill

W*inston Churchill (1874–1965), English author, statesman, and orator, has been prominent in British life since 1899, when he went to South Africa as a reporter to cover the Boer War. In 1900 he was elected to Parliament as a Conservative, but by 1906 had joined the Liberal party as a supporter of free trade. During the First World War he served as head of the Admiralty and later in other important military posts. After the war Churchill returned to the Conservative party and was Chancellor of the Exchequer in the second Baldwin ministry (1924– 1929). In May, 1940, after the Germans had successfully invaded Norway, Neville Chamberlain was forced to resign as prime minister, and the British people turned to the veteran Churchill to lead them through the dark days ahead. In June, 1940, he addressed the House of Commons and later the same speech was broadcast to the nation. His words came to the ears of the Empire at its darkest hour, but this famous speech, which has become known under the title, "Their Finest Hour," did much to calm his people and to steel them for the great task ahead. In reading the concluding section of this address note (1) the balance sheet of favorable and unfavorable factors which Churchill outlined, (2) the part he expected the Dominions and the United States to play in the struggle, (3) the parallel he drew with the First World War, (4) the war aims he stated, (5) his concept of what the Battle of Britain would mean for the future, and (6) the stirring admonition to the British people with which he concluded the passage.*

From: A PARLIAMENTARY SPEECH BY WINSTON CHURCHILL

We may now ask ourselves: In what way has our position worsened since the beginning of the war? It has worsened by the fact that the Germans have conquered a large part of the coast line of Western Europe, and many small countries have been overrun by them. This aggravates the possibilities of air attack and adds to our naval preoccupations. It in no way diminishes, but on the contrary definitely increases, the power of our long-distance blockade. Similarly, the entrance of Italy into the war increases the power of our long-distance blockade. We have stopped the worst leak by that. We do not know whether military resistance will come to an end in France or not, but should it do so, then of course the Germans will be able to concentrate their forces, both military and industrial, upon us. But for the reasons I have given to the House these will not be found so easy to apply. If invasion has become more imminent, as no doubt it has, we, being relieved from the task of maintaining a large army in France, have far larger and more efficient forces to meet it.

If Hitler can bring under his despotic control the industries of the countries he has conquered, this will add greatly to his already vast armament output. On the other hand, this will not happen immediately, and we are now assured of immense, continuous and increasing support in supplies and munitions of all kinds from the United States; and especially of aeroplanes and pilots from the Dominions and across the oceans, coming from regions which are beyond the reach of enemy bombers.

I do not see how any of these factors can operate to our detriment on balance before the winter comes; and the winter will impose a strain upon the Nazi regime, with almost all Europe writhing and starving under its cruel heel, which, for all their ruthlessness, will run them very hard. We must not forget that from the moment when we declared war on the 3rd of September it was always possible for Germany to turn all her Air Force upon this country, together with any other devices of invasion she might conceive, and that France could have done little or nothing to prevent her doing so. We have, therefore, lived under this danger, in principle and in a slightly modified form, during all these months. In the meanwhile, however, we have enormously improved our methods of defense, and we have learned what we had no right to assume at the beginning, namely, that the individual aircraft and the individual British pilot have a sure and definite superiority. Therefore, in casting up this dread balance-sheet and contemplating our dangers with a disillusioned eye, I see great reason for intense vigilance and exertion, but none whatever for panic or despair.

During the first four years of the last war the Allies experienced nothing but disaster and disappointment. That was our constant fear: one blow after another, terrible losses, frightful dangers. Everything miscarried. And yet at the end of those four years the morale of the Allies was higher than that of the Germans, who had moved from one aggressive triumph to another, and who stood everywhere triumphant invaders of the lands into which they had broken. During that war we repeatedly asked ourselves the question: How are we going to win? and no one was able ever to answer it with much precision, until at the end, quite suddenly, quite unexpectedly, our terrible foe collapsed before us, and we were so glutted with victory that in our folly we threw it away.

We do not yet know what will happen in France or whether the French resistance will be prolonged, both in France and in the French Empire overseas. The French Government will be throwing away great opportunities and casting adrift their future if they do not continue the war in accordance with their Treaty obligations, from which we have not felt able to release them. The House will have read the historic declaration in which, at the

Winston Churchill, *Blood, Sweat and Tears*, G. P. Putnam's Sons, New York, 1941, 312–313. Courtesy of G. P. Putnam's Sons.

desire of many Frenchmen—and of our own hearts—we have proclaimed our willingness at the darkest hour in French history to conclude a union of common citizenship in this struggle. However matters may go in France or with the French Government, or other French Governments, we in this Island and in the British Empire will never lose our sense of comradeship with the French people. If we are now called upon to endure what they have been suffering, we shall emulate their courage, and if final victory rewards our toils they shall share the gains, aye, and freedom shall be restored to all. We abate nothing of our just demands; not one jot or tittle do we recede. Czechs, Poles, Norwegians, Dutch, Belgians have joined their causes to our own. All these shall be restored.

What General Weygand called the Battle of France is over. I expect that the Battle of Britain is about to begin. Upon this battle depends the survival of Christian civilization. Upon it depends our own British life, and the long continuity of our institutions and our Empire. The whole fury and might of the enemy must very soon be turned on us. Hitler knows that he will have to break us in this Island or lose the war. If we can stand up to him, all Europe may be free and the life of the world may move forward into broad, sunlit uplands. But if we fail, then the whole world, including the United States, including all that we have known and cared for, will sink into the abyss of a new Dark Age made more sinister, and perhaps more protracted, by the lights of perverted science. Let us therefore brace ourselves to our duties, and so bear ourselves that, if the British Empire and its Commonwealth last for a thousand years, men will still say, "This was their finest hour."

United States Strategic Bombing Survey

In November, 1944, the United States Secretary of War established the United States Strategic Bombing Survey to study the effects of aerial attacks upon Germany preparatory to planning strikes against Japan. In August, 1945, President Truman requested that a study be made of the effects of air attacks upon Japan. The Survey, thereupon, reconstructed much of wartime Japanese military planning, as well as Japan's over-all program and the background of her entry into the war. In addition, the Survey studied and reported upon the impact of the war on Japan. The Medical Division of the Survey, among other tasks, undertook to prepare a report on the effects of atomic bombs on health and medical services in Hiroshima and Nagasaki. A portion of this report, published in 1947, is reproduced here. In reading the selection note (1) the status of medical care before the attack, (2) the situation in Hiroshima immediately prior to the bombing, (3) the immediate effects of the raid, (4) the fate of medical facilities in the two cities, (5) the reaction of the population following the bombing, (6) the restoration of medical services following the disaster, (7) the efforts to deal with the dead, the wounded, the ill, and the essential sanitary services, (8) the effects on medical personnel in the two cities, and (9) the implications for civilization's future in this report.

From: REPORT OF THE EFFECTS OF ATOMIC BOMBS ON HEALTH AND MEDICAL SERVICES

In order to appreciate the effects of the atomic bombs on Hiroshima and Nagasaki one must realize something of the character and extent of medical institutions in the two cities. In addition, it is important for one to realize the magnitude of the destructive forces since they so completely surpass all previous concepts of destruction that one might have when thinking in terms of ordinary incendiary or high-explosive bombing.

STATUS OF MEDICAL CARE PRIOR TO BOMBING

Generally speaking, the Japanese are not accustomed to good medical care as one uses the term in light of practice in the Western world. Hospitals are usually available to only those who are able to pay and the average Japanese citizen has never been educated to the value and use of hospitals. Though the number of physicians per unit of population compares favorably with that in the United States, the average physician is poorly trained and the character of medicine which he practices is far below Western standards. Even the licensed physicians resort to unconventional and unscientific methods which have their origin in Far-Eastern religion and superstition. In addition, the government licenses a group of "persons engaged in the traditional methods of treatment," such as acupuncture, massage, and moxa. There are also a large number of unlicensed cultists who treat persons by means of faith healing. Both the licensed and unlicensed cultists have fairly large followings, particularly in the rural population and the lower classes.

The average Japanese hospital is a small private hospital which consists of 10 to 50 beds. Actually, the term "beds" is used loosely in this respect since few of them have western-style beds. The rooms in such hospitals are very much like rooms in Japanese homes with tatami floors and beds made by spreading bedding (Futon) upon the floor. It is thus impossible to give an accurate bed capacity, this figure actually representing the number that can be crowded into the available space. On the other hand, the larger city institutions and university hospitals are usually well equipped, of modern construction and use western beds throughout. Despite this fact, there are in every city large numbers of these small Japanese-style hospitals. Too, a large percentage of the population never go to hospitals, but are born, have their illnesses and babies, and die in their own homes. Most of the births in Japan are attended by midwives.

Hiroshima and Nagasaki did not differ from the usual medium-sized Japanese city. Hiroshima had two Army hospitals and an Army-Navy relief hospital in addition to the civilian institutions. The Red Cross Hospital and the Communications Hospital were modern structures and were the better institutions of the city. In addition there were many small Japanese hospitals scattered over the city. In the spring of 1945 a medical college was started in Hiroshima and the first class had matriculated. Though no school building was available they were being taught in one of the local hospitals at the time of the bombing. The supply of doctors and nurses seemed up to Japanese standards and it was thought that the city was well provided with medical care.

The situation in Nagasaki differed from Hiroshima in that it possessed one of the finest medical centers in Japan. The University Hospital was the pride of the city and was reputed to be second to none in Japan except the Imperial University Hospital in Tokyo. It was a large modern unit consisting of many buildings and contained about 500 beds. This number represented more than three-quarters of the hospital facilities in the city. The Medical College was located near the hospital and had a large staff of well-trained teachers. There were

---

"The Effects of Atomic Bombs on Health and Medical Services in Hiroshima and Nagasaki," in United States, *The United States Strategic Bombing Survey*, Washington, D. C., 1947, 2–4; 10; 19–21. Courtesy of the Department of the Air Force.

in adition a tuberculosis sanatorium and many small private and industrial hospitals. Here too, the number of physicians and nurses seemed to be adequate in comparison to other Japanese cities.

Since most of the other large cities of Japan had been subjected to demolition and incendiary raids during late 1944 and 1945 it was natural for Nagasaki and Hiroshima to expect similar treatment. Hiroshima contained no large war industries and had been bombed on one previous occasion only. At that time a single B-29 had dropped several demolition bombs on a suburban district, but there was little damage done. Nagasaki had experienced demolition bombing on several occasions but these raids were directed at key industrial plants. On 1 August 1945, 6 bombs were dropped on the University Hospital hitting the operating room and laboratories and resulting in the death of 3 students and 30–40 other casualties. Many patients were then evacuated as an air-raid precaution. The fact that Hiroshima had been so completely spared of bombing apparently gave rise to some rumors that the city was being saved for some "fantastic" weapon. Several survivors relate having heard such rumors. There was, however, no real reason to suspect that any fate other than that experienced by other cities was in store for it. Accordingly, the officials proceeded with the creation of large firebreaks. This work was started in March 1945 and continued until the time of the atomic bombing. Thousands of homes were thus destroyed and their occupants were required to leave the city. It was estimated by the Prefectural Health Officer that 150,000 people were evacuated from Hiroshima from March to August 1945, of whom probably 10,-000 had returned. Similar preparations were being carried out in Nagasaki but they appear to have been on a somewhat smaller scale.

THE ATOMIC BOMBING

It was upon the previously-described conditions that the atomic bombs were dropped on Hiroshima on 6 August and on Nagasaki three days later. In order to appreciate the conditions at the time of the blast and immediately thereafter it will be well to reconstruct the scene in Hiroshima as best it can be determined from talking with survivors.

The morning of 6 August 1945 began bright and clear. At about 0700 there was an air-raid alarm and a few planes appeared over the city. Many people within the city went to prepared air-raid shelters, but since alarms were heard almost every day the general population did not seem to have been greatly concerned. About 0800 an all-clear was sounded after the planes had disappeared. At this hour of the morning many people were preparing breakfast. This fact is probably important since there were fires in charcoal braziers in many of the homes at this time. Some of the laboring class were at work but most of the downtown business people had not gone to work. Consequently, a large percentage of the population was in their homes and relatively few were in the more strongly constructed business buildings.

After the all-clear sounded persons began emerging from air-raid shelters and within the next few minutes the city began to resume its usual mode of life for that time of day. It is related by some survivors that they had watched planes fly over the city. At about 0815 there was a blinding flash. Some described it as brighter than the sun, others likened it to a magnesium flash. Following the flash there was a blast of heat and wind. The large majority of people within 3,000 feet of ground zero were killed immediately. Within a radius of about 7,000 feet almost every Japanese house collapsed. Beyond this range and up to 15,000–20,000 feet many of them collapsed and others received serious structural damage. Persons in the open were burned on exposed surfaces, and within 3,000–5,000 feet many were burned to death while others received severe burns through their clothes. In many instances clothing burst into spontaneous flame and had to be beaten out. Thousands of people were pinned beneath collapsed buildings or injured by flying debris. Flying glass particularly produced many non-lethal injuries at greater distances from the center of the blast. Details relative to the nature of the injuries and the distances at which they occurred are discussed in the [following chapter], but the foregoing presentation was necessary for one to appreciate the state of the population immediately after the bomb exploded.

Shortly after the blast fires began to spring up over the city. Those who were able made a mass exodus from the city into the outlying hills. There was no organized activity. The people appeared stunned by the catastrophe and rushed about as jungle animals suddenly released from a cage. Some few apparently attempted to help others from the wreckage, particularly members of their family or friends. Others assisted those who were unable to walk alone. However, many of the injured were left trapped beneath collapsed buildings as people fled by them in the streets. Pandemonium reigned as the uninjured and slightly injured fled the city in fearful panic. Teams which had been previously organized to render first aid failed to form and function. Those closer to ground zero were largely demobilized due to injuries and death. However, there were physically intact teams on the outskirts of the city which did not function. Panic drove these people from the city just as it did the injured who could walk or be helped along. Much of the city's fire-fighting equipment was damaged beyond use so that soon the conflagrations were beyond control.

In Nagasaki a similar but slightly less catastrophic picture occurred. The blast was not centered over the main business section of the city but was up the valley about 2 miles. There were large industrial plants, hospitals, the medical school and partially built-up residential areas near the ground zero. The terrain in this area was uneven with large hills which shielded certain areas. Due to the shielding factor and the distance of the explosion from the center of the city, Nagasaki was less completely destroyed than Hiroshima and the panic was apparently less.

THE FATE OF MEDICAL FACILITIES

The fate of the hospitals in Hiroshima is particularly interesting in the light of this chaos and destruction. Many of the smaller hospitals and clinics were located in the center of the city and were of typical Japanese construction. For instance, the Shima Surgical Hospital was only 100 feet from ground zero. It was partly

brick but largely wooden construction. The blast blew it flat, and it is believed that all of the occupants were killed immediately. The remains of the building burned, and the spot is now a mass of flattened rubble. The Tada Hospital was partly reinforced concrete and partly wooden construction. Located at 2,600 feet from ground zero it was completely demolished, and the only remnants were the concrete foundation and the gutted and broken concrete portions of the building. The exact fate of its occupants could not be definitely determined but it is believed that they were all killed by the blast and succeeding fire. Another building of medical nature which was located near the center of the blast was the Japan Red Cross Office Building. It was only 740 feet from ground zero and was almost completely demolished. The windows, window casements, and doors were blown out and even the concrete structure was broken by the downward thrust of the blast. The building was then gutted by fire and all occupants perished. The Hiroshima Army Hospitals No. 1 and No. 2 were located within 1,500–2,000 feet of ground zero. It is reported that 80 percent of the personnel and all of the patients (500 in No. 1 and 650 in No. 2) were killed. The ultimate fate of the surviving 20 percent of the personnel is not known, but on the basis of other experiences at this distance it is probable that a large percentage of them died of injuries or radiation effects. The hospital buildings collapsed and burned. The Red Cross Hospital, which was the city's largest and best hospital, was located 4,860 feet from ground zero. The basic structure of the building, which is reinforced concrete, remained virtually intact. However, steel window casements were blown out or twisted and torn on the side near the blast and the interior was seriously damaged by falling plaster, broken partitions, and falling ceilings. There were 90 percent casualties of the occupants of this building and the damage was so great that the hospital ceased operation for several weeks after the bombing. It did, however, serve as a first-aid station and out-patient clinic in the interim. Practically all instruments and supplies in this hospital were completely destroyed or damaged beyond repair. The Hiroshima Communications Hospital was located at a similar distance from the ground zero, 4,900 feet. It, too, was of reinforced-concrete construction. Though the concrete framework of the building remained intact it suffered even more severe damage than did the Red Cross Hospital. Steel window casements were blown out, partitions blown down, and all of the contents were damaged beyond repair. It was later reoccupied as were most of the buildings which were left standing. An example of a hospital located at greater distance from ground zero is the Army-Navy Relief Hospital. It was 10,400 feet from the ground zero and sustained considerable damage. The building was stucco and two floors in height. Though it did not collapse, it was seriously damaged. Most of the tile roof was broken and blown off, window frames were broken and blown out, and in a few places walls were crushed. The principal injuries to the occupants of this hospital were due to flying glass and other missiles. Many smaller hospitals and clinics were destroyed in similar manner, depending upon their distance from the center of the blast. Since practically all of these buildings were of wooden construction they were either blown down and/or burned shortly thereafter. There was little evidence of their existence to one who came into the area later. It has been impossible to trace the fate of their occupants but it is felt that it coincided to some extent with the fate of other persons in Japanese-type homes at similar distances from ground zero. Actually the incidence of flash burns was probably lower, since few of them would have been outdoors, but the secondary injuries were probably higher. Inasmuch as they were already ill and many no doubt were helpless, the mortality rate surely exceeded that of the general population at comparable distances.

Thus it may be said of Hiroshima that essentially all of the civilian hospitals and 2 large Army hospitals were located within 5,000 feet of ground zero and were functionally completely destroyed. Those within 3,000 feet were totally destroyed and the mortality rate of the occupants was practically 100 percent. Two large hospitals of reinforced concrete construction were located 4,860 and 4,900 feet from the ground zero. The basic structures remained erect but there was such severe interior damage that neither was able to continue operation as a hospital. The casualty rate in these 2 hospitals was approximately 90 percent. Hospitals and clinics beyond 7,000–10,000 feet often remained standing but were badly damaged and there were many casualties due to flying glass and other missiles.

The destruction of hospitals in Nagasaki was even more outstanding than that in Hiroshima. Since the Nagasaki University Hospital contained over three-quarters of the hospital beds in the city it represented the bulk of the city's hospital facilities. The center of the hospital grounds was only 2,400 feet from ground zero and from a functional standpoint the hospital was completely obliterated. Most of the buildings were of reinforced-concrete construction but a great deal of wood was used in interior construction and fittings. The basic structure of all these buildings remained essentially intact but there was severe damage otherwise. The blast effects were very severe and almost every building was gutted by fire. The mortality rate of occupants of this hospital was at least 80 percent, two-thirds being killed outright. The Nagasaki Medical College was located even closer to ground zero, being only 1,700 feet distant. A large portion of the buildings were of inflammable nature but a few small buildings were constructed of reinforced concrete. The wooden buildings were blown down and subsequently consumed by flames. The concrete structures remained erect but were completely gutted by fire. Of the 850 medical students present 600 were killed and 12 of the 16 professors were also lost. The third- and fourth-year medical students escaped by virtue of the fact that they were elsewhere at the time of the bomb blast. Almost all of the other occupants of the buildings were killed outright. All medical equipment and supplies in the medical college buildings were completely destroyed by blast and fire. The Nagasaki Tuberculosis Sanatorium was located across the valley from the college and the hospital but was only 2,600 feet from ground zero. Since the buildings were all of wooden construction they were completely destroyed by blast and fire. It was reported that all of the patients and other occupants of the sanatorium were killed. Except the 2 hospitals mentioned above there were no others of any size located within Nagasaki, although there were many small private hospitals and clinics of typical Japanese construction, scattered throughout the city. The fate of these buildings and their occupants corresponded in general to that of buildings of similar construction at comparable distances from the bomb in Hiroshima. However, there was an additional factor of the hills shielding some structures in Nagasaki. In Hiroshima the effective zone was entirely flat and hills on the outskirts of the city were so distant that they did not interfere with the effects of the bomb to any appreciable extent. On the other hand, in Nagasaki many structures that would otherwise have suffered much more severe damage were partially or completely protected from the bomb effects by hills.

In summary, it may be said of the hospital facilities in Nagasaki that over 80 percent of the hospital beds and the Medical College were located within 3,000 feet of ground zero and were completely destroyed. Reinforced-concrete buildings within this range remained standing but were completely gutted by fire; buildings of wooden construction were completely destroyed by fire and blast; the mortality rate of occupants of this group of buildings was about 75–80 percent.

RESTORATION OF HOSPITALS AFTER BOMBING

An amazing feature of the atomic bombings to one going into the areas later was the poor recuperative powers of the population towards the restoration of all types of facilities. Though this was probably less so in the medical field than in others it was still alarmingly apparent. The panic of the people immediately after the bombing was so great that Hiroshima was literally deserted. It was apparently less true of Nagasaki and this was probably due to the fact that the city was less completely destroyed, but the same apathy was there. The colossal effects of the bombs and the surrender following shortly thereafter seemed to have completely stunned the people. The effects of the typhoons of September and early October may have contributed to this psychological reaction.

Since the most outstanding feature of the

atomic bombs was the high rate of human casualties, it was natural that this was the greatest problem in the areas following the bombing. But even in this regard the progress was astoundingly slow and haphazard. Other evidences of restoration were almost completely absent. For instance, at the time the Medical Division visited Hiroshima, 3 months after the bombing, the first street car was beginning operation, people wandered aimlessly about the ruins, and only a few shacks had been built as evidence of reoccupation of the city. No system for collection of night soil or garbage had been instituted. Leaking water pipes were seen all over the city with no evidence of any attention. It was reported that following the bombing several days were required for disposal of the dead and then they were simply piled into heaps and burned without attempts at identification or enumeration. Street cars were burned as a method of cremating the bodies within. All in all, there appeared to be no organization and no initiative.

The care of the wounded immediately after the bombing was essentially nil in Hiroshima. Beyond the sphere of family ties there seemed to be little concern for their fellow man. It is true that essentially all of the medical supplies were destroyed by the bombing, and that there were no hospitals and little with which to work. For the first 3 days there was no organized medical care. At the end of this time the Prefectural Health Department was successful in getting a portion of the surviving physicians together and to begin ministering to the wounded who remained in the city. Up until this time all nursing and medical care had been on an individual basis. The more seriously injured were placed in the few remaining public buildings on the outskirts of the city. Many of them died but many seriously burned cases remained. Small stocks of medical supplies which had been stored in caves outside the city were brought out but were soon exhausted. With all medical supplies gone and practically none being brought in the treatment of the injured seems to have consisted largely of offering a place of refuge. There is no doubt that many died who might have been saved by modern, competent medical care. As time elapsed many of the small hospitals and clinics were able to reopen and offer some help. Japanese medical authorities and other scientists visited the city in order to appraise the nature and extent of the damage but they did not contribute materially to the care of the sick and injured. Finally, medical teams consisting of medical students and physicians were sent into the area from the larger cities such as Tokyo, Osaka and Kyoto. They assisted materially in administering medical care but were handicapped by the overwhelming size of the task and the lack of supplies. The Red Cross Hospital was cleared of wreckage and finally reopened without any repair of the building. In many respects it was fortunate that such a large proportion of the injured fled to nearby towns and villages. Except for Kure which had been largely destroyed by incendiary bombing, the facilities in these areas were relatively intact.

Soon after American occupation forces entered the area some medical supplies were made available. A medical unit representing the Surgeon General of the United States Army was assigned to the project. The task of this unit was largely investigative in nature but they did assist the Japanese authorities in organizing and directing medical relief for the bomb victims. The American physicians did not treat any of the cases. In the first place they arrived so late (about 1 October) that deaths from radiation had practically ceased. Secondly, they did not have supplies and personnel to perform a thorough study of methods of treatment. Thirdly, it was apparently felt that investigation of the nature of the casualties was more important. And finally, with these facts in mind the Americans had a clear understanding with the Japanese that they would assume no responsibility for the treatment of cases but would merely consult with and advise the Japanese whenever necessary. In time a large rayon factory in Ujina and other buildings were taken over by the Japanese Government and utilized as hospitals. Some of the injured found their way to distant cities for treatment and other groups were officially transferred by the Japanese Government to medical centers in Osaka, Kyoto, and Tokyo for study and treatment.

Most of the fatalities due to flash burns and secondary injuries occurred within a few days after the bombing. The peak of deaths due to radiation effects was not reached until late August or the early part of September. Very few cases suffering from radiation died after 1 October and deaths due to other causes had practically ceased by this time. Thus during October the essential medical care was directed almost exclusively toward burn cases, most of which were flash burns. A large number were still in hospitals but the vast majority of these patients could be treated as out-patients. By 1 November adequate hospital space was available but it was still of emergency nature and medical supplies were inadequate. Many of the burns remained unhealed. Inadequate medical care, poor nutrition, and secondary infection were important factors in this delayed healing.

The effects of the atomic bombing of Nagasaki were very similar to those in Hiroshima. Even though it followed the bombing of Hiroshima by 3 days, wartime secrecy, general confusion and the short elapse of time did not allow the population of Nagasaki any particular advantage from the previous experience. The psychological reaction of the people was essentially the same and the chaos in the city seems to have been almost as great. A very important difference between the two cities was that Nagasaki was not so completely destroyed. Further, the bomb blast was centered over a more industrial area and the character of the buildings resulted in less extensive fires. But from the medical standpoint the bombing was particularly catastrophic because the bulk of the city's hospital facilities were located within a radius of 3,000 feet of the center of the explosion. The destruction of the University Hospital and the Medical College was so great that the buildings left standing could not be reoccupied even for emergency medical care. Other hospitals and clinics, including the Tuberculosis Sanatorium, had burned to a heap of ashes. The only remaining facilities were small private clinics and hospitals and many of them were seriously damaged. Essentially no organized medical care was carried out for several days after the bombing. The Shinkosen hospital was established in an old school building for the care of bomb victims, but it was woefully inadequate. At one time it harbored over 500 victims. Fortunately, there was a large medical depot at Omura, 20 miles away. Such large stocks of supplies were on hand here that Nagasaki did not suffer in this respect as did Hiroshima. Another school building was converted into an infectious disease hospital.

At the time the Allied Military Government entered Nagasaki, about 1 October, the population was found to be apathetic and profoundly lethargic. Even at this time the collection of garbage and night soil had not been reestablished, restoration of other public utilities was lacking and the hospital facilities were inadequate. Through the initiative of the Military Government, a system of reporting infectious diseases was instituted, the collection of garbage and night soil was reestablished, and attempts were made to increase the supply of safe water. A survey of the remaining hospitals and clinics at this time by Captain Horne of American Military Government revealed such obvious inadequacies that the survey was not even completed. A perusal of the incomplete report reveals that there were many small private hospitals remaining, most of which were damaged and without satisfactory potential value even if they were repaired. In the face of the inadequacy of the Shinkosen Hospital, and the absence of other facilities in Nagasaki, bomb victims were transferred to the Omura Naval Hospital where the conditions were much better. The Shinkosen Hospital has now been evacuated and abandoned.

When Nagasaki was visited by the Medical Division, about three months after the bombing, conditions were still very primitive. A visit to the Infectious Disease Hospital revealed that the school building in which it was located had been seriously damaged by bombing and no repairs had been made. The roof was partially destroyed, there were no window panes and the building was filthy. All of the patients, both male and female, were in adjacent beds in the same ward. Members of their families were present and were going in and out at will. The hospital had a capacity of 35 beds and contained 21 patients; 18 cases of dysentery and 3 cases of typhoid fever, at the time of the visit. There were no isolation precautions in practice. The only medicine and supplies were

those furnished by the Military Government. Because of these conditions the Military Government had taken over a Japanese Army hospital of 103 beds and 12 bassinets and was converting it for use as a Japanese civilian hospital. It was expected to be available very shortly thereafter. The Omura General Hospital (formerly a Naval hospital) was in excellent condition and was being used for the care of atomic bomb victims. Thus, it may be seen that by 1 November some semblance of medical care and sanitary procedures had been reestablished in Nagasaki but the facilities were still inadequate. The entire program had to be directed and forced by the Americans though they did not enter the area until nearly 2 months after the bombing.

The devastating effects of the atomic bombs upon medical facilities can be appreciated in the light of the foregoing presentation. Not only were the existing facilities almost completely destroyed but there was extreme apathy toward the restoration of hospitals and the care of the injured.

EFFECTS ON MEDICAL PERSONNEL

It was almost impossible to get any accurate information relative to the number of doctors, nurses and other medical personnel in the area prior to bombing, the number injured and killed, or even the number actually present at the time of the visit by the Medical Division. Data obtained from various sources showed extreme variation and were often unreliable. Naturally, the medical personnel in general met the same fate as others located at the same distances from the bomb. The number of casualties also probably bore a direct relationship to the fate of hospitals since medical personnel would be concentrated at those institutions and roughly in proportion to the size of the hospital or clinic.

The number of physicians in Hiroshima prior to the bombing has been variously estimated from 200 to 298. The former figure was supplied to the Medical Division by the Prefectural Health Officer and the latter figure was included in an address by the Prefectural Governor on 9 September 1945. The actual figures probably fall between these two extremes. Regardless of the total number it is known that the casualty rate among this group was very high. About 90 percent were casualties, and 60 of these physicians were killed. One month later only 30 physicians were able to perform their usual duties.

The Hiroshima Prefectural Medical College was started in the spring of 1945 and the first class had matriculated. As a result of the bombing the hospital was demolished and one member of the faculty was killed and another injured. The number of students killed and injured could not be determined.

Prior to the bombing there were 1,780 nurses in Hiroshima. Of these, 1,654 were killed or injured on 6 August. Consequently, the city suffered greatly because of the lack of nurses and many untrained volunteers had to be pressed into service in caring for the injured.

The experience in Nagasaki was very similar to that in Hiroshima. The exact number of physicians in the city prior to the bombing could not be determined but there were probably about 200–250 in 1944. This number may have decreased slightly in 1945 as a result of actual bombing and the effects of partial evacuation of the city in preparation for raids. Due to the different character of the two cities it would at first appear that the loss of medical personnel would have been proportionately less in Naga-saki. However, a factor which counterbalanced this fact to some extent was that the largest number and best of the medical personnel were concentrated in the medical school and the University Hospital, both of which were completely destroyed with a large percentage of their occupants. Actual investigation as of 1 November revealed that there were about 120 physicians in Nagasaki. So apparently the city did fare better than Hiroshima which had less than half that many physicians at about the same time.

The damage to the Nagasaki Medical College and University Hospital has already been described. Reports reveal that 600 of the 850 medical students were killed and some others may have died later. Of the survivors practically every one was injured and at least half had radiation sickness later. There were 16 of the 20 faculty members present at the time of the bombing and 12 of them were killed and the others injured.

The casualty rate among nurses in Nagasaki could not be accurately determined. There were 683 nurses in the city on 1 November but it is not known how many of those had come in after the bombing. The percentage of fatalities and injuries probably closely paralleled that of the physicians but no accurate figures are available to support this supposition. . . .

Barbara Ward

Barbara Ward (1914–   ) is a well-known English economist, lecturer and writer who is deeply concerned with the challenges to Western Civilization being made by the new nations emerging from the former colonial empires. In The Rich Nations and the Poor Nations she describes the historical forces which have brought about the impressive development of the West, and the reasons why comparable changes have not occurred in the backward nations. In reading the two chapters from this remarkable book note (1) the four revolutions which have most affected western life; (2) the influence of equality upon nationalism; (3) the historical roots of the revolutions in the West; (4) the extent of the wealth which these revolutions have created and their future potential; (5) the differences these revolutions have created between the West and the rest of the world; (6) the reasons given for Western complacency about this gap; (7) the attitude of the Communist bloc toward the problems of the backward nations as contrasted with that of the West; (8) the program outlined which the West might adopt to assist the developing nations; (9) the discussion of freedom and equality as factors in revolutions; and (10) the glorious message of the closing paragraphs.

From: THE RICH NATIONS AND THE POOR NATIONS

THE RICH NATIONS

I suppose we are all aware of the fact that we live in the most catastrophically revolutionary age that men have ever faced. Usually one thinks of a revolution as one event or at least as one interconnected series of events. But we are in fact living with ten or twenty such revolutions—all changing our ways of life, our ways of looking at things, changing everything out of recognition and changing it fast.

What I want to do here is to trace some of these revolutions in their effect on our environment and on the way we live. And since I cannot deal with all of them, I have chosen four which seem to me to weave their way in and out of our lives at every point.

Now, the first and perhaps the most perva-

sive of these revolutions begins in the field of ideas. This is hardly surprising since ideas are the prime movers of history. Revolutions usually begin with ideas and it is by our ideas that we change the way we live, the way we organize society, the way we manipulate material things. So let us begin with a revolutionary idea now at work from one end of the world to the other: the revolution of equality—equality of men and equality of nations. This is a bald statement. It cannot be treated exhaustively. There is simply not time to explore all the implications of man's equality with man. For one thing, no society yet knows fully what it means by such equality. Is it to be only a levelling? Does it imply indifference to excellence? Can it be combined with reasonable lines of command and control? And, since someone must rule, if all

Barbara Ward. *The Rich Nations and the Poor Nations* (New York: W. W. Norton and Company, Inc., 1962), **pp.** 13–36; 137–159. Reprinted with the permission of the author.

supposedly extraneous obstacles to equality were removed—birth, land, wealth, inheritance —would rule by brain and ability alone create a 'meritocracy,' a 'Mandarinate' of refined intelligence, finally more unequal than a system demanding less rigorous and inflexible methods of recruiting the governing group? These are all fascinating questions to pursue and many of them are strictly relevant to the great international questions of our day. For instance, the recruitment of leaders among the dispossessed in the name of equality is a great strength for Communism, since in all developing nations the dispossessed make up the vast majority. But there must be limits set to our discussion and here we are concerned primarily with equality as a force making for social, economic, and national change.

We know that men's passionate desire to see themselves as the equals of other human beings without distinctions of class or sex or race or nationhood is one of the driving forces of our day. And I believe it is a tap root of modern nationalism. I do not, of course, minimize the other roots of nationalism: the sense of community, the common tongue, the shared history. But when nations look out on the international arena, much of the strength of their nationalism comes from the sense that they are as good as their neighbours and ought to have the same rights; in other words, equality. The whole United Nations with its 'one state, one vote,' reflects this egalitarian nationalism and 'the right to self-determination,' the most cutting edge of nationalism as old empires dissolve, is in essence the new peoples' claim to national equality with the older states. For this reason, nationalism today comes to us in great measure in the form of equality—the equality of nations one with each other, the equality of esteem and prestige which comes from not being run by other nations. This is one of the great drives of our world. And when we discuss nationalism, I think it is legitimate to unite it with the idea of equality.

The second revolution also concerns ideas: the idea of progress, of the possibility of material change leading to a better world, not hereafter, but here and now. This worldliness, if you like, this emphasis on the goods and opportunities of this world, is another radical force at work in our world.

The third revolution is a biological revolution: the sudden vast increase in the rate at which the human race is multiplying upon the face of the earth.

The fourth and perhaps the most pervasive of all the revolutions of our day is the application of science and saving—or capital—to all the economic processes of our life. In fact, the application is much wider. We have begun to apply science and reason to nearly all our forms of living, to administration, to office management, to politics, to sociology, even to culture and to art.

These four revolutions—of equality, of this-worldliness, of rising birth-rates, and of driving scientific change—all started in the North Atlantic arena, in those nations which lie around the North Atlantic Ocean. Britain, Western Europe, and North America have, by working and expanding together, created a quite new kind of human society. A sort of mutation has occurred and we in the Atlantic area no longer share a continuous way of life with under-developed and emerging peoples, because in their societies none of the revolutions has been fully at work. They have had little idea of equality. There was in the past no great urge for general material progress. The pressure of population followed a strict rotation of famine and feast and had little of the explosive burst that we have seen in our day. Above all, traditional societies did very little saving and had virtually no science. By the same token, these changes which cut us off from all earlier forms of social organization have created in the Atlantic world what can only be called a new kind of human community.

I do not know whether one would say of this new society that it is demonstrably happier. Sometimes I think people wonder whether it can be said to be more civilized. But there is one thing which is absolutely certain. It is sensationally richer. What has happened around the North Atlantic is that a ring of societies has come into being with more wealth, more economic resources at its disposal, then has ever before been known in human history. This is the profoundly revolutionary change to which all the subsidiary re-volutions have contributed. And, since all na-tions have not yet come within the scope of this revolution, or rather this series of revolu-tions, and since all of them without exception desire to do so, the distinction between rich nations and poor nations is one of the great dominant political and international themes of our century.

How have these four revolutions, working together, produced the mutation of a quite new kind of society: the wealthy or affluent society? How is it that, remoulding the tradi-tional forms of social order, they have devel-oped a form of society so different from any that went before? Let us begin with the revo-lution of equality. It has its roots in two pro-found traditions of Western society: the Greek view of law and the Judeo-Christian vision of souls all equal in the sight of God. For the Greek, the essence of citizenship, what distinguished the *polis*—the city-state—from the barbarians outside, was that men lived in the Greek city according to laws which they themselves had helped to frame. This was not a full vision of equality; slaves and women were excluded. But the citizen enjoyed equality with his fellows before the law and the law was the final shield of his integrity and equality against the threat of tyranny; either the tyranny of a single leader or the possibly more dangerous threat of an arbitrary majority. Here in its first emergence in history could be found a definition of the 'rights of man' in terms of his rights against a dangerously sovereign government.

The other mood of equality is expressed in Christian metaphysics, in the vision of souls standing equal in the sight of God. During the Middle Ages, cathedral and church were the educators of the common man and a favourite theme in those days was the 'Doom,' or Last Judgment, carved above the portals of cathe-drals or painted on the humbler walls of parish churches. From these panoramas of bliss and misery men received with vivid emotional force the sense of human equality. Among those called to bliss would be the shepherd, the peasant, the woodman, the carpenter, while those descending with tortured faces to everlasting misery were all too often kings,

princes, dukes, and bishops as well. Here, expressed with the most dramatic sense of contrast, is the profound root of equality: the belief that souls are equal before God and that, therefore, their equality is innate, meta-physical, and independent of the vanities of class, race, or culture. Clearly, once you im-plant an idea as revolutionary as this in the soil of society, you can have no conception of the luxuriance and diversity of the growth that may follow. And one consequence in our Western civilization is especially worth exa-mining. It is the emergence to a dominant position in society of men and groups who have never achieved a political 'break-through' in any other civilization.

Since the beginning of history, you can say in shorthand that the dominant rulers have been the kings and the priests. They were flanked by the warriors, and often, as in the early Middle Ages in Europe, warriors were rewarded for their services with fiefs of land. Or, as in India, land revenue was allotted to court officials and advisers as a source of in-come. Thus the political leadership of the community came to be monopolized by the court and by landed men. In such societies —and most traditional societies resemble this pattern—the merchant was of necessity a marginal figure. To this day, in parts of Latin America and Asia, this old, more or less feudal pattern persists. But as the Middle Ages un-folded in Europe a different picture began to appear. Owing to the division of power be-tween Pope and Emperor at the head of so-ciety, the possibility of a plurality of powers opened up for the whole social order. Sub-sidiary groups—nations, cities, communes, corporations—grasped the power needed for their operations, defined it in terms of law, and defended it in the name of equal rights. In such a society the merchant was able to exercise real power and to enjoy real security for his work, his trade, and his savings. The charters given to cities defined his rights of self-government and, as early as the fourteenth century, the sov-ereign called him into consultation—through parliament—before trying to tax his wealth for national purposes.

These developments gave the cities with their merchants and bankers and rising middle classes an independence they enjoyed no-where else. There was never any figure in Delhi or Canton who had the status, influence, and rights, of the Lord Mayor of London or the Burgomaster of Ghent. And without the self-confidence and security of the merchant class the later evolution of capitalist society would have been inconceivable.

But of course the leaven of equality did not cease to operate once it had raised the middle classes to effective influence. It worked right on through the rest of society and it works on to this day. In England's Civil War it was John Lilburne, a soldier on the more extreme wing in Cromwell's Army, who gave classic expression to the drive which would dominate politics for the next four hundred years. 'The poorest he that is in England has a life to live as the richest he.' This was Lilburne's phrase and ever since it has been the motive power of revolutions beyond number. It underlies the growth of socialism, the cutting edge of trade union organization, the emancipation of the workers in the wake of the middle classes, the whole concept of the modern welfare state. We do not see the end of the process for, as I suggested earlier, we do not know what the ultimate stage of equality may be. Is it level equalness? Is it equal chance and opportunity? Is it conceivably a society ruled by love, not force?

We do not know. But we *do* know that the leaven of equality has worked through every stratum of our society, emancipating new classes and letting loose new political forces onto the great stage of history. Now we have to ask the question: What in the main have these new classes asked for in claiming their emancipation? At this point we meet the second of our revolutionary ideas: the idea of what one might call this-worldliness, of immense interest in *this* world, in its processes, in its laws and construction, in the ways in which it can be set to work and made over according to human ends and purposes—in a word, the world as an arena of work and effort where needs and dreams can be satisfied.

These ideas spring essentially from our triple inheritance: Greek thought, Judaism, and Christianity. It was in the Greek vision of law that science acquired its fundamental confi-dence in a material universe predictable and orderly enough to be explored. From the Judeo-Christian religious inheritance came the idea that the whole of creation is God's work, and as such must be of immense interest and value. 'Call thou no thing unclean' was the divine instruction to Peter and, in spite of the temptations of religious pessimism, Christianity has never dismissed as 'illusion' what comes from the hand of God. Other societies have lacked this essential insight into the value of created things. In Hindu culture, for instance, the world is *Maya*, illusion, a fevered dance of fleeting appearances which mask the pure reality of uncreated being.

But perhaps the sharpest break in Western tradition from the basic ideas of other civilizations lies in its vision of reality as an unfolding drama, as an immense dialogue between God and man crowned at some inconceivable end in an outcome of fulfilment and bliss. All archaic societies feel themselves bound to a 'melancholy wheel' of endless recurrence. Seasons, the life cycle, planetary order, all revealed the return of things to their origins, and life swung round in the orbit fixed by destiny. Marcus Aurelius, wisest of Roman emperors, believed that at forty a man had experienced all there was to experience. No vision of reality as progressing forward to new possibilities, no sense of the future as better and fuller than the present, tempered the underlying fatalism of ancient civilization. It is only in the Jewish and Christian faith that a Messianic hope first breaks upon mankind. In Christianity, the hope is expressed in religious terms of deliverance and salvation. But over the centuries the idea became transmuted into this-worldly terms, in fact into the dominant idea of progress, of getting forward, of being able to see hope ahead, and of working for a better future, not hereafter, but here and now.

Now let us examine the effect of this respect for material things, coupled with a Messianic hope of the future, upon one aspect of Western society—upon its economic system. As the Middle Ages ended and the merchants felt their status and their opportunities increase, they found in the Christian tradition those elements which best suited their outlook and condition. Opposing the luxuries of the courts and the loudly alleged idleness of monastic living, they preached a gospel of work, praising the religious value of what men did in the counting house, in the workshop, in farm and field, and looking forward to the coming of the Kingdom in terms of work, effort, and material success. No one can doubt that, as a result, an immense charge of energy was added to the urge to work and produce at the beginning of the capitalist era.

But there were still limits to the merchant's materialism. As workers, they stood out against an idle and luxurious world. To acquire wealth was one thing; to spend it in riotous living quite another. So, instead, they accumulated capital and set it working further. This restraint was one of the roots of saving on a large scale without which sufficient capital might never have been accumulated for the modern economic system. Work, austerity, and an increasingly secularized version of the Messianic hope were thus the ferments of a new society, the portents of a revolutionary age when the desire for better things and 'the revolution of rising expectations'—to use Mr. Adlai Stevenson's phrase—would engulf the whole world.

Before we leave these mutations in the Western idea, we should also examine the extent to which equality and material progress have enlarged the concept of the nation. Undoubtedly today the main drives behind the idea of nationhood, especially in the emergent territories, are equality and material progress. Nevertheless nationalism as such is so deeply rooted in human affairs that we must make a brief detour to examine it in its own terms. It begins with the tribe. The tribe is the oldest of human associations, a total community bound by links of kinship and blood, all too often propelled into action by the sense of having competing interests with other tribes, which it fights for hunting fields and grazing areas and, when conflict becomes insoluble, involves in tragic wars of extermination.

In large parts of Africa, this original organization of mankind remains and, as the collapse of the Congo has shown, easily reverts to violence and destruction. But in other continents wider forms of political organization have developed. We move on from the tribe to congeries of tribes and to the union of different tribes under conquering dynasties or empires. In these wider states the sense of blood kinship is lessened. Wars of imperial conquest take the place of wars of tribal extermination. Professional armies arise in place of a people armed *en masse*. In large parts of Asia and for long years under the Roman Empire in Europe, wars changed the leadership of the state and the distribution of power, but the life of the peasants and villages and country towns continued with relatively little disturbance. Throughout northern India, for instance, after the collapse of organized imperial rule, Rajput princes fought each other continuously while the villagers took virtually no part in the wars.

This relative discontinuity between rulers and ruled began to end when, towards the end of the Middle Ages, a new sense of blood brotherhood and cohesion was restored to the political community in Western Europe. At that time Europe began to reacquire an almost tribal sense of the state. It had been dynastic. The Plantagenets, the Capets, were symbols and leaders of their peoples but, owing to the coincidence of language and frontiers in Western Europe, people began to discover again a sense of kinship based upon what they came to feel was almost common blood, an organic family unity. So the nation-state has in it some element of the tribe, operating at a more elaborate and a more organized level.

Now this almost tribal concept of the nation had extremely important effects both in the development of the modern economy and in the development of the West's relations with the rest of the world. Modern capitalist society needs a certain scale of market if it is to gain anything from the division of labour and the diversification of work and product. The nation-state provided a framework cohesive enough to act as an enlarged market. Merchants felt that they had a common unit in which to work. They moved on from the highly restricted market of the village, the estate, or the river valley to the larger market of the nations. And they moved on with all the more vigour and all the more drive because they were competing with other nations who were developing their own markets in the same sense: British merchants competing with French merchants, French with Dutch, Dutch with Portuguese, and so forth. The nation defined the market and then, reciprocally, the interests of the market helped to underline the exclusiveness of nationhood.

The effect was not limited to Western Europe. Out of the intense rivalry came the great thrust which led to the colonial control of most of the world by these same Western nations. Arabs, after all, had been out trading in Asia for generations before the Westerners arrived. But the trade was peaceful and did not impinge much on local politics. What the Westerners brought with them was a fierce competitive determination to cut other nations off from the profits of the new oriental trade. This led to the struggle for the control of the seas. And, if one follows the process closely in such areas as Indonesia or India, one can see how the determination of the Dutch to throw everybody else out, or the determination of the British not to allow the French to maintain a foothold, afterwards led to the kind of jockeying and maneuvering and backing of local rulers that, little by little, brought about the extension of Western colonial control to the whole area.

At this point it should be easier to understand why modern nationalism has such deep roots in the ideas of equality and material progress. The Western traders-turned-rulers in Asia took their fierce exclusive nationalism into societies still loosely united as dynastic or imperial states. There they settled down to make money, to trade, to build up export industries, and to set in motion some of the economic processes which underpin the modern economy. They carried with them a concern for progress, for material well-being, for this worldliness, all unknown in Eastern lands. They began to spur local peoples to think in this same sense.

At the same time, they created a nationalist reaction against their own nationalist pretensions. By ruling other groups in the name of their own national interests, they taught these groups to see themselves as nations and to claim equality for their own rights. There was no 'nationalism' in India until Britain aroused it by teaching Indians the ideals of nationhood and at the same time denying them the rights of national self-determination. Material progress and equality have been the great spurs to nationalism throughout the colonial world, and the reason is simply that it was in the mood of national self-assertion and economic advantage that Westerners established and maintained their rule.

Now let us turn to the third of the revolutions that have created the metamorphosis of Western society. From the eighteenth century onwards new medical sciences and steady advances in public sanitation, coupled with the crowding of more and more people into the new cities, lengthened life and set in process an explosion of the birth-rate. In the West, on the whole, this explosion has proved a boost to growth, a boost to wealth, a boost to economic development. The reason is, in the main, that the creation and expansion of the modern economic system came into being while the explosion of population was still in its early stages. In fact, as population grew the economy could grow with it. There was a time in the eighteenth century when it looked as though a shortage of manpower would set a definite limit to the growth of economy. In nineteenth-century America massive immigration was one of the great spurs to economic growth. In the nineteen-twenties and -thirties, the Depression coincided, earlier in Britain and later in America, with a considerable falling off in the birth-rate. Today, once again, it seems certain that some aspects of American growth are greatly stimulated by its spurt in population. So, on the whole, economic growth and growth in population have gone together in the West. That they have not done so in the East is one of the world's great problems. But in the West the dilemma of population outstripping resources has not occurred. On the contrary, an expanding manpower, absorbed into an expanding economic system, has provided labour for the production of goods and a consumers' market for their sale.

Now we come to the last of our revolutions, the most pervasive of all, that of capital and science, and the application of both to our economic processes.

Now, capital is saving; and saving means

not consuming. But there is no point in delay-ing or cutting back consumption unless, at some point, the saving made will result in more consumption later on. For example, it takes more effort, time, and input to produce a better seed or to develop a better plough. But in the end you are rewarded with a better harvest; in other words, consumption can go up as a result of the extra effort.

The trouble with traditional society is quite simply this: man's knowledge of how material things behave is still very limited. He has not yet developed the habits and tools of science and experiment to explore all the ways in which matter can be changed and manipu-lated. There are few ways known of making better seeds; not very much has been tried in the way of constructing better ploughs; better ploughs have to wait on more refined tech-niques for dealing with iron ore; and experi-ments with iron ore have in turn to wait on finding a substitute for charcoal. In short, the heat of wood, the energy of wind and water, the speed of a horse, the skill of the hand still represent the outer limits of a very restricted technology,

The great change that occurred in the eighteenth century was above all an enormous expansion in the techniques and technologies to which savings could be devoted. This change came about because of the revolution-ary change we have already discussed: the West's steadily increasing interest in material things, in this worldliness, and in the purpos-ive exploration of physical reality.

We take this attitude so entirely for granted that it is easy to forget how recent it is and how entirely its origins lie in our Western society. The scientific spirit, drawing on the Greek sense of law and the Judeo-Christian respect for the handiwork of God, is perhaps the most profoundly distinguishing feature of our civilization. Science could hardly arise in Hindu society since one does not devote a lifetime to exploring an illusion. It did not arise in China, for in spite of orderly govern-ment, rational rule, and intense intellectual in-terest stretching back through millennia into the past, the dominant Confucian class turned its back on science and preferred instead the consideration of human relations and urbane life.

But in the West, the aftermath of the Wars of Religion was to turn educated opinion to the examination of material things in which, it was hoped, the clash of dogma could be left behind. As a result, in the seventeenth and eighteenth centuries, all over Western Eu-rope, especially in Britain, the inventors and experimenters set to work to explore matter and improve technology. They revolutionized the use of iron. They transformed textile ma-chinery. They invented the steam engine. The age of the railways and the factory system opened up ahead.

An emancipated and self-confident mer-chant class, with a strongly developed credit system, had savings to pour into these new technologies. They were joined by enlight-ened gentleman farmers and by sturdy self-reliant artisans, all ready to experiment and back the experiments with their own—and other people's—savings. This combination of new technology and expanded saving made possible great increases in productivity. Much more could be produced by each pair of hands in each working hour. The surplus could be reinvested in further expansion. This process depended on keeping general consumption low. The mass of workers did not at first profit from the new system. Herded into the towns, ignorant, unorganized, they contributed the massive new saving by working for wages which were much lower than their true pro-ductivity. But the savings were made by en-trepreneurs who invested them to expand the whole scale of the economy.

Out of this massive 'primitive accumulation' came what one might call a 'break-through' to a new type of economy where, with fresh capital applied to all the processes of produc-tion, the expansion of each helped the expan-sion of all with a sort of internal momentum which finally put the economy into orbit as the new type of advanced, capitalized, industrial-ized, technological society that we see around us in the West today.

These then, are the four revolutions that have transformed traditional society to give us the modern world. It is above all in the North Atlantic community that all of them have in fact started, grown, interacted upon each other, and come together to create a quite new kind of society. First, the 'break-through' came in Britain. Then it followed in countries resembling Britain in basic social pre-conditions: the dominance of the merchant class, the relative openness of society, the pressure upwards of new social groups—merchants, workers, and farmers—and the basic attitudes of scientific interest and material ambition. Especially in empty lands settled by Europeans overseas, and above all in the United States, there occurred a mutual flow of capital, a mutual interdependence of trade which meant that all these lands helped to draw each other up the spiral of expanding production: Britain sparking growth in Europe; British and European investment spurring expansion in the United States. As early as the 1870s, the North Atlantic countries were providing over sixty percent of the foreign capital loaned in these areas and were together engrossing something like seventy percent of world trade.

The degree to which this interdependence stimulated the expansion of new wealth can, I think, be shown perhaps better by our failures than by our successes. This Atlantic society can still be wealthier than any known to man, in spite of the fact that it has contrived in the seventy to a hundred years of its interdependence to fight two wars of such appalling, such drastic, such monstrous destruction that one might have conceived that no people on earth could have recovered their wealth after such an outpouring of waste and carnage. But no; this interdependent community, even interdependent when fighting within itself, has been able to drag itself out of these holocausts and to achieve levels of wealth and well-being even greater than anything that went before. This, I think, is the most startling measure of the effectiveness of the new methods of science, the new methods of technology, the whole new field of saving applied to the production of wealth.

Nor is the story finished. On the contrary; at the present moment this group of wealthy countries—Great Britain, the white Dominions of the British Commonwealth, the United States, and Western Europe—represent a capacity, not only for present wealth but for future wealth of which we really have no very clear sense. Changes in technology are becoming more frequent and drastic. New frontiers

open up in energy, in chemicals, in ever wider applications of science to production. Above all, we do not produce at full stretch. The scale of our reserves is illustrated by the fact that we only put our productive machine fully to work when, in war, we are all vowed to destruction. Our most productive periods are those in which we are destroying most fully what we make. And from this folly, we are not yet released, owing to the fabulous weight of our armament programs.

So this enormously wealthy community of nations is growing wealthier and could grow wealthier still. But at the same time it is not now having a comparable effect on the rest of the world. In the nineteenth century, a portion of the capital that went out in search of profits from this growing wealthy community did go out to the colonies, to India, to the Far East, to Latin America; and part of the growth of the Atlantic world was in some measure sparked by buying the raw materials of less developed countries overseas. But in the twentieth century, this kind of interdependence between an industrial centre and the producers of raw materials on the fringe has tended to weaken. In the last twenty or thirty years, the West has grown much more rapidly in internal production than it has in its need for imports. We are no longer, in the hopeful nineteenth-century sense, necessarily dragging up the rest of the world in our wake. The automatic stimulus we give to growth overseas is now much less than it was even seventy years ago; and this is because of a very profound change in our industrial processes. We apply science so much more freely through changed technology that the art of the substitute has come to a quite new effectiveness. Very often the imported raw materials on which we used to depend can now be produced within our own frontiers. One thinks of artificial rubber, new fabrics for textiles, petro-chemicals, conceivably even *ersatz* chocolate. And so we no longer automatically exercise the same pull of development on the outside world as we did in our early days of growth and wealth. We have been filling the gap with extraordinary economic assistance. But we do not look on this 'job' as a settled commitment. It is still a precarious expedient; and in any case it is too small.

Then there is another big change which alters the relationship. It is quite simply that the West has completed its 'break-through' to modernization and the emergent countries have not. Above all, they have not completed the first, hard, even merciless, phase of early saving.

To begin the whole process of saving is a massive task. A sort of momentum has to be achieved. All parts of the economy have to be affected if the economic pattern as a whole is to change. A little modification here, a little development there, may transform parts of the economy, but it is only when the flood of change begins to run right through society that you get that actual 'break-through' to a new type of productive economy which has occurred in the West. But naturally, this 'break-through' occurring in a traditional society, demands an immense amount of capital. You have to begin to modify almost everything; education, farming, transport, power, industry—all have to change. This means that capital is required not in little amounts, but on a massive scale. And yet society, being under-developed, is still too poor for savings on such a scale. This is the paradox of the phase which Marx called 'primitive accumulation'—the first great effort of saving which has to be achieved if the new momentum is to begin. The Western colonial impact on the rest of the world did not create such a momentum. It created partial modernization: the beginnings of modern education and industry, some cash farming directed to export markets, some ports, some transport, some beginnings of modern administration. But all this did not amount to the full momentum of sustained growth.

The result is that the gap between those Western lands that are already 'in orbit' in their economic life, and those that are not yet off the ground, is tending at the moment to grow wider, not narrower. We in the West have long completed our first phase of primitive accumulation; we have a machine in being to use for further expansion; and, incidentally, we contrived to acquire that machine while our population was still at a relatively low level. Now that we are 'in orbit,' our own wealth can multiply by compound interest because we are already wealthy. This,

after all, is a cycle we recognize very well in family life. It is very much easier for a rich man to invest and grow richer than for the poor man to begin investing at all. And this is also true of nations. Nations that are not yet through the 'sound barrier' of saving are tending to get poorer with the added complication that their populations are meanwhile going steadily up.

So our world today is dominated by a complex and tragic division. One part of mankind has undergone the revolutions of modernization and has emerged on the other side to a pattern of great and increasing wealth. But most of the rest of mankind has yet to achieve any of the revolutions; they are caught off balance before the great movement of economic and social momentum can be launched. Their old traditional world is dying. The new radical world is not yet born. This being so, the gap between the rich and the poor has become inevitably the most tragic and urgent problem of our day. . . .

NOT BY BREAD ALONE

All the great revolutions of our contemporary world had their origin round the North Atlantic. The revolution by which equality has become a driving force in political life, the new concern with material things, the absorption in scientific analysis, the spurt of growth in the world's population, the whole transformation of our economic system by the application of technology and capital: all these vast changes were launched in the North Atlantic arena. Yet if you look at these Atlantic nations today they make the strange impression of not being particularly concerned with the revolutions they have wrought. The changes have been unleashed on mankind. Blindly, blunderingly, with immense impact and immense confusion, they are remarking the face of the earth. But can one say that the Western powers follow their course with any intimate concern? Do they see them as direct projections of the Western way of life or accept responsibility for the fact that it was the Western colonial system that chiefly set in motion the present world-wide movement of revolutionary change?

Is it not strange to care so little for what we

have launched; to lose interest in our inventions just when they are beginning to have their maximum impact? And if one asks why we behave in this way, I suppose some of the answers are not entirely comfortable. It seems to be a law of life that when you become rich you tend to become complacent. What is the Biblical phrase? 'They sat down to eat and they rose up to play.' Since the post-war economic revival in the West, the feeling has become fairly general that things are not going too badly. Elections have been fought on the slogan: 'You never had it so good'; great nations have been lulled with the promise of 'peace and prosperity.' The once militant working class substitutes 'I'm all right, Jack' for 'workers of the world, unite.' This mood of ease and complacency inevitably limits our ability to understand the needs and hungers of the millions who have not yet found their way into the modern world. To be rich and be complacent invites the nemesis of such a condition—which is by indifference and by a narrowing of the heart to lose contact with the urgent desires of the great mass of one's fellow men. This constriction of pity can happen to individual men and women. History has always shown it. Today perhaps we see a new phenomenon: rich communities succumbing to the same limitation of human understanding.

But there is another more subtle reason that helps to explain why we are not as interested as we might be in all the revolutions we have launched. We simply cannot, out of our own experience, measure their truly daunting difficulties. All of them happened in the Western world under the conditions of maximum convenience. The West was relatively underpopulated; it was immensely well endowed with the resources that are needed for the new kind of economy. Iron ore and coal were plentiful for the launching of industry. The great plains of North America and Southern Russia quickly began to pour out food for the new industrial millions.

But perhaps the chief reason for our overconfidence is to be found in the mechanism by which, in the main, the Western breakthrough to sustained growth was accomplished. In the critical early stages of change, the profit motive proved to be an immensely powerful engine of growth. Its success implanted deeply in the minds of many of us the idea that the greatest good of the greatest number can be achieved provided each individual or company or even nation vigorously pursues its own self-interest. The strength of the case lies in the fact that, up to a point and under certain conditions, the premise may well be right. Competition in a free market has produced enormous gains in wealth and efficiency. In fact, we are living today through another such burst of growth as the tariff barriers go down inside the Common Market. But equally the conditions in Western Europe between the wars showed that if each nation pursued its own self-interest by a wrong route —in this case by constantly increasing its protective tariffs—the end result was not the good of all but the ruin of each. Nor has the Common Market come about by the unguided pressure of local interests. On the contrary, it has been an act of high statesmanship, pursued by dedicated political leaders and purposefully formulated by planners associated with M. Jean Monnet—surely one of the most quietly and effectively revolutionary groups the world has ever known.

In other words, there are conditions in which the unchecked pursuit of self-interest is an excellent guide to socially desirable action. There are also conditions when it is not. But the West still has a certain bias towards believing in its general efficacy, without regard to the framework within which it is to act. We tend to have a Micawberish attitude towards life, a feeling that so long as we do not get too excited something is certain to turn up. Yet if we look back over history I do not think the experience of other generations teaches us precisely this lesson. On the contrary, it suggests that not the Micawbers, but those who will, and want, and work, are more likely to see their plans and visions realized. It is, therefore, a disturbing reflection that in our own day the amount of effort, interest, preparation, and sheer slogging hard work which the Communists tend to put into the task of building *their* version of world order very greatly exceeds what we are ready to do or the sacrifices we are prepared to make. Even more obviously, their vision of a world brotherhood made one by Communism outstrips the scale of our imagination. The West thinks only marginally in terms of the whole world, the whole family of man. Each group tends to concentrate on its own parochial interests. There is apparently no energy comparable to the world-wide ambitions that set the Communists to work from one end of our planet to the other.

If we are to face the vast gap between the rich nations and the poor, between the nations round the Atlantic area which have been through their modernizing revolutions and the searching nations all around the world who seek desperately to make the same transition, perhaps the first decision we have to make is to abandon the fallacy that, somewhere, somehow, everything is going to turn out all right. We have to be ready to be as foresighted, as determined, as ready to work and to go on working, as are our busy Communist comrades. We must be prepared to match them, policy for policy, vision for vision, ideal for ideal.

I must confess that I can see no inherent reason why such a re-dedication of ourselves to great tasks should be impossible. We have the resources available; we have more resources at our disposal than any group of nations in the history of man. And it is hard to believe that we have run out of the moral energy needed to make the change. Looking at our society I certainly do not feel that it already presents such an image of the good life that we can afford to say that we have contributed all that we can to the vision of a transfigured humanity. Our uncontrollably sprawling cities, our shapeless suburbia, our trivial pursuits—quiz shows, TV, the golf games—hardly add up to the final end of man. We can do better than this. We also have the means to do better. If we do not feel the need there is only one explanation. We no longer have the vital imagination for the task.

Let us suppose, however, that we slough off our innate complacency. What ought we to try to do? What should be our aim in the challenging testing-period that lies ahead when the aspirations of the poor nations are going to become more and more urgent? For let us have no doubt about this. So far we have been living through the more comfortable phase of transformation in the under-developed areas;

we have seen them during a time when their concentrated effort to get rid of colonialism gave them political unity and a sense of national purpose which they may well lack now that independence is achieved. Now that they are running their own affairs, all the grim problems of life face them in the raw: their bounding birth-rates, their lack of capital, their desperate poverty, and, above all, the rising expectations of their own people. Every leader who has led his nation to the overthrow of Western influence or colonial rule is now faced with the stark problem: 'What next?' Whether he is a Nasser in Egypt, a Kasim in Iraq, an Azikiwe in Nigeria, a Nkrumah in Ghana, or even—in a more hopeful setting—a Nehru in India, he still must answer the question. There are no evasions now, no blaming it on the West—though that temptation continues—no looking for outside scapegoats. So, by a paradox, the post-colonial period is more tense, dangerous, and uncertain than the colonial struggle itself.

What can we do? What sort of policies can help the developing nations in the crucial years that lie ahead? And if I give you something of a shorthand answer, it is because we have already discussed a number of the crucial changes that must be made. Let us be clear first of all over the general aim. During the next twenty to thirty years we hope to see a majority of the developing nations pass through the sound-barrier of sustained growth. Moreover, we want these societies to have political elbow-room with a measure of autonomy for different groups and political power organized on a plural basis. We do not specify institutions or ideologies; but we hope for open societies in an open world. How shall we set about it?

The first point to make is that some general strategy is needed. And strategy is inseparable from a sustained effort through time. The rhythm of growth is not the rhythm of annual budgets and appropriations. Unless the Western nations bring themselves to accept the need for five- and ten-year programs, they will even waste what they do spend, for it will not be geared into a genuine strategy of growth.

The next point is that the scale of aid must be adequate. Patchy development, a little here, a little there, does not lead to sustained growth. In every developing economy, there comes a time when, for perhaps two decades, a 'big push' is needed to get the economy off the launching-pad and into orbit.

Not all nations come to that point at the same time. There seems to be a certain pattern of progress and expansion, and different economies are ranged at different points along the line. First there is a phase that one might call the 'pre-investment' phase. Nearly everything needed for a 'big push' in investment is still lacking. Educated people are not available, training is minimal, capital overheads or infra-structure—power, transport, harbours, housing—have still to be built. At this stage, the country must be prepared for a later plunge into investment and help with education and training, investment in infra-structure, surveys of resources, and some preliminary planning, are the great needs.

But at the next stage—where such countries as India or Brazil or Mexico now stand—the big investments begin to pay off. The ground is laid, rapid growth can be secured. It is at this point that large-scale capital aid from abroad can offset local poverty and lack of capital, thereby sparing governments the cruel choice of using totalitarian methods to compel people to save. Of all the countries at this stage of growth, I would say that India is the most important. The framework of a functioning economy is already built. But its ambitious capital plans are gravely endangered by a critical shortage of foreign exchange. In any Western development-strategy for the next decade, I myself would hope to see something like a billion dollars a year reserved for India's foreign exchange bill. If India can achieve its break-through, it is not only a question of India's preparedness. Nearly half the people living in the under-developed areas will be on their way to the modern world. If one adds Pakistan, more than half the problem of under-development could be met there in the Indian subcontinent.

Given that we accept the philosophy of a 'big push' in aid and investment, once the pre-conditions of growth have been realized, where should the capital be directed? It is quite impossible to define a general strategy since each country varies so much in its capacities, in its endowment of resources, in the scale of its internal market, and its export prospects. But perhaps one or two general points are worth making here. The first is that investment in education must continue to receive strong emphasis. Recent studies suggest that between sixty and fifty per cent of the gains in productivity made in the West in the last half-century spring from better trained minds, from more research, and more systematic use of the economy's brain-power. At present, most of the developing economies are only in the very first stages of the needed advance in education. Africa is strewn with societies where not more than ten per cent of the people are literate, where perhaps only one per cent ever reach secondary levels of schooling. The final tragic consequence of these standards can be seen in the Congo which became independent with perhaps not more than a dozen people with university degrees. No modern economy can be built on this basis.

A second critical area is that of farming. Modernized agriculture is, as we have seen, indispensable to the creation of general momentum in the economy. There are two separate needs: to encourage the structural changes which modern agriculture demands—the land reforms, the consolidation of holdings, the building of an influential co-operative movement; and to ensure a sufficient flow of capital into farming. The great variety of modern techniques, new fertilizers, new seed, new methods in planting and tilling, are nearly all costly. So is the scale of credit needed to launch a successful cooperative system. So last of all are the agricultural extension systems without which the farmer cannot learn what new opportunities are open to him. In the past, agriculture has been all too often the last on the government's priority list. Modern experience suggests it should be moved to the top.

The third area of expansion—industry—shows such universal variety that most generalizations have little value. However, one or two comments have some validity. One can say that industrialization will proceed more rapidly if a mistaken sense of national prestige does not precipitate large and costly mistakes in planning, such as investing in an integrated steel-works where there is neither iron ore nor coking-coal. Programs will lead to a better use of resources if capital is recognized for what it is in all developing economies: extremely scarce. Its price should be high, even if this idea upsets the more usual concept that basic services should be kept cheap in order to stimulate growth.

Another aspect of the same problem is that since foreign exchange is the scarcest of all forms of capital, it may be necessary, by high import duties or by auctioning import licences, or by other measures, to ensure that the entrepreneur who gets his hands on foreign exchange pays for its full value. This approach may contradict another tendency—to overvalue a developing nation's currency so that its exports will buy a maximum amount of foreign supplies. But, then, the way to development is, as Professor Benjamin Higgins once remarked, 'paved with vicious circles.'

A developing government should aim its policies at ensuring the quickest rate of capital accumulation. Profits should be strongly encouraged, in public as in private enterprise, and tax-systems arranged so that all the incentives are towards their reinvestment. This again does not always arouse much enthusiasm among planners brought up to believe in the inherent immorality of profits and ready to run essential public services on a 'no profit, no loss' basis. But profits are one of the chief means by which resources can be put at the disposal of the investors in society and, as we have seen, are a major source of investment in Soviet Russia.

When it comes to the actual content of industrial policy, it must fit local conditions. Most countries can begin to produce locally some of the goods they import, provided protection is given. The 'beer, boots, and bricks' stage of consumer industry only awaits a determined government and some local entrepreneurial talent. But large-scale industry depends upon the availability of crucial raw materials. And it depends, too, upon the scale of the internal market. Five large steel-plants in India, where over four hundred million people make up the market and where iron ore and coking-coal are available, make per-

fect sense. East Europe's proliferation of steel-mills after 1948 did not. Clearly, developing governments would be well advised to look round and see whether by customs unions or common markets with their neighbours they may not increase the size and efficiency of their industrial units without risk of over-production.

To all these changes—in education, in farming, in industry—there are more than economic consequences. Investment in men, investment in new techniques, investment in new forms of activity, all widen and strengthen the managerial and professional class and increase the training and scope of the manual worker. That gradual extension of the middle class to cover more and more of the nation's citizens is set in motion. With it goes a brighter hope of rational politics and civil rights.

These, then, are some of the elements in a broad strategy of modernization. But I think we have to realize that we in the Western world are not now organized to accomplish anything of the kind. It may be true that for nearly a hundred years we have been a kind of inter-connected economy, taking some seventy per cent of each other's foreign investment, engrossing nearly seventy per cent of world trade, and affecting each other radically by the shifts and changes in our economic policy. But here Mr. Micawber has reigned; here, above all, we have assumed that if everybody pursues his own national interest to the limit, the outcome will somehow be to the advantage of everybody else. But this is very far from being generally true. Everyone's decision in 1929—as the recession deepened —to cut imports and push exports reduced world trade by three-quarters in nine months. The recession itself had been in some measure sparked by the fact that between 1925 and 1929 Britain did not dare reflate its economy for fear of losing its foreign reserves and America dared not deflate its wild boom for fear of attracting even more of the world's gold. Now if we think that this unreconciled opposite pull between domestic and foreign interest is a thing of the past, let us remember that all through 1960 we saw comparable pressures between the German mark and the dollar. In short, we have not yet worked out the policies and institutions needed to overcome the conflicting interests in our interdependent Atlantic world. In fact, only once did we have such a policy: during the Marshall Plan when for a time, owing to America's generosity and leadership, the nations of the Atlantic area walked in step towards common goals.

Today, I believe we have to revive the Marshall spirit if we are to have any hope of dealing—and dealing in time—with the problem of our obligations to the underdeveloped areas. Once again, I can suggest only in short-hand terms some of the policies we should undertake if we were a genuine community of rich nations dedicated to the task of creating the prosperity and the well-being of the developing world. And perhaps I should add, in parenthesis, that in doing so we should expand our own well-being as well. To me, one of the most vivid proofs that there is a moral governance in the universe is the fact that when men or governments work intelligently and far-sightedly for the good of others, they achieve their own prosperity too. Take our Western experience with the welfare state. We did not plan to do it as a good stroke of business. It was a moral decision with ancient antecedents. Yet one of the consequences has been to reduce business risks. Mass consumption, secured by social security, enables the economy to avoid the booms and collapses of the old economy.

I believe we should see the same outcome if in the world economy we could determine to build up the purchasing power of the poorer nations. We should find that, once again, our own prosperity had been helped by the underpinning of world consumption and by the creation of a world economy free from the ups and downs, the uncertainties and incoherences, of the system as we know it today.

'Honesty is the best policy' used to be said in Victorian times. I would go further. I would say that generosity is the best policy and that expansion of opportunity sought for the sake of others ends by bringing well-being and expansion to oneself. The dice are not hopelessly loaded against us. Our morals and our interests—seen in true perspective—do not pull apart. Only the narrowness of our own interests, whether personal or national, blinds us to this moral truth.

What then should we do? Our first step must be a commitment. All the wealthy nations must accept a common obligation to provide capital and technical assistance to the under-developed areas. Britain, Canada, Australia, Western Europe: we must all begin to do our share. Let us be quite clear about one thing. The reason why there is trouble over the American balance of payments is nothing to do with the inherent strength of the American economy, which is vast. It is nothing to do with the American trade balance, which is favourable. It has something to do, admittedly, with the American export of capital. But, above all, it is created by the fact that America is carrying far more than its fair burden both of the defence of the free world and of aid to the developing nations. And before we can hope to have a functioning Atlantic economy the other member nations must play their part. A suggested one per cent of national income is a fair criterion; and, incidentally, I consider that Germany, so generously rebuilt after the war and so generously forgiven the enormous destruction which Hitler created, might be in the forefront of those who accept this obligation.

This commitment is, however, only the beginning of the matter. Such a common purpose needs the proper institutional form. I believe we should attempt to build up in our Atlantic world some of the institutions which make it possible for us to co-operate *within* the national community. I think we should have an Atlantic Reserve Bank. I think we should develop common strategies for development and investment both inside and outside the Atlantic arena. I think we should take a long, hard look at our trade policies, particularly the prices we pay for primary products. At present they do not, as they once did, pull up the rest of the world behind us. On the contrary, they tend to widen the gap. And for all this I think we need to expand our present Atlantic Organization for Economic Development into as many institutions—banks, development funds, trade groups, common markets, statistical services, and, above all, common policy-making organs—which might be needed to knit our interdependent economy into an integrated whole.

If we did this, I think we should do more than simply provide ourselves with the means to work out a strategy for the developing world; we should be creating the economic pre-conditions of a functioning world order. After all, we know that inside our domestic society we cannot survive in peace without law and welfare. It is upon these two pivots that the health of a community depends. Is our narrow interdependent world so different? Should we not be trying to create in the world at large the basic pre-conditions of a peaceful society?

We recognize the principles more or less inside our own domestic community. We do not have private wars. The rich do indeed contribute to the advancement of the poor. And while I am not concerned here with the whole great issue of world law and of disarmament, I am deeply concerned with the second aspect of good order: the ability of the rich to recognize their obligations and to see that in an interdependent world—and Heaven knows our interdependence cannot be denied when we all stand under the shadow of atomic destruction—the principles of the general welfare cannot stop at the limits of our frontiers. It has to go forward; it has to include the whole family of man.

And having said so much, I begin to wonder whether there are any forces inside our comfortable, cosy, complacent Western world that will make us accept this challenge and see that we now face thirty to forty years of world-building on a scale never known in human history, since all our forefathers lived without the community of science, the speed of transport, the whole interconnectedness of the modern globe. What will spur us to face this kind of decision? Facts? The facts are there. We cannot wish away the great revolution of modernization that is sweeping round the world; we cannot say it would be easier or more pleasant if it had not happened. Perhaps so; but we started the revolution and we can hardly ignore the forces that we unleashed upon the world.

Should we be guided by fear? Fear can

indeed be the beginning of wisdom. Those who can live comfortably and without perturbation under the hideous threat of atomic destruction do not seem to me to be very wise. But blind fear is not a constructive force. Fear will serve us only if it drives us on to find a way out of our fears. And there is only one: to leave behind our present community of potential annihilation and build a community of moral purpose in its place. In such a world public law would take the place of private violence and the general welfare would be accepted over and above the particular interests of particular communities; above all, mankind would discover, beneath the clash of ideology, some minimum standards of trust rooted in the fact that we are all men, that we all stand under the judgment of history, and that we all love and seek to live and know that we must die.

It is just because the task before us is the positive task of building a peaceful home for the human family that I doubt whether realism or fear is enough to set us to work. We need resources of faith and vision as well. Do we have them? Or have the revolutions of our day, while increasing our physical powers, damped down the ardours of our spirit?

I do not believe it. Every one of the revolutions we have discussed goes beyond our material concerns and offers a challenge to the quality of our mind and spirit. The equality of men which is such a driving force all round the world sprang originally from the Western sense that men, as souls of infinite metaphysical value, stand equal before the throne of God. And if we feel this equality of man as a profound, moral fact, can we really be content to see men hungry, to see men die, to see men continue in starvation and ill-health when we have the means to help them? Is this our concept of equality? If it is, do we not betray our faith?

Then, again, our concern with worldly things is not mere materialism. It has in it an essential element of religious insight. God looked on his universe and found it good. The materials offered us in farm and factory can be set to work to create a community in which no one need starve or go naked and unhoused. We can 'redeem the time' by setting matter to work for the greater good of all our brothers, who are all mankind. The Christian God who bade His followers feed the hungry and heal the sick and took His parables from the homely round of daily work gave material things His benediction. It has not faded because material things are more abundant now.

Science itself—this vision of an orderly world in which matter does not respond to chaotic promptings but to some vast harmony of universal law—is in no way incompatible with a vision of moral order in which it can be the tool of a better life for all mankind. Science has removed us from the heaviest bondage of the past: the fact that material resources were always too scarce to match even the greatest goodwill. Only a hundred years ago, if we had wished to give covering, food, shelter, and a simple education to the mass of mankind, we could not have done so because our material means were not equal to the task. What science has done has been to set us free. It has delivered us from the bondage of our material poverty and opened a great area of choice where vision and will can operate because they have the physical means at hand.

Science, understood in this sense, is indeed a means of liberty. Perhaps you have wondered why I have not mentioned freedom as the greatest revolution of our time. Quite frankly, the reason is that I am not sure whether it *is* one of the spreading revolutions of this century. There are times when I feel that, in our Western world, freedom rather resembles the Biblical talent that was put in a napkin and buried in the ground. We have it—but do we use it? On the issue of freedom, the revolutions of our day are all ambiguous. The revolution of equality does not necessarily imply freedom. All prisoners in a jail are equal. But they are not free. The revolution of science offers the means of freedom. But it can be used as well for making dictatorship more efficient and war more dire. And materialism, misunderstood as a false overconcern with the things of this world, a false worship of 'the idols of the market place and the idols of the tribe,' can create the reverse of true freedom if men and women become more and more entangled in their own clamant and un-

assuageable wants. Our revolutions will not do our work for us. They can yield us freedom or its opposite. The outcome depends on us, and I sometimes wonder whether we have made any very fundamental attempt to interpret the revolutions of our time in the light of freedom. Have we measured the margin of choice given us by our new capital resources, our new technology, our new ability to create the means of wealth? Have we understood that this liberty of action must be used? It cannot, it must not be left to rust with us. And given our ability to assist in the process of modernization, have we really grasped its relevance to the grand question of our time: whether the developing world society will be closed or open, slave or free?

After all, constitutional liberty is a sophisticated concept. Between Magna Charta and our present-day democracy there lie eight hundred years of experience and feeling our way. I am not a determinist. I do not believe that economic forces necessarily create political forms. On the contrary, I believe freedom to have been one of the innate formative ideas of our Western way of life. But equally I observe that its incorporation in concrete institutions did presuppose some economic and social changes. The emergence of a strong middle class after the Middle Ages helped to secure rights and liberties to a larger and larger group of articulate and responsible citizens. In the nineteenth century, the growth of wealth and the spread of literacy encouraged the extension of democratic privileges even further, and complete adult suffrage and complete adult literacy arrived at about the same time.

I think it is probably a safe assumption that something of the same pattern must be expected in emergent societies; though they need not wait so long since models of change already exist. A strong expanding professional and managerial class, a strong thrust of literacy, and the expanding resources both presuppose are almost certainly pre-conditions of political development in freedom. We are, I think, irrational when we suddenly expect those who emerge from primitive societies to seize our concepts of liberty intact, forgetting the long intervening history of our own experiments. If we are not to be disappointed, I think we must seek with new energy and commitment to fill in the historical gap. We need to be far more active in the way of economic aid, capital investment, and educational assistance. We need to work with far more purpose to create the framework of general literacy and personal responsibility. We need to be far more imaginative in showing that we regard the right of nations to govern themselves as only the first, essential, but preliminary, step in creating the conditions in which nations can be truly free. But the next step is equally vital: to give concrete substance to the experience of national liberty and not permit it to become a time of lessening opportunity and hope.

But I have the impression that when we talk so confidently of liberty, we are unaware of the awful servitudes that are created by the ancient enemies of mankind: the servitude of poverty when means are so small that there is literally no choice at all; the servitude of ignorance when there are no perspectives to which the mind can open because there is no education on which the mind can begin to work; the servitude of ill-health which means that the expectation of life is almost too short to allow for any experience of freedom, and the years that *are* lived are dragged out without the health and strength which are themselves a liberation.

Because we have interpreted freedom in too narrow a sense and assumed that people will find the outer form of freedom natural when none of its actual substantial content has been realized, there has been something empty about our advocacy of the free way of life. What is the free way of life to a tribal society which does not know whether it can eat next week? What is the free way of life to an ancient society where illiteracy bars most people from any of the benefits of freedom? What, above all, can freedom be said to mean when the nations who talk of it most incessantly seem to have so little awareness of its wider moral dimensions? Am I free if my brother is bound by hopeless poverty and ignorance? Am I a prophet of the free way of life if I reveal perfect indifference to the plight of the man who has 'fallen among thieves,' the man whom the good Samaritan helped while the others passed him by?

If we want to spread the revolution of liberty round the world to complete and reconcile the other great revolutions of our day, we have to re-examine its moral content and ask ourselves whether we are not leaving liberty as a wasted talent and allowing other forces, not friendly to liberty, to monopolize the great vision of men working in brotherhood to create a world in which all can live. But God is not mocked. We reap what we sow and if freedom for us is no more than the right to pursue our own self-interest—personal or national—then we can make no claim to the greatest vision of our society: 'the glorious liberty of the sons of God.' Without vision we, like other peoples, will perish. But if it is restored, it can be as it always has been the profoundest inspiration of our society, and can give our way of life its continuing strength.

John Fitzgerald Kennedy

John Fitzgerald Kennedy (1917–1963), the 35th President of the United States, was the first to be born in the twentieth century. In many ways he epitomized the new generation of Americans who rose to national prominence after the close of World War II. He was the grandson of Irish immigrants to Boston, the son of a self-made business tycoon, and himself a cum laude graduate of Harvard University. He served as a naval officer in World War II, was awarded the Purple Heart, and, soon after his return to civilian life, began a career in politics. He was elected to the House of Representatives from Massachusetts, then to the United States Senate from the same state and, in 1960, to the presidency. He was assassinated on November 22, 1963, and his tragic death temporarily eclipsed the leadership of the new breed in politics. His Inaugural Address, delivered from the east front of the Capitol, is a masterpiece of elocution and soon became a credo for the younger generation of Americans. It also served as a pledge to the new nations which he intended as a counter statement to the more doctrinaire pronouncements of the Soviets. In reading the address note (1) the groups to which he addresses his pledges and the spirit and content of each; (2) the nature of the request to those nations who would make themselves our enemies; (3) evidences of the President's familiarity with our Western Heritage; (4) the character of the struggle he asks all Americans to join; (5) the immortal challenge he presents to his fellow Americans and to the citizens of the world; and (6) the almost prophetic comments about his own part in the new world he envisages.

From: PRESIDENT KENNEDY'S INAUGURAL ADDRESS, January 20, 1961

Vice President Johnson, Mr. Speaker, Mr. Chief Justice, President Eisenhower, Vice President Nixon, President Truman, Reverend Clergy, fellow citizens:

We observe today not a victory of party but a celebration of freedom—symbolizing an end as well as a beginning—signifying renewal as well as change. For I have sworn before you and Almighty God the same solemn oath our forebears prescribed nearly a century and three quarters ago.

The world is very different now. For man holds in his mortal hands the power to abolish all forms of human poverty and all forms of human life. And yet the same revolutionary beliefs for which our forebears fought are still at issue around the globe—the belief that the rights of man come not from the generosity of the state but from the hand of God.

We dare not forget today that we are the heirs of that first revolution. Let the word go forth from this time and place, to friend and foe alike, that the torch has been passed to a new generation of Americans—born in this century, tempered by war, disciplined by a hard and bitter peace, proud of our ancient heritage—and unwilling to witness or permit the slow undoing of those human rights to which this nation has always been committed, and to which we are committed today at home and around the world.

Let every nation know, whether it wishes us well or ill, that we shall pay any price, bear any burden, meet any hardship, support any friend, oppose any foe to assure the survival and the success of liberty.

This much we pledge—and more.

To those old allies whose cultural and spiritual origins we share, we pledge the loyalty of faithful friends. United, there is little we cannot do in a host of cooperative ventures. Divided, there is little we can do—for we dare not meet a powerful challenge at odds and split asunder.

To those new states whom we welcome to the ranks of the free, we pledge our word that

John F. Kennedy. *Public Papers of the Presidents of the United States.* John F. Kennedy . . . (Washington: United States Government Printing Office, 1962), pp. 1–3.

one form of colonial control shall not have passed away merely to be replaced by a far more iron tyranny. We shall not always expect to find them supporting our view. But we shall always hope to find them strongly supporting their own freedom—and to remember that, in the past, those who foolishly sought power by riding the back of the tiger ended up inside.

To those peoples in the huts and villages of half the globe struggling to break the bonds of mass misery, we pledge our best efforts to help them help themselves, for whatever period is required—not because the communists may be doing it, not because we seek their votes, but because it is right. If a free society cannot help the many who are poor, it cannot save the few who are rich.

To our sister republics south of our border, we offer a special pledge—to convert our good words into good deeds—in a new alliance for progress—to assist free men and free governments in casting off the chains of poverty. But this peaceful revolution of hope cannot become the prey of hostile powers. Let all our neighbors know that we shall join with them to oppose aggression or subversion anywhere in the Americas. And let every other power know that this Hemisphere intends to remain the master of its own house.

To that world assembly of sovereign states, the United Nations, our last best hope in an age where the instruments of war have far outpaced the instruments of peace, we renew our pledge of support—to prevent it from becoming merely a forum for invective—to strengthen its shield of the new and the weak—and to enlarge the area in which its writ may run.

Finally, to those nations who would make themselves our adversary, we offer not a pledge but a request: that both sides begin anew the quest for peace, before the dark powers of destruction unleashed by science engulf all humanity in planned or accidental self-destruction.

We dare not tempt them with weakness. For only when our arms are sufficient beyond doubt can we be certain beyond doubt that they will never be employed.

But neither can two great and powerful groups of nations take comfort from our present course—both sides overburdened by the cost of modern weapons, both rightly alarmed by the steady spread of the deadly atom, yet both racing to alter that uncertain balance of terror that stays the hand of mankind's final war.

So let us begin anew—remembering on both sides that civility is not a sign of weakness, and sincerity is always subject to proof. Let us never negotiate out of fear. But let us never fear to negotiate.

Let both sides explore what problems unite us instead of belaboring those problems which divide us.

Let both sides, for the first time, formulate serious and precise proposals for the inspection and control of arms—and bring the absolute power to destroy other nations under the absolute control of all nations.

Let both sides seek to invoke the wonders of science instead of its terrors. Together let us explore the stars, conquer the deserts, eradicate disease, tap the ocean depths and encourage the arts and commerce.

Let both sides unite to heed in all corners of the earth the command of Isaiah—to "undo the heavy burdens . . . (and) let the oppressed go free."

And if a beach-head of cooperation may push back the jungle of suspicion, let both sides join in creating a new endeavor, not a new balance of power, but a new world of law, where the strong are just and the weak secure and the peace preserved.

All this will not be finished in the first one hundred days. Nor will it be finished in the first one thousand days, nor in the life of this Administration, nor even perhaps in our lifetime on this planet. But let us begin.

In your hands, my fellow citizens, more than mine, will rest the final success or failure of our course. Since this country was founded, each generation of Americans has been summoned to give testimony to its national loyalty. The graves of young Americans who answered the call to service surround the globe.

Now the trumpet summons us again—not as a call to bear arms, though arms we need—not as a call to battle, though embattled we are—but a call to bear the burden of a long twilight struggle, year in and year out, "rejoicing in hope, patient in tribulation"—a struggle against the common enemies of man: tyranny, poverty, disease and war itself.

Can we forge against these enemies a grand and global alliance, North and South, East and West, that can assure a more fruitful life for all mankind? Will you join in that historic effort?

In the long history of the world, only a few generations have been granted the role of defending freedom in its hour of maximum danger. I do not shrink from this responsibility—I welcome it. I do not believe that any of us would exchange places with any other people or any other generation. The energy, the faith, the devotion which we bring to this endeavor will light our country and all who serve it—and the glow from that fire can truly light the world.

And so, my fellow Americans: ask not what your country can do for you—ask what you can do for your country.

My fellow citizens of the world: ask not what America will do for you, but what together we can do for the freedom of man.

Finally, whether you are citizens of America or citizens of the world, ask of us here the same high standards of strength and sacrifice which we ask of you. With a good conscience our only sure reward, with history the final judge of our deeds, let us go forth to lead the land we love, asking His blessing and His help, but knowing that here on earth God's work must truly be our own.

NOTE: The President spoke at 12:52 P.M. from a platform erected at the east front of the Capitol. Immediately before the address the oath of office was administered by Chief Justice Warren.

The President's opening words "Reverend Clergy" referred to His Eminence Richard Cardinal Cushing, Archbishop of Boston; His Eminence Archbishop Iakovos, head of the Greek Archdiocese of North and South America; the Reverend Dr. John Barclay, pastor of the Central Christian Church, Austin, Tex.; and Rabbi Dr. Nelson Glueck, President of the Hebrew Union College, Cincinnati, Ohio.

The Communist Party of the Soviet Union

The Communist Party over the years has sought to guide the development of society in harmony with what its leadership has believed to be the basic doctrines of Marx and Lenin. Since the party is committed to conscious control and direction of society, it has stressed outlines of intentions more than accurate descriptions of goals accomplished. Each new program, it is thought, is made necessary by completion of tasks and objectives outlined in the previous program or programs. The student should be aware that the party defines certain terms precisely and not infrequently in ways quite different from the manner in which non-communists use them. Socialism and communism provide examples; often, the two terms are confused and used interchangeably by non-communists. The Soviets, for example, believe that they have built a socialist society in Russia following their victory in the 1917 revolution; the socialist state, it is argued, is dominated by the dictatorship of the proletariat. Communism will prevail when the state withers away (the state being defined as the political agent of class domination) and there remains only administration of government, and each person will labor according to his abilities and receive rewards in accordance with his needs. The 22nd Party Congress of 1961 is of particular interest for a number of reasons. For example, the Congress endorsed a policy of coexistence with the West and promised a greater diffusion of power and responsibility among the workers. In reading this selection note (1) how the party placed the communist movement in an historical setting and gave it a universal quality; (2) the party's interpretation of contemporary nationalist movements; (3) its program for colonial and former colonial peoples; (4) reasons for endorsing a policy of coexistence with capitalism; (5) how the party defined communism; (6) what it regarded as its prime tasks in the development of a communist society; (7) evidences of concern for improving standards and levels of living for the masses; (8) proposals for democratizing government; (9) the part education is expected to play in society; (10) what role the party envisages for itself in the promotion of education, science, and the arts; (11) the party's conception of its world mission; (12) the rhetoric employed in the document; and (13) aspects of the program that give it a strong propagandistic appeal.

From: THE PROGRAMME OF THE COMMUNIST PARTY OF THE SOVIET UNION

INTRODUCTION

The Great October Socialist Revolution ushered in a new era in the history of mankind, the era of the downfall of capitalism and the establishment of communism. Socialism has triumphed in the Soviet Union and has achieved decisive victories in the People's Democracies; socialism has become the practical cause of hundreds of millions of people, and the banner of the revolutionary movement of the working class throughout the world.

More than a hundred years ago Karl Marx and Frederick Engels, the great teachers of the proletariat, wrote in the Communist Manifesto: "A spectre is haunting Europe, the spectre of communism." The courageous and selfless struggle of the proletarians of all countries brought mankind nearer to communism. First dozens and hundreds of people, and then thousands and millions, inspired by the ideals of communism, stormed the old world. The Paris Commune, the October Revolution,

the socialist revolutions in China and in a number of European and Asian countries are the major historical stages in the heroic battles fought by the international working class for the victory of communism. A tremendously long road, a road drenched in the blood of fighters for the happiness of the people, a road of glorious victories and temporary reverses, had to be traversed before *communism, which was once no more than a dream, became the greatest force of modern times, a society that is being built up over vast areas of the globe.*

In the early twentieth century the centre of the international revolutionary movement shifted to Russia. Russia's heroic working class, led by the Bolshevik Party headed by Vladimir Ilyich Lenin, became its vanguard. The Communist Party inspired and led the socialist revolution; it was the organiser and leader of the first workers' and peasants' state in history. The brilliant genius of Lenin, the great teacher of the working people of the

The Programme of the Communist Party of the Soviet Union Adopted by the 22nd Congress of the C.P.S.U. October 31, 1961. Soviet Booklet, no. 83 (London: Soviet Books, 1961), pp. 5–7; 32–36; 39; 41–44; 46–48; 50–55; 61–70; 77–90; 92–93.

world, whose name will live forever, illumines mankind's road to communism.

On entering the arena of political struggle, the Leninist Communist Party raised high the banner of revolutionary Marxism over the world. Marxism-Leninism became a powerful ideological weapon for the revolutionary transformation of society. At every historical stage the Party, taking guidance from the theory of Marx, Engels and Lenin, accomplished the tasks scientifically formulated in its Programmes.

In adopting its *first Programme* at its Second Congress in 1903, the Bolshevik Party called on the working class and all working people of Russia to fight for the overthrow of the tsarist autocracy and then of the bourgeois system and for the establishment of the dictatorship of the proletariat. In February 1917 the tsarist régime was swept away. In October 1917 the proletarian revolution abolished the capitalist system so hated by the people. *A socialist country came into being for the first time in history. The creation of a new world began.*

The first Programme of the Party had been carried out.

Adopting its *second Programme* at its Eighth Congress in 1919, the Party promulgated the task of building a socialist society. Treading on unexplored ground and overcoming difficulties and hardships, the Soviet people under the leadership of the Communist Party put into practice the plan for socialist construction drawn up by Lenin. *Socialism triumphed in the Soviet Union completely and finally.*

The second Programme of the Party had likewise been carried out.

The gigantic revolutionary exploit accomplished by the Soviet people has roused and inspired the masses in all countries and continents. A mighty purifying thunderstorm marking the spring-time of mankind is raging over the earth. *The socialist revolutions in European and Asian countries have resulted in the establishment of the world socialist system.* A powerful wave of national liberation revolutions is sweeping away the colonial system of imperialism.

One-third of mankind is building a new life under the banner of scientific communism. The first contingents of the working class to shake off capitalist oppression are facilitating victory for fresh contingents of their class brothers. The socialist world is expanding; the capitalist world is shrinking. Socialism will inevitably succeed capitalism everywhere. Such is the objective law of social development. Imperialism is powerless to check the irresistible process of emancipation.

Our epoch, whose main content is the transition from capitalism to socialism, is an epoch of struggle between the two opposing social systems, an epoch of socialist and national liberation revolutions, of the breakdown of imperialism and the abolition of the colonial system, an epoch of the transition of more and more peoples to the socialist path, of the triumph of socialism and communism on a world-wide scale. The central factor of the present epoch is the international working class and its main creation, the world socialist system.

Today the Communist Party of the Soviet Union (C.P.S.U.) is adopting its third Programme, a programme for the building of communist society. The new Programme is a constructive generalisation of the experience of socialist development; it takes account of the experience of the revolutionary movement throughout the world and, giving expression to the collective opinion of the Party, defines the main tasks and principal stages of communist construction.

The supreme goal of the Party is to build a communist society on whose banner will be inscribed: "From each according to his ability, to each according to his needs." The Party's motto, "Everything for the sake of man, for the benefit of man," will be put into effect in full.

The Communist Party of the Soviet Union, true to proletarian internationalism, always follows the militant slogan "Working men of all countries, unite!". *The Party regards communist construction in the U.S.S.R. as the Soviet people's great internationalist task,* in keeping with the interests of the world socialist system as a whole and with the interests of the international proletariat and all mankind.

Communism accomplishes the historic mission of delivering all men from social inequality, from every form of oppression and exploitation, from the horrors of war, and proclaims *Peace, Labour, Freedom, Equality, Fraternity* and *Happiness* for all the peoples of the world. . . .

THE NATIONAL LIBERATION MOVEMENT

The world is experiencing a period of stormy national liberation revolutions. Imperialism suppressed the national independence and freedom of the majority of the peoples and put the fetters of brutal colonial slavery on them, but *the rise of socialism marks the advent of the era of emancipation of the oppressed peoples.* A powerful wave of national liberation revolutions is sweeping away the colonial system and undermining the foundations of imperialism. Young sovereign states have arisen, or are arising, in one-time colonies or semi-colonies. Their peoples have entered a new period of development. They have emerged as makers of a new life and as active participants in world politics, as a revolutionary force destroying imperialism.

But the struggle is not yet over. The peoples who are throwing off the shackles of colonialism have attained different degrees of freedom. Many of them, having established national states, are striving for economic and durable political independence. The peoples of those formally independent countries that in reality depend on foreign monopolies politically and economically are rising to fight against imperialism and reactionary pro-imperialist regimes. The peoples who have not yet cast off the chains of colonial slavery are conducting a heroic struggle against their foreign enslavers.

The young sovereign states do not belong either to the system of imperialist states or to the system of socialist states. But the overwhelming majority of them have not yet broken free from world capitalist economy even though they occupy a special place in it. They constitute that part of the world which is still being exploited by the capitalist monopolies. As long as they do not put an end to their economic dependence on imperialism, they will be playing the role of a "world countryside," and will remain objects of semi-colonial exploitation.

The existence of the world socialist system and the weakening of imperialism offer the peoples of the newly-free countries the prospect of a national renascence, of ending age-long backwardness and poverty, and achieving economic independence.

The national interests demand the eradication of the remnants of colonialism, the elimination of the roots of imperialist power, the ousting of foreign monopolies, the founding of a national industry, the abolition of the feudal system and its survivals, the implementation of radical land reforms with the participation of the entire peasantry and in its interests, the pursuit of an independent foreign policy of peace, the democratisation of the life of society and the strengthening of political independence. All patriotic and progressive forces of the nation are interested in the solution of national problems. That is the basis on which they can be united.

Foreign capital will retreat only before a broad union of patriotic, democratic forces pursuing an anti-imperialist policy. The pillars of feudalism will crumble only under the impact of a general democratic movement. Only far-reaching agrarian reforms and a broad peasant movement can sweep away the remnants of medievalism that fetter the development of the productive forces, and solve the acute food problem that faces the peoples of Asia, Africa, and Latin America. Political independence can be made secure only by a people that has won democratic rights and freedoms and is taking an active part in governing the state.

Consistent struggle against imperialism is a paramount condition for the solution of national tasks. Imperialism seeks to retain one-time colonies and semi-colonies within the system of capitalist economy and perpetuate their under-privileged position in it. *U. S. imperialism is the chief bulwark of modern colonialism.* . . .

What can capitalism bring them?

Capitalism is the road of suffering for the people. It will not ensure rapid economic progress nor eliminate poverty; social inequality will increase. The capitalist development of the countryside will ruin the peasantry still more. The workers will be fated either to engaging in back-breaking labour to enrich the capitalists, or to swelling the ranks of the disinherited army of the unemployed. The petty bourgeoisie will be crushed in competition with big capital. The benefits of culture and education will remain out of reach of the people. The intelligentsia will be compelled to sell its talent.

What can socialism bring the peoples?

Socialism is the road to freedom and happiness for the peoples. It ensures rapid economic and cultural progress. It transforms a backward country into an industrial country within the lifetime of one generation and not in the course of centuries. Planned socialist economy is an economy of progress and prosperity by its very nature. Abolition of the exploitation of man by man does away with social inequality. Unemployment disappears completely. Socialism provides all peasants with land, helps them to develop farming, combines their labour efforts in voluntary co-operatives and puts modern agricultural machinery and agronomy at their disposal. Peasant labour is made more productive and the land is made more fertile. Socialism provides a high material and cultural standard of living for the working class and all working people. Socialism lifts the people out of darkness and ignorance and gives them access to modern culture. The intelligentsia is offered ample opportunities for creative effort for the benefit of the people.

It is for the peoples themselves to decide which road they will choose. In view of the present balance of the world forces and the actual feasibility of powerful support from the world socialist system, the peoples of the former colonies can decide this question in their own interest. Their choice will depend on the balance of the class forces. The non-capitalist road of development is ensured by the struggle of the working class and the masses of the people, by the general democratic movement, and meets the interests of the absolute majority of the nation. . . .

The socialist countries are sincere and true friends of peoples fighting for their liberation and of those that have freed themselves from imperialist tyranny, and render them all-round support. They stand for the abolition of all forms of colonial oppression and vigorously promote the strengthening of the sovereignty of the states rising on the ruins of colonial empires.

The C.P.S.U. considers fraternal alliance with the peoples who have thrown off the colonial or semi-colonial yoke to be a cornerstone of its international policy. This alliance is based on the common vital interests of world socialism and the world national liberation movement. The C.P.S.U. regards it as its internationalist duty to assist the peoples who have set out to win and strengthen their national independence, all peoples who are fighting for the complete abolition of the colonial system. . . .

PEACEFUL COEXISTENCE AND THE STRUGGLE FOR WORLD PEACE

The C.P.S.U. considers that the chief aim of its activity in the field of foreign policy is to provide peaceful conditions for the building of a communist society in the U.S.S.R. and developing the world socialist system, and together with the other peace-loving peoples to deliver mankind from a world war of extermination. . . .

Peaceful coexistence of the socialist and capitalist countries is an *objective necessity* for the development of human society. *War cannot and must not serve as a means of settling international disputes.* Peaceful coexistence or disastrous war—such is the alternative offered by history. Should the imperialist aggressors nevertheless venture to start a new world war, the peoples will no longer tolerate a system which drags them into devastating wars. They will sweep imperialism away and bury it.

Peaceful coexistence implies renunciation of war as a means of settling international disputes, and their solution by negotiation; equality, mutual understanding and trust between countries; consideration for each other's interests; non-interference in internal affairs; recognition of the right of every people to solve all the problems of their country by themselves; strict respect for the sovereignty and territorial integrity of all countries; promotion of economic and cultural co-operation on the basis of complete equality and mutual benefit.

Peaceful coexistence serves as a basis for the peaceful competition between socialism and capitalism on an international scale and constitutes a specific form of class struggle between them. As they consistently pursue the policy of peaceful coexistence, the socialist countries are steadily strengthening the positions of the world socialist system in its competition with capitalism. Peaceful coexistence affords more favourable opportunities for the struggle of the working class in the capitalist countries and facilitates the struggle of the peoples of the colonial and dependent countries for their liberation. Support for the principle of peaceful coexistence is also in keeping with the interests of that section of the bourgeoisie which realises that a thermonuclear war would not spare the ruling classes of capitalist society either. The policy of peaceful coexistence is in accord with the vital interests of all mankind, except the big monopoly magnates and the militarists.

The Soviet Union has consistently pursued, and will continue to pursue, the policy of the peaceful coexistence of states with different social systems.

The Communist Party of the Soviet Union advances the following *tasks in the field of international relations:*

to use, together with the socialist countries, peaceful states and peoples, every means of preventing world war and providing conditions for the complete banishment of war from the life of society;

to pursue a policy of establishing sound international relations, and work for the disbandment of all military blocs opposing each other, the discontinuance of the "cold war" and the propaganda of enmity and hatred among the nations, and the abolition of all air, naval, rocket, and other military bases on foreign territory;

to work for general and complete disarmament under strict international control;

to strengthen relations of fraternal friendship and close co-operation with the countries of Asia, Africa, and Latin America which are fighting to attain or consolidate national independence, with all peoples and states that advocate the preservation of peace;

to pursue an active and consistent policy of improving and developing relations with all capitalist countries, including the United States of America, Great Britain, France, the Federal Republic of Germany, Japan, and Italy, with a view to safeguarding peace;

to contribute in every way to the militant solidarity of all contingents and organisations of the international working class, which oppose the imperialist policy of war;

steadfastly to pursue a policy of consolidating all the forces fighting against war. All the organisations and parties that strive to avert war, the neutralist and pacifist movements and the bourgeois circles that advocate peace and normal relations between countries will meet with understanding and support on the part of the Soviet Union;

to pursue a policy of developing international co-operation in the fields of trade, cultural relations, science, and technology;

to be highly vigilant with regard to the aggressive circles, which are intent on violating peace; to expose, in good time, the initiators of military adventures; to take all necessary steps to safeguard the security and inviolability of our socialist country and the socialist camp as a whole. . . .

THE TASKS OF THE COMMUNIST PARTY OF THE SOVIET UNION IN BUILDING A COMMUNIST SOCIETY

The building of a communist society has become an immediate practical task for the Soviet people. The gradual development of socialism into communism is an objective law; it has been prepared by the development of Soviet socialist society throughout the preceding period. . . .

Communism is a classless social system with one form of public ownership of the means of production and full social equality of all members of society; under it, the all-round development of people will be accompanied by the growth of the productive forces through continuous progress in science and technology; all the springs of co-operative wealth will flow more abundantly, and the great principle "From each according to his ability, to each according to his needs" will be implemented. Communism is a highly organised society of free, socially conscious working people in which public self-government will be established, a society in which labour for the good of society will become the prime vital requirement of everyone, a necessity recognised by one and all, and the ability of each person will be employed to the greatest benefit of the people.

A high degree of communist consciousness, industry, discipline, and devotion to the public interest are qualities typifying the man of communist society. . . .

The C.P.S.U. being a party of scientific communism, proposes and fulfils the tasks of communist construction in step with the preparation and maturing of the material and spiritual prerequisites, considering that it would be wrong to jump over necessary stages of development, and that it would be equally wrong to halt at an achieved level and thus check progress. The building of communism must be carried out by successive stages.

In the current decade (1961–70) the Soviet Union, in creating the material and technical basis of communism, will surpass the strongest and richest capitalist country, the U.S.A., in production per head of population; the people's standard of living and their cultural and technical standards will improve substantially; everyone will live in easy circumstances; all collective and state farms will become highly productive and profitable enterprises; the demand of Soviet people for well-appointed housing will, in the main, be satisfied; hard physical work will disappear; the U.S.S.R. will have the shortest working day.

The material and technical basis of communism will be built up by the *end of the second decade* (1971–80), ensuring an abundance of material and cultural values for the whole population; Soviet society will come close to a stage where it can introduce the principle of distribution according to needs, and there will

be a gradual transition to one form of ownership—public ownership. Thus, *a communist society will in the main be built in the U.S.S.R.* The construction of communist society will be fully completed in the subsequent period.

The majestic edifice of communism is being erected by the persevering effort of the Soviet people—the working class, the peasantry and the intelligentsia. The more successful their work, the closer the great goal—communist society.

THE TASKS OF THE PARTY IN THE ECONOMIC FIELD AND IN THE CREATION AND PROMOTION OF THE MATERIAL AND TECHNICAL BASIS OF COMMUNISM

The main economic task of the Party and the Soviet people is to create *the material and technical basis of communism* within two decades. This means complete electrification of the country and perfection on this basis of the techniques, technologies, and organisation of social production in all the fields of the national economy; comprehensive mechanisation of production operations and a growing degree of their automation; widespread use of chemistry in the national economy; vigorous development of new, economically effective branches of production, new types of power and new materials; all-round and rational utilisation of natural, material and labour resources; organic fusion of science and production, and rapid scientific and technical progress; a high cultural and technical level for the working people; and substantial superiority over the more developed capitalist countries in productivity of labour, which constitutes the most important prerequisite for the victory of the communist system. . . .

The Development of Industry, Building, and Transport, and their Role in Creating the Productive Forces of Communism

The creation of the material and technical basis of communism, the task of making Soviet industry technologically the best and strongest in the world call for the further development of heavy industry. On this basis, all the other branches of the national economy—agriculture, the consumer goods industries, the building industry, transport and communications, as well as the branches directly concerned with services for the population—trade, public catering, health, housing, and communal services—will be technically re-equipped.

A first-class heavy industry, the basis for the country's technical progress and economic might, has been built up in the Soviet Union. The C.P.S.U. will continue to devote unflagging attention to the growth of heavy industry and its technical progress. The main task of heavy industry is to meet all the needs of the country's defence and to ensure the development of industries producing consumer goods, so as to satisfy better and in full the requirements of the people, the vital demands of Soviet man, and to effect the development of the country's productive forces.

With these aims in view, the C.P.S.U. plans the following increases in *total industrial output:*

within the current 10 years, by approximately 150 per cent, exceeding the level of U. S. industrial output;

within 20 years, by not less than 500 per cent, leaving the present overall volume of U. S. industrial output far behind.

To achieve this, it is necessary to raise *productivity of labour* in industry by more than 100 per cent within 10 years, and by 300–350 per cent within 20 years. In 20 years' time labour productivity in Soviet industry will exceed the present level of labour productivity in the U. S. A. by roughly 100 per cent, and considerably more in terms of per-hour output, due to the reduction of the working day in the U. S. S. R. . . .

The C.P.S.U. will concentrate its efforts on ensuring a rapid increase in the output of *consumer goods.* The growing resources of industry must be used more and more to fully meet all the requirements of Soviet people and to build and equip enterprises and establishments catering to the household and cultural needs of the population. Along with the accelerated development of all branches

of the light and food industries, the share of consumer goods in the output of heavy industry will also increase. More electricity and gas will be supplied to the population.

The growth of the national economy will call for the accelerated development of *all transport facilities.* The most important tasks in the sphere of transport are: expansion of transport and road construction to meet in full the requirements of the national economy and the population in all modes of transport; further modernisation of the railways and other transport systems; a considerable increase in the speed of rail, sea and river traffic; the co-ordinated development of all types of transport as components of a single transport network. The share of transport by pipelines will be increased.

A single deep-water system will link the main inland waterways of the European part of the U. S. S. R.

A ramified network of modern roads will be built throughout the country. The automobile fleet will increase sufficiently to fully meet freight and passenger requirements; car hire centres will be organised on a large scale. Air transport will becomes a means of mass passenger traffic extending to all parts of the country.

Up-to-date *jet* engineering will develop rapidly, above all in air transport, as well as in space exploration.

All means of *communication* (post, radio and television, telephone and telegraph) will be developed still more. All regions of the country will have reliable communications and a link-up system of television stations.

Full-scale communist construction calls for a more rational *geographic distribution* of the industries in order to have social labour and ensure the comprehensive development of areas and the specialisation of their industries, do away with the overpopulation of big cities, facilitate the elimination of essential distinctions between town and countryside, and further even out the economic levels of different parts of the country.

To gain time, priority will be given to developing easily exploited natural resources that provide the greatest economic effect.

The industry in the areas to the *east of the*

Urals, where there are immense natural riches, raw material and power resources, will expand greatly. . . .

The maximum acceleration of scientific and engineering progress is a major national task which calls for daily effort to reduce the time spent on designing new machinery and introducing it in industry. It is necessary to promote in every way the initiative of economic councils, enterprises, social organisations, scientists, engineers, designers, workers and collective farmers in creating and applying new technical improvements. Of utmost importance is the material and moral stimulation of mass invention and rationalisation movements, of enterprises, shops, state and collective farms, teams, and innovators who master the production of new machinery and utilise it skilfully.

The Party will do everything to *enhance the role of science* in the building of communist society; it will encourage research to discover new possibilities for the development of the productive forces, and the rapid and extensive application of the latest scientific and technical achievements; a decisive advancement in experimental work, including research directly at enterprises, and the efficient organisation of scientific and technical information and of the whole system of studying and disseminating progressive Soviet and foreign methods. Science will itself in full measure become a direct productive force.

The constant *improvement in the technology* of all industries and production branches is a requisite for their development. Technological progress will make man's labour easier, facilitate substantial intensification and acceleration of production and give it the highest degree of precision, will facilitate the standardisation of mass production items and maximum use of production lines. Machining will be supplemented and, when necessary, replaced by chemical methods, the technological use of electricity, electrochemistry, etc.; radio-electronics, semiconductors and ultrasound will occupy a more and more important place in production techniques. The construction of new, technically up-to-date enterprises will proceed side by side with the reconstruction of those now in existence and the replacement and modernisation of their equipment. . . .

New techniques and the reduction of the working day call for *a higher level in the organisation of work.* Technical progress and better organisation must be fully utilised to increase labour productivity and reduce production costs at every enterprise. This implies a higher rate of increase in labour productivity as compared with the rate of growth of wages, better rate-fixing, prevention of loss of working time, and operation on a profitable basis in all sectors of production.

Most important will be the systematic improvement of the qualifications of those working in industry and other branches of the economy in connection with technical progress. The planned training, instruction and rational employment of those released from various jobs and transferred to other jobs due to mechanisation and automation are essential.

Existing enterprises will be improved and developed into enterprises of communist society. Typical of this process will be new machinery, high standards of production organisation and efficiency through increased automation of production operations and the introduction of automation into control; an improvement of the cultural and technical standards of the workers, the increasing fusion of physical and mental labour and the growing proportion of engineers and technicians in every industrial enterprise; the expansion of research, and closer links between enterprises and research institutes; promotion of the emulation movement, the application of the achievements of science and the best forms of labour organisation and best methods of raising labour productivity, the extensive participation of workers' collectives in the management of enterprises, and the spreading of communist forms of labour.

The Development of Agriculture and Social Relations in the Countryside

Along with a powerful industry, a flourishing, versatile and highly productive agriculture is an imperative condition for the building of communism. The Party is organising a great development of productive forces in agriculture, which will make it possible to accomplish two basic, closely related tasks: (a) to build up an abundance of high-quality food products for the population and of raw materials for industry, and (b) to effect the gradual transition of social relations in the Soviet countryside to communist relations and eliminate, in the main, the distinctions between town and country.

The chief means of achieving progress in agriculture and satisfying the growing needs of the country in farm produce are comprehensive mechanisation and consistent *intensification:* high efficiency of crop farming and stock-breeding based on science and progressive experience in all collective and state farms, a steep rise in the yielding capacity of all crops and greater output per hectare with the minimum outlay of labour and funds. On this basis, it is necessary to achieve an uninterrupted growth of agricultural production in keeping with the needs of society. Agriculture will approach the level of industry in technical equipment and the organisation of production; farm labour will turn into a variety of industrial labour, and the dependence of agriculture upon the elements will decrease considerably, and ultimately drop to a minimum.

The development of virgin and disused land and establishment of new large-scale farms, the reorganisation of the machine and tractor stations, the sale of implements of production to the collective farms, introduction of new planning procedures, and the enhancement of material incentives for agricultural workers—all constituted an important stage in the development of agriculture. The Party will continue to devote considerable attention to the development of agriculture in the virgin and disused land development areas.

The further advance of the countryside to communism will proceed through the development and improvement of the two forms of socialist farming—the collective and state farms.

The *collective farm system* is an integral part of Soviet socialist society. It is a way charted by V. I. Lenin for the gradual transition of the peasantry to communism; it has stood the test of history and conforms to the distinctive features of the peasantry.

Collective farming accords in full with the level and needs of the development of modern productive forces in the countryside, and makes possible effective use of new machinery and the achievements of science, and rational employment of manpower. The collective farm blends the personal interests of the peasants with common, nation-wide interests, individual with collective interest in the results of production, and offers extensive opportunities for raising the incomes and the well-being of peasants on the basis of growing labour productivity. It is essential to make the most of the possibilities and advantages of the collective farm system. By virtue of the social form of its economy—its organisational structure and its democratic groundwork—which will develop more and more, the collective farm ensures that production is run by the collective farmers themselves, that their creative initiative is enhanced and that the collective farmers are educated in the communist spirit. The collective farm is a school of communism for the peasantry.

Economic advancement of the collective farm system creates conditions for the gradual *rapprochement* and, in the long run, also for the merging of collective farm property and the property of the whole people into one communist property.

The *state farms,* which are the leading socialist agricultural enterprises, play an ever increasing role in the development of agriculture. The state farms must serve the collective farms as a model of progressive, scientifically-managed, economically profitable social production of high efficiency and labour productivity.

The C.P.S.U. proceeds from the fact that the further consolidation of the *unbreakable alliance of the working class and the collective farm peasantry* is of crucial political, social and economic importance for the building of communism in the U. S. S. R.

In order to satisfy fully the requirements of the entire population and of the national economy in agricultural produce, the task is to increase the *aggregate volume of agricultural production* in 10 years by about 150 per cent, and in 20 years by 250 per cent. Agricultural output must keep ahead of the growing de-

THE COMMUNIST PARTY OF THE SOVIET UNION • 871

mand. In the first decade the Soviet Union will outstrip the United States in output of the key agricultural products per head of population. . . .

To ensure high, stable, steadily increasing harvests, to deliver agriculture from the baneful effects of the elements, especially droughts, to steeply raise land fertility, and to rapidly advance livestock breeding, it is necessary:

to effect a scientifically expedient distribution of agriculture by natural and economic zones and districts, and a more thorough and stable *specialisation* of agriculture with priority given to the type of farm product where the best conditions for it exist and the greatest saving in outlay is achieved;

to introduce on all collective and state farms a *scientifically motivated system of land cultivation and animal husbandry* consistent with local conditions and with the specialisation of each farm, ensuring the most effective use of the land and the most economically expedient combination of branches, the best structure of crop acreage with the substitution of high-yielding and valuable crops for crops of little value and those giving low yields; to ensure that every collective and state farm master the most advanced methods of crop farming with the application of efficient crop rotation and sow high-grade seed only; to build up reliable fodder resources in all districts and to introduce the foremost stock-breeding techniques in collective and state farms;

to effect a rational *introduction of chemicals* in all branches of agriculture, to meet all its needs in mineral fertilisers and chemical and biological means of combating weeds, blights, diseases and plant and animal pests, and to ensure the best use of local fertilisers in all collective and state farms;

to apply broadly biological achievements, and especially microbiology, which is assuming ever greater importance for the improvement of soil fertility;

to carry through a far-flung *irrigation programme:* to irrigate and water millions of hectares of new land in the arid areas and improve existing irrigated farming; to expand field-protective afforestation, building of water reservoirs, watering of pastures and me-

lioration of overmoist land; and to combat systematically the water and wind erosion of soil. Considerable attention will be devoted to the conservation and rational use of forests, water reservoirs, and other natural resources, and to their re-stocking and development.

The Party will promote the development of *agricultural science,* focus the creative efforts of scientists on the key problems of agricultural progress, and work for the practical application and extensive introduction of the achievements of science and progressive production experience in crop farming and stock-breeding. Research institutions and experimental stations are to become important links in agricultural management, and scientists and specialists must become the direct organisers of farm production. Each region or group of regions of the same zonal type should have agricultural research centres, with their own large-scale farms and up-to-date material and technical resources, to work out recommendations for collective and state farms applicable to the given district. Agricultural research and educational establishments and institutions must be chiefly located in rural areas and be directly associated with farm production, so that students may learn while working and work while learning. . . .

THE TASKS OF THE PARTY IN IMPROVING THE LIVING STANDARDS OF THE PEOPLE

The heroic labour of the Soviet people has produced a powerful and versatile economy. There is now every possibility to improve rapidly the living standards of the entire population—the workers, peasants, and intellectuals. The C.P.S.U. puts forward the historically important task of *achieving in the Soviet Union a living standard higher than that of any of the capitalist countries.*

This task will be effected by: (a) raising individual payment according to the quantity and quality of work done, coupled with reduction of retail prices and abolition of taxes paid by the population; (b) increase of the public consumption fund intended for the satisfaction of the requirements of members of society irrespective of the quantity and quality of their labour, that is, free of charge (education, medical treatment, pensions, maintenance of children at children's institutions, transition to cost-free use of public amenities, etc.).

The rise of the real incomes of the population will be outstripped by a rapid increase in the amount of commodities and services, and by extensive construction of dwellings and cultural and service buildings.

Soviet people will be more prosperous than working people in the developed capitalist countries even if average incomes are equal, because in the Soviet Union the national income is distributed in the interests of all members of society and there are no parasitical classes as in the bourgeois countries who appropriate and squander immense wealth plundered from millions of working people.

The Party acts upon Lenin's thesis that communist construction must be based upon the principle of material incentive. In the coming twenty years payment according to one's work will remain the principal source for satisfying the material and cultural needs of the working people.

The disparity between high and comparatively low incomes must be steadily reduced. Increasingly greater numbers of unskilled personnel will become skilled, and the diminishing difference in proficiency and labour productivity will be accompanied by a steady reduction of disparities in the level of pay. As the living standard of the entire population rises, low income levels will approach the higher, and the disparity between the incomes of peasants and workers, low-paid and high-paid personnel and of the populations of different parts of the country, will gradually shrink.

At the same time, as the country advances towards communism, personal needs will be increasingly met out of public consumption funds, whose rate of growth will exceed the rate of growth of payments for labour. The transition to communist distribution will be completed after the principle of distribution according to one's work will outlive itself, that is, when there will be an abundance of material and cultural wealth and labour will become a prime necessity of life for all members of society.

(*a*) *Provision of a high level of income and consumption for the whole population. Expansion of trade.*

The national income of the U. S. S. R. in the next ten years will increase nearly 150 per cent, and about 400 per cent in twenty years. The real income per head of population will increase by more than 250 per cent in twenty years. In the first decade already the real incomes of all factory, professional and office workers (including public funds) per employed person will, on the average, be almost doubled, and the incomes of the low-paid brackets of factory and office workers will increase approximately 3-fold. Thus, by the end of the first decade there will be no low-paid brackets of factory and office workers in the country.

By virtue of higher rates of growth of the labour productivity of collective farmers their real incomes will grow more rapidly than the incomes of factory workers, and will, on an average per employed person, more than double in the next ten years and increase more than fourfold in twenty years.

The wages of such numerically large sections of the Soviet intelligentsia as engineers and technicians, agronomists and stockbreeding experts, teachers, medical and cultural workers, will rise considerably.

As the incomes of the population grow, *the general level of popular consumption will rise rapidly.* The entire population will be able adequately to satisfy its need in high-quality and varied foodstuffs. The share of animal products (meat, fats, dairy produce), fruit, and high-grade vegetables in popular consumption will rise substantially in the near future. The demand of all sections of the population for high-quality consumer goods—attractive and durable clothes, footwear and goods improving and adorning the daily life of Soviet people, such as comfortable modern furniture, up-to-date domestic goods, a wide range of goods for cultural purposes, etc.—will be amply satisfied. Production of motorcars will be considerably extended to service the population.

Output of consumer goods must meet the growing consumer demand in full, and must conform to its changes. Timely output of goods in accordance with the varied demand of the population, with consideration for local, national and climatic conditions, is an imperative requirement for all the consumer industries.

Soviet trade will be further developed as a necessary condition to meeting the growing requirements of the people. Good shopping facilities will be made available throughout the country, and progressive forms of trading will be widely applied. The material and technical basis of Soviet trade—the network of shops, warehouses, refrigerators and vegetable stores—will be extended.

Consumer co-operatives, which are to improve trade in the countryside and to organise sales of surplus agricultural produce, will develop. Collective-farm trade will lose none of its importance.

An abundance of material and cultural benefits for the whole population will be attained in the course of the second decade, and material prerequisites will be created for the transition in the period to follow to the communist principle of distribution according to need.

(*b*) *Solution of the housing problem and improvement of living conditions.* The C.P.S.U. sets the task of solving the most acute problem in the improvement of the well-being of the Soviet people—the housing problem. In the course of the first decade an end will be put to the housing shortage in the country. Families that are still housed in overcrowded and substandard dwellings, will get new flats. At the end of the second decade, every family, including newlyweds, will have a comfortable flat conforming to the requirements of hygiene and cultural living. Peasant houses of the old type will, in the main, give place to new modern dwellings, or—whenever possible—they will be rebuilt and appropriately improved. In the course of the second decade housing will gradually become rent-free for all citizens.

Town building, architecture and planning aimed at designing modern, comfortable towns and communities, industrial projects, dwellings and public buildings economical to build and to maintain, are acquiring great importance. Towns and communities must constitute a rational and comprehensive organisation of industrial zones, residential areas, public and cultural institutions, communal services, transport, engineering equipment and power sources ensuring the best possible conditions for labour, life and leisure.

An extensive programme of public-service construction and of improvements in all towns and workers' estates will be carried out in the coming period, which will involve completion of their electrification, the necessary gasification, provision of telephone communications, public transport facilities, waterworks, sewerage, and measures for the further improvement of sanitary conditions in towns and other populated localities, including tree planting, pond building, and effective measures to combat air, soil and water pollution. Well-appointed small and middle-size towns will be increasingly developed, making for better and healthier living conditions.

Public transport facilities (tramways, buses, trolley-buses, and subways) will become free in the course of the second decade, and at the end of it such public amenities as water, gas, and heating will also be free.

(*c*) *Reduction of working hours and the further improvement of working conditions.* In the coming ten years the country will go over to a *six-hour working day* with one day off a week, or *a 35-hour working week* with two days off, and on underground jobs and enterprises with harmful working conditions to a five-hour working day or a 30-hour five-day working week.

By virtue of a corresponding rise in labour productivity, transition to a still shorter working week will be begun in the second decade.

The Soviet Union will thus have the world's shortest and, concurrently, the most productive and highest-paid working day. Working people will have much more leisure time, and this will add to their opportunities of improving their cultural and technical level.

The length of the annual paid holidays of working people will be increased together with the reduction of the working day. Gradually the minimum length of leave for all industrial, professional and office workers will increase to three weeks and subsequently to one month. Paid holidays will be gradually extended also to collective farmers.

All-round measures to make working conditions healthier and lighter constitute an important task in improving the well-being of the people. Modern means of labour safety and hygiene designed to prevent occupational injuries and diseases will be introduced at all enterprises. Night shifts will be gradually abolished at enterprises, save those where round-the-clock operation is required by the production process or the need to service the population.

(*d*) *Health services and measures for increased longevity.* The socialist state is the only state which undertakes to protect and continuously improve the health of the whole population. This is provided for by a system of social, economic and medical measures. There will be an extensive programme designed to prevent and sharply reduce diseases, wipe out mass infectious diseases and further increase longevity.

The needs of the urban and rural population in all forms of highly-qualified *medical services* will be met in full. This will call for the extensive building of medical institutions, including hospitals and sanatoria, the equipment of all medical institutions with modern appliances, and regular medical check-ups for the entire population. Special emphasis must be laid on extending in town and country the network of mother-and-child health institutions (maternity homes, medical consultation centres, children's health homes and hospitals, forest schools, etc.).

In addition to the existing free medical services, accommodation of sick persons at sanatoria and the dispensing of medicines will become gratuitous.

In order to afford the population an opportunity to rest in an out-of-town environment, holiday homes, boarding-houses, country hotels, and tourist camps will be built, where working people will be accommodated at a reasonable charge or by way of a bonus, as well as at a discount or gratis.

The Party considers it a most important task to ensure the education from early childhood of a sound young generation harmoniously developed physically and spiritually. This calls for utmost encouragement of all forms of mass sport and physical training, specifically at schools, and for drawing greater and greater sections of the population, particularly the youth, into sports.

(*e*) *Improvement of family living conditions and of the position of women. Maintenance of children and incapacitated people at public expense.* The remnants of the unequal position of women in domestic life must be totally eliminated. Social and living conditions must be provided to enable women to combine happy motherhood with increasingly active and creative participation in social labour and social activities, and in scientific and artistic pursuits. Women must be given relatively lighter and yet sufficiently well-paid jobs. Maternity leave will be extended.

It is essential to provide conditions to reduce and lighten the domestic work of women, and later to make possible the replacement of domestic work by public forms of satisfying the daily needs of the family. Up-to-date inexpensive domestic machinery, appliances, and electrical devices will be made extensively available for this purpose; the needs of the population in service establishments will be fully met in the next few years.

The extension of *public catering*, including canteens at enterprises, institutions, and in big dwelling houses, until it meets the demands of the population, calls for special attention. The service at catering establishments and the quality of catering must be radically improved, so that meals at public catering establishments should be tasty and nourishing and should cost the family less than meals cooked at home. Price reductions in public catering will keep ahead of price reductions for foodstuffs in the shops. By virtue of all this public catering will be able to take precedence over home cooking within ten to fifteen years.

The transition to free public catering (mid-day meals) at enterprises and institutions, and for collective farmers at work, will begin in the second decade.

A happy childhood for every child is one of the most important and noble aspects of communist construction. The development of a ramified network of children's institutions will make it possible for more and more families, and in the second decade for every family, to keep children and adolescents free of charge at children's establishments if they so desire. The Party considers it essential that everything should be done to fully meet in the next few years the demand in children's pre-school institutions.

In town and country there will be: full and cost-free satisfaction of the population's need in nurseries, kindergartens, playgrounds, day-care schools and young pioneer camps; the mass provision of an extensive network of boarding-schools with free maintenance of children; free hot meals at all schools, introduction of after-school hours with free dinners for school children, and free issue of uniforms and school supplies.

In keeping with the growth of the national income, the organs of state, the trade unions, and the collective farms will in the course of the twenty years gradually undertake maintenance of all citizens incapacitated through old age or disability. Sickness and disability grants and old-age pensions will be extended to collective farmers; old-age and disability pensions will be steadily raised. The number of comfortable homes for old people and invalids providing free accommodation for all applicants will be greatly increased in town and country.

By fulfilling the tasks set by the Party for the improvement of the well-being of the people, the Soviet Union will make considerable headway towards the practical realisation of the communist principle of distribution according to need.

At the end of the twenty years public consumption funds will total about half of the aggregate real income of the population. This will make it possible to effect at public expense:

free maintenance of children at children's institutions and boarding-schools (if parents wish);

maintenance of disabled people;

free education at all educational establishments;

free medical services for all citizens, including the supply of medicines and the treatment of sick persons at sanatoria;

rent-free housing and free communal services;

free municipal transport facilities;

free use of some types of public services;

steady reduction of charges for and partially free use of holiday homes, boarding-houses, tourist camps and sports facilities;

increasingly broad provision of the population with benefits, privileges and scholarships (grants to unmarried mothers, mothers of many children, scholarships for students);

gradual introduction of free public catering (midday meals) at enterprises and institutions, and for collective farmers at work.

The Soviet state will thus demonstrate to the world a truly full satisfaction of the growing material and cultural requirements of man. The living standards of Soviet people will improve all the faster, the faster the productive forces of the country develop and labour productivity grows, and the more broadly the creative energy of the Soviet people comes into play.

The set programme can be fulfilled with success under conditions of peace. Complications in the international situation and the resultant necessity to increase defence expenditures may hold up the fulfilment of the plans for raising the people's standard of living. An enduring normalisation of international relations, reduction of military expenditures and, in particular, the realisation of general and complete disarmament under an appropriate agreement between countries, would make it possible greatly to surpass the plans for raising the people's standard of living.

The fulfilment of the grand programme of improving the living standards of the Soviet people will have a world-wide historic impact. The Party calls on the Soviet people to work perseveringly, with inspiration. Every one of the working people of the Soviet Union must do his duty in the building of a communist society and in the effort to fulfil the programme for the improvement of the people's standard of living. . . .

The Soviets and Development of the Democratic Principles of Government

The role of the Soviets, which are an all-inclusive organisation of the people embodying their unity, will grow as communist construction progresses. The Soviets, which combine the features of a government body and a mass organisation of the people, operate more and more like social organisations, with the masses participating extensively and directly in their work.

The Party considers it essential to perfect the forms of popular representation and promote the democratic principles of the Soviet electoral system.

In nominating candidates for election to the Soviets, it is necessary to guarantee the widest and fullest discussion of the personal qualities and suitability of the candidates at meetings and in the press in order to ensure the election of the worthiest and most authoritative of them.

To improve the work of the Soviets and bring fresh forces into them, it is advisable that at least one-third of the total number of deputies to a Soviet should be elected anew each time so that *fresh millions of working people may learn to govern the state.*

The Party considers *systematic renewal of the leading bodies* necessary to bring a wider range of able persons into them and rule out abuses of authority by individual government officials. It is advisable to introduce the principle that the leading officials of the Union, republican and local bodies should be elected to their offices, as a rule, for not more than three consecutive terms. In those cases when the personal talents of the official in question are generally believed to make his further activity within a leading body useful and necessary, his re-election may be allowed. His election shall be considered valid if not a simple majority, but at least three-quarters of the votes are cast in his favour. . . .

An effort should be made to ensure that the salaried government staffs are reduced, that ever larger sections of the people learn to take part in administration and that work on government staffs eventually cease to constitute a profession.

While every executive must be held strictly and personally responsible for the job entrusted to him, it is necessary consistently to exercise the principle of collective leadership at all levels of the government and economic apparatus. . . .

THE TASKS OF THE PARTY IN THE SPHERES OF IDEOLOGY, EDUCATION, INSTRUCTION, SCIENCE, AND CULTURE

Soviet society has made great progress in the socialist education of the masses, in the moulding of active builders of socialism. But even after the socialist system has triumphed there persist in the minds and behaviour of people survivals of capitalism, which hamper the progress of society.

In the struggle for the victory of communism, ideological work becomes an increasingly powerful factor. The higher the social consciousness of the members of society, the more fully and broadly their creative activities come into play in the building of the material and technical basis of communism, in the development of communist forms of labour and new relations between people, and, consequently, the more rapidly and successfully the building of communism proceeds.

The Party considers that the paramount task in the ideological field in the present period is to educate all working people in a spirit of ideological integrity and devotion to communism, and cultivate in them a communist attitude to labour and the social economy; to eliminate completely the survivals of bourgeois views and morals; to ensure the all-round, harmonious development of the individual; to create a truly rich spiritual culture. Special importance is attached by the Party to the moulding of the rising generation.

The moulding of the new man is effected through his own active participation in communist construction and the development of communist principles in the economic and social spheres, under the influence of the educational work carried out by the Party, the state, and various social organisations, work in which the press, radio, cinema, and television play an important part. As communist forms of social organisation are created, communist ideas will become more firmly rooted in life and work and in human relations, and people will develop the ability to enjoy the benefits of communism in a rational way. Joint planned labour by the members of society, their daily participation in the management of state and public affairs, and the development of communist relations of comradely co-operation and mutual support recast the minds of people in a spirit of collectivism, industry, and humanism.

Increased communist consciousness of the people furthers the ideological and political unity of the workers, collective farmers, and intellectuals, and promotes their gradual fusion into a single collective of the working people of communist society.

The Party sets the following tasks:

In the Field of Development of Communist Consciousness

(*a*) *The Shaping of a Scientific World Outlook.* Under socialism and at a time when a communist society is being built, when spontaneous economic development has given way to the conscious organisation of production and social life as a whole, and when theory is daily translated into practice, it is of prime importance that a scientific world outlook be developed in all working people of Soviet society on the basis of Marxism-Leninism, an integral and harmonious system of philosophical, economic, social and political views. The Party calls for the education of the population as a whole in the spirit of scientific communism and strives to ensure that all working people fully understand the course and perspectives of world development, that they take a correct view of international and domestic events and consciously build their life on communist lines. Communist ideas and communist deeds should blend organically in the behaviour of every person and in the activities of all collectives and organisations.

The theoretical elaboration and timely practical solution of new problems raised by life are essential to the successful advance of society to communism. Theory must continue to illumine the road of practice, and help detect and eliminate obstacles and difficulties hindering successful communist construction. The Party regards it as one of its most important duties to further elaborate Marxist-Leninist

theory by studying and generalising new phenomena in the life of Soviet society and the experience of the world revolutionary working-class and liberation movements, and creatively to combine the theory and practice of communist construction.

(*b*) *Labour Education.* The Party sees the development of a communist attitude to labour in all members of society as its chief educational task. Labour for the benefit of society is the sacred duty of all. Any labour for society, whether physical or mental, is honourable and commands respect. Exemplary labour and management in the social economy should serve to educate all working people.

Everything required for life and human progress is created by labour. Hence every able-bodied man must take part in creating the means which are indispensable for his life and work and for the welfare of society. Anyone who received any benefits from society without doing his share of work, would be a parasite living at the expense of others.

It is impossible for a man in communist society not to work, for neither his social consciousness, nor public opinion would permit it. Work according to one's ability will become a habit, a prime necessity of life, for every member of society.

(*c*) *The Affirmation of Communist Morality.* In the course of transition to communism, the moral principles of society become increasingly important; the sphere of action of the moral factor expands and the importance of the administrative control of human relations diminishes accordingly. The Party will encourage all forms of conscious civic self-discipline leading to the assertion and promotion of the basic rules of the communist way of life.

The Communists reject the class morality of the exploiters; in contrast to the perverse, selfish views and morals of the old world, they promote communist morality, which is the noblest and most just morality, for it expresses the interests and ideals of the whole of working mankind. Communism makes the elementary standards of morality and justice, which were distorted or shamelessly flouted under the rule of the exploiters, inviolable rules for relations both between individuals and between peoples. Communist morality encompasses the fundamental norms of human morality which the masses of the people evolved in the course of millennia as they fought against vice and social oppression. The revolutionary morality of the working-class is of particular importance to the moral advancement of society. As socialist and communist construction progresses, communist morality is enriched with new principles, a new content.

The Party holds that *the moral code of the builder of communism* should comprise the following principles:

devotion to the communist cause; love of the socialist motherland and of the other socialist countries;

conscientious labour for the good of society —he who does not work, neither shall he eat;

concern on the part of everyone for the preservation and growth of public wealth;

a high sense of public duty; intolerance of actions harmful to the public interest;

collectivism and comradely mutual assistance: one for all and all for one;

humane relations and mutual respect between individuals—man is to man a friend, comrade and brother;

honesty and truthfulness, moral purity, modesty, and unpretentiousness in social and private life;

mutual respect in the family, and concern for the upbringing of children;

an uncompromising attitude to injustice, parasitism, dishonesty, careerism and money-grubbing;

friendship and brotherhood among all peoples of the U. S. S. R.; intolerance of national and racial hatred;

an uncompromising attitude to the enemies of communism, peace and the freedom of nations;

fraternal solidarity with the working people of all countries, and with all peoples.

(*d*) *The Promotion of Proletarian Internationalism and Socialist Patriotism.* The Party will untiringly educate Soviet people in the spirit of proletarian internationalism and will vigorously promote the international solidarity of the working people. In fostering the Soviet people's love of ther country, the Party maintains that with the emergence of the world socialist system the patriotism of the members of socialist society is expressed in devotion and loyalty to their own country and to the entire community of socialist countries. Socialist patriotism and socialist internationalism necessarily imply proletarian solidarity with the working class and all working people of all countries. The Party will continue perseveringly to combat the reactionary ideology of bourgeois nationalism, racialism, and cosmopolitanism.

(*e*) *All-Round and Harmonious Development of the Individual.* In the period of transition to communism, there are greater opportunities of *educating a new man, who will harmoniously combine spiritual wealth, moral purity and a perfect physique.*

All-round development of the individual has been made possible by historic social gains—freedom from exploitation, unemployment and poverty, from discrimination on account of sex, origin, nationality or race. Every member of society is provided with equal opportunities for education and creative labour. Relations of dependence and inequality between people in public affairs and in family life disappear. The personal dignity of each citizen is protected by society. Each is guaranteed an equal and free choice of occupation and profession with due regard to the interests of society. As less and less time is spent on material production, the individual is afforded ever greater opportunities to develop his abilities, gifts, and talents in the fields of production, science, engineering, literature, and the arts. People will increasingly devote their leisure to public pursuits, cultural activities, intellectual and physical development, scientific, technical and artistic endeavour. Physical training and sports will become part and parcel of the everyday life of people.

(*f*) *Elimination of the Survivals of Capitalism in the Minds and Behaviour of People.* The Party considers it an integral part of its work of communist education to combat manifestations of bourgeois ideology and morality, and the remnants of private-owner psychology, superstitions, and prejudices.

The general public, public opinion, and extensive criticism and self-criticism must play a big role in combating survivals of the past and manifestations of individualism and selfishness. Comradely censure of antisocial behaviour will gradually become the principal means of doing away with manifestations of bourgeois views, customs and habits. The power of example in public affairs and in private life, in the performance of one's public duty, acquires tremendous educational significance.

The Party uses ideological media to educate people in the spirit of a scientific materialist world conception, to overcome religious prejudices without insulting the sentiments of believers. It is necessary to conduct regularly broad atheistic propaganda on a scientific basis, to explain patiently the untenability of religious beliefs, which were engendered in the past when people were overawed by the elemental forces and social oppression and did not know the real causes of natural and social phenomena. This can be done by making use of the achievements of modern science, which is steadily solving the mysteries of the universe and extending man's power over nature, leaving no room for religious inventions about supernatural forces.

(g) *The Exposure of Bourgeois Ideology.* The peaceful coexistence of states with different social systems does not imply any easing of the ideological struggle. The Communist Party will go on *exposing the antipopular, reactionary nature of capitalism* and all attempts to paint bright pictures of the capitalist system.

The Party will *steadfastly propagate the great advantages of socialism and communism over the declining capitalist system.*

The Party advances the scientific ideology of communism in contrast to reactionary bourgeois ideology. Communist ideology, which expresses the fundamental interests of the working class and all working people, teaches them to struggle, to live and work, for the happiness of all. It is the most humane ideology. Its ideals are to establish truly human relations between individuals and peoples, to deliver mankind from the threat of wars of extermination, and bring about universal peace and a free, happy life for all men on earth.

In the Field of Public Education

The transition to communism implies training that will make people communist-minded and highly-cultured, people fitted for both physical and mental labour, for active work in various social, governmental, scientific, and cultural spheres.

The system of public education is so organised as to ensure that the instruction and education of the rising generation are closely bound up with life and productive labour, and that the adult population can combine work in the sphere of production with further training and education in keeping with their vocations and the requirements of society. Public education along these lines will make for the moulding of harmoniously developed members of communist society and for the solution of a cardinal social problem, namely, the elimination of substantial distinctions between mental and physical labour.

The main tasks in the field of instruction and education are:

(a) *Introduction of Universal Compulsory Secondary Education.* In the next decade compulsory secondary general and polytechnical eleven-year education is to be introduced for all children of school age, and eight-year education for young people engaged in the national economy who have not had the appropriate schooling; in the subsequent decade every one will have the opportunity to receive a complete secondary education. Universal secondary education is guaranteed by the development of general and polytechnical education, professional training combined with socially useful labour of school children to the extent of their physical capacity, and a considerable expansion of the network of all types of general schools, including evening schools, which provide a secondary education in off-work hours.

Secondary education must furnish a solid knowledge of the fundamentals of the basic sciences, an understanding of the principles of the communist world outlook, and a labour and polytechnical training in accordance with the rising level of science and engineering, with due regard to the needs of society and to the abilities and inclinations of the students, as well as the moral, aesthetic and physical education of a healthy rising generation.

In view of the rapid progress of science and engineering, the system of industrial, professional and vocational training should be improved continuously, so that the skills of those engaged in production may develop together with their better general education in the social and natural sciences and with the acquisition of specialised knowledge in engineering, agronomy, medicine, and other fields.

(b) *The Public Upbringing of Children of Pre-School and School Age.* The communist system of public education is based on the public upbringing of children. The educational influence which the family exerts on children must be brought into ever greater harmony with their public upbringing.

The growing number of pre-school institutions and boarding-schools of different types will fully meet the requirements of all working people who wish to give their children of pre-school and school age a public upbringing. The importance of the school, which is to cultivate love of labour and knowledge in children and to raise the younger generation in the spirit of communist consciousness and morality, will increase. An honourable and responsible role in this respect falls to teachers, and to the Young Communist League and Young Pioneer organisations.

In the Field of Science

Under the socialist system of economy, scientific and technical progress enables man to employ the riches and forces of nature most effectively in the interests of the people, to discover new forms of energy and to create new materials, to develop means of weather control, and to master outer space. Application of science in production becomes a decisive factor for the rapid growth of the productive forces of society. Scientific progress and the introduction of scientific achievements into the economy will remain an object of special concern to the Party.

Most important are the following tasks:

(a) *Development of Theoretical Investigations.* The further perspectives of scientific and technical progress depend in the present period primarily on the achievements of *the key branches of natural science.* A high level of development in *mathematics, physics, chemistry, and biology* is a necessary condition for the advancement and the effectiveness of the technical, medical, agricultural, and other sciences.

Theoretical research will be promoted to the utmost, primarily in such decisive fields of technical progress as electrification of the whole country, comprehensive mechanisation and automation of production, transport and communications, the application of chemistry to the leading branches of the national economy, industrial uses of atomic energy. This applies to:

studying the power and fuel balance of the country, finding the best ways and means of utilising the natural sources of power, working out the scientific fundamentals of a single power grid, discovering new power sources and developing methods of direct conversion of thermal, nuclear, solar, and chemical energy into electric power, and solving problems related to control of thermonuclear reactions;

working out the theory and principles of designing new machines, automatic and telemechanical systems, intensively developing radioelectronics, elaborating the theoretical foundations of computing, control and information machines, and technically improving them;

investigating chemical processes, working out new, more efficient technologies and creating inexpensive high-quality artificial and synthetic materials for all branches of the national economy: mechanical engineering, building, the manufacture of household goods and mineral fertilisers, and creating new preparations for use in medicine and agriculture;

improving existing methods and devising new, more effective methods of prospecting minerals and making comprehensive use of natural wealth.

Big advances are to be made in the development of all the biological sciences in order successfully to solve medical problems and achieve further progress in agriculture. The main tasks to be solved by these sciences in the interests of mankind are: ascertainment of the essence of the phenomena of life, the biological laws governing the development of the organic world, study of the physics and chemistry of living matter, elaboration of various methods of controlling vital processes, in particular, metabolism, heredity and directed changes in organisms. It is essential to develop more broadly and deeply the Michurin line in biology, which is based on the proposition that conditions of life are primary in the development of the organic world. Medicine must concentrate on discovering means of preventing and conquering cancer, virulent, cardiovascular, and other dangerous diseases. It is important to study and extensively use micro-organisms in the economy and the health services, among other things for the production of foods and feedstuffs, vitamins, antibiotics and enzymes, and for the development of new agricultural techniques.

Artificial earth satellites and spaceships have, by enabling man to penetrate into outer space, provided great opportunities of discovering new natural phenomena and laws and of investigating the planets and the sun.

In the age of rapid scientific progress, the elaboration of the philosophical problems of modern natural science on the basis of dialectical materialism, the only scientific method of cognition, becomes still more urgent.

There must be intensive development of research work in the *social sciences,* which constitute the scientific basis for the guidance of the development of society. Most important in this field is the study and theoretical generalisation of the experience gained in communist construction; investigation of the key objective laws governing the economic, political and cultural progress of socialism and its development into communism, and elaboration of the problems of communist education.

The task of economic science is to generalise new phenomena in the economic life of society, and to work out the national economic problems whose solution promotes successful communist construction. Economists must concentrate on finding the most effective ways of utilising material and labour resources in the economy, the best methods of planning and organising industrial and agricultural production, and elaborating the principles of a rational distribution of the productive forces and

of the technical and economic problems of communist construction.

The investigation of the problems of world history and contemporary world development must disclose the law-governed process of mankind's advance towards communism, the change in the balance of forces in favour of socialism, the aggravation of the general crisis of capitalism, the break-up of the colonial system of imperialism and its consequences, and the upsurge of the peoples' national liberation movement.

It is important to study the historical experience of the Communist Party and the Soviet people, tried and proved successful in practice, the objective laws of development of the world socialist system and the world Communist and working-class movement.

It is essential, in the future as well, to firmly defend and develop dialectical and historical materialism as the science of the most general laws of development of nature, society and human thinking.

The social sciences must continue to struggle with determination against bourgeois ideology, against Right-wing Socialist theory and practice, against revisionism and dogmatism; they must uphold the purity of the principles of Marxism-Leninism.

(b) *Ties Between Science and Production.* Close ties with the creative labour of the people and practical communist construction are an earnest of a fruitful development of science.

In conformity with the requirements of economic and cultural development, it is essential to extend and improve the network of research institutions, including those attached to the central bodies directing economic development and those attached to the economic councils, and the network of research laboratories and institutes at the major industrial plants and in farming areas; to develop research at higher educational establishments; to improve the geographical distribution of research institutions and higher educational establishments, and to ensure the further development of science in all the Union republics and major economic areas.

The research institutions must plan and co-ordinate their work in the most important fields of research in accordance with the plans of economic and cultural development. The role of the collective opinion of scientists in directing scientific work will increase. Free comradely discussions promoting the creative solution of pressing problems are an essential condition for scientific development.

The Party will adopt measures to extend and improve the material facilities of science and to enlist the most capable creative forces in scientific pursuits.

It is a point of honour for Soviet scientists to consolidate the advanced positions which Soviet science has won in major branches of knowledge and to take *a leading place in world science* in all the key fields.

In the Field of Cultural Development, Literature and Art

Cultural development during the full-scale construction of communist society will constitute the closing stage of a great cultural revolution. At this stage all the necessary ideological and cultural conditions will be created for the victory of communism.

The growth of the productive forces, progress in engineering and in the organisation of production, increased social activity of the working people, development of the democratic principles of self-government, and a communist reorganisation of everyday life depend in very large measure on the cultural advancement of the population.

Absorbing and developing all the best that has been created by world culture, communist culture will be a new, higher stage in the cultural progress of mankind. It will embody the versatility and richness of the spiritual life of society, and the lofty ideals and humanism of the new world. It will be the culture of a classless society, a culture of the entire people, of all mankind.

(*a*) *All-Round Advancement of the Cultural Life of Society.* In the period of transition to communism, creative effort in all fields of culture becomes particularly fruitful and accessible to all members of society. Soviet literature, music, painting, cinema and theatre, television and all the other arts, will attain higher standards in their ideological make-up

and artistry. People's theatres, mass amateur art, technical invention and other forms of creative endeavour by the people will become widespread. The advancement of artistic and creative activities among the masses will ensure the appearance of new gifted writers, artists, musicians, and actors. The development and enrichment of the arts are based on a combination of mass amateur endeavour and professional art.

The Party will work unremittingly to ensure that literature, art, and culture flourish, that every individual is given full scope to apply his abilities, that the people are educated aesthetically and develop a fine artistic taste and cultural habits. The artistic element will ennoble labour still more, make living conditions more attractive, and lift man up spiritually.

To provide the material basis for cultural development on a grand scale:

book publishing and the press will be vigorously developed, and the printing and paper industries will be expanded accordingly;

there will be more libraries, lecture halls and reading-rooms, theatres, houses of culture, clubs, and cinemas;

the country-wide radio diffusion network will be completed; television stations covering all industrial and agricultural areas will be built;

people's universities, people's theatrical companies, and other amateur cultural organisations will be widely developed;

a large network of scientific and technical laboratories and of art and cinema studios will be provided for the use of all who have the inclination and ability.

The Party considers it necessary to distribute cultural institutions evenly throughout the country in order gradually to bring the cultural standard of the countryside level with that of the town and achieve rapid cultural progress in all the newly-developed areas.

(*b*) *Enhancement of the Educational Role of Literature and Art.* Soviet literature and art, imbued with optimism and dynamic communist ideas, are great factors in ideological education and cultivate in Soviet people the qualities of builders of a new world. They must be a source of joy and inspiration to millions of people, express their will, their sentiments and ideas, enrich them ideologically and educate them morally.

The highroad of literature and art lies through the strengthening of their bond with the life of the people, through faithful and highly artistic depiction of the richness and versatility of socialist reality, inspired and vivid portrayal of all that is new and genuinely communist, and exposure of all that hinders the progress of society.

In the art of socialist realism, which is based on the principles of partisanship and kinship with the people, bold pioneering in the artistic depiction of life goes hand in hand with the cultivation and development of the progressive traditions of world culture. Writers, artists, musicians, theatrical workers, and film makers have every opportunity of displaying creative initiative and skill, using manifold forms, styles, and genres.

The Communist Party shows solicitude for the proper development of literature and art and their ideological and artistic standards, helps social organisations and literary and art associations in their activities.

(*c*) *The Expansion of International Cultural Relations.* The Party considers it necessary to expand the Soviet Union's cultural relations with the countries of the socialist system and with all other countries for the purpose of pooling scientific and cultural achievements and of bringing about mutual understanding and friendship among the peoples.

COMMUNIST CONSTRUCTION IN THE U.S.S.R. AND CO-OPERATION OF THE SOCIALIST COUNTRIES

The C.P.S.U. regards communist construction in the Soviet Union as a component of the building of communist society by the peoples of the entire world socialist system.

The fact that socialist revolutions have taken place at different times and that the economic and cultural levels of the countries concerned are dissimilar, predetermines the non-simultaneous completion of socialist construction in these countries and their non-simultaneous entry into the period of the full-scale construction of communism. Nev-

ertheless, the fact that the socialist countries are developing as members of a single world socialist system and utilising the objective laws and advantages of this system *enables them to reduce the time necessary for the construction of socialism and offers them the prospect of effecting the transition to communism more or less simultaneously, within one and the same historical epoch.*

The first country to advance to communism facilitates and accelerates the advance of the entire world socialist system to communism. In building communism, the peoples of the Soviet Union are breaking new roads for mankind, testing their correctness by their own experience, bringing out difficulties, finding ways and means of overcoming them, and selecting the best forms and methods of communist construction. . . .

The C.P.S.U., in community with the Communist parties of the other socialist countries, regards the following as its tasks:

in the *political* field, the utmost strengthening of the world socialist system: promotion of fraternal relations with all the socialist countries on lines of complete equality and voluntary co-operation; political consolidation of the countries of the socialist community for joint struggle against imperialist aggressors, for universal peace and for the complete triumph of communism;

in the *economic* field, expansion of trade between the socialist countries; development of the international socialist division of labour; increasing co-ordination of long-range economic plans of the socialist countries to ensure a maximum saving of social labour and an accelerated development of the world socialist economy; the promotion of scientific and technical co-operation;

in the *cultural* field, steady development of all forms of cultural co-operation and intercourse between the peoples of the socialist countries; exchanges of cultural achievements; encouragement of joint creative efforts by scientists, writers and artists; extensive measures to ensure the mutual enrichment of national cultures and bring the mode of life and the spiritual quality of the socialist nations closer together.

The C.P.S.U. and the Soviet people will do

everything in their power to support all the peoples of the socialist community in the construction of socialism and communism.

THE PARTY IN THE PERIOD OF FULL-SCALE COMMUNIST CONSTRUCTION

As a result of the victory of socialism in the U.S.S.R. and the consolidation of the unity of Soviet society, the Communist Party of the working class has become the vanguard of the Soviet people, a Party of the entire people, and extended its guiding influence to all spheres of social life. The Party is the brain, the honour and the conscience of our epoch, of the Soviet people, the people effecting great revolutionary transformations. It looks keenly into the future and shows the people scientifically motivated roads along which to advance, arouses titanic energy in the masses and leads them to the accomplishment of great tasks.

The period of full-scale communist construction is characterised by a further *enhancement of the role and importance of the Communist Party* as the leading and guiding force of Soviet society.

Unlike all the preceding socio-economic formations, communist society does not develop spontaneously, but as a result of the conscious and purposeful efforts of the masses led by the Marxist-Leninist Party. The Communist Party, which unites the foremost representatives of the working class, of all working people, and is closely connected with the masses, which enjoys unbounded prestige among the people and understands the laws of social development, provides proper leadership in communist construction as a whole, giving it an organised, planned and scientifically based character.

The enhancement of the role of the Party in the life of Soviet society in the new stage of its development derives from:

the growing scope and complexity of the tasks of communist construction, which call for a higher level of political and organisational leadership;

the growth of the creative activity of the masses and the participation of fresh millions of working people in the administration of state affairs and of production;

the further development of socialist democracy, the enhancement of the role of social organisations, the extension of the rights of the Union republics and local organisations;

the growing importance of the theory of scientific communism, of its creative development and propaganda, the necessity for improving the communist education of the working people and struggling to overcome the survivals of the past in the minds of the people.

There must be a new, higher stage in the development of the Party itself and of its political, ideological, and organisational work that is in conformity with the full-scale building of communism. The Party will continuously improve the forms and methods of its work, so that its leadership of the masses, of the building of the material and technical basis of communism, of the development of society's spiritual life will keep pace with the growing requirements of the epoch of communist construction.

Being the vanguard of the people building a communist society, the Party must also be in the van in the organisation of internal Party life and serve as an example and model in developing the most advanced forms of public communist self-government.

Undeviating observance of the Leninist standards of Party life and the principle of collective leadership, enhancement of the responsibility of Party organs and their personnel to the Party rank and file, promotion of the activity and initiative of all Communists and of their participation in elaborating and realising the policy of the Party, and the development of criticism and self-criticism are a law of Party life. This is an imperative condition of the ideological and organisational strength of the Party itself, of the unity and solidarity of Party ranks, of an all-round development of inner-Party democracy and an activisation on this basis of all Party forces, and of the strengthening of ties with the masses.

The cult of the individual, and the violations of collectivism in leadership, of inner-Party democracy and socialist legality arising out of it, are incompatible with the Leninist principles of Party life. The cult of the individual belittles the role of the Party and the masses and hampers the development of the ideological life of the Party and the creative activity of the working people. . . .

Such is the programme of work for communist construction which the Communist Party of the Soviet Union has mapped out.

The achievement of communism in the U.S.S.R. will be the greatest victory mankind has ever won throughout its long history. Every new step made towards the bright peaks of communism inspires the working masses in all countries, renders immense moral support to the struggle for the liberation of all peoples from social and national oppression, and brings closer the triumph of Marxism-Leninism on a world-wide scale.

When the Soviet people will enjoy the blessings of communism, new hundreds of millions of people on earth will say: "We are for communism!" It is not through war with other countries, but by the example of a more perfect organisation of society, by rapid progress in developing the productive forces, the creation of all conditions for the happiness and wellbeing of man, that the ideas of communism win the minds and hearts of the masses.

The forces of social progress will inevitably grow in all countries, and this will assist the builders of communism in the Soviet Union.

The Party proceeds from the Marxist-Leninist proposition: history is made by the people, and communism is a creation of the people, of its energy and intelligence. The victory of communism depends on people, and communism is built for people. Every Soviet man brings the triumph of communism nearer by his labour. The successes of communist construction spell abundance and a happy life to all, and enhance the might, prestige and glory of the Soviet Union.

The Party is confident that the Soviet people will accept the new Programme of the C.P.S.U. as their own vital cause, as the greatest purpose of their life and as a banner of nation-wide struggle for the building of communism. The Party calls on all Communists, on the entire Soviet people—all working men and women, collective farmers and workers by brain—to apply their energies to the successful fulfilment of the historic tasks set forth in this Programme.

Under the tried and tested leadership of the Communist Party, under the banner of Marxism-Leninism, the Soviet people have built socialism.

Under the leadership of the Party, under the banner of Marxism-Leninism, the Soviet people will build communist society.

The party solemnly proclaims: the present generation of Soviet people shall live in communism!

Contemporary Civilization

The first world war exerted a profound moral shock upon the people of the West. The twentieth century had dawned as a century of hope, but the war, followed by the eclipse of idealism and the spread of materialism, quickly dispelled that hope. Some critics of contemporary civilization attacked the barrenness implicit in materialism, while others sought to re-evaluate the role of pragmatic realism in effecting society's reformation. Facing the collapse of an older moral order undergirded by a Christian ethic now challenged by an expanding science with universal pretentions, philosophers (both professional and amateur) sought a way of rescuing the individual from meaninglessness. Abandoning the centuries-old search for an answer to the question, "What is man?" these restless seekers shifted the locus of attention from finding man's place in the proper niche in the biological order of life to learning about those qualities of his existence which made him a unique being. The new query, echoing the cry of a few ancients and moderns, pointedly and persistently asked, "Who am I?" Both secular and religious answers began to appear. Meanwhile, in the confusions of aims and objectives produced by wars, economic dislocations, and moral insecurities, religious leaders reexamined the bases of their faith. Religious thought and conviction underwent modification toward a restatement of primary Christian dogma with its emphasis upon original and corporate sin and the necessity of depending on the redemptive power of God, on the one hand, and on the other toward explorations of religious affirmation and commitment in a world which no longer needed nor believed in the continued existence of God.

Thomas Stearns Eliot

T S. Eliot (1888–1965) was one of the more influential poets and critics of the period following the First World War. He was born in St. Louis, Missouri, attended Harvard, the Sorbonne, and Oxford. In 1914, he became an expatriate, a practice common among artists and literary men during the first decades of the twentieth century. In 1927 he renounced his American citizenship to become a British subject. Eliot reacted with disgust against the sterility and sordidness of modern materialistic civilization, but he sought surcease in religion as a practical escape from materialism rather than follow some of his fellows into radical politics, sensualism in art, or retreat into the unconscious. His interest in religion helps to explain some of the symbolism so frequently found in Eliot's poetry. In reading these selections note (1) Eliot's tone of frustration and defeat, (2) his characterization of modern society, (3) what hopes he held out for contemporary society, and (4) his conclusions concerning man's ultimate destiny.

THE HOLLOW MEN

Mistah Kurtz—he dead.

A penny for the Old Guy.

I

We are the hollow men
We are the stuffed men
Leaning together
Headpiece filled with straw. Alas!
Our dried voices, when
We whisper together
Are quiet and meaningless
As wind in dry grass

Or rats' feet over broken glass
In our dry cellar

Shape without form, shade without colour,
Paralysed force, gesture without motion;

Those who have crossed
With direct eyes, to death's other Kingdom
Remember us—if at all—not as lost
Violent souls, but only
As the hollow men
The stuffed men.

II

Eyes I dare not meet in dreams
In death's dream kingdom
These do not appear:
There, the eyes are
Sunlight on a broken column
There, is a tree swinging
And voices are
In the wind's singing
More distant and more solemn
Than a fading star.

Let me be no nearer
In death's dream kingdom
Let me also wear
Such deliberate disguises
Rat's coat, crowskin, crossed staves
In a field
Behaving as the wind behaves
No nearer—

Not the final meeting
In the twilight kingdom

III

This is the dead land
This is cactus land
Here the stone images
Are raised, here they receive
The supplication of a dead man's hand
Under the twinkle of a fading star.

T. S. Eliot, *Collected Poems of T S. Eliot*, Harcourt, Brace and Company, Inc., New York, 1936, 99–105. Courtesy of Harcourt, Brace and Company, Inc.

Is it like this
In death's other kingdom
Waking alone
At the hour when we are
Trembling with tenderness
Lips that would kiss
Form prayers to broken stone.

IV

The eyes are not here
There are no eyes here
In this valley of dying stars
In this hollow valley
The broken jaw of our lost kingdoms

In this last of meeting places
We grope together
And avoid speech
Gathered on this beach of the tumid river

Sightless, unless
The eyes reappear
As the perpetual star
Multifoliate rose
Of death's twilight kingdom
The hope only
Of empty men.

V

*Here we go round the prickly pear
Prickly pear prickly pear*

*Here we go round the prickly pear
At five o'clock in the morning.*

Between the idea
And the reality
Between the motion
And the Act
Falls the Shadow

For Thine is the Kingdom

Between the conception
And the creation
Between the emotion
And the response
Falls the Shadow

Life is very long

Between the desire
And the spasm
Between the potency
And the existence
Between the essence
And the descent
Falls the Shadow

For Thine is the Kingdom

For Thine is
Life is
For Thine is the

*This is the way the world ends
This is the way the world ends
This is the way the world ends
Not with a bang but a whimper.*

Sigmund Freud

$\mathcal{S}$igmund Freud (1856–1939), the founder of psycho-
analysis, was born in Moravia; he studied medicine at
the Universities of Vienna and Paris and spent most of his
life in practice and research at Vienna. Freud, in assigning
prime importance to the non-rational, unconscious forces
within the personality as determinants of behavior, effected
a revolution in the way we have come to view man. As he
explored the personality in depth he developed three concepts to help explain observed phenomena: (1) the id—the
unconscious self containing instinctual drives or impulses
repressed and submerged from consciousness, (2) the
super-ego—representing one's conscience, the collection of
conscious and unconscious values derived from the culture
which restricts and condemns the impulses of the id, and
(3) the ego—the conscious self which tries to maintain a
balance between the id and the super-ego. With these

basic assumptions Freud developed techniques for healing mental ills, explored the relationships between psychic and physical functions of the body, and expanded his analysis of the individual psyche to an analysis of society. He argued that psychoneurotic symptoms in the individual result from a failure to derive satisfaction of instinctual desires. In Civilization and its Discontents (1930) Freud taught that as civilization advances, social controls indispensable to group life increasingly limit areas of action leading to satisfaction of instinctual urges; hence, as civilization progresses, discontents mount. He thought that the tendency to aggression, an innate independent instinct, constituted the most powerful obstacle to culture; but that civilization checks aggression by evoking a sense of guilt within society. "If civilization," he concluded, "is an inevitable course of development from the group of the family to the group of humanity as a whole, then an intensification of the sense of guilt—resulting from the innate conflict of ambivalence, from the eternal struggle between the love and the death trends—will be inextricably bound up with it, until perhaps the sense of guilt may swell to a magnitude that individuals can hardly support." In reading the selections note (1) Freud's answer to the question, "What is the purpose of life?" (2) his definition of happiness and the various means of achieving it, (3) his explanation of the common hostility to civilization, (4) the relation of instinctual renunciation to cultural evolution, (5) his explanation of how culture arose and what determined its course, (6) the significance to culture of transferring the value of being loved to the act of loving, (7) the cause of the rift between aim-inhibited love and sensual love, (8) his argument supporting the contention that aggression is an independent instinct and the threat it poses to civilization, (9) his discussion of communism and its remedy for curbing aggression, (10) his judgment of the possibilities of checking the aggression instinct, (11) his analogy between the process of cultural evolution and individual development, (12) the role of the cultural super-ego, (13) his suggestions for the analysis of society and the obstacles to such an analysis, and (14) his answer to the question whether and to what extent culture can master the instinct of aggression.

From: CIVILIZATION AND ITS DISCONTENTS

II

The question, 'What is the purpose of human life?' has been asked times without number; it has never received a satisfactory answer; perhaps it does not admit of such an answer. Many a questioner has added that if it should appear that life has no purpose, then it would lose all value for him. But these threats alter nothing. It looks, on the contrary, as though

As translated by Joan Riviere in Sigmund Freud, *Civilization and its Discontents*, New York: Doubleday & Company, Inc., 1958, 15–24; 28–32; 41–53; 56–67; 76–78; 99–105.

one had a right to dismiss this question, for it seems to presuppose that belief in the superiority of the human race with which we are already so familiar in its other expressions. Nobody asks what is the purpose of the lives of animals, unless peradventure they are designed to be of service to man. But this, too, will not hold, for with many animals man can do nothing— except describe, classify and study them; and countless species have declined to be put even to this use, by living and dying and becoming extinct before men had set eyes upon them. So again, only religion is able to answer the question of the purpose of life. One can hardly go wrong in concluding that the idea of a purpose in life stands and falls with the religious system.

We will turn, therefore, to the less ambitious problem, what the behaviour of men themselves reveals as the purpose and object of their lives, what they demand of life and wish to attain in it. The answer to this can hardly be in doubt: they seek happiness, they want to become happy and to remain so. There are two sides to this striving, a positive and a negative; it aims on the one hand at eliminating pain and discomfort, on the other at the experience of intense pleasures. In its narrower sense the word 'happiness' relates only to the last. Thus human activities branch off in two directions—corresponding to this double goal—according to which of the two they aim at realizing, either predominantly or even exclusively.

As we see, it is simply the pleasure-principle which draws up the programme of life's purpose. This principle dominates the operation of the mental apparatus from the very beginning; there can be no doubt about its efficiency, and yet its programme is in conflict with the whole world, with the macrocosm as much as with the microcosm. It simply cannot be put into execution, the whole constitution of things runs counter to it; one might say the intention that man should be 'happy' is not included in the scheme of 'Creation.' What is called happiness in its narrowest sense comes from the satisfaction—most often instantaneous—of pent-up needs which have reached great intensity, and by its very nature can only be a transitory experience. When any condition desired by the pleasure-principle is protracted, it results in a feeling only of mild comfort; we are so constituted that we can only intensely enjoy contrasts, much less intensely states in themselves. Our possibilities of happiness are thus limited from the start by our very constitution. It is much less difficult to be unhappy. Suffering comes from three quarters: from our own body, which is destined to decay and dissolution, and cannot even dispense with anxiety and pain as danger-signals; from the outer world, which can rage against us with the most powerful and pitiless forces of destruction; and finally from our relations with other men. The unhappiness which has this last origin we find perhaps more painful than any other; we tend to regard it more or less as a gratuitous addition, although it cannot be any less an inevitable fate than the suffering that proceeds from other sources.

It is no wonder if, under the pressure of these possibilities of suffering, humanity is wont to reduce its demands for happiness, just as even the pleasure-principle itself changes into the more accommodating reality-principle under the influence of external environment; if a man thinks himself happy if he has merely escaped unhappiness or weathered trouble; if in general the task of avoiding pain forces that of obtaining pleasure into the background. Reflection shows that there are very different ways of attempting to perform this task; and all these ways have been recommended by the various schools of wisdom in the art of life and put into practice by men. Unbridled gratification of all desires forces itself into the foreground as the most alluring guiding principle in life, but it entails preferring enjoyment to caution and penalizes itself after short indulgence. The other methods, in which avoidance of pain is the main motive, are differentiated according to the source of the suffering against which they are mainly directed. Some of these measures are extreme and some moderate, some are one-sided and some deal with several aspects of the matter at once. Voluntary loneliness, isolation from others, is the readiest safeguard against the unhappiness that may arise out of human relations. We know what this means: the happiness found along this path is that of peace. Against the dreaded outer world one can defend oneself only by turning away in some other direction, if the difficulty is to be solved single-handed. There is indeed another and a better way: that of combining with the rest of the human community and taking up the attack on nature, thus forcing it to obey human will, under the guidance of science. One is working then with all for the good of all. But the most interesting methods for averting pain are those which aim at influencing the organism itself. In the last analysis all pain is but sensation; it only exists in so far as we feel it, and we feel it only in consequence of certain characteristics of our organism.

The crudest of these methods of influencing the body, but also the most effective, is the chemical one: that of intoxication. I do not think anyone entirely understands their operation, but it is a fact that there are certain substances foreign to the body which, when present in the blood or tissues, directly cause us pleasurable sensations, but also so change the conditions of our perceptivity that we become insensible of disagreeable sensations. The two effects not only take place simultaneously, they seem to be closely bound up with each other. But there must be substances in the chemical composition of our bodies which can do the same, for we know of at least one morbid state, that of mania, in which a condition similar to this intoxication arises without any drug being absorbed. Besides this, our normal mental life shows variations, according to which pleasure is experienced with more or less ease, and along with this goes a diminished or increased sensitivity to pain. It is greatly to be regretted that this toxic aspect of mental processes has so far eluded scientific research. The services rendered by intoxicating substances in the struggle for happiness and in warding off misery rank so highly as a benefit that both individuals and races have given them an established position within their libido-economy. It is not merely the immediate gain in pleasure which one owes to them, but also a measure of that independence of the outer world which is so sorely craved. Men know that with the help they can get from 'drowning their cares' they can at any time slip away from the oppression of reality and find a refuge in a world of their own where painful feelings do not enter. We are aware that it is just this property which constitutes the danger and injuriousness of intoxicating substances. In certain circumstances they are to blame when valuable energies which could have been used to improve the lot of humanity are uselessly wasted. . . .

Another method of guarding against pain is by using the libido-displacements that our mental equipment allows of, by which it gains so greatly in flexibility. The task is then one of transferring the instinctual aims into such directions that they cannot be frustrated by the outer world. Sublimation of the instincts lends an aid in this. Its success is greatest when a man knows how to heighten sufficiently his capacity for obtaining pleasure from mental and intellectual work. Fate has little power against him then. This kind of satisfaction, such as the artist's joy in creation, in embodying his phantasies, or the scientist's in solving problems or discovering truth, has a special quality which we shall certainly one day be able to define metapsychologically. Until then we can only say metaphorically it seems to us 'higher and finer,' but compared with that of gratifying gross primitive instincts its intensity is tempered and diffused; it does not overwhelm us physically. The weak point of this method, however, is that it is not generally applicable; it is only available to the few. It presupposes special gifts and dispositions which are not very commonly found in a sufficient degree. And even to these few it does not secure complete protection against suffering; it gives no invulnerable armour against the arrows of fate, and it usually fails when a man's own body becomes a source of suffering to him.

This behaviour reveals clearly enough its aim—that of making oneself independent of the external world, by looking for happiness in the inner things of the mind; in the next method the same features are even more marked. The connection with reality is looser still; satisfaction is obtained through illusions, which are recognized as such, without the discrepancy between them and reality being allowed to interfere with the pleasure they give. These illusions are derived from the life of phantasy which, at the time when the sense of reality developed, was expressly exempted from the demands of the reality-test and set apart for the purpose of fulfilling wishes which would be very hard to realize. At the head of these phantasy-pleasures stands the enjoyment of works of art which through the agency of the artist is opened to those who cannot themselves create. Those who are sensitive to the influence of art do not know how to rate it high enough as a source of happiness and consolation in life. Yet art affects us but as a mild narcotic and can provide no more than a temporary refuge for us from the hardships of life; its influence is not strong enough to make us forget real misery.

Another method operates more energetically and thoroughly; it regards reality as the source of all suffering, as the one and only enemy, with whom life is intolerable and with whom therefore all relations must be broken off if one is to be happy in any way at all. The hermit turns his back on this world; he will have nothing to do with it. But one can do more than that; one can try to re-create it, try to build up another instead, from which the most unbearable features are eliminated and replaced by others corresponding to one's own wishes. He who in his despair and defiance sets out on this path will not as a rule get very far; reality will be too strong for him. He becomes a madman and usually finds no one to help him in carrying through his delusion. It is said, however, that each one of us behaves in some respect like the paranoiac, substituting a wish-fulfilment for some aspect of the world which is unbearable to him, and carrying this delusion through into reality. When a large number of people make this attempt together and try to obtain assurance of happiness and protection from suffering by a delusional transformation of reality it acquires special significance. The religions of humanity, too, must be classified as mass-delusions of this kind. Needless to say, no one who shares a delusion recognizes it as such.

I do not suppose that I have enumerated all the methods by which men strive to win happiness and keep suffering at bay, and I know, too, that the material might have been arranged differently. One of these methods I have not yet mentioned at all—not because I had forgotten it, but because it will interest us in another connection. How would it be possible to forget this way of all others of

practising the art of life! It is conspicuous for its remarkable capacity to combine characteristic features. Needless to say, it, too, strives to bring about independence of fate—as we may best call it—and with this object it looks for satisfaction within the mind, and uses the capacity for displacing libido which we mentioned before, but it does not turn away from the outer world; on the contrary, it takes a firm hold of its objects and obtains happiness from an emotional relation to them. Nor is it content to strive for avoidance of pain—that goal of weary resignation; rather it passes that by heedlessly and holds fast to the deep-rooted, passionate striving for a positive fulfilment of happiness. Perhaps it really comes nearer to this goal than any other method. I am speaking, of course, of that way of life which makes love the centre of all things and anticipates all happiness from loving and being loved. This attitude is familiar enough to all of us; one of the forms in which love manifests itself, sexual love, gives us our most intense experience of an overwhelming pleasurable sensation and so furnishes a prototype for our strivings after happiness. What is more natural than that we should persist in seeking happiness along the path by which we first encountered it? The weak side of this way of living is clearly evident; and were it not for this, no human being would ever have thought of abandoning this path to happiness in favour of any other. We are never so defenceless against suffering as when we love, never so forlornly unhappy as when we have lost our love-object or its love. But this does not complete the story of that way of life which bases happiness on love; there is much more to be said about it. . . .

III

Our discussion of happiness has so far not taught us much that is not already common knowledge. Nor does the prospect of discovering anything new seem much greater if we go on with the problem why it is so hard for mankind to be happy. We gave the answer before, when we cited the three sources of human sufferings, namely, the superior force of nature, the disposition to decay of our bodies, and the inadequacy of our methods of regulating human relations in the family, the community and the state. In regard to the first two, our judgment cannot hesitate: it forces us to recognize these sources of suffering and to submit to the inevitable. We shall never completely subdue nature; our body, too, is an organism, itself a part of nature, and will always contain the seeds of dissolution, with its limited powers of adaptation and achievement. The effect of this recognition is in no way disheartening; on the contrary, it points out the direction for our efforts. If we cannot abolish all suffering, yet a great deal of it we can, and can mitigate more; the experience of several thousand years has convinced us of this. To the third, the social source of our distresses, we take up a different attitude. We prefer not to regard it as one at all; we cannot see why the systems we have ourselves created should not rather ensure protection and well-being for us all. To be sure, when we consider how unsuccessful our efforts to safeguard against suffering in this particular have proved, the suspicion dawns upon us that a bit of unconquerable nature lurks concealed behind this difficulty as well—in the shape of our own mental constitution.

When we start to consider this possibility, we come across a point of view which is so amazing that we will pause over it. According to it, our so-called civilization itself is to blame for a great part of our misery, and we should be much happier if we were to give it up and go back to primitive conditions. I call this amazing, because—however one may define culture—it is undeniable that every means by which we try to guard ourselves against menaces from the several sources of human distress is a part of this same culture.

How has it come about that so many people have adopted this strange attitude of hostility to civilization? In my opinion, it arose from a background of profound long-standing discontent with the existing state of civilization, which finally crystallized into this judgement as a result of certain historical happenings. I believe I can identify the last two of these; I am not learned enough to trace the links in the chain back into the history of the human species. At the time when Christianity conquered the pagan religions some such antagonism to culture must already have been actively at work. It is closely related to the low estimation put upon earthly life by Christian doctrine. The earlier of the last two historical developments was when, as a result of voyages of discovery, men came into contact with primitive peoples and races. To the Europeans, who failed to observe them carefully and misunderstood what they saw, these people seemed to lead simple, happy lives—wanting for nothing—such as the travellers who visited them, with all their superior culture, were unable to achieve. Later experience has corrected this opinion on many points; in several instances the ease of life was due to the bounty of nature and the possibilities of ready satisfaction for the great human needs, but it was erroneously attributed to the absence of the complicated conditions of civilization. The last of the two historical events is especially familiar to us; it was when people began to understand the nature of the neuroses which threaten to undermine the modicum of happiness open to civilized man. It was found that men become neurotic because they cannot tolerate the degree of privation that society imposes on them in virtue of its cultural ideals, and it was supposed that a return to greater possibilities of happiness would ensue if these standards were abolished or greatly relaxed.

And there exists an element of disappointment, in addition. In the last generations man has made extraordinary strides in knowledge of the natural sciences and technical application of them, and has established his dominion over nature in a way never before imagined. The details of this forward progress are universally known: it is unnecessary to enumerate them. Mankind is proud of its exploits and has a right to be. But men are beginning to perceive that all this newly won power over space and time, this conquest of the forces of nature, this fulfilment of age-old longings, has not increased the amount of pleasure they can obtain in life, has not made them feel any happier. The valid conclusion from this is merely that power over nature is not the only condition of human happiness, just as it is not the only goal of civilization's efforts, and there is no ground for inferring that its technical progress is worthless from the standpoint of happiness. It prompts one to exclaim: is it not then a positive pleasure, an unequivocal gain in happiness, to be able to hear, whenever I like, the voice of a child living hundreds of miles away, or to know directly a friend of mine arrives at his destination that he has come well and safely through the long and troublesome voyage? And is it nothing that medical science has succeeded in enormously reducing the mortality of young children, the dangers of infection for women in childbirth, indeed, in very considerably prolonging the average length of human life? And there is still a long list one could add to these benefits that we owe to the much-despised era of scientific and practical progress—but a critical, pessimistic voice makes itself heard, saying that most of these advantages follow the model of those 'cheap pleasures' in the ancedote. One gets this enjoyment by sticking one's bare leg outside the bedclothes on a cold winter's night and then drawing it in again. If there were no railway to make light of distances my child would never have left home, and I should not need the telephone to hear his voice. If there were no vessels crossing the ocean my friend would never have embarked on his voyage, and I should not need the telegraph to relieve my anxiety about him. What is the use of reducing the mortality of children when it is precisely this reduction which imposes the greatest moderation on us in begetting them, so that taken all round we do not rear more children than in the days before the reign of hygiene, while at the same time we have created difficult conditions for sexual life in marriage and probably counteracted the beneficial effects on natural selection? And what do we gain by a long life when it is full of hardship and starved of joys and so wretched that we can only welcome death as our deliverer? . . .

We have obtained a clear impression of the general picture presented by culture through adopting the common view as to which aspects of human life are to be called cultural; but it is true that so far we have discovered nothing that is not common knowledge. We have, however, at the same time guarded ourselves against accepting the misconception that civilization is synonymous with becoming perfect, is the path by which man is ordained to reach perfection. But now a certain point of view presses for consideration; it will lead perhaps in another direction. The evolution of culture seems to us a peculiar kind of process passing over humanity, of which several aspects strike us as familiar. We can describe this process in terms of the modifications it effects on the known human instinctual dispositions, which it is the economic task of our lives to satisfy. Some of these instincts become absorbed, as it were, so that something appears in place of them which in an individual we call a character-trait. The most remarkable example of this process is found in respect of the anal erotism of young human beings. Their primary interest in the excretory function, its organs and products, is changed in the course of their growth into a group of traits that we know well—thriftiness, orderliness and cleanliness—valuable and welcome qualities in themselves, which, however, may be intensified till they visibly dominate the personality and produce what we call the anal character. How this happens we do not know; but there is no doubt about the accuracy of this conclusion. Now, we have seen that order and cleanliness are essentially cultural demands, although the necessity of them for survival is not particularly apparent, any more than their suitability as sources of pleasure. At this point we must be struck for the first time with the similarity between the process of cultural development and that of the libidinal development in an individual. Other instincts have to be induced to change the conditions of their gratification, to find it along other paths, a process which is usually identical with what we know so well as sublimation (of the aim of an instinct), but which can sometimes be differentiated from this. Sublimation of instinct is an especially conspicuous feature of cultural evolution; this it is that makes it possible for the higher mental operations, scientific, artistic, ideological activities, to play such an important part in civilized life. If one were to yield to a first impression, one would be tempted to say that sublimation is a fate which has been forced upon instincts by culture alone. But it is better to reflect over this a while longer. Thirdly and lastly, and this seems most important of all, it is impossible to ignore the extent to which civiliza-tion is built up on renunciation of instinctual gratifications, the degree to which the existence of civilization presupposes the non-gratification (suppression, repression or something else?) of powerful instinctual urgencies. This 'cultural privation' dominates the whole field of social relations between human beings; we know al-ready that it is the cause of the antagonism against which all civilization has to fight. It sets hard tasks for our scientific work, too; we have a great deal to explain here. It is not easy to understand how it can become possible to withhold satisfaction from an instinct. Nor is it by any means without risk to do so; if the deprivation is not made good economically, one may be certain of producing serious dis-orders.

But now, if we wish to know what use it is to us to have recognized the evolution of culture as a special process, comparable to the normal growth of an individual to maturity, we must clearly attack another problem and put the question: what are the influences to which the evolution of culture owes its origin, how did it arise and what determined its course?

IV

This task seems too big a one; one may well confess oneself diffident. Here follows what little I have been able to elicit about it.

Once primitive man had made the discovery that it lay in his own hands—speaking literally —to improve his lot on earth by working; it cannot have been a matter of indifference to him whether another man worked with him or against him. The other acquired the value of a fellow-worker, and it was advantageous to live with him. Even earlier, in his ape-like prehis-tory, man had adopted the habit of forming families: his first helpers were probably the members of his family. One may suppose that the founding of families was in some way con-nected with the period when the need for genital satisfaction, no longer appearing like an occasional guest who turns up suddenly and then vanishes without letting one hear anything of him for long intervals, had settled down with each man like a permanent lodger. When this happened, the male acquired a motive for keep-ing the female, or rather, his sexual objects, near him; while the female, who wanted not to be separated from her helpless young, in their interests, too, had to stay by the stronger male. In this primitive family one essential feature of culture is lacking: the will of the father, the head of it, was unfettered. I have endeavoured in *Totem und Tabu* to show how the way led from this family-life to the succeed-ing phase of communal existence in the form of a band of brothers. By overpowering the father, the sons had discovered that several men united can be stronger than a single man. The totemic stage of culture is founded upon the restrictions that the band were obliged to im-pose on one another in order to maintain the new system. These taboos were the first 'Right' or law. The life of human beings in common therefore had a twofold foundation, *i.e.* the compulsion to work, created by external neces-sity, and the power of love, causing the male to wish to keep his sexual object, the female, near him, and the female to keep near her that part of herself which has become detached from her, her child. Eros and Ananke were the parents of human culture, too. The first result of culture was that a larger number of human beings could then live together in common. And since the two great powers were here co-operating together, one might have expected that further cultural evolution would have proceeded smoothly towards ever greater mas-tery over the external world, as well as towards greater extension in the numbers of men sharing the life in common. Nor is it easy to understand how this culture can be felt as anything but satisfying by those who partake of it.

Before we go on to enquire where the dis-turbances in it arise, we will let ourselves di-gress from the point that love was one of the founders of culture and so fill a gap left in our previous discussion. We said that man, having found by experience that sexual (genital) love afforded him his greatest gratification, so that it became in effect a prototype of all happiness to him, must have been thereby impelled to seek his happiness further along the path of sexual relations, to make genital erotism the central point of his life. We went on to say that in so doing he becomes to a very dangerous degree dependent on a part of the outer world, namely, on his chosen love-object, and this exposes him to most painful sufferings if he is rejected by it or loses it through death or defection. The wise men of all ages have consequently warned us emphatically against this way of life; but in spite of all it retains its attraction for a great number of people.

A small minority are enabled by their constitution nevertheless to find happiness along the path of love; but far-reaching mental transformations of the erotic function are necessary before this is possible. These people make themselves independent of their object's acquiescence by transferring the main value from the fact of being loved to their own act of loving; they protect themselves against loss of it by attaching their love not to individual objects but to all men equally, and they avoid the uncertainties and disappointments of genital love by turning away from its sexual aim and modifying the instinct into an impulse with an *inhibited aim*. The state which they induce in themselves by this process—an unchangeable, undeviating, tender attitude—has little superficial likeness to the stormy vicissitudes of genital love, from which it is nevertheless derived. It seems that Saint Francis of Assissi may have carried this method of using love to produce an inner feeling of happiness as far as anyone; what we are thus characterizing as one of the procedures by which the pleasure-principle fulfils itself has in fact been linked up in many ways with religion; the connection between them may lie in those remote fastnesses of the mind where the distinctions between the ego and objects and between the various objects become matters of indifference. From one ethical standpoint, the deeper motivation of which will later become clear to us, this inclination towards an all-embracing love of others and of the world at large is regarded as the highest state of mind of which man is capable. Even at this early stage in the discussion I will not withhold the two principal objections we have to raise against this view. A love that does not discriminate seems to us to lose some of its own value, since it does an injustice to its object. And secondly, not all men are worthy of love.

The love that instituted the family still retains its power; in its original form it does not stop short of direct sexual satisfaction, and in its modified form as aim-inhibited friendliness it influences our civilization. In both these forms it carries on its task of binding men and women to one another, and it does this with greater intensity than can be achieved through the interest of work in common. The casual and undifferentiated way in which the word 'love' is employed by language has its genetic justification. In general usage the relation between a man and a woman whose genital desires have led them to found a family is called love; but the positive attitude of feeling between parents and children, between brothers and sisters in a family, is also called love, although to us this relation merits the description of aim-inhibited love or affection. Love with an inhibited aim was indeed originally full sensual love and in men's unconscious minds is so still. Both of them, the sensual and the aim-inhibited forms, reach out beyond the family and create new bonds with others who before were strangers. Genital love leads to the forming of new families; aim-inhibited love to 'friendships', which are valuable culturally because they do not entail many of the limitations of genital love—for instance, its exclusiveness. But the interrelations between love and culture lose their simplicity as development proceeds. On the one hand, love opposes the interests of culture; on the other, culture menaces love with grievous restrictions.

This rift between them seems inevitable; the cause of it is not immediately recognizable. It expresses itself first in a conflict between the family and the larger community to which the individual belongs. We have seen already that one of culture's principal endeavours is to cement men and women together into larger units. But the family will not give up the individual. The closer the attachment between the members of it, the more they often tend to remain aloof from others, and the harder it is for them to enter into the wider circle of the world at large. That form of life in common which is phylogenetically older, and is in childhood its only form, resists being displaced by the type that becomes acquired later with culture. Detachment from the family has become a task that awaits every adolescent, and often society helps him through it with pubertal and initiatory rites. One gets the impression that these difficulties form an integral part of every process of mental evolution—and indeed, at bottom, of every organic development, too.

The next discord is caused by women, who soon become antithetical to cultural trends and spread around them their conservative influence—the women who at the beginning laid the foundations of culture by the appeal of their love. Women represent the interests of the family and sexual life; the work of civilization has become more and more men's business; it confronts them with ever harder tasks, compels them to sublimations of instinct which women are not easily able to achieve. Since man has not an unlimited amount of mental energy at his disposal, he must accomplish his tasks by distributing his libido to the best advantage. What he employs for cultural purposes he withdraws to a great extent from women and his sexual life; his constant association with men and his dependence on his relations with them even estrange him from his duties as husband and father. Woman finds herself thus forced into the background by the claims of culture, and she adopts an inimical attitude towards it.

The tendency of culture to set restrictions upon sexual life is no less evident than its other aim of widening its sphere of operations. Even the earliest phase of it, the totemic, brought in its train the prohibition against incestuous object-choice, perhaps the most maiming wound ever inflicted throughout the ages on the erotic life of man. Further limitations are laid on it by taboos, laws and customs, which touch men as well as women. Various types of culture differ in the lengths to which they carry this; and the material structure of the social fabric also affects the measure of sexual freedom that remains. We have seen that culture obeys the laws of psychological economic necessity in making the restrictions, for it obtains a great part of the mental energy in needs by subtracting it from sexuality. Culture behaves towards sexuality in this respect like a tribe or a section of the population which has gained the upper hand and is exploiting the rest to its own advantage. Fear of a revolt among the oppressed then becomes a motive for even stricter regulations. A high-water mark in this

type of development has been reached in our Western European civilization. Psychologically it is fully justified in beginning by censuring any manifestations of the sexual life of children, for there would be no prospect of curbing the sexual desires of adults if the ground had not been prepared for it in childhood. Nevertheless there is no sort of justification for the lengths beyond this to which civilized society goes in actually denying the existence of these manifestations, which are not merely demonstrable but positively glaring. Where sexually mature persons are concerned, object-choice is further narrowed down to the opposite sex and most of the extragenital forms of satisfaction are interdicted as perversions. The standard which declares itself in these prohibitions is that of a sexual life identical for all; it pays no need to the disparities in the inborn and acquired sexual constitutions of individuals and cuts off a considerable number of them from sexual enjoyment, thus becoming a cause of grievous injustice. The effect of these restrictive measures might presumably be that all the sexual interest of those who are normal and not constitutionally handicapped could flow without further forfeiture into the channel left open to it. But the only outlet not thus censured, heterosexual genital love, is further circumscribed by the barriers of legitimacy and monogamy. Present-day civilization gives us plainly to understand that sexual relations are permitted only on the basis of a final, indissoluble bond between a man and woman; that sexuality as a source of enjoyment for its own sake is unacceptable to it; and that its intention is to tolerate it only as the hitherto irreplaceable means of multiplying the human race.

This, of course, represents an extreme. Everyone knows that it has proved impossible to put it into execution, even for short periods. Only the weaklings have submitted to such comprehensive interference with their sexual freedom, and stronger natures have done so only under one compensatory condition, of which mention may be made later. Civilized society has seen itself obliged to pass over in silence many transgressions which by its own ordinances it ought to have penalized. This does not justify anyone, however, in leaning towards the other side and assuming that, because it does not achieve all it aims at, such an attitude on the part of society is altogether harmless. The sexual life of civilized man is seriously disabled, whatever we may say; it sometimes makes an impression of being a function in process of becoming atrophied, just as organs like our teeth and our hair seem to be. One is probably right in supposing that the importance of sexuality as a source of pleasurable sensations, *i.e.*, as a means of fulfilling the purpose of life, has perceptibly decreased. Sometimes one imagines one perceives that it is not only the oppression of culture, but something in the nature of the function itself, that denies us full satisfaction and urges us in other directions. This may be an error; it is hard to decide.

V

Psycho-analytic work has shown that these frustrations in respect of sexual life are especially unendurable to the so-called neurotics among us. These persons manufacture substitute-gratifications for themselves in their symptoms, which, however, are either painful in themselves or become the cause of suffering owing to the difficulties they create with the person's environment and society at large. It is easy to understand the latter fact, but the former presents us with a new problem. But culture demands other sacrifices besides that of sexual gratifications.

We have regarded the difficulties in the development of civilization as part of the general difficulty accompanying all evolution, for we have traced them to the inertia of libido, its disinclination to relinquish an old position in favour of a new one. It is much the same thing if we say that the conflict between civilization and sexuality is caused by the circumstance that sexual love is a relationship between two people, in which a third can only be superfluous or disturbing, whereas civilization is founded on relations between larger groups of persons. When a love-relationship is at its height no room is left for any interest in the surrounding world; the pair of lovers are sufficient unto themselves, do not even need the child they have in common to make them happy. In no other case does Eros so plainly betray the core

of his being, his aim of making one out of many; but when he has achieved it in the proverbial way through the love of two human beings, he is not willing to go further.

From all this we might well imagine that a civilized community could consist of pairs of individuals such as this, libidinally satisfied in each other, and linked to all the others by work and common interests. If this were so, culture would not need to levy energy from sexuality. But such a desirable state of things does not exist and never has existed; in actuality culture is not content with such limited ties as these; we see that it endeavours to bind the members of the community to one another by libidinal ties as well, that it makes use of every means and favours every avenue by which powerful identifications can be created among them, and that it exacts a heavy toll of aim-inhibited libido in order to strengthen communities by bonds of friendship between the members. Restrictions upon sexual life are unavoidable if this object is to be attained. But we cannot see the necessity that forces culture along this path and gives rise to its antagonism to sexuality. It must be due to some distrubing influence not yet detected by us.

We may find the clue in one of the so-called ideal standards of civilized society. It runs: 'Thou shalt love thy neighbour as thyself'. It is world-renowned, undoubtedly older than Christianity which parades it as its proudest profession, yet certainly not very old; in historical times men still knew nothing of it. We will adopt a naïve attitude towards it, as if we were meeting it for the first time. Thereupon we find ourselves unable to suppress a feeling of astonishment, as at something unnatural. Why should we do this? What good is it to us? Above all, how can we do such a thing? How could it possibly be done? My love seems to me a valuable thing that I have no right to throw away without reflection. It imposes obligations on me which I must be prepared to make sacrifices to fulfil. If I love someone, he must be worthy of it in some way or other. (I am leaving out of account now the use he may be to me, as well as his possible significance to me as a sexual object; neither of these two kinds of relationship between us come into question where the injunction to love my neighbour is concerned.)

He will be worthy of it if he is so like me in important respects that I can love myself in him; worthy of it if he is so much more perfect than I that I can love my ideal of myself in him; I must love him if he is the son of my friend, since the pain my friend would feel if anything untoward happened to him would be my pain—I should have to share it. But if he is a stranger to me and cannot attract me by any value he has in himself or any significance he may have already acquired in my emotional life, it will be hard for me to love him. I shall even be doing wrong if I do, for my love is valued as a privilege by all those belonging to me; it is an injustice to them if I put a stranger on a level with them. But if I am to love him (with that kind of universal love) simply because he, too, is a denizen of the earth, like an insect or an earthworm or a grass-snake, then I fear that but a small modicum of love will fall to his lot, and it would be impossible for me to give him as much as by all the laws of reason I am entitled to retain for myself. What is the point of an injunction promulgated with such solemnity, if reason does not recommend it to us?

When I look more closely I find still further difficulties. Not merely is this stranger on the whole not worthy of love, but, to be honest, I must confess he has more claim to my hostility, even to my hatred. He does not seem to have the least trace of love for me, does not show me the slightest consideration. If it will do him any good, he has no hesitation in injuring me, never even asking himself whether the amount of advantage he gains by it bears any proportion to the amount of wrong done to me. What is more, he does not even need to get an advantage from it; if he can merely get a little pleasure out of it, he thinks nothing of jeering at me, insulting me, slandering me, showing his power over me; and the more secure he feels himself, or the more helpless I am, with so much more certainty can I expect this behaviour from him towards me. If he behaved differently, if he showed me consideration and did not molest me, I should in any case, without the aforesaid commandment, be willing to treat him similarly. If the high-sounding ordinance had run, 'Love thy neighbour as thy neighbour loves thee', I should not take objection to it. And there is a second commandment that seems to me even more incomprehensible, and arouses still stronger opposition in me. It is: 'Love thine enemies'. When I think it over, however, I am wrong in treating it as a greater imposition. It is at bottom the same thing.

I imagine now I hear a voice gravely adjuring me: 'Just because thy neighbour is not worthy of thy love, is probably full of enmity towards thee, thou shouldst love him as thyself'. I then perceive the case to be like that of *Credo quia absurdum.*

Now it is, of course, very probable that my neighbour, when he is commanded to love me as himself, will answer exactly as I have done and reject me for the same reasons. I hope he will not have the same objective grounds for doing so, but he will hope so as well. Even so, there are variations in men's behaviour which ethics, disregarding the fact that they are determined, classifies as 'good' and 'evil'. As long as these undeniable variations have not been abolished, conformity to the highest ethical standards constitutes a betrayal of the interests of culture, for it puts a direct premium on wickedness. One is irresistibly reminded here of an incident in the French Chamber when capital punishment was being discussed; the speech of a member who had passionately supported its abolition was being applauded with loud acclamation, when suddenly a voice was heard calling out from the back of the room, '*Que messieurs les assassins commencent!*'

The bit of truth behind all this—one so eagerly denied—is that men are not gentle, friendly creatures wishing for love, who simply defend themselves if they are attacked, but that a powerful measure of desire for aggression has to be reckoned as part of their instinctual endowment. The result is that their neighbour is to them not only a possible helper or sexual object, but also a temptation to them to gratify their aggressiveness on him, to exploit his capacity for work without recompense, to use him sexually without his consent, to seize his possessions, to humiliate him, to cause him pain, to torture and to kill him. *Homo homini lupus;* who has the courage to dispute it in the face of all the evidence in his own life and in history? This aggressive cruelty usually lies in wait for some provocation, or else it steps into the service of some other purpose, the aim of which might as well have been achieved by milder measures. In circumstances that favour it, when those forces in the mind which ordinarily inhibit it cease to operate, it also manifests itself spontaneously and reveals men as savage beasts to whom the thought of sparing their own kind is alien. Anyone who calls to mind the atrocities of the early migrations, of the invasion by the Huns or by the so-called Mongols under Jenghiz Khan and Tamerlane, of the sack of Jerusalem by the pious Crusaders, even indeed the horrors of the last world war, will have to bow his head humbly before the truth of this view of man.

The existence of this tendency to aggression which we can detect in ourselves and rightly presume to be present in others is the factor that disturbs our relations with our neighbours and makes it necessary for culture to institute its high demands. Civilized society is perpetually menaced with disintegration through this primary hostility of men towards one another. Their interests in their common work would not hold them together; the passions of instinct are stronger than reasoned interests. Culture has to call up every possible reinforcement in order to erect barriers against the aggressive instincts of men and hold their manifestations in check by reaction-formations in men's minds. Hence its system of methods by which mankind is to be driven to identifications and aim-inhibited love-relationships; hence the restrictions on sexual life; and hence, too, its ideal command to love one's neighbour as oneself, which is really justified by the fact that nothing is so completely at variance with original human nature as this. With all its striving, this endeavour of culture's has so far not achieved very much. Civilization expects to prevent the worst atrocities of brutal violence by taking upon itself the right to employ violence against criminals, but the law is not able to lay hands on the more discreet and subtle forms in which human aggressions are expressed. The time comes when every one of us has to abandon the illusory anticipations with which in our youth we regarded our fellow-men, and when we realize how much hardship and suffering we have been caused in life through their ill-will. It would be unfair, however, to reproach culture with trying to eliminate all disputes and competition from human concerns. These things are undoubtedly indispensable; but opposition is not necessarily enmity, only it may be misused to make an opening for it.

The Communists believe they have found a way of delivering us from this evil. Man is wholeheartedly good and friendly to his neighbour, they say, but the system of private property has corrupted his nature. The possession of private property gives power to the individual and thence the temptation arises to ill-treat his neighbour; the man who is excluded from the possession of property is obliged to rebel in hostility against the oppressor. If private property were abolished, all valuables held in common and all allowed to share in the enjoyment of them, ill-will and enmity would disappear from among men. Since all needs would be satisfied, none would have any reason to regard another as an enemy; all would willingly undertake the work which is necessary. I have no concern with any economic criticisms of the communistic system; I cannot enquire into whether the abolition of private property is advantageous and expedient. But I am able to recognize that psychologically it is founded on an untenable illusion. By abolishing private property one deprives the human love of aggression of one of its instruments, a strong one undoubtedly, but assuredly not the strongest. It in no way alters the individual differences in power and influence which are turned by aggressiveness to its own use, nor does it change the nature of the instinct in any way. This instinct did not arise as the result of property; it reigned almost supreme in primitive times when possessions were still extremely scanty; it shows itself already in the nursery when possessions have hardly grown out of their original anal shape; it is at the bottom of all the relations of affection and love between human beings—possibly with the single exception of that of a mother to her male child. Suppose that personal rights to material goods are done away with, there still remain prerogatives in sexual relationships, which must arouse the strongest rancour and most violent enmity among men and women who are otherwise equal. Let us suppose this were also to be removed by instituting complete liberty in sexual life, so that the family, the germ-cell of culture, ceased to exist; one could not, it is true, foresee the new paths on which cultural development might then proceed, but one thing one would be bound to expect, and that is, that the ineffaceable feature of human nature would follow wherever it led.

Men clearly do not find it easy to do without satisfaction of this tendency to aggression that is in them; when deprived of satisfaction of it they are ill at ease. There is an advantage, not to be undervalued, in the existence of smaller communities, through which the aggressive instinct can find an outlet in enmity towards those outside the group. It is always possible to unite considerable numbers of men in love towards one another, so long as there are still some remaining as objects for aggressive manifestations. I once interested myself in the peculiar fact that peoples whose territories are adjacent, and are otherwise closely related, are always at feud with and ridiculing each other, as, for instance, the Spaniards and the Portuguese, the North and South Germans, the English and the Scotch, and so on. I gave it the name of 'narcissism in respect of minor differences', which does not do much to explain it. One can now see that it is a convenient and relatively harmless form of satisfaction for aggressive tendencies, through which cohesion amongst the members of a group is made easier. The Jewish people, scattered in all directions as they are, have in this way rendered services which deserve recognition to the development of culture in the countries where they settled; but unfortunately not all the massacres of Jews in the Middle Ages sufficed to procure peace and security for their Christian contemporaries. Once the apostle Paul had laid down universal love between all men as the foundation of his Christian community, the inevitable consequence in Christianity was the utmost intolerance towards all who remained outside of it; the Romans, who had not founded their state on love, were not given to lack of religious toleration, although religion was a concern of the state, and the state was permeated through and through with it. Neither was it an unaccountable chance that the dream of a German world-dominion evoked a complementary movement towards anti-Semitism; and it is quite intelligible that the attempt to establish a new communistic type of culture in Russia should find psychological support in the persecution of the bourgeois. One only wonders, with some concern, however, how the Soviets will manage when they have exterminated their bourgeois entirely.

If civilization requires such sacrifices, not only of sexuality but also of the aggressive tendencies in mankind, we can better understand why it should be so hard for men to feel happy in it. In actual fact primitive man was better off in this respect, for he knew nothing of any restrictions on his instincts. As a set-off against this, his prospects of enjoying his happiness for any length of time were very slight. Civilized man has exchanged some part of his chances of happiness for a measure of security. We will not forget, however, that in the primal family only the head of it enjoyed this instinctual freedom; the other members lived in slavish thraldom. The antithesis between a minority enjoying cultural advantages and a majority who are robbed of them was therefore most extreme in that primeval period of culture. With regard to the primitive human types living at the present time, careful investigation has revealed that their instinctual life is by no means to be envied on account of its freedom; it is subject to restrictions of a different kind but perhaps even more rigorous than is that of modern civilized man.

In rightly finding fault, as we thus do, with our present state of civilization for so inadequately providing us with what we require to make us happy in life, and for the amount of suffering of a probably avoidable nature it lays us open to—in doing our utmost to lay bare the roots of its deficiencies by our unsparing criticisms, we are undoubtedly exercising our just rights and not showing ourselves enemies of culture. We may expect that in the course of time changes will be carried out in our civilization so that it becomes more satisfying to our needs and no longer open to the reproaches we have made against it. But perhaps we shall also accustom ourselves to the idea that there are certain difficulties inherent in the very nature of culture which will not yield to any efforts at reform. Over and above the obligations of putting restrictions upon our instincts, which we see to be inevitable, we are imminently threatened with the dangers of a state one may call 'la *misère psychologique'* of groups. This danger is most menacing where the social forces of cohesion consist predominantly of identifications of the individuals in the group with one another, whilst leading personalities fail to acquire the significance that should fall to them in the process of group-formation. The state of civilization in America at the present day offers a good opportunity for studying this injurious effect of civilization which we have reason to dread. But I will resist the temptation to enter upon a criticism of American culture; I have no desire to give the impression that I would employ American methods myself. . . .

VIII

What means does civilization make use of to hold in check the aggressiveness that opposes it, to make it harmless, perhaps to get rid of it? Some of these measures we have already come to know, though not yet the one that is apparently the most important. We can study it in the evolution of the individual. What happens in him to render his craving for aggression innocuous? Something very curious, that we should never have guessed and that yet seems simple enough. The aggressiveness is introjected, 'internalized'; in fact, it is sent back where it came from, *i.e.*, directed against the ego. It is there taken over by a part of the ego that distinguishes itself from the rest as a super-ego, and now, in the form of 'conscience,' exercises the same propensity to harsh aggressiveness against the ego that the ego would have liked to enjoy against others. The tension between the strict super-ego and the subordinate ego we call the sense of guilt; it manifests itself as the need for punishment. Civilization therefore obtains the mastery over the dangerous love of aggression in individuals by enfeebling and disarming it and setting up an institution within their minds to keep watch over it, like a garrison in a conquered city.

As to the origin of the sense of guilt, analysts have different views from those of the psychologists; nor is it easy for analysts to explain it either. First of all, when one asks how a sense of guilt arises in anyone, one is told something one cannot dispute: people feel guilty (pious people call it 'sinful') when they have done something they know to be 'bad.' But then one sees how little this answer tells one. Perhaps after some hesitation one will add that a person who has not actually committed a bad act, but has merely become aware of the intention to do so, can also hold himself guilty; and then one will ask why in this case the intention is counted as equivalent to the deed. In both cases, however, one is presupposing that wickedness has already been recognized as reprehensible, as something that ought not to be put into execution. How is this judgement arrived at? One may reject the suggestion of an original—as one might say, natural—capacity for discriminating between good and evil. Evil is often not at all that which would injure or endanger the ego; on the contrary, it can also be something that it desires, that would give it pleasure. An extraneous influence is evidently at work; it is this that decides what is to be called good and bad. Since their own feelings would not have led men along the same path, they must have had a motive for obeying this extraneous influence. It is easy to discover this motive in man's helplessness and dependence upon others; it can best be designated the dread of losing love. If he loses the love of others on whom he is dependent, he will forfeit also their protection against many dangers, and above all he runs the risk that this stronger person will show his superiority in the form of punishing him. . . .

Just as a planet circles round its central body while at the same time rotating on its own axis, so the individual man takes his part in the course of humanity's development as he goes on his way through life. But to our dull eyes the play of forces in the heavens seems set fast in a never-varying scheme, though in organic life we can still see how the forces contend with one another and the results of the conflict change from day to day. So in every individual the two trends, one towards personal happiness and the other towards unity with the rest of humanity, must contend with each other; so must the two processes of individual and of cultural development oppose each other and dispute the ground against each other. This struggle between individual and society, however, is not derived from the antagonism of the primal instincts, Eros and Death, which are probably irreconcilable; it is a dissension in the camp of the libido itself, comparable to the contest between the ego and its objects for a share of the libido; and it does eventually admit of a solution in the individual, as we may hope it will also do in the future of civilization—however greatly it may oppress the lives of individuals at the present time.

The analogy between the process of cultural evolution and the path of individual development may be carried further in an important respect. It can be maintained that the community, too, develops a super-ego, under whose influence cultural evolution proceeds. It would be an enticing task for an authority on human systems of culture to work out this analogy in specific cases. I will confine myself to pointing out certain striking details. The super-ego of any given epoch of civilization originates in the same way as that of an individual; it is based on the impression left behind them by great leading personalities, men of outstanding force of mind, or men in whom some one human tendency has developed in unusual strength and purity, often for that reason very disproportionately. In many instances the analogy goes still further, in that during their lives—often enough, even if not always—such persons are ridiculed by others, ill-used or even cruelly done to death, just as happened with the primal father who also rose again to become a deity long after his death by violence. The most striking example of this double fate is the figure of Jesus Christ, if indeed it does not itself belong to the realm of mythology which called it into being out of a dim memory of that primordial event. Another point of agreement is that the cultural super-ego, just like that of an individual, sets up high ideals and standards, and that failure to fulfil them is punished by both with 'anxiety of conscience'. In this particular, indeed, we come across the remarkable circumstance that the mental processes concerned here, are actually more familiar to us and more accessible to consciousness when they proceed from the group than they can be in the individual. In the latter, when tension arises, the aggressions of the super-ego voicing its noisy reproaches are all that is perceived, while its injunctions themselves often remain unconscious in the background. If we bring them to the knowledge of consciousness we find that they coincide with the demands of the prevailing cultural super-ego. At this point the two processes, that of the evolution of the group and the development of the individual, are always firmly mortised together, so to speak. Consequently many of the effects and properties of the super-ego can be more easily detected through its operations in the group than in the individual.

The cultural super-ego has elaborated its ideals and erected its standards. Those of its demands which deal with the relations of human beings to one another are comprised under the name of ethics. The greatest value has at all times been set upon systems of ethics, as if men had expected them in particular to achieve something especially important. And ethics does in fact deal predominantly with the point which is easily seen to be the sorest of all in any scheme of civilization. Ethics must be regarded therefore as a therapeutic effort: as an endeavour to achieve something through the standards imposed by the super-ego which had not been attained by the work of civilization in other ways. We already know—it is what we have been discussing—that the question is how to dislodge the greatest obstacle to civilization, the constitutional tendency in men to aggressions against one another; and for that very reason the commandment to love one's neighbour as oneself—probably the most recent of the cultural super-ego's demands—is especially interesting to us. In our investigations and our therapy of the neuroses we cannot avoid finding fault with the super-ego of the individual on two counts: in commanding and prohibiting with such severity, it troubles too little about the happiness of the ego, and it fails to take into account sufficiently the difficulties in the way of of obeying it—the strength of instinctual cravings in the id and the hardships of external environment. Consequently in our therapy we often find ourselves obliged to do battle with the super-ego and work to moderate its demands. Exactly the same objections can be made against the ethical standards of the cultural super-ego. It, too, does not trouble enough about the mental constitution of human beings; it enjoins a command and never asks whether or not it is possible for them to obey it. It presumes, on the contrary, that a man's ego is psychologically capable of anything that is required of it—that his ego has unlimited power over his id. This is an error; even in so-called normal people the power of controlling the id cannot be increased beyond certain limits. If one asks more of them, one produces revolt or neurosis in individuals or makes them unhappy. The command to love our neighbours as ourselves is the strongest defence there is against human aggressiveness and it is a superlative example of the unpsychological attitude of the cultural super-ego. The command is impossible to fulfil; such an enormous inflation of love can only lower its value and not remedy the evil. Civilization pays no heed to all this; it merely prates that the harder it is to obey, the more laudable the obedience. The fact remains that anyone who follows such preaching in the present state of civilization only puts himself at a disadvantage beside all those who set it at naught. What an overwhelming obstacle to civilization aggression must be if the defence against it can cause as much misery as aggression itself! 'Natural' ethics, as it is called, has nothing to offer here beyond the narcissistic satisfaction of thinking oneself better than others. The variety of ethics that links itself with religion brings in at this point its promises of a better future life. I should imagine that as long as virtue is not rewarded in this life ethics will preach in vain. I too think it unquestionable that an actual change in men's attitude to property would be of more help in this direction than any ethical commands; but among the Socialists this proposal is obscured by new idealistic expectations disregarding human nature, which detract from its value in actual practice.

It seems to me that the point of view which seeks to follow the phenomena of cultural evolution as manifestations of a super-ego promises to yield still further discoveries. I am coming quickly to an end. There is one question, however, which I can hardly ignore. If the evolution of civilization has such a far-reaching similarity with the development of an individual, and if the same methods are employed in both, would not the diagnosis be justified that many systems of civilization—or epochs of it—possibly even the whole of humanity—have become 'neurotic' under the pressure of the civilizing trends? To analytic dissection of these neuroses therapeutic recommendations might follow which could claim a great practical interest. I would not say that such an attempt to apply psycho-analysis to civilized society would be fanciful or doomed to fruitlessness. But it behoves us to be very careful, not to forget that after all we are dealing only with analogies, and that it is dangerous, not only with men but also with concepts, to drag them out of the region where they originated and have matured. The diagnosis of collective neuroses, moreover, will be confronted by a special difficulty. In the neurosis of an individual we can use as a starting-point the contrast presented to us between the patient and his environment which we assume to be 'normal'. No such background as this would be available for any society similarly affected; it would have to be supplied in some other way. And with regard to any therapeutic application of our knowledge, what would be the use of the most acute analysis of social neuroses, since no one possesses power to compel the community to adopt the therapy? In spite of all these difficulties, we may expect that one day someone will venture upon this research into the pathology of civilized communities.

For various reasons, it is very far from my intention to express any opinion concerning the value of human civilization. I have endeavoured to guard myself against the enthusiastic partiality which believes our civilization to be the most precious thing that we possess or could acquire, and thinks it must inevitably lead us to undreamt-of-heights of perfection. I can at any rate listen without taking umbrage to those critics who aver that when one surveys the aims of civilization and the means it employs, one is bound to conclude that the whole thing is not worth the effort and that in the end it can only produce a state of things which no individual will be able to bear. My impartiality is all the easier to me since I know very little about these things and am sure only of one thing, that the judgements of value made by mankind are immediately determined by their desires for happiness; in other words, that those judgements are attempts to prop up their illusions with arguments. I could understand it very well if anyone were to point to the inevitable nature of the process of cultural development and say, for instance, that the tendency to institute restrictions upon sexual life or to carry humanitarian ideals into effect at the cost of natural selection is a developmental trend which it is impossible to avert or divert, and to which it is best for us to submit as though they were natural necessities. I know, too, the objection that can be raised against this: that tendencies such as these, which are believed to have insuperable power behind them, have often in the history of man been thrown aside and replaced by others. My courage fails me, therefore, at the thought of rising up as a prophet before my fellow-men, and I bow to their reproach that I have no consolation to offer them; for at bottom this is what they all demand—the frenzied revolutionary as passionately as the most pious believer.

The fateful question of the human species seems to me to be whether and to what extent the cultural process developed in it will succeed in mastering the derangements of communal life caused by the human instinct of aggression and self-destruction. In this connection, perhaps the phase through which we are at this moment passing deserves special interest. Men have brought their powers of subduing the forces of nature to such a pitch that by using them they could now very easily exterminate one another to the last man. They know this—hence arises a great part of their current unrest, their dejection, their mood of apprehension. And now it may be expected that the other of the two 'heavenly forces,' eternal Eros, will put forth his strength so as to maintain himself alongside of his equally immortal adversary.

Jean Anouilh

Jean Anouilh (1910–   ), present-day French Existentialist playwright, has expressed some of the pessimism characteristic of so much of modern continental European thinking. Existentialism, a new name for an old philosophy, has provided in recent years an intellectual framework for literary and religious expression, especially in contemporary Europe. Perhaps the crisis of modern Western man, as exemplified in Germany and France since 1919, has con tributed heavily to making of this movement one of the strongest and saddest reactions to chaos, confusion, and disillusionment. Anouilh's works are marked by an insistent posing of ultimate questions concerning the nature of life and society in a time when all values have been challenged in the most ruthless fashion. Antigone, first produced in Paris in 1944, has had the distinction, for obvious reasons, of being produced both in German-occupied and in liberated France. The play, however, represents far more than a mere document of French politics; it treats of deep-seated conflicts of human and social motivation. In reading Antigone, note (1) how the author uses and adapts the classic theme and form, (2) what Creon is made to represent, (3) the character and aims of Antigone, (4) the conflict within Antigone's personality, (5) the nature and meaning of Ismene's plea to Antigone, (6) the double standard of conduct under which Creon is willing to act, (7) the contrast between Creon's and Antigone's religious beliefs, (8) Creon's defence of his rule, (9) Creon's definition of life, (10) the central theme of the play, and (11) evidences of existentialism.

ANTIGONE

CAST

Chorus	First Guard
Antigone	Second Guard
Nurse	Third Guard
Ismene	Messenger
Haemon	Page
Creon	Eurydice

THE SETTING

A gray cloth cyclorama, semi-circular, hangs at the back of the set. At the bottom of the cyclorama, a stair, of three steps, sweeps in a semi-circle. Downstage, right and left, two archways. The curtains part in the center for entrance and exit.

A table stands left of center-stage, with matching chairs set at either end. A small stool is placed right of the chair at the right of the table.

ANTIGONE

ANTIGONE, *her hands clasped round her knees, sits on the top step. The* THREE GUARDS

sit on the steps, in a small group, playing cards. The CHORUS *stands up on the top step.* EURYDICE *sits on the top step, just left of center, knitting. The* NURSE *sits on the second step, left of* EURYDICE. ISMENE *stands in front of arch, left, facing* HAEMON, *who stands left of her.* CREON *sits in the chair at right end of the table, his arm over the shoulder of his* PAGE, *who sits on the stool beside his chair. The* MESSENGER *is leaning against the downstage portal of the right arch.*

The curtain rises slowly; then the CHORUS *turns and moves downstage.*

CHORUS. Well, here we are.

These people that you see here are about to act out for you the story of Antigone.

That thin little creature sitting by herself, staring straight ahead, seeing nothing, is Antigone. She is thinking. She is thinking that the instant I finish telling you who's who and what's what in this play, she will burst forth as the tense, sallow, wilful girl who would never listen to reason and who is about to rise up alone against Creon, her uncle, the King.

As translated and adapted by Lewis Galantiere from the play by Jean Anouilh in *Antigone*, Random House, New York, 1946. Reprinted by permission of Random House, Inc. Copyright, 1946.

Another thing that she is thinking is this: she is going to die. Antigone is only twenty years old. She would much rather live than die. But there is no help for it. When you are on the side of the gods against the tyrant, of Man against the State, of purity against corruption—when, in short, your name is Antigone, there is only one part you can play; and she will have to play hers through to the end.

Mind you, Antigone doesn't know all these things about herself. I know them because it is my business to know them. That's what a Greek Chorus is for. All that she knows is that Creon will not allow her dead brother to be buried; and that in spite of Creon, she must bury him. Antigone doesn't think, she acts; she doesn't reason, she feels. And from the moment the curtain went up, she began to feel that inhuman forces were whirling her out of this world, snatching her away from her sister, Ismene, whom you see smiling and chatting with that young man, making her an instrument of the gods in a way she cannot fathom but that she will faithfully pursue.

You have never seen inhuman forces at work? You will, tonight.

(CHORUS *turns and indicates* HAEMON.)

The young man talking to Ismene—to the pliant and reasonable Ismene—is Haemon. He is the King's son, Creon's son. Antigone and he are engaged to be married. You wouldn't have thought she was his type. He likes dancing, sports, competition; he likes women, too. Now look at Ismene again. She is certainly more beautiful than Antigone. She is the girl you'd think he'd go for. Well . . . there was a ball one night. Ismene wore a new evening dress. She was radiant. Haemon danced every dance with her; he wouldn't look at any other girl. And yet, that same night, before the dance was over, suddenly he went in search of Antigone, found her sitting alone—like that, with her arms clasped round her knees—and asked her to marry him. It didn't seem to surprise Antigone in the least. She looked up at him out of those solemn eyes of hers, then smiled sort of sadly; and she said "yes." That was all. Well, here is Haemon expecting to marry Antigone. He won't, of course. He didn't

know, when he asked her, that the earth wasn't made to hold a husband of Antigone, and that this princely distinction was to earn him no more than the right to die sooner than he might otherwise have done.

(CHORUS *turns toward* CREON.)

That gray-haired, powerfully built man sitting lost in thought, with his little Page at his side, is Creon, the King. His face is lined. He is tired. He practices the difficult art of a leader of men. When he was younger, when Oedipus was King and Creon was no more than the King's brother-in-law, he was different. He loved music, bought rare manuscripts, was a kind of art patron. He used to while away whole afternoons in the antique shops of this city of Thebes. But Oedipus died. Oedipus' sons died. Creon's moment had come. He took over the kingdom.

(CHORUS *moves downstage. Reflects a moment.*)

I'll tell you something about Creon. He has a tendency to fool himself. This leader of men, this brilliant debater and logician, likes to believe that if it were not for his sense of responsibility, he would step down from the throne and go back to collecting manuscripts. But the fact is, he loves being King. He's an artist who has always believed that he could govern just as well as any man of action could; and he's quite sure that no god nor any man can tell him anything about what is best for the common people.

Creon has a wife, a Queen. Her name is Eurydice. There she sits, the gentle old lady with the knitting, next to the Nurse who brought up the two girls. She will go on knitting all through the play, till the time comes for her to go to her room and die. She is a good woman, a worthy, loving soul. But she is no help to her husband. Creon has to face the music alone. Alone with his Page, who is too young to be of any help.

The others? Well, let's see.

(*He points toward the* MESSENGER.)

That pale young man leaning against the wall is the Messenger. Later on, he will come running in to announce that Haemon is dead.

He has a premonition of catastrophe. That's what he is brooding over. That's why he won't mingle with the others.

As for those three pasty-faced card players —they are the guards, members of Creon's police force. They chew tobacco; one smells of garlic, another of beer; but they're not a bad lot. They have wives they are afraid of, kids who are afraid of them; they're bothered by the little day-to-day worries that beset us all. At the same time—they are policemen: eternally innocent, no matter what crimes are committed; eternally indifferent, for nothing that happens can matter to them. They are quite prepared to arrest anybody at all, including Creon himself, should the order be given by a new leader.

That's the lot. Now for the play.

Oedipus, who was the father of the two girls, Antigone and Ismene, had also two sons, Eteocles and Polynices. After Oedipus died, it was agreed that the two sons should share his throne, each to reign over Thebes in alternate years.

(*Gradually, the lights on the stage have been dimmed.*)

But when Eteocles, the elder son, had reigned a full year, and time had come for him to step down, he refused to yield up the throne to his younger brother. There was civil war. Polynices brought up allies—six foreign princes; and in the course of the war he and his foreigners were defeated, each in front of one of the seven gates of the city. The two brothers fought, and they killed one another in single combat just outside the city walls. Now Creon is King.

(CHORUS *is leaning, at this point, against the left proscenium arch. By now the stage is dark, with only the cyclorama bathed in dark blue. A single spot lights up the face of* CHORUS.)

Creon has issued a solemn edict that Eteocles, with whom he had sided, is to be buried with pomp and honors, and that Polynices is to be left to rot. The vultures and the dogs are to bloat themselves on his carcass. Nobody is to go into mourning for him. No gravestone is to be set up in his memory. And above all, any person who attempts to give him religious burial will himself be put to death.

It is against this blasphemy that Antigone rebels. What is for Creon merely the climax of a political purge, is for her an outrage against her dead brother which swells and grows until she perceives that it is an offense against God and against all men.

(*The light on* CHORUS *vanishes and* CHORUS *disappears through the left arch.*)

(*It is dawn, gray and ashen, in a house asleep.* ANTIGONE *steals in from out-of-doors, through the arch right. She is carrying her sandals in her hand. She pauses, looking off through the arch, taut, listening, then turns and moves across downstage. As she reaches the table, she sees the* NURSE *approaching through the arch left. She runs quickly towards the exit. As she reaches the steps, the* NURSE *enters through arch and stands still when she sees* ANTIGONE.)

NURSE. Where have you been?

ANTIGONE. Nowhere. It was beautiful. The whole world was gray when I went out. And now—you wouldn't recognize it. It's like a post card: all pink, and green and yellow. You'll have to get up earlier, Nurse, if you want to see a world without color.

NURSE. It was still pitch black when I got up. I went to your room, for I thought you might have flung off your blanket in the night. You weren't there.

ANTIGONE. (*Comes down the steps.*) The garden was lovely. It was still asleep.

NURSE. You hadn't slept in your bed. I couldn't find you. I went to the back door. You'd left it half open.

ANTIGONE. The fields were wet. They were waiting for something to happen. The whole world was breathless, waiting. I can't tell you what a roaring noise I seemed to make as I went up the road. I took off my sandals and slipped into a field. (*She moves down to the stool and sits.*)

NURSE. (*Kneels at* ANTIGONE's *feet to chafe them and put on the sandals.*) You'll do well to wash your feet before you go back to bed, Miss.

ANTIGONE. I'm not going back to bed.

NURSE. Don't be a fool! You get some sleep! And me, getting up to see if she hasn't flung off her blanket; and I find her bed cold and nobody in it!

ANTIGONE. Do you think that if a person got up every morning like this, it would be just as thrilling every morning to be the first girl out-of-doors?

(NURSE *puts* ANTIGONE's *left foot down, lifts her other foot and chafes it.*)

NURSE. Morning my grandmother! It was night. It still is. And now, my girl, you'll stop trying to squirm out of this and tell me what you were up to. Where've you been?

ANTIGONE. That's true. It was still night. There wasn't a soul out-of-doors but me who thought that it was morning.

NURSE. Oh, my little flibberty-gibbet! Just can't imagine what I'm talking about, can she? Go on with you! I know that game. Where have you been, wicked girl?

ANTIGONE (*soberly*). No. Not wicked.

NURSE. You went out to meet someone, didn't you? Deny it if you can.

ANTIGONE. Yes. I went out to meet someone.

NURSE. A lover?

ANTIGONE. Yes, Nurse. Yes, the poor dear. I have a lover.

NURSE. (*Stands up; bursting out.*) Ah, that's very nice now, isn't it? Such goings-on! You, the daughter of a king, running out to meet lovers. And we work our fingers to the bone for you, we slave to bring you up like young ladies! (*She sits on chair right of table.*) You're all alike, all of you. Even you—who never used to stop to primp in front of a looking-glass, or smear your mouth with rouge, or dindle and dandle to make the boys ogle you, and you ogle back. How many times I'd say to myself, "Now that one, now: I wish she was a little more of a coquette—always wearing the same dress, her hair tumbling round her face. One thing's sure," I'd say to myself, "none of the boys will look at her while Ismene's around, all curled and cute and tidy and trim. I'll have this one on my hands the rest of my life." And now, you see? Just like your sister, after all. Only worse: a hypocrite. Who is the lad? Some little scamp, eh? Somebody you can't bring home and show to your family, and

say, "Well, this is him, and I mean to marry him and no other." That's how it is, is it? Answer me!

ANTIGONE (*smiling faintly*). That's how it is. Yes, Nurse.

NURSE. Yes, says she! God save us! I took her when she wasn't that high. I promised her poor mother I'd make a lady of her. And look at her! But don't you go thinking this is the end of this, my young 'un. I'm only your nurse and you can play deaf and dumb with me; I don't count. But your uncle Creon will hear of this! That, I promise you.

ANTIGONE (*a little weary*). Yes. Creon will hear of this.

NURSE. And we'll hear what he has to say when he finds out that you go wandering alone o'nights. Not to mention Haemon. For the girl's engaged! Going to be married! Going to be married, and she hops out of bed at four in the morning to meet somebody else in a field.

ANTIGONE. Please, Nurse, I want to be alone.

NURSE. And if you so much as speak of it, she says she wants to be alone!

ANTIGONE. Nanny, you shouldn't scold, dear. This isn't a day when you should be losing your temper.

NURSE. Not scold, indeed! Along with the rest of it, I'm to like it. Didn't I promise your mother? What would she say if she was here? "Old Stupid!" That's what she'd call me. "Old Stupid. Not to know how to keep my little girl pure! Spend your life making them behave, watching over them like a mother hen, running after them with mufflers and sweaters to keep them warm and eggnogs to make them strong; and then at four o'clock in the morning snoring in your bed and letting them slip out into the bushes." That's what she'd say, your mother. And I'd stand there, dying of shame if I wasn't dead already. And all I could do would be not to dare look her in the face; and "That's true," I'd say. "That's all true what you say, Your Majesty."

ANTIGONE. Nanny, dear. Dear Nanny. Don't cry. You'll be able to look Mamma in the face when it's your time to see her. And she'll say, "Good morning, Nanny. Thank you for my little Antigone. You did look after her so well." She knows why I went out this morning.

NURSE. Not to meet a lover?

ANTIGONE. No. Not to meet a lover.

NURSE. Well, you've a queer way of teasing me, I must say! Not to know when she's teasing me! (*Rises to stand behind* ANTIGONE.) I must be getting awfully old, that's what it is. But if you loved me, you'd tell me the truth. You'd tell me why your bed was empty when I went along to tuck you in. Wouldn't you?

ANTIGONE. Please, Nanny, don't cry any more. (ANTIGONE *turns partly towards* NURSE, *puts an arm up to* NURSE's *shoulder. With her other hand,* ANTIGONE *caresses* NURSE's *face.*) There, now, my sweet red apple. Do you remember how I used to rub your cheeks to make them shine? My dear, wrinkled red apple! I didn't do anything tonight that was worth sending tears down the little gullies of your dear face. I am pure, and I swear that I have no other lover than Haemon. If you like, I'll swear that I shall never have any other lover than Haemon. Save your tears, Nanny, save them, Nanny dear; you may still need them. When you cry like that, I become a little girl again; and I mustn't be a little girl today. (ANTIGONE *rises and moves upstage.*)

(ISMENE *enters through arch left. She pauses in front of arch.*)

ISMENE. Antigone! What are you doing up at this hour? I've just been to your room.

NURSE. The two of you, now! You're both going mad, to be up before the kitchen fire has been started. Do you like running about without a mouthful of breakfast? Do you think it's decent for the daughters of a king? (*She turns to* ISMENE.) And look at you with no wraps on, and the sun not up! I'll have you both on my hands with colds before I know it.

ANTIGONE. Nanny dear, go away now. It's not chilly, really. Summer's here. Go make us some coffee. Please, Nanny, I'd love some coffee. It would do me so much good.

NURSE. My poor baby! Her head's swimming, what with nothing on her stomach, and I stand here like an idiot when I could be getting her something hot to drink. (NURSE *exits.*)

(*A pause.*)

ISMENE. Aren't you well?

ANTIGONE. Of course I am. Just a little tired.

I got up too early. (ANTIGONE *sits on chair, suddenly tired.*)

ISMENE. I couldn't sleep, either.

ANTIGONE. Ismene, you ought not to go without your beauty sleep.

ISMENE. Don't make fun of me.

ANTIGONE. I'm not, Ismene, truly. This particular morning, seeing how beautiful you are makes everything easier for me. Wasn't I a miserable little beast when we were small? I used to fling mud at you, and put worms down your neck. I remember tying you to a tree and cutting off your hair. Your beautiful hair! How easy it must be never to be unreasonable with all that smooth silken hair so beautifully set round your head.

ISMENE (*abruptly*). Why do you insist upon talking about other things?

ANTIGONE (*gently*). I am not talking about other things.

ISMENE. Antigone, I've thought about it a lot.

ANTIGONE. Have you?

ISMENE. I thought about it all night long. Antigone, you're mad.

ANTIGONE. Am I?

ISMENE. We cannot do it.

ANTIGONE. Why not?

ISMENE. Creon will have us put to death.

ANTIGONE. Of course he will. That's what he's here for. He will do what he has to do, and we will do what we have to do. He is bound to put us to death. We are bound to go out and bury our brother. That's the way it is. What do you think we can do to change it?

ISMENE. (*Releases* ANTIGONE's *hand; draws back a step.*) I don't want to die.

ANTIGONE. I'd prefer not to die, myself.

ISMENE. Listen to me, Antigone. I thought about it all night. I always think things over, and you don't. You are impulsive. You get a notion in your head and you jump up and do the thing straight off. And if it's silly, well, so much the worse for you. Whereas, *I* think things out.

ANTIGONE. Sometimes it is better not to think too much.

ISMENE. I don't agree with you! (ANTIGONE *looks at* ISMENE, *then turns and moves to chair behind table.* ISMENE *leans on end of table top.*

toward ANTIGONE.) Oh, I know it's horrible. And I pity Polynices just as much as you do. But all the same, I sort of see what Uncle Creon means.

ANTIGONE. I don't want to "sort of see" anything.

ISMENE. Uncle Creon is the king. He has to set an example!

ANTIGONE. Example! Do you call that edict an example? Polynices is cheated out of his rights. He makes war. Creon sides against him, and he is killed. After which Creon insists that Polynices must rot and putrefy and be mangled by dogs and birds, with no priest to bury him. And you talk to me of examples!

ISMENE. Oh, Antigone, you don't understand!

ANTIGONE. What in God's name is there to understand? Except that a man's body lies rotting, unburied. And that he is my brother. And that I must bury him.

ISMENE. But Creon won't let us bury him. And he is stronger than we are. He has made himself king.

ANTIGONE. (*Sits on chair.*) I am not listening to you.

ISMENE. (*Kneels on stool, facing* ANTIGONE.) You must! You know how Creon organizes things. His mob will come running, howling as it runs. A thousand arms will seize our arms. A thousand breaths will breathe into our faces. Like one single pair of eyes, a thousand eyes will stare at us. We'll be driven in a tumbrel through their hatred, through the smell of them and their cruel roaring laughter. We'll be dragged to the scaffold for torture, surrounded by guards with their idiot faces all bloated, their animal hands clean-washed for the sacrifice, their beefy eyes squinting as they stare at us. And we'll know that no shrieking and no begging will make them understand that we want to live. And we shall suffer, we shall feel pain rising in us until it becomes so unbearable that we *know* it must stop. But it won't stop; it will go on rising and rising, like a screaming voice. Oh, I can't, I can't, Antigone!

(*A pause.*)

ANTIGONE. How well you have thought it all out.

ISMENE. I thought of it all night long. Didn't you?

ANTIGONE. Oh, yes.

ISMENE. I'm an awful coward, Antigone.

ANTIGONE. So am I. But what has that to do with it?

ISMENE. But, Antigone! Don't you want to go on living?

ANTIGONE. Go on living! Who was it that was always the first out of bed because she loved the touch of the cold morning air on her bare skin? Who was always the last to bed because nothing less than infinite weariness could wean her from the lingering night?

ISMENE. (*Clasps* ANTIGONE's *hands, in a sudden rush of tenderness.*) Antigone! Darling little sister!

ANTIGONE (*repulsing her*). No! For heaven's sake! Don't paw me! And stop sniveling! You say you've thought it all out. The howling mob—the torture—the fear of death. . . . They've made up your mind for you. Is that it?

ISMENE. Yes.

ANTIGONE. All right. They're as good excuses any any.

ISMENE. (*Turns to* ANTIGONE.) Antigone, be sensible. It's all very well for men to believe in ideas and die for them. But you are a girl!

ANTIGONE. Don't I know I'm a girl? Haven't I spent my life cursing the fact that I was a girl?

ISMENE (*with spirit*). Antigone! You have everything in the world to make you happy. All you have to do is reach out for it. You are going to be married; you are young; you are beautiful. . . .

ANTIGONE. I am not beautiful.

ISMENE. Yes, you are! Not the way other girls are. But it's always you that the little tough boys turn to look back at when they pass us in the street. And when you go by, the little girls stop talking. They stare and stare at you, until we've turned a corner.

ANTIGONE. (*A faint smile.*) "Little tough boys—little girls."

ISMENE (*challengingly*). And what about Haemon?

(*A pause.*)

ANTIGONE. I shall see Haemon this morning. I'll take care of Haemon. Go back to bed now.

Ismene. The sun is coming up, and, as you can see, there is nothing I can do today. Our brother Polynices is as well guarded as if he had won the war and were sitting on his throne.

ISMENE. What are you going to do?

NURSE. (*Calls from off-stage.*) Come along, my dove. Come to breakfast.

ANTIGONE. I don't feel like going to bed. However, if you like, I'll promise not to leave the house till you wake up.

ISMENE. And you will listen to reason, won't you? You'll let me talk to you about this again? Promise?

ANTIGONE. I promise. I'll let you talk. I'll let all of you talk. Go to bed, now. You're white with weariness. (ISMENE *goes to arch and exits.* NURSE *enters through arch, speaking as she enters.*)

NURSE. Come along, my dove. I've made you some coffee and toast and jam. (*She turns toward arch as if to exit.*)

ANTIGONE. I'm not really hungry, Nurse.

(NURSE *stops, looks at* ANTIGONE, *then moves behind her.*)

NURSE (*very tenderly*). Where is your pain?

ANTIGONE. Nowhere, Nanny dear. But you must keep me warm and safe, the way you used to do when I was little. Nanny! Stronger than all fever, stronger than any nightmare, stronger than the shadow of the cupboard that used to turn into a dragon on the bedroom wall. Give me your hand, Nanny, as if I were ill in bed, and you sitting beside me.

NURSE. My sparrow, my lamb! What is it that's eating your heart out?

ANTIGONE. Oh, it's just that I'm a little young still for what I have to go through. But nobody but you must know that.

NURSE. (*Places her other arm around* ANTIGONE's *shoulder.*) A little young for what, my kitten?

ANTIGONE. Nothing in particular, Nanny. Just—all this. Oh, it's so good that you are here. I can hold your callused hand, your hand that is so prompt to ward off evil. You are very powerful, Nanny.

NURSE. What is it you want me to do for you, my baby?

ANTIGONE. There isn't anything to do, except put your hand like this against my cheek. (*She places the* NURSE's *hand against her cheek. A pause, then, as* ANTIGONE *leans back, her eyes shut.*) There! I'm not afraid any more. Not afraid of the wicked ogre, nor of the sandman, nor of the dwarf who steals little children. (*A pause.* ANTIGONE *resumes on another note.*) Nanny. . . .

NURSE. Yes?

ANTIGONE. My dog, Puff. . . .

NURSE. (*Straightens up, draws her hand away.*) Well?

ANTIGONE. Promise me that you will never scold her again.

NURSE. Dogs that dirty up a house with their filthy paws deserve to be scolded.

ANTIGONE. And promise me that you will talk to her. That you will talk to her often.

NURSE. (*Turns and looks at* ANTIGONE.) Me, talk to a dog!

ANTIGONE. Yes. But mind you: you are not to talk to her the way people usually talk to dogs. You're to talk to her the way I talk to her.

NURSE. I don't see why the both of us have to make fools of ourselves. So long as you're here, one ought to be enough.

ANTIGONE. But if there was a reason why I couldn't go on talking to her . . .

NURSE (*interrupting*). Couldn't go on talking to her! And why couldn't you go on talking to her? What kind of poppycock . . . ?

ANTIGONE. And if she got too unhappy, if she moaned and moaned, waiting for me with her nose under the door the way she does when I'm out all day, then the best thing, Nanny, might be to have her mercifully put to sleep.

NURSE. Now what *has* got into you this morning? (HAEMON *enters through arch.*) Running round in the darkness, won't sleep, won't eat—(ANTIGONE *sees* HAEMON.) and now it's her dog she wants killed. I never . . .

ANTIGONE (*interrupting*). Nanny! Haemon is here. Go inside, please. And don't forget that you've promised me. (NURSE *goes to arch and exits.* ANTIGONE *rises.*) Haemon, Haemon! Forgive me for quarreling with you last night. (*She crosses quickly to* HAEMON *and they embrace.*) Forgive me for everything. It was all my fault. I beg you to forgive me.

HAEMON. You know that I've forgiven you.

You had hardly slammed the door, your perfume still hung in the room, when I had already forgiven you. (*He holds her in his arms and smiles at her. Then draws slightly back.*) You stole that perfume. From whom?

ANTIGONE. Ismene.

HAEMON. And the rouge? and the face powder? and the dress? Whom did you steal them from?

ANTIGONE. Ismene.

HAEMON. And in whose honor did you get yourself up so elegantly?

ANTIGONE. I'll tell you everything. (*She draws him closer.*) Oh, darling, what a fool I was! To waste a whole evening! A whole, beautiful evening!

HAEMON. We'll have other evenings, my sweet.

ANTIGONE. Perhaps we won't.

HAEMON. And other quarrels, too. A happy love is full of quarrels, you know.

ANTIGONE. A happy love, yes. Haemon, listen to me.

HAEMON. Yes?

ANTIGONE. Don't laugh at me this morning. Be serious.

HAEMON. I am serious.

ANTIGONE. And hold me tight. Tighter than you have ever held me. I want all your strength to flow into me.

HAEMON. There! With all my strength.

(*A pause.*)

ANTIGONE (*breathless*). That's good. (*They stand for a moment, silent and motionless.*) Haemon! I wanted to tell you. You know—the little boy we were going to have when we were married?

HAEMON. Yes?

ANTIGONE. I'd have protected him against everything in the world.

HAEMON. Yes, dearest.

ANTIGONE. Oh, you don't know how I should have held him in my arms and given him my strength. He wouldn't have been afraid of anything. Our little boy, Haemon! His mother wouldn't have been very imposing: her hair wouldn't always have been brushed; but she would have been strong where he was concerned, so much stronger than all those real mothers with their real bosoms and their aprons round their middle. You believe that, don't you, Haemon?

HAEMON (*soothingly*). Yes, yes, my darling.

ANTIGONE. And you believe me when I say that you would have had a real wife?

HAEMON. Darling, you are my real wife.

ANTIGONE (*pressing against him and crying out*). Haemon, you loved me! You did love me that night, didn't you? You're sure of it!

HAEMON (*rocking her gently*). What night, my sweet?

ANTIGONE. And you are very sure, aren't you, that that night, at the dance, when you came to the corner where I was sitting, there was no mistake? It was me you were looking for? It wasn't another girl? And you're sure that never, not in your most secret heart of hearts, have you said to yourself that it was Ismene you ought to have asked to marry you?

HAEMON (*reproachfully*). Antigone, you are idiotic. You might give me credit for knowing my own mind. It's you I love, and no one else.

ANTIGONE. But you love me as a woman—as a woman wants to be loved, don't you? Your arms round me aren't lying, are they? Your hands, so warm against my back—they're not lying? This warmth, this confidence, this sense that I am safe, secure, that flows through me as I stand here with my cheek in the hollow of your shoulder: they are not lies, are they?

HAEMON. Antigone, darling, I love you exactly as you love me. With all of myself.

(*They kiss.*)

ANTIGONE. I'm sallow, and I'm scrawny. Ismene is pink and golden. She's like a fruit.

HAEMON. Look here, Antigone. . . .

ANTIGONE. Ah, dearest, I am ashamed of myself. But this morning, this special morning, I must know. Tell me the truth! I beg you to tell me the truth! When you think about me, when it strikes you suddenly that I am going to belong to you—do you have the feeling that —that a great empty space is being hollowed out inside you, that there is something inside you that is just—dying?

HAEMON. Yes, I do, I do.

(*A pause.*)

ANTIGONE. That's the way I feel. And another thing. I wanted you to know that I

should have been very proud to be your wife
—the woman whose shoulder you would put
your hand on as you sat down to table, ab-
sent-mindedly, as upon a thing that belonged
to you. (*After a moment, draws away from
him. Her tone changes.*) There! Now I have
two things more to tell you. And when I have
told them to you, you must go away instantly,
without asking any questions. However strange
they may seem to you. However much they
may hurt you. Swear that you will!

HAEMON (*beginning to be troubled*). What
are these things that you are going to tell me?

ANTIGONE. Swear, first, that you will go
away without one word. Without so much as
looking at me. (*She looks at him, wretchedness
in her face.*) You hear me, Haemon. Swear it,
please. This is the last mad wish that you will
ever have to grant me.

(*A pause.*)

HAEMON. I swear it, since you insist. But I
must tell you that I don't like this at all.

ANTIGONE. Please, Haemon. It's very serious.
You must listen to me and do as I ask. First,
about last night, when I came to your house.
You asked me a moment ago why I wore
Ismene's dress and rouge. It was because I
was stupid. I wasn't very sure that you loved
me as a woman; and I did it—because I
wanted you to take me. I wanted to be your
wife before. . . .

HAEMON. Oh, my darling. . . .

ANTIGONE. (*Shuts him off.*) You swore you
wouldn't ask any questions. You swore, Haemon. (*Turns her face away and goes on in a
hard voice.*) As a matter of fact, I'll tell you
why. I wanted to be your wife last night because I love you that way very—very strongly.
And also because—Oh, my darling, my darling, forgive me; I'm going to cause you quite
a lot of pain. (*She draws away from him.*) I
wanted it also because I shall never, never be
able to marry you, never! (HAEMON *is stupefied and mute; then he moves a step toward
her.*) Haemon! You took a solemn oath! You
swore! Leave me quickly. Tomorrow—tomorrow the whole thing will be clear to you. Even
before tomorrow: this afternoon. If you please,
Haemon, go now. It is the only thing left that
you can do for me if you still love me. (*A

pause as* HAEMON *stares at her. Then he turns
and goes out through the arch.* ANTIGONE
*stands motionless, then moves to chair at end
of table and lets herself gently down on it.
In a mild voice, as of calm after storm.*) Well,
it's over for Haemon, Antigone.

(ISMENE *enters through arch, pauses for
a moment in front of it when she sees*
ANTIGONE, *then crosses behind table.*)

ISMENE. I can't sleep. I'm terrified. I'm so
afraid that even though it is daylight, you'll
still try to bury Polynices. Antigone, you remember what Polynices was like. He was our
brother, of course. But he's dead; and he never
loved us. He was a bad brother. He was like
an enemy in this house. He never thought of
you. Why should you think of him? What if
he does have to lie rotting in a field? It's
Creon's doing, not ours. Don't try to change
things. You can't bury Polynices. I'm older
than you are and I won't let you!

ANTIGONE. You are too late, Ismene. When
you first saw me this morning, I had just come
in from burying him. (ANTIGONE *exits through
arch.*)

(*The lighting, which by this time has
reached a point of early morning sun, is
quickly dimmed out, leaving the stage
bathed in a light-blue color.*)

(ISMENE *runs out after* ANTIGONE.)

(*On* ISMENE's *exit the lights are brought
up suddenly to suggest a later period of
the day.*)

(CREON *and* PAGE *enter through curtain
upstage.* CREON *stands on the top step;
his* PAGE *stands at his right side.*)

CREON. A private of the guards, you say?
One of those standing watch over the body?
Show him in.

(*The* PAGE *crosses to arch and exits.*
CREON *moves down to end of table.*)

(PAGE *re-enters, preceded by the* FIRST
GUARD, *livid with fear.* PAGE *remains on
upstage side of arch.* GUARD *salutes.*)

GUARD. Private Jonas, Second Battalion.
CREON. What are you doing here?
GUARD. It's like this, Chief. Soon as it hap-

pened, we said: "Got to tell the Chief about this before anybody else spills it. He'll want to know right away." So we tossed a coin to see which one would come up and tell you about it. You see, Chief, we thought only one man better come because, after all, you don't want to leave the body without a guard. Right? I mean, there's three of us on duty, guarding the body.

CREON. What's wrong about the body?

GUARD. Chief, I've been seventeen years in the service. Volunteer. Wounded three times. Two citations. My record's clean. I know my business and I know my place. I carry out orders. Sir, ask any officer in the battalion; they'll tell you. "Leave it to Jonas. Give him an order; he'll carry it out." That's what they'll tell you, Chief. Jonas, that's me—that's my name.

CREON. What's the matter with you, man? What are you shaking for?

GUARD. By rights it's the corporal's job, Chief. I've been recommended for a corporal but they haven't put it through yet. June, it was supposed to go through.

CREON. (Interrupts.) Stop chattering and tell me why you are here. If anything has gone wrong I'll break all three of you.

GUARD. Nobody can say we didn't keep our eye on that body. We had the two o'clock watch—the tough one. You know how it is, Chief. It's nearly the end of the night. Your eyes are like lead. You've got a crick in the back of your neck. There's shadows, and the fog is beginning to roll in. A fine watch they give us! And me, seventeen years in the service. But we was doing our duty, all right. On our feet, all of us. Anybody says we were sleeping is a liar. First place, it was too cold. Second place . . . . (CREON makes a gesture of impatience.) Yes, Chief. Well, I turned round and looked at the body. We wasn't only ten feet away from it, but that's how I am. I was keeping my eye on it. (Shouts.) Listen, Chief, I was the first man to see it! Me! They'll tell you. I was the one let out that yell!

CREON. What for? What was the matter?

GUARD. Chief, the body! Somebody had been there and buried it. (CREON comes down a step on the stair. The GUARD becomes more frightened.) It wasn't much, you understand.

With us three there, it couldn't have been. Just covered over with a little dirt, that's all. But enough to hide it from the buzzards.

CREON. By God, I'll . . . ! (He looks intently at the GUARD.) You are sure that it couldn't have been a dog, scratching up the earth?

GUARD. Not a chance, Chief. That's kind of what we hoped it was. But the earth was scattered over the body just like the priests tell you you should do it. Whoever did that job knew what he was doing, all right.

CREON. Who could have dared? (He turns and looks at the GUARD.) Was there anything to indicate who might have done it?

GUARD. Not a thing, Chief. Maybe we heard a footstep—I can't swear to it. Of course we started right in to search, and the corporal found a shovel, a kid's shovel no bigger than that, all rusty and everything. Corporal's got the shovel for you. We thought maybe a kid did it.

CREON. (To himself.) A kid! (He looks away from the GUARD.) I broke the back of the rebellion; but like a snake, it is coming together again. Polynices' friends, with their gold, blocked by my orders in the banks of Thebes. The leaders of the mob allied to envious princes. And the temple priests, always ready for a bit of fishing in troubled waters. A kid! I can imagine what he is like, their kid: a baby-faced killer, creeping in the night with a toy shovel under his jacket. (He looks at his PAGE.) Though why shouldn't they have corrupted a real child? There is something, now, to soften the hearts and weaken the minds of the populace! Very touching! Very useful to them, an innocent child. A martyr. A real white-faced baby of fourteen who will spit with contempt at the guards who kill him. A free gift to their cause: the precious, innocent blood of a child on my hands. (He turns to the GUARD.) They must have accomplices in the Guard itself. Look here, you. Who knows about this?

GUARD. Only us three, Chief. We flipped a coin, and I came right over.

CREON. Right. Listen, now. You will continue on duty. When the relief squad comes up, you will tell them to return to barracks. You will uncover the body. If another attempt is made to bury it, I shall expect you to make an arrest and bring the person straight to me. And you will keep your mouths shut. Not one word of this to a human soul. You are all guilty of neglect of duty, and you will be punished; but if the rumor spreads through Thebes that the body received burial, you will be shot—all three of you.

GUARD (*excitedly*). Chief, we never told nobody, I swear we didn't! Anyhow, I've been up here. Suppose my pals spilled it to the relief; I couldn't have been with them and here, too. That wouldn't be my fault if they talked. Chief, I've got two kids. You're my witness, Chief, it couldn't have been me. I was here with you. I've got a witness! If anybody talked, it couldn't have been me! I was . . .

CREON (*interrupting*). Clear out! If the story doesn't get round, you won't be shot. (*The* GUARD *salutes, turns and exits, on the run.* CREON *turns and paces upstage, then comes down to end of the table.*) A child! (*He looks at* PAGE.) Come here, my lad. (PAGE *crosses to side of* CREON. CREON *puts his hand on* PAGE's *shoulder.*) Would you defy me with your little shovel? (PAGE *looks up at* CREON.) Of course you would. You would do it, too. (*A pause.* CREON *looks away from* PAGE *and murmurs.*) A child! (CREON *and* PAGE *go slowly upstage center to top step.* PAGE *draws aside the curtain, through which* CREON *exits with* PAGE *behind him.*)

(*As soon as* CREON *and* PAGE *have disappeared,* CHORUS *enters and leans against the upstage portal of arch, left. The lighting is brought up to its brightest point to suggest mid-afternoon.* CHORUS *allows a pause to indicate that a crucial moment has been reached in the play, then moves slowly downstage center. He stands for a moment silent, reflecting, and then smiles faintly.*)

CHORUS. The spring is wound up tight. It will uncoil of itself. That is what is so convenient in tragedy. The least little turn of the wrist will do the job. Anything will set it going: a glance at a girl who happens to be lifting her arms to her hair as you go by; a feeling when you wake up on a fine morning that you'd like a little respect paid to you today, as if it were as easy to order as a second cup of coffee; one question too many, idly thrown out over a friendly drink—and the tragedy is on.

The rest is automatic. You don't need to lift a finger. The machine is in perfect order; it has been oiled ever since time began, and it runs without friction. Death, treason and sorrow are on the march; and they move in the wake of storm, of tears, of stillness. Every kind of stillness. The hush when the executioner's axe goes up at the end of the last act. The unbreathable silence when, at the beginning of the play, the two lovers, their hearts bared, their bodies naked, stand for the first time face to face in the darkened room, afraid to stir. The silence inside you when the roaring crowd acclaims the winner—so that you think of a film without a sound-track, mouths agape and no sound coming out of them, a clamor that is no more than a picture; and you, the victor, already vanquished, alone in the desert of your silence. That is tragedy.

Tragedy is clean, it is firm, it is flawless. It has nothing to do with melodrama—with wicked villains, persecuted maidens, avengers, sudden revelations and eleventh-hour repentances. Death, in a melodrama, is really horrible because it is never inevitable. The dear old father might so easily have been saved; the honest young man might so easily have brought in the police five minutes earlier.

In a tragedy, nothing is in doubt and everyone's destiny is known. That makes for tranquillity. There is a sort of fellow-feeling among characters in a tragedy: he who kills is as innocent as he who gets killed: it's all a matter of what part you are playing. Tragedy is restful; and the reason is that hope, that foul, deceitful thing, has no part in it. There isn't any hope. You're trapped. The whole sky has fallen on you, and all you can do about it is to shout.

Don't mistake me: I said "shout": I did not say groan, whimper, complain. That, you cannot do. But you can shout aloud; you can get all those things said that you never thought you'd be able to say—or never even knew you had it in you to say. And you don't say these things because it will do any good to say them: you know better than that. You say them for their own sake; you say them because you learn a lot from them.

In melodrama, you argue and struggle in the hope of escape. That is vulgar; it's practical. But in tragedy, where there is no temptation to try to escape, argument is gratuitous: it's kingly.

(*Voices of the* GUARDS *and scuffling sounds heard through the archway.* CHORUS *looks in that direction, then in a changed tone.*)

The play is on. Antigone has been caught. For the first time in her life, little Antigone is going to be able to be herself.

(CHORUS *exits through arch.*)

(*A pause, while the off-stage voices rise in volume, then the* FIRST GUARD *enters, followed by* SECOND *and* THIRD GUARDS, *holding the arms of* ANTIGONE *and dragging her along. The* FIRST GUARD, *speaking as he enters, crosses swiftly to end of the table. The* TWO GUARDS *and* ANTIGONE *stop downstage.*)

FIRST GUARD (*recovered from his fright*). Come on, now, Miss, give it a rest. The Chief will be here in a minute and you can tell him about it. All I know is my orders. I don't want to know what you were doing there. People always have excuses; but I can't afford to listen to them, see. Say, if we had to listen to all the people who want to tell us what's the matter with this country, we'd never get our work done. (*To the* GUARDS.) You keep hold of her and I'll see that she keeps her face shut.

ANTIGONE. They are hurting me. Tell them to take their dirty hands off me.

FIRST GUARD. Dirty hands, eh? The least you can do is try to be polite, Miss. Look at me: I'm polite.

ANTIGONE. Tell them to let me go. I shan't run away. My father was King Oedipus. I am Antigone.

FIRST GUARD. King Oedipus' little girl! What do you know about that! Listen, Miss, the night watch never picks up a lady, but they say, you better be careful; I'm sleeping with the police commissioner.

(*The* GUARDS *laugh.*)

ANTIGONE. I don't mind being killed, but I don't want them to touch me.

FIRST GUARD. Yeah? And what about stiffs, and dirt, and such like? You wasn't afraid to touch them, was you? "Their dirty hands!" Take a look at your own hands. (ANTIGONE, *handcuffed, smiles despite herself as she looks down at her hands. They are grubby.*) Guess you must have lost your shovel, didn't you? Had to go at it with your fingernails the second time, I guess. By God, I never saw such nerve! I turn my back for about five seconds; I ask a pal for a chew; I say "thanks"; I get the tobacco stowed away in my cheek—the whole thing don't take ten seconds; and there she is, clawing away like a hyena. Right out in broad daylight! And boy! did she scratch and kick when I grabbed her! Straight for my eyes with them nails she went. And yelling something fierce about, "I ain't finished yet; let me finish!" She ain't got all her marbles!

SECOND GUARD. I pinched a nut like that the other day. Right on the main square, she was, histin' up her skirts and showing her behind to anybody wanted to take a look.

FIRST GUARD. Listen, we're going to get a bonus out of this. What do you say we throw a party, the three of us?

SECOND GUARD. At the old woman's? Behind Market Street?

THIRD GUARD. Suits me. Sunday would be a good day. We're off duty Sunday. What do you say we bring our wives?

FIRST GUARD. Nix. Let's have some fun this time. Bring *your* wife, there's always something goes wrong. First place, what do you do with the kids? Bring them, they always want to go to the can just when you're right in the middle of a game of cards or something. Say, listen. Who would have thought an hour ago that us three would be talking about throwing a party right now? The way I felt when the old man was interrogatin' me, we'd be lucky if we got off with being docked a month's pay. I want to tell you, I was scared.

SECOND GUARD. You sure we're going to get a bonus?

FIRST GUARD. Yeah. Something tells me this is big stuff.

THIRD GUARD (*to* SECOND GUARD). What's-his-name, you know—in the Third Battalion? He got an extra month's pay for catching a fire-bug.

SECOND GUARD. If we get an extra month's pay, I vote we throw the party at the Arabian's.

FIRST GUARD. You're crazy! He charges twice as much for liquor as anybody else in town. Unless you want to go upstairs, of course. Can't do that at the old woman's.

THIRD GUARD. Say, we can't keep this from our wives, no matter how you figure it. You get an extra month's pay, and what happens? Everybody in the battalion knows it, and your wife knows it too. They might even line up the battalion and give it to you in front of everybody, so how could you keep your wife from finding out?

FIRST GUARD. Well, we'll see about that. If they do the job out in the barracks-yard—of course that means women, kids, everything.

ANTIGONE. I should like to sit down, if you please.

(*A pause, as the* FIRST GUARD *thinks it over.*)

FIRST GUARD. Let her sit down. But keep hold of her. (*The two* GUARDS *start to lead her towards the chair at end of table. The curtain upstage opens, and* CREON *enters, followed by his* PAGE. FIRST GUARD *turns and moves upstage a few steps, sees* CREON.) 'Tenshun! (*The three* GUARDS *salute.* CREON, *seeing* ANTIGONE *handcuffed to* THIRD GUARD, *stops on the top step, astonished.*)

CREON. Antigone! (*To the* FIRST GUARD.) Take off those handcuffs! (FIRST GUARD *crosses above table to left of* ANTIGONE.) What is this? (CREON *and his* PAGE *come down off the steps.*)

(FIRST GUARD *takes key from his pocket and unlocks the cuff on* ANTIGONE'S *hand.* ANTIGONE *rubs her wrist as she crosses below table toward chair at end of table.* SECOND *and* THIRD GUARDS *step back to front of arch.* FIRST GUARD *turns upstage toward* CREON.)

FIRST GUARD. The watch, Chief. We all came this time.

CREON. Who is guarding the body?

FIRST GUARD. We sent for the relief.

(CREON *comes down.*)

CREON. But I gave orders that the relief was to go back to barracks and stay there! (ANTIGONE *sits on chair at left of table.*) I told you not to open your mouth about this!

FIRST GUARD. Nobody's said anything, Chief. We made this arrest, and brought the party in, the way you said we should.

CREON (*to* ANTIGONE). Where did these men find you?

FIRST GUARD. Right by the body.

CREON. What were you doing near your brother's body? You knew what my orders were.

FIRST GUARD. What was she doing? Chief, that's why we brought her in. She was digging up the dirt with her nails. She was trying to cover up the body all over again.

CREON. Do you realize what you are saying?

FIRST GUARD. Chief, ask these men here. After I reported to you, I went back, and first thing we did, we uncovered the body. The sun was coming up and it was beginning to smell, so we moved it up on a little rise to get him in the wind. Of course you wouldn't expect any trouble in broad daylight. But just the same, we decided one of us better keep his eye peeled all the time. About noon, what with the sun and the smell, being the wind dropped, and I wasn't feeling none too good, I went over to my pal to get a chew. I just had time to say "thanks" and stick it in my mouth, when I turned round and there she was, clawing away at the dirt with both hands. Right out in broad daylight! Wouldn't you think when she saw me come running, she'd quit and beat it out of there? Not her! She went right on digging as fast as she could, as if I wasn't there at all. And when I grabbed her, she scratched and bit and yelled to leave her alone, she hadn't finished yet, the body wasn't all covered yet, and the like of that.

CREON (*to* ANTIGONE). Is this true?

ANTIGONE. Yes, it is true.

FIRST GUARD. We scraped the dirt off as fast as we could, then we sent for the relief and we posted them. But we didn't tell them a thing, Chief. And we brought in the party so's you could see her. And that's the truth, so help me God.

CREON (*to* ANTIGONE). And was it you who covered the body the first time? In the night?

ANTIGONE. Yes, it was. With a toy shovel we used to take to the seashore when we were children. It was Polynices' own shovel; he had cut his name in the handle. That was why I left it with him. But these men took it away; so the next time, I had to do it with my hands.

FIRST GUARD. Chief, she was clawing away like a wild animal. Matter of fact, first minute we saw her, what with the heat haze and everything, my pal says, "That must be a dog," he says. "Dog!" I says, "That's a girl, that is!" And it was.

CREON. Very well. (*Turns to the* PAGE.) Show these men to the anteroom. (*The* PAGE *crosses to the arch, stands there, waiting.* CREON *moves behind the table. To the* FIRST GUARD.) You three men will wait outside. I may want a report from you later.

FIRST GUARD. Do I put the cuffs back on her, Chief?

CREON. No. (*The three* GUARDS *salute, do an about-face and exit through arch right.* PAGE *follows them out. A pause.*) Had you told anybody what you meant to do?

ANTIGONE. No.

CREON. Did you meet anyone on your way —coming or going?

ANTIGONE. No, nobody.

CREON. Sure of that, are you?

ANTIGONE. Perfectly sure.

CREON. Very well. Now listen to me. You will go straight to your room. When you get there, you will go to bed. You will say that you are not well and that you have not been out since yesterday. Your nurse will tell the same story. (*He looks toward arch, through which the* GUARDS *have exited.*) And I'll dispose of those three men.

ANTIGONE. Uncle Creon, you are going to a lot of trouble for no good reason. You must know that I'll do it all over again tonight.

(*A pause. They look one another in the eye.*)

CREON. Why did you try to bury your brother?

ANTIGONE. I owed it to him.

CREON. I had forbidden it.

ANTIGONE. I owed it to him. Those who are not buried wander eternally and find no rest. Everybody knows that. I owe it to my brother

to unlock the house of the dead in which my father and my mother are waiting to welcome him. Polynices has earned his rest.

CREON. Polynices was a rebel and a traitor, and you know it.

ANTIGONE. He was my brother, and he was a human being. Who, except you, wants my brother's body to rot in a field? Does God want that? Do the people want it?

CREON. God and the people of Thebes are not concerned in this. You heard my edict. It was proclaimed throughout Thebes. You read my edict. It was posted up on the city walls.

ANTIGONE. Of course I did.

CREON. You knew the punishment I decreed for any person who attempted to give him burial.

ANTIGONE. Yes, I knew the punishment.

CREON. Did you by any chance act on the assumption that a daughter of Oepidus, a daughter of Oedipus' stubborn pride, was above the law?

ANTIGONE. No, I did not act on that assumption.

CREON. Because if you had acted on that assumption, Antigone, you would have been deeply wrong. Nobody has a more sacred obligation to obey the law than those who make the law. You are a daughter of law-makers, a daughter of kings, Antigone. You must observe the law.

ANTIGONE. Had I been a scullery maid washing my dishes when that law was read aloud to me, I should have scrubbed the greasy water from my arms and gone out in my apron to bury my brother.

CREON. What nonsense! If you had been a scullery maid, there would have been no doubt in your mind about the seriousness of that edict. You would have known that it meant death; and you would have been satisfied to weep for your brother in your kitchen. But you! You thought that because you come of the royal line, because you were my niece and were going to marry my son, I shouldn't dare have you killed.

ANTIGONE. You are mistaken. Quite the contrary. I never doubted for an instant that you would have me put to death.

(*A pause, as* CREON *stares fixedly at her.*)

CREON. The pride of Oedipus! Oedipus and his headstrong pride all over again. I can see your father in you—and I believe you. Of course you thought that I should have you killed! Proud as you are, it seemed to you a natural climax in your existence. Your father was like that. For him as for you human happiness was meaningless; and mere human misery was not enough to satisfy his passion for torment. (*He sits on stool behind the table.*) You come of people for whom the human vestment is a kind of strait-jacket: it cracks at the seams. You spend your lives wriggling to get out of it. Nothing less than a cosy tea-party with death and destiny will quench your thirst. The happiest hour of your father's life came when he listened greedily to the story of how, unknown to himself, he had killed his own father and dishonored the bed of his own mother. Drop by drop, word by word, he drank in the dark story that the gods had destined him, first to live and then to hear. How avidly men and women drink the brew of such a tale when their names are Oedipus—and Antigone! And it is so simple, afterwards, to do what your father did, to put out one's eyes and take one's daughter begging on the highways.

Let me tell you, Antigone: those days are over for Thebes. Thebes has a right to a king without a past. My name, thank God, is only Creon. I stand here with both feet firm on the ground; with both hands in my pockets; and I have decided that so long as I am king—being less ambitious than your father was—I shall merely devote myself to introducing a little order into this absurd kingdom; if that is possible.

Don't think that being a king seems to me romantic. It is my trade; a trade a man has to work at every day; and like every other trade, it isn't all beer and skittles. But since it is my trade, I take it seriously. And if, tomorrow, some wild and bearded messenger walks in from some wild and distant valley—which is what happened to your dad—and tells me that he's not quite sure who my parents were, but thinks that my wife Eurydice is actually my mother, I shall ask him to do me the kindness to go back where he came from; and I shan't let a little matter like that persuade me to order my wife to take a blood test and the police

to let me know whether or not my birth certificate was forged. Kings, my girl, have other things to do than to surrender themselves to their private feelings. (*He looks at her and smiles.*) Hand *you* over to be killed! (*He rises, moves to end of table and sits on the top of table.*) I have other plans for you. You're going to marry Haemon; and I want you to fatten up a bit so that you can give him a sturdy boy. Let me assure you that Thebes needs that boy a good deal more than it needs your death. You will go to your room, now, and do as you have been told; and you won't say a word about this to anybody. Don't fret about the guards; I'll see that their mouths are shut. And don't annihilate me with those eyes. I know that you think I am a brute, and I'm sure you must consider me very prosaic. But the fact is, I have always been fond of you, stubborn though you always were. Don't forget that the first doll you ever had came from me. (*A pause.* ANTIGONE *says nothing, rises and crosses slowly below the table toward the arch.* CREON *turns and watches her; then*) Where are you going?

ANTIGONE. (*Stops downstage. Without any show of rebellion.*) You know very well where I am going.

CREON. (*After a pause.*) What sort of game are you playing?

ANTIGONE. I am not playing games.

CREON. Antigone, do you realize that if, apart from those three guards, a single soul finds out what you have tried to do, it will be impossible for me to avoid putting you to death? There is still a chance that I can save you; but only if you keep this to yourself and give up your crazy purpose. Five minutes more, and it will be too late. You understand that?

ANTIGONE. I must go bury my brother. Those men uncovered him.

CREON. What good will it do? You know that there are other men standing guard over Polynices. And even if you did cover him over with earth again, the earth would again be removed.

ANTIGONE. I know all that. I know it. But that much, at least, I can do. And what a person can do, a person should do.

(*Pause.*)

CREON. Tell me, Antigone, do you believe all that flummery about religious burial? Do you really believe that a so-called shade of your brother is condemned to wander forever homeless if a little earth is not flung on his corpse to the accompaniment of some priestly abracadabra? Have you ever listened to the priests of Thebes when they were mumbling their formula? Have you ever watched their dreary sullen faces while they were preparing the dead for burial—skipping half the gestures required by the ritual, swallowing half their words, hustling the dead into their graves out of fear that they might be late for lunch?

ANTIGONE. Yes, I have seen all that.

CREON. And did you never say to yourself as you watched them, that if someone you really loved lay dead under the shuffling, mumbling ministrations of the priests, you would scream aloud and beg the priests to leave the dead in peace?

ANTIGONE. No, Creon. There is God and there are His priests. They are not the same thing. You are not free to do with men as you wish—not even when they are dead.

CREON. And you are going to stop me, are you?

ANTIGONE. Yes, I am going to stop you.

(*A pause as they stand looking at one another.*)

CREON. You must want very much to die. You look like a trapped animal.

ANTIGONE. Stop feeling sorry for me. Do as I do. Do your job. But if you are a human being, do it quickly.

CREON. (*Takes a step toward her.*) I want to save you, Antigone.

ANTIGONE. You are the King, and you are all-powerful. But that you cannot do.

CREON. You think not?

ANTIGONE. Neither save me nor stop me.

CREON. Prideful Antigone!

ANTIGONE. Only this can you do: have me put to death.

CREON. Have you tortured, perhaps?

ANTIGONE. Why would you do that? To see me cry? To hear me beg for mercy? Or swear whatever you wish, and then begin over again?

(*A pause.*)

CREON. You listen to me. You have cast me for the villain in this little play of yours, and yourself for the heroine. And you know it, you damned little mischief-maker! But don't you drive me too far! If I were one of your preposterous little tyrants that Greece is full of, you would be lying in a ditch this minute with your tongue pulled out and your body drawn and quartered. But you can see something in my face that makes me hesitate to send for the guards and turn you over to them. Instead, I let you go on arguing; and you taunt me, you take the offensive. (*He grasps her left wrist.*) What are you driving at, you she-devil?

ANTIGONE. Let me go. You are hurting my arm.

CREON (*gripping her tighter*). I will not let you go.

ANTIGONE. (*Moans.*) Oh!

CREON. I was a fool to waste words. I should have done this from the beginning. (*He looks at her.*) I may be your uncle; but we are not a particularly affectionate family. Are we, eh? (*Through his teeth as he twists.*) Are we? (CREON *propels* ANTIGONE *round below him to his side.*) What fun for you, eh? To be able to spit in the face of a King who has all the power in the world; a man who has done his own killing in his day; who has killed people just as pitiable as you are—and who is still soft enough to go to all this trouble in order to keep you from being killed.

(*A pause.*)

ANTIGONE. Now you are squeezing my arm too tightly. It doesn't hurt any more.

(CREON *stares at her, then drops her arm.*)

CREON. I shall save you yet. (*He goes below the table to the chair at the end of table, takes off his coat and places it on the chair.*) God knows, I have things enough to do today without wasting my time on an insect like you. But urgent things can wait. I am not going to let politics be the cause of your death. For it is a fact that this whole business is nothing but politics: the mournful shade of Polynices, the decomposing corpse, the sentimental weeping and the hysteria that you mistake for heroism, nothing but politics.

Look here. I may not be soft, but I'm fastidious. I like things clean, ship-shape, well scrubbed. Don't think that I am not just as offended as you are by the thought of that meat rotting in the sun. In the evening, when the breeze comes in off the sea, you can smell it in the palace, and it nauseates me. But I refuse even to shut my window. The people of Thebes have got to have their noses rubbed into it a little longer. My God! If it was up to me, I should have had them bury your brother long ago as a mere matter of public hygiene. I admit that what I am doing is childish. But it is by childish tricks like this that men are governed. And if the feather-headed rabble I govern are to understand what's what, that stench has got to fill the town for a month!

ANTIGONE. (*Turns to him.*) You are a loathsome man!

CREON. I agree. My trade forces me to be. We could argue whether I ought or ought not to follow my trade; but once I take on the job, I must do it properly.

ANTIGONE. Why do you do it at all?

CREON. My dear, I woke up one morning and found myself King of Thebes. God knows, there were other things I loved in life more than power.

ANTIGONE. Then you should have said no.

CREON. Yes, I could have done that. Only, I felt that it would have been cowardly. I should have been like a workman who turns down a job that has to be done. So I said yes.

ANTIGONE. So much the worse for you, then. I didn't say yes. I can say no to anything I think vile, and I don't have to count the cost. But because you said yes to your lust for power, all that you can do, for all of your crown, your trappings, and your guards—all that you can do is to have me killed.

CREON. Listen to me.

ANTIGONE. If I want to. I don't have to listen to you if I don't want to. There is nothing you can tell me that I don't know. Whereas I can tell you a thousand things that you don't know. You stand there, drinking in my words. (*She moves behind chair.*) Why is it that you don't call your guards? I'll tell you why. You want to hear me out to the end; that's why.

CREON. You amuse me.

ANTIGONE. Oh, no, I don't. I frighten you.

That is why you talk about saving me. Everything would be so much easier if you had a docile, tongue-tied little Antigone living in the palace. But you are going to have to bury Polynices or put me to death today—one of the two—and you know it. And that's what frightens you.

CREON. Very well. I am afraid, then. Does that satisfy you? I am afraid that if you insist upon it, I shall have to have you killed. And I don't want to.

ANTIGONE. I don't have to do things that I think are wrong. If it comes to that, you didn't really want to leave my brother's body unburied, did you? Say it! Admit that you didn't.

CREON. I have said it already.

ANTIGONE. But you did it just the same. And now, though you don't want to do it, you are going to have me killed. And you call that being a king!

CREON. Yes, I call that being a king.

ANTIGONE. Poor Creon! My nails are broken, my fingers are bleeding, my arms are covered with the welts left by the paws of your guards—but I am a queen!

CREON. Then why not have pity on me, and live? Isn't your brother's corpse, rotting there under my windows, payment enough for peace and order in Thebes?

ANTIGONE. What have I to do with your slave's peace and your barbarian's order? No, Creon! You said yes, and made yourself King. Now you will never stop paying.

CREON. But God in Heaven! Won't you try to understand me! I'm trying hard enough to understand you! There had to be one man who said yes. Somebody had to agree to captain the ship. She had sprung a hundred leaks; she was loaded to the waterline with crime, ignorance, poverty. The wheel was swinging with the wind. The crew refused to work and were looting the cargo. The officers were building a raft, ready to slip overboard and desert the ship. The mast was splitting, the sails were beginning to rip. Every man-jack on board was about to drown—and only because the only thing they thought of was their own skins and their cheap little day-to-day traffic. Was that a time, do you think, for playing with words like yes and no? You grab the wheel, you right the ship in the face of a mountain of water. You shout an order, and if one man refuses to obey, you shoot straight into the mob. Into the mob, I say! The beast as nameless as the wave that crashes down upon your deck, as nameless as the whipping wind. The thing that drops when you shoot may be someone who poured you a drink the night before; but it has no name. And you, braced at the wheel, you have no name, either. Nothing has a name—except the ship, and the storm. (*A pause as he looks at her.*) Now do you understand?

ANTIGONE. I am not here to understand. Not what you call understand. I am here to say no to you, and bury Polynices.

CREON. It is easy to say no.

ANTIGONE. Not always.

CREON. It is easy to say no. To say yes, you have to sweat and roll up your sleeves and plunge both hands into life up to the elbows. It is easy to say no, even if saying no means death. All you have to do is to sit still and wait. Wait to go on living; wait to be killed. That is the coward's part. *No* is one of your man-made words. Can you imagine a world in which trees say *no* to the sap? In which beasts say *no* to hunger or to propagation? Animals are good, simple, tough. They move in droves, nudging one another onwards, all traveling the same road. Some of them keel over; but the rest go on; and no matter how many may fall by the wayside, there are always those few left who go on bringing their young into the world, traveling the same road with the same obstinate will, unchanged from those who went before.

ANTIGONE. Animals, eh, Creon! What a king you could be if only men were animals!

(*A pause.* CREON *turns and looks at her.*)

CREON. You despise me, don't you? (ANTIGONE *is silent.* CREON *goes on, as if to himself.*) Strange. Again and again, I have imagined myself holding this conversation with a pale young man I have never seen in the flesh. He would have come to assassinate me, and would have failed. I would be trying to find out from him why he wanted to kill me. But with all my logic and all my powers of debate, the only think I could get out of him would be that he despised me. Who would have thought that that white-faced boy would turn out to be you? And that the debate would arise out of something so meaningless as the burial of your brother?

ANTIGONE. (*Repeats contemptuously.*) Meaningless!

CREON. (*Earnestly, almost desperately.*) And yet, you must hear me out. My part is not a heroic one, but I shall play my part. I shall have you put to death. Only before I do, I want to make one last appeal. I want to be sure that you know what you are doing as well as I know what I am doing. Antigone, do you know what you are dying for? Do you know the sordid story to which you are going to sign your name in blood, for all time to come?

ANTIGONE. What story?

CREON. The story of Eteocles and Polynices, the story of your brothers. You think you know it, but you don't. Nobody in Thebes knows that story but me. And it seems to me, this afternoon, that you have a right to know it, too. (*A pause as* ANTIGONE *moves to chair and sits.*) It's not a pretty story. (*He turns, gets stool from behind the table and places it between the table and the chair.*) You'll see. (*He looks at her for a moment.*) Tell me, first. What do you remember about your brothers? They were older than you, so they must have looked down on you. And I imagine that they tormented you—pulled your pigtails, broke your dolls, whispered secrets to each other to put you in a rage.

ANTIGONE. They were big and I was little.

CREON. And later on, when they came home wearing evening clothes, smoking cigarettes, they would have nothing to do with you; and you thought they were wonderful.

ANTIGONE. They were boys and I was a girl.

CREON. You didn't know why, exactly, but you knew that they were making your mother unhappy. You saw her in tears over them; and your father would fly into a rage because of them. You heard them come in, slamming doors, laughing noisily in the corridors—insolent, spineless, unruly, smelling of drink.

ANTIGONE (*staring outward*). Once, it was very early and we had just got up. I saw them coming home, and hid behind a door. Polynices was very pale and his eyes were shining. He was so handsome in his evening clothes. He saw me, and said: "Here, this is for you"; and he gave me a big paper flower that he had brought home from his night out.

CREON. And of course you still have that flower. Last night, before you crept out, you opened a drawer and looked at it for a time, to give yourself courage.

ANTIGONE. Who told you so?

CREON. Poor Antigone! With her night-club flower. Do you know what your brother was?

ANTIGONE. Whatever he was, I know that you will say vile things about him.

CREON. A cheap, idiotic bounder, that is what he was. A cruel, vicious little voluptuary. A little beast with just wit enough to drive a car faster and throw more money away than any of his pals. I was with your father one day when Polynices, having lost a lot of money gambling, asked him to settle the debt; and when your father refused, the boy raised his hand against him and called him a vile name.

ANTIGONE. That's a lie!

CREON. He struck your father in the face with his fist. It was pitiful. Your father sat at his desk with his head in his hands. His nose was bleeding. He was weeping with anguish. And in a corner of your father's study, Polynices stood sneering and lighting a cigarette.

ANTIGONE. That's a lie.

(*A pause.*)

CREON. When did you last see Polynices alive? When you were twelve years old. *That's* true, isn't it?

ANTIGONE. Yes, that's true.

CREON. Now you know why. Oedipus was too chicken-hearted to have the boy locked up. Polynices was allowed to go off and join the Argive army. And as soon as he reached Argos, the attempts upon your father's life began— upon the life of an old man who couldn't make up his mind to die, couldn't bear to be parted from his kingship. One after another, men slipped into Thebes from Argos for the purpose of assassinating him, and every killer that we caught always ended by confessing who had put him up to it, who had paid him to try it. And it wasn't only Polynices. That is really what I am trying to tell you. I want you to know what went on in the back room, in the kitchen of politics; I want you to know what took place in the wings of this drama in which you are burning to play a part.

Yesterday, I gave Eteocles a State funeral, with pomp and honors. Today, Eteocles is a saint and a hero in the eyes of all Thebes. The whole city turned out to bury him. The schoolchildren emptied their piggy-banks to buy wreaths for him. Old men, orating in quavering, hypocritical voices, glorified the virtues of the great-hearted brother, the devoted son, the loyal prince. I made a speech myself; and every temple priest was present with an appropriate show of sorrow and solemnity in his stupid face. And military honors were accorded the dead hero.

Well, what else could I have done? People had taken sides in the civil war. Both sides couldn't be wrong; that would be too much. I couldn't have made them swallow the truth. Two gangsters was more of a luxury than I could afford. (*He pauses for a moment.*) And this is the whole point of my story. Eteocles, that virtuous brother, was just as rotten as Polynices. That great-hearted son had done his best, too, to procure the assassination of his father. That loyal prince had also offered to sell out Thebes to the highest bidder.

Funny, isn't it? Polynices lies rotting in the sun while Eteocles is given a hero's funeral and will be housed in a marble vault. Yet I have absolute proof that everything that Polynices did, Eteocles had plotted to do. They were a pair of blackguards—both engaged in selling out Thebes, and both engaged in selling out each other; and they died like the cheap gangsters they were, over a division of the spoils.

But, as I told you a moment ago, I had to make a martyr of one of them. I sent out to the holocaust for their bodies; they were found clasped in one another's arms—for the first time in the lives, I imagine. Each had been spitted on the other's sword, and the Argive cavalry had trampled them down. They were mashed to a pulp, Antigone. I had the prettier of the two carcasses brought in, and gave it a State funeral; and I left the other to rot. I didn't know which was which. And I assure you, I didn't care. (*Long silence, neither looking at the other.*)

ANTIGONE. (*In a mild voice.*) Why do you tell me all this?

(*Another pause.*)

CREON. (*Relaxed in the belief that he has defeated her, speaks with pompous self-satisfaction.*) You hold a treasure in your hands, Antigone—life, I mean. (*He picks up his coat from the chair, puts it on.*) And you were about to throw it away. Would it have been better to let you die a victim to that obscene story? Don't think me fatuous if I say that I understand you; and that at your age I should have done the same thing. A moment ago, when we were quarreling, you said I was drinking in your words. I was. But it wasn't you I was listening to; it was a lad named Creon who lived here in Thebes many years ago. He was thin and pale, as you are. His mind, too, was filled with thoughts of self-sacrifice. Go find Haemon. And get married quickly, Antigone. Be happy. Life is not what you think it is.

Life is a child playing round your feet, a tool you hold firmly in your grip, a bench you sit down upon in the evening, in your garden. People will tell you that that's not life, that life is something else. They will tell you that because they need your strength and your fire, and they will want to make use of you. Don't listen to them. Believe me, the only poor consolation that we have in our old age is to discover that what I have just said to you is true. Life is nothing more than the happiness that you get out of it.

ANTIGONE. (*Murmurs, lost in thought.*) Happiness. . . .

CREON. (*Suddenly a little self-conscious.*) Not much of a word, is it?

ANTIGONE (*quietly*). What kind of happiness do you foresee for me? Paint me the picture of your happy Antigone. What are the unimportant little sins that I shall have to commit before I am allowed to sink my teeth into life and tear happiness from it? Tell me: to whom shall I have to lie? Upon whom shall I have to fawn? To whom must I sell myself? Whom do you want me to leave dying, while I turn away my eyes?

CREON. Antigone, be quiet.

ANTIGONE. Why do you tell me to be quiet when all I want to know is what I have to do to be happy? You tell me that life is so wonderful. I want to know what I have to do in order to be able to say that myself.

CREON. Do you love Haemon?

ANTIGONE. Yes, I love Haemon. The Haemon I love is hard and young, faithful and difficult to satisfy, the way I am. But if what I love in Haemon is to be worn away like a stone step by the tread of the thing you call life, the thing you call happiness; if Haemon reaches the point where he stops growing pale with fear when I grow pale, stops thinking that I must have been killed in an accident when I am five minutes late, stops feeling that he is alone on earth when I laugh and he doesn't know why—if he too has to learn to say yes to everything—why, no, then, no! I do not love Haemon!

CREON. You don't know what you are talking about!

ANTIGONE. I do know what I am talking about! It is you who have lost your way and don't know what to say. I am too far away from you now, talking to you from a kingdom you can't get into, with your quick tongue and your hollow heart. (*Laughs.*) I laugh, Creon, because I see suddenly what a transparent hypocrite you are. Creon, the family man! Creon, the contented sitter on benches, in the evening, in his garden! Creon, desecrating the dead while he tries to fob me off with platitudes about happiness!

CREON. It is your happiness, too, Antigone!

ANTIGONE. I spit on your happiness! I spit on your idea of life—that life that must go on, come what may. You are all like dogs that lick everything they smell. You with your promise of a humdrum happiness—provided a person doesn't ask too much of life. I want everything of life, I do; and I want it now! I want it total, complete: otherwise I reject it! If life must be a thing of fear and lying and compromise; if life cannot be free, gallant, incorruptible—then, Creon, I choose death!

CREON. Scream on, daughter of Oedipus! Scream on, in your father's own voice!

ANTIGONE. In my father's own voice, yes! The voice of a king who died to purify his people, whereas you live to make them vile. You've told me that you'd like to bury Polynices, but that there are political reasons why —what was that horrible thing you said?— why that stench has got to fill the town for a month. I have nothing to do with your politics. Tell me why I can't bury him.

CREON. Because it's my order.

ANTIGONE. The order of a coward King who makes war upon the dead!

CREON. Be quiet, I say!

ANTIGONE. Why do you want me to be quiet? Because you know that I am right? Do you think I can't tell from your face that what I'm saying is true? Of course, it's true. But no, you can't admit it; because you have to growl and defend the bone that you call politics.

CREON. (*Grasps her by her arms.*) Shut up! If you could see how ugly you are, shrieking those words!

ANTIGONE. Yes, I am ugly! Father was ugly, too. (CREON *releases her arms, turns and moves away. Stands with his back to AN-TIGONE.*) But father became beautiful. And do you know when? (*She follows him to behind the table.*) At the very end. When all his questions had been answered. When he could no longer doubt that he *had* killed his own father; that he *had* gone to bed with his own mother. When he was absolutely certain that he had to die if the plague was to be lifted from his people. Then he was at peace; then he could smile, almost; then he became beautiful. . . . Whereas you! Look at yourself, Creon! That never-extinguished glint of fear and suspicion in the corner of your eye—that ever-present crease in the corner of your power-loving mouth. Creon, you spoke the word a moment ago: the smelly kitchen of politics. That's where you were fathered and pupped—in a filthy kitchen!

CREON. (*Turns to her.*) I order you to shut up! Do you hear me!

ANTIGONE. *You* order me? Cook! Do you really believe that you can give me orders?

CREON. Antigone! The anteroom is full of people! Do you want them to hear you?

ANTIGONE. Open the doors! Let us make sure that they can hear me!

CREON. By God! You shut up, I tell you!

(ISMENE *enters through arch.*)

ISMENE. (*Distraught.*) Antigone!

ANTIGONE. (*Turns to* ISMENE.) You, too? What do you want?

ISMENE. Oh, forgive me, Antigone. I've come back. I'll go with you now.

ANTIGONE. Where will you go with me?

ISMENE. (*To* CREON.) Creon! If you kill her, you'll have to kill me, too. I was with her. I helped her bury Polynices.

ANTIGONE. Oh, no, Ismene! You had your chance to come with me in the black night, creeping on your hands and knees. You had your chance to claw up the earth with your nails, as I did; to get yourself caught like a thief, as I did. And you refused it.

ISMENE. Not any more. If you die, I don't want to live. I'll do it alone tonight.

ANTIGONE. You hear that, Creon? (*She turns round toward* CREON.) The thing is catching! Who knows but that lots of people will catch the disease from me! What are you waiting for? Call in your guards! Come on, Creon! Show a little courage! It only hurts for a minute! Come on, cook!

CREON. (*Turns toward arch and calls.*) Guard!

(GUARDS *enter through arch.*)

ANTIGONE. (*In a great cry of relief.*) At last, Creon!

(CHORUS *enters through left arch.*)

CREON. (*To the* GUARDS.) Take her away! (CREON *goes up onto top step.*)

(GUARDS *grasp* ANTIGONE *by her arms, turn and hustle her towards the arch right and exit.*)

(ISMENE *mimes horror, backs away towards the arch left, then turns and runs out through the arch.*)

(*A long pause, as* CREON *moves slowly downstage.*)

CHORUS. (*Behind* CREON. *Speaks in a deliberate voice.*) You are out of your mind, Creon. What have you done?

CREON. (*His back to* CHORUS.) She had to die.

CHORUS. You must not let Antigone die. We shall carry the scar of her death for centuries.

CREON. She insisted. No man on earth was strong enough to dissuade her. Polynices was a mere pretext. When she had to give up that pretext, she found another one—that life and happiness were tawdry things and not worth possessing. She was bent upon only one thing: to reject life and to die.

CHORUS. You say so, Creon. But it is not the truth.

CREON. What do you want me to do for her? Condemn her to live?

HAEMON. (*Calls from off-stage.*) Father! (HAEMON *enters through arch right.* CREON *turns toward him.*)

CREON. Haemon, forget Antigone. Forget her, my dearest boy.

HAEMON. How can you talk like that?

CREON. (*Grasps* HAEMON *by the hands.*) I did everything I could to save her, Haemon. I used every argument. I swear I did. The girl doesn't love you. She could have gone on living for you; but she refused. She wanted it this way; she wanted to die.

HAEMON. Father! The Guards are dragging Antigone away! You've got to stop them! (*He breaks away from* CREON.)

CREON. (*Looks away from* HAEMON.) I can't stop them. It's too late. Antigone has spoken. The story is all over Thebes. I cannot save her now.

CHORUS. Creon, you must find a way to keep Antigone from being put to death.

CREON. I cannot.

CHORUS. You must recall your edict. You must order the burial of Polynices.

CREON. Too late. The law must be obeyed. I can do nothing.

HAEMON. But, Father, you are master in Thebes!

CREON. I am master under the law. Not above the law.

HAEMON. But you made that law yourself. What you ordained, you can repeal. You cannot let Antigone be taken from me.

CREON. I cannot do anything else, my poor boy. She must die and you must live.

HAEMON. Live, you say! Live a life without Antigone? A life in which I am to go on admiring you as you busy yourself about your kingdom; go on admiring you as you make your persuasive speeches and strike your attitudes? Not without Antigone. I love Antigone. She never struck a pose and waited for me to admire her. Mirrors meant nothing to her. She never looked at herself. She looked at me, and expected me to be somebody. And I was—when I was with her. Do you think I am not going after her? I will not live without Antigone!

CREON. Haemon—you will have to resign yourself to life without Antigone. (*He moves to left of* HAEMON.) Sooner or later there comes a day of sorrow in each man's life when he must cease to be a child and take up the burden of being a man. That day has come for you.

HAEMON. (*Backs away a step.*) That giant strength, that courage. That massive god who used to pick me up in his arms and shelter me from shadows and monsters—was that you, Father? Was it of you I stood in awe? Was that man you?

CREON. Yes, Haemon, that was me.

HAEMON. Then you are not that man today. For if you were, you'd know that your enemies are abroad in every street. You'd know that the people are stirring and murmuring against you. You cannot put Antigone to death. She will not have been dead an hour before shame will sit on every Theban doorstep and horror will fill every Theban heart. Already the people are full of fear and anger because you have not buried Polynices. If you kill Antigone, they will hate you!

CREON. Silence! That edict stands!

HAEMON. (*Stares at* CREON *for a moment.*) I tell you again that I will not live without Antigone. (*Turns and goes quickly out through arch.*)

CHORUS. Creon, the gods have a way of punishing injustice.

CREON (*contemptuously*). The gods!

CHORUS. Creon, that boy is wounded to death.

CREON. We are all wounded to death.

(FIRST GUARD *enters through arch right, followed by* SECOND *and* THIRD GUARDS *pulling* ANTIGONE *along with them.*)

FIRST GUARD. Chief, the people are crowding into the palace!

ANTIGONE. Creon, you are going to kill me

let that be enough. I want to be alone until it is over.

CREON. Empty the palace! Guards at the gates! (CREON *quickly crosses toward the arch and exits. Two* GUARDS *release* ANTIGONE *and exit behind* CREON. CHORUS *goes out through arch left.*)

(*The lighting dims so that only the area about the table is lighted. The cyclorama is covered with a dark blue color. The scene is intended to suggest a prison cell, filled with shadows and dimly lit.*)

(ANTIGONE *moves to stool and sits. The* FIRST GUARD *stands upstage. He watches* ANTIGONE, *and as she sits, he begins pacing slowly downstage, then upstage.*)

(*A pause.*)

ANTIGONE. (*Turns and looks at the* GUARD.) It's you, is it?

GUARD. What do you mean, me?

ANTIGONE. The last human face that I shall see. (*A pause as they look at one another, then* GUARD *paces upstage; turns and crosses behind table.*) Was it you that arrested me this morning?

GUARD. Yes, that was me.

ANTIGONE. You hurt me. There was no need for you to hurt me. Did I act as if I was trying to escape?

GUARD. Come on now, Miss. It was my business to bring you in. I did it. (*A pause. He paces to and fro upstage. Only the sound of his boots is heard.*)

ANTIGONE. How old are you?

GUARD. Thirty-nine.

ANTIGONE. Have you any children?

GUARD. Yeah. Two.

ANTIGONE. Do you love your children?

GUARD. What's that got to do with you? (*A pause. He paces upstage and downstage.*)

ANTIGONE. How long have you been in the Guards?

GUARD. Since the war. I was in the army. Sergeant. Then I joined the Guards.

ANTIGONE. Does one have to have been an army sergeant to get into the Guards?

GUARD. Supposed to be. Either that or on special detail. But when they make you a guard, you lose your stripes.

ANTIGONE. (*Murmurs.*) I see.

GUARD. Yes. Of course, if you're a guard, everybody knows you're something special; they know you're an old non-com. Take pay, for instance. When you're a guard you get your pay, and on top of that you get six months' extra pay, to make sure you don't lose anything by not being a sergeant any more.

ANTIGONE. (*Barely audible.*) I see.

GUARD. That's what I'm telling you. That's why sergeants, now, they don't like guards. Maybe you noticed they try to make out they're better than us? Promotion, that's what it is. In the army, anybody can get promoted. All you need is good conduct. Now in the Guards, it's slow, and you have to know your business—like how to make out a report and the like of that. But when you're a non-com in the Guards, you've got something that even a sergeant-major ain't got. For instance. . . .

ANTIGONE. (*Breaking him off.*) Listen.

GUARD. Yes, Miss.

ANTIGONE. I'm going to die soon. (*The* GUARD *looks at her for a moment, then turns and moves away.*)

GUARD. For instance, people have a lot of respect for guards, they have. A guard may be a soldier, but he's kind of in the civil service, too.

ANTIGONE. Do you think it hurts to die?

GUARD. How would I know? Of course, if somebody sticks a sabre in your gut and turns it round, it hurts.

ANTIGONE. How are they going to put me to death?

GUARD. Well, I'll tell you. I heard the proclamation, all right. There isn't much that gets away from me. It seems that they don't want to dirty up. . . . Wait a minute. How did that go now? (*He stares into space and recites from memory.*) "In order that our fair city shall not be pol-luted with her sinful blood, she shall be im-mured—immured." That means, they shove you in a cave and wall up the cave.

ANTIGONE. Alive?

GUARD. Yes. . . . (*He moves away a few steps.*)

ANTIGONE. (*Murmurs.*) O tomb! O bridal bed! Alone! (ANTIGONE *sits there, a tiny figure in the middle of the stage. You would say she felt a little chilly. She wraps her arms around herself.*)

GUARD. Yep! Outside the southeast gate of the town. In the Cave of Hades. In broad daylight. Some detail, eh, for them that's on the job! First they thought maybe it was a job for the army. Now it looks like it's going to be the Guards. There's an outfit for you! Nothing the Guards can't do. No wonder the army's jealous.

ANTIGONE. A pair of animals.

GUARD. What do you mean, a pair of animals?

ANTIGONE. When the winds blow cold, all they need do is to press close against one another. I am all alone.

GUARD. Say, is there anything you want? I can send out for it, you know.

ANTIGONE. You are very kind. (*A pause.* ANTIGONE *looks up at the* GUARD.) Yes, there is something I want. I want you to give someone a letter from me, when I am dead.

GUARD. How's that again? A letter?

ANTIGONE. Yes, I want to write a letter; and I want you to give it to someone for me.

GUARD. (*Straightens up.*) Hey, wait a minute. Take it easy. It's as much as my job is worth to go handing out letters from prisoners.

ANTIGONE. (*Removes a ring from her finger and holds it out toward him.*) I'll give you this ring if you will do it.

GUARD. Is it gold? (*He takes the ring from her.*)

ANTIGONE. Yes, it is gold.

GUARD. (*Shakes his head.*) Uh-uh. No can do. Suppose they go through my pockets. I might get six months for a thing like that. (*He stares at the ring, then glances off right to make sure that he is not being watched.*) Listen, tell you what I'll do. You tell me what you want to say, and I'll write it down in my book. Then afterwards, I'll tear out the pages and give them to the party, see? If it's in my handwriting, it's all right.

ANTIGONE. (*Winces.*) In your handwriting? (*She shudders slightly.*) No. That would be awful. The poor darling! In your handwriting.

GUARD. (*Offers back the ring.*) O.K. It's no skin off my nose.

ANTIGONE (*quickly*). Of course, of course. No, keep the ring. But hurry. Time is getting short. Where is your notebook? (*The* GUARD *pockets the ring, takes his notebook and pencil from his pocket, puts his foot up on chair, and rests the notebook on his knee, licks his pencil.*) Ready? (*He nods.*) Write, now. "My darling. . . ."

GUARD. (*Writes as he mutters.*) The boy friend, eh?

ANTIGONE. "My darling. I had to die, and perhaps you will not love me any more. . . ."

GUARD. (*Mutters as he writes.*) ". . . will not love me any more."

ANTIGONE. "Perhaps it would have been simple to accept life. . . ."

GUARD. (*Repeats as he writes.*) ". . . to accept life. . . ."

ANTIGONE. "But it was not for myself. And now, it's so dreadful here alone. I am afraid . . . (*She glances wildly about.*) And these shadows. . . ."

GUARD. (*Looks at her.*) Wait a minute! How fast do you think I can write?

ANTIGONE. (*Takes hold of herself.*) Where are you?

GUARD. (*Reads from his notebook.*) ". . . dreadful here alone. I am afraid. . . ."

ANTIGONE. No. Scratch that out. Nobody must know that. They have no right to know. It's as if they saw me naked and touched me, after I was dead. Scratch it all out. Just write: "Forgive me."

GUARD. (*Looks at* ANTIGONE.) I cut out everything you said there at the end, and I put down, "Forgive me"?

ANTIGONE. Yes. "Forgive me, my darling. but it wasn't for myself. I love you." (*She murmurs, as* GUARD *writes.*) No, it wasn't for myself.

GUARD. (*Finishes the letter.*) ". . . I love you." (*He looks at her.*) Is that all?

ANTIGONE. That's all.

GUARD. (*Straightens up, looks at notebook.*) Damn funny letter.

ANTIGONE. I know.

GUARD. (*Looks at her.*) Who is it to? (*A sudden roll of drums begins and continues until after* ANTIGONE *exits. The* FIRST GUARD *pockets the notebook and shouts at* ANTIGONE.) O.K. That's enough out of you! Come on!

(*At the sound of the drum roll,* SECOND *and* THIRD GUARDS *enter through the right arch.* ANTIGONE *rises.* GUARDS *seize her and exit with her.*)

(*The lighting moves up to suggest late afternoon.*)

(CHORUS *enters.*)

CHORUS. And now it is Creon's turn.

(MESSENGER *runs through the arch right.*)

MESSENGER. The Queen . . . the Queen! Where is the Queen?

CHORUS. What do you want with the Queen? What have you to tell the Queen?

MESSENGER. News to break her heart. Antigone had just been thrust into the cave. They hadn't finished heaving the last blocks of stone into place when Creon and the rest heard a sudden moaning from the tomb. A hush fell over us all, for it was not the voice of Antigone. It was Haemon's voice that came forth from the tomb. Everybody looked at Creon; and he howled like a man demented: "Take away the stones! Take away the stones!" The slaves leaped at the wall of stones, and Creon worked with them, sweating and tearing at the blocks with his bleeding hands. Finally a narrow opening was forced, and into it slipped the smallest guard.

Antigone had hanged herself by the cord of her robe, by the red and golden twisted cord of her robe. The cord was round her neck like a child's collar. Haemon was on his knees, holding her in his arms and moaning, his face buried in her robe. More stones were removed, and Creon went into the tomb. He tried to raise Haemon to his feet. I could hear him begging Haemon to rise to his feet. Haemon was deaf to his father's voice, till suddenly he stood up of his own accord, his eyes dark and burning. Anguish was in his face, but it was the face of a little boy. He stared at his father. Then suddenly he struck him—hard; and he drew his sword. Creon leapt out of range. Haemon went on staring at him, his eyes full of contempt—a glance that was like a knife, and that Creon couldn't escape. The King stood trembling in the far corner of the tomb, and Haemon went on staring. Then, without a word, he stabbed himself and lay down beside Antigone, embracing her in a great pool of blood.

(*A pause as* CREON *and* PAGE *enter through arch on the* MESSENGER's *last words.* CHORUS *and the* MESSENGER *both turn to look at* CREON, *then the* MESSENGER *exits through curtain.*)

CREON. I have had them laid out side by side. They are together at last, and at peace. Two lovers on the morrow of their bridal. Their work is done.

CHORUS. But not yours, Creon. You have still one thing to learn. Eurydice, the Queen, your wife. . . .

CREON. A good woman. Always busy with her garden, her preserves, her sweaters—those sweaters she never stopped knitting for the poor. Strange, how the poor never stop needing sweaters. One would almost think that was all they needed.

CHORUS. The poor in Thebes are going to be cold this winter, Creon. When the Queen was told of her son's death, she waited carefully until she had finished her row, then put down her knitting calmly—as she did everything. She went up to her room, her lavender-scented room, with its embroidered doilies and its pictures framed in plush; and there, Creon, she cut her throat. She is laid out now in one of those two old-fashioned twin beds, exactly where you went to her one night when she was still a maiden. Her smile is still the same, scarcely a shade more melancholy. And if it were not for that great red blot on the bed linen by her neck, one might think she was asleep.

CREON. (*In a dull voice.*) She, too. They are all asleep. (*Pause.*) It must be good to sleep.

CHORUS. Tomorrow they will sleep sweetly in the ground, Creon. You will bury them tomorrow. You who would not bury Polynices today will bury Eurydice and Haemon tomorrow. And Antigone, too. (*Pause.*) The gods take a hand in every game, Creon. Even politics.

CREON. (*Nodding soberly.*) The gods!

CHORUS. And now you are alone, Creon.

CREON. Yes, all alone. (*He remains lost in thought as the hour strikes. To* PAGE.) What time was that?

PAGE. Five o'clock, Sir.

CREON. What have we on at five o'clock?

PAGE. Cabinet meeting, Sir.

CREON. Cabinet meeting. Well, we might as well go along to it. (CREON *and* PAGE *exit slowly through arch left and* CHORUS *moves downstage.*)

CHORUS. And there we are. All those who were meant to die have died. Those who believed one thing, those who believed the contrary thing, and even those who believed nothing at all, yet were caught up in the web without knowing why. All dead: stiff, useless, rotting.

Creon was the most rational, the most plausible of tyrants. But like all tyrants, he refused to distinguish between the things that are Caesar's and the things that are God's. Now and again, in the three thousand years since the first Antigone was heard of, someone has had to come forward to remind men of this distinction. And whether we say that the result is Christianity, or popular revolution, or underground resistance, the cause is always the same—a passionate belief that moral law exists, and a passionate regard for the sanctity of human personality.

Well, Antigone is calm tonight. She has played her part.

(*Three* GUARDS *enter, resume their places on steps as at the rise of the curtain, and begin to play cards.*)

A great melancholy wave of unrest now settles down upon Thebes, upon the empty palace, upon Creon, who can now begin to long for his own death.

Only the guards are left, and none of this matters to them. It's no skin off their noses. They go on playing cards.

(CHORUS *walks toward the arch left as the curtain falls.*)

Jean-Paul Sartre

Jean-Paul Sartre (1905–   ) is a French author, play-wright, and philosopher. He served in the French army at the outbreak of World War II, was captured by the enemy, and held as a prisoner in Germany for nine months. When released, he returned to Paris and participated in the Resistance Movement. He is considered an outstanding exponent of one of the varied manifestations of Existentialism. (See above p. 907) His analysis as outlined here seems to fit in well with his own personal experiences. Originally a lecture delivered in 1945 at the Club Maintenant in Paris, the essay was later published as L'Existentialisme est un humanisme, from which this translation was made. In it he sets forth the basic principles of the Existentialists as he interprets them and offers answers to some of the criticisms leveled against them. In reading the selection note (1) the criticisms of Existentialism which Sartre seeks to refute; (2) the two kinds of Existentialism he identifies; (3) the arguments he presents for placing existence before essence; (4) his comments about man's control over his being; (5) the relationship he develops between individual decisions and the molding of humanity; (6) the Existentialist interpretation of anguish and abandonment; (7) Sartre's treatment of human freedom; (8) the Existentialist concept of total commitment; (9) its relationship to absolute truth; and (10) the extent to which Sartre argues that Existentialism is a humanist philosophy.

From: Existentialism

I should like on this occasion to defend existentialism against some charges which have been brought against it.

First, it has been charged with inviting people to remain in a kind of desperate quietism because, since no solutions are possible, we should have to consider action in this world as quite impossible. We should then end up in a philosophy of contemplation; and since contemplation is a luxury, we come in the end to a bourgeois philosophy. The communists in particular have made these charges.

On the other hand, we have been charged with dwelling on human degradation, with pointing up everywhere the sordid, shady, and slimy, and neglecting the gracious and beautiful, the bright side of human nature; for example, according to Mlle. Mercier, a Catholic critic, with forgetting the smile of the child. Both sides charge us with having ignored human solidarity, with considering man as an isolated being. The communists say that the main reason for this is that we take pure subjectivity, the *Cartesian I think*, as our starting point; in other words, the moment in which man becomes fully aware of what it means to him to be an isolated being; as a result, we are unable to return to a state of

Jean-Paul Sartre, *Existentialism* as translated by Bernard Frechtman (New York: Philosophical Library, 1947), pp. 11–61. Reprinted with the permission of The Philosophical Library and Methuen and Co. Ltd.

solidarity with the men who are not ourselves, a state which we can never reach in the *cogito*.

From the Christian standpoint, we are charged with denying the reality and seriousness of human undertakings, since, if we reject God's commandments and the eternal verities, there no longer remains anything but pure caprice, with everyone permitted to do as he pleases and incapable, from his own point of view, of condemning the points of view and acts of others.

I shall try today to answer these different charges. Many people are going to be surprised at what is said here about humanism. We shall try to see in what sense it is to be understood. In any case, what can be said from the very beginning is that by existentialism we mean a doctrine which makes human life possible and, in addition, declares that every truth and every action implies a human setting and a human subjectivity.

As is generally known, the basic charge against us is that we put the emphasis on the dark side of human life. Someone recently told me of a lady who, when she let slip a vulgar word in a moment of irritation, excused herself by saying, "I guess I'm becoming an existentialist." Consequently, existentialism is regarded as something ugly; that is why we are said to be naturalists; and if we are, it is rather surprising that in this day and age we cause so much more alarm and scandal than does naturalism, properly so called. The kind of person who can take in his stride such a novel as Zola's *The Earth* is disgusted as soon as he starts reading an existentialist novel; the kind of person who is resigned to the wisdom of the ages—which is pretty sad—finds us even sadder. Yet, what can be more disillusioning than saying "true charity begins at home" or "a scoundrel will always return evil for good?"

We know the commonplace remarks made when this subject comes up, remarks which always add up to the same thing: we shouldn't struggle against the powers-that-be; we shouldn't resist authority; we shouldn't try to rise above our station; any action which doesn't conform to authority is romantic; any effort not based on past experience is doomed to failure; experience shows that man's bent is always toward trouble, that there must be a strong hand to hold him in check, if not, there will be anarchy. There are still people who go on mumbling these melancholy old saws, the people who say, "It's only human!" whenever a more or less repugnant act is pointed out to them, the people who glut themselves on *chansons réalistes;* these are the people who accuse existentialism of being too gloomy, and to such an extent that I wonder whether they are complaining about it, not for its pessimism, but much rather its optimism. Can it be that what really scares them in the doctrine I shall try to present here is that it leaves to man a possibility of choice? To answer this question, we must re-examine it on a strictly philosophical plane. What is meant by the term *existentialism?*

Most people who use the word would be rather embarrassed if they had to explain it, since, now that the word is all the rage, even the work of a musician or painter is being called existentialist. A gossip columnist in *Clartés* signs himself *The Existentialist,* so that by this time the word has been so stretched and has taken on so broad a meaning, that it no longer means anything at all. It seems that for want of an advance-guard doctrine analogous to surrealism, the kind of people who are eager for scandal and flurry turn to this philosophy which in other respects does not at all serve their purposes in this sphere.

Actually, it is the least scandalous, the most austere of doctrines. It is intended strictly for specialists and philosophers. Yet it can be defined easily. What complicates matters is that there are two kinds of existentialist; first, those who are Christian, among whom I would include Jaspers and Gabriel Marcel, both Catholic; and on the other hand the atheistic existentialists, among whom I class Heidegger, and then the French existentialists and myself. What they have in common is that they think that existence precedes essence, or, if you prefer, that subjectivity must be the starting point.

Just what does that mean? Let us consider some object that is manufactured, for example, a book or a paper-cutter: here is an object which has been made by an artisan whose inspiration came from a concept. He referred to the concept of what a paper-cutter is and likewise to a known method of production, which is part of the concept, something which is, by and large, a routine. Thus, the paper-cutter is at once an object produced in a certain way and, on the other hand, one having a specific use; and one can not postulate a man who produces a paper-cutter but does not know what it is used for. Therefore, let us say that, for the paper-cutter, essence—that is, the ensemble of both the production routines and the properties which enable it to be both produced and defined—precedes existence. Thus, the presence of the paper-cutter or book in front of me is determined. Therefore, we have here a technical view of the world whereby it can be said that production precedes existence.

When we conceive God as the Creator, He is generally thought of as a superior sort of artisan. Whatever doctrine we may be considering, whether one like that of Descartes or that of Leibnitz, we always grant that will more or less follows understanding or, at the very least, accompanies it, and that when God creates He knows exactly what He is creating. Thus, the concept of man in the mind of God is comparable to the concept of paper-cutter in the mind of the manufacturer, and, following certain techniques and a conception, God produces man, just as the artisan, following a definition and a technique, makes a paper-cutter. Thus, the individual man is the realisation of a certain concept in the divine intelligence.

In the eighteenth century, the atheism of the *philosophes* discarded the idea of God, but not so much for the notion that essence precedes existence. To a certain extent, this idea is found everywhere; we find it in Diderot, in Voltaire, and even in Kant. Man has a human nature; this human nature, which is the concept of the human, is found in all men, which means that each man is a particular example of a universal concept, man. In Kant, the result of this universality is that the wild-man, the natural man, as well as the bourgeois, are circumscribed by the same definition and have the same basic qualities. Thus, here too the essence of man precedes the historical existence that we find in nature.

Atheistic existentialism, which I represent, is more coherent. It states that if God does not exist, there is at least one being in whom existence precedes essence, a being who exists before he can be defined by any concept, and that this being is man, or, as Heidegger says, human reality. What is meant here by saying that existence precedes essence? It means that, first of all, man exists, turns up, appears on the scene, and, only afterwards, defines himself. If man, as the existentialist conceives him, is undefinable, it is because at first he is nothing. Only afterward will he be something, and he himself will have made what he will be. Thus, there is no human nature, since there is no God to conceive it. Not only is man what he conceives himself to be, but he is also only what he wills himself to be after this thrust toward existence.

Man is nothing else but what he makes of himself. Such is the first principle of existentialism. It is also what is called subjectivity, the name we are labeled with when charges are brought against us. But what do we mean by this, if not that man has a greater dignity than a stone or table? For we mean that man first exists, that is, that man first of all is the being who hurls himself toward a future and who is conscious of imagining himself as being in the future. Man is at the start a plan which is aware of itself, rather than a patch of moss, a piece of garbage, or a cauliflower; nothing exists prior to this plan; there is nothing in heaven; man will be what he will have planned to be. Not what he will want to be. Because by the word "will" we generally mean a conscious decision, which is subsequent to what we have already made of ourselves. I may want to belong to a political party, write a book, get married; but all that is only a manifestation of an earlier, more spontaneous choice that is called "will." But if existence really does precede essence, man is responsible for what he is. Thus, existentialism's first move is to make every man aware of what he is and to make the full responsibility of his existence rest on him. And when we say that a man is responsible for himself, we do not only mean that he is responsible for his own individuality, but that he is responsible for all men.

The word subjectivism has two meanings,

and our opponents play on the two. Subjectivism means, on the one hand, that an individual chooses and makes himself; and, on the other, that it is impossible for man to transcend human subjectivity. The second of these is the essential meaning of existentialism. When we say that man chooses his own self, we mean that every one of us does likewise; but we also mean by that that in making this choice he also chooses all men. In fact, in creating the man that we want to be, there is not a single one of our acts which does not at the same time create an image of man as we think he ought to be. To choose to be this or that is to affirm at the same time the value of what we choose, because we can never choose evil. We always choose the good, and nothing can be good for us without being good for all.

If, on the other hand, existence precedes essence, and if we grant that we exist and fashion our image at one and the same time, the image is valid for everybody and for our whole age. Thus, our responsibility is much greater than we might have supposed, because it involves all mankind. If I am a workingman and choose to join a Christian trade-union rather than be a communist, and if by being a member I want to show that the best thing for man is resignation, that the kingdom of man is not of this world, I am not only involving my own case—I want to be resigned for everyone. As a result, my action has involved all humanity. To take a more individual matter, if I want to marry, to have children; even if this marriage depends solely on my own circumstances or passion or wish, I am involving all humanity in monogamy and not merely myself. Therefore, I am responsible for myself and for everyone else. I am creating a certain image of man of my own choosing. In choosing myself, I choose man.

This helps us understand what the actual content is of such rather grandiloquent words as anguish, forlorness, despair. As you will see, it's all quite simple.

First, what is meant by anguish? The existentialists say at once that man is anguish. What that means is this: the man who involves himself and who realizes that he is not only the person he chooses to be, but also a lawmaker who is, at the same time, choosing all mankind as well as himself, can not help escape the feeling of his total and deep responsibility. Of course, there are many people who are not anxious; but we claim that they are hiding their anxiety, that they are fleeing from it. Certainly, many people believe that when they do something, they themselves are the only ones involved, and when someone says to them, "What if everyone acted that way?" they shrug their shoulders and answer, "Everyone doesn't act that way." But really, one should always ask himself, "What would happen if everybody looked at things that way?" There is no escaping this disturbing thought except by a kind of double-dealing. A man who lies and makes excuses for himself by saying "not everybody does that," is someone with an uneasy conscience, because the act of lying implies that a universal value is conferred upon the lie.

Anguish is evident even when it conceals itself. This is the anguish that Kierkegaard called the anguish of Abraham. You know the story: an angel has ordered Abraham to sacrifice his son; if it really were an angel who has come and said, "You are Abraham, you shall sacrifice your son," everything would be all right. But everyone might first wonder, "Is it really an angel, and am I really Abraham? What proof do I have?"

There was a madwoman who had hallucinations; someone used to speak to her on the telephone and give her orders. Her doctor asked her, "Who is it who talks to you?" She answered, "He says it's God." What proof did she really have that it was God? If an angel comes to me, what proof is there that it's an angel? And if I hear voices, what proof is there that they come from heaven and not from hell, or from the subconscious, or a pathological condition? What proves that they are addressed to me? What proof is there that I have been appointed to impose my choice and my conception of man on humanity? I'll never find any proof or sign to convince me of that. If a voice addresses me, it is always for me to decide that this is the angel's voice; if I consider that such an act is a good one, it is I who will choose to say that it is good rather than bad.

Now, I'm not being singled out as an Abraham, and yet at every moment I'm obliged to perform exemplary acts. For every man, everything happens as if all mankind had its eyes fixed on him and were guiding itself by what he does. And every man ought to say to himself, "Am I really the kind of man who has the right to act in such a way that humanity might guide itself by my actions?" And if he does not say that to himself, he is masking his anguish.

There is no question here of the kind of anguish which would lead to quietism, to inaction. It is a matter of a simple sort of anguish that anybody who has had responsibilities is familiar with. For example, when a military officer takes the responsibility for an attack and sends a certain number of men to death, he chooses to do so, and in the main he alone makes the choice. Doubtless, orders come from above, but they are too broad; he interprets them, and on this interpretation depend the lives of ten or fourteen or twenty men. In making a decision he can not help having a certain anguish. All leaders know this anguish. That doesn't keep them from acting; on the contrary, it is the very condition of their action. For it implies that they envisage a number of possibilities, and when they choose one, they realize that it has value only because it is chosen. We shall see that this kind of anguish, which is the kind that existentialism describes, is explained, in addition, by a direct responsibility to the other men whom it involves. It is not a curtain separating us from action, but is part of action itself.

When we speak of forlornness, a term Heidegger was fond of, we mean only that God does not exist and that we have to face all the consequences of this. The existentialist is strongly opposed to a certain kind of secular ethics which would like to abolish God with the least possible expense. About 1880, some French teachers tried to set up a secular ethics which went something like this: God is a useless and costly hypothesis; we are discarding it; but, meanwhile, in order for there to be an ethics, a society, a civilization, it is essential that certain values be taken seriously and that they be considered as having an *a priori* existence. It must be obligatory, *a priori,* to be honest, not to lie, not to beat your wife, to have children, etc., etc. So we're going to try a little device which will make it possible to show that values exist all the same, inscribed

in a heaven of ideas, though otherwise God does not exist. In other words—and this, I believe, is the tendency of everything called reformism in France—nothing will be changed if God does not exist. We shall find ourselves with the same norms of honesty, progress, and humanism, and we shall have made of God an outdated hypothesis which will peacefully die off by itself.

The existentialist, on the contrary, thinks it very distressing that God does not exist, because all possibility of finding values in a heaven of ideas disappears along with Him; there can no longer be an *a priori* Good, since there is no infinite and perfect consciousness to think it. Nowhere is it written that the Good exists, that we must be honest, that we must not lie; because the fact is we are on a plane where there are only men. Dostoievsky said, "If God didn't exist, everything would be possible." That is the very starting point of existentialism. Indeed, everything is permissible if God does not exist, and as a result man is forlorn, because neither within him nor without does he find anything to cling to. He can't start making excuses for himself.

If existence really does precede essence, there is no explaining things away by reference to a fixed and given human nature. In other words, there is no determinism, man is free, man is freedom. On the other hand, if God does not exist, we find no values or commands to turn to which legitimize our conduct. So, in the bright realm of values, we have no excuse behind us, nor justification before us. We are alone, with no excuses.

That is the idea I shall try to convey when I say that man is condemned to be free. Condemned, because he did not create himself, yet, in other respects is free; because, once thrown into the world, he is responsible for everything he does. The existentialist does not believe in the power of passion. He will never agree that a sweeping passion is a ravaging torrent which fatally leads a man to certain acts and is therefore an excuse. He thinks that man is responsible for his passion.

The existentialist does not think that man is going to help himself by finding in the world some omen by which to orient himself. Because he thinks that man will interpret the omen to suit himself. Therefore, he thinks that man, with no support and no aid, is condemned every moment to invent man. Ponge, in a very fine article, has said, "Man is the future of man." That's exactly it. But if it is taken to mean that this future is recorded in heaven, that God sees it, then it is false, because it would really no longer be a future. If it is taken to mean that, whatever a man may be, there is a future to be forged, a virgin future before him, then this remark is sound. But then we are forlorn.

To give you an example which will enable you to understand forlornness better, I shall cite the case of one of my students who came to see me under the following circumstances: his father was on bad terms with his mother, and, moreover, was inclined to be a collaborationist; his older brother had been killed in the German offensive of 1940, and the young man, with somewhat immature but generous feelings, wanted to avenge him. His mother lived alone with him, very much upset by the half-treason of her husband and the death of her older son; the boy was her only consolation.

The boy was faced with the choice of leaving for England and joining the Free French Forces—that is, leaving his mother behind—or remaining with his mother and helping her to carry on. He was fully aware that the woman lived only for him and that his going-off—and perhaps his death—would plunge her into despair. He was also aware that every act that he did for his mother's sake was a sure thing, in the sense that it was helping her to carry on, whereas every effort he made toward going off and fighting was an uncertain move which might run aground and prove completely useless; for example, on his way to England he might, while passing through Spain, be detained indefinitely in a Spanish camp; he might reach England or Algiers and be stuck in an office at a desk job. As a result, he was faced with two very different kinds of action: one, concrete, immediate, but concerning only one individual; the other concerned an incomparably vaster group, a national collectivity, but for that very reason was dubious, and might be interrupted en route. And, at the same time, he was wavering between two kinds of ethics. On the one hand, an ethics of sympathy, of personal devotion;

on the other, a broader ethics, but one whose efficacy was more dubious. He had to choose between the two.

Who could help him choose? Christian doctrine? No. Christian doctrine says, "Be charitable, love your neighbor, take the more rugged path, etc., etc." But which is the more rugged path? Whom should he love as a brother? The fighting man or his mother? Which does the greater good, the vague act of fighting in a group, or the concrete one of helping a particular human being to go on living? Who can decide *a priori*? Nobody. No book of ethics can tell him. The Kantian ethics says, "Never treat any person as a means, but as an end." Very well, if I stay with my mother, I'll treat her as an end and not as a means; but by virtue of this very fact, I'm running the risk of treating the people around me who are fighting, as means; and, conversely, if I go to join those who are fighting, I'll be treating them as an end, and, by doing that, I run the risk of treating my mother as a means.

If values are vague, and if they are always too broad for the concrete and specific case that we are considering, the only thing left for us is to trust our instincts. That's what this young man tried to do; and when I saw him, he said, "In the end, feeling is what counts. I ought to choose whichever pushes me in one direction. If I feel that I love my mother enough to sacrifice everything else for her—my desire for vengeance, for action, for adventure—then I'll stay with her. If, on the contrary, I feel that my love for my mother isn't enough, I'll leave."

But how is the value of a feeling determined? What gives his feeling for his mother value? Precisely the fact that he remained with her. I may say that I like so-and-so well enough to sacrifice a certain amount of money for him, but I may say so only if I've done it. I may say "I love my mother well enough to remain with her" if I have remained with her. The only way to determine the value of this affection is, precisely, to perform an act which confirms and defines it. But, since I require this affection to justify my act, I find myself caught in a vicious circle.

On the other hand, Gide has well said that a mock feeling and a true feeling are almost indistinguishable; to decide that I love my mother and will remain with her, or to remain with her by putting on an act, amount somewhat to the same thing. In other words, the feeling is formed by the acts one performs; so, I can not refer to it in order to act upon it. Which means that I can neither seek within myself the true condition which will impel me to act, nor apply to a system of ethics for concepts which will permit me to act. You will say, "At least, he did go to a teacher for advice." But if you seek advice from a priest, for example, you have chosen this priest; you already knew, more or less, just about what advice he was going to give you. In other words, choosing your adviser is involving yourself. The proof of this is that if you are a Christian, you will say, "Consult a priest." But some priests are collaborating, some are just marking time, some are resisting. Which to choose? If the young man chooses a priest who is resisting or collaborating, he has already decided on the kind of advice he's going to get. Therefore, in coming to see me he knew the answer I was going to give him, and I had only one answer to give: "You're free, choose, that is, invent." No general ethics can show you what is to be done; there are no omens in the world. The Catholics will reply, "But there are." Granted—but, in any case, I myself choose the meaning they have.

When I was a prisoner, I knew a rather remarkable young man who was a Jesuit. He had entered the Jesuit order in the following way: he had had a number of very bad breaks; in childhood, his father died, leaving him in poverty, and he was a scholarship student at a religious institution where he was constantly made to feel that he was being kept out of charity; then, he failed to get any of the honors and distinctions that children like; later on, at about eighteen, he bungled a love affair; finally, at twenty-two, he failed in military training, a childish enough matter, but it was the last straw.

This young fellow might well have felt that he had botched everything. It was a sign of something, but of what? He might have taken refuge in bitterness or despair. But he very wisely looked upon all this as a sign that he was not made for secular triumphs, and that only the triumphs of religion, holiness, and faith were open to him. He saw the hand of God in all this, and so he entered the order. Who can help seeing that he alone decided what the sign meant?

Some other interpretation might have been drawn from this series of setbacks; for example, that he might have done better to turn carpenter or revolutionist. Therefore, he is fully responsible for the interpretation. Forlornness implies that we ourselves choose our being. Forlornness and anguish go together.

As for despair, the term has a very simple meaning. It means that we shall confine ourselves to reckoning only with what depends upon our will, or on the ensemble of probabilities which make our action possible. When we want something, we always have to reckon with probabilities. I may be counting on the arrival of a friend. The friend is coming by rail or street-car; this supposes that the train will arrive on schedule, or that the street-car will not jump the track. I am left in the realm of possibility; but possibilities are to be reckoned with only to the point where my action comports with the ensemble of these possibilities, and no further. The moment the possibilities I am considering are not rigorously involved by my action, I ought to disengage myself from them, because no God, no scheme, can adapt the world and its possibilities to my will. When Descartes said, "Conquer yourself rather than the world," he meant essentially the same thing.

The Marxists to whom I have spoken reply, "You can rely on the support of others in your action, which obviously has certain limits because you're not going to live forever. That means: rely on both what others are doing elsewhere to help you, in China, in Russia, and what they will do later on, after your death, to carry on the action and lead it to its fulfillment, which will be the revolution. You even *have* to rely upon that, otherwise you're immoral." I reply at once that I will always rely on fellow-fighters insofar as these comrades are involved with me in a common struggle, in the unity of a party or a group in which I can more or less make my weight felt; that is, one whose ranks I am in as a fighter and whose movements I am aware of at every moment. In such a situation, relying on the unity and will of the party is exactly like counting on the fact that the train will arrive on time or that the car won't jump the track. But, given that man is free and that there is no human nature for me to depend on, I can not count on men whom I do not know by relying on human goodness or man's concern for the good of society. I don't know what will become of the Russian revolution; I may make an example of it to the extent that at the present time it is apparent that the proletariat plays a part in Russia that it plays in no other nation. But I can't swear that this will inevitably lead to a triumph of the proletariat. I've got to limit myself to what I see.

Given that men are free and that tomorrow they will freely decide what man will be, I can not be sure that, after my death, fellow-fighters will carry on my work to bring it to its maximum perfection. Tomorrow, after my death, some men may decide to set up Fascism, and the others may be cowardly and muddled enough to let them do it. Fascism will then be the human reality, so much the worse for us.

Actually, things will be as man will have decided they are to be. Does that mean that I should abandon myself to quietism? No. First, I should involve myself; then, act on the old saw, "Nothing ventured, nothing gained." Nor does it mean that I shouldn't belong to a party, but rather that I shall have no illusions and shall do what I can. For example, suppose I ask myself, "Will socialization, as such, ever come about?" I know nothing about it. All I know is that I'm going to do everything in my power to bring it about. Beyond that, I can't count on anything. Quietism is the attitude of people who say, "Let others do what I can't do." The doctrine I am presenting is the very opposite of quietism, since it declares, "There is no reality except in action." Moreover, it goes further, since it adds, "Man is nothing else than his plan; he exists only to the extent that he fulfills himself; he is therefore nothing else than the ensemble of his acts, nothing else than his life."

According to this, we can understand why our doctrine horrifies certain people. Because often the only way they can bear their wretchedness is to think, "Circumstances have been against me. What I've been and done doesn't show my true worth. To be sure, I've had no great love, no great friendship, but that's because I haven't met a man or woman who was worthy. The books I've written haven't been very good because I haven't had the proper leisure. I haven't had children to devote myself to because I didn't find a man with whom I could have spent my life. So there remains within me, unused and quite viable, a host of propensities, inclinations, possibilities, that one wouldn't guess from the mere series of things I've done."

Now, for the existentialist there is really no love other than one which manifests itself in a person's being in love. There is no genius other than one which is expressed in works of art; the genius of Proust is the sum of Proust's works; the genius of Racine is his series of tragedies. Outside of that, there is nothing. Why say that Racine could have written another tragedy, when he didn't write it? A man is involved in life, leaves his impress on it, and outside of that there is nothing. To be sure, this may seem a harsh thought to someone whose life hasn't been a success. But, on the other hand, it prompts people to understand that reality alone is what counts, that dreams, expectations, and hopes warrant no more than to define a man as a disappointed dream, as miscarried hopes, as vain expectations. In other words, to define him negatively and not positively. However, when we say, "You are nothing else than your life," that does not imply that the artist will be judged solely on the basis of his works of art; a thousand other things will contribute toward summing him up. What we mean is that a man is nothing else than a series of undertakings, that he is the sum, the organization, the ensemble of the relationships which make up these undertakings.

When all is said and done, what we are accused of, at bottom, is not our pessimism, but an optimistic toughness. If people throw up to us our works of fiction in which we write about people who are soft, weak, cowardly, and sometimes even downright bad, it's not because these people are soft, weak, cowardly, or bad; because if we were to say, as Zola did, that they are that way because of heredity, the workings of environment, society, because of biological or psychological determinism, people would be reassured. They would say, "Well, that's what we're like, no one can do anything about it." But when the existentialist writes about a coward, he says that this coward is responsible for his cowardice. He's not like that because he has a cowardly heart or lung or brain; he's not like that on account of his physiological makeup; but he's like that because he has made himself a coward by his acts. There's no such thing as a cowardly constitution; there are nervous constitutions; there is poor blood, as the common people say, or strong constitutions. But the man whose blood is poor is not a coward on that account, for what makes cowardice is the act of renouncing or yielding. A constitution is not an act; the coward is defined on the basis of the acts he performs. People feel, in a vague sort of way, that this coward we're talking about is guilty of being a coward, and the thought frightens them. What people would like is that a coward or a hero be born that way.

One of the complaints most frequently made about *The Ways of Freedom* can be summed up as follows: "After all, these people are so spineless, how are you going to make heroes out of them?" This objection almost makes me laugh, for it assumes that people are born heroes. That's what people really want to think. If you're born cowardly, you may set your mind perfectly at rest; there's nothing you can do about it; you'll be cowardly all your life, whatever you may do. If you're born a hero, you may set your mind just as much at rest; you'll be a hero all your life; you'll drink like a hero and eat like a hero. What the existentialist says is that the coward makes himself cowardly, that the hero makes himself heroic. There's always a possibility for the coward not to be cowardly any more and for the hero to stop being heroic. What counts is total involvement; some one particular action or set of circumstances is not total involvement.

Thus, I think we have answered a number of the charges concerning existentialism. You see that it can not be taken for a philosophy of quietism, since it defines man in terms of

action; nor for a pessimistic description of man—there is no doctrine more optimistic, since man's destiny is within himself; nor for an attempt to discourage man from acting, since it tells him that the only hope is in his acting and that action is the only thing that enables a man to live. Consequently, we are dealing here with an ethics of action and involvement.

Nevertheless, on the basis of a few notions like these, we are still charged with immuring man in his private subjectivity. There again we're very much misunderstood. Subjectivity of the individual is indeed our point of departure, and this for strictly philosophic reasons. Not because we are bourgeois, but because we want a doctrine based on truth and not a lot of fine theories, full of hope but with no real basis. There can be no other truth to take off from than this: *I think; therefore, I exist.* There we have the absolute truth of consciousness becoming aware of itself. Every theory which takes man out of the moment in which he becomes aware of himself is, at its very beginning, a theory which confounds truth, for outside the Cartesian *cogito,* all views are only probable, and a doctrine of probability which is not bound to a truth dissolves into thin air. In order to describe the probable, you must have a firm hold on the true. Therefore, before there can be any truth whatsoever, there must be an absolute truth; and this one is simple and easily arrived at; it's on everyone's doorstep; it's a matter of grasping it directly.

Secondly, this theory is the only one which gives man dignity, the only one which does not reduce him to an object. The effect of all materialism is to treat all men, including the one philosophizing, as objects, that is, as an ensemble of determined reactions in no way distinguished from the ensemble of qualities and phenomena which constitute a table or a chair or a stone. We definitely wish to establish the human realm as an ensemble of values distinct from the material realm. But the subjectivity that we have thus arrived at, and which we have claimed to be truth, is not a strictly individual subjectivity, for we have demonstrated that one discovers in the *cogito* not only himself, but others as well.

The philosophies of Descartes and Kant to the contrary, through the *I think* we reach our own self in the presence of others, and the others are just as real to us as our own self. Thus, the man who becomes aware of himself through the *cogito* also perceives all others, and he perceives them as the condition of his own existence. He realizes that he can not be anything (in the sense that we say that someone is witty or nasty or jealous) unless others recognize it as such. In order to get any truth about myself, I must have contact with another person. The other is indispensable to my own existence, as well as to my knowledge about myself. This being so, in discovering my inner being I discover the other person at the same time, like a freedom placed in front of me which thinks and wills only for or against me. Hence, let us at once announce the discovery of a world which we shall call intersubjectivity; this is the world in which man decides what he is and what others are.

Besides, if it is impossible to find in every man some universal essence which would be human nature, yet there does exist a universal human condition. It's not by chance that today's thinkers speak more readily of man's condition than of his nature. By condition they mean, more or less definitely, the *a priori* limits which outline man's fundamental situation in the universe. Historical situations vary; a man may be born a slave in a pagan society or a feudal lord or a proletarian. What does not vary is the necessity for him to exist in the world, to be at work there, to be there in the midst of other people, and to be mortal there. The limits are neither subjective or objective, or, rather, they have an objective and a subjective side. Objective because they are to be found everywhere and are recognizable everywhere; subjective because they are *lived* and are nothing if man does not live them, that is, freely determine his existence with reference to them. And though the configurations may differ, at least none of them are completely strange to me, because they all appear as attempts either to pass beyond these limits or recede from them or deny them or adapt to them. Consequently, every configuration, however individual it may be, has a universal value.

Every configuration, even the Chinese, the Indian, or the Negro, can be understood by a Westerner. "Can be understood" means that by virtue of a situation that he can imagine, a European of 1945 can, in like manner, push himself to his limits and reconstitute within himself the configuration of the Chinese, the Indian, or the African. Every configuration has universality in the sense that every configuration can be understood by every man. This does not at all mean that this configuration defines man forever, but that it can be met with again. There is always a way to understand the idiot, the child, the savage, the foreigner, provided one has the necessary information.

In this sense we may say that there is a universality of man; but it is not given, it is perpetually being made. I build the universal in choosing myself; I build it in understanding the configuration of every other man, whatever age he might have lived in. This absoluteness of choice does not do away with the relativeness of each epoch. At heart, what existentialism shows is the connection between the absolute character of free involvement, by virtue of which every man realizes himself in realizing a type of mankind, an involvement always comprehensible in any age whatsoever and by any person whosoever, and the relativeness of the cultural ensemble which may result from such a choice; it must be stressed that the relativity of Cartesianism and the absolute character of Cartesian involvement go together. In this sense, you may, if you like, say that each of us performs an absolute act in breathing, eating, sleeping, or behaving in any way whatever. There is no difference between being free, like a configuration, like an existence which chooses its essence, and being absolute. There is no difference between being an absolute temporarily localised, that is, localised in history, and being universally comprehensible.

This does not entirely settle the objection to subjectivism. In fact, the objection still takes several forms. First, there is the following: we are told, "So you're able to do anything, no matter what!" This is expressed in various ways. First we are accused of anarchy; then they say, "You're unable to pass judgment on others, because there's no reason to prefer one configuration to another"; finally they tell us, "Everything is arbitrary in this choosing of yours. You take something from one pocket and pretend you're putting it into the other."

These three objections aren't very serious. Take the first objection. "You're able to do anything, no matter what" is not to the point. In one sense choice is possible, but what is not possible is not to choose. I can always choose, but I ought to know that if I do not choose, I am still choosing. Though this may seem purely formal, it is highly important for keeping fantasy and caprice within bounds. If it is true that in facing a situation, for example, one in which, as a person capable of having sexual relations, of having children, I am obliged to choose an attitude, and if I in any way assume responsibility for a choice which, in involving myself, also involves all mankind, this has nothing to do with caprice, even if no *a priori* value determines my choice.

If anybody thinks that he recognizes here Gide's theory of the arbitrary act, he fails to see the enormous difference between this doctrine and Gide's. Gide does not know what a situation is. He acts out of pure caprice. For us, on the contrary, man is in an organized situation in which he himself is involved. Through his choice, he involves all mankind, and he can not avoid making a choice: either he will remain chaste, or he will marry without having children, or he will marry and have children; anyhow, whatever he may do, it is impossible for him not to take full responsibility for the way he handles this problem. Doubtless, he chooses without refering to pre-established values, but it is unfair to accuse him of caprice. Instead, let us say that moral choice is to be compared to the making of a work of art. And before going any further, let it be said at once that we are not dealing here with an aesthetic ethics, because our opponents are so dishonest that they even accuse us of that. The example I've chosen is a comparison only.

Having said that, may I ask whether anyone has ever accused an artist who has painted a picture of not having drawn his inspiration from rules set up *a priori?* Has anyone ever asked, "What painting ought he to make?" It is clearly understood that there is no definite painting to be made, that the artist is engaged in the making of his painting, and that the painting to be made is precisely the painting he will have made. It is clearly understood that there are no *a priori* aesthetic values, but that there are values which appear subsequently in the coherence of the painting, in the correspondence between what the artist intended and the result. Nobody can tell what the painting of tomorrow will be like. Painting can be judged only after it has once been made. What connection does that have with ethics? We are in the same creative situation. We never say that a work of art is arbitrary. When we speak of a canvas of Picasso, we never say that it is arbitrary; we understand quite well that he was making himself what he is at the very time he was painting, that the ensemble of his work is embodied in his life.

The same holds on the ethical plane. What art and ethics have in common is that we have creation and invention in both cases. We can not decide *a priori* what there is to be done. I think that I pointed that out quite sufficiently when I mentioned the case of the student who came to see me, and who might have applied to all the ethical systems, Kantian or otherwise, without getting any sort of guidance. He was obliged to devise his law himself. Never let it be said by us that this man—who, taking affection, individual action, and kindheartedness toward a specific person as his ethical first principle, chooses to remain with his mother, or who, preferring to make a sacrifice, chooses to go to England—has made an arbitrary choice. Man makes himself. He isn't ready made at the start. In choosing his ethics, he makes himself, and force of circumstances is such that he can not abstain from choosing one. We define man only in relationship to involvement. It is therefore absurd to charge us with arbitrariness of choice.

In the second place, it is said that we are unable to pass judgment on others. In a way this is true, and in another way, false. It is true in this sense, that, whenever a man sanely and sincerely involves himself and chooses his configuration, it is impossible for him to prefer another configuration, regardless of what his own may be in other respects. It is true in this sense, that we do not believe in progress. Progress is betterment. Man is always the same. The situation confronting him varies. Choice always remains a choice in a situation. The problem has not changed since the time one could choose between those for and those against slavery, for example, at the time of the Civil War, and the present time, when one can side with the Maquis Resistance Party, or with the Communists.

But, nevertheless, one can still pass judgment, for, as I have said, one makes a choice in relationship to others. First, one can judge (and this is perhaps not a judgment of value, but a logical judgment) that certain choices are based on error and others on truth. If we have defined man's situation as a free choice, with no excuses and no recourse, every man who takes refuge behind the excuse of his passions, every man who sets up a determinism, is a dishonest man.

The objection may be raised, "But why mayn't he choose himself dishonestly?" I reply that I am not obliged to pass moral judgment on him, but that I do define his dishonesty as an error. One can not help considering the truth of the matter. Dishonesty is obviously a falsehood because it belies the complete freedom of involvement. On the same grounds, I maintain that there is also dishonesty if I choose to state that certain values exist prior to me; it is self-contradictory for me to want them and at the same state that they are imposed on me. Suppose someone says to me, "What if I want to be dishonest?" I'll answer, "There's no reason for you not to be, but I'm saying that thats' what you are, and that the strictly coherent attitude is that of honesty."

Besides, I can bring moral judgment to bear. When I declare that freedom in every concrete circumstance can have no other aim than to want itself, if man has once become aware that in his forlornness he imposes values, he can no longer want but one thing, and that is freedom, as the basis of all values. That doesn't mean that he wants it in the abstract. It means simply that the ultimate meaning of the acts of honest men is the quest for freedom as such. A man who belongs to a communist or revolutionary union wants concrete goals; these goals imply an abstract desire for freedom; but this freedom is wanted in something concrete. We want freedom for freedom's sake and in every particular circumstance. And in wanting freedom we discover that it depends entirely on the freedom of others, and that the freedom of others depends on ours. Of course, freedom as the definition of man does not depend on others, but as soon as there is involvement, I am obliged to want others to have freedom at the same time that I want my own freedom. I can take freedom as my goal only if I take that of others as a goal as well. Consequently, when, in all honesty, I've recognized that man is a being in whom existence precedes essence, that he is a free being who, in various circumstances, can want only his freedom, I have at the same time recognized that I can want only the freedom of others.

Therefore, in the name of this will for freedom, which freedom itself implies, I may pass judgment on those who seek to hide from themselves the complete arbitrariness and the complete freedom of their existence. Those who hide their complete freedom from themselves out of a spirit of seriousness or by means of deterministic excuses, I shall call cowards; those who try to show that their existence was necessary, when it is the very contingency of man's appearance on earth, I shall call stinkers. But cowards or stinkers can be judged only from a strictly unbiased point of view.

Therefore though the content of ethics is variable, a certain form of it is universal. Kant says that freedom desires both itself and the freedom of others. Granted. But he believes that the formal and the universal are enough to constitute an ethics. We, on the other hand, think that principles which are too abstract run aground in trying to decide action. Once again, take the case of the student. In the name of what, in the name of what great moral maxim do you think he could have decided, in perfect peace of mind, to abandon his mother or to stay with her? There is no way of judging. The content is always concrete and thereby unforeseeable; there is always the element of invention. The one thing that counts is knowing whether the inventing that has been done, has been done in the name of freedom.

For example, let us look at the following two cases. You will see to what extent they correspond, yet differ. Take *The Mill on the Floss*. We find a certain young girl, Maggie Tulliver, who is an embodiment of the value of passion and who is aware of it. She is in love with a young man, Stephen, who is engaged to an insignificant young girl. This Maggie Tulliver, instead of heedlessly preferring her own happiness, chooses, in the name of human solidarity, to sacrifice herself and give up the man she loves. On the other hand, Sanseverina, in *The Charterhouse of Parma*, believing that passion is man's true value, would say that a great love deserves sacrifices; that it is to be preferred to the banality of the conjugal love that would tie Stephen to the young ninny he had to marry. She would choose to sacrifice the girl and fulfill her happiness; and, as Stendhal shows, she is even ready to sacrifice herself for the sake of passion, if this life demands it. Here we are in the presence of two strictly opposed moralities. I claim that they are much the same thing; in both cases what has been set up as the goal is freedom.

You can imagine two highly similar attitudes: one girl prefers to renounce her love out of resignation; another prefers to disregard the prior attachment of the man she loves out of sexual desire. On the surface these two actions resemble those we've just described. However, they are completely different. Sanseverina's attitude is much nearer that of Maggie Tulliver, one of heedless rapacity.

Thus, you see that the second charge is true and, at the same time, false. One may choose anything if it is on the grounds of free involvement.

The third objection is the following: "You take something from one pocket and put it into the other. That is, fundamentally, values aren't serious, since you choose them." My answer to this is that I'm quite vexed that that's the way it is; but if I've discarded God the Father, there has to be someone to invent values. You've got to take things as they are.

Moreover, to say that we invent values means nothing else but this: life has no meaning *a priori*. Before you come alive, life is nothing; it's up to you to give it a meaning, and value is nothing else but the meaning that you choose. In that way, you see, there is a possibility of creating a human community.

I've been reproached for asking whether existentialism is humanistic. It's been said, "But you said in *Nausea* that the humanists were all wrong. You made fun of a certain kind of humanist. Why come back to it now?" Actually, the word humanism has two very different meanings. By humanism one can mean a theory which takes man as an end and as a higher value. Humanism in this sense can be found in Cocteau's tale *Around the World in Eighty Hours* when a character, because he is flying over some mountains in an airplane, declares, "Man is simply amazing." That means that I, who did not build the airplanes, shall personally benefit from these particular inventions, and that I, as man, shall personally consider myself responsible for, and honored by, acts of a few particular men. This would imply that we ascribe a value to man on the basis of the highest deeds of certain men. This humanism is absurd, because only the dog or the horse would be able to make such an over-all judgment about man, which they are careful not to do, at least to my knowledge.

But it can not be granted that a man may make a judgment about man. Existentialism spares him from any such judgment. The existentialist will never consider man as an end because he is always in the making. Nor should we believe that there is a mankind to which we might set up a cult in the manner of Auguste Comte. The cult of mankind ends in the self-enclosed humanism of Comte, and, let it be said, of fascism. This kind of humanism we can do without.

But there is another meaning of humanism. Fundamentally it is this: man is constantly outside of himself; in projecting himself, in losing himself outside of himself, he makes for man's existing; and, on the other hand, it is by pursuing transcendent goals that he is able to exist; man, being this state of passing-beyond, and seizing upon things only as they bear upon this passing-beyond, is at the heart, at the center of this passing-beyond. There is no universe other than a human universe, the universe of human subjectivity. This connection between transcendency, as a constituent element of man—not in the sense that God is transcendent, but in the sense of passing beyond—and subjectivity, in the sense that man is not closed in on himself but is always present in a human universe, is what we call existentialist humanism. Humanism, because we remind man that there is no law-maker other than himself, and that in his forlornness he will decide by himself; because we point out that man will fulfill himself as man, not in turning toward himself, but in seeking outside of himself a goal which is just this liberation, just this particular fulfillment.

From these few reflections it is evident that nothing is more unjust than the objections that have been raised against us. Existentialism is nothing else than an attempt to draw all the consequences of a coherent atheistic position. It isn't trying to plunge man into despair at all. But if one calls every attitude of unbelief despair, like the Christians, then the word is not being used in its original sense. Existentialism isn't so atheistic that it wears itself out showing that God doesn't exist. Rather, it declares that even if God did exist, that would change nothing. There you've got our point of view. Not that we believe that God exists, but we think that the problem of His existence is not the issue. In this sense existentialism is optimistic, a doctrine of action, and it is plain dishonesty for Christians to make no distinction between their own despair and ours and then to call us despairing.

George Orwell

George Orwell (1903–1950), a brilliant English political author, wrote satirical novels of his own times and the problems facing Western Civilization. An intellectual who hated both communism and totalitarianism in any form, he wrote 1984 as a warning to western industrial countries of the forces already at work within them that could destroy individualism, freedom, and democracy as they now exist. This modern classic describes a negative Utopia which is more than a denunciation of Hitler's Germany or of Stalin's Russia. It suggests a society which could also emerge in the West if these forces are not curtailed. To Orwell, his imaginary country, Oceania, contains many features already characteristic of western capitalistic democracies. The selection which follows is from the last chapter and contains a dramatic conversation between the protagonist of the Party, O'Brien, and a beaten rebel, Winston Smith, who personifies the last hold-out for the way of life characteristic in the West before 1950. In reading the selection note (1) the use of torture devices adapted from modern science and technology; (2) the relationship between the past and Party control of memory and documents; (3) the Party's control of truth; (4) the comparison between the Party's method of obliterating deviationists and earlier techniques; (5) the nature and position of Big Brother; (6) the three stages in Smith's reintegration into the Party; (7) the basic principles of the Party; (8) the Party's sole purpose in gaining power; (9) *the final break-down of Smith's resistance; and (10) the description of Smith's character and existence after his absorption into the Party.*

From: 1984

He was lying on something that felt like a camp bed, except that it was higher off the ground and that he was fixed down in some way so that he could not move. Light that seemed stronger than usual was falling on his face. O'Brien was standing at his side, looking down at him intently. At the other side of him stood a man in a white coat, holding a hypodermic syringe.

Even after his eyes were open he took in his surroundings only gradually. He had the impression of swimming up into this room from some quite different world, a sort of underwater world far beneath it. How long he had been down there he did not know. Since the moment when they arrested him he had not seen darkness or daylight. Besides his memories were not continuous. There had been times when consciousness, even the sort of consciousness that one has in sleep, had stopped dead and started again after a blank interval. But whether the intervals were of days or weeks or only seconds, there was no way of knowing.

With that first blow on the elbow the nightmare had started. Later he was to realize that all that then happened was merely a preliminary, a routine interrogation to which nearly all prisoners were subjected. There was a long range of crimes—espionage, sabotage, and the like—to which everyone had to confess as a matter of course. The confession was a formality, though the torture was real. How many times he had been beaten, how long the beatings had continued, he could not remember. Always there were five or six men in black uniforms at him simultaneously. Sometimes it was fists, sometimes it was truncheons, sometimes it was steel rods, sometimes it was boots. There were times when he rolled about the floor, as shameless as an animal, writhing his body this way and that in an endless, hopeless effort to dodge the kicks, and simply inviting more and yet more kicks, in his ribs, in his belly, on his elbows, on his shins, in his groin, in his testicles, on the bone at the base of his spine. There were times when it went on and on until the cruel, wicked, unforgivable thing seemed to him not that the guards continued to beat him but that he could not force himself into losing consciousness. There were times when his nerve so forsook him that he began shouting for mercy even before the beating began, when the mere sight of a fist drawn back for a blow was enough to make him pour forth a confession of real and imaginary crimes. There were other times when he started out with the resolve of confessing nothing, when every word had to be forced out of him between gasps of pain, and there were times when he feebly tried to compromise, when he said to himself: "I will confess, but not yet. I must hold out till the pain becomes unbearable. Three more kicks, two more kicks, and then I will tell them what they want." Sometimes he was beaten till he could hardly stand, then flung like a sack of potatoes onto the stone floor of a cell, left to recuperate for a few hours, and then taken out and beaten again. There were also longer periods of recovery. He remembered them dimly, because they were spent chiefly in sleep or stupor. He remembered a cell with a plank bed, a sort of shelf sticking out from the wall, and a tin washbasin, and meals of hot soup and bread and sometimes coffee. He remembered a surly barber arriving to scrape his chin and crop his hair, and businesslike, unsympathetic men in white coats feeling his pulse, tapping his reflexes, turning up his eyelids, running harsh fingers over him in search of broken bones, and shooting needles into his arm to make him sleep.

The beatings grew less frequent, and be-

Nineteen Eighty-Four by George Orwell. Copyright, 1949 by Harcourt, Brace & World, Inc. Reprinted by permission of Brandt & Brandt. *1984, A Novel* (New York: The New American Library, 1961. Originally published in 1949 by Secker and Warburg Ltd.), pp. 198–245. Used with the permission also of Miss Sonia Brownell and Secker and Warburg Ltd.

came mainly a threat, a horror to which he could be sent back at any moment when his answers were unsatisfactory. His questioners now were not ruffians in black uniforms but Party intellectuals, little rotund men with quick movements and flashing spectacles, who worked on him in relays over periods which lasted—he thought, he could not be sure—ten or twelve hours at a stretch. These other questioners saw to it that he was in constant slight pain, but it was not chiefly pain that they relied on. They slapped his face, wrung his ears, pulled his hair, made him stand on one leg, refused him leave to urinate, shone glaring lights in his face until his eyes ran with water; but the aim of this was simply to humiliate him and destroy his power of arguing and reasoning. Their real weapon was the merciless questioning that went on and on hour after hour, tripping him up, laying traps for him, twisting everything that he said, convicting him at every step of lies and self-contradiction, until he began weeping as much from shame as from nervous fatigue. Sometimes he would weep half a dozen times in a single session. Most of the time they screamed abuse at him and threatened at every hesitation to deliver him over to the guards again; but sometimes they would suddenly change their tune, call him comrade, appeal to him in the name of Ingsoc and Big Brother, and ask him sorrowfully whether even now he had not enough loyalty to the Party left to make him wish to undo the evil he had done. When his nerves were in rags after hours of questioning, even this appeal could reduce him to sniveling tears. In the end the nagging voices broke him down more completely than the boots and fists of the guards. He became simply a mouth that uttered, a hand that signed whatever was demanded of him. His sole concern was to find out what they wanted him to confess, and then confess it quickly, before the bullying started anew. He confessed to the assassination of eminent Party members, the distribution of seditious pamphlets, embezzlement of public funds, sale of military secrets, sabotage of every kind. He confessed that he had been a spy in the pay of the Eastasian government as far back as 1968. He confessed that he was

a religious believer, an admirer of capitalism, and a sexual pervert. He confessed that he had murdered his wife, although he knew, and his questioners must have known, that his wife was still alive. He confessed that for years he had been in personal touch with Goldstein and had been a member of an underground organization which had included almost every human being he had ever known. It was easier to confess everything and implicate everybody. Besides, in a sense it was all true. It was true that he had been the enemy of the Party, and in the eyes of the Party there was no distinction between the thought and the deed.

There were also memories of another kind. They stood out in his mind disconnectedly, like pictures with blackness all round them.

He was in a cell which might have been either dark or light, because he could see nothing except a pair of eyes. Near at hand some kind of instrument was ticking slowly and regularly. The eyes grew larger and more luminous. Suddenly he floated out of his seat, dived into the eyes, and was swallowed up.

He was strapped into a chair surrounded by dials, under dazzling lights. A man in a white coat was reading the dials. There was a tramp of heavy boots outside. The door clanged open. The waxen-faced officer marched in, followed by two guards.

"Room 101," said the officer.

The man in the white coat did not turn round. He did not look at Winston either; he was looking only at the dials.

He was rolling down a mighty corridor, a kilometer wide, full of glorious, golden light, roaring with laughter and shouting out confessions at the top of his voice. He was confessing everything, even the things he had succeeded in holding back under the torture. He was relating the entire history of his life to an audience who knew it already. With him were the guards, the other questioners, the men in white coats, O'Brien, Julia, Mr. Charrington, all rolling down the corridor together and shouting with laughter. Some dreadful thing which had lain embedded in the future had somehow been skipped over and had not happened. Everything was all right, there was no more pain, the last detail of his life was laid bare, understood, forgiven.

He was starting up from the plank bed in the half-certainty that he had heard O'Brien's voice. All through his interrogation, although he had never seen him, he had had the feeling that O'Brien was at his elbow, just out of sight. It was O'Brien who was directing everything. It was he who set the guards onto Winston and who prevented them from killing him. It was he who decided when Winston should scream with pain, when he should have a respite, when he should be fed, when he should sleep, when the drugs should be pumped into his arm. It was he who asked the questions and suggested the answers. He was the tormentor, he was the protector, he was the inquisitor, he was the friend. And once— Winston could not remember whether it was in drugged sleep, or in normal sleep, or even in a moment of wakefulness—a voice murmured in his ear: "Don't worry, Winston; you are in my keeping. For seven years I have watched over you. Now the turning point has come. I shall save you, I shall make you perfect." He was not sure whether it was O'Brien's voice; but it was the same voice that had said to him, "We shall meet in the place where there is no darkness," in that other dream, seven years ago.

He did not remember any ending to his interrogation. There was a period of blackness and then the cell, or room, in which he now was had gradually materialized round him. He was almost flat on his back, and unable to move. His body was held down at every essential point. Even the back of his head was gripped in some manner. O'Brien was looking down at him gravely and rather sadly. His face, seen from below, looked coarse and worn, with pouches under the eyes and tired lines from nose to chin. He was older than Winston had thought him; he was perhaps forty-eight or fifty. Under his hand there was a dial with a lever on top and figures running round the face.

"I told you," said O'Brien, "that if we met again it would be here."

"Yes," said Winston.

Without any warning except a slight movement of O'Brien's hand, a wave of pain flooded his body. It was a frightening pain, because he could not see what was happening, and he had the feeling that some mortal injury was being done to him. He did not know whether the thing was really happening, or whether the effect was electrically produced; but his body was being wrenched out of shape, the joints were being slowly torn apart. Although the pain had brought the sweat out on his forehead, the worst of all was the fear that his backbone was about to snap. He set his teeth and breathed hard through his nose, trying to keep silent as long as possible.

"You are afraid," said O'Brien, watching his face, "that in another moment something is going to break. Your especial fear is that it will be your backbone. You have a vivid mental picture of the vertebrae snapping apart and the spinal fluid dripping out of them. That is what you are thinking, is it not, Winston?"

Winston did not answer. O'Brien drew back the lever on the dial. The wave of pain receded almost as quickly as it had come.

"That was forty," said O'Brien. "You can see that the numbers on this dial run up to a hundred. Will you please remember, throughout our conversation, that I have it in my power to inflict pain on you at any moment and to whatever degree I choose. If you tell me any lies, or attempt to prevaricate in any way, or even fall below your usual level of intelligence you will cry out with pain, instantly. Do you understand that?"

"Yes," said Winston.

O'Brien's manner became less severe. He resettled his spectacles thoughtfully, and took a pace or two up and down. When he spoke his voice was gentle and patient. He had the air of a doctor, a teacher, even a priest, anxious to explain and persuade rather than to punish.

"I am taking trouble with you, Winston," he said, "because you are worth trouble. You know perfectly well what is the matter with you. You have known it for years, though you have fought against the knowledge. You are mentally deranged. You suffer from a defective memory. You are unable to remember real events, and you persuade yourself that you remember other events which never happened. Fortunately it is curable. You have never cured yourself of it, because you did not choose to. There was a small effort of the will that you were not ready to make. Even now, I am well aware, you are clinging to your disease under the impression that it is a virtue. Now we will take an example. At this moment, which power is Oceania at war with?"

"When I was arrested, Oceania was at war with Eastasia."

"With Eastasia. Good. And Oceania has always been at war with Eastasia, has it not?"

Winston drew in his breath. He opened his mouth to speak and then did not speak. He could not take his eyes away from the dial.

"The truth, please, Winston. *Your* truth. Tell me what you think you remember."

"I remember that until only a week before I was arrested, we were not at war with Eastasia at all. We were in alliance with them. The war was against Eurasia. That had lasted for four years. Before that—"

O'Brien stopped him with a movement of the hand.

"Another example," he said. "Some years ago you had a very serious delusion indeed. You believed that three men, three one-time Party members named Jones, Aaronson, and Rutherford—men who were executed for treachery and sabotage after making the fullest possible confession—were not guilty of the crimes they were charged with. You believed that you had seen unmistakable documentary evidence proving that their confessions were false. There was a certain photograph about which you had a hallucination. You believed that you had actually held it in your hands. It was a photograph something like this."

An oblong slip of newspaper had appeared between O'Brien's fingers. For perhaps five seconds it was within the angle of Winston's vision. It was a photograph, and there was no question of its identity. It was *the* photograph. It was another copy of the photograph of Jones, Aaronson, and Rutherford at the Party function in New York, which he had chanced upon eleven years ago and promptly destroyed. For only an instant it was before his eyes, then it was out of sight again. But he had seen it, unquestionably he had seen it! He made a desperate, agonizing effort to wrench the top half of his body free. It was impossible to move so much as a centimeter in any direction. For the moment he had even forgotten the dial. All he wanted was to hold the photograph in his fingers again, or at least to see it.

"It exists!" he cried.

"No," said O'Brien.

He stepped across the room. There was a memory hole in the opposite wall. O'Brien lifted the grating. Unseen, the frail slip of paper was whirling away on the current of warm air; it was vanishing in a flash of flame. O'Brien turned away from the wall.

"Ashes," he said. "Not even identifiable ashes. Dust. It does not exist. It never existed."

"But it did exist! It does exist! It exists in memory. I remember it. You remember it."

"I do not remember it," said O'Brien.

Winston's heart sank. That was doublethink. He had a feeling of deadly helplessness. If he could have been certain that O'Brien was lying, it would not have seemed to matter. But it was perfectly possible that O'Brien had really forgotten the photograph. And if so, then already he would have forgotten his denial of remembering it, and forgotten the act of forgetting. How could one be sure that it was simply trickery? Perhaps that lunatic dislocation in the mind could really happen: that was the thought that defeated him.

O'Brien was looking down at him speculatively. More than ever he had the air of a teacher taking pains with a wayward but promising child.

"There is a Party slogan dealing with the control of the past," he said. "Repeat it, if you please."

" 'Who controls the past controls the future; who controls the present controls the past,' " repeated Winston obediently.

" 'Who controls the present controls the past,' " said O'Brien, nodding his head with slow approval "Is it your opinion, Winston, that the past has real existence?"

Again the feeling of helplessness descended upon Winston. His eyes flitted toward the dial. He not only did not know whether "yes" or "no" was the answer that would save him from pain; he did not even know which answer he believed to be the true one.

O'Brien smiled faintly. "You are no metaphysician, Winston," he said. "Until this moment you had never considered what is meant by existence. I will put it more precisely. Does the past exist concretely, in space? Is there somewhere or other a place, a world of solid objects, where the past is still happening?"

"No."

"Then where does the past exist, if at all?"

"In records. It is written down."

"In records. And——?"

"In the mind. In human memories."

"In memory. Very well, then. We, the Party, control all records, and we control all memories. Then we control the past, do we not?"

"But how can you stop people remembering things?" cried Winston, again momentarily forgetting the dial. "It is involuntary. It is outside oneself. How can you control memory? You have not controlled mine!"

O'Brien's manner grew stern again. He laid his hand on the dial.

"On the contrary," he said, "*you* have not controlled it. That is what has brought you here. You are here because you have failed in humility, in self-discipline. You would not make the act of submission which is the price of sanity. You preferred to be a lunatic, a minority of one. Only the disciplined mind can see reality, Winston. You believe that reality is something objective, external, existing in its own right. You also believe that the nature of reality is self-evident. When you delude yourself into thinking that you see something, you assume that everyone else sees the same thing as you. But I tell you, Winston, that reality is not external. Reality exists in the human mind, and nowhere else. Not in the individual mind, which can make mistakes, and in any case soon perishes; only in the mind of the Party, which is collective and immortal. Whatever the Party holds to be truth *is* truth. It is impossible to see reality except by looking through the eyes of the Party. That is the fact that you have got to relearn, Winston. It needs an act of self-destruction, an effort of the will. You must humble yourself before you can become sane."

He paused for a few moments, as though to allow what he had been saying to sink in.

"Do you remember," he went on, "writing in your diary, 'Freedom is the freedom to say that two plus two make four'?"

"Yes," said Winston.

O'Brien held up his left hand, its back toward Winston, with the thumb hidden and the four fingers extended.

"How many fingers am I holding up, Winston?"

"Four."

"And if the Party says that it is not four but five—then how many?"

"Four."

The word ended in a gasp of pain. The needle of the dial had shot up to fifty-five. The sweat had sprung out all over Winston's body. The air tore into his lungs and issued again in deep groans which even by clenching his teeth he could not stop. O'Brien watched him, the four fingers still extended. He drew back the lever. This time the pain was only slightly eased.

"How many fingers, Winston?"

"Four."

The needle went up to sixty.

"How many fingers, Winston?"

"Four! Four! What else can I say? Four!"

The needle must have risen again, but he did not look at it. The heavy, stern face and the four fingers filled his vision. The fingers stood up before his eyes like pillars, enormous, blurry, and seeming to vibrate, but unmistakably four.

"How many fingers, Winston?"

"Four! Stop it, stop it! How can you go on? Four! Four!"

"How many fingers, Winston?"

"Five! Five! Five!"

"No, Winston, that is no use. You are lying. You still think there are four. How many fingers, please?"

"Four! Five! Four! Anything you like. Only stop it, stop the pain!"

Abruptly he was sitting up with O'Brien's arm round his shoulders. He had perhaps lost consciousness for a few seconds. The bonds that had held his body down were loosened. He felt very cold, he was shaking uncontrollably, his teeth were chattering, the tears were rolling down his cheeks. For a moment he clung to O'Brien like a baby, curiously comforted by the heavy arm round his shoulders. He had the feeling that O'Brien was his protector, that the pain was something that came from outside, from some other source, and that it was O'Brien who would save him from it.

"You are a slow learner, Winston," said O'Brien gently.

"How can I help it?" he blubbered. "How can I help seeing what is in front of my eyes? Two and two are four."

"Sometimes, Winston. Sometimes they are five. Sometimes they are three. Sometimes they are all of them at once. You must try harder. It is not easy to become sane."

He laid Winston down on the bed. The grip on his limbs tightened again, but the pain had ebbed away and the trembling had stopped, leaving him merely weak and cold. O'Brien motioned with his head to the man in the white coat, who had stood immobile throughout the proceedings. The man in the white coat bent down and looked closely into Winston's eyes, felt his pulse, laid an ear against his chest, tapped here and there; then he nodded to O'Brien.

"Again," said O'Brien.

The pain flowed into Winston's body. The needle must be at seventy, seventy-five. He had shut his eyes this time. He knew that the fingers were still there, and still four. All that mattered was somehow to stay alive until the spasm was over. He had ceased to notice whether he was crying out or not. The pain lessened again. He opened his eyes. O'Brien had drawn back the lever.

"How many fingers, Winston?"

"Four. I suppose there are four. I would see five if I could. I am trying to see five."

"Which do you wish: to persuade me that you see five, or really to see them?"

"Really to see them."

"Again," said O'Brien.

Perhaps the needle was at eighty—ninety. Winston could only intermittently remember why the pain was happening. Behind his screwed-up eyelids a forest of fingers seemed to be moving in a sort of dance, weaving in and out, disappearing behind one another and reappearing again. He was trying to count them, he could not remember why. He knew only that it was impossible to count them, and that this was somehow due to to the mysterious identity between five and four. The pain died down again. When he opened his eyes it was to find that he was still seeing the same thing. Innumerable fingers, like moving trees, were still streaming past in either direction, crossing and recrossing. He shut his eyes again.

"How many fingers am I holding up, Winston?"

"I don't know. I don't know. You will kill me if you do that again. Four, five, six—in all honesty I don't know."

"Better," said O'Brien.

A needle slid into Winston's arm. Almost in the same instant a blissful, healing warmth spread all through his body. The pain was already half-forgotten. He opened his eyes and looked up gratefully at O'Brien. At sight of the heavy, lined face, so ugly and so intelligent, his heart seemed to turn over. If he could have moved he would have stretched out a hand and laid it on O'Brien's arm. He had never loved him so deeply as at this moment, and not merely because he had stopped the pain. The old feeling, that at bottom it did not matter whether O'Brien was a friend or an enemy, had come back. O'Brien was a person who could be talked to. Perhaps one did not want to be loved so much as to be understood. O'Brien had tortured him to the edge of lunacy, and in a little while, it was certain, he would send him to his death. It made no difference. In some sense that went deeper than friendship, they were intimates; somewhere or other, although the actual words might never be spoken, there was a place where they could meet and talk. O'Brien was looking down at him with an expression which suggested that the same thought might be in his own mind. When he spoke it was in an easy, conversational tone.

"Do you know where you are, Winston?" he said.

"I don't know. I can guess. In the Ministry of Love."

"Do you know how long you have been here?"

"I don't know. Days, weeks, months—I think it is months."

"And why do you imagine that we bring people to this place?"

"To make them confess."

"No, that is not the reason. Try again."

"To punish them."

"No!" exclaimed O'Brien. His voice had changed extraordinarily, and his face had suddenly become both stern and animated. "No! Not merely to extract your confession, nor to punish you. Shall I tell you why we have brought you here? To cure you! To make you sane! Will you understand, Winston, that no one whom we bring to this place ever leaves our hands uncured? We are not interested in those stupid crimes that you have committed. The Party is not interested in the overt act: the thought is all we care about. We do not merely destroy our enemies; we change them. Do you understand what I mean by that?"

He was bending over Winston. His face looked enormous because of its nearness, and hideously ugly because it was seen from below. Moreover it was filled with a sort of exaltation, a lunatic intensity. Again Winston's heart shrank. If it had been possible he would have cowered deeper into the bed. He felt certain that O'Brien was about to twist the dial out of sheer wantonness. At this moment, however, O'Brien turned away. He took a pace or two up and down. Then he continued less vehemently:

"The first thing for you to understand is that in this place there are no martyrdoms. You have read of the religious persecutions of the past. In the Middle Ages there was the Inquisition. It was a failure. It set out to eradicate heresy, and ended by perpetuating it. For every heretic it burned at the stake, thousands of others rose up. Why was that? Because the Inquisition killed its enemies in the open, and killed them while they were still unrepentant; in fact, it killed them because they were unrepentant. Men were dying because they would not abandon their true beliefs. Naturally all the glory belonged to the victim and all the shame to the Inquisitor who burned him. Later, in the twentieth century, there were the totalitarians, as they were called. There were the German Nazis and the Russian Communists. The Russians persecuted heresy more cruelly than the Inquisition had done. And

they imagined that they had learned from the mistakes of the past; they knew, at any rate, that one must not make martyrs. Before they exposed their victims to public trial, they deliberately set themselves to destroy their dignity. They wore them down by torture and solitude until they were despicable, cringing wretches, confessing whatever was put into their mouths, covering themselves with abuse, accusing and sheltering behind one another, whimpering for mercy. And yet after only a few years the same thing had happened over again. The dead men had become martyrs and their degradation was forgotten. Once again, why was it? In the first place, because the confessions that they had made were obviously extorted and untrue. We do not make mistakes of that kind. All the confessions that are uttered here are true. We make them true. And, above all, we do not allow the dead to rise up against us. You stop imagining that posterity will vindicate you, Winston. Posterity will never hear of you. You will be lifted clean out from the stream of history. We shall turn you into gas and pour you into the stratosphere. Nothing will remain of you: not a name in a register, not a memory in a living brain. You will be annihilated in the past as well as in the future. You will never have existed."

Then why bother to torture me? thought Winston, with a momentary bitterness. O'Brien checked his step as though Winston had uttered the thought aloud. His large ugly face came nearer, with the eyes a little narrowed.

"You are thinking," he said, "that since we intend to destroy you utterly, so that nothing that you say or do can make the smallest difference—in that case, why do we go to the trouble of interrogating you first? That is what you were thinking, was it not?"

"Yes," said Winston.

O'Brien smiled slightly. "You are a flaw in the pattern, Winston. You are a stain that must be wiped out. Did I not tell you just now that we are different from the persecutors of the past? We are not content with negative obedience, nor even with the most abject submission. When finally you surrender to us, it must be of your own free will. We do not destroy the heretic because he resists us; so long as he resists us we never destroy him. We convert him, we capture his inner mind, we reshape him. We burn all evil and all illusion out of him; we bring him over to our side, not in appearance, but genuinely, heart and soul. We make him one of ourselves before we kill him. It is intolerable to us that an erroneous thought should exist anywhere in the world, however secret and powerless it may be. Even in the instant of death we cannot permit any deviation. In the old days the heretic walked to the stake still a heretic, proclaiming his heresy, exulting in it. Even the victim of the Russian purges could carry rebellion locked up in his skull as he walked down the passage waiting for the bullet. But we make the brain perfect before we blow it out. The command of the old despotisms was 'Thou shalt not.' The command of the totalitarians was 'Thou shalt.' Our command is *Thou art.* No one whom we bring to this place ever stands out against us. Everyone is washed clean. Even those three miserable traitors in whose innocence you believed—Jones, Aaronson, and Rutherford—in the end we broke them down. I took part in their interrogation myself. I saw them gradually worn down, whimpering, groveling, weeping—and in the end it was not with pain or fear, only with penitence. By the time we had finished with them they were only the shells of men. There was nothing left in them except sorrow for what they had done, and love of Big Brother. It was touching to see how they loved him. They begged to be shot quickly, so that they could die while their minds were still clean."

His voice had grown almost dreamy. The exaltation, the lunatic enthusiasm, was still in his face. He is not pretending, thought Winston; he is not a hypocrite; he believes every word he says. What most oppressed him was the consciousness of his own intellectual inferiority. He watched the heavy yet graceful form strolling to and fro, in and out of the range of his vision. O'Brien was a being in all ways larger than himself. There was no idea that he had ever had, or could have, that O'Brien had not long ago known, examined, and rejected. His mind *contained* Winston's mind. But in that case how could it be true that O'Brien was mad? It must be he, Winston, who was mad. O'Brien halted and looked down at him. His voice had grown stern again.

"Do not imagine that you will save yourself, Winston, however completely you surrender to us. No one who has once gone astray is ever spared. And even if we chose to let you live out the natural term of your life, still you would never escape from us. What happens to you here is forever. Understand that in advance. We shall crush you down to the point from which there is no coming back. Things will happen to you from which you could not recover, if you lived a thousand years. Never again will you be capable of ordinary human feeling. Everything will be dead inside you. Never again will you be capable of love, or friendship, or joy of living, or laughter, or curiosity, or courage, or integrity. You will be hollow. We shall squeeze you empty, and then we shall fill you with ourselves."

He paused and signed to the man in the white coat. Winston was aware of some heavy piece of apparatus being pushed into place behind his head. O'Brien had sat down beside the bed, so that his face was almost on a level with Winston's.

"Three thousand," he said, speaking over Winston's head to the man in the white coat.

Two soft pads, which felt slightly moist, clamped themselves against Winston's temples. He quailed. There was pain coming, a new kind of pain. O'Brien laid a hand reassuringly, almost kindly, on his.

"This time it will not hurt," he said. "Keep your eyes fixed on mine."

At this moment there was a devastating explosion, or what seemed like an explosion, though it was not certain whether there was any noise. There was undoubtedly a blinding flash of light. Winston was not hurt, only prostrated. Although he had already been lying on his back when the thing happened, he had a curious feeling that he had been knocked into that position. A terrific, painless blow had flattened him out. Also something had happened inside his head. As his eyes regained their focus he remembered who he was, and where he was, and recognized the face that was gazing into his own; but somewhere or other there was a large patch of emptiness, as though a piece had been taken out of his brain.

"It will not last," said O'Brien. "Look me in the eyes. What country is Oceania at war with?"

Winston thought. He knew what was meant by Oceania, and that he himself was a citizen of Oceania. He also remembered Eurasia and Eastasia; but who was at war with whom he did not know. In fact he had not been aware that there was any war.

"I don't remember."

"Oceania is at war with Eastasia. Do you remember now?"

"Yes."

"Oceania has always been at war with Eastasia. Since the beginning of your life, since the beginning of the Party, since the beginning of history, the war has continued without a break, always the same war. Do you remember that?"

"Yes."

"Eleven years ago you created a legend about three men who had been condemned to death for treachery. You pretended that you had seen a piece of paper which proved them innocent. No such piece of paper ever existed. You invented it, and later you grew to believe in it. You remember now the very moment at which you first invented it. Do you remember that?"

"Yes."

"Just now I held up the fingers of my hand to you. You saw five fingers. Do you remember that?"

"Yes."

O'Brien held up the fingers of his left hand, with the thumb concealed.

"There are five fingers there. Do you see five fingers?"

"Yes."

And he did see them, for a fleeting instant, before the scenery of his mind changed. He saw five fingers, and there was no deformity. Then everything was normal again, and the old fear, the hatred, and the bewilderment came crowding back again. But there had been a moment—he did not know how long, thirty seconds, perhaps—of luminous certainty, when each new suggestion of O'Brien's had filled up a patch of emptiness and become absolute truth, and when two and two could have been three as easily as five, if that were

what was needed. It had faded out before O'Brien had dropped his hand; but though he could not recapture it, he could remember it, as one remembers a vivid experience at some remote period of one's life when one was in effect a different person.

"You see now," said O'Brien, "that it is at any rate possible."

"Yes," said Winston.

O'Brien stood up with a satisfied air. Over to his left Winston saw the man in the white coat break an ampoule and draw back the plunger of a syringe. O'Brien turned to Winston with a smile. In almost the old manner he resettled his spectacles on his nose.

"Do you remember writing in your diary," he said, "that it did not matter whether I was a friend or an enemy, since I was at least a person who understood you and could be talked to? You were right. I enjoy talking to you. Your mind appeals to me. It resembles my own mind except that you happen to be insane. Before we bring the session to an end you can ask me a few questions, if you choose."

"Any question I like?"

"Anything." He saw that Winston's eyes were upon the dial. "It is switched off. What is your first question?"

"What have you done with Julia?" said Winston.

O'Brien smiled again. "She betrayed you, Winston. Immediately—unreservedly. I have seldom seen anyone come over to us so promptly. You would hardly recognize her if you saw her. All her rebelliousness, her deceit, her folly, her dirtymindedness—everything has been burned out of her. It was a perfect conversion, a textbook case."

"You tortured her."

O'Brien left this unanswered. "Next question," he said.

"Does Big Brother exist?"

"Of course he exists. The Party exists. Big Brother is the embodiment of the Party."

"Does he exist in the same way as I exist?"

"You do not exist," said O'Brien.

Once again the sense of helplessness assailed him. He knew, or he could imagine, the arguments which proved his own nonexistence; but they were nonsense, they were only a play on words. Did not the statement, "You do not exist," contain a logical absurdity? But what use was it to say so? His mind shriveled as he thought of the unanswerable, mad arguments with which O'Brien would demolish him.

"I think I exist," he said wearily. "I am conscious of my own identity. I was born, and I shall die. I have arms and legs. I occupy a particular point in space. No other solid object can occupy the same point simultaneously. In that sense, does Big Brother exist?"

"It is of no importance. He exists."

"Will Big Brother ever die?"

"Of course not. How could he die? Next question."

"Does the Brotherhood exist?"

"That, Winston, you will never know. If we choose to set you free when we have finished with you, and if you live to be ninety years old, still you will never learn whether the answer to that question is Yes or No. As long as you live, it will be an unsolved riddle in your mind."

Winston lay silent. His breast rose and fell a little faster. He still had not asked the question that had come into his mind the first. He had got to ask it, and yet it was as though his tongue would not utter it. There was a trace of amusement in O'Brien's face. Even his spectacles seemed to wear an ironical gleam. He knows, thought Winston suddenly, he knows what I am going to ask! At the thought the words burst out of him:

"What is in Room 101?"

The expression on O'Brien's face did not change. He answered drily:

"You know what is in Room 101, Winston. Everyone knows what is in Room 101."

He raised a finger to the man in the white coat. Evidently the session was at an end. A needle jerked into Winston's arm. He sank almost instantly into deep sleep.

"There are three stages in your reintegration," said O'Brien. "There is learning, there is understanding, and there is acceptance. It is time for you to enter upon the second stage."

As always, Winston was lying flat on his back. But of late his bonds were looser. They still held him to the bed, but he could move his knees a little and could turn his head from side to side and raise his arms from the elbow. The dial, also, had grown to be less of a terror. He could evade its pangs if he was quick-witted enough; it was chiefly when he showed stupidity that O'Brien pulled the lever. Sometimes they got through a whole session without use of the dial. He could not remember how many sessions there had been. The whole process seemed to stretch out over a long, indefinite time—weeks, possibly—and the intervals between the sessions might sometimes have been days, sometimes only an hour or two.

"As you lie there," said O'Brien, "you have often wondered—you have even asked me—why the Ministry of Love should expend so much time and trouble on you. And when you were free you were puzzled by what was essentially the same question. You could grasp the mechanics of the society you lived in, but not its underlying motives. Do you remember writing in your diary, 'I understand *how;* I do not understand *why*'? It was when you thought about 'why' that you doubted your own sanity. You have read *the book*, Goldstein's book, or parts of it, at least. Did it tell you anything you did not know already?"

"You have read it?" said Winston.

"I wrote it. That is to say, I collaborated in writing it. No book is produced individually, as you know."

"Is it true, what it says?"

"As description, yes. The program it sets forth is nonsense. The secret accumulation of knowledge—a gradual spread of enlightenment—ultimately a proletarian rebellion—the overthrow of the Party. You foresaw yourself that that was what it would say. It is all nonsense. The proletarians will never revolt, not in a thousand years or a million. They cannot. I do not have to tell you the reason; you know it already. If you have ever cherished any dreams of violent insurrection, you must abandon them. There is no way in which the Party can be overthrown. The rule of the Party is forever. Make that the starting point of your thoughts."

He came closer to the bed. "Forever!" he repeated, "And now let us get back to the question of 'how' and 'why.' You understand well enough *how* the Party maintains itself in power. Now tell me *why* we cling to power. What is our motive? Why should we want power? Go on, speak," he added as Winston remained silent.

Nevertheless Winston did not speak for another moment or two. A feeling of weariness had overwhelmed him. The faint, mad gleam of enthusiasm had come back into O'Brien's face. He knew in advance what O'Brien would say: that the Party did not seek power for its own ends, but only for the good of the majority. That it sought power because men in the mass were frail, cowardly creatures who could not endure liberty or face the truth, and must be ruled over and systematically deceived by others who were stronger than themselves. That the choice for mankind lay between freedom and happiness, and that, for the great bulk of mankind, happiness was better. That the Party was the eternal guardian of the weak, a dedicated sect doing evil that good might come, sacrificing its own happiness to that of others. The terrible thing, thought Winston, the terrible thing was that when O'Brien said this he would believe it. You could see it in his face. O'Brien knew everything. A thousand times better than Winston, he knew what the world was really like, in what degradation the mass of human beings lived and by what lies and barbarities the Party kept them there. He had understood it all, weighed it all, and it made no difference: all was justified by the ultimate purpose. What can you do, thought Winston, against the lunatic who is more intelligent than yourself, who gives your arguments a fair hearing and then simply persists in his lunacy?

"You are ruling over us for our own good," he said feebly. "You believe that human beings are not fit to govern themselves, and therefore—"

He started and almost cried out. A pang of pain had shot through his body. O'Brien had pushed the lever of the dial up to thirty-five.

"That was stupid, Winston, stupid!" he said. "You should know better than to say a thing like that."

He pulled the lever back and continued:

"Now I will tell you the answer to my question. It is this. The Party seeks power entirely for its own sake. We are not interested in the good of others; we are interested solely in power. Not wealth or luxury or long life or happiness; only power, pure power. What pure power means you will understand presently. We are different from all the oligarchies of the past in that we know what we are doing. All the others, even those who resembled ourselves, were cowards and hypocrites. The German Nazis and the Russian Communists came very close to us in their methods, but they never had the courage to recognize their own motives. They pretended, perhaps they even believed, that they had seized power unwillingly and for a limited time, and that just round the corner there lay a paradise where human beings would be free and equal. We are not like that. We know that no one ever seizes power with the intention of relinquishing it. Power is not a means; it is an end. One does not establish a dictatorship in order to safeguard a revolution; one makes the revolution in order to establish the dictatorship. The object of persecution is persecution. The object of torture is torture. The object of power is power. Now do you begin to understand me?"

Winston was struck as he had been struck before, by the tiredness of O'Brien's face. It was strong and fleshy and brutal, it was full of intelligence and a sort of controlled passion before which he felt himself helpless; but it was tired. There were pouches under the eyes, the skin sagged from the cheekbones. O'Brien leaned over him, deliberately bringing the worn face nearer.

"You are thinking," he said, "that my face is old and tired. You are thinking that I talk of power, and yet I am not even able to prevent the decay of my own body. Can you not understand, Winston, that the individual is only a cell? The weariness of the cell is the vigor of the organism. Do you die when you cut your fingernails?"

He turned away from the bed and began strolling up and down again, one hand in his pocket.

"We are the priests of power," he said. "God is power. But at present power is only a word so far as you are concerned. It is time for you to gather some idea of what power means. The first thing you must realize is that power is collective. The individual only has power in so far as he ceases to be an individual. You know the Party slogan 'Freedom is Slavery.' Has it ever occurred to you that it is reversible? Slavery is freedom. Alone—free—the human being is always defeated. It must be so, because every human being is doomed to die, which is the greatest of all failures. But if he can make complete, utter submission, if he can escape from his identity, if he can merge himself in the Party so that he *is* the Party, then he is all-powerful and immortal. The second thing for you to realize is that power is power over human beings. Over the body—but, above all, over the mind. Power over matter— external reality, as you would call it—is not important. Already our control over matter is absolute."

For a moment Winston ignored the dial. He made a violent effort to raise himself into a sitting position, and merely succeeded in wrenching his body painfully.

"But how can you control matter?" he burst out. "You don't even control the climate or the law of gravity. And there are disease, pain, death—"

O'Brien silenced him by a movement of the hand. "We control matter because we control the mind. Reality is inside the skull. You will learn by degrees, Winston. There is nothing that we could not do. Invisibility, levitation— anything. I could float off this floor like a soap bubble if I wished to. I do not wish to, because the Party does not wish it. You must get rid of those nineteenth-century ideas about the laws of Nature. We make the laws of Nature."

"But you do not! You are not even masters of this planet. What about Eurasia and Eastasia? You have not conquered them yet."

"Unimportant. We shall conquer them when it suits us. And if we did not, what difference would it make? We can shut them out of existence. Oceania is the world."

"But the world itself is only a speck of dust. And man is tiny—helpless! How long has he been in existence? For millions of years the earth was uninhabited."

"Nonsense. The earth is as old as we are, no older. How could it be older? Nothing exists except through human consciousness."

"But the rocks are full of the bones of extinct animals—mammoths and mastodons and enor-

mous reptiles which lived here long before man was ever heard of."

"Have you ever seen those bones. Winston? Of course not. Nineteenth-century biologists invented them. Before man there was nothing. After man, if he could come to an end, there would be nothing. Outside man there is nothing."

"But the whole universe is outside us. Look at the stars! Some of them are a million light-years away. They are out of our reach forever."

"What are the stars?" said O'Brien indifferently. "They are bits of fire a few kilometers away. We could reach them if we wanted to. Or we could blot them out. The earth is the center of the universe. The sun and the stars go round it."

Winston made another convulsive movement. This time he did not say anything. O'Brien continued as though answering a spoken objection:

"For certain purposes, of course, that is not true. When we navigate the ocean, or when we predict an eclipse, we often find it convenient to assume that the earth goes round the sun and that the stars are millions upon millions of kilometers away. But what of it? Do you suppose it is beyond us to produce a dual system of astronomy? The stars can be near or distant, according as we need them. Do you suppose our mathematicians are unequal to that? Have you forgotten doublethink?"

Winston shrank back upon the bed. Whatever he said, the swift answer crushed him like a bludgeon. And yet he knew, he *knew*, that he was in the right. The belief that nothing exists outside your own mind—surely there must be some way of demonstrating that it was false. Had it not been exposed long ago as a fallacy? There was even a name for it, which he had forgotten. A faint smile twitched the corners of O'Brien's mouth as he looked down at him.

"I told you, Winston," he said, "that metaphysics is not your strong point. The word you are trying to think of is solipsism. But you are mistaken. This is not solipsism. Collective solipsism, if you like. But that is a different thing; in fact, the opposite thing. All this is a digression," he added in a different tone.

"The real power, the power we have to fight for night and day, is not power over things, but over men." He paused, and for a moment assumed again his air of a schoolmaster questioning a promising pupil: "How does one man assert his power over another, Winston?"

Winston thought. "By making him suffer," he said.

"Exactly. By making him suffer. Obedience is not enough. Unless he is suffering, how can you be sure that he is obeying your will and not his own? Power is in inflicting pain and humiliation. Power is in tearing human minds to pieces and putting them together again in new shapes of your own choosing. Do you begin to see, then, what kind of world we are creating? It is the exact opposite of the stupid hedonistic Utopias that the old reformers imagined. A world of fear and treachery and torment, a world of trampling and being trampled upon, a world which will grow not less but *more* merciless as it refines itself. Progress in our world will be progress toward more pain. The old civilizations claimed that they were founded on love and justice. Ours is founded upon hatred. In our world there will be no emotions except fear, rage, triumph, and self-abasement. Everything else we shall destroy—everything. Already we are breaking down the habits of thought which have survived from before the Revolution. We have cut the links between child and parent, and between man and man, and between man and woman. No one dares trust a wife or a child or a friend any longer. But in the future there will be no wives and no friends. Children will be taken from their mothers at birth, as one takes eggs from a hen. The sex instinct will be eradicated. Procreation will be an annual formality like the renewal of a ration card. We shall abolish the orgasm. Our neurologists are at work upon it now. There will be no loyalty, except loyalty toward the Party. There will be no love, except the love of Big Brother. There will be no laughter, except the laugh of triumph over a defeated enemy. There will be no art, no literature, no science. When we are omnipotent we shall have no more need of science. There will be no distinction between beauty and ugliness. There will be no curiosity, no employment of the process of life. All competing pleasures will be destroyed. But always—do not forget this, Winston—always there will be the intoxication of power, constantly increasing and constantly growing subtler. Always at every moment, there will be the thrill of victory, the sensation of trampling on an enemy who is helpless. If you want a picture of the future, imagine a boot stamping on a human face—forever."

He paused as though he expected Winston to speak. Winston had tried to shrink back into the surface of the bed again. He could not say anything. His heart seemed to be frozen. O'Brien went on:

"And remember that it is forever. The face will always be there to be stamped upon. The heretic, the enemy of society, will always be there, so that he can be defeated and humiliated over again. Everything that you have undergone since you have been in our hands—all that will continue, and worse. The espionage, the betrayals, the arrests, the tortures, the executions, the disappearances will never cease. It will be a world of terror as much as a world of triumph. The more the Party is powerful, the less it will be tolerant; the weaker the opposition, the tighter the despotism. Goldstein and his heresies will live forever. Every day, at every moment, they will be defeated, discredited, ridiculed, spat upon—and yet they will always survive. This drama that I have played out with you during seven years will be played out over and over again, generation after generation, always in subtler forms. Always we shall have the heretic here at our mercy, screaming with pain, broken up, contemptible—and in the end utterly penitent, saved from himself, crawling to our feet of his own accord. That is the world that we are preparing, Winston. A world of victory after victory, triumph after triumph after triumph: an endless pressing, pressing, pressing upon the nerve of power. You are beginning, I can see, to realize what that world will be like. But in the end you will do more than understand it. You will accept it, welcome it, become part of it."

Winston had recovered himself sufficiently to speak. "You can't!" he said weakly.

"What do you mean by that remark, Winston?"

"You could not create such a world as you have just described. It is a dream. It is impossible."

"Why?"

"It is impossible to found a civilization on fear and hatred and cruelty. It would never endure."

"Why not?"

"It would have no vitality. It would disintegrate. It would commit suicide."

"Nonsense. You are under the impression that hatred is more exhausting than love. Why should it be? And if it were, what difference would that make? Suppose that we choose to wear ourselves out faster. Suppose that we quicken the tempo of human life till men are senile at thirty. Still what difference would it make? Can you not understand that the death of the individual is not death? The Party is immortal."

As usual, the voice had battered Winston into helplessness. Moreover he was in dread that if he persisted in his disagreement O'Brien would twist the dial again. And yet he could not keep silent. Feebly, without arguments, with nothing to support him except his inarticulate horror of what O'Brien had said, he returned to the attack.

"I don't know—I don't care. Somehow you will fail. Something will defeat you. Life will defeat you."

"We control life, Winston, at all its levels. You are imagining that there is something called human nature which will be outraged by what we do and will turn against us. But we create human nature. Men are infinitely malleable. Or perhaps you have returned to your old idea that the proletarians or the slaves will arise and overthrow us. Put it out of your mind. They are helpless, like the animals. Humanity is the Party. The others are outside—irrelevant."

"I don't care. In the end they will beat you. Sooner or later they will see you for what you are, and then they will tear you to pieces."

"Do you see any evidence that this is happening? Or any reason why it should?"

"No. I believe it. I *know* that you will fail. There is something in the universe—I don't know, some spirit, some principle—that you will never overcome."

"Do you believe in God, Winston?"

"No."

"Then what is it, this principle that will defeat us?"

"I don't know. The spirit of Man."

"And do you consider yourself a man?"

"Yes."

"If you are a man, Winston, you are the last man. Your kind is extinct; we are the inheritors. Do you understand that you are *alone?* You are outside history, you are nonexistent." His manner changed and he said more harshly: "And you consider yourself morally superior to us, with our lies and our cruelty?"

"Yes, I consider myself superior."

O'Brien did not speak. Two other voices were speaking. After a moment Winston recognized one of them as his own. It was a sound track of the conversation he had had with O'Brien, on the night when he had enrolled himself in the Brotherhood. He heard himself promising to lie, to steal, to forge, to murder, to encourage drug taking and prostitution, to disseminate veneral diseases, to throw vitriol in a child's face. O'Brien made a small impatient gesture, as though to say that the demonstration was hardly worth making. Then he turned a switch and the voices stopped.

"Get up from that bed," he said.

The bonds had loosened themselves. Winston lowered himself to the floor and stood up unsteadily.

"You are the last man," said O'Brien. "You are the guardian of the human spirit. You shall see yourself as you are. Take off your clothes."

Winston undid the bit of string that held his overalls together. The zip fastener had long since been wrenched out of them. He could not remember whether at any time since his arrest he had taken off all his clothes at one time. Beneath the overalls his body was looped with filthy yellowish rags, just recognizable as the remnants of underclothes. As he slid them to the ground he saw that there was a three-sided mirror at the far end of the room. He approached it, then stopped short. An involuntary cry had broken out of him.

"Go on," said O'Brien. "Stand between the wings of the mirror. You shall see the side view as well."

He had stopped because he was frightened. A bowed, gray-colored, skeletonlike thing was coming toward him. Its actual appearance was frightening, and not merely the fact that he knew it to be himself. He moved closer to the glass. The creature's face seemed to be protruded, because of its bent carriage. A forlorn, jailbird's face with a nobby forehead running back into a bald scalp, a crooked nose and battered-looking cheekbones above which the eyes were fierce and watchful. The cheeks were seamed, the mouth had a drawn-in-look. Certainly it was his own face, but it seemed to him that it had changed more than he had changed inside. The emotions it registered would be different from the ones he felt. He had gone partially bald. For the first moment he had thought that he had gone gray as well, but it was only the scalp that was gray. Except for his hands and a circle of his face, his body was gray all over with ancient, ingrained dirt. Here and there under the dirt there were the red scars of wounds, and near the ankle the varicose ulcer was an inflamed mass with flakes of skin peeling off it. But the truly frightening thing was the emaciation of his body. The barrel of the ribs was as narrow as that of a skeleton; the legs had shrunk so that the knees were thicker than the thighs. He saw now what O'Brien had meant about seeing the side view. The curvature of the spine was astonishing. The thin shoulders were hunched forward so as to make a cavity of the chest, the scraggy neck seemed to be bending double under the weight of the skull. At a guess he would have said that it was the body of a man of sixty, suffering from some malignant disease.

"You have thought sometimes," said O'Brien, "that my face—the face of a member of the Inner Party—looks old and worn. What do you think of your own face?"

He seized Winston's shoulder and spun him round so that he was facing him.

"Look at the condition you are in!" he said. "Look at this filthy grime all over your body. Look at the dirt between your toes. Look at that disgusting running sore on your leg. Do you know that you stink like a goat? Probably you have ceased to notice it. Look at your emaciation. Do you see? I can make my thumb and forefinger meet around your bicep. I could snap your neck like a carrot. Do you know that you have lost twenty-five kilograms since you have been in our hands? Even your hair is coming out in handfulls. Look!" He plucked at Winston's head and brought away a tuft of hair. "Open your mouth. Nine, ten, eleven teeth left. How many had you when you came to us? And the few you have left are dropping out of your head. Look here!"

He seized one of Winston's remaining front teeth between his powerful thumb and forefinger. A twinge of pain shot through Winston's jaw. O'Brien had wrenched the loose tooth out by the roots. He tossed it across the cell.

"You are rotting away," he said; "you are falling to pieces. What are you? A bag of filth. Now turn round and look into that mirror again. Do you see that thing facing you? That is the last man. If you are human, that is humanity. Now put your clothes on again."

Winston began to dress himself with slow stiff movements. Until now he had not seemed to notice how thin and weak he was. Only one thought stirred in his mind: that he must have been in this place longer than he had imagined. Then suddenly as he fixed the miserable rags round himself a feeling of pity for his ruined body overcame him. Before he knew what he was doing he had collapsed onto a small stool that stood beside the bed and burst into tears. He was aware of his ugliness, his gracelessness, a bundle of bones in filthy underclothes sitting weeping in the harsh white light; but he could not stop himself. O'Brien laid a hand on his shoulder, almost kindly.

"It will not last forever," he said. "You can escape from it whenever you choose. Everything depends on yourself."

"You did it!" sobbed Winston. "You reduced me to this state."

"No, Winston, you reduced yourself to it. That is what you accepted when you set yourself up against the Party. It was all contained in that first act. Nothing has happened that you did not foresee."

He paused, and then went on:

"We have beaten you, Winston. We have broken you up. You have seen what your body is like. Your mind is in the same state. I do not think there can be much pride left in you. You have been kicked and flogged and insulted, you have screamed with pain, you have rolled on the floor in your own blood and vomit. You have whimpered for mercy, you have betrayed everybody and everything. Can you think of a single degradation that has not happened to you?"

Winston had stopped weeping, though the tears were still oozing out of his eyes. He looked up at O'Brien.

"I have not betrayed Julia," he said.

O'Brien looked down at him thoughtfully. "No," he said "no; that is perfectly true. You have not betrayed Julia."

The peculiar reverence for O'Brien, which nothing seemed able to destroy, flooded Winston's heart again. How intelligent, he thought, how intelligent! Never did O'Brien fail to understand what was said to him. Anyone else on earth would have answered promptly that he *had* betrayed Julia. For what was there that they had not screwed out of him under the torture? He had told them everything he knew about her, her habits, her character, her past life; he had confessed in the most trivial detail everything that had happened at their meetings, all that he had said to her and she to him, their black-market meals, their adulteries, their vague plottings against the Party—everything. And yet, in the sense in which he intended the word, he had not betrayed her. He had not stopped loving her; his feeling toward her had remained the same. O'Brien had seen what he meant without the need for explanation.

"Tell me," he said, "how soon will they shoot me?"

"It might be a long time," said O'Brien. "You are a difficult case. But don't give up hope. Everything is cured sooner or later. In the end we shall shoot you."

He was much better. He was growing fatter and stronger every day, if it was proper to speak of days.

The white light and the humming sound were the same as ever, but the cell was a little more comfortable than the others he had been in. There were a pillow and a mattress on the plank bed, and a stool to sit on. They had

given him a bath, and they allowed him to wash himself fairly frequently in a tin basin. They even gave him warm water to wash with. They had given him new underclothes and a clean suit of overalls. They had dressed his varicose ulcer with soothing ointment. They had pulled out the remnants of his teeth and given him a new set of dentures.

Weeks or months must have passed. It would have been possible now to keep count of the passage of time, if he had felt any interest in doing so, since he was being fed at what appeared to be regular intervals. He was getting, he judged, three meals in the twenty-four hours; sometimes he wondered dimly whether he was getting them by night or by day. The food was surprisingly good, with meat at every third meal. Once there was even a packet of cigarettes. He had no matches, but the never-speaking guard who brought his food would give him a light. The first time he tried to smoke it made him sick, but he persevered, and spun the packet out for a long time, smoking half a cigarette after each meal.

They had given him a white slate with a stump of pencil tied to the corner. At first he made no use of it. Even when he was awake he was completely torpid. Often he would lie from one meal to the next almost without stirring, sometimes asleep, sometimes waking into vague reveries in which it was too much trouble to open his eyes. He had long grown used to sleeping with a strong light on his face. It seemed to make no difference, except that one's dreams were more coherent. He dreamed a great deal all through this time, and they were always happy dreams. He was in the Golden Country, or he was sitting among enormous, glorious, sunlit ruins, with his mother, with Julia, with O'Brien—not doing anything, merely sitting in the sun, talking of peaceful things. Such thoughts as he had when he was awake were mostly about his dreams. He seemed to have lost the power of intellectual effort, now that the stimulus of pain had been removed. He was not bored; he had no desire for conversation or distraction. Merely to be alone, not to be beaten or questioned, to have enough to eat, and to be clean all over, was completely satisfying.

By degrees he came to spend less time in sleep, but he still felt no impulse to get off the bed. All he cared for was to lie quiet and feel the strength gathering in his body. He would finger himself here and there, trying to make sure that it was not an illusion that his muscles were growing rounder and his skin tauter. Finally it was established beyond a doubt that he was growing fatter; his thighs were now definitely thicker than his knees. After that, reluctantly at first, he began exercising himself regularly. In a little while he could walk three kilometers, measured by pacing the cell, and his bowed shoulders were growing straighter. He attempted more elaborate exercises, and was astonished and humiliated to find what things he could not do. He could not move out of a walk, he could not hold his stool out at arm's length, he could not stand on one leg without falling over. He squatted down on his heels, and found that with agonizing pains in thigh and calf he could just lift himself to a standing position. He lay flat on his belly and tried to lift his weight by his hands. It was hopeless; he could not raise himself a centimeter. But after a few more days—a few more mealtimes—even that feat was accomplished. A time came when he could do it six times running. He began to grow actually proud of his body, and to cherish an intermittent belief that his face also was growing back to normal. Only when he chanced to put his hand on his bald scalp did he remember the seamed, ruined face that had looked back at him out of the mirror.

His mind grew more active. He sat down on the plank bed, his back against the wall and the slate on his knees, and set to work deliberately at the task of re-educating himself.

He had capitulated; that was agreed. In reality, as he saw now, he had been ready to capitulate long before he had taken the decision. From the moment when he was inside the Ministry of Love—and yes, even during those minutes when he and Julia had stood helpless while the iron voice from the telescreen told them what to do—he had grasped the frivolity, the shallowness of his attempt to set himself up against the power of the Party. He knew now that for seven years the Thought Police had watched him like a beetle under a magnifying glass. There was no physical act, no word spoken aloud, that they had not noticed, no train of thought that they had not been able to infer. Even the speck of whitish dust on the cover of his diary they had carefully replaced. They had played sound tracks to him, shown him photographs. Some of them were photographs of Julia and himself. Yes, even . . . He could not fight against the Party any longer. Besides, the Party was in the right. It must be so: how could the immortal, collective brain be mistaken? By what external standard could you check its judgments? Sanity was statistical. It was merely a question of learning to think as they thought. Only—!

The pencil felt thick and awkward in his fingers. He began to write down the thoughts that came into his head. He wrote first in large clumsy capitals:

FREEDOM IS SLAVERY.

Then almost without a pause he wrote beneath it:

TWO AND TWO MAKE FIVE.

But then there came a sort of check. His mind, as though shying away from something, seemed unable to concentrate. He knew that he knew what came next, but for the moment he could not recall it. When he did recall it, it was only by consciously reasoning out what it must be; it did not come of its own accord. He wrote:

GOD IS POWER.

He accepted everything. The past was alterable. The past never had been altered. Oceania was at war with Eastasia. Oceania had always been at war with Eastasia. Jones, Aaronson, and Rutherford were guilty of the crimes they were charged with. He had never seen the photograph that disproved their guilt. It had never existed; he had invented it. He remembered remembering contrary things, but those were false memories, products of self-deception. How easy it all was! Only surrender, and everything else followed. It was like swimming against a current that swept you backwards however hard you struggled, and then suddenly deciding to turn round and go with the current instead of opposing it. Nothing had changed except your own attitude; the predestined thing happened in any case. He hardly knew why he had ever rebelled. Everything was easy, except—!

Anything could be true. The so-called laws of Nature were nonsense. The law of gravity was nonsense. "If I wished," O'Brien had said, "I could float off this floor like a soap bubble." Winston worked it out. "If he *thinks* he floats off the floor, and if I simultaneously *think* I see him do it, then the thing happens." Suddenly, like a lump of submerged wreckage breaking the surface of water, the thought burst into his mind: "It doesn't really happen. We imagine it. It is hallucination." He pushed the thought under instantly. The fallacy was obvious. It presupposed that somewhere or other, outside oneself, there was a "real" world where "real" things happened. But how could there be such a world? What knowledge have we of anything, save through our own minds? All happenings are in the mind. Whatever happens in all minds, truly happens.

He had no difficulty in disposing of the fallacy, and he was in no danger of succumbing to it. He realized, nevertheless, that it ought never to have occurred to him. The mind should develop a blind spot whenever a dangerous thought presented itself. The process should be automatic, instinctive. *Crimestop* they called it in Newspeak.

He set to work to exercise himself in crimestop. He presented himself with propositions—"the Party says the earth is flat," "the Party says that ice is heavier than water"—and trained himself in not seeing or not understanding the arguments that contradicted them. It was not easy. It needed great powers of reasoning and improvisation. The arithmetical problems raised, for instance, by such a statement as "two and two make five" were beyond his intellectual grasp. It needed also a sort of athleticism of mind, an ability at one moment to make the most delicate use of logic and at the next to be unconscious of the crudest logical errors. Stupidity was as necessary as intelligence, and as difficult to attain.

All the while, with one part of his mind, he wondered how soon they would shoot him. "Everything depends on yourself," O'Brien had said; but he knew that there was no conscious act by which he could bring it nearer. It might be ten minutes hence, or ten years. They might keep him for years in solitary confinement; they might send him to a labor camp; they might release him for a while, as they sometimes did. It was perfectly possible that before he was shot the whole drama of his arrest and interrogation would be enacted all over again. The one certain thing was that death never came at an expected moment. The tradition—the unspoken tradition: somehow you knew it, though you never heard it said—was that they shot you from behind, always in the back of the head, without warning, as you walked down a corridor from cell to cell.

One day—but "one day" was not the right expression; just as probably it was in the middle of the night: once—he fell into a strange, blissful reverie. He was walking down the corridor, waiting for the bullet. He knew that it was coming in another moment. Everything was settled, smoothed out, reconciled. There were no more doubts, no more arguments, no more pain, no more fear. His body was healthy and strong. He walked easily, with a joy of movement and with a feeling of walking in sunlight. He was not any longer in the narrow white corridors of the Ministry of Love; he was in the enormous sunlit passage, a kilometer wide, down which he had seemed to walk in the delirium induced by drugs. He was in the Golden Country, following the foot track across the old rabbit-cropped pasture. He could feel the short springy turf under his feet and the gentle sunshine on his face. At the edge of the field were the elm trees, faintly stirring, and somewhere beyond that was the stream where the dace lay in the green pools under the willows.

Suddenly he started up with a shock of horror. The sweat broke out on his backbone. He had heard himself cry aloud:

"Julia! Julia! Julia, my love! Julia!"

For a moment he had an overwhelming hallucination of her presence. She had seemed to be not merely with him, but inside him. It was as though she had got into the texture of his skin. In that moment he had loved her far more than he had ever done when they were together and free. Also he knew that somewhere or other she was still alive and needed his help.

He lay back on the bed and tried to compose himself. What had he done? How many years had he added to his servitude by that moment of weakness?

In another moment he would hear the tramp of boots outside. They could not let such an outburst go unpunished. They would know now, if they had not known before, that he was breaking the agreement he had made with them. He obeyed the Party, but he still hated the Party. In the old days he had hidden a heretical mind beneath an appearance of conformity. Now he had retreated a step further: in the mind he had surrendered, but he had hoped to keep the inner heart inviolate. He knew that he was in the wrong, and he preferred to be in the wrong. They would understand that—O'Brien would understand it. It was all confessed in that single foolish cry.

He would have to start all over again. It might take years. He ran a hand over his face, trying to familiarize himself with the new shape. There were deep furrows in the cheeks, the cheekbones felt sharp, the nose flattened. Besides, since seeing himself in the glass he had been given a complete new set of teeth. It was not easy to preserve inscrutability when you did not know what your face looked like. In any case, mere control of the features was not enough. For the first time he perceived that if you want to keep a secret you must also hide it from yourself. You must know all the while that it is there, but until it is needed you must never let it emerge into your consciousness in any shape that could be given a name. From now onwards he must not only think right; he must feel right, dream right. And all the while he must keep his hatred locked up inside him like a ball of matter which was part of himself and yet unconnected with the rest of him, a kind of cyst.

One day they would decide to shoot him. You could not tell when it would happen, but a few seconds beforehand it should be possible to guess. It was always from behind, walk-ing down a corridor. Ten seconds would be enough. In that time the world inside him could turn over. And then, suddenly, without a word uttered, without a check in his step, without the changing of a line in his face— suddenly the camouflage would be down and bang! would go the batteries of his hatred. Hatred would fill him like an enormous roaring flame. And almost in the same instant bang! would go the bullet, too late, or too early. They would have blown his brain to pieces before they could reclaim it. The heretical thought would be unpunished, unrepented, out of their reach forever. They would have blown a hole in their own perfection. To die hating them, that was freedom.

He shut his eyes. It was more difficult than accepting an intellectual discipline. It was a question of degrading himself, mutilating himself. He had got to plunge into the filthiest of filth. What was the most horrible, sickening thing of all? He thought of Big Brother. The enormous face (because of constantly seeing it on posters he always thought of it as being a meter wide), with its heavy black mustache and the eyes that followed you to and fro, seemed to float into his mind of its own accord. What were his true feelings toward Big Brother?

There was a heavy tramp of boots in the passage. The steel door swung open with a clang. O'Brien walked into the cell. Behind him were the waxen-faced officer and the black-uniformed guards.

"Get up," said O'Brien. "Come here."

Winston stood opposite him. O'Brien took Winston's shoulders between his strong hands and looked at him closely.

"You have had thoughts of deceiving me," he said. "That was stupid. Stand up straighter. Look me in the face."

He paused, and went on in a gentler tone:

"You are improving. Intellectually there is very little wrong with you. It is only emotionally that you have failed to make progress. Tell me, Winston—and remember, no lies; you know that I am always able to detect a lie—tell me, what are your true feelings toward Big Brother?"

"I hate him."

"You hate him. Good. Then the time has

come for you to take the last step. You must love Big Brother. It is not enough to obey him; you must love him."

He released Winston with a little push toward the guards.

"Room 101," he said.

At each stage of his imprisonment he had known, or seemed to know, whereabouts he was in the windowless building. Possibly there were slight differences in the air pressure. The cells where the guards had beaten him were below ground level. The room where he had been interrogated by O'Brien was high up near the roof. This place was many meters underground, as deep down as it was possible to go.

It was bigger than most of the cells he had been in. But he hardly noticed his surroundings. All he noticed was that there were two small tables straight in front of him, each covered with green baize. One was only a meter or two from him; the other was further away, near the door. He was strapped upright in a chair, so tightly that he could move nothing, not even his head. A sort of pad gripped his head from behind, forcing him to look straight in front of him.

For a moment he was alone, then the door opened and O'Brien came in.

"You asked me once," said O'Brien, "what was in Room 101. I told you that you knew the answer already. Everyone knows it. The thing that is in Room 101 is the worst thing in the world."

The door opened again. A guard came in, carrying something made of wire, a box or basket of some kind. He set it down on the further table. Because of the position in which O'Brien was standing, Winston could not see what the thing was.

"The worst thing in the world," said O'Brien, "varies from individual to individual. It may be burial alive, or death by fire, or by drowning, or by impalement, or fifty other deaths. There are cases where it is some quite trivial thing, not even fatal."

He had moved a little to one side, so that Winston had a better view of the thing on the table. It was an oblong wire cage with a handle on top for carrying it by. Fixed to the front of it was something that looked like a fencing mask, with the concave side outwards. Although it was three or four meters away from him, he could see that the cage was divided lengthways into two compartments, and that there was some kind of creature in each. They were rats.

"In your case," said O'Brien, "the worst thing in the world happens to be rats."

A sort of premonitory tremor, a fear of he was not certain what, had passed through Winston as soon as he caught his first glimpse of the cage. But at this moment the meaning of the masklike attachment in front of it suddenly sank into him. His bowels seemed to turn to water.

"You can't do that!" he cried out in a high cracked voice. "You couldn't, you couldn't! It's impossible."

"Do you remember," said O'Brien, "the moment of panic that used to occur in your dreams? There was a wall of blackness in front of you, and a roaring sound in your ears. There was something terrible on the other side of the wall. You knew that you knew what it was, but you dared not drag it into the open. It was the rats that were on the other side of the wall."

"O'Brien!" said Winston, making an effort to control his voice. "You know this is not necessary. What is it that you want me to do?"

O'Brien made no direct answer. When he spoke it was in the schoolmasterish manner that he sometimes affected. He looked thoughtfully into the distance, as though he were addressing an audience somewhere behind Winston's back.

"By itself," he said, "pain is not always enough. There are occasions when a human being will stand out against pain, even to the point of death. But for everyone there is something unendurable—something that cannot be contemplated. Courage and cowardice are not involved. If you are falling from a height it is not cowardly to clutch at a rope. If you have come up from deep water it is not cowardly to fill your lungs with air. It is merely an instinct which cannot be disobeyed. It is the same with the rats. For you, they are unendurable. They are a form of pressure that you cannot withstand, even if you wish to. You will do what is required of you."

"But what is it, what is it? How can I do it if I don't know what it is?"

O'Brien picked up the cage and brought it across to the nearer table. He set it down carefully on the baize cloth. Winston could hear the blood singing in his ears. He had the feeling of sitting in utter loneliness. He was in the middle of a great empty plain, a flat desert drenched with sunlight, across which all sounds came to him out of immense distances. Yet the cage with the rats was not two meters from him. They were enormous rats. They were at the age when a rat's muzzle grows blunt and fierce and his fur brown instead of gray.

"The rat," said O'Brien, still addressing his invisible audience, "although a rodent, is carnivorous. You are aware of that. You will have heard of the things that happen in the poor quarters of this town. In some streets a woman dare not leave her baby alone in the house, even for five minutes. The rats are certain to attack it. Within quite a small time they will strip it to the bones. They also attack sick or dying people. They show astonishing intelligence in knowing when a human being is helpless."

There was an outburst of squeals from the cage. It seemed to reach Winston from far away. The rats were fighting; they were trying to get at each other through the partition. He heard also a deep groan of despair. That, too, seemed to come from outside himself.

O'Brien picked up the cage, and, as he did so, pressed something in it. There was a sharp click. Winston made a frantic effort to tear himself loose from the chair. It was hopeless: every part of him, even his head, was held immovably. O'Brien moved the cage nearer. It was less than a meter from Winston's face.

"I have pressed the first lever," said O'Brien. "You understand the construction of this cage. The mask will fit over your head, leaving no exit. When I press this other lever, the door of the cage will slide up. These starving brutes will shoot out of it like bullets. Have you ever seen a rat leap through the air? They will leap onto your face and bore straight into it. Sometimes they attack the eyes first. Sometimes they burrow through the cheeks and devour the tongue."

The cage was nearer; it was closing in. Winston heard a succession of shrill cries which appeared to be occurring in the air above his head. But he fought furiously against his panic. To think, to think, even with a split second left—to think was the only hope. Suddenly the foul musty odor of the brutes struck his nostrils. There was a violent convulsion of nausea inside him, and he almost lost consciousness. Everything had gone black. For an instant he was insane, a screaming animal. Yet he came out of the blackness clutching an idea. There was one and only one way to save himself. He must interpose another human being, the *body* of another human being, between himself and the rats.

The circle of the mask was large enough now to shut out the vision of anything else. The wire door was a couple of hand-spans from his face. The rats knew what was coming now. One of them was leaping up and down; the other, an old scaly grandfather of the sewers, stood up, with his pink hands against the bars, and fiercely snuffed the air. Winston could see the whiskers and the yellow teeth. Again the black panic took hold of him. He was blind, helpless, mindless.

"It was a common punishment in Imperial China," said O'Brien as didactically as ever.

The mask was closing on his face. The wire brushed his cheek. And then—no, it was not relief, only hope, a tiny fragment of hope. Too late, perhaps too late. But he had suddenly understood that in the whole world there was just *one* person to whom he could transfer his punishment—*one* body that he could thrust between himself and the rats. And he was shouting frantically, over and over:

"Do it to Julia! Do it to Julia! Not me! Julia! I don't care what you do to her. Tear her face off, strip her to the bones. Not me! Julia! Not me!"

He was falling backwards, into enormous depths, away from the rats. He was still strapped in the chair, but he had fallen through the floor, through the walls of the building, through the earth, through the oceans, through the atmosphere, into outer space, into the gulfs between the stars— always away, away, away from the rats. He was light-years distant, but O'Brien was still standing at his side. There was still the cold touch of wire against his cheek. But through the darkness that enveloped him he heard another metallic click, and knew that the cage door had clicked shut and not open.

The Chestnut Tree was almost empty. A ray of sunlight slanting through a window fell yellow on dusty tabletops. It was the lonely hour of fifteen. A tinny music trickled from the telescreens.

Winston sat in his usual corner, gazing into an empty glass. Now and again he glanced up at a vast face which eyed him from the opposite wall. BIG BROTHER IS WATCHING YOU, the caption said. Unbidden, a waiter came and filled his glass up with Victory Gin, shaking into it a few drops from another bottle with a quill through the cork. It was saccharine flavored with cloves, the specialty of the café.

Winston was listening to the telescreen. At present only music was coming out of it, but there was a possibility that at any moment there might be a special bulletin from the Ministry of Peace. The news from the African front was disquieting in the extreme. On and off he had been worrying about it all day. A Eurasian army (Oceania was at war with Eurasia; Oceania had always been at war with Eurasia) was moving southward at terrifying speed. The mid-day bulletin had not mentioned any definite area, but it was probable that already the mouth of the Congo was a battlefield. Brazzaville and Leopoldville were in danger. One did not have to look at the map to see what it meant. It was not merely a question of losing Central Africa; for the first time in the whole war, the territory of Oceania itself was menaced.

A violent emotion, not fear but a sort of undifferentiated excitement, flared up in him, then faded again. He stopped thinking about the war. In these days he could never fix his mind on any one subject for more than a few moments at a time. He picked up his glass and drained it at a gulp. As always, it made him shudder and even retch slightly. The stuff was horrible. The cloves and saccharine, themselves disgusting enough in their sickly way, could not disguise the flat oily smell; and what was worst of all was that the smell of gin, which dwelt with him night and day, was inextricably mixed up in his mind with the smell of those—.

He never named them, even in his thoughts, and so far as it was possible he never visualized them. They were something that he was half aware of, hovering close to his face, a smell that clung to his nostrils. As the gin rose in him he belched through purple lips. He had grown fatter since they released him, and had regained his old color—indeed, more than regained it. His features had thickened, the skin on nose and cheekbones was coarsely red, even the bald scalp was too deep a pink. A waiter, again unbidden, brought the chessboard and the current issue of the *Times,* with the page turned down at the chess problem. Then, seeing that Winston's glass was empty, he brought the gin bottle and filled it. There was no need to give orders. They knew his habits. The chessboard was always waiting for him, his corner table was always reserved; even when the place was full he had it to himself, since nobody cared to be seen sitting too close to him. He never even bothered to count his drinks. At irregular intervals they presented him with a dirty slip of paper which they said was the bill, but he had the impression that they always undercharged him. It would have made no difference if it had been the other way about. He had always plenty of money nowadays. He even had a job, a sinecure, more highly paid than his old job had been.

The music from the telescreen stopped and a voice took over. Winston raised his head to listen. No bulletin from the front, however. It was merely a brief announcement from the Ministry of Plenty. In the preceding quarter, it appeared, the Tenth Three-Year Plan's quotas for bootlaces had been overfulfilled by ninety-eight per cent.

He was examined the chess problem and set out the pieces. It was a tricky ending, involving a couple of knights. "White to play and mate in two moves." Winston looked up at the portrait of Big Brother. White always mates, he thought with a sort of cloudy mysticism. Always, without exception, it is so arranged. In no chess problem since the beginning of the world has black ever won. Did it not symbolize the eternal, unvarying triumph of Good over Evil? The huge face gazed back at him, full of calm power. White always mates.

The voice from the telescreen paused and added in a different and much graver tone: "You are warned to stand by for an important announcement at fifteen-thirty. Fifteen-thirty! This is news of the highest importance. Take care not to miss it. Fifteen-thirty!" The tinkling music struck up again.

Winston's heart stirred. That was the bulletin from the front; instinct told him that it was bad news that was coming. All day, with little spurts of excitement, the thought of a smashing defeat in Africa had been in and out of his mind. He seemed actually to see the Eurasian army swarming across the never-broken frontier and pouring down into the tip of Africa like a column of ants. Why had it not been possible to outflank them in some way? The outline of the West African coast stood out vividly in his mind. He picked up the white knight and moved it across the board. *There* was the proper spot. Even while he saw the black horde racing southward he saw another force, mysteriously assembled, suddenly planted in their rear, cutting their communications by land and sea. He felt that by willing it he was bringing that other force into existence. But it was necessary to act quickly. If they could get control of the whole of Africa, if they had airfields and submarine bases at the Cape, it would cut Oceania in two. It might mean anything: defeat, breakdown, the redivision of the world, the destruction of the Party! He drew a deep breath. An extraordinary medley of feelings—but it was not a medley, exactly; rather it was successive layers of feeling, in which one could not say which was undermost—struggled inside him.

The spasm passed. He put the white knight back in its place, but for the moment he could not settle down to serious study of the chess problem. His thoughts wandered again. Almost unconsciously he traced with his finger in the dust on the table:

$$2 + 2 = 5.$$

"They can't get inside you," she had said. But they could get inside you. "What happens to you here is *forever*," O'Brien had said. That was a true word. There were things, your own acts, from which you could not recover. Something killed in your breast; burnt out, cauterized out.

He had seen her; he had even spoken to her. There was no danger in it. He knew it as though instinctively that they now took almost no interest in his doings. He could have arranged to meet her a second time if either of them had wanted to. Actually it was by chance that they had met. It was in the Park, on a vile, biting day in March, when the earth was like iron and all the grass seemed dead and there was not a bud anywhere except a few crocuses which had pushed themselves up to be dismembered by the wind. He was hurrying along with frozen hands and watering eyes when he saw her not ten meters away from him. It struck him at once that she had changed in some ill-defined way. They almost passed one another without a sign; then he turned and followed her, not very eagerly. He knew that there was no danger, nobody would take any interest in them. She did not speak. She walked obliquely away across the grass as though trying to get rid of him, then seemed to resign herself to having him at her side. Presently they were in among a clump of ragged leafless shrubs, useless either for concealment or as protection from the wind. They halted. It was vilely cold. The wind whistled through the twigs and fretted the occasional, dirty-looking crocuses. He put his arm round her waist.

There was no telescreen, but there must be hidden microphones; besides they could be seen. It did not matter, nothing mattered. They could have lain down on the ground and done *that* if they had wanted to. His flesh froze with horror at the thought of it. She made no response whatever to the clasp of his arm; she did not even try to disengage herself. He knew now what had changed her. Her face was sallower, and there was a long scar, partly hidden by the hair, across her forehead and temple; but that was not the change. It was that her waist had grown thicker and, in a surprising way, had stiffened. He remembered how once, after the explosion of a rocket bomb, he had helped to drag a corpse out of some ruins, and had been astonished not only by the incredible weight of the thing, but by its rigidity and awkwardness to handle, which made it seem more like stone than flesh. Her body felt like that. It occurred to him that the texture of her skin would be quite different from what it had once been.

He did not attempt to kiss her, nor did they speak. As they walked back across the gate she looked directly at him for the first time. It was only a momentary glance, full of contempt and dislike. He wondered whether it was a dislike that came purely out of the past or whether it was inspired also by his bloated face and the water that the wind kept squeezing from his eyes. They sat down on two iron chairs, side by side but not too close together. He saw that she was about to speak. She moved her clumsy shoe a few centimeters and deliberately crushed a twig. Her feet seemed to have grown broader, he noticed.

"I betrayed you," she said badly.

"I betrayed you," he said.

She gave him another quick look of dislike.

"Sometimes," she said, "they threaten you with something—something you can't stand up to, can't even think about. And then you say, 'Don't do it to me, do it to somebody else, do it to so-and-so.' And perhaps you might pretend, afterwards, that it was only a trick and that you just said it to make them stop and didn't really mean it. But that isn't true. At the time when it happens you do mean it. You think there's no other way of saving yourself and you're quite ready to save yourself that way. You *want* it to happen to the other person. You don't don't give a damn what they suffer. All you care about is yourself."

"All you care about is yourself," he echoed.

"And after that, you don't feel the same toward the other person any longer."

"No," he said, "you don't feel the same."

There did not seem to be anything more to say. The wind plastered their thin overalls against their bodies. Almost at once it became embarrassing to sit there in silence; besides, it was too cold to keep still. She said something about catching her Tube and stood up to go.

"We must meet again," he said.

"Yes," she said, "we must meet again."

He followed irresolutely for a little distance, half a pace behind her. They did not speak again. She did not actually try to shake him off, but walked at just such a speed as to prevent his keeping abreast of her. He had made up his mind that he would accompany her as far as the Tube station, but suddenly this process of trailing along in the cold seemed pointless and unbearable. He was overwhelmed by a desire not so much to get away from Julia as to get back to the Chestnut Tree Café, which had never seemed so attractive as at this moment. He had a nostalgic vision of his corner table, with the newspaper and the chessboard and the ever-flowing gin. Above all, it would be warm in there. The next moment, not altogether by accident, he allowed himself to become separated from her by a small knot of people. He made a half-hearted attempt to catch up, then slowed down, turned and made off in the opposite direction. When he had gone fifty meters he looked back. The street was not crowded, but already he could not distinguish her. Any one of a dozen hurrying figures might have been hers. Perhaps her thickened, stiffened body was no longer recognizable from behind.

"At the time when it happens," she had said, "you do mean it." He had meant it. He had not merely said it, he had wished it. He had wished that she and not he should be delivered over to the——.

Something changed in the music that trickled from the telescreen. A cracked and jeering note, a yellow note, came into it. And then—perhaps it was not happening, perhaps it was only a memory taking on the semblance of sound—a voice was singing:

*"Under the spreading chestnut tree
I sold you and you sold me—"*

The tears welled up in his eyes. A passing waiter noticed that his glass was empty and came back with the gin bottle.

He took up his glass and sniffed at it. The stuff grew not less but more horrible with every mouthful he drank. But it had become the element he swam in. It was his life, his death, and his resurrection. It was gin that sank him into stupor every night, and gin that revived him every morning. When he woke, seldom before eleven hundred, with gummed-up eyelids and fiery mouth and a back that seemed to be broken, it would have been impossible even to rise from the horizontal if it had not been for the bottle and teacup placed beside the bed overnight. Through the mid-day hours he sat with glazed face, the bottle handy, listening to the telescreen. From fifteen to closing time he was a fixture in the Chestnut Tree. No one cared what he did any longer, no whistle woke him, no telescreen admonished him. Occasionally, perhaps twice a week, he went to a dusty, forgotten-looking office in the Ministry of Truth and did a little work, or what was called work. He had been appointed to a sub-committee of a sub-committee which had sprouted from one of the innumerable committees dealing with minor difficulties that arise in the compilation of the Eleventh Edition of the Newspeak dictionary. They were engaged in producing something called an Interim Report, but what it was that they were reporting on he had never definitely found out. It was something to do with the question of whether commas should be placed inside brackets, or outside. There were four others on the committee, all of them persons similar to himself. There were days when they assembled and then promptly dispersed again, frankly admitting to one another that there was not really anything to be done. But there were other days when they settled down to their work almost eagerly, making a tremendous show of entering up their minutes and drafting long memoranda which were never finished—when the argument as to what they were supposedly arguing about grew extraordinarily involved and abstruse, with subtle hagglings over definitions, enormous digressions, quarrels—threats, even, to appeal to higher authority. And then suddenly the life would go out of them and they would sit round the table looking at one another with extinct eyes, like ghosts fading a cock-crow.

The telescreen was silent for a moment. Winston raised his head again. The bulletin! But no, they were merely changing the music. He had the map of Africa behind his eyelids. The movement of the armies was a diagram: a black arrow tearing vertically southward, and a white arrow tearing horizontally eastward, across the tail of the first. As though for reassurance he looked up at the imperturbable face in the portrait. Was it conceivable that the second arrow did not even exist?

His interest flagged again. He drank another mouthful of gin, picked up the white knight, and made a tentative move. Check. But it was evidently not the right move, because—

Uncalled, a memory floated into his mind. He saw a candlelit room with a vast white-counterpaned bed, and himself, a boy of nine or ten, sitting on the floor, shaking a dice box and laughing excitedly. His mother was sitting opposite him and also laughing.

It must have been about a month before she disappeared. It was a moment of reconciliation, when the nagging hunger in his belly was forgotten and his earlier affection for her had temporarily revived. He remembered the day well, a pelting, drenching day when the water streamed down the window pane and the light indoors was too dull to read by. The boredom of the two children in the dark, cramped bedroom became unbearable. Winston whined and grizzled, made futile demands for food, fretted about the room, pulling everything out of place and kicking the wainscoting until the neighbors banged on the wall, while the younger child wailed intermittently. In the end his mother had said. "Now be good, and I'll buy you a toy. A lovely toy—you'll love it"; and then she had gone out in the rain, to a little general shop which was still sporadically open near by, and comes back with a cardboard box containing an outfit of Snakes and Ladders. He could still remember the smell of the damp cardboard. It was a miserable outfit. The board was cracked and the tiny wooden dice were so ill-cut that they would hardly lie on their sides. Winston looked at the thing sulkily and without interest. But then his mother lit a piece of candle and they sat down on the floor to play. Soon he was wildly excited and shouting with laughter as the tiddlywinks climbed hopefully up the ladders and then came slithering down the snakes again, almost back to the starting point. They played eight games, winning four each. His tiny sister, too young to understand what the game was about, had sat propped up against a bolster, laughing because the others were laughing. For a whole afternoon they had all been happy together, as in his earlier childhood.

He pushed the picture out of his mind. It was a false memory. He was troubled by false memories occasionally. They did not matter so long as one knew them for what they were. Some things had happened, others had not happened. He turned back to the chessboard and picked up the white knight again. Almost in the same instant it dropped onto the board with a clatter. He had started as though a pin had run into him.

A shrill trumpet call had pierced the air. It was the bulletin! Victory! It always meant victory when a trumpet call preceded the news. A sort of electric thrill ran through the café. Even the waiters had started and pricked up their ears.

The trumpet call had let loose an enormous volume of noise. Already an excited voice was gabbling from the telescreen, but even as it started it was almost drowned by a roar of cheering from outside. The news had run round the streets like magic. He could hear just enough of what was issuing from the telescreen to realize that it had all happened as he had foreseen: a vast seaborne armada secretly assembled, a sudden blow in the enemy's rear, the white arrow tearing across the tail of the black. Fragments of triumphant phrases pushed themselves through the din: "Vast strategic maneuver—perfect co-ordination—utter rout—half a million prisoners—complete demoralization—control of the whole of Africa—bring the war within measurable distance of its end—victory—greatest victory in human history—victory, victory, victory!"

Under the table Winston's feet made convulsive movements. He had not stirred from his seat, but in his mind he was running, swiftly running, he was with the crowds outside, cheering himself deaf. He looked up against the portrait of Big Brother. The colossus that bestrode the world! The rock against which the hordes of Asia dashed themselves in vain! He thought how ten minutes ago—yes, only ten minutes—there had still been equivocation in his heart as he wondered whether the news from the front would be of victory or defeat. Ah, it was more than a Eurasian army that had perished! Much had changed in him since the first day in the Ministry of Love, but the final, indispensable, healing change had never happened, until this moment.

The voice from the telescreen was still pouring forth its tale of prisoners and booty and slaughter, but the shouting outside had died down a little. The waiters were turning back to their work. One of them approached with the gin bottle. Winston, sitting in a blissful dream, paid no attention as his glass was filled up. He was not running or cheering any longer. He was back in the Ministry of Love, with everything forgiven, his soul white as snow. He was in the public dock, confessing everything, implicating everybody. He was walking down the white-tiled corridor, with the feeling of walking in sunlight, and an armed guard at his back. The long-hoped-for bullet was entering his brain.

He gazed up at the enormous face. Forty years it had taken him to learn what kind of smile was hidden beneath the dark mustache. O cruel, needless misunderstanding! O stubborn, self-willed exile from the loving breast! Two gin-scented tears trickled down the sides of his nose. But it was all right, everything was all right, the struggle was finished. He had won the victory over himself. He loved Big Brother.

Dietrich Bonhoeffer

Dietrich Bonhoeffer (1906–1945) was born and reared in Germany in an intellectual and academic atmosphere. He studied at the University of Berlin, concentrating in theology. Among those who made an indelible impression upon him was the German theologian, Karl Barth. A pastorate in Barcelona, Spain (1928–29) and a year of study at Union Theological Seminary, New York (1930) preceded a teaching assignment in Berlin which the Nazis ended in 1936. By the mid-thirties Bonhoeffer had clearly indicated his break with the national Church in Germany, and with the publication of The Cost of Discipleship (1937) and Gemeinsames Leben (1938) his name and views became well known throughout Germany. During a lecture tour in 1939 in the United States, American friends implored him to seek sanctuary in their country, but he thought his future role, despite his alienation from the current German government, should be played out in his native land. The Nazis, suspicious of his anti-Hitler connections, arrested Bonhoeffer in April, 1943 and hanged him two years later as World War II was coming to an end. Since he was prevented by his early death from systematically working out the theses advanced in these Letters and Papers, post World War II German intellectuals are inclined to minimize Bonhoeffer's achievements as a theologian while paying more attention to such figures as Karl Barth, Martin Buber, and Rudolf Bultmann. Yet Bonhoeffer's influence upon contemporary theology, especially in America, has been impressive. In the United States, Reinhold Niebuhr sparked in the 1930's and 1940's a revival of orthodoxy in Protestant theology. Niebuhr, writing under the spell cast by the great depression, almost universal war, and threats of atomic annihilation, breathed a pessimistic mood of tragic despair and resignation which seem not to suit the more optimistic mood prevalent in the 1950's and 1960's. Radical theology is increasingly supplanting neo-orthodoxy especially among the younger intellectuals for theological as well as non-theological reasons. Among the sources which the proponents of radical theology have found fruitful are Bonhoeffer's Letters and Papers from Prison. In reading the following selection note (1) his reasons for saying that men cannot be religious anymore; (2) questions he raises for a religionless Christianity; (3) what he suggests should be the chief concerns of the religionless Christian; (4) his views respecting the "death of God"; (5) the nature of his criticism of Barth and Bultmann; (6) his explanation for the increased popularity of psychotherapy and his judgment of it; and (7) his prescription for his fellows and for the Church.

Dietrich Bonhoeffer. *Letters and Papers from Prison,* ed. by Eberhard Bethge; tr. by Reginald H. Fuller (New York: The Macmillan Company, 1953. Paperback edn., 1962), pp. 162–69; 194–200; 211–15; 217–20; 222–27; 235–40. Reprinted with the special permission of the Macmillan Company.

From: LETTERS AND PAPERS FROM PRISON

April 30, 1944. The thing that keeps coming back to me is, what *is* Christianity, and indeed what *is* Christ, for us to-day? The time when men could be told everything by means of words, whether theological or simply pious, is over, and so is the time of inwardness and conscience, which is to say the time of religion as such. We are proceeding towards a time of no religion at all: men as they are now simply cannot be religious any more. Even those who honestly describe themselves as "religious" do not in the least act up to it, and so when they say "religious" they evidently mean something quite different. Our whole nineteen-hundred-year-old Christian preaching and theology rests upon the "religious premise" of man. What we call Christianity has always been a pattern—perhaps a true pattern—of religion. But if one day it becomes apparent that this *a priori* "premise" simply does not exist, but was an historical and temporary form of human self-expression, i.e., if we reach the stage of being radically without religion—and I think this is more or less the case already, else how is it, for instance, that this war, unlike any of those before it, is not calling forth any "religious" reaction?—what does that mean for "Christianity"?

It means that the linchpin is removed from the whole structure of our Christianity to date, and the only people left for us to light on in the way of "religion" are a few "last survivals of the age of chivalry," or else one or two who are intellectually dishonest. Would they be the chosen few? Is it on this dubious group and none other that we are to pounce, in fervour, pique, or indignation, in order to sell them the goods we have to offer? Are we to fall upon one or two unhappy people in their weakest moment and force upon them a sort of religious coercion?

If we do not want to do this, if we had finally to put down the western pattern of Christianity as a mere preliminary stage to doing without religion altogether, what situation would result for us, for the Church? How can Christ become the Lord even of those with no religion? If religion is no more than the garment of Christianity—and even that garment has had very different aspects at different periods—then what is a religionless Christianity? Barth, who is the only one to have started on this line of thought, has still not proceeded to its logical conclusion, but has arrived at a positivism of revelation which has nevertheless remained essentially a restoration. For the religionless working man, or indeed, man generally, nothing that makes any real difference is gained by that. The questions needing answers would surely be: What is the significance of a Church (church, parish, preaching, Christian life) in a religionless world? How do we speak of God without religion, i.e., without the temporally-influenced presuppositions of metaphysics, inwardness, and so on? How do we speak (but perhaps we are no longer capable of speaking of such things as we used to) in secular fashion of God? In what way are we in a religionless and secular sense Christians, in what way are we the *Ekklesia,* "those who are called forth," not conceiving of ourselves religiously as specially favoured, but as wholly belonging to the world? Then Christ is no longer an object of religion, but something quite different, indeed and in truth the Lord of the world. Yet what does that signify? What is the place of worship and prayer in an entire absence of religion? Does the secret discipline, or, as the case may be, the distinction (which you have met with me before) between penultimate and ultimate, at this point acquire fresh importance. . . .

The Pauline question whether circumcision is a condition of justification is to-day, I consider, the question whether religion is a condition of salvation. Freedom from circumcision is at the same time freedom from religion. I often ask myself why a Christian instinct frequently draws me more to the religionless than to the religious, by which I mean not with any intention of evangelizing them, but rather, I might almost say, in "brotherhood." While I often shrink with religious people from speaking of God by name—because that Name somehow seems to me here not to ring true, and I strike myself as rather dishonest (it is especially bad when others start talking in religious jargon: then I dry up completely and feel somehow oppressed and ill at ease)—with people who have no religion I am able on occasion to speak of God quite openly and as it were naturally. Religious people speak of God when human perception is (often just from laziness) at an end, or human resources fail: it is really always the *Deus ex machina* they call to their aid, either for the so-called solving of insoluble problems or as support in human failure—always, that is to say, helping out human weakness or on the borders of human existence. Of necessity, that can only go on until men can, by their own strength, push those borders a little further, so that God becomes superfluous as a *Deus ex machina*. I have come to be doubtful even about talking of "borders of human existence." Is even death to-day, since men are scarcely afraid of it any more, and sin, which they scarcely understand any more, still a genuine borderline? It always seems to me that in talking thus we are only seeking frantically to make room for God. I should like to speak of God not on the borders of life but at its centre, not in weakness but in strength, not, therefore, in man's suffering and death but in his life and prosperity. On the borders it seems to me better to hold our peace and leave the problem unsolved. Belief in the Resurrection is not the solution of the problem of death. The "beyond" of God is not the beyond of our perceptive faculties. The transcendence of theory based on perception has nothing to do with the transcendence of God. God is the "beyond" in the midst of our life. The Church stands not where human powers give out, on the borders, but in the centre of the village. That is the way it is in the Old Testament, and in this sense we still read the New Testament far too little on the basis of the Old. The outward aspect of this religionless Christianity, the form it takes, is something to which I am giving much thought, and I shall be writing to you about it again soon. It may be that on us in particular, midway between East and West, there will fall an important responsibility. . . .

May 5th 1944. A bit more about "religionlessness." I expect you remember Bultmann's paper on the demythologizing of the New Testament? My view of it to-day would be not that he went too far, as most people seem to think, but that he did not go far enough. It is not only the mythological conceptions, such as the miracles, the ascension and the like (which are not in principle separable from the conceptions of God, faith and so on) that are problematic, but the "religious" conceptions themselves. You cannot, as Bultmann imagines, separate God and miracles, but you do have to be able to interpret and proclaim *both* of them in a "non-religious" sense. Bultmann's approach is really at bottom the liberal one (i.e. abridging the Gospel), whereas I seek to think theologically.

What do I mean by "interpret in a religious sense"? In my view, that means to speak on the one hand metaphysically, and on the other individualistically. Neither of these is relevant to the Bible message or to the man of to-day. Is it not true to say that individualistic concern for personal salvation has almost completely left us all? Are we not really under the impression that there are more important things than bothering about such a matter? (Perhaps not more important than the matter itself, but more than bothering about it.) I know it sounds pretty monstrous to say that. But is it not, at bottom, even biblical? Is there any concern in the Old Testament about saving one's soul at all? Is not righteousness and the kingdom of God on earth the focus of everything, and is not Romans 3.14 ff., too, the culmination of the view that in God alone is righteousness, and not in an individualistic doctrine of salvation? It is not with the next world that we are concerned, but with this world as created and preserved and set subject to laws and atoned for and made new. What is above the world is, in the Gospel, intended to exist *for* this world—I mean that not in the anthropocentric sense of liberal, pietistic, ethical theology, but in the Bible sense of the creation and of the incarnation, crucifixion, and resurrection of Jesus Christ.

Barth was the first theologian to begin the criticism of religion,—and that remains his really great merit—but he set in its place the positivist doctrine of revelation which says in effect, "Take it or leave it": Virgin Birth, Trinity or anything else, everything which is an equally significant and necessary part of the whole, which latter has to be swallowed as a whole or not at all. That is not in accordance with the Bible. There are degrees of perception and degrees of significance, i.e. a secret discipline must be re-established whereby the *mysteries* of the Christian faith are preserved from profanation. The positivist doctrine of revelation makes it too easy for itself, setting up, as in the ultimate analysis it does, a law of faith, and mutilating what is, by the incarnation of Christ, a gift for us. The place of religion is taken by the Church—that is, in itself, as the Bible teaches it should be—but the world is made to depend upon itself and left to its own devices, and that is all wrong.

I am thinking over the problem at present how we may reinterpret in the manner "of the world"—in the sense of the Old Testament and of John 1.14—the concepts of repentance, faith, justification, rebirth, sanctification and so on. . . .

June 8th 1944. The movement beginning about the thirteenth century (I am not going to get involved in any arguments about the exact date) towards the autonomy of man (under which head I place the discovery of the laws by which the world lives and manages in science, social and political affairs, art, ethics and religion) has in our time reached a certain completion. Man has learned to cope with all questions of importance without recourse to God as a working hypothesis. In questions concerning science, art, and even ethics, this has become an understood thing which one scarcely dares to tilt at any more. But for the last hundred years or so it has been increasingly true of religious questions also: it is becoming evident that everything gets along without "God," and just as well as before. As in the scientific field, so in human affairs generally, what we call "God" is being more and more edged out of life, losing more and more ground.

Catholic and Protestant historians are agreed that it is in this development that the great defection from God, from Christ, is to be discerned, and the more they bring in and make use of God and Christ in opposition to this trend, the more the trend itself considers itself to be anti-Christian. The world which has attained to a realization of itself and of the laws which govern its existence is so sure of itself that we become frightened. False starts and failures do not make the world deviate from the path and development it is following; they are accepted with fortitude and detachment as part of the bargain, and even an event like the present war is no exception. Christian apologetic has taken the most varying forms of opposition to this self-assurance. Efforts are made to prove to a world thus come of age that it cannot live without the tutelage of "God." Even though there has been surrender on all secular problems, there still remain the so-called ultimate questions—death, guilt—on which only "God" can furnish an answer, and which are the reason why God and the Church and the pastor are needed. Thus we live, to some extent, by these ultimate questions of humanity. But what if one day they no longer exist as such, if they too can be answered without "God"? We have of course the secularized off-shoots of Christian theology, the existentialist philosophers and the psychotherapists, who demonstrate to secure, contented, happy mankind that it is really unhappy and desperate, and merely unwilling to realize that it is in severe straits it knows nothing at all about, from which only they can rescue it. Wherever there is health, strength, security, simplicity, they spy luscious fruit to gnaw at or to lay their pernicious eggs in. They make it their object first of all to drive men to inward despair, and then it is all theirs. That is secularized methodism. And whom does it touch? A small number of intellectuals, of degenerates, of people who regard themselves as the most important thing in the world and hence like looking after themselves. The ordinary man who spends his everyday life at work, and with his family, and of course with all kinds of hobbies and other interests too, is not affected. He has neither time nor inclination for thinking about his intellectual despair and regarding his modest share of happiness as a trial, a trouble or a disaster.

The attack by Christian apologetic upon the adulthood of the world I consider to be in the first place pointless, in the second ignoble, and in the third un-Christian. Pointless, because it looks to me like an attempt to put a grown-up man back into adolescence, i.e. to make him dependent on things on which he is not in fact dependent any more, thrusting him back into the midst of problems which are in fact not problems for him any more. Ignoble, because this amounts to an effort to exploit the weakness of man for purposes alien to him and not freely subscribed to by him. Un-Christian, because for Christ himself is being substituted one particular stage in the religiousness of man, i.e. a human law. Of this more later.

But first a word or two on the historical situation. The question is, Christ and the newly matured world. It was the weak point of liberal theology that it allowed the world the right to assign Christ his place in that world: in the dispute between Christ and the world it accepted the comparatively clement peace dictated by the world. It was its strong point that it did not seek to put back the clock, and genuinely accepted the battle (Troeltsch), even though this came to an end with its overthrow.

Overthrow was succeeded by capitulation and an attempt at a completely fresh start based on consideration of the Bible and Reformation fundamentals of the faith. Heim sought, along pietist and methodist lines, to convince individual man that he was faced with the alternative "either despair or Jesus." He gained "hearts." Althaus, carrying forward the modern and positive line with a strong confessional emphasis, endeavoured to wring from the world a place for Lutheran teaching (ministry) and Lutheran worship, and otherwise left the world to its own devices. Tillich set out to interpret the evolution of the world itself—against its will—in a religious sense, to give it its whole shape through religion. That was very courageous of him, but the world unseated him and went on by itself: he too sought to understand the world better than it understood itself, but it felt entirely *mis*understood, and rejected the imputation. (Of course the world does need to be understood better than it understands itself, but not "religiously," as the religious socialists desired.) Barth was the first to realize the mistake that all these efforts (which were all unintention-

ally sailing in the channel of liberal theology) were making in having as their objective the clearing of a space for religion in the world or against the world.

He called the God of Jesus Christ into the lists against religion, *"pneuma* against *sarx."* That was and is his greatest service (the second edition of his Epistle to the Romans, in spite of all its neo-Kantian shavings). Through his later dogmatics, he enabled the Church to effect this distinction in principle all along the line.) It was not that he subsequently, as is often claimed, failed in ethics, for his ethical observations—so far as he has made any—are just as significant as his dogmatic ones; it was that he gave no concrete guidance, either in dogmatics or in ethics, on the non-religious interpretation of theological concepts. There lies his limitation, and because of it his theology of revelation becomes positivist, a "positivism of revelation," as I put it.

The Confessing Church has to a great extent forgotten all about the Barthian approach, and lapsed from positivism into conservative restoration. The important thing about that Church is that it carries on the great concepts of Christian theology, but that seems all it will do. There are, certainly, in these concepts the elements of genuine prophetic quality (under which head come both the claim to truth and the mercy you mention) and of genuine worship, and to that extent the message of the Confessing Church meets only with attention, hearing and rejection. But they both remain unexplained and remote, because there is no interpretation of them.

People like, for instance, Schültz, or the Oxford Group, or the Berneucheners, who miss the "movement" and "life," are dangerous reactionaries, retrogressive because they go straight back behind the approach of revelation theology and seek for "religious" renewal. They simply do not understand the problem at all, and what they say is entirely beside the point. There is no future for them (though the Oxford people would have the biggest chance if they were not so completely devoid of biblical substance).

Bultmann would seem to have felt Barth's limitations in some way, but he misconstrues them in the light of liberal theology, and hence goes off into the typical liberal reduction process (the "mythological" elements of Christianity are dropped, and Christianity is reduced to its "essence"). I am of the view that the full content, including the mythological concepts, must be maintained. The New Testament is not a mythological garbing of the universal truth; this mythology (resurrection and so on) is the thing itself—but the concepts must be interpreted in such a way as not to make religion a pre-condition of faith (cf. circumcision in St. Paul). Not until that is achieved will, in my opinion, liberal theology be overcome (and even Barth is still dominated by it, though negatively), and, at the same time, the question it raises be genuinely taken up and answered—which is not the case in the positivism of revelation maintained by the Confessing Church.

The world's coming of age is then no longer an occasion for polemics and apologetics, but it is really better understood than it understands itself, namely on the basis of the Gospel, and in the light of Christ.

You ask whether this leaves any room for the Church, or has it gone for good? And again, did not Jesus himself use distress as his point of contact with men, whether as a consequence the "methodism" I have so frowned upon is not right after all? . . .

July 8th 1944. A short time ago I sent you a letter containing some very theoretical philosophizing on the subject of heat. During the past few days I've had a taste of it myself, and I'm feeling as though I were in an oven. I am wearing only a shirt I bought one day with you and a pair of shorts. But I don't complain about it, for I can imagine how much worse it must be for you, and how frivolous my remarks on the subject must have seemed to you. So let me try and squeeze a few thoughts out of my sweating brain, and let you have them. Who knows, perhaps we shan't have to write much longer! The other day I came across a wonderful phrase in Euripides, in a scene of reunion after long absence: "So then, to meet again is a god."

Now a few more thoughts on our theme. Marshalling the biblical evidence requires more lucidity and concentration than I am capable of at the moment. Let's wait a few more days until it gets cooler. I haven't forgotten I owe you something about the non-religious interpretation of biblical terminology. But let me start to-day with a few preliminary observations.

When God was driven out of the world, and from the public side of human life, an attempt was made to retain him at least in the sphere of the "personal," the "inner life," the private life. And since every man still has a private sphere, it was thought the he was most vulnerable at this point. The secrets known by a man's valet, that is, to put it crudely, the area of his intimate life—from prayer to his sexual life—have become the hunting ground of modern psychotherapists. In this way they resemble, though quite involuntarily, the dirtiest gutter journalists. Think of the newspapers which specialize in bringing to light the most intimate details about prominent people. They practise social, financial and political blackmail on their victims: the psychotherapists practise religious blackmail. Forgive me, but I cannot say less about them.

From the sociological point of view this is a revolution from below, a revolt of inferiority. Just as the vulgar mentality is never satisfied until it has seen some highly placed personage in his bathing attire, or in other compromising situations, so it is here. There is a kind of malicious satisfaction in knowing that everyone has his weaknesses and nakednesses. In my contacts with the outcasts of society, its pariahs, I have often noticed how mistrust is the dominant motive in their judgements of other people. Every act of a person of high repute, be it never so altruistic, is suspected from the outset. Incidentally, I find such outcasts in all ranks of society. In a flower garden they grub around for the dung on which the flowers grow. The less responsible a man's life, the more easily he falls a victim to this attitude.

This irresponsibility and absence of bonds has its counterpart among the clergy in what I should call the "priestly" snuffing around in the sins of men in order to catch them out. It is as though a beautiful house could only be known after a cobweb had been found in the furthermost corner of the cellar, or as though a good play could only be appreciated after one had seen how the actors behave off-stage. It is the same kind of thing you find in the novels of the last fifty years, which think they have only depicted their characters properly when they have described them in bed, or in films where it is thought necessary to include undressing scenes. What is clothed, veiled, pure and chaste is considered to be deceitful, disguised and impure, and in fact only shows the impurity of the writers themselves. Mistrust and suspicion as the basic attitude of men is characteristic of the revolt of inferiority.

From the theological point of view the error is twofold. First, it is thought that a man can be addressed as a sinner only after his weaknesses and meannesses have been spied out. Second, it is thought that man's essential nature consists of his inmost and most intimate background, and that is defined as his "interior life"; and it is in these secret human places that God is now to have his domain!

On the first point it must be said that man is certainly a sinner, but not mean or common, not by a long chalk. To put the matter in the most banal way, are Goethe or Napoleon sinners because they were not always faithful husbands? It is not the sins of weakness, but the sins of strength, which matter here. It is not in the least necessary to spy out things. The Bible never does so. (Sins of strength: in the genius, *hybris,* in the peasant, the breaking of the order of life—is the Decalogue a peasant ethic?—in the bourgeois, fear of free responsibility. Is this correct?)

On the second point it must be said that the Bible does not recognize our distinction of outer and inner. And why should it? It is always concerned with *anthropos teleios,* the *whole* man, even where, as in the Sermon on the Mount, the Decalogue is pressed home to refer to inward disposition. It is quite unbiblical to suppose that a "good intention" is enough. What matters is the whole good. The discovery of inwardness, so-called, derives from the Renaissance, from Petrarch perhaps. The "heart" in the biblical sense is not the inward life, but the whole man in relation to God. The view that man lives just as much from outwards to inwards as from inwards to outwards is poles apart from the view that his essential nature is to be understood from his intimate background.

This is why I am so anxious that God should not be relegated to some last secret place, but that we should frankly recognize that the world and men have come of age, that we should not speak ill of man in his worldliness, but confront him with God at his strongest point, that we should give up all our clerical subterfuges, and our regarding of psychotherapy and existentialism as precursors of God. The importunity of these people is far too unaristocratic for the Word of God to ally itself with them. The Word of God is far removed from this revolt of mistrust, this revolt from below. But it reigns. . . .

July 16, 1944. On the historical side I should say there is *one* great development which leads to the idea of the autonomy of the world. In theology it is first discernible in Lord Herbert of Cherbury, with his assertion that reason is the sufficient instrument of religious knowledge. In ethics it first appears in Montaigne and Bodin with their substitution of moral principles for the ten commandments. In politics, Machiavelli, who emancipates politics from the tutelage of morality, and founds the doctrine of "reasons of state." Later, and very differently, though like Machiavelli tending towards the autonomy of human society, comes Grotius, with his international law as the law of nature, a law which would still be valid, *etsi deus non daretur.* The process is completed in philosophy. On the one hand we have the deism of Descartes, who holds that the world is a mechanism which runs on its own without any intervention of God. On the other hand there is the pantheism of Spinoza, with its identification of God with nature. In the last resort Kant is a deist, Fichte and Hegel pantheists. All along the line there is a growing tendency to assert the autonomy of man and the world.

In natural science the process seems to start with Nicolas of Cusa and Giordano Bruno with their "heretical" doctrine of the infinity of space. The classical cosmos was finite, like the created world of the middle ages. An infinite universe, however it be conceived, is self-subsisting *etsi deus non daretur.* It is true that modern physics is not so sure as it was about the infinity of the universe, but it has not returned to earlier conceptions of its finitude.

There is no longer any need for God as a working hypothesis, whether in morals, politics or science. Nor is there any need for such a God in religion or philosophy (Feuerbach). In the name of intellectual honesty these working hypotheses should be dropped or dispensed with as far as possible. A scientist or physician who seeks to provide edification is a hybrid.

At this point nervous souls start asking what room there is left for God now. And being ignorant of the answer they write off the whole development which has brought them to this pass. As I said in an earlier letter, various emergency exists have been devised to deal with this situation. To them must be added the *salto mortale* back to the Middle Ages, the fundamental principle of which however is heteronomy in the form of clericalism. But that is a counsel of despair, which can be purchased only at the cost of intellectual sincerity. It reminds one of the song:

It's a long way back to the land of childhood
But if only I knew the way!

There isn't any such way, at any rate not at the cost of deliberately abandoning our intellectual sincerity. The only way is that of Matthew 18.3, i.e. through repentance, through *ultimate* honesty. And the only way to be honest is to recognize that we have to live in the world *esti deus non daretur*. And this is just what we do see—before God! So our coming of age forces us to a true recognition of our situation *vis à vis* God. God is teaching us that we must live as men who can get along very well without him. The God who is with us is the God who forsakes us (Mark 15.34). The God who makes us live in this world without using him as a working hypothesis is the God before whom we are ever standing. Before God and with him we live without God. God allows himself to be edged out of the world and on to the cross. God is weak and powerless in the world, and that is exactly the way, the only way, in which he can be with us and help us. Matthew 8.17 makes it crystal clear that it is not by his omnipotence that Christ helps us, but by his weakness and suffering.

This is the decisive difference between Christianity and all religions. Man's religiosity makes him look in his distress to the power of God in the world; he uses God as a *Deus ex machina*. The Bible however directs him to the powerlessness and suffering of God; only a suffering God can help. To this extent we may say that the process we have described by which the world came of age was an abandonment of a false conception of God, and a clearing of the decks for the God of the Bible, who conquers power and space in the world by his weakness. This must be the starting point for our "worldly" interpretation. . . .

July 18th 1944. The poem about Christians and Unbelievers embodies an idea you will recognize: "Christians range themselves with God in his suffering; that is what distinguishes them from the heathen." As Jesus asked in Gethsemane, "Could ye not watch with me one hour?" That is the exact opposite of what the religious man expects from God. Man is challenged to participate in the sufferings of God at the hands of a godless world.

He must therefore plunge himself into the life of a godless world, without attempting to gloss over its ungodliness with a veneer of religion or trying to transfigure it. He must live a "worldly" life and so participate in the suffering of God. He *may* live a worldly life as one emancipated from all false religions and obligations. To be a Christian does not mean to be religious in a particular way, to cultivate some particular form of asceticism (as a sinner, a penitent or a saint), but to be a man. It is not some religious act which makes a Christian what he is, but participation in the suffering of God in the life of the world.

This is *metanoia*. It is not in the first instance bothering about one's own needs, problems, sins, and fears, but allowing oneself to be caught up in the way of Christ, into the Messianic event, and thus fulfilling Isaiah 53. Therefore, "believe in the Gospel," or in the words of St. John the Baptist, "Behold the lamb of God that taketh away the sin of the world." (By the way, Jeremias has recently suggested that in Aramaic the word for "lamb" could also mean "servant"—very appropriate, in view of Isaiah 53). This being caught up into the Messianic suffering of God in Jesus Christ takes a variety of forms in the New Testament. It appears in the call to discipleship, in Jesus' table fellowship with sinners, in conversions in the narrower sense of the word (e.g. Zacchaeus), in the act of the woman who was a sinner (Luke 7), an act which she performed without any specific confession of sin, in the healing of the sick (Matthew 8.17, see above), in Jesus' acceptance of the children. The shepherds, like the wise men from the east, stand at the crib, not as converted sinners, but because they were drawn to the crib by the star just as they were. The centurion of Capernaum (who does not make any confession of sin) is held up by Jesus as a model of faith (cf. Jairus). Jesus loves the rich young man. The eunuch (Acts 8), Cornelius (Acts 10) are anything but "existences over the abyss." Nathanael is an Israelite without guile (John 1.47). Finally, Joseph of Arimathaea and the women at the tomb. All that is common between them is their participation in the suffering of God in Christ. That is their faith. There is nothing of religious asceticism here. The religious act is always something partial, faith is always something whole, an act involving the whole life. Jesus does not call men to a new religion, but to life. What is the nature of that life, that participation in the powerlessness of God in the world? More about that next time, I hope.

Just one more point for to-day. When we speak of God in a non-religious way, we must not gloss over the ungodliness of the world, but expose it in a new light. Now that it has come of age, the world is more godless, and perhaps it is for that very reason nearer to God than ever before.

Forgive me putting it all so clumsily and badly. . . . We have to get up nearly every night at 1.30, which is not very good for work like this.

CHRISTIANS AND UNBELIEVERS

Men go to God when they are sore bestead,
Pray to him for succour, for his peace, for
bread,

For mercy for them sick, sinning or dead:
All men do so, Christian and unbelieving.

Men go to God when he is sore bestead,
Find him poor and scorned, without shelter or
bread,

Whelmed under weight of the wicked, the
weak, the dead:
Christians stand by God in his hour of griev-
ing.

God goeth to every man when sore bestead,
Feedeth body and spirit with his bread,
For Christians, heathens alike he hangeth
dead:
And both alike forgiving.

July 21st 1944. [Written after the news of the failure of the attempt to assassinate Hitler on the 20th July.] All I want to do to-day is to send you a short greeting. I expect you are often thinking about us, and you are always pleased to hear we are still alive, even if we lay aside our theological discussion for the moment. It's true these theological problems are always occupying my mind, but there are times when I am just content to live the life of faith without worrying about its problems. In such moods I take a simple pleasure in the text of the day, and yesterday's and to-day's were particularly good (July 20th: Psalm 20.8: Romans 8:31; 21.7: Psalm 23.1: John 10.24). Then I go back to Paul Gerhardt's wonderful hymns, which never pall.

During the last year or so I have come to appreciate the "worldliness" of Christianity as never before. The Christian is not a *homo religiosus*, but a man, pure and simple, just as Jesus was man, compared with John the Baptist anyhow. I don't mean the shallow thisworldliness of the enlightened, of the busy, the comfortable or the lascivious. It's something much more profound than that, something in which the knowledge of death and resurrection is ever present. I believe Luther lived a this-worldly life in this sense. I remember talking to a young French pastor at A. thirteen years ago. We were discussing what our real purpose was in life. He said he would like to become a saint. I think it is quite likely he did become one. At the time I was very much impressed, though I disagreed with him, and said I should prefer to have faith, or words to that effect. For a long time I did not realize how far we were apart. I thought I could acquire faith by trying to live a holy life, or something like it. It was in this phase that I wrote *The Cost of Discipleship*. To-day I can see the dangers of this book, though I am prepared to stand by what I wrote.

Later I discovered and am still discovering up to this very moment that it is only by living completely in this world that one learns to believe. One must abandon every attempt to make something of oneself, whether it be a saint, a converted sinner, a churchman (the priestly type, so-called), a righteous man or an unrighteous one, a sick man or a healthy one. This is what I mean by worldliness—taking life in one's stride, with all its duties and problems, its successes and failures, its experiences and helplessness. It is in such a life that we throw ourselves utterly in the arms of God and participate in his sufferings in the world and watch with Christ in Gethsemane. That is faith, that is *metanoia,* and that is what makes a man and a Christian (cf. Jeremiah 45). How can success make us arrogant or failure lead us astray, when we participate in the sufferings of God by living in this world? . . .

August 3rd 1944. I am enclosing the outline of a book I have planned. I don't know whether you will be able to make anything of it, but I believe you already have some idea what I am driving at. I only hope I shall be given the peace and strength to finish it. The Church must get out of her stagnation. We must move out again into the open air of intellectual discussion with the world, and risk shocking people if we are to cut any ice. I feel obliged to tackle this question myself as one who, though a "modern" theologian, is still aware of the debt we owe to liberal theology. There will not be many of the younger men who combine both trends in themselves. What a lot I could do with your help! But even when we have talked things over and clarified our minds, we still need to pray, for it is only in the spirit of prayer that a work like this can be begun and carried through.

OUTLINE FOR A BOOK

I should like to write a book not more than 100 pages long, and with three chapters.

1. A Stocktaking of Christianity.
2. The Real Meaning of the Christian Faith.
3. Conclusions.

Chapter 1 to deal with:

(*a*) The coming of age of humanity (along the lines already suggested). The insuring of life against accident, ill-fortune. If elimination of danger impossible, at least its minimization. Insurance (which although it thrives upon accidents, seeks to mitigate their effects), a western phenomenon. The goal, to be independent of nature. Nature formerly conquered by spiritual means, with us by technical organization of various kinds. Our immediate environment not nature, as formerly, but organization. But this immunity produces a new crop of dangers, i.e. the very organization.

Consequently there is a need for spiritual vitality. What protection is there against the danger of organization? Man is once more faced with the problem of himself. He can cope with every danger except the danger of human nature itself. In the last resort it all turns upon man.

(*b*) The decay of religion in a world that has come of age. "God" as a working hypothesis, as a stop-gap for our embarrassments, now superfluous (as already intimated).

(*c*) The Protestant Church. Pietism as the last attempt to maintain evangelical Christianity as a religion. Lutheran orthodoxy—the attempt to rescue the Church as an institution for salvation. The Confessing Church and the theology of revelation. A δὸς μοὶ ποῦ στῶ over against the world, involving a "factual" interest in Christianity. Art and science seeking for a foundation. The over-all achievement of the Confessing Church: championing ecclesiastical interests, but little personal faith in Jesus Christ. "Jesus" disappearing from sight. Sociologically, no effect on the masses—interest confined to the upper and lower middle classes. Incubus of traditional vocabulary, difficult to understand. The decisive factor: the

Church on the defensive. Unwillingness to take risks in the service of humanity.

(d) Public morals—as evidenced by sexual behavior.

Chapter 2

(a) "Worldliness" and God.

(b) What do we mean by "God"? Not in the first place an abstract belief in his omnipotence, etc. That is not a genuine experience of God, but a partial extension of the world. Encounter with Jesus Christ, implying a complete orientation of human being in the experience of Jesus as one whose only concern is for others. This concern of Jesus for others the experience of transcendence. This freedom from self, maintained to the point of death, the sole ground of his omnipotence, ominiscience and ubiquity. Faith is participation in this Being of Jesus (incarnation, cross and resurrection). Our relation to God not a religious relationship to a supreme Being, absolute in power and goodness, which is a spurious conception of transcendence, but a new life for others, through participation in the Being of God. The transcendence consists not in tasks beyond our scope and power, but in the nearest thing to hand. God in human form, not, as in other religions, in animal form—the monstrous, chaotic, remote and terrifying—nor yet in abstract form—the absolute, metaphysical, infinite, etc.—nor yet in the Greek divine-human of autonomous man, but man existing for others, and hence the Crucified. A life based on the transcendent.

(c) This is the starting point for the reinterpretation of biblical terminology. (Creation, fall, atonement, repentance, faith, the new life, the last things.)

(d) Cultus. (Details to follow later, in particular on cultus and religion.)

(e) What do we really believe? I mean, believe in such a way as to stake our whole lives upon it? The problem of the Apostles' Creed? "What must I believe?" the wrong question. Antiquated controversies, especially those between the different confessions. The Lutheran versus Reformed, and to some extent, the Catholic versus Protestant controversy. These divisions may at any time be revived with passion, but they no longer carry real conviction. Impossible to prove this, but necessary to take the bull by the horns. All we can prove is that the faith of the Bible and Christianity does not stand or fall by these issues. Barth and the Confessing Church have encouraged us to entrench ourselves behind the "faith of the Church," and evade the honest question, what is our real and personal belief? Hence lack of fresh air, even in the Confessing Church. To say, "It's the Church's faith, not mine," can be a clericalist subterfuge, and outsiders always regard it as such. Much the same applies to the suggestion of the dialectical theologians that we have no control over our faith, and so it is impossible for us to say what we do believe. There may be a place for such considerations, but they do not release us from the duty of being honest with ourselves. We cannot, like the Catholics, identify ourselves *tout court* with the Church. (This incidentally explains the popular complaint about Catholic insincerity.) Well then, what do we really believe? Answer, see (b), (c) and (d).

Chapter 3

Consequences

The Church is her true self only when she exists for humanity. As a fresh start she should give away all her endowments to the poor and needy. The clergy should live solely on the free-will offerings of their congregations, or possibly engage in some secular calling. She must take her part in the social life of the world, not lording it over men, but helping and serving them. She must tell men, whatever their calling, what it means to live in Christ, to exist for others. And in particular, our own Church will have to take a strong line with the blasphemies of *hybris*, power-worship, envy and humbug, for these are the roots of evil. She will have to speak of moderation, purity, confidence, loyalty, steadfastness, patience, discipline, humility, content and modesty. She must not underestimate the importance of human example, which has its origin in the humanity of Jesus, and which is so important in the teaching of St. Paul. It is not abstract argument, but concrete example which gives her word emphasis and power. I hope to take up later this subject of example, and its place in the New Testament. It is something we have well-nigh forgotten. Further: the question of revising the creeds (the Apostles' Creed). Revision of Christian apologetics. Reform of the training for the ministry and the pattern of clercial life.

All this is very crude and sketchy, but there are certain things I want to say simply and clearly, things which we so often prefer to ignore. Whether I shall succeed or not is another matter, and I shall certainly find it difficult without your help. But I hope in this way to do something for the sake of the Church of the future. . . .

INDEX